TOTTENHAM HOTSPUR

THE COMPLETE RECORD

TOTTENHAM HOTSPUR

THE COMPLETE RECORD

BOB GOODWIN

First published in Great Britain in 2007 by The Breedon Books Publishing Company Limited, Breedon House, 3 The Parker Centre, Derby, DE21 4SZ.

This edition published in Great Britain in 2011 by The Derby Books Publishing Company Limited, 3 The Parker Centre, Derby, DE21 4SZ.

ISBN 978-1-85983-846-4

Printed and bound in Poland

www.polskabook.co.uk

CONTENTS

FOREWORD

By Daniel Levy,
Chairman, Tottenham Hotspur FC

We are immensely proud of our history at Tottenham Hotspur and this marvellous reflective tome fully illustrates and carefully records that great tradition.

From my perspective, you can never have too much information about this club and this latest edition of what is a meticulously researched book will sit well on the shelf of every Spurs supporter with a sense of the past and a quest for knowledge.

It is so comprehensive that it serves two main purposes – the ability to answer just about every question there can be on past games together with evoking a warm glow as readers look back on a succession of great games and moments in this club's fortunes.

To date, our club has been on a journey through football that has involved many great events as we have set records all along the way. Our marvellous past also provides the current side with targets to strive to match or even surpass and that in itself perpetuates the demand that the future can also be golden.

So while this book allows us to wallow in nostalgia and the glory of our past, it must also inspire us to even greater things. I take great pride in my role as chairman but also appreciate that I have inherited the task of striving to ensure that tomorrow must always be better than yesterday. A near impossible task, such is our great history, but that challenge is always there.

Enjoy this book. Its detail is immense on a past that other clubs can only envy. Now we must ensure that greater statistics are written; that the next chapters are even more triumphal as the name Tottenham Hotspur marches on.

Dedication

In memory of Ian Scott.

INTRODUCTION

It's always a pleasure when the publishers ask me to update the *Complete Record*, but that's even more so after a season like the last one. To see Spurs competing in the Champions League and making such a wonderful job of it added a little bounce to the task of recording events that are not always so exciting. It reinforces my view that appreciation of the good times only comes when you've been through the bad ones.

There are several comments I've made in all previous editions of the *Complete Record*, and there's no harm in repeating them again.

I try to use official club data where possible, but that is not always possible and even where it is I like to get verification when I can. The *Tottenham & Edmonton Weekly Herald* always provided a mine of information going back to the club's earliest days, but it disappeared many years back. Where the *Herald* could not assist, I have looked at many other sources and, if there was a conflict formed a view as to which was correct, leaning towards the club records unless they were clearly wrong.

I try to get the information in this book as accurate as possible, but I'm not foolish enough to think there will not be mistakes. The only way I can correct them is if people tell me about them so please, if you spot one, write to me care of the publishers. Chris Gray has been good enough to do that in the past, and I'm extremely grateful to him for that.

I've been compiling my records on Spurs now for the best part of 45 years and could never have done that without the support and help of so many friends, acquaintances and public servants. It is impossible for me to name them individually, and I would not want to offend by forgetting anyone. However, there are some who always deserve a mention. Carolyn Tingay, 'Ossie', the staff of Bruce Castle Museum and the British Library and Spurs' custodian extraordinaire, Andy Porter. Thanks to all.

I must also thank Tottenham Hotspur for giving the *Complete Record* its blessing and all at DB Publishing for their hard work. I may provide the information, but they have the task of putting it into a readable format. They do a marvellous job.

Bob Goodwin
London
May 2011

THE TOTTENHAM HOTSPUR STORY

Tottenham Hotspur! A unique name for a unique club, but why Hotspur? Why not Rovers or Albion, Wanderers or Athletic? Where does the name originate and why should a football club carry such an unusual and unlikely title?

In the early 1880s Tottenham, Middlesex, bore little resemblance to the densely populated part of North London it has since become. On the very fringes of London, it was still a suburb, but the coming of the railways had seen an explosion in the population. As land in the centre of London was bought up to enable the railway companies to build their stations and railways lines, so they were obliged to provide cheap travel into the city for the masses who were forced to move out in search of somewhere to live. What, not long before, had been a series of villages with a few grand houses and plenty of agricultural land, was soon submerged as the tentacles of the city reached out in all directions.

As the population increased, so did the demand for schools and recreational facilities. There was still enough open land in Tottenham, not least the marshes that remain today, to provide the space needed for those that wanted to play sport, and, while Tottenham Grammar School was well established, several private schools sprung up to cater for those able to afford the fees.

Among these was St John's Middle Class School, a Scottish Presbyterian Academy run by Mr William Cameron situated in Tottenham High Road, just opposite Bill Nicholson Way. In 1880 some of the boys from St John's, along with a few friends from the Grammar School, got together to form the Hotspur Cricket Club. Exactly why the name Hotspur was chosen is lost in the mists of time, but the commonly accepted story is that two of the boys, Hamilton and Lindsay Casey, were studying the reign of King Henry IV and had been enthralled by the battlefield deeds of Sir Henry Percy, eldest son of the 1st Earl of Northumberland. The Earl was head of the Percy family and one of the most powerful men in the country.

The Percy family was originally based in North Yorkshire but, tasked with the job of protecting the King's realm from attacks by the Scots, its influence soon spread to Northumberland with Alnwick becoming its seat of power. Knighted at the age of 13, Sir Henry Percy grew up with a sword in his hand, first tasting battle at the age of 14 and rapidly building himself a reputation as a heroic knight with his assaults on the Scottish hordes. His attacks were marked by the speed and fury with which they were carried out, and it was this that led the Scots to give him the 'Hotspur' nickname by which history knows him.

Doubtless part of the plot by which Henry IV deposed his brother, Richard II, in 1399, the Percys' soon fell out with the new king and led a rebellion that climaxed with the

Battle of Shrewsbury in 1403. Lacking the expected support of the Welsh rebel Owen Glyndwr, Hotspur took the battle to the king, but his outnumbered and outmanoeuvred army was defeated with Hotspur meeting a glorious end.

His historical reputation established, Hotspur was introduced to a new audience by his immortalisation in William Shakespeare's Richard II and Henry IV, and there was no better name for a schoolboys' club to take onto the cricket battlefield. This was all the more so for the boys of St John's and Tottenham Grammar, as the Percy family, albeit far removed from that of Harry Hotspur, had been big landowners in Tottenham, many of the boys lived in or around Northumberland Park and knew Percy House, the High Road home of the local YMCA.

The cricket club played for two years on a field owned by Captain Delano, uncle of two of the members. Few details of its results have survived but evidently the boys enjoyed their time together, and as the 1882 cricket season drew to a close they looked to find another pastime that would keep them together during the winter months.

Football was becoming an increasingly popular sport. The Royal Engineers and the Old Etonians, FA Cup winner's only a few years earlier, played in the locality and many junior clubs had sprung up to try and emulate these early football heroes. The precise turn of events is uncertain but legend has it that at the behest of Robert Buckle, John Anderson and Ham (also know as Sam) Casey, a meeting of the cricket club was called and it was decided to take up football. Ham Casey may have been the driving force behind the move. He is the only one of the early members known to have played football before, having turned out for a local club known as the Radicals in the 1881–82 season.

The earliest known records of the club, perhaps the very first, are six torn and faded pages of what appears to be the original club book. Written by honorary treasurer Lindsay Casey, they show that the football club's initial funds, 5 shillings (25p), were provided by the cricket club and supplemented by sixpence (2.5p) subscriptions from Ham Casey, Edward Beaven and Fred Dexter. Those subscriptions were paid on 5 September 1882, so that date has come to be recognised as the official date that the Hotspur Football Club came into being. Further subscriptions were soon paid by John Thompson, Bobby Buckle, Tom Anderson, Stuart Leaman, Lindsay Casey, Edward Wall, John Anderson and Philip Thompson, all members of the cricket club. The first non-cricket club member to join was D. Davies. He paid a subscription of one shilling (5p), as did Charles Iverson, William Lovell and John Fisher. R. Hewlett paid 1s 6d (7.5p) and Tom Bumberry 1s 3d (1.2p). John Thompson occupied the position of honorary secretary, with Bobby Buckle elected captain and Ham Casey vice-captain.

The money received was quickly expended on the purchase of wood for goal posts (2s 6d [12.5p]), flag poles (1s [5p]) and other essentials such as flags, tacks, white paint and tape. The goal posts were made by the father of the Casey brothers and painted blue and white. The major outlay was not incurred until 30 September when 6s 6d (32.5p) was paid for a football. This is the first ball the club purchased, but it has been said that the elder brother of the Caseys had already donated one. On the same day as the ball was bought, Spurs played their first match. It was not the most inspiring of results, a 0–2 defeat against the Radicals. They had been playing for a year or two with players slightly older than the 13 and 14 year olds that made up Spurs. Sadly, this defeat is the only game recorded in the club book. The only other known result from that first season was a 1–8 defeat at the hands of Latymer, a school side from Edmonton, on 6 January 1883.

It might have been expected that the young Hotspurs would use Captain Delano's field for their football matches, but that was not to be. Tottenham Marshes provided more than enough free accommodation for them, together with other local clubs Park, Star and Radicals, and Northumberland Park station was nearby with a station master good enough to allow them to store the goalposts there.

Playing on a public space was not without its problems though. Apart from gangs of local bullies who frequented the marshes and taunted the Hotspur members, the players often had to literally fight to keep their painstakingly marked-out pitch from teams who preferred to take by force what they were not willing to prepare themselves. At the end of their first season the Hotspur boys decided that, if they were going to enjoy their sport, adult help was needed. They approached John Ripsher, an iron works clerk who lived with his brother in Northumberland Park. He was warden of Tottenham YMCA, took bible classes at the Parish Church of All Hallows and was already a popular figure among the local boys. He readily agreed to assist.

Evidently the boys decided to concentrate on football. There is no record of the cricket club playing any matches in 1883 and the football club book records that in May and June 1883 the assets of the cricket club were sold off, Ripsher paying 5s 3d (27p) to acquire some of them.

At Ripsher's suggestion, John Randall, a former Radicals player and clerk in Edmonton County Court, called a meeting of the Hotspur Football Club in the basement kitchen of the YMCA. Ripsher took the chair and set out how the 21 boys present could put their club on a formal footing. At the end of the meeting Ripsher was appointed president, a position he was to hold throughout the club's formative years. John Randall was elected captain with Billy Harston his deputy, along with a committee comprised of Tom Bumberry, Billy Herbert, Fred Dexter and Billy Tyrell. Subscriptions were payable on or before 8 September 1883, matches were to be played at the Park Lane end of Tottenham Marshes and all members were requested to wear the club colours of navy blue with a scarlet shield on the left bearing the letter 'H'.

Spurs' first season as an organised club started in great style with a 9–0 thrashing of Brownlow Rovers, the first Spurs match to be reported in the *Tottenham & Edmonton Weekly Herald*. Although the line up was not mentioned, it was recalled some years later by Billy Harston as Leaman; Tyrell and Dexter; Casey and Lovis; Lomas, Cottrell, Watson, Fisher, Harston and Buckle. Note: two half-backs and six forwards. Although commended in *The Herald* for his performance, Harston made no reference to Jack Jull, a former St John's pupil who had moved on to boarding school and was to prove Spurs' first real star.

The whole season proved a success, with Spurs winning 15 of their 20 known games and enough members for them to field a second team regularly. The only sour note came when Spurs were asked to leave the YMCA after a council member, investigating noise in the basement, was struck by a soot-covered football.

With nowhere for the boys to meet, Ripsher persuaded the Vicar of Tottenham, Revd

Wilson, to allow them the use of 1 Dorset Villas, Northumberland Park, as their headquarters. The only condition was that they attended church every Wednesday evening. At about the same time Spurs changed their name to Tottenham Hotspur for no reason other than to avoid confusion with a slightly more established club, London Hotspur.

Playing success continued in 1884–85 but, more than that, Spurs were already starting to build a reputation for themselves. Football fans were making their way to the marshes specifically to watch Spurs in action, having heard of the entertaining football they played. At the end of the season Spurs cancelled their final game so they could got to the Kennington Oval and watch Blackburn Rovers beat Queen's Park for the second successive season to retain the FA Cup. The young Spurs were clearly impressed with Rovers' performance, deciding to adopt their blue and white halves as a sign of respect for the Lancashire club.

Spurs' progress continued in 1885–86 with over 100 goals scored in 37 games and just 51 conceded. The season also saw Spurs make their first foray into Cup competition, the London Association Cup. Their first ever Cup tie was on 17 January 1886 when they met St Albans, a London business house team, in the first round. Despite being up against much older and more experienced opponents, they pulled off a surprise 5–2 victory in front of no less than 400 spectators on the marshes. They did not fare so well in the next round, going down 0–8 to the Casuals, but even to play such a famous outfit showed how much Spurs had developed in just a few years.

While all looked rosy on the pitch, off it Spurs were still getting themselves in hot water. They had dutifully attended church every Wednesday evening, but when some of the boys

The first known picture of Spurs taken at Stonebridge Lock on the Marshes on 17 October 1885. Back row, left to right: R. Amos, L. Brown, T. Wood, T.W. Bumberry, J. Anderson, John Ripsher (president), H.D. Casey. Middle row: J.H. Thompson, W.C. Tyrell, F. Lovis, J. Jull, H. Goshawk, W. Hillyer, S. Leaman, F. Bayne, J. Randall. Front row: J.G. Randall, R. Buckle, G.F. Burt, G. Bush, P. Moss, W. Mason, W. Harston, F. Cottrell, H. Bull.

were caught playing cards during the service Revd Wilson asked them to vacate Dorset Villas. Again, it was Ripsher who came to their rescue. He could not have approved of their antics but appreciated that 'boys will be boys' and was not about to desert his charges. He arranged facilities at the Red House in Tottenham High Road. The building still stands today, on the corner of Tottenham High Road and Bill Nicholson Way, opposite Rudolph's and for many years now part of the club offices.

In 1886–87 Spurs continued to build a name for themselves. They went out of the London Association Cup in the first round to Upton Park, but in the East End Cup victories over Phoenix, Park and St Luke's saw them through to a semi-final meeting with London Caledonians at Millwall's North Greenwich ground. On the appointed day the teams arrived to find the playing surface in such a terrible state that they agreed it was not good enough for so important a Cup tie. With a good number of spectators present, they played a friendly that the Calies won 2–0. The semi-final was rearranged for a week later on Tottenham Marshes, but the Calies failed to appear. Spurs promptly kicked off, scored a goal and claimed their place in the Final, but the organising committee ordered them to play again, and this time the exiled Scots notched the only goal.

Spurs' continuing success and the reputation they now had for playing an entertaining game brought new problems. Up to 4,000 fans were making their way to the marshes to watch them. The pitch was fenced off to prevent encroachment, but there was nothing Spurs could do about some of the coarse remarks, mud and even rotten vegetables hurled at their opponents by unruly spectators. Complaints were common and some clubs made it clear they would not visit Spurs unless the situation improved, but what could Spurs do? They could not stop people gathering on public land.

There was only one solution. A private ground would allow them to control spectators, even to charge an admission fee. It was a major gamble and there were plenty who felt the public would not pay for what they had become accustomed to watching for free, but Bobby Buckle, Jack Jull, Ham Casey and Secretary Frank Hatton persuaded the doubters it was a gamble worth taking. A site was found off Northumberland Park. Part of it was already occupied by the Foxes club, but for £10 a season Spurs could rent a pitch used by a tennis club in the summer.

The first match played on the new ground was a B team fixture against Stratford St Johns in the London Junior Cup on 6 October 1888. It was followed a week later by the visit of Old Etonians in the London Senior Cup. The big crowd they drew to Northumberland Park witnessed a fine performance by Spurs. They lost 2–8 to the team that had been FA Cup finalists five years earlier but only after the old boys had scored five goals without reply in the second half, as their strength and experience proved too much for Spurs. The whole season proved another success with the move to a private ground vindicated. Crowds were nowhere near the levels that had congregated on the marshes, but they were enough to more than cover the costs involved.

Over the next few seasons Spurs' progress continued at a steady rate, but it could have been more rapid. They played in what Cup competitions they could but the vast bulk of their matches were of the friendly variety. Gates invariably increased when there was something at stake, and it was obvious that bigger strides could be made if regular competitive football was available.

The Football League had proved a success since it began in 1888, but it was made up of the professional clubs from the Midlands and North. The men who ran the game in London and the South remained rooted in the past of the Old Boys' clubs, implacably opposed to professionalism and determined to maintain a vice-like grip on those they controlled. Woolwich Arsenal rebelled in 1891 and decided to pay their players, only to find they were immediately expelled from the London FA and banned from all Cup competitions. When they floated the idea of a league for London and the South they received overwhelming support from the 26 clubs invited to a meeting. Spurs were one of the clubs in favour but not among the 12 elected to form the League. It mattered not, as pressure from the London FA quickly made the clubs, concerned they would suffer the same penalties as Arsenal, pull out.

Spurs remained keen to secure regular competitive football, and when John Oliver, president of Westminster Criterion, sponsored the formation of the Southern Alliance for 1892–93, they were one of 10 founder members. Wearing a new red and blue kit, they took the competition seriously to begin with, but the same could not be said of their rivals, who really were of a level lower than Spurs. While Spurs completed their fixtures to finish third in the competition, most of the other clubs did not even play all their games. It was a pity the competition was not a success, for Spurs were attracting increasingly-better players to their ranks, evidenced by the fact the famous Casuals only managed to beat them 1–0 in the London Senior Cup before a Northumberland Park crowd of 3,000. At least it brought Spurs into contact with Oliver, a man who was to prove highly influential to Spurs' future.

Spurs' increasing standing was recognised by their invitation to participate in the inaugural FA Amateur Cup competition, a competition introduced because it was now recognised amateur clubs had little chance of winning the FA Cup. Spurs defeated Vampires in the first round and were drawn to meet Clapham Rovers in the next, but a typical example of the intransigent and backward-looking attitude of the London FA meant the game never took place.

Ernie Payne was a competent left-winger with Fulham but rarely able to get a game with them. Invited to play for Spurs, he called in at Fulham to collect his kit, only to find it had all disappeared. Spurs had no problem providing shirt, shorts and socks, but no suitable boots were available so they gave him 10 shillings (50p) to buy a pair. Fulham took exception to this and complained to the London FA, accusing Spurs of poaching and professionalism. The poaching charge was dismissed, but Spurs were found guilty of misconduct. Buying the boots was regarded as 'an unfair inducement' to persuade Payne to play for Spurs. They were suspended for two weeks with Northumberland Park closed for the same length of time.

The decision was ridiculed in most quarters, but it did give Spurs a lot of positive publicity. If the London FA intended to make an example of Spurs, their plan backfired as public support for the club was overwhelming. Some 2,000 attended when the ground was re-opened for the visit of Crusaders in the London Charity Cup and 6,000 were reported to have gathered when Spurs visited Southampton St Mary's on Boxing Day.

Not everybody was quite so impressed. When Millwall Athletic resurrected plans for a Southern League in early 1894, they did not even invite Spurs to the meetings that saw the Southern League formed. This was no surprise, for a bitter rivalry between the two clubs had already developed.

Spurs in 1894–95. Back row, left to right: E.E. Stuart (referee), D. Goodall, P. Hunter, L. Burrows, J. Welham, C. Ambler, J. Julian, E. Payne, A. Norris (trainer), R. Buckle. Front row: W. Shepherd, A. Cubberley, J. Jull, J. Eccles.

One man who had begun to take a close interest in developments at Tottenham was John Oliver. He had a burning ambition to see a London club good enough to challenge the powerful Football League clubs and believed Spurs could be that club. A wealthy man, he was able to attract quality players with the offer of jobs in his East End carpet-making factory. At the club's 1894 annual meeting, Oliver was elected president with Ripsher given the honorary title of club president, a more than deserved reward for the support that had so often saved Spurs in their infant days.

Oliver's first act was to pay for the erection of a stand at Northumberland Park. Spurs now had the ground to themselves but the only previous 'stand' had been one or two wagons. The new stand, with dressing rooms underneath and seating for 100, was partially blown down shortly after it went up but soon repaired. Oliver also secured Spurs' first trainer Arthur Norris, at a salary of 10 shillings (50p) per week.

As the standard of players attracted to Spurs increased, so performances improved. In the Amateur Cup they overcame Old Harrovians, City Ramblers, Romford, London Welsh and Beeston, before going out to the holders and eventual runners-up Old Carthusians. In their first venture into the FA Cup they beat West Herts, Wolverton and Clapton, before succumbing to Luton Town. Spurs were not only competing with the best clubs in the South, they were beating them, but if they were to go any further the shackles imposed by the London FA had to be thrown off and that meant following the likes of Arsenal, Millwall and Southampton in paying players.

It was a major step and not without its opponents. Most could see that professionalism was the only way forward but many were concerned about the financial implications. The club's committee, confident of Norris's financial support, were wholeheartedly behind the idea. A meeting was called for 16 December 1895, two days after Spurs had secured a place in the first round proper of the FA Cup, at The Eagle pub in Chesnut Road. The proposal was put by Bobby Buckle – player, committee member, secretary, treasurer or auditor since the club's formation – that the committee's recommendation to adopt professionalism should be accepted. The meeting took much longer than expected, with vociferous early opposition and the debate at times getting very heated, but when it came to the vote there was only one member against, although a few abstained.

Two immediate results of the decision were Spurs' withdrawal from the Amateur Cup (they had been due to meet Chesham in the first round having been exempted from the qualifying competition), and the dispatch of trainer Norris to Scotland with instructions to secure new players. He returned with centre-forward J. Logan and full-back John Montgomery. Montgomery and Charles Lanham were the only professionals that played in the first-round FA Cup tie at Stoke in February 1896 when Spurs lost 0–5.

The decision to turn professional also had an immediate impact on the opposition Spurs met. They could no longer continue meeting their old amateur foes. If they were to pay the wages quality players expected they had to attract the paying public, and the best way to do that was to entice football's big names to Northumberland Park. That in itself presented a problem, as the top clubs would only play if they received a sufficient financial guarantee. Reading, Middlesbrough, Burslem Port Vale, Swindon Town and even Aston Villa were persuaded to visit Northumberland Park, but Spurs could never be sure their opponents would field their top stars and, even if they did, that crowds would be big enough to pay the visitors and leave money in hand. Regular competitive football was the only answer.

When the Football League decided to increase its size in 1896, Spurs were quick to put their name forward. There were three places available in the Second Division, but Spurs were to be disappointed. Of the 10 applicants, they finished joint bottom with Macclesfield with just two votes. It could not have been a big surprise. Woolwich Arsenal was the only London club in the League, they had always struggled financially and the northern and midland clubs were not keen on expensive trips to London.

Spurs fared much better with an application to join the Southern League. Their obvious strength and ambition was recognised with election straight into the First Division. To mark the event Spurs changed their colours from the red and blue worn since 1892–93 to chocolate and gold.

Spurs finished fourth in the Southern League in 1896–97, a more than reasonable performance, but not so satisfactory was finishing bottom of the United League. However, of more importance were the financial affairs. The Northumberland Park ground was not possessed of the best facilities and many of the clubs Spurs were playing just did not have great appeal for the paying public. Even when clubs such as Nottingham Forest and Blackburn Rovers were persuaded to visit for friendlies, gates were not sufficient to cover the visitors' guarantee. Losses were being incurred.

Spurs turned to Charles Roberts, a trooper in the Herts Yeomanry and well-known fundraiser for help. He organised a Military Tournament at Northumberland Park in June 1897 that raised over £100 for the club. It was not enough to cover the losses but at least provided renewed confidence and allowed the signing of many experienced players such as Joe Cullen, Sandy Hall, Joe Knowles, Bob Tannahill, David Black, Bob Stormont, Bill Joyce and the Welsh international John L. Jones.

Results improved in 1897–98, with Spurs finishing third in the Southern League and second in the United League. They might have fared even better had Spurs supporters not taken the law into their own hands after a United League meeting with Luton Town in February 1898. The Luton tactics had been reprehensible and the referee too weak to do anything about them, but that was no excuse for the spectators to attack the Luton players and the referee. The punishment was the closure of Northumberland Park for a fortnight.

While playing affairs were left to the professionals, behind the scenes Charles Roberts was working on the finances. He decided capital was needed, and the only way to raise it was for the club to become a limited company. The committee members could not be expected to finance the club, and he was sure supporters, residents and local tradesmen would be only too pleased to invest a few pounds to support their local club. The committee accepted Roberts's advice and a meeting was arranged for 2 March 1898. Again, it was Bobby Buckle who was called upon to propose the resolution. It was passed without dissent, John Oliver, Roberts, Buckle, Ralph Bullock and John Thompson being elected the first directors of Tottenham Hotspur Football & Athletic Company Limited, with Frank Brettell secretary-manager. Brettell, who had played for Everton and served on their committee, was tempted away from Bolton Wanderers, where he had been their secretary and built many useful contacts. The share issue proved a major disappointment. Eight thousand shares were offered to the public but in the first year only 1,558 were taken up.

The new players signed in the 1897 close season certainly proved popular with the crowds. Ten thousand turned up for a meeting with Millwall Athletic in September 1897 and 12,000 for an FA Cup tie with Luton Town in the November. Northumberland Park was claimed to have a capacity of 30,000 but that was wildly optimistic. Breaking point arrived on Good Friday 1898 when near on 15,000 packed into the ground for a United League fixture with Woolwich Arsenal. About 80 people foolishly decided to climb on the roof of a refreshment bar to get a view of events. Most of them were lucky but five were still slightly injured when the bar collapsed.

When the season was over, Brettell set to work strengthening the playing staff. Putting his northern connections to good use, he persuaded Bob Cain, Harry Erentz, James McNaught, Jimmy Melia, Tom Smith and John Cameron to sign for Spurs. They were all quality players, some of them destined to have a major impact on the club, but their arrival was not to have an immediate effect – at least not in League performances. Spurs finished the 1898–99 season seventh in the Southern League, third in the United and Thames & Medway Leagues. It was in the FA Cup, though, where Spurs really began to make a mark. After seeing off Wolverton, Clapton and Luton Town (after two replays) in the qualifying rounds, Newton Heath were the opponents in the first-round proper. The club later to find fame as Manchester United were clear favourites, and all the more so after securing a 1–1 draw at Northumberland Park, but Spurs pulled off a major surprise, producing a stunning performance to win the Clayton replay 5–3. Another major Football League scalp was taken when Sunderland were beaten 2–1 before Stoke put an end to Spurs' hopes in the third round.

In February 1899 Brettell announced he would be leaving Spurs to take the manager's job at Portsmouth. It was another unwanted blow to Spurs, for in November 1898 John

Spurs in 1897–98. Back row, left to right: H.D. Casey, L. Burrows, J. Cullen, R. Buckle, J. Montgomery, J. Campbell (trainer), Mr R. Bullock. Middle row: R.Tannahill, A. Hall, J.L. Jones, R. Stormont, D. Black. Front row: J. Davidson, W. Joyce, T. Meade.

Oliver had stood down as club chairman. Oliver had guided Spurs through some trying times and his importance to the club's development cannot be overstated. It was later learned that his businesses were in severe financial difficulty and he fell on such hard times that Spurs held a benefit match for him. He never did realise his ambition of building a London team that could challenge the powerful clubs of the Football League, but within a couple of years he could look on as the club he had done so much for not only took on football's big names but actually beat them.

Spurs had a ready-made replacement for Oliver in Charles Roberts, but finding a successor for Brettell was reckoned to be a harder job. As it transpired the man to do it was already at Northumberland Park. Although there were many applicants, the directors decided to ask John Cameron, only 26 and a valuable player, to take on the manager-secretary's role and combine it with playing. Cameron's role as secretary of the Association Footballers' Union meant he was not only well qualified to take on the administrative side of the job but well known to many players who might be tempted to Tottenham.

The summer of 1899 was a busy time for Spurs. They decided to change their colours to blue and white in tribute to Preston North End's 1888–89 double winners – 'The Invincibles' – and put Cameron's contacts to good use, securing the services of George Clawley, Ted Hughes, Sandy Tait, David Copeland, John Kirwan, Tom Morris and Tom Pratt. The major development, though, was the conclusion of the long-running search for a new ground on which to play. Ever since the refreshment stand collapsed during the Woolwich Arsenal game two years earlier, the Spurs executive had been hunting for a new ground. There was minimal room for them to develop Northumberland Park, and as it was held on lease there was little point spending money on a ground they did not own.

The prospective site was the size Spurs needed and perfectly situated just off Tottenham High Road. Negotiations were swiftly conducted with the owners, and as soon as they were concluded work began to turn the nursery land into a football ground. In just four months the ground was prepared for its first event, another fundraising Military Tournament in August 1899. The official opening of the ground came the following month with a visit from Notts County.

The new ground demanded a heavy investment and, with the directors prepared to make available the money needed, it was left to the men on the pitch to justify the confidence in the future the directors clearly held. They did not let the club down.

Southampton had won the Southern League title for three successive seasons. They were favourites to make it four in a row, but right from the start of the campaign Spurs were determined to challenge them. Eleven of the first 13 matches were won (although the results of two later expunged when clubs withdrew from the League) as the title battle became a three-horse race between Southampton, Spurs and Portsmouth. As the season wore on Southampton looked to be favourites, but they became distracted by their FA Cup run and Spurs took advantage. It went to the last match of the season but a 2–1 victory at New Brompton left Spurs three points ahead of Portsmouth and nine clear of Southampton. It gave Spurs their first-ever trophy and the title 'Flower of the South'.

In a year, Cameron had put together a powerful team, but even as the season was finishing he knew he would have to change it. Topscorer Tom Pratt, 54 goals in 60 games, was unable to settle in London and returned to Preston North End. Sandy Brown was signed from Portsmouth as his replacement.

Hampered by injuries to some of their most influential players and unable to find a settled combination, Spurs began their defence of the Southern League title in poor style. By Christmas any realistic hope of retaining it had disappeared. The focus for the season became the FA Cup.

In the first round Spurs were drawn against Preston North End. The match was delayed due to the death of Queen Victoria, fortunate for Spurs as when it took place David Copeland had just about recovered from an injury that had plagued him for months. Preston had knocked Spurs out of the FA Cup in the previous season so Spurs were keen to gain revenge, but prospects looked bleak when an edge-of-the-box shot from Preston full-back Johnny McMahon after half an hour found its way past the unsighted Clawley. Spurs attacked relentlessly for the rest of the game, but while Pratt was giving his former teammates a torrid time Sandy Brown was having a miserable match. Brown was not a gifted footballer, but he was not a man to give up. It took a 'superhuman' effort from Brown to get to a Kirwan cross with nine minutes left and take the tie to a replay.

Jimmy McNaught, Spurs' indefatigable centre-half, was injured and had to miss the replay, with Ted Hughes deputising, but at least Jack L. Jones was fit to return. Only 6,000 locals turned out for the replay, so confident were they of victory, but Spurs took a surprise lead through Cameron after only six minutes and then played a superb counter-attacking game that saw Brown add two more before the interval. In the second half he completed his hat-trick, the final 4–2 scoreline hardly doing Spurs justice.

FA Cup holders Bury were the visitors in the second round. Playing away from home held no fears for them; they had been drawn away in all their ties the previous season before outclassing Southampton 4–0 in the Final at the Crystal Palace and had beaten the

Wednesday in Sheffield in the first round. It took them only two minutes to take the lead at White Hart Lane, but Brown equalised before the break and pounced again early in the second half to put Spurs ahead. Bury piled on the pressure, but the Spurs defence held out.

Having put out two Football League sides it might have been expected that a visit to fellow Southern Leaguers Reading in the third round would hold no fear for Spurs, but they were more than fortunate to take the Berkshire men back to White Hart Lane for a replay. Reading were a hard, physical team who had no qualms about playing to their strengths. From the kick-off they imposed themselves on their more skilful visitors, and it was no surprise when they took the lead after 15 minutes. Spurs had their chances but whenever an opening presented itself they hesitated, expecting a crunching challenge, and the chance was lost. Only in the early stages of the second half did Spurs play anything like they could, and it was during this spell that Kirwan equalised. For the rest of the game Reading had the better of things, and it was only thanks to Dame Fortune that Spurs lived to fight another day. There was little time left when a shot from the left slipped from Clawley's grasp. With the ball heading for the net Sandy Tait punched clear. It was a clear penalty but the referee had been unsighted and, despite consulting his linesman amid furious Reading demands for a spot-kick, his decision was a goal-kick.

The decision knocked the fight out of Reading, not only for the few minutes of the game that remained but for the replay too. Spurs were never threatened and ran out easy winners, with two goals from Brown adding to one from Copeland.

The draw for the semi-final had been made before Spurs met Reading for the second time, with West Bromwich Albion the winners' opponents. Their officials were interested observers at the replay and immediately after the game surprisingly persuaded the Spurs directors to agree to the match taking place at Villa Park on Easter Monday. An army of Spurs supporters made their way to Birmingham and were treated to a fine exhibition of football as it should be played. From the outset Spurs' swift passing and movement gave them the upper hand, but they had to wait until early in the second half before getting their reward, with Brown nodding home Kirwan's cross. Ten minutes later the game was all but over as Brown grabbed his second, and before the final whistle blew he had taken his tally to four.

Since the Football League had been formed in 1888 no outsider had managed to lift the FA Cup. Southampton had reached the Final in 1900 but been well and truly put in their place by Bury. The prospect of a Southern League club, and one from London at that, breaking the stranglehold was just one of the factors that attracted a world-record crowd of 114,815 to the Crystal Palace for one of the best Cup Finals seen till then. The match and replay are fully reported in the Matches to Remember section and all that need be said here is that lifting the trophy for the first time was no more than Spurs deserved. Over the two games they were clearly the better team and in Sandy Brown, 15 goals in the competition, a record to this day, they had just the man to put the finishing touch to the pacy, skilful and above all entertaining football of those around him.

After two years of success, expectations were high that Spurs would now establish themselves as the best club outside the Football League, but it was not to be. They started 1901–02 well enough but defeats over the Christmas period at the hands of the top teams,

OFFICIAL PROGRAMME. PRICE 1d.

Tottenham Hotspur Football and Athletic Company, Limited.

PROGRAMME.

PIANOS.

PIANOS Tuned and Repaired by best Workmen.

PIANOS PACKED, REMOVED OR WAREHOUSED.

W. SAVILLE & CO., BRUCE GROVE.

FRIENDLY.] [SEPTEMBER 2nd, 1901.

TOTTENHAM HOTSPUR.

RIGHT WING. GOAL. LEFT WING.

CLAWLEY 1

BACKS.

ERENTZ 2 TAIT 3

HALF-BACKS.

MORRIS 4 HUGHES 5 JONES 6

FORWARDS.

SMITH 7 CAMERON 8 BROWN 9 COPELAND 10 KIRWAN 11

Referee:—Mr. F. H. KING.

12 BELL 13 HOUSTON 14 LORN 15 WALKER 16 PORTEOUS

FORWARDS.

17 HOGG 18 BUICK 19 KEY

HALF-BACKS.

20 BAIRD 21 ALLAN

BACKS.

22 McWATTIE

LEFT WING. GOAL. RIGHT WING.

HEART OF MIDLOTHIAN,

(SCOTTISH CUP HOLDERS.)

Any alteration taking place in the Players' names, a Board will be sent round the ground corresponding with Nos. on the Programme.

PIANOS.

200 PIANOS to select from. TUNINGS FREE. Delivery Free. Send for Price List Free.

W. SAVILLE & Co.,

TOTTENHAM, WOOD GREEN, WALTHAMSTOW, PLUMSTEAD, &c.

Programmes but this, as they are NOT Official.

The programme from Spurs' opening match of the 1901–02 season when they entertained their Cup-winning counterparts from Scotland, Heart of Midlothian.

Southampton and Portsmouth, left them off the pace. Southampton knocked them out of the FA Cup in a first-round second reply and a resurgence in League form was brought to an end by a late season spell of four draws and one defeat in five games that saw them finish five points behind champions Portsmouth.

They slipped back to fourth in the Southern League the following season, although some satisfaction came in the FA Cup. After a poor 0–0 draw with West Bromwich Albion in the first round before a record White Hart Lane crowd of 25,641, Spurs pulled off a surprise by going to The Hawthorns for the replay and returning with a fine 2–0 victory. Bristol City provided stubborn opposition in the second round before a single goal from Vivian J. Woodward took Spurs through. The third round paired Spurs with Aston Villa, a team at the peak of their form. Another big crowd assembled at White Hart Lane and the ground record only remained intact because the weather kept many away. Villa gave a masterful performance, perhaps the best seen at White Hart Lane, but

Photographs from Spurs' draw with Reading on 23 March 1901 as they appeared in the following week's issue of *The King*.

THE ASSOCIATION CUP.

READING v. TOTTENHAM HOTSPUR.

THIS MATCH WAS PLAYED AT READING ON SATURDAY LAST, AND RESULTED IN A DRAW. 14,000 SPECTATORS WATCHED THE GAME.

THE SPURS HAVE A FREE KICK QUITE NEAR TO THE READING GOAL.

"HALF-TIME," WHEN READING WAS ONE GOAL AND TOTTENHAM HOTSPUR NIL.

Spurs put up a real fight and Villa were grateful to leave on the right end of a 3–2 scoreline.

In 1903–04 Spurs were runners-up in both the Southern and London Leagues, and took top spot in the Western League, but again it was the FA Cup that provided national exposure, although not all of it for the right reasons. After another great away performance gave them a 2–1 victory at Everton, the second-round draw dictated that Aston Villa should again visit Tottenham. This time the ground record was smashed as 32,000, hopeful Spurs would do better than 12 months earlier, crammed in. The gates were closed half an hour before kick-off – the first time that had happened in the club's history – but too many had already been admitted. Even before kick-off it was obvious there was little chance of the game going ahead without interruption. Barely 15 minutes had elapsed, with Villa one up, when the game was held up for the first time, and when it was stopped again a few minutes later FA Secretary F.J. Wall strolled out to confer with the referee. They decided the game was no longer a Cup tie but the crowd did not hear of this until half-time, 35 minutes after kick-off and after only 20 minutes play. Pandemonium ensued, with the crowd flooding on to the pitch and further play impossible. Spurs were fined £350 with the FA ordering the replay should take place in Birmingham. John 'Bristol' Jones grabbed a surprise winner at Villa Park, but Spurs met their match in the next round, going out to League champions Sheffield Wednesday in a replay.

For the next few years Spurs maintained a position in the upper reaches of the Southern League and flirted with further FA Cup glory, but overall it was not a time of great success, at least not in the trophy sense. Fortunately, Spurs continued to play the style of football for which they had become renowned and, while everybody wanted success, winning had yet to become the be-all and end-all. John Cameron was a man who wanted the game played in the right fashion and was not prepared to resort to the aggressive tactics that some clubs found brought short-term success. For Cameron, the game was about entertainment, about putting together a group of footballers who played the game as a team, passing the ball and overcoming the opposition with skill. It was, in part, this attitude that proved influential in persuading Vivian J. Woodward to play for Spurs. The best centre-forward in the country, Woodward was an architect by profession and avowed amateur, who rejected numerous efforts to entice him into the professional ranks. He believed in playing the game in the Corinthian spirit and had winning become more important than playing, he would soon have found a club who shared his principles.

While Spurs were not garnering trophies, no pressure was put on Cameron. His commitment to the club was never questioned and everyone knew he was working hard to create a team as good as the ones that had won the Southern League and FA Cup. To allow Cameron to concentrate wholly on footballing matters, Arthur Turner was appointed secretary in August 1906, so it was a major shock when, in March 1907, Cameron announced he was giving up the manager's position. Even more of a shock came when he put his decision down to 'differences with the directorate'.

Another shock was the appointment of Cameron's successor. The position had been advertised and any number of experienced managers and players were believed to be in the running, so the announcement that a commercial traveller was to be given the job seemed a most peculiar one. Fred Kirkham had never played the game at a high level and was only

A corner being taken against Brighton & Hove Albion as Spurs lead at White Hart Lane in the match played on 20 January 1906.

known in football circles as a referee, albeit one of the best. He had taken charge of the 1902 and 1906 FA Cup Finals plus several internationals, but seemed to have few qualifications to manage a football club. His appointment proved short-lived. Unpopular with players and supporters, the directors were quick to realise their mistake, but with more important matters to deal with it was not until July 1908 that an agreement was reached on the remainder of Kirkham's contract and his departure announced.

It was decided not to seek a replacement, a surprise in view of the more important matters that had exercised the minds of the board over the preceding few months.

For some time Spurs had been growing increasingly frustrated by the ultra-conservative attitude of the Southern League. While the Football League had been forging ahead, expanding and proving itself the country's premier competition, the Southerners had been content to plod along, those in charge content to keep their own little empires in place and with no concern for the good of the game in general. In 1905 Clapton Orient and the newly-formed Chelsea had been rejected by the Southern League but welcomed into the Football League. In 1907 Fulham, Southern League champions for two years, had defected after plans to merge the two Leagues were defeated by the Southerners.

When, in February 1908, a Spurs proposal that would have taken the Southern League forward failed to find a seconder, the Spurs board decided enough was enough. They would seek to join the Football League. Queen's Park Rangers and Bradford followed suite with the Southern League, largely at Millwall's urging, retaliating by resolving the three club's conduct was objectionable and demanding their resignation. When they refused, the rules were changed so they could be expelled.

The meetings of the two Leagues were both set for 27 May 1908. The Southern League brought theirs forward so the two clashed exactly. Bradford had resigned, but Spurs and QPR refused to do so and were both expelled. At the Football League meeting Spurs were competing with Chesterfield, Grimsby Town, Lincoln City, Bradford and Boston United for three places. Spurs finished fifth in the poll. QPR were taken back into the Southern League but forced to play all their matches in mid-week, while Spurs were quietly told they could return but only in the Second Division.

Spurs clung to the hope the Football League would adopt a Third Division, but when that was dashed they faced an uncertain future. One season, at least, without League football could put them out of business. Hope was revived when financially-troubled Stoke resigned from the Football League and pledged their support to Spurs, but by the time a special Football League meeting was held on 29 June they had changed their minds. They were too late to withdraw their resignation and went into a ballot with Spurs, Lincoln, Rotherham Town and Southport. In the first ballot Spurs and Lincoln got 17 votes each, Stoke six, and Rotherham and Southport nil. A second ballot ended with Spurs and Lincoln getting 20 votes each. The decision went to the management committee, who voted five to three in Spurs' favour.

Spurs began their Football League career against FA Cup holders Wolverhampton Wanderers at White Hart Lane. After only six minutes, Vivian J. Woodward got Spurs' first Football League goal in a 3–0 win. It was a great start but only a portent of what was to come. Spurs battled for promotion with Bolton Wanderers, West Bromwich Albion, Birmingham and Derby County in a contest that went to the last week of the season. In Spurs' final game at Derby they needed victory or nothing more than a 1–1 draw. A Booby Steel goal proved enough to give Spurs the point needed.

To celebrate promotion Spurs undertook an ambitious tour of Argentina with one game in Uruguay. On the way back one of the Spurs players used the ship's parrot as a prop when dressing up as Long John Silver for a fancy dress contest. As a souvenir of the occasion the parrot was given to Spurs.

If Spurs believed they would find life in the First Division easy, they soon learned otherwise. Badly hit by Woodward's decision to quit Spurs and return to Chelmsford, they struggled from the start and it was only with the signing of Percy Humphreys from Chelsea in December 1909 that escaping relegation began to look a possibility. Humphreys had only become available when Chelsea persuaded Woodward to play for them, a blow more bitter to Spurs than Woodward's original 'retirement'. Humphreys's goals gave Spurs hope, but again Spurs' fate went to the last game of the season. Chelsea were the visitors and the situation was simple: a draw or victory would see Spurs safe and Chelsea relegated, a Chelsea win and Spurs would be down. Thirty-five thousand squeezed into White Hart Lane and saw Jimmy Windridge give Chelsea the lead, but Billy Minter equalised before half-time. In the second half the game swayed from end to end with Woodward causing untold problems for the Spurs defenders, but when a winner came it was from the foot of Humphreys.

For the next four years Spurs continued to find life in the top flight hard going. They were never at real risk of going down but continued to hover around the lower reaches of the table, avoiding relegation regarded as a success. The directors came in for much haranguing. Having shown determination to escape the Southern League, they were accused of lacking ambition, particularly when it came to signing quality players. Survival seemed the peak of their ambition, whereas supporters had loftier aims.

Although it may have been a way of deflecting criticism, at least one positive step was taken with the appointment of a manager. Peter McWilliam, formerly of Newcastle United,

Midfield action from Sheffield Wednesday's visit to White Hart Lane on 7 September 1912.

a Scottish international with a big reputation in the game as a player, was given the job in January 1913. He had hardly been able to get to work in prising open the purse strings when a threat every bit as great as relegation reared its ugly head.

At the end of the 1912–13 season Woolwich Arsenal had been relegated. Controlled by Henry Norris they had struggled for years, hampered by the facilities at their Plumstead ground. Norris had tried to merge Arsenal with Fulham, intending to make Craven Cottage the merged club's home while utilising Arsenal's First Division status, but his plans had been thwarted by the League. Relegation combined with Second Division football was a recipe for disaster and simply made the need to find a new ground even more urgent. When word got out that Norris had found his new site at Highbury, Spurs were more than concerned. Competition from Clapton Orient and West Ham United was acceptable but Arsenal on their doorstep something altogether different. Chelsea and Clapton Orient shared Spurs' worries but despite their combined efforts there was nothing anybody could do to thwart Norris's plans. Arsenal moved to Highbury in 1913. Spurs were in the First Division, Arsenal the Second. So long as that remained the position Spurs would retain the upper hand, but if the roles were reversed anything might happen.

It very nearly changed within a year, Spurs finishing 17th in 1913–14 while Arsenal only missed promotion on goal average. Spurs would have to improve quickly if their worst nightmare was not to be realised.

Any plans Spurs may have had for making their position secure were soon put into cold storage with the outbreak of World War One and, indeed, Spurs were grateful for the close proximity of Highbury, using it for many of their home games after White Hart Lane had been taken over as a gasmask factory. Such neighbourliness was obviously appreciated by Spurs, but when the conflict with Germany came to an end the conflict in north London took another twist.

When War broke out in August 1914 the government wanted life to continue much as normal. Despite the losses in the trenches football continued, although all clubs were quickly hit by their young men joining up, Spurs harder than most. After just one season the Football League was suspended, but that one season had been more than enough for Spurs. They had finished bottom of the table.

With hostilities over, the Football League decided to increase the First Division by two clubs. This had happened twice before. In 1898 Blackburn Rovers and Newcastle United had been due for relegation but were elected back into the First Division. In 1905 it was Bury and Notts County who were reprieved. In 1919 Spurs expected the same thing would happen. Derby County and Preston North End, the top two in the Second Division of 1914–15, would go up, Spurs and Chelsea, the bottom two in the First Division, would stay up. That it did not was down to the manoeuvrings of Henry Norris.

Arsenal were £60,000 in debt, a vast sum in those days, and Norris had personally invested £125,000 (about £4 million in today's money) in them. His only chance of turning their fortunes around was to get them in the First Division. When he began canvassing for Arsenal to be promoted, Spurs did not take him seriously, at least not seriously enough. He aimed his attack solely at Spurs, basing it purely and simply on Arsenal having been members of the Football League longer than Spurs.

It was not an argument that seemed to have any chance of success. Arsenal had finished the last League season in sixth place (in fact it was fifth, but the error was only realised years later). Wolverhampton Wanderers and Birmingham had been fourth and fifth. They had both been in the League longer than Arsenal, and Wolves had been founder members. If longevity of membership rather than performances on the field was the measure, they both had a much better claim than Arsenal.

As soon as the League meeting started in March 1919 it was obvious all was not right. In the past, all clubs seeking election had gone into a simple ballot with the top four promoted. League President, and friend of Norris, John McKenna of Liverpool suggested something different.

Chelsea were in the ballot. They had finished one point ahead of Spurs and one behind Manchester United, but it had transpired during the war that United's 2–0 defeat of Liverpool in April 1915 had been fixed as part of a betting scandal. If the score had been reversed then Chelsea would have been safe and United in the relegation spot. McKenna suggested Chelsea should be re-elected without a vote. Nobody objected – they were sure to garner enough votes. He then proposed Derby and Preston should be elected. Again this was agreed without a vote. That left Spurs, Arsenal, Barnsley, Wolves, Nottingham Forest, Birmingham and Hull City to contest the final place with all votes still to be cast.

If Charles Roberts had not realised by now how comprehensively he had been outmanoeuvred by Henry Norris, he did when McKenna made a long speech urging the meeting to vote for Arsenal. His advice was followed. Arsenal got 18 votes to Spurs' five. No logical explanation was ever given for McKenna's handling of the meeting or his unprecedented plea in support of Arsenal, but the damage was done. Not only had Arsenal bulldozed their way on to Spurs' territory, they had now taken Spurs' First Division place.

Spurs were bitterly angry at events, but there was little they could do other than what Arsenal could not do and that was win promotion on the pitch. Ever since his appointment Peter McWilliam had been working away at building a team, and as soon as players began to return he redoubled his efforts to get them fit and play in the style he wanted. The injustice of Spurs' relegation led the directors to promise the support that had often been lacking before, but McWilliam hardly needed it. The only new players of significance were half-back Bert Smith, who had first come to McWilliam's attention as a war-time guest, and a local youngster of immense talent, Jimmy Dimmock. The 1919–20 season started with a 5–0 win at Coventry and continued in the same vein as Spurs strolled to the Second Division title, with a record 70 points and a place back where they belonged.

As if winning the Second Division so convincingly did not prove what a terrible mistake the League had made barely 12 months earlier, Spurs went on to emphasise it in 1920–21. They did not start in the best fashion but as the season wore on settled down to finish the season sixth, their highest-ever League position. It was in the FA Cup, though, that the real impression was made.

Bristol Rovers were easily beaten 6–2 in the first round, followed by Bradford City 4–0 with Jimmy Seed netting a hat-trick in the second, both matches being at White Hart Lane. In the third round Spurs visited Third Division Southend United and for 60 minutes looked to be going out of the competition. Southend took an early lead but that was pegged back by a Jimmy Cantrell equaliser, only for Bert Smith to concede a penalty shortly before the interval. Albert Fairclough went to take the kick but the referee was not happy the ball was on the spot. He re-positioned it and refused to let Fairclough adjust it. Put off by the referee's actions, Fairclough put the kick wide. Southend remained on top for the early stages of the second half, but as they tired Spurs began to play and eventually took control, three more goals giving a somewhat flattering 4–1 scoreline.

The best match of the previous season's competition had come in the fourth round when Aston Villa had visited White Hart Lane. A titanic tussle Spurs looked like edging was settled by an own-goal by Tommy Clay, a terrible miskick he was never to forget. Villa had gone on to win the trophy and were now called upon to visit Spurs in the fourth round again. Fifty-two thousand packed White Hart Lane for a contest even better than the previous season's and one talked about for years after. Again it was decided by one goal but this time it came from the foot of Jimmy Banks, a blistering drive in the 23rd minute that gave the Villa 'keeper no chance.

The semi-final pitted Spurs against Preston North End at Hillsborough. Spurs controlled the match to win 2–1 but a more balanced refereeing performance would have seen a scoreline that truly reflected Spurs' dominance. Jimmy Banks netted midway through the first half only for the referee to disallow it for a foul on Jimmy Seed and bring play back for a free-kick to Spurs. Shortly after that a free-kick into the Preston box saw the ball find its way into the net, but the referee disallowed it for reasons he refused to explain and then Jimmy Dimmock crashed the ball against the bar when only a few yards out. Early in the second half Banks was clearly brought down in the box. Even the Preston players accepted it was a penalty, but not according to the referee. Spurs were growing increasingly frustrated when brilliant inter-passing between Grimsdell and Dimmock ended with Grimsdell

FA Cup winners 1921. Back row, left to right: W. Minter (trainer), T. Clay, B. Smith, A. Hunter, C. Walters, R. McDonald. Front row: J. Banks, J. Seed, A. Grimsdell, J. Cantrell, H. Bliss, J. Dimmock.

suddenly cutting the ball back to Bert Bliss, who hooked it home. Even the referee could find no reason to disallow that one. Bliss then all but wrapped the game up with a second goal, only for Spurs to let Preston pull one back near the end. Even then Preston showed little hope of taking the game to a replay, and Spurs had the chances to add to their total before the final whistle saw Spurs through to their second FA Cup Final.

Second Division Wolverhampton Wanderers beat Cardiff City in an Old Trafford replay to win the other semi-final and provide the opposition for Spurs at a sodden Stamford Bridge in front of King George V and the Duke of York. Reported in Matches to Remember, Jimmy Dimmock made himself the hero of thousands with the only goal of the game as Spurs brought the FA Cup back to the south for the first time since winning it in 1901.

With promotion and the FA Cup won in two years, all that remained for McWilliam's men was that elusive Football League title. They got as close as they ever could in 1921–22, although for much of the season they looked anything but Championship challengers. It was not until Christmas that they began to find any form, but then they set out on a run that took them up to second. They were rarely a challenger to champions Liverpool but second was the highest placing of a London team since the League had been formed.

The return to form coincided with the FA Cup. After seeing off Brentford, Watford, Manchester City and Cardiff City, a semi-final pairing with Preston at Hillsborough kindled thoughts of Spurs becoming the first club to retain the trophy since Blackburn Rovers in 1891. That they did not was as much down to another controversial refereeing decision as their Lancashire opponents. Spurs led at the break with a single goal from Seed, scant reward for their territorial dominance. Preston were allegedly given champagne at half-time, but, true or not, they were a different team in the second period and deserved their equaliser. Play was pretty even then, but Spurs looked to have regained the advantage when a typical Bliss thunderbolt found its mark, only for the referee to disallow the goal claiming to have blown for a Preston player, lying uninjured in the centre circle, to receive treatment before Bliss's shot crossed the line. Before Spurs had recovered from the setback, Preston snatched the winner.

The 1922 semi-final was the swansong for McWilliam's team. Clay, Dimmock, Grimsdell, Seed and Smith remained but those around them moved on, and while many replacements were brought in they, by and large, were not of the same quality. The directors steadfastly refused to pay out large fees for players, preferring to believe local youngsters should be found or bargains secured. They did make money available sometimes, and McWilliam was able to secure some fine players, notable among them Jack Elkes and Frank Osborne, but, while he always had the nucleus of a good team, he was unable to turn it into another great team. The attitude of the directors led to McWilliam making an arrangement with Northfleet United whereby talented Spurs youngsters were farmed out to the Kent/Southern League side to gain experience and learn the 'Tottenham way'. It was an arrangement from which Spurs were to reap rich rewards, but not before McWilliam had moved on.

Only occasionally did Spurs look capable of mounting a serious title challenge. Early in October 1925 they found themselves top of the table, but then Arthur Grimsdell's leg was broken at Leicester and the challenge crumbled. Just over 12 months later they reached top spot again, but any hopes of going on to greater things were destroyed when the director's parsimony saw McWilliam depart.

£850 a year was not a big salary for the manager of a First Division club, and when Second Division Middlesbrough approached McWilliam in December 1926, offering to

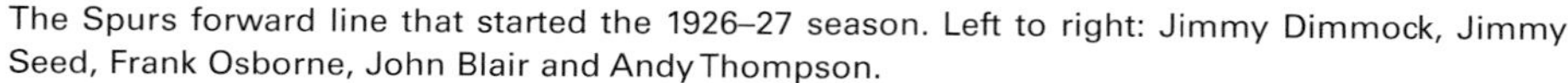
The Spurs forward line that started the 1926–27 season. Left to right: Jimmy Dimmock, Jimmy Seed, Frank Osborne, John Blair and Andy Thompson.

almost double his pay, he was tempted. He was a loyal man though and had no desire to leave Tottenham, but when he asked for his salary to be increased to £1,000 a year the board refused. McWilliam had little option. Despite being paid weekly so he could be dismissed on a week's notice, McWilliam tendered three months' notice. There was plenty of time for the Spurs board to see sense, but they would not change their minds and McWilliam departed.

Billy Minter, over 20 years at the club, was given the task of replacing McWilliam. A Spurs man through and through, he had spent six years as trainer and knew the players as well as anyone. He had been greatly impressed by a young Welsh lad, a product of the Northfleet nursery, Taffy O'Callaghan, and when Jimmy Seed was injured Minter handed him the job of standing in for the England international. O'Callaghan was like a breath of fresh air, his sudden darts from midfield, incisive passing and ability to shoot equally well with either foot lifting a crowd and team still dejected by McWilliam's departure. A certain star of the future, O'Callaghan kept Seed out of the team, which was no good for a man approaching his mid-30s. Seed made his unhappiness known but there was little he could do. Players in those days had no power, with the 'retain and transfer' system weighted in the clubs' favour. He successfully applied for the manager's job at Aldershot but Spurs refused to let him leave – they had already decided to use him as a makeweight in a deal to sign 'Darkie' Lowdell from Sheffield Wednesday. Seed departed for Sheffield in August 1927, leaving O'Callaghan the midfield maestro. At only 20 he was inexperienced and still learning the game and, not surprisingly, as the season wore on and he became better known, he began to flag.

At Easter Spurs were seventh with 35 points from the same number of games. Sheffield Wednesday looked doomed, 11 points behind Spurs with two games in hand but bottom of the table. The clubs met twice over Easter. Wednesday won 3–1 at White Hart Lane and 4–2 at Hillsborough, Seed scoring in both games and playing superbly. Spurs finished the season with one point from four games and left for a tour of Holland. When they got back they had been relegated. Inspired by Seed, Wednesday had collected 17 points from their last 10 games. They led a cluster of clubs on 39 points. Spurs had 38 and Middlesbrough 37. While Spurs spent the next five years in the Second Division, Seed led Wednesday to successive League titles.

Spurs may have been unlucky to be relegated but really it was the culmination of several years' poor management on the part of the directors. Sadly, relegation did little to alter their attitude. Investment in new players remained woefully inadequate, cheap signings of players past their best or that other clubs did not want. The only player of real quality signed was former England centre-forward Ted Harper, a £5,500 signing from Sheffield Wednesday in March 1929. Harper was an immediate success, scoring 11 goals in as many games, but was injured for the start of the 1929–30 season. With only 12 points from the opening 15 games, relegation to Division Three became a real concern and the pressure affected Billy Minter's health so much that in November 1929 he resigned. Bury's Percy Smith was Minter's successor.

With Harper returning and finding the net regularly Spurs pulled away from the relegation zone, while Smith assessed the players at his disposal. It did not take him long to recognise wholesale changes were needed. At last a Spurs manager succeeded in persuading the directors to compete in the transfer market. Dick Rowley, Ireland's centre-forward, was signed from Southampton and Welsh international Willie Davies arrived from Aston Villa. They were joined by full-backs Bert Hodgkinson from Barnsley and Bert Lyons from Clapton Orient, and the Reading centre-half Tom Messer.

As 1930–31 progressed, the investment Smith had secured looked like reaping its rewards. Everton were far and away the best team in the Second Division and it soon became a fight between Spurs and West Bromwich Albion for second spot. Ted Harper, with 28 goals in 34 games, was in cracking form, but as the season drew to a climax he was injured. Young George Hunt, a brave but raw 20-year-old picked up from Chesterfield and very much one for the future, was called up as Harper's replacement. Hunt scored five goals in eight games but lacked Harper's guile and experience, and in Harper's absence Spurs collected only four points from six games, allowing West Bromwich Albion to pip them for the runners'-up place.

Smith continued to ring the changes as he looked to find that winning combination. Players were signed and then discarded, youngsters from the Northfleet nursery promoted. Slowly a team began to take shape, but it was not until October 1932 that all the pieces of the jigsaw fell into place. After playing Oldham Athletic on the first of the month, Spurs were fourth from bottom with six points from eight games. Radical changes were needed and Smith made them. The experienced Willie Davies and Jimmy Brain were dropped, youngsters George Greenfield and Les Howe called up. The turnaround was startling. Preston North End were beaten 6–2, Burnley 4–1, Southampton 5–0, Millwall 4–1 and Port Vale 4–0. Playing with the freshness and innocence of youth, skill, determination and trickery, but most of all speed that saw them labelled the 'Greyhounds', Spurs surged up the table.

7 October 1933: George Hunt flashes the ball home as Spurs beat Sunderland 3–1 at White Hart Lane.

The only setback came in December when George Greenfield, a youngster of exceptional talent tipped for England honours, broke his leg. Smith moved quickly to sign the only player able to fill Greenfield's boots, Willie Hall of Notts County. The impetus was only disturbed for a short time, but with Stoke City leading the table from the start it went to the end of the season before Spurs secured that vital second place.

Having built his team, Smith made few additions to his squad for the return to the top flight. Many critics thought this a mistake. Defensively Spurs might be alright but the forwards were lightweight and would soon be mastered by First Division defenders. There was no doubt Spurs did not possess the big, strong attackers most clubs preferred. None of the regular forward line, Jimmy McCormick, Willie Hall, George Hunt, Taffy O'Callaghan or Willie Evans, were over 5ft 8in, but Spurs relied on speed, quick passing and movement, not brawn. Smith's belief in his players looked to be well placed when Spurs led the League in November 1933, but Christmas and Boxing Day defeats at the hands of Huddersfield Town proved the turning point, and at the end of the season they had to settle for third place.

Still, there was promise of great things to come, but 1934–35 was a disaster from beginning to end. Spurs tried to continue the style that had been so successful months earlier, but that could only be done with a settled team and fit players. Injuries so decimated Spurs that they were rarely able to field the same team in successive games with one player after another succumbing to injury, often long term. Even when Smith tried to shore things up with new signings, they soon became victims of the injury jinx. Every area of the team suffered, with no less than 36 players being used. Spurs spent the whole season in the lower reaches of the table eventually finishing rock bottom, three points behind Leicester City.

As with any struggling club, rumours abounded as to the cause of the problems. Most of the players who had taken the club to promotion and third in the League were home-grown or cheaply-acquired youngsters. The directors felt this justified their long-held belief that it was not necessary to spend vast amounts on ready-made stars and put the cheque book away again. A favourite story of the critics was that the directors had interfered in Smith's selections. That was strongly denied, but it was the reason Smith gave for his departure in April 1935.

Jack Tresadern, famous for being captain of West Ham United in the first Wembley FA Cup Final, took over from Smith. He had three years in charge, but they were years of few highs and many lows. In the League there was nothing to enthuse about, Spurs doing little more than coasting along in the top half of the table without ever making a serious promotion challenge. The only respite came in the FA Cup with Spurs reaching the sixth round in each year of Tresadern's reign and at least giving supporters something to dream about.

The most memorable of the Cup runs came in 1937. In the third round Spurs had to visit First Division Portsmouth. Pompey were on a hot streak and clear favourites, but a Johnny Morrison hat-trick inspired Spurs to a remarkable 5–0 victory that had even those at the game double checking the papers to make sure their eyes had not been playing tricks. Jimmy McCormick got the only goal to see off Plymouth Argyle in the next round and then scored to secure a 1–1 draw at Everton in the fifth. The replay was one of those games that has gone down in FA Cup folklore. With six minutes remaining Everton were 3–1 up and had just been awarded a penalty when a linesman flagged for a foul throw by Joe Mercer. The referee brought play back, and from the re-taken throw in Morrison pulled one back. Joe Meek then grabbed an equaliser and Morrison snatched the winner with the last kick of the game. A new record for White Hart Lane was set when 71,913 turned up for the sixth-round clash with Preston North End, only for Spurs to rediscover their League form and go down 1–3.

In 1938 Spurs overcame Blackburn Rovers, New Brighton and Chesterfield, before another White Hart Lane record attendance of 75,038 saw Sunderland ruin Spurs' dreams with a 1–0 victory.

A little success in the FA Cup was welcome but climbing out of the Second Division was all that really mattered and, under Tresadern, Spurs seemed as far away from doing that as ever. Rumours were soon circulating that Peter McWilliam would return, and no sooner had Treasdern handed in his notice in April 1938 to join Plymouth Argyle than McWilliam was back in his old office.

McWilliam never had the time to work his magic again, being in charge for just one full season before World War Two broke out. He had no real opportunity to build a team but at least laid the foundations for future success by promoting from the Northfleet nursery future stars such as Ron Burgess, Bill Nicholson, Freddie Cox, Les Bennett, Ted Ditchburn and Les Medley.

McWilliam continued as manager during the early years of the war, but both he and his wife suffered ill health and in June 1942 he resigned. In August 1942 secretary Arthur Turner was given the manager's job for the rest of the war. Despite the extra burdens thrust on him by the death of chairman Charles Roberts in July 1943, and having Arsenal as guests at White Hart Lane after Highbury was commandeered for use as a First Aid post and Air-Raid Precaution centre, he did a remarkable job, ensuring Spurs fulfilled their fixtures and always put a full XI on the field. He even had some success, Spurs winning the Football League South in 1943–44 and 1944–45.

Former Arsenal winger Joe Hulme was Spurs' next manager, appointed in January 1946 as football began to return to normal. With the country still recovering from the ravages of war, it was a difficult time for everyone and football was no exception. The experienced players of pre-war days were past their best and the up-and-coming talent had missed out on years of coaching. Spurs were luckier than most. Many of their players had come up

Saunders, the West Bromwich Albion goalkeeper, waits and hopes as Len Duquemin fires in a piledriver during the FA Cup fourth-round tie on 24 January 1948. Spurs won the game 3–1 and reached the semi-final before going out to Blackpool.

through Northfleet and knew each other's strengths and weaknesses. They had also been schooled in the Tottenham style, the emphasis on skill, teamwork and entertainment.

Under Hulme, Spurs hovered around the promotion places without really looking like promotion material, but he did take them closer to their first Wembley appearance than they had ever managed before. In 1948 Spurs beat Bolton Wanderers, West Bromwich Albion, Leicester City and Southampton, before meeting Blackpool in a Villa Park semi-final. With stars like Stan Mortensen, Harry Johnston and Stan Matthews, Blackpool were favourites but Spurs got within four minutes of pulling off a shock win. Len Duquemin put Spurs ahead mid-way through the second half, and they looked like holding out until Mortensen beat four players in a 30-yard run before firing past Ted Ditchburn from an almost impossible angle. In extra-time Blackpool's greater class came to the fore and a Mortensen brace proved too much for Spurs.

Getting out of the Second Division had become the only thing that mattered to the Spurs directors, and when it was clear they would not achieve that target in 1948–49 Hulme was sacked. Given the circumstances Hulme had not done a bad job at all, and he has, perhaps, not been given the credit he deserved for guiding Spurs through difficult times and assembling a squad that was to bring so much glory to the club. Hulme had tried without success to sign Alf Ramsey for Spurs. After his departure Ramsey was signed, but it was the arrival of a young, innovative new manager that was to see Spurs set new standards of footballing excellence.

Arthur Rowe, Tottenham-born former Spurs centre-half of the 1930s and a Northfleet product, was the man given the task of taking Spurs back to the top flight. A true footballing half-back, injury had forced Rowe's retirement from playing in April 1939, and he accepted a coaching post in Hungary, but the war meant a swift return. Serving as an army physical training instructor he coached the army football team and when demobbed secured the Chelmsford City manager's job. In four years he had made Chelmsford the country's outstanding non-League team.

Apart from Ramsey, Rowe had the same players as Hulme, but the big difference was that Rowe operated to a simple philosophy. It came to be known as 'Push and Run': push the ball to a teammate, run into space to take a pass. It was as simple as that, at least in theory. The only requirement was possession. With it you could score and the opposition could not. That meant not giving the ball away, not holding on to it so a player could be dispossessed and moving the ball quickly from one player to another over short distances so there was less chance of interceptions. That demanded ball control, passing ability and accuracy. From there would flow teamwork – attacking as a team and defending as a team. Fortunately Rowe inherited just the players to do that, intelligent players, receptive to new ideas and prepared to execute them.

From his very first game in charge – a 4–1 win at Brentford – Rowe's tactics proved a success. Spurs led the Second Division from start to finish and proved far superior to their rivals. A 2–0 win at Queen's Park Rangers on 1 April 1950 secured promotion, a goalless draw with Hull City on Easter Friday the Second Division Championship. Spurs should have gone on to set a new record number of points in a season but with the job done they eased up, collecting only one point in their last five games but still finishing nine clear of Sheffield Wednesday, Sheffield United and Southampton.

The master goalkeeper Ted Ditchburn goes full length to turn a shot round the post. The gable atop the old West Stand bore many different decorations during its 73 years of existence.

'Push and Run' had worked perfectly and not only against Second Division opposition. In the FA Cup Spurs won at First Division Stoke City and then gave another top-flight outfit, Sunderland, a footballing lesson and a 5–1 hammering.

Spurs had no fear entering the 1950–51 season but got a nasty shock in their first game as Blackpool won 4–1 at White Hart Lane. A goal down at Bolton Wanderers in the next game, it took a 50-yard dribble, not what Rowe preached, and terrific cross-shot from new signing Peter Murphy to pull Spurs level. In the second half Spurs raised themselves a gear and scored three more. 'Push and Run' would work against the country's best team, but it had to be played with more pace. It took another seven games before Spurs had really become accustomed to the demands of First Division football, but they then set off on a run of eight successive victories that included a 6–1 defeat of Stoke City, a 5–1 success over Portsmouth and culminated in a quite astonishing 7–0 drubbing of Newcastle United when Spurs, without their great captain Ron Burgess, literally played their exalted opponents, Joe Harvey, Jackie Milburn and George Robledo included, off the pitch.

Huddersfield Town brought Spurs down to earth with a 3–2 defeat, but by the end of the year Spurs were back to their best and leading the Football League for the first time in 25 years. Huddersfield put Spurs out of the FA Cup in the third round but against everyone else they just kept rolling on. 14 April 1951 was marked down as Championship-winning day but again Huddersfield proved Spurs' bogey team, winning 2–0. Their success put the big day back by two weeks and the visit of Sheffield Wednesday, when a goal from Len Duquemin a minute before the break proved enough to bring the Football League title to White Hart Lane for the first time.

In two years Rowe had moulded a group of talented players into the most exciting and effective team in the country, instilling in them the belief he had in how simply and effectively the game could be played if his maxim of 'Keep it quick, keep it simple' was followed. The style he preached and then perfected was to change the pattern of play not just of English teams, but of teams worldwide. One of the young coaches Rowe had influenced in his short spell in Hungary was Gusztav Sebes, who went on to manage the Magical Magyars side of the early 50s, who gave England a footballing lesson at Wembley in 1953.

Rowe's 'Push and Run' team contained some of the best footballers to don a Spurs shirt – Ron Burgess, Ted Ditchburn, Alf Ramsey, Eddie Baily – but while they were truly-outstanding individuals, the strength of the team lay in the way everybody played their part in making the whole machine function as a unit. They all had their roles to fill but each knew how to do that so their colleagues could fulfil their own role with ease.

Prior to the 1951–52 season Rowe stated he did not expect Spurs to retain their title. For two years he had been able to field a settled side as serious injuries were avoided, but he knew that could not go on forever. He was proved right even before the season kicked-off, centre-half Harry Clarke picking up an injury in training. Further injuries disrupted the team and, while a place near the top of the table was maintained, the zest of the previous two years was missing. Rowe's team relied on movement and players knowing what each other would do. His players could never stand still; they always had to be looking for space,

The players and club officials proudly display the Football League trophy in 1951. Back row, left to right: Arthur Rowe (manager), A. Ramsey, C. Withers, S. McClellan, D. Uphill, Cecil Poynton (trainer), Dr A.E. Tughan. Middle row: H.E. Taylor (director), C. Brittan, L. Duquemin, T. Ditchburn, F. Dewhurst-Hornsby (director), H. Clarke, L. Bennett, R. Jarvis (secretary). Front row: F. Wale (director), Rt Hon Lord Morrison (president), W. Nicholson, F.J. Bearman (chairman), R. Burgess, G. Wagstaffe-Simmons (vice-chairman), W.J. Heryet (director). On ground: L. Medley, A. Willis, E. Baily, W. Walters.

moving around wherever they could find it, confident cover would be in place. As injuries hit, the replacements knew the theory but did not have time to learn how to put it into practice. Added to that, the team were growing old but bringing in new blood was difficult for the same reason.

Four defeats in five games in the weeks leading up to Christmas effectively knocked Spurs out of the title race, and when being knocked out of the FA Cup by Newcastle United was sandwiched between defeats at the hands of the League leaders Manchester United and Arsenal Spurs had little left to play for than pride. That was one thing Rowe instilled into his players that injuries and poor results could not knock out of them. They went through the last 12 games of the season unbeaten to overhaul Arsenal and Portsmouth, finishing four points behind Manchester United.

Spurs may have given up their title to United, but if United thought Spurs were mere also-rans they were soon reminded otherwise. At the end of the season both clubs embarked on North American tours. They met twice in two days, first in Toronto, then in New York. Spurs won the first game 5–0 in exhilarating style. United's pride was stung and in the second they took an early lead, determined to justify their new champion status. Spurs took it all in their stride and then gave an exhibition of 'Push and Run' at its absolute best to run out 7–1 winners.

Sadly there was to be no repeat. Apart from age and injuries, opponents had now worked out how to counter Spurs' tactics. It was easy really: tight marking. Space and time on the ball were essential to 'Push and Run'. Cut down the space, cut down the time and Spurs could not function. The best way to do that was to get close to your man. Deny him space, deny him time.

1952–53 proved the swansong for Rowe's great team. It had taken Spurs out of the Second Division and delivered the League title. All that was left now was the FA Cup and a first trip to Wembley. A more determined effort could not have been made, but eventually Spurs fell short even closer to the Twin Towers than Joe Hulme's team five years earlier.

Only against Halifax Town in the fifth round did Spurs get through at the first time of asking. Replays were needed to dispose of both Tranmere Rovers and Preston North End and two before Birmingham City were seen off at Molineux. In the semi-final Spurs again had to travel to Villa Park and again their opponents were Blackpool. Bill Perry put Blackpool ahead in the first half, but Len Duquemin equalised early in the second. Spurs were looking the better team, but as the final whistle approached both seemed to have settled for extra-time. There were only seconds to go when a free-kick was given against Eddie Baily for handball. Baily was not best pleased, and as he stood arguing with the referee Blackpool took the kick. Baily was out of position, but Alf Ramsey took the ball off Bill Perry and the danger seemed over. All Ramsey had to do was kick the ball into the stand, but he hesitated, decided to play it back to Ditchburn, then slipped. Jackie Mudie was on the ball in a flash to slip it past Ditchburn. As soon as Spurs restarted the match, the final whistle went and with it 'Push and Run'.

For the next couple of years Rowe worked tirelessly trying to halt the decline. It was difficult for him to accept that players who had served him so well were no longer good enough, and it was always with the greatest reluctance that he accepted their time was over.

What was even more difficult though was finding the players to replace them. There were some good youngsters available: Tony Marchi, Tommy Harmer, Alfie Stokes, Ron Reynolds, but they needed time to gain experience and, just as today, time was not always to be had.

1954–55 began poorly and by mid-November Spurs were one off the bottom with relegation a distinct possibility. Ron Burgess had departed for Swansea Town, Les Bennett for West Ham United and Bill Nicholson had said himself he was no longer good enough. The heart of Rowe's team had gone. A transplant was urgently needed.

Rowe identified the man he wanted in Danny Blanchflower, the strong-willed, straight-talking Irishman who wanted away from Aston Villa but had a £40,000 price tag. Rowe got the board to sanction an offer of £28,000, matching the figure put forward by Arsenal who were as desperate for Blanchflower as Spurs. When Rowe persuaded the board to up Spurs' offer by £2,000, Arsenal failed to match it, Villa accepted and the opening to the most glorious chapter in Spurs' history began. At last they had a true captain again, a man who could lead by example, make decisions and play a bit.

Blanchflower's signing was Rowe's last major contribution as Spurs manager. The pressure had taken its toll, and by April 1955 Rowe was too ill to work and his assistant Jimmy Anderson took up temporary charge. Rowe's contract ran through to January 1956, but he knew it would be some time before he could return. A Spurs man to the core, he resigned so the club could get on with planning for the future.

Initially that future lay in the hands of Jimmy Anderson who had been with the club since 1908. Schooled in the Tottenham way, there was probably no one who knew the club, its traditions and its demands better.

Anderson's reign started with one point from six games, five from the next nine, and Spurs adrift at the foot of the table. No matter what combination Anderson tried, little was going right. It was only with the signings of Maurice Norman and Bobby Smith that League results improved, but it was the last week of the season before a dour, goalless draw at Cardiff in the penultimate game saw Spurs safe.

While the League was a miserable battle from start to finish, the FA Cup provided relief and even the possibility of a Wembley appearance. Boston United, Middlesbrough and Doncaster Rovers were seen off with little difficulty before West Ham United visited White Hart Lane in the sixth round. Spurs were 0–2 and 1–3 down, but a fighting performance eventually enabled them to force in a replay in a truly memorable match. The second game proved just as exciting as the first, with Spurs winning 2–1.

Spurs had been lucky so far in not drawing First Division opposition, but the luck deserted them for the semi-final, not because their opponents were First Division Manchester City but because the venue was Villa Park, scene of Spurs' exits in both 1948 and 1953. Again they were to leave Birmingham with the bitter taste of defeat, but things might have been different had Anderson shown more faith in little Tommy Harmer. The midfield maestro had been almost ignored for the past three or four years but for the fifth-round meeting with Doncaster had been called up and asked to play in an unaccustomed role on the left. Harmer had been outstanding, but a week before the semi-final Portsmouth had bullied him out of the game. Anderson was worried City's Roy Paul would do the same so dropped Harmer and called up Dave Dunmore, normally a centre-forward. If Bill Leivers had not cleared Dunmore's shot off the line in the opening minutes Anderson's decision may have been vindicated, but he did, and without Harmer's promptings Spurs posed little threat. Bobby Johnstone got the only goal of the game and again Villa Park had proved the graveyard of Spurs' Wembley dreams.

Harmer was soon recalled and suddenly the team were transformed from relegation candidates to title contenders. They spent the whole of 1956–57 chasing Manchester United, but the 'Busby Babes' were the outstanding team of the time. Spurs were rarely able to get close to them and had to settle for second place. While Harmer caught the eye in attack, behind him captain Tony Marchi proved a defensive rock, so much so that he became the target of rich Italian clubs who could offer wages far above those permitted in England. When Juventus offered £35,000 for his transfer, Spurs could not refuse.

Just how vital a player Marchi had become was apparent as soon as the 1957–58 season got under way, with Spurs leaking goals at an alarming rate. Any hopes of improving on the previous season's second place soon disappeared as Anderson shuffled his players before finding the right defensive blend. When he did, performances improved rapidly. With Blanchflower outstanding and Bobby Smith rattling in the goals, they soon began to climb the table to finish third. Blanchflower was voted Footballer of the Year, and Smith equalled Ted Harper's 1931 record of 36 League goals in a season.

Anderson seemed to be set to lead Spurs to greater glories, only for Cliff Jones to break his leg in pre-season training for 1958–59. Another poor start increased the pressure on him and as his health suffered he stood down. His time in charge may have been a period of ups and downs, but he had made some great signings and given an opportunity to some fine home-produced talent. The rewards of his hard work were yet to be reaped.

Bill Nicholson, who had been appointed coach on his retirement from playing, took over. A 10–4 defeat of Everton in his first match was just a foretaste of the glory times that were to come eventually, but before then he had a tough time of it as Spurs loitered around the relegation zone. They finished 18th but again suffered embarrassment in the FA Cup. Just as in 1955 with York City and 1957 with Bournemouth & Boscombe Athletic, they went out to a Third Division side, this time the giant killers being Norwich City.

Nicholson did not need long to size up where Spurs' weaknesses lay and eradicate them. In March 1959 he signed Dave Mackay and in the summer Bill Brown. Their impact, particularly that of Mackay, was immediate. Spurs started 1959–60 in fine style, unbeaten in the first 12 games. Half of them were draws, four at White Hart Lane, and it was home results that were to cost Spurs dear come the end of the season. The title race developed into a battle between Spurs and Wolverhampton Wanderers, with Burnley hanging in there just waiting for the others to slip up. As well as Spurs were doing, Nicholson could still see room for improvement, and when the chances came to sign John White and Les Allen he wasted no time in getting the board to sanction his actions. Right to the end of March the odds on securing the title looked good, but as the season drew to a climax the pressure began to tell. Fulham and Luton Town left north London with a point each, then, over Easter, Manchester City and Chelsea both took the two on offer. Just as Wolves seemed certain to take their third successive title and the first leg of the fabled double, Spurs gave their performance of the season, winning 3–1 at Molineux. Wolves did win the FA Cup, but Burnley pipped them for the title.

Spurs and Nicholson learned a lot that season, most importantly the pressure that comes with battling for the top prizes. Captain Danny Blanchflower learned something more: that the double could be done, and he believed Spurs could become the first team to pull it off since Aston Villa in 1897.

Spurs started 1960–61 beating Everton 2–0 at White Hart Lane. It was a competent performance with little sign of what was to come. As the season got into full stride, so did the team, winning, winning and winning again as all comers were swept aside by a tidal wave of electrifying football, breathless in its efficiency, exhilarating in its execution. The first 11 games were won, and Spurs went another five before suffering their first defeat against Sheffield Wednesday, the only team posing any sort of challenge. At the turn of the year they were 10 points ahead of Wolves, with the title almost won. They could now turn their attention to the FA Cup.

Two goals from Les Allen and another from Terry Dyson were enough to see off Charlton Athletic 3–2 in the third round before Crewe Alexandra visited White Hart Lane in the fourth. Almost 12 months earlier, Crewe had visited for a replay at the same stage of the competition and returned to Cheshire on the receiving end of a 13–2 thrashing. Determined not to suffer the same fate again, their tactics were somewhat crude, but Nicholson's team were not only capable of playing thrilling football, they could mix it with the toughest when they had to. Goals from Dyson, Smith, Mackay, Allen and Cliff Jones saw them through 5–2. At Villa Park a John Neal own-goal and one from Jones gave Spurs a 2–0 win and a trip to Sunderland in the sixth round. An early header from Jones should have been followed by more but Spurs relaxed, let Sunderland back in and were grateful for a second chance. Any complacency was banished for the replay, Allen, Smith, Mackay and

Cliff Jones leaps high to reach a cross in the game with Chelsea on 18 April 1960 but is unable to get quite high enough to get his shot on target.

The goal that won the League. Les Allen's volley flies past Sheffield Wednesday's Peter Springett on 17 April 1961 to give Spurs the first leg of the impossible double.

Dyson with two getting the goals as they made sure of getting through to their fourth FA Cup semi-final since the war. After three semi-final defeats there, Villa Park was not the venue they wanted, but even their bogey ground could not dent their belief in themselves. Burnley were not the easiest of opponents, but after two goals from Smith, Spurs shut up shop until the last minute when Jones netted a third.

With Spurs at last through to their first Wembley appearance, it was time for the League to take precedence again. Since the Cup run had started, League performances had taken a dip and Sheffield Wednesday were only four points adrift. Defeat at home to Newcastle United and a draw with Fulham meant Spurs' lead was reduced to three, but any thoughts they would crumble under the pressure were banished as four straight wins left them needing only two more points to take the title. It was all set up for Sheffield Wednesday's visit to White Hart Lane on 17 April. Spurs had enthralled the country with the pure quality of their football, but for one night quality had to accept second place to passion and determination.

Much as Spurs were determined to secure the title in front of their own fans, so Wednesday were not prepared to simply play the supporting role. Victory, and it was still possible for them to pinch the title. On a night that set the nerve ends jangling, White Hart Lane was silenced on 30 minutes when a Don Megson free-kick rebounded back to him and he beat Bill Brown to give Wednesday the lead. This was not part of the script, and it was almost torn up three minutes from the interval when a Keith Ellis header thudded against Brown's post, but within a minute Terry Dyson out-jumped Megson to nod on a Peter Baker clearance. Smith flicked the ball over Peter Swan's head and smashed it into the back of the net. The celebrations were still in full swing when Les Allen connected with a Maurice Norman knockdown to put Spurs ahead. It proved to be the winning goal, and at the final whistle the pitch was invaded by delirious fans who refused to leave until Blanchflower and the rest of the team had appeared in the directors' box to take the adulation.

The first part of the double completed, the focus now turned to the FA Cup Final and the meeting with Leicester City. The match is reported in Matches to Remember. It was not the best of Cup Finals, but victory left no doubt that Spurs were the best team in the country, and it proved nothing is impossible. For so long the myth had built up that the double could never be achieved. Spurs had exploded that myth.

Spurs were undoubtedly the best team in the British Isles, but football's horizons had expanded since the mid-50s. The European Cup was now the measure of greatness. For five years it had been the exclusive property of Real Madrid but had now gone to Benfica. It

Danny Blanchflower addresses the crowd having just collected the League Championship Trophy after the last League game of the season against West Bromwich Albion on 29 April 1961.

Double winners. Back row, left to right: Ron Henry, Maurice Norman, Bill Brown, Bobby Smith, Peter Baker. Front row: John White, Les Allen, Danny Blanchflower, Terry Dyson, Cliff Jones, Dave Mackay.

would take a special team to wrest the trophy from the Portuguese champions, but Spurs were very nearly the team to do so.

Spurs' first European campaign began with a preliminary round trip to the Polish mining city of Zabrze. Against Gornik they were quickly taught that European club football was very different from what they were used to domestically. They could not go away from home and play their normal attacking game. Discipline and resilience were demanded, not conceding goals the first priority. Spurs were four down well into the second half with only a late rally giving them two goals and hope for the second leg. The return game was the first of what were to become famous European nights under the White Hart Lane floodlights. The experienced Poles set out to defend their lead but were quickly overwhelmed by the power of Spurs' football. Within 20 minutes the tie was back on level terms, by half-time Spurs held a 7–5 advantage and in the second period they controlled the game, three more goals giving them an 8–1 victory and warning the rest of Europe of what was to come.

Against Feyenoord in the first leg of the first round, Spurs were without Mackay, Smith and Allen. The lesson learned, they absorbed the home-team's early attacks, took the sting out of the game and then struck on the counter to win 3–1. The job done, they took it easy in the second leg, content with a 1–1 draw. Dukla Prague were the opponents in the second round. A 0–1 defeat in the first leg was evidence Spurs had got to grips with the demands of two-leg football, a 4–1 victory in the second that they need fear no one.

In the semi-final Spurs were paired with Benfica. They needed to be at their peak for the first leg in the Stadium of Light but were well below par. A goal down after five minutes and two behind at the break, Spurs had to sacrifice their new-found defensive pragmatism in the second half and take the game to the Portuguese. Smith pulled one back early in the second period, but rather than revert to defensive mode Spurs continued to pour forward, looking for a second goal. They had the chances but not the luck and were then caught by a third Benfica goal. In the final minute Smith looked to have scored a perfectly good goal but, even though there were two defenders on the line, his effort was ruled out for offside.

The 'Tottenham Roar' was never more needed than in the second leg, all the more so when Benfica scored after 15 minutes leaving Spurs to get three to force a play-off. Eight minutes after Benfica's goal, Jimmy Greaves had the ball in the net only for an offside flag to catch the referee's eye. Smith did pull one back before the interval, and only two minutes after the restart Blanchflower slotted home a penalty to give Spurs renewed hope. Much as Spurs battered the Benfica defence for the remaining 43 minutes, the nearest they got to the crucial third was a blistering drive from Dave Mackay that hit the bar and shook the posts to their foundations.

Despite the defeat, Spurs had shown they could match the best Europe had to offer. All they needed was another chance. They did not have long to wait.

In the League Spurs were always chasing Burnley but, reinforced by the signing of English football's greatest scorer, Jimmy Greaves, they slowly reeled in the Lancashire club only for Alf Ramsey's Ipswich Town to make a late run and pinch the title.

Spurs quest for the FA Cup began at Birmingham City's St Andrews, and they looked to have the tie won when they led 3–0 at half-time. In the second half the Blues battled back to grab an unlikely draw allowing Birmingham manager Gill Merrick to claim Spurs were 'only a first-half team'. That being so, Spurs were in trouble in the replay, a goal down after 50 seconds and the scores level at half-time. Merrick was made to eat his words in the second half as they added three goals and conceded only one. If the visit to Plymouth Argyle in the fourth round kindled hopes of a giant killing for the locals, they were soon disappointed as Spurs ran out easy 5–1 winners, and it was almost as comfortable in the fifth round as Spurs won 4–2 at West Bromwich Albion. Having accounted for two of Birmingham's clubs, Spurs completed the set in the sixth round, beating Aston Villa 2–0 at White Hart Lane.

For the semi-final Spurs at last got away from Villa Park, Hillsborough being the venue for their meeting with Manchester United. Fitted in between the two meetings with Benfica, Spurs controlled the match from the outset, and the 3–1 scoreline was more than a little flattering to United. In the other semi-final Burnley beat Fulham to set up what was expected to be one of the best Cup Finals for years. Burnley had finished second in the League, a point ahead of Spurs, and had the chance of revenge for the previous year's semi-final defeat. As Newcastle United were the only club to have successfully retained the FA Cup in modern times, Burnley were slight favourites. The match is reported in Matches to Remember.

Winning the FA Cup not only gave Spurs another trophy, but it also provided another chance to test themselves against Europe's best, this time in the European Cup-winners' Cup. The first round meetings with Rangers were billed as the 'Championship of Britain', but they were uneven contests with Spurs winning 5–2 in London and 3–2 in Glasgow. In the first leg of the second round they gave their worst European performance, grateful to Bill Brown that they returned home from Slovan Bratislava with nothing worse than a two

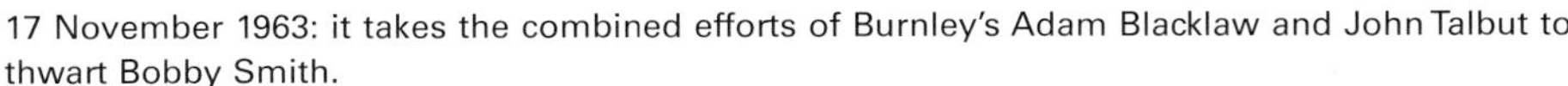

17 November 1963: it takes the combined efforts of Burnley's Adam Blacklaw and John Talbut to thwart Bobby Smith.

goal deficit to retrieve. The Spurs crowd was reckoned to be worth a goal advantage, but if anything their passion worked to Slovan's advantage in the second leg. Encouraged to throw everything at their opponents, Spurs started with a display of frenzied football that saw the visitors' goal bombarded but no real chances created. Spurs had forgotten the slick, intelligent football that had served them so well, and had it not been for the post and some excellent saves from Brown they could have been out of the competition before half-time. It was only when Dave Mackay broke the deadlock that Spurs reverted back to their normal game. It immediately reaped dividends, Greaves and Smith giving Spurs an overall lead before the interval. In a nine-minute spell of superb football in the second half, Greaves, Jones and White finished off the Czechs.

Spurs' opponents in the semi-final were the talented but limited OFK Belgrade. Even before the first leg in Belgrade the Yugoslavs had decided they could not outplay Spurs. Their only hope was to bully and intimidate, literally to kick Spurs out of the game. Such an attitude reflected badly on the OFK scouts, who should have known that, while Spurs were lauded for their quality football, they could play as rough as the best of them and still let their class shine through. It was 25 minutes before Spurs responded to the rough-house tactics of their hosts. A brutal foul by Maric on Smith led to a Spurs free-kick. As the players jostled for position in the OFK box, Maric was suddenly laid out cold, Smith, the alleged perpetrator of the deed, ready to take on all-comers. When the kick was eventually taken, Smith was the target of the vengeful home players, but he still managed to lay the ball off for White to put Spurs ahead. They would have gone into the interval in the lead had the referee not given in to the baying home supporters and awarded OFK a penalty when the ball ricocheted on to Mackay's arm. As the second half unfolded the Yugoslavs continued their nasty tactics and looked to have been rewarded with far more than they could ever have hoped for when Greaves was sent off after lashing out at his assailant. If OFK had achieved their objective it did them no good. Spurs continued to dominate and grabbed a winner with 20 minutes left through Terry Dyson. They won the second leg 3–1, but it was not one of their more glorious performances. As referee Sorensen put it, 'In the second half both teams seemed more interested in each other than the ball.'

For the Final, Spurs had to make the short trip to Rotterdam and a meeting with the Cup holders, Athletico Madrid. Nicholson knew he needed his men at their best, but he had problems even before the team flew out. Mackay and White were both doubtful with injuries and skipper Blanchflower was still troubled by a knee problem that had afflicted him since the second meeting with Rangers and caused him to be out of the team as often as in. White passed a late fitness test, but Mackay failed his. Tony Marchi was the automatic replacement but, as good a player as he was, the loss of Mackay was a body blow, particularly to Nicholson. His pre-match team talk was downbeat and gloomy, concentrating on the strengths of the Spaniards and forgetting what a tremendous team he had built for Spurs. Fortunately Blanchflower did not forget and, after Nicholson had left the dressing room, gave his own pep-talk, reminding his teammates that they were every bit as good as their opponents. They proved to be even better, as reported in Matches to Remember.

Defeating Athletico Madrid had been essential if Spurs were to continue their European exploits. Burnley had, at last, managed to beat them in the FA Cup, and while Spurs had

Alan Gilzean bursts through the Sheffield United defence to get in his shot on 27 December 1965.

matched Everton for most of the season a late collapse had allowed the Merseysiders to take the title. As it was, their defence of the European Cup-winners' Cup lasted only two games. Drawn against Manchester United, Spurs' 2–0 home win made them favourites, but the whole tie was ruined after just eight minutes of the second game. With United a goal up, Mackay had his leg broken in a tackle with Noel Cantwell. There were no substitutes so Spurs had to play practically the whole game with only 10 men. They held out until the last two minutes when Bobby Charlton got United's fourth of the night against Greaves's solitary strike.

The defeat was bad enough, but the loss of Mackay for the best part of two years was an even greater blow. Blanchflower had, although not known at the time, played his last game, and without the two half-backs Spurs began to lose their way. Nicholson was not going to suffer the same problem Arthur Rowe had been unable to overcome, a team growing old. He recognised the need to rebuild but his plans were thrown into disarray in the summer of 1964 when one of the players he intended to build a new team around, John White, was tragically killed by lightning on a north London golf course. While keeping Spurs near the top of English football, it took Nicholson time to get together a new team that could add more honours to the trophy list and do it in the way their traditions demanded. England won the World Cup with a functional team in which hard work was as important, if not more so, than skill and flair. That was not good enough for Spurs, winning was important but it had to be done the right way.

Nicholson showed great bravery in making difficult decisions, allowing players who had done so much to make Spurs the best leave and paying out large sums to secure their replacements. His hard work came to fruition in 1966–67. The season began well, an early exit from the Football League Cup, a competition Spurs had previously scorned, regrettable

Tottenham Hotspur celebrate after beating Chelsea in the 1967 FA Cup Final at Wembley 2–1.
msi

but not viewed with any great sadness. They topped the table in October but then picked up just one point in six games, leaving too much to do to overhaul Manchester United. The FA Cup became the sole target for the season. Spurs had the luck of the draw in the early rounds, being drawn out of the bag against Second Division sides Millwall, Portsmouth, Bristol City and Birmingham City in the early rounds and overcoming them all with little difficulty. It was only at the semi-final stage that Spurs met a top Division club, Nottingham Forest at Hillsborough. Forest were the nearest challengers to Manchester United in the League, but a 25-yard goal from Greaves after half an hour put Spurs in charge. Frank Saul added a second against the run of play midway through the second half, and although Forest pulled one back it was too late and Spurs were through to their fifth FA Cup Final, where they met Chelsea. The first all-London Final is reported in Matches to Remember.

Three FA Cups in seven years was a remarkable achievement and playing in every one of those Finals was Dave Mackay. For many the Scot had been written off after having his leg broken at Old Trafford in the European Cup-winners' Cup. Even more had decided his career was over when his leg was broken again in his comeback game for the reserves, but Mackay was a man who should never be written off. His mere presence inspired those around him, and there was no more fitting reward than for him to lead Spurs up Wembley's steps to collect the trophy and his third winners' medal.

The European nights of the early 60s had gone down in legend, but the legend was not enhanced with the European Cup-winners' Cup campaign of 1967–68. Leading Hadjuk Split 2–0 from the first leg in Yugoslavia, Spurs raced into a 3–0 lead by half-time in the return leg but then thought the job was done. Hadjuk pulled two goals back and even a fourth for Spurs was not the end of the scoring as the visitors grabbed a last-minute penalty. The message was clear, in European games nothing could be taken for granted, every game had to be played out to the last minute. It was not a message Spurs were to heed. They returned from Olympique Lyonnais bruised and battered after a thuggish performance from the French with a one goal deficit. Alan Mullery was sent off in the first game and suspended for the second, but Spurs still had more than enough class to ensure a safe passage to the next round. Two up at half-time, the French twice pulled a goal back, but each time Spurs scored another to maintain the advantage. They had chances to put the result beyond doubt, failed to take them and were caught by a killer blow 10 minutes from time, eventually going out on the away-goals rule.

For the next three years Spurs failed to make any sort of impression despite Nicholson's constant forays into the transfer market. The only time success looked even possible was in 1968–69 when they got to the semi-final of the Football League Cup before losing to Arsenal. All the time football was changing, avoiding defeat all that mattered and entertainment way down the list of priorities. Hard work and rigid systems now took over, individual brilliance a luxury few clubs could afford. It was not the way Nicholson was prepared to go. He recognised Spurs would have to adapt, but he was not prepared to give up the traditions that had made Spurs a great club. Spurs' players would have to work as hard as their opponents and then let their superior skills come to the fore.

Matters came to a head in January 1970 when Spurs were beaten by a Crystal Palace side short on skill but full of commitment in the FA Cup. It was a gutless performance by Spurs and not one Nicholson could tolerate. He wielded the axe, dropping established stars Jimmy Greaves, Alan Gilzean, Joe Kinnear and Cyril Knowles and replacing them with hungry youngsters, not as talented but prepared to give their all. The lesson learned, Gilzean, Kinnear and Knowles recovered their places and went on to help the club lift more trophies. Only Greaves did not get his place back, the greatest goalscorer Spurs have had departing for West Ham United in a deal that saw Martin Peters, one of the new breed of skilful, hard-working footballers, joining Spurs.

Peters was not a player who grabbed attention on the pitch. It was only as events were analysed that his contribution became apparent, and it was realised how much work he put in and how much he brought out the best in other players. That was particularly the case with Martin Chivers, who blossomed into the country's best centre-forward under the subtle promptings of Peters and the more noticeable urgings of Alan Mullery and Steve Perryman.

The true measure of a team has always been how well it performs in the marathon of a Football League campaign, how it picks up points consistently, perhaps not always playing to its best but grinding out results week after week. Spurs found it difficult to maintain a solid level of performance week in, week out, but when it came to Cup ties they always managed to raise their game.

Spurs had no time for the Football League Cup when it was first introduced, but as the competition gained credibility, first with the Final moving to Wembley, then with automatic entry to the UEFA Cup for the winners, it began to offer a realistic route to further glory.

In 1970–71 Spurs beat Swansea City, Sheffield United, West Bromwich Albion and Coventry City to reach the semi-final, where they were drawn against Bristol City. A 1–1 draw at Ashton Gate should have been enough to see Spurs through to the Final, but at White Hart Lane the Second Division strugglers played well above their lowly status, and it was only extra-time goals from Chivers and Jimmy Pearce that saw off their brave challenge. Their opponents at Wembley were Aston Villa, Third Division conquerors of Manchester United in the other semi-final. Spurs should have been hot favourites but already two Third Division clubs had won the trophy at Wembley, Queen's Park Rangers in 1967 and Swindon Town in 1969, both overcoming First Division opposition. Spurs did not join their number, as reported in Matches to Remember.

There were two months between beating Bristol City and meeting Aston Villa, and in that time Spurs had made steady progress towards another Wembley outing. In the FA Cup they had disposed of Sheffield Wednesday, Carlisle United and Nottingham Forest. After beating Villa they went to Anfield in the sixth round and took Liverpool back to White Hart Lane having not lost an FA Cup replay at home for 60 years. That record fell thanks to an inspired performance from Liverpool 'keeper Ray Clemence.

Football League Cup winners, FA Cup quarter-finalists and third in the League, all-in-all 1970–71 was a good season but the next, at least from the Cup angle, was to be even better. Spurs again reached the sixth round of the FA Cup, fell one game short of Wembley in the Football League Cup but found success in the UEFA Cup.

The Icelandic outfit Keflavik were brushed aside 15–1 on aggregate before Spurs accounted for Nantes, Rapid Bucharest and Unizale Textile Arad to face AC Milan in the semi-final. Success in so many competitions caused the inevitable fixture chaos and injury problems. Spurs were so short of men for the first leg meeting with the Italians that Nicholson was forced to recall Mullery from a loan spell with Fulham. After the match

Spurs against Liverpool, 4 September 1971. It looks as if the ball is going in but in fact Ray Clemence has pulled off another superb save to deny Martin Chivers and Alan Gilzean.

Spurs' playing resources were depleted even more as Milan showed the most cynical side of Italian football. From the start their only concern was to defend, and if they could injure a few opponents in doing so, so much the better. Spurs were taught every trick in the book and matters only got worse after Milan had taken a shock lead through Romeo Benetti. How Spurs managed to keep their cool was almost as big a mystery as where they might get a goal from. Try as they might there seemed no way through, but, just as despair was about to set in, up stepped Steve Perryman, not once but twice, to fire home from the edge of the area.

For Spurs to make the Final they would have to produce their finest European display. That they did was largely down to Mullery. In the first leg he gave a majestic performance, controlling the midfield, breaking up the rare Italian advances and always urging Spurs forward. In the second leg he raised himself to even greater heights, cracking home from 20 yards after only seven minutes and then masterminding a fantastic rearguard action breached only by a penalty 20 minutes from time. The Final with Wolverhampton Wanderers is reported in Matches to Remember.

In 1972–73 the defence of the UEFA Cup began with a 12–3 demolition of Lyn Oslo followed by victories over Olympiakos Piraeus, Red Star Belgrade and Vitoria Setúbal. Spurs lost the first leg of the semi-final with Liverpool 0–1 at Anfield, but Peters made the aggregate scores level early in the second half of the second leg, only for Steve Heighway to snatch a breakaway goal to leave Spurs needing to score twice more to go through. Peters got one 20 minutes from time, but Ray Clemence was again in outstanding form and much as Spurs bombarded the Liverpool goal they just could not get the vital third and went out on the away-goals rule.

In the FA Cup Spurs went out to Derby County in a fourth-round replay, one of the most dramatic Cup ties seen at White Hart Lane for many years. Spurs were 3–1 up with five minutes left, only for Derby to force the match into extra-time and then go on to win 5–3.

It was again the Football League Cup that kept the Spurs' honours board engraver busy. Huddersfield Town and Middlesbrough were victims in the early rounds with Liverpool overcome in a fifth-round replay that started in a torrential downpour. The rain lasted for 15 minutes but in that time Spurs gave a scintillating exhibition of football to race into a three-goal lead Liverpool were never going to retrieve. In the semi-final Wolves had the opportunity to avenge their UEFA Cup defeat of the previous season, but, just like in the UEFA Cup, Spurs did the hard work by winning the first leg at Molineux. Although Wolves took the return leg to extra-time, Chivers got the clincher. The Final with Norwich City, reported in Matches to Remember, was not one of Wembley's most memorable occasions.

Winning the Football League Cup meant Spurs again qualified for the UEFA Cup and enhanced their reputation as a Cup side. Winning a Cup had now become their only realistic hope of qualifying for Europe. In the League, performances had steadily declined and there might have been dark mutterings around White Hart Lane had the Cup runs not provided consolation. That seemed unlikely to continue in 1973–74 with early exits in the FA and Football League Cups to Leicester City and Queen's Park Rangers, but there was still the UEFA Cup.

Grasshoppers, Aberdeen, Dinamo Tbilisi, IFC Cologne and Lokomotive Leipzig were all defeated but none of them too convincingly. Spurs were not the power they had been and Feyenoord, newly-crowned Dutch champions, were by no means an easy proposition in the Final. In all the previous rounds Spurs had the advantage of being drawn away in the first leg. They knew what they would have to do in the second and could rely upon the crowd to help them do it. Spurs had to play the first leg of the Final at White Hart Lane. They pushed Feyenoord back from the first whistle, but it was six minutes before the break when Mike England glanced home a Ray Evans free-kick. The celebrations had hardly subsided when Wim van Hanegem curled a 20-yard free-kick round the wall for an equaliser. The confidence could be seen to drain from Spurs. The Dutch began to control the game and there was more than a slice of luck when Spurs got back in front on the hour mark. A hopeful free-kick into the visitors' penalty box intended for England's head was sliced into his own net by Joop van Daele. Spurs should have increased their lead, but as the game drew to a close they looked to have settled for taking a one-goal lead to Rotterdam, only for Theo de Jong to grab an equaliser with four minutes left.

If Spurs were to lift the trophy they would have to produce a performance every bit as good as when they won the European Cup-winners' Cup in Rotterdam 21 years before. They started confidently enough, but midway through the first half what appeared to be a good goal by Chris McGrath was disallowed for offside. The Spurs players accepted the decision, but up on the terraces mayhem broke out. The rival supporters were separated by little more than flimsy fencing and as fighting broke out attention was diverted from what was happening on the pitch. When baton-welding police decided to intervene, a riot

With a little help from Keith Osgood, John Duncan climbs above Phil Thompson and John Toshack to reach a corner on 22 March 1975. Spurs lost 0–2 but a final game defeat of Leeds United saw them retain their First Division place.

developed and many in the crowd were so engrossed in watching that they barely noticed Wim Rijsbergen put Feyenoord ahead in the 42nd minute. The fighting continued during the break with Bill Nicholson called from the dressing room to appeal to the Spurs fans for calm. It did little good. Most of the Spurs support had been cleared from the ground by the time Peter Ressel got the decisive second for Feyenoord.

The rioting led to UEFA ordering Spurs to play their next two home European games at least 250 kilometres from White Hart Lane. It was not a penalty that would have any immediate effect because the defeat against Feyenoord meant Spurs had not qualified for Europe.

Bill Nicholson had been finding it hard to cope with the changing face of football. A firm believer in entertaining, loyalty and playing the game for its own sake, he had become disenchanted with the attitude of players, the press and the authorities. He knew Spurs needed a transformation if they were to retain their place in football's elite, but he would not be party to the illegal activities that were threatening to destroy the game he loved. The trouble in Rotterdam made Nicholson wonder whether it was really all worthwhile. When Spurs opened 1974–75 with four straight defeats he decided it was not and resigned. It was a sad end to a truly brilliant era made all the sadder by the way the Spurs directors, who had basked in the glory Nicholson worked so hard to achieve, just said thank you and waved him on his way.

Nicholson wanted Danny Blanchflower to succeed him, but the directors, perhaps conscious of how Matt Busby's shadow continued to hang over Manchester United, had other ideas. They appointed Terry Neill, best known as the former captain of Arsenal. It was not a decision that met with much approval on the terraces or in the dressing room. Neill seemed determined to make his mark by discarding those who had served Spurs, and Nicholson, so well and bringing in his own men. The problem was his men were not as good as those he allowed to leave. It was only when Neill turned to 'the old guard' that escaping relegation looked possible, but it took a last match defeat of Leeds United to make Spurs safe. Results improved in 1976–77, and Spurs even reached the semi-final of the Football League Cup, but performances were still poor and the future seemed more likely to be concerned with avoiding the drop than challenging at the top. When Arsenal's double-winning manager Bertie Mee resigned in June 1976, it was with almost embarrassing haste that Neill quit Spurs to replace Mee.

A brave man was needed to follow Neill, and, while managing Spurs was still one of the most prestigious jobs in the game, there seemed few of those around. The task was given to first-team coach Keith Burkinshaw, a run-of-the-mill lower Division player whose only managerial experience had been gained with Workington and Scunthorpe United but who had the players' support. He showed he had no fear by immediately persuading Nicholson to return as consultant. Even with Nicholson's help there was little Burkinshaw could do to arrest the decline that had set in at White Hart Lane. Spurs were simply not good enough for the top flight, and at the end of his first season in charge they were relegated.

The same fate had befallen Manchester United three years earlier. They had bounced back at the first attempt, using their year in the Second Division to rebuild and develop a team that was to take them to further honours. It was hoped Spurs could do the same. They did, but it was only a goalless draw at Southampton in the last game of the season that saw them pip Brighton & Hove Albion for the third promotion place on goal difference. Getting back to the First Division was what mattered most, but Burkinshaw had achieved that playing football in the best traditions of Tottenham Hotspur, football that excited and gave free rein to talented individuals such as Glenn Hoddle and Neil McNab.

Taking Spurs back to the First Division was only the start for Burkinshaw. For him it was no good for Spurs to simply make up the numbers, he was determined to rediscover the Glory Days, to win trophies and rediscover Spurs' fame, not for what they had done but for what they were doing now. To do that Spurs needed the best players available and for Burkinshaw that did not simply mean the best players in the country, but the best in the world. Barely had the 1978 World Cup come to an end than Burkinshaw had the opportunity to turn his thoughts into deeds. Osvaldo Ardiles, midfield star of Argentina's winning team, was available and wanted to play in England. Burkinshaw wasted no time jetting to Buenos Aires. He returned with not only Ardiles but also Ricardo Villa, a bit-part player in the World Cup but reckoned by many to be even better than Ardiles. At just over £700,000 the signing of the two Argentines was a bargain and, if not immediately, heralded the dawn of a new and glorious era for Spurs.

Villa did not find it easy adapting to English football, but Ardiles fitted in perfectly, linking with Hoddle to form one of the most exciting and attractive midfields in the game. Alone they could not turn Spurs into challengers for the big prizes but slowly Burkinshaw began to assemble a squad that could best utilise their unique talents. The big money signings of Garth Crooks and Steve Archibald meant Spurs now had two lightning-quick strikers to take advantage of the chances Ardiles and Hoddle created, but it was the development of two bargain signings from non-League football, Graham Roberts and Tony Galvin, that proved the turning point.

Roberts made his breakthrough in December 1980. Galvin's, due to Ardiles playing for Argentina in the Gold Cup, came the following month in the FA Cup third-round meeting with Queen's Park Rangers. Hull City, Coventry City and Exeter City were all defeated at White Hart Lane, putting Spurs through to a semi-final meeting at Hillsborough with Wolverhampton Wanderers. Archibald gave Spurs an early lead but Wolves were quickly back on level terms through Kenny Hibbitt. Spurs controlled the first half, led at the interval thanks to a Hoddle free-kick, easily repelled Wolves' attacks in the second half and seemed through to the Final when referee Clive Thomas intervened. With only 20 seconds remaining, Hoddle tackled Hibbitt on the edge of the box and clearly won the ball. Not so, decided Thomas. Hoddle had fouled Hibbitt and more than that he had done so in the penalty area. Thomas was the only person in the ground who thought so,

Ossie Ardiles races clear of his marker in the match against Aston Villa on 26 April 1980.

Steve Archibald holds off Aston Villa's Kenny Swain as Spurs take another step towards a Wembley return by beating Villa 1–0 on 13 February 1982.

but his was the decision that mattered. Willie Carr put the spot-kick away, and although 30 minutes extra-time were played a winner never seemed likely. If Spurs made a mistake in the first game it was to funnel back and allow Wolves to come at them in the second half. The same mistake would not be made in the Highbury replay. Spurs controlled the game for practically the entire 90 minutes, two goals from Crooks and a 30-yard rocket from Villa nothing more than Spurs deserved.

The build-up to the Final against Manchester City was dominated by tales of Ardiles's desire to appear in an FA Cup Final. City did their best, particularly in the first game, to ruin his big day, but in the end his dream was realised thanks to his great pal Ricky Villa, as reported in Matches to Remember.

Reinforced by the signings of Ray Clemence and Paul Price, Spurs embarked on their centenary season of 1981–82 with realistic hopes of lifting at least one of the four trophies available to them. The Football League remained the priority but to the two domestic Cups Spurs could again add the European Cup-winners' Cup, and they did not have to play their first two home games away from White Hart Lane. The penalty imposed after the Rotterdam troubles of 1974 had been lifted as part of UEFA's 25th anniversary amnesty.

The European campaign began with victories over Ajax, Dundalk and Eintracht Frankfurt but culminated in defeat at the hands of Barcelona. The first leg of the semi-final witnessed one of the most brutal displays by a foreign team at White Hart Lane. The Spaniards had no interest in playing football, their only objective was not to concede. Using every trick in the book, they got their reward with a 1–1 draw, a terrible blunder by Clemence gifting them a lead only retrieved in the dying seconds by Roberts. In the second leg Barcelona showed no desire to attack, content to sit back on the away goal and secure their place in the Final already booked for their own Nou Camp stadium. That they pinched a goal early in the second half did them no credit.

Spurs went one step further in the Football League Cup, overcoming Manchester United, Wrexham, Fulham, Nottingham Forest and West Bromwich Albion to meet Liverpool at Wembley in what was now renamed the Milk Cup. After a 10th-minute goal from Archibald, Spurs held out until three minutes from time before Ronnie Whelan equalised. The pressure exerted by Liverpool had its effect in extra-time. Spurs rarely threatened and conceded two more goals to sample defeat for the first time in a major domestic Cup Final.

Spurs had maintained a position near the top of the League, but the sheer volume of Cup games, injuries and inexperienced reserves eventually took its toll, leaving them fourth but at least qualified for the UEFA Cup. As the final month of the season approached, they were left with only the FA Cup to play for. They beat Arsenal, Leeds United, Aston Villa, Chelsea and Leicester City to reach the Final and expected Ossie Ardiles to be released from Argentina's World Cup preparations for the meeting with Queen's Park Rangers. Unfortunately the Falklands War intervened. Ardiles was unable to return, and when it came to the day Burkinshaw decided it would not be right to risk Ricky Villa before a worldwide audience. The two games with Rangers are reported in Matches to Remember.

Over two years Burkinshaw's team, built around Hoddle and Ardiles, had delivered entertainment and success. It was a considerable blow when Ardiles decided he could not return to England after the events in the South Atlantic, but it was made all the worse when Hoddle fell victim to injury. The team was badly affected, suffering early exits from the European Cup-winners' Cup, FA Cup and Milk Cup. Even finishing high enough in the League to qualify for Europe again seemed unlikely, until a run of nine victories in the last 12 games secured a place in the UEFA Cup.

Burkinshaw had not been helped by events off the pitch. Rebuilding the West Stand at White Hart Lane cost far more than expected, and while Spurs were not in serious financial difficulty, there was a lack of funds to buy players. The club was controlled by the Wale family, large but not majority shareholders. Chairman Sidney Wale was opposed to the rebuilding plans, and when his views were ignored he resigned. The financial problems and Wale's departure combined to put Spurs at the forefront of big changes in English football.

By and large football clubs had been the plaything of rich men prepared to bankroll a club for the local kudos, knowing that when they wanted to sell a ready buyer would appear. Businessmen were now eyeing up football, regarding it as an opportunity to make money and willing to take a chance.

As a private company, the Spurs directors had the power to veto the transfer of any shares, thus ensuring they remained in control. What they could not prevent was the sale of shares and with them vital voting rights. Irving Scholar, a Monte Carlo-based millionaire property developer and long-time Spurs fan, saw his chance and with the support of another property developer, Paul Bobroff, made his move. The coup was bloodless, and by December 1982 Scholar and his colleagues were in control. They had big plans for the club, looking to raise money on the Stock Exchange and make it the cornerstone of a leisure empire. In October 1983 £3.8 million was raised as Tottenham Hotspur plc was successfully floated on the Stock Exchange, the first football club to do so.

The new regime had its own ideas on how a football club should be run, and they were very different to what Keith Burkinshaw had been used to. As the season progressed, it became clear the differences were incompatible and a parting of the ways was inevitable. In April 1984 it was announced Burkinshaw would be leaving at the end of the season. By then Spurs were through to the semi-final of the UEFA Cup, having knocked out Drogheda United, Ajax, Bayern Munich and Austria Vienna. There could be no more fitting tribute to Burkinshaw than to win the trophy and that provided the perfect incentive for Spurs to overcome Hadjuk Split and set up a Final against Anderlecht. The two legs of the Final are reported in Matches to Remember and provided a truly dramatic climax to Burkinshaw's reign. The football may not have been of the free-flowing style Burkinshaw favoured, but it provided another glorious chapter in Spurs' history.

Clive Allen celebrates scoring against his former club Queen's Park Rangers at White Hart Lane on 15 September 1984.

Burkinshaw's replacement was not one of the many big names bandied about but a relative unknown as his assistant and former youth-team coach, Peter Shreeves. Despite early exits from the domestic Cups, his time in charge started well with Spurs and Everton leading the League. Progress was also made in the UEFA Cup with SC Braga, Brugge and Bohemians of Prague defeated to give Spurs a fourth-round meeting with Real Madrid. The Spaniards were not the team they had been but still the most attractive name in European football and, as it transpired, too strong for Spurs. In the first leg at White Hart Lane an own-goal by Perryman was all it took for Spurs to lose their record of never being beaten at home in a European game, and in the second leg Perryman was sent off as Spurs tried everything to retrieve the deficit but had to be content with just avoiding defeat. After surrendering the trophy injuries began to hit, and Spurs had to be content with third place in the League.

Shreeves's second season saw a fall off in performances and results. No impression was made in the FA or Milk Cups and a drop to 10th in the League was not good enough for a board that not only wanted success as much as the fans but also had shareholders to answer to. Shreeves was replaced by David Pleat, a manager who had proved at Luton Town that he could produce good, attractive football with limited resources.

At Spurs he found financial muscle and quickly set about reshaping the squad he inherited. Early success in the League could not be maintained as progress in the Cups again caused a backlog of fixtures that just proved too much to handle. Still, third place was not to be sniffed at and the Cups again promised some tangible reward for the season's efforts. With Clive Allen the sole striker in front of a fluid, attack-minded midfield, Spurs reached the semi-final of the Littlewoods Cup before going out to Arsenal in a replay. In the FA Cup they went one step further, seeing off Scunthorpe United, Crystal Palace, Newcastle United, Wimbledon and Watford on the road to Wembley and a meeting with Coventry City.

It was Coventry's first major Cup Final. For Spurs it was their eighth in the FA Cup alone. The match proved to be one of the best Finals ever. Spurs took the lead in the second minute when Allen nodded home Chris Waddle's near-post cross. It was his 49th goal of the season. Only seven minutes later Coventry were level as Dave Bennett bundled the ball home, but five minutes before the break Gary Mabbutt got on the end of a Hoddle free-kick to give Spurs a half-time lead. The game had already produced some superb flowing football, but the second half was to be even better. Both teams played with a freedom usually missing in such big games as play ebbed and flowed. Coventry seemed to have a particularly cavalier attitude, perhaps accepting the age-old advice to just go out and enjoy themselves, and fully deserved their equaliser from Keith Houchen's diving header on the hour mark. Both teams had chances to grab the winner, but when the decisive goal finally came it was another example of how cruel football can be. As Lloyd McGrath broke down the right, his forwards were well covered, but when Mabbutt stuck out a leg to clear the near-post cross, the ball struck his thigh, ballooned over Clemence and finished in the far corner of the net.

Hoddle made his last appearance for Spurs in the Final. After 12 fantastic years he decided to test himself on the continent with Monaco. It was always going to be difficult to replace the man around whom the team had revolved for so long, but matters were made worse with the 1987–88 season only a couple of months old when Pleat departed. Allegations about his private life were first raised in the summer, but when they re-surfaced his position became untenable.

The obvious replacement was Terry Venables who had just left Barcelona having taken them to the Spanish title and European Cup Final. He quickly accepted the position but was unable to take up the post immediately. While his arrival was awaited, the team lost all sense

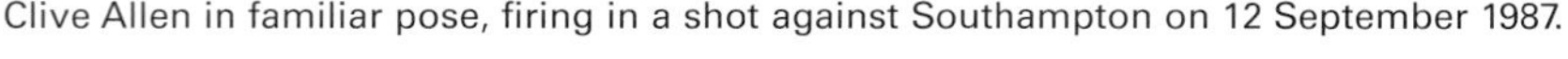
Clive Allen in familiar pose, firing in a shot against Southampton on 12 September 1987.

of direction and the season rapidly deteriorated, culminating in defeat at Third Division Port Vale in the FA Cup.

Venables began to assemble the players he wanted in the summer of 1988, splashing out £2 million for both Paul Gascoigne and Paul Stewart. Gascoigne made an immediate impact, lifting the club not only with his ability but also his sense of fun and obvious love of the game. As a settled squad began to take shape, hopes for the future rose, never more so than when Gary Lineker was signed in June 1989. The prospect of Lineker finishing off the approach work of Gascoigne and Waddle was enough to give any defence the jitters, but it was not to be. Olympique Marseille offered £4.25 million for Waddle. Although a vast sum, Spurs were a club known for buying not selling, so it was more than a surprise when they announced it was an offer too good to refuse. Not so surprising was that Spurs found it difficult to compensate for the loss of such a key player. All the pre-season promise soon evaporated, and it was only a late run that took Spurs to third in the League.

Spurs were remarkably quiet on the transfer front in the summer of 1990, and only a couple of weeks into the new season the *The Sunday Times* revealed why. Spurs were in deep financial trouble. £20 million in debt, the grand plans on flotation that ancillary businesses would provide money for investment in the football club had backfired. It was the football club that was keeping the other businesses afloat. Rumours abounded; the banks were going to pull the plug and send Spurs to the wall, the soon to be disgraced publishing magnate Robert Maxwell was going to buy the club, Gascoigne, Lineker and anyone else worth a few bob would be sold. As speculation grew, results were affected and the situation grew increasingly desperate.

The situation called for a knight in shining armour to ride to the rescue, but who would want to and on what terms? Qualifying for Europe might attract someone prepared to take a risk, but Spurs were not going to win the League. Their only hope was the FA Cup. Form-wise, success in the competition seemed a forlorn hope, but the year did end in '1' and that had always been good to Spurs in the past – 1901, 1921, 1951, 1961, 1971, 1981 had all seen Spurs collect one trophy or another.

Spurs began their FA Cup campaign with a 1–0 win at Blackpool, but Gascoigne was injured. Wrapped in cotton wool he continued to play, proving the hero in victories over Oxford United, Portsmouth and Notts County, but treatment could not be left any longer. He went for an operation, and it became a question of whether he could recover in time for the semi-final meeting with Arsenal, League leaders and hot favourites to secure their second double. It was a match so many people wanted to attend that for the first time an FA Cup semi-final was staged at Wembley.

Gascoigne took his place against Arsenal, far from fit but an inspiration simply by being on the field. He knew he could not last the full 90 minutes, but even if he was only able to play for a short time, he was going to make every second count. Five minutes had elapsed when Spurs were awarded a free-kick 30 yards out. There were few with the audacity, let alone the ability, to beat David Seaman from that distance, but Gascoigne was one of them. As his shot flew past the England 'keeper, hope became belief. Five minutes later Gascoigne linked with Paul Allen to set up a goal for Lineker. Belief now became conviction. Arsenal pulled one back before half-time, but Lineker added another in the second half. Conviction

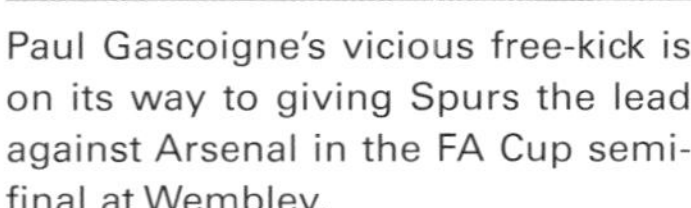
Paul Gascoigne's vicious free-kick is on its way to giving Spurs the lead against Arsenal in the FA Cup semi-final at Wembley.

Minutes later Gary Lineker pokes out a leg to put Spurs two up.

now became reality. The dream that Spurs might still be saved remained. Everything now depended on beating Nottingham Forest in the Final. Gascoigne would be available but a deal had already been done to sell him to Lazio. His last appearance for Spurs, and arguably his most important, is reported in Matches to Remember.

Securing the trophy against all the odds gave everyone connected with Spurs an immediate lift, but the cold light of day soon brought people back to earth. Spurs may have won the Cup, but Gascoigne had suffered a serious cruciate ligament injury and his

Paul Gascoigne's 30-yard free-kick rockets into the net after only five minutes of the first FA Cup semi-final to be staged at Wembley on 14 April 1991.

£8.5 million transfer to Lazio was put on ice. No deal would be completed until he had proved his fitness and then only at a reduced price.

Ever since Spurs' money problems first surfaced, Venables had been trying to put together a rescue package. He did not have the funds to take over the club himself, but he did have a top-class reputation in football and was prepared to risk his own money if the right 'partner' could be found. When a partner did appear it was something of a surprise. Alan Sugar, the electronics magnate, was well-known as a self-made multi-millionaire, but he was not regarded as someone who had even the slightest interest in the national game. The Venables–Sugar partnership was labelled 'The Dream Ticket'. It soon became 'The Nightmare Union'.

Initially the pairing appeared to work well, Sugar, the chairman, looking after the finances, while Venables, the chief executive, took care of the football side. It was too much to expect Venables to also handle team affairs so Peter Shreeves was appointed first-team coach on a one-year contract. It was a difficult role for Shreeves. Money was found to sign Gordon Durie, but he was expected to work with Venables's players and, even then, without the best of them, Gascoigne. It would have been unfair to expect too much from Shreeves. Spurs did reach the Rumbelows League Cup semi-final before going out to Nottingham Forest, but he did little to help his cause when, with Spurs slipping towards the relegation dogfight, he adopted long-ball tactics so alien to Spurs' traditions. They were not good enough to prevent Spurs tumbling out of the European Cup-winners' Cup in the third round to Feyenoord but at least ensured Spurs retained a place in the top flight for the start of the FA Premiership.

Shreeves departed after 12 months with Doug Livermore and Ray Clemence appointed first-team coaches and Venables resuming control of team affairs. Sugar had done a fine job in turning round the financial situation, and with Gascoigne's move to Italy completed and Lineker departing for Japan Venables found himself with the funds to start rebuilding the team. Darren Anderton and Teddy Sheringham were signed and Spurs again reached the FA Cup semi-final, Arsenal taking revenge for their defeat at the same stage two years earlier. In the League Spurs climbed to eighth and the future was viewed with optimism but, as so often with Spurs, those hopes were to be shattered. On the eve of the Cup Final Venables was sacked by Sugar amid allegations of bungs and backhanders.

With claims and counterclaims flying around, litigation hogging the headlines and both sides claiming they were in the right, the club was once again thrown into turmoil. Ossie Ardiles was lured from West Bromwich Albion as manager but took on a near-impossible job. With both manoeuvring for position the Sugar–Venables feud rumbled on, the players were unhappy and to cap it all the FA began an investigation into allegations Sugar had made against Venables. The 1993–94 season did not start too badly, but when Sheringham was injured results took a turn for the worse. With the problems he faced it is difficult to criticise Ardiles, but it was only in the last but one match of the season that Spurs made sure they would not finish in a relegation spot.

Venables was eventually forced to concede defeat in his battle with Sugar. It had cost both men dearly, but the club would have paid an even greater penalty had it not been for Sugar's tenacity and refusal to accept what he considered an injustice. The FA's investigation, with which Sugar co-operated fully, resulted in charges being laid against Spurs that during the Scholar/Venables era illegal payments had been made to players. Sugar did not fight the charges, as he had provided much of the evidence himself, but was shocked when the FA sanctions of a £600,000 fine, 12 point deduction for the 1994–95 season and exclusion from the FA Cup were announced. It was a vicious penalty out of all proportion to the charges and not only a kick in the teeth for honesty and openness but also ignored the fact that those individuals who had been responsible for the misdemeanours had long since departed. Four clubs were to be relegated at the end of the season, and the penalty guaranteed Spurs would be one of them.

Spurs' appeal saw the points deduction reduced to six, the fine increased to £1.5 million and the FA Cup ban remained. It was not a decision Sugar could accept. He would resort to the courts if necessary but in the meantime reinforced his commitment to Spurs by making the money available to sign the Romanian World Cup stars Ilie Dumitrescu and Gica Popescu, and Germany's Jürgen Klinsmann, the world's number-one striker.

With the arrival of three such talented players, Ardiles had the most potent attacking force a manager could ask for. Darren Anderton, Nick Barmby and Dumitrescu were all goal makers as well as scorers, while Sheringham and Klinsmann were the perfect strike partnership. Ardiles knew Spurs' traditions demanded football that was exciting to watch. That meant the emphasis had to be on attack, but he went too far and forgot that football is also about defending. For two months Spurs fans watched some of the most breathtaking football, but all too often it was the opposition who reaped the benefit of Ardiles's attacking plans. A 2–5 defeat at Manchester City was followed by a 1–3 reverse that saw Notts County turf Spurs out of the Coca-Cola Cup and the more vociferous Spurs fans were calling for Ardiles to go. Sugar gave in to their demands, a decision he later admitted was wrong. Steve Perryman, Ardiles's assistant, took charge of the team for one game before he too was sacked as the manager's job went to former England captain Gerry Francis.

Like David Pleat, Francis had built his reputation at small clubs, Bristol Rovers and Queen's Park Rangers, but unlike Pleat he had based success on a rigid system in which each player had a job to do, and if they failed to do it they would be replaced. It was not difficult for any coach to recognise that Spurs needed to tighten up defensively. Francis did that by replacing Dumitrescu with David Howells. The improvement was immediate, and while Spurs were not dazzling all and sundry with the brilliance of their football, they were still capable of turning it on, but more importantly they were getting results.

It was not only on the pitch that life got better for Spurs. Sugar's refusal to accept the verdict of the FA's Appeals Committee resulted in an arbitration panel reviewing the decision. It decided the FA had gone outside its powers in deducting points and banning Spurs from the FA Cup. The fine remained, but the other penalties were reversed. The decision came just in time for the third round of the FA Cup, and for a while it looked as if Spurs would rub salt into the FA's wounds, but in the semi-final they were overwhelmed by Everton.

A season that began with relegation a certainty ended with Spurs just missing out on a UEFA Cup spot, but even before the season closed they were to suffer another setback. Klinsmann's partnership with Sheringham had proved a great success. The German was the nucleus around which next season's title challenge would be based, but it was not going to be the Premiership title he aimed for. He wanted another tilt at the Bundeslegia and invoked a clause in his contract that allowed him to join Bayern Munich. With Popescu and Barmby also departing, a promising squad was suddenly weakened.

1995–96 and 1996–97 proved to be miserable seasons, not only in terms of results but also in the quality of football produced. While Newcastle United, Manchester United, even Arsenal, were playing the type of football for which Spurs were renowned, Spurs were going backwards. Flair and imagination were replaced by functionality, exciting players by hard workers, youngsters of potential by men who had done a job for Francis in the past but were now living off past glories. Passing and movement were eschewed in favour of long balls played into space in the hope willing runners could make something of them. Avoiding defeat became the height of ambition, victory welcome but more hoped for than planned. The Bosman decision promised an influx of foreign talent but, while other clubs were quick to seize the opportunities it offered, Sugar was not going to waste his money on 'Carlos Kickaballs'.

When Teddy Sheringham, frustrated by Francis's 'direct' style, packed his bags for Manchester United, the voices of discontent grew. As if to pacify them, Francis signed David Ginola, a charismatic Frenchman and darling of Kevin Keegan's exciting Newcastle team, and Les Ferdinand, another Francis old boy but one of the most potent strikers in the game. Ginola proved an instant hit but Ferdinand was soon struck by injury. As Spurs struggled the disquiet increased, and Francis resigned.

For a man reluctant to buy foreign players, it was surprising Sugar should look abroad for the man to revive Spurs' flagging fortunes. Even more surprising was that he should entrust the job to a little-known coach from Switzerland. Christian Gross had been successful with Grasshoppers Zurich, but he was unheard of in England and his limited English was instantly ridiculed by the media. Appointed Head Coach rather than manager, he was under pressure from day one with stories the players had no respect for him, and he had little say in the signing of players. He certainly worked hard, but it would have taken a miracle run to the top of the League for Gross to be accepted and given the opportunity to make a success of the job. He endured a miserable 10 months at White Hart Lane before Sugar spared him further pain by relieving him of his job. David Pleat had returned to Spurs as director of football and was given temporary control of the team while the hunt began for a new coach.

Sugar had come in for a lot of flak since his fallout with Venables, some of it merited, much of it not. He was a businessman, not a football man, and never understood the unique nature of the football industry. Regarded by many as an opportunist who had only become involved with Spurs because of the benefits it could bring his other businesses, he was not the most approachable of people, could be unnecessarily rude and would certainly have benefitted from a little PR training. Criticism was not something he took well, and often he would vent his anger with attacks on the football authorities, players and supporters and threaten to sell the club to anyone who would pay the price he wanted.

For many the appointment of Gross's successor was seen as a sign Sugar was about to go, but before leaving he would get revenge on those who had been most critical of him: the supporters.

George Graham was a man who would always be associated with Arsenal. A member of their double-winning team of 1971, he had won six major trophies as manager at Highbury before a 'bungs' scandal saw him banned from the game for a year. Having sacked Venables for alleged financial chicanery, hypocritical was a word that sprang quickly to mind. Worse than that, though, was that Graham was perceived as the arch-disciple of defensive football, a man whose team would grind out results with a sterile brand of football that even bored his own club's fans. If Sugar hoped to divide Spurs fans, then Graham's appointment certainly succeeded.

To have any hope of acceptance, Graham had to make an immediate impression, preferably by winning a trophy and not ditching David Ginola. The French ace was always regarded as an exciting talent, but he was an entertainer and hardly renowned for grafting. The antithesis of the type of player Graham favoured, Ginola would have his work cut out to impress Graham, but equally Graham would have little chance of winning over the fans if he discarded their favourite.

The Worthington Cup, devalued by the growth of European football and many clubs just fielding their reserve sides, always provided Graham's best hope. Spurs had already got past Brentford by the time Graham took over and had little difficulty seeing off Northampton Town, a weak Liverpool team and a Manchester United reserve team. Wimbledon proved much sterner opposition in the semi-final, with a Steffen Iversen goal all that divided the sides over two legs. Leicester City provided the opposition for Spurs' last visit to the soon-to-be-demolished Wembley. Save for the result, the match, reported in Matches to Remember, was not one to live long in the memory, but the victory it provided at least went some way to quietening those who still opposed Graham's appointment. Those detractors may have been silenced even more had the referee penalised a blatant handball by Newcastle United's Nikos Dabizas in the FA Cup semi-final at Old Trafford, but he did not and Newcastle went on to secure the victory they deserved in extra-time.

Apart from Steffen Freund, a midfield destroyer who strangely went on to become a cult figure with the fans, the team that won the Worthington Cup had all been with Spurs when Graham took over. It included Ginola, who seemed determined to show Graham he was well worth his place. Ginola performed so well throughout the season that he was voted Player of the Year by both the Footballer Writers' and Professional Footballers Associations.

A trophy in his first season may have lifted some of the pressure on Graham, but it was to prove short-lived. The 1999–2000 season saw Spurs going backwards in more ways than one. Beaten by First Division Fulham in the Worthington Cup, humiliated by Newcastle United in the FA Cup and little more than making up the numbers in the Premier League, even the UEFA Cup proved a miserable disappointment. After beating Zimbru Chisinau 3–0 in the first-round first leg, Spurs ground out a boring and embarrassing goalless draw in the second leg. In the second round against IFC Kaiserslautern an Iversen penalty gave Spurs a first-leg lead, but instead of trying to snatch a crucial away goal in the second, Graham left out Ginola and concentrated on preventing the Germans from scoring. An ultra-defensive performance looked like succeeding until two goals in the last two minutes saw them out of the competition.

The fragile relationship between Graham and the fans was put under fresh strain in the summer of 2000 when Ginola left for Aston Villa, with the anger only partially placated by the signing of Sergei Rebrov for £11 million. Rebrov was a class act, but at Dynamo Kiev he played just behind Andrei Shevchenko. At Spurs he was expected to fulfil an out-and-out striker's role, and in a team that concentrated on defence, he found it difficult to adapt. He was not helped by poor results, with Spurs again dumped out of the Worthington Cup by a First Division side, this time at home to Birmingham City, and mid-table was the best Spurs could hope for in the League.

When it was announced that Sugar, after months of speculation, had finally agreed to sell a controlling interest in Spurs to ENIC, an investment company funded by Bahamas-based billionaire, Joe Louis, time seemed to be running out for Graham. When Spurs found themselves two down at Charlton Athletic in the FA Cup fourth round it looked to have expired, but a remarkable turnaround saw them score four in the second half to go through. Stockport County were beaten in round five and with a trip to West Ham United in the sixth round a year ending in '1' might still prove Graham's salvation.

During the build up to the Upton Park clash ENIC's takeover of Spurs was completed, again raising question marks over Graham's position. Daniel Levy, the man in day-to-day control of ENIC, was a life-long Spurs fan and quick to let supporters know how much ENIC appreciated the history and traditions of Spurs and how they were determined to take Spurs back to the top of the football tree, playing the style of football for which it had become famous.

When West Ham were beaten to set up a semi-final meeting with Arsenal, Graham must have thought his job was safe until at least the end of the season, but within a week he was dismissed for allegedly disclosing details of private discussion with the new board to the press.

David Pleat took temporary control of the team and was expected to remain in charge for the semi-final, but with less than a week to go Glenn Hoddle was installed as the new manager. Hoddle had done well managing Swindon Town and Chelsea and was far from a failure as England coach until the press decided to castigate him for some ill-advised comments made months earlier. Southampton gave him the opportunity to rebuild his reputation, but he was always likely to jump at the chance of returning to his spiritual home.

Hoddle had no time to get to know the players before the semi-final and there was little he could do to influence events on the day. Despite an early goal from Gary Docherty, Spurs were outclassed by their greatest rivals far more than the 1–2 scoreline would suggest, although things might have been different if Sol Campbell had not departed the game early because of injury.

Campbell's importance to Spurs could not be over-emphasised. He was approaching the peak of his career and was the defensive rock around whom Hoddle could build a team, but he never got the opportunity to do so as at the end of the season Campbell walked out on Spurs to join Arsenal.

At Chelsea Hoddle had assembled a team of experienced, quality players aiming for quick success while developing younger players for the future. He tried the same thing with Spurs, signing proven performers like Teddy Sheringham, Gus Poyet and Christian Ziege, giving a chance to Ledley King, Simon Davies, Matt Etherington and Anthony Gardner. More importantly, he got Spurs playing a passing game again, the emphasis on attack. In his first full season League results improved only slightly, but in the Cups Spurs again made their mark.

Torquay United, Tranmere Rovers, Fulham, Bolton Wanderers and Chelsea were all beaten on the way to Spurs' first visit to the Millennium Stadium for the Worthington Cup Final against Blackburn Rovers. Going into the game as favourites, Spurs held the advantage early on and should have scored, before Blackburn went ahead in the 25th minute when Ben Thatcher deflected a Keith Gillespie shot to Matt Jansen, who beat Neil Sullivan from eight yards. Eight minutes later Spurs were level as Les Ferdinand found space down the right. He cut the ball back for Ziege to side-foot home. Spurs had not played well in the first half. They had never settled into their stride, stuttering forward rather than sweeping down, attacks breaking down on the edge of the box and few real opportunities being created. They did not improve in the second period, rarely able to get past Rovers hard-working midfield, unable to find space on the flanks. Poyet did rattle the bar from 10 yards on the hour mark but that was the nearest Spurs came to a second goal. Rovers were no better than Spurs, working hard but creating little. The winning goal came with 20 minutes to go, and it was, like the game, a scrappy affair. Jansen pressed King and poked the ball through to Andy Cole, whose half-hit shot found a way past Sullivan. Only in the final minutes did Spurs look like rescuing the game, but even when Sheringham was hauled down in the box referee Graham Poll waved played on.

The FA Cup did not provide any consolation, Chelsea getting revenge for their 5–1 trouncing in the second leg of the Worthington Cup semi-final with an easy 4–0 success in the sixth round at White Hart Lane.

There was definite promise for the future, and early in the 2002–03 season Spurs even topped the table, but it did not last. The signing of Robbie Keane raised expectations, but too many of Hoddle's signings had been short term. No matter how much he tinkered with formations and personnel Spurs were ponderous, lacking in pace and someone able to produce the unexpected. It was a frustrating time, particularly as Hoddle had a man who might make the difference at the club. Sadly, he clearly had no time for club-record signing Sergei Rebrov. Never given a chance, Rebrov was marginalised before being shipped out on long-term loan to Fenerbahce in January 2003. It was terrible waste, not only of money but of talent. Burnley knocked Spurs out of the Worthington Cup in the third round, and when Southampton put them out of the FA Cup at the same stage it just became a case of getting the season over and done with as quickly as possible.

Hoddle recognised that his plan of signing experienced men to bring quick rewards had not worked, and in the summer of 2003 he set about rebuilding his squad, saying farewell to the likes of Sheringham, Ferdinand and Freund and bringing in younger blood in the shape of Helder Postiga, Bobby Zamora and Freddie Kanoute, but he was given no time to see them settle in. Four points in the first three games was just about acceptable, but three successive defeats, the last at home to Southampton, proved too much and Hoddle was sacked.

Again David Pleat was the man deputed to hold the fort while a new manager was found, but this time it was not a short-term role. Daniel Levy decided not to appoint the first man available. The board would take their time, look at the whole management structure and plan for the very long term. It did not make things easy for Pleat. He quickly ditched

Hoddle's favoured five at the back and for a while results improved, but there was always an air of uncertainty over the club, and from November 2003 onwards it was just a case of keeping things ticking over while the board finalised its plans. Early exits from both Cup competitions, a mid-table place in the League and another season had been wasted.

Come the end of the season though and Levy was ready with his new plans, a blueprint for the future based whole-heartedly on the continental system and not the halfway house that had been flirted with in the past. Frank Arnesen, the experienced and well-connected technical director of PSV Eindhoven, was appointed sporting director, responsible for all footballing aspects of the club save team selection and coaching. Those responsibilities fell on the shoulders of head coach Jacques Santini, the former French national manager, and his first assistant Martin Jol.

Between them a revolution in the playing staff was brought about, an incredible 13 new players from all over Europe being signed before the summer transfer window closed. Most of those players were destined for an immediate place in the first-team squad, Paul Robinson, Pedro Mendes, Erik Edman, Nourredine Naybet, Noe Pamarot, Thimothee Atouba, Michael Carrick and Sean Davis. Others such as Marton Fulop, Calum Davenport and Reto Ziegler were looked upon as players for the future. Despite most of the signings being foreigners the squad still had a solid British core with Ledley King, Jermain Defoe and Robbie Keane.

With so many new arrivals, and more arriving in January, 2004–05 was never going to be much more than a season for bedding in the new players, hoping to snatch a UEFA Cup spot and perhaps making an impact in the FA or Carling Cup, but hardly had the season got into full swing than Spurs were rocked by news Santini was leaving because of family problems back home in France. Levy's new structure, designed to provide continuity, was immediately put to the test. Jol was promoted to head coach with Chris Hughton his first assistant. Liverpool put Spurs out of the Carling Cup and Newcastle did the same in the FA Cup. In the League Spurs had been in the running for a UEFA Cup place but fell short by three points.

The influx of players continued in the summer of 2005 but not under the direction of Arnesen. He was tempted away by the promise of unlimited funds at Roman Abramovich's Chelsea. The focus remained on promising young English talent, Tom Huddlestone, Aaron Lennon and Jermaine Jenas, supplemented by the experience of Edgar Davids and Paul Stalteri.

Victory at Portsmouth, the first time in five years Spurs had won their opening fixture, augured well for the 2005–06 season. Finishing high enough in the League to qualify for the UEFA Cup was the realistic target but, perhaps helped by early exits from the Carling and FA Cups, the dream of a top four Champions League spot became increasingly possible as the season wore on. With Chelsea, Manchester United and Liverpool way out in front, the race for the last place developed into a battle between Spurs and Arsenal. It went to the very last day. Victory at West Ham United and no matter what Arsenal did Spurs would clinch fourth, but it was not to be. An overnight virus laid low more than half the squad. The players gave their best, of that there can be no doubt, but many of them were clearly suffering badly and West Ham won 2–1, while Arsenal secured the three points they needed.

Spurs continued their climb back to the top in 2006–07. There were no early exits from the Cup competitions as progress was made to the semi-final of the Carling Cup and the sixth round of the FA Cup, but it was the UEFA Cup that held out real promise of further honour. Spurs won their first eight matches in the competition, accounting for Slavia Prague, Besiktas, Club Bruggge, Bayer Leverkusen, Dinamo Bucharest and Braga, before losing out to holders Seville after some poor refereeing decisions had gone against them.

The burden of so many Cup games was reflected in the League as Spurs again trailed behind the Big Four of Manchester United, Chelsea, Liverpool and Arsenal, but a late season run was enough to take Spurs up to fifth spot in the table. No better than the previous season but with the Cup successes taken into account a further improvement.

Although there were suggestions Martin Jol was not seeing the players he wanted arrive, large fees were paid out to secure the likes of Darren Bent, Gareth Bale and Younes Kaboul. With young players of undoubted quality joining, Spurs again looked set to seriously challenge for a regular place at the top of English football but, not for the first time, managed to wreck all hope of that with no outside help. With qualification for the Champions League rapidly becoming a demand rather than an aspiration, defeat in the first two games of the 2007–08 season saw the panic button pushed. All of a sudden Martin Jol was not the man to take Spurs forward; he had done all he could. Further progress demanded a top managerial name, a continental manager with experience of Champions League football. Amid never-ending stories of secret approaches to some of Europe's best, results were not going to improve. When the club secretary and one of the directors were caught making a not-so-secret approach to Juande Ramos, the coach of Sevilla, Jol's position became untenable. With the fans behind him, he would not resign, but it was just a question of time before the axe fell. It did so in October 2007.

As so often the case when a new manager arrives, results picked up as Ramos settled to his task. Assisted by trusted confidantes who followed him from Spain, he soon led Spurs to mid-table security. At the same time progress was made to the Carling Cup Final and Ramos's reputation as a man who knew how to win cup competitions enhanced as Jonathan Woodgate's extra-time winner defeated Chelsea. Further cup success almost followed in the UEFA Cup. Having won the competition for the last two years with Sevilla, Ramos almost pulled off an unlikely hat-trick as Spurs gave what was probably their best performance under Ramos to recover from a 0–1 first-leg defeat at home to PSV Eindhoven in the last 16 and reverse the score-line in Holland before going out on penalties. With the Cup exploits at an end, performances and results tailed off as Spurs finished the season almost as badly as it had begun but another trophy had been won, the new coach had settled and money was made available for Ramos to move Spurs forward again.

Big money was spent on bringing in Roman Pavlyuchenko, Luka Modric, Heurelho Gomes, Vedran Corluka and Giovani dos Santos but it was not only foreign players that were invested in. The core of the team remained English and was added to with the signing of David Bentley. Ramos was certainly given the tools to do the job, but his plans were severely damaged when Manchester United's long-term pursuit of Dimitar Berbatov came to an end with a mega offer accepted just as the transfer window closed. The loss of such a gifted player was a setback, but it should not have plunged the team into an immediate relegation spiral. From the very first game the team was lacking organisation and direction, Ramos lacking ideas. In less than 12 months under Ramos Spurs had won a trophy but in all other respects had gone backwards. Chairman Daniel Levy knew a change had to be made and made quickly. It would cost money, but nothing compared to what relegation would cost. By the time Levy had a replacement for Ramos in place, eight League games had been played, two draws and six defeats. Ramos was sacked but more than that, little more than four years after its introduction, the continental management structure it had taken Spurs so long to decide was the way forward was ditched. Along with Ramos and his coaching staff, Damien Comolli was shown the exit door.

Levy decided to replace the Sporting Director/first-team coach concept with a traditional English manager, and in Harry Redknapp he could not have found a more traditional English manager. Redknapp's influence was immediate and impressive. With the leadership and inspiration so lacking under Ramos, Spurs quickly began to move away from the foot of the table while also making progress in the UEFA and Carlings Cups. Indeed, the latter competition provided another day out at Wembley with Spurs drawing 0–0 with Manchester United before losing on penalties in a Final that, with a little bit of luck, they could have won. Having seemed certainties for relegation, Spurs finished the 2008–09 season in the top half of the table, only two points away from qualification for the Europa League.

Redknapp had bought his coaching staff of Kevin Bond and Joe Jordan with him from Portsmouth. During the course of the season he tempted Pascal Chimbonda, Robbie Keane and Jermain Defoe back to White Hart Lane, the latter from Portsmouth. In the summer he added Sebastien Bassong, Peter Crouch and Niko Kranjcar to the staff, the last two also

Harry Redknapp Action Images / Carl Recine

Peter Crouch scores Tottenham's first goal against Manchester City to secure Champions League Football.
REUTERS/Nigel Roddis

Peter Crouch (unseen) heads his goal past Manchester City goalkeeper Marton Fulop, 5 May, 2010.
REUTERS/Eddie Keogh

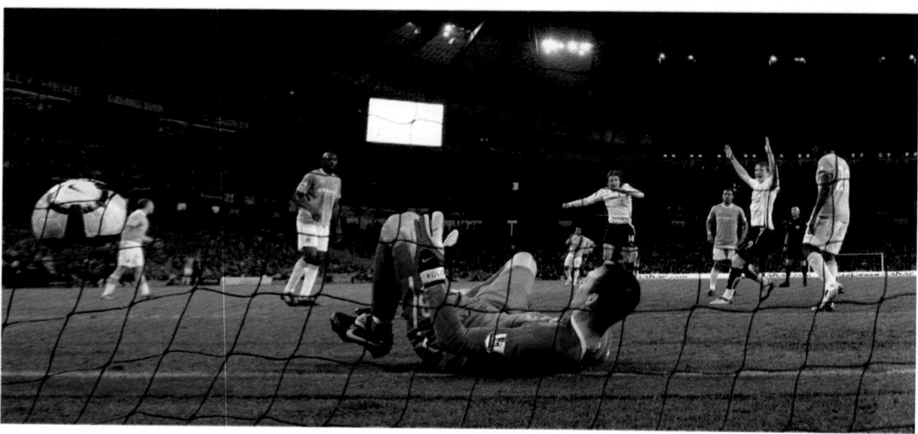

signed from Portsmouth. In the January transfer window Younes Kaboul also returned to Spurs from Portsmouth. Redknapp liked people he knew around him.

Including an opening-day success over Liverpool, Spurs started the 2009–10 season with four successive victories, but defeats to Manchester United, Chelsea and Arsenal soon dispelled all thoughts of winning the Barclays Premier League. As had been the case so often in the past, Spurs just seemed incapable of taking points from the title challengers. However, Liverpool's power was continuing to wane, and as Spurs did not have the distraction of UEFA Cup football fourth place became a realistic target. Manchester City, with their Arab billions, emerged as the principal challengers for the final Champions League spot, and as the season moved into its last few weeks City became favourites as Spurs focussed their attention on the FA Cup. Defeat to Portsmouth in the semi-final might have finished Spurs' season, but as it was immediately followed by victories over Arsenal and Chelsea belief that a top-four finish was not beyond Spurs was suddenly rekindled. Spurs were called on to visit Manchester City with only a trip to relegated Burnley to follow. Defeat at Eastlands would not end the Champions League dream but, as Spurs had proved in the past, nothing could ever be taken for granted. In a performance that showed Redknapp had instilled the resilience and belief that turns potential into triumph, a Peter Crouch goal secured the three points and the place at Europe's top table Bill Nicholson had always believed Spurs needed.

For Spurs' first venture into Europe's restructured premier competition, few changes were made. Apart from the experienced William Gallas being snapped up after his release by Arsenal, the only major purchase was Rafael Van der Vaart, and that was a last-second signing when Real Madrid suddenly announced he could leave. Spurs' last European Cup game had been a semi-final second leg against Benfica in April 1962. It had taken them nearly 50 years to secure another tilt at the competition. Not required to play in the qualifying rounds, Spurs

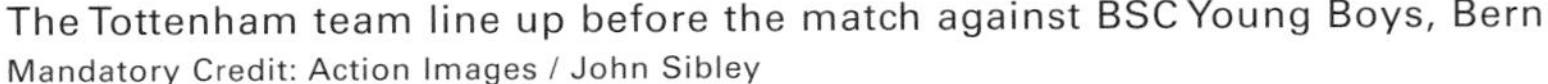
The Tottenham team line up before the match against BSC Young Boys, Bern.
Mandatory Credit: Action Images / John Sibley

Rafael van der Vaart. Action Images / Paul Childs

went straight into the Play-offs for the right to compete in the Champions League group stages but were very nearly out of the whole competition before it had begun. After 30 minutes of the first leg, they were three goals down to BSC Young Boys of Berne. If Spurs did not know it before, they knew then that the Champions League was a step above what they had been used to. Fortunately, goals by Sebastien Bassong and Roman Pavlyuchenko set Spurs up to overcome the Swiss League runners-up over the two legs and led to some of the most unforgettable performances from Spurs' teams in many years.

Tottenham's team lineup before the match v Inter Milan at the San Siro Stadium, Milan.
Action Images / Andrew Couldridge

Grouped alongside Werder Bremen, Twente Enschede and Internazionale, third place and a drop into the Europa League would not have been viewed as failure. Having drawn in Germany and beaten the Dutch at White Hart Lane, the visit to the San Siro to meet Inter was regarded as the true test of how far Spurs had come, and could go. By half-time, and reduced to 10 men after Heurelho Gomes's red card, they had been outclassed and were four goals down, the offensive tactics that had served them well against lesser opposition exposed by the European champions. In the second half a more controlled but still attacking attitude reaped dividends. Gareth Bale scored a hat-trick as he gave a performance that put him at the top of the wanted list of every club in Europe. Spurs did not win, they did not draw, but in the last few minutes they had Inter panicking. It showed that Spurs had nothing to fear from Europe's best, and that view was reinforced when Inter left White Hart Lane on the receiving end of a marvellous Spurs team performance and a 3–1 scoreline. Spurs' reward for winning their group was a return to the San Siro to meet AC Milan. A stubborn, defensive performance that showed a different side to Spurs' game looked like producing a goal-

Tottenham team group photo before the first leg game against AC Milan.
Action Images / Andrew Couldridge

So often did Gareth Bale burst past Inter's Brazilian full-back Maicon in the Champions League meeting at White Hart Lane that well before the end of the game the chant 'Taxi for Maicon!' was echoing around the ground.
Action Images / John Sibley

Rafael van der Vaart scores a goal against Inter Milan during their Champions League match at White Hart Lane, 2 November 2010.
REUTERS/Dylan Martinez

The Tottenham side to face Real Madrid in the Champions League quarter-final first leg.
Action Images / Andrew Couldridge

less draw until 10 minutes from the end when Peter Crouch popped up with a winner. It was a result that ranked amongst the best in the club's history.

Another disciplined performance in the return leg that ended 0-0 saw Spurs through to the quarter-finals and the end of what was becoming an improbable dream. Spurs had seen off the best Italy could offer but were unable to repeat the heroics against Real Madrid. Again reduced to 10 men when Peter Crouch got his marching orders early on in the Santiago Bernabeau, the Spanish giants were just too powerful for Spurs and well worth their 4–0 first-leg lead. In the return leg a mistake by Gomes allowed Real to win 1–0. It was an inglorious end to a wonderful adventure.

While Spurs had been doing so well against Europe's elite, performances in domestic competition had not been so praiseworthy. Always hovering around the title contenders, too often Spurs were unable to master the lesser lights, particularly at home where they lost only once but drew nine games. The home form was to costs Spurs dear at the final reckoning. If just three of the draws had been turned into victories, fourth place might have been snatched from Arsenal. As it was, Spurs had to be content with fifth and entry to the Europa League.

Where Spurs go from here depends on many factors. If they can keep the management and playing staff together there is no reason why Champions League qualification cannot be secured again, but Spurs have reached the stage where it is not only results that will determine the club's future. With plans for the rebuilding of White Hart Lane to provide a near 60,000 capacity stadium shelved because demanded alterations meant the project was not financially viable and West Ham United winning the contest to take over the Olympic Stadium site after the 2012 Olympic Games, Spurs must produce revised plans that will provide a stadium fit for a club with genuine ambitions to be the best.

GROUNDS

Tottenham Marshes

The Hotspur Football Club played its first home games on Tottenham Marshes, an area of marshland to the east of the London Liverpool Street to Cambridge/Stansted Airport railway line. The exact location of the original ground is unknown, and trying to identify it today is like pointing to the multitude of pitches on Hackney Marshes and saying 'so-and-so played over there'!

On crossing the railway line at Northumberland Park station, the industrial units to the right occupy the site of Asplins Farm. This property was owned in the early 1880s by Captain William Delano, and it was on one of his fields that the Hotspur Cricket Club had played.

Opposite the site of the farm, Park Lane (as it was then, it is now Marsh Lane) curved to the right and ran down to a Water Pumping Station. When Bobby Buckle, the last surviving founder member, was asked in the 1950s where it was that the club had originally played, he indicated it was roundabout the curve in Park Lane, between the railway line and the River Lea. This would indicate that the pitch was what is now part of the Victoria Line depot. It would also be consistent with reports that at the August 1883 meeting it was resolved to play matches at the Park Lane end of the Marshes.

However, about half a mile from the station and standing on the River Lea is Stonebridge Lock and the earliest known photograph of Spurs, which was owned by Buckle, carries the notation that it was taken there. It might be strange if the players walked so far from the area of the marshes they had marked out for their pitch to have the photo taken, but, of course, they could have played anywhere on the marshes and it is more than likely they played on more than one site.

Northumberland Park

Identifying the site of Spurs' second ground – the first private one – is not so difficult. It was off Northumberland Park, just behind a small nursery with the main access point being a passageway between numbers 69 and 75. The field was large enough for two football pitches and Spurs had Foxes FC as neighbours. During the summer months the pitch, for which Spurs initially paid £10 a season, was used for tennis, indeed it was originally known as Northumberland Tennis Field, so there can be little doubt it must have provided an excellent playing surface.

The first Spurs game played at Northumberland Park was a B-team fixture against Stratford St John's in the London Junior Cup on 6 October 1888, with the first team making

Spurs' defence crowds out Newton Heath's attackers in an FA Cup tie at Northumberland Park on 28 January 1899. Spurs looked to be out of the competition after a 1–1 draw but pulled off an astonishing 5–3 victory in the replay.

its new 'home' debut a week later against the Old Etonians in the London Senior Cup. It was not an auspicious start, as Spurs were beaten 8–2, but it was only in the second half that the visitors took control and scored five goals. Three of those fell to the England international A.T.B. Dunn. He so peppered the Spurs goal with powerful shots that an old black shed that stopped the ball disappearing from the ground immediately became known as the 'Dunn Shed'.

Initially Spurs did little to improve the ground; there were few reasons to do so. They did not own it, had no idea how spectators would react to having to pay to watch their football and, frankly, could not afford to carry out any work. The pitch was roped off, but it was not until 1891 that trestles were provided so spectators had something to stand on other than grass, the only 'stand' being an old wagon that provided a seat and elevated view for a few lucky spectators.

One step they had to take was to extend some hoardings around the ground to prevent the public obtaining a cheap view of matches. The owner of some adjacent land installed a platform on his land, charging 2d for its use – 1d less than Spurs charged for admission. When Spurs put their hoarding up the enterprising neighbour promptly replaced his platform with a wagon and hitched horses to it so the wagon could be moved along and an unobstructed view obtained. This necessitated Spurs paying a couple of lads to patrol the fence with a tarpaulin stretched between two poles until the cheapskates tired of their little game.

In 1893 Spurs took over the whole of the ground, building a new entrance from Waggon-Horse Lane and constructing an enclosure along the eastern side of the ground, for which an extra 2d admission was charged. The rent rose to £17 a year, although it did not stay at that level for long. As Spurs' fame and popularity increased, so did the rent.

A year later the first grandstand on the ground was erected. A wooden construction financed by new Chairman John Oliver, it was designed by a Mr English and built by the local firm of Messrs Knight and Son. It held 350 people, 100 of them seated, with facilities for the press. Under the grandstand were dressing rooms illuminated by oil lamps, which

A fine view of the Park Lane end of White Hart Lane during Spurs' first match on their new ground against Notts County on 4 September 1899.

were necessary as little natural light got through to them. Admission to the ground was increased to 6d with a further 6d for access to the grandstand, which a Mr Clarke was paid £1 a week to look after. The grandstand was fully opened by the end of October 1894, but on 22 December 1894 it was out of use. The shutters on the stand had been left open overnight and when a strong gale struck in the morning the corrugated roof and its supporting timbers were uplifted and deposited 30 to 40 yards away. The stand was quickly rebuilt and presumably Mr Clarke lost his £1 a week!

While expenditure was kept to a minimum, the ground was gradually improved. Banking was provided along the sides and behind the goals, so even those at the back of the ground could view proceedings without craning their necks too much and mobile stands were provided to add a few more seats. Spurs were on short-term leases and if not renewed money would just be wasted.

1896 saw the ropes around the pitch replaced with iron railings, which allowed the enclosure to be extended. The railings and a large flagstaff that was erected at the same time had previously seen service at Woolwich Arsenal's old Invicta ground in Plumstead. The railings did not last long, soon being replaced by white wooden fencing. New dressing rooms were provided in the grandstand and for the first time turnstiles were installed at the main entrance, replacing the old table that had previously been used.

Northumberland Park was claimed to have a capacity of anything between 20,000 and 30,000, but crowds never got anywhere near those figures. Had they done so the ground could never have coped. Five thousand spectators attended for the first time on 15 December 1894 when Spurs entertained Luton Town in the FA Cup, with five figures being breached for the first time in September 1897 for a friendly with Millwall Athletic. A couple of months later another FA Cup tie with Luton Town attracted 12,000 and it was already being claimed the ground could hold no more. When the refreshment stand collapsed during the United League game with Arsenal on 8 April 1898 with an estimated 15,000 present, it was clear breaking point had been passed. It was perhaps partly because of a desire to limit attendances that admission prices were increased whenever large crowds were expected, notably for FA Cup ties – the most attractive fixtures. Twelve thousand people paid £237 in December 1898 for Luton Town's visit, 13,721 paid £419 when Newton Heath visited in the first round in January 1899 and the receipts record was set at £681 for an attendance of 12,371 against Sunderland in the second round a month later.

Capacity was not the only problem Spurs had to contend with. The main entrance to Northumberland Park was small, and, with spectators normally only arriving minutes before the advertised kick-off time, gaining entry, and exiting, was always fraught with difficulties. Spurs tried to alleviate the access problem by enlarging the Waggon-Horse Lane entrance, but an adjoining landowner made such unreasonable demands for his co-operation that the idea had to be abandoned.

The incident in the Woolwich Arsenal game left Spurs with little option but to seek a new ground, but it was about a year before a new site was found and that only just after they had agreed a new five-year lease on Northumberland Park.

White Hart Lane

How Spurs came to move to White Hart Lane was related several years later by chairman Charles Roberts. He told how, in about January 1899, an apprentice cooper told him a new football club was going to start up playing on land at the rear of the White Hart in Tottenham High Road. Roberts went to see the landlord of the public house, who claimed a new football club was his idea. He had never heard of Spurs but had recently moved from a public house near a football ground in Millwall and knew how good football fans could be for his business. He would have no objection to Spurs moving on to the land provided that was acceptable to his landlords, the brewers Charringtons.

Roberts and Bobby Buckle lost no time in approaching Charringtons, who intended to use the land for housing, and persuading them to grant Spurs a lease. It was for 21 years, with the only conditions the brewers imposed that Spurs should guarantee gates of 1,000 for first-team games and 500 for reserves. Roberts and Buckle had no difficulty with that.

Spurs now had two grounds and no money to do anything with them, but no sooner had they reached an agreement with Charringtons than they were offered a tidy sum by their Northumberland Park landlord to surrender their lease so houses could be built on the ground. A deal was negotiated before news of Spurs' impending move could leak out. Spurs now had one ground and some money to get it ready for a new season.

The former landlord of the White Hart, George Beckwith, had been running a nursery business, known both as Beckwith's Nursery and Tottenham Nursery, from the land behind his premises for many years, and it was covered with many well-built greenhouses. John Over, groundsman of Edmonton Cricket Club and the man who prepared the wicket for the first Test Match on British soil against the Australians in 1880, was given the task of supervising the demolition of the greenhouses and laying out the playing surface. It was a job and a half, with tons of concrete having to be blown up and disposed of before the pitch could be laid, while at the same time work was in hand to move the old stands from Northumberland Park and build new ones. The ground was expected to have a capacity of

Top: April 1952 and work begins on a total relaying of the playing surface.

Left: construction underway on the East Stand in July 1934.

Right: July 1934: the cockerel that adorned the West Stand being cleaned up before its removal to the East Stand.

Below: An artist's impression of how White Hart Lane would look on completion of Archibald Leitch's new East Stand.

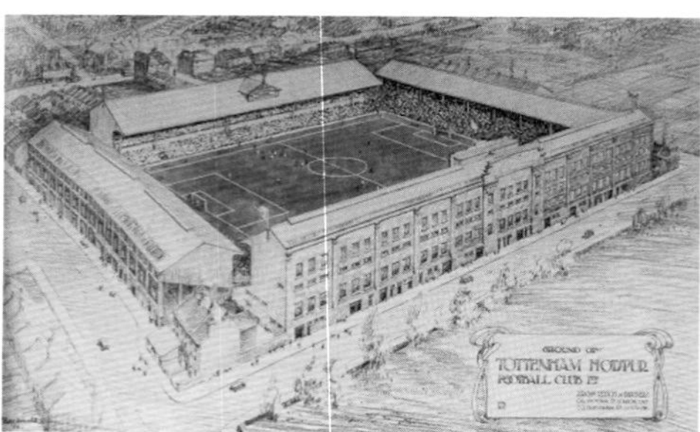

about 30,000, with one stand running the length of the ground and a covered section providing seating for 2,500.

The public were invited to suggest a name for the new ground but few responded. Percy Park, with its obvious connection to Harry Hotspur, was one. Another was Rowel Park, a rowel being the wheel at the end of a horseman's spur. Perhaps one of the most interesting was Gilpin Park, a reference to the central character of William Cowper's comic poem *The Diverting History of John Gilpin*, which told of a linen draper's attempt to spend an anniversary holiday with his family at The Bell in Edmonton. None of these names were accepted, and when the ground opened the club initially referred to it as Hotspur Ground, but it soon came to be known as simply White Hart Lane.

The first event to be held on the ground was a Military Tournament on 7 August 1899, when about 5,000 people attended to watch such events as 'Lemon Cutting', 'Balaclava Melee' and 'Cleaving the Turk's Head'. The first football match played there was on 22 August when the Stripes met the Whites in a public practice match. This was quickly followed by two more club games and a trial match for local juniors hoping to make the step up.

The official opening took place on 4 September 1899 with a visit from Notts County. Five thousand people assembled to see Spurs win 4–1, David Copeland getting a hat-trick. Two of his goals came in the second half when County's half-back Walter Bull, who joined Spurs five years later, played in goal after 'keeper Bob Suter had been injured. The crowd was more than doubled five days later for the first competitive match against Queen's Park Rangers in the Southern League.

Over the next few years the ground was improved and the capacity increased, with the three stands on the west side merged into one, further roofing provided to extend the covered accommodation and banking provided at both ends. Part of the White Hart was demolished so the entrance to the ground, which is now Bill Nicholson Way, could be doubled in size. The expenditure was not inconsequential and there was a lot more Spurs wanted to do but, as with Northumberland Park, there was little point laying out large sums of money when the ground was held on lease. In 1905 Spurs negotiated the purchase of the freehold from Charringtons for £8,900 and the acquisition of land on Paxton Road for a further £2,600, which would give them the whole block between Paxton Road and Park Lane. Five thousand new £1 shares were offered to help towards the purchase price, but, as with the original share issue, the take up was not great. Only 2,000 shares were subscribed to, but Spurs were able to find the funds to complete the purchases and erect a large bank at the Paxton Road end, taking the capacity up to 40,000.

Spurs had a ground that was probably the best in the Southern League, but they had loftier ambitions. When they secured election to the Football League in 1908 they knew further improvements were essential. Archibald Leitch, the pre-eminent architect of football stands and grounds, was appointed to come up with proposals for redevelopment of the ground, starting with the main West Stand. No less than seven designs for the stand were proposed by Leitch, and it was only after promotion to the First Division had been secured in May 1909 that one was settled upon.

The largest stand to have been built on a British football ground to that time, it ran the whole length of the ground. In two tiers, the top section provided seating for 5,300, the lower a standing enclosure taking 6,000 spectators, with the whole stand roofed over. From the outside the stand looked nothing more than functional, a large structure covered in corrugated cladding with a few oblong windows and a wide staircase in the centre. From the pitch it was far more attractive, with a magnificent mock-Tudor gable emblazoned with the club name and, from November 1909, surmounted by a copper cockerel and ball made by a former player from Spurs' amateur days, W.J. Scott. Work only began on demolition of the old stand in June 1909 but the new stand was open for Spurs' home debut in the First Division against Manchester United on 11 September 1909. The stand was slightly altered in 1934, with the 10 lattice roof supports being replaced by five solid columns, but it then remained practically unaltered until demolished in 1980.

While the West Stand was being built, the central section of the East stand was roofed over and that roofing was extended for the length of the ground two years later, with the wooden terracing replaced by concrete. With the banking at the two ends doubled in size, by the time of World War One the ground could comfortably hold 50,000.

The 1921 FA Cup success provided the money for a two-tierd covered terrace to be built at the Paxton Road end, with the Park Lane end similarly rebuilt two years later. Archibald Leitch was responsible for the design of both. Capacity remained at about 50,000 with 80 percent under cover.

The East Stand was now the only single-storey construction, but Spurs could do little to rebuild it. There was a row of terraced houses behind the stand, and although Spurs bought them with demolition the intention laws to help overcome a housing shortage made it impossible for them to do so until 1934. With alternative accommodation or compensation provided to the residents, Leitch was given the job of completing his redevelopment of the ground. He designed a majestic double-decker stand, but with the lower section in two tiers it appeared almost a triple-decker. The top level was fitted with 4,983 seats, the middle tier, soon known as 'the Shelf', and the lower terrace held over 18,000, while the whole structure was topped by a 109-seat 'crow's nest' press box that was never actually to be used by the press. The stand was officially opened for the visit of Aston Villa on 22 September 1934, taking the estimated capacity of White Hart Lane to 80,000, of which 60,000 were under cover. In February 1935 over 70,000 passed through the turnstiles for the first time to see Spurs play Bolton Wanderers in the fifth round of the FA Cup and the record attendance, 75,038, was recorded for another FA Cup tie, against Sunderland in March 1938.

There was no major development over the next few years. Floodlight poles appeared in 1953 with the first official floodlit match taking place against Racing Club de Paris on 29 September 1953. The floodlights were upgraded in 1957, necessitating the removal of the cockerel to the East stand, and a complete new system, with pylons in the four corners of the ground, was installed in 1961. 1962 saw the rear section of the Park Lane stand fitted with seats, and a year later the same addition was made at the Paxton Road end, which was linked up with the West Stand in 1968. New floodlights were installed in 1972 and the following year the corner between the West and Park Lane stands filled with more seats.

Leitch's West Stand witnessed its last Spurs match against Crystal Palace on 12 November 1980. Within days, work began on its demolition and 15 months later, 6 February 1982, its replacement was officially opened for the visit of Wolverhampton

A floodlit White Hart Lane as it is today.

Wanderers. The first part of an ambitious plan to redevelop the whole stadium as football moved into a new era, the stand only provided 6,500 seats but it incorporated 72 private executive boxes and other office and corporate facilities.

The cost of the West Stand went way over budget and put Spurs in the financial difficulties that eventually saw the club taken over and floated on the Stock Market. It was not until 1988 that further substantial work on the ground began, but it did not start well, with the opening match of the 1988–89 season postponed at the last minute because safety works had not been completed. The following summer the 'crow's-nest' was demolished as the East Stand roof was replaced to match that on the West Stand, the floodlight pylons were taken down with spotlights on the East and West Stands replacing the old lights and part of 'the Shelf' was converted into another 36 executive boxes.

In 1992 seats were installed on the lower terraces of both the East and South stands, and a year later the lower North terrace was similarly seated. The plan to link all four stands and provide an all-seated wrap-around arena was further advanced in 1994, with 'the Shelf' giving way to seats and the South Stand demolished. Rebuilding of the South Stand was completed a year later, with the first Jumbotron screen installed, and in 1998 refurbishment of the North Stand was completed with a second Jumbotron screen.

Minor alterations continued to be made, but as the 21st century got underway it was increasingly obvious that if Spurs were to harbour realistic dreams of competing at the highest level of the domestic game, let alone on the international stage, a new ground could no longer be something that was just talked about every few years. It had to become fact. With a capacity only just above 36,000 and rivals rebuilding, moving or announcing plans to do so, Spurs were in danger of being permanently left behind.

A season ticket waiting list of around 22,000 proved that a vastly larger stadium could be filled easily, and in October 2008 detailed plans were at last announced for one that could accommodate near three times that number and provide true world class facilities. Perhaps of more importance for many, the Northumberland Development Project plans did not simply involve a new stadium, not even a new stadium based in Tottenham but a new stadium that would be built barely 200yds north of the current one, taking Spurs closer to the site of the old Northumberland Park ground.

The plans provided real hope, but in order to get all the necessary planning approvals, revisions were necessary. Those revisions added greatly to the cost. Two years after first producing their plans, Spurs were forced to announce that £50 million of extra costs, taking the total cost to around £450 million, made the whole project unviable.

There was an alternative. Bidders were being sought to take over the 80,000 capacity Olympic stadium site at Stratford after the 2012 Olympic Games. Five miles from White Hart Lane, it had many attractions but one major drawback, a running track. Spurs were thrown into competition with West Ham United who were content to take on the stadium, reduce the capacity but retain the athletics track. Spurs' proposal was to totally demolish the Olympic Stadium and rebuild with a 60,000 capacity but, crucially, no facilities for athletics. They would be provided by funding the rebuilding of the Crystal Palace athletics stadium at the National Sports' Centre. The politics of the situation meant Spurs had little chance, and it was no surprise when a unanimous decision of the Olympic Park Legacy Company went in the Hammers' favour.

For Spurs, it was back to the drawing board. Back to the search for a new 'World Famous Home of the Spurs'.

General view of White Hart Lane,
Tottenham Hotspur v Slavia Prague
UEFA Cup third round second leg,
February 2008.
Action Images / Paul Harding

MATCHES TO REMEMBER

1901 FA Cup Final v Sheffield United

0 April 1901 at Crystal Palace

A world-record crowd of 114,815 assembled at the old Crystal Palace ground to see if Spurs could become the first club from outside the Football League to win the FA Cup since the League had been established in 1888.

'Nudger' Needham, United's England star, won the toss and chose to defend the southern end, leaving Spurs to kick-off with the sun and wind in their eyes. United had the best of the early exchanges, Needham dominating play with raking passes to his wingers and Harry Erentz was soon called upon to make an exceptional clearance as George Hedley bore down on goal. Spurs looked nervous and unsure of themselves, but as the game settled they began to find their passing rhythm. Jack Kirwan and David Copeland jinked their way down the wing, Sandy Brown laid Kirwan's cross off for John Cameron only for the linesman to flag for offside. Hedley got in a good shot to call George Clawley into action for the first time and Erentz twice headed away yards from his line before United took the lead. Twelve minutes had gone when Fred Priest collected from 'Oakey' Field and fired past the unsighted Clawley.

For the next 20 minutes United controlled the game, but the Spurs defence did not allow them a clear-cut opening, and with just over 30 minutes gone Spurs struck back. A free-kick for a foul by Harry Thickett on Kirwan was flighted into the penalty area, and Brown rose to guide his header past Bill Foulke. The rest of the first half saw a tremendous struggle for control, Bert Lipsham firing just over and Foulke making a brilliant one-handed save from Tom Smith. Clawley was the busier of the two 'keepers, but he only had to deal with long-range efforts, whereas Spurs' close passing cut through the United defence to create the better openings.

Just a small part of the vast crowd, a world record 114,815, at Crystal Palace.

Five minutes into the second half Spurs took the lead. Kirwan set Cameron free and, as Brown's marker moved across to tackle Cameron, the Spurs secretary-manager rolled the ball to Brown whose rasping shot beat Foulke all ends up and thundered off the bar into the back of the net. Barely had a minute elapsed before the scores were level again, with a goal that today would have the pundits screaming for video replays. From the kick-off, Lipsham, looking offside, got away and fired in a shot that Clawley fumbled. As Walter Bennett rushed in to charge the goalkeeper, Clawley managed to push the ball out of play. The linesman signalled a corner, Clawley placed the ball for a goal-kick but referee Kingscott marched back to the centre circle. Despite being well behind play he decided the ball had crossed the line from Lipsham's shot.

The decision took much of the heart out of Spurs and even United seemed embarrassed. Both teams strove to get the upper hand but play was remarkably even, United perhaps having the majority of it but Spurs creating the better chances. Brown missed one glorious opportunity and Kirwan allowed Thickett to rob him when he should at least have got his shot away. In the last 10 minutes Spurs tired and United sensed the game was there for the taking, but Clawley repelled all their attacks and so the game went to a replay.

27 April 1901 replay at Burnden Park

Prior to the Final, the FA had decided a replay would take place at Goodison Park the following week, but Liverpool objected as they had a game at Anfield that day so the game was switched to Burnden Park, a decision that did not find favour with Spurs or United.

The two teams were the same as for the first game, but there was a vast difference in the attendance. As Bolton station was being rebuilt, the Lancashire and Yorkshire Railway refused to offer cheap fares. A fair contingent made their way from Sheffield, but few Spurs supporters were able to make the six-hour journey from London and most of the 20,470 who witnessed the game were locals.

With the wind behind them Spurs started the match in fine form, one attack after another penning United in their own half. Needham halted a promising move by Copeland and Brown, Thickett did the same to repulse Brown and Cameron, and Copeland seemed set to score when Harry Johnson nicked the ball off him. Foulke was called on to save Copeland's header and then pull off smart saves to deny Brown and Kirwan. Spurs were

George Clawley comes out to clear a free-kick into the Spurs box.

totally in control but for all their superiority the first goal would not come. Too often the opening was there for a shot but they would pass instead, trying to score the perfect goal.

United had been criticised for their physical approach in the first game. They had been quite restrained in the replay but as Spurs domination grew the Cutlers again resorted to the rough stuff. It was the only way for United to get into the game and it worked. A flowing move between Priest, Hedley, Field and Lipsham was only halted at the last second by Jack Jones, and Johnson then sent a shot just over the bar. Needham now began to exert control, pushing forward and fashioning three excellent chances for his forwards, but none of them could capitalise. With five minutes to the break, Needham again burst forward. Dribbling past Tom Morris, he fed Lipsham, who laid the ball into Priest's pass and United were ahead. Spurs' heads dropped, and it was only thanks to sterling work by Clawley, Erentz and Sandy Tait that United did not go in at the interval more than one goal up.

Spurs began the second half determined to retrieve the deficit and for 10 minutes battered away at the Sheffield defence. They got through a couple of times, only to find Foulke at his sharpest. With 10 minutes gone a great pass out of defence from Tait found Copeland. The inside-forward rounded Thickett, interchanged passes with Brown and then spread the ball out to Smith. He quickly moved the ball on to Cameron, who struck it from distance to put Spurs back level.

A terrific struggle now ensued, with Spurs again taking control. Brown twice broke through but Foulke blocked his first effort and the second went just the wrong side of the post. There was just over a quarter of an hour left when Needham made his first mistake of the two matches, only half clearing Cameron's shot to Smith who coolly slotted home. There was no holding Spurs now. Their control was absolute but the killer third did not come until seven minutes from time, when Brown headed home from a corner. In the remaining minutes Spurs could have added to their total, but 3–1 was enough to see their name etched on 'the Little Tin Idol' for the first time.

Spurs: Clawley; Erentz, Tait; Morris, Hughes, Jones; Smith, Cameron, Brown, Copeland, Kirwan.
Sheffield United: Foulke; Thickett, Boyle; Johnson, Morren, Needham; Bennett, Field, Hedley, Priest, Lipsham.

1921 FA Cup Final v Wolverhampton Wanderers

23 April 1921 at Stamford Bridge
With rain having fallen practically non-stop since 6am, the Stamford Bridge pitch was sodden when Spurs and Wolves took their places for the presentation of the teams to the King. As George V met the players, a torrential downpour fell, and by the time the teams lined up for the kick-off pools of water were laying all over the pitch. Hardly conducive to the fast-flowing football that had taken Spurs to the Final it may have been, but Spurs were not going to let the conditions dictate.

From the kick-off they got the ball down and kept it on the floor, continually seeking out their wingers Jimmy Banks and Jimmy Dimmock and showing a remarkable ability to judge whether the ball was going to hold up in the puddles or zip across the greasy

Bert Bliss threatens the Wolves goal with an over-head kick.

surface. Dimmock had the first opening but fired his shot wide, and after Wolves had made their first sortie into Spurs' half Jimmy Seed won a corner that Banks sent across and Jimmy Cantrell headed just over. With Arthur Grimsdell and Bert Smith controlling the midfield, the Spurs forwards were seeing plenty of the ball and combining well, the Wolves defence under constant pressure. It seemed just a matter of time before the Wolves goal fell and that almost happened midway through the half. Grimsdell sent Dimmock on another dribble down the wing that was only stopped at the expense of a corner. When the ball was played into the middle Bert Bliss executed a perfect bicycle kick and the ball seemed destined for the net when George Marshall appeared from nowhere to head off the line. Wolves seldom threatened Alex Hunter's goal, only Sammy Brooks, a Fanny-Walden clone later to play for Spurs, posing any sort of danger. How the Wolves goal remained intact at half-time was more a matter of luck than judgement.

Arthur Grimsdell provides a young supporter with a moment he would never forget as he leaves Stamford Bridge with the trophy.

Rain had continued to fall throughout the first half and the pitch resembled a quagmire, but as the teams emerged for the second period the sun came out. Wolves were at last seen to good effect, 'Tansey' Lea threatening until Tommy Clay dispossessed and then swinging in a beautiful cross that none of his forwards could reach. Almost 65 minutes had elapsed when Bliss found Dimmock with Val Gregory and Maurice Woodward in close proximity. Getting the ball under control in an instant, Dimmock strode past Gregory, but as he advanced on Woodward he played the ball too far in front of him. Woodward moved in but as he went to clear slipped and just played the ball back to Dimmock. Twenty-five yards out and advancing on the angle of the box, Dimmock hit a swift, oblique shot that skimmed across the surface, just past the despairing dive of Noel George and into the far corner of the net.

Spurs almost got a second minutes later, as Banks was sent haring in on goal only to be brought down just outside the box. Bliss blasted the resultant free-kick wide. Brooks then got through and looked almost certain to grab the equaliser until Clay charged him down. A lovely move involving the entire Spurs forward line ended with Banks and George colliding as the 'keeper rushed out and the ball went harmlessly wide. A second goal for Spurs was sure to end the contest, and it almost came when Banks swung the ball from his wing over to the opposite wing. Dimmock connected with the ball sweetly, only to see his drive strike the crossbar and fly over.

As the final whistle approached Wolves at last began to exert some pressure. The heavy conditions had taken their toll on Spurs' short-passing game and they were visibly tiring. Hunter now came to the fore, one rush from his line and plunge at the feet of George Edmonds saving an almost certain goal. Just before the end Arthur Potts seemed in a good position, but Bob MacDonald rushed across to clear the danger and Spurs hung on to bring the Cup back to London for the first time since winning it in 1901.

Spurs: Hunter; Clay, MacDonald; Smith, Walters, Grimsdell; Banks, Seed, Cantrell, Bliss, Dimmock.

Wolverhampton Wanderers: George; Woodward, Marshall; Gregory, Hodnett, Riley; Lea, Burrill, Edmonds, Potts, Brooks.

1961 FA Cup Final v Leicester City

6 May 1961 at Wembley Stadium

With that elusive double within their grasp, Spurs went into the FA Cup Final as hot favourites, but also under enormous pressure. Not that anyone would have guessed that as they tore into Leicester from the start as if determined to have the game over and done with before it had begun. With Dave Mackay and Danny Blanchflower pushed right up, they spent the first five minutes camped in the Leicester half and should have taken the lead in the third minute, but John White blasted the easiest chance of the game over from seven yards out. A goal then and no doubt Spurs would have relaxed and given one of their better performances, but while they continued to do the bulk of the pressing (four clear-cut chances were carved out), Leicester began to push them back, although not troubling Bill Brown in the Spurs goal.

Danny Blanchflower hoists the FA Cup, and the 'Impossible Dream' has become reality.

What is commonly regarded as the turning point came after 19 minutes. Len Chalmers and Bobby Smith tussled for the ball, and as Chalmers came away with it Les Allen went into the tackle. There was nothing unfair about the challenge, the referee did not give a free-kick, but Allen caught Chalmers on the shin, and as he went down Chalmers twisted his knee and crumpled to the turf, another victim of the Wembley Cup Final jinx. After lengthy treatment he resumed, but he was a hobbling passenger, first playing on the right wing then the left. The injury seemed to upset Spurs as much as it inspired Leicester. While Allen was clearly put off his normal game, Leicester, as is so often the case, raised theirs. They now had nothing to lose, while defeat to 10 men would be a miserable climax to Spurs' season-long efforts.

Spurs remained on top, but they were not playing well. Blanchflower was finding Hugh McIlmoyle a real handful and Mackay never got into his gargantuan stride. Apart from Cliff Jones, the Spurs forward line seemed slow and devoid of ideas. It was the unsung stalwarts, Maurice Norman, Peter Baker and Ron Henry, who were proving the heroes. White had another opening but put his shot into the side netting and when Jones did side-foot past Gordon Banks from Terry Dyson's cross the joy was short-lived, as the linesman waved his flag. Jones was clearly onside as he ran through the Leicester rearguard, but it was not the first, and would not be the last, time Jones was not only too fast for his defender but also the officials.

As the second half unfolded, it was still Spurs creating all the chances. Allen so badly mishit a shot it nearly hit the corner flag and Dyson headed over an open goal, but Spurs kept plugging away and got their reward with the first move of real quality. Sixty-nine minutes had elapsed when a passage of play involving seven passes ended with Dyson finding Smith. In a flash Smith turned in a yard of space, beat a defender and lashed a vicious shot past Banks. The pressure could be seen to lift from Spurs and they at last began to play like real champions. Moments after the opener Dyson contrived to head over the bar when standing almost beneath it, but with just 15 minutes left he made up for that error, racing in from the touchline to meet Smith's cross and bury the ball in the back of the net.

The game was all but over now. Leicester's determined efforts had taken their toll and Spurs strolled through the last few minutes. They could have had at least two more goals, but the two they had were more than enough.

Spurs: Brown; Baker, Henry; Blanchflower, Norman, Mackay; Jones, White, Smith, Allen, Dyson.

Leicester City: Banks; Chalmers, Norman; McLintock, King, Appleton; Riley, Walsh, McIlmoyle, Keyworth, Cheesebrough.

1962 FA Cup Final v Burnley

5 May 1962 at Wembley Stadium

This was expected to be the Cup Final for the connoisseur. Ipswich Town may have won the Football League title, but Spurs and Burnley were reckoned to be the best pure-footballing sides in the country. Separated by only a point over the League season, they both played in the classic style, building attacks through midfield with pacy wingers, skilful strikers and full rein given to individual talents. The match lived up to most of the expectations but as a contest fell short of what many had hoped for. That was all due to Jimmy Greaves. Prior to the match he had attempted to lift the dressing-room tension by announcing he would score in the fourth minute. He disappointed, but only because he scored a minute earlier than he predicted.

Barely had the crowd settled than Bill Brown drop-kicked the ball into the centre circle. Bobby Smith flicked the ball to his right and there was Greaves, racing onto it and heading straight for goal. So quick was he that the ball got left behind him and the chance appeared to have been lost, but in a flash he turned, retrieved the ball, rounded Tommy Cummings and slid his shot past the startled Adam Blacklaw. It was the perfect start and left Burnley chasing the game for nigh on 80 minutes.

They responded in typical fashion, pushing forward, looking to get their speedy wingers John Connolly and Gordon Harris into the game, Ray Pointer ever waiting to latch onto the delicate passes of Jimmy McIlroy. At times their build-up play was beautiful, but it rarely threatened. Peter Baker and Ron Henry tied down the outside men, Maurice Norman dominated Pointer so much the centre-forward spent much of his time drifting out to the wing just hoping to see the ball and Dave Mackay rampaged through midfield snuffing out every threat before it developed. Beside him Danny Blanchflower gave an imperious performance, working tirelessly on Burnley's perceived weak link, centre-half Cummings.

Burnley did fashion some chances – Bill Brown had to punch a vicious 25-yarder from Brian Miller clear and pluck a bullet-like header from Jimmy Robson out of the air – but the better ones were falling to Spurs. Greaves had a thunderbolt tipped over by Blacklaw who then managed to push a wickedly-deceptive cross from John White from under his bar at the last second.

Burnley finished the first half on the attack and started the second in the same fashion. Five minutes had gone when White's pass to Mackay fell short of its target. Pointer nipped

Danny Blanchflower's perfect penalty makes sure Spurs have retained their grip on the FA Cup.

Cliff Jones, Dave Mackay and Jimmy Greaves lead the parade after the defeat of Burnley.

in, pinched the ball and pushed it out to Harris, who beat Baker before crossing for Robson to stab past Brown. If Burnley thought they were back in the game, less than 30 seconds later they were back to square one. From the restart the ball was fed out to White who raced down the left flank and floated the ball into the Burnley goalmouth. Miller looked favourite to clear, but Smith got there first, killed the ball, swivelled and in the same movement lashed the ball past Blacklaw. The goal was a killer. Much as Burnley tried they rarely posed a threat again, and eight minutes from time they were killed off. Greaves slipped a reverse pass to Terry Medwin who found White. Another immaculate cross saw Smith challenge Blacklaw. The ball broke to Medwin, whose shot was going in until Cummings stuck out a hand. Blanchflower took the penalty. As Blacklaw plunged to the right the ball went to the left and Spurs became only the second club since the turn of the century to retain the trophy.

Spurs: Brown; Baker, Henry; Blanchflower, Norman, Mackay; Medwin, White, Smith, Greaves, Jones.

Burnley: Blacklaw; Angus, Elder; Adamson, Cummings, Miller; Connolly, McIlroy, Pointer, Robson, Harris.

1963 European Cup-winners' Cup Final v Atletico Madrid

15 May 1963 at Feyenoord Stadium, Rotterdam

With Danny Blanchflower's words of encouragement still ringing in their ears and 4,000 fans singing the *Glory, Glory Hallelujah* battle anthem, Spurs took to the field in Rotterdam confident they would carve another niche in football history. 90 minutes later

The celebrations are about to begin as Spurs pose with the European Cup-winners' Cup.

The two captains exchanging pennants.

John White's shot rockets past Madinabeytia for Spurs' second goal.

they had succeeded in doing just that, producing a brilliant exhibition of football to brush aside the holders and become the first British club to win a European trophy. They did it without the heartbeat of Bill Nicholson's team, Dave Mackay, but with a new hero in the unlikely shape of little Terry Dyson, a man who played the match of his life when it was most needed.

Atletico were on £360 a man to retain the trophy and in the first two minutes showed they were prepared to resort to any tactics to secure their bonus. The first time Bobby Smith challenged for the ball he was sent sprawling from behind by Jorge Griffa and as he lay on the turf was stamped on by his assailant. If any more incentive was needed, Griffa had provided it. Spurs knew immediately that avoiding injury would mean playing their short-passing game at its swiftest.

For 15 minutes Spurs prodded and probed at the Spaniard's defence before ripping it to shreds with a move of stunning simplicity and breathtaking speed. It started with John White and Danny Blanchflower winning the ball in midfield and finding Smith, who had dropped deep to escape his marker. His pass to Cliff Jones sent the winger haring down the right wing before whipping over an inch-perfect cross for Jimmy Greaves to meet on the half-volley and direct just inside the post.

Spurs kept the pressure on with Blanchflower and Dyson going close, but in the 32nd minute Greaves's cross was dummied by Smith, and Dyson cut the ball back to White. On the edge of the box, he brought it down in an instant and fizzed a left-footed shot through the Spanish defence and into the top corner of the net.

Spurs cruised through the rest of the first half but as the second began were suddenly facing a different proposition. Atletico were not going to give up the trophy without a fight and tore into Spurs with a vengeance. They got an immediate reward, barely 50 seconds having gone when Ron Henry handled Antonio Chuzo's shot to stop a certain goal. Enrique Collar tucked away the spot-kick to herald a period of sustained pressure on Spurs' goal. Ramiro Rodriguez missed by inches, Chuzo went within a whisker of finding the net and in five minutes the Spaniards won four corners. Spurs were rocking but Maurice Norman stood out like a colossus while Blanchflower coolly and calmly organised his men.

The pressure was intense but all of a sudden it was lifted as Dyson collected a clearance from defence, flicked the ball over Feliciano Rivilla and sent a curving lob into the centre. A cross or a shot, it matters not. The ball sailed over Edgardo Madinabeytia's head and dipped just under the bar. The match was three-quarters over but for Atletico the game was up. Their fire fizzled out as Spurs regained total control and swept their deflated opponents aside. With 10 minutes to go Greaves pounced on another Dyson cross to volley his second, and in the final moments Dyson advanced 40 yards with the defence retreating in front of him. He looked up, saw he had no one to pass to so just hammered the ball into the top corner.

Spurs: Brown; Baker, Henry; Blanchflower, Norman, Marchi; Jones, White, Smith, Greaves, Dyson.

Atletico Madrid: Madinabeytia; Rivilla, Rodriquez; Ramiro, Griffa, Glaria; Jones, Adelardo, Chuzo, Mendonca, Collar.

1967 FA Cup Final v Chelsea

20 May 1967 at Wembley Stadium

The first all-London FA Cup Final, the 'Cockney Cup Final', was billed as a clash of styles with the pundits looking forward to seeing how the classic, close-passing and carefully-constructed football of Spurs would fare against the hurried, energetic and hard-running new style of Chelsea. It turned out to be a nothing sort of contest, as Spurs elegantly ambled their way through 90 minutes rarely under threat and, even when Chelsea pulled a goal back, in almost embarrassing control.

From the opening minutes Spurs played with an elegance and silkiness that suited Wembley's fabled wide-open spaces, passing the ball around, unhurried and playing their own game deep in the heart of the Chelsea defence, just probing for one slip or sign of weakness. They played with variety and subtleness, looking to cut through Chelsea down the flanks one minute, knocking over a tantalising cross for Alan Gilzean to knock down the next, then trying to slip the ball through the channels for Jimmy Greaves to run on to. Chelsea, on the other hand, had only one attacking weapon, the high ball aimed from any part of the pitch towards Tony Hateley, hoping, not expecting, the big man might beat Mike England and create some havoc. There was never much chance of that, as England dominated Hateley from start to finish. In direct comparison Gilzean was leading Marvin Hinton a merry dance, his oft overlooked strength too much for Hinton, his deft flicks from head and foot always causing panic in the Chelsea back line. Even Chelsea's one player of true quality, Charlie Cooke, was so well shackled he gave up trying to dribble his way through and resorted to the long, hopeful cross that only found England's head.

Cooke was the one man Bill Nicholson had marked out as a danger, but he had a simple way of nullifying the threat. Dave Mackay had always been seen as the marauding half-back pushing Spurs forward, while Alan Mullery played deeper, providing the defensive strength.

Jimmy Greaves and Terry Venables are first to realise Jimmy Robertson's shot has just given Spurs the lead.

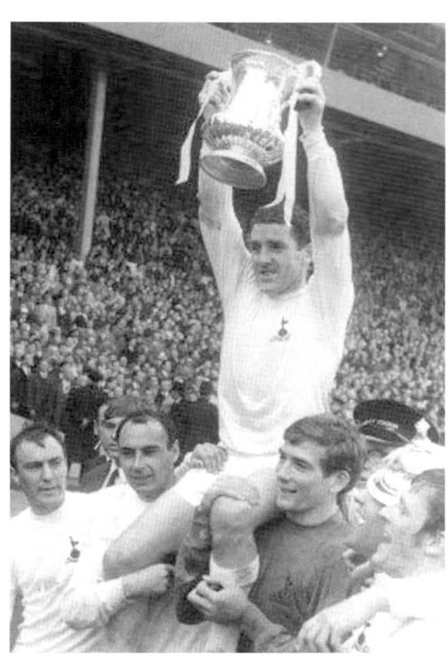

Dave Mackay has two hands on the Cup but still safely clutches his third winners' medal.

Nicholson just switched them round: Mackay held back to provide cover for Cyril Knowles, while Mullery was given free rein to steam forward whenever the opportunity arose. It worked perfectly, with Mullery forcing John Boyle and Tommy Baldwin deep, leaving plenty of space for young Joe Kinnear to race into.

It was from one of Mullery's forward sorties that Spurs took the lead just before half-time. They had gone close several times before, a Gilzean flick setting up Frank Saul only for Alan Harris to block the shot, Peter Bonetti flying across goal to get both hands to a Jimmy Robertson blockbuster and tip the ball round the post. There was nothing Bonetti

Tottenham Hotspur celebrate after winning the 1967 FA Cup Final against Chelsea at Wembley

could do though, as Mullery advanced on a retreating Chelsea defence and let fly from 30 yards. The shot would have gone in had Ron Harris not got in the way, but all he managed to do was divert the ball to Robertson whose first-time, low volley fizzed just inside the post. It was no more than Spurs deserved. Only twice had Chelsea threatened, Pat Jennings dealing confidently with long-range efforts from John Hollins.

As the second half unfolded Spurs' grip on the game tightened, their control almost total. Like a well-oiled machine they continued to push Chelsea back, another goal sure to come. That second goal arrived in the 67th minute. A typical burst down the wing from Knowles resulted in Hollins putting the ball out for a throw-in. Mackay hurled one of his long throws to the edge of the box, Robertson slipped the ball on to Saul who swivelled on a sixpence and despatched a perfectly-placed shot past Bonetti.

The game was won and Spurs eased up, content to play the ball around while the clock ran down. Even when Chelsea pulled one back four minutes from time, Jennings misjudging his punch at a Boyle cross, the ball striking Bobby Tambling and ricocheting in, Spurs did not allow themselves to be flustered. There was no hoofing the ball to the far corners of Wembley. Controlled possession was the order of the day, just as it had been at the start.

Spurs: Jennings; Kinnear, Knowles; Mullery, England, Mackay; Robertson, Greaves, Gilzean, Venables, Saul.

Chelsea: Bonetti; Harris, McCreadie; Hollins, Hinton, Harris; Cooke, Tambling, Hateley, Baldwin, Boyle.

1971 League Cup Final v Aston Villa

27 February 1971 at Wembley Stadium

With Queen's Park Rangers and Swindon Town of the Third Division having previously beaten First Division sides to win the Football League Cup at Wembley, Spurs knew their meeting with the more famous, but still Third Division, Aston Villa was going to be no Saturday afternoon stroll. Villa had a new tradition to maintain, while Spurs had no desire to join West Bromwich Albion and Arsenal on the roll of shame. That they did not was largely down to the professionalism of Steve Perryman and the opportunism of Martin Chivers.

Spurs knew that in terms of pure football technique they were vastly superior to Vill, but, as is always the case when big clubs face clubs from lower down the football ladder, they expected Villa would try to bridge the gap in class with sheer hard work and effort. If Spurs' class was to tell, they would have to compete for every ball just as hard as their Midlands' opponents.

For the first 20 minutes the expectation seemed unlikely to turn to reality. Spurs began as if victory would be little more than a stroll. They bossed the opening period, showing off their skills and looking for all the world as if they could score at will. The problem was they failed to score. They had the chances: Alan Gilzean twice put easy headers wide, Martin Peters shot tamely into John Dunn's hands when the 'keeper would have been beaten by even a half-hit shot and Chivers shot wide when scoring seemed the easier option. Villa seemed to realise that

Bill Nicholson joins two-goal scorer Martin Chivers and skipper Alan Mullery in showing the Football League Cup to the fans.

if they continued to let Spurs ride rough shod over them it was inevitable a chance would eventually be taken. Their only hope was to attack, to get Spurs on the back foot. All Spurs' mastery would count for nought if the finishing touch continued to elude them, while one flash of genius, one lucky break, might just be enough for Villa to lift the Cup.

Villa began to look for that lucky break. Chico Hamilton and Willie Anderson attacked Cyril Knowles instead of letting him race past them on the overlap. Pat McMahon pushed up on to Joe Kinnear, forcing Alan Mullery deeper and deeper to cover. The wily old stager Andy Lochhead began to use all his guile to master the inexperienced Peter Collins. The flash of genius almost came as the second half opened when Hamilton seized on a mistake by Knowles, cut into the middle and with all the space he wanted unleashed a dipping drive from 25 yards. Pat Jennings could do little as the ball clipped the bar and went over.

As the second half went on Villa dominated more and more, Spurs concentrating on defence and grateful the ever-reliable Phil Beal was playing at his best. Even he could do little, though, on the hour mark. As Collins and Jennings went for a high ball, Lochhead gave Collins a little nudge. It was subtle but effective. Jennings, Collins and Lochhead collided, and while Spurs waited for the whistle Lochhead hooked the ball towards an empty net. Spurs' experienced internationals appealed for a foul that was not to be given, grateful that young Perryman obeyed the old adage of playing to the whistle and appeared from nowhere to clear off the line.

At last Spurs were stirred into action. Mullery realised they would never win if he spent his time defending and began do what he was best at, attack. With 17 minutes left he burst forward and chipped the ball up to Chivers. His nod down found Gilzean, but there was no room for a shot so he pushed the ball in the direction of the inrushing Jimmy Neighbour. The

Tottenham Hotspur's Alan Mullery with the League Cup trophy
Action Images / MSI

opening was there and Neighbour got enough power into his shot, but it lacked conviction and was too close to Dunn. The 'keeper had little difficulty in parrying the ball but could not push it out of the danger area, and it fell perfectly for Chivers to hammer home.

Spurs now poured forward and three minutes later Chivers finished Villa off with a goal that showed just why he was regarded as England's best centre-forward. Again Mullery was at the centre of the move, finding Chivers in a crowded goalmouth with a perfect chip. Chivers took the ball down, twisted past one opponent, side-stepped another, and as the whole Villa defence went one way, he fired a fierce low drive the other. It was a cracking goal, a goal that deserved to seal another Cup Final success.

Spurs: Jennings; Kinnear, Knowles; Mullery, Collins, Beal; Gilzean, Perryman, Chivers, Peters, Neighbour.

Aston Villa: Dunn; Bradley, Aitken; Godfrey, Turnbull, Tiler; McMahon, Rioch, Lochhead, Hamilton, Anderson.

1972 UEFA Cup Final v Wolverhampton Wanderers

3 May 1972 at Molineux – first leg

Having accounted for teams from Iceland, France, Romania and Italy, the prospect of meeting another team of proven European pedigree in the Final was a mouth-watering one for Spurs, but unfortunately the Hungarians of Ferencvaros lost out to Wolverhampton Wanderers in the semi-final. Although it meant two English clubs met in the Final of a European competition for the first time, some of the gloss was taken away by facing familiar opponents.

Spurs had opened the season with a 2–2 draw with Wolves in the League and finished three places and four points above them. There was not a lot to choose between the teams, but Spurs were favoured by having the first leg at Molineux, a stadium that had witnessed some stirring European games in the later 50s when Wolves had been at their peak and invited some of the continent's best over for floodlit friendlies.

As with all two-leg ties when they were away first, Spurs knew the priority was to return with a result that would make them favourites for the second leg. A draw would be good, even a one-goal defeat acceptable, but Bill Nicholson was not a man who could put out a purely-defensive team. An away goal, even victory, would make the second leg so much easier.

The match almost opened in dramatic style as Martin Chivers hit the angle of post and crossbar after barely five minutes, but the first half soon settled down to a battle for midfield mastery. Wolves did most of the attacking, but Spurs' defence looked solid. The only incident of note in the first 45 minutes came with 20 minutes on the clock. Pat Jennings rushed out of his box to kick clear and then had to race back to his line to tip over Danny Hegan's half-volley from the halfway line.

Wolves began the second half in determined mood, and for the first 10 minutes Spurs were penned back in their own box. The home team won four corners and caused several scares in the Spurs defence, but only once did Jennings have to really distinguish himself, going down at his near post to block a John Richards shot from six yards. With 12 minutes gone the vital breakthrough Spurs had been hoping for arrived. Mike England launched a free-kick from deep inside his own half into the Wolves penalty box. Chivers, who had been rather anonymous thus far, raced across in front of Frank Munro, rose majestically and thumped his header past Phil Parkes.

The goal inspired Wolves to a period of sustained attacking, but Jennings did not look like being beaten, until the 72nd minute when the quick-thinking Richards slipped a free-kick on the edge of the Spurs box to Jim McCalliog. Spurs were still organising their defensive wall and half expected referee Bakhramov, the man who as linesman had allowed Geoff Hurst's crucial goal in the 1966 World Cup Final, to order the kick to be retaken, but he did not and McCalliog had no difficulty slipping the ball past Jennings.

Bill Nicholson responded by sending on John Pratt for Ralph Coates to bolster the defence, but the move almost immediately backfired as Pratt deflected a cross towards his own goal. Jennings did well to keep the ball out. Wolves threw men forward in search of another goal but three minutes from time were caught out by a classic counter-attack. Mullery robbed John McAlle deep in Spurs' half and fed the ball out to Chivers, loitering on

Alan Mullery throws himself full length to connect with Martin Chivers's long throw to give Spurs the lead before crashing into Phil Parkes.

Alan Mullery hoisted high by his teammates after collecting the UEFA Cup. He then did a solo lap of honour – but retained a firm grip on the trophy.

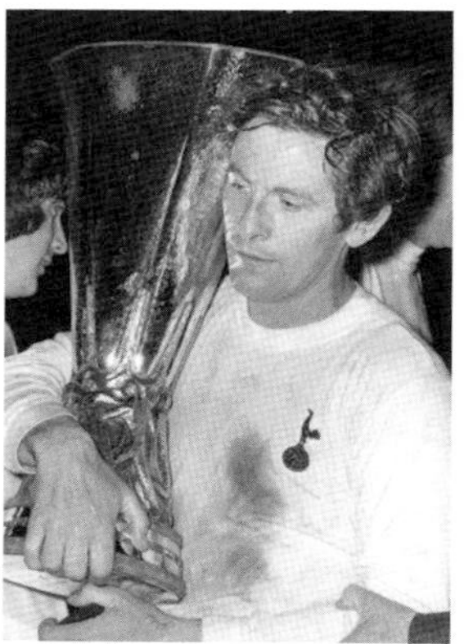

the touchline just inside the Wolves half. He advanced a dozen paces and from over 30 yards hit a scorching shot drive that gave Parkes no chance.

Wolverhampton Wanderers: Parkes; Shaw, Taylor; Hegan, Munro, McAlle; McCalliog, Hibbitt, Richards, Dougan, Wagstaffe.

Spurs: Jennings; Kinnear, Knowles, Mullery, England, Beal; Gilzean, Perryman, Chivers, Peters, Coates (Pratt).

17 May 1972 at White Hart Lane – second leg

Spurs' 68th competitive game of a long hard season that had seen them finish sixth in the League, reach the sixth round of the FA Cup and the semi-final of the League Cup, and it showed. The tiredness and fatigue was obvious in all the players. All bar one that was. Alan Mullery had missed more than half the season with a pelvic strain. He thought he was fit to return, but Bill Nicholson had not agreed so Mullery had gone on loan to Fulham, only to be recalled for the UEFA Cup semi-final with AC Milan due to an injury crisis. He had been outstanding against the Italians, played every game since his return and was now about to add the final touch to his Spurs career.

Spurs began the game as if determined to make sure the trophy was theirs before the weariness took its toll, not prepared to defend their first-leg advantage but looking to add to it and ensure no late comeback from the visitors. Mullery and Steve Perryman took a firm grip in midfield while Martin Peters hovered just behind the ever-dangerous Alan Gilzean and Martin Chivers probing for the opening. Twice Gilzean glided past the Wolves defence to go close with headers, but it was almost 30 minutes before Spurs got their reward. Peters took a free-kick out on the left and floated it towards the near post, a regular move aiming for the head of Gilzean or Chivers. This time the kick fell short, but as it dropped towards the six-yard box Mullery appeared from nowhere and flung himself at the ball. His got his head to it just as Phil Parkes clattered into him. As the ball zipped into the net, Mullery knew little about it, knocked out cold by Parkes's challenge.

Mullery soon recovered and continued to play superbly as Spurs controlled the game, but that all changed five minutes from the break. Danny Hegan tried a shot from outside the box, Mullery charged it down, but the ball spun out to David Wagstaffe who rifled it past Pat Jennings.

The second half could not have been much different from the first. Spurs seemed to have decided attack was no longer the best form of defence. They sat back, surrendered the midfield and soaked up the pressure. Wolves needed no invitation to go forward, but it was only with the introduction of Mike Bailey, the club captain who had been out injured since January, on the hour mark that they began to believe they could win the game. They pressed forward for the rest of the match, but on those rare occasions they managed to get past Spurs' defence Jennings was there to defy them.

At the final whistle Spurs had become the first winners of the UEFA Cup and the first British club to win two European trophies. Alan Mullery collected the trophy, and while his teammates sought the sanctuary of the dressing room he set off on a lone lap of honour around White Hart Lane. Lone that was except for the 4,000 delirious Spurs supporters who had invaded the pitch and accompanied him.

Spurs: Jennings; Kinnear, Knowles; Mullery, England, Beal; Gilzean, Perryman, Chivers, Peters, Coates.

Wolverhampton Wanderers: Parkes; Shaw, Taylor, Hegan. Munro, McAlle; McCalliog, Hibbitt (Bailey), Richards, Dougan (Curran), Wagstaffe.

1973 League Cup Final v Norwich City

3 March 1973 at Wembley Stadium

Cup Finals are expected to be occasions when what matters most is winning, when both teams go out on to a perfect pitch in front of a massive crowd at an historic stadium to display their football at its best. Unfortunately, Norwich City went into this game with only one objective, not to be embarrassed. Having lost their last five games, the First Division newcomers were struggling near the foot of the table. Their total lack of confidence was evident, even before the first whistle blew, as they lined up in a 4–4–2 formation. It was obvious any entertainment would have to be provided by Spurs.

Spurs certainly did their best to oblige, but they always found it difficult to raise their game above the mediocre level to which Norwich dragged them. They started with every intention of turning on the style but were soon bogged down as Norwich smothered Spurs' most creative player, Martin Peters, and matched the midfield engine room of John Pratt and Steve Perryman for endeavour. Their were few incidents of note in the goalless first half:

Norwich 'keeper Kevin Keelan pulls off a good save from Jimmy Pearce's shot.

Duncan Forbes hacked a Peters header off the line, Kevin Keelan made one good save from Alan Gilzean and Mike England went close with a couple of efforts. At the other end Norwich created only one opening, Forbes turning the chance wide. With Martin Chivers shackled by Forbes and a minimum of space for Spurs' attackers to exploit, Spurs tried to draw Norwich out of their defensive shell as the break approached. They passed the ball around at the back and in midfield, but Norwich could not be tempted forward. The most notable event came after 20 minutes, when Pratt twisted his knee and had to be replaced by Ralph Coates.

The second half continued much the same as the first, Norwich defending deep and Spurs lacking the guile to break them down. Jimmy Pearce hooked one shot just wide, scraped the post from a Peters cross and clipped a Gilzean flick against a post, but as time ran down a replay began to look almost certain. Seventy-two minutes had elapsed when the stalemate was at last broken. Chivers hurled a long throw into the Norwich box. For the umpteenth time Forbes rose to head the ball but merely deflected it across the box to Gilzean. He could do no more than head it back towards England on the edge of the box, but the big Welshman was unable to reach it. Following up was Coates, who slammed the ball along the ground, past Keelan and in at the foot of a post to make him the first substitute to score at Wembley.

Norwich had no choice now if they had any desire to win their first trophy, but still refused to make any real effort to attack. Spurs could have just played out time but they tried to add to the score, Chivers hooking a shot fractionally wide and Cyril Knowles thumping one against an upright. Only in the last couple of minutes did Norwich make any real effort to equalise, Forbes heading inches wide.

The match was not one to live long in the memory, but the victory at least maintained Spurs' record of never losing in a Final. Nine Finals, nine victories.
Spurs: Jennings; Kinnear, Knowles; Pratt (Coates), England, Beal; Gilzean, Perryman, Chivers, Peters, Pearce.
Norwich City: Keelan; Payne, Butler; Stringer, Forbes, Briggs; Livermore, Blair (Howard), Cross, Paddon, Anderson.

1981 FA Cup Final v Manchester City

9 May 1981 at Wembley Stadium
As the 100th FA Cup Final approached, attention focussed on the first appearance at Wembley of Spurs' two Argentine stars, Ossie Ardiles and Ricky Villa. Along with Glenn Hoddle they were expected to provide the midfield creativity that would set up the chances for the quicksilver strikers Garth Crooks and Steve Archibald to put Manchester City to the sword. City, though, had other ideas. Their midfield quartet of Tommy Hutchison, Steve MacKenzie, Paul Power and Gerry Gow were given the job of disrupting Spurs' fluency and imposing City's own hard-running style on the Final. They did it to great effect, Gow in particular relishing the idea of shackling Ardiles, no matter what that took. Conditions should have been ideal for Spurs, rain having made the surface slick, but if anything it counted against them as the ball skidded over the pitch, judging the weight of a pass difficult.

City began the game by making their intentions clear, hurtling into the tackle, muscling through Spurs' midfield. They won four corners in the first five minutes as Spurs were pushed back, surprised by the energy and commitment City showed. Spurs were given no time on the ball, no chance to get their passing game going and their artistry to flourish. It was 20 minutes before Spurs threatened, but then the game exploded into a flurry of activity. It started as Joe Corrigan plunged among the boots to fall on a Graham Roberts header from Steve Perryman's long free-kick, continued as he flung himself to his left to tip away Tony Galvin's shot and then raced out to foil Garth Crooks, and concluded with City taking the lead. Dave Bennett won the ball, played a one-two with Kevin Reeves and released the ball to Ray Ranson. Reeves had moved out of the middle, but Hutchison ran into the space and met Ranson's cross with a diving header from 12 yards that Milija Aleksic could only wave an arm at. Thirty minutes had gone with City in control, and the first half continued in much the same way, Crooks and Archibald isolated as Spurs were unable to get the ball, let alone hold on to it.

As the second half commenced it was clear Keith Burkinshaw had given his men a real talking to at half-time. Crooks curled a shot wide of Corrigan's post and Ardiles, having danced his way into the City area, was about to strike the equaliser when Bobby McDonald got in a last-gasp tackle. Spurs were on top now, but City were still dangerous on the break and should have gone two up just before the hour mark. Reeves cut through Spurs' defence and found MacKenzie unmarked in front of goal. He had all the time he needed and more to control the ball before walking it into the net, but chose instead to stab at the ball and watch in horror as it struck the outside of the post.

Villa was having a poor time: easily dispossessed, unable to run and find his own men with passes, and barely on the fringes of the game. After 68 minutes Burkinshaw decided a change had to be made and Villa was withdrawn, Garry Brooke taking his place. As Villa trudged to the tunnel, head bowed, despondent, Brooke provided Spurs with a new spark. He almost equalised within minutes of coming on as Archibald took the ball wide of Corrigan and cut it back. Brooke's first shot was blocked and Corrigan was back in position to collect the second. Desperation was beginning to creep into Spurs' play, but with 10 minutes left their pressure finally paid off. Gow fouled Ardiles again 30 yards out. Ardiles tapped the free-kick to Perryman who rolled it to Hoddle. Hutchison recognised the danger and stepped from City's defensive wall. Hoddle's curling shot looked to be going wide until it deflected off Hutchison's shoulder and past Corrigan.

Spurs had been looking the stronger side, but as the game went into extra-time both sides suffered with Wembley's famous cramp, and as the final whistle went they were just grateful of the chance for a rest before a second meeting.

Spurs: Aleksic; Hughton, Miller, Roberts, Perryman, Villa (Brooke); Ardiles, Archibald, Galvin, Hoddle, Crooks.

Manchester City: Corrigan; Ranson, McDonald; Reid, Power, Caton; Bennett, Gow, MacKenzie, Hutchison (Henry), Reeves.

14 May 1981 at Wembley Stadium – Replay

Football has always been a game of highs and lows, but for Ricky Villa the contrasting emotions he experienced in the space of five days could not have been greater. Having trooped miserably around the Wembley pitch, a study in abject misery, on the Saturday, he

Tottenham's Ricky Villa scores the first goal in the 1981 FA Cup Final Replay.
Action Images / Sporting Pictures / Joe Mann

Ricky Villa scores the third goal after a mazy run through the City defence.
Action Images / Sporting Pictures / Joe Mann

returned the following Thursday to end the night the hero, dancing about the stadium with the world's most famous trophy in his grasp.

Spurs knew that if they were to have any chance of winning the replay they had to compete with City's tigerish midfield far more than they had in the first game. From the kick-off they showed they were up for the challenge, and they continued in the same vein, giving City as good as they got and eventually triumphing due to their greater flair and skill.

The game started with a flourish, Ossie Ardiles freeing Garth Crooks down the right and Villa smashing the cross at goal only to see it strike Steve Archibald. Two minutes later Chris Hughton cleared Steve MacKenzie's shot off the line. Another four minutes and Spurs were back in the City area. Ardiles wriggled through their defence and shot, but the ball hit Archibald's heel. The Scot reacted quicker than anyone around him and fired in a venomous shot. Joe Corrigan did well to block the effort, but all he could do was parry the ball. It fell perfectly for Villa to control and rifle home. Eight minutes gone and the match had already produced as much excitement as the first. Three minutes later and the match moved to another level. A City free-kick was pumped into the Spurs area. Graham Roberts half-cleared, Tommy Hutchison nodded the ball to MacKenzie and his 20-yard volley flew past Milija Aleksic. A minute later Glenn Hoddle curled a free-kick around City's wall only to see it strike the post.

Spurs continued to match City's work rate and then let their superior skill tell, but Corrigan was proving a formidable barrier, thwarting Spurs time after time – two superb saves from Villa standing out. It seemed only a matter of time before Spurs scored again, but when the next goal came it was Aleksic fishing the ball out of the net. The second half was five minutes old when Dave Bennett chased a long ball into the Spurs box and went down under a challenge from Hughton and Paul Miller. Referee Hackett pointed to the spot and Kevin Reeves had no trouble converting the penalty.

It was tough on Spurs to go behind, but they did not let it affect them and pulled level on 70 minutes. A Spurs corner was cleared to the edge of the box. Hoddle delicately chipped the ball back, Archibald pulled it down and was about to let fly when Crooks poked out his left foot to jab the ball past Corrigan. The game was already being viewed as one of the most memorable of recent years but the best was yet to come. Seven minutes later Tony Galvin made another of his familiar bursts down the wing. Confronted by Ray Ranson and Tommy Caton, he checked back and rolled the ball to Villa. The big man advanced, beat Caton, then Ranson, then Caton again. As Corrigan came out Villa seemed to hesitate, but he was just waiting for Corrigan to commit himself, and as the big 'keeper went down Villa guided the ball under his body and into the net. It was a fantastic goal, as good as any ever seen at Wembley and a fitting finale to the Final in the Year of the Cockerel.

Spurs: Aleksic; Hughton, Miller, Roberts, Villa, Perryman; Ardiles, Archibald, Galvin, Hoddle, Crooks.

Manchester City: Corrigan; Ranson, McDonald (Tueart); Reid, Power, Caton; Bennett, Gow, MacKenzie, Hutchison, Reeves.

1982 FA Cup Final v Queen's Park Rangers

22 May 1982 at Wembley Stadium

After another long, tiring season in which they had reached the League (Milk) Cup Final, the European Cup-winners' Cup semi-final and finished fourth in the League, Spurs almost limped into the FA Cup Final. Tony Galvin, only just returned from injury, was clearly not fully fit, and Steve Perryman only able to play with the aid of painkillers. With Ossie Ardiles at home preparing for the World Cup Finals and refused permission to return for the Final because of the Falklands War, Spurs were desperate for the boost the presence of Ricky Villa would provide, but as events in the South Atlantic took a turn for the worse Keith Burkinshaw decided he could not risk last year's hero in the full glare of a worldwide audience. Micky Hazard replaced Ardiles and Graham Roberts was moved into midfield to take Villa's place, while Paul Price deputised at the back.

Even without their talismen Spurs should have been too powerful for their Second Division opponents, but while they had the chances to win the game comfortably they were never able to lift themselves and truly impose their superior quality on a team that fought for every minute. Under Terry Venables's management Rangers were organised and effective, but any plans he had for winning the game were sabotaged in the first minute when his star striker, Clive Allen, picked up an injury. Allen continued until early in the second half but never posed a threat.

Rangers' policy seemed one of containment, snatching a goal on the break the height of their ambition. Gary Waddock was detailed to follow Glenn Hoddle everywhere and Rangers' midfield creator, Tony Currie, was given a role just in front of the back four, so robbing Rangers of the one man who might create an opening. The deployment allowed Micky Hazard free rein to push forward, thus ensuring Spurs always had the upper hand.

For almost the entire 90 minutes of normal time it was Spurs on the attack. If the finishing had matched the build-up play they would have won comfortably. More than enough openings were created: Garth Crooks skimmed the crossbar with a curling left-footer, Hoddle whistled a free-kick just wide, Steve Archibald blazed a good chance over the bar. When they did manage to find the target they found Peter Hucker in inspired form in the Rangers' goal. He made first-class saves from Archibald, Hoddle, Crooks and Garry Brooke, and in the last minute dived at Perryman's feet to thwart the Spurs skipper. Only once had Ray Clemence been called into serious action, leaping across goal to pluck a Simon Stainrod hook out of the air.

Spurs at last got the goal their season-long efforts deserved four minutes into the second period of extra-time. Hoddle won a 50/50 tackle with Waddock, played a quick one-two with Roberts and just managed to get his shot away as he fell. The ball glanced off Currie's left leg just enough to leave Hucker stranded. Only now did Rangers make any concerted effort to attack. With five minutes remaining, Stainrod hurled a long throw into Spurs' box. Bob Hazell flicked the ball on at the near post and Terry Fenwick steamed in at the far post to head into the roof of the net.

Spurs: Clemence; Hughton, Miller, Price, Hazard (Brooke), Perryman; Roberts, Archibald, Galvin, Hoddle, Crooks.

Queen's Park Rangers: Hucker; Fenwick, Gillard; Waddock, Hazell, Roeder; Currie, Flanagan, Allen (Micklewhite), Stainrod, Gregory.

27 May 1982 at Wembley Stadium – Replay

Spurs were unchanged for the replay: Villa was, again, left to watch from the sidelines, while Rangers were weakened by the absence of the injured Allen and their suspended captain Glenn Roeder. Spurs seemed to realise Rangers would be at their most vulnerable in the early stages and set out to gain an early advantage with a series of swift attacks on the Rangers goal. Only six minutes had gone when the pressure paid dividends. Graham Roberts dispossessed Simon Stainrod in the centre circle and charged forward. He brushed aside Bob Hazell and advanced into the penalty box, only to be cut down by Tony Currie. There was not the slightest doubt it was a penalty and even less doubt Glenn Hoddle would tuck the spot-kick away. He swept it low and firm inside Peter Hucker's left-hand post as the hero of the first match went the other way.

One up so quickly, Spurs might have expected Rangers to crumble while they could at last let loose the fast, flowing, football that seemed to be pent up inside them just waiting to burst out, but it was not to be. Spurs were simply unable to find any rhythm. Their play was ponderous, lacking in confidence and too often shuddering to a halt just when it should have been piercing the Rangers defence. Their was little to remember in the rest of the first half as the game settled to a midfield stalemate, Spurs always the better team, Rangers at times struggling to hold them but rarely looking as if they would concede the killer second goal.

It all changed in the second half. Terry Venables had obviously torn into his team and they emerged to give Spurs a torrid 45 minutes. For the first time in the tie, Spurs' defence

Glenn Hoddle scores the winning goal from the penalty spot.
Action Images / Sporting Pictures / Trevor Jones

was given a thorough examination, and Ray Clemence, slowed by a first-half knock, was called upon to show all his class. Three minutes had gone when a bad back pass by Roberts was picked up by Currie. He released Gary Micklewhite, who rounded Paul Price and chipped the ball in for Stainrod to beat Clemence, but his header went over the bar. Clemence was continually called into action, making agile saves from Stainrod and Waddock, but he could only look on helplessly after missing Stainrod's cross to see Paul Miller and Steve Perryman scramble John Gregory's header away.

Rangers' commitment to attack was total, which meant they were always susceptible to a quick breakaway. Just such a situation arose in the 57th minute, but Hucker made a fine save from Steve Archibald. Rangers immediately resumed where they had left off, camped in Spurs' half. Stainrod's fearsome shot hit Roberts and deflected towards the top corner, but Clemence went full length to fingertip the ball away. A minute later, a Gregory effort hit the bar. Rangers fully deserved an equaliser, and it seemed certain to arrive with 13 minutes left. Currie delayed his cross until Hazell had thundered into the area, but Miller dived in to block the Rangers centre-half just three yards out. As the final whistle drew nearer Rangers' desperation grew, they threw everyone at Spurs and very nearly paid the penalty in the final minute when Archibald clipped the post.

When the whistle went, Spurs had retained the Cup, reward for a season of endeavour mixed with disappointment, but Rangers were the heroes, applauded off the field by the Spurs fans as loudly as by their own supporters.

Spurs: Clemence; Hughton, Miller, Price, Hazard (Brooke), Perryman; Roberts, Archibald, Galvin, Hoddle, Crooks.

Queen's Park Rangers: Hucker; Fenwick, Gillard; Waddock, Hazell, Neill; Currie, Flanagan, Micklewhite (Burke), Stainrod, Gregory.

1984 UEFA Cup Final v Anderlecht

9 May 1984 at Stadion Constant Vanden Stock, Brussels – first leg

If Spurs' players needed any incentive to go out and win the UEFA Cup for the second time, it came with the news manager Keith Burkinshaw was leaving at the end of the season. A popular figure ever since joining the club as a coach, Burkinshaw had led his men to some of the most successful days in their playing careers, members of a team revered for their fabulous football and second only to the double winners in terms of winning trophies.

Anderlecht were expected to be formidable opponents, recognised as one of Europe's top teams, technically gifted and unbeaten at home in 10 years of European football. Spurs would need to be at their best to get anything from the first leg and preferably at their strongest. There was little chance of that. Ossie Ardiles had returned early from his loan at Paris St Germain but suffered one injury after another and Glenn Hoddle, the player Burkinshaw had built his team around, had been out since March. At best one of them might be available for the second leg.

Anderlecht had put three goals past Nottingham Forest in the semi-final, and Spurs knew they would need a superb defensive performance if they were to have any hope of overcoming the Cup holders in the second leg. Graham Roberts and Paul Miller, in particular, were required to be at their absolute best if they were to keep the Belgian's dangerous forwards away from Tony Parks. The young 'keeper had done such a good job as stand-in for the injured Ray Clemence that, although Clemence was fit enough to take his place on the bench, Parks could not be left out.

Paul Miller can just be seen between Steve Archibald (8) and Mark Falco (9) as he powers home his header to give Spurs the lead in Brussels.

In an intimidating, compact stadium, Spurs produced more than a superb defensive performance. They stunned the Belgians not only with their determination and commitment, but also with their technical ability and swift, precise counter-attacking. There were times when they even outplayed their hosts. Twice in the first half Mark Falco had great chances to put Spurs ahead but each time missed the target. Early in the second period he saw his shot cleared off the line. He might have regretted those misses, but in the 58th minute Paul Miller silenced the 85% of the crowd made up of home fans. Micky Hazard floated a corner into the box, and Miller muscled his way through to send a bullet-like header past Jacky Munaron.

Anderlecht were stung into action and launched attack after attack, but the whole Spurs back line rose to the challenge, repelling all the hosts could throw at them. Falco could have made the tie safe but blasted over from a rare breakaway. Spurs looked like holding out for one of their best-ever away results, but with five minutes left Anderlecht got an equaliser. Frank Arnesen got in a powerful shot; Parks did well to get his hands to the ball but could only parry it to Morten Olsen, who whipped it home. A draw was still a great result, and Spurs returned home confident they would complete the job in the second leg.

Anderlecht: Munaron; Grun, de Greef, Czerniatinski (Vercauteren), de Groote; Scifo, Vandereycken, Hofkens, Vandenbergh (Arnesen), Olsen, Larsen.

Spurs: Parks; Thomas, Hughton; Roberts, Miller, Perryman; Hazard, Archibald, Falco, Stevens (Mabbutt), Galvin.

23 May 1984 at White Hart Lane – second leg

Neither Glenn Hoddle nor Ossie Ardiles were fit enough to return for the second leg, and to make things even worse for Spurs a booking in the first leg meant captain Steve Perryman was suspended and could not take up his almost mandatory position.

The match was pulsating from start to finish, muscular aggression, determination and commitment mixed with some delicate skills from both sides. Not surprisingly as the home team, Spurs had most of the play, but Anderlecht, with their sharp, incisive football, were always dangerous on the break. Spurs tried to put the game beyond Anderlecht with some early pressure but seemed inhibited and weighed down with the pressure of expectation. They created few real openings: a Steve Archibald volley over the bar, a Gary Mabbutt shot blocked, while the best chance of the half fell to the visitors as Tony Parks was forced to rush from his line to clear from a clean through Alex Czerniatinski. The second half started in similar fashion, but on the hour mark White Hart Lane was stunned as the Belgians took the lead. Morten Olsen created the opening for Czerniatinski, who finished with a sweet right-footed chip past Parks.

For the next 15 minutes Spurs pounded the Anderlecht defence. Munaron made two flying saves from Archibald, but as the clock ticked down there seemed no way through. With 77 minutes gone, Spurs, growing increasingly desperate and needing something different, Burkinshaw threw Ardiles on in place of first-leg hero Paul Miller. The little man inspired Spurs to one last effort as an incredible spell of pressure followed. With seven minutes left Archibald, the one man who might just have the beating of Munaron, saw another effort wonderfully saved at the expense of a corner. When the flag-kick came

Graham Roberts celebrates after scoring a late equalising goal.
Action Images / Sporting Pictures / Joe Mann

in, Ardiles hit the bar from six yards out. The ball was cleared but sent straight back in by Hazard, and Graham Roberts bustled his way through to take the ball down on his chest and crash in the equaliser. Falco almost snatched the trophy in injury time but Wim Hofkens cleared his header off the line.

Penalty saving hero Tony Parks gets his hands on the trophy after a night of high drama at White Hart Lane.

In extra-time both teams were tired and cautious. One mistake and the match could be lost. The longer it went the more both teams seemed to have settled for penalties. Never a satisfactory way to settle one game, let alone a major competition, two things penalties do provide are drama and the chance for an unlikely hero to emerge.

Roberts, Spurs' stand-in skipper who had proved a colossus in defence and attack, took the first kick and hammered it home. Morten Olsen was next up, but Parks flew to his left to push his shot away. Falco, Gary Stevens and Archibald then netted for Spurs with Michel de Groote, Franky Vercauteren and Enzo Scifo replying. Danny Thomas

Tottenham's Graham Roberts lifts the UEFA Cup trophy.
Action Images / Sporting Pictures / Joe Mann

stepped forward to win the trophy but held his head in horror as Munaron saved. Parks had already made one great save, but now he had to do it again if sudden death penalties were to be avoided. Anderlecht substitute Arnor Gudjohnsen hit his shot sweetly, but instead of going to his left as he had for the previous penalties, Parks dived to his right, blocked the shot and then set out on a wheel of delight as he realised he had won the UEFA Cup.

Spurs: Parks; Thomas, Hughton; Roberts, Miller (Ardiles), Mabbutt (Dick); Hazard, Archibald, Falco, Stevens, Galvin.

Anderlecht: Munaron; Grun, de Greef, Czerniatinski (Brylle), de Groote, Vercauteren; Vandereycken, Hofkens, Scifo, Olsen, Arnesen (Gudjohnsen).

1991 FA Cup Final v Nottingham Forest

18 May 1991 at Wembley Stadium

Paul Gascoigne was expected to embellish the biggest day in the domestic football calendar with a performance that would hog the headlines not only on the back pages of the Sunday papers, but the front pages too. Hog the headlines he did, but not for a Cup-winning show.

As the teams came out it was obvious Gascoigne was high on adrenaline, a nervous bundle of energy who could not wait to make his mark as Spurs went for a record eighth FA Cup success. He made it within a minute, high up on Gary Parker's midriff. The foul merited a booking, and if referee Milford had dished one out Gascoigne may have calmed down. He failed to do so and Gascoigne continued to steam around the pitch trying to do everything. In the 15th minute he was back on the edge of his box as Forest full-back Gary Charles looked for a gap. There was little danger, but Gascoigne hurled himself at Charles with a high and late, but not malicious, challenge. After treatment, Gascoigne took up his defensive position. The free-kick was in the 'D', perfect for Stuart Pearce. Forest positioned Lee Glover on the end of Spurs' defensive wall, and as Pearce moved up to strike the ball he turned Gary Mabbutt, making just enough space for Pearce's shot to thunder through and past Erik Thorstvedt. As Forest celebrated Gascoigne collapsed. He had seriously damaged his knee and was stretchered off.

The loss of Gascoigne could have proved too much, but Spurs were not a one-man team and now they had to win the trophy as payback for the way Gascoigne had worked minor miracles to take Spurs to Wembley. Eight minutes after Forest had taken the lead, Gary Lineker nipped through the Forest defence to poke the ball home, only to be given offside, wrongly as replays later showed. Ten minutes after that he was set free by a Paul Stewart pass. One on one with the 'keeper, he rounded Mark Crossley only to be brought down. There was no one better to take a penalty than Lineker, but he put his shot too close to Crossley who clawed the ball away. Spurs spent the rest of the first half probing for another opening, but one would not come.

As soon as the game restarted, David Howells was called upon to clear Roy Keane's shot off the line. It signalled the beginning of 15 minutes pressure by Spurs that was to turn the match. In the 54th minute Nayim found Paul Allen. The little midfielder scurried hard to

Paul Stewart scores the equaliser v Nottingham Forest in the 1991 FA Cup Final.
Action Images

the right of the Forest penalty, spotted Stewart racing up outside and played the ball perfectly into his path. Stewart controlled the ball, advanced a few strides and drilled his shot across Crossley and in at the post.

Spurs continued to control the game, but it was only in the last few minutes of normal time that another goal looked like coming. Paul Walsh looped a header over Crossley, but

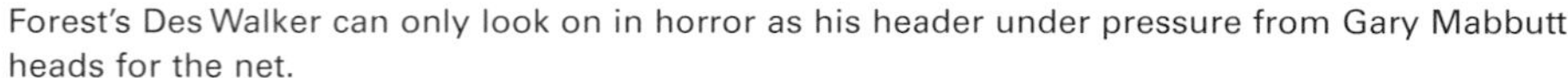
Forest's Des Walker can only look on in horror as his header under pressure from Gary Mabbutt heads for the net.

The Tottenham Hotspur players celebrate with the Cup after beating Nottingham Forest 2–1.
Action Images / MSI

the ball landed on top of the bar and in the last minute a flying leap from Crossley denied Howells a winner. Extra-time was only four minutes old when another Walsh header was tipped over. Nayim's corner was floated to the near post where Stewart back-headed across goal. If Des Walker had not gone for the ball Gary Mabbutt would have applied the finishing touch. Walker got his head to the ball but could only head it into the roof of his own net. The game was won and all that remained was for the Spurs players to deliver the Cup and a medal to Gascoigne in his hospital bed.

Spurs: Thorstvedt; Edinburgh, Van den Hauwe; Sedgley, Howells, Mabbutt; Stewart, Gascoigne (Nayim), Samways (Walsh), Lineker, Allen.

Nottingham Forest: Crossley; Charles, Pearce; Walker, Chettle, Keane; Crosby, Parker, Clough, Glover (Laws), Woan (Hodge).

Tottenham Hotspur's Gary Mabbutt raises the trophy.
Action Images / Sporting Pictures

1999 Worthington Cup Final v Leicester City

21 March 1999 at Wembley Stadium

The Worthington Cup may have lost much of its importance with the expansion of the European Champions Cup into the Champions League and many of the 'big' clubs fielding less than full-strength teams, but it still provided a route into European competition and, as Bill Nicholson had said, Spurs just had to be playing in Europe. For one man, though, it meant more than that. George Graham desperately needed to win some silverware if he was to have any chance of being accepted by most Spurs supporters.

In a way it was ironic that Spurs' opponents should be Leicester City. Martin O'Neill had built a solid, dependable team based on hard work, commitment and occasional flashes of skill, just the type of team Graham had spent his managerial career striving to fashion.

Spurs were favourites, if only because in David Ginola they had the man who could turn a game with one flash of brilliance. Unfortunately, Ginola was also a player who could be frustrated and drift out of games if shackled. O'Neill knew that and his plans were based around stifling the Frenchman. Rob Ullathorne was given the job of man-marking Ginola while Neil Lennon, Robbie Savage and Matt Elliott were deputed to cover, one of them always ready to step in if Ginola got free. It all contributed to a stagnant match, bogged down in midfield and with few incidents of note.

Spurs began by trying to get the ball out to Ginola at every opportunity, but Ullathorne stuck to his man like a limpet. Without Ginola's creativity Spurs had little else to offer. Darren Anderton had the ability but could find no space, while Leicester always had defence uppermost in their minds. Ginola's back-heel did give Anderton a glimpse of an opening, but he was closed down before he could shoot. Apart from that the only time either goal came under threat in the first half was six minutes before the break, when Kasey Keller had little difficulty dealing with a Steffen Iversen header. Early in the second half Ullathorne left Ginola for a moment and fired in a firm shot. Ian Walker should have dealt with it comfortably, but he fumbled the ball and only just retrieved it before Tony Cottee pounced.

The game sparked into life for a few minutes just after the hour mark but not for any goalmouth excitement. Justin Edinburgh and Savage went for a loose ball in midfield. Edinburgh got there first. Savage did not need to continue with his challenge, but he did and caught Edinburgh late. Edinburgh responded by slapping his assailant. It was a nothing blow but Savage held his face as if he had received a full-blown punch. Edinburgh was sent off, Savage booked.

Anderton dropped back to fill in for Edinburgh and Iversen was pulled back into midfield. Leicester may have had the numerical superiority, but they made little attempt to take advantage of it, seemingly content to wait for extra-time. Spurs sensed their only hope of victory was to score in the 90 minutes, but their best chance seemed to have disappeared with 10 minutes to go when Iversen shot into the side netting. The match had just gone into injury time when Steve Carr showed the courage to dribble past Cottee and Ian Marshall deep in his own area before finding Les Ferdinand, who switched the ball to Iversen. The young Norwegian knocked the ball past Steve Walsh and powered down the wing after it.

Allan Neilson scores against Leicester City with a diving header minutes before the final whistle of the Worthington Cup Final at Wembley, March 21.
Action Images / Reuters

He had too much pace for Walsh but from a wide angle could do no more than hit a cross-cum-shot into the Leicester box. Keller blocked but the ball looped up into the air, and Alan Nielsen, the only Spurs player with the energy to keep up with Iversen, plunged to head home.

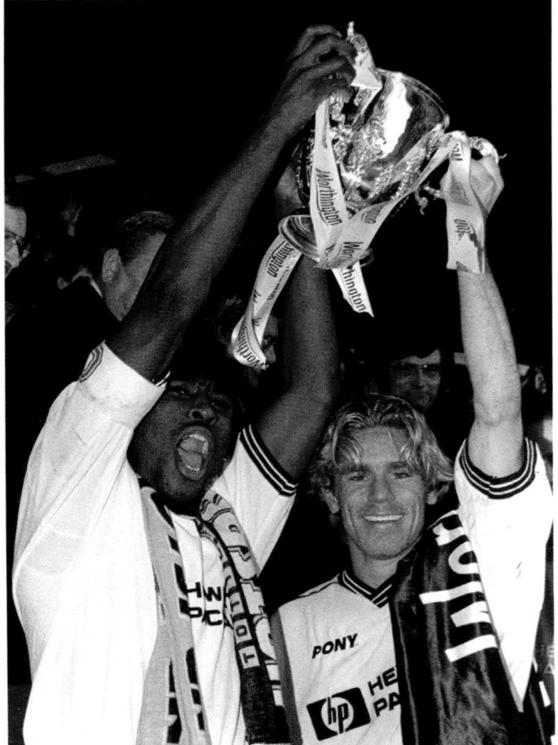

It was not a performance Spurs could be particularly proud of, but victory meant a return to the UEFA Cup and the chants of 'One-nil to the Tottenham' must have been music to one man's ears.

Spurs: Walker; Carr, Edinburgh; Freund, Vega, Campbell; Ginola (Sinton), Nielsen, Anderton; Ferdinand, Iversen.

Leicester City: Keller; Taggart, Ullathorne; Elliott, Walsh, Izzet; Lennon, Savage (Zagorakis), Heskey (Marshall), Cottee, Guppy.

Sol Campbell lifts the Worthington Cup with teammate Allan Neilson at Wembley.
Reuters / Action Images

2008 Carling Cup Final v Chelsea

24 February 2008 at Wembley Stadium

In beating Chelsea on Spurs first visit to the new Wembley Stadium, Juande Ramos's reputation as a Cup-winning coach was reinforced by a success that owed much to his ability to make the changes that can alter the course of a game.

Under Jose Mourinho, Chelsea's expensively assembled stars had been moulded into a team that won matches, a team that put winning at the top of the agenda with entertainment very much a secondary consideration. Attack early on, grab a goal, then shut up shop was the order of the day. If further goals came along, all well and good, but they only needed to be sought out when not already ahead. Mourinho had gone, but there was little reason for his successor, Avram Grant, to change Mourinho's winning formula. It was a formula that would have bought about another success had Ramos not shown the tactical nous needed to derail the Chelsea machine.

With a fantastic, flag-waving support that drowned out the West Londoner's fans, Spurs took the game to Chelsea from the first minute as Robbie Keane snapped up a poor pass by Juliano Belletti to fire in a shot diverted wide by John Terry. From the resulting corner Ledley King, playing his first game for a month, only just failed to reach Dimitar Berbatov's header. It set the tone for the first half-hour as Spurs continued to attack, while Chelsea were content to simply hold on to a goalless score-line.

A Steed Malbranque corner that saw a back-header from Pascal Chimbonda bounce on top of the Chelsea crossbar was quickly followed by a mis-directed Berbatov header from Keane's cross going wide when he was left free in the box.

When Chelsea did, at last, get into an offensive position, Jonathan Woodgate easily snuffed out the threat from a Shaun Wright-Phillips cross before making his way forward to emphasise Spurs' aerial threat by getting on the end of a perfectly flighted Jermaine Jenas free-kick. Steed Malbranque had a shot easily saved by Peter Cech before Frank Lampard had Chelsea's first shot at goal. It had taken them 30 minutes and was hardly worth the effort.

Spurs had been by far the better team. Their football was quick, the passing neat and fluent and, even though Chelsea had an extra man in midfield, Spurs dominated possession. It was a situation Chelsea were not unfamiliar with. Having ridden out the storm, now was the time for Chelsea to grab what had all too often proved the decisive first goal. That was exactly what they did.

Didier Zokora fouled compatriot Didier Drogba on the edge of Spurs' penalty area. Drogba took the free-kick and put it well over Paul Robinson's bar. It was to prove nothing more than a sighter. With 37 minutes gone, a clumsy Zokora challenge saw Drogba crumble to the floor again. From almost the same position as his first effort, Drogba bent his free-kick around the wall and past a flat-footed Robinson.

The goal took the sting out of Spurs' play, while Chelsea retreated back into their shell and awaited half-time. Berbatov did have an opening just before the break, but slipped as he and Ricardo Carvalho went for Keane's pass.

Dimitar Berbatov scores the first goal for Tottenham Hotspur from the penalty spot.
Action Images / Michael Regan

Dimitar Berbatov sends the 'keeper the wrong way.
Action Images / Tony O'Brien

Jonathan Woodgate scores the second goal for Tottenham Hotspur.
Action Images / Alex Morton

Tottenham Hotspur celebrate victory with champagne and the Carling Cup.
Action Images / Alex Morton

The second half started as the first had, Spurs trying to create openings but Chelsea happy to pull everyone back and stifle the game.

With an hour gone Ramos took off Chimbonda and introduced Tom Huddleston's passing skills in midfield. It meant Malbranque moving to full-back but, with no Chelsea forward prepared to take him on, the Frenchman was as free to continue attacking as he had been prior to the break.

After 10 minutes the substitution paid dividends. Aaron Lennon, rejuvenated by Huddlestone's ability to release him down the left, swapped roles and hit a diagonal pass across the pitch to the far side of the penalty area. As Huddlestone took the ball down Wayne Bridge's juggling of it with his hand was spotted by the linesman. There was no arguing that it was a clear penalty and even less arguing about the nonchalant way Berbatov sent Cech in one direction and the ball in the other.

For the rest of normal time it was back to how it had been with Spurs dominating and Chelsea trying to kill the game. Only one real chance was created. With 81 minutes gone, a quick through ball from Keane sent Zokora through from the half-way line. Anybody else and a goal would have been a near certainty but Zokora's prowess lay in breaking up play, not rounding a world-class 'keeper and rolling the ball into an empty net. As he advanced on goal doubt crept in. Rather than going past Cech, he shot from the edge of the box. The ball struck Cech on the head. It rebounded to Zokora, but his second effort was way off target.

Into extra-time and only four minutes had elapsed when Spurs got the goal their play and attitude deserved. Jenas floated a free-kick into the box from the left. Woodgate, playing only his fifth game since signing from Middlesbrough, escaped his marker and got his head to the ball before Cech. It hit the Chelsea 'keeper, rebounded into Woodgate's face and bounced into the net.

Only now did Chelsea show any attacking intent. Younes Kaboul was brought on in place of Keane to strengthen the back line as Chelsea began to hurl the ball forward in the hope Drogba and Nicholas Anelka could pinch an undeserved equaliser. In fact, Chelsea created little, Robinson only being called upon to make one serious save from Salomon Kalou before the final whistle.

Spurs: Robinson; Chimbonda (Huddlestone), Hutton, Zokora, Woodgate, King, Malbranque (Tainio), Jenas, Berbatov, Keane (Kaboul), Lennon
Chelsea: Cech; Belletti, Carvalho, Terry, Bridge, Mikel (Cole J.), Wright-Phillips (Kalou), Essien (Ballack), Lampard, Anelka, Drogba.

100 GREAT PLAYERS

n the following pages appear profiles of 100 players who have appeared for Spurs since the club's foundation in 1882.

It is not a list of the 'Top 100' or best-known players, but a selection of some of the great names who have served the club so well. Many of the players will be household names, others well known to the older generation of supporters, and some players from the dim and distant past whose contributions to laying the foundations of the club we have today have become lost in the mists of time.

A few words of explanation are appropriate.

Transfer fees are always notoriously difficult to ascertain. These days figures are often released, but in past years there would rarely be any official announcement of how much had been paid or received. Journalists would make their educated guesses and were often remarkably accurate, but just as often their estimates would be totally incorrect. The figures given are those that are generally accepted as being pretty close to the mark, but they should not be regarded as authoritative in any way.

The debut given for each player is the first game they played in what would today be regarded as a major competitive game, not necessarily the player's first appearance in what is generally accepted as a first-team game.

ALLEN, Clive Darren (1984–88)

Striker, 5ft 10in, 12st 3lb

Born: Stepney, East London, 20 May 1961

Signed from Queen's Park Rangers, August 1984, £700,000

Transferred to Bordeaux (France), March 1988, £1,000,000

Also played for: Queen's Park Rangers, Arsenal, Crystal Palace, Bordeaux, Manchester City, Chelsea, West Ham United, Millwall, England

Spurs record:

Debut: 25 August 1984 v Everton (FL) (a) won 4–1

Appearances: League 97(8), FA Cup 11(1), League Cup 13(1), Europe 3(1), others 32(7)

Goals: League 60, FA Cup 9, League Cup 13, Europe 2, others 29

■ Following in the footsteps of his double-winning father Les was never going to be easy for Clive Allen, but while he never won the trophies his father did he left as indelible a mark on Spurs' history for his individual exploits as Les did as a member of the club's greatest team.

Allen began his career with Queen's Park Rangers, notching 34 goals in 55 games, before becoming the youngest player transferred for a seven-figure fee when he joined Arsenal for £1.25 million in June 1980. It was a move that might have scuppered any chance of him gracing White Hart Lane on a regular basis, but his stay at Highbury was incredibly short. Within a couple of months he was off to Crystal Palace, Terry Neill acceding to Palace manager Terry Venables's demands for Allen in exchange for Kenny Sansom. Two months later Venables went to Queen's Park Rangers, and Allen struggled in his one season at Selhurst Park before returning to Loftus Road.

Allen quickly rediscovered his goalscoring form and led the line as Rangers progressed to the 1982 FA Cup Final, but the joy of playing in a Wembley Final was short-lived. Injured in the first 10 minutes, he had to go off and missed the replay, won for Spurs by Glenn Hoddle's penalty.

On returning from England's 1984 tour to South America, Allen became, along with John Chiedozie, one of new manager Peter Shreeves's first signings. He made a great start, scoring two goals on his debut, and his partnership with

Mark Falco looked full of promise, until Allen sustained a groin injury in December 1984. It was almost a year before he returned, but signs of what was to come were apparent in the last three games of 1985–86 as Allen found the net five times.

The following season every touch of the ball turned to goals for Allen. Right from an opening-day hat-trick at Aston Villa, he could do no wrong, but it was when David Pleat decided to play with an attacking, fluid five-man midfield that Allen's goalscoring reached new levels. Ironically, it was the arrival of Nico Claesen that proved the catalyst. The Belgian had proved very successful as a lone striker in the 1986 World Cup, and Pleat secured his transfer intending to play him if not in place of then alongside Allen. As it transpired, Allen flourished as the sole attacker supported by Hoddle, Chris Waddle, Paul Allen, Steve Hodge and Ossie Ardiles or Tony Galvin. In 54 matches he scored 49 goals, an incredible total that beat Jimmy Greaves's 1962–63 record of 42.

Everything that made Allen a natural goalscorer was encapsulated in that one season. Not a player with great dribbling ability or pace, while he had a powerful long-range shot Allen often appeared to do little outside the penalty area, but he was there to finish off other's hard work, and when the ball was near goal he was supreme. No matter how it arrived, he had the ability to get it under control instantly, twist away from his marker and find just enough space to get in a shot that usually found the target. His great strength, though, was an uncanny ability to know where the ball was going to end up irrespective of where it seemed to be heading. Often he would hold his run into the box as if he knew a cross was going to deflect off a defender's boot to land at his feet. When it did, he was lethal, reacting instantly and guiding the ball into the net in a manner reminiscent of Greaves.

The last of his 49 goals came in the 1987 FA Cup Final, a near-post header in the first two minutes, but again Wembley did not prove a happy venue as Coventry City went on to win the most entertaining Final for years. Small consolation came with both the PFA and FWA Player of the Year awards.

1986–87 proved the peak of Allen's Spurs career. A marked man, he started the new season well enough, but with supplier-in-chief Hoddle departed and off-field distractions taking their toll on the team his form took a turn for the worse. The arrival of Venables promised to rejuvenate him, but the man who had twice invested heavily in Allen's talents soon made it known he was not part of his plans. He moved to Bordeaux and later played for Manchester City, Chelsea, West Ham United and Millwall, giving him a total of seven London clubs. He added another in 1997, as kicker for the London Monarchs in the World League of American Football, aiming to put the ball over a bar he had proved so adept at putting it under.

ALLEN, Leslie William (1959–1965)

Centre or inside-forward, 5ft 10in, 10st 3lb

Born: Dagenham, Essex,
4 September 1937
Signed from Chelsea December 1959, in exchange for Johnny Brooks. Transferred to Queen's Park Rangers, July 1965, £21,000
Also played for: Chelsea, Queen's Park Rangers

Spurs record:

Debut: 19 December 1959 v Newcastle United (FL) (h) won 4–0

Appearances: League 119, FA Cup 15, Europe 3, others 10

Goals: League 47, FA Cup 13, Europe 1, others 14

■ In four years with Chelsea, Les Allen had scored 11 goals in 44 League games, but with Ron Tindall and Jimmy Greaves ahead of him in the pecking order he did not look to have much of a future in West London. At 22 his career appeared to have stalled, but within 18 months of joining Spurs it zoomed to new heights as Allen became an ever-present member of the double-winning team.

It was a typically shrewd piece of business when Bill Nicholson offered former England international Johnny Brooks in exchange for Allen, who had been an amateur on Spurs' books before signing for Chelsea in December 1959. Nicholson had been in charge for just over a year and was already turning things around but knew he needed more firepower. Brooks was a popular player who could be exciting and effective, but at other times he was inconsistent and drifted out of games. Allen was not eye-catching, but he was dependable and could always be relied upon to give everything for the full 90 minutes. Having started as an out-and-out centre-forward, he was also more likely to score than Brooks and his arrival was sure to take some of the goalscoring burden off the shoulders of Bobby Smith and Cliff Jones.

Allen did not find the net on his debut but netted 13 in his next eight games, including five in the 13–2 FA Cup annihilation of Crewe Alexandra. By the end of the season he had scored 15 goals in 19 matches. Nicholson's ability to spot an unappreciated talent was again to pay rich dividends.

Allen fitted perfectly into the style of play Nicholson demanded of his team. He was strong, had excellent ball control and liked to move the ball around quickly. His intelligent linking of defence and attack was just what Nicholson wanted, his tireless work in closing down space and defending from the front crucial to Spurs' success, and when an opening presented itself he knew how to make the most of it. Playing behind Smith, Allen had time and space and was able to move into the box late to feed off the crosses supplied by Jones and Terry Dyson, or pick up the pieces from a Smith knockdown. He was also able to hold back and use his excellent passing ability to create chances.

Ever present in the double season, he scored 27 goals, second only to Smith, including the one that clinched the League title against Sheffield Wednesday – a superb right-foot volley that sent a packed White Hart Lane into raptures. Like Peter Baker and Ron Henry, Allen was one of the unsung heroes of the double winners, often overlooked by those on the outside but truly appreciated by their teammates.

That Allen was a class footballer was beyond doubt. If he lacked in anything it was confidence, often deferring to his more exalted colleagues. With a bit more belief in his own ability, a little arrogance if you like, he might have enjoyed even more success.

Allen collected an England Under-23 cap in February 1961, but that was the nearest he got to full international honours. The chances of going further on the international scene were not helped by the arrival in November 1961 of Jimmy Greaves, the only player who could

improve Nicholson's great team. Greaves was expected to take Allen's place, but it was actually Bobby Smith who found himself out of the team at first, Allen taking his number-nine shirt and partnering Greaves. For the next two years Allen competed with Smith for the central role, partnering Greaves as often as Smith did but losing out when trophies were at stake: the 1962 FA Cup Final and the following year's European Cup-winners' Cup Final.

It was only with the arrival of Alan Gilzean in December 1964 that Allen became surplus to requirements, and in the summer of 1965 he was allowed to move to Queen's Park Rangers for a £21,000 fee.

At Loftus Road he helped a young Rangers side climb from the Third to the First Division in successive seasons and become the first Third Division side to win the Football League Cup on the first occasion the Final was held at Wembley. Allen moved into management with Rangers in December 1968, later managing Swindon Town and in Greece before leaving football entirely to work in the car industry back home in Essex.

ALLEN, Paul Kevin (1985–94)

Midfield, 5ft 7in, 11st

Born: Aveley, Essex, 26 August 1962
Signed from West Ham United, June 1985, £400,000
Transferred to Southampton, September 1993, £550,000
Also played for: West Ham United, Southampton, Luton Town, Stoke City, Swindon Town, Bristol City, Millwall, Purfleet

Spurs record:

Debut: 17 August 1985 v Watford (FL) (h) won 4–0
Appearances: League 276(16), FA Cup 26(1), League Cup 42(2), Europe 6(1), others 94(7)
Goals: League 23, FA Cup 1, League Cup 4, others 3

■ Nephew of Les and cousin of Clive, Paul Allen may never have received the personal glory heaped upon his relatives, but to those Spurs' supporters who watched him in the late 80s and early 90s he was every bit as important to Spurs as the two goalscorers. As part of the famous football family, Allen was earmarked for fame

even before he signed for West Ham United, and he soon lived up to the billing, establishing himself in their first team by the age of 18 and at only 17 years and 256 days old becoming the youngest player in FA Cup Final history when he played against Arsenal in 1980. He may well have become the youngest scorer in an FA Cup Final too, had it not been for a cynical 'professional foul' by Arsenal's former Spurs defender Willie Young when clear on goal.

Moving smoothly through from England Youth to Under-21 level, Allen's whole-hearted commitment and ceaseless running soon attracted the attention of the bigger clubs, and with West Ham struggling at the wrong end of the table a move to a club more likely to garner football's trophies seemed inevitable. With his contract coming to an end in the summer of 1985, it came down to a choice between Spurs, Arsenal and Liverpool, Allen choosing to join Clive at White Hart Lane with the £400,000 fee being set by a tribunal.

Chris Waddle joined Spurs at the same time, and, while the Geordie grabbed the headlines, Allen settled to the task of establishing himself and battening down the right side of midfield. It took him time to settle and there were some supporters who doubted the wisdom of his signing, but worries over the health of his daughter were not well known, and it was only as those concerns receded that Allen really began to show his worth.

With a unique scampering run, Allen worked his socks off for the Spurs cause, shuttling backwards and forwards down the right flank, one minute racing past his marker to set up an opening, the next scurrying back to provide support for his full-back. He never gave less than 100 percent, cajoling his teammates to follow his example and urging the crowd to get behind the team. Allen may not have had the flair of some, but what he lacked in skill (and he possessed a fair amount) he more than made up for with a fierce determination to give his all for the full 90 minutes, which often put his more lauded colleagues to shame. This was particularly so in away games. While some would retreat into their shell, Allen would rise to the challenge, taking the battle to the opposition.

Allen became one of Spurs' most consistent performers, his contribution often overlooked by the pundits but fully appreciated by his coaches and teammates. A member of the side that lost to Coventry City in the 1987 FA Cup Final, he was selected for the England B tour at the end of the 1988–89 season but injury forced his withdrawal. He never got another chance to perform at international level but deservedly picked up an FA Cup-winners' medal against Nottingham Forest in 1991. The loss of Paul Gascoigne seemed to galvanise Allen into giving that little bit more, and it was his break from deep in midfield that set up the opening for Paul Stewart's crucial equaliser.

Consistent, reliable and a fixture in the team, Allen seemed set to finish his career at Spurs but the arrival of Ossie Ardiles with his dream of packing the team with skill and flair saw Allen out of favour. Never given an opportunity to show Ardiles just what he had to offer, Allen was allowed to move to Southampton in September 1993 for £550,000.

Those supporters who regularly travel to away games see a side of players not apparent to those who only watch the team at home. When Spurs went to the Dell a couple of months after Allen's departure, those travelling fans showed how much they appreciated Allen's efforts. Despite losing 0–1 to the Saints, the travelling Spurs support remained in place at the final whistle, not to applaud Spurs for their efforts but to chant the name of Paul Allen. There could be no better display of the esteem in which he was held.

ANDERTON, Darren Robert (1992–2004)

Forward, 6ft 1in, 12st 7lb

Born: Southampton, Hampshire, 3 March 1972
Signed from Portsmouth, June 1992, £2,000,000
Transferred to Birmingham City, August 2004, released
Also played for: Portsmouth, Birmingham City, Wolverhampton Wanderers, AFC Bournemouth, England

Spurs record:

Debut: 15 August 1992 v Southampton (a) drew 0–0
Appearances: League 273(26), FA Cup 26(2), League Cup 30(1), others 60(9)
Goals: League 34, FA Cup 6, League Cup 8, others 18

■ To many people, Terry Venables's £2 million signing of Darren Anderton was a gamble. The youngster had played barely 18 months of First Division football, and while he clearly possessed ability it was still a lot of money to lay out on a 20-year-old some viewed as a bit of an old-fashioned winger.

Anderton had made his name as the outstanding performer for Portsmouth as they made their way to the 1992 FA Cup semi-finals and proved the star of the battles with Liverpool that they were unfortunate to lose on penalties. Venables was always regarded as a good judge of young players and not afraid to back his judgement with big money, so while others dithered he moved quickly to secure Anderton's services in June 1992.

With Portsmouth, Anderton played out wide, tracking back when needed but very much an attacking player, a real handful for any full-back with his pace and trickery. Since the departure of Chris Waddle, Spurs had been lacking pace and guile on the flanks. Anderton was expected to fill the void.

Initially he struggled, not helped by a niggling injury that took some time to diagnose and the inevitable comparisons with Waddle, but, as he overcame his injury problems and found his feet in the top flight, there were signs he would more than justify Venables's investment.

Principally operating on the right, Anderton had a coltish style of running and the ability to beat his marker before swinging in dangerous crosses, just the type of service demanded by Teddy Sheringham. When he got into his stride there were few full-backs who could keep up with him, but once clear he did not just hammer the ball into the middle. He was an intelligent player and would hold the ball up until making a calculated pass or rolling the ball into the path of a colleague.

Anderton was not just a winger in the old sense of the word. There was far more to his game. His incredible stamina allowed him to work back and defend, and he also had a penchant for moving into midfield, where his passing could come to the fore or he could show the range of his shooting.

Shortly after joining Spurs, Anderton made his England Under-21 debut and in March 1994 collected his first full cap against Denmark in Venables's first game as England coach, giving a performance that marked him out as a natural for football at the highest level.

In 1994–95 Anderton, along with Nick Barmby, Jurgen Klinsmann, Ilie Dumitrescu and Teddy Sheringham, was lauded as one of Ossie Ardiles's 'Famous Five', the attacking gems in a team that only knew how to go forward. When results turned against Ardiles and he was sacked, Anderton found himself having to show his controlled and defensive qualities in the more rigid midfield Ardiles's replacement Gerry Francis preferred. Now established as an England regular, even a £5 million approach from Manchester United would not tempt Spurs to part with Anderton. That approach came at what proved to be the peak of Anderton's career.

Injured early in the 1995–96 season, he only recovered just in time for Euro '96 and proved himself one of the stars of the competition, but from then on he suffered one injury after another and for two years made only sporadic appearances. The press cruelly labelled him 'Sicknote', a tag that was to remain with him for the rest of his career. The injuries took their toll, and Anderton no longer had the pace to beat his marker, and perhaps no longer had the desire to take on his opponent for fear of suffering further injuries. The work ethic remained as strong as ever though, particularly useful as Anderton adapted to a more central role, providing the ammunition for his strikers with passes played through the defence rather than crosses from out wide, and he played a full part in helping Spurs lift the Worthington Cup in 1999.

When fit, Anderton remained as near an automatic choice as one could be, but he was unavailable too often and, despite being on a 'pay-as-you-play' deal when his contract expired in the summer of 2004, he was released. He moved to Birmingham City but played there for only one season before joining one of his former Spurs and England managers, Glenn Hoddle, at Wolves. After a year at Molineux, Anderton brought a memorable career to a close with two years at Bournemouth.

ARCHIBALD, Steven (1980–88)

Striker, 5ft 10in, 11st 2lb

Born: Glasgow, 27 September 1956
Signed from Aberdeen, May 1980, £800,000
Transferred to Barcelona (Spain), July 1984, £1,250,000
Also played for: East Stirling, Clyde, Aberdeen, Barcelona, Blackburn Rovers, Hibernian, Espanyol, St Mirren, Scotland

Spurs record:

Debut: 16 August 1980 v Nottingham Forest (FL) (h) won 2–0
Appearances: League 128(3), FA Cup 17(1), League Cup 18, Europe 22, others 25(2)
Goals: League 58, FA Cup 5, League Cup 7, Europe 7, others 18

■ At £800,000 Steve Archibald became Spurs' most expensive signing and the most expensive player to join an English club from a Scottish one when Keith Burkinshaw signed him from Aberdeen in May 1980. He had only been a full professional for just over two years, having preferred to complete his apprenticeship as a Rolls-Royce mechanic before taking the plunge into professional sport, but he soon showed his future lay on the football field rather than under the bonnet of a car as he led Aberdeen to the Scottish title before his move to Spurs.

At White Hart Lane he was joined by another new signing in Garth Crooks, but there was none of the usual nonsense about players taking time to get to know each other. Right from the off Crooks and Archibald struck up a marvellous, and highly productive, rapport.

The slim Scot was an instinctive scorer, ever on the lookout for the merest hint of a chance and rapier like in his execution. He was not the tallest of players and not built like most central strikers, but he had a strength and determination that surprised many. No matter who the opponent, Archibald would not allow them to put him off his game. They could knock him down as often as they liked, but he would just pick himself up and punish them in the best possible way – with a goal.

Playing right up against his marker, Archibald could take the ball down and turn in a split second, firing in an instant shot or subtly manoeuvring a better opening for himself or a teammate. With Glenn Hoddle and Ossie Ardiles prompting from behind, Tony Galvin rampaging down the wing and Crooks flitting here and there and dragging defenders out of position, Archibald was able to concentrate on doing what he was best at, finding the back of the net.

In his first season Archibald rattled in 25 goals and led the line as a year ending in '1' again saw the FA Cup find a home at White Hart Lane. He did not score in the Final against Manchester City or in the two games against Queen's Park Rangers in 1982, but he did find the target in that year's League Cup Final, giving Spurs an early lead against Liverpool in a game that they only surrendered in the last few minutes. A regular in the Scotland squad, he played in all three of their games in the 1982 World Cup.

The 1981–82 and 1982–83 seasons were not the best for Archibald in terms of goalscoring, but he was a marked man now and proved his worth to the team with unselfish hold-up play, often seeming to get almost, but not quite, as much pleasure from creating goals as scoring himself. Archibald's aim in life was to score, and the joy on his face as he would turn away, one arm pointing to the skies as he took the applause, was clear for all to see.

Very much his own man, Archibald sometimes seemed a loner, sullen and wrapped up in his own little world, but he was a perfectionist, and when things did not go right he blamed himself, even when the blame lay elsewhere. This public persona did him few favours in August 1983 when Archibald was injured in a game with Coventry. He felt he could not continue, but Spurs had already used their substitute, and when Burkinshaw insisted Archibald play on he made his displeasure known. It was a display of indiscipline the manager could not allow to go unpunished, and Archibald found himself on the sidelines for half a dozen games. When he returned he seemed more determined than ever to prove Burkinshaw had been wrong to question his commitment to the cause. His desire was never more apparent as he cracked in 28 goals and played a full part in lifting the UEFA Cup.

The damage had been done though, and his rift with Burkinshaw was never going to be healed. When Barcelona made a £1.25 million bid for his services he was allowed to leave.

In Spain Archibald proved just as popular with the Catalan fans as he had with the Spurs faithful. The Nou Camp regulars may not have adapted the chorus of 'We'll take more care of you, Archibald, Archibald' that used to echo around White Hart Lane, but as he helped their club win the Spanish title and reach the European Cup Final they found their own way of acknowledging the value of a truly stylish goalscorer.

ARDILES, Osvaldo Cesar (1978–91)

Midfielder, 5ft 6in, 9st 10lb

Born: Cordoba, Argentina, 3 August 1952
Signed from Huracan (Argentina), July 1978, £325,000
Transferred to Queen's Park Rangers, August 1988, free
Also played for: Red Star Cordoba, Cordoba Instituto, Belgrano, Huracan, Paris St Germain, Blackburn Rovers, Queen's Park Rangers, Fort Lauderdale Strikers, Argentina

Spurs record:

Debut: 19 August 1978 v Nottingham Forest (FL) (a) drew 1–1
Appearances: League 222(16), FA Cup 32, League Cup 31(1), Europe 8(1), others 92(15)
Goals: League 16, FA Cup 4, League Cup 3, Europe 2, others 12

■ When Ossie Ardiles starred for Argentina as they won the World Cup in 1978, Spurs fans could only dream of what it would be like to have his fabulous talent in a team that had just returned to the First Division. Within two months the dream became reality, and for the next 10 years Ardiles graced the white shirt with a distinction few have matched.

Ardiles's signing, for a more than reasonable £325,000, was regarded as a major coup for Keith Burkinshaw but also something of a gamble. His ability was undoubted but some questioned whether an apparently frail midfielder, 5ft 6in and little more than 10st, could stand the rigours of English football. He soon proved nobody need have any fears on that score. The Latin flair was immediately apparent but so too was a willingness to work

hard, support colleagues and accept the defensive responsibilities expected of all players in the hurly-burly of the Football League. He did more than that though, showing that skill and guile could dovetail with hard work and elevate football to a new level.

With Argentina, Ardiles played as the link between a tough, uncompromising defence and a fast moving, fluid attack that liked the ball played through the defence to run on to. He picked the ball up from his defenders or goalkeeper and worked it through midfield before making the final killer pass. He was expected to do the same for Spurs, but, with the man-marking he was now subjected to and midfields more congested than he had been used to, it was soon realised that he would have to adapt his game. He still accepted the ball from colleagues even when surrounded by two or three opponents, confident in his own ability to retain possession, but he now looked to play quickfire, tight, short passes. He still took the opportunity to run with the ball when he could, displaying a unique ability to keep his body between ball and opponent, with the ball just out of his opponent's reach yet under perfect control, and he still found time and space when none seemed to exist.

Ardiles came into a team that was not yet of the highest calibre but with his 'apprentice' Glenn Hoddle beside him, they provided the base around which Burkinshaw could construct a great team. The arrival of the quicksilver Steve Archibald and Garth Crooks at last gave Spurs strikers to fully exploit the opportunities Ardiles and Hoddle created. In 1981 Ardiles won his first honour with Spurs, the FA Cup, his eventual domination of the abrasive Gerry Gow as important to the victory as the glorious winning goal by Ricky Villa.

He collected a runners'-up medal in the 1982 League (Milk) Cup but missed the FA Cup Final due to events in the South Atlantic. Having returned to Argentina to prepare for the World Cup Finals, he was hopeful of being released for the Final but the Falklands War intervened.

A patriotic man, Ardiles did not feel it wise to return to England once the conflict was over. He joined Paris St Germain on loan but things did not go well, and within a few months he was back at White Hart Lane, welcomed home by Spurs fans, and football fans in general, with open arms. His immediate return was short-lived. In his fourth game back he broke his shin, the first of a series of injuries that plagued the rest of his playing days. He rarely managed a lengthy run of games and had to settle for a bit part in the 1984 UEFA Cup success. It was only in 1987 that he got back to his best, making another Wembley appearance in the FA Cup Final.

With the arrival of Terry Venables, Ardiles departed. He ran down his career with Blackburn Rovers, Queen's Park Rangers and Fort Lauderdale Strikers before making the expected move into management that eventually saw him return to his spiritual home with dreams of building a team that played football the way he did as a player.

BAILY, Edward Francis (1945-56)

Inside-forward, 5ft 7in, 10st

Born: Clapton, East London, 6 August 1925

Died: Welwyn Garden City, Hertfordshire, 13 October 2010
Signed from amateur, February 1946
Transferred to Port Vale, January 1956, £6,000
Also played for: Port Vale, Nottingham Forest, Leyton Orient, England

Spurs record:

Debut: 4 January 1947 v West Bromwich Albion (FL) (h) won 2–0
Appearances: League 297, FA Cup 29, others 56**
*(*Includes one abandoned)*
Goals: League 64, FA Cup 5, others 21

■ The 'Cheeky Chappie' of the 'Push and Run' team, Eddie Baily was a local talent taken under Spurs' wing as a 14-year-old. There were no youth teams in the 1930s and 40s as we know them today, but Spurs had the foresight to arrange for promising youngsters to play for Tottenham Juniors before placing them with one of the many junior nursery clubs in the area.

Baily played for the Juniors and was registered as an amateur with Spurs while

placed with Finchley. Called up to the forces during World War Two, Spurs allowed his registration to lapse under the mistaken belief he had been reported as missing in action, and when he was demobbed in 1945, Baily, having heard nothing from Spurs, signed for Chelsea. Fortunately it did not take much to persuade Chelsea to release his registration when they were told the facts, a decision they probably came to regret.

Baily signed professional for Spurs in October 1946. Within 12 months he was in the first team and quickly established himself as a regular, taking over from Johnny Jordan when the latter moved to Italy. A typical Cockney character off the pitch, Baily was like a Cockney sparrow on it, flitting between defence and attack, picking up the ball and seeking out the openings.

A natural footballer with wonderful vision, Baily was one of the most important cogs in Arthur Rowe's great 'Push and Run' team. When he played well, so did the team. If he was off form or lacking in confidence (a permanent trait as he was his own worst critic), the team struggled. He epitomised everything that made the team so successful; the principles of 'make it quick, make it simple' did not need to be taught to him, it was exactly how he had always played the game.

The demands of 'Push and Run' placed considerable burdens on Baily and the other inside-forward, Les Bennett. They were expected to do so much hard work, dribbling, passing, shooting and covering back. For Baily it was perfect as he thrived on the responsibility. Always on the move, never resting for a second to admire his work but looking for the space to receive the ball again and already eyeing up what he was going to do next, Baily just loved the continual involvement.

His first-time passing was immaculate. He was a good dribbler, able to beat his man in one quick move and lay the ball off – short if that was most effective or long if the opportunity was there. He also possessed a fierce, accurate shot and put it to good use with his fair share of goals. He could cover back too, and while tackling was never his forte he knew how to hold the opposition up by cutting off the angles.

For three years, the most successful in the club's history till then, he was almost ever present, thrilling the Spurs crowd as much with the pleasure he clearly got from playing the game in the way he believed it should be as with the results he helped secure.

At his best there were few inside-forwards to compare with him. He played for England B three times and won his first full cap against Spain in the 1950 World Cup Finals in Brazil, collecting nine caps in total. He should have won more but never really did himself justice on the international stage. He was not the most confident of players by nature and needed time to build a rapport with those around him, but even in the 1950s time was a luxury.

After 10 years and over 300 games, Baily was allowed to move to Port Vale as Jimmy Anderson began to rebuild Spurs following the resignation of Rowe. He spent only nine months in the Potteries before Nottingham Forest realised he still had plenty to offer and proved one of their most influential performers as they won promotion back to the First Division. He finished his playing career at Leyton Orient where he moved onto the coaching staff and helped them reach the First Division for the only time in their history.

In October 1963 Baily returned to Spurs as assistant manager to his former teammate Bill

Nicholson. In 11 years he built a fine reputation as a coach, a disciplinarian who demanded the absolute maximum from his men, but a man who still believed in playing football with a flourish, with the same broad smile he had painted on the teams he played in.

BAKER, Peter Russell Barker (1952–65)

Full-back, 5ft 10in, 10st 8lb

Born: Hampstead, London, 10 December 1931

Signed from amateur, October 1952

Transferred to Durban United, (South Africa) May 1965, free

Also played for: Durban United, Addington, Durban Spurs

Spurs record:

Debut: 18 April 1953 v Sunderland (a) drew 1–1

Appearances: League 299, FA Cup 27, Europe 16, others 58(2)*

*(*Includes one abandoned match)*

Goals: League 3

■ In every great team there are great players. They grab the headlines and get the plaudits. But every great team also has those less-recognised players, the solid, dependable performers without whom the stars would not have the stage on which to flaunt their talents.

Peter Baker and his full-back partner Ron Henry were the latter sort of players, never at the top of the list when the double-winning team was named but every bit as important as the likes of Danny Blanchflower, Dave Mackay and Bobby Smith. They formed one of the best full-back partnerships of their time. They were recognised by their teammates as the cornerstone upon which success was based, although it was only with the benefit of hindsight that their importance was recognised by those watching from the terraces.

Baker was one of the longest-serving members of the early 1960s team and no overnight success. He joined Spurs as an 18-year-old amateur in the summer of 1949 while playing for Enfield but did not make the move into the professional ranks until October 1952. By the end of his first season he had made his League debut, but Alf Ramsey was still firmly ensconced as first-choice right-back, and Baker knew he had to bide his time if he was ever to establish himself.

He might have expected to get his chance when Ramsey decided to take the manager's job at Ipswich Town, but, while Baker was recognised as a player of enormous potential, the veteran Charlie Withers was initially given Ramsey's old place. When Baker did get the chance of a few games he did not perform as well as hoped, trying too much to emulate the Ramsey style, a style it had taken years to develop. When big Maurice Norman was signed, Baker had to be content with a role in the reserves, and it was only when Norman was injured that Baker got another chance. This time he grabbed it with both hands. Showing calmness and confidence that belied his lack of top-level experience, Baker now played his own game and did so well that when Norman was fit he could only get back in the team by switching to centre-half.

The emergence of Johnny Hills during the 1957–58 season put Baker's place in jeopardy, but he saw off the challenge and by the time Bill Nicholson was appointed manager in October 1958 the number-two shirt was once again Baker's property. He kept it for another seven years, missing only one game in 1960–61 and very few

more in the next three seasons as the FA Cup and European Cup-winners' Cup were added to the double.

Baker was a cool, efficient player who did his job as simply as possible. Not that it was a simple job to do. A full-back was expected to take care of his opposing winger and support his half-back. In return his half-back would cover the full-back. Baker's problem was that in front of him he had Danny Blanchflower, a man who never did what was expected of him. Baker was frequently left alone, confronting both his opposing winger and inside-forward. Fortunately he was well equipped to handle the problem.

Baker's positional sense was first class, and if, on rare occasions, that let him down he was quick enough to recover before any damage could be done. The problem of Blanchflower's wanderings meant Baker could never hurtle into challenges, so he perfected the art of shepherding opponents out to the touchline and away from the danger area, until cover was in place or a well-timed tackle put the ball out of play. When he got the ball he did the simple thing, a quick pass to Blanchflower or, if he was unavailable, inside to John White or down the wing to Cliff Jones. The unsung hero had done his job, now it was up to the superstars to do theirs.

Although well into his 30s, Baker looked as if he could go on for a few more years, but the arrival of Cyril Knowles in May 1964, as Nicholson began to build another trophy-winning team, signalled the end of Baker's Spurs career. Nicholson valued him enough to want him to stay, but when the chance came of building a new life for himself in South Africa, Nicholson allowed Baker to leave. He emigrated in 1965 and initially played for Durban United. After playing he coached for a while before going into business.

BEAL, Philip (1960–75)

Defender, 5ft 10in, 11st 11lb

Born: Godstone, Surrey, 8 January 1945
Signed from amateur, January 1962
Transferred to Brighton & Hove Albion, July 1975, free
Also played for: Brighton & Hove Albion, Los Angeles Aztecs, Memphis Rogues, Chelmsford City, Crewe Alexandra, Oxford City, Woking

Spurs record:

Debut: 16 September 1963 v Aston Villa (FL) (a) won 4–2
Appearances: League 330(3), FA Cup 30, League Cup 27, Europe 30, others 62(1)
Goals: League 1

■ If ever there was a Spurs player who deserved the title 'Mr Dependable', that player was Phil Beal. In over 400 games he rarely made a mistake, proving one of the most reliable and trustworthy defenders the club ever had.

Signed as a 17-year-old, he worked his way through the youth structure, a defensive half-back who played the game as simply as possible. When he made his debut it was in place of Danny Blanchflower, a player more renowned for his attacking ability, but Beal knew he could never replace the irrepressible Irishman and stuck to playing his own game.

For a couple of years he made steady progress without really getting a lengthy run in the team, but his opportunity came in late 1965. Maurice Norman had been playing at full-back, but he broke his leg and Beal was called in to cover for

him. He settled in the position well, and when Norman was forced to retire he seemed destined to make the place his own. Unfortunately injury then hit Beal. He broke his arm in January 1967, just before the FA Cup run began. It not only cost him an FA Cup-winners' medal but also his place in the team, as Joe Kinnear took the chance Beal's absence gave him.

Kinnear was not as defensively strong as Beal, but he was superior going forward. In an era when over-lapping full-backs were needed to compensate for the demise of out-and-out wingers as the game became more defensive, Kinnear was the better choice.

Beal may not have been first choice in any position but his versatility and willingness to fill any role saw him playing regularly, and when Dave Mackay left for Derby County Beal was the obvious choice to take on the second defensive role now demanded of a half-back.

Alongside big Mike England, Beal had the job of covering for both England and his full-backs. He proved perfectly suited to the role as his positional play and ability to spot danger before a real threat developed came to the fore. If an attacker seemed likely to get through, his speed allowed him to get back and make a tackle from which he would frequently emerge with the ball. When Bill Nicholson felt an opponent needed special attention, Beal would be given the job of man-marker. He would stick to his target like glue and there were few who managed to get the better of him.

A fixture in the team, he helped Spurs lift the League Cup in 1971 and 1973, the UEFA Cup in 1972 and collected a losers' medal in the 1974 UEFA Cup. Perhaps the greatest compliment that can be paid Beal is to say that his value was most appreciated on the rare occasions he was absent.

As a defender pure and simple, Beal rarely got the chance to score – he never even went forward for corners or free-kicks – but he did get his name on the scoresheet once and no one present will ever forget the goal. It came against Queen's Park Rangers in January 1969. A corner to the visitors ended with Beal emerging from a crowd of players on the edge of his box with the ball at his feet. As he moved away from goal he had few options, all his teammates bar Jimmy Greaves were behind him and his only option was to go forward. As he crossed the halfway line the crowd looked on in shock. As he continued to move forward panic set in. What would happen when he lost the ball and was not back to defend? When he passed to Greaves, relief set in. Surely Beal would turn tail and rush back to the safety of his own half. No. He continued his run, collected a return pass from Greaves and from the edge of the Rangers box whacked the ball home off the underside of the bar. For a few seconds there was silence, even Beal did not seem to know what to do. Then the celebrations began.

Following Nicholson's resignation and the arrival of Terry Neill, Beal found himself out of favour as Neill decided to give younger players their chance and brought in his own men. As Spurs struggled against relegation in the spring of 1975, Beal and some of the other more experienced players were recalled. They all played their part in the final few games when just enough points were secured to avoid the drop. At the end of the season Beal was released. He joined Brighton & Hove Albion, spent a year there and then moved to America, where he first played for Los Angeles Aztecs, scoring on his debut for them!

BENNETT, Leslie Donald (1939–55)

Inside-forward, 5ft 11in, 11st

Born: Wood Green, North London, 10 January 1918

Died: Hackney, East London 29 April 1999

Signed from amateur, May 1939

Transferred to West Ham United, December 1954, free

Also played for: West Ham United, Clacton Town, Romford

Spurs record:

Debut: 31 August 1946 v Birmingham City (FL) (h) lost 1–2

Appearances: League 273, FA Cup 22, others 84**
*(*Includes one abandoned match)*

*Goals: League 103, FA Cup 14, others 52***
*(**Includes 1 in an abandoned match)*

■ As a member of Arthur Rowe's 'Push and Run' team, Les Bennett achieved considerable success, winning the Second and First Division titles in

1950 and 1951, but had it not been for World War Two there can be little doubt his career would have reached even greater heights.

A Wood Green lad, he was a schoolboy star in local football and taken under Spurs' wing from an early age. After playing for Tottenham Juniors, he was placed with the Northfleet United nursery, which helped produce so many Spurs stars of the future, before making the move to the professional ranks at White Hart Lane in May 1939.

Before his career could get under way, war broke out, but at least the disruption that followed, with normal football suspended and players returning home to prepare for defending their country, gave Bennett an early opportunity to show his talents. He made an impressive first-team debut in November 1939, scoring a hat-trick against Charlton Athletic in a Football League South game.

Soon called up to serve his country, while undertaking his army training in Devon he guested for Torquay United, and when serving in Northern Ireland he played for Distillery, even representing the Northern Ireland Regional League against the League of Ireland. Most of his military service was in Egypt, Burma and India, too far from home for him to make more than a handful of appearances for Spurs in the wartime competitions.

On being demobbed in March 1946 he immediately established himself as first-choice inside-right and made his first Football League appearance in the opening game of the 1946–47 season. At 28 he had lost his best years to the war, but he still had enough time to carve a niche for himself in Spurs' history and make football fans wonder about what might have been.

Bennett possessed every attribute an inside-forward needed. Tall and well balanced, he had the pace and long stride to take him away from a man, the close control to beat his marker in a confined space and a hunger for hard work. He knew just when to hold on to the ball, when to release it and when to strike for goal. He perfected the art of dummying to make a pass and then slipping past his opponent. He also had a flair for the unpredictable that would create openings from nothing and an elegance about his play that was almost balletic.

There was no finer sight than to see Bennett picking up the ball and striding through the midfield before spraying it out to the wing or slipping a short pass through a defence.

He also possessed fine dribbling ability, a talent that might have been out of place in a team based on the principle of passing the ball quickly, but Bennett was the one player given the freedom to run with the ball when he thought it best.

There were times when 'Push and Run' could be too fast, when the quick, simple passes out of defence would see the ball moving from one end of the pitch to the other so quickly that players were left trailing in its wake. That was when Bennett would take his time, a few extra touches. Then, when players had caught up with play, the impetus would be resumed. There were also times when heavy pitches would slow down Spurs' play, the ball bogged down in the mud instead of zipping across the surface. Bennett would then take control, his running with the ball keeping Spurs moving forward.

Bennett scored over 100 goals in League football alone, testament to his ability to find space and get into goalscoring positions, but if he had one fault it was that he was sometimes too hurried in his shooting. A little more calm, and he would have scored many more.

Bennett was a stalwart of the 'Push and Run' side, an automatic choice, and when he was absent through injury the team lacked something special. He deserved to play for England and was often on the fringe of selection, but with competition from the likes of Ivor Broadis, Raich Carter and Wilf Mannion the nearest he got to a cap was to be 12th man on one occasion.

By 1954 Rowe's great team was breaking up, and with Bennett in the veteran class Johnny Brooks was signed to fill the midfield role Bennett had occupied so superbly. Bennett was allowed to join West Ham United, where he spent a year before dropping into the non-League game as manager of Clacton Town and Romford.

BLANCHFLOWER, Robert Dennis (1954–64)

Half-back, 5ft 10ins, 10st 7lb

Born: Belfast, 10 February 1926

Died: Cobham, Surrey, 9 December 1993

Signed from Aston Villa, December 1954, £30,000

Retired, June 1964

Also played for: Connsbrook, Bloomfield United, Glentoran, Barnsley, Aston Villa, Northern Ireland

Spurs record:

Debut: 11 December 1954 v Manchester City (FL) (a) drew 0–0

Appearances: League 337, FA Cup 33, Europe 12, others 54(1)

Goals: League 15, FA Cup 4, Europe 2, others 6

■ Many footballers have left an indelible mark on football's history, most for their performances on the pitch, some for their managerial skills and others their tactical innovations. Few have left their mark because of the man they were. Danny Blanchflower is one of that select band.

A boy from Belfast, he moved to England to ply his trade, became one of the greatest footballers this country has produced, proved footballers can be more than just overgrown boys kicking a ball around and built a reputation as a deep thinker, with real passion for the game he played and wrote about so well. Frequently controversial, there were many who disagreed with his views but none who did not respect them.

His whole ethos on the game is summed up in one quotation that will always be pure Blanchflower: 'The game is about glory. It's about doing things in style, with a flourish, about going out and beating the other lot, not waiting for them to die of boredom.'

Blanchflower began his career with Glentoran, moved to Barnsley and then joined Aston Villa, the £15,000 fee ample evidence of how much his playing talents were recognised, even though he had already shown his rebellious side by upsetting Barnsley manager Angus Seed with demands to use a ball in training.

At Villa Park Blanchflower flourished on and off the pitch. On it his talents shone through. Off it he began espousing his views on the game and how it should be played in the media. He was not afraid to speak his mind, a trait that endeared him to some but upset others. After three years with Villa, Blanchflower felt the club did not match his ambitions. He was 28 and apart from international caps had little to show for his hard work. He wanted to win trophies and to leave his mark. His transfer request granted, Villa placed a record £40,000 fee on his head. Only two clubs were prepared to pay anywhere near that figure: Spurs and Arsenal.

With Bill Nicholson past his best, Arthur Rowe was desperate for Blanchflower. He had heard the stories but recognised a kindred spirit and knew he and Blanchflower shared the same vision of the game. £30,000 secured Blanchflower's signature, the best £30,000 Rowe ever spent.

From his very first game in a Spurs shirt, Blanchflower showed the superlative skills that made him the country's premier attacking wing-half. Always demanding the ball, everything he did was simplicity itself, whether playing a short pass to his inside-forward, dropping a long ball into the stride of his opposite winger or arrowing a defence-splitting pass to his forwards.

His great strength lay in his attacking play, and he was not renowned for defending, but

while he often got caught upfield he did not totally forget his defensive job. He was not a player for the thunderous tackle, á la Dave Mackay, but preferred to break up attacks with swift interceptions or jockey opponents into areas from which they could cause no harm.

Perhaps Blanchflower's greatest skill, though, was in captaincy. He replaced Alf Ramsey in the role before his first season in London was over, but he lost the job in 1956 when his decisions to push forward Maurice Norman near the end of the FA Cup semi-final with Manchester City and Tony Marchi in a League game with Huddersfield Town failed to bring the rewards similar decisions had reaped previously. Reinstated soon after Bill Nicholson assumed the managerial reins, their relationship was in no small way responsible for the club's greatest successes.

Blanchflower was an inspirational captain, leading from the front, encouraging, always there to back his colleagues and representing them off the field with style and intelligence. More than that, he had the ability to take Nicholson's ideas onto the pitch and put them into action, changing them if needed, knowing he had Nicholson's full support.

When he was into his late 30s the trophies he had left Villa to find came, with the double in 1961, the FA Cup in 1962 and the European Cup-winners' Cup in 1963. He also collected the Player of the Year award in 1957 and 1961.

Injury brought Blanchflower's playing career to a close in 1964. He then built a new career as a journalist; controversial, forceful and innovative as ever, he was respected by his peers as someone who really knew the game.

When Nicholson retired he lobbied unsuccessfully for Blanchflower to succeed him. The Spurs board did not follow Nicholson's advice but Blanchflower did later have spells as manager of Chelsea and Northern Ireland.

On the international stage, Blanchflower won 56 caps for Northern Ireland, captaining them in their vain but glorious World Cup campaign of 1958.

BRIGGS, Stanley (1891–98)

Half-back, 6ft 3in, 13st 10lb

Born: Stamford Hill, North London, 7 February 1872

Died: Canada, September 1935
Also played for: Folkestone, Hermitage, Tottenham, Clapton, Corinthians, Evesham Wanderers, Friars, London Caledonians, Millwall Athletic, Richmond Association, Upton Park, Woolwich Arsenal, Shepherds Bush

Spurs record:

Debut: 13 October 1894 v West Herts (FAC) (h) won 3–2
Appearances: Southern League 7, FA Cup 10, others 95
Goals: Southern League 1, others 10

■ At a time when professional football was coming to be accepted, even in London where opposition to players being paid was most deep-rooted, Stanley Briggs was one of those players more than good enough to make a living from playing but who preferred to remain loyal to his amateur principles.

Born in Stamford Hill and a contemporary of the players who first formed Spurs, Briggs was sent to Folkestone for schooling and first played for his school, Grove House, although not at football but at rugby. A particularly well-built lad, by the age of 14 he was a regular for

the Folkestone rugby club, but, when one of his schoolmates was injured playing the oval ball game, the school bowed to parental pressure and dropped rugby in favour of the association game. Returning to London, Briggs joined Hermitage, a club that became Tottenham FC and proved a short-lived rival to Spurs, but was clearly destined for better things, and in January 1892 he threw in his lot with Spurs.

He made his first appearance for Spurs that month in a friendly with Westminster Criterion, occupying the centre-half berth he was to fill for the best part of six years. Not that a centre-half in those days bore much resemblance to what would pass as a central-defender now. Football was still a game of two full-backs, three half-backs and five forwards. Briggs had the job of patrolling the middle of the park, blocking the rushes of three attackers, covering for his full-backs and getting forward to support his forwards. It was a demanding role but one he was ideally suited to. A strapping 6ft 3in tall, he was perfectly built for his height and a tireless worker, well able to take the knocks. He possessed a fierce long-range shot and his height meant he was always a danger in the opposition's area.

When Briggs joined Spurs they were at a crossroads. The boys who had founded the club were drifting away. If progress was to be made and Spurs were not to just disappear like others had done, fresh blood was needed – players able to take Spurs to the next level. Briggs was exactly the type of player needed, and he was soon made Spurs' captain. League competition in the Southern Alliance was experienced for the first time, and Spurs made their debut in the FA and Amateur Cups. They were making their mark and so was Briggs. In his early 20s he showed a maturity well beyond his years, and as his reputation grew so did that of Spurs.

Professional clubs soon recognised Briggs was a rare talent, and he received numerous offers to join the paid ranks but rebuffed them all. He believed football was a sport, not a job. He did, however, accept invitations to make guest appearances for other clubs, Millwall Athletic, the Corinthians and London Caledonians among them. Whenever he turned out, gates would increase. Briggs even signed Football League forms for Woolwich Arsenal in October 1893, although he made only two appearances for them the following season, preferring to play for Spurs or Clapton.

He became one of the most well-known players in London amateur football, a regular for both London and Middlesex. Having done much to establish Spurs as one of the South's up-and-coming clubs, it was unfortunate that he objected to the members' decision in 1895 to adopt professionalism. At the meeting to decide the issue he was one of the few players to speak out against the resolution, so it was no surprise when he decided to concentrate his efforts on playing for Clapton. He still made a few appearances for Spurs, but they were more out of loyalty than desire.

Had Briggs decided to make football his career, he would almost certainly have played for England. He did play in an international trial match in February 1899, but that was the nearest he got to an international cap, although the FA XI he captained on its tour of Germany and Bohemia in November 1899 was regarded in many quarters as an unofficial England team.

In late 1901 Briggs took over a hotel in Shepherds Bush and was persuaded to turn out for the Shepherds Bush club, not in his recognised position but as goalkeeper. He finished his career in West London before emigrating to Canada.

BROWN, Alexander (1900–02)

Centre-forward, 5ft 10in, 11st 6lb

Born: Glenbuck, Ayrshire, 7 April 1879
Signed from Portsmouth, May 1900
Transferred to Portsmouth, May 1902
Also played for: Glenbuck Athletic, Kilsyth Wanderers, Edinburgh St Bernards, Preston North End, Portsmouth, Middlesbrough, Luton Town, Kettering, Scotland

Spurs record:

Debut: 1 September 1900 v Millwall (SL) (h) lost 0–3
Appearances: Southern League 46, FA Cup 11, others 56
Goals: Southern League 30, FA Cup 15, others 51

■ Sandy Brown was a Spurs player for only two years, but 96 goals in only 113 appearances, particularly the 15 he scored as Spurs won the FA Cup in 1901, more than merit his inclusion in any list of Spurs legends.

Born in the Ayrshire mining village of Glenbuck that also produced Sandy Tait, Brown began his football career with local clubs before moving to Edinburgh as a 16-year-old and signing professional terms for the St Bernards Club. Scotland was the favoured hunting ground of English clubs looking for recruits, and within a year Brown was on the move to England, signing for Preston North End. In two seasons in Lancashire he scored 18 goals in 42 games, a hard-running, bustling style of centre-forward, only 5ft 10in but a handful for any defence, and his departure was greeted with regret by Preston fans.

Brown moved to Portsmouth, a new club emerging from the wreckage of the Royal Artillery, Portsmouth, and a popular and successful outfit who had infringed their amateur status by taking their players away for special training before a Cup tie. He was one of the first signings of Frank Brettell, the former Spurs manager who had lost many friends when

he persuaded several highly-prized Northern-based players to follow him south to Spurs a year earlier. He lost a few more with the news of Brown's move.

Brown was an instant success on the South coast, his 19 goals in 23 games helping the new club finish runners-up to Spurs in the Southern League. Top scorer for Spurs as they won their first major honour was Tom Pratt, and when he made it clear he wanted to return to Preston North End John Cameron immediately moved to secure Brown as his replacement.

He did not score in his first couple of games, but once he began to adapt to his new teammates' style, the goals began to flow and the departure of the popular Pratt was soon forgotten. Brown was not a particularly stylish or elegant forward, and he often looked lazy and disinterested, but his job was to score goals and when the opening was there he would come alive. He rarely joined in build-up play but did not need to. With players like Cameron, John Kirwan and David Copeland doing the hard work, all Brown had to do was finish off the openings they created. How the goals came about did not matter; he could hit the ball powerfully with either foot, chip home delicately from close range or bundle both the 'keeper and ball into the net. One part of his game that could never be questioned was his bravery. If there was a chance of scoring he would put his body in there, ignoring the knocks and flying boots, only satisfied when the ball was in the net.

It was in the FA Cup that Brown really made his mark at Spurs. He scored in every round of the competition, including all four in the semi-final victory over West Bromwich Albion, both goals in the Final at the Crystal Palace and the final killer goal in the Burnden Park replay that at last saw off Sheffield United's challenge. Fifteen goals in eight games, a record then and one that stands to this day.

Little changed for Brown in the 1901–02 season. Although he was now a marked man, he still rattled home the goals as Spurs finished second to Portsmouth in the Southern League, although the FA Cup proved a disappointment. In three first-round games against Southampton he was unable to find the target once.

Some consolation came for him on the international stage but even that was to be short-lived. After playing for the Anglo-Scots against the Home Scots in an international trial in March 1902, he was selected for the full Scotland team against England on 5 April 1902, an ill-fated match subsequently declared void due to the Ibrox Disaster. Brown did not get a further chance to be one of Spurs' Scottish internationals, returning to Portsmouth at the end of the season.

He stayed for just a year at his old club and then enjoyed two successful years at Middlesbrough, at last winning his international cap against England in April 1904. Twelve months later he joined Luton Town and continued to find the back of the net regularly before finishing his career in 1907–08 with Kettering.

BROWN, William Dallas Fyfe (1959–67)

Goalkeeper, 6ft 1in, 10st 2lb

Born: Arbroath, Angus, 8 October 1931
Died: Simoce, Ontario, Canada, 1 December 2004
Signed from Dundee, June 1959, £16,500
Transferred to Northampton Town, October 1966, nominal fee

Also played for: Carnoustie Panmure, Dundee, Northampton Town, Toronto Falcons, Scotland

Spurs record:

Debut: 22 August 1959 v Newcastle United (FL) (a) won 5–1

Appearances: League 222, FA Cup 23, Europe 17, others 30

■ As a schoolboy, Bill Brown had a trial for Scotland at outside-left – the number 11 on his back. Fortunately for Spurs, the selectors decided he was not up to the required standard. The next time he was invited for a trial he wore a different coloured jersey to his teammates with just a single '1' on the reverse. This time he was deemed good enough and his future as a goalkeeper was determined.

Brown's first senior club was Dundee, who he helped win the Scottish League Cup in 1952. Representative honours began with an

appearance for Scotland B against England in February 1956, and he played eight times for the Scottish League but a full cap eluded him. Tommy Younger was the established 'keeper for the Scots, and Brown had to be content with standing by as Younger's reserve on no less than 22 occasions, before winning his first full cap against France in Scotland's last match of the 1958 World Cup Finals in Sweden. His fourth cap came against England in April 1959 when Brown was the star of the show, even though the Scots lost. It was his performance that day that convinced Bill Nicholson he was the 'keeper he had been looking for.

The legendary Ted Ditchburn had at last reached the end of his remarkable career, and although Ron Reynolds had proved a capable deputy Nicholson did not think he was quite good enough for the team he wanted to build. It took a cheque for £16,500, a hefty fee in those days, to persuade Dundee to part with Brown. He soon proved a worthwhile successor to Ditchburn, and Nicholson later regarded Brown's signing as one of his best.

Brown was tremendously athletic, able to move quickly from one side of his goal to the other and with a remarkable reach. His handling was immaculate, no doubt a legacy of the basketball he used to excel at in school. That was also apparent in his distribution of the ball. More often than not he would eschew the long punt downfield that might give the ball back to the opposition in favour of an accurate throw to one of his own team, quickly turning defence into attack.

Lean and wiry, Brown was not heavily built. Although over six foot tall, it meant that if he had a weakness it was his lack of physique. He could be susceptible to high crosses and heavy challenges, but with big Maurice Norman in front of him that was not a problem. Brown would leave Norman to deal with the physical stuff while he focussed on his positioning, ready to pick up the pieces.

There was none of the showman about Brown. He believed his job was simple and that was the way he did it, no fuss, no playing to the crowd. It meant he was one of the less lauded members of the team, but those who watched him closely noted his studied concentration. Even when the ball was down the other end of the field he would be pacing his area, watching every move and organising his defenders. It was a crucial part of his game, for he would frequently spend ages without the ball anywhere near him as Spurs dominated their opponents but would suddenly have to spring into action when danger threatened.

Solid, reliable and confident in his own ability, Brown inspired confidence in his defenders and never was this more apparent than during Spurs' early European exploits. Spurs were used to dominating games, over-running opponents with the power of their attacking play. Against top-quality European opposition they were often on the back foot, under pressure and at risk of being overwhelmed. It was then that Brown came to the fore, organising his defence, calming them and pulling off one inspiring save after another.

Almost ever present through the successes of the early-60s in the League, FA Cup and European Cup-winners' Cup, it was only with the arrival of Pat Jennings and his precocious talents that Brown's place in the team came under threat. For a couple of seasons he vied with the young Irishman for the number-one shirt, but eventually Nicholson recognised Jennings represented Spurs' future. In October 1966 Brown's great service to Spurs was recognised with a cut-price transfer to Northampton. He only remained with the Cobblers till the end of the season when he joined Toronto Falcons and eventually settled in Canada.

BUCKLE, Robert (1882–95)

Inside-forward

Born: Tottenham, North London, 17 October 1868

Died: Mitcham, Surrey, 14 April 1959

Spurs record:

Appearances: others 54

Goals: others 28

■ Bobby Buckle was one of the Tottenham Grammar School pupils responsible for Spurs being founded in 1882. A 13-year-old lad, born locally, there is no record of him playing for the cricket club which preceded Spurs, but he was

certainly around when the decision was taken to abandon cricket in favour of the winter game. He is one of the first boys recorded as having paid their 6d (2.5p) season subscriptions in September 1882 and the club's first captain.

Records of Spurs' first season are scant to say the least, only two games being known and the teams that played in them lost in the mists of time. As match details become known, Buckle is revealed as the club's first outside-left, present in practically every game for which a team line up is known and a consistent scorer. He remained a regular performer for 10 years, years when the foundations for one of the world's greatest clubs were laid and when the style of football always associated with Spurs was developed. Even when he stopped playing, Buckle continued to support the club. He was present when all the momentous decisions were taken and more often than not a backer, if not proposer, of the resolutions concerned.

On the playing side Buckle was a speedy little winger, much like his successors Fanny Walden and Terry Dyson. He had the simple job of getting his head down, haring down the wing and banging the ball into the middle for one of the two centre-forwards, then the norm, to turn into goal. If the ball was on the opposite wing, he was expected to move more into the centre ready to pick up any balls that went right across goal and have a shot himself. There was little trickery to his play, as the art of dribbling was a Scottish trait, and pace and strength were his main attributes. He needed to be strong too. The toughest men on the pitch were full-backs, and they revelled in the rough treatment they were allowed to mete out to anyone who tried to go past them. With his speed, Buckle came in for a lot of rough play, but it did not stop him; he was a ceaseless worker and frequently praised for his bravery.

Most of the games Buckle is known to have played were friendlies, but as Spurs progressed to competitive matches Buckle was invariably there. He was a member of the first Spurs team to play a Cup tie, against the London business house, St Albans, in the London Association Cup in October 1885, and he played in every round of the East End Cup the following season when Spurs reached the semi-final before being defeated in a replay by London Caledonians. He also played when Spurs made their debut in the London and Middlesex Senior Cups.

For most of his Spurs playing career Buckle had Billy Harston as his inside-forward. The pair of them developed a remarkable understanding, linking well and proving a continual threat. They helped establish a style of play followed in later years by the likes of David Copeland and Jack Kirwan, or Bert Bliss and Jimmy Dimmock.

Off the pitch Buckle was a true leader. A member of the committee that ran the club from its early days till it became a limited company, he also served as treasurer and secretary. He was one of the main proponents of the move to a private ground in 1888, and in 1895 he put forward and spoke eloquently in favour of the resolution to adopt professionalism. It was his proposal that a limited company should be incorporated to run the club in 1898, and he was one of the original directors elected. A year later it was he and chairman Charles Roberts who persuaded the brewers Charringtons to grant Spurs a lease on the ground behind the White Hart pub that has since been known as White Hart Lane.

A solicitor's clerk in the city, it was not until 1900, when he left the Tottenham area after marrying, that Buckle's immediate association with the club came to an end, but he continued to support it from a distance. At the celebration dinners of both 1901 and 1921 he was the man selected to propose the toast to the Cup-winning teams. One can only wonder at the pride and joy he must have felt when the club he helped create and did so much to establish won the Football League in 1951.

BULL, Walter (1904–09)

Half-back, 5ft 9in, 12st 8lb

Born: Nottingham, 19 December 1874
Died: Nottingham, 28 July 1952
Signed from Notts County, May 1904, £300
Transferred to Heanor United, June 1910, released
Also played for: Nuncargate, Newstead Byron, St Andrews Church, Notts County, Heanor United

Spurs record:

Debut: 8 October 1904 v Bristol Rovers (SL) (a) lost 1–3
*Appearances: League 12, FA Cup 15, others 159**
*(*Includes one abandoned match)*
Goals: FA Cup 1, others 14

■ After 10 years with Notts County, Walter Bull had built a big reputation for himself and was rated one of the most accomplished, although perhaps not most talented, footballers in the game when Spurs secured his services in May 1904. Surprisingly for a player of his standing, he had not made an international appearance, although he had played in an England international trial match and turned out for the Football League against their Scottish counterparts in March 1901.

Signing such a well-known stalwart of football's oldest League club was regarded as a considerable coup for Spurs, a Southern League club that was still living on the glory of winning the FA Cup three years earlier, but it was not to be without its difficulties. As Notts County held Bull's Football League registration and Spurs were in the Southern League, Spurs did not have to pay County a transfer fee, at least not until Spurs joined the Football League. That was not until 1908, by which time Bull had become Spurs' captain and an essential member of the team. When the time did come for a fee to be paid, Spurs offered £175 – £25 less than County were demanding. A compromise proved impossible, so Spurs had to wait for the Football Association to adjudicate on the issue. It ordered Spurs to pay County £300, not only far more than County were demanding but a really hefty fee for a 34-year-old and a true indication of how highly Bull was rated.

Bull had started his County career as a winger, but he occupied almost every position for them before settling in at half-back, which was to bring him such fame. He even played in goal when circumstances demanded, one such occasion being the first match at White Hart Lane when Spurs entertained Notts County. Suter, the County 'keeper, was injured early in the second half and Bull took over from him between the sticks. He was reported as performing well, although unable to stop Spurs scoring three goals.

A big, brawny fellow, Bull was renowned for being a real tough nut. Subtlety was certainly not one of his attributes, just as tenacity definitely was. He played in the middle of the pitch, hunting down the ball, breaking up attacks and setting his own forwards on the offensive. He was far from being the quickest of players and not one for nipping in swiftly to intercept a pass. His great strength was in using his weight and build to his advantage, muscling opponents off the ball and overpowering lesser men by his mere presence.

Although a player of 30 something might be considered 'over the hill' in today's football, that was regarded as the peak age for most players in the early 1900s, and for four years Bull proved he was worth every penny of the fee Spurs eventually had to pay for him, an inspiring captain in a pretty average team. With Spurs competing in two League competitions, Bull did not play in every game, no player did, but he played the vast majority of Southern League games and Cup ties. He also played in three more England trials and was first reserve several times but never collected the cap he probably deserved.

It was only with the arrival of Danny Steel in May 1906 that Bull's place came under threat, but he did not give it up easily. Steel was 10 years younger than Bull, but it was a full 18 months before he began to get the upper hand.

With Bull unable to play, first because of the argument with Notts County over his transfer fee and then because of injury, Steel seemed to have won the battle as Spurs embarked on their first season in the Football League, 1908–09, but Bull was recalled to add his experience, alongside Steel, for the last dozen games of the season as Spurs fought successfully to secure promotion to the First Division.

A member of the committee when the Players' Union was first formed in 1907, Bull had to be content with playing in the reserves in 1909–10 and in June 1910 left Spurs to join Heanor United. The following April he went to coach in Buenos Aires, having previously visited Argentina with Spurs' touring party in 1909. On his return in July 1912 he replaced former Notts County and Spurs teammate Herbert Chapman as manager of Northampton Town, although he only held the post for a couple of months before quitting.

BURGESS, William Arthur Ronald (1938–54)

Half-back, 5ft 11in, 11st

Born: Cwm, South Wales, 9 April 1917
Died: Swansea, South Wales, 14 February 2005
Signed from amateur, August 1938
Transferred to Swansea Town, May 1954, free
Also played for: Cwm Villa, Northfleet United, Swansea Town, Wales

Spurs record:

Debut: 4 February 1939 v Norwich City (FL) (a) won 2–1
Appearances: League 301, FA Cup 27, others 179*
*(*Includes one abandoned match)*
Goals: League 16, FA Cup 1, others 46

■ The greatest accolade that could be paid to any Spurs player was to be described by Bill Nicholson as having all the requirements of the perfect footballer. That was how he described Ron Burgess, left-half and captain of Arthur Rowe's 'Push and Run' team.

A human dynamo, Burgess led Spurs from the Second Division to the League title playing a 'make it quick, make it simple' style of football that was as revolutionary as the fluid possession football introduced by the Magical Magyars of Hungary in 1953 was to be. It is incredible to think that it was only due to a stroke of luck that Burgess even made a career in football instead of spending a life of toil down the pits of his native South Wales.

It was while playing in his usual inside-forward position that Burgess was spotted by Spurs playing for his junior side, Cwn Villa. Invited to play for the Tottenham Juniors, less than a year after arriving in London he was told Spurs did not think he would make the grade. Before returning home, Burgess called in to White Hart Lane for what he expected to be the last time to watch the A team. They were a man short, and at the last minute Burgess was roped in to play at right-half, a position he had never played before in his life. The rest, as they say, is history. He was outstanding in his new role, scored twice, and was the star of the show. Two days later he was asked to join Spurs' nursery club at Northfleet. Twelve months later, having helped Northfleet United win the double of Kent Senior League and Kent Senior Cup, he signed as a professional, but before he had even played a paid game for Northfleet he was taken on the full-time staff at White Hart Lane.

Burgess made his Spurs debut in February 1939 and immediately made a position in the team his own. Allowing for the war years when military service meant he was rarely available, he hardly missed a game for 15 years.

In the six months or so before World War Two broke out he was marked out as a player to watch and a future star. With the outbreak of war, he was far from London but never short of a game, as every club near where he was stationed would clamour for his services as a guest. In November 1939 he won his first Welsh 'cap' playing in a wartime international against England, at only 22 years old and with barely 20 League games to his name. He played in a total of 10 wartime internationals and made numerous other representative appearances. After the war he just went from strength to strength, captaining his country, missing only two internationals in eight years, becoming the first Welshman to play for the Football League and being acknowledged as the finest half-back in the country with his selection for Great Britain against Europe in May 1947.

A powerhouse of a player, Burgess was the engine room of the team. Never slacking for a minute, he was an inspirational leader, driving his side on and leading by example, but also able to get the best out of his colleagues with a quiet word of encouragement here or a bellowed demand there. His incredible stamina and desire to attack were what caught the eye most, but he had skill in abundance, slick passing ability and a thunderous shot. His ball control was immaculate, he could strike the ball equally well with either foot, get up for headers and head the ball powerfully. He could also defend when he had to, tackling with strength and determination, never knowing when he was beaten. As Nicholson said – the perfect footballer.

A Spurs team without Burgess became almost unthinkable, but age catches up with everyone. Not long after winning his 32nd full cap in May 1954, Burgess was offered the player-coach's job with Swansea Town with the promise of elevation to the manager's role. The chance to make a new career was too good to turn down, and although there were many who thought he could have played on at the top level for a year or two more Spurs agreed to let him leave, and with more than a few words of thanks.

Burgess was not finished with his service to Spurs though. After four years with Swansea he became manager of Watford where he discovered and nurtured Pat Jennings, who was then transferred to Spurs.

BURROWS, Lycurgus (1894–98)

Full-back, 5ft 10in, 12st 10lb

Born: Ashton-under-Lyne, Lancashire, 26 June 1875
Died: Gosforth, Northumberland, 23 August 1952
Also played for: Melrose, Woolwich Polytechnic, Woolwich Arsenal, Sheffield United

Spurs record:

Debut: 3 November 1894 v Wolverton (FAC) (h) won 5–3
Appearances: Southern League 27, FA Cup 12, others 79
Goals: Southern League 1, others 2

■ Lancashire-born Lycurgus Burrows began his football career as a youngster with the Melrose club of Govan near Glasgow. He played for his school team in Sheffield when his family moved there, and when London became the family home he turned out for Woolwich Polytechnic. It was there the 17-year-old was spotted by Woolwich Arsenal and signed on amateur terms. That was in January 1892, not long after the South London club had taken the plunge into professionalism. A tall, surprisingly-cultured full-back, it was soon apparent he was capable of holding down a place in their team, even after they joined the League in 1893, but his age and the feeling paid players had to be given priority over amateurs meant he was given few chances.

Burrows was not happy playing for Arsenal's reserves, and when he made his feelings known Spurs were quick to offer him the chance of donning their colours. He played his first game in October 1894, and although he missed the next two he played in every other game that season. It was the season that saw Spurs make their first venture into the FA Cup, and he helped Spurs make their mark in a national competition for the first time. Burrows did not play in the first qualifying round match with West Herts, but he did play in the other four FA Cup games that season as Spurs progressed to the fourth qualifying round before going out to Luton Town.

He began the following season, 1894–95, as first-choice right-back but was then afflicted by a serious and debilitating illness that, at times, raised serious concerns over his future well-being and meant he played few more games before the season ended.

That was the season when the momentous decision to turn professional was made but Spurs did not go out and sign a full team of professionals. They signed a few but basically tried to keep the nucleus of the amateur players together, although some of them were paid. Such was the faith Spurs had in Burrows that no thought was given to securing a replacement for him, and when he recovered full fitness he was straight back in the team. Over the next couple of years he proved himself as one of the best defenders in the South, making a name for himself as Spurs, having joined the Southern League in 1896, really began to build their own reputation.

Burrows was a well-built lad, 5ft 10in tall, 12st 10lb in weight and strong with it. He needed to be, as the full-back position was one of the toughest on the field in late Victorian times. Almost always having to cope with a speedy winger, a full-back needed pace, but that alone was not enough. Half-backs were more attackers than defenders and would often be left upfield with their defence susceptible to a quick counter-attack. A good full-

back, therefore, needed fine positional sense and the ability to contain opponents while cover was organised. Consequently, most full-backs gained a reputation for being 'hard men', but this also meant they were fair game for hefty challenges themselves.

Burrows was perfectly suited for the full-back role, tall, strong, quick and able to look after himself. What made him stand out was that he was unlike the vast majority of players in his position in that he was never content just to defend. Not for him the big boot into the stand. He was cultured, preferring to get the ball under control and pass it to a colleague, frequently opting to send it down the line and so release his own winger. It made him one of London football's premier full-backs, and he was frequently selected to represent London, a great honour in those days.

While very much regarded as a Spurs player, Burrows remained registered with Woolwich Arsenal and played 10 Football League games for them between 1894 and 1896.

In December 1897 Burrows announced he was moving back to Sheffield for business reasons. No longer part of Spurs' long-term plans, he played a few more games before the season was over and then departed, having done much to help establish Spurs as one of the most up-and-coming clubs in the South.

On returning to Sheffield he signed for Sheffield United, but as business took over his life he played few games for the Blades.

CAMERON, John (1898–1907)

Inside-forward, 5ft 10in, 11st 4lb

Born: Ayr, 13 April 1872
Died: Glasgow, 20 April 1935
Signed from Everton, May 1898
Also played for: Ayr Parkhouse, Queen's Park, Everton, Scotland

Spurs record:

Debut: 10 September 1898 v Bedminster (SL) (h) drew 1–1
Appearances: Southern League 117, FA Cup 25, others 147**
*(*Includes one abandoned)*
Goals: Southern League 43, FA Cup 7, others 89

■ When Frank Brettell became Spurs' first secretary-manager in March 1898, he was expected to use his contacts in the North to secure new players. One of his first signings turned out to be one of the most important Spurs ever made.

John Cameron had played for Ayr Parkhouse and Queen's Park before moving to Liverpool to work as a clerk in Cunard's offices. He signed for Everton but maintained his association with the famous Glasgow amateurs, who were credited as being his club when he won an international cap in March 1896. His amateur status caused problems with teammates, who were concerned a player whose livelihood did not depend on performances could not be as committed as those for whom it did. Pressure was exerted and eventually Cameron relented, joined the paid ranks and slowly began to establish himself.

Originally a centre-forward, in his last year on Merseyside Cameron played at inside-forward with some success. Brettell believed Cameron was not only the man to create chances for centre-forward Bill Joyce, but would also contribute a fair number of goals himself. He worked hard to persuade Cameron to move down to London, his task being made easier when Everton placed Cameron on the transfer

list, a decision that may have had more to do with his post as secretary of the newly-formed Association Football Players' Union than his football ability.

Brettell's belief proved well founded. In his first season Cameron scored a total of 35 goals, only three less than Joyce, as Spurs finished third in the three League competitions they played in (Southern, Western and Thames and Medway), and reached the competition proper of the FA Cup for the first time.

Cameron was typical of many Scottish inside-forwards of the time, slim, pacy and with a natural dribbling ability, but he was an intelligent player who knew when to hold the ball and when to employ his excellent passing skills. He linked well with his winger, Tom Bradshaw, and his half-back, Bob Stormont. The trio took no time in establishing a rapport that was to serve Spurs well, but it was Cameron who caught the eye most.

An articulate man, while Cameron was making his mark with Spurs fans for his football skills he was impressing the club's directors as a man with leadership and administrative abilities. When Brettell resigned in February 1899 they looked no further than Cameron for his replacement, appointing him as the club's first and only player-manager-secretary. At 26 it was a considerable burden for one so young, but one he accepted with relish, and it took him no time to confirm the wisdom of his appointment.

Signing top-quality players in George Clawley, David Copeland, John Kirwan, Tom Pratt, Sandy Tait, Tom Morris and Ted Hughes, and quickly shaping them into a fine, attacking team combining the strength and hard work of players like Hughes, Morris and Jack L. Jones with the speed, pace and ball skills of Copeland, Kirwan and Cameron himself, he quickly made an impact. In his first full season in charge, Spurs won the Southern League title for the only time, finishing three points ahead of Portsmouth. It was the first major success in the club's history and earned the team the name 'Flower of the South'.

The following season, having replaced Pratt with Sandy Brown, Cameron took Spurs one step further on the way to fame with their victory in the FA Cup, the final replay at Burnden Park showing Cameron's tactical nous at its best. In the first half Spurs dominated Sheffield United, with the ball channelled out to the wingers, Kirwan and Tom Smith, who hugged the touchlines. Their football was intricate and pleasing to the eye but with no end result. A goal down at half-time, Cameron realised the tactics had to be changed. He instructed Smith and Kirwan to move more infield where they could support the inside-forwards. The move worked a treat. Within 10 minutes of the restart Cameron scored the all-important equaliser; 20 minutes later it was his shot that Bill Foulke parried into the path of Tom Smith and Spurs were ahead.

CAMPBELL, Sulzeer Jeremiah (1991–2001)

Central-defender, 6ft 2in, 14st 4lb

Born: Newham, 18 September 1974
Signed from trainee, September 1992
Transferred to Arsenal, July 2001, contract expired
Also played for: Arsenal, Portsmouth, Notts County, Newcastle United, England

Spurs record:

Debut: 5 December 1992 v Chelsea (sub) (FL) (h) lost 1–2
Appearances: League 246(9), FA Cup 29(2), FL Cup 28, Europe 2, others 39(12)*
*(*Includes one abandoned)*
Goals: League 10, FA Cup 1, FL Cup 4, others 3

■ Throughout the 1990s Sol Campbell was the rock around whom Spurs should have built a great team. That they failed to do, with the result that Campbell took his immense talents to another corner of North London.

Campbell was an outstanding prospect as a youngster, and from the minute he stepped up for his League debut as a substitute against Chelsea in December 1992 it was obvious he was destined for the very top. Big and strong, he was playing in midfield but even then looked ideally suited to a central-defensive role. As it was, he first secured a regular place at full-back where his pace and willingness to thrust forward were a valuable weapon, while his speed of recovery and ability to shepherd an opponent away from the danger areas could not be faulted.

Although frequently employed in the centre of defence, it was only with Gary Mabbutt's retirement that Campbell moved there permanently, and he was soon seen at his majestic best.

Packed with solid muscle, his mere physical presence was enormous. Standing over 6ft 2in and with a terrific spring in his leap, even from a standing position he would tower above a ruck of players to get his head to the ball, while his near 14st meant players who could out-muscle him were rare indeed. He possessed pace enough to catch even the most fleet-footed of forwards and a tackle that was not only strong and solid but timed to perfection, so that he did not simply put the ball out of play but more often than not won it cleanly.

It was not the power and strength of his game that made Campbell stand out though. He had a remarkable composure, confidence in his own ability and a surprising amount of skill, often advancing from deep positions to set out on an attacking foray.

First called up for England in May 1996, he was soon as dominant on the international stage as at club level, and was one of the stars of the 1998 World Cup.

For Spurs, Campbell was the bedrock of the defence, turning in one outstanding performance after another, coveted by every club in the country and many abroad. He seemed totally committed to the Spurs cause, frequently playing when not fully fit and throwing himself at the ball as if his life depended on it.

As club captain he led Spurs to success in the 1999 Worthington Cup Final and collected 40 England caps, but that was not sufficient for Campbell. He wanted to win trophies on a regular basis and to compete against the best in the Champions League. With the continual chopping and changing of managers, there was little prospect of his ambitions being satisfied with Spurs.

Campbell did not hide his feelings. There were many who could sympathise with him, who, if he had packed his bags and taken himself off to Real Madrid, Barcelona, or even Liverpool or Manchester United, would have thanked him for his past services and wished him well, but Campbell did not do that.

As his contract ran down in 2000–01, he appeared to toy with the club, making all the right noises of how he wanted to achieve success with Spurs but all the time refusing to sign the best contract the club had ever offered a player. He played his last match in a Spurs shirt in the FA Cup semi-final at Old Trafford, turning out when clearly far from fit and departing the action early.

With the benefit of the Bosman ruling, Campbell allowed his contract to expire and then announced he was joining Arsenal. For many supporters it was a kick in the teeth, an act of betrayal by one they had for so long identified as the very heart and soul of Spurs. To lose their captain, their inspiration, was bad enough but to lose him to Arsenal was too much. In an instant Campbell turned from hero to less than zero.

Over at Highbury Campbell won his medals, two League titles, two FA Cups, and he even scored in a Champions League Final, but at White Hart Lane he has still not been forgiven.

Perhaps, in time, people will recall Campbell at his best in a lily-white shirt, a master defender who never gave anything but total commitment while out on the pitch.

CANTRELL, James (1912–23)

Centre-forward, 5ft 9in, 11st 8lb

Born: Sheepbridge, nr Chesterfield, Derbyshire, 7 May 1882
Died: Basford, Nottinghamshire, 31 July 1960
Signed from Notts County, October 1912
Transferred to Sutton Town, October 1923, free
Also played for: Bulwell Red Rose, Bulwell White Star, Carey United, Hucknall Constitutional, Aston Villa, Notts County, Sutton Town

Spurs record:
Debut: 19 October 1912 v Manchester United (FL) (a) lost 0–2
Appearances: League 159, FA Cup 15, others 20
Goals: League 74, FA Cup 10, others 11

■ Jimmy Cantrell first caught the eye as a young inside-forward with Aston Villa, scoring 23 goals in 52 appearances over four years, but his chances were limited at Villa Park. He moved to Notts County where, moved to centre-forward and the focal point of the team, he continued a scoring ratio of a goal every other match and built a reputation as one of the best centre-forwards in the game. Top scorer in each of his three full seasons with County, he was enviously eyed by many other clubs.

In October 1912 he played for Notts County at White Hart Lane. Spurs had made a miserable start to the season with only two points from six matches. Things did not get any better, but at least they did not suffer another defeat as the game was abandoned with 10 minutes to go due to fog. County were leading 3–1, and Cantrell had scored two of the goals. Within a week Spurs had paid a big, but undisclosed, fee to secure Cantrell's services.

It was a positive move and a sign the Spurs directors were prepared to lay out big money for a top player, but results did not improve and for the whole season Spurs struggled. The story was the same for the next two years, and it was no surprise when Spurs were relegated at the end of the war-disrupted 1914–15 season. It had been a miserable time for Spurs followers, but at least Cantrell had proved one of the bright spots. He scored regularly, if not enough to make up for the deficiencies in defence, and was always very

popular. Without his goals Spurs would have gone down sooner, but it remains a matter of conjecture how much personal success he may have enjoyed had he been playing in a good team. Certainly international honours may have been expected to come his way, but as it was he never got closer to a cap then being picked as a reserve several times.

During World War One Cantrell returned to the Midlands. He guested for Notts County and rattled in the goals. When normal football resumed he was 37, and it was thought he would have little to offer. In fact, the immediate post-war years turned out to be his best.

He had never been a bustling type of centre-forward. Although physically strong and weighing 11 and a half stone, he was only 5ft 9in tall and not one for making heavy challenges. He was more an artist, relying on craft and subtlety and preferring to find the target with a carefully-placed shot rather than trying to break the back of the net with power. He had lost practically all the pace he possessed as a young man but more than made up for that with guile and experience. The skill was still there, and, if anything, the lack of pace only emphasised what a good footballer he was. He took more than his fair share of over-physical challenges from defenders who could not match him for skill but had a dogged determination to carry on and let his talent come to the fore.

In 1919–20 he led the line as Spurs swept all before them in winning the Second Division with a record 70 points after being cruelly thrown out of the expanded First Division to accommodate Arsenal. Only the young Bert Bliss outscored Cantrell, and many of Bliss's goals were down to the intelligent, unselfish play of Cantrell.

Back in the First Division his place came under threat from Charlie Wilson early in the 1920–21 season, but Cantrell would not give up his place without a fight, and although not the power he had once been he was reinstated up front before Christmas and played in every match as Spurs went on to lift the FA Cup at Stamford Bridge.

As age eventually took its toll and he found it harder to shake off injuries, Cantrell was called upon less, but when he made his last appearance for Spurs in April 1923 he was only a couple of weeks short of his 41st birthday, the oldest player to appear for Spurs in the Football League.

Six months later he joined Sutton Town, where he finished his career in May 1925. An all-round sportsman, he later became a golf professional.

CHIVERS, Martin Harcourt (1967–80)

Striker, 6ft 1in, 13st 12lb

Born: Southampton, Hampshire, 27 April 1945
Signed from Southampton, January 1968, £125,000
Transferred to Servette (Switzerland), £80,000
Also played for: Southampton, Servette, Norwich City, Brighton & Hove Albion, Dorchester Town, Vard, Barnet, England

Spurs record:

Debut: 17 January 1968 v Sheffield Wednesday (FL) (a) won 2–1
Appearances: League 268(10), FA Cup 22(2), League Cup 33, Europe 32, others 47(1)
Goals: League 118, FA Cup 11, League Cup 23, Europe 22,
others 28

■ Martin Chivers was fortunate to play alongside Ron Davies in his early days with Southampton, for there was no better tutor in the art of centre-forward play than the famous Welsh international. Davies was one of the best headers of the ball ever, and Chivers certainly learned from him, but, whereas heading was Davies's great talent, it was just one of the many attributes Chivers possessed.

In six years with Southampton Chivers scored 97 goals in 175 appearances, won 12 England Under-23 caps and was recognised as one of the country's outstanding young talents. When Bill Nicholson decided Chivers was the man to lead Spurs' attack he had to fork out a record £125,000 and allow 1967 FA Cup Final hero Frank Saul to move in part exchange. The outlay seemed justified in Chivers's first game as he scored the winning goal, a 30-yard volley with just four minutes left in a 2–1 defeat of Sheffield Wednesday, Spurs' first victory at Hillsborough since 1937. Ten days later Chivers went one better, scoring both goals as Spurs drew 2–2 at Manchester United in the FA Cup third round. A large chunk of the transfer fee had already been repaid.

As Chivers settled in to a forward line that included Jimmy Greaves and Alan Gilzean, and learned what playing for a club with Spurs traditions meant, his career suffered a setback when he sustained a serious knee injury against Nottingham Forest in September 1968. It put him out of action for the rest of the season. When he returned he lacked confidence, pulling out of physical challenges, and was a shadow of his former self. Nicholson persevered but eventually had to leave Chivers out and tell him to study the play of Geoff Hurst. Nicholson always found Chivers a difficult player but knew that if he could find that one little thing to make Chivers perform as Nicholson knew he could, he would have a great talent on his hands.

The turning point came in October 1970. The departure of Jimmy Greaves had thrown the main goalscoring burden on Chivers's shoulders. He had scored 12 goals in 18 games when Stoke City visited White Hart Lane. Chivers was up against Dennis Smith, a tough, uncompromising defender with little regard for the niceties of the game. Just the sort of player Chivers would normally wilt against. Spurs were two up and defending a corner with Chivers and Smith loitering in the centre circle. The ball broke from defence and appeared to be heading for the touchline just inside the Stoke half. Smith seemed well in control as the pair of them moved towards the ball, but suddenly Chivers accelerated. He hit Smith with a perfectly fair shoulder charge that was so powerful Smith was sent tumbling 10 yards and did not stop till he was off the pitch. Chivers picked up the ball, advanced a couple of paces and curled the sweetest of 30-yarders around Gordon Banks. It was a proclamation of what was to come.

For the next four years Chivers was outstanding, far and away the best striker in the country, arguably the best in the world. The power, pace and strength that had been hidden for too long came to the fore. When Chivers got the ball and turned on goal it was the defenders that wilted now. Chivers was not only about aggression though. He had incredible balance, ball control and unexpected subtlety.

In the 1971 Football League Cup Final he scored both goals against Aston Villa, the first a poacher's goal as he poked home a rebound after John Dunn had parried a Jimmy Neighbour shot, the second driven home after taking down a high ball, controlling it and turning in a tight circle. A year later he got both goals in the first leg of the UEFA Cup Final at Molineux, the first a powerful header, the second a 35-yard strike from the touchline no 'keeper could have saved. Four goals, all totally different but encompassing every aspect of the goalscorer's art.

There were still times when Chivers seemed casual, even lazy. Teammates like John Pratt, who were not endowed with the same gifts and had to rely on hard work, often found this infuriating.

On the international stage Chivers collected 13 goals while winning 24 caps but was unable to make up for the shortcomings in the England team. He played his last game in the World Cup qualifying draw with Poland at Wembley that saw the end of Alf Ramsey's England reign.

Having won another League Cup-winners' tankard in 1973 and played in the UEFA Cup Final of 1974, Chivers left Spurs to join Servette, returning to England and flirting with management before settling to life as a hotelier in Hertfordshire.

CLAWLEY, George (1899–1907)

Goalkeeper, 6ft 1in, 12st 7lb

Born: Odd Rode, Scholar Green, Staffordshire, 10 April 1875
Died: Southampton, Hampshire, 16 July 1920
Signed from Stoke, May 1899
Transferred to Southampton, May 1903
Also played for: Crewe Alexandra, Stoke, Southampton St Marys

Spurs record:

Debut: 2 September 1899 v Millwall (FL) (a) won 3–1
Appearances: Southern League 83, FA Cup 12, others 90*
*(*Includes one abandoned match)*

■ Unlike the modern era, when an opponent going anywhere near a goalkeeper is likely to result in a free-kick, 'keepers in the late Victorian period received scant, if any, protection. They were fair game for the roughest of challenges, frequently facing two or three onrushing forwards and ending up bruised and battered. It meant that no matter how good they were technically, bravery was their most important asset. George Clawley was a man endowed with more courage than most. Added to that, he was a top-quality custodian.

Clawley started out with Crewe Alexandra but was quickly spotted by Stoke and, still only 19, signed for a £10 transfer fee. In no time he established himself as first choice, and Potters fans were far from happy when Clawley led a flood of players away from Stoke in the summer of 1896. Clawley moved to Southampton, adding the final piece to the team they had been building. In his first season in Hampshire they won the Southern League for the first time, and the following season, with Clawley captain, not only retained their title but reached the FA Cup semi-final, a more than creditable performance for a Southern League side.

Clawley seemed to be settled in Hampshire, playing for the county and the Southern League, so it was surprising that Southampton allowed him to return to Stoke in the summer of 1898. Stoke were a better team now than the one he had left and his arrival, as captain, made them even better. They were never strong enough to be a serious challenger for the Football League title, but the FA Cup only involves a few games, and they did well in the competition. On the way to the semi-final, where they lost to Derby County, they beat Spurs in the third round. They won comfortably enough by 4–1, but on the few occasions Spurs threatened Clawley impressed. His performance was noted by Spurs' newly-appointed secretary-manager John Cameron.

Stoke's financial difficulties were well known, and at the first opportunity Cameron made sure Spurs made an offer for Clawley's services Stoke could not refuse. Joe Cullen had been Spurs' first-choice 'keeper for two years, but Cameron felt he was getting past his best and Clawley was not only a better 'keeper but a long-term prospect.

Clawley impressed from his first game at White Hart Lane, but after no more than eight Southern League games he broke his leg in a Southern District Combination fixture with Queen's Park Rangers in October 1899. It put him out of the game for six months and, although he returned before the season was over, it meant he missed out on a Southern League Championship medal.

Compensation came the following season when Clawley played practically every game, only missing a few competitive matches when Cameron decided to rest players prior to the FA Cup ties. He at last got past the semi-final stage of the FA Cup and played a full part in the two games with Sheffield United that finally saw a Southern club win the trophy again.

Clawley was everything one would expect a goalkeeper to be. At 6ft 1in he was taller than most and, weighing in at 12 and a half stone, well built enough to handle the buffetings. He had a fantastic reach that he put to particularly good use in plucking crosses out of the air and

a hefty kick that frequently reached the halfway line, a more than good distance in those days. He was brave to the point of recklessness, but his great forte was coming out to face an inrushing forward. If he was unable to get his hands to the ball he was more than happy using his feet, in many respects a sweeper-keeper in the mould of modern 'keepers. He was also calm, never panicking and instilling confidence in his defenders.

He was generally recognised as one of the absolute best in his position, and it was always a surprise he missed out on the major representative honours. He was certainly good enough to play for England, but the nearest he got was playing in an international trial at White Hart Lane in March 1903.

At the end of the 1902–03 season Clawley returned to Southampton and was their regular 'keeper as they won the Southern League the next season. He remained with Southampton until retiring in 1907 to run the Wareham Arms in Southampton.

CLAY, Thomas (1913–29)

Full-back, 5ft 10in, 11st 10lb

Born: Leicester, 19 November 1892
Died: Southend, Essex, 21 February 1949
Signed from Leicester Fosse, January 1914
Also played for: Leicester Fosse, Northfleet United, England

Spurs record:

Debut: 17 January 1914 v Oldham Athletic (FL) (h) won 3–1
*Appearances: League 318, FA Cup 33, others 156**
*(*Includes one abandoned match)*
Goals: League 23, FA Cup 1, others 13

■ Tommy Clay was a star of youth football tipped to reach the very top when he signed for his home-town team, Leicester Fosse. He went on to prove the tipsters right, starring for Fosse, representing his country and providing Spurs with 15 years' wonderful service.

He joined Fosse as an 18-year-old in April 1911, made his Football League debut at the end of October that year and played every match till the end of the season. In almost three years as a first-team regular at Leicester, Clay displayed remarkable style and ability for such a young and inexperienced player, particularly as he was playing in a struggling Second Division side.

He was marked out by several bigger clubs as one for the future, which was fortunate for Spurs. While others just kept their eye on him, Peter McWilliam moved in to sign him. McWilliam was particularly impressed by Clay's performances in two first-round FA Cup ties in January 1914. In the first match at Filbert Street, the teams drew 5–5 in a quite astonishing game. Straight after winning the replay 2–0, McWilliam knew he had to act quickly before someone else stepped in and persuaded cash-strapped Fosse to release Clay.

From the first time he pulled on a white shirt it was obvious Spurs had signed a special player, but, unfortunately for Clay, he had switched from a poor Second Division team to one struggling in the First Division.

He was practically ever present in the 1914–15 season that ended with Spurs relegated and played throughout the war years, but it was when normal football resumed that he really came to the fore. Cruelly refused their rightful place in the First Division to accommodate Arsenal when the Division was expanded in

1919, the next season was expected to be a difficult one for Spurs. Appointed captain, Clay led the team as it romped away with the Second Division title at the first attempt, and he collected his first cap against Wales in March 1920. The only disappointment for Clay came in the sixth-round FA Cup tie with Aston Villa at White Hart Lane, when Spurs really were thought to have a great chance of getting through to the semi-final for the first time since 1901. Clay made one of those awful mistakes that every player dreads but few have to face. He completely mishit a clearance and sliced the ball into his own net for the only goal of the game.

Clay handed over the captaincy to Arthur Grimsdell for the following season so did not have the honour of lifting the FA Cup after Spurs had beaten Wolverhampton Wanderers at Stamford Bridge, but he was one of the stars of the run to the Final. Jimmy Dimmock will always be remembered as the hero of the Final, but Clay more than made up for his mistake against Villa, with an immaculate performance on an atrocious pitch against a fast-moving Wolves attack.

After the war, Clay was without doubt one of the finest full-backs of his time. Consistent and always in control, he was quick and strong in the tackle with an astute tactical brain – particularly when it came to exploiting the old offside law – but his greatest asset was his immaculate passing. He scorned the long punt downfield or the hurried clearance into the crowd and firmly believed in attacking from the back. That meant using the ball, not giving it away, which in turn demanded coolness when in possession – for which full-backs were not normally known. His passes were accurate and precise, with the ball played carefully so his teammates could take it under control instantly.

Throughout the first half of the 1920s he was irreplaceable for Spurs, won four more caps and represented the Football League. Even when his pace began to go he was still worth a place in the team, if only for his experience and positional sense.

In May 1929 Spurs decided not to retain Clay's services as a player but they did not just let him go. He was appointed player-coach at Spurs' nursery club of Northfleet United, where he worked for two years before becoming trainer/coach to St Albans City and later coaching in Holland.

Clay's talents were not only as a full-back. In March 1921 'keepers Bill Jacques and Alex Hunter were both injured, and Clay filled in between the posts at Sunderland, keeping a clean sheet as Spurs won 1–0. A good class cricketer, he was invited for trials by Leicestershire, and although he was not taken on he later coached the sport as well as football.

CLEMENCE, Raymond Neal MBE (1981–91)

Goalkeeper, 6ft, 12st 9lb

Born: Skegness, Lincolnshire, 5 August 1948

Signed from Liverpool, August 1981, £300,000

Retired, March 1988

Also played for: Scunthorpe United, Liverpool, England

Spurs record:

Debut: 29 August 1981 v Middlesbrough (FL) (a) won 3–1

Appearances: League 240, FA Cup 25, League Cup 38, Europe 27, others 77

Goals: others 1

■ Allowing Pat Jennings to leave and placing his trust in the promising but ultimately unconvincing Barry Daines was perhaps the one serious mistake Keith Burkinshaw made in his managerial career. Daines, Mark Kendall and Milija Aleksic all had their moments, but none of them proved an adequate replacement for the legendary Irishman. It was not until Ray Clemence arrived at White Hart Lane in August 1981 that Spurs again had a goalkeeper who was worth his weight in points.

Clemence had begun his career with Scunthorpe United but played only 50 senior games, many of them behind Burkinshaw, before joining Liverpool. He spent 14 years at Anfield, years when Liverpool dominated British football. Once established in the team he was rarely absent and missed only six League games in 11 seasons – testament to his consistency and fitness. He amassed over 650 appearances, winning five Football League titles,

three European Cups, two UEFA Cups, the FA Cup, the Football League Cup and 56 England caps. Many more caps would have come his way were he not competing with Peter Shilton.

Clemence was 33 when he joined Spurs, but if Burkinshaw had learned one lesson from the Jennings episode it was that age does not matter when it comes to goalkeepers, when most outfield players would be thinking of retirement, 'keepers were just coming to their best.

Clemence made his Spurs debut at Wembley in the 1981 FA Charity Shield against Aston Villa. In his first few games he looked ill at ease and suspect, but it takes time for a 'keeper to build a rapport with those in front of him, and as Clemence became more familiar with his colleagues so he began to impress. In his early days with Spurs the most obvious attribute he possessed was his organisational ability. Perhaps it was the respect his experience engendered; perhaps it was his persistent nagging and barking out of instructions. Whatever it was, the defence visibly improved, everybody knowing their job and Clemence making sure they did it.

Clemence had not joined Spurs to see out his career on easy street, he still possessed a fierce determination to add to his collection of trophies and expected everyone around him to have the same desire. He brought with him the professional attitude for which Liverpool were so well known and transplanted it at Tottenham. Confident in his own ability, he inspired confidence in those around him with his calm authority, positional sense and consistency. When all else failed he still had his sharp reflexes and bravery to fall back on and continued to prove an excellent shot-stopper.

Clemence did make mistakes, every 'keeper does, but he only let them affect him by making him ever more determined to make up for them.

In his first season in London he helped Spurs retain the FA Cup and reach the League (Milk) Cup Final, where he looked like thwarting his old friends from Merseyside until constant Liverpool pressure eventually wore Spurs down in extra-time. Injury meant he missed out on the 1984 UEFA Cup success, but he returned the following season looking as good as ever, as Spurs, at last, had a team that seriously challenged for the League title.

In 1985 he completed 1,000 first-class games and was still playing as well as ever in 1987 when he played for Spurs in the FA Cup Final against Coventry City, before receiving an MBE for services to football in the Queen's Birthday Honours List. Looking as if he would play well into his 40s, Clemence picked up a knee injury at Norwich City in October 1987. It turned out to be much worse than first expected, and after struggling to return Clemence had to admit defeat and was forced to retire.

He accepted the post of goalkeeping coach at Spurs before moving up to manage the reserve XI. When Alan Sugar and Terry Venables took over Spurs in 1991, Clemence worked with Doug Livermore as first-team coach, but left in 1993 following Venables's fall out with Sugar. Clemence spent a short time at Barnet as general manager before accepting an invitation from Venables to join the England coaching set up, where he continues to work as much a fixture behind the scenes as he was between the posts, now passing on his experience to Spurs' own Paul Robinson.

Like his illustrious predecessor, Jennings, Clemence once scored for Spurs. Unlike Jennings, it was not in front of a massive crowd with an effort from his own box but from a penalty against a Guernsey FA XI in April 1985.

CONN, Alfred James (1974–77)

Forward, 5ft 8in, 11st 5lb

Born: Kirkcaldy, Fife, 5 April 1952
Signed from Rangers, June 1974, £140,000
Transferred to Celtic, April 1977, £80,000
Also played for: Musselburgh Windsor, Rangers, Celtic, Hercules Alicante, Pittsburgh Spirit, San Jose Earthquakes, Hartford Hellions, Heart of Midlothian, Blackpool, Motherwell, Scotland

Spurs record:

Debut: 2 September 1974 v Middlesbrough (FLC) (sub) (h) lost 0–4
Appearances: League 35(3), FA Cup 2, League Cup 1(2), others 11(5)
Goals: League 6, League Cup 1, others 3

■ Alfie Conn played barely 40 competitive matches in three years at White Hart Lane, hardly enough to qualify as a 'legend', but the mid-1970s were a miserable time for Spurs, and for those fans who had the pleasure of watching Conn at his best, infrequent though that was, he was the one bright spot.

Conn, whose father played for Hearts and Scotland in the 1950s, joined Leeds United as an apprentice, but his contract was cancelled so he could return to Scotland, where he joined Rangers. He made his debut as a 16-year-old, helped Rangers win the Scottish League Cup in 1971, the European Cup-winners' Cup a year later and the Scottish Cup in 1973, and he was regarded as one of the brightest talents in Scotland for some time.

He joined Spurs in June 1974, Bill Nicholson's last signing and perhaps his most frustrating. His only appearance under Nicholson was as substitute in a 0–4 League Cup defeat at home to Middlesbrough, probably Spurs' worst showing in a season of mediocre performances and Nicholson's last match in charge.

Under Terry Neill, Conn made one substitute appearance in a League game before being called up to stand in for Martin Chivers for a third-round FA Cup replay with Nottingham Forest in January 1975, Brian Clough's first match in charge of Forest. Another abysmal performance left Spurs with just a relegation struggle to face for the rest of the season, but Conn retained his place for the next game and what a full League debut he made.

Away to Newcastle, he scored twice in the first half as Spurs took a 4–0 lead and completed his hat-trick to help Spurs return from the North East 5–2 winners, the result of the season. After that he could not be left out, but Conn was not a striker; he was an inside-forward from the old Scottish school more suited to creating chances from midfield and coming through to support the front men than playing with his back to goal and tightly marked.

With Chivers's return, Conn was able to play deeper and show the full range of skills that made him both exciting and exasperating. With his long flowing locks and shirt flapping, he looked a rebel, and it was easy to see why Nicholson had been reluctant to play him. He did not conform to the clean-cut, hard-working team player Nicholson believed in.

A natural showman, Conn was always prepared to take on one man after another, his

magical dribbling skills getting fans out of their seats, always expecting something different, something exciting. Much as he thrilled, the end product was too often missing, the ball being lost or Conn trying to do too much on his own.

Although he lifted the whole club, results continued to go against Spurs with relegation seemingly certain. It would have been easy for Neill to drop Conn but that would have incurred the wrath of fans, who had pinned all hope of avoiding the drop on Conn.

Conn justified his retention with a dazzling performance, and crucial goal, in a relegation four-pointer with Chelsea in April 1975, but in the next game, at Highbury, he showed the frustrating side of his game when he missed an easy opening that would have given Spurs a draw and not left them needing a point from the last game against Leeds United.

In the match against the European Cup finalists, Conn turned in probably his best performance in a Spurs shirt, totally beguiling the Leeds defence with his trickery. He scored the crucial fourth goal after a mazy dribble past three men and then endeared himself to the full-house crowd by sitting on the ball in midfield. That very act probably summed up Conn. He would do anything to entertain.

Conn had impressed so much in his few games that at the end of the season he played for Scotland in the home internationals, but they were to be his only full caps.

Although he spent another two years at White Hart Lane, he was never able to reach the same heights again. His style of play led to him receiving many knocks and he was rarely fully fit for more than a few games. He was, perhaps, too much of an individual, a luxury in a team doing well but a liability in one, like Spurs, that was struggling for results.

In March 1977 he joined Celtic on loan, with the move being made permanent once he had proved his fitness. He played for Celtic in their 1977 Scottish Cup Final success and helped them to the Scottish League title in 1977 and 1979.

COPELAND, David Campbell (1899–1905)

Inside or centre-forward, 5ft 7in, 11st 5lb

Born: Ayr, Scotland, 7 April 1875
Died: Erdington, Birmingham, 16 November 1931
Signed from Bedminster, May 1899
Transferred to Chelsea, May 1905
Also played for: Ayr Parkhouse, Walsall, Bedminster, Chelsea, Glossop, Walsall

Spurs record:

Debut: 2 September 1899 v Millwall (SL) (a) won 3–1
Appearances: Southern League 144, FA Cup 20, others 136*
*(*Includes one abandoned match)*
Goals: Southern League 50, FA Cup 3, others 53

■ One of the many Scots who moved down to England to earn a living playing football, David Copeland was only 24 when he joined Spurs in the summer of 1899, but he already had a wealth of experience. Having joined Walsall from his home town Ayr Parkhouse in October 1893, he had played well over 100 games for them before spending a season with Spurs' Southern League rivals, Bedminster.

Copeland began his career as a winger but, although only 5ft 7in tall, it was as a tough little centre-forward that he made his name, scoring an incredible 21 goals in 28 outings in Walsall's Midland League campaign of 1895–96. At Bedminster he was the star of what was otherwise a poor team.

He played in either the inside-forward position or at centre-forward for Walsall and Bedminster, but when John Cameron signed him for Spurs the plan was to make him the focal point of the attack. Copeland made his first few appearances in a Spurs shirt at centre-forward and found the net regularly, but Tom Pratt was not proving so effective at inside-left. Cameron decided to switch the pair of them round, a move that was to prove a master stroke.

With Copeland striking up an instant rapport with his wing partner John Kirwan, the pair of them set up the chances and Pratt put them away, while Copeland still contributed a

goodly number of goals himself. As Spurs secured the Southern League title for the first and only time in their history in 1899–1900, Pratt top scored with 24, while Copeland was not far behind with 17.

Unfortunately, Copeland was injured when Spurs began their defence of the title in the 1900–01 season, and it was not until January 1901 that he was fit enough to resume. In his absence, Spurs' attacking play had suffered badly. New centre-forward Sandy Brown had shown he had the ability to put away the chances, but without Copeland far fewer of them were being created.

Any hopes of retaining the title had been dashed, but Copeland's return at least coincided with the FA Cup run, and even though it was clear he was not fully fit he was soon proving as influential as before, feeding Kirwan and setting up the chances for Brown. Rested for many League games so as not to overburden him, he played every game as Spurs went on to lift the trophy, getting stronger as the season drew to a close and producing his best performances in the Cup ties.

For the next four years Copeland was rarely absent, forming a partnership with Kirwan that matched that of Bobby Buckle and Billy Harston from the 1880s. It was one of the most effective in the country and instrumental in keeping Spurs at the forefront of Southern football.

Copeland was a hard-working inside-forward, who busied himself in winning the ball and then using it intelligently. He was forever looking for the ball, harrying his opposing half-back and not afraid to go into the tackle in order to secure it. Setting Kirwan free was his favoured tactic but he was adept at sliding the ball through for his centre-forward or running with the ball himself and making his own shooting opportunities.

Had Copeland been Irish there can be no doubt he and Kirwan would have played together at international level, but as a Scot the nearest Copeland ever got to playing for his country was playing in a Scottish international trial match in March 1903, another of the Spurs Scottish contingent who seemed to suffer because of the selectors preference for rewarding home-based players.

Copeland remained with Spurs until May 1905 when he and Kirwan were tempted away by the newly-formed Chelsea. He played a full part in helping them establish themselves in the Football League, was appointed captain in September 1906 but shortly after broke his leg and had to retire at the end of the season. An attempted comeback with Glossop failed but in 1910 he turned out a few times for Walsall again.

Copeland settled in Birmingham but still maintained a close relationship with Spurs. Whenever they played in the Midlands he would meet the team, escort them from station to ground and watch the match from the touchline, often acting as assistant trainer.

CROOKS, Garth Anthony OBE (1980–85)

Striker, 5ft 8in, 11st 6lb

Born: Stoke-on-Trent, Staffordshire, 10 March 1958
Signed from Stoke City, July 1980, £650,000
Transferred to West Bromwich Albion, July 1985, £100,000
Also played for: Stoke City, Manchester United, West Bromwich Albion, Charlton Athletic

Spurs record:

Debut: 16 August 1980 v Nottingham Forest (FL) (h) won 2–0
Appearances: League 121(4), FA Cup 21, League Cup 19(1), Europe 15(1), others 42(14)
Goals: League 48, FA Cup 9, League Cup 9, Europe 9, others 31

■ When Ian Moores moved from Stoke City to Spurs in September 1976, Garth Crooks followed him into Stoke's first team. Almost four years later he again followed Moores, this time moving to White Hart Lane. An England Under-21 international, Crooks had helped Stoke return to the First Division in 1979 and was looked upon as one of the most promising young strikers in the game. At one time Moores had been viewed in the same way, but he had proved a disappointment at Spurs. Crooks was to prove a major success.

At £650,000, Crooks cost £150,000 less than another new signing he was to partner up front, Steve Archibald. New signings who had never played together before might be expected to take some time to gel, but from their very first game together it was clear Crooks and Archibald were not only made for each other but made for Spurs. In their first three games Spurs scored eight goals, with Crooks getting four of them. At last, Spurs had strikers to apply the finishing touches to the approach play of Ossie Ardiles and Glenn Hoddle.

Crooks was a real live wire, forever moving, looking for space and pulling his marker out of position. Lightning quick off the mark and with reflexes to match, Crooks loved to spin off his defender and surge into the space behind him to collect a delicate chip over the top by Hoddle or pick up a penetrative through pass from Ardiles. When he got the opening he was a true opportunist, happy to take a first-time shot and more often than not getting his effort on target. He was not just a goalscorer though. He worked solidly for the full 90 minutes, harrying defenders, forcing them to make mistakes, cutting off the goalkeeper and generally making a thorough nuisance of himself. He kept defenders on their toes, and if they slackened for a moment he would be away, his pace making him hard to catch. Although not the biggest of players, he had a strength that made it difficult to knock him over, shielded the ball well and was no slouch in the air. While Archibald was the artist, Crooks was the worker, but no one recognised more than Archibald how many of his goals were thanks to the efforts of Crooks.

For two years Crooks was one of the first names on the team sheet, only absent when injured, and helped Spurs to FA Cup success in 1981 and 1982 and the League (Milk) Cup Final in 1982. He scored many important goals, but none were more valuable than those he scored in the 1981 FA Cup run. In the semi-final replay against Wolverhampton Wanderers at Highbury, Crooks scored with a fine header to put Spurs ahead early in the game and then ran from the halfway line on to Hoddle's threaded pass to hammer home the second from the edge of the Wolves box. While Ricky Villa's amazing winner in the Final replay overshadowed all that went before, Spurs were beginning to waiver at 1–2 down after outplaying Manchester City, when Hoddle chipped a half-cleared corner back into the box. Archibald took the ball down in an instant, but before he could pull his leg back to get in his shot Crooks had struck to flash the ball past Joe Corrigan, put Spurs level and set the scene for Villa's heroics.

In three seasons Crooks scored over 50 goals, but with Mark Falco emerging Alan Brazil signed and Crooks going through one of those goal droughts all strikers suffer, he found himself out of favour and even loaned out to Manchester United. The arrival of Clive Allen seemed to signify the end of Crooks's Spurs career, but when Allen was injured Crooks returned, showing much of his old sparkle and that he still had something to offer.

In August 1985 Crooks left to join West Bromwich Albion but returned to London within a couple of years, creating and scoring many of the goals that helped Charlton Athletic stave off relegation from the First Division.

In November 1990 Crooks gave up playing after failing to overcome a back injury. He also stood down as chairman of the Professional Footballers Association, an organisation he had served well for several years. Popular and articulate, it was thought he would make a new career for himself as one of football's top administrators, but he decided instead to join the BBC, where he continues to work as one of their top presenters and interviewers.

CUBBERLEY, Archibald William (1892–95)

Inside-forward

Born: Bermondsey, South London, 1 February 1875

Died: Brentwood, Essex, 1958

Also played for: Asplin Rovers, Park, Lansdown

Spurs record:

Debut: 13 October 1894 v West Herts (FAC) (h) won 3–2

Appearances: FA Cup 5, others 44

Goals: FA Cup 1, others 6

■ One of the first Spurs players to win representative honours, Archie Cubberley was an exceptionally-talented young inside-forward who could have reached the very top and certainly gone as far as his brother Stanley, had injury not brought his career to a cruel early end.

While born in South London, Cubberley's family, which eventually saw him with eight brothers and sisters, moved to Edmonton when he was still little more than a baby. He began his football career while at school and first came to local prominence playing for one of Tottenham's premier junior clubs, Asplin Rovers.

His first recorded appearance for Spurs was in September 1892, when they met Polytechnic in their opening game of the Southern Alliance, a competition sponsored by John Oliver, chairman of Westminster Criterion and a future Spurs chairman. An attempt had been made earlier that year to form a Southern League. Spurs had failed to win election to the new competition, finishing bottom of the poll with just one vote, but the proposed competition had failed to get off the ground. The Southern Alliance was a poor substitute, but at least it provided Spurs with regular competitive games for the first time.

In that first season Cubberley is known to have made three more appearances for Spurs in the Southern Alliance and one in a friendly match, but records of most games from that time have proved impossible to trace. Although he is known to have continued to turn out for Asplin Rovers, it is likely he also played in many more games for Spurs.

Early in October 1893 Cubberley threw in his lot with Spurs on a permanent basis and was a regular throughout the season. It was a season in which Spurs really began to make their name, and Cubberley was one of those most responsible for their rise in stature. A ball-playing inside-right, he loved to embark on mazy dribbles, but he also appreciated the value of teamwork and formed a fine partnership with Louis Sykes, angling pin-point passes into the path of the speedy winger.

Cubberley played in practically every game and was a great favourite with the increasingly-large crowds making their way to Northumberland Park to watch the up-and-coming club in action. Spurs were invited to compete in the first Amateur Cup competition, and Cubberley proved to be one of the star performers in their first-round defeat of Vampires in November 1893. They went no further in the competition, unable to meet Clapham Rovers in the next round when their ground was closed as a result of the 'Payne's Boots Affair'.

For the 1894–95 season Spurs were strengthened with the arrival of some quality, experienced players, such as Jimmy Eccles, Donald Goodall, Peter Hunter and Ly Burrows, but Cubberley was still there and still impressing.

He helped Spurs reach the fourth qualifying round of the FA Cup for the first time before they went out to Luton Town, and in November 1894 he was selected to play for Middlesex against Kent. At only 18 he gave a performance of maturity far beyond his years.

Cubberley seemed set for a long and successful football career, but, sadly, on Christmas Day of that year he sustained a knee injury in a friendly with a Sheffield & District League XI at Northumberland Park. He tried to return a month later but the injury was far worse than first thought, and after a long struggle he had to give up hope of returning to Spurs.

The injury did not only bring an early end to his Spurs career. So serious was it that he was even unable to hold down a regular job. A benefit match was arranged for him between players from local junior clubs at Northumberland Park on Boxing Day 1895, but atrocious weather conditions saw few spectators attend and he received little over £3 from the gate receipts. Fortunately this was supplemented by some generous donations from local sportsmen and supporters.

Although any hopes of playing at the highest level were dashed, Cubberley still had a passion for football, and he eventually returned to playing junior football in the Tottenham area with Park, Lansdowne and Asplin Rovers, even playing in goal for Rovers.

It was a real shame Cubberley never had the opportunity to fulfil his enormous potential. He was widely regarded as a better player than his younger brother Stan, who played for Cheshunt and spent several years with Leeds City in their Football League days.

DEFOE, Jermain Colin (2004–)

Striker, 5ft 7in, 10st 10lb

Born: Beckton, East London,
7 October 1982
Signed from West Ham United, February 2004, £7,000,000
Also played for: West Ham United, AFC Bournemouth, Portsmouth, England

Spurs record:

Debut: 7 February 2004 v Portsmouth (FL) (h) won 4–3
Appearances: League 85(35), FA Cup 7(4), League Cup 8(2), Europe 2(3), Others 16(9)
Goals: League 39, FA Cup 5, League Cup 9, Europe 3, others 21

■ With tremendous pace and the single-minded determination to find the back of the net all great goalscorers need, Jermain Defoe was marked out as a future star of the game even before making the breakthrough into senior football.

While an Eastender, he was one of the most promising youngsters on the books of Charlton Athletic when West Ham United targeted him. Even though he had not played a single game for Charlton, a furious tug-of-war broke out over his services. West Ham eventually won and signed him as a scholar in 1999, but they had to pay Charlton substantial compensation.

He quickly justified the Hammers' outlay and within a year had scored on his senior debut, but West Ham decided he needed to gain experience lower down the League ladder, and in October 2000 he was loaned to AFC Bournemouth. His impact was immediate and headline grabbing. The 18-year-old scored in 10 successive League games, a feat never achieved before or since, and finished the season with 19 goals.

Back at Upton Park, Defoe soon showed he had what it takes to score at the top level, but, as West Ham allowed their best young talent to leave, he alone was unable to keep them in the top flight, and at the end of 2002–03 they were relegated. Supremely confident in his own ability, Defoe angered West Ham fans when he demanded a transfer immediately after their fate was sealed, but when it was refused he buckled down to helping their fight for a return to the Premiership. Fifteen goals in 22 games showed that he was too good for First Division football, and his frustration showed with three red cards by Christmas 2003. David Pleat rescued him from his West Ham misery in February 2004, laying out £7 million to secure his signature and allowing Bobby Zamora to move in the opposite direction. In total Defoe had scored 41 goals in 105 appearances for the Hammers.

A goal on his debut against Portsmouth showed Spurs had secured another bright young English talent, and within two months Defoe had made his full England debut to follow his 23 Under-21 caps. While he found the target regularly for Spurs, Defoe found the transition to international level more difficult, although he has not been helped by too often only getting brief substitute appearances, expected to perform the miracles others have failed to produce in ever-changing formations. Without doubt one of England's few true natural goalscorers, Defoe was ridiculously left out of the 2006 World Cup squad as Sven-Goran Eriksson opted to take the advice of Arsene Wenger and select the untried Arsenal youngster Theo Walcott.

At 5ft 7in Defoe does not have the build of most strikers, but what he lacks in physique he more than makes up for with his instinctive positioning, ability to find space and uncanny sense of knowing where the goal is even when he cannot see the target. A born predator, even the most imposing of defenders find it impossible to shackle Defoe. To take their eye off him for a second runs the risk of Defoe bursting clear and causing havoc.

Playing right up against the last defender, Defoe's speed off the mark is a continual threat as he looks for the ball played through for him to run on to, but he is not just a player who can finish off the chances created for him by others. Comfortable with the ball at his feet, he creates chances for himself, running at defenders and committing them before getting in an effort that is usually on target.

A clinical finisher, as adept at finishing with a perfectly placed pass into the net as a fiercely struck shot that beats the 'keeper for power, Defoe is at his most potent when he knows his place in the team is secure, and he does not need to score in every game to justify his selection, but with Martin Jol preferring one big man and one small man as his perfect striking combination Defoe has found himself battling with Robbie Keane to partner Dimitar Berbatov at the forefront of Spurs' attack. Keane has often won the battle, but Defoe remains a perennial threat, ensuring the competition for places that make the difference between clubs near the top of the tree and those collecting the silverware.

A clinical finisher, as adept at scoring with a perfectly placed pass into the net as a fiercely struck shot that beats the 'keeper for power, Defoe is at his most potent when he knows his place in the team is secure, when he does not to score in every game to justify his selection. Under Martin Jol, Defoe found himself competing with Robbie Keane to partner Dimitar Berbatov at the cutting edge of Spurs' attack. With Keane winning the contest and Defoe not content with brief substitute appearances, he was unwilling to extend his contract, so when Portsmouth made a £9 million offer for Defoe in January 2008, it was an offer that in financial terms Spurs could not refuse and in playing terms Defoe had to accept. Back with the man who had first given him his chance at West Ham, Harry Redknapp, Defoe quickly settled at Fratton Park, confident he was first choice. The transfer meant he missed out on Spurs' 2008 Carling Cup success, and the fact he had played for Spurs in the FA Cup deprived him of the chance to play a part in Portsmouth's success in that competition.

With Redknapp having taken over at White Hart Lane in October 2008, he quickly recognised that a badly mis-firing attack desperately needed a striker of Defoe's calibre. Barely a year after leaving White Hart Lane, Defoe was back but was soon struck by injury and played little during 2007–08. The following season he was back scoring regularly, but the arrival of Rafael Van der Vaart has frequently seen Spurs play with just one out-and-out striker, and all too often that has left Defoe warming the bench again.

DIMMOCK, James Henry (1918–31)

Outside-left, 5ft 10in, 11st 6lb

Born: Edmonton, North London, 5 December 1900
Died: Enfield, Middlesex, 23 December 1972
Signed from amateur, May 1919

Transferred to Thames, August 1931, released
Also played for: Park Avenue, Gothic Works, Edmonton Ramblers, Thames, Clapton Orient, Ashford Town, Tunbridge Wells Rangers, England

Spurs record:

Debut: 4 October 1919 v Lincoln City (FL) (a) drew 1–1
Appearances: League 400, FA Cup 38, others 55
Goals: League 100, FA Cup 12, others 26

■ Jimmy Dimmock's name was written indelibly into Spurs' history for far more than one goal, albeit a goal that won the FA Cup. He was one of the finest players ever to appear for Spurs, a local lad who fulfilled every boy's dream of starring for his local club, idolised by young and old alike.

Edmonton-born Dimmock was a schoolboy star who played for several local clubs but was always closely watched by Spurs. He was first associated with the club during World War One while still at school and signed as an amateur immediately after he turned 18. As World War One was still coming to an end and clubs were not running reserve sides, Spurs allowed Dimmock to play for Clapton Orient. He was soon showing the talents that were to make him so special, and within six months Spurs had signed him to a professional contract to ward off interest from Orient and Arsenal.

He made his League debut in October 1919 when Jimmy Chipperfield was injured, returned to the reserves for a while but when called up a month later to stand in for Chipperfield again he performed so well that he made the outside-left berth his and kept it for the next 12 years. Untouched by too much coaching, Dimmock was a natural winger. He got the ball, faced his full-back, beat him and headed for the touchline before delivering a cross. It was simple and perfect for the style of football played by Spurs in the immediate post-war years. With Bert Bliss inside him, Arthur Grimsdell behind and Jimmy Cantrell at centre-forward, Dimmock had the perfect players to take advantage of his wing play. They thrived on the chances he created as Spurs strolled to the Second Division title.

Spurs did not find it quite so easy in the top Division, but for Dimmock the step up was no problem. He flourished against the best players in the country, showing that he was a player destined for the highest honours. The first of those came on 9 April 1921 when he lined up alongside Bliss and Grimsdell for England against Scotland. A fortnight later, on a rain-sodden Stamford Bridge, he burst through the Wolves defence to score with a scorching left-foot drive from the edge of the area to bring the FA Cup back to the South for the first time since Spurs had won it in 1901. Still only 20, Dimmock was a star.

In 1921–22 he helped Spurs to the semi-final of the FA Cup and second place in the Football League, the highest Spurs had ever managed, but for the next few years Spurs struggled to impress, mid-table being the best they could do and relegation the worst. Throughout it all Dimmock was there, thrilling fans week in, week out.

A natural genius, stylish and elegant, he was blessed with every attribute a winger needed: speed, vision, two good feet and mesmeric dribbling skills. His balance was perfect. He could stop dead in his tracks, feint to go one way and then move the other as his marker tackled empty space. Inside or out, it mattered not. Outside he would make for the touchline before firing in a dangerous centre; inside he would head for goal before unleashing a vicious shot with either foot. His control of the ball was absolute. It seemed to be tied to his boots as he set out on long mazy dribbles, beating his man, then going back to do so again. It may not always have been effective, but the crowd loved it, and to Dimmock entertaining the paying punter was what mattered.

As Spurs struggled, Dimmock became increasingly popular, the one player who could lift the fans as well as the team. It placed an extra burden on his slim shoulders, but he revelled in the responsibility, increasing his goal output and becoming the first Spurs player to score 100 Football League goals.

Despite his consistently-brilliant performances for Spurs, Dimmock won nothing like the number of caps he deserved. He added only two more to the one he collected in 1921 and had to wait until 1926 for them, playing against Wales and Belgium. It was a meagre reward for one so talented.

As he entered his 30s, the buffetings Dimmock had taken from opponents who could only stop him by foul means began to take effect. He still had the skill but had lost the quick burst of speed that was so important. In modern times he might have moved into a midfield role, but in the 30s few players strayed far from the roles in which they had made their name. At the end of the 1930–31 season Dimmock was released. He was gone but never forgotten.

DITCHBURN, Edwin George (1939–59)

Goalkeeper, 6ft 1in, 12st 9lb

Born: Gillingham, Kent, 24 October 1921
Died: Wickham Market, Suffolk, 26 December 2005
Signed from amateur, May 1939
Transferred to Romford, April 1959, free
Also played for: Northfleet Paper Mills, Northfleet United, Romford, Brentwood Town, England

Spurs record:

Debut: 31 August 1946 v Birmingham City (FL) (h) lost 1–2
Appearances: League 419, FA Cup 34, others 122*
*(*Includes one abandoned match)*

■ Spurs' pre-war Northfleet United nursery team was responsible for producing many future White Hart Lane stars. They travelled

from all over the country to the Medway town for their football education, but Ted Ditchburn, one of Northfleet's finest products, did not have so far to travel. He was born only a few miles away in Gillingham, worked for one of the paper mills in the town as a boy and was spotted by Spurs playing for Northfleet Paper Mills.

Ditchburn spent only a year playing for Northfleet before moving up to White Hart Lane, a young talent tipped for the very top, but within weeks of his arrival his career was put on hold by the outbreak of World War Two. It cost him seven years of top-flight football. He was rarely available to turn out for Spurs in wartime games, but at least he got plenty of experience playing with and against experienced pros for the RAF and Football Association, and he even made two appearances for England in wartime internationals. Quite a feat for someone who had yet to make his Football League debut.

When normal football resumed, Ditchburn found himself first-choice 'keeper and set about making up for lost time. He missed one match in each of the first two seasons of post-war football and then went five seasons without missing a senior game. He set a record of 247 consecutive League appearances plus 22 in FA Cup ties, a record that will probably never be surpassed. During that sequence he helped Spurs win the Second Division title in 1949–50 and the Football League the following season.

Athletic and perfectly built for a 'keeper at over 6ft and nearly 13st, Ditchburn was supremely confident in his own ability. He frequently took the ball at shoulder height, disdaining the orthodox wisdom of getting his body behind the ball, but knowing he was in charge and emphasising that to opponents. When the ball was in the air he was always positive, quickly making his mind up and strong enough to fight his way through the most crowded of goalmouths before leaping to catch the ball high above those around him. If he had one weakness it was with his punching, ironic for the son of a boxer who had practised the pugilist's art himself, but with his great strength and reach he rarely needed to punch. Quick to get down and throw himself across goal, he was a great shot-stopper and his courage was beyond question. In fact, he seemed to relish the last second dive at an onrushing forward, timing his plunge to perfection to get his hands to the ball just as boot was about to make contact with leather. It was enough to discourage the best of attackers.

He had a mighty kick but used it sparingly, preferring the quick, accurate throw, usually to Alf Ramsey or Les Medley. It was perfect for Spurs' 'Push and Run' style that relied on possession of the ball being retained, allowing attacks to be built from the back, Ditchburn the last line of defence and the first of attack.

For 12 years Ditchburn was remarkably consistent, setting new standards of reliability and fitness. In the mid-50s he was injured a few times, giving Ron Reynolds the opportunity to stake his claim for the 'keeper's jersey, but Ditchburn always returned, his mere presence enough to boost team and fans alike.

Despite his wartime internationals Ditchburn won few representative honours in peacetime, far fewer than he should. That had little to do with his performances and was more down to the legendary figures he was competing with, such as Frank Swift and Bert Williams.

Ditchburn won his first England cap against Switzerland in December 1948 after making five appearances for the Football League, but in the next eight years he collected only five further caps and played once more for the League.

After almost 20 years of splendid service to Spurs, Ditchburn left in April 1959 with a record of 418 League appearances to his credit. How many more he would have added to that total were it not for the war will always be a matter of conjecture. He joined Romford, where he played for six years, and then played a few games for Brentwood Town before retiring.

DUNCAN, John Pearson (1974–79)

Striker, 5ft 11in, 11st 4lb

Born: Dundee, 22 February 1949
Signed from Dundee, October 1974, £150,000
Transferred to Derby County September 1978, £160,000
Also played for: Dundee, Derby County, Scunthorpe United

Spurs record:

Debut: 26 October 1974 v Luton Town (FL) (a) drew 1–1
Appearances: League 101(2), FA Cup 7, League Cup 10, others 21(4)
Goals: League 53, FA Cup 2, League Cup 7, others 13

■ As a schoolboy in his native Dundee, John Duncan stood on the Dens Park terraces and watched Alan Gilzean in action. A few years later he followed Gilzean's footsteps, first into the Dundee team, then to White Hart Lane. Although not as elegant or as lauded as Gilzean, Duncan proved an effective goalscorer and one of the most popular Spurs players in the late 1970s.

In eight years with Dundee, Duncan notched over 100 goals for the Dark Blues, was twice substitute for Scotland and scored both the Scottish League's goals against the Football League in March 1973. Ambitious to prove he could make the grade in English football and enhance his international prospects, Duncan requested a transfer in October 1974, and Terry Neill was quick to splash out £150,000 to make Duncan his first signing for a struggling Spurs team.

Duncan did not score on his debut but netted twice against Stoke City in his next game to immediately make himself a fans' favourite, and that was how he continued, top scoring in the League as Spurs struggled successfully to avoid the dreaded drop. As Spurs continued to rebuild in 1975–76, Duncan became the focal point of Spurs' attack, an ever-present threat to opposing defenders with a total of 25 goals testimony to his prowess.

Duncan was not the greatest of footballers, but he was lethal when the ball was in the box, a real penalty-box predator. He looked awkward and ungainly, sometimes seeming to fall over the ball but somehow just able to retain control.

Not a big player, he had strength, stamina and determination, and was adept at shielding the ball and turning his marker.

What he lacked in style he made up for with anticipation and an uncanny positional sense that would take him almost unnoticed into the most dangerous of positions. He was not blessed with great ball control but could take the ball down and get in an instant shot. He did not have great pace, but his speed of thought and reactions gave him the advantage. He did not possess a particularly powerful shot, but, even though he often seemed to scuff his shot or just

get a toe end to the ball, he knew how to get the ball on target. He could strike with either foot and was no slouch when it came to heading.

Just when Spurs seemed set to be a force again and calls for Duncan to be found a place in the Scotland team were increasing, Neill walked out on the club. To make matters worse, Duncan suffered a serious back injury that was to afflict him for the rest of his career. It was a big blow for Spurs.

Without Duncan's predatory instincts they struggled from the start of the 1976–77 season, and it was no surprise when they eventually went down, the shortage of goals as contributory a factor as the porous defence.

Duncan returned to play his part in the Second Division campaign that followed, top scoring as Spurs returned to the top flight at the first time of asking and maintaining his record of more than a goal every two games. Injury still restricted his appearances though, which led (his popularity as strong as ever) to the terrace chant of 'Duncan is back, Duncan is back. Hello, hello.'

Back in the First Division Spurs started poorly as Keith Burkinshaw sought to integrate Ossie Ardiles and Ricky Villa into his team. Following a 0–7 defeat at Liverpool, Derby County offered £160,000 for Duncan's transfer. It was an offer Burkinshaw considered too good to refuse. It seemed a strange decision at the time. Colin Lee, Ian Moores, Chris Jones and Gerry Armstrong were all on the books, but all bar Lee were suffering with their own injury problems, and none of them had a goalscoring record to compare with Duncan's. Burkinshaw was undoubtedly proved right in taking the money on offer. In three years at the Baseball Ground his back problems meant Duncan played barely 40 games.

Duncan finished his playing career with Scunthorpe United, where he made a bright start to his managerial career but was cruelly sacked with promotion from the Fourth Division almost assured. He proved adept at working for clubs with limited financial muscle, managing Hartlepool United and leading Chesterfield to the Fourth Division title, but he was unable to lead Ipswich Town back to the top flight. He returned to Chesterfield and guided them to the FA Cup semi-final in 1997, almost to the Final itself, before they went out to Middlesbrough.

DUQUEMIN, Leonard Stanley (1945–57)

Centre-forward, 5ft 11in, 11st 11lb

Born: Cobo, Guernsey, 17 July 1924
Died: Buckhurst Hill, Essex, 20 April 2003
Signed from amateur, January 1946
Transferred to Bedford Town November 1958, free
Also played for: Guernsey Rangers, Vauxbelet, Bedford Town, Hastings United, Romford

Spurs record:

Debut: 30 August 1947 v Sheffield Wednesday (FL) (h) won 5–1
Appearances: League 275, FA Cup 33, others 66*
*(*Includes one abandoned match)*
Goals: League 114, FA Cup 20, others 53

■ Not many players from the Channel Islands have made it in the Football League, and Len Duquemin was one of the first. He grew up in Guernsey under the yoke of Nazi occupation during World War Two, working in a monastery and playing for the Vauxbelet club. When the war was over, a long-standing Spurs supporter on the island recommended Duquemin to Spurs. It was a big step for the 21-year-old centre-forward when he arrived at White Hart Lane for a trial in

December 1945, but he quickly proved it was a wise decision. He impressed greatly in his trial games, was signed to amateur forms and made his debut in a Football League South match at Fulham two months later. Within nine months of arriving in London he was on the professional staff.

Duquemin did not get a chance when football returned to normal in 1946–47, manager Joe Hulme preferring the experienced George Foreman and the younger but speedier Charlie Rundle, but after defeat in the opening two games of August 1947 Duquemin was given his opportunity against Sheffield Wednesday. He scored in a 5–1 win and netted five more goals in his next four games. Tommy Lawton had just been made available by Chelsea and Spurs had been strongly linked with him, but Hulme decided to put his faith in Duquemin. It was a decision time was to prove absolutely correct, albeit long after Hulme had departed, as 'the Duke' led the line when Spurs won the Second Division in 1949–50 and immediately followed up with the Football League title, but it was almost vindicated much earlier.

The FA Cup third-round tie at Bolton in January 1948 was played on a mudbath of a pitch. Both sides struggled and after 90 minutes there was no score. Few appeared to have the energy for extra-time, but barely had the match re-started than Duquemin gathered the ball in the centre circle. He literally ploughed his way through the mud, dummied two players and then, as the Bolton defence converged, found the corner of the goal. In the dying seconds of the game he threw himself full length into the mud and boots to get a second. It was the start of a run that took Spurs to within four minutes of Wembley before they lost to Blackpool.

Duquemin had his limitations and throughout his career had to suffer stories of how Spurs were looking to replace him. He was not particularly skilful, rarely did anything unexpected and with his chunky build often appeared a bit overweight. He lacked pace and sometimes seemed behind the play, but the positives more than made up for the negatives. His greatest assets were his willingness to work hard for the benefit of the team and his determination. He had a real whole-hearted approach to his job, working tirelessly, putting himself in where the knocks were hardest and holding the ball up for his colleagues before finding one of them with a well-placed pass. Duquemin never stood still. He was always on the move, looking for space in which to receive the ball or get through for a crack at goal. Neat and tidy, he believed in playing the game simply and that was what he did, proving that simplicity could be just as effective as anything more flamboyant. He may not have been as skilful as many of his colleagues, he may not have got the plaudits he deserved, but he was the perfect centre-forward for the 'Push and Run' team. He created as many chances, if not more, for his teammates than they made for him. No matter what happened he always exhibited the same stoical expression. Whether he had just been clattered to the ground or scored a match-winning goal, he just got on with his job.

Duquemin scored over 100 League goals for Spurs, none more important than the one against Sheffield Wednesday at White Hart Lane on 28 April 1951. After good work by Ron Burgess, Eddie Baily wriggled his way through the visitors' defence. His pass found Les Medley, who immediately moved the ball on for Duquemin to stride onto and fire home. It gave Spurs the League Championship for the first time in their history.

As Arthur Rowe's great team began to break up, so Duquemin's place came under threat. Dave Dunmore's arrival in February 1954 was expected to spell the end of Duquemin's Spurs career, but he typically fought back and then saw off the challenge of Alfie Stokes before eventually losing out to Bobby Smith. Duquemin remained with Spurs until November 1958, when he moved on to Bedford Town, leading the scoring charts as they won the Southern League in 1959.

ELKES, Albert John (1923–29)

Inside-forward or centre-half, 6ft, 12st 6lb

Born: Snedshill, Salop, 31 December 1894
Died: Rayleigh, Essex, 22 January 1972
Signed from Southampton, May 1923, £1,000
Transferred to Middlesbrough August 1929, released

Also played for: Wellington Town, Wellington St Georges, Stalybridge Celtic, Shifnal Town, Birmingham, Southampton, Middlesbrough, Watford, Stafford Rangers, Oakengates Town

Spurs record:

Debut: 8 September 1923 v Middlesbrough (FL) (h) won 2–1

Appearances: League 191, FA Cup 10, others 12

Goals: League 50, FA Cup 1, others 6

■ Former miner Jack Elkes was one of those players who got the chance of a top-flight football career thanks to world conflict. Just prior to the outbreak of World War One, he had taken the plunge into professional football with Stalybridge Celtic, but once war broke out he had to content himself with playing for Shifnal Town. It was there he was spotted by Birmingham and taken onto their staff as, like all clubs, they began to prepare for football getting back to normal. He made 16 appearances for the Blues in the 1919–20 season as they finished third, 14 points behind Spurs, in the Second Division, but only a couple the following season as they won the title. He started the following campaign as first-choice inside-left and scored six goals in the opening four games, but when Birmingham began to struggle he found himself out of the team.

With Birmingham desperate for quality wingers, Elks and half-back George Getgood were transferred to Southampton, then in the Third Division South, in exchange for Saints' Fred Foxall and Joe Barratt, a very unusual four-player exchange deal. Elkes was an immediate hit, scoring twice on his debut against Southend United at the Dell, but in the next match, also against Southend, he suffered the misfortune of breaking his collarbone. He played no further part in Southampton's successful promotion campaign, but the following season, as they consolidated their Second Division place, Elkes began to blossom. At the end of the season Spurs manager Peter McWilliam offered Southampton £1,000 for Elkes's transfer, an offer too good for the Saints to refuse.

Although Spurs had paid a reasonably-large fee for Elkes, he did not go straight into the first team and it was not until the fifth match of 1923–24 that he was called up to replace the injured 'Tich' Handley. Elkes was a totally different style of player to Handley, who was a no-nonsense, hard-working little terrier who liked to run with the ball. The most notable difference was in size. Elkes was 6ft, not far short of 13st, far bigger than most inside-forwards of his day, and with his upright stance he seemed even taller. He, too, could run with the ball, but whereas Handley scampered around, Elkes strolled through the game, elegant and long-striding. He had great dribbling skill and his height and strength made him very difficult to dispossess, but he was not one dimensional. He liked to mix up his play, dribbling through one minute and then showing his excellent passing skills with a ball swept out to his winger or a piercing pass through to his centre-forward.

Spurs began Elkes's first season at White Hart Lane reasonably well, but as the season wore on their form dipped. From Boxing Day 1923 to the end of the season they secured only three victories. Elkes, though, was outstanding and close to international honours with two appearances in England trial games before the season was over

Spurs' weakness was in defence. Because of his size and fierce determination to win, it was often suggested Elkes might be more effective if tried in a more defensive role. In pre-season training for

1924–25 he was tried at centre-half, a position he had occupied in his early days with Wellington Town. He clearly had the physique for the job but there were concerns the forward line would be deprived of its most creative element. In the first couple of League games all went well, with two wins, five goals and none conceded, but when the next five games yielded just two draws and only one goal, Elkes was moved back to where he was most effective. He remained in the inside-forward position for the next two years as Spurs continued to occupy a mid-table position. He also remained on the fringe of the England team, playing for the Football League twice, again appearing in an international trial, and he was a member of the FA party that toured Australia in 1925.

With the signing of John Blair in April 1926, Elkes was again moved into the back line for 1926–27. He spent the whole season there, coping well with the burliest of centre-forwards and skilful enough to spark attacks from deep in his own half. In his new role he was good enough to play for the League and appear in yet another international trial, this time as a centre-half. For his last two years at Spurs Elkes reverted to inside-forward, but he could not stop Spurs being relegated in 1928 and, by now approaching 35, was released in April 1929. He was immediately snapped up by Middlesbrough, managed by Peter McWilliam, and played in over 100 games in four years on Teesside before joining Watford.

ENGLAND, Harold Michael MBE (1966–75)

Centre-half, 6ft 2in, 13st 3lb

Born: Greenfield, North Wales, 2 December 1941
Signed from Blackburn Rovers, August 1966, £95,000
Transferred to Seattle Sounders, May 1975 released
Also played for: Blackburn Rovers, Seattle Sounders, Cardiff City, Wales

Spurs record:

Debut: 20 August 1966 v Leeds United (FL) (h) won 3–1
Appearances: League 300, FA Cup 32, League Cup 30, Europe 35, others 37
Goals: League 14, FA Cup 2, Europe 3, others 1

■ When Maurice Norman broke his leg playing against a Hungarian XI in a friendly match in November 1965, Spurs lost the best central-defender in the club, and one of the best in the country. To secure a replacement Bill Nicholson had to ask his directors to sign a cheque for £95,000, a British record for a defender. That was just enough to persuade newly-relegated Blackburn Rovers to release their Welsh centre-half Mike England, widely acknowledged as the best youngster around in his position.

England had joined Blackburn as a 17-year-old and played for them at outside-right, half-back and centre-forward before settling into the back line. A schoolboy teammate of Ron Davies, he collected 11 Welsh Under-23 caps before stepping up to the full team, and by the time of his move to Spurs in August 1966, only a few days before the opening of the season, he had 20 full caps to his name.

England went straight into the team, and, although it did take him a while to settle to his new surroundings and teammates, it was clear Nicholson had again spent Spurs' money well and secured a giant around whom a solid defence could be built. He was everything a defensive kingpin in the 60s and 70s needed to be: 6ft 2in tall, over 13st in weight, ruggedly

built and never happier than when involved in a physical battle with a bustling opponent. His most obvious strength was in the air, but it was not merely his height that meant few centre-forwards out jumped him. He had a tremendous ability to leap high combined with the timing that allowed him to meet the ball at its highest. His aerial power was only part of his armoury. For such a big man he was quick over the ground and when given the time showed the control and skill on the ball he had learned as a young winger. He could also hit some lovely long passes and was particularly adept at dropping free-kicks into the most dangerous of areas.

In England's first season at White Hart Lane he played a full part in the club reaching the FA Cup Final, where he gave a truly immaculate performance, totally dominating Tony Hateley, who, pre-match, had been rated Chelsea's biggest threat to Spurs.

Although England will always be remembered as one of the best, if not the best, centre-halves to wear a Spurs shirt, his aerial strength was a frequently-potent weapon at attacking set plays, and when the situation demanded it he would be pushed forward as an extra striker. When Martin Chivers was injured in 1968–69 England was asked to replace him. In his first game up front his physical presence created havoc in the Sunderland defence. He gave a magnificent display and after he had created three goals for Jimmy Greaves the last 10 minutes saw Greaves and co spurning chances until England had scored the goal he deserved. Having done that, he set up a fourth for Greaves. Although Greaves thrived with England beside him, the defence suffered and England had to return to where he was most needed.

Rarely absent, England built a terrific understanding with Pat Jennings, knowing when to take control and clear the ball with a massive header and when to leave it for Jennings to come and claim. For the best part of nine years they provided Spurs with a solid core to the defence.

Although an ankle injury caused England to miss the 1971 League Cup Final, he returned to help Spurs win the 1972 UEFA Cup and the 1973 League Cup. He also played in the 1974 UEFA Cup Final, scoring the opening goal in the first leg of the Final against Feyenoord with a glancing header and panicking Joop van Daele into slicing the ball into his own net for Spurs' second.

On the international stage England continued to represent Wales, winning another 24 caps as a Spurs player. He captained his country on many occasions and proved himself to be one of the best central-defenders in Europe.

Continually having to overcome ankle injuries, England began to find it tough as Spurs struggled against relegation in 1974–75. In March 1975 he suddenly announced he was retiring, but then went to play for Seattle Sounders in the US before returning for a season with Cardiff City. Back in America he represented Team America in the 1976 Bi-Centennial Tournament with England, Brazil and Italy.

In May 1980 he was appointed manager of Wales and led his country for seven and a half seasons, desperately unlucky not to take the principality to the final stages of the World Cup or European Championships.

EVANS, William (1930–37)

Winger, 5ft 6in, 12st 11lb

Born: Wannllwyd, nr Ebbw Vale, 7 November 1912

Died: Ponders End, London, 22 July 1976

Signed from amateur, May 1931

Transferred to Fulham, May 1937, released

Also played for: Barnet, Hayward Sports, Fulham, Wales

Spurs record:

Debut: 7 November 1931 v Swansea Town (FL) (h) won 6–2

Appearances: League 178, FA Cup 17, others 8

Goals: League 78, FA Cup 8, others 10

■ Spurs' team of the early 1930s was nicknamed 'the Greyhounds' because of the speed of the forward line. Fastest of them all was Willie Evans, a whippet-like winger with a sledgehammer shot.

Sixteen-year-old Evans had played for Ebbw Vale Schools as an inside-forward but football seemed to have passed him by when he took a job

in the pits, until he was invited to join the Tottenham Juniors. Signed as an amateur, Spurs arranged for him to play a few games for Barnet before quickly moving him on to Hayward Sports in Enfield, where he switched to the outside-right role and developed so rapidly that he was soon collecting minor representative honours, playing for the Spartan League, Middlesex and the London FA. So well did he play in one game for the Southern Counties that he was told he would be in the next England amateur international team, until he pointed out he was Welsh!

When Haywards Sports folded in May 1931, Evans signed professional forms for Spurs and made his Football League debut within six months, on his 19th birthday, against Swansea Town at White Hart Lane. After six games without a win and with both Walter Bellamy and Jimmy Smailes disappointing, manager Percy Smith decided to give Evans his chance. Within seven minutes his speed and control set up a goal for Willie Davies, and before half-time he had created a second for Taffy O'Callaghan. In the second half he scored twice himself and would have had a third, as Spurs won 6–2, had the referee not disallowed a thunderous shot from outside the area because of the 'keeper being impeded.

A fortnight later Evans did not score but gave another outstanding performance as the Spurs crowd witnessed another goal feast, with Spurs beating Port Vale 9–3. Evans was in the team to stay. In 1932–33 he scored an incredible 29 goals from wide on the right, only centre-forward George Hunt surpassing him, as Spurs climbed out of the Second Division after five years. The following season he scored another 19, helping Spurs to third place in the First Division. It was in these two seasons that Percy Smith's team built on pace and power, and with a shoot-on-sight attitude they devastated teams with their attacking power and won their canine nickname.

Along with Hunt, Evans was the offensive star. Pace was his most obvious weapon and few full-backs could stay with him as he pushed the ball past them or hared after a pass from his inside partner Willie Hall. Every time he got the ball a buzz went round the crowd. There was more to his game, though, than mere speed. He had excellent control and an appreciation of his colleagues, Hunt in particular profiting from Evans's ability to hit in early and dangerous crosses, sometimes in the air but often drilled across low. The power of his shooting frequently surprised, Evans unafraid to take on shots from long range with both feet and normally making the 'keeper work.

Even when Spurs were decimated by injuries in 1934–35 and finished bottom of the table, Evans performed to the same high level that came to be expected of him and led the club's scoring charts. His all-round ability was put to good use when Smith was left desperately short of players, with Evans playing a couple of games at inside-forward.

Relegation cost Percy Smith his job, but his replacement, Jack Tresadern, decided to build a new team around the talents of Evans and Willie Hall. Sadly, his plans suffered the worst possible setback when Evans suffered a serious knee injury against Aston Villa on his 24th birthday in November 1936. A cartilage operation was needed, but when Spurs learned it had not been a success and another one was necessary with no guarantee it would cure the problem they decided to release Evans. Fulham took a chance on him but the second operation was a failure, and Evans was forced to retire in May 1938. He was only 25.

He had failed to realise his full potential but had still reached legendary status.

Evans collected his first Welsh cap against Northern Ireland in December 1932, and he had taken his total to six and established himself in the Welsh team when struck by the injury that finished his career.

GALVIN, Anthony (1978–88)

Wide midfield, 5ft 9in, 11st 5lb

Born: Huddersfield, Yorkshire, 12 July 1956
Signed from Goole Town, January 1978, £30,000
Transferred to Sheffield Wednesday, August 1987, £130,000
Also played for: Goole Town, Sheffield Wednesday, Swindon Town, Republic of Ireland

Spurs record:

Debut: 3 February 1979 v Manchester City (FL) (h) lost 0–3
Appearances: League 194(7), FA Cup 23(1), League Cup 20(3), Europe 25, others 88(14)
Goals: League 20, FA Cup 2, League Cup 3, Europe 6, others 16

■ In the early 1980s, to see Tony Galvin making tracks down the wing was a heart-warming sight for Spurs supporters and a reminder that football is not only about artistry. Hard work plays just as important a part in a successful side, and while the outrageously talented may grab the headlines it is only thanks to the non-stop efforts of their less-gifted teammates that the stars have the platform on which to shine.

Although he played for Yorkshire and England Schools, Galvin was a latecomer to professional football. He obtained a Bachelor of Arts degree in Russian Studies at Hull University and had started a Teacher Training course when spotted by Spurs playing for Northern Premier League side Goole Town. Signed for what proved a bargain £30,000 in January 1978, he completed his training course before signing as a full-time professional that summer.

The wisdom of getting his professional qualifications was soon apparent as a back injury restricted Galvin in his early days at White Hart Lane. He played a few games late in the 1979–80 season, but it was getting on for three years before he made his mark.

With Ossie Ardiles playing for Argentina in the Gold Cup in Uruguay and Ricky Villa still unable to find his best form or position for Spurs, Galvin replaced Villa during a sterile 0–0 draw at Queen's Park Rangers in the FA Cup in January 1981. With Villa injured, Galvin kept his place for the replay and had one of those nights when everything fell into place.

He set up Spurs' first goal, scored the second, hit the bar and generally added a new dimension to the play with his natural inclination to stick to the touchline. Even when Ardiles returned and Villa recovered from injury, Galvin retained his place, already an integral part of a team that was to take Spurs to new successes.

Spectators always knew what they were going to get with Galvin. His style of play was simple and direct, based on a never-ending willingness to work. He patrolled the wing as if the whole length of the pitch was his personal domain, working back in defence then springing forward with lung-bursting runs from deep in his own half to the corner flag.

He did not have a particularly sharp turn of speed and few tricks, but once he had played the ball in front of him he had the pace and strength to get by his man and stay there, taking the ball down to the byline before crossing on the run or turning back to find Glenn Hoddle or Ardiles on the edge of the box.

Once Galvin had established his role in the team he proved impossible to displace and became a crucial element in Spurs' successes of the early 1980s. He played in every remaining FA Cup tie in 1980–81, excelling in the first of the Final games with Manchester City when City's aggressive midfield overwhelmed the Hoddle-Ardiles axis. Always available, he provided an alternative outlet for the defence, holding the ball up and taking the attack to City, Wembley's famed wide-open spaces seemingly made for him and the cramp-inducing turf having no effect.

He did not miss a match in the following season's runs to both the FA and League (Milk) Cup Finals and played a full part in the club winning the UEFA Cup in 1983–84.

The European games saw Galvin give some of his best performances, his hard work in both defence and attack and his stamina often surprising opponents, who could not believe how he could be running as hard in the last minute as he had been in the first.

Qualifying through his grandfather, Galvin played for the Republic of Ireland, winning his first cap against Holland in September 1982 and collecting a total of 20 as a Spurs player.

Always happy to give everything for the cause, most memories of Galvin revolve around his attacking sorties, but there were many occasions when it was in dropping back to bolster the defence that his value to the team was most apparent.

In August 1987, with injuries beginning to take their toll, Galvin was transferred to Sheffield Wednesday, with Spurs making a nice £100,000 profit on the deal. He spent two difficult years at Hillsborough before becoming Ardiles's first signing for Swindon Town, where he became assistant manager and later followed Ardiles to Newcastle United.

GASCOIGNE, Paul John (1988–91)

Midfield, 5ft 10in, 11st 7lb

Born: Gateshead, Tyne and Wear, 27 May 1967
Signed from Newcastle United, July 1988, £2,000,000
Transferred to Lazio (Italy), June 1992, £5,500,000
Also played for: Newcastle United, Lazio, Rangers, Middlesbrough, Everton, Burnley, Gansu Tianma, Boston United, England

Spurs record:

Debut: 3 September 1988 v Newcastle United (FL) (a) drew 2–2
Appearances: League 91(1), FA Cup 6, League Cup 13(1), others 29(3)
Goals: League 19, FA Cup 6, League Cup 8, others 13

■ Few footballers could make the country want to wrap their arms around them and wipe away the tears, but Paul Gascoigne did that when he realised a booking in the 1990 World Cup semi-final meant he would miss the Final if England overcame Germany. In a matter of seconds he turned from a football star to national icon.

When Gascoigne signed from Newcastle United in July 1988 he was already hailed as the midfield genius to build the England team around. The only concern was the devil-may-care attitude that some regarded as indiscipline, but which also endeared him to supporters who craved the type of character all but driven from the game.

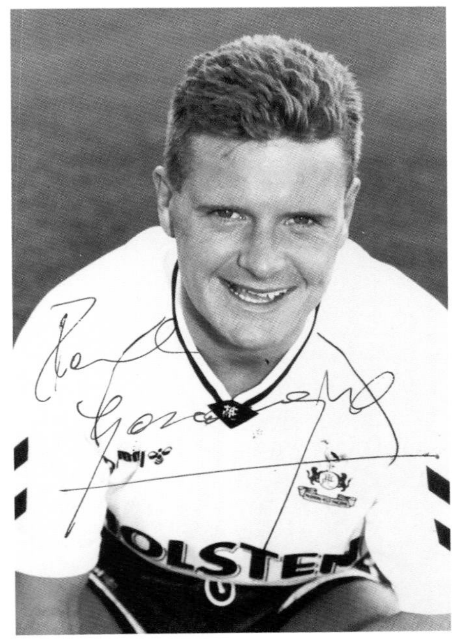

Terry Venables had little difficulty harnessing Gascoigne's care-free spirit for the benefit of Spurs. He gave Gascoigne his head and let him get on with his game. The result was that for three years Spurs fans watched Gascoigne at his absolute best as he developed into one of the most exciting talents in European football, a midfield maestro who had it all, and a lot more.

Supremely confident, Gascoigne was involved in every minute of a game. Always demanding the ball, he would drop deep to receive it or throw himself into a tackle to win it. If he did not have the ball he worked hard to get it, tracking back, harrying the opposition, waiting for the instant he could nip in and pinch it.

His range of passing was complete. Quick one-touch exchanges, long-raking balls or inch-perfect killer passes, Gascoigne could play them all equally well. He could score goals too, simple ones from a few yards, the spectacular from distance. Strong and able to withstand the most desperate of lunges, his great forte was his dribbling ability. Bursting from midfield with a sudden injection of pace and switching the ball between feet, he could throw opponents off balance with a dip of the shoulder or a quick shuffle. It was the winger's lost art supplanted into the most congested area of the pitch.

Within a fortnight of his first senior game for Spurs, Gascoigne had won his first full cap, but his willingness to take risks in his desire to entertain and an attitude that was too often childish when things did not go his way raised doubts about whether he could be trusted at the highest level. In the build up to the 1990 World Cup Finals he at last showed a sense of maturity that convinced Bobby Robson he could not be left out. On the world stage Gascoigne blossomed and proved himself as a star of the tournament.

The success made 'Gazza' a household name, public property, every move scrutinised and publicised. His only escape was on the pitch, in front of millions, but he was at home, where he was at his most comfortable and doing what he loved.

In early 1991 the off-field pressures were exacerbated by a serious stomach-muscle injury just as news broke of Spurs' deepening financial crisis: even Gascoigne's sale might not be enough to save the club; FA Cup success was essential. Gascoigne rose to the challenge and almost single-handedly took Spurs to the Final. He scored two goals against both Oxford United and Portsmouth, the winner against Notts County and then, barely a month after an operation to repair his stomach muscles, gave the performance of his Spurs career against Arsenal in the Wembley semi-final. After barely four minutes he seized the ball for a free-kick 30 yards out. It was an impossible position to score from. Only Gascoigne would have had the audacity to try, but he hit the ball with such venom that it flashed past David Seaman into the net. Six minutes later his deft lay off set Paul Allen away, and Gary Lineker put Spurs two up. By half-time Gascoigne was struggling, but he had done his job and Spurs held on to reach their ninth FA Cup Final.

That Final should have been the peak of Gascoigne's Spurs career, but it proved a disaster. The weight of expectation was enormous, and he was hyped up beyond belief. Lucky to stay on the field after a first-minute assault on Nottingham Forest's Gary Parker, only 15 minutes had gone when he hacked down Gary Charles. Stuart Pearce scored from the free-kick but worse followed as Gascoigne crumpled to the ground, a cruciate-ligament injury putting him out of the game and wrecking his planned £8.5 million move to Lazio.

It was a full year before Gascoigne's move to Italy could go through, but he was never quite the same player again. He picked up a fair few medals with Rangers, but spells with Middlesbrough, Everton and Burnley just made one think of what might have been. At least Spurs fans will always remember what was.

GIBBONS, Albert Henry (1937–38 and 1940–46)

Centre-forward, 5ft 9in, 11st 5lb

Born: Fulham, West London,
10 April 1914
Died: Johannesburg, South Africa, 4 July 1986
Signed from amateur March, 1937
Transferred to Brentford, July 1938, amateur and Bradford Park Avenue, December 1945, amateur
Also played for: Hayes, Uxbridge, Kingstonian, Brentford, Bradford Park Avenue

Spurs record:

Debut: 16 September 1937 v Sheffield Wednesday (FL) (a) won 3–0
Appearances: League 27, FA Cup 6, others 115
Goals: League 13, FA Cup 5, others 91

■ Even before World War Two, an amateur needed to be a truly-outstanding footballer if he was to hope to claim a regular place in a Football League team. Jack Gibbons was just such a footballer.

An RAF aircraftsman based at Barnes, he played for the senior amateur clubs in West London, but it was his performances for the RAF that grabbed Spurs' attention, and he was signed to amateur forms in March 1937.

A bustling type of inside or centre-forward, it was a surprise when Gibbons was called up for his Football League debut in September 1937. Spurs had been badly hit by early season injuries, and when Andy Duncan was added to the roll the choice was between Gibbons and the experienced George Hunt. Hunt was still a popular figure, even though he was unable to displace Johnny Morrison from his favoured central role, but they were too similar to be paired together. It was a brave move for manager Jack Tresadern to give Gibbons his chance, but it paid immediate dividends. Spurs had won only one of their five League games, but Gibbons and Morrison hit it off immediately, both scoring in a 3–0 win at Sheffield Wednesday.

Gibbons did not look back and quickly established himself as first-choice inside-left, adding the touch of power and dash to the forward line that had been missing. Not that aggression was all his game was about. He knew when to use his strength and when to call on his more subtle skills, particularly when in front of goal. In his first season he found the back of the net 18 times in 33 appearances, second only to Morrison in Spurs' goalscoring chart. He might have outscored Morrison had the RAF not had first call on his services and the experience he gained playing top-level football seen him called up for the England amateur team. There were times when his lack of full-time training was obvious, most notably when he was called upon to play two or more games in a week, and Spurs made frequent efforts to persuade him to join the professional ranks, but he was fully committed to the RAF.

Spurs had spent two seasons in the Second Division but Tresadern had been patiently building a team, and while never really serious contenders for promotion they finished fifth in Gibbons's first season, reaching the sixth round of the FA Cup. With the return of Peter McWilliam as manager, they seemed set to make a real challenge for promotion with Gibbons a major part of the plans.

It was therefore a considerable blow when, in August 1938, it was announced Gibbons would not be re-signing for Spurs. His Commanding Officer did not think it convenient – he would have to restrict his footballing activities to RAF matches. Even more of a blow came two months later when Gibbons signed for Brentford, apparently his Commanding Officer happy with that as they were the local club.

Things did not go so well for Gibbons with Brentford. Despite the fact they were struggling against relegation from the First Division, Gibbons made only 11 appearances and it was no surprise when, in August 1939, it leaked out that he was returning to Spurs. Of course, the activities of a certain German dictator put paid to any hope of Gibbons leading Spurs back to the top flight.

When he should have been at his footballing peak Gibbons was fighting a more serious battle, but he was at least able to play for Spurs in wartime competition and give a taste of what might have been. Playing at centre-forward he scored an incredible 91 goals in only 115 matches, proving himself one of the most potent marksmen in the game. It may not have been football as strong as that before the war or what was to follow, but, with all players missing the training that made the difference between professionals and amateurs, it at least showed what Gibbons could have achieved playing with equals.

As football began to return to normal, Spurs again harboured hopes of Gibbons re-appearing in their League side, but in December 1945 he accepted a job that was too good to turn down working in Bradford. At first he played for Bradford Park Avenue as an amateur, but in May 1946 he finally accepted the opportunity to be paid for playing football. He returned to Brentford after a year, became their manager and, strangely for someone who, when at his best, had treated football as a hobby, then spent the rest of his life travelling the world as a coach.

GILZEAN, Alan John (1964–75)

Forward, 6ft, 12st 4lb

Born: Coupar Angus, Perthshire, 23 October 1938

Signed from Dundee, December 1964, £72,500

Transferred to Highland Park (South Africa) July 1975, released

Also played for: Dundee Violet, Dundee, Highland Park, Scotland

Spurs record:

Debut: 19 December 1964 v Everton (FL) (h) drew 2–2

Appearances: League 335(8), FA Cup 40, League Cup 27(1), Europe 27(1), others 62(5)

Goals: League 93, FA Cup 21, League Cup 6, Europe 13, others 40

■ The sight of Alan Gilzean's balding pate, rising from among a clutch of defenders to delicately flick the ball on for Jimmy Greaves or Martin Chivers, will be an enduring memory for those Spurs patrons who had the privilege of watching 'The King of White Hart Lane' in action. For almost 10 years Gilzean's subtle attacking play provided the ammunition for Spurs' greatest scorers to fire home the goals that garnered the silverware to fill the trophy cabinet.

Gilzean had been a key figure in the Dundee teams that won the Scottish League in 1961–62 and reached the semi-final of the European Champion's Cup the following season. In seven years he scored over 160 goals for the Dark Blues, but like so many of the talented players Dundee produced he became disenchanted with a club that seemed satisfied with its lot. Only on a short-term contract because Dundee refused to release his registration, several clubs including Sunderland and Torino were interested in signing him, but Dundee resisted all offers. In November 1964 Gilzean scored twice for a Scotland XI in a memorial match for John White at White Hart Lane. It was enough to convince Bill Nicholson that Gilzean was the man he wanted to spearhead the new team he was determined to build, as the double side broke up. Dundee would not release Gilzean cheaply, and it took a cheque for £72,500 to secure his signature.

With Dundee, Gilzean had been the strong, bustling spearhead they relied on for goals. At Spurs Greaves was the principal scorer, and Gilzean quickly adapted his style to suit the pace and quicksilver reactions of the little man. The two of them formed a devastating partnership, with Gilzean the focal point of the attack and Greaves picking up the pieces from the havoc Gilzean created. He still put himself about and netted his fair share of goals, but power was supplemented by subtlety and guile. In the 1967 FA Cup Final he gave a master class in centre-forward play, totally dominating Marvin Hinton and creating the space that led to the goals by Frank Saul and Jimmy Robertson that won Spurs the trophy.

When Martin Chivers was signed from Southampton early in 1968 Gilzean's place seemed under threat. Chivers was bigger and more powerful than Gilzean, more like Bobby Smith who had formed such a deadly

combination with Greaves. Gilzean's Spurs career, though, was far from over. He again adapted, this time moving from the central position out wide, from where he could move into the danger area with late runs. Gilzean worked so well with Chivers that eventually it was Greaves who found himself out of the team and on his way to West Ham United, while Gilzean and Chivers went on to lead Spurs to Football League Cup success in 1971 and 1973 and victory in the UEFA Cup in 1972.

Gilzean's great strength was his aerial power, but there was more to 'Gilly' than just an ability to get his head to the ball. He could get power behind his headers when needed, but it was the way he could guide the ball into the perfect place with a delicate deflection that he will be most remembered for. This was never more apparent than when he stationed himself at the near post and, with the minimum of space in which to get any elevation, would climb high to get on the end of a Martin Chivers long throw and flick the ball into the middle for Martin Peters to run on to. He was no slouch on the floor, protecting the ball with his body while he caressed it gently before laying it off. Gilzean did not look particularly powerful, but he had a strength few defenders could match and a stamina that was surprising for someone who often looked older than he actually was. Never the fastest of players, what he lacked in pace he more than made up for with speed of thought and cunning that helped him find time and space.

Gilzean won his first Scottish cap against Norway in November 1963 and collected 17 as a Spurs player, but for Scots fans he will always be remembered for the winning goal he scored against England in April 1964, a typically-deft near-post header.

Gilzean's Spurs career came to an end in June 1974 on an end-of-season tour to Mauritius. He scored seven goals in three games against Mauritius Select XIs, including a hat-trick in the last that was followed by his teammates carrying him around the pitch on a lap of honour. Fortunately Spurs fans had their chance to show their appreciation of his service the following November, when he scored in his Testimonial against Red Star Belgrade.

GINOLA, David Desire Marc (1997–2000)

Winger, 6ft 1in, 11st 10lb

Born: Gassin, France, 25 January 1967
Signed from Newcastle United, July 1997, £2,500,000
Transferred to Aston Villa, July 2000, £3,000,000
Also played for: OGC Nice, Toulon, Matra Racing, Brest Amorique, Paris Saint-Germain, Newcastle United, Aston Villa, Everton, France

Spurs record:

Debut: 10 August 1997 v Manchester United (PL) (h) lost 0–2
Appearances: League 100, FA Cup 11, League Cup 13, Europe 2(1), others 23(2)
Goals: League 13, FA Cup 5, League Cup 4, others 2

■ David Ginola first came to the attention of English football fans in March and April 1994, when he played for Paris Saint-Germain against Arsenal in the European Cup-winners' Cup semi-final. It led to stories that he would sign for Arsenal but there was never any chance of that. Ginola was far too much of a flair player for a club managed by George Graham, who still believed defence was all that mattered.

Instead, Ginola joined Newcastle United where Kevin Keegan gave him the freedom to flourish in a team that came so close to winning the League, before another manager who believed in the ethos of hard work, Kenny Dalglish, decided flair had to be sacrificed for functionality.

It was rather a surprise when Gerry Francis laid out £2.5 million to sign Ginola for Spurs in July 1997. Francis had quickly dismantled Ossie Ardiles's team of attacking talents and adopted the pragmatic approach of building a team to do a job. Results had improved, but the football being played was far from exciting.

Spurs fans have always demanded a hero, a star on whom they could pin their hopes. From his very first game it was clear Ginola was to be that man. With the Gallic good looks, a physique many a movie star would envy and the graceful poise of a dancer, he added a sense of style and panache even before he got on the ball.

Ginola was regarded as a winger when he joined Spurs, a player who would beat his man and provide the crosses for Les Ferdinand, who joined at the same time and also from Newcastle, to feed off. He did that, but he also showed there was a lot more to his game, often playing as a second striker or dropping back to a midfield position where time on the ball was at a premium. Most of his games for Spurs were played out on the wing, and it is testament to his ability that even in that position he was invariably the most influential player on the pitch.

When in possession Ginola would glide over the surface, the ball under control but temptingly close to his marker, inviting the lunging tackle that would miss the ball by inches as Ginola nicked it away before speeding off. His exquisite ball control and perfect balance enabled him to take the ball close in on an opponent before a sudden drag back or quick flick took him past his man.

Ginola arrived with the reputation of being a typical continental. When things were going his way he would be demanding the ball, trying all his tricks and dominating matches. When things went against him or he just did not fancy it, he would disappear, complain at every decision that did not go his way and blame anyone but himself if anything went wrong. Early in his first season, though, with Spurs struggling, Francis gone and Christian Gross installed in his place, Ginola seemed to realise that if relegation was to be avoided he would have to buckle down and contribute fully. He showed a side of his game not seen too often in the past, working back, encouraging his teammates, even making tackles! The returning Jurgen Klinsmann may have got much of the credit, but in truth it was the performances of Ginola that did most to keep Spurs up.

With the arrival of George Graham as manager there was a risk Ginola would be sidelined, but the arch disciple of defensive football seemed to realise that leaving out the fans' favourite would definitely alienate the 50 percent of Spurs supporters who were prepared to give Graham a chance to prove he could change his ways. Ginola rose to the challenge and, despite Graham's continual criticism of his work rate and penchant for substituting him, played his part in helping Spurs lift the Worthington Cup in 1999. His outstanding performances were recognised with both the PFA and FWA Player of the Year awards.

Ginola was never a consistent scorer, but when he did score they were not simple goals. Just like the man himself, his goals were something special. He could find the back of the net with perfectly-placed shots after cutting in from the wing, as he did against Liverpool in March 1998, he could hammer home a vicious first-time volley, as he did against Leeds United in the FA Cup in February 1999, or he could finish with a simple push past the 'keeper after a mazy dribble past four men, as he did in the FA Cup at Barnsley in March 1999. Every goal was a stunner and every one of them just another reason to remember one of the most thrilling players Spurs have had in the last few years.

GREAVES, James Peter (1961–79)

Inside-forward, 5ft 8in, 10st 8lb

Born: East Ham, London, 20 February 1940
Signed from AC Milan (Italy) December 1961, £99,999
Transferred to West Ham United, March 1970, part-exchange value £54,000
Also played for: Chelsea, AC Milan, West Ham United, Barnet, Chelmsford City, Brentwood Town, Woodford Town, England

Spurs record:

Debut: 16 December 1961 v Blackpool (FL) (h) won 5–2
Appearances: League 322, FA Cup 36, League Cup 8, Europe 14, others 40*
*(*Includes one abandoned match)*
Goals: League 220, FA Cup 32, League Cup 5, Europe 9, others 40

■ There are few words that can adequately describe the genius of Jimmy Greaves, Spurs' greatest goalscorer and the finest British football has ever seen. Three hundred and six goals in 420 games is a truly-phenomenal record, but it is frightening to think how many he may have scored if Spurs manager Arthur Rowe had not fallen ill early in 1955. Greaves had been expected to sign for Spurs on leaving school, but in Rowe's absence Chelsea nipped in and persuaded Greaves to join them. It was another six years before he donned the white shirt he had always been destined to grace.

Greaves made his League debut for Chelsea in August 1957. It was at White Hart Lane, and he scored, the first in a long line of debut goals. For club, for country, in one competition after another, when Greaves made his first appearance he would inevitably score.

With 132 goals in 169 games over four years at Stamford Bridge, Greaves topped the wanted list of every Italian club planning for the day their League lifted its embargo on foreign players. That came in June 1961, but Greaves spent a miserable six months at AC Milan, unable to accept the way they demanded total domination of a player's life. His unhappiness came to an end in December 1961 when Bill Nicholson laid out £99,999 to secure the only player he thought could improve the double-winning side.

Greaves scored a wonderful hat-trick on his debut and, as so often, Nicholson was proved right. At the end of the season he played in his first FA Cup Final and scored the opener within three minutes, a typical piece of opportunism, as he collected a pass from Bobby Smith, spun one way, then the other and left three defenders for dead as he slipped the ball home. A year later he went one better, netting twice in the European Cup-winners' Cup Final.

For eight years Greaves was simply outstanding, breaking one record after another. Scoring was his job and that was all he concentrated on. There was no haring round the pitch hunting the ball, and no marking an opponent or trying to tackle. Greaves spent his time quietly drifting around as if disinterested, apparently putting in little effort but all the while working away to find that yard of space he could exploit in an instant. When the chance of a goal came along the master goalscorer would come alive.

Scoring is the most difficult art in football, but for Greaves it was easy. His anticipation was incredible, moving into position as if he knew where a misplaced pass or deflection would deposit the ball, his reactions razor-sharp and his initial burst of pace enough to take him away from any defender. When he got the ball his control was immaculate, his balance perfect and his coolness unsurpassable. In one-on-one situations there was only one winner as a little feint took the ball out of the 'keeper's reach before the deftest of touches guided it home. It looked easy but it disguised how much hard work he really put in. Most players would stand back and watch a shot. Not Greaves, he would follow the ball in, waiting for the rebound, ready to apply the final touch. When that time came, Greaves knew precision was best, side footing the ball home rather than blasting it.

Greaves scored the majority of his goals from inside the box, but he did more work outside the area than given credit for. Frequently on the end of the roughest treatment, he was always available for a pass, always looking for the opening that would allow him to turn and show his close control as defenders were left in his wake. He scored many spectacular goals, but perhaps the most memorable came in October 1968 against Leicester City. Collecting a Pat Jennings punt wide on the right, just inside the Leicester half, he had the ball under control and the first defender beaten in one movement. He then weaved his way past three more opponents, dummied Peter Shilton and slipped the ball home. For several weeks Spurs' programme cover pictured Greaves applying the finishing touch as four defenders could be seen in the background at varying stages of recovering their feet.

Greaves scored 44 goals in 57 appearances for England but missed the 1966 World Cup success as he continued to recover from hepatitis. Some consolation came a year later as Spurs beat Chelsea in the 1967 Cockney Cup Final.

He left Spurs for West Ham United in March 1970 as part of the Martin Peters transfer and retired from the top flight a year later. In October 1972 he became the first Spurs player of modern times to be granted a testimonial. A crowd of 45,799 turned out to see Greaves score inside three minutes.

GRIMSDELL, Arthur (1911–29)

Half-back, 5ft 10in, 12st 2lb

Born: Watford, Hertfordshire, 23 March 1894

Died: Watford, Hertfordshire, 12 March 1963

Signed from Watford, April 1912, £500 (with Walter Tattersall)

Transferred to Clapton Orient, August 1929

Also played for: Watford St Stephens, St Albans City, Watford, Clapton Orient, England

Spurs record:

Debut: 20 April 1912 v Bolton Wanderers (FL) (h) won 1–0

Appearances: League 324, FA Cup 36, others 58

Goals: League 26, FA Cup 1, others 11

■ When Spurs signed Arthur Grimsdell from Watford in April 1912 he was a raw 18-year-old former-schoolboy star. He grew to be captain of England, the finest half-back in the country and, at the time, possibly the finest the country had produced.

Barely past his 17th birthday when he made his debut for Southern League Watford, Grimsdell was soon first-choice centre-half and attracting the attention of several Football League clubs. Spurs were quick to move in for him when they learned Watford were having money troubles and secured his services,

together with those of Walter Tattersall, for a bargain £500.

When he arrived at White Hart Lane Grimsdell was regarded as one for the future, but he was plunged straight into the League side and did not look out of his depth. He began the following season as reserve centre-half but was called up to the first team in December 1912, just before Peter McWilliam was appointed manager. McWilliam had been an exceptional half-back himself and soon recognised that, while Grimsdell possessed great defensive qualities, his attacking prowess meant he had the potential to be every bit as good as McWilliam had been.

Given the freedom to roam where his instincts took him, Grimsdell developed in leaps and bounds. By November 1913, still well short of his 20th birthday, he was playing in an international trial and on the fringes of the England team, but as Spurs struggled in 1914–15 and McWilliam sought to strengthen the defence, Grimsdell found himself out of the team. One of the first to enlist, he was not available to Spurs throughout World War One, but when he returned he had developed from a strapping youth to a powerful man, determined to make up for lost time, and he collected his first international honour in the Victory internationals of April and May 1919.

With Spurs cruelly denied their rightful place in the First Division, McWilliam set about building a team to take them straight back up, and Grimsdell was at the centre of it. As they stormed away with the Second Division title Grimsdell dominated play from midfield, forever looking to attack and showing the power of his long-range shooting with an incredible 14 goals.

Appointed club captain in December 1919, he led Spurs back into the top flight, to FA Cup success in 1921 and two years later to their highest finish, second, in the Football League – his reputation growing all the time. Forever involved in the thick of the action, Grimsdell was masterful in defence, but he believed attack was the best form of defence, and it was in going forward that he really excelled. His strength in the tackle, determination and aggression were his most obvious qualities, but he also had terrific skill on the ball and a fine tactical brain. He was an exceptional captain for both club and country, refusing to accept defeat and inspiring his men to keep going to the end. His mere presence seemed to lift his teams to a higher level.

Grimsdell was at the peak of his power in January 1924 when he suffered a knee-ligament injury in an FA Cup tie with Crystal Palace. The injury proved to be far more serious than first thought and rumours circulated that his career was over, but just as Grimsdell was a fighter on the pitch, so he was off it. It took the best part of a year but eventually he fought his way back, and as he returned to his best so did Spurs. Leading the First Division and at last looking like a team that really could win the League title, disaster struck at Leicester in October 1925 when Grimsdell broke his leg.

It was a measure of his importance to the team that without their inspiration Spurs tumbled down the table, rapidly turning from Championship contenders to relegation strugglers. It was not until April 1927 that he returned again, but the injuries had taken their toll, and although he continued to don the white shirt he had worn with so much distinction for another two years he was never quite the same player again.

Released in April 1929, he joined Clapton Orient as player/secretary/manager but after only a year moved into coaching schoolboys before leaving the game altogether.

HALL, George William (1932–44)

Inside-forward, 5ft 7in, 10st 7lb

Born: Newark, Nottinghamshire, 12 March 1912
Died: Newark, Nottinghamshire, 22 May 1967
Signed from Notts County, November 1930
Retired, February 1944
Also played for: Ransome & Miles, Notts County, England

Spurs record:

Debut: 24 December 1932 v Notts County (FL) (a) lost 0–3
Appearances: League 205, FA Cup 20, others 151
Goals: League 27, FA Cup 2, others 16

■ In George Greenfield Spurs had uncovered a schemer of rare talent. In the dozen matches the inside-forward had played by early December 1932 Spurs had scored an amazing 42 goals, with Greenfield's promptings behind many of them and his contribution being six. They were well poised in the promotion battle and at last looked to have a team capable of escaping the Second Division. When Greenfield broke his leg at Fulham that month it was viewed as a disaster.

Manager Percy Smith knew that if the momentum was not to be lost he would have to find an immediate replacement. He wasted no time in swooping for Willie Hall, a 20-year-old with Notts County and the one inside-forward

rated every bit as exciting a prospect as Greenfield.

Hall fitted into the Spurs pattern of play immediately, and at the end of the season Spurs went up as runners-up to Stoke City. Within a year of joining Spurs, Hall had made his England debut, completing a meteoric rise.

A schoolboy star in Nottingham, Hall had been playing for the works team of Ransome & Miles before joining Notts County. He made his debut for them in the champion's last Third Division South match of 1930–31, spent 18 months with County and six with Spurs in the Second Division, and then found himself playing in the First Division. His international debut was in December 1933 against France at White Hart Lane, an outing that meant Spurs had to pay Notts County another £500.

Hall provided the perfect link between defence and attack. Always looking for the ball and quite happy to work back to get it, he dovetailed perfectly with Willie Evans, knowing exactly how and when to release the flying winger and possessing the precision passing Evans thrived upon. Passing was not Hall's only strength though. He also possessed the ability to dribble his way through a defence as good as any winger and weaved magical patterns in midfield before releasing the killer ball. George Hunt, in particular, thrived on Hall's ability to hold the ball and attract players to him while Hunt waited for the right moment to burst through, knowing Hall would play the ball perfectly into his run.

Hall's position as the centre of Spurs' attacking movements cost him and the club dear in November 1934. Already badly hit by injuries, Spurs were not having the best of times, but things got a lot worse when three Manchester City players went in to tackle Hall at the same time. It left him crumpled on the ground and resulted in a cartilage operation that kept him out of the team for almost five months. By the time he was fit to return to League action Spurs were all but relegated, and while performances, and results, improved with him back there was nothing he could do to save them.

While Spurs struggled unsuccessfully to get out of the Second Division again, Hall continued to shine. His outstanding performances led to selection for the Football League against their Irish counterparts in October 1937 and an England recall against Northern Ireland later that month. All told, Hall made 10 full England appearances for England, but the most remarkable was that against Northern Ireland at Old Trafford in November 1938. Hall was never a consistent scorer, but against the Irish he combined to devastating effect with Stan Matthews and scored five goals, including the fastest hat-trick in international football.

Just when Hall should have been reaching his peak, World War Two broke out. He was rejected by the services because of injuries sustained playing football and served in the police war reserve in London, which meant he was available to play for Spurs. In the early years of the war he was the most regular performer, playing week in, week out in whatever position needed filling, often full-back. Whatever it was that had prevented him joining the forces, Hall seemed perfectly fit for football until late in 1943 when he was struck down by a serious leg disease. It forced him to retire in February 1944 and in later years to have the lower parts of both legs amputated. Despite the handicap he remained in football for several years as a coach and manager with Clapton Orient, Chelmsford City and Chingford Town. One of the first footballers to be the subject of a *This is Your Life* programme, Hall was never forgotten at White Hart Lane and for many years was vice-President of the Spurs Supporters Club.

HARMER, Thomas Charles (1949–60)

Inside-forward, 5ft 6in, 8st 9lb

Born: Hackney, East London, 2 February 1928
Died: Edmonton, north London, 25 December 2008
Signed from amateur, August 1948
Transferred to Watford, October 1960, £5,000
Also played for: Watford, Chelsea, Hastings United

Spurs record:

Debut: 8 September 1951 v Bolton Wanderers (FL) (h) won 2–1
Appearances: League 205, FA Cup 17, others 51(2)
Goals: League 47, FA Cup 4, others 18

■ Throughout his football career little Tommy Harmer was known as the 'Charmer' and never

could there have been a more appropriate nickname for a player who totally enchanted spectators with his absolute mastery of a football.

A product of Tottenham Juniors, Harmer was a featherweight as a boy and remained one all his career, rarely tipping the scales at much over nine stone. Such a frail physique held him back in his early days as there were concerns whether he could handle the robust nature of professional football. Everything from special diets to special training was tried in an effort to make him fill out, but Harmer was a wisp of a lad and eventually it just had to be accepted that nothing could change that.

From his earliest appearances in a Spurs shirt Harmer had an army of admirers. Those who frequented the A and reserve-team games immediately took him to their hearts. Even as Spurs lifted the Second Division and Football League titles in successive seasons, they pressed for him to be given the chance to show his skills in the League side, but Arthur Rowe's vision of 'Push and Run' called for instant passing with players holding the ball for the minimum of time. Les Bennett had the freedom to run with the ball and Rowe did not feel the team could accommodate two players who might slow the attacking play so vital to Spurs' success.

Harmer had been a professional for three years before he got his chance against League leaders Bolton Wanderers in September 1951. The cheer that greeted the announcement of his inclusion in the team was as great as those that marked the two goals Spurs scored and surpassed only by the applause reserved for Harmer at the end of the 90 minutes. In the one game he had shown everything that made him such a wonderful talent. Supremely confident, he produced all the little flicks and feints, the ball-juggling skills and mesmeric dribbling that were his trademarks.

Even while being feted as a true star of the future, there were those who wondered how he would cope with winter's muddy pitches and heavy challenges. Rowe was among them and once Eddie Baily was fit to return Harmer found himself back in the reserves. So it was for the next few years, as he flitted in and out of the team, rarely getting a run of more than half-a-dozen games. He often sought a transfer but Spurs refused, perhaps worried that given the chance elsewhere he would return to haunt them.

When Rowe resigned in the summer of 1956 his replacement Jimmy Anderson realised that the players who had done so much for the club in the early 50s were now past their best and fresh blood was needed. Even then, it was only after Baily left in early 1956 that Harmer was really given a chance, and then it came more by luck than planning. Struggling at the wrong end of the table, it was almost in desperation that Harmer was called up to face Doncaster Rovers in the FA Cup in February 1956. He was asked to play out wide on the right, hardly the best place to influence a game, but Harmer was superb and it was down to his prompting that Spurs progressed to the semi-final.

Still the doubts persisted. Anderson decided Harmer was not strong enough to face Manchester City strongman Roy Paul in the Villa Park semi-final and left him out in favour of Dave Dunmore. It was a mistake that probably cost Spurs their first visit to Wembley but not one Anderson was to repeat.

Harmer was soon reinstated and for the next four years dazzled opponents and fans alike with the sheer magic of his football. With Danny Blanchflower beside him and Bobby Smith leading the line, Harmer's artistry lit up White Hart Lane. At times one wondered why there had ever been doubts about his ability to handle the rigours of top-flight football as he flitted past the toughest opponents and skated across the heaviest surfaces, but at others he could be bullied out of a game and heavy pitches could nullify his skills.

Much as Bill Nicholson appreciated Harmer's talents, he felt a more direct, hard-running lieutenant was needed alongside Blanchflower and found that man in John White. With 1960–61 starting so well and Harmer not content with reserve-team football, Nicholson allowed him to move to Watford where he played for two years before a final brief spell with Chelsea.

In later years Harmer was often seen at games or attending functions for old players. He was a lovely, engaging character ever willing to talk about football and Spurs in particular. 'Harmer the Charmer' – as a player, as a man.

HARPER, Edward Cashfield (1928–32)

Centre-forward, 5ft 11in, 11st 10lb

Born: Sheerness, Kent, 22 August 1902
Died: Blackburn, Lancashire, 22 July 1959
Signed from Sheffield Wednesday November 1927, £5,500
Transferred to Preston North End December 1931, £5,000 (with Dick Rowley)
Also played for: Whitstable Town, Sheppey United, Blackburn Rovers, Sheffield Wednesday, Preston North End, England

Spurs record:

Debut: 16 March 1929 v Clapton Orient (FL) (a) won 3–2
Appearances: League 63, FA Cup 4, others 11
Goals: League 62, FA Cup 1, others 20

■ A veritable goalscoring machine, Ted Harper spent less than three years with Spurs, netting an astonishing 62 goals in just 63 League outings. It was nothing unusual for the Sheerness-born centre-forward. Throughout his career he scored with such regularity it is hard to believe he won only one England cap until one realises that scoring was the only real footballing talent he possessed.

Harper first attracted attention as an 18-year-old, netting over 100 goals in one season of Kent League football, but he decided to complete his apprenticeship as a shipwright before taking the plunge into professional football with Blackburn Rovers in May 1923. Immediately given his chance in their League team, he netted on his debut and finished his season with 18 goals but started 1924–25 poorly and eventually found himself out of the team. When Blackburn began the following season with three defeats, Harper was recalled. He netted five in a 7–1 defeat of Newcastle that set him off on a rampage through opposing defences. He finished the season with 43 goals, a Football League record only surpassed after the change in the offside law, and played against Scotland in April 1926.

Harper took his total to 106 goals in 144 League games before a £4,400 move to Sheffield Wednesday. A hat-trick on his debut augured well, but Wednesday were a relegation-haunted outfit and Harper was not a player at his best in a struggling team. In a little over 15 months he added 13 goals and 18 games to his League total but was not prepared to accept reserve-team football and demanded a transfer in February 1929.

Relegated from the First Division nine months earlier, Spurs had shown little likelihood of making an immediate return. Minimal expenditure on inferior players had been the order of the day from the Spurs directors, their reluctance to sanction any investment in quality players well known and blamed for the club's slide. At last they were persuaded to open the cheque book and hand over £5,000 to bring Harper to White Hart Lane.

Harper's impact was immediate: a goal on his debut followed by 10 more in another 10 outings. It was a great start and just the fillip Spurs needed, but a cartilage injury in pre-season put Harper on the sidelines as 1929–30 got under way. He returned to score 14 goals in his next 19 games, but it was in 1931–32 that he really delivered the goods for Spurs. He scored 36 goals in only 30 League appearances, setting a record for Spurs that was not equalled until Bobby Smith came along in 1957–58 and was only beaten by Jimmy Greaves.

Harper was a goalscorer, pure and simple. He had great positional sense, seeming to drift into the perfect position without even realising himself what he was doing. It was a natural instinct, a talent that cannot be taught. He could finish with either foot or with his head and displayed a sense of bravery verging on the reckless. When the ball was within range of goal he came alive but that in itself was his weakness. It was only when there was a chance of scoring that he showed any interest in what was going on. The rest of the time he made little contribution.

An ungainly figure, he possessed strength and a good burst of pace, but in football skills he was sadly lacking, his ball control was poor, he lacked trickery in his dribbling, his passing left a great deal to be desired, and he failed to bring other players into the game. For all his faults, though, Harper could score goals and, at the time, that was what Spurs needed.

His reputation as a scorer meant Harper was always a marked man, the recipient of rough and often unfair challenges. Combined with his willingness to go in where it hurt, he was often injured, and it was injury that not only prevented him setting a season scoring record for Spurs that was unlikely to be beaten but may also have cost Spurs promotion. Injured at Swansea in March 1931, he missed six of the last eight games. In his absence Spurs picked up only four points to finish three points behind second-placed West Bromwich Albion.

Young George Hunt deputised for Harper in those six games, and, although he lacked Harper's experience, manager Percy Smith decided Hunt's all-round game was what Spurs needed. Harper was consigned to the reserves until moving to Preston North End in December 1931. The following season he rattled in 43 goals for Preston, leaving him with the record of having scored most goals in a season for three different clubs.

HARSTON, William Robert (1883–1892)

Forward

Born: Edmonton, North London, December 1867
Died: Tottenham, North London, 30 August 1953
Also played for: Tottenham College, Broadwater

Spurs record:

Appearances: others 40
Goals: others 13

■ While Billy Harston was not one of the 11 schoolboys who founded the Hotspur Football Club in 1882 or one of the seven members that were known to join the club during its first season, he was certainly one of the 21 lads who attended a meeting at the Tottenham Young Men's Christian Association in the High Road in August 1883 when steps were taken to put the club on a more formal footing under the guidance of John Ripsher. A 15-year-old apprentice engineer at a Brass Works and Iron Foundry, it is almost certain Harston had played for Spurs in their first season, for it is unlikely the meeting would have elected a newcomer as vice-captain to John Randall.

Spurs' opening game of the 1883–84 season was on 6 October, and it is the first match for which a team line up has been recorded, the details being recalled several years later by Harston who captained the side in the absence of Randall. He appeared in the inside-left position with Bobby Buckle, his wing partner. It was a partnership that was to serve Spurs marvellously well for the best part of 10 years as the club moved from infancy through adolescence and into adult life.

With records of the club's early matches almost non-existent, it is impossible to tell how many games Harston played, but he seems to have appeared in most of them, and he was certainly in those that marked a landmark in the club's development.

The first Cup competition Spurs entered was the London Association Cup, and in October 1885 they were drawn at home in the first round to St Albans, not the modern day Hertfordshire club from the town of the same name but the team run by a London business house. Spurs won the game 5–2 with Harston scoring once and evidently one of the stars of the show, as he and Billy Mason were carried shoulder high from the pitch by some of the 400 spectators. Spurs did not do so well in the second round, beaten at home 0–8 by the Casuals, but even taking to the pitch with such a famous club was a measure of how much progress had been made in such a short space of time.

In following years Spurs entered the East End, London Senior, Middlesex Senior and Luton Charity Cups, and Harston was always there, with his ever-trusty partner Bobby Buckle. The pair were a permanent fixture, one rarely taking to the pitch without the other.

By all accounts they were both small but an exceptional pairing, Buckle being the fleet-footed winger, Harston the hard-working inside-forward, whose job was to set Buckle free and then follow up ready to feed off the cross that was bound to come.

In the dim and distant days of Spurs' early history it was quite normal to play with two centre-forwards and two wingers. It meant inside-forwards had a lot of ground to cover, but Harston, apparently, relished the responsibility and particularly loved to run from deep with the ball before releasing Buckle.

Apart from Jack Jull, Buckle and Harston were to be the longest-serving early members, doing more than most to help lay the foundations for a style of play that was to be followed for years to come, by the likes of Copeland and Kirwan, Bliss and Dimmock, Baily and Medley.

In the late 1880s Harston attended Tottenham College and played for their football team on a few occasions, but he continued to turn out for Spurs until 1892. By then Spurs were really making a name for themselves and beginning to attract some of London's top amateur players. Harston had done his bit for Spurs and switched to playing for another local team, Broadwater, who he assisted for some time.

Harston lived all his life in Tottenham and continued to be associated with Spurs for many years after he finished playing. A guest at the banquets in 1901 and 1921 to celebrate winning the FA Cup, he was a regular at White Hart Lane and up to his death in August 1953 worked as a press box steward. He was certainly the last player from those days on Tottenham Marshes to still have an active involvement with the club, only his old pal, Bobby Buckle, being known to survive him.

HENRY, Ronald Patrick (1954–67)

Full-back, 5ft 11in, 11st 13lb

Born: Shoreditch, London, 17 August 1934

Signed from amateur, January 1955

Retired, May 1969

Also played for: Harpenden Town, Redbourne, England

Spurs record:

Debut: 12 April 1955 v Huddersfield Town (FL) (a) lost 0–1

Appearances: League 247, FA Cup 23, Europe 17, others 51(4)

Goals: League 1, others 1

■ Every great team has its unsung heroes, the hard-working, no-nonsense players who, because they got on with their jobs in a quiet and effective manner, allowed the more

flamboyant stars to catch the eye and receive the adulation. Ron Henry was just such a player, a Spurs stalwart in every sense of the word.

Seemingly passed over by Luton Town and Wolverhampton Wanderers, Henry was playing for Redbourne when spotted by Spurs and taken on the books as an a amateur in March 1953, but it was almost two years later before he joined the professional staff and began the slow process of working his way through the ranks.

Originally a winger but now playing at half-back, he made his Football League debut in April 1955 playing at centre-half in the absence of Harry Clarke, but after the one game it was back to the reserves.

Moving to left-back, he settled in the reserve team, a competent if not outstanding performer. Mel Hopkins was the established left-back, one of the best in the country and an automatic choice. Henry made a few appearances when the Welshman was away on international duty or injured, his only sustained run being towards the end of 1958–59 when Hopkins was injured playing for Wales. At first Henry kept the position, but once Hopkins was fully recovered he was again ahead of Henry, and it seemed Henry would have to content himself with the role of Hopkins's permanent understudy.

However, in November 1959, again while playing for his country, Hopkins broke his nose. Henry was called up, no doubt fully expecting his first-team tenure to be short-lived again, but this time he was not prepared to relinquish his place so easily.

As Bill Nicholson's coaching and forays into the transfer market began to have an effect, so Henry blossomed. Selected ahead of Hopkins on merit, his confidence increased, and he began to show that he was good enough to make a contribution to the best team any manager had ever assembled. He may not have had the long-legged stride, the pace or the attacking instincts of Hopkins, but he did have a cool head, an intelligent footballing brain and a good strong tackle.

He knew just where to position himself to intercept dangerous passes, when to go in for a tackle and when to hold back, shepherding his man to where he could do no harm before moving in to dispossess. When he got the ball he was neat and tidy, finding a colleague with a simple pass, making himself available to take the ball back and looking for another simple layoff to set Spurs going forward. There was nothing fancy about Henry, everything was simplicity itself and that meant errors were rare.

Throughout the double season Henry's name appeared on the team sheet for every game as he collected League Championship and FA Cup-winners' medals. In 1961–62 he missed only one game, allowing his permanent understudy Mel Hopkin a rare outing in the number-three shirt, and collected another FA Cup-winners' medal. In 1962–63 he was again an ever present, now ending the season with a European Cup-winners' medal. Only in 1963–64 was he absent for any length of time, and that due to injury, before another season in which he missed only one game. Henry's name had become a byword for reliability and consistency.

At club level Henry won just about everything, but he was not so fortunate on the international scene. He collected just one England cap, against France in February 1963. It was Alf Ramsey's first match in charge and few could have dreamt of the glory Ramsey would lead his team to a little over three years later as England lost 1–5. Henry probably deserved another chance, but Ray Wilson was in his prime and opportunity did not knock again. He was left to do what he was best at and that was to turn in one consistent performance after another for Spurs.

As wingers began to disappear from the game and over-lapping full-backs were expected do their job, Nicholson signed Cyril Knowles. After a season helping the youngster settle in, Knowles took his place, but Henry was not lost to Spurs. He dropped down to the reserves, giving them the benefit of his experience and helping the likes of Joe Kinnear to prepare for League action. When he did hang up his boots he coached the juniors and, after a spell running a nursery, then returned to coach at Spurs' School of Excellence. One of his pupils there was his grandson Ronnie.

HODDLE, Glenn (1975–87)

Midfield, 6ft 1in, 11st 6lb

Born: Hayes, Middlesex, 27 October 1957
Signed from apprentice, April 1975
Transferred to Monaco, July 1987, £750,000
Also played for: Monaco, Chelsea, Swindon Town, England

Spurs record:

Debut: 30 August 1975 v Norwich City (sub) (FL) (h) drew 2–2
Appearances: League 370(7), FA Cup 47(1), League Cup 44, Europe 17(4), others 88(12)
Goals: League 88, FA Cup 11, League Cup 10, Europe 1, others 22

■ The term 'The most naturally-gifted footballer of his generation' is one of those over-used clichés, but in the case of Glenn Hoddle it is an understatement. Hoddle was not just the most naturally-gifted player of his generation, he was the most naturally-gifted of many generations.

Living in Harlow, he was noted by Spurs as a schoolboy, but it was only after playing in a local junior Cup Final in front of Martin Chivers that he was invited to train with Spurs. Chivers and Ray Evans had gone along to present the trophies and Chivers mentioned Hoddle's name when he got back to White Hart Lane. Only 11, he was outstanding even then, and so he continued as he moved up through the ranks, with Spurs signing him to apprentice and professional forms at the first opportunity. As he developed, anyone who watched him play knew that here was a special talent.

Hoddle made his League debut as a substitute in August 1975 but Terry Neill was still finding his feet at Spurs and was not going to risk giving an 18-year-old free rein. It was not until February 1976 that Hoddle started his first League game, and he announced his arrival with the type of goal, against Stoke City, he was to become renowned for, beating England 'keeper Peter Shilton with a perfectly-placed long-range volley.

Neill soon departed to be replaced by Keith Burkinshaw, who immediately showed his confidence in Hoddle's talents by installing him as the midfield playmaker, the player around whom everything would revolve. It was a heavy burden for one so young, and with Spurs relegated in 1977 it might have appeared one too demanding, but Hoddle needed time to develop and Burkinshaw time to assemble the right players around Hoddle. That one season sojourn in the hustle and bustle of the Second Division probably did more to bring Hoddle on than several seasons in the First. He learned there were times when he had to dig in and work before class would tell, and class was one thing Hoddle had in abundance.

Tall, slim, elegant, perfectly balanced and with a bearing that just screamed confidence, Hoddle simply oozed class. There seemed

nothing he could not do with a football, whether it was playing quick-fire one-twos, threading it through a massed defence, juggling it in the tightest of corners, bending it round a defensive wall, chipping it into a few feet of space or dropping it inch perfect into the stride of a colleague. Hoddle never played a long ball in his life, but he hit a multitude of 40 and 50-yard passes. He could dribble, not with pace but with grace, poise and a sway of the body that would send opponents the wrong way.

Hoddle could score too, and what goals he scored. If it were ever possible to compile a Spurs top 20 goals of all time, Hoddle would have several entrants – his edge of the box volley after a slick one-two with Ossie Ardiles against Manchester United in August 1979, his first-time sledgehammer against Nottingham Forest two months later, when Gerry Armstrong and Chris Jones nodded on a Milija Aleksic punt, his delicate inch-perfect lob from the angle of the area at Watford in September 1983, his parting gift to Spurs fans as he feinted and shimmied his way through the Oxford United defence in April 1987, the list is endless.

Hoddle made his last appearance for Spurs in the 1987 FA Cup Final. Defeat was not the way he wanted to leave, but he more than many had given the fans good times with the FA Cup in 1981 and 1982, the League (Milk) Cup Final in 1982 and, although he missed the Final because of injury, the UEFA Cup in 1984.

Hoddle won 53 full England caps, a reasonable number but barely half of what he should have collected. Too often England managers preferred to ignore his ability to turn a game with one flash of genius in favour of blood, sweat and hard work.

After Spurs, Hoddle took his talents to Monaco where his vision and skills found a new adoring audience to appreciate his artistry before embarking on a managerial career with Swindon Town, Chelsea, England, Southampton, a return home to Spurs and Wolverhampton Wanderers.

HOPKINS, Melvyn (1952–64)

Full-back, 5ft 11in, 10st 6lb

Born: Ystraad Rhondda, Wales, 7 November 1934

Signed from amateur, May 1952

Transferred to Brighton & Hove Albion, October 1964, £5,000

Also played for: Brighton & Hove Albion, Canterbury City, Ballymena, Bradford Park Avenue, Wales

Spurs record:

Debut: 11 October 1952 v Derby County (FL) (a) drew 0–0

Appearances: League 219, FA Cup 20, Europe 1, others 31

Goals: others 1

■ Although Manchester United also had their eyes on the gangly young full-back with Ystraad Boys Club, when Spurs offered Mel Hopkins a trial in February 1951 he was quick to take up the offer. With Arthur Rowe's great 'Push and Run' team on the way to the Football League title, what 17-year-old from the valleys would not want the chance to mix with some of the country's top stars, even if only for a few days? Hopkins stayed for more than a few days. It was to be over 13 years before he left Spurs, and by then he had himself become a star, a Welsh international and one of the best full-backs ever to play for Spurs.

Arthur Willis and Charlie Withers were competing for the left-back spot when Hopkins arrived. They had pretty much shared the position since 1949 but were both getting on, and Rowe knew they would have to be replaced soon. Hopkins was just the man to do that, but even Rowe was surprised at the speed with which he progressed. He made his first appearance in October 1952 and played again in the last match of the season but had to bide his time before he could be regarded as a regular.

By 1955 Hopkins had made the number-three shirt his property. Even as Spurs struggled in the mid 50s he stood out as one of the country's outstanding young talents and, as first Jimmy Anderson and then Bill Nicholson turned things around, he moved on to establish himself as a player any club would want in their team.

Slender and a fraction under six foot tall, Hopkins had the appearance of a giant spider, all arms and legs, but he possessed terrific pace

and when he got into his stride a surprising grace. Always keen to join the attack, he often pushed up ahead of his winger, overlapping in a manner yet to become a feature of football, but he had such a remarkable ability to recover he was rarely caught out of position. Defensively he showed great composure, tenacity and strength in the tackle, while his height was put to good use in the air.

Hopkins broke into the Welsh team for the first time in April 1956 against Northern Ireland and was soon first choice for his country, although it was his international duties that were to cost him his place at Spurs and eventually see him miss out on the club's greatest successes. Injured against Israel in February 1958, Ron Henry stepped in and at first Hopkins was unable to get his place back. It was only after that summer's World Cup, when the Welsh proved the surprise team of the tournament, that Hopkins returned to the team, but he was not so fortunate when a kick in the face from Scotland's Ian St John rearranged his nose in November 1959. Henry stepped in again, but now he was there to stay, not as eye-catching but as consistent as Hopkins himself had been. Henry rarely missed a game, so Hopkins got few opportunities over the next five years and had to content himself with a role as a reserve for his club while an automatic choice for his country, taking his total of caps as a Spurs player to 34.

Hopkins was first-choice cover for either full-back position and from 1961 to 1964 played roughly half his games on the right and half on the left. While he would have been an automatic choice for any other team, in Henry and Peter Baker Spurs were blessed with two of the most consistent and reliable backs around. Hopkins never let the team down whenever he was called upon, but if Baker and Henry were available it was the reserve side for Hopkins. Understandably frustrated, he did ask for a transfer, but he was so highly appreciated by Nicholson that all requests were refused.

Cyril Knowles arrived in the summer of 1964 and soon proved he had what it took to establish himself at White Hart Lane. Hopkins was now allowed to leave. In October 1964 he moved to Brighton & Hove Albion and helped them collect the Fourth Division title before moving on to play for Canterbury City, Ballymena and Bradford Park Avenue.

HOWE, Leslie Francis (1930–46)

Utility, 5ft 10in, 10st 8lb

Born: Bengeo, Hertfordshire, 5 March 1912

Died: Tottenham, North London, 23 February 1999

Signed from amateur, August 1930

Retired, June 1946

Also played for: Northfleet United

Spurs record:

Debut: 26 December 1930 v Southampton (FL) (a) won 3–0

*Appearances: League 165, FA Cup 17, others 103**

*(*Includes one abandoned match)*

Goals: League 26, FA Cup 2, others 19

■ Les Howe was one of those players who gave their whole playing career and more to one club without ever becoming a real star or receiving the credit they deserved for their years of loyal service.

Although born in Hertfordshire, Howe moved to Tottenham when he was a boy and was always destined to become a Spurs player.

He attended the local Lancastrian School, represented Tottenham, London and England at Schoolboy level and played for the local junior club, Tottenham Argyle, before coming under Spurs' wing with the Tottenham Juniors. Signed as an amateur, he spent a season with both Enfield and the Northfleet United nursery club before signing as a professional and moving on to the White Hart Lane staff in August 1930.

Howe received a surprise call-up for his League debut against Southampton on Boxing Day 1930, replacing right-half Harry Skitt who had been injured against Saints the previous day. Centre-half or right-half were becoming Howe's recognised positions at the time, but he had already shown his versatility. He had played a couple of games in the London FA Charity Cup and in the second of those, against Ilford, had spent part of the game on the right wing and scored a hat-trick.

Against Southampton, Howe performed competently if not spectacularly as Spurs won 3–0 to reverse Christmas Day's 1–3 defeat. He would have retained his place for the following day's fixture at Reading but picked up an injury himself. This allowed Wally Alsford a chance to stake his claim as Skitt's replacement and Howe only played two more League games that season, although he did play in the London FA Charity Cup Final, this time at centre-forward.

Howe then spent another season with Northfleet United, usually occupying one of the forward positions before returning to White Hart Lane. When he was called up for first-team action again in October 1932 it was at outside-right. Spurs had started the season poorly and Willie Davies seemed to have lost all his confidence. Wholesale changes were made for the match at Preston North End, and they worked a treat. Spurs won 6–2, the first of eight wins in nine games. Howe kept his place until Christmas 1932 when injury forced him out and let Davies back in. As Spurs battled to finish second and secure promotion, Howe got a few more games at the end of the season, now at inside-right, the position he occupied in a few games the following season.

It was in 1934–35, as injuries decimated Spurs and led to their relegation, that Howe really established himself as a first-team regular,

but even then he continued to turn out in a variety of positions: inside-forward, right-wing, half-back and centre-half. His career continued in similar vein over the next few years. Most of his games were at right-half, but when injuries or poor form struck manager Jack Tresadern knew he could switch Howe to fill in, safe in the knowledge he would never let the team down.

There was nothing special about Howe's footballing talents. He was a good, solid all-round player, perhaps best at half-back where his strength and willingness to work came to the fore. Always ready to push forward, he could knit the midfield together and with a powerful shot contribute a fair number of goals. On the wing he was not the speediest or trickiest of wingers, but he knew how to find that crucial yard of space to whip the ball in, while at centre-forward he could hold the ball up and trouble the most accomplished of defenders.

With Ron Burgess developing rapidly, Howe found himself out of favour as war threatened and may have been allowed to leave had hostilities not broken out. When service demands allowed, he continued to serve Spurs well throughout the war years, occupying any position needed. Overall he played in every outfield position and even had a go in goal in an emergency.

Throughout the time Howe played, players specialised and rarely played in anything other than their recognised position. Howe was an exception, a player competent enough to fill any role, if not outstanding in one and priceless for that versatility.

Howe might have continued with Spurs after the war but an injury in September 1945 proved complicated, and after fighting hard to overcome it he had to accept he was never going to be fit enough for League football again. Given a free transfer, he coached Edmonton Borough and later managed Enfield, continuing to live in Tottenham until he passed away.

HOWELLS, David Glyn (1985–97)

Midfield, 5ft 11in, 11st 10lb

Born: Guildford, Surrey, 15 December 1967
Signed from trainee, January 1985
Transferred to Southampton, July 1998, free
Also played for: Southampton, Bristol City, Hartley Wintney, Havant & Waterlooville

Spurs record:

Debut: 22 February 1986 v Sheffield Wednesday (FL) (a) won 2–1
Appearances: League 238(39), FA Cup 17(4), FL Cup 26(5), Europe 6, others 62(26)
Goals: League 22, FA Cup 1, FL Cup 4, others 13

■ David Howells was one of those players whose value to the team was only fully appreciated when he was absent; he was the type who gave a good, solid display week in, week out with little fuss and even less recognition but whose name would be among the first on the team sheet.

He was a home-produced player, a central striker, who worked his way through the youth ranks scoring regularly. With little reserve-team action behind him, he was given a surprise Football League debut against Sheffield Wednesday in February 1986, replacing the out-of-form Clive Allen as Spurs sought to halt a depressing run of League results that had seen them pick up only one point in six games and not score a single goal. Eighteen years earlier Spurs had given a Hillsborough debut to another centre-forward, Martin Chivers, and he had scored the winner in a 2–1 victory. Howells was not to score anywhere near as many goals for Spurs as Chivers, but he did just as well on his debut, ramming home a Paul Allen cross to give Spurs three points away from home for the first time in three months.

Howells did not make the first team again that season and played only once in 1986–87, but he gradually established himself as a member of the first-team squad without ever really looking like finding a permanent position up front. Although good in the air and with an eye for goal, he was not a powerful attacker and lacked the pace that was becoming increasingly important.

With the signing of Paul Stewart, Howells chances looked even more limited, but Terry Venables saw in Howells the vision, awareness, hard work and passing ability that made him ideally suited to play in midfield. Operating alongside Paul Gascoigne, Howells provided stability, a solid base from which his more exalted colleague could work his magic, safe in the knowledge Howells would be covering for him.

Howells was not just a defensive player though. He read the game well, brought other players into the action and had an eye for the killer ball. He retained the goalscorer's instinct, venturing forward with late runs into the box and contributing some valuable goals.

It was his overall play that caught the eye. Always aware of what was going on around him,

he knew just when to go forward, when to hold back and when to cover for a teammate who had ventured forward. It was the unglamorous side of the game but a role that someone had to fulfil, and Howells was happy to do that.

His value to the team was perhaps best illustrated in that memorable FA Cup semi-final with Arsenal in 1991. While much was made of how Gascoigne carried an injury into the game, Howells was quietly rushed back from injury himself and played a crucial role in battening down the left side of midfield and restricting Lee Dixon's dangerous forward sorties. Despite having been out of action for three months, he completed the full 90 minutes in what was one of the most important games in Spurs' history, tiring visibly towards the end but giving everything for the club he had always supported.

In the Final, too, he rose to the early loss of Gascoigne by increasing his work rate and helping lay the solid base that allowed Vinny Samways and Nayim to apply the more subtle talents that eventually overcame Nottingham Forest.

Gascoigne's injury and subsequent departure should have allowed Howells to really establish himself in the Tottenham Hall of Fame, but persistent niggling injuries all too often saw him sidelined. It was not what Howells needed with Ossie Ardiles now installed as manager.

Just when he appeared to be back to full fitness, Ardiles's dream of building a team for which attack was not the best form of defence, but the only one, really began to take shape, and Howells found Gica Popescu occupying his favoured central-midfield role.

It was a frustrating time for Howells. Popescu was a highly-talented player but clearly struggling to adapt to the pace of English football. Many believe that had Howells been given the role of holding player in midfield, the protection he would have afforded an often undermanned defence would have allowed the array of attacking talent Ardiles had assembled to fulfil the dream.

With Ardiles's departure and the arrival of the pragmatic Gerry Francis, Howells was reinstated. He played a vital role in helping steady the ship as Francis imposed a more realistic style before further injury problems saw him given a free transfer and a move to Southampton

HUGHES, Edward (1899–1908)

Half-back, 5ft 8in, 11st 4lb

Born: Ruabon, Clwyd, Wales 1876
Died: Tottenham, North London, 6 June 1936
Signed from Everton, July 1899
Transferred to Clyde, July 1908
Also played for: Formby, Everton, Clyde, Wales

Spurs record:

Debut: 7 October 1899 v Brighton United (SL) (h) won 6–1
Appearances: Southern League 151, FA Cup 31, others 130(1)*
*(*Includes one abandoned match)*
Goals: Southern League 9, FA Cup 2, others 9

■ In the latter years of the 19th century Everton must have been blessed with an abundance of outstanding half-backs, for in three years on Merseyside Ted Hughes managed only eight Football League games. They all came in early 1899, and while Hughes may not have done enough to keep his place in the Everton team he obviously made an impression on the Welsh

selectors. In March of that year, despite having returned to Everton's reserve ranks, he picked up his first two caps, playing alongside his future Spurs captain John L. Jones.

One of Hughes's colleagues at Everton had been John Cameron, who had moved to Spurs in May 1898 and been appointed manager in February 1899. When his initial season in charge came to an end, one of Cameron's first moves was to bring Hughes to North London. It was a signing that was to prove one of the best in Cameron's nine years as manager.

At about the same time as Hughes arrived, Spurs also signed Tom Morris. With Jones, Bob Stormont and James McNaught already on the staff, they had five top-flight half-backs and initially Hughes had to battle with Morris to be first reserve to the other three. Even when Hughes did make his Southern League debut, it did not count and nor did his second appearance. The first was against Brighton United in October 1899 and the second two months later against Cowes, but both those clubs were to withdraw from the League before the season was over with their records expunged.

Hughes spent the majority of his first season doing duty with the reserves and that was how he started the 1900–01 campaign, but as Cameron shuffled his team around trying to find the right combination, Hughes began to establish himself playing in any of the half-back positions and sometimes at full-back.

His big break came in February 1901. Centre-half McNaught was injured in the first-round FA Cup tie with Preston North End and Hughes was called upon to fill in for the captain in the replay. So well did he perform that McNaught was unable to recover his place, and when he did get back in the team it was so Hughes could be rested for future FA Cup matches.

As Hughes grew in confidence, so his performances got better and better. With McNaught and Stormont keeping the pressure on he could not relax, but at least he knew he did not need to impress in every game just to keep his place.

It was no surprise that Hughes's sterling performances earned him a recall to the Welsh team in March 1901. He collected a total of 12 caps as a Spurs player, although that would have been 13 if Spurs had not withdrawn him from a match against England in March 1903 because the Welsh FA refused to insure him against injury.

Providing the solid base in the centre of midfield, Hughes went on to help Spurs lift the FA Cup for the first time, giving a particularly outstanding performance in the semi-final with West Bromwich Albion at Villa Park when he totally snuffed out any threat from Albion's central-striking trio.

A tireless worker, Hughes was perhaps best known for his defensive qualities, his ability in the air being particularly notable, but half-backs in his day were not just defenders. They were true midfielders expected to cover back when under attack but spring forward on the offensive as soon as their team was in possession. Hughes was a fine defender, knowing just when to hold off and when to launch into a hard tackle that invariably saw him emerge with the ball. He was often called upon to fill in at full-back where his pace and positional sense came to the fore but was at his happiest going forward, picking up the pieces and never afraid to unleash a powerful shot.

For eight years he was a regular performer, helping Spurs develop the attacking play that has always been their trademark and doing much to establish them as one of the outstanding teams in the Southern League.

Reaching the veteran stage, he was released in the summer of 1908 just as Spurs won election to the Football League. He moved to Scotland where he played for a year with Clyde but soon returned to London, running a public house in Enfield Highway until the end of World War One. He then emigrated to the US but returned to Tottenham later in life, where he remained until passing away in June 1936.

HUGHTON, Christopher William Gerard (1978–90)

Full-back, 5ft 7in, 10st 10lb

Born: Forest Gate, East London, 11 December 1958
Signed from part-time professional, June 1979
Transferred to West Ham United, December 1990, free

Also played for: West Ham United, Brentford, Republic of Ireland

Spurs record:

Debut: 29 August 1979 v Manchester United (FLC) (h) won 2–1
Appearances: League 293(4), FA Cup 34(2), League Cup 33(2), Europe 29(1), others 96(5)
Goals: League 12, FA Cup 1, League Cup 2, Europe 4, others 3

■ Even as a youngster Chris Hughton displayed the innate common sense he exhibits today as First Assistant to Head Coach Martin Jol. Having trained with Spurs from his schoolboy days, he had the chance to join the professional staff but decided to spend a couple of years as a part-time pro, while he completed his apprenticeship as a lift engineer before embarking on the rocky road to football stardom.

He took the plunge in the summer of 1979 and within a couple of months had made his first-team debut in a League Cup tie with Manchester United. This was to be the beginning of a career that was destined for the very top and the start of a period in Spurs' history that was to see them garner silverware, as Keith Burkinshaw fashioned another exciting, attacking team to follow in the traditions of his predecessors.

Full-back had proved a problem position for Burkinshaw. Colin Lee, a central-striker, had been tried at right-back but was not up to the job, and Gordon Smith, continually beset by injury, had proved a disappointment after signing from Aston Villa.

From his very first game it was obvious Hughton was the answer to the problem, as he took to top-level football as if he had been playing it for years. Once in the team he was there to stay, an integral part of the teams that won the FA Cup in 1981 and 1982, reached the League (Milk) Cup Final and European Cup-winners' Cup semi-final in 1982, before ending Burkinshaw's reign with the UEFA Cup in 1984.

In his early days Hughton had been a winger, but Spurs had realised his best position was at full-back, where his searing pace would prove most effective on the overlap. Although naturally right-footed, he played most of his

career on the left, developing a perfect understanding with Tony Galvin that created chance after chance for the strikers. While pace, timing and an ability to deliver accurate crosses were Hughton's greatest assets going forward, he was no slouch dribbling with the ball and on the edge of the box could play the perfect one-two before cutting the ball back.

Offensively there was something of the Robert Carlos about Hughton. Similarly built, they both revelled in the attacking side of the game but, whereas Carlos is famed for his power-packed shooting, Hughton preferred to get in close and beat the 'keeper with accuracy and subtlety.

Defensively Hughton was probably the superior of the two, less likely to lunge in, more aware of his defensive responsibilities and quicker to get back in position. He preferred to jockey his opponent into a cul-de-sac before nipping in to take the ball and set Spurs going forward with a simple pass.

Although Hughton continued to turn in one consistent performance after another and was recognised as one of the best full-backs in the country, his position came under threat with the arrival of Mitchell Thomas in May 1986.

Thomas followed David Pleat from Luton Town and was immediately installed in the number-three shirt. It left Hughton to compete with Danny Thomas and Gary Stevens on the right, and with injuries taking their toll Hughton's appearances were limited.

His considerable value as a squad member was amply proved in March 1987 when Danny Thomas suffered the cruel injury that was to end his career. Although Stevens was initially given the job of replacing Thomas, Hughton soon stepped in and helped Spurs to another Wembley appearance against Coventry City. Although up against the tricky David Bennett, Hughton gave another polished performance in what was one of the best Cup Finals for years.

Hughton's mother was Irish, and he accepted the invitation to play for the Republic, making his first international appearance against the US just two months after making his debut for Spurs. In some respects it is a pity he decided to throw in his lot with the Republic so quickly, for there can be no doubt that if he had waited a while the call would have come from England. As it was, he went on to collect 50 caps as a Spurs player and was a member of the Republic's successful team in the 1988 European Championships.

While never a regular again, Hughton continued to serve Spurs until November 1990 when he joined West Ham United. He helped them to promotion from the Second Division and then joined Brentford, helping them lift the Third Division title.

Hughton returned to Spurs as a coach under Ossie Ardiles and worked with Christian Gross, George Graham, Glenn Hoddle, Jacques Santini and as Martin Jol's assistant until being dismissed with the Dutchman in October 2007. Hughton then joined the coaching staff at Newcastle United, frequently standing in as manager during a chaotic time that saw the Geordie club up for sale and one manager after another unable to stop the club's decline. Hughton quickly became the one constant, the only member of the management staff who could be relied upon. Caretaker manager at the start of the 2009-10 season, Hughton's success in making Newcastle front-runners in the race for promotion, saw him given the manager's job on a permanent basis. He led Newcastle back to the Premier League and, despite limited funds being provided by a reluctant owner, was doing a marvellous job establishing the club back in the top flight when he was cruelly sacked in December 2010. There can be no doubt Hughton has the potential to make a real impact as a manager and will soon be given the opportunity to do so.

HUNT, George Samuel (1930–37)

Centre-forward, 5ft 8in, 10st 13lb

Born: Barnsley, Yorkshire, 22 February 1910
Died: Bolton, Lancashire, 19 September 1996
Signed from Chesterfield, September 1929, £1,000
Transferred to Arsenal, October 1937, £1,000
Also played for: Chesterfield, Arsenal, Bolton Wanderers, Sheffield Wednesday, England

Spurs record:

Debut: 20 September 1930 v Stoke City (FL) (a) lost 1–2

Appearances: League 185, FA Cup 13, others 7
Goals: League 125, FA Cup 13, others 10

■ In the mid 1920s Spurs had a reputation as a wealthy club who were not prepared to pay out

big fees to secure the top-class players that might turn them into serious title challengers. This refusal to invest was largely responsible for their relegation in 1928. It was only towards the end of the following campaign that the policy was relaxed with the signing of former England centre-forward Ted Harper. At £5,000 he was a bargain but still a considerable sum to the Spurs directors.

While Harper was justifying his fee, manager Percy Smith knew he was not a long-term signing. With an eye to the future, he persuaded the directors to relax the purse strings again so he could pay £1,000 to sign George Hunt from Chesterfield in June 1930.

Hunt was a rough, rumbustious 20-year-old known as the 'Chesterfield Tough', who had scored nine goals in 14 games for Chesterfield in his one season of professional football. Smith was not the only manager to have spotted his talent. Herbert Chapman was keen on taking Hunt to Highbury but, fortunately for Spurs, decided to hold his hand while some of the rough edges were smoothed out before making an offer.

Hunt was a player who knew his own worth. He had refused to sign for Barnsley, Sheffield United and Port Vale because they were not prepared to offer the money he thought he merited. Spurs had no such problem, Hunt even accepting he could not expect a first-team place immediately. He was being signed because he had the potential Spurs could work on.

Hunt made his Spurs debut earlier than anyone expected, stepping in at the last minute against Stoke City when Harper was ruled out by injury. He acquitted himself reasonably well but the lack of subtlety was obvious.

Back with the reserves, Hunt proved himself a prolific scorer if not the most accomplished of players. Spurs eventually had to accept that, while they could improve Hunt's all-round game, they could not take away the very attributes that made him so effective.

As the 1930–31 season approached its climax with Spurs in the promotion scrap, Hunt was called upon when Harper was injured again. He scored five goals in eight games, but his lack of experience and totally different style to that of Harper cost Spurs dear. Six games without a win left them just outside the promotion places.

Percy Smith, though, had seen enough to realise Hunt was the player he could build a team around. While Harper began the following campaign, a 0–4 defeat at Wolverhampton Wanderers on the opening day showed injuries had deprived him of all confidence.

Hunt was recalled and as the team began to play to his strengths so the goals began to flow. At 5ft 8in he was far from the biggest of players, but he had no fear and was quite happy to throw his 10 and a half stone of solid muscle into the toughest of challenges, often showing a total disregard for his own safety if there was the sniff of a goal. Tenacious and a glutton for hard work for every minute of the game, he continually harried and chased defenders, often overstepping the mark with his challenges but prepared to accept the retribution without complaint.

With a sprinter's speed off the mark and an unquenchable thirst for goals, there was no more exciting sight than Hunt picking up the ball and dashing full speed for goal, brushing off defenders and then unleashing a rocket-like shot.

With Taffy O'Callaghan, Willie Hall and Willie Evans providing the ammunition, Hunt banged in the goals, hitting 33 in 1932–33 as the team, dubbed 'The Greyhounds', at last secured promotion and enough to see him win three England caps.

Back in the top flight Hunt scored 32 goals as Spurs secured third place, their best League position for years, but in 1934–35 the punishment he and his opponents had inflicted on his body began to take its toll. Slowing noticeably, he was unable to save Spurs from relegation, and with injuries continually leaving him on the sidelines he found his place taken by Johnny Morrison.

Still a hero to supporters who remembered him at his best, he appeared to be returning to something like his old form as he recovered from a cartilage operation early in 1936–37. Spurs were reported to have turned down several offers for him when it was suddenly announced Hunt was joining Arsenal as a replacement for Ted Drake. It was not a popular decision.

Hunt only remained at Highbury for six months but did enough in that time to help Arsenal win the League title before moving on to Bolton Wanderers.

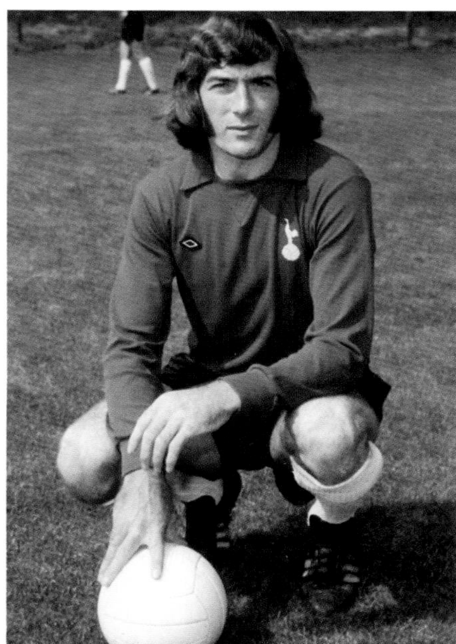

JENNINGS, Patrick Anthony MBE (1964–77 and 1983–86)

Goalkeeper, 6ft, 12st 6lb

Born: Newry, County Down, 12 June 1945
Signed from Watford, June 1964, £27,000
Transferred to Arsenal, August 1977, £45,000
Also played for: Newry United, Newry Town, Watford, Arsenal, Northern Ireland

Spurs record:

Debut: 22 August 1964 v Sheffield United (FL) (h) won 2–0
Appearances: League 473, FA Cup 43, League 39, Europe 36, others 82(3)*
*(*Includes one abandoned match)*
Goals: others 1

■ Few Spurs fans fortunate enough to have watched both Ted Ditchburn and Pat Jennings can agree who was the best. Bill Nicholson refused to choose. Those who only saw Jennings can but wonder how good Ditchburn was if he even came close to matching the man most regard as the best goalkeeper the world has seen.

Jennings honed his talents in the rough, tough arena of Gaelic football before turning to football. Spotted by former Spurs great Ron Burgess, the Watford manager, in a youth tournament, Watford paid £6,000 to sign Jennings in May 1963.

Just 18, Jennings was thrown into senior action immediately, playing all Watford's 52 competitive games in 1963–64 – an early sign of the consistency that became a byword to his career. Although raw and with much to learn, Nicholson had no compunction paying £27,000 to bring Jennings to Spurs, confident he had just the man to succeed double winner Bill Brown.

Jennings was to prove one of Nicholson's finest signings, up there alongside Dave Mackay, although in his first couple of seasons some doubted he would make the grade. He was nervous and lacking in confidence, not helped by a section of the crowd who had difficulty accepting anyone could replace Brown. At times the barracking got so bad that Nicholson appealed for Jennings to be given a chance.

With the double side breaking up, the high standards set by an outstanding team were not being met. It changed with the arrival of Mike England, the big Welshman instilling confidence in Jennings who, in turn, inspired the defence.

Jennings gave an immaculate performance in the 1967 FA Cup Final, never putting a foot wrong and showing he had found belief in his own ability when, with Chelsea pressing for a late equaliser, he plucked a dangerous cross from the air with one massive hand, a movement that was to become a trademark.

Jennings blossomed now, taking the goalkeeper's art to new levels. To his natural height, the strength gained from working in a timber yard before joining Watford and the ability to leap high developed in the Gaelic game, he added a positional sense second to none and the finest judgement, knowing exactly when to come and when to stay on his line. Calm under pressure, he dominated his six-yard box, organising his defenders and taking charge of every situation.

The master of angles, Jennings knew just where to position himself to leave the minimum target to aim for and would judge to perfection the moment to plunge forward and whip the ball away or smother a shot. When the orthodox did not work, Jennings could call on his fantastic reflexes, whether plunging low to tip the ball round the post or flying across goal to push it over the bar.

His distribution was excellent, either bowling the ball out accurately to his full-backs or launching giant kicks downfield that were so powerful he once stunned himself as the ball bounced on the edge of Manchester United's penalty area and sailed over Alex Stepney's head into the net in the 1967 FA Charity Shield game.

Over 10 years Jennings reached the peak of his profession, helping Spurs win the League Cup in 1971 and 1973 and the UEFA Cup in 1974, picking up the FWA and PFA Player of the Year awards and collecting an MBE. Remarkably consistent, he rarely missed a game, setting a record number of appearances for Spurs surpassed only by Steve Perryman.

Throughout his Spurs career he turned in many magnificent performances, few better than the one at Anfield in March 1973 that saw him save penalties from Kevin Keegan and Tommy Smith in front of the Kop, the second even having the referee applauding. He made some truly stunning saves, one of the best against Newcastle United in the 1976 League Cup semi-final first leg. He could only have seen Tommy Craig's venomous edge of the box volley at the last second. If Jennings had not arched his back and launched himself to tip it over the bar, the ball would have gone through the net and punched a hole in the stand behind.

Jennings suffered a rare injury during the disastrous 1976–77 season that contributed to Spurs relegation. Barry Daines did well as his stand-in, and Keith Burkinshaw decided Daines was the better long-term prospect. Burkinshaw later admitted the decision was a mistake.

Jennings joined Arsenal where he played for nine years, continuing to display a master craftsman's talent and picking up more silverware.

He returned to Spurs in 1985 as cover for Ray Clemence but primarily to keep fit for the World Cup, at the end of which he retired with a world-record 119 caps to his name and ever since has worked on the Spurs coaching staff.

JONES, Clifford William (1957–78)

Winger, 5ft 7in, 10st 7lb

Born: Swansea, Glamorgan, 7 February 1935

Signed from Swansea Town, February 1958, £35,000

Transferred to Fulham, October 1968, £5,000

Also played for: Swansea Town, Fulham, Kings Lynn, Bedford Town, Wealdstone, Cambridge City, Wingate, Wales

Spurs record:

Debut: 22 February 1958, v Arsenal (FL) (a) drew 4–4

Appearances: League 314(4), FA Cup 35(4), League Cup 2, Europe 19, others 38(2)

Goals: League 135, FA Cup 16, League Cup 1, Europe 7, others 15

■ There were the times he skimmed across the White Hart Lane mudbath of a pitch as fast as a top-class sprinter, ball at his feet, perfectly under control, defenders trailing in his wake.

Then there were those soaring leaps as he came hurtling in from the wing to climb high above friend and foe alike, meet the ball full on the forehead and send it, rocket like, into the back of the net.

Not to mention those moments of sheer madness when he would fling himself low into a posse of flying boots in the six-yard box in the hope, however forlorn, of getting the faintest of touches to deflect the ball home.

All these, and more, make up the inspiring memories that made Cliff Jones so revered in his 10 years at Spurs. Ten years in which he was a crucial element of the team that took Spurs to the peak at home and in Europe.

The Jones footballing family were well known in Swansea, Cliff's father Ivor and uncle Bryn Welsh internationals, uncles Emlyn and Bert, cousin Ken and brother Bryn playing for League clubs. His Uncle Bryn was the most famous, having joined Arsenal from Wolverhampton Wanderers for a record £14,000, but Cliff was to elevate the family name to a new level following his £35,000 move from Swansea Town to Spurs in February 1958.

Not that his first few matches held out much promise of what was to come. He took time to settle and was fortunate the team was playing well and able to carry him. At the end of the season he went to the World Cup in Sweden where, back among players he knew well, he began to rediscover his form, but on his return he broke a leg in pre-season training.

It was December before he was fit to return. By then, Bill Nicholson had replaced Jimmy Anderson as manager, but Spurs were having a tough time of things. A team that had finished third was now struggling to stay out of the bottom three. It would be wrong to say Jones turned Spurs' season around, but as full fitness returned he began to show the pace, skill and talent that had led Spurs to lay out such a big fee and never looked back.

With Nicholson strengthening the team with players of quality, such as John White and Dave Mackay, Jones was given the freedom to roam where he could do most damage. He was not a winger in the old sense of the word, hugging the touchline, beating his full-back and content to cross the ball. He could play that way, but Jones was unorthodox. Although right-footed, he spent most of his time on the left, picking up the ball deep in midfield, running straight at the defence, beating opponents with speed, a dip of the shoulder and a sudden swerve while heading straight for goal. Then he would turn, confusing defenders, before slipping the ball to Bobby Smith or Les Allen or unleashing a fierce, accurate shot.

Jones netted an incredible 25 goals in 42 League and Cup appearances in 1959–60 as the double-winning team took shape, and when all the pieces of the jigsaw fell into place he proved himself one of the outstanding stars of that unforgettable team. Reportedly the subject of £80,000 and £100,000 offers from Athletico Madrid and Juventus, there was no amount of money that would persuade Nicholson to release Jones. He was simply priceless.

A member of the teams that won the FA Cup in 1962 and European Cup-winners' Cup in 1963, Jones gave some of his finest performances on the European stage, his mere name on the team sheet instilling fear in the opposition. Never knowing what to expect, he would terrorise opponents with his pace and control and stun them as he responded to the roughest of challenges, sometimes pure thuggery, by simply bouncing up and going back for more. He was outstanding against Athletico Madrid, creating the first two goals and running the Madrid defenders ragged for the full 90 minutes.

Jones's bravery was legendary, and it often left him with some nasty injuries, but it took something serious to keep him out of the team. That happened in 1965–66 when he missed most of the season, but he returned to collect a third FA Cup-winners' medal in 1967 – the first player to do so without playing, as the unused substitute in the defeat of Chelsea.

Although the knocks and age began to slow Jones, he still turned out regularly until October 1969 when his great service to Spurs was rewarded with a cut-price transfer to Fulham. He signed off in the best possible way, with a goal against Manchester United.

JONES, John Leonard (1897–1904)

Half-back, 5ft 10in, 12st 8lb

Born: Rhuddlan, nr Rhyl, 1866
Died: Sunderland, County Durham, 24 November 1931

Signed from Sheffield United, May 1897
Transferred to Watford, May 1904
Also played for: Rhuddlan, Bootle, Stockton, Grimsby Town, Sheffield United, Watford, Worcester City, Wales

Spurs record:

Debut: 4 September 1897 v Sheppey United (SL) (a) drew 1–1
Appearances: Southern League 135, FA Cup 31*, others 171*
*(*Includes one abandoned match)*
Goals: Southern League 7, FA Cup 1, others 8

■ Spurs' signing of Jack Jones in May 1897 caused quite a stir in football circles of the time. It was not quite 15 years since a group of schoolboys had founded Spurs, they had played only one season of competitive League football, and yet here they were enticing Wales's regular left-half away from one of the country's oldest and best-established clubs, Sheffield United.

Jones may not have been in the first flush of youth, he was over 31, but most players of his day were at their peak at that age, and if age were a disadvantage it was more than compensated for by the wealth of experience he had gathered. He had never been a regular with the Blades but in three years had played a fair number of games for them, originally in either the inside-forward or winger position, and in his last season as cover for Rab Howell, Tommy Morren and 'Nudger' Needham – possibly the best half-back trio in the country.

Spurs did not have a manager when Jones signed so it is not surprising that, as he was the most accomplished and experienced player on the books, the Spurs directors chose to install Jones as captain. He shouldered the burden admirably and over the next few years led the club to heights those schoolboys could never have dreamed of.

He began his Spurs career at centre-half, exerting his influence throughout the team and helping pull together and mould into an effective combination a group of players who had been strangers until they assembled for the start of the season. Spurs had discarded practically all those who had served them in 1896–97 and signed an entirely new team from all corners of the country.

From his very first game it was obvious that Jones was a cut above most of the players Spurs had previously employed. Well built and hard working, his experience stood out as he controlled play with astute positional sense and excellent organisational skills. He let the ball do the hard work, passing it around smoothly while never being afraid to display his individual abilities with a sudden surge through midfield, ball at his feet. He rarely looked rushed and it was only when up against the top teams such as Southampton and Bristol City that he had to step up a gear.

In his first season he only missed three competitive matches, all because he was playing for Wales, the first Spurs player to win international recognition. Spurs finished third in the Southern League and second in the United League, an improvement on the previous season and proof Spurs were making headway.

The summer again saw wholesale changes as manager Frank Brettell, appointed in March 1898, used his connections in the North to bring another crop of experienced players to Northumberland Park. Jones was one of only three first-team regulars retained, the others being Bob Stormont and Willie Joyce. Among the newcomers was Jim McNaught from Newton Heath, a ball-playing centre-half best known for his defensive qualities. His arrival allowed Jones to move to the right where his attacking instincts could be given free rein.

Although Spurs did little better in the Leagues than they had before, finishing third in the Southern, United and Thames & Medway Leagues, they began to make a name for themselves in the FA Cup. For the first time they reached the competition proper then beat Newton Heath 5–3 in an amazing first-round replay at Clayton and Sunderland at home, before unluckily going out to Stoke. It was at Stoke that Jones gave one of his best performances for Spurs, driving his men on even when Spurs were 1–4 down.

By now John Cameron had taken over as manager. Using his contacts in the North and the Association Football Players' Union, he strengthened the team further and the Southern League title was won in 1900.

Among Cameron's signings were Ted Hughes and Tom Morris. With Jones, McNaught and Stormont, Spurs had five top-class half-backs and Jones looked to be one of the unlucky ones until Stormont was injured in the first-round FA Cup tie with Preston North End. Jones replaced him for the replay and Spurs never looked back. Jones dovetailed perfectly with David Copeland and Jack Kirwan, the Welshman, Scotsman and Irishman forming the perfect left-wing trio. Their ability to work together played no small part in taking Spurs to the FA Cup Final in 1901, culminating in Jones becoming the first Spurs captain to lift the trophy.

That was the peak of his career, but he continued to serve Spurs for another three years before leaving to join Watford, shortly after taking his number of caps as a Spurs player to 12.

JULL, John Charles (1883–1897)

Full-back

Born: Edmonton, North London, June 1867
Died: Stoke Newington, North London, 22 December 1920

Spurs record:
Debut: 13 October 1894 v West Herts (FAC) (h) won 3–2
Appearances: FA Cup 8, others 153
Goals: others 24

■ If all the 'stars' that have played for Spurs were put in a chronological list, Jack Jull would be up there at the very top. Even in the days when the Spurs players had to cart the goalposts from the station manager's office at Northumberland Park, mark out their pitch on the marshes and fight off the local yobs to keep it, Jull stood out as a player of special ability.

Although not recorded as one of the founders in 1882, Jull was a former pupil of Mr Cameron's at St Johns Middle Class School, which was situated just opposite what is now the main entrance to White Hart Lane. His father was landlord of the George & Vulture in Tottenham High Road and had sent Jull away to boarding school, but when he was home he obviously renewed acquaintance with his old schoolmates.

He is first known to have played for Spurs against Brownlow Rovers in October 1883, the opening match of the season and the first game to be reported in the local *Herald*. Jull was singled out as one of Spurs' best players in their 9–0 victory, along with Bobby Buckle, Billy Harston and Ham Casey. That was to become a common occurrence as Jull played in practically all the early matches, for which even part of a team line up has been discovered.

Elected captain for the 1884–85 season, Jull usually occupied the right-back position, but he was capable of playing wherever needed and was undoubtedly the best all-round player with the club. He once turned out at centre-forward in a friendly against Iona in October 1889 and responded with five of Spurs' goals in a 10–0 victory.

Right-back was his recognised position, though, and he was ideally suited to the role. Tall, very well built and strong, he had the pace and mobility to handle the trickiest of wingers and the power to deal with the more robust of opponents when called upon to cover the centre of defence. He apparently led by example and was described by one of London's foremost amateur half-backs and a frequent Spurs teammate, Stanley Briggs, as 'one of the finest captains and most fearless'. Coming from someone who was himself regarded as an excellent skipper, leading the FA touring party to Germany and Bohemia in 1899 and playing under some of the top professional captains, that was some accolade. One story displaying Jull's attitude comes from Spurs' first visit to Luton Town in December 1887. As the captain's tossed up the Luton man commented on how small some of the Spurs players were. Jull's retort was said to be 'Wait until after the match, old man, before you say any more; schoolboys or not, we can beat you'. Spurs won 2–1.

Jull was a real cornerstone of the club, playing regularly for 12 years as Spurs developed from a bunch of schoolboys playing their scratch games for fun to one of London's premier footballing forces. At every stage of their progress he was there, playing in their first-ever Cup tie, against St Albans in the London Senior Cup in October 1885, their first-ever League game, against Polytechnic in the Southern Alliance in September 1892, their first Amateur Cup tie, against Vampires in November 1893 and their first FA Cup game against West Herts in October 1894.

It was not only on the playing side that his influence was felt. He was a real guiding light, serving on the committee that ran the club in its earliest days and giving his full support to all the major decisions that were taken, such as the move to a private ground at Northumberland Park and the step into professionalism.

Jull also played for the Tottenham district team and London, and became the first Spurs player to collect a major representative honour when he played for Middlesex against Surrey at Guildford in February 1891.

He captained Spurs from 1884 until 1896, only giving up the role after the decision in December 1895 to pay players. He continued as captain till the end of the season and was then made a life member and President of the club, the first person to be given that honour and followed only by Bill Nicholson.

Jull still assisted Spurs for a couple of years and even turned out in two United League games in April 1897. He also played for Old Tottonians and the Spurs 'Old Crocks', a selection of some of the earliest players who would get together at the end of the season to play local opposition for charity.

When his playing days were over Jull continued to live in Tottenham, working as a rate collector, and was a frequent visitor to White Hart Lane right up to his death in December 1920.

KEANE, Robert David (2002–)

Forward, 5ft 9in, 12st 2lb

Born: Dublin, Eire, 8 July 1980
Signed from Leeds United, August 2002, £7,000,000
Also played for: Crumlin United, Wolverhampton Wanderers, Coventry City, Internazionale, Leeds United, Liverpool, Celtic, West Ham United, Republic of Ireland

Spurs record:

Debut: 15 September 2002 v West Ham United (FL) (h) won 3–2
Appearances: League 126 (35), FA Cup 12(4), League Cup 10(4), Europe 8(1), others 19(7)
Goals: League 65, FA Cup 9, League Cup 5, Europe 4, others 13

■ It is difficult to believe Robbie Keane is still only 27, so much has he crammed into his football career. A target for many of England's biggest clubs while still a schoolboy in Dublin, Keane decided to join Wolverhampton Wanderers, reasoning he had a better chance of making the breakthrough lower down the

League ladder. His decision was vindicated as he burst on to the scene as a 17-year-old rattling in 29 goals in 87 appearances for Wolves before a £6 million move to Coventry City in August 1999. He successfully transferred his talents to the top-flight and again the country's big names were casting envious glances in his direction, but while they hesitated Internazionale of Milan swooped with a £13 million offer Coventry could not refuse.

Keane seemed to have the prefect stage for his blossoming talents, but Inter had a miserable start to the 2000–01 season. Manager Marcello Lippi was soon sacked and his replacement, Marco Tardelli, made it clear Keane was not to be part of his plans. Free-spending Leeds United were quick to make their move, taking Keane on loan for the rest of the season with a view to a permanent £12 million deal. While his Italian sojourn may not have been the most successful, Keane's class shone through at Elland Road and nine goals in 20 games ensured Leeds made the transfer permanent at the first opportunity.

Keane should have reached the heights with Leeds but for some reason his career began to stagnate. Whether it was the Yorkshire club's desire for instant success that saw them spending huge sums on strikers or the fact Keane's game is about far more than just scoring goals, he began to struggle to hold down a regular place, finding himself on the periphery far too often.

With Leeds's well-publicised financial problems, Keane was deemed surplus to requirements as the 2002–03 season got underway, but Glenn Hoddle saw in him just the type of talented forward Spurs fans have always taken to their hearts. The £7 million fee was not a gamble for a player barely 22 but who had already garnered terrific experience and proved on the international as well as domestic stage that given his head he could be a huge success.

With his friendly Irish character and willingness to work for the cause, it took Keane no time to become a firm favourite at White Hart Lane, his cartwheel celebration followed by the imaginary firing of an arrow from his bow or rapid fire salvo from his two six guns the signature on almost every goal. Not quite all though, for Keane has too much respect for followers of his old clubs to celebrate in the same way when he scores against them.

Never an out-and-out striker, there were times when Keane's position seemed under threat with the signing of pure goalscorers such as Helder Postiga, Bobby Zamora, Fredi Kanoute and Jermain Defoe, but Keane simply responded to the challenge by showing that not matter who he was paired with he could adapt his game to get the best out of his partner, while still making his own unique contribution.

Keane is not one of those players who loiter around the opposition area waiting for his opportunity. He is a player who always wants the ball, willing to drop deep to find it and not afraid to do his fair share of defending. Never happier than when he has the ball at his feet, he can run at a defender, but there are times when he perhaps holds the ball too long, missing the opportunity to make the killer pass or running up a cul-de-sac, but these are more than compensated for by openings his pacy running and trickery create.

With the arrival of Dimitar Berbatov, Keane's game rose to a new level, the two of them striking up an immediate and almost telepathic understanding. Always full of the promise of goals, the Bulgarian's promptings turned that promise into reality with Keane hitting 21 goals in the 2006–07 and 23 the following season. When Liverpool publicly declared their interest in signing him, Keane was quick to let it be known he wanted to sign for his boyhood idols. He left for Anfield in July 2008 with Spurs collecting a reported £19 million but did not have a happy time on Merseyside. Unable to reproduce his White Hart Lane form and with Spurs struggling without him and Berbatov, it was still a surprise that he and Liverpool accepted Spurs offer to resign him barely six months after his departure and at a greatly reduced fee. While Keane played his part in helping Spurs escape from what had seemed a serious relegation battle, his time in Liverpool seemed to have taken that vital little spark from his game. While Keane could never be criticised for his attitude and willingness to work for the team, the goals were not flowing and within a year of his return he was loaned out to Celtic. The signing of Rafael Van der Vaart in August 2010 saw Keane drop down the pecking list, and with few opportunities he was allowed to join West Ham on loan, the Eastenders having an option to sign him permanently had they successfully avoided relegation. Keane made his debut for the Republic of Ireland in March 1998 and now has over 100 caps to his name, captains his country and leads the all-time list of goalscorers for the Republic.

KING, Ledley Brenton (1998–)

Central Defender, 6ft 2in, 14st 5lb

Born: Bow, East London,
12 October 1980
Signed from trainee, July 1998
Also played for: England

Spurs record:

Debut: 1 May 1999 v Liverpool (sub) (FL) (a) lost 2–3
Appearances: League 190(3), FA Cup 1(1), League Cup 15, Europe 6, others 23(3)
Goals: League 7, FA Cup 3, League Cup 1

■ To lose their captain, a player at the peak of his powers around whom so many plans for the future could be built, would be a painful blow for any club. When that player was an international regular of the calibre of Sol Campbell and there was not even the compensation of a few million in the bank, that loss could be shattering. Luckily for Spurs, when Campbell decided to take his enormous talents a few miles down the road to Highbury they already had a ready-made replacement in Ledley King, a player who may have lacked Campbell's presence and experience but in pure footballing terms was probably a better player.

King had been with Spurs from his schooldays, and as he worked his way through the youth ranks his outstanding ability was obvious to all. Given his debut at Anfield in May 1999, the prospect of King pairing up with Campbell in the centre of defence promised a solid backbone that could lead Spurs to future success, but George Graham's reluctance to trust in youth and continual niggling injuries held King back. When he did get a proper

chance again it was in midfield, his ball-winning qualities and physical presence providing a defensive solidity in front of the back four and his simple but effective passing freeing up his more offence-minded colleagues.

Following Campbell's departure, King's versatility was vividly illustrated by his deployment across the back line and in the holding midfield role. Wherever he was asked to play, full-back, central-defence or midfield, King excelled, showing a maturity and calmness well beyond his years, but central-defence always seemed the position he was destined to make his own.

King made his debut for the England Under-21s in September 1999 and played 13 games at that level, all in central-defence, before collecting his first full cap as a substitute against Italy in March 2002. At full international level he again played in both defence and midfield, but if confirmation of his best position was needed it came in the opening game of Euro 2004 in Portugal. With injuries decimating England's back line, King was called up for only his sixth cap in the opening game against holders France. Up against Thierry Henry, King gave a masterful performance and totally dominated the Arsenal star.

The French coach Jacques Santini had a first-hand view of King at his best in that game, and when he took over at Spurs there was never any doubt that the centre of defence was where he saw King playing. Appointed club captain, under first Santini and then Martin Jol, King's reputation as one of the country's best defenders continued to be enhanced, and he was a certainty for England's World Cup squad in 2006 until the curse of the metatarsal struck and put him out of the running.

Tall and strong, King is perfectly built for one of the most physically demanding positions on the pitch, but so are many defenders. What sets King apart from the rest is the calm air of authority his every move exudes. Whether it is manoeuvring himself out of the tightest of corners or using his terrific pace to cover for a beaten colleague, he is always totally in command, confident in his own abilities. Positionally astute and a fine reader of the game, King knows just how to shepherd his man away from danger, his eye fixed on the ball just waiting for the perfect moment to nip and come away with it. When he does get the ball it is rarely lashed hurriedly away. King is quite happy to keep it under control until he can play the ball to a colleague or launch his own forward sortie.

Unfortunately the injury problems that have all too often plagued King struck again in the 2006–07 season. On the treatment table for much of the season his calm assurance was sadly missed at times, as Spurs struggled to improve their League performances while making a determined assault on the FA, Carling and UEFA Cups. Rushed back because of an injury crisis for the round-eight second leg UEFA Cup clash with Seville, King was far from match fit, but his mere presence raised the level of optimism. He could do nothing to keep Spurs interest in the competition alive but did help Spurs finish the season well enough to take fifth place in the League and qualify for another tilt at the UEFA Cup.

KINNEAR, Joseph Patrick (1965–80)

Full-back, 5ft 9in, 11st 4lb

Born: Dublin, Eire, 27 December 1947
Signed from amateur, February 1965
Transferred to Brighton & Hove Albion, August 1975
Also played for: St Albans City, Brighton & Hove Albion, Dunstable Town, Republic of Ireland

Spurs record:

Debut: 8 April 1966 v West Ham United (FL) (h) lost 1–4
Appearances: League 190(7), FA Cup 24, League Cup 20, Europe 18, others 40(3)
Goals: League 2, others 4

■ As a seven-year-old, Joe Kinnear moved from Dublin to Watford and soon became one of the local schoolboy football stars, playing for Watford and Hertfordshire Schools. Turned down after a trial with his local club, he played as an amateur for St Albans City while doing an apprenticeship in the printing trade, and it was at St Albans that he was spotted by Spurs.

Initially taken on as an amateur while he continued his apprenticeship, Kinnear worked

his way quickly through the junior and reserve ranks and gave up ideas of a future in the printing trade to sign professional for Spurs in February 1965. By then he had settled at right-back, having previously played in the half-back line.

Kinnear made his debut in April 1966 against West Ham United. It was not an auspicious start, as Spurs were hammered 1–4, but Kinnear was not to blame and retained his place for the rest of the season.

Phil Beal began the following season in the number-two shirt, but injury to Alan Mullery gave Kinnear another chance, and he looked to be developing well until a thigh injury put him out. He had to wait until the end of February, just after winning his first Republic of Ireland cap, for another chance. Beal broke his arm playing against Manchester City, Kinnear stepped in and never looked back.

He played in the 1967 FA Cup Final against Chelsea and was the youngest and most inexperienced player on view – not that you would have guessed it. He gave a superb performance, calm, unflustered, totally in control and aiding the attack with his overlapping runs. Even when the wing wizard Charlie Cooke tried his luck on the left, Kinnear kept him well in check.

Bill Nicholson always regarded the Cup Final as Kinnear's best performance in a Spurs shirt, and it certainly established him as first-choice right-back, releasing Beal to fill the left-half position left vacant by Dave Mackay's departure for Derby County.

Compact, quick and hard tackling, Kinnear relished the one-on-one battle with a tricky winger, but wingers were a dying breed, their demise accelerated by England's 1966 World Cup success. It meant a full-back had to be capable of more than just defending, they had to get forward, fill the space previously occupied by their own wingman and join the attacking play more than ever before.

Kinnear was perfectly suited to the role, that quintessential Irish devil-may-care attitude seeing him bombing down the wing at every opportunity, always available for the pass out wide and accurately getting the ball back into the danger area.

Not that he neglected his defensive duties. With the similarly attack-minded Cyril Knowles on the opposite flank, he knew there were times when he had to curb his attacking instinct lest a quick counter-attack caught Spurs short at the back, but when he did advance he knew he had the pace and energy to get back quickly. Many a time he would slide into a tackle with perfect timing to block a cross or emerge with the ball at his feet.

Just when Kinnear had made the right-back position his own, he suffered a broken leg against Leeds United in January 1969. It was almost a year before he was fit to return, but 18 months later he was back to his best.

In his absence, Ray Evans had staked his claim for a starting position, but Kinnear's experience won him the nod in 1970–71 and Kinnear played in every game of the Football League Cup run that culminated in Spurs lifting the trophy for the first time after beating Aston Villa.

For the next couple of years Kinnear vied with Evans for a place in the team, and while Evans was frequently preferred Kinnear always fought back, collecting winners' medals in the 1972 UEFA Cup and 1973 League Cup Finals.

1973–74 was a miserable season for Kinnear. Injuries, loss of form and the continual pressure from Evans saw him spend most of the season in the reserves, and the following season was little better. Kinnear's days as the regular number two were over, but when Spurs were at their lowest ebb, battling against relegation, he answered the call, playing a full part in the fight to avoid the drop that only succeeded in a last-day defeat of Leeds United.

With Terry Neill looking to make his mark, Kinnear was transferred to Brighton & Hove Albion in August 1975, where he played for a year before embarking on a long coaching and managerial career that saw him travelling the world.

KIRWAN, John Francis (1899–1905)

Outside-left, 5ft 7in, 10st 8lb

Born: Wicklow, Ireland, 12 December 1872
Died: Hendon, Middlesex, 9 January 1959
Signed from Everton, May 1899
Transferred to Chelsea, May 1905
Also played for: Southport Central, Everton, Chelsea, Clyde, Leyton, Ireland

Spurs record:

Debut: 2 September 1899 v Millwall (SL) (a) won 3–1
Appearances: Southern League 157, FA Cup 24, others 160(1)
Goals: Southern League 41, FA Cup 2, others 55

■ John Kirwan had won an All Ireland medal at Gaelic Football before deciding to cross the sea in the summer of 1897 and try his hand at professional football with Southport Central in the Lancashire League. He impressed immediately, with Football League clubs taking an interest and Everton and Blackburn Rovers bidding for his services. A major argument developed between the two of them as to who he should play for, and it was only settled when he opted to join Everton. He was officially transferred to them in February 1898 and appeared regularly in their Football League team throughout the 1898–99 season.

However, he was not happy in Liverpool, and when John Cameron, who had played with Kirwan for a couple of months before his move to Spurs, got to learn of this he was quick to offer Kirwan the chance of joining him in London. Kirwan was just as quick to accept it.

Again his impact was immediate. Initially playing outside Cameron but soon partnered by David Copeland, he proved a devastating little winger, incredibly popular with the Spurs crowd and instantly taken to their hearts.

With pace and trickery he used to run at his full-back and torment the life out of him, with his feints and little tricks. His opponent would never know what Kirwan was going to do next. He would make the same move two or three times, but just as his marker thought he knew what was coming Kirwan would pull another trick out of the bag and leave his man on the seat of his pants. Nimble of foot, he had the ability to head in one direction before stopping dead in his tracks and going off in another, and when past his man covering defenders could never be sure what he was going to do. He was unorthodox in that he did not finish a run down the wing with a hopeful punt into the centre like so many of his contemporaries. He would take a second to consider his options and, if a pass to his centre-forward was not on, cut

the ball back to the edge of the box for Copeland or Cameron to burst onto.

Kirwan needed his trickery for he was not the biggest of men, and when defenders did get to him he took some really hard challenges, but when clattered to the ground he just picked himself up and got on with the game, confident that skill would tell.

One of the stars of the team that won the Southern League Championship in 1900, Kirwan was responsible for many of the goals scored by Tom Pratt but chipped in with quite a few of his own, netting a total of 20 as Spurs not only won their first major title but finished second in the Southern District Combination. It was no surprise when he collected his first Irish cap against Wales in February 1900.

Having really made his mark in Southern football, Kirwan's talents were then seen on the national stage as Spurs went on to win the FA Cup the following season. Ever present throughout the run to the Final, Kirwan was at his absolute best in the Villa Park semi-final. Sandy Brown took the plaudits with all four Spurs goals, but it was the first two, both set up by Kirwan, that were to prove so decisive.

Over the next few years Spurs were unable to repeat their earlier triumphs, but Kirwan continued to dazzle – spectators prepared to pay their money just to see him perform. All the time his partnership with Copeland continued to develop. It was almost as if they had a telepathic understanding, seeming to know what each was going to do as if they had played together all their lives.

Kirwan took his total of Irish caps as a Spurs player to 12, and it is just unfortunate Copeland was a Scot. Together on the international stage they would certainly have flourished.

Almost regarded as indispensable, it was a considerable surprise to all at White Hart Lane when, in 1905, Kirwan and Copeland were enticed away, becoming the first major signings of West London's newly-formed club Chelsea. Kirwan in particular was highly instrumental in helping Chelsea finish third in their first season in the Football League and secure promotion in their second.

Kirwan later played for Clyde and Leyton before embarking on a coaching career that took him to Holland and Italy, but he always retained one souvenir of his time with Spurs. At the final whistle of the 1901 FA Cup Final replay, he was first to grab the ball and kept it until his death.

KLINSMANN, Jurgen (1994–95 and 1997–98)

Striker, 6ft 2in, 12st 13lb

Born: Goppingen, West Germany, 30 July 1974
Signed from Monaco (France), July 1994, £2,000,000
Transferred to Bayern Munich, July 1994, £1,300,000
Signed from Sampdoria (Italy), December 1997, £175,000
Retired, July 1998
Also played for: TB Gingen, SV Geislingen, Stuttgart Kickers, Vfb Stuttgart, Internazionale, Monaco, Bayern Munich, Sampdoria, Orange County Blue Stars, Germany

Spurs record:

Debut: 20 August 1994 v Sheffield Wednesday (PL) (a) won 4–3
Appearances: League 56, FA Cup 9, League Cup 3, others 3
Goals: League 29, FA Cup 5, League Cup 4, others 4

■ Spurs are a club named after a knight, Harry Hotspur, son of the Duke of Northumberland who was famously slain at the Battle of Shrewsbury in 1403. Like most clubs they have at one time or another needed a saviour, a knight in shining armour. Twice, Jurgen Klinsmann proved to be that man.

In the summer of 1994 Spurs were in a desperate situation, financial irregularities under the Venables regime seeing them banned from the FA Cup and given a 12 point deduction even before the League season began. Gloom and despondency hung heavy over White Hart Lane. It was all the more astonishing, therefore, that Spurs Chairman Alan Sugar was somehow able to persuade Klinsmann to join Spurs. Perhaps it was the opulent surroundings of Sugar's yacht moored in Monaco harbour where the deal was done, perhaps it was the money or perhaps, as

Klinsmann himself suggested, it was the challenge of playing for a famous but beleaguered club. Whatever the reason, his signing was hailed a coup as big as that of Ossie Ardiles and Ricky Villa 16 years earlier.

A World Cup winner in 1990, Klinsmann, a true superstar of the European game, had already played in his native Germany, in Italy and in France and was keen to sample football in the Premiership, but there was one fear. He had a reputation as a 'diver', a man who would fall over at the slightest touch, particularly if there was a chance of winning a penalty.

It was a fear Klinsmann turned into an attribute. At his first press conference he asked the assembled hacks for directions to the nearest diving school, immediately winning over the public with his charm and sense of humour.

On the pitch Klinsmann started in the perfect way with a cracking header against Sheffield Wednesday followed by an exaggerated celebratory dive to the touchline before being stretchered off after a sickening clash of heads. It was the first of several scintillating performances from Ardiles's 'Famous Five' of Klinsmann, Teddy Sheringham, Nick Barmby, Darren Anderton and Ilie Dumitrescu, but not all ended so well.

The football was brilliant but results were not, and Ardiles was dismissed to be replaced by Gerry Francis. Ardiles's devil-may-care football gave way to Francis's more pragmatic 'results first, performance second' style, but the change had little effect on Klinsmann.

A natural goalscorer, Klinsmann continued to find the back of the net regularly, forming a devastating partnership with Teddy Sheringham. Klinsmann was all action, forever on the move, wandering wherever there was space, just waiting for the moment to burst into action. Although 30 years old, he still possessed that vital burst of pace, that little edge and all-important killer instinct. Equally proficient with either foot or head, he could finish with simple knock-ins from a few yards, searing volleys from 20 or delicate chips past even the best-positioned 'keeper.

His most outstanding attribute, though, was his attitude. For a man some critics had labelled a mercenary, he worked tirelessly from start to finish, harassing defenders, pressurising goalkeepers, encouraging those around him. And he did it all with a smile, clearly enjoying every minute and relishing a fantastic rapport with the fans.

With the points deduction and FA Cup ban replaced with a fine, Klinsmann almost made it a fairytale first season, but hopes of a Wembley visit were dashed by Everton in the FA Cup semi-final. Worse was to follow, with Klinsmann, much to Sugar's chagrin, announcing he was returning to Germany to join Bayern Munich. He wanted to win the Bundeslegia before retiring.

While Spurs struggled to find a replacement, Klinsmann captained Germany to the 1996 European Championship and won the Bundeslegia title he so yearned for before joining Sampdoria. Late in 1997 he found himself out of the team and was concerned for his international place with the 1998 World Cup on the horizon. He had already announced he would be retiring after the competition. Spurs were having a bad time again, finding goals hard to come by and not safe from relegation. In December 1997 Klinsmann returned to White Hart Lane.

He was not the power he had been, but his return gave the whole club a lift. Showing flashes of his old brilliance, he helped Spurs pull clear of the relegation zone, scoring six goals in his last three games. Four of them came in his last-but-one outing against Wimbledon at Selhurst Park, when he gave a master class in finishing. Each goal was different, each was clinical and each was as joyously celebrated as if it was the first he had ever scored.

KNOWLES, Cyril Barry (1964–77)

Full-back, 6ft, 13st 13lb

Born: Fitzwilliam, Yorkshire, 13 July 1944
Died: Middlesbrough, Cleveland, 31 August 1991
Signed from Middlesbrough May 1964, £45,000
Retired May 1976
Also played for: Middlesbrough, England

Spurs record:

Debut: 22 August 1964 v Sheffield United (FL) (h) won 2–0
Appearances: League 401(1), FA Cup 42, League Cup 32(1), Europe 30, others 62*
*(*Includes one abandoned match)*
Goals: League 15, FA Cup 1, Europe 1, others 3

■ The thought of replacing a member of the double-winning team must have been a daunting prospect for any footballer, let alone a 20-year-old virtual unknown, but in Cyril Knowles Bill Nicholson found the perfect successor to Ron Henry.

Knowles had been a left-winger when associated with Manchester United and Wolverhampton Wanderers, but both decided he would not make the grade. He did not give hope of a career in the game but contented himself with playing for local clubs, Hemsworth and Monckton Colliery Welfare, while working with the pit ponies at Fitzwilliam Colliery until Middlesbrough acceded to his request for a trial and decided he was worth taking on.

They decided his height and willingness to get involved made him more suited to a position at the back, and although he was predominantly left-footed he made his Football League debut at right-back in April 1963. He rapidly established himself and with Nicholson appreciating that Henry, Peter Baker and Mel

Hopkins were all reaching the veteran stage he moved to secure Knowles's signature in May 1964.

Knowles had only played 39 senior games but still cost £45,000. That was a substantial sum for an unproven talent, but it proved to be another excellent piece of business with the fee repaid many times over.

Knowles went straight into the team, replacing Baker on the right, and, although rough around the edges, he soon had the fans behind him with his mixture of daring attacking forays and rugged defensive work. After one season he switched to the left, where he was to spend the rest of his career, recognised as one of the best left-backs in the country and the best to play for Spurs.

Fiercely competitive, Knowles had no fear when it came to tackling, going in hard with power, determination and total commitment. He had great confidence in his own ability, happy to get the ball under control and dribble away from danger, even when seemingly trapped in his own box. More than once he was seen to trap the ball on his goalline before, with colleagues screaming at him to whack it into row Z, dummying and tricking his way past opponents until he was ready to pass it up field.

Then he would turn to Pat Jennings or Mike England with an enormous grin on his face as if he enjoyed giving them heart attacks.

Going forward was where Knowles most caught the eye, sweeping down the wing with arms raised, taking the ball in full stride and hitting over the most perfect of crosses. No matter what the angle he had the knack of dropping the ball in just the right area for the likes of Martin Chivers, Alan Gilzean or Martin Peters to come on to it and connect with full force.

On those occasions that a first-time cross was not possible, he would call on his old winger's tricks, nutmegging a defender before going past him or turning the ball back to his right foot and chipping it into the box.

Stylish and elegant, Knowles was a beautiful footballer to watch but there was more. He played the game as if it was the only thing he ever wanted to do, loving every minute of it, laughing and joking but still with passion. It endeared him to the crowd and he had an incredible rapport with those on the terraces who knew that Knowles appreciated their support.

A member of the teams that won the FA Cup in 1967, the League Cup in 1971 and 1973, and the UEFA Cup in 1972, he won six England Under-23 caps but only four at full level. It was a miserly total for a player who deserved so many more, but he was first in competition with one of the best over-lapping full-backs ever in Terry Cooper and then lost out to Emlyn Hughes.

A knee injury in December 1973 put Knowles on the sidelines and gave Terry Naylor the chance to stake his claim for the number-three shirt, but following Nicholson's retirement in September 1974 Knowles was recalled. Despite suffering with the injury, his experience proved invaluable as Spurs battled the spectre of relegation, never more so than on that fateful evening in April 1974 when Spurs had to beat Leeds United to stay up. Knowles was superb, crowning a masterful display with two goals, one a typical free-kick from the edge of the area, the other a calmly-taken penalty.

After retiring because of problems with his knee, Knowles went into management. When he returned to White Hart Lane with his Torquay United and Hartlepool United teams for League Cup ties, the refrains of 'Nice One Cyril' echoed round the ground, testament to a special player and a special man.

LINEKER, Gary Winston OBE (1989–92)

Striker, 5ft 11in, 12st 2lb

Born: Leicester, 30 November 1960
Signed from Barcelona, July 1989, £1,200,000
Transferred to Grampus Eight (Japan) May 1992, £900,000
Also played for: Leicester City, Everton, Barcelona, Grampus Eight, England

Spurs record:

Debut: 19 August 1989 v Luton Town (FL) (h) won 2–1
Appearances: League 105, FA Cup 9, League Cup 16, Europe 8, others 24(3)
Goals: League 67, FA Cup 3, League Cup 8, Europe 2, others 10

■ England's premier goalscorer of the 1980s, Gary Lineker was desperately unlucky not to beat Bobby Charlton's 49 international goals, finishing just one short having played in 80 internationals compared to Charlton's 106.

Often disparagingly referred to as a penalty-box predator, Lineker may not have scored many spectacular goals but score goals he did, and at a rate many more lauded marksman envied.

He first made his name with Leicester City, operating out wide where his blistering pace made him dangerous, but it was when he switched to a central role that his career blossomed, his coolness in the box and knack of finding space evident even in a struggling team.

It was no surprise when Everton snapped him up for a cool £800,000 in June 1985 and 40 goals the following season made him a certainty for England's 1986 World Cup campaign, when he really came to the fore.

England were struggling in the group stage, victory over Poland essential if they were not to return home early. A Lineker hat-trick saw England through, and with goals against Paraguay and Argentina following he finished the competition with the coveted Golden Boot.

Now an international star, Everton could not resist a £2.75 million offer from Terry Venables's Barcelona, and within weeks of returning from Mexico Lineker was off to Catalonia's capital. With his easy-going personality and willingness to adapt to the Spanish way of life, he soon became popular with Barcelona's fans, even if unable to deliver the Spanish title they craved.

A bout of hepatitis left Lineker below par for the 1988 European Championships, and when fit to return he found himself out of favour with Barca's new coach Johan Cruyff. It was fan power that restored Lineker to the team but in a wide position, where he was not at his most effective.

His acceptance of the situation enhanced his reputation as a true professional, but when Venables offered him the chance of playing in his favoured role for Spurs he did not take much persuading.

The £1.2 million fee was a snip for Spurs, although Lineker's White Hart Lane career did not start in the blaze of goals expected. It took him six matches to get off the mark, but once he began to settle in his class was obvious. He scored 24 League goals in his first season to continue where he had left off at Everton, top of the First Division scoring chart.

Lineker's pace remained his greatest asset but his all-round game had matured. He was as quick as ever but now it was over a distance of a few yards only, just enough to get him away from an opponent. He had learned the knack of dragging his marker into areas of no danger and then spinning away to utilise the space behind. His reading of the game had been refined so he knew just were to position himself to have the best chance of getting a shot in on goal and his anticipation was second to none. He gave defenders no time to relax, a split-second lapse would see him in the clear.

Lineker always did his most potent work in the box, rarely joining in build-up play, but he was a goalscorer, not a creator, and did his job to perfection. Whatever angle the ball came to him, he always seemed to get it under control, perhaps not totally but enough to get in his shot. He was not always the cleanest striker of the ball, but more often than not the shot would be on target and he often managed to find a shot when goalkeepers least expected one. In one-on-one situations with a 'keeper it was rare for Lineker not to come out on top.

In his second season with Spurs he suffered, as the whole team did, from the rumours about the club's financial problems, but he kept sticking the goals away, none more important than the two in the FA Cup semi-final with Arsenal. The first was toe-poked home from two yards, the second, just as Arsenal were beginning to get on top, blasted past David Seaman from 15 yards after Lineker had run at the Arsenal defence.

Lineker did not score in the Final against Nottingham Forest. He should have, but his penalty was saved by Mark Crossley and when he did get the ball in the net it was wrongly disallowed for offside.

Lineker's final season was overshadowed with concerns for his son George, who was suffering from cancer, but the England captain continued as the true professional he was, netting 33 goals before departing at the end of the season to become England's ambassador to the Japanese J League with Nagoya Grampus Eight.

LUDFORD, George Albert (1936–50)

Forward or half-back, 5ft 7in, 10st 12lb

Born: Barnet, Hertfordshire, 22 March 1915
Died: Enfield, Middlesex, 2 January 2001
Signed from amateur, May 1936
Also played for: Enfield, Northfleet United

Spurs record:

Debut: 29 August 1936 v West Ham United (FL) (a) lost 1–2
Appearances: League 77, FA Cup 6, others 192
Goals: League 8, FA Cup 1, others 83

■ If ever there was an example of a player whose career was ruined by the war, that man is George Ludford. Had Hitler not embarked on his attempt to conquer Europe, Ludford may well have conquered the English football world.

A schoolboy centre-forward, Ludford was taken on to the White Hart Lane groundstaff on leaving school as a 16-year-old in May 1931. He spent two years playing for Tottenham Juniors, an outstanding prospect tipped for the very top, had a brief spell with Enfield and was then sent down to the Northfleet United nursery.

As soon as they could, Spurs signed Ludford to amateur forms as he continued his football education down in Kent. In 1935–36 he scored an incredible 101 goals as Northfleet won the Kent League, so it was no surprise when he was taken on the professional staff in May 1936.

Ludford made his League debut in the opening game of the following season. He had made quite an impression in the pre-season trial games, but it was still something of a surprise that he should be preferred to the more experienced Willie Hall. It was thought he would be quicker off the mark than Hall and less inclined to hold the ball, but it was perhaps a step up too soon for Ludford. He had rarely played at inside-forward. His inexperience was obvious and, hard as he worked, nothing would go right for him.

He did not play again that season and only once in 1937–38. It was not until April 1939 that he got anything like a sustained run in the first team. This was not due to lack of ability on Ludford's part, he scored six goals in 10 first-team outings and was banging them in for the reserves. It was just that Johnny Morrison was doing the same for the first team.

Ludford played in the first two games of 1939–40 but both were drawn, and when Morrison was recalled for the third game he scored a hat-trick in a 4–3 win at West Bromwich Albion. It looked like Ludford would have to wait a while longer if he was to stake a claim to a regular starting place, but then war intervened.

Morrison remained first choice for the number-nine shirt, but Ludford got more chances, if not at centre-forward then on the left wing and once even at half-back. As call-ups began to have a greater effect, Ludford played more and more, and between 1940 and 1943 he was the most regular performer, usually at centre-forward or in either of the wing positions.

Ludford was a touch on the small size for the number-nine berth, being only 5ft 7in tall, but he was a chunky, well-built player able to handle the rough treatment centre-forwards received and to dish it out himself. He had a good burst of pace and neat ball control and knew how to finish. In 170 wartime matches he netted 76 goals, more than good going, even allowing for the often disorganised conditions. In 1943–44 and 1944–45 service demands meant he was not always available to play for Spurs. He would make every effort to turn out, but if it were impossible any club near where he was stationed would ask him to guest for them.

With the war coming to a close, Ludford began to play regularly again in the transitional 1945–46 season, now at right-half. His speed off the mark had gone but his football ability remained, as did his willingness to work hard. He played regularly in the first post-war season, missing only one game, but with Bill Nicholson moved from centre-half to right-half Ludford found himself in the reserves.

He accepted the position without complaint, providing experience and guidance to the up-and-coming youngsters in the reserves but ever ready to step up when needed, even playing a few games at left-back towards the tail end of 1948–49. He made four appearances in the Second Division Championship side of 1949–50 but that was the end of his first-team career.

For the rest of his playing days, Ludford turned out with the reserves and juniors, moving on to the coaching staff in 1954 and a year later taking on the manager's job at Enfield.

In total Ludford served Spurs for 24 years, never a star but a regular in the dark days of war and a tremendously-loyal, if often unsung, servant to the club.

MABBUTT, Gary Vincent MBE (1982–99)

Midfield or defender, 5ft 9in, 12st 9lb

Born: Bristol, 23 August 1961
Signed from Bristol Rovers July 1992, £120,000
Released, June 1998
Also played for: Bristol Rovers, England

Spurs record:

Debut: 28 August 1982 v Luton Town (FL) (h) drew 2–2
Appearances: League 458(19), FA Cup 46(2), League Cup 60(2), Europe 22(3), others 143(23)*
*(*Includes one abandoned)*
Goals: League 27, FA Cup 5, League Cup 2, Europe 4, others 15

■ One of the most versatile players ever to play for Spurs, Gary Mabbutt was a snip at £120,000 when signed from Bristol Rovers in July 1982. He had played in just about every outfield

position for Rovers and although primarily regarded as a defender or defensive midfielder, his best position had yet to be determined. Such was his all round ability that it was only after four years at White Hart Lane that he finally settled as a central-defender.

That he ever even played professional football was a testament to Mabbutt's character. As a 17-year-old he had been diagnosed with diabetes, but he had fought to overcome it, just as he had to fight to overcome injuries later in his career that may have proved too much for a lesser man.

When Mabbutt joined Spurs he was not expected to go straight into a team that had just won the FA Cup for the second successive year, but to take time to find his feet in the top flight. As it was, injuries and the exile to France of Ossie Ardiles after the Falklands War meant Mabbutt made his debut in the FA Charity Shield with Liverpool and from that very first game it was obvious he was a player who would have no difficulty making the step up.

Operating in midfield, he covered every inch of the Wembley turf, chasing and harrying, biting into the tackle and laying the ball off with quick, accurate passes. Not that he contented himself with the defensive side of the game. At every opportunity he pushed forward, joining in the attacking play and showing what a menace he could be to opposing defences.

For the first few months midfield seemed to be his position, even though he made his England debut in October 1982 on the right of defence and played up front for Spurs, but he soon showed he could do a more than competent job wherever he was needed and it almost became a case of whoever was injured, Mabbutt would fill in.

A member of the UEFA Cup-winning team in 1984, Mabbutt looked like he was becoming the perfect substitute, but when Paul Miller was injured in November 1985 he was given a run in the centre of defence. Although Miller later returned and Mabbutt had to revert to midfield, David Pleat had seen enough, and when he was appointed manager in May 1986 he paired Mabbutt with Richard Gough.

It looked the perfect combination, Gough tall and commanding, Mabbutt tidying up the pieces, and while the fluid forward line grabbed the glory, it was Gough and Mabbutt who provided the solid defence that did so much to take Spurs to the 1987 FA Cup Final. When Mabbutt grabbed Spurs' second goal, a day of joy looked likely, but it all turned to disaster when Mabbutt's deflection looped over Ray Clemence for Coventry City's winner.

When Gough returned to Scotland far too early, Mabbutt came into his own. Appointed captain, he adopted the mantle of defensive kingpin. Cool, calm and reliable, he was not the tallest of players but he had a spring in his leap and perfect timing that allowed him to dominate even the tallest of strikers. He never knew when he was beaten, often pulling off the cleanest of tackles when even getting a challenge in looked impossible, and he excelled in organising those around him.

While often linked with moves to other clubs, Mabbutt showed great loyalty to Spurs, and it was nothing more than he deserved when he led the team up the Wembley steps to collect the FA Cup in 1991.

While Mabbutt's versatility was a godsend for Spurs, it probably did him few favours at international level, and he won nothing like the number of caps he deserved. However, when qualification for the 1992 European Championships looked in serious doubt, it was Mabbutt that Graham Taylor turned to for the final crucial games against Turkey and Poland, and he did not let his country down.

In November 1993 Mabbutt was on the end of a particularly-vicious elbow from Wimbledon's Justin Fashanu. It fractured his cheekbone and put him out of the game for three months, but Mabbutt showed his character to come back as good as ever. Even a broken leg sustained at Blackburn in the opening game of the 1996–97 season did not defeat Mabbutt. It took him a full year to return, but he battled back to give Spurs a 16th year of great service. Released in May 1998, there were several clubs interested in signing him, but, restricted by a knee injury, he retired in January 1999.

MACKAY, David Craig (1958–68)

Half-back, 5ft 8in, 11st 6lb

Born: Musselburgh, Midlothian, 13 November 1934

Signed from Heart of Midlothian, March 1959, £30,000

Transferred to Derby County, July 1968, £5,000

Also played for: Slateford Athletic, Newtongrange Star, Hutcheson Vale, Heart of Midlothian, Derby County, Swindon Town, Scotland

Spurs record:

Debut: 21 March 1959 v Manchester City (FL) (h) won 3–1

Appearances: League 268, FA Cup 33, Europe 17, others 44(2)

Goals: League 42, FA Cup 4, Europe 5, others 12

■ There are stars and heroes, legends and myths. Then there is Dave Mackay. Signed from Heart of Midlothian in March 1959 after Mel Charles had, to Bill Nicholson's relief, turned down Spurs for Arsenal, Mackay went on to become probably the greatest player ever to don a Spurs shirt – a legend at White Hart Lane in his playing days and a legend even now.

After playing in Scottish junior football, Mackay joined Hearts as a 17-year-old. In seven years he won everything Scottish football had to offer, the League, the Cup and the League Cup,

played for Scotland at Under-23 and full international level and also appeared for the Scottish League. If the Mackay trophy cabinet was already beginning to creak, he was soon to need a bigger one.

From his very first game in a Spurs shirt it was obvious Mackay would have no trouble settling into English football, even if it was faster than he had been used to. His obvious desire to win, total commitment and willingness to lead by example had the Spurs fans behind him from the start, as they saw in Mackay the embodiment of everything they dreamt of being.

Mackay was not a particularly big man, but he had a presence about him that added an extra couple of inches to his height, and even more to his barrel-like chest and trunk-like thighs. As he took to the pitch he would puff out his chest as if throwing out a challenge, daring anyone to mess with him.

Mackay was a terrific footballer with every skill a player needed. His ball control was immaculate, his passing accurate and he had vision, spotting openings even before his colleagues realised they were there. He could score, too, with viciously-struck volleys from the edge of the box or delicate chips over the 'keeper. Any lack of pace was more than compensated for by his reading of the game and positional play. His pure footballing ability alone would have been enough to make Mackay a star, but it was the physical side of his game that gave him that something extra and for which he will always be renowned.

His strength was incredible, his stamina, hard work and crunching tackles the stuff of legend, his determination and love of the game obvious. With his handclapping and encouragement, he lifted those around him, driving them to new levels and his team to ever-greater heights.

Mackay hardly missed a game during the double-winning season, helped Spurs retain the FA Cup in 1962 and was the powerhouse behind the drive to the European Cup-winners' Cup Final in 1963. Injury forced him to miss the Final, a blow of more concern to Bill Nicholson than all the big names in the Athletico Madrid side.

The Cup-winners' Cup was not a competition that was particularly kind to Mackay. It was in the second match of Spurs' attempt to retain the trophy that Mackay had his leg broken by Manchester United's Noel Cantwell at Old Trafford in December 1963. The loss of Spurs' driving force was a big blow, but worse was to follow in September 1964 when, just as Mackay was beginning to recover his fitness, his leg was broken again in a reserve match with Shrewsbury Town.

In the 60s many players failed to recover from breaking their leg once. Breaking it twice was viewed as the end of a player's career. Not for Dave Mackay. The fierce determination he had shown in playing now came to the fore off the pitch. It took him nearly another year, but, come the start of the 1965–66 season, Mackay was back, maybe a fraction slower than he had been but otherwise every bit as good as before and now even more inspirational.

Taking over as captain on Danny Blanchflower's retirement, Mackay dropped back to play alongside the centre-half, but he still moved forward when the opportunity arose, still went into those thundering, bone-shaking challenges, still bossed the game and lifted his team. He led Spurs to FA Cup success in 1967 and played for another year before being released to join Derby County.

Anyone who thought Mackay would settle for a couple of years' quiet retirement could not have been more mistaken. He led Brian Clough's young Derby side to promotion, at last picking up the one honour he had missed out on, the FWA Player of the Year award.

Mackay helped Derby establish themselves in the top flight before embarking on a long managerial career that saw him working throughout England and the Near East, the highlight being to take Derby to the League title in 1974–75.

MARCHI, Anthony Vittorio (1949–57 and 1959–65)

Half-back, 6ft, 11st 4lb

Born: Edmonton, North London, 21 January 1933

Signed from amateur, June 1950 – Torino £20,000 July 1959

Transferred to Lanerossi Vicenza (Italy) July 1957, £35,000 – Northampton Town, June 1965, player-manager

Also played for: Lanerossi, Torino

Spurs record:

Debut: 22 April 1950 v Grimsby Town (FL) (h) lost 1–2

*Appearances: League 232, FA Cup 16, Europe 12, others 57**

*(*Includes one abandoned match)*

Goals: League 7, others 3

■ The most unenviable position for any player in Spurs' double-winning season must have been that of 'first reserve'. For a player of Tony Marchi's calibre, a player who had been there when Spurs had won the Football League title for the only other time in their history, had captained the club and would have walked into any other side, that must have been even more frustrating. That Marchi accepted the situation without public complaint reflects tremendous credit on a player who spent his best years in the shadow of Danny Blanchflower and Dave Mackay.

A schoolboy prodigy, Marchi won every representative honour going before joining Spurs as an amateur in July 1948. After only a couple of

games for the reserves he was called up for his League debut in April 1950 against Grimsby Town, a match Spurs lost but after which they received the Second Division Championship shield, and three months later signed his first professional contract.

Tall and composed, Marchi was ideally suited to either of the half-back positions, but Arthur Rowe's 'Push and Run' team possessed the ideal pairing of Ron Burgess and Bill Nicholson. Marchi had to show considerable patience before wresting the left-half position from the more experienced Colin Brittan following Burgess's departure, but by the end of the 1954–55 season he had firmly established himself in the role.

As Spurs rebuilt following the break up of Rowe's great team, Marchi proved a solid, dependable presence, full of skill and vision, strong and commanding. With an inbuilt calmness and assurance, he always seemed to have time, never flustered and was always in control of the situation. He became an automatic choice and with his natural leadership qualities was appointed club captain, leading Spurs to second place in the First Division in 1956–57 and picking up an England B cap against Scotland in February 1957 on the way.

Still only 24, Marchi looked set for a long career in the lily-white shirt, but in the summer of 1957 Juventus offered Spurs £42,000 for his transfer. It was an offer even Spurs could not afford to turn down, with the money and opportunity to make a name for himself in his father's home country too much for Marchi to refuse. Reluctantly, Spurs let him leave, but not before they had ensured the transfer contained a proviso that if Marchi was to be transferred outside of Italy, Spurs would have first option on his services.

Marchi was never to play for Juventus. Although the Italians lifted their ban on foreign players, they limited clubs to one player each. Juventus had just signed John Charles and Marchi was therefore loaned out, first to Lanerossi, then to Torino. Even in a struggling Lanerossi side, Marchi stood out, and within weeks of making the move to Italy he was expected to be called up for the Italian national team, but his appearance for England B prevented that.

After two years in Italy Marchi was anxious to return home. Arsenal, who had tried to sign him as a schoolboy, were keen, but Spurs invoked their contractual rights and re-signed Marchi for a bargain £20,000 in July 1959. With Dave Mackay signed to play at left-half, Marchi was looked upon as a likely replacement for the veteran Danny Blanchflower, but the brilliant Irishman had other ideas. Whether it was the threat of losing his place to his old skipper or not, Blanchflower lifted his game to new heights. Neither he nor Mackay could be left out so Marchi had to be content with that 'first-reserve' role.

Marchi played just six games in the double season but over the next few years appeared in roughly half of Spurs' games as injuries and age began to get the better of Blanchflower and Mackay suffered a twice-broken leg, never once letting the side down. It was as stand-in for Mackay that Marchi won his only club honour, giving a near-perfect performance in the European Cup-winners' Cup Final against Athletico Madrid.

By the time Blanchflower decided to call it a day and retire, a new generation of young talent in the shape of Phil Beal and Alan Mullery was coming through as Bill Nicholson looked to build a new team. With Mackay recovering from his misfortunes, Marchi was allowed to move to Northampton Town in June 1965 as player-manager.

MEDLEY, Leslie Dennis (1938–53)

Outside-left, 5ft 7in, 11st 11lb

Born: Edmonton, North London, 3 September 1920
Died: London, Ontario, Canada, 22 February 2001
Signed from amateur, February 1939
Retired, May 1953
Also played for: Tottenham Juniors, Northfleet United, Harwich & Parkeston, Toronto Greenbacks, Ulster United, Randfontein, England

Spurs record:

Debut: 5 January 1946 v Brentford (FAC) (h) drew 2–2
Appearances: League 150, FA Cup 14, others 89
Goals: League 45, FA Cup 1, others 28

■ Les Medley followed a well-trodden route through Tottenham Juniors and Northfleet United before joining the White Hart Lane professional staff in February 1939. He had not made the breakthrough into the first team when World War Two broke out, but the demands of war gave him an early opportunity to show his prowess and he played regularly for a year from October 1939, his pacy, direct wing play auguring well for the future.

Service in the RAF saw Medley posted to Canada where he met and married a local girl. They returned to the UK as the war drew to a close, and Medley soon established himself as first-choice outside-left, but Mrs Medley was unable to settle and in November 1946 they returned to Canada. It was a blow to Spurs as Medley had begun to settle in top-flight football and looked certain to fulfil his early potential.

While Medley was playing for Toronto Greenbacks and Ulster United, Spurs had difficulty filling his old position. Les Stevens and Ernie Jones were both competent wingers but neither possessed the dash or goalscoring threat of Medley. When Medley decided Canada was not the place for him and let it be known he was returning to London, Spurs were quick to assure him he would be more than welcome back.

He returned to Spurs in January 1948 but much of his fitness had been lost, and it was not until April 1949 that he started to make his mark again. It was then that manager Joe Hulme switched Eddie Baily from inside-right to inside-left and paired him with Medley. It was a move that was to prove a masterstroke. The Baily/Medley combination flourished immediately, the two of them dovetailing perfectly as they cut a swath down the left wing, fast interpassing and quick running, leaving a trail of devastation as they swiftly turned defence into attack. With Ron Burgess providing midfield support, the trio developed a triangular understanding on the left flank to rival that of Grimsdell, Bliss and Dimmock in the 1920s. Together they became one of the most important components of the 'Push and Run' team that won the Second and First Division titles in successive seasons in 1950 and 1951.

Medley was a player with pace, skill and trickery, quite able to take the ball up to an opponent, beat him with nimble footwork and leave him for dead, but that meant holding on to the ball, slowing play down and Arthur Rowe's philosophy was based on players moving the ball around quickly, not holding it. Medley had no difficulty adapting to Rowe's demands, happy to lay the ball off, run into a space to receive a return pass and then do the same thing again until he had worked himself into the perfect position to cross the ball or strike for goal. His play with Baily epitomised everything Rowe believed in – pace, movement, precision and the ball doing the work.

As good as anyone when it came to orthodox wing play, Medley possessed an exceptional burst of pace and a natural bodyswerve. Whether advancing on his full-back, pushing the ball beyond him or playing slick one-twos with Baily, Medley would send his marker one way before bursting past him. While he could hare down the line like most of his contemporaries before crossing, he would just as often cut inside, a move both unexpected and effective.

It was this unpredictability that made Medley stand out. Unlike most wingers he did not loiter around on his touchline waiting for the ball to be given to him. He wanted to be involved all the time, and if that meant dropping back to his own box or crossing to the opposite flank that was just what he would do. Wherever the action was, Medley would be found. It made him an impossible man to tie down and meant he popped up in the most unexpected positions, a crucial factor in his amassing so many goals. In the promotion season of 1950 he top scored with 18 goals and added another 11 as the title was won in 1951.

In the top Division, Medley was soon recognised as the most effective left-winger in the country and was selected for England against Wales in November 1950. It was to be the first of six full caps he collected, four of which came with Eddie Bailey as his inside-forward partner, and Medley was never on the losing side. He also played for the Football League and the Rest of the United Kingdom.

An automatic choice for Spurs for four seasons, Medley decided to retire at the end of the 1952–53 season. He went back to Canada, although he later played and coached in South Africa.

MIDDLEMISS, Herbert (1907–20)

Outside-left, 5ft 10in, 11st 5lb

Born: New Benwell, Newcastle, 19 December 1888
Died: Brixham, Devon, 28 June 1941
Signed from Stockport County, September 1907, £250
Transferred to Queen's Park Rangers, June 1920, released
Also played for: Stalybridge Rovers, Queen's Park Rangers

Spurs record:

Debut: 16 November 1907 v Brentford (SL) (h) won 1–0
Appearances: League 248, FA Cup 17, others 94 (*Includes three abandoned matches)*
Goals: League 52, FA Cup 3, others 35

■ Bert Middlemiss was a young winger playing as an amateur with Stalybridge Rovers in the Lancashire Combination early in the 1907–08 season, when word got out that Spurs manager Fred Kirkham was casting his eyes over him. Second Division Stockport County had a close relationship with Stalybridge and moved quickly to sign Middlemiss to a professional contract, knowing that if Spurs wanted to sign him before the end of the season they would have to pay Stockport a transfer fee.

Outside-left was proving a problem position for Spurs. Alf Whyman, Arthur Pickett and Harry Stansfield had all been tried in the position but were not a success, so Kirkham had little difficulty persuading his directors to fork out a fee of about £250 to secure Middlemiss's signature. It proved to be a more than satisfactory piece of business.

Middlemiss went straight in to Spurs' Southern League team and made an immediate impression with his bursts down the wing and powerful shooting. Initially he played too much as an individual and tired easily, but with professional training he developed rapidly, realising he could not do it all on his own and learning to pace himself so he could be as effective at the end of the game as the start.

He barely missed a game in his first season, one of the few bright spots in a Spurs team that did not have a particularly successful time, seventh being the lowest position Spurs finished in their 12 seasons competing in the Southern League.

Spurs were elected to the Football League in 1908 and among the players they signed for the step up in grade was Bobby Steel. Steel played at inside-left and immediately struck up a fine understanding with Middlemiss, coaxing his young partner along, knowing just when to release the ball to make the most of Middlemiss's pace and generally giving Middlemiss the benefit of his experience.

Once Middlemiss had the ball at his feet his only thought was to attack. He was not a great dribbler or one for trickery, but he did have an abundance of pace and a variety to his play that meant defenders often did not know what he was going to do until it was too late. Sometimes he would push the ball past his man and hare for the goal-line before sending over accurate crosses for the likes of Vivian Woodward and Billy Minter to feed off. At other times he would cut inside and head for goal before unleashing a powerful shot. He scored 13 goals as Spurs won promotion in their first Football League season, a total only surpassed by Minter and Woodward.

It was no more than Middlemiss deserved when he was selected to play for the South against the North in the January 1909 international trial. Although he did not win selection for the end of season internationals, he did well enough to be marked down as one for the future.

Spurs did not find life easy in the First Division, but Middlemiss continued to impress with one consistent performance after another. Rarely absent, he was one of the few players from the Southern League days who were really comfortable in the top flight, and his explosive bursts were one of the rare bright spots in an otherwise nondescript time.

As Spurs struggled to make their mark, some of the bigger clubs cast envious eyes at Middlemiss, but there was never any chance of Spurs allowing him to leave – relegation would have been guaranteed without his goals and the chances he created for others. He was selected for three more international trials but was never quite able to make the England team.

Middlemiss missed very few games between Spurs elevation to the League and the outbreak of World War One, but when hostilities began he went to work in the Midlands. Rarely able to get to Spurs for games, he made a few appearances for Birmingham and Coventry City, but when he returned to Spurs he was clearly out of condition.

It took most of the first post-war season for Middlemiss to get his fitness back, but by then Jimmy Dimmock had emerged as Spurs' long-term outside-left. Middlemiss played just four games after the war, all as a replacement for Fanny Walden, before being released. He joined Queen's Park Rangers and played for the Third Division South side for a year before retiring.

MINTER, William James (1907–26)

Inside-forward, 5ft 10in, 11st 7lb

Born: Woolwich, South London, 16 April 1888
Died: Tottenham, North London, 21 May 1940
Signed from Reading, March 1908
Also played for: Norwich City, Woolwich Arsenal, Reading

Spurs record:

Debut: 7 March 1908 v Millwall (SL) (h) lost 1–2
Appearances: League 248, FA Cup 19, others 76*
*(*Includes 4 abandoned)*
Goals: League 95, FA Cup 6, others 55

■ Although Billy Minter was born in Woolwich, his talents were largely overlooked by his local club, much to Spurs' benefit.

After playing a couple of games for Norwich City and an unsuccessful three months with Woolwich Arsenal, Minter took his talents to Reading, where he immediately exhibited the skills that were to prove so valuable to Spurs.

In his first season in Berkshire, 1906–07, he led Reading's Southern League scoring list and was well on the way to repeating the feat when Spurs moved to sign him, and teammate Ernie Coquet, in March 1908.

Spurs were going through a poor spell when Minter arrived. Results were not good and the quality of football poor. Manager Fred Kirkham had made continual changes but with little effect. The defence was not too bad but the forward line weak in the extreme. Only Vivian Woodward was anything like a regular scorer, but with the internationals season about to begin he would not be available for many games.

The club was already bound to record its worst-ever finish in the Southern League and, as it was already lobbying for admission to the

Football League, results had to improve if there was to be any hope of that being achieved.

Minter found the net on his debut against Millwall, the first of four goals in nine games, and helped bring about a degree of consistency that secured a reasonable end to the season.

With election to the Football League, Spurs allowed many of the players who had proved inadequate to depart, but Minter was regarded as one of the younger talents on whom the future could be built. The experienced Doug McFarlane was signed from Burnley to play at centre-forward, with Vivian Woodward moving to inside-right and Minter expected to cover for Woodward, particularly early in the season when the great amateur would still be playing cricket.

McFarlane proved a disappointment from the start. Minter played a few games at centre-forward but he was not really comfortable there and eventually Woodward resumed his old position with Minter inside. It was a combination that worked well, Woodward scored 18 goals and Minter 16 as promotion to the First Division was secured.

Woodward's decision to quit senior football in the summer of 1909 was a big blow to Spurs, but Minter continued to perform and score consistently. As Spurs struggled to maintain their position in the top echelon they relied more and more on him to provide the goals, and he did not let the club down. For the three seasons from 1909–10 he was top scorer, and it was only with the arrival of Jimmy Cantrell and Bert Bliss that the scoring burden was lifted from his shoulders.

Minter was not an exceptional talent but a good, solid, dependable footballer. He was well built, worked hard in support of his centre-forward, and played the game simply and neatly. There was no great pace, no explosive shooting and no sublime dribbling skills, but he had strength and an eye for goal. In the penalty box he could be lethal, seeing the openings and finishing with a well-placed shot.

With the start of World War One, Spurs were hard hit by players joining the forces, and although Minter played through the season there was nothing he could do to prevent relegation. Joining up himself he only played a few games in the early wartime competitions, but when he returned in early 1919 he had not lost any of his abilities, scoring nine goals in the same number of matches.

With Spurs in the Second Division after the war, Minter began 1919–20 at centre-half but soon reverted to his normal inside-right role. He played 20 games as Spurs ran away with the Second Division before losing his place to Jimmy Banks. With the signing of Jimmy Seed, Minter decided to retire from playing in 1920 to take on the role of trainer.

MORRIS, Thomas (1899–1913)

Half-back, 5ft 10in, 11st 9lb

Born: Grantham, Lincolnshire, 9 February 1875
Died: Uxbridge, Middlesex, 25 April 1942
Signed from Gainsborough Trinity, July 1899
Retired, May 1912
Also played for: Grantham Rovers, Gainsborough Trinity

Spurs record:

Debut: 9 September 1899 v Queen's Park Rangers (SL) (h) won 1–0
Appearances: League 63, FA Cup 39, others 424***
*(*Includes two abandoned matches, **Includes one abandoned match)*
Goals: League 2, FA Cup 1, others 45

■ One of the most important, if unsung, figures in helping Spurs develop from a promising Southern League side to Southern League champions, FA Cup winners and on to become an established Football League outfit, Tom Morris was a well-experienced professional when John Cameron signed him for Spurs in May 1899.

Having played for Grantham Rovers in his home town, he had moved on to Gainsborough Trinity, then a Second Division Football League club, and built such a solid reputation for himself that several First Division clubs were said to be interested in securing his services. Fortunately, Cameron proved remarkably adept at persuading quality players to make what might have appeared a downward move by signing for a Southern League outfit. Morris was among half-a-dozen or so top-flight performers he persuaded to join Spurs at their new White Hart Lane ground as he sought to fashion a team for his first full year as player-manager.

Cameron knew full well that the half-back line provided the engine room of the team and recognised the importance of having a surfeit of players capable of controlling the middle of the field, players who could both defend and attack. In Jack Jones, Bob Stormont and James McNaught he already had three of the best outside the Football League. By adding Morris and Ted Hughes he ensured adequate back-up and competition for places.

Morris fitted Cameron's idea of a half-back perfectly. He was powerfully built and indefatigable, working tirelessly both in defence and attack. He played right across the half-back line and even made a few appearances at inside-forward, but most of his games were played at right-half where he could get the ball and feed his inside-forward or winger yet provide cover for his full-back.

Settling in immediately, Morris played in 24 games as the Southern League title was won in 1899–1900, chipping in five goals with his powerful shooting, and played in practically every match of the Southern District Combination campaign in which Spurs finished second. He started at right-half, moved to the centre when James McNaught was injured but soon returned to the right where his attacking instincts were best put to use. His solid performances caught the eye of the international selectors and resulted in him being selected for the South against the North in the international trial match of March 1900.

Injury in the first match of the following campaign saw Morris out of the team, and when he recovered Ted Hughes had begun to stake a claim for a regular place. It took Cameron some time to shuffle his pack before finding the best combination and that meant Morris playing on the right. In that position he played in every match of the successful FA Cup campaign of 1901, when his value to the team was most apparent.

Possessing limitless energy, Morris never seemed to slacken, covering every inch of the ground, supporting his forwards whenever the opportunity arose and working back when the pressure was on. It was in defence that he was most noticeable, getting in his tackles, winning the ball and then bursting forward or laying it off simply to his more gifted colleagues.

Throughout the early part of the 20th century Morris provided the solid backbone around which the Spurs team was built. After the FA Cup success Spurs went into decline and struggled to make much of an impression, but Morris continued to shine, playing in another international trial in January 1903. That he did not win a call-up to the England team was due to the selectors preferring the outstanding William Johnson of Sheffield United.

When Spurs made the move up to the Football League in 1908 Morris was still there, the sole survivor from 1901 and the man who holds the record of Southern League appearances for Spurs.

He displayed remarkable longevity and consistency, and was well into his 30s before his standards began to slip. Early in the 1910–11 season he was left out, and although he played a few games after that, including a couple at full-back, his first-team career was over.

He remained on the playing staff, usually assisting the reserves, until the summer of 1913 when he took up a position on the ground staff. Apart from serving with the Footballers' Battalion during World War One and on Air Raid Precaution duties during World War Two, he continued to work for the club until his death in April 1942.

MULLERY, Alan Patrick MBE (1963–72)

Midfield, 5ft 9in, 12st 4lb

Born: Notting Hill, West London, 23 November 1941

Signed from Fulham, March 1964, £72,500
Transferred to Fulham, July 1972, £65,000
Also played for: Fulham, England

Spurs record:

Debut: 21 March 1964 v Manchester United (FL) (h) lost 2–3
Appearances: League 313, FA Cup 33, League Cup 18, Europe 10, others 55*
*(*Includes one abandoned match)*
Goals: League 25, FA Cup 1, Europe 4, others 9

■ It is a testament to Alan Mullery the man that Alan Mullery the footballer was a success at Spurs, for in replacing Danny Blanchflower he had the most difficult, if not impossible, job in the game. To succeed as he did shows he was not only an exceptionally-good footballer but a man of tremendous character.

Mullery made his name at Fulham, a homely club known for its friendliness, where he did the donkey work in midfield for Johnny Haynes. In six years and over 200 appearances he had shown himself as one of the best young talents in the game, with three England Under-23 caps to his name.

When Blanchflower's knee gave way in November 1963, Bill Nicholson knew he had to secure a replacement. The choice was between Mullery and Mike Bailey of Charlton Athletic. Nicholson liked the way Mullery rarely missed a game, but the decision was made for Nicholson, who was also looking to replace Peter Baker, when Mullery made it clear he would not play at full-back. Signed in March 1964 for £72,500, Mullery knew his own mind, something Nicholson liked and something he had in common with the man he was succeeding.

There the similarities ended. Whereas Blanchflower was tall, elegant and stylish, Mullery was stocky, full of non-stop action and hard work. He did not possess the cool, calm assurance of the Irishman, but he did have enthusiasm, a desire for hard work and an ability to inspire those around him by his own example.

It took time for Mullery's qualities to be recognised by Spurs' regulars, but Alf Ramsey had no such problem. Selected for England's 1964 summer tour to South America, Mullery ricked his neck shaving on the day the party was due to depart and had to miss the trip, but come December he collected his first cap against Holland.

Winning over the England manager was easy compared to the difficulties Mullery faced at White Hart Lane. So accustomed had supporters become to Blanchflower's sublime talents that many resented Mullery and his own style. Often the butt of vitriolic comments from the terraces, many a lesser man would have

demanded a transfer but Mullery was determined to win the crowd over. Many managers would have considered 'resting' him, but Nicholson valued Mullery's contribution highly and never considered leaving him out.

As football changed with hard work increasingly important, Mullery's value began to win some recognition, but the turning point came with the 1967 FA Cup Final. He had an outstanding game, hunting down the ball, harrying the Chelsea midfield and bursting forward at every opportunity. It was his charge at the Chelsea defence just before half-time that led to Spurs' first goal. Having made ground as Chelsea retreated and covered every pass, Mullery's only option was to have a pop at goal. Ron Harris got his foot in the way of the shot but the ball ballooned up and fell perfectly for Jimmy Robertson to tuck away. As the game drew to a close and Chelsea pressed for an equaliser, Mullery worked ceaselessly to keep them out and win the first club honour of his career.

The Cup Final not only changed Mullery's club career, it had a similar effect on his international fortunes too. Four days after the Final he won his second cap and immediately established himself as Nobby Stiles's successor, playing regularly and having an outstanding tournament in the 1970 Mexico World Cup.

Now accepted as an inspirational figure and possessing the same determination to succeed, Mullery was Dave Mackay's natural successor as Spurs' captain when the great Scot left.

Mullery skippered Spurs to victory in the 1971 Football League Cup Final, but in October that year he suffered a serious pelvic injury. Out of action for over six months, he thought he was fit to return, but Nicholson had other ideas. Mullery demanded the chance to prove he was right and went to Fulham on loan.

It looked like the end of his Spurs career, but in April 1972 he was recalled, as an injury crisis left Spurs short for the first leg of the UEFA Cup semi-final with AC Milan. Mullery looked as good as ever and in the second leg scored a 30-yard screamer to secure Spurs' place in the Final. The second leg of the Final proved to be Mullery's last appearance for Spurs, and he went out with a bang, throwing himself full length to head home the crucial goal that secured the trophy.

At the end of the game Mullery collected the trophy. With fans streaming on to the pitch and the other players seeking the sanctuary of the dressing room, he embarked on a solo lap of honour. It was all so different to how his Spurs career had started.

NICHOLSON, William Edward OBE (1938–55)

Half-back, 5ft 9in, 11st 7lb

Born: Scarborough, Yorkshire, 26 January 1919

Died: Potters Bar, Hertfordshire, 23 October 2004

Signed from amateur, August 1938

Also played for: Scarborough Working Men's Club, Scarborough Young Liberals, Northfleet United, England

Spurs record:

Debut: 22 October 1938 v Blackburn Rovers (FL) (a) lost 1–3

Appearances: League 318, FA Cup 27, others 50*

*(*Includes one abandoned match)*

Goals: League 6, others 1

■ In the 125 years since Spurs were formed, nobody comes close to matching Bill Nicholson for his contribution to the club's success, let alone the dedication he showed over 68 years. He may not have been around when Bobby Buckle and his schoolboy pals laid the foundations for the Tottenham style, when John Cameron's team lifted the FA Cup, when Peter McWilliam's stormed through the Second Division and won the FA Cup or when Percy Smith's 'Greyhounds' thrilled fans with their fast-paced attacking, but he was there when Arthur Rowe's 'Push and Run' team stunned football with the simplicity of their game and he was there to guide Spurs to previously unattainable heights.

Nicholson came down from Scarborough for a trial in March 1936. He gave up his job as a laundry boy to join the groundstaff, spent two years at the Northfleet United nursery and signed professional in August 1938.

Originally a left-back, his League debut came in October 1938, and he spent most of his first season understudying Bill Whatley, only playing when the Welshman was injured or on international duty. The start of 1939–40 saw Nicholson as first choice, but when war broke out he joined the Durham Light Infantry and was hardly seen at White Hart Lane until demobbed in February 1946. By then, Vic Buckingham had staked a claim to the number-three shirt but centre-half was proving a problem, and Nicholson was given the job of shackling opposing centre-forwards.

He performed well enough and occupied the position in the first season of post-war football but was not the tallest of players, and as 1947–48 started he was moved to right-half, where his strong tackling and simple distribution of the ball would be most effective.

Nicholson was an unfussy player, cutting down the space available to his opposing inside-forward, snapping into the tackle, working out the angles and intercepting before danger threatened. Once he had the ball he rarely held on to it, a few quick strides and then it was released. It was an attitude that fitted perfectly with Arthur Rowe's 'Push and Run' philosophy that demanded continual movement from ball and player.

Nicholson missed only three games in the Second Division-winning season of 1949–50 and only one as the Football League title was won for the first time in 1951. Although not regarded as one of the most gifted footballers in Rowe's team, he was regarded, along with Ron Burgess, Alf Ramsey and Eddie Baily, as one of the four 'greats' in the team. He played a crucial role, providing the solid base in midfield that allowed Burgess to press forward so effectively, Ramsey to concentrate on controlling the right flank and Baily to perform his full range of tricks.

It was not only at White Hart Lane that Nicholson's attributes were recognised. He won his first representative honour in January 1950 when he played for England B against Switzerland, but it was not to be the start of the long international career his performances merited. He appeared for the Football League, won two more England B caps and was a member of England's 1950 World Cup squad, but he was to win only one full England cap. That came against Portugal at Goodison Park in May 1951 when, remarkably, he scored with his first kick of the match. He seemed set to make himself an England regular, but after being selected for the game against Austria in November 1951 he was forced to withdraw through injury. He was not to get another chance as Billy Wright made the position his own.

Nicholson anchored the Spurs midfield until the 1954–55 season when, approaching the veteran stage, he realised he was past his best, and he himself made it clear to Rowe that a replacement had to be secured. The result was the signing of Danny Blanchflower and the beginning of a new era in Spurs' history that saw Nicholson lead Spurs to previously unimagined glories.

NORMAN, Maurice (1955–66)

Defender, 6ft 1in, 12st 2lb

Born: Mulbarton, Norfolk, 8 May 1934
Signed from Norwich City, November 1955, £18,000
Retired, June 1967
Also played for: Mulbarton, Norwich City, England

Spurs record:

Debut: 5 November 1955 v Cardiff City (FL) (h) drew 1–1
Appearances: League 357, FA Cup 37, Europe 17, others 43
Goals: League 16, FA Cup 2, Europe 1

■ Another player Spurs spotted at an early stage in his career who went on to great things, Maurice Norman had played only 35 League games for Norwich City when Spurs swooped to sign him in November 1955 at a cost of £18,000, plus winger Johnny Gavin.

A strapping six-footer, Norman had begun his career as a centre-half but Norwich had switched him to right-back. Harry Clarke still commanded the number-five shirt at White Hart Lane, but Alf Ramsey had departed for Ipswich Town without a long-term successor and Norman was regarded as the man who could fill his boots.

For such a big and powerful man, Norman was quite at home out on the flank. His positional sense was excellent, his tackling strong and his speed surprising. He spent the best part of a year developing his game before injury left him on the sidelines for six months. When fit to return he found Peter Baker had made the right-back spot his own and Norman had to settle for a few games at left-back and centre-half.

It was not until a third of the way through the 1957–58 season, with Spurs only four places off the bottom, that Norman took over the centre-half role from Clarke's successor John Ryden. He immediately injected a strength and sense of resolution in the defence that had been sadly missing. By the end of the season Spurs had climbed to third and Norman had won himself a place in the England squad for the 1958 World Cup Finals.

Norman did not play in Sweden but on his return developed into an essential part of the double-winning team, the defensive rock around which Bill Nicholson built the greatest team in Spurs' history.

To his height Norman added a superb physique, a quiet determination and a footballing ability often overlooked because of the quality of those around him. Strong and resolute in the tackle, his experience at

full-back had taught him the art of positional play and the importance of accurate distribution of the ball once he had won it. With two half-backs such as Danny Blanchflower and Dave Mackay forever pushing forward, his great discipline and concentration were needed lest Spurs were caught by a quick counter-attack. More than once Spurs would be caught short of numbers at the back, a through ball about to cut them open when a long leg from Norman would snake out and stifle the threat.

Not that Norman was just a defender. He was one of the first centre-halves to push forward regularly for set plays, and although he did not score many goals himself his strength in the air and mere presence unsettled opposing defences and created many openings for the likes of Bobby Smith, Les Allen and Jimmy Greaves. He enjoyed the chance to attack and would often emerge from defence with his long, loping stride, apparently all arms and legs, seeking the angle to lay the ball off before hurrying back to his defensive station.

Norman missed only one game in the double season of 1961 and, after helping Spurs retain the FA Cup in 1962, at last won his first England cap against Peru in May 1962, the last warm up game before the World Cup. Displacing Peter Swan and seeing off the challenge of Brian Labone, Norman established himself as England's first choice in the centre of defence, winning a total of 23 full caps until another tall, gangling man mountain in the shape of Jack Charlton appeared.

A European Cup-winners' Cup winners' medal was added to Norman's impressive trophy collection in 1963, and he continued to provide the solid centre to Spurs defence for another two years, as Nicholson began to develop a new team to secure more silverware for the trophy cabinet.

With Peter Baker departing and Cyril Knowles needed to replace the veteran Ron Henry, Norman was switched back to the right of defence at the start of the 1965–66 season. With Laurie Brown playing in the centre, the move may have extended Norman's career, but, sadly, Norman broke his leg in five places in a friendly against a Hungarian Select XI in November 1965. For two years he fought a desperate battle to recover, but in the end he had to admit defeat and retire.

O'CALLAGHAN, Eugene (1926–35 and 1940–44)

Inside-forward, 5ft 8in, 11st 10lb

Born: Ebbw Vale, 6 October 1906
Died: Fulham, London, 4 July 1956
Signed from amateur, August 1926
Transferred to Leicester City, March 1935, £2,250
Also played for: Victoria United, Ebbw Vale Corinthians, Barnet, Northfleet United, Leicester City, Fulham, Wales

Spurs record:

Debut: 15 January 1927 v Everton (FL) (a) won 2–1
Appearances: League 252, FA Cup 11, others 50
Goals: League 92, FA Cup 6, others 23

■ The late 1920s and early 1930s were not exactly the most exciting times to be a Spurs supporter. With a brief exception it was a period of averageness, a time when Spurs were neither mediocre nor inspiring. Throughout it all one of the few pleasures was watching Taffy O'Callaghan in action.

A Welsh Schoolboy international, Eugene O'Callaghan was working down the pits and

playing for Ebbw Vale reserves when he was spotted by Spurs' Welsh scout and signed to amateur forms in September 1924. Taken on the groundstaff, he had a brief spell with Barnet, followed by a year at the Northfleet United nursery before signing his first professional contract in August 1926.

O'Callaghan immediately impressed with the reserves but there were concerns that, while 5ft 8ins, he weighed barely 11 and a half stone and was too easily brushed off the ball. His first-team debut was against Everton in January 1927 when Jimmy Seed went down with flu, and although O'Callaghan looked timid to begin with by the end of the match his confidence had blossomed.

He did not get another chance for a month. Frank Osborne had been out injured with Jimmy Blair occupying Osborne's centre-forward berth. With Osborne recovered Blair took the inside-right position O'Callaghan had filled, but then got himself sent off against Huddersfield Town at the end of January. When Blair was suspended for a month, and with Seed now injured, O'Callaghan was recalled. He took his chance well, displaying some pretty footwork and luring players to him before playing clever little passes to his colleagues. Spurs' attacking play had become predictable and boring, O'Callaghan added an exciting new dimension to their game.

Billy Minter had now taken over as manager from Peter McWilliam, and he decided O'Callaghan was to be the new creative force in his team. Such was his confidence in the young Welshman he allowed Seed, midfield maestro since his arrival in April 1919, to leave for Sheffield Wednesday just before the 1927–28 season started. That turned out to be a bad decision.

Although O'Callaghan justified Minter's faith with his skilful performances and top scored with 24 League and Cup goals, he lacked experience and no matter how well he played could not inspire a less than average Spurs team as they hovered around the lower reaches of the First Division table, along with Sheffield Wednesday. In the last few weeks of the season Seed inspired Wednesday to a run of great results. Victory in the last match of the season saw Wednesday escape relegation with Spurs going down instead.

Spurs did not fare very well in the Second Division and things only got worse when O'Callaghan suffered a cartilage injury in November 1929. He missed the rest of the season and when fit enough to return Minter had resigned to be replaced by Percy Smith.

Smith realised O'Callaghan was a great talent, but he needed the right players around him. Despite being a lightweight, O'Callaghan possessed great stamina and bravery, prepared to take on the toughest of defenders and not easily muscled off the ball. He had terrific enthusiasm, chasing every ball and often creating chances out of what appeared the most hopeless of situations. Those factors alone were enough to make him a crowd favourite, but he had more. His passing was neat and accurate, he could use both feet, he was forever coming up with unexpected little tricks, and he could score goals.

Gradually Smith got together a team who could play one touch football at great pace. It was perfect for O'Callaghan, who pinged the ball around, playing it into space and knowing someone would get on the end of his pass. As he pulled the strings, Spurs finished 1932–33 as runners-up in Division Two and the following season rose to third in the First Division.

1934–35, though, was a disaster, as continual injuries devastated the team. O'Callaghan suffered as much as anyone, but Smith seemed to place much of the blame for Spurs' predicament on O'Callaghan and the two fell out. Even then it was a surprise when O'Callaghan was allowed to leave for Leicester City in March 1935. His departure did nothing to help Spurs, just as his arrival at Filbert Street did little to help Leicester. Both clubs were relegated at the end of the season.

While Spurs remained in the Second Division until 1950, O'Callaghan, who had won 11 Welsh caps in his Spurs days, at least helped Leicester back into the top flight before moving to Fulham.

During World War Two O'Callaghan appeared as a guest for Spurs on 22 occasions. While not the player he had been, his appearances rekindled fond memories for those who had seen him at his best.

OSBORNE, Frank Raymond (1923–31)

Forward, 5ft 10in, 10st 7lb

Born: Wynberg, South Africa, 14 October 1896

Died: Epsom, Surrey, 8 March 1988

Signed from Fulham, January 1924, £1,500

Transferred to Southampton, June 1931, £450

Also played for: Netley, Bromley, Fulham, Southampton, England

Spurs record:

Debut: 19 January 1924 v Newcastle United (FL) (h) won 2–0

Appearances: League 210, FA Cup 9, others 10

Goals: League 78, FA Cup 4, others 5

■ The son of a Royal Army Medical Corps colonel, Frank Osborne was born in South Africa and did not come to England until well into his teens. He joined his local club in Hampshire, Netley, but the outbreak of World War One saw him follow his father into the RAMC. On leaving the army he played for the well-known amateurs Bromley and in

November 1921, already 25, he signed for Fulham.

He went straight into their Second Division team, scoring on his debut and sparking a run of seven successive victories that kept Fulham in the promotion pack. Fulham were unable to maintain the momentum and in an effort to recapture their form Osborne was moved around the forward line, playing in every position except outside-left. He started the next season at centre-forward and did so well he won his first cap against Ireland in October 1922, but was later switched to the right wing and again impressed so much that his second cap against France in May 1923 saw him playing at outside-right.

Fulham began 1923–24 terribly and continued in the same vein. The whole season was destined to be one long battle against relegation, not helped by dire financial problems. When Peter McWilliam made a £3,000 offer for Osborne in January 1924 it was one Fulham could not afford to turn down, particularly as Osborne wanted to go.

Osborne made his first appearance in a Spurs shirt for the reserves against Arsenal and scored two goals with fine individual efforts, as good a debut as anyone could hope for. It was a performance that provided a silver lining to what was otherwise a miserable day, as the first team were beaten in the FA Cup at Second Division Crystal Palace

With Alex Lindsay banging in the goals from centre-forward and Fanny Walden still the established outside-right, Osborne began his First Division career at inside-right. He performed well enough, as Spurs won at Newcastle, but they played another 11 games that season, and he was not on the winning side once more. It was obvious Osborne would take time to settle, especially as Walden's form was erratic, and, even when on song, he was such an unpredictable winger that he did not make life easy for his inside partner.

As it turned out, Osborne and Walden never had a chance to build an understanding. The veteran winger was injured in pre-season and Osborne started 1924–25 in his place, collecting another England cap, against Belgium, in December 1924.

Osborne could be effective on the wing, he had pace and trickery and usually put in dangerous crosses, but Spurs did not have a good team. Under pressure for large parts of games, Osborne was too often left isolated for long periods. He needed to be more involved to have a real impact.

In October 1925 he was moved to centre-forward. Spurs had started the season with four wins on the trot, but Lindsay had broken his hand, young Billy Lane was not experienced enough and Harry Hargreaves totally off form. The move looked a masterstroke, particularly when Osborne netted three successive hat-tricks against Liverpool, Leicester City and West Ham United. He found the back of the net regularly all season, scoring 27 goals in total. It was no surprise when he was selected for England again, scoring a hat-trick against Belgium in May 1926 from the centre-forward position.

Not powerfully built, Osborne knew his limitations and did not attempt to play a physical game. He relied on sound positional sense and his natural dribbling skills, dropping off to find space, collecting the ball and facing the defence head on. Once within range of goal he was cool and unhurried, often relying on accuracy to place his shots on target but with a powerful shot when needed.

When Billy Minter took over as manager from Peter McWilliam in February 1927 he moved Osborne back to the flank, but he was not to stay there long. After Jimmy Blair had been granted his demand for a transfer, Osborne returned to the centre where he struck up a fine understanding with Taffy O'Callaghan. The two of them led the scoring list, but they could not prevent Spurs being relegated in 1927–28.

In the Second Division Osborne continued to prove himself as Spurs' premier marksman, but as first Minter and then Percy Smith searched for that winning combination, Osborne was moved around the front line and eventually found himself in the reserves.

It was not what a player coming to the end of his career needed. In June 1931 he moved to Southampton where he played for two years. He then returned to Fulham, initially as a director but later as team manager, general manager and secretary-manager.

PARKS, Anthony (1979–88)

Goalkeeper 1979–88, 5ft 11in, 10st 8lb

Born: Hackney, East London, 28 January 1963
Signed from apprentice, September 1980
Transferred to Brentford, July 1988, £60,000
Also played for: Oxford United, Gillingham, Brentford, Queen's Park Rangers, Fulham, West Ham United, Falkirk, Blackpool, Burnley, Doncaster Rovers, Barrow, Scarborough, Halifax Town

Spurs record:

Debut: 10 May 1982 v West Ham United (FL) (a) drew 2–2
Appearances: League 37, FA Cup 5, League Cup 1, Europe 5(1), others 24(16)

■ If a man can become a legend as a result of just one game, then Tony Parks is that man. One moment of inspiration, some would say good fortune, and Parks wrote his name forever in the annals of Spurs' history.

It all happened one May evening in 1984. Spurs had drawn the first leg of the UEFA Cup Final with Anderlecht 1–1 in Brussels and went into the second leg as favourites to prise the

trophy away from the holders. The match was Keith Burkinshaw's last in charge and all the plans were based around another night of glorious European football at White Hart Lane, ending with Burkinshaw getting his hands on a final piece of silverware.

Those plans were rudely interrupted by the visitors. Anderlecht proved stubborn opponents, and when Alex Czerniatinski deservedly put them ahead with an hour gone, the evening looked like ending in bitter disappointment.

The game only changed with the introduction of Ossie Ardiles 15 minutes from time. The little Argentine inspired a relentless bombardment of the visitors' goal. With only seven minutes left, Steve Archibald saw his shot wonderfully saved by Jacques Munaron in the Anderlecht goal. There was no time to bemoan the effort, as the ball was played back into the box. Ardiles got his toe to the ball, it struck the crossbar but fell perfectly for Graham Roberts to grab the equaliser.

Thirty minutes extra-time could not produce a winner, so the match went to penalties. In Munaron Anderlecht had a top-class 'keeper, a Belgian international with World Cup experience. For Spurs there was Parks, a 21-

year-old with barely 30 first-team games to his credit.

After Graham Roberts had put the first spot-kick away, another experienced international, the Dane Morten Olsen, stepped up for Anderlecht. His shot was firm enough, but Parks went full length to turn it away. Mark Falco, Gary Stevens and Steve Archibald all converted for Spurs, Kenny Brylle, Enzo Scifo and Frankie Vercauteren did likewise for Anderlecht. It was left for Danny Thomas to put the final kick away and give Spurs the trophy, but he shot straight at Munaron.

It all rested now on Parks and Arnor Gudjohnsen. As half the crowd watched with their eyes closed, the Icelandic international struck his penalty well enough, but Parks flung himself to his right, got both hands to the ball and pushed it away. It was a few seconds before Parks realised what he had done and the next thing he knew he was buried by celebrating teammates.

Parks was a local lad who worked his way through the ranks to understudy Ray Clemence. So consistent and injury-free was the former England 'keeper that Parks had few opportunities until Clemence was injured at Fulham in January 1984. Parks played for a couple of months and did all that was asked of him, but as soon as Clemence was fit, Parks was back in the reserves. When Clemence severed a finger tendon in training late in March, Parks was called up again. He put in some creditable performances, none more so than in the two UEFA Cup semi-final games with Hadjuk Split, when he pulled off some stunning saves. Clemence was fit enough to return for the meetings with Anderlecht, indeed he sat on the bench in both games, but Parks had done enough to justify his place on merit.

Having sampled the sweet taste of glory, Parks found himself back as second choice, as first Peter Shreeve and then David Pleat sought to emulate Burkinshaw's successes. It was not until October 1987, when Clemence sustained the injury that led to his eventual retirement, that Parks had another chance to stake his claim to the number-one spot. It could not have come at a worse time, with the fallout from Pleat's departure and the hiatus before Terry Venables's arrival. With the whole team shorn of confidence, Parks failed to impress Venables. There were times when he pulled off some great saves, but all too often he looked lacking in the basics of his trade.

With the arrival of Bobby Mimms, Parks was released and joined former captain Steve Perryman at Brentford, where he was one of the stars of the Bees progress to the sixth round of the FA Cup in 1989. He then moved around the lower levels of football before taking up coaching and returned to Spurs as goalkeeping coach in November 2008.

PAYNE, Ernest George (1893–99)

Outside-left, 5ft 9in, 11st 6lb

Born: Fulham, West London, 1876
Also played for: Old Sherbrookians, Fulham, Bush Hill Rovers

Spurs record:

Debut: 13 October 1894 v West Herts (FAC) (h) won 3–2
Appearances: Southern League 20, FA Cup 14, others 103
Goals: Southern League 5, FA Cup 6, others 53

■ Ernie Payne was a fast, direct winger, who always posed a threat with his shooting as much as with his orthodox style of wing play. He would merit more than an honourable mention in any history of Spurs for the quality of his football, but what elevates him to a more notable position were the events that followed his first game for Spurs and the effect they had on the whole direction the club took in the 1890s.

Payne was a West London lad who, after playing for his old school team, had joined Fulham. Although rated highly enough, he was given few opportunities to play for them and when invited to turn out for Spurs against Old St Marks in a London Senior Cup match on 21 October 1893 he readily accepted.

On the morning of the game, Payne called in at Fulham's ground as he made his way to Tottenham with the intention of collecting his playing gear. He found it had all disappeared and so arrived at Northumberland Park bereft of any kit, hoping Spurs would be able to provide it. Shirt, knickers, socks and pads were quickly found, but boots proved a problem. Despite trying on every available pair, none fitted. Payne was given 10 shillings and pointed in the direction of the nearest sports outfitter.

When Fulham heard what had happened they complained to the London FA, accusing Spurs of 'poaching' and 'professionalism'. The complaint was heard within two weeks. Spurs were found not guilty of the poaching charge, but the disciplinary committee decided that giving Payne 10 shillings was an unfair inducement to persuade him to play for Spurs and misconduct. Despite an appeal, Spurs were suspended for two weeks and Payne for one.

The conduct of Fulham and the London FA to the whole business was typical of the short-sighted and petty-minded attitude that had already left football in London trailing in the wake of the Lancashire clubs, who had openly adopted professionalism. The southern authorities seemed more interested in keeping clubs under their control and petty infractions of out-dated rules than developing the game. While the decision thrust Spurs into the limelight, with the public and sporting press supporting them far more than the authorities, the decision festered with Spurs for two years and eventually led to the momentous decision to pay their players.

Payne, meanwhile, became a regular for Spurs as the publicity the 'Payne's Boots Affair' generated led to an increased level of interest in the club. He did not completely throw in his lot with Spurs until February 1894, but when he did he announced his permanent arrival with four goals in a 5–1 defeat of Polytechnic and finished the season with eight goals in 10 appearances. His new-found fame soon saw him playing for London and Middlesex.

As Payne developed an understanding with Jimmy Eccles and Peter Hunter, his fast-raiding play from either wing and smart finishing became a crucial element of Spurs' game.

Spurs were really beginning to make a name for themselves now. They entered the FA Cup for the first time in 1894–95 and got through to the fourth qualifying round before going out to Luton Town in a replay and fared even better in the FA Amateur Cup. Their first venture into the competition had come to a swift end after only one game because their London FA suspension coincided with their next fixture, but in 1894–95 they battled through to the second round proper before meeting their match in the Old Carthusians.

When the decision was taken in December 1895 to turn professional, Payne was one of the players who decided to take up the offer of paid football. He was almost ever present throughout Spurs' first season of Southern League football, one of the few pre-professional players still in the first team and out-scored only by Bob 'Topsy' Clements.

The arrival of Frank Brettell as Spurs' first manager saw wholesale changes to the playing staff in the summer of 1897. Among the signings was David Black, a former Scottish international who scored for Wolverhampton Wanderers in the 1896 FA Cup Final. Vastly more experienced and, frankly, a better player than Payne, he rarely missed a game.

Payne was to make few more senior appearances but he had, albeit perhaps unwittingly, done his bit to help Spurs' progress from being local amateurs to a team of national prominence. He continued to turn out for the reserves until March 1898, when a knee injury forced him out of top-level football.

PERRYMAN, Stephen John MBE (1969–90)

Midfield or defender, 5ft 8in, 10st 10lb

Born: Ealing, West London, 21 December 1951

Signed from apprentice, January 1969

Transferred to Oxford United, March 1986, £50,000

Also played for: Oxford United, Brentford, England

Spurs record:

Debut: 27 September 1969 v Sunderland (FL) (h) lost 0–1

Appearances: League 654(2), FA Cup 69, League Cup 66, Europe 63(1), others 162(5)*

*(*Includes one abandoned match)*

Goals: League 31, FA Cup 2, League Cup 3, Europe 3, others 12

■ In their 125-year history, Spurs have had some of the world's most talented and exciting footballers, some of the greatest names in the game, but never have they had a more loyal, reliable or self-sacrificing player than Steve Perryman. In almost 17 seasons in the first team he missed no more than a handful of games, setting standards of consistency and a number of appearances that will never be beaten.

Perryman joined Spurs straight from school in 1967, having been the club's guest at the 1967 FA Cup Final. Little more than two years later he was playing alongside many of the stars he had watched at Wembley and did not look out of place.

An all-action dynamo, Perryman was originally called up in September 1969 to add bite and aggression to a midfield that had the skills but needed someone to win the ball. Closing down opponents and snapping into the tackle, he performed the job admirably, breaking up attacks before they threatened and laying the ball off simply and quickly to the likes of Alan Mullery and Martin Peters.

After 20 or so games Perryman was rested, but results took a turn for the worse and he was recalled, never to be left out again unless injured – as indispensable a player as it was possible to have.

Perryman won his first trophy as a member of the team that lifted the Football League Cup in 1971, his scurrying back to clear Andy Lochead's effort off the line with the scores level a perfect example of his never giving up, even when the cause looked hopeless.

Perryman's ceaseless hard work, willingness to give all for the team and refusal to accept defeat were what caught the eye most, but there was far more to his game. He was a gifted playmaker in his own right, playing tidy, concise passes and with the vision to spot and play the killer pass at just the right moment. He was never a prolific scorer but could always be relied upon to chip in one or two goals a season, usually crucial ones such as the two half volleys he struck from the edge of the box to overcome AC Milan in the first leg of the 1972 UEFA Cup semi-final.

After the UEFA Cup success of 1972, Perryman won his first England Under-23 cap and looked set for a long international career, but despite winning the League Cup in 1973, Spurs were on a downward slope. With Perryman taking over the captaincy following Peters's departure, he found himself holding together a team fighting relegation.

In a desperate attempt to avoid the drop, Keith Burkinshaw moved Perryman to the centre of defence. His lack of inches meant he was not the strongest in the air, but he made up for that with his shrewd positional play, natural reading of the game and ability to organise those around him. The position also gave him more time on the ball, allowing him to see the whole game and spark attacks from deeper positions. Operating alongside Keith Osgood, he brought an air of composure and assurance to the back line but it was not enough to keep Spurs up. Few would have blamed Perryman had he decided to leave, but he showed his loyalty and led Spurs back to the First Division at the first attempt.

The emergence of Graham Roberts saw Perryman move to full-back for the most successful period of his career. Still sprightly, pushing forward at every opportunity and creating chances from out wide, he captained Spurs to FA Cup success in 1981 and 1982, and the 1982 League (Milk) Cup Final.

In June 1982, the Football Writers' Association's Player of the Year, Perryman at last added an England cap to his 17 Under-23 caps when he played against Iceland.

Perryman continued to give everything for Spurs for another four years and collected a UEFA Cup-winners' medal in 1984. He only played in the first leg of the Final as he was suspended for the second, but such was the esteem in which he was held by teammates that Ossie Ardiles insisted Perryman should have his medal.

A truly great professional, Perryman's Spurs career came to an end in March 1986. He joined Oxford United, played there for two months and then managed Brentford and Watford, before returning to White Hart Lane as assistant manager to Ardiles in July 1993.

Sadly he was not to enjoy the same success as a coach. Although he appreciated Ardiles's dream of building a great attacking team in the best traditions of Spurs, he knew a solid defensive base was essential but was unable to influence Ardiles enough. When Ardiles was sacked, Perryman took over for one game but was then dismissed himself.

PETERS, Martin Stanford MBE (1969–75)

Midfield, 5ft 11in, 11st 10lb

Born: Plaistow, East London, 8 November 1943

Signed from West Ham United March 1970, £200,000

Transferred to Norwich City, March 1975, £50,000

Also played for: West Ham United, Norwich City, Sheffield United, Gorleston Town, England

Spurs record:

Debut: 21 March 1970 v Coventry City (FL) (h) lost 1–2

Appearances: League 189, FA Cup 16, League Cup 23, Europe 32, others 28

Goals: League 46, FA Cup 5, League Cup 12, Europe 13, others 11

■ When Sir Alf Ramsey described Martin Peters as being '10 years ahead of his time', he burdened one of England's 1966 World Cup heroes with a label he was never able to shake off. It was an invitation for the wags on the terraces to unleash their sarcastic humour, but for anyone who watched Peters for any length of time it was an apt description of a consummate professional footballer, a player with such fine football skills that no matter what age he played in, no matter what fancy formation might be employed, he would embellish the game with subtlety and style.

Spurs supporters were privileged to watch Peters at the peak of his career, although there were many who only realised just how good and important to the team he was once he had departed.

A product of the West Ham Academy, Peters began his career as an orthodox wing-half, shuttling back and forth between penalty boxes, supporting his inside-forward and full-back. As football changed he developed into the complete midfield player, working back inside his own box, supporting his strikers and weighing in with more than his fair share of goals.

A member of West Ham's European Cup-winners' Cup-winning team of 1965, he made his England debut in May 1966 in the warm-up games for the World Cup Finals and played in all bar the first match of the tournament, scoring in the Final with West Germany.

His West Ham colleagues Bobby Moore, the England captain, and Geoff Hurst, the hat-trick hero of the Final, became lauded as the stars of the tournament, and Peters, undoubtedly the more reserved and private of the three, was often left in the shadows. It was not something he complained of, in fact he probably preferred it that way, but he was the more ambitious of the trio, and when he decided West Ham's ambitions did not match his own, he made his feelings known.

Bill Nicholson was an admirer of Peters, and when he heard Peters wanted a move to a club more geared to winning trophies he was quick to move in with a record £200,000 offer. It was a difficult deal for Nicholson. West Ham demanded Jimmy Greaves in part-exchange. It was not easy for Nicholson to release England's greatest goalscorer, but in Peters he saw an experienced player who could create and score goals and still had youth on his side.

Peters was signed just before deadline day in March 1970 and made his debut against Coventry City. It was not an easy game for Peters, replacing a man who was a hero to so many, but, although Spurs lost, Peters signed on with a typical headed goal.

He settled quickly to the Spurs style, adding a beautiful, silky touch to the build-up play. Elegant in everything he did, Peters's technical skills were beyond question, but what was not always noticed was the amount of hard work he put in, covering the pitch from one end to the other. He had great vision and fine appreciation of space, appearing from nowhere with perfectly-timed runs into the danger area. With an ability to time his leaps to perfection and a spring that took him even higher than might be expected from his near six foot, ghosting in with late blindside runs became his trademark.

Peters developed a perfect understanding with Martin Chivers and Alan Gilzean, the three of them being particularly strong in the air and the Chivers long throw to the near post, flicked on by Gilzean and headed home by Peters, a well-known but impossible to stop ploy.

Peters's ambitions to collect silverware were fulfilled at White Hart Lane with the Football League Cup in 1971 followed by the UEFA Cup in 1972. He was the natural choice to take over the captaincy when his former England colleague Alan Mullery left for Fulham, and he captained Spurs to the League Cup victory in 1973 and the 1974 UEFA Cup Final.

An England regular, Peters won 34 caps as a Spurs player but, following the departure of Bill Nicholson and the arrival of the brash young Terry Neill, found himself one of the victims of Neill's over eagerness to make his mark. He had given Spurs five years of great service and could have gone on to give many more, but Neill decided to sweep away the old hands.

Peters was moved on to Norwich City for a bargain £60,000. They got six years invaluable service from him before he finished his playing career with Sheffield United, taking his total of League outings to over 700.

He returned to Spurs in August 1998 and for four years was director responsible for supporter liaison, as elegant and stylish as he had been as a player.

PRATT, John Arthur (1969–86)

Midfield, 5ft 8in, 10st 3lb

Born: Hackney, East London, 26 June 1948
Signed from amateur, November 1965
Transferred to Portland Timbers, free
Also played for: Portland Timbers

Spurs record:

Debut: 24 March 1969 v Arsenal (FL) (a) lost 0–1
Appearances: League 307(24), FA Cup 23(5), League Cup 27(4), Europe 24(1), others 81(11)
Goals: League 39, FA Cup 2, League Cup 7, Europe 1, others 15

■ It is strange how football fans whinge and whine at the most gifted of players when they appear to lack commitment but forgive all when they see one bit of magic, yet they slaughter those who may not have an over-abundance of skill but give their all for every minute of every game.

John Pratt was not the greatest of footballers, he would not claim to be, but he was a player totally committed to Spurs, a player who, in today's parlance, 'played for the shirt'. Sadly, there were those who claimed to be Spurs supporters that never got off his back. Fortunately, for those who did appreciate his qualities, he never let his detractors get the upper hand.

Former Spurs winger Terry Medwin spotted Pratt playing for Brentford's youth team and recommended him to Spurs. Initially a centre-half, Pratt never grew big enough to fill that berth, but height and build were not so important at wing-half and Pratt soon moved to that position.

He signed professional for Spurs in May 1965 and made his debut at Highbury in March 1969, playing alongside Peter Collins as Spurs were hit by injuries to Mike England and Phil Beal. Ray Evans also made his debut and the two youngsters did remarkably well in a makeshift defence, only a thunderous strike from well outside the box giving Arsenal the points. Pratt played most of the remaining games that season but in the new season found himself on the fringes of the first team.

It was only following the abysmal FA Cup exit to Crystal Palace that Pratt got another real chance. Bill Nicholson reacted angrily to the defeat, considering some of the established players were taking things too easy. He dropped Alan Gilzean, Jimmy Greaves, Joe Kinnear and Cyril Knowles, replacing them with some of the youngsters. Pratt was given Greaves's number-eight shirt, but he had to step down with the arrival of Martin Peters.

Pratt continued to work away and eventually got his reward with a regular place in the starting line up following Alan Mullery's return to Fulham, only to sustain an injury in the first 20 minutes of the 1973 Football League Cup Final with Norwich City. Small consolation came in the 1974 UEFA Cup Final when he played in both legs.

The mid-70s to the end of the decade was not the best of times for Spurs, but things would have been a lot worse were it not for Pratt's performances. No matter how much criticism he came in for he never hid, he was always leading from the front, not afraid to exhort to greater effort those with more skill or honours than he. One thing he could not abide was gifted players not prepared to put in the hard work that would allow their skills to flourish.

Pratt himself worked ceaselessly and gave everything he had. Whether it was snapping into a tackle, hustling back to cover in defence or tearing forward to support the attack, he never stopped trying. There were occasions when he got things terribly wrong, normally when he tried to do too much, but at other times he surprised with what he could do, a defence-splitting pass or instant exchange of one-twos to carve out an opening.

Often overlooked are the goals Pratt contributed: a stunning, swerving 25-yarder against Wolverhampton Wanderers in the first leg of the League Cup semi-final in December 1972, a delicate lob to secure three points at Coventry City in February 1973. There were many more. Pratt was only outscored by John Duncan in the 1975–76 season.

Pratt did not take kindly to Spurs' relegation in 1977, but the Second Division campaign that followed was one of his best. Ever present, he contributed seven goals, his two edge-of-the-box volleys at Notts County in January 1978 being particularly memorable.

Back in the First Division he found his place taken by Ricky Villa as the season got under way, but he was recalled after the 0–7 drubbing at Liverpool to add a bit of steel to midfield. Without Pratt doing the dirty work, Ossie Ardiles and Glenn Hoddle would not have been half as effective.

Reaching his 30s, Pratt was released in May 1980 and spent three years with Portland Timbers before returning to Spurs as youth-team coach. Elevated to reserve-team coach, he moved up to assistant manager under Peter Shreeve, until the pair of them were dismissed in May 1986.

Pratt is still a regular at White Hart Lane, working on the hospitality side, a friendly, approachable man who is perhaps more appreciated now than when he was playing.

RAMSEY, Sir Alfred Ernest (1949–55)

Full-back, 5ft 10in, 11st 6lb

Born: Dagenham, Essex
22 January 1920
Died: Ipswich, Suffolk, 28 April 1999
Signed from Southampton, May 1949, £21,000
Also played for: Southampton, England

Spurs record:

Debut: 20 August 1949 v Brentford (FL) (a) won 4–1
Appearances: League 226, FA Cup 24, others 33
Goals: League 24, others 6

■ Alf Ramsey was responsible for the introduction of a new phrase into football's

dictionary: 'the cultured full-back'. Until Ramsey came on the scene, full-backs had, with notable exceptions such as Tommy Clay, been men whose job was simply to defend, to dispossess their opponent and, unless a simple pass was on, kick the ball as far as possible. It mattered not whether that meant into row Z or to the other end of the field, so long as it was away from the danger area they had done their job. Ramsey changed all that.

Although an Essex boy, he first made his name in Hampshire. Serving in the army, he played centre-half for his battalion in a pre-season practice match against Southampton in 1943. His team lost 1–10, but a week later they beat Southampton's reserves 4–1 and the Saints had seen enough to invite Ramsey to sign amateur forms. Within a year he was a professional.

In those wartime games Ramsey usually played centre-half, sometimes centre-forward, but eventually settled at right-back, wresting the position from England's Bill Ellerington. Ramsey played for England B and the Football League before winning his first full cap against Switzerland in December 1948, but early in 1949 injury let Ellerington back in. At 29 Ramsey could not afford reserve-team football and asked for a transfer.

Ever since the war, Joe Hulme had been quietly assembling a talented squad at Spurs. He had been keen to sign Ramsey but all approaches had been rebuffed. When Arthur Rowe replaced Hulme he had better luck, but it took £21,000, a record for a full-back, to persuade Southampton to let Ramsey leave.

Ramsey was the last piece of Hulme's jigsaw. Whether Spurs would have had the same success under Hulme as they were to have under Rowe will never be known, but what is certain is that Ramsey was everything Rowe believed a full-back should be, and the perfect man to put Rowe's theories on how the game should be played into practice.

Almost ever present from his debut in August 1949 through to March 1955, Ramsey was one of the true stars of the 'Push and Run' side that captivated football on their way to the Second Division title in 1950 and then stunned the game as the League Championship was secured a year later.

Not for Ramsey was the hurried clearance of his contemporaries. Everything he did was calm and meticulous, his thinking so advanced he knew what he was going to do with the ball not the next time he got it but the time after that. Nicknamed 'the General', he commanded Spurs from the back, taking control of situations and dictating the play.

He knew as well as Rowe that possession was all-important, simple short passing being the way to retain it. He developed the ploy of moving into space when Ted Ditchburn got the ball, making himself available for a throw rather than leaving Ditchburn to launch the ball forward and probably give it away. Even before receiving the ball Ramsey had decided what he was going to do with it and would execute his pass to perfection. Whether over five yards or 25 yards, his passes were accurate to the inch and played so carefully his teammate would always have instant control.

Ramsey applied the same philosophy to taking penalties. Instead of blasting the ball he always placed it just out of the 'keeper's reach. It made him one of the most successful penalty takers of his time.

While not the quickest of defenders, not the strongest, not the tightest marker and not fast on the turn, Ramsey had a studied approach to the game, using this to develop a positional sense that cut out danger before weaknesses could be exposed.

After winning the League title in 1951 and finishing runners-up the following year, the 'Push and Run' side's ambition was to take Spurs to Wembley for the first time. They got as close as the semi-final in 1953 when, with only seconds to go and drawing 1–1 with Blackpool, Ramsey dispossessed Bill Perry. He had the time and space to hit the ball to any corner of the ground but instead tried to play it back to Ditchburn, slipped and let in Jackie Mudie for the winner. It was gutting, but Ramsey said he would have tried the same pass again. For him, it was the only way to play football.

Ramsey won 31 caps as a Spurs player, captained Spurs following Ron Burgess's departure and led England in the absence of Billy Wright. A great thinker on the game, he left Spurs in August 1955 to manage Ipswich Town and, after taking them from the Third Division North to the Football League title, led England to their greatest football achievement in 1966.

ROBERTS, Graham Paul (1979–88)

Defender or midfield, 5ft 10in, 12st 12lb

Born: Southampton, Hampshire, 3 July 1959

Signed from Weymouth, May 1980, £35,000

Transferred to Rangers, December 1986, £450,000

Also played for: Dorchester Town, Weymouth, Rangers, Chelsea, West Bromwich Albion, Enfield, Slough Town, Stevenage Borough, Chesham United, England

Spurs record:

Debut: 4 October 1980 v Stoke City (FL) (sub) (a) won 3–2

Appearances: League 200(9), FA Cup 27, League Cup 24(1), Europe 25(1), others 81(6)

Goals: League 23, FA Cup 2, League Cup 5, Europe 5, others 10

■ Graham Roberts is the perfect example of a player rejected by professional clubs who never gave up hope and eventually reached the heights.

Released by Southampton, AFC Bournemouth and Portsmouth, Roberts played for Dorchester Town before moving on to Weymouth. It was while with the Alliance League club that Bill Nicholson got talking to a football fan at Swindon railway station, who expressed the view that Roberts was Weymouth's best young player.

Nicholson was quick to follow up the lead and obviously shared the stranger's view, persuading Keith Burkinshaw to move for Roberts in May 1980. West Bromwich Albion were also interested, but £20,000 and a game at Weymouth were enough to secure Roberts's transfer. With the friendly worth up to £15,000, the transaction was a record for non-League football. For Spurs, it was an absolute bargain.

Within 12 months the former shipyard fitter's mate was a cult hero, spitting out two teeth at Wembley after a kick in the mouth from Chris Hughton and helping Spurs lift the FA Cup.

Roberts's progress was quite astounding. He made only a few, brief substitute appearances before his full League debut at Anfield in December 1980, replacing injured Paul Miller in central-defence. Tough and combative, his obvious lack of fear made an immediate impression.

Initially Roberts played anywhere across the back line, but it was soon apparent his best position was in the centre, alongside Miller. The two of them formed a fearsome partnership, not the prettiest in pure footballing terms, but hard, physical and effective. They played a big part in taking Spurs to the 1981 FA Cup Final, particularly in the sixth-round tie with Exeter City. The West Country team were proving stubborn opposition until first Roberts and then Miller showed Spurs' attacking stars how to score.

Winning the FA Cup in his first season was a fairytale for Roberts, although a week before the Final his participation looked in doubt. Caught by a stray Cyrille Regis elbow, he was knocked out for a full five minutes and carried from The Hawthorns pitch, but it would have taken a lot more to deprive him of his big day.

Roberts had come a long way in a short time, but there were still setbacks to endure. Midway through 1981–82 he was pushed into midfield to provide steel and ball-winning qualities, a move that gave Paul Price a run alongside Miller. Roberts was unable to get his old place back and missed the Football League (Milk) Cup Final, but with Ossie Ardiles's return to Argentina for World Cup preparations, Roberts resumed his midfield role. He scored an amazing hat-trick against Southampton in December 1981 before settling down as the midfield strongman. Not that Roberts contented himself with defensive work. He loved to push forward and have a crack at goal, and it was his unexpected run at the heart of the Queen's Park Rangers defence in the 1982 FA Cup Final replay, ended by Tony Currie's foul, that set up the Glenn Hoddle penalty, by which Spurs retained the trophy.

Roberts missed the start of the following season due to injury, but once fit he resumed his partnership with Miller and took his career a step further with his first England cap in May 1983.

In defence or midfield, Roberts could be relied on for whole-hearted endeavour. Whether facing one of the top strikers, competing with football's midfield hard men or hurling himself into a crowded penalty area in search of a goal, it was the same. He went in hard for the ball, prepared to hand out a few knocks and take them in return.

The peak of Roberts's Spurs career came in May 1984 when, with Steve Perryman suspended, he was handed the captaincy for the second leg of the UEFA Cup Final against Anderlecht. On a night when Spurs struggled against the Belgians, Roberts lifted himself to new heights and dragged his weary teammates with him. It was Roberts who grabbed the vital equaliser six minutes from the end of normal time, brushing aside friend and foe to get to the ball first, then stepping forward to lash home the crucial first spot-kick.

Roberts stayed with Spurs for another two years, the tough centre of a team that at last began to look as if it might lift the League title, until the arrival of David Pleat. He signed Richard Gough and made it clear his plans for Spurs did not include Roberts.

A transfer to Rangers followed, where he enjoyed the same cult status he had at Spurs until falling out with manager Graeme Souness. Roberts returned to England with Chelsea and later played for West Bromwich Albion before starting a varied and eventful managerial career.

ROWE, Arthur Sydney (1930–38)

Centre-half, 5ft 9in, 12st 8lb

Born: Tottenham, North London, 1 September 1906
Died: Norbury, South London, 5 November 1993
Signed from amateur, May 1929, Retired, April 1939
Also played for: Cheshunt, Northfleet United, England

Spurs record:

Debut: 10 October 1931 v Burnley (FL) (h) won 2–1
Appearances: League 182, FA Cup 19, others 9

■ Alongside Bill Nicholson and Steve Perryman, Arthur Rowe is rightly regarded as one of the most loyal servants Spurs have ever had. Born little more than a goal-kick from White Hart Lane, he was a Spurs fan from the time he was first able to squeeze under a turnstile to the end of his days. Playing for and managing the club were not jobs to him, they were an honour.

Taken under Spurs' wing at 15, he signed as an amateur in 1923, played for the nursery clubs at Cheshunt and Northfleet, and joined the White Hart Lane staff in May 1929.

It was two years before he made his League debut. Manager Percy Smith was under a lot of pressure with rumours of his imminent dismissal and made seven changes for Burnley's visit in October 1931. Alf Messer, a bruiser of a centre-half, had missed a game with illness but his replacement, Tommy Cable, had been poor. Rowe was given his chance and gave a creditable performance. His inexperience showed but a 1–1 draw was an improvement on what had gone before.

Messer returned but had not fully recovered, and Rowe was recalled, keeping his place even when Messer was fully fit. Messer was a strong, hard-tackling defender, who used his height and strength to great effect, but only in marking his opponent and getting the ball away from his area. He was purely destructive. Rowe was totally different, a footballing centre-half who believed in playing his way out of trouble. In some respects he was a throwback to the early years of the

century when centre-halves had been true half-backs, not out and out defenders whose only concern was to stop goals.

As the season progressed, Rowe improved immensely, growing in confidence and adding a touch of class to an ever-changing back line. The critics still had plenty to moan about, but Rowe was exempt from their acidic comments.

Smith's rebuilding job came to fruition in 1932–33, despite a wobble in the last few games. Rowe missed only one match as Spurs at last escaped the Second Division, finishing second to Stoke City.

Back in the top flight Rowe looked every bit the cultured footballing centre-half: cool, confident, always trying to play constructively, never hacking the ball away but looking to start attacks with controlled football from defence. He collected an England cap against France at White Hart Lane in December 1933 as Spurs finished the season in third place, a far cry from the shambolic outfit when he had made his debut.

The future for Rowe and Spurs looked promising, but 1934–35 was a disaster from start to finish, one injury after another devastating the team. Rowe was crucial to holding things together, but when he was injured in December 1934 the team collapsed, with relegation a certainty long before the season ended.

Although Rowe was fit to return at the start of the following season, he was never the same player again, in and out of the team as one injury after another took its toll. A cartilage problem proved the final straw. It took him a full season to recover from an operation to correct it, but he had suffered so much muscle wastage that in April 1939 he decided it was time to retire.

He took to coaching, destined to return to Spurs and breathe new life not only into the club he had graced as a player but into English football in general.

SEED, James Marshall (1919–27)

Inside-forward, 5ft 10in, 11st 9lb

Born: Blackhill, Co Durham, 25 March 1895
Died: Farnborough, Kent, 16 July 1966
Signed from Mid-Rhondda, February 1920
Transferred to Sheffield Wednesday, August 1927
Also played for: Whitburn, Sunderland, Mid-Rhondda, Sheffield Wednesday, England

Spurs record:

Debut: 5 April 1920 v Wolverhampton Wanderers (FL) (a) won 3–1
Appearances: League 229, FA Cup 25, others 31
Goals: League 65, FA Cup 12, others 8

■ The German gassing of British trenches during World War One was responsible for the deaths of thousands of troops and deeply affected many more young men for the rest of their lives. One of those to suffer was Jimmy Seed, fortunately not too severely, but enough to make Sunderland decide it was doubtful he would be able to resume a promising career that had seen him score 80 goals in one season for Whitburn before joining the Roker club.

Invited to play for Mid-Rhondda, he secured a free transfer from Sunderland and was soon pulling the strings in their midfield, no ill effects from the gas attack apparent.

Spurs manager Peter McWilliam had been tipped off about the promise of Ton Pentre's 'Darkie' Lowdell. He went to watch Lowdell in a match against Mid-Rhondda in February 1920, but so taken was he by Seed's performance that it was Seed, not Lowdell, he immediately signed for Spurs.

Spurs were romping away with the Second Division title with a team that seemed unbeatable, but McWilliam recognised there was always room for improvement. Seed played a few games in the reserves before being elevated to the League XI and certainly brought something different to Spurs' play. Jimmy Banks had been playing inside-right. He was a direct player, getting the ball, heading for goal, and not always appreciating he had other players around him.

Seed was more a linkman, taking the ball off his defenders, looking round and seeking out colleagues in a better position than he. If none were available he had no fear of keeping the ball, more than competent at dribbling past his man and opening play up before seeking to pass.

Along with Arthur Grimsdell and Jimmy Dimmock, he was one of the truly-outstanding stars of the team that lifted the FA Cup in 1921,

forever probing and looking for the weak link in a defence. It was unfortunate Fanny Walden was injured early in the Cup run, for he and Seed had quickly developed a fine understanding, often indulging in a game of 'keep ball' as the two of them inter-passed down the wing with neat one-twos before remembering there were others waiting to join in. On the slippery Stamford Bridge surface the pair would have had a field day.

Seed's outstanding performance for Spurs that day led to him being selected for England against Belgium in May 1921, the first of five caps he was to win as a Spurs player.

Spurs followed the FA Cup success of 1921 by finishing runners-up in the First Division a year later, but after that they spent the rest of the early 20s pottering along in mid-table. Throughout that time Seed masterminded the Spurs attack, developing an almost telepathic understanding with Grimsdell, not only linking with the captain as they pushed the team forward but covering for him when Grimsdell's forward sorties sometimes left him out of position.

With his shrewd tactical brain, almost every attacking move flowed through Seed with him often on the end of them. His passing and creation of chances for others were well known but he was no slouch at finishing off moves as well. He scored 17 goals in 1920–21, 13 in 1921–22 and an incredible 19 in 1924–25. Seed could finish in whatever fashion most appropriate, passing the ball home from close range, blasting it from distance or getting on the end of a well-placed cross with a powerful header.

He seemed set for several more years of service to Spurs when he sustained a serious ankle injury late in 1926. It gave young Taffy O'Callaghan the chance to stake a claim to the main creative role in the team and he did so well manager Billy Minter decided to let Seed leave when Sheffield Wednesday made an approach in August 1927. Lowdell joined Spurs as part of the deal but the decision must rank alongside the departure of Pat Jennings as one of the worst made by Spurs.

Near the end of 1927–28 Spurs were seventh and Wednesday bottom of the table, seemingly doomed. As Spurs slumped, Wednesday, with Seed captain, staged a miraculous late run. While Spurs were relegated, Wednesday stayed up and while Spurs languished in the Second Division, Seed led Wednesday to successive League titles.

When he finished playing, Seed went into management with Clapton Orient before managing Charlton Athletic for 23 years, helping them achieve so much that one of the stands at The Valley still bears his name.

SHERINGHAM, Edward Paul (1992–97 and 2001–03)

Striker, 6ft, 12st 8lb

Born: Highams Park, 2 April 1966
Signed from Nottingham Forest, August 1992, £2,100,000
Transferred to Manchester United, August 1997, £3,500,000
Signed from Manchester United, May 2001, free
Transferred to Portsmouth, July 2003, released
Also played for: Millwall, Aldershot, Djurgaarden (Sweden), Nottingham Forest, Manchester United, Portsmouth, West Ham United, England

Spurs record:

Debut: 30 August 1992 v Ipswich Town (FL) (a) drew 1–1
Appearances: League 230 (6), FA Cup 21, FL Cup 20 (1), others 30(1)*
*(*Includes one abandoned match)*
Goals: League 97, FA Cup 14, FL Cup 13, others 20

A £2.1 million signing from Nottingham Forest, Teddy Sheringham was one of those players just born to wear the white shirt of Spurs. An artist of delicate talents, he brought to Spurs and England a new dimension in centre-forward play, a goalscorer as recognised for his ability to create openings for others as he was for applying the finishing touch himself.

Sheringham started his career with Millwall, scoring 111 goals in eight seasons to make him their record scorer before moving to Nottingham Forest in July 1991. At Millwall he had learned to take care of himself in the hard, physical world of long-ball football, with Forest he had to adapt to the passing style demanded of Brian Clough's sides. He found the target regularly for Forest, but when Terry Venables offered him the opportunity to sign for the club he had supported as a boy Sheringham had no hesitation in agreeing the move. It was a transfer that was to have long-term repercussions for Venables and Clough, with allegations of cash bungs in brown paper bags leading to an FA investigation.

Millwall and Forest had relied heavily on Sheringham's scoring knack for the bulk of their goals. When he arrived at Spurs in August 1992 those talents were desperately needed, as Spurs had only scored twice in their opening four League games. As Sheringham settled in the goals began to flow, and by the end of the season he had netted 21 for Spurs, with a single for Forest making him the Premiership's top scorer, and won his first England cap against Poland, but it was not just his scoring that caught the eye. Dropping deep, he linked midfield and attack, creating as many goals as he scored.

With the departure of Venables and the arrival of Ossie Ardiles with his passion for attacking football, Sheringham was expected to flourish, but while Spurs struggled at the wrong end of the table he could only look on as injury

left him on the sidelines. He played in just 21 games but still scored 15 goals to lead Spurs' scoring chart.

When Jurgen Klinsmann was signed, much of the goalscoring burden was lifted from Sheringham's shoulders, and he was given more freedom to show the full range of his talents. He struck up an immediate and highly-productive rapport with the German captain, dropping deep to utilise the space between midfield and attack that defenders hate to stray into and displaying a perceptive appreciation of how to unlock defences.

In all he did Sheringham displayed class and a delicate touch, whether it was leaping high to flick the ball on, floating passes out to the wing or finishing with a perfect chip over the 'keeper. Klinsmann prospered beside him and was later to acknowledge Sheringham as the best strike partner he ever had.

Following Klinsmann's departure, Sheringham was paired with Chris Armstrong and responsible for many of the youngster's goals, while with England he formed a devastating partnership with Alan Shearer, his performances in Euro '96 showing that, even at the highest leve, intelligence and skill were just as important as pace and power.

The brightest star at White Hart Lane, it was more than a shock when Sheringham announced in mid 1997 that he wanted to leave. At 31, he was concerned that if he saw out his career with Spurs he would never win a major club honour.

Alex Ferguson recognised Sheringham's unique abilities, paying £3.5 million to sign him as replacement for Eric Cantona. Sheringham did not have the best of first seasons at Old Trafford, as United failed to collect any silverware, but in 1998–99 he played an outstanding part as they secured the Treble, scoring in the FA Cup Final then coming off the bench to grab a last-minute equaliser and set up the injury-time winner in the Champions League Final. Two more Premiership titles were won before Sheringham was released in May 2001.

By then, Glenn Hoddle was in charge at White Hart Lane. Much as he had done at Chelsea, Hoddle wanted experienced, intelligent footballers to help in his quest for immediate success while young players were developed. Sheringham was one of the first he turned to.

At an age when most strikers have retired to nurse their bruises, Sheringham relished his position as the elder statesman of the team, showing he still possessed the same sweet skills even if he found it difficult to keep going for the full 90 minutes. In two years he took his appearances for Spurs past the 250 mark and his goal tally to well over 100, before moving to Portsmouth.

SMITH, Bertram (1916–29)

Half-back, 5ft 7in, 11st 4lb

Born: Higham, Kent, 7 March 1892
Died: Biggleswade, Bedfordshire, September 1969
Signed from Huddersfield Town, August 1919, free
Transferred to Northfleet United, May 1930, released
Also played for: Vanbrugh Park, Crawford United, Metrogas, Huddersfield Town, Sheppey United, Young Boys, England

Spurs record:

Debut: 30 August 1919 v Coventry City (FL) (a) won 5–0
Appearances: League 291, FA Cup 28, others 52
Goals: League 9, FA Cup 1, others 3

■ As often happened during the war years, players who might otherwise never have met got to play together in service games and looked to do each other a favour. So it was with Bert Bliss and Bert Smith. Bliss was well established at Spurs when he joined up, but Smith was still pretty much an unknown who had spent two years with Huddersfield Town, mainly in their reserves. They played together during World War One, and as Smith was a Kent boy, and would not be returning to Yorkshire, when on leave Bliss recommended him to Spurs.

Smith made his first appearance for Spurs in December 1916 against Arsenal, but it was not until 1918–19 that he played again. A goalscoring inside-forward with Huddersfield (he had scored 26 goals for their reserves in 1913–14), Spurs were already well served in that position, but Peter McWilliam knew the half-back line needed strengthening. He gave Smith a couple of games at right-half and was impressed enough to arrange his transfer. It was another smart piece of business by McWilliam.

Smith was given a starting place at right-half when the 1919–20 Second Division campaign opened and took to it as if born to the position. With his strength and 90-minute game, he covered acres of ground, clamping down hard on his opposing inside-forward with swift but sure tackling and pushing up with his attack. There was nothing fancy about Smith, he did the simple things but did them to perfection. The international selectors were quick to notice him, and he played in an international trial in February 1920.

He did not win an immediate international call-up, but that may have been due to the fact that when Charlie Rance was injured later that month Smith was moved to centre-half. He looked just as at home there and occupied the role for the rest of the season as Spurs stormed away with the Second Division title.

Back in the First Division, Smith returned to his more accepted role and really blossomed with Jimmy Seed in front of him. The pair dovetailed perfectly, with Smith winning the ball and feeding Seed, who knew he could concentrate on opening up defences with Smith sure to be covering for him. Arthur Grimsdell was another who benefitted from Smith's solid reliability. It gave him the confidence to rampage forward, sure in the knowledge that Smith would fill any holes he left behind.

Not that Smith was purely a defensive player. He had excellent ball control, an abundance of skill and relished the chance to join the attack. He may not have scored many goals, but when the chance arose he could still unleash a fearsome shot.

Smith was not the type of player to grab the headlines but a real team player, content to do his job while others received all the attention. His dependability was recognised with two England caps, the first against Scotland in April 1921, just before the FA Cup Final, when he appeared alongside clubmates Bliss, Grimsdell and Jimmy Dimmock.

The 1921 Cup Final saw Smith at his best, as he ploughed his way through the Stamford Bridge mud nullifying all the efforts of the Wolves inside-forwards to get their attack rolling and working ceaselessly to set his own forwards free. Dimmock may have garnered all the glory with his winning goal, but without Smith's mountain of work he would have had few opportunities.

Smith played for the Football League against their Scottish counterparts in February 1922 and won another England cap against Wales the following month, but that was the full extent of his individual honours.

As McWilliam's great side of the immediate post-war years broke up, Smith remained the solid cornerstone of the Spurs team until January 1927, when he lost his place to Harry Skitt. He remained with Spurs until May 1930, making the occasional appearance, and then took up a coaching role with the nursery club at Northfleet.

Following a brief spell at Sheppey United, Smith coached the Young Boys club in Switzerland and continued to be involved in football for the rest of his life, working for Harwich and Parkeston, Stevenage Town and Hitchin Town, where he finished his working life as groundsman.

SMITH, Robert Alfred (1955–64)

Centre-forward, 5ft 10in, 12st 11lb

Born: Lingdale, North Yorkshire, 22 February 1933
Died: Enfield, Middlesex, 18 September 2010"
Signed from Chelsea, December 1955, £18,000
Transferred to Brighton & Hove Albion, May 1964, £5,000
Also played for: Redcar United, Chelsea, Brighton & Hove Albion, Hastings United, Banbury United, England

Spurs record:

Debut: 24 December 1955 v Luton Town (FL) (h) won 2–1
Appearances: League 271, FA Cup 32, Europe 14, others 41(1)
Goals: League 176, FA Cup 22, Europe 10, others 43

■ There is a commonly-used term in English football, 'a typical old-fashioned English centre-forward'. For anyone who watched football in the 1950s and 60s, it means a big, bustling striker, hurtling into defenders and goalkeepers like a

human battering ram, bulldozing his way to goal without a care for the pain he was inflicting or suffering.

When the phrase is used in the Spurs context one name springs to mind, that of Bobby Smith. The description is apt but does not really do Smith justice. He was a big, bustling striker, he did bulldoze his way through defences and if there was a chance of scoring he cared not a jot for the risk of injury, but he was much more than that. He was a skilful centre-forward who relied as much on guile and subtlety as sheer-brute strength. He had to be to establish a place in the finest football team the country had produced.

Smith first made his name with Chelsea but was unable to displace a Chelsea legend, Roy Bentley, and when Jimmy Anderson made an approach in December 1955 Smith was languishing in their reserves. At the time Spurs were in dire straits, one place off the bottom of the table and struggling to score. Although his obvious lack of subtlety led some to doubt whether he was a Spurs type of player, his goals helped avoid the drop and almost turned the season right round as the club reached the FA Cup semi-final.

With Danny Blanchflower and Tommy Harmer pulling the strings in midfield and Terry Medwin providing the crosses, Smith embarked on a goal-scoring rampage. In 1957–58 he equalled Ted Harper's Spurs record of 36 League goals in a season, added 57 more in the next two seasons and, at the end of August 1960, celebrated passing George Hunt's record 125 League, and 138 total, goals with a superb hat-trick against Blackpool. The first was a towering header, the second a crashing drive and the third precisely slotted home after controlling the ball and creating room for the shot.

Smith went on to top score in the double-winning side, two goals in the FA Cup semi-final against Burnley seeing him carried off the pitch by jubilant Spurs fans and a deft piece of control, sudden turn on the proverbial sixpence and flashing drive providing the all-important first goal against Leicester City in the Final. Vital as those goals were, his most important of the season probably came in the League match with Sheffield Wednesday, Spurs' only challengers, at White Hart Lane in mid-April 1960. Spurs were expected to clinch the title in style, but Wednesday were not prepared to accept the inevitable without a battle. Their tough tackling upset Spurs' rhythm and they deservedly took the lead with a Don Megson goal. Up against the rugged Peter Swan it was just the type of physical battle Smith relished, but when he struck it was with a combination of craft and power. Terry Dyson beat Swan to a long clearance and headed the ball to Smith. He flicked the ball over Megson's head and hit an unstoppable first-time volley into the roof of the net. A minute later Les Allen grabbed Spurs' second and the title was won.

With the arrival of Jimmy Greaves, much of the goalscoring weight was taken off Smith's broad shoulders. He was still the aggressive spearhead of the attack, but now he could concentrate his strength and commitment on unsettling defences, while Greaves hovered around picking up the pieces. Although not always first choice to partner Greaves, the pair of them formed a devastating partnership, with Greaves the first to admit that much of his success was down to the unselfish work of Smith.

This was particularly so when Spurs sampled European football, Smith's apparent rumbustious style unknown to continental defenders, but concealing a well thought out plan. The uncertainty of what they could expect gave Smith the upper hand even before a match had started, and he was not shy in loudly announcing what a hard time an opponent could expect.

Smith scored Spurs' first goal in the 1962 FA Cup Final and netted four as they marched to European Cup-winners' Cup success in 1963. He garnered 13 in 15 England games, many of them alongside Greaves, but eventually the physical strain he put on his body began to take its toll. Never one to cry off, there were many occasions when he took to the field despite injury, the most well known being the 1961 FA Cup Final when he nipped away from the team hotel on the morning of the match for a pain-killing injection.

After hammering his niche into Spurs' history, Smith departed for Brighton & Hove Albion in May 1964.

STEEL, Daniel (1906–12)

Centre-half, 5ft 9in, 10st 5lb

Born: Newmilns, Ayrshire, 2 May 1884
Died: Marylebone, London,
29 April 1931
Signed from Rangers, May 1906
Transferred to Third Lanark, July 1912
Also played for: Newmilns, Airdrie, Rangers, Third Lanark, Clapton Orient

Spurs record:

Debut: 1 December 1906 v Reading (SL) (h) won 2–0
Appearances: League 131, FA Cup 13, others 67*
*(*Includes three abandoned matches)*
Goals: League 3, others 3

■ Within a couple of months of joining Airdrie, after impressing with his home-town team of Newmilns, Danny Steel had made such a name for himself as a youngster of great potential that he had been signed on by Rangers. Although he played in two junior internationals, his career otherwise came to a full stop with the Scottish giants. Rarely able to get past the reserve team, he made only three senior appearances in two years.

With his prospects in Glasgow poor, he was persuaded to join Spurs in May 1906 but, at first, a reserve place seemed the best he could hope for at White Hart Lane. Steel was recognised as a half-back, but the stalwarts of the 1901 team, Tom Morris and Ted Hughes,

despite getting on, were still more than good enough and Walter Bull was in a class of his own.

Steel had to wait until October 1906 to make his senior debut. It came in a Western League fixture at West Ham United, but it was not a particularly auspicious beginning as Spurs lost 0–5. His Southern League debut did not come until December 1906, and in total he made only 10 first-team appearances in his first season, but he had shown enough with the reserves for Spurs to believe he provided ideal cover for any of the half-back positions and was certainly too good to allow to leave.

Steel's big chance came in November 1907 when Bull suffered a knee injury that was to see him sidelined for some months. Steel stepped up and performed more than creditably. With pace and persistence, he fed his forwards well and, while not as aggressive in attack as Bull, the more he played the more confident he became in getting up to support the front line.

So well did Steel perform that, when Bull was fit to return, Steel initially retained his centre-half role with Bull tried at inside-forward. It was not the ideal position for the highly-influential Bull. He was soon reinstated in the centre of midfield but not at Steel's expense. Steel was shifted to the right, with Tom Morris the unlucky man left out.

When Spurs entered the Football League in 1908–09 Bull was expected to occupy the central half-back position, but the dispute with Notts County over how much Spurs should pay for his Football League registration left him unable to play. Steel really seized the opportunity to make the position his own. With his brother, Bobby, signed to add some creativity from inside-forward, Danny was able to concentrate on what he did best, patrolling the middle of the park, winning the ball and making it available to his forwards.

Appointed captain of the side, Steel exhibited an air of authority in all that he did, a commanding influence with class obvious in every touch of the ball. He could tackle strongly, was always capable of finding time and space, and passed the ball with simple but pinpoint accuracy.

Steel played in every game as Spurs finished their first season in the Football League with promotion from the Second Division as runners-up to Bolton Wanderers. They found life much harder in the First Division but with his simple and effective style, his non-stop running and encouragement of his colleagues, Steel was one of the few players who really looked cut out for the top level.

He missed only two games in 1909–10 but towards the end of the following season found his place coming under threat from the emerging talents of young Charlie Rance. Steel was 5ft 9in and although height was not a pre-requisite for a centre-half in those days it was a useful tool. Rance was over 6ft tall with a bearing that made him seem even taller.

In 1911–12 Steel reverted to right-half, from where he continued to exert his influence on proceedings, but at the end of the season he was released and went back to Scotland with Third Lanark, where he played for two years before returning to London with Clapton Orient.

Steel never collected a representative honour in his time with Spurs. He played for the Anglo-Scots against the Home Scots in three international trials, in 1908, 1910 and 1912, without making the breakthrough, perhaps a victim of the Scottish selectors' reluctance to pick players earning their living South of the border.

STEEL, Robert Loudoun (1908–16)

Inside-forward and centre-half, 5ft 10in, 11st 9lb

Born: Newmilns, Ayrshire, 25 June 1888
Died: Winchmore Hill, North London, 28 March 1972
Signed from Port Glasgow Athletic, June 1906
Released, May 1919
Also played for: Newmilns, Kilwinning, Greenock Morton, Port Glasgow Athletic, Gillingham

Spurs record:

Debut: 1 September 1908 v Wolverhampton Wanderers (FL) (h) won 3–0
Appearances: League 230, FA Cup 19, others 68*
*(*Includes three abandoned matches)*
Goals: League 41, FA Cup 5, others 16

■ The youngest of the three Steel brothers, like his siblings Danny and Alex, Bobby began his career with his home-town club before moving on to greater things, first in Scotland and then down South.

He arrived at Spurs from Port Glasgow Athletic in May 1908 just as Spurs were in the midst of applying for election to the Football League. William Bulloch joined Spurs from Port Glasgow at the same time, and the Scottish club, known as the Undertakers, demanded a £700 transfer fee for the two players, but eventually an Inter-League tribunal fixed the fee at £450. Bulloch never made the first team at White Hart Lane, but Steel went on to give Spurs seven years great service and more than justified the fee on his own.

Making his debut in Spurs' first-ever Football League fixture, against Wolverhampton Wanderers on 1 September 1908, Steel immediately impressed with his mastery of the ball and his penchant for hard work. Like many Scottish inside-forwards of his day, he loved to run with the ball and possessed superb dribbling skills, but unlike many of his contemporaries he also appreciated the advantages of slick passing and quick inter-play.

He quickly developed an understanding with his wing partner Bert Middlemiss and centre-forward Vivian Woodward, the pair of them thriving on the service Steel provided. He created many of the opportunities they capitalised on and weighed in with his fair share of goals, netting 12 as Spurs secured promotion from the Second Division at the first attempt. He missed only one match in that 1908–09 season, having been laid low with flu when he returned to Scotland to play for the Anglo-Scots against the Home Scots in the international trial match. Despite having spent the previous day in bed, he turned out in the trial but was clearly far from well and failed to do himself justice.

With Spurs in the First Division he became one of the club's star performers, week in and week out a model of consistency and reliability, and continued to exert his influence from inside-forward until late in December 1912.

At that time he was injured, but instead of taking time to recover he tried to continue playing in order to impress the newly-appointed manager, Peter McWilliam. It was a bad mistake, for the injury severely affected Steel's performances, and it was no surprise when he was dropped with the emerging Bert Bliss taking his place.

Out of the team for the rest of the season, a reserve role looked the best Steel could hope for, but when Charlie Rance was injured in pre-season training in August 1913, Steel was asked to occupy the centre-half berth previously so well filled by brother Danny. It was expected to be a short-term role, but Rance was so seriously injured he was out for several months.

Fortunately for Spurs, Steel found a new lease of life in the deeper position, displaying defensive qualities that had not been apparent before. He also found the extra space and opportunity to face the play more to his liking and did so well that when Rance recovered he could not get back in the team. Even when Spurs, badly hit by the call to arms, were struggling in 1914–15, Steel added experience and battling qualities to the ultimately-unsuccessful bid to avoid relegation.

With normal football suspended in 1915, Steel's versatility was called upon in the first season of the London Football Combination when he occupied any position needed, playing at centre-forward, outside-left, half-back and even left-back.

After joining the services, Steel was not available to Spurs for the rest of the war. When he returned in 1919 McWilliam decided there was no place for Steel and released him. At first Steel took to refereeing in the Southern League, but in December 1919 his brother, Alex, persuaded him to sign for Gillingham, where he played until the end of the season.

The Steel brothers hold a unique place in Spurs' history. Alex, who had previously played for Newmilns, Ayr United and Manchester City, signed for Spurs in January 1910. When he was called up for his only senior game for Spurs, against Bradford City that month, it was the only time Spurs have ever fielded three brothers in a League game.

TAIT, Alexander Gilchrist (1899–1908)

Full-back, 5ft 9in, 11st 10lb

Born: Glenbuck, Ayrshire, 1873
Died: Croydon, Surrey, 6 April 1949
Signed from Preston North End, May 1899
Released Transferred to Leyton, May 1908

Also played for: Glenbuck Athletic, Ayr, Royal Albert, Rangers, Motherwell, Preston North End, Leyton

Spurs record:

Debut: 2 September 1899 v Millwall (SL) (a) won 3–1

Appearances: Southern League 205, FA Cup 36**, others 177****

*(*Includes one abandoned match, **Includes one abandoned match, ***Includes two abandoned matches)*

*Goals: Southern League 3, others 7*****

*(****Includes one in an abandoned match)*

■ Dave Mackay and Graham Roberts have reputations as being truly-hard football men, but can there ever have been a more fiercesome-looking player than Alexander Tait? The moustachioed Scot was known as one of the toughest full-backs in the game around the turn of the century, a big, strong, imposing character who played the game hard but fairly.

Tait hailed from Glenbuck, a Scottish mining village famed for the number of top-class footballers it produced, and left school as a lad to work down the pit, where he led the ponies. One of 13 children, Tait rapidly progressed from playing for his local team through Ayr, Royal Albert and Rangers to Motherwell, where he came under scrutiny from the English clubs.

Enticed to Preston North End in the summer of 1894, he spent five years in Lancashire building a reputation as one of the best full-backs in the country, but it was after John Cameron had persuaded him to join Spurs in May 1899 that his stock rose to such a level that many a commentator openly regarded him as the best left-back in the country.

From his very first game Tait endeared himself to Spurs' supporters with his whole-hearted commitment and ferocious play. If the ball was there to be won he showed not a moment's hesitation in throwing himself into the challenge, not concerned whether he took his opponent with the ball or risked injuring himself. He was soon dubbed with the nickname 'Terrible Tait', not for any nasty reason but because the sight of him rushing toward an opponent put fear into the bravest of men.

The sliding tackle was a particular forte of Tait's. He would launch himself across the heaviest of surfaces, intent on getting his foot to the ball and not just to put it out of play. Frequently he would hook his foot around the ball and emerge with it under control while some poor opponent got a taste of mud and grass.

Despite his formidable reputation, and obvious relish, for the physical side of the game Tait was not a dirty player. On the contrary, he was regarded as one of the fairest players around. Opponents always knew they were in for a hard game when up against him, but they also knew that, come what may, Tait would play by the rules and spirit of the game. There was no nastiness in his play, and he was never booked throughout his career.

If Tait had one shortcoming it was a lack of pace. Up against a flying winger he could be exposed, but it rarely happened. Tait compensated with a remarkable ability to read the game, to know a split second before anyone else what was going to happen and to get himself in position. It proved particularly useful when his half-back Jack Jones decided to go on one of his attacking forays, for Tait would position himself to cover any threat that might come from the area usually occupied by the Welsh international.

In his first season with Spurs Tait played in every game of the successful Southern League campaign, the only player to do so, and in 1901 played every match of the FA Cup success. In both the Final and the replay Tait did a more than excellent job in keeping Sheffield United's England winger Bert Lipsham quiet, although if a linesman had possessed better eyesight Tait might have been the villain of Spurs' early exit from the competition. In the third-round tie at Reading, Tait did not have one of his better games. With only a few minutes remaining and the score one-all, George Clawley half stopped a Reading shot. As the ball headed for the net, Tait rushed up and punched it away. It was a clear handball, but the referee was unsighted and his linesman convinced Tait had not used his hand.

Although there were times when Tait's high standards slipped and he was left out, he remained the cornerstone of Spurs' defence until 1907–08, when he lost out to another rugged defender, Ollie Burton. At the end of that season he was released and joined Leyton, later managing them and the short-lived Croydon Common.

Despite playing over 400 games for Spurs, Tait only scored seven goals, and three of those came in one game. In January 1901 Spurs entertained a German Association XI. So outclassed were the visitors that by half-time Spurs were 5–0 up. Spurs made wholesale positional changes for the second half, with Tait, his full-back partner Jimmy Melia and goalkeeper David Haddow being played as forwards. Tait grabbed his hat-trick as Spurs, part of the time with Jack Kirwan in goal but often with no one filling the role, went on to win 9–6.

VILLA, Julio Ricardo (1978–88)

Midfield or forward, 6ft, 12st 5lb

Born: Buenos Aires, Argentina, 18 August 1952

Signed from Racing Club, June 1978, £375,000

Transferred to Fort Lauderdale Strikers, June 1983, released

Also played for: Quilmes, Athletico Tucuman, Racing Club, Fort Lauderdale Strikers, Deportivo Cali, Defensa y Justicia, Buenos Aires, Argentina

Spurs record:

Debut: 19 August 1978 v Nottingham Forest (FL) (a) drew 1–1

Appearances: League 124(9), FA Cup 21, League Cup 15(1), Europe 8(1), others 43(2)

Goals: League 18, FA Cup 3, League Cup 3, Europe 1, others 15

■ If ever there was a player who experienced the ups and downs of a footballer's life it was Ricky Villa. In the space of five days the Argentinian went from the despair of forlornly traipsing round the Wembley pitch to the joy of being a hero, the scorer of the greatest goal ever to win an FA Cup Final.

The big, bearded Argentinian joined Spurs in June 1978. Although the most expensive player transferred from one Argentinian club to another, and actually costing Spurs more than his compatriot, he was regarded in some quarters as something of a makeweight in the deal that saw Ossie Ardiles arrive at White Hart Lane. In fact Villa was a superbly-talented footballer in his own right, who many knowledgeable pundits thought might make the greater impact.

In the end, Ardiles did prove the more successful of the two, but Villa will be remembered by many as the man who made their dreams come true.

He began life at White Hart Lane with a bang, scoring on his debut at Nottingham Forest, but he soon fell victim to injury, a problem that was to plague his whole career at Spurs, and the vexed question of how he could best fit into Spurs' system. His favoured position was central-midfield, where he could be involved all the time and support the strikers, but that was the domain of Ardiles and Glenn Hoddle. Out wide he did not possess the pace to take people on and would be out of the game for long spells. He was big enough to cause trouble to any defence if played up front but was not a natural scorer.

The result was that Villa never really settled into one regular position, injuries to others often dictating that he played where he was needed, not where he could be at his best, and frequently occupying the substitutes' bench.

There were times he would be totally anonymous, and others when his abilities shone

out like a beacon. Despite his size and sometimes ponderous style, Villa was a lovely footballer who, while he could use his strength and bulk to his advantage, possessed deceptive skills for such a big man.

At his best he would run at players, the ball under total control, tricking his way through with a sudden switch of the ball from one foot to the other and back again, impossible to dispossess. He had a remarkably-deft touch and unorthodoxy about his play that meant nobody knew what he was going to do next.

Villa played over 120 Football League games for Spurs, but it was the FA Cup that brought out the best out of him and it is his exploits in that competition in 1980–81 for which he will always be remembered.

The competition did not begin well for him, as he limped off in the third-round tie at Queen's Park Rangers with another injury. He did not return until the first semi-final meeting with Wolverhampton Wanderers, but in the replay had one of those nights when he could do no wrong. Garth Crooks scored twice, but it was Villa who controlled the game, crowning his performance with a superb left-foot shot from 25 yards after cutting in from the wing.

As the Final with Manchester City approached, Villa found himself competing with young Garry Brooke for a place in the team. Keith Burkinshaw plumped for the more experienced Villa, but he had a nightmare game, within 70 minutes was replaced by Brooke and cut a sorry sight as he tearfully headed for the dressing room, his big day ruined.

It would have been all too easy for Burkinshaw to have left Villa out of the replay, but his decision to stick by him was vindicated in a fashion none could have imagined. After only seven minutes Villa lashed home a loose ball to put Spurs ahead. The confidence that had flooded out of him five days earlier returned with renewed vigour, but it was another 70 minutes before he won the game with the best individual goal seen at Wembley.

Taking the ball from Tony Galvin on the left, he weaved his way past four defenders, feinted to shoot and then slipped the ball past Joe Corrigan. His dash across the Wembley pitch into the arms of Burkinshaw will be remembered for ever.

Sadly, Villa was never to reach such heights again. Omitted from the 1982 FA Cup Final team because of the Falklands conflict, he left Spurs in June 1983 for Fort Lauderdale Strikers. He may not have had a long and glorious career with Spurs, but his five seconds of pure magic will never be forgotten.

WADDLE, Christopher Roland (1985–89)

Forward, 6ft, 11st 5lb

Born: Gateshead, Tyne and Wear, 14 December 1960

Signed from Newcastle United, July 1985, £590,000

Transferred to Olympique Marseille, July 1989, £4,250,000

Also played for: Tow Law Town, Newcastle United, Olympique Marseille, Sheffield Wednesday, Falkirk, Bradford City, Sunderland, Burnley, Torquay United, England

Spurs record:

Debut: 17 August 1985 v Watford (FL) (h) won 4–0

Appearances: League 137(1), FA Cup 14, League Cup 21, others 41(4)

Goals: League 33, FA Cup 5, League Cup 4, others 11

■ When Chris Waddle bamboozled Graham Roberts before swerving a perfect shot past Ray Clemence to give Newcastle United the lead at White Hart Lane in December 1984, it was obvious the Geordies had unearthed another special talent. Spurs recovered to win that game, but Waddle's performance was so outstanding that Spurs chairman Irving Scholar decided then and there he was determined to add Waddle to the long list of supreme footballers who have embellished Spurs' history.

It was Waddle's first season of top-level football, but he had settled to it like a natural and before the season was over had been selected for England. A local lad, he had replaced Kevin Keegan in the hearts of the Toon Army with his scintillating bursts down the wing, but with his contract coming to an end the powers that be at St James' Park were not prepared to give Waddle the contract he deserved. Feeling unwanted at Newcastle but with Spurs prepared to give him what he wanted, it was not difficult for Scholar to persuade Waddle to make the move to London, the £590,000 fee being set by an FA tribunal.

Waddle's Spurs career started in perfect fashion with two goals against Watford, but it did not continue so well. He struck up an immediate rapport with Glenn Hoddle, but at Newcastle Waddle had been the focal point of the team, whatever system they played. At Spurs, Hoddle was the fulcrum of everything that happened, and Waddle was expected to stick to the left wing. The restrictions often left him on the periphery of the game. Too keen to impress when he did get the ball, he tended to hold on to it for too long, running into blind alleys and losing possession.

It was a frustrating time for Waddle and Spurs supporters. His ability to beat a man in the most confined of spaces, to skip past lunging challenges, to run with the ball at pace with his unique hunched-shoulders style and play the most telling of passes into the danger area were there for all to see, but were seen only in flashes.

He could be devastatingly effective on the wing, a prime example being the way he twisted and turned past the Coventry City defence to set up Clive Allen for the opening goal in the 1987 FA Cup Final, and when played as a striker he showed the coolness and eye for a chance of the most clinical finishers, but Waddle needed to be involved for the entire 90 minutes.

It was the departure of Hoddle for Monaco that gave Waddle the chance to show the full range of his talents, although even then not without its difficulties. Expected to assume the mantle of midfield maestro in 1987–88, injuries held him back and the departure of David Pleat badly affected the whole team in 1987–88. The burden proved too much for Waddle alone to carry.

When Terry Venables assumed control and signed Paul Gascoigne, he allowed Waddle the freedom to go where he felt he could do the most damage. With Gascoigne the centre of attention and dominating midfield, Waddle was able to flourish. His natural winger's talents brought a new dimension to the midfield as he ran at defences from deep, cutting inside or out and bringing his trickery to the most dangerous of areas, the penalty box.

Waddle had won his first England cap in March 1985 and continued to appear regularly for his country, transferring to the international stage the freedom he so enjoyed at White Hart Lane. By the summer of 1989 he was widely regarded as one of the shining lights in the national team, his goal-making and goal-taking talents sure to make him a star of the 1990 World Cup.

Such was his standing that Olympique Marseille offered Spurs £4.5 million for his transfer. It was an enormous fee, surpassed only by those paid for Diego Maradona and Ruud Gullit. Gary Lineker was due to arrive at Spurs and the prospect of Gascoigne and Waddle setting up the chances for England's number-one goalscorer was mouth-watering, but such an offer was too good for Spurs to turn down, particularly in their, as yet undisclosed, financial predicament.

Equally, the chance to set himself up for life and perform regularly in the top European competitions was too good an opportunity for Waddle to pass up. He took his talents to France, helping Marseille win three French titles and reach the European Cup Final, leaving Spurs fans to dream of what might have been.

WALDEN, Frederick Ingram (1912–26)

Winger, 5ft 2in, 8st 9lb

Born: Wellingborough, Northamptonshire, 1 March 1888

Died: Northampton, 3 May 1949

Signed from Northampton Town, April 1913, £1,700

Transferred to Northampton Town, May 1926, released

Also played for: White Cross, All Saints, Wellingborough Redwell Stars, Wellingborough Town, Northampton Town, England

Spurs record:

Debut: 19 April 1913 v Woolwich Arsenal (FL) (h) drew 1–1

*Appearances: League 214, FA Cup 22, others 87**

*(*Includes one abandoned match)*

Goals: League 21, FA Cup 4, others 21

■ At 5ft 2in Fanny Walden was one of the smallest players ever to grace the professional game, and probably the smallest to play for England; however, it was not his lack of stature that secured for him a place in the annals of football history but the wonderful skills he brought to a game that showed size is not all that matters.

Nicknamed 'Fanny' by his schoolmates in Wellingborough after the lady who ran their favourite corner shop, Walden made his name

locally with Wellingborough Town, but it was when he joined Northampton Town that he began to rise to real prominence. Initially he played at inside-forward, then moved to the centre and scored a hat-trick on his debut in that position, but it was soon obvious his most effective position was out on the right wing.

With space to demonstrate his amazing skills, in no time he was proving a big attraction, playing for the Southern League and selected for England against the South in the international trial match of March 1913.

His manager at Northampton had been the legendary Herbert Chapman, and when Chapman joined Leeds City in the summer of 1912 he wanted to take Walden with him. Northampton would not let Walden leave, but Chapman kept making bids, knowing his former club were in dire financial straits and would have to succumb eventually. Such was Walden's popularity that a 'Save Fanny Walden Fund' was started. All sorts of schemes were tried to raise funds, including subscription lists and appeals to shoe and boot manufacturers. Two huge clock faces to show the progress of the fund were erected outside the Town Hall and lemonade bottles with holes in the neck for the insertion of coins were even left all over the town. It all proved in vain. Although £600 was raised, Northampton just could not turn down £1,700 when Spurs manager Peter McWilliam made his move in April 1913.

Never had Spurs laid out more money to sign a player, but from his very first game in a Spurs shirt it was clear why McWilliam, and Chapman, had been so keen to sign the winger. Signed after the transfer deadline, Walden's first game was for the reserves, but the Football League allowed him to make his League debut against Woolwich Arsenal, as the result would have no bearing on the critical relegation issues. In both games he exhibited the magical dribbling skills that so endeared him to football followers.

For the two years prior to the Football League being suspended because of World War One, Walden dazzled with the brilliance of his wing play, displaying a never-ending repertoire of tricks that would have crowds purring as opponents were left chasing shadows. He collected his first England cap in April 1914 and would doubtless have won many more if the war had not intervened and robbed the game of seeing one of its finest wingers during his peak years.

When football got back to normal after the conflict Walden resumed where he had left off, sparkling on Spurs' right wing and creating many of the goals that helped Spurs walk away with the Second Division title in 1919–20.

There seemed nothing Walden could not do with a football at his feet. With a full-back tight on him, he could juggle the ball, while twisting and turning like an eel, before accelerating away; with one who stood off he would feint to go one way or the other, waiting for that instant of commitment, before slipping the ball past his man, hurdling a lunging tackle and regaining possession. It was not unknown for Walden to play the ball one side of a man and run off the pitch, onto the cinder track, and back to avoid a clumsy challenge.

In the 1920 FA Charity Shield meeting with West Bromwich Albion at White Hart Lane, Walden gave a remarkable performance against Jesse Pennington, one of England's finest full-backs. Towards the end of the game Walden made Pennington look such a fool for the umpteenth time that the Baggies star turned to the crowd and threw his arms in the air in genuine surrender.

Desperately unlucky to miss the 1921 FA Cup success because of a cartilage injury, Walden collected another England cap in March 1922, but while he continued to weave his touchline magic until returning to Northampton in May 1926, he was not to win any further honours in his football career.

There were still awards to come though. A useful county cricketer with Northamptonshire throughout his football career, he later became a first-class umpire and stood in 11 Test matches.

WHITE, John Anderson (1959–64)

Inside-forward, 5ft 8in, 10st 8lb

Born: Musselburgh, Midlothian, 28 April 1937
Died: Crews Hill, Middlesex, 21 July 1964
Signed from Falkirk, October 1959
Also played for: Bonnyrigg Rose Athletic, Alloa Athletic, Falkirk, Scotland

Spurs record:

Debut: 17 October 1959 v Sheffield Wednesday (FL) (a) lost 1–2

Appearances: League 183, FA Cup 19, Europe 17, others 14

Goals: League 40, FA Cup 1, Europe 6, others 6

■ For those football fans fortunate enough to have seen him play, hearing of John White's tragic death, struck by lightning while sheltering under a tree from a thunderstorm on an Enfield golf course, was one of those moments when the world stands still. For several minutes, as the awful news sank in, misty pictures of a master craftsman at work flooded forth from the memory.

At only 27 and still far from the peak of his career, White was one of those truly-outstanding footballers for whom no accolade can be too high.

One of the most crucial elements of the double-winning team, White was the man who made the team tick, the conduit through which the grace and style of Danny Blanchflower and Cliff Jones was allied to the power and strength of Dave Mackay and Bobby Smith, to produce a football team unlike any ever seen before.

White joined Spurs for £20,000 in October 1959 from Falkirk, a pale, waif-like inside-forward just beginning to establish himself in the Scotland team. Several English clubs had looked at him but hesitated because of his apparently frail appearance and concerns about his stamina. With both Mackay and Blanchflower recommending White, Bill Nicholson contacted his army sports office (White was doing his National Service at the time), and received confirmation that White was a cross-country runner of some ability. That was enough for Nicholson.

At first White played at inside-left, but, while he chipped in his share of goals, he was not a regular scorer. With the arrival of Les Allen, White moved out to the right wing where he partnered the magical Tommy Harmer. The two of them were similar, both gifted with immaculate ball control and pin-point accuracy in their passing, but while Harmer possessed and displayed a range of tricks that thrilled the crowds, White, with just as many tricks, preferred to play the game simply. While Harmer would juggle with the ball to draw the applause, White would find the killer pass.

Spurs fans did not see the best of White in his early outings. Completing his National Service in Berwick, he was not training with his teammates and facing a 700 mile round trip for home games. When he was able to move down to London the improvement was plain for all to see.

White and Harmer worked well together, but while Nicholson wanted entertainment he knew results were just as important. White had the edge over Harmer in terms of effectiveness, being faster, more direct and happiest moving the ball on with quick passing, while Harmer's love of dribbling tended to slow play down.

Harmer was left out, with White given the number-eight shirt, and as the double season unfolded the wisdom of Nicholson's decision was never in doubt. With his perfect balance, incisive passing and ceaseless promptings, White made the whole team operate smoothly. He was not an eye-catching player or one for the spectacular, but as the ball hit the back of the net a quick analysis of the move that had led to the goal would invariably show White had been involved somewhere along the line.

Short or long, his passes were inch perfect. He could run with the ball at pace, shielding it from an opponent until the precise second came to release it. When he wanted to he could catch a defender's attention with a decoy run, opening up space for a teammate, but when he did not want to be seen he had the uncanny ability to slip into space unnoticed, which earned him the nickname of 'The Ghost'. Perhaps best remembered for the chances he created for others, when he had a sight of goal his shooting was unerringly accurate.

Ever present in the double-winning team, White helped Spurs retain the FA Cup in 1962 and collect the European Cup-winners' Cup in 1963. He took his talents onto the international stage, winning a total of 18 caps as a Spurs player and being one of the few non-Englishmen to represent the Football League.

As Nicholson's great side began to break up, White remained destined to be an integral part of the new team he was building, until Mother Nature intervened. We can never know what might have been, but we do know that for five years White Hart Lane was graced by one of the finest inside-forwards British football ever produced.

WOODWARD, Vivian John (1900–09)

Centre-forward, 5ft 11in, 11st

Born: Kennington, South London, 3 June 1879
Died: Ealing, London, 31 January 1954
Signed as amateur, March 1901
Retired, May 1909
Also played for: Clacton Town, Colchester Town, Harwich & Parkeston, Chelmsford, Chelsea, England

Spurs record:

Debut: 6 April 1901 v Bristol City (SL) (h) won 1–0
Appearances: League 27, FA Cup 24, others 142**
*(*Includes one abandoned match)*
Goals: League 18, FA Cup 5, others 73

■ In the early years of the 20th century there was still a place for amateur footballers at the top level, but they had to be someone special to play alongside hardened professionals. Vivian J. Woodward was not merely such a man, he was also an exceptionally-gifted player held in enormous respect by those who relied on the game for their living.

Woodward began a career that was to reach the heights with Ascham College, but it was when he joined Chelmsford that Spurs started to take an interest in him. In April 1901 he was invited to play for Spurs reserves as they fulfilled a Southern League fixture, while the first XI were rested for the forthcoming FA Cup semi-final. Within two years he was established as first-choice centre-forward, with three England caps and four goals to his name.

Many amateurs of his time still held to the old-fashioned idea of getting the ball and running as far as possible with it before being dispossessed. That was not for Woodward. He could dribble as smartly as any winger, but he also appreciated that success only came through the combined efforts of a team. He would hold on to the ball when he had to but preferred to progress with quick passing.

Most of his contemporaries relied on sheer brute strength, but Woodward, tall and slim, was not built for hard, physical battles. He relied on skill, avoiding the attentions of his marker with nifty footwork, superior ball control and pace. He could kill a ball in an instant, at the same time swaying away from a tackle and despatching a perfect pass before sprinting away to collect the return ball. For Spurs he had a strike rate of one goal every other game, showing great calmness in the box, the master of feigning to shoot one way, waiting for the 'keeper to commit himself and then placing the ball in the opposite corner. He could finish with a viciously-powerful shot when needed but, like everything he did, preferred subtlety to power.

An elegant figure amid the hustle and bustle, Woodward was often the target of harsh, sometimes downright dirty, treatment, but he never let such tactics get the better of him and never retaliated. For him it was a sign he was winning, and even when his own teammates decided to seek a little retribution for him it was Woodward who would intervene. Foul play was a nonsense, and he would have none of it. It was just one of the factors that made him such a popular figure, frequently referred to as 'Sir' by colleagues, opponents and referees alike.

As Woodward's fame increased so did that of Spurs. Any number of Football League clubs would have given two of their best players to secure his services, but Woodward remained loyal to Spurs, repaying some of the loyalty they showed him. While he was crucial to Spurs' plans, they appreciated he had his business as an architect to attend to, and he could rarely make himself available for midweek matches, while if there were occasions when Chelmsford or Essex needed him for important games, so be it.

Apart from those demands, there were also his international obligations. He made a total of 23 appearances for England, many as captain, scoring 28 goals. He also played 67 times for the England and United Kingdom amateur teams, captaining the UK to success in the 1908 and 1912 Olympics. Added to that he was often called upon to play in less important representative games and, as one of the game's finest exponents, was in demand to join tours abroad organised to help spread football throughout the world.

Scorer of Spurs' first Football League goal against Wolverhampton Wanderers in September 1908, Woodward made 27 League appearances that season, finishing top scorer with 18 goals as promotion was secured. With Spurs looking forward to their first season in Division One, Woodward shocked football in June 1909 with the announcement he was giving up top-flight football to play again for Chelmsford. It was a big blow to Spurs, only surpassed four months later with the news Woodward had changed his mind and was returning to League football with Chelsea.

Despite his success, Woodward never collected a top domestic honour, although he did have the chance. Unable to play any part in Chelsea's progress to the 1915 FA Cup Final because he had enlisted in the Footballers' Battalion shortly after World War One began, he was given leave to play in the Final but refused the chance as he did not consider it fair that he should replace one of the men who had taken Chelsea that far.

It was typical of Woodward – a true gentleman of the game.

MANAGERS AND HEAD COACHES

Frank Brettell

Secretary-manager 14 March 1898 to 17 February 1899.

■ Spurs' first secretary-manager Frank Brettell was appointed in February 1898, just prior to a meeting called to decide whether the club should move to limited company status. He took up the post the following month, by which time the limited company had been formed.

A native of Liverpool, Brettell had been one of the founders of Everton, usually playing in the forward line, sometimes at half-back, and serving on the committee in their first season. He worked as a reporter on the *Liverpool Echo* and formed a close relationship with Liverpool when they were formed after Everton's move to Goodison Park. In 1895 Brettell joined Bolton Wanderers as club secretary and proved adept not only at the administrative side of the game but also in persuading good quality players to join the Trotters.

The announcement of his move to Spurs was well received, a respected official from the Football League's northern stronghold expected to attract top-quality players to Northumberland Park. Joining with the season in full swing, it was not until the summer that he could put his connections to good use, but he did not disappoint, signing players of the calibre of Bob Cain, Jim McNaught, Tom Smith, Kenny McKay and John Cameron. Although he held the title of manager, the role was very different from the modern one. He did select the team, but most of the day-to-day work with the players was left to trainer W. Brierley, and the bulk of Brettell's time was expended on his secretarial duties.

In February 1899 Brettell tendered his resignation having accepted a substantially higher package to become secretary-manager of the Portsmouth club, rising from the ruins of Royal Artillery (Portsmouth). His notice expired on 1 April 1899, but Spurs allowed him to leave early and his last match was a United League fixture at Southampton on 15 February. Brettell may have been in charge of Spurs for less than a year, but he was to leave a lasting legacy in the form of his successor.

Brettell helped Portsmouth secure election to the Southern League and served them as manager until 1901 and secretary until April 1903. He then joined Plymouth Argyle, a club about to make the move from amateur to professional, led them into the Southern League and used all his old contacts to build the west country club a reasonable squad before retiring in 1906.

John Cameron

Player, secretary-manager 17 February 1899 to 16 March 1907.

■ Immediately Frank Brettell handed in his resignation, Spurs advertised the vacancy, but they could hardly have looked at any of the applicants before deciding his successor at the club, who was already there.

John Cameron had been one of Frank Brettell's first signings for Spurs in May 1898, a skilful Scottish inside-forward who had previously played in the central position and retained an eye for goal. He was to become one of Spurs' finest inside-forwards and is profiled in 100 Great Players for his time as a player.

At Everton, Cameron had been one of the leaders of efforts to establish a players' union. He was the first secretary of the Association Footballers' Union, forerunner of today's Professional Footballers' Association and, while not one of its best-known members, had a considerable influence on its early works. At Spurs he linked up with two members of the Unions' Management Committee, James McNaught and Tom Bradshaw. Cameron clearly had a flair for administrative duties, was well respected by his fellow players and knew many players through his Union work.

His managerial career could not have started in more impressive style, with Spurs winning the Southern League in 1900 and the FA Cup the following year. The demise of the Players' Union in 1901 allowed Cameron more time to concentrate his efforts solely on Spurs, but he was still in demand in the wider circles of football, writing regularly in newspapers and often called upon for his views on important football topics of the day.

In 1901–02 he led Spurs to second in the Southern, Western and London Leagues, but, although Spurs won the London League the following season, results dipped as Cameron played less and less, his influence on the pitch clearly missed. The Western League was won in the 1903–04 season, but it was now rare for Cameron to don his football togs, his managerial and secretarial duties more then enough to keep him busy. He effectively ran the club on a day-to-day basis, responsible for everything from organising matches to selling tickets.

Cameron kept Spurs up with the top four or five clubs in Southern football, but without it ever really looking as if the Southern League title could be bought to north London again. On the national stage the third (equivalent to today's fifth) round of the FA Cup was reached in 1903, 1904 and 1906, but that was the best that could be achieved. However, winning was not all that mattered in those days. Football was still, first and foremost, entertainment, and Cameron always insisted Spurs played in an entertaining way. Cameron was very much the architect of the style of football for which Spurs have always been known, taking the fast passing, attacking style, first developed by the likes of Bobby Buckle and Billy Harston, refining it and laying the basis of all that followed. Attack was always the order of the day, and while results may not have gone Spurs' way there were few days when spectators would leave the ground complaining about the quality of football they had witnessed.

In July 1906 the directors decided to ease the burden on Cameron by dividing the posts of secretary and manager and appointing Arthur Turner as secretary. Spurs did not start the season well. They gradually moved up among the top half-dozen in the Southern League, but while there was no pressure on Cameron it was known that behind the scenes there were disagreements between him and the directors. Cameron had become inextricably part of Spurs, and it came as a surprise when he suddenly announced in March 1907 that he had resigned, placing the blame for his departure on 'differences with the directorate'.

Cameron did not look for another job in football immediately. Instead he took to journalism and was responsible for not only writing but also publishing the first history of Spurs in 1908, *The White Hart's Souvenir of the Spurs Entry to the English League*. He also coached and while working with the Dresden club was one of the British coaches famously interned at the Ruhleben camp near Berlin in 1915. After the war Cameron had a year, August 1918 to August 1919, as manager of Ayr United before returning to football journalism.

Fred Kirkham

Manager 22 April 1907 to 20 July 1908.

■ Immediately John Cameron's resignation was announced, Spurs advertised the position. They had many applicants, well-known managers and players throwing their hat in the ring, but it is doubtful whether more than one referee applied for the post.

Fred Kirkham was a commercial traveller by occupation and well known as a referee, having officiated in the FA Cup Finals of 1902 and 1906 and several international matches, but quite what his qualifications were to be manager of a football club is not clear. He was said to command the respect of players and thus to be a man who could control them, but any referee should have those qualities. It was suggested he would be a good judge of players, but referees only see them for 90 minutes once a week. What do they know of training and tactics, how players conduct themselves off the pitch and how to get the best out of them? Still, Kirkham was the man appointed, and on a five-year contract at £350 a year. The appointment was made on 18 April 1907, five days after Kirkham had refereed Spurs 0–0 draw with Watford, although not announced until four days later.

Kirkham only had two matches in charge at the end of the season, but the second saw him collect a trophy as Spurs beat Southampton to win the Southern Charity Cup. It was the high point of his short time in charge, quite a contrast with a player he immediately released, inside-forward Herbert Chapman, who set out on one of football's most glorious managerial careers with his first position at Northampton Town.

One of Kirkham's first actions was to change the training regime. Previously players only had to report in the morning. He demanded they should be in both morning and afternoon. If this was expected to have a beneficial effect on

performances it did not work. Spurs did not start the 1907–08 season badly, but they were inconsistent and, worse, the quality of football, even when they won, was not good. Although Spurs did reach third in the Southern League at the start of December, they did not stay there for long and it was clear all was not well.

In November 1907 Kirkham was strongly censured for improper remarks to the referee after Spurs' match with Brighton & Hove Albion on 19 October 1907. In February 1908 the directors met the players amid rumours of a lack of harmony between players and management, and at the end of that month three players were charged with a breach of training regulations. James Gray and Bob Walker were suspended; the third, unidentified, player censured. Within a couple of weeks Walker and Gray were suspended for a second time and did not play for Spurs again.

By then it was all but public knowledge Kirkham was on his way out, but Spurs' departure from the Southern League and application to join the Football League demanded all the director's attentions, and it was some time before they were able to agree terms for Kirkham's departure.

It was at the Annual General Meeting of the club on 20 July 1908 that it was announced

Kirkham's resignation had been received that morning. The shareholders made their pleasure well known with a sustained round of applause. Chairman Charles Roberts was rather more circumspect. He expressed the hope Kirkham 'would obtain a position in the commercial world such as he was used to in the 17 years before he joined the Spurs'!

Peter McWilliam

Manager 26 December 1912 to 28 February 1927 and 14 May 1938 to 15 June 1942.

■ Following Fred Kirkham's departure, the Spurs directors decided not to appoint a replacement but to take on responsibility for the scouting and signing of players and team selection themselves. It was a strange decision as Spurs were about to embark on their first campaign in the Football League but one that seemed vindicated with promotion secured at the first time of asking. Having made it to the top flight, Spurs did not find it easy, but it was not until November 1912, after three draws and 10 defeats in the first 13 League games and with the shareholders in open revolt, that the directors decided a full-time manager was needed.

The man selected was Peter McWilliam, one of the great half-backs of the game, former Scotland captain and the heartbeat of the great Newcastle United team that won three League titles and reached four FA Cup Finals, winning one, between 1905 and 1910. As a manager, he was to be every bit as successful as he had been as a player.

McWilliam took up his post on Boxing Day 1912 and immediately set about building a team that played the style of attacking football that had made his name as a player and Spurs' fans demanded. Relegation was avoided in his first season and a definite improvement witnessed in 1913–14, only undermined by an end of season slump that saw one win in the last nine games. There was little McWilliam could do in 1914–15 as the demands of war ravaged his playing staff and left Spurs bottom of the table, but he kept working during the War, searching out talent and planning for the future. By the time normal football resumed, McWilliam had assembled a squad of players good enough for the First Division, but the shenanigans of 1919 saw Spurs relegated. They were far too good for the Second Division and almost walked to the title in 1920 with a record 70 points, six clear of Huddersfield Town.

McWilliam had brought in some of the great names in Spurs' history: Fanny Walden, Tommy Clay, Bert Smith, and combined them with the likes of Arthur Grimsdell, Bert Bliss and Jimmy Dimmock to produce a team that at times played football to absolute perfection. With the addition of Jimmy Seed and Charlie Walters, he took Spurs a step higher in 1920–21 with FA Cup success, and the following season they almost reached the pinnacle, finishing second to Liverpool in the Football League.

McWilliam was a real players' manager with a simple philosophy on how to do his job. He did not waste time and effort coaching players, telling them what to do or making them play to a system, he just surrounded himself with quality footballers and let them get on with playing the game. If they were good enough to be in the team, they did not need instructions from him. When the offside rule was changed in 1925, McWilliam did not even discuss it with his players, confident Jimmy Seed would

quickly realise he would need to drop deep to take advantage of the space that would suddenly be available.

He possessed all the attributes a great manager needed. He had an uncanny ability to spot talent others had not seen, the classic example being Cecil Poynton, an average half-back who had never played anywhere else when McWilliam suddenly selected him at left-back. McWilliam told him he would soon find his feet and so he did, going on to give Spurs many years' service. He had great determination to get the men he wanted, one famous story surrounding the signing of Jimmy Seed. When word leaked out Spurs were interested in the Mid-Rhondda inside-forward, the local supporters threatened to lynch McWilliam if he went within a mile of their man. McWilliam wore glasses and a false beard to watch Seed, then signed him after the game before anyone realised he had even been in the vicinity. He also had a long-term view of his job and was responsible for Spurs adopting Northfleet United as its nursery club in 1923. It was a far-sighted arrangement from which Spurs were to benefit for well over 20 years, with numerous players learning the basics of their trade, and the Tottenham way, down in Kent.

It was a policy that saved Spurs a fortune, something the director appreciated. Their refusal to spend big money for top players meant McWilliam struggled to keep Spurs at the top of football's tree after the early successes of the 1920s, but he continued to turn out teams that played football with freedom and style.

In December 1926 Middlesbrough offered McWilliam the job as their manager on £1,500 a year compared with the £850 Spurs were paying him. McWilliam wanted to stay with Spurs, he asked for another £150 a year, but such was the short-sighted parsimony of the Spurs' board they refused. McWilliam's resignation was tendered and accepted in January 1927. He gave three months' notice, more than enough time for the board to change their mind, but it was not to be, and he left at the end of February 1927. While McWilliam took Boro into the First Division twice and kept them there, Spurs struggled.

McWilliam stayed with Middlesbrough until his dismissal in March 1934, even turning down an offer to succeed Herbert Chapman as Arsenal manager when Chapman died, but he did join Arsenal as chief scout. As Spurs fortunes ebbed and flowed there were continual rumours of his return, and in May 1935 it was announced he was taking over from Percy Smith, but Arsenal refused to release him from his contract.

In March 1938 McWilliam agreed to return to Spurs, but an announcement was delayed for a month, until Jack Tresadern resigned to take over at Plymouth Argyle. McWilliam did not have enough time before the outbreak of World War Two to work his magic again, but in the year he promoted the likes of Bill Nicholson, Ron Burgess and Freddie Cox, players who were to have such a profound effect on Spurs' fortunes after the war, from the Northfleet nursery. With both McWilliam and his wife suffering from illness, he resigned in June 1942.

Billy Minter

Manager 28 February 1927 to 20 November 1929.

■ Billy Minter's career as one of Spurs' most effective inside-forwards either side of World War One is detailed in 100 Great Players. The signing of Jimmy Seed in February 1920 consigned Minter to the reserves, and at the end of the season he decided to retire from playing. Appointed trainer in August 1920, he was responsible for the fitness of the teams that won the FA Cup in 1921 and came as close as Spurs had ever been to securing the Football League title in 1922 when they finished second. He remained as trainer, even playing a couple of friendly games in an emergency, until being asked to replace Peter McWilliam as manager.

Minter was officially appointed on 1 February 1927 but did not take up the reins fully until the 27th of the month, spending the intervening period being given a crash course in management by McWilliam. There was little time for him to make any impact as Spurs finished the season just below the midpoint in the First Division, his major decision being to give young Taffy O'Callaghan a chance in place of Jimmy Seed.

Minter faced a difficult task in following McWilliam with the team his predecessor had built breaking up and the board reluctant to invest in suitable replacements. Taking what was expected to be the first-choice starting 11, they had a team good enough for the First Division, if not Championship material. The problem, evident even before the season got under way, was that they did not have enough talent and experience in the back-up players. Injuries and lack of form would leave the team struggling.

That was just what happened, although it was only in the last three months of the season that it all went wrong. When Spurs went to Huddersfield for the sixth round of the FA Cup, they were sitting safe in mid-table, 29 points from an equal number of games. Trounced 1–6 at Huddersfield, they won the next game but the rot had set in. They collected only seven points from their last 12 games and finished the season early to embark on a trip to Holland. With four teams each two points behind them and a decent goal average they appeared safe, but they were not. The now departed Jimmy Seed inspired Sheffield Wednesday to a miracle run, and with three of their opponents picking up the two points they needed Spurs found themselves one place off bottom and relegated. While seven clubs finished just a point above them, there was only one below, McWilliam's Middlesbrough.

McWilliam led Middlesbrough back up at the first attempt, but Minter was not so fortunate. After finishing 10th in 1928–29 Spurs began the next season abysmally. With an horrendous injury list, 15 points from 12 games and a relegation battle looming, the stresses and strains proved too much and his health suffered. Shy and modest at the best of times, he knew the job was beyond him and in November 1929 resigned. A Spurs man to the core, he took on the post of assistant secretary, a role he fulfilled until his death in May 1940.

Percy Smith

Manager 4 January 1930 to 18 April 1935.

■ Spurs had over 100 applicants to replace Billy Minter and decided to take their time in reaching a decision. At least eight applicants were interviewed, and it was not until January 1930 that Percy Smith was announced as the new incumbent.

Smith had played for Preston North End and Blackburn Rovers, a member of the latter's Championship sides of 1911–12 and 1913–14. He retired in 1920 to manage Nelson and had been manager of Bury since May 1927 before applying for the job at White Hart Lane.

Going out of the FA Cup to Manchester City in a third-round replay was not the best start for Smith, but he could not complain about his first League game, a 6–1 demolition of Blackpool. There were only four points between Spurs and the bottom of the Second Division when Smith arrived, but he began to get the team playing together and persuaded the board to release some money, allowing him to sign Willie Davies and Dick Rowley, not the biggest of names but both internationals and a definite improvement on what he had inherited. Smith guided Spurs to mid-table safety in his first season and, with few additions to his squad, third place in 1930–31, promotion only missed because of a late season injury that deprived Smith of goalscorer-in-chief Ted Harper.

Smith continued his rebuilding and reaped the reward in 1932–33 when a team full of

power and pace nicknamed 'the Greyhounds' secured promotion. The team was built to provide the best service to George Hunt with Taffy O'Callaghan and Willie Evans not only the main providers but regular goalscorers themselves. The team played at speed from start to finish, whether relying on slick one-touch passing or players breaking with the ball and dribbling downfield. The team was reckoned too lightweight for the First Division, but Smith's confidence in his men was fully justified with Spurs finishing third in the First Division in 1933–34.

Spurs should have gone on from there to greater things, but 1934–35 proved a disaster. It did not start too well, but a sudden spate of injuries decimated the playing strength and left Spurs just above the relegation battlers. After Boxing Day, results were abysmal: Spurs went 16 League games without a victory and plunged to the bottom of the table. By April 1935 relegation was a certainty.

For some time all had not been well between the board and Smith. As injuries took their toll, Smith, dissatisfied with the available reserves, wanted to sign new players but the board were simply not prepared to sanction the spending of money. When a new player was signed it was not someone Smith wanted, and the first he knew of it was when he read it in the press. Wally Hardinge was appointed reserve-team coach in January 1935, ostensibly to whip the reserves into shape, but it was almost public knowledge he was there to step into the breech if Smith departed.

Once relegation was all but confirmed, the board notified Smith they were going to make management changes. It is not clear exactly what their plans were, but Smith's reaction was to immediately hand in his resignation. It was to take effect from the end of the season, but there was little point in him serving out his notice, and he left on 18 April.

Hardinge took charge of the team for the final three League games of the season, among the favourites to get the job permanently until it was prematurely announced Peter McWilliam was returning.

Jack Tresadern

Manager 1 July 1935 to 21 April 1938

■ With Peter McWilliam unable to secure his release from Arsenal, Spurs advertised the position and received over 200 applicants. Eight were interviewed, and in June 1935 it was announced John 'Jack' Tresadern had been successful.

Tresadern had started his football career with his local club West Ham United, appearing for them in the famous 'White Horse' FA Cup Final of 1923, the first at Wembley, and collecting one England cap. A part-timer, when his job as a shipping clerk moved to Burnley Tresadern joined the local club, but he only stayed there a short time, accepting the position of player-manager with Northampton Town in May 1925. A broken leg in December 1926 brought his playing career to an end, but he continued as Northampton manager until October 1930 when he joined Crystal Palace.

At the time of his move to Spurs, Tresadern was recognised as one of the most 'promising' young managers in the game. Unfortunately Spurs' position demanded more than promise, and, with the ever-present shadow of McWilliam, Tresadern needed to make an

immediate impact. Things started well enough as Spurs competed with the likes of Charlton Athletic, Leicester City and Sheffield United for promotion come Christmas 1935, but results took a turn for the worse in the second half of the season and fifth was their final position. The next two seasons were pretty similar, promotion a realistic possibility but hope fading as the season wore on. Only in the FA Cup was any real success tasted, Spurs reaching the sixth round in each of Tresadern's three seasons in charge.

At times Tresadern got Spurs playing with real quality and results followed, but he faced the same old problem of injuries depriving him of his best men and inadequate reserves. He was always searching for reinforcements but like his predecessors had to labour under the handicap of a board that was not prepared to invest much of Spurs' huge wealth on reinforcements. Too often he identified the men he needed, but the directors baulked at the fees demanded.

In March 1938 rumours began, not for the first time, that Tresadern was about to resign and McWilliam had agreed to return. They were promptly denied, but Tresadern knew the writing was on the wall. Plymouth Argyle were looking for a new manager, and in early April 1938 Tresadern made a late but successful application for the post. He was offered a substantially higher salary at Plymouth, given a three-year contract as opposed to the 12-month ones he had with Spurs, and viewed the job as 'definitely better', but he also commented that at Plymouth he would be in total control, whereas at Spurs the 'directors had a voice in the selection of the team'.

At the same time as announcing Tresadern's departure, Spurs also announced McWilliam would be returning, but not immediately. He was not able to start until mid-May, and in the interim chief scout and assistant team manager Ben Ives took charge of the first team.

Arthur Turner

Secretary-manager August 1942 to January 1946.

■ When Peter McWilliam resigned in June 1942 Spurs decided not to seek a replacement until they knew what would be happening, football-wise, the following season. Along with all the other clubs in London, they had been in dispute with the Football League over the structure of war-time football and for the 1941–42 season had formed their own London War League.

When the dispute was resolved, with the London clubs returning to the Football League, the directors decided there was just too much uncertainty over the future to appoint a long-term successor to McWilliam. They decided instead to make Arthur Turner secretary-manager for the rest of the war.

Turner had joined Spurs in July 1906 as secretary, having filled the same post with his home-town club Rotherham County, and was respected as one of the most diligent and effective administrators in the game. An accountant by profession, he was an expert in tax and rating law and over the years helped Spurs make considerable savings in those areas.

Turner's job as manager bore little resemblance to that of McWilliam. He was not concerned with training the players, scouting for new signings or deciding tactics. In theory, his job was relatively simple: to get 11 players together every Saturday. In practice, it was far from simple. With service demands, travel restrictions and communication problems, every club had difficulty putting a full team in the field. Starting matches one or two players short or calling for last-minute volunteers from the crowd was not uncommon. The fact Spurs started all their war-time matches with a full complement of players was testament to Turner's organisational abilities.

Not only did he put out a full team in every game, but he even managed to get together a winning team. In 1942–43 Spurs were runners-up in the Football League South, and the following two seasons they won it. Turner, ably assisted by coaches George Hardy, Jimmy Anderson and Joe Hulme, did a remarkable job throughout the war, but as the conflict drew to a close and football began to plan for the future it was clear Turner could not continue to look after the team and perform his secretarial duties, which were made all the more burdensome by Arsenal's use of White Hart Lane when Spurs were away.

Joe Hulme

Manager January 1946 to 3 March 1949.

■ As the transitional 1945–46 season got under way, with players returning from military

service and guest players returning to their clubs, Spurs struggled. From early December 1945 they lost eight out of 10 games, and the directors decided a full-time team manager was required if Spurs were to make any impact when normal League football resumed. The job was given to Joe Hulme, initially until the end of the season but with a view to the appointment becoming permanent if Hulme decided it was a job he wanted.

Hulme had made his name with Arsenal, one of Herbert Chapman's first major signings for the Gunners, when joining from Blackburn Rovers in February 1926, having previously played for York City. At Highbury, Hulme, known for his blistering, famous runs down the wing, won three Football League titles, played in four FA Cup Finals, twice collecting a winners' medal, and collected nine England caps. Transferred to Huddersfield Town in January 1938, he made his last appearance in that season's FA Cup, the first player to appear in five FA Cup Finals. Hulme had joined Spurs as part-time assistant to Arthur Turner in February 1944, was moved up to chief coach and in October 1945 appointed assistant manager and secretary.

Hulme had just over three years in charge, years in which he laid the groundwork for future success but failed to achieve it himself. The only taste of success he enjoyed was in the FA Cup of 1948, when Spurs got within four minutes of their first Wembley appearance before Blackpool equalised, going on to win the game in extra-time. Like all clubs, hopes were high in the early post-War years, but while Spurs were always in the top half of the table, promotion rarely seemed within their reach and, having been in the Second Division too long, promotion was all that mattered.

Hulme had assembled a more than decent squad, most of the players home-developed. At times the team could be thrilling to watch, but at others it seemed slow and uncertain, lacking that certain something that turns a team from a competent one to something special. Hulme knew there were weaknesses, particularly in defence, where he needed not only a top-class full-back but a man who could organise the defence. He identified the perfect man in Alf Ramsey, but all his efforts to sign the England full-back were rebuffed by Southampton.

In December 1948 Hulme was admitted to hospital with abdominal trouble. He resumed his duties in early March 1949 but immediately on his return received a letter from the directors saying that if his health was not up to the strains of the job he should resign. He replied that he was perfectly fit, to which the directors responded by giving him a month's notice.

Assistant manager Jimmy Anderson, who had been in charge of the team since Hulme's admission to hospital, was given the job of running the team until a new man was appointed.

Arthur Rowe

Manager 4 May 1949 to July 1955.

■ Arthur Rowe's career as a cultured, footballing centre-half with Spurs is detailed in 100 Great Players. When injury brought his playing career to an end, he decided to make a new career as a coach, and began it in 1939 when he embarked on a lecture tour as football coach to the Hungarian government. The outbreak of World War Two forced him to return home early, but not before he had made a big impression on Gusztav Sebes, a young Hungarian coach who went on to manage the 'Magical Magyars' side of the early 1950s that gave England a footballing lesson at Wembley in 1953.

Rowe got his first managerial experience during the war with the Army football team and, as the war came to an end, successfully applied for the manager's job at Chelmsford City. He led them to the Southern League title in 1945–46 and quickly developed a reputation as an innovative coach with simple but effective ideas on how the game should be played and an ability to communicate those ideas to the players so they were put into practice.

With Joe Hulme's departure, Rowe was immediately identified as one of the favourites for the job at White Hart Lane and his appointment was announced on 4 May 1949. It was a couple of weeks before he could tidy up affairs at Chelmsford and devote all his time to Spurs, but that did not stop him sanctioning the signings of Alf Ramsey and Billy Rees. While other new signings were expected, they were the only two made before the new season got under way, and as it got into full swing it soon became

apparent no more new men were required.

The change in Spurs' fortunes was brought about not so much by the men in the team but by the way those men played the game. Rowe's philosophy was simple. It was all about possession, keeping the ball, passing it around, always giving the man with the ball more than one passing option. With his famous motto of 'Make it quick, make it simple', Rowe's brand of 'Push and Run' football was the very essence of how the game should be played, talented players working to a simple system aimed at scoring goals and entertaining crowds.

'Push and Run' revolutionised the game and took Spurs to heights rarely dreamt of before, the Second Division title in 1949–50 followed by the League Championship for the first time 12 months later. In 1953 they got even closer to Wembley than in 1948, a goal in the last few seconds again putting them out at the semi-final stage.

Having taken Spurs to the heights, Rowe found it much harder to keep them there. If he had a failing it was loyalty to players who had served him well but were past their best. As results suffered so did Rowe. His love of Spurs knew no bounds, and he worked ceaselessly to make them a power again but the worry only made him ill. He suffered a breakdown in January 1954, returned to White Hart Lane in July that year but was again taken into hospital in April 1955. By July 1955 Rowe knew he would not be fit to return to the pressures of management for some time and resigned. It was not because it was best for him, but because it was best for the club.

Jimmy Anderson

18 April 1955 to 11 October 1959.

■ Jimmy Anderson joined Spurs' groundstaff as a 15-year-old in 1908, going on to become one of the club's most loyal, dedicated and unsung servants. When he first reported for duty at White Hart Lane, Anderson was principally concerned with the upkeep of the stands and pitch, one of his earliest jobs helping groundsman John Over remove weeds from the playing surface. Unable to make the grade as a player, he continued working behind the scenes

but was involved in the playing side, initially as a trainer. He then moved on to the coaching staff, both at White Hart Lane and the Northfleet United nursery, and managed the reserve team before being appointed assistant manager to Joe Hulme in October 1946. He retained the role on Arthur Rowe's arrival, taking charge of first-team affairs when Rowe was taken ill. With an unparalleled knowledge of Spurs and the players, it was no surprise when Anderson was asked to assume the managerial reins on Rowe's resignation.

Ever since winning the League in 1951, Spurs had been on the decline, gradual at first but now accelerating. Anderson knew radical changes were needed, but bringing in the players he wanted was not an easy task. His first season in charge was one of continual struggle in the League, punctuated only by a run to another unsuccessful FA Cup semi-final. It started with only one point from the first 12 and Spurs rock bottom of the table. They remained in a relegation spot until early 1956 but slowly clawed their way up the table, although it was only a final day defeat of Sheffield United that ensured Spurs survived on points and did not have to rely on goal average.

The turnaround in 1956–57 was quite astounding, with Spurs pushing Manchester United's 'Busby Babes' all the way to the title, and while it took time to compensate for the loss of Tony Marchi, third place the following season was no disgrace. Anderson had bought well in the transfer market, signing Maurice Norman, Bobby Smith and Cliff Jones, and given a chance to home-produced players like Ron Henry, Peter Baker and Terry Dyson. Prospects for the future looked bright, but all the promise evaporated as Spurs started 1958–59 in miserable fashion. With nine points from 11 games Anderson decided it was time to resign.

Bill Nicholson

Manager 11 October 1958 to 13 September 1974.

■ On Jimmy Anderson's resignation there was one obvious candidate to succeed him, Bill Nicholson, and the board had no hesitation in turning to a man who had already given Spurs 22 years of great service.

A fine half-back, even as a first-team regular, Nicholson had shown a keen interest in coaching and been marked out as a manager of the future. While still playing, he obtained his FA Coaching badge at the first attempt and took charge of the Cambridge University team. When, in 1954, he persuaded manager Arthur Rowe he was no longer up to First Division football and a younger man should be given a chance, Nicholson was appointed to the coaching staff, initially still with a playing contract. With Anderson's promotion to manager, Nicholson was made first-team coach and was soon helping England manager Walter Winterbottom with the Under-23 team. In July 1957, credited with having done much to turn the team around in 1956–57, Nicholson was promoted to assistant manager, and on the morning of 11 October 1958 was asked to take over as manager. Nicholson could not have asked for a better start as that afternoon Spurs played Everton at White Hart Lane and won 10–4. It was a sign of some great times to come. Not that those times were just around the corner, Spurs spent the rest of 1958–59 flirting with the relegation zone, only pulling clear as the season came to an end.

In 1959–60 Nicholson turned a struggling team into Championship contenders. Spurs finished third, only dropping out of the title race in the last few games, but all the time Nicholson was assembling the players that were to form not only Spurs' finest team but one of the best English football has ever seen. He got together the perfect combination of youth and experience, home produced and expensively acquired talent, and in 1960–61 led Spurs to what many regarded as the impossible dream, the League and FA Cup double.

He followed that with third place in the League, the semi-finals of the European Cup and the FA Cup again the following season and the European Cup-winners' Cup in 1962–63. It was a true purple patch in Spurs' history, but not just for the trophies that were won. Nicholson's team played football that was as perfect as it could be. Great players allowed to show their skills, playing with pace and fluidity, attacking all the time and most importantly entertaining. It was football that did not simply follow the traditions set by John Cameron, Peter McWilliam and Arthur Rowe, it set new standards for all those that followed to try and emulate.

Not that Nicholson was content with what he had achieved. Having taken Spurs to the peak, he was determined to keep them there, if not take them even higher. It meant dismantling the double-winning team, but Nicholson had no qualms about that, only the best was good enough for Spurs. With the total backing of the board, Nicholson rebuilt, won the FA Cup again in 1967 and then rebuilt once more, rewarded with the League Cup in 1971 and 1973 and the UEFA Cup in 1972.

Throughout his time as manager, Nicholson insisted on his teams playing football the 'Tottenham way'. He wanted to win but that alone was never enough. There was a proper way to play and that meant remembering that the supporters were the most important people in football, they were the people who paid the players' wages, the people who were there to be entertained. No matter how much other teams resorted to defensive or 'professional' tactics to get results, Nicholson would not compromise his principles. While he was in charge Spurs would play his way, 'the Glory, Glory Way'.

It was perhaps this attitude that led to Nicholson quitting. In 1973–74 he knew the team was not good enough, wholesale changes were needed but football had changed dramatically. No longer were players happy to just play the game, they wanted more and more and they had the power to get what they wanted. Becoming disenchanted with the game he had given his life to, the breaking point came with the troubles at the 1974 UEFA Cup Final in Rotterdam when the supporters, the people who meant so much to Nicholson, disgraced Spurs' name. With defeat in the first four matches of the 1974–75 season, Nicholson decided he had had enough. He resigned. Despite the board, players and supporters doing all they could to persuade him to change his mind, his decision was final. He remained just until his replacement was appointed.

After leaving Spurs, Nicholson took a well-deserved rest from football, but he was not away from the game for long, returning to scout for West Ham in their European campaign of 1975–76. A year later he was back where he belonged, at White Hart Lane. When Keith Burkinshaw was appointed manager his first 'signing' was that of Nicholson, persuading him to return in July 1976 as consultant. In that wide-ranging role he provided invaluable support to everybody at the club, responsible for unearthing some real gems in Tony Galvin, Graham Roberts and Gary Mabbutt, and in May 1991 was made Club President. Even in his last few years Nicholson could be found in his office more often than not and hardly missed a game at White Hart Lane, frequently making his way there after standing out in the bitter cold of the training ground watching a youth-team game.

When Nicholson passed away in October 2004 the club lost its most dedicated and influential servant, but his legacy will never fade.

Terry Neill

Manager 13 September 1974 to 30 June 1976.

■ When Bill Nicholson resigned he made it clear that the man to succeed him was Danny Blanchflower, but the board had other ideas. They did appoint a loquacious former Northern Ireland captain and a man who had captained a north London side, but it was not the man who had famously led Spurs to the double. Instead they went for Terry Neill, manager of Hull City and Northern Ireland and a former captain of Arsenal.

It was a strange decision and not one popular with the fans. Nicholson was a man with a deep passion for Spurs, who avoided the limelight and let the team do the talking for him. Neill was just the opposite, laid back, ever ready to talk to the media and, seemingly, viewing the position as just another job.

His arrival did see an immediate improvement in results with the first two games under his management won, but that did not last and Spurs were soon in deep trouble, with relegation increasingly probable. He tried to improve matters by bringing in his own men, discarding some of the more established players and relying on youngsters, but it was not a policy that worked. Spurs were on a downward slide and, while still recognised as a big club, attracting real quality players was not easy. It was only in the final few games, when Neill turned to the experienced men whose days at

White Hart Lane seemed numbered, that results took a turn for the better and staying up seemed a possibility. It went right to the final game of the season, European Cup finalists Leeds United at home. Nothing less than victory would suffice and on a night that rivalled the Glory, Glory nights of European matches for noise and commitment it was two of the recalled stars, Cyril Knowles and Martin Chivers, who proved the match winners.

Having avoided the drop, the only way was up, and, while the 1975–76 season started almost as badly as the previous one, Neill's policy of introducing fresh young talent eventually began to pay off. A finishing place of ninth, together with a run to the League Cup semi-final, was far better than many had anticipated.

Any hopes Neill would take the club on were shattered in May 1976. For many, Neill's time with Spurs had always been viewed as just a training ground for his return to Highbury, and so it proved. Within days of Arsenal announcing that Bertie Mee had decided to retire, Neill resigned and was immediately installed at Highbury.

Keith Burkinshaw

Manager 14 July 1976 to 31 May 1984.

■ Neill's departure again saw many top names touted as successor, but for the board it was a choice between first-team coach Keith Burkinshaw and youth-team boss Pat Welton. Burkinshaw had built a good rapport with the senior players and their support proved decisive.

A hard-working, dependable half-back in his playing days, Burkinshaw made one first-team appearance in four years with Liverpool before moving on to Workington and Scunthorpe United. He played well over 400 games for the two clubs and first sampled a manager's life with a five-month spell at Workington followed by 10 months in a caretaker capacity at Scunthorpe. When released by Scunthorpe he coached in Zambia, then returned to join the coaching staff at Newcastle United, where he spent seven years before being sacked in May 1975 as part of cost-cutting measures. As soon as news of Burkinshaw's dismissal reached Terry Neill's ears, he was in contact and quick to offer Burkinshaw the senior coaching role at White Hart Lane. It was undoubtedly the most important signing Neill made for the club.

He went on to become second only to Bill Nicholson in terms of bringing trophies to White Hart Lane, but there was little indication of the impact he would have during his early days in charge. Spurs had been on a downward slope for several years. Under Neill the slide had accelerated with experienced and quality players leaving and their replacements full of potential but young and raw. Burkinshaw paid the price with his first season ending in relegation. Perhaps realising they were as much to blame as anybody, the directors stood by Burkinshaw, a decision that was to reap rich rewards.

Burkinshaw was a firm believer in the quality, attacking football for which Spurs have always been renowned. Under his guidance young talent such as Glenn Hoddle and Neil McNab developed rapidly, and Spurs played their way out of the Second Division at the first attempt, but Burkinshaw knew that alone was not enough. To recapture their former position, Spurs needed to be competing with the best, winning silverware, and that meant securing the best players, real world-class stars.

The opportunity to do just that came even before Argentina had finished celebrating its 1978 World Cup success when Burkinshaw heard Ossie Ardiles, their midfield maestro, was interested in playing in England. In what was one of the most amazing transfer coups of all time, Burkinshaw persuaded Ardiles and his compatriot, Ricky Villa, to sign for Spurs. It was a courageous move but a sure sign Burkinshaw was prepared to take a calculated gamble to take Spurs back to the very top. The signing of the two Argentines had an immediate effect, but it alone was not enough. Burkinshaw backed his judgment with big money again to sign Garth Crooks and Steve Archibald, but his management was not all about buying readymade stars. Bargain buys and home-produced youngsters were given their chance with players such as Graham Roberts, Mark Falco, Chris Hughton, Mike Hazard and Tony Galvin all given the opportunity to show they were good enough.

The result was a team that rekindled old glories, winning the FA Cup in 1981 and retaining the trophy the following year while also reaching the League (Milk) Cup Final and finishing fourth in the League.

Burkinshaw was similar to Nicholson in many ways, a straight-talking, gritty Yorkshireman who respected his players, treating them like men and demanding the same level of commitment he displayed himself. Not for him the television appearances and punditry. He was at home on the training pitch or out and about watching potential recruits.

A manager in the old mould, he expected to manage the club from top to bottom, but Spurs new owners had other ideas. Burkinshaw was not prepared to accept their plans for a continental system where he would coach but do little else. In April 1984 he announced he would leave at the end of the season and went out on the perfect note, Tony Parks' dramatic penalty save winning the UEFA Cup.

Peter Shreeves

Manager 22 June 1984 to 13 May 1986 and 22 July 1991 to 15 May 1992.

■ Promoting from within had proved successful with Keith Burkinshaw, and the principle was followed on his departure, with Peter Shreeves moving up from assistant manager to the number-one job. A former Reading player, Shreeves had joined Spurs in October 1974 as youth-team coach and been promoted to reserve-team manager three years later.

Appointed Burkinshaw's assistant in late 1980, Shreeves had played a big part in the successes of the early 1980s and sought to continue in the Burkinshaw style, his first signings of Clive Allen and John Chiedozie evidence that he intended to follow the attacking policy that had paid rich dividends. His first season started with a 4–1 victory at eventual champions Everton and, while early exits from the Milk and FA Cups were not ideal, they at least allowed Shreeves to focus on retaining the UEFA Cup and the chase for the League title. Even though the services of Allen were lost due to injury, Spurs got through to the fourth round of the UEFA Cup before going out to Real Madrid and battled with Everton for top spot until the final few weeks of the season when a glut of fixtures, injuries and miserable

home form saw Spurs fade into third place, equal on points with Liverpool but 13 behind the other Merseyside club.

The summer of 1986 saw Shreeves reinforce his attacking options with the signings of Paul Allen and Chris Waddle, but it was in defence that Spurs were lacking. Again the two domestic Cups provided no sustained interest, and with the events of Heysel meaning no European competition a drop to 10th in the League saw the season viewed as a failure.

With the new management at White Hart Lane desperate for success and keen to have a 'big-name' manager in charge, Shreeves was sacked. It was tough on Shreeves. Following Burkinshaw was never going to be easy, and Shreeves had to work with a board still trying to develop its blueprint for the running of a modern football club while answerable to a PLC. Shreeves never really had the time in which to make his impression on the team, but he had taken Spurs to a higher place in the League than his predecessor, and he had done it playing the type of football Spurs fans wanted to see.

Shreeves went on to work as assistant manager at Queen's Park Rangers and Watford before returning to Spurs in July 1991 as the Sugar–Venables combination set about rebuilding the club. Again Shreeves took on an unenviable task. He had little money to play with, Paul Gascoigne was out for the season and Terry Venables was an ever present figure as much in the foreground as the background. Only on a one-year contract, Shreeves adopted an over-cautious approach and at times sacrificed Spurs' passing game for a long ball approach that drew unfavourable comparisons to the football played in his previous time in charge. The semi-final of the Rumbelows League Cup was reached, but there was little to cheer about in the other competitions. At the end of the season Shreeves's contract was not renewed.

David Pleat

Manager 16 May 1986 to 23 October 1987. Caretaker manager 5 September 1998 to 4 October 1998, 16 March 2001 to 1 April 2001 and 21 September 2003 to 15 May 2004.

■ In almost eight years as manager of Luton Town, David Pleat had performed minor miracles taking a small Bedfordshire club with limited funds into the First Division and keeping them there. Regarded as one of the most up-and-coming managers in the game, innovative, comfortable in the ever-increasing media glare and a firm believer in playing stylish football, he had long been regarded as a man who could reach the very peak given the right backing.

Taking over from Peter Shreeves, he had his own firm ideas on how he wanted the team to play, and it was one based very much on skill and pace. Paul Miller and Graham Roberts had been terrific players for Spurs, hard uncompromising defenders, but hardly the most cultured. They both departed with Richard Gough and Gary Mabbutt installed as the central-defensive pairing, two players who could defend with the best of them but who could also play constructive football from deep. Mark Falco had proved a strong, under-rated striker, but he lacked the pace and guile of Clive Allen.

Ever receptive to new ideas, Pleat had noted how successful Belgium had been in the 1986

World Cup, playing with five in midfield supporting one man up front. He introduced the system to Spurs, even signing the Belgian's lone striker Nico Claesen, but then finding he already had the perfect man for the job in Allen. It was a system other teams found hard to come to terms with. It took some time for the players to adapt to, but as the 1986–87 season progressed they settled to it, and while winning the title was never a realistic dream the two domestic Cups were both within reach. In the Littlewoods Cup Spurs reached the semi-final before going out to Arsenal, and in the FA Cup they got all the way to Wembley only to fall to Coventry City in one of the most entertaining Finals for years.

The future was full of rich promise, but in the summer of 1987 stories began to circulate about Pleat's private life. He looked to have ridden out the storm, but when Spurs struggled as they tried to cope with the departure of Glenn Hoddle the stories resurfaced. Pleat could handle the attention from the sports media, but with his personal life under scrutiny he decided to resign in October 1987.

Pleat returned to the game with Leicester City in the summer of 1988 and went on to manage Luton Town and Sheffield Wednesday, before returning to Spurs as Director of Football in January 1998 to provide support for Christian Gross. When Gross was sacked in September 1998 Pleat took over as caretaker manager for a month and did so again for a couple of weeks in March 2001 when George Graham was given his marching orders.

The dismissal of Glenn Hoddle in September 2001 saw Pleat again put in charge of team affairs, but this time it was until the end of the season as chairman Daniel Levy decided to spend all the time he needed deciding on a total restructuring of the managerial and coaching departments. It was a difficult job for Pleat. While the fans were not happy to write off the season so quickly, he was expected to keep the club ticking over with little opportunity to plan for the future and knowing his own job was likely to be in jeopardy. He did as well as could be expected, making sure the club remained in the Premiership, blooding some promising young players and persuading the board to sign Jermaine Defoe.

As almost expected, Levy's revamp did see Pleat surplus to requirements, and in July 2005 he stood down as director of football.

Terry Venables

23 November 1987 to 22 July 1991

■ Spurs could have been in real problems following David Pleat's departure in October 1987. League clubs had agreed not to approach each other's managers during the season and any manager worth his salt was already in a job. Fortunately Terry Venables had just stood down as manager of Barcelona. A former Spurs player, Venables also played for Chelsea, Queen's Park Rangers and Crystal Palace, began coaching while at Selhurst Park and managed Palace and Rangers before being tempted to Barcelona. Having led Barca to the Spanish title and European Cup Final, he was not only the obvious candidate but the perfect man for the job. Chairman Irving Scholar was quick to fly out to America where Venables was on holiday and had little difficulty persuading him to return to English football.

Venables had personal affairs to attend to and was unable to take the helm for a month, so in the interim Pleat's assistant Trevor Hartley and first-team coach Doug Livermore were put in charge, Livermore taking on sole responsibility when Hartley departed. It was not a good time. The team was dispirited, lacking leadership, and by the time Venables arrived any hope of improving on the previous season had already disappeared. It was just a question of planning for the future.

Venables had made his name at Palace and Rangers by bringing through young talent, giving them their head and building a team. At White Hart Lane the demands were higher, but Venables still believed in youth only now he had the resources to go out and buy players rather than having to develop them. Never afraid to pay big money to secure the talent he wanted, he invested heavily in players of the calibre of Paul Gascoigne, Paul Stewart, Erik Thorstvedt and Gary Lineker, and while no trophies were garnered it seemed just a question of time.

A popular figure, feted by the press for his forward thinking ideas and approachable personality, liked by the fans for his openness, publicly stated desire to give them the football they desired and willingness to sign the players who could provide that, Venables endeared himself to the Spurs fans even more when news broke of the club's financial plight in late 1990. With rumours players would have to be sold and the banks would let the club go under, he had a tough enough job just managing the team but added to his burdens when he decided to get involved in efforts to save the club. With all the pressures he did remarkably well to lead the team to FA Cup success in 1991 before joining with Alan Sugar to put together a rescue package.

Taking the position of chief executive, Venables invested all he had, and a lot he borrowed, to fulfil an ambition of running a club from top to bottom, but the dream was not to last for long. Taking charge of all footballing aspects of the club, he gave Peter Shreeves the role of manager for one season, but when that was not successful he assumed control of team affairs himself, with Doug Livermore appointed first-team coach. With Sugar having straightened out the finances, Venables was able to start rebuilding again. Teddy Sheringham, Darren Anderton and Neil Ruddock were signed, but they took time to settle, and it was only in the second half of the 1992–93 season that Spurs began to produce the performances they should always have been capable of. The FA Cup semi-final and a final place of eighth in the Premier League were a definite improvement.

Action Images

Once again hopes were raised that the future would see Spurs back at the top, but even before the season had reached its conclusion they were dramatically shattered. Amid allegations of bungs, backhanders and other dodgy dealings, Venables was removed from his position by Sugar and, after an acrimonious but short-lived battle, forced to relinquish his interest in the club.

Ossie Ardiles

19 June 1993 to 1 November 1994.

■ The fallout from the Sugar–Venables bust up initially saw Sugar painted the villain of the piece. With the fans railing behind Venables, Sugar needed to appoint as manager a man the fans would get behind, someone who had a special place in the hearts of all Spurs supporters. The man he chose was Ossie Ardiles, one of the finest midfield players to have donned the lilywhite shirt.

On leaving Spurs, Ardiles played briefly for Queen's Park Rangers and Fort Lauderdale Strikers before taking his first steps in management at Swindon Town. Combining the best of British and South American styles, he led Swindon to promotion via the Play-offs in 1990, only to see all his efforts bought to nought as financial irregularities deprived Swindon of their place in the First Division. Ardiles had done enough to establish his reputation and moved to Newcastle United but departed the financially-stricken club after less than a year as they struggled at the foot of the Second Division. West Bromwich Albion gave Ardiles the chance to rebuild his career, but when Spurs came knocking Ardiles had no hesitation returning home.

He walked into a club in turmoil. Venables was still fighting his sacking, the fans were firmly behind their departed saviour, several of the players were in open revolt and to cap it all the FA was investigating the club's affairs. Many a bigger man would have shied away, but Ardiles was never one to shirk a challenge. He set about the job with relish, signing the type of skilful players he thought would produce the flowing football he believed in and demanding his team play with a sense of freedom. His first season started well enough, but when Teddy Sheringham was injured Ardiles had no adequate replacement. The football was still neat and based on skill not brawn, the build up play was smooth, but the end product was lacking. The season became one of fighting against the drop, an objective only achieved with victory at Oldham in the penultimate League game.

With four clubs to be relegated, the FA's decision in June 1994 to ban Spurs from the FA Cup and deduct 12 points meant they were certainties for the drop. While Sugar fought the FA, Ardiles was given the freedom to secure the players that would at least see Spurs go down with a bang and not a whimper: Ilie Dumitrescu, Gica Popescu and Jurgen Klinsmann, not just big names, true international stars.

The season began in a flurry of goals as Ardiles's team of attacking talents gelled from the start. Ardiles had an unshakeable belief in playing the 'beautiful game', a team loaded with offensive-minded players, attacking from every part of the field, outscoring the opposition. For two months the football was exhilarating, some of the most exciting Spurs had produced in years, but football is about results as much as performances. Going forward Spurs could be unstoppable, their football the stuff of dreams. Defensively they could be a nightmare. The results were not good enough, but Ardiles refused to compromise his principles. Sugar had enough on his hands battling the football authorities; the last thing he wanted was a battle with fans who were now beginning to call for Ardiles's head. Defeat at Notts County in the Coca-Cola Cup proved the final straw, and Ardiles was sacked. It was a sad end to what had promised so much.

Gerry Francis

Manager 15 November 1994 to 19 November 1997.

■ Steve Perryman, Ardiles's assistant, took over for one game hoping he might be offered the role permanently, but he was too closely associated with Ardiles and passed over in favour of Gerry Francis.

The former England captain had made his name as a player with Queen's Park Rangers before moving into management with Exeter City, Bristol Rovers and Rangers. Francis did a fine job with the west London club, leading them to fifth place in the Premier League in 1992–93 and building a team that played some lovely football, but Rangers have never been a wealthy club, too often having to sell their big names. Francis was frustrated and, with Rangers having made a poor start to the season, felt threatened by rumours Rodney Marsh was to be appointed chief executive. He resigned and within a few days was unveiled as the new manager at White Hart Lane.

Francis's success with Rangers had been based on his ability to organise, to settle on a system of play that suited the available players and bringing through players who suited the system. At Spurs, Francis quickly realised that all that was lacking was a little organisation, particularly in defence. David Howells, a steadying influence, was recalled in favour of the less disciplined Dumitrescu and the defenders were made to realise their first job was to defend. In little time results improved. Steady progress was made up the League, seventh place a more than creditable finish, and

with Sugar winning his battle with the FA and getting Spurs back in the FA Cup there was even hope of winning the trophy again, until Everton exposed Spurs' lack of depth in the Elland Road semi-final.

The season petered out after the defeat against Everton and was brought to a sad end with the news Klinsmann was leaving for Bayern Munich. He was soon followed out of the club by Popescu and Nicky Barmby. Money was made available for replacements, but the quality of Francis's signings did not compare with those who had departed. Chris Armstrong was a willing young striker but not a patch on Klinsmann, Clive Wilson nothing but a short-term signing and the only way Ruel Fox could get out of Newcastle United's reserves was to leave. With Dumitrescu eventually banished to West Ham United, his replacement Andy Sinton, a Sheffield Wednesday reserve, and Darren Anderton suffering continual injury problems the football became functional, devoid of excitement, avoiding defeat all that mattered. Ambition seemed sadly lacking, and while Francis became adept at finding excuses and promising things would improve his inability to look the camera in the eye in his media interviews said much, while his signings belied his words. Mid-table finishes in 1995–96 and 1996–97 and no impression in the Cups were not good enough. Jimmy Greaves found the perfect words to describe Spurs under Francis – 'Wimbledon with fans'. Teddy Sheringham became so frustrated with the long-ball game Francis imposed he departed for Manchester United

Francis eventually realised Spurs' supporters demand a little magic and signed David Ginola, but as fine a player as he was, the Frenchman alone was not enough. Les Ferdinand, like Sinton and Wilson one of Francis's Rangers' old boys, was another big money signing but was not successful. Francis had been given every opportunity and plenty of money, but under his control Spurs had just slipped further and further behind their rivals. As they hovered just above the relegation places the pressure mounted and Francis resigned, with reserve-team coach Chris Hughton taking over for a few days until a new man was appointed.

Christian Gross

Head Coach 25 November 1997 to 5 September 1998.

■ Alan Sugar's experience with the likes of Jurgen Klinsmann, Gica Popescu and Ilie Dumitrescu had soured his view of foreign footballers. With the Bosman decision promising an influx of the continent's top names, Sugar had famously announced he was not going to waste money on 'Carlos Kickaballs'. It was therefore something of a surprise that the next man he entrusted with rebuilding Spurs' fortunes should be a foreigner and even more of a surprise that it should be someone only serious students of the continental game would know.

Former Swiss international Christian Gross was coach of Grasshoppers Zurich, hardly one of the game's giants, but he had done a good job in his four years in charge, taking Grasshoppers to the Swiss Cup, two League titles and the league stage of the European Cup, and he was highly regarded in Europe for his coaching ability.

Sadly, the popular press had little time for a man they did not know and even less time to bother finding out his credentials. Instantly nicknamed 'Christian Who', they ridiculed him from his first press conference. Slated for declaring he had travelled to White Hart Lane as many supporters do, by public transport, criticised for his lack of perfect English and questioned as to how such an unknown could secure the respect of highly-paid professionals, he was not given a chance.

Isolated by the Home Office refusing to grant a work permit to his fitness coach and right-hand man Fritz Schmid, Gross was a man who believed in hard work and everyone pulling together. That was certainly what Spurs needed in their situation and nobody could have worked harder than Gross himself. That he failed to communicate his ideas to the players is undeniable, but he arrived with only one job in mind, to save Spurs from relegation, and that he achieved, albeit only in the final few matches of the season and after the return of Jurgen Klinsmann.

Throughout the close season of 1998 Gross faced renewed criticism for his failure to lure players to the club, his only signing being the unfortunate Paolo Tramezzani. Defeated in the first two games, Spurs won the third at Everton, but Sugar had already decided to spare Gross further criticism and relieved him of his duties.

Gross returned to Switzerland and in June 1999 took over at Basel. He has led them to two Swiss Cups, three League titles and sustained runs in the Champions League, re-establishing his reputation and perhaps raising questions of how he might have succeeded in England had he been given a proper chance.

George Graham

5 October 1998 to 16 March 2001.

■ Having tried a former Spurs hero, a former England captain and an unknown Swiss coach, it was hard to know where Alan Sugar might turn next in his efforts to find a manager to reverse the decline that had taken place ever since he had assumed control of the club. Sugar was coming under increasing pressure. He did not like it and frequently threatened to sell up. To many Spurs supporters his next appointment was viewed as the final snub before he carried out the threat.

Of all the men he turned to, George Graham had by far the best track record. A double winner as a player, as a manager he had won the FA Cup, the League Cup twice, the European Cup-winners' Cup and twice collected the League title. Unfortunately all that success had come with Arsenal and most of it playing a brand of football totally alien to the traditions Peter McWilliam, Arthur Rowe and Bill Nicholson had done so much to establish. On top of that, Graham had been banned from football after being convicted of taking 'bungs'. For many Spurs supporters it represented the final sell-out.

If Sugar thought the appointment would divide Spurs fans it was a resounding success, if he thought it would result in a trophy being won he was right, if he thought it would lead to a return to the 'glory days' he was terribly wrong.

For Graham to have any chance of being accepted by the Spurs faithful he had to make an immediate impression, and that meant winning something. His best chance of doing that was in the Worthington Cup, a competition already greatly devalued by the bigger clubs fielding severely weakened teams. In its old guise of the League Cup it had provided Graham's first success at Highbury, and it was to provide his first and only success at White Hart Lane. Graham almost ended his first season in charge with a Cup double, but Newcastle United exposed Spurs' weaknesses in the FA Cup semi-final.

Graham firmly believed in 'building from the back'. If the defence did not concede a goal matches could not be lost, and if the forwards managed to nick one, they could be won. For him the priority was always defending, even if that meant packing the midfield with players who rarely ventured into the opposition penalty box. It was a philosophy that had brought him success in the past, but football had changed. Attack was now the order of the day, but Graham could not, or would not, change. Signing players like Steffen Freund, Tim Sherwood, Oyvind Leonhardsen, Chris Perry and Ben Thatcher, competent performers but hardly exciting, was indicative of his attitude. Only David Ginola provided any flair, and Graham made his dislike of the Frenchman obvious but dare not discard him if he did not want the fans in open revolt.

Under Graham Spurs' defence-dominated slide towards lower mid-table mediocrity continued. Their reputation for playing stylish football was tarnished, at home and abroad; the stupefying performance away to Zimbru Chisinau in the UEFA Cup of 1999–2000 was an embarrassment to a club that had once illuminated the European game.

With the ENIC takeover and their public pronouncements that they wanted a return to Spurs traditional style, Graham's days were numbered. His removal was almost certain. It was just a question of how long he could hold on. Having taken Spurs to another FA Cup semi-final, he seemed safe till the end of the season, but when he revealed to the press ENIC were not making available the type of money for new signings he wanted he was dismissed. Only days from the meeting with Arsenal at Old Trafford it was a strange decision, but many fans were just pleased to see the back of 'the man in a raincoat'.

Glenn Hoddle

Manager 2 April 2001 to 21 September 2003.

■ When George Graham was sacked David Pleat again stood in as caretaker manager and was expected to fill the role till the end of the season, but less than a week before the FA Cup semi-final Glenn Hoddle was persuaded to return to his spiritual home.

A knee injury having ended his top-flight playing career at Monaco, Hoddle had taken to management with Swindon Town and led them to promotion to the Premier League. He then took over at Chelsea, laying the foundations for the success they subsequently achieved under Ruud Gullit and Gianluca Vialli, before taking on the England coach's job in May 1996. Far from a failure at international level, he was sacked in February 1999 when the press began a witch-hunt based on comments he had made about the disabled months earlier. Southampton gave him the chance to rebuild his reputation, and he was doing a good job when the chance came to take over at White Hart Lane.

He had no time to influence the team before the semi-final, when Spurs were totally outplayed by Arsenal, and it was obvious what an enormous job Hoddle had taken on, a job made all the more difficult when Sol Campbell deserted them for Arsenal. Hoddle's success with Chelsea had been based on signing top-quality players who had perhaps passed the peak of their careers but still had plenty to offer, and who knew what it took to win titles and Cups and could be supplemented by younger, hungrier players. He applied the same approach at Spurs, and it was a policy that almost brought instant success, but Blackburn Rovers beat Spurs in the 2002 Worthington Cup Final and their bogey side, Chelsea, put them out of the FA Cup in the sixth round. Out of the Cups and with the older players tiring, the season faded, but ninth in the League was still an improvement, and at least Spurs were beginning to play football again.

Hoddle remained true to his beliefs in the 2002–03 season and Spurs started well, even leading the League at one time. It was not a position anyone could have expected them to maintain, but a place in the upper reaches of the table seemed likely until another end of season collapse saw them drop to 10th. Hoddle changed tact in the summer of 2003, bringing in younger players like Helder Postiga and Bobby Zamora, but as they struggled to settle results were simply not good enough. In some respects Hoddle was like Ardiles: he believed in playing football in a particular way, an attacking way, and he could not accept that he was wrong. Spurs needed a defensive midfielder, someone who could hold the side together under pressure, but that was not the type of player Hoddle wanted. After six games Spurs had just four points. Coupled with the results from the tail-end of the previous season, the board decided Hoddle was not going to be the Messiah they had originally envisaged and he was sacked. Hoddle may not have been a success as manager, but he had at least rekindled a belief in Spurs' traditional style.

Jacques Santini

Head coach 1 July 2004 to 5 November 2004

■ Having dispensed with Glenn Hoddle's services, the Spurs board decided to review the

whole management and coaching structure. While they sought out the best advice, both at home and abroad, David Pleat took control of team affairs. Originally he might have expected that to be a short-term appointment, but he ended up in charge for the rest of the season as the board took all the time they needed before determining their future plans.

It was not until May 2004 that the board announced they were introducing a continental system with a director of football heading the signing and development of players and a head coach responsible for training and selection of the first-team squad. Frank Arnesen was paraded as the director of football, but it was not until the following month that the new head coach was revealed. When it came the announcement was a surprise, not because Jacques Santini was given the job but because he was manager of France and they were just about to defend their European title in Portugal.

Santini was one of the game's most respected coaches, having worked with CA Lisieux, Toulouse, Lille, St Etienne, Sochaux, Lyon and the French Football Academy. He had taken over the full French team two years earlier and done a fine job rebuilding his country's reputation after their debacle in the 2000 World Cup.

Along with Arnesen and Santini, a whole flood of players arrived at White Hart Lane in the summer of 2004. Some of them did not stay for long but all outlasted Santini. After just 13 games Santini decided to return to France for 'personal reasons'.

In such a short time Santini had no opportunity to make his mark, and it would not be fair to pass judgement on him. Results were mixed and there were complaints he was not adventurous enough, but with no previous experience of English football, a new structure still to find its feet and a squad of players from all over the globe getting to know each other it is not surprising his first objective was to get a few points on the board while he settled in.

Martin Jol

Head coach 8 November 2004 to 25 October 2007

■ Santini's departure provided an immediate test of Spurs' new management structure. Martin Jol had been appointed First Assistant to Santini in June 2004 with the expectation that, in time, he would

move up to the senior position, but it was never envisaged he would have to take on the senior position within six months.

Jol had started his football career with his home-town club, ADO Den Haag, and played for Bayern Munich and Twente before becoming familiar to English fans as a tough-tackling midfielder with West Bromwich Albion and Coventry City. He wound down his career back at ADO Den Haag, then went into coaching with the amateurs of ADO Den Haag and Scheveningen before moving into top-flight coaching with Roda JC Kerkrade and RKC Waalwijk. At RKC he worked minor miracles on one of the tightest budgets in the Dutch League, leading RKC into the upper reaches of the League and European competition and building a reputation as one of the most talented up-and-coming coaches in the country.

Taking control at White Hart Lane, Jol did not have the best of starts with three successive League defeats and an early exit from the Carling Cup, but as he began to exert his influence results improved. At one time UEFA Cup qualification seemed a realistic target, but Spurs had to settle for a mid-table finish plus a run to the sixth round of the FA Cup.

Spurs' new structure went through a further testing time in the summer of 2005 with Frank Arnesen departing for Chelsea. Until a replacement could be found, Jol shouldered the extra burden and reinforced his belief that Spurs should have a core of young English players with the signing of Tom Huddlestone, Jermaine Jenas and Aaron Lennon. Jol's reputation had, in part, been built on his ability to spot and develop young talent, and there can be no doubt Spurs' youngsters progressed in leaps and bounds under his guidance.

In 2005–06 Jol continued to take Spurs forward, fifth place in the League at last seeing Spurs back in the UEFA Cup and only a mystery virus that debilitated half the squad hours before the final match of the season at West Ham depriving Spurs of a place in the Champions League for the first time. Europe's premier competition may have proved a step too far too soon for Jol's developing team, but in the 2006–07 UEFA Cup campaign Jol showed that he had assembled a squad that could cope with the demands of European football as Spurs advanced to the last eight before going out to holders Seville.

With runs to the semi-final of the Carling Cup, the sixth round of the FA Cup and their European exploits, the demands proved too great for Spurs to challenge in the League, but fifth place in the final reckoning gave Spurs another season of improvement and the belief that the breakthrough into the Champions League was not too far away.

The continuing improvement in Spurs' fortunes under Jol's guidance has saw his popularity with Spurs' supporters continue to rise, but that was not simply down to results. The quality football Spurs demand was still there but reinforced by a definite appreciation that success requires skill to be interwoven with hard work.

With his outwardly calm appearance, sense of humour and acceptance that not all decisions will go your way, Jol proved himself a man who could cope with the lows as well as the highs, but defeat in the first two games of the 2007–08 season suddenly saw him under pressure. Stories began to circulate that he was unhappy with the influence of Director of Football, Damien Comolli, that the Spurs' hierarchy had decided Jol had taken Spurs as far as he could and he was not the man to take them to the next level. The speculation led to poor results that in turn bred further speculation.

Jol's friendly, easy-going but forthright style, coupled with the improvement in performances and results he had overseen, had made him popular among the Spurs support. While fearful that there might be something in them, little credence was given to stories of his impending departure until club secretary John Alexander and director Paul Kemsley were caught negotiating with Juande Ramos. The Sevilla manager readily admitted that Spurs had made him a 'dizzying offer'. Despite the fans' support, Jol's position quickly became untenable, his departure just a matter of time. Even then it was surprising that news of his dismissal only emerged as Spurs were being beaten at home by Getafe in a UEFA Cup tie.

Juande Ramos

Head coach 27 October 2007 to 25 October 2008

■ In two years with Sevilla, Juan de la Cruz Ramos Cano had built a fine reputation as an innovative, attack-minded coach expected to make his mark with one of Europe's top teams. Forced to retire from playing due to injury, having appeared as a midfielder in the lower reaches of Spanish football with Elche, Alcoyano, Linares, Eldense, Alicante and Denia, Ramos took up his first coaching post with Alcoyano in 1993. He moved quickly up the coaching ladder with one season at both Levante and Logrones, his success in taking Logrones into the top flight of Spanish football tempting Barcelona to find a role for him. After a season in charge of their B team and another with Lleida, Ramos took over at Rayo Vallecano. In three seasons he led Madrid's least fashionable club from the second division to la Liga and the semi-finals of the UEFA Cup before departing for Real Betis. Espanyol and Malaga followed, with Ramos out of top-flight football for a year before being asked to take over at Sevilla. They had qualified for European competition for the first time under Joaquin Caparros, but President Jose Maria del Nido decided Caparros had taken them as far as he could; Ramos's European experience with Vallecano was needed if Sevilla were to make a name in Europe.

Fortunate to find an exciting group of young and largely home-produced players who had grown up together, Ramos did not disappoint his new employer. The UEFA Cup was won in 2006 and retained in 2007, with the Copa del Rey, UEFA and Spanish Supercups also finding homes in the Sevilla trophy cabinet. With third place in la Liga in 2006-07 securing Sevilla entry to the Champions League for the first time, Ramos's star was certainly in the ascendancy.

Tempted by what was reportedly one of the highest managerial salaries on offer, Ramos arrived at White Hart Lane in October 2007 with Spurs in the relegation zone. With the speculation at an end, results slowly improved as Ramos tightened up a defence that had been porous and lacking

in confidence while at the same time giving free rein to an attack that with the likes of Dimitar Berbatov and Aaron Lennon was always going to score goals. Ramos enhanced the Cup-winning reputation he had built in Spain as Spurs celebrated their first visit to the new Wembley Stadium with Carling Cup success against Chelsea while also getting through to the last 16 of the UEFA Cup before unluckily exiting the competition to PSV Eindhoven on penalties.

Finishing mid-table in the League and winning a Cup competition that provided entry to European football again was a more than satisfactory first season for Ramos, and things might have been better still were it not for an end-of-season fall-off in results. Even with the departure of star forward Berbatov, it was not expected Spurs would take a giant step backward in 2008–09, but that was exactly what happened. Two draws in the eight League games with only an unexpected Carling Cup victory at Newcastle to lift the gloom, and Ramos was dismissed without even completing a full year in charge.

Harry Redknapp

Manager 26 October 2008 -

■ Having played for West Ham United, AFC Bournemouth and Brentford, Harry Redknapp joined the legion of English professionals winding down their careers in the US, where he got his first real experience of coaching during four seasons with Seattle Sounders. Back home in England, he joined Bournemouth as David Webb's assistant manager, kept the post when Webb was dismissed and took on the manager's job in October 1983. Redknapp spent nine years at Dean Court, developing the skills that were to serve him well as he worked on a shoestring budget that demanded innovative coaching, man-management

skills and an ability to spot the bargain signing.

Having done as much as anyone could at Bournemouth, Redknapp returned to West Ham, initially as Billy Bonds assistant before taking over from his old teammate in August 1994. Over the course of seven years he turned what had been a struggling club into a top half of the table side, even securing UEFA Cup football. He seemed set to continue with West Ham for years to come until his readiness to talk honestly with supporters saw the board take exception to some reported comments and relieve him of his job.

Redknapp was only out of the game for a short time, taking on the Director of Football role at Portsmouth and then stepping in as manager when Graham Rix was dismissed in March 2002. Little over 12 months later, Redknapp led Portsmouth into the Premier League just as West Ham were going in the opposite direction. Under his guidance Portsmouth were just settling to top-flight football when he fell out with club owner Milan Mandaric over the appointment of a Director of Football. Not prepared to play second fiddle, Redknapp promptly resigned. Within weeks he was unveiled as Southampton's new manager, charged with saving the Saints from relegation, a task that proved beyond even Redknapp's talents.

Halfway through the following season, 2005–06, Redknapp returned to Portsmouth as they struggled at the wrong end of the table. He led them away from relegation, consolidated their Premier League status and in 2008 guided Pompey to FA Cup success, their first major trophy for near 60 years.

With two points out of a possible 24 and a battle against relegation a near certainty, Redknapp was one of the few managers Spurs could turn to with any real confidence that their top flight status might be saved. Such was the belief in his talents that Spurs paid Portsmouth £5 million compensation to secure Redknapp's services. It was to prove money well spent.

Redknapp's influence was immediate as his mere presence lifted the whole atmosphere. Confident, relaxed and approachable, he gave the impression of being a man in control. He knew what needed to be done and how that would be achieved. Spurs climbed steadily away from the drop zone while also making progress in the Carling and UEFA Cups. Manchester United and the lottery of spot-kicks proved too much for Spurs in the Carling Cup, and Shakhtar Donetsk might have been overcome in Europe had Redknapp not decided to keep the first-team regulars back for the more important Premier League games.

Having achieved the primary objective of guiding Spurs away from relegation, Redknapp's attention turned to taking Spurs forward. He lived up to his reputation of being a transfer market wheeler-dealer as he restructured the squad, although while he had been known in the past for snapping up often unknown foreign talent at bargain prices, with Spurs his targets were well-known, established performers, often men he had worked with in the past.

Never one for dour, defensive football, Redknapp loves to have players with real attacking ability around him, but if he feels the situation calls for it he has no fear of being a little less adventurous than supporters might want. Never afraid to make holding on to what has been won his priority, Redknapp's tactics were more often right than wrong as his first full season in charge saw him achieve something none of his predecessors had managed; qualification for the Champions League.

In Europe's premier competition Redknapp enhanced his reputation as Spurs stunned the continent's elite with performances that surprised even him. He realised that Spurs did not have the players, and would not be allowed by the fans, to stifle the opposition in the hope of snatching a one-goal victory. Home or away, attack was the only option. At times it may have looked naïve, three down to Young Boys after 30 minutes, four down to Inter by half-time, but even then Spurs always looked capable of coming back.

Spurs' success under Redknapp's guidance has led to the inevitable speculation. As one of the few Englishmen at the top of the domestic game, he has been thrust forward as the obvious successor to Fabio Capello as England manager, while clubs with vastly more resources than Spurs and a demand for instant success have cast covetous glances in his direction. Hopefully Redknapp knows that his services are appreciated at White Hart Lane and that what he can achieve there will leave an indelible mark on Spurs' history.

1896-97

SOUTHERN LEAGUE

Manager: None

Did you know that?

Spurs' prospects of winning their first Cup, the Wellingborough Charity Cup, were not helped when four players, Devlin, McElhaney, Milliken and Wilson, were suspended in the days leading up to the Final for allegedly not trying in recent matches.

Match No.	Date			Opponents		Result	Scorers	Attendar
1	Sep	5	A	Sheppey United	D	3-3	Crump, Milliken, R.Clements	2,(
2		12	A	Wolverton	L	0-1		1,(
3	Oct	3	A	Gravesend United	W	3-1	Newbigging, R.Clements, Payne	1,8
4		10	H	Chatham	L	2-3	Minter, Middlemiss	5,(
5		17	H	Gravesend United	W	4-0	McElhaney, Milliken 2, R.Clements	3,(
6		24	A	Royal Ordnance*	W	2-1	Almond, Payne	5
7		31	A	Chatham	W	2-1	McElhaney, Milliken 2	5,(
8	Nov	7	H	Sheppey United	W	3-2	McElhaney, R.Clements, Briggs	3,(
9		14	H	Swindon Town	W	3-1	Devlin, Milliken, Newbigging	2,(
10		28	H	Millwall Athletic	L	1-3	Fleming	6,(
11	Dec	5	A	Reading	L	1-2	Payne	3,5
12		25	A	Millwall Athletic	W	4-0	McElhaney, R.Clements 2, Payne	6,(
13	Jan	9	A	Swindon Town	L	0-1		2,(
14	Feb	13	H	Northfleet	W	5-0	Robertson, R.Clements 3, Stirling (og)	3,(
15		20	A	New Brompton	L	1-2	R.Clements	2,(
16	Mar	6	A	Northfleet	L	0-2		2,(
17		20	H	Reading	D	4-4	Almond, McElhaney, Wilson, R.Clements	4,(
18		27	H	New Brompton	W	2-0	Wilson, R.Clements	2,(
19		29	A	Southampton St Marys	D	1-1	R.Clements	3,(
20	Apr	1	H	Wolverton	W	2-0	McElhaney, Crump	2,(
21		8	H	Southampton St Marys	D	2-2	Wilson, R.Clements	3,(

*Result expunged on Royal Ordnance's resignation from the League

Appearanc

Goa

United League

No.	Date			Opponents		Result	Scorers	Attendance
1	Sep	19	A	Millwall Athletic	L	5-6	Crump 2, Newbigging 2, R.Clements	6,(
2	Nov	2	A	Rushden	L	0-2		1,(
3		9	A	Woolwich Arsenal	L	1-2	Devlin	2,(
4	Jan	30	A	Wellingborough	D	2-2	Burrows (pen), R.Clements	1,2
5	Feb	25	H	Woolwich Arsenal	D	2-2	Devlin, R.Clements	2,(
6		27	H	Loughborough	L	1-2	Payne	4,(
7	Mar	4	H	Rushden	W	5-1	Briggs, Newbigging, Milliken, Allen, Crump	
8		13	H	Luton Town	L	1-2	Devlin	7,(
9		15	A	Kettering Town	D*	1-1	Milliken	2
10	Apr	3	H	Millwall Athletic	L	1-3	Milliken	5,(
11		10	A	Luton Town	L	1-2	Newbigging	2,5
12		13	A	Kettering Town	L	2-5	Wilson, Draper (og)	3
13		17	H	Kettering Town	D	1-1	R.Clements	
14		19	H	Wellingborough	D	1-1	Lanham	3,(
15		27	A	Loughborough	L	2-3	R.Clements, Hobson	

Appearanc

Goa

FA Cup

Round	Date			Opponents		Result	Scorers	Attendance
Q1	Dec	12	H	Old Stepehns	W	4-0	Newbigging, R.Clements 2, Payne	1,5
Q2	Jan	6	H	Maidenhead	W	6-0	Crump 2, McElhaney, Newbigging 2, Payne	2,0
Q3		16	A	Luton Town	L	0-3		5,0

Appearanc

Goa

Wellingborough Charity Cup

Round	Date			Opponents		Result	Scorers	Attendance
Pr	Nov	19	H	Gravesend United	W	3-2	Almond, Fleming 2	1,0
R1	Dec	16	A	Wolverton	W	2-0	McElhaney, Lanham	
SF	Apr	5	N*	Rushden	W#	2-1	McElhaney (pen), R.Clements	1,0
F		29	A	Wellingborough	L	0-2		

*played at Wellingborough #after extra-time

Appearanc

Goa

Almond W	Ambler CJ	Briggs SS	Brown S	Burrows L	Clements RW	Collins JS	Cook HJ	Crump WH	Devlin J	Fleming W	Hatfield T	Hobson	Hunter PJ	Jull JC	Jull TE	Lanham CH	Latham F	Mair J	Markham ES	McElhaney R	Milligan A	Milliken J	Montgomery J	Newbigging WM	Payne EG	Regan CD	Robertson A	Shepherd WJ	Wilson F	own-goals
	1			2	10	4		6	5											7		8	3	9	11					
5	1			2	10			6	4							7						8	3	9	11					
	1	5		2	10			6	4											7		8	3	9	11					
	1	5		2	10			6	4											7		8	3	9	11					
5	1			2	10			6	4											7		8	3	9	11					
5	1			2	10			6	4											7		8	3	9	11					
5	1			2	10	4		6	8											7		9	3		11					
5	1	4		2	10			6	8											7		9	3		11					
5	1			2	10			6	4											7		8	3	9	11					
5	1			2	10			6	4	9										7		8	3		11					
5	1			2	10				4	11								6		7		8	3		9					
5	1			2	10			6	4											7		8	3	9	11					
	1			2	10			6	4									5		7			3	9	11					
5	1			2	10			6	4											7		8	3		11		9			
5	1			2	10			6	4							8				7		9	3		11					
5	1			2	10			6	4													8	3	7	11					
5	1			2	10			6	4											7		8	3		11				9	
5	1	6			10			11	4										2	7			3		8				9	
	1	6			10			11	4										2	7		8	3						9	
5		6			10			11	4		1								2	7		8	3						9	
5	1				10			6	4											7		8	3		11				9	
16	20	6	0	17	21	2	0	20	21	2	1	0	0	0	0	2	0	2	3	19	0	19	21	10	19	0	1	0	5	
2		1			14			2	1	1										6		6		2	5		1		3	1

Almond W	Ambler CJ	Briggs SS	Brown S	Burrows L	Clements RW	Collins JS	Cook HJ	Crump WH	Devlin J	Fleming W	Hatfield T	Hobson	Hunter PJ	Jull JC	Jull TE	Lanham CH	Latham F	Mair J	Markham ES	McElhaney R	Milligan A	Milliken J	Montgomery J	Newbigging WM	Payne EG	Regan CD	Robertson A	Shepherd WJ	Wilson F	own-goals
	1	5		2	10			6	4											7		8	3	9	11					
	1	5		2	10	6			4											7		8	3	9	11					
5	1			2	10	4		6	8											7		11	3	9						
	1			2	10			6	4							9				7		8	3		11					
5	1			2	10			6	4											7		8	3	9	11					
5	1			2	10			6	4									3		7		8		9	11					
	1	6		2	10			11	5													8	3	7		4				
5	1			2	10			6	4											7		8	3		11					
	1				10			11	4									6	2	7		8	3	9						
5	1	6		2	10				4											7		8	3		11				9	
	1	5			10			6	4									3		7				8	11				9	
		5			10			11	4		1							6	3	7		8							9	
				2	10			6						7		8	1	4					3	9	11					
	1			2	10			6						7		8		4					3	9	11					
					10			7				11	8		2		1	6					3	9				4		
5	12	6	0	11	15	2	0	13	12	0	1	1	1	2	1	3	2	7	2	11	0	11	12	11	10	1	0	1	3	
		1		1	5			3	3			1				1						3		4	1				1	1

Almond W	Ambler CJ	Briggs SS	Brown S	Burrows L	Clements RW	Collins JS	Cook HJ	Crump WH	Devlin J	Fleming W	Hatfield T	Hobson	Hunter PJ	Jull JC	Jull TE	Lanham CH	Latham F	Mair J	Markham ES	McElhaney R	Milligan A	Milliken J	Montgomery J	Newbigging WM	Payne EG	Regan CD	Robertson A	Shepherd WJ	Wilson F	own-goals
5	1	6		2	10				4											7		8	3	9	11					
5	1			2	10			4	6											7		8	3	9	11					
5	1			2	10			4	6											7		8	3	9	11					
3	3	1	0	3	3	0	0	2	3	0	0	0	0	0	0	0	0	0	0	3	0	3	3	3	3	0	0	0	0	
					2			2												1				3	2					

Almond W	Ambler CJ	Briggs SS	Brown S	Burrows L	Clements RW	Collins JS	Cook HJ	Crump WH	Devlin J	Fleming W	Hatfield T	Hobson	Hunter PJ	Jull JC	Jull TE	Lanham CH	Latham F	Mair J	Markham ES	McElhaney R	Milligan A	Milliken J	Montgomery J	Newbigging WM	Payne EG	Regan CD	Robertson A	Shepherd WJ	Wilson F	own-goals
5	1			2	10			6	4	9										7		8	3		11					
		5					2	11	4		1					8		6		7		10	3	9						
	1	5			10			6	4											7		8	3	11					9	
	1	5	7		10			11					8								2		3	9			6			
1	3	3	1	1	3	0	1	4	3	1	1	0	1	0	0	1	0	1	0	3	1	3	4	3	1	0	1	0	1	
1					1					2						1				2										

League Table

	P	W	D	L	F	A	Pts
Southampton St Marys	20	15	5	0	63	18	35
Millwall Athletic	20	13	5	2	63	24	31
Chatham	20	13	1	6	54	29	27
TOTTENHAM HOTSPUR	20	9	4	7	43	29	22
Gravesend United	20	9	4	7	35	34	22
Swindon Town	20	8	3	9	33	37	19
Reading	20	8	3	9	31	49	19
New Brompton	20	7	2	11	32	42	16
Northfleet	20	5	4	11	24	46	14
Sheppey United	20	5	1	14	34	47	11
Wolverton	20	2	0	18	17	74	4

UNITED LEAGUE	P	W	D	L	F	A	Pts
Millwall Athletic	14	11	1	2	43	22	23
Luton Town	14	10	1	3	52	16	21
Woolwich Arsenal	14	6	3	5	28	34	15
Loughborough	14	6	1	7	29	31	13
Rushden	14	6	1	7	25	42	13
Kettering Town*	14	4	4	6	23	24	10
Wellingborough	14	3	3	8	17	39	9
TOTTENHAM HOTSPUR	14	1	4	9	25	34	6

*Two points deducted

1897-98

SOUTHERN LEAGUE

Manager: Frank Brettell from March

Did you know that?

Jack Jones became the first Spurs player to appear in an international match when he played for Wales against Ireland on 19 February 1898. He went on to win another 11 caps as a Spurs player.

Match No.	Date			Opponents	Result		Scorers	Attendan
1	Sep	4	A	Sheppey United	D	1-1	Joyce	2,0
2		18	H	Southampton	W	2-0	Davidson 2	6,0
3		25	H	Millwall Athletic	W	7-0	Tannahill, Davidson, Meade 3, Joyce, Black	10,0
4	Oct	2	A	New Brompton	L	0-1		4,0
5		9	H	Gravesend United	W	2-0	Hartley 2	2,0
6		23	A	Southampton	L	1-4	Tannahill	10,0
7	Nov	6	A	Reading	D	3-3	Tannahill, Joyce, Black	4,0
8		13	H	Bristol City	D	2-2	Burrows, Black	9,0
9		27	A	Bristol City	L	1-3	Devlin, Milliken, Newbigging	2,0
10	Dec	18	A	Wolverton	W	2-1	Joyce, Stormont	1,5
11	Jan	15	H	Northfleet	W	4-0	Hartley, Joyce 3	2,0
12		22	H	Wolverton	W	7-1	Davidson 2, Joyce 4, Hartley	3,0
13		29	A	Chatham	L	2-4	Black, Joyce	2,5
14	Feb	5	A	Swindon Town	L	0-3		4,0
15		19	A	Northfleet	W	3-1	Joyce 2, Black	2,0
16		26	H*	Reading	D	1-1	Jones	5,5
17	Mar	5	A	Gravesend United	W	2-1	Hartley 2	3,0
18		19	H	Sheppey United	W	4-0	Joyce 4	2,8
19	Apr	2	H	New Brompton	W	3--1	Joyce 1, Black 2	4,0
20		9	H	Chatham	W	2-1	Hartley, Black	3,0
21		11	H	Swindon Town	W	2-0	Meade, Stormont	5,0
22		16	A	Millwall Athletic	L	1-3	Meade	3,0

*played at East Ferry Road, Millwall

Appearance

Goa

United League

1	Sep	16	H	Kettering Town	D	1-1	R.Clements	2,0
2		29	A	Loughborough	W	2-1	Tannahill, Stormont	
3	Oct	11	A	Luton Town	L	0-5		
4		16	A	Millwall Athletic	W	1-0	Jones	8,0
5	Dec	4	H	Wellingborough	W	5-0	Tannahill, Joyce, Stormont 2, Black	1,0
6		25	A	Woolwich Arsenal	W	3-2	Joyce 2, Stormont	6,0
7	Jan	1	A	Rushden	L	2-5	Hartley 2	1,5
8		8	H	Rushden	W	3-1	Hartley 3	4,0
9		10	A	Kettering Town	L	2-4	Joyce 2 (1 pen)	1,5
10		19	A	Southampton	D	2-2	Tannahill, Joyce (pen)	3,0
11	Feb	3	H	Luton Town	D	2-2	Stormont, Joyce	4,0
12	Mar	12	H	Millwall Athletic	W	3-2	Jones (pen), Davidson, Black	8,0
13		24	H	Loughborough	W	5-0	Joyce 2, Stormont, Black 2	3
14		28	H	Southampton	W	7-0	Hartley, Joyce 4, Stormont, Black	3,0
15	Apr	8	H	Woolwich Arsenal	D	0-0		15,0
16		23	A	Wellingborough	D	2-2	Stormont, Black	

Appearance

Goa

FA Cup

Q1	Oct	30	H*	2nd Coldstream Guards	W	7-0	Hall, Crump, Meade 2, Joyce, Stormont, Black	4,0
Q2	Nov	20	H	Luton Town	L	3-4	Joyce 2, Black	12,0

*Spurs drawn away but played at home by mutual consent

Appearance

Goa

Black DG	Briggs SS	Burrows L	Clements RW	Crump WH	Cullen J	Davidson JW	Downie E	Hall AR	Hargreaves E	Hartley JM	Jones JL	Joyce W	Knowles J	Madden J	Meade TG	Montgomery J	Payne EG	Stormont R	Tannahill R
11					1	10		6			5	9	2		8	3		4	7
11		2		6	1	8		4			5				9	3		10	7
11		2			1	8		4			5	10			9	3		6	7
11		2			1	8		4			5	10	3		9			6	7
11		2			1	8		4		9	5	10	3					6	7
11		2			1	8		4		10	5	9	3					6	7
11	5				1			4			6	9	2		8	3		10	7
11		2		6	1			4			5	9	3		8			10	7
11		2		6		8		4			5	9	3					10	7
11		2		6	1	8		4		7	5	9	3					10	
					1	8		4		7	5	9	2	10		3		6	11
				11	1	8	4			10	5	9	2			3		6	7
7				11	1	8		4		10	5	9	2			3		6	
11				6	1	8		4		7	5		2		9	3		10	
11				6	1	8	5	4		7		9	2			3		10	
11				6	1	8		4		7	5	9	2			3		10	
11				6	1	8		4		7	5	9	2			3		10	
11				6	1		5	4		7		9	2		8	3		10	
11					1	8	6	4		7	5	9	2			3		10	
11		2			1	8	6	4		7	5			9		3		10	
11					1		6	4		7	5	9	2		8	3		10	
11		2			1		6	4		7	5	9	3		8			10	
20	1	10	0	11	21	17	7	21	0	15	20	19	19	2	10	15	0	22	11
8		1				5				7	1	20			5			2	3

Black DG	Briggs SS	Burrows L	Clements RW	Crump WH	Cullen J	Davidson JW	Downie E	Hall AR	Hargreaves E	Hartley JM	Jones JL	Joyce W	Knowles J	Madden J	Meade TG	Montgomery J	Payne EG	Stormont R	Tannahill R
11		2	10		1	8		4			5	9	3					6	7
11		2		6	1	8		4			5	10	3					9	7
11		2			1	8		4	7	9	5	10				3		6	
11		2		6	1	8		4			5	9	3					10	7
11		2		6		8		4			5	9	3					10	7
11		2		6	1	8		4		7	5	9	3					10	
11		2		6	1	8		4		7	5	9	3					10	
11					1	8		4		7	5	9	2	10		3		6	
11					1	8		4		7	5	9	2	10		3		6	
				11	1	8		4		10	5	9	2			3		6	7
11				6	1	8		4		7	5	9	2			3		10	
11		2		6	1	8		4		7	5	9	3					10	
11					1		6	4		7	5	9	2	8		3		10	
11				6	1		5	4		7		9	2	8		3		10	
11		2		6	1	8		4		7	5	9	3					10	
11		2		6	1		3	4		8	5	9					7	10	
15	0	10	1	11	15	13	3	16	1	12	15	16	14	4	0	7	1	16	5
6			1			1				6	2	13						8	3

Black DG	Briggs SS	Burrows L	Clements RW	Crump WH	Cullen J	Davidson JW	Downie E	Hall AR	Hargreaves E	Hartley JM	Jones JL	Joyce W	Knowles J	Madden J	Meade TG	Montgomery J	Payne EG	Stormont R	Tannahill R
11		2		6	1			4			5	9			8	3		10	7
11		2		6	1			4		8	5	9	3					10	7
2	0	2	0	2	2	0	0	2	0	1	2	2	1	0	1	1	0	2	2
2				1				1				3			2			1	

League Table

	P	W	D	L	F	A	Pts
Southampton	22	18	1	3	53	18	37
Bristol City	22	13	7	2	67	33	33
TOTTENHAM HOTSPUR	22	12	4	6	52	31	28
Chatham	22	12	4	6	50	34	28
Reading	22	8	7	7	39	31	23
New Brompton	22	9	4	9	37	37	22
Sheppey United	22	10	1	11	40	49	21
Gravesend United	22	7	6	9	28	39	20
Millwall Athletic	22	8	2	12	48	45	18
Swindon Town	22	7	2	13	36	48	16
Northfleet	22	4	3	15	29	60	11
Wolverton	22	3	1	18	28	82	7

UNITED LEAGUE	P	W	D	L	F	A	Pts
Luton Town	16	13	2	1	49	11	28
TOTTENHAM HOTSPUR	16	8	5	3	40	27	21
Woolwich Arsenal	16	8	5	3	35	24	21
Kettering Town	16	9	1	6	28	25	19
Rushden	16	7	1	8	24	26	15
Southampton*	16	6	3	7	23	28	13
Millwall Athletic	16	4	4	8	27	27	12
Wellingborough	16	3	3	10	17	41	9
Loughborough	16	1	2	13	8	42	4

*Two points deducted

1898-99

SOUTHERN LEAGUE

Manager: Frank Brettell until February then John Cameron

Did you know that?

Spurs' last match at Northumberland Park was a United League fixture with Woolwich Arsenal on 29 April 1899. A crowd of 5,000, far larger than anticipated, paying £113 assembled to say farewell to the old ground. The South Londoners needed victory to secure second place in the League but Spurs won 3–2 to pip them for third place.

Match No.	Date		Opponents		Result		Scorers	Attendan
1	Sep	10	H	Bedminster	D	1-1	Cameron	5,0
2		17	H	Sheppey United	W	3-2	Cameron 3	4,5
3		24	H	Warmley	W*	7-1	Smith 3, McKay, Joyce 3	4,0
4	Oct	8	H	Chatham	W	2-0	Smith, Cameron	10,0
5		26	A	Millwall Athletic	L	2-4	Smith 2	14,0
6	Nov	5	H	Reading	W	3-0	McKay, Cameron, Bradshaw	12,0
7		26	A	Royal Artillery	W	3-2	Joyce 3	5,0
8	Dec	3	A	Bristol City	L	1-2	Joyce	6,0
9		17	A	Sheppey United	L	2-3	McKay, Penney (og)	9
10		24	A	Warmley	W*	5-1	Smith, Hartley, Joyce, Cameron, Bradshaw	2,0
11		26	A	Southampton	D	1-1	Smith	16,0
12		31	A	Swindon Town	L	3-4	Cameron 3	6,0
13	Jan	7	H	Royal Artillery	W	1-0	McKay	3,5
14		14	A	Gravesend United	L	2-4	Joyce 2	3,5
15		21	A	Brighton United	W	1-0	Bradshaw	2,0
16	Feb	4	A	Reading	L	0-2		3,0
17		18	H	Bristol City	W	3-2	McKay, Hartley, Bradshaw	6,0
18	Mar	13	A	New Brompton	D	1-1	Joyce	3,0
19		18	H	New Brompton	W	3-0	Smith 2, Rule	3,0
20		25	H	Brighton United	L	1-3	Joyce	2,5
21		31	H	Southampton	L	0-1		8,5
22	Apr	1	H	Gravesend United	W	3-0	Joyce, Leech 2	4,0
23		3	H	Swindon Town	D	1-1	Cameron	4,5
24		8	A	Chatham	L	0-1		3,0
25		15	A	Bedminster	L	0-1		1,5
26		22	H	Millwall Athletic	W	3-1	Joyce, Cameron, Bradshaw	7,0

*result expunged on Warmley's resignation from League

Appearanc

Go

FA Cup

Q1	Oct	29	H*	Wolverton	W	4-0	McKay, Joyce, Cameron, Bradshaw	3,0
Q2	Nov	19	A	Clapton	D	1-1	Bradshaw	7,0
Q2r		23	H	Clapton	W	2-1	Cameron 2	2,5
Q3	Dec	10	H	Luton Town	D	1-1	Joyce	12,0
Q3r		14	A	Luton Town	D	1-1	Meade	4,0
Q3r		19	N#	Luton Town	W	2-0	Cameron, Bradshaw	8,0
R1	Jan	28	H	Newton Heath	D	1-1	Joyce	13,7
R1r	Feb	1	A	Newton Heath	W	5-3	Jones, McNaught, Smith, Hartley, Joyce	6,0
R2		11	H	Sunderland	W	2-1	Cameron, Bradshaw	12,3
R3		25	A	Stoke	L	1-4	Bradshaw	25,0

*Spurs drawn away but played at home by mutual consent

#played at Tufnell Park

Appearanc

Go

Atherton TH	Bradshaw TH	Cain R	Cameron J	Cullen J	Downie E	Erentz HB	Hall AR	Hartley JM	Hickson	Hudson	Jones JL	Joyce W	Kerry	Leech W	Markham ES	McKay K	McNaught JR	Meade TG	Melia J	Payne EG	Rule AG	Smith T	Stormont R	Waller WH	Own-goal
	11	3	10	1		2					4	9				8	5					7	6		
	11	3	10	1		2					6	9				8	5					7	4		
	11	3	10	1		2					4	9				8	5					7	6		
		3	10	1		2					4	9				8	5			11		7	6		
	11	3	10	1		2					4	9				8	5					7	6		
	11	3	10	1		2					4	9				8	5					7	6		
	11	3	10	1		2					4	9				8	5					7	6		
	11	3	10	1		2					4	9				8	5					7	6		
	11	3		1		4					5	10				8		9	2			7	6		
	11	3	10	1		2		8			4	9					5					7	6		
	11	3	10	1		2		8			4	9					5					7	6		
	11	3	10	1		5					4	9				8			2			7	6		
	11	3	10	1		5					4					8		9	2			7	6		
	11		10	1		2	4					9				8		5	3			7	6		
	11	3	10			4	5					9				8			2			7	6	1	
	11	3	10				5				4	9					2	8				7	6		
	11	3	10	1				9			4					8	5		2			7	6		
	11	3	10	1		2					4	9					5	8				7	6		
8	11	3	10	1		4											5		2		9	7	6		
	11	3	8	1		4						10					5		2		9	7	6		
	11	3	10			4						9					5		2		8	7	6	1	
		2	10	1	6	4						9		11		8	5		3			7			
	9	2	10	1	6	4								11		8	5		3			7			
	9	3	10	1	4	2								11		8	5					7	6		
8	11		10	1	4	3						9		6			5		2			7			
	11	3	10			4						9				8	5		2			7	6	1	
2	24	24	25	22	4	24	3	3	0	0	16	21	0	4	0	18	21	5	13	1	3	26	23	3	
	5		12					2				14		2		5					1	10			1

Atherton TH	Bradshaw TH	Cain R	Cameron J	Cullen J	Downie E	Erentz HB	Hall AR	Hartley JM	Hickson	Hudson	Jones JL	Joyce W	Kerry	Leech W	Markham ES	McKay K	McNaught JR	Meade TG	Melia J	Payne EG	Rule AG	Smith T	Stormont R	Waller WH	Own-goal
	11	3	10	1							4	9				8	5		2			7	6		
	11	3	10	1		2					4	9				8	5					7	6		
	11	3	10	1		2					4	9				8	5					7	6		
	11	3	10	1		4					5	9				8			2			7	6		
	11	3		1		4					5	10				8		9	2			7	6		
	11	3	10	1		2					4	9				8	5					7	6		
	11	3	10	1		2					4	9				8	5					7	6		
		3	10	1		2		9			4	11				8	5					7	6		
	11	3	10	1		2					4	9				8	5					7	6		
	11	3	10	1		2		8			4	9					5					7	6		
0	9	10	9	10	0	9	0	2	0	0	10	10	0	0	0	9	8	1	3	0	0	10	10	0	
	5		5					1			1	4				1	1	1				1			

League Table

	P	W	D	L	F	A	Pts
Southampton	24	15	5	4	54	24	35
Bristol City	24	15	3	6	55	33	33
Millwall Athletic	24	12	6	6	59	35	30
Chatham	24	10	8	6	32	23	28
Reading	24	9	8	7	31	24	26
New Brompton	24	10	5	9	38	30	25
TOTTENHAM HOTSPUR	24	10	4	10	40	36	24
Bedminster	24	10	4	10	35	39	24
Swindon Town	24	9	5	10	43	49	23
Brighton United	24	9	2	13	37	48	20
Gravesend United	24	7	5	12	42	52	19
Sheppey United	24	5	3	16	23	53	13
Royal Artillery	24	4	4	16	17	60	12

1898-99 Cont.

Match No.	Date		Opponents		Result		Scorers	Attendance
United League								
1	Sep	5	H	Luton Town	W	1-0	McKay	1,0
2		19	A	Luton Town	W	4-3	Cameron 2, Joyce 2	
3	Oct	12	A	Brighton United	W	2-1	Cameron, Joyce	2
4		10	H	Southampton	W	4-0	Smith, McKay, Cameron, Bradshaw	7,0
5		15	A	Bristol City	W	1-0	Cameron	8,0
6	Nov	9	A	Reading	L	0-1		
7		12	H	Bristol City	W	2-1	McKay, Cameron	7,0
8	Dec	5	H	Kettering Town	W	3-0	Joyce 2, Bradshaw	2,0
9	Jan	23	H	Reading	D	1-1	Bradshaw	2,0
10	Feb	15	A	Southampton	L	1-2	Joyce	
11		20	A	Rushden	L	1-2	McKay	
12		27	A	Kettering Town	W	1-0	McNaught	
13	Mar	4	A	Millwall Athletic	L	1-2	Erentz	10,0
14		11	A	Woolwich Arsenal	L	1-2	Meade	6,0
15		27	H	Rushden	D	0-0		1,0
16	Apr	4	H	Brighton United	W	3-0	Cameron (pen), Bradshaw, Caldwell (og)	3,0
17		17	A	Wellingborough	L	1-3	Joyce	
18		24	H	Wellingborough	W	5-2	Cain, Atherton, Hartley 3	8
19		26	H	Millwall Athletic	L	1-3	Cameron	2,5
20		29	H	Woolwich Arsenal	W	3-2	Smith, Joyce, Ord (og)	5,0
								Appearanc
								Goa

Match No.	Date		Opponents		Result		Scorers	Attendance
Thames & Medway League								
1	Sep	3	H	Thames Ironworks	W	3-0	McKay, Cameron, Bradshaw	3,0
2		27	A	Sheppey United	W	3-2	Joyce (pen), Cameron, McKay	5
3	Oct	3	H	Gravesend United	W	3-1	Joyce, Cameron, McKay	2,5
4		17	H	New Brompton	W	2-1	Smith, McKay	6,0
5		26	A	Dartford	W	3-2	Bradshaw, Cameron, McKay	5
6	Nov	2	A	Royal Engineers	W	6-2	McKay 5, McNaught	1
7	Jan	2	A	Chatham	L	0-5		
8		9	H	Chatham	L	0-4		2,5
9		16	H	Sheppey United	W	3-0	Hartley, Cameron, Bradshaw	1,5
10	Feb	6	H	Grays United	W	2-1	Atherton, Leech	4
11	Mar	8	A	Gravesend United	W	3-0	Atherton, Cameron, Bradshaw	2,0
12		16	A	Thames Ironworks	L	1-2	Joyce	2,0
13		20	H	Royal Engineers	L	1-2	Hartley	
14		22	A	Grays United	L	0-1		
15	Apr	10	A	New Brompton	L	4-5	Smith, Atherton, Cameron, Leech	
16		13	H	Dartford	W	9-0	Joyce 5, Cameron 2, Leech 2	
								Appearanc
								Goa

mbler CJ	Atherton TH	Bradshaw TH	Cain R	Cameron J	Cullen J	Downie E	Erentz HB	Hall AR	Hartley JM	Hickson	Hudson	Jones JL	Joyce W	Kerry	Leech W	Markham ES	McKay K	McNaught JR	Meade TG	Melia J	Payne EG	Rule AG	Smith T	Stormont R	Waller WH	Own-goals
		11	3	10								4	9				8	5		2			7	6		
			2	10	1		3	6	7			4	9				11	5						8		
		11	3	10	1		2					4	9				8	5					7	6		
		11	3	10	1		2					4	9				8	5					7	6		
		11	2	10	1		3					4	9				8	5					7	6		
		11	3	10	1		2		4				9				8	5					7	6		
		11	3	10	1		2					4	9				8	5					7	6		
		11	3	10	1		2	4				5	9				8						7	6		
		11	3	10	1	6	4	5					9			2	8						7			
		11	3	10	1		2		8			4	9		6					5			7			
		11		10	1		4		7			5	9			3	8			2				6		
		11	3	10	1		4					5	9					8		2			7	6		
		11	3	10	1		4						9				8	5		2			7	6		
		11	3	10	1		2					4						5	8			9	7	6		
		11	3	10		5	4						9				8			2			7	6		
	8	9	3	10	1	4	2								11			5					7	6		
	10	11	3		1	4	2						9					5	8				7	6		
	9	11	3	10	1	5	4		8											2			7	6		
		11	3	10		6	4						9				8	5		2			7		1	
		11	3	10	1		4						9				8	5		2			7	6		
	3	19	19	19	17	6	19	3	5	0	0	11	17	0	2	2	14	14	2	9	0	1	18	17	1	
	1	4	1	8			1		3				8				4	1	1				2			2

mbler CJ	Atherton TH	Bradshaw TH	Cain R	Cameron J	Cullen J	Downie E	Erentz HB	Hall AR	Hartley JM	Hickson	Hudson	Jones JL	Joyce W	Kerry	Leech W	Markham ES	McKay K	McNaught JR	Meade TG	Melia J	Payne EG	Rule AG	Smith T	Stormont R	Waller WH	Own-goals
		11	3	10				1				4	9				8	5		2			7	6		
		11	2	10	1		3					4	9				8	5					7	6		
		11	3	10	1		2					4	9				8	5					7	6		
		11	3	10	1		2					4	9				8	5					7	6		
		11	3	10	1							4	9				8	5		2			7	6		
		11	3	10	1							4	9				8	5		2			7	6		
		11			1		3		9			4	5		10		8			2			7	6		
		11	3	10	1		4		9			5					8			2			7	6		
	5	9		8		6	3	4	7	10					11					2						
	8					5		4	7	10	9			6	11	3				2						
	8	11	3	10	1		2					4	9					5					7	6		
	8	11	3	10	1		2					5	9					4					7	6		
	8	11	3	10	1		4	6	7	9								5		2						
	8	9	3	10	1	4			7						11			5		2				6		
	8	9	3	10	1	4									11			5		2			7	6		
	8		3	10	1	4			7				9		11	2		5						6		
	8	14	13	14	13	5	9	4	7	3	1	10	10	1	6	2	8	12	0	10	0	0	11	13	0	
	3	4		9					2				8		4		10	1					2			

League Table

UNITED LEAGUE	P	W	D	L	F	A	Pts
Millwall Athletic	20	14	3	3	42	19	31
Southampton	20	12	1	7	53	32	25
TOTTENHAM HOTSPUR	20	11	2	7	36	25	24
Woolwich Arsenal	20	10	4	6	40	30	24
Bristol City	20	11	0	9	43	31	22
Reading	20	8	5	7	36	25	21
Brighton United	20	10	1	9	41	42	21
Wellingborough	20	7	1	12	32	40	15
Kettering Town*	20	8	1	11	25	38	15
Rushden	20	6	1	13	26	45	13
Luton Town	20	2	3	15	24	71	7

*Two points deducted

THAMES MEDWAY LEAGUE	P	W	D	L	F	A	Pts
New Brompton	16	12	2	2	48	14	26
Chatham	16	12	1	3	39	11	25
Gravesend United	16	11	0	5	48	21	22
TOTTENHAM HOTSPUR	16	10	0	6	43	28	20
Thames Ironworks	16	9	0	7	22	25	18
Sheppey United	16	7	1	8	31	31	15
Royal Engineers	16	3	2	11	24	55	8
Grays United	16	2	2	12	11	34	6
Dartford	16	2	0	14	21	68	4

1899-1900

SOUTHERN LEAGUE

Manager: John Cameron

Did you know that?

Chairman Charles Roberts performed the ceremonial kick-off when White Hart Lane was officially opened with a friendly against Notts County on 4 September 1899.

Match No.	Date			Opponents	Result		Scorers	Attendance
1	Sep	2	A	Millwall	W	3-1	Copeland, Kirwan 2	12,00
2		9	H	Queen's Park Rangers	W	1-0	Smith	11,00
3		16	A	Chatham	W	3-2	Morris, Pratt, Kirwan	4,00
4		23	H	Reading	W	2-1	Smith 2	9,00
5	Oct	2	H	Gravesend United	W	4-0	Pratt, Copeland 2, Cameron	1,80
6		7	H	Brighton United	W*	6-1	J.L.Jones, Copeland 2, Kirwan 3	6,00
7		14	A	Bedminster	L	1-2	Copeland, Kirwan 2	3,00
8		21	H	Bristol Rovers	W#	1-0	Pratt	4,00
9	Nov	4	H	Thames Ironworks	W	7-0	Morris 2, Pratt 3, Copeland, Kirwan	7,00
10	Dec	2	A	Swindon Town	W	2-0	Pratt, Cameron	3,00
11		9	H	Bristol City	D	2-2	Copeland, Kirwan	5,00
12		16	A	Cowes	W^	6-1	Smith 2, Pratt, Copeland 3	50
13		25	H	Portsmouth	W	3-0	Pratt, Copeland, Kirwan	14,00
14		26	A	Southampton	L	1-3	Cameron	9,00
15		31	H	Millwall	W	2-1	Cameron, Pratt	10,00
16	Jan	6	A	Queen's Park Rangers	D	0-0		8,00
17		13	H	Chatham	W	2-1	Smith, Pratt (pen)	4,50
18		20	A	Reading	W	1-0	Cameron	2,00
19	Feb	3	A	Sheppey United	W	4-1	Cameron, Pratt 2, Morris	2,00
20		10	A	Brighton United	W*	3-0	Pratt 3 (1 pen)	1,80
21		17	H	Bedminster	W	5-2	Pratt 3, Kirwan 2	7,00
22		24	A	Bristol Rovers	D	2-2	Copeland, Hyde	3,00
23	Mar	3	A	Portsmouth	L	0-1		7,00
24		10	A	Thames Ironworks	D	0-0		9,00
25		19	H	Bristol Rovers	W	5-1	Morris, Cameron 2, Stormont, Kirwant	2,00
26		24	H	New Brompton	W	1-0	Pratt	5,00
27		31	A	Gravesend United	W	6-2	Cameron 2, Pratt 2, Copeland 2	2,00
28	Apr	7	H	Swindon Town	W	3-0	Smith, Pratt, Copeland	7,00
29		13	H	Southampton	W	2-0	Cameron 2	15,00
30		14	A	Bristol City	L	0-3		4,00
31		16	H	Sheppey United	W	3-0	Hyde, Pratt, Kirwan	4,50
32		28	A	New Brompton	W	2-1	Cameron, Copeland	3,00

*result expunged on Brighton United's resignation from League ^result expunged as Cowes disbanded

#abandoned after 55 mins - fog

Appearance

Goa

Southern District Combination

Match No.	Date			Opponents	Result		Scorers	Attendance
1	Sep	18	H	Portsmouth	W	2-0	Cameron, Kirwan	4,00
2	Oct	9	A	Reading	L	1-2	Morris	
3		16	H	Millwall	L	1-2	Cameron	6,00
4		23	A	Queen's Park Rangers	W	3-1	Cameron 3	
5		30	H	Reading	W	3-0	Smith, Cameron, Copeland	3,00
6	Nov	6	H	Chatham	W	6-0	Morris (pen), Smith, Pratt 3, Cameron, Copeland, Kirwan	
7		15	A	Bristol City	D	3-3	Smith, Copeland, Kirwan	3,00
8		20	H	Queen's Park Rangers	W	3-1	Copeland, Kirwan 2	2,00
9	Dec	4	A	Chatham	W	1-0	Copeland	
10	Jan	8	H	Southampton	W	3-2	Cameron, Pratt, Durber (og)	
11		17	A	Portsmouth	D	2-2	Smith, Pratt	4,00
12	Mar	12	H	Bristol City	W	2-0	Cameron, Kirwan	3,00
13	Apr	17	H	Woolwich Arsenal	W	4-2	Smith, Pratt 2, Kirwan	4,00
14		24	A	Woolwich Arsenal	L*	1-2	Pratt	50
15		26	A	Millwall	D	0-0		2,00
16		30	A	Southampton	W	4-1	Hyde, Roberts 2, Leigh (og)	10

*abandoned after 75 mins - bad language - result stood

Appearance

Goa

FA Cup

Match No.	Date			Opponents	Result		Scorers	Attendance
R1	Jan	27	A	Preston North End	L	0-1		3,00

Appearance

Goa

Ambler CJ	Cameron J	Clawley G	Copeland DC	Crump H	Erentz HB	Haddow D	Hughes E	Hyde LJ	Jones J	Jones JL	Kirwan JF	McNaught JR	Melia J	Morris T	Pratt TP	Raby WJ	Roberts JW	Rule AG	Smith T	Stormont R	Tait AG	Waller WH	Own-goals
	10	1	9		2					4	11	5			8				7	6	3		
	10	1	9		2					6	11	5		4	8				7		3		
	10	1	9		2					6	11	5		4	8				7		3		
	10	1	9		2					6	11	5		4	8				7		3		
	10	1	9		2					6	11	5		4	8				7		3		
	10	1	9		2		6			4	11			5	8				7		3		
	10	1	9		2					5	11			4	8				7	6	3		
	8	1	10							4	11		2	5	9				7	6	3		
	8		10							4	11		2	5	9				7	6	3	1	
	8		10			1				4	11		2	5	9				7	6	3		
	8		10			1				4	11		2	5	9				7	6	3		
	8		10		2	1	4				11	5			9				7	6	3		
	8		10		2	1				4	11	5			9				7	6	3		
	8		10		2	1				4	11	5			9				7	6	3		
	8				2	1	6	11		4	10	5			9				7		3		
	8		10		2	1				4	11	5			9				7	6	3		
			10		2	1					11	5		4	9			8	7	6	3		
	8		10		2	1		11				5		4	9				7	6	3		
	8		10		2	1					11	5		4	9				7	6	3		
	8		10			1					11	5	2	4	9				7	6	3		
			10			1					11	5	2	4	9			8	7	6	3		
	8		10			1		11		4		5	2		9				7	6	3		
	8		10			1					11	5	2	4		7		9		6	3		
	8					1		11			7	5	2	4		10		9		6	3		
	8					1		7		6	11	5	2	4	9					10	3		
	8				2	1				6	11	5		4	9				7	10	3		
	8		10			1					11	5	2	4	9				7	6	3		
	8		10			1					11	5	2	4	9				7	6	3		
	8		10			1					11	5	2	4	9				7	6	3		
	8		10			1					11	5	2	4	9				7	6	3		
	8		10		2	1		7		4	11	5			9					6	3		
	8	1	10		2					6	11	5		4	9				7		3		
0	30	9	28	0	18	22	3	6	0	20	30	26	14	24	30	2	0	4	28	25	32	1	
	13		17					2		1	13			5	24				7	1			

Ambler CJ	Cameron J	Clawley G	Copeland DC	Crump H	Erentz HB	Haddow D	Hughes E	Hyde LJ	Jones J	Jones JL	Kirwan JF	McNaught JR	Melia J	Morris T	Pratt TP	Raby WJ	Roberts JW	Rule AG	Smith T	Stormont R	Tait AG	Waller WH	Own-goals
	10	1	9		2					6	11	5		4	8				7		3		
	9	1			2		6	11		4				5	8	10			7		3		
	10	1	9		2					5	11			4	8				7	6	3		
	8	1	10							4	11		2	5	9				7	6	3		
1	8		10							4	11		2	5	9				7	6	3		
1	8		10		2					4	11			5	9				7	6	3		
	8		10			1				4	11		2	5	9				7	6	3		
	8		10			1				4	11		2	5	9				7	6	3		
	8		10			1					11	4	2	5				9	7	6	3		
	8		10		2	1		11		4	7	5			9					6	3		
	8		10		2	1					11	5		4	9				7	6	3		
	9					1		7		6	11	5	2	4		8				10	3		
	8		10		2	1				4	11	5			9				7	6	3		
	8		10		2	1				6	11	5		4	9				7		3		
		1		6	2		3	11				5		4		10	9	8	7				
	8	1	10		2		3	11	6	5				4			9		7				
2	15	6	13	1	10	8	3	5	1	13	13	8	6	14	12	3	2	2	14	11	14	0	
	9		5					1			7			2	8		2		5				

Ambler CJ	Cameron J	Clawley G	Copeland DC	Crump H	Erentz HB	Haddow D	Hughes E	Hyde LJ	Jones J	Jones JL	Kirwan JF	McNaught JR	Melia J	Morris T	Pratt TP	Raby WJ	Roberts JW	Rule AG	Smith T	Stormont R	Tait AG	Waller WH	Own-goals
	8		10		2	1					11	5		4	9				7	6	3		
0	1	0	1	0	1	1	0	0	0	0	1	1	0	1	1	0	0	0	1	1	1	0	

League Table

	P	W	D	L	F	A	Pts
TOTTENHAM HOTSPUR	28	20	4	4	67	26	44
Portsmouth	28	20	1	7	59	29	41
Southampton	28	17	1	10	70	33	35
Reading	28	15	2	11	41	28	32
Swindon Town	28	15	2	11	50	42	32
Bedminster	28	13	2	13	44	45	28
Millwall	28	12	3	13	36	37	27
Queen's Park Rangers	28	12	2	14	50	58	26
Bristol City	28	9	7	12	44	47	25
Bristol Rovers	28	11	3	14	46	55	25
New Brompton	28	9	6	13	39	49	24
Gravesend United	28	10	4	14	38	58	24
Chatham	28	10	3	15	38	58	23
Thames Ironworks	28	8	5	15	30	45	21
Sheppey United	28	3	7	18	24	66	13

SOUTHERN DISTRICT COMBINATION

	P	W	D	L	F	A	Pts
Millwall	16	12	2	2	30	10	26
TOTTENHAM HOTSPUR	16	10	3	3	39	18	23
Portsmouth	16	8	2	6	28	18	18
Woolwich Arsenal	16	8	1	7	27	22	17
Southampton	16	6	2	8	24	29	14
Bristol City	16	5	3	8	25	32	13
Reading	16	4	4	8	16	28	12
Chatham	16	5	2	9	12	35	12
Queen's Park Rangers	16	4	1	11	19	28	9

1900-01

SOUTHERN LEAGUE

Manager: John Cameron

Did you know that?

Not only did Alexander 'Sandy' Brown score in every round of the FA Cup, but his total of 15 goals in the campaign remains a record to this day.

Match No.	Date			Opponents	Result		Scorers	Attendance
1	Sep	1	H	Millwall	L	0-3		13,40
2		15	H	Chatham	W*	5-0	Smith, Cameron, Brown 3	3,00
3		22	A	Bristol City	D	1-1	Stormont	9,00
4		29	H	Swindon Town	W	2-0	Smith, Stormont	7,00
5	Oct	6	A	Watford	L	1-2	Brown	7,00
6		20	A	Queen's Park Rangers	L	1-2	Brown	5,00
7		27	H	West Ham United	D	0-0		5,00
8	Nov	10	A	New Brompton	W	2-1	Cameron, Brown	3,00
9		24	A	Reading	L	1-3	Morris	5,00
10	Dec	1	H	Kettering Town	W	1-0	Morris	4,00
11		15	A	Millwall	W	2-1	Cameron, Brown	8,00
12		25	H	Portsmouth	W	4-1	Smith, Brown, J.L.Jones, Kirwan	12,00
13		26	A	Southampton	L	1-3	Cameron	10,00
14	Jan	12	A	Swindon Town	D	1-1	Brown	2,50
15		19	H	Watford	W	7-0	Smith, Brown, J.L.Jones 2, Kirwan 2, Cother (og)	10,00
16		26	H	Bristol Rovers	W	4-0	Morris (pen), Cameron, Copeland 2	6,00
17	Feb	16	A	West Ham United	W	4-1	Brown, Stormont 2, Hyde	5,00
18	Mar	2	H	New Brompton	W	2-1	Brown, Copeland	4,50
19		9	A	Bristol Rovers	L	0-1		5,00
20		16	H	Reading	W	1-0	Hughes	5,00
21		30	H	Queen's Park Rangers	W	4-1	Copeland 2, Kirwan, Hyde	4,00
22	Apr	3	A	Gravesend United	L	1-2	Stormont	80
23		5	H	Southampton	W	1-0	Hughes	12,00
24		6	H	Bristol City	W	1-0	Burton	5,00
25		24	A	Portsmouth	L	0-4		3,00
26		25	H	Luton Town	W	3-2	Melia, Moffatt 2	4,00
27		27	H	Gravesend United	W	5-0	Burton, Fortnum, Woodward 2, Hyde (pen)	5,00
28		29	H	Luton Town	W	4-2	Hawley 2, Moffatt, Kirwan	4,00
29		30	A	Kettering Town	D	1-1	A.E.Jones	4,00

*result expunged due to Chatham's withdrawal from the League

Appearance
Goa

Western League

Match No.	Date			Opponents	Result		Scorers	Attendance
1	Nov	17	H	Portsmouth	W	8-1	McNaught 2, A.E.Jones, Morris, Brown 2, Cameron, Kirwan	5,00
2		26	H	Bristol City	W	4-1	A.E.Jones 2, Morris, Kirwan	3,00
3	Dec	5	A	Swindon Town	W	1-0	Cameron	4,00
4		8	A	Millwall	D	1-1	Kirwan	7,00
5		10	H	Bristol Rovers	W	6-0	Morris 2 (2 pens), Smith, Brown 3 (1 pen)	
6		22	H	Southampton	W	2-0	McNaught, Cameron	5,00
7	Feb	18	H	Reading	W	3-2	Smith, Copeland, Kirwan	3,00
8		27	H	Swindon Town	W	5-0	Hughes, Cameron 2, Copeland 2	1,00
9	Mar	6	A	Reading	D	1-1	J.L.Jones	1,00
10		11	A	Southampton	D	1-1	Brown	
11		18	A	Queen's Park Rangers	D	1-1	Stormont	1,00
12		27	A	Bristol City	L	1-4	A.E.Jones	
13	Apr	13	H	Millwall	W	1-0	Cameron	10,00
14		15	H	Queen's Park Rangers	D	2-2	A.E.Jones, Woodward	1,20
15		17	A	Portsmouth	L	0-1		2,50
16		22	A	Bristol Rovers	L	0-4		50

Appearance
Goa

FA Cup

Round	Date			Opponents	Result		Scorers	Attendance
R1	Feb	8	H	Preston North End	D	1-1	Brown	15,22
R1r		13	A	Preston North End	W	4-2	Brown 3, Cameron	6,00
R2		23	H	Bury	W	2-1	Brown 2	20,25
R3	Mar	23	A	Reading	D	1-1	Kirwan	14,41
R3r		28	H	Reading	W	3-0	Brown 2, Copeland	11,6C
SF	Apr	8	N*	West Bromwich Albion	W	4-0	Brown 4	46,00
F		20	N#	Sheffield United	D	2-2	Brown 2	114,81
Fr		27	N^	Sheffield United	W	3-1	Smith, Brown, Cameron	20,47

*played at Villa Park #played at Crystal Palace ^played at Burnden Park

Appearance
Goa

nson WC	Berry F	Brown A	Buckingham WF	Burton JH	Cameron J	Clawley G	Copeland DC	Erentz HB	Finch P	Fortnum W	Haddow D	Hawley A	Hudson EG	Hughes E	Hyde LJ	Jones AE	Jones JL	Kirwan JF	Leigh AK	McNaught JR	Melia J	Moffatt J	Moles WJ	Morris T	Pangbourne T	Sands	Smith T	Stevens RC	Stormont R	Tait AG	Woodward VJ	Own-goal
		9			8	1												11		5	2			4	10		7		6	3		
		9			8	1		4								5	6	11			2						7		10	3		
		9			8	1		4						3			6	11		5	2						7		10			
		9			8	1		4									6	11		5	2						7		10	3		
		9			8	1											6	11		5	2			4			7		10	3		
		9			10	1		2									4	11		5					8		7		6	3		
		9			8	1		2						6			4	11		5							7		10	3		
		9			8	1		2						4	11	7				10				5					6	3		
		9			10	1		2						4		7		11		5				8					6	3		
					10	1		2						4		7		11		5		9		8					6	3		
		9			7	1		2						4			10	11		5				8					6	3		
		9				1		2						4			10	11		5				8			7		6	3		
		9			7	1		2						4			10	11		5				8					6	3		
		9			8	1	10	2						6	11					4				5			7			3		
		9			8	1		2						3			10	11		5				4			7		6			
					8	1	9	2									10	11		5				4			7		6	3		
		9			8	1		2						5	11		6							4			7		10	3		
		9			8	1	10	2							11					5				4			7		6	3		
		9			8	1	10	2						5			11							4			7		6	3		
		9			8	1	10	2						5			6	11						4			7			3		
					9	1	8	2						5	7		10	11						4					6	3		
3	7		6	4							1				11	8				5	2	9							10			
		9			8	1	10	2						5			6	11						4			7			3		
			8		1								3	11		7			5	2	10							6		9		
4			6							8	1		10		11					5	2	9	7					3				
			6	4							1	8			11	7					2	9	5					3	10			
5			6	4						8	1				11	7					2							3	10		9	
			6			1	10					8		5				11			2	9		4			7			3		
		9	6			1	10					8		2		7		11		5				4						3		
4	1	20	6	4	21	25	9	20	0	2	4	3	1	18	10	8	17	19	0	20	11	6	2	19	2	0	17	3	23	22	2	
		12		2	5		5			1		2		2	3	1	3	5			1	3		3			4		5		2	1

nson WC	Berry F	Brown A	Buckingham WF	Burton JH	Cameron J	Clawley G	Copeland DC	Erentz HB	Finch P	Fortnum W	Haddow D	Hawley A	Hudson EG	Hughes E	Hyde LJ	Jones AE	Jones JL	Kirwan JF	Leigh AK	McNaught JR	Melia J	Moffatt J	Moles WJ	Morris T	Pangbourne T	Sands	Smith T	Stevens RC	Stormont R	Tait AG	Woodward VJ	Own-goal
		9			10	1		2						4		7		11		5				8					6	3		
		9			10	1		2						4		7		11		5				8					6	3		
					9	1		2						4		7	10	11		5				8					6	3		
		9			7	1		2						4			10	11		5				8					6	3		
		9				1								4			10	11		5	2			8			7		6	3		
		9			7	1		2						4			10	11		5				8					6	3		
		9			8		10	2			1				11	5								4			7		6	3		
					9		10	2			1			5	11	8								4			7		6	3		
		9			8		10	2			1			5			11							4			7		6	3		
		9				1	10	2						5			8	11						4			7		6	3		
		9			8	1	10	2							7		6	11						4					5	3		
3			6						8		1	7			11	9				5	2		4						10			
		9			10	1		2						6		8		11		5				4			7			3		
			6	4				2			1				11	8			7	5		10								3	9	
			6	4							1				11	7					2	9	5			8		3	10			
	7			4							1	10			11	8				5	2	9						3	6			
1	1	10	3	3	10	9	5	12	1	0	7	2	0	10	7	10	7	9	1	10	4	3	2	12	0	1	6	2	14	13	1	
		6			6		3							1		5	1	3		3				4			2		2		1	

nson WC	Berry F	Brown A	Buckingham WF	Burton JH	Cameron J	Clawley G	Copeland DC	Erentz HB	Finch P	Fortnum W	Haddow D	Hawley A	Hudson EG	Hughes E	Hyde LJ	Jones AE	Jones JL	Kirwan JF	Leigh AK	McNaught JR	Melia J	Moffatt J	Moles WJ	Morris T	Pangbourne T	Sands	Smith T	Stevens RC	Stormont R	Tait AG	Woodward VJ	Own-goal
		9			8	1	10	2										11		5				4			7		6	3		
		9			8	1	10	2						5			6	11						4			7			3		
		9			8	1	10	2						5			6	11						4			7			3		
		9			8	1	10	2						5			6	11						4			7			3		
		9			8	1	10	2						5			6	11						4			7			3		
		9			8	1	10	2						5			6	11						4			7			3		
		9			8	1	10	2						5			6	11						4			7			3		
		9			8	1	10	2						5			6	11						4			7			3		
0	0	8	0	0	8	8	8	8	0	0	0	0	0	7	0	0	7	8	0	1	0	0	0	8	0	0	8	0	1	8	0	
		15			2		1											1									1					

League Table

	P	W	D	L	F	A	Pts
Southampton	28	18	5	5	58	26	41
Bristol City	28	17	5	6	54	27	39
Portsmouth	28	17	4	7	56	32	38
Millwall	28	17	2	9	55	32	36
TOTTENHAM HOTSPUR	28	16	4	8	55	33	36
West Ham United	28	14	5	9	40	28	33
Bristol Rovers	28	14	4	10	46	35	32
Queen's Park Rangers	28	11	4	13	43	48	26
Reading	28	8	8	12	24	25	24
Luton Town	28	11	2	15	43	49	24
Kettering Town	28	7	9	12	33	46	23
New Brompton	28	7	5	16	34	51	19
Gravesend United	28	6	7	15	32	85	19
Watford	28	6	4	18	24	52	16
Swindon Town	28	3	8	17	19	47	14

WESTERN LEAGUE	**P**	**W**	**D**	**L**	**F**	**A**	**Pts**
Portsmouth	16	11	2	3	26	22	24
Millwall	16	9	5	2	33	14	23
TOTTENHAM HOTSPUR	16	8	5	3	37	19	21
Queen's Park Rangers	16	7	4	5	39	25	18
Bristol City	16	6	4	6	25	26	16
Reading	16	5	5	6	24	29	15
Southampton	16	5	2	9	20	29	12
Bristol Rovers	16	4	1	11	18	42	9
Swindon Town	16	2	2	12	19	35	6

1901-02

SOUTHERN LEAGUE

Manager: John Cameron

Did you know that?

White Hart Lane hosted an international match for the first time on 21 September 1901, with England beating Germany 12–0 in an amateur international.

Match No.	Date		Opponents		Result		Scorers	Attendance
1	Sep	7	H	Millwall	W	2-0	Cameron, Brown	13,50
2		14	H	Queen's Park Rangers	W	2-0	Cameron, Copeland	9,00
3		21	A	Reading	D	1-1	Morris (pen)	8,00
4	Oct	5	A	Bristol Rovers	W	2-1	Smith, Brown	7,00
5		12	H	New Brompton	W	3-1	Brown, Kirwan 2	8,00
6		19	A	Northampton Town	L	1-3	Smith	5,00
7		26	H	Watford	W	8-1	Cameron 2, Brown 3, Copeland 2, Kirwan	7,50
8	Nov	2	A	West Ham United	W	1-0	Jones	17,50
9		9	A	Wellingborough	W	1-0	Brown	4,50
10		23	A	Swindon Town	W	3-1	Morris, Cameron 2	3,00
11	Dec	7	A	Kettering Town	W	2-0	Cameron, Kirwan	1,20
12		21	A	Millwall	D	1-1	Kirwan	4,00
13		25	H	Portsmouth	L	1-2	Cameron	14,00
14		26	A	Southampton	L	0-1		11,00
15		28	A	Queen's Park Rangers	W	3-0	Brown 3	13,00
16	Jan	4	H	Reading	W	4-2	Hughes, Cameron, Copeland, Kirwan	9,00
17		18	H	Bristol Rovers	W	1-0	Cameron	6,00
18	Feb	1	H	Northampton Town	W	1-0	Kirwan	3,00
19		8	A	Watford	W	3-0	Brown, Copeland	2,50
20		15	H	West Ham United	L	1-2	Copeland	9,00
21		22	H	Wellingborough	W	3-0	Brown, Copeland 2	6,00
22	Mar	8	H	Swindon Town	W	7-1	Cameron, Brown 3, Copeland 2, Kirwan	4,00
23		15	A	Brentford	L	1-2	Smith	11,00
24		22	H	Kettering Town	W	4-0	Smith, Copeland 3	3,00
25		28	H	Southampton	D	2-2	Hughes, Kirwan	21,30
26		29	A	Luton Town	D	0-0		3,00
27		31	A	Portsmouth	L	0-1		13,40
28	Apr	5	A	New Brompton	D	0-0		5,00
29		12	H	Luton Town	D	0-0		6,00
30		26	H	Brentford	W	3-0	Morris (pen), Brown 2	3,00
								Appearances
								Goals

FA Cup

R1	Jan	25	H	Southampton	D	1-1	Copeland	24,23
R1r		29	A	Southampton	D	2-2	Hughes 2	12,03
R1r	Feb	3	N*	Southampton	L	1-2	Kirwan	7,00
								Appearances
								Goals

*played at Elm Park, Reading

Southern Charity Cup

SF	Apr	23	A	Woolwich Arsenal	D	0-0		3,00
SFr		29	H	Woolwich Arsenal	W	2-1	Copeland, Coles (og)	2,00
								Appearances
								Goals

arlow J	Brown A	Burton JH	Cameron J	Clawley G	Copeland DC	Erentz HB	Fitchie TT	Gilhooley P	Griffiths FJ	Haig-Brown AR	Hughes E	Hyde LJ	Jones JL	Kirwan JF	McNaught JR	Moles WJ	Montgomery G	Morris T	Smith T	Soulsby T	Stephenson JW	Stevens RC	Tait AG	Woodward VJ	Own-goal
	9		8	1	10	2					6			11	5			4	7				3		
	9		8	1	10	2		7			3		6	11	5			4							
		4	9	1	10	2		8			3		6	11				5	7						
	9			1	10	2		8			5		6	11				4	7				3		
	9			1	10	2		8			5		6	11				4	7				3		
			9	1	10	2		8			5		6	11				4	7				3		
	9		8	1	10	2							6	11	5			4	7				3		
	9		8	1	10	2					5		6	11				4	7				3		
3	9			1	10	2					5		6	11				4	7				3		
	9		8	1	10	2							6	11	5			4	7				3		
	9		8	1	10	2					5		6	11				4	7				3		
			8		10	2		7	1		5		6	11				4					3	9	
	9		8		10	2			1		5		6	11				4	7				3		
	9		8		10	2			1		5		6	11				4	7				3		
	9		10			2		8	1		4		6	11	5				7				3		
	9		8		10	2			1		5		6	11				4	7				3		
	9		8		10	2		7	1		5		6	11				4					3		
	9		8		10	2		7	1		4		6	11	5								3		
	9		8		10	2		7	1		6			11	5			4					3		
	9		8		10	2			1	7	4		6	11	5								3		
	9	6		1	10	2						11			5			4	7				3	8	
	9		8	1	10	2				7	6			11	5			4					3		
3	9			1	10	2					4			11	5			6	7				3		
	9		8	1	10	2						11	6		5			4	7				3		
	9		8	1	10	2					5		6	11				4	7				3		
	9		8	1	10	2							6	11	5			4	7				3		
	9		8	1	10	2							6	11	5			4	7				3		
0			8		9	2					3		6	11	5	1		4	7						
	9			1	10	2	8				4		6	11	5				7			3			
	9		8	1	10	2							6	11	5			4	7				3		
3	26	2	24	20	29	30	1	10	9	2	23	2	25	28	17	1	0	26	23	0	0	1	26	2	
	18		11		13						2		1	9				3	4						

arlow J	Brown A	Burton JH	Cameron J	Clawley G	Copeland DC	Erentz HB	Fitchie TT	Gilhooley P	Griffiths FJ	Haig-Brown AR	Hughes E	Hyde LJ	Jones JL	Kirwan JF	McNaught JR	Moles WJ	Montgomery G	Morris T	Smith T	Soulsby T	Stephenson JW	Stevens RC	Tait AG	Woodward VJ	Own-goal
	9		8		10	2			1		4		6	11	5				7				3		
	9		8		10	2		7	1		4		6	11	5								3		
	9		8		10	2		7	1		4		6	11	5								3		
0	3	0	3	0	3	3	0	2	3	0	3	0	3	3	3	0	0	0	1	0	0	0	3	0	
					1						2			1											

arlow J	Brown A	Burton JH	Cameron J	Clawley G	Copeland DC	Erentz HB	Fitchie TT	Gilhooley P	Griffiths FJ	Haig-Brown AR	Hughes E	Hyde LJ	Jones JL	Kirwan JF	McNaught JR	Moles WJ	Montgomery G	Morris T	Smith T	Soulsby T	Stephenson JW	Stevens RC	Tait AG	Woodward VJ	Own-goal
8			9	1	10	2					6			11	5			4	7				3		
	9		8	1	10	2					6			11	5			4	7				3		
1	1	0	2	2	2	2	0	0	0	0	2	0	0	2	2	0	0	2	2	0	0	0	2	0	
					1																				1

League Table

	P	W	D	L	F	A	Pts
Portsmouth	30	20	7	3	67	24	47
TOTTENHAM HOTSPUR	30	18	6	6	61	22	42
Southampton	30	18	6	6	71	28	42
West Ham United	30	17	6	7	45	28	40
Reading	30	16	7	7	57	24	39
Millwall	30	13	6	11	46	31	32
Luton Town	30	11	10	9	31	36	32
Kettering Town	30	12	5	13	44	39	29
Bristol Rovers	30	12	5	13	43	39	29
New Brompton	30	10	7	13	39	38	27
Northampton Town	30	11	5	14	53	65	27
Queen's Park Rangers	30	9	6	15	34	55	24
Watford	30	9	4	17	36	58	22
Wellingborough	30	9	3	18	34	72	21
Brentford	30	7	6	17	34	61	20
Swindon Town	30	2	3	25	17	92	7

1901-02 CONT.

Match No.	Date			Opponents	Result		Scorers	Attendance
Western League								
1	Sep	9	H	Reading	W	4-0	Morris (pen), Cameron, Brown 2	4,00
2		28	H	Southampton	W	5-0	Hughes, Cameron, Copeland 2, Kirwan	11,00
3		30	A	Queen's Park Rangers	W	3-1	Morris, Copeland, Kirwan	4,00
4	Oct	7	H	Millwall	W	3-1	Brown 2, Kirwan	5,00
5		14	H	West Ham United	W	2-1	Cameron, Copeland	7,00
6		21	H	Bristol Rovers	W	4-1	McNaught, Cameron	5,00
7	Nov	11	H	Swindon Town	W	6-0	Morris, Woodward 2, Copeland, Kirwan 2	2,20
8		16	A	Portsmouth	L	1-3	Brown	16,00
9		18	A	Bristol Rovers	W	4-0	Morris, Smith, Brown, Kirwan	60
10	Dec	9	H	Queen's Park Rangers	W	3-2	Brown, Smith, Kirwan	2,50
11	Jan	11	A	Southampton	L	1-5	Cameron	6,00
12		15	A	Reading	D	1-1	Gilhooley	
13	Feb	17	A	Millwall	W	3-1	Barlow, Cameron 2	2,00
14	Mar	10	A	West Ham United	D	1-1	Brown	3,00
15		17	H	Portsmouth	D	0-0		4,00
16	Apr	9	A	Swindon Town	W	1-0	Copeland	
								Appearances
								Goals

Match No.	Date			Opponents	Result		Scorers	Attendance
London League								
1	Sep	16	A	Woolwich Arsenal	W	2-0	Gilhooley, Brown	4,00
2	Nov	4	H	Woolwich Arsenal	W	4-0	Barlow, Brown 3, Copeland	4,00
3	Dec	16	A	West Ham United	L	1-3	Gilhooley	2,00
4	Jan	6	A	Millwall	D	1-1	Smith	2,00
5	Feb	10	H	Queen's Park Rangers	L	1-5	Brown	1,50
6	Mar	24	H	Millwall	D	1-1	Cameron	1,00
7	Apr	14	A	Queen's Park Rangers	W	2-1	Hughes, Cameron	
8		21	H	West Ham United	D	2-2	Brown	2,00
								Appearances
								Goals

Barlow J	Brown A	Burton JH	Cameron J	Clawley G	Copeland DC	Erentz HB	Fitchie TT	Gilhooley P	Griffiths FJ	Haig-Brown AR	Hughes E	Hyde LJ	Jones JL	Kirwan JF	McNaught JR	Moles WJ	Montgomery G	Morris T	Smith T	Soulsby T	Stephenson JW	Stevens RC	Tait AG	Woodward VJ	Own-goal
	9		8		10	2		7	1				6	11	5			4			3				
		6	9	1	10	2		8			5			11				4	7				3		
		6	9	1	10	2		8			5			11				4	7				3		
	9	6			10	2		8	1		5			11				4	7				3		
	9		8	1	10	2		7			5		6	11				4					3		
8	9	6	10			2			1					11	5			4	7				3		
8					10				1		6			11	5			4	7		2		3	9	
	9		8	1	10	2					5		6	11				4	7				3		
8	9			1	10	2					5		6	11				4	7				3		
	9			1	10	2		8			5		6	11				4	7				3		
	9		10			2		8	1		3		6	11	5			4	7						
	9	4			10	2		8	1			11	6					5	7				3		
8		3	9		10	2		7	1		4		6	11	5										
	9		8	1	10	2							6	11	5			4	7				3		
7	9		8	1	10	2					4		6	11	5								3		
	9		8	1	10	2					4	11	6		5				7		3				
5	12	6	11	9	14	15	0	9	7	0	12	2	11	14	8	0	0	13	12	0	3	0	12	1	
1	9		7		6			1			1			9				4	2					2	

Barlow J	Brown A	Burton JH	Cameron J	Clawley G	Copeland DC	Erentz HB	Fitchie TT	Gilhooley P	Griffiths FJ	Haig-Brown AR	Hughes E	Hyde LJ	Jones JL	Kirwan JF	McNaught JR	Moles WJ	Montgomery G	Morris T	Smith T	Soulsby T	Stephenson JW	Stevens RC	Tait AG	Woodward VJ	Own-goal
	9			1	10	2		8			3		6	11			5	4	7						
8	9			1	10	2					5		6	11				4	7				3		
			9	1	10	2		8			3		6	11	5			4		7					
	9				10			8	1		2		6	11	5			4	7		3				
8	9	6			10	2		7	1					11	5			4					3		
10			9	1							4	11	6		5			8	7		2		3		
	9		8	1	10	2					4		6	11	5				7		3				
	9			1	10	2		8			5		6	11				4	7				3		
3	6	1	3	6	7	6	0	5	2	0	7	1	7	7	5	0	1	7	6	1	3	0	4	0	
1	7		2		1			2			1								1						

League Table

	P	W	D	L	F	A	Pts
Portsmouth	16	13	1	2	53	16	27
TOTTENHAM HOTSPUR	16	11	3	2	42	17	25
Reading	16	7	3	6	29	22	17
Millwall	16	8	1	7	25	29	17
Bristol Rovers	16	8	0	8	25	31	16
Southampton	16	7	1	8	30	28	15
West Ham United	16	6	2	8	30	20	14
Queen's Park Rangers	16	5	1	10	17	43	11
Swindon Town	16	0	2	14	8	53	2

LONDON LEAGUE	**P**	**W**	**D**	**L**	**F**	**A**	**Pts**
West Ham United	8	5	1	2	18	9	11
TOTTENHAM HOTSPUR	8	3	3	2	15	13	9
Millwall	8	2	4	2	9	13	8
Queen's Park Rangers	8	2	2	4	11	14	6
Woolwich Arsenal	8	2	2	4	9	13	6

1902-03

SOUTHERN LEAGUE

Manager: John Cameron

Did you know that?

Charlie Williams was given a fearful time by the Woolwich Arsenal supporters when Spurs reserves visited Plumstead in October 1902. As the teams came off at the end of the game, one of his detractors could not resist having at final pop at the 'keeper. Williams was suspended for two weeks after punching his abuser on the nose.

Match No.	Date			Opponents	Result		Scorers	Attendance
1	Sep	6	H	Queen's Park Rangers	D	0-0		13,000
2		20	H	Wellingborough	W	6-1	Houston, J.Jones, Cameron, Copeland, Kirwan, Dartnell (og)	8,000
3		27	A	Bristol Rovers	L	2-3	J.Jones 2	12,000
4	Oct	4	H	Northampton Town	W	2-0	Morris (pen), Copeland	8,000
5		11	A	Watford	W	2-1	Houston	4,000
6		18	H	Brentford	W	3-1	Smith	5,000
7		25	A	Millwall	L	0-2		12,000
8	Nov	1	H	West Ham United	D	1-1	Copeland	9,000
9		22	H	Swindon Town	W	2-0	Gilhooley, Kirwan	5,500
10	Dec	6	H	Luton Town	D	1-1	Gilhooley	4,500
11		20	A	Queen's Park Rangers	W	4-0	Hughes, Woodward 2, Kirwan	7,000
12		25	H	Portsmouth	D	2-2	Dryburgh, Warner	23,000
13		26	A	Southampton	W	1-0	Kirwan	12,000
14	Jan	3	A	Wellingborough	W	2-0	Warner, Kirwan	3,000
15		5	H	New Brompton	W	3-1	Tait (pen), Warner, Copeland	3,000
16		10	H	Bristol Rovers	W	3-0	Warner 2, Woodward	11,000
17		17	A	Northampton Town	L	1-3	Woodward	4,000
18		24	H	Watford	D	1-1	Kirwan	6,000
19		31	A	Brentford	D	1-1	Copeland	4,000
20	Feb	14	A	West Ham United	L	0-1		10,000
21	Mar	14	H	Kettering Town	W	4-0	Hughes 2 (1 pen), Dryburgh, Warner	7,000
22		21	A	Luton Town	L	0-3		6,000
23		28	H	Reading	W	2-0	Warner, Copeland	4,000
24	Apr	4	A	Reading	D	0-0		5,000
25		10	H	Southampton	W	2-1	Warner, Copeland	20,000
26		11	A	New Brompton	L	0-3		4,000
27		13	A	Portsmouth	L	0-2		12,000
28		14	H	Millwall	W	2-0	Cameron, Copeland	8,000
29		22	A	Swindon Town	L	0-2		3,000
30		25	A	Kettering Town	L	0-1		2,000
								Appearances
								Goals

FA Cup

R1	Feb	7	H	West Bromwich Albion	D	0-0		25,641
R1r		11	A	West Bromwich Albion	W	2-0	Dryburgh (pen), Woodward	32,000
R2		21	H	Bristol City	W	1-0	Woodward	18,750
R3	Mar	7	H	Aston Villa	L	2-3	Woodward, Copeland	24,500
								Appearances
								Goals

Southern Charity Cup 1901-02

F	Sep	8	N*	West Ham United	W	2-1	Houston, Kirwan	6,000
								Appearances
								Goals

*played at the Manor Ground, Plumstead

Southern Charity Cup

R1	Nov	24	H	Reading	D	1-1	Kirwan	3,000
R1r	Jan	14	A	Reading	L	2-3	Houston, Quinn	1,500
								Appearances
								Goals

Barlow J	Brown C	Bugg JW	Burton JH	Burton O	Cameron J	Chalmers J	Clawley G	Copeland DC	Dryburgh W	Erentz HB	Fredericks GH	Gilhooley P	Haig-Brown AR	Houston R	Hughes E	Jones JL	Jones JT	Kirwan JF	Moles WJ	Morris T	Quinn D	Rainbird HA	Stephenson JW	Steven	Tait AG	Warner AC	Watson J	Williams CA	Woodward VJ	Own-goal
							1	10		2				9	5	6	8	11		4					3	7				
					8		1	10		2				9	5	6	7	11		4					3					
					8		1	10		2				9	5	6	7	11		4					3					
			4		8		1	10		2				9		6	7	11		5					3					
							1	10		2		7		9	5	6	8	11		4					3					
			4				1	10		2		7		9		6	8	11		5							3			
					8		1	10		2				9	5	6	7	11		4					3					
9	4				8		1	10		2					5	6	7	11							3					
9	4				8		1	10		2		7				6		11		5							3			
8							1	10		2		7			5	6		11		4							3		9	
	4						1	10				7			5	6		11							3	8	2		9	
	4						1	10	7							6		11		5					3	8	2		9	
	4						1	10	7							6		11		5					3	8	2		9	
	4		6				1	10	7	2								11		5					3	8			9	
9	4		6				1	10	7	2								11		5					3	8				
	4		6				1	10	7	2								11		5					3	8			9	
	4		6			11	1	10	7	2										5					3	8			9	
	4		6					10	7	2				9	5			11							3	8		1		
	4				8		1	10		2						6		11		5					3	7			9	
					9	11	1		7		10	8			5	6				4					3		2			
							1	10	7	2					5			11		4					3	8	6		9	
					10	11	1		7	2					5	6				4						8	3		9	
	4					11	1	10	7	2					6					5					3	8			9	
			5				1	10	7	2				9				11		4					3	8	6			
			6				1	10	7						5			11		4					3	8	2		9	
			6		9		1	10	7	2					4			11		5						8	3			
			6		9		1	10	7	2					4			11		5					3	8				
					9		1	10		2			7		4			11		5					3	8	6			
			3		9		1	10		2			7		4			11		5						8	6			
					9		1	10	7	2					4	6		11		5					3	8				
4	12	0	12	0	14	4	29	28	16	25	1	6	2	9	19	17	8	26	0	27	0	0	0	0	24	20	14	1	12	
			1		2			8	2			2		3	3		4	6		2					1	8			4	1

Barlow J	Brown C	Bugg JW	Burton JH	Burton O	Cameron J	Chalmers J	Clawley G	Copeland DC	Dryburgh W	Erentz HB	Fredericks GH	Gilhooley P	Haig-Brown AR	Houston R	Hughes E	Jones JL	Jones JT	Kirwan JF	Moles WJ	Morris T	Quinn D	Rainbird HA	Stephenson JW	Steven	Tait AG	Warner AC	Watson J	Williams CA	Woodward VJ	Own-goal
					8		1	10	7						5	6		11		4					3		2		9	
					10		1		7			8			5	6		11		4					3		2		9	
					8		1	10	7						5	6		11		4					3		2		9	
					8		1	10	7						5	6		11		4					3		2		9	
0	0	0	0	0	4	0	4	3	4	0	0	1	0	0	4	4	0	4	0	4	0	0	0	0	4	0	4	0	4	
								1	1																				3	

Barlow J	Brown C	Bugg JW	Burton JH	Burton O	Cameron J	Chalmers J	Clawley G	Copeland DC	Dryburgh W	Erentz HB	Fredericks GH	Gilhooley P	Haig-Brown AR	Houston R	Hughes E	Jones JL	Jones JT	Kirwan JF	Moles WJ	Morris T	Quinn D	Rainbird HA	Stephenson JW	Steven	Tait AG	Warner AC	Watson J	Williams CA	Woodward VJ	Own-goal
							1	10		2		7		9	5	6	8	11		4					3					
0	0	0	0	0	0	0	1	1	0	1	0	1	0	1	1	1	1	1	0	1	0	0	0	0	1	0	0	0	0	
														1				1												

Barlow J	Brown C	Bugg JW	Burton JH	Burton O	Cameron J	Chalmers J	Clawley G	Copeland DC	Dryburgh W	Erentz HB	Fredericks GH	Gilhooley P	Haig-Brown AR	Houston R	Hughes E	Jones JL	Jones JT	Kirwan JF	Moles WJ	Morris T	Quinn D	Rainbird HA	Stephenson JW	Steven	Tait AG	Warner AC	Watson J	Williams CA	Woodward VJ	Own-goal
	4				8		1	10		2					5	6	7	11									3		9	
			6			11						8		9					4		10	7	2	5			3	1		
0	1	0	1	0	1	1	1	1	0	1	0	1	0	1	1	1	1	1	1	0	1	1	1	1	0	0	2	1	1	
														1				1			1									

League Table

	P	W	D	L	F	A	Pts
Southampton	30	20	8	2	83	20	48
Reading	30	19	7	4	72	30	45
Portsmouth	30	17	7	6	69	32	41
TOTTENHAM HOTSPUR	30	14	7	9	47	31	35
Bristol Rovers	30	13	8	9	46	34	34
New Brompton	30	11	11	8	37	35	33
Millwall	30	14	3	13	52	37	31
Northampton Town	30	12	6	12	39	48	30
Queen's Park Rangers	30	11	6	13	34	42	28
West Ham United	30	9	10	11	35	49	28
Luton Town	30	10	7	13	43	44	27
Swindon Town	30	10	7	13	38	46	27
Kettering Town	30	8	11	11	33	40	27
Wellingborough	30	11	3	16	36	56	25
Watford	30	6	4	20	35	87	16
Brentford	30	2	1	27	16	84	5

1902-03 CONT.

Match No.	Date			Opponents	Result		Scorers	Attendance
Western League								
1	Sep	13	A	Southampton	D	1-1	Houston	7,00
2		15	H	Millwall	W	4-3	Hughes, J.L.Jones, Cameron, Barlow	5,00
3		22	A	Queen's Park Rangers	W	2-0	J.Jones, Kirwan	5,00
4		29	H	Reading	W	2-1	Cameron, Copeland	
5	Oct	13	H	Bristol Rovers	L	0-1		6,50
6		29	A	Reading	L	0-3		
7	Nov	3	H	Queen's Park Rangers	W	3-0	J.Jones, Barlow 2	
8		8	H	Portsmouth	D	0-0		11,00
9		29	A	Portsmouth	D	2-2	Barlow 2	9,00
10	Dec	27	H	Southampton	D	0-0		20,00
11	Jan	28	A	Millwall	D	1-1	Copeland	2,00
12	Feb	16	H	West Ham United	W	1-0	Rainbird	4,00
13		23	A	Bristol Rovers	L	0-2		2,00
14	Mar	9	A	Brentford	D	0-0		2,00
15		19	A	West Ham United	D	0-0		
16		26	H	Brentford	W	4-0	Gilhooley, Houston 2, Fredericks	1,00
								Appearances
								Goals

Match No.	Date			Opponents	Result		Scorers	Attendance
London League								
1	Oct	6	A	Brentford	W	5-1	Morris (pen), J.Jones 3, Copeland	1,50
2		20	A	West Ham United	D	0-0		4,00
3	Nov	17	A	Woolwich Arsenal	L	1-2	Morris (pen)	4,00
4	Dec	1	H	Woolwich Arsenal	W	1-0	Warner	4,00
5		15	H	West Ham United	W	4-0	Tait (pen), Hughes (pen), Barlow, Kirwan	3,00
6	Jan	12	H	Brentford	W	1-0	Warner	
7	Mar	2	A	Millwall	W	3-0	J.Burton, Houston 2	1,00
8		16	A	Queen's Park Rangers	L	0-1		3,00
9		23	H	Millwall	W	1-0	Chalmers	1,50
10		30	H	Queen's Park Rangers	W	3-0	Hughes (pen), Copeland, Chalmers	2,50
								Appearances
								Goals

arlow J	Brown C	Bugg JW	Burton JH	Burton O	Cameron J	Chalmers J	Clawley G	Copeland DC	Dryburgh W	Erentz HB	Fredericks GH	Gilhooley P	Haig-Brown AR	Houston R	Hughes E	Jones JL	Jones JT	Kirwan JF	Moles WJ	Morris T	Quinn D	Rainbird HA	Stephenson JW	Steven	Tait AG	Warner AC	Watson J	Williams CA	Woodward VJ	Own-goals
					7		1	10		2				9	5	6	8	11		4					3					
			4		8			10		2					5	6		11								7	3	1		
			4				1	10		2		7		9		6	8	11		5					3					
			6		8		1	10		2				9	5		7	11		4					3					
					10		1			2		7			5	6	8	11		4					3				9	
			4		8		1	10						9		6		11		5			2		3	7				
	4		5		8		1	10		2						6	7	11							3					
					8		1	10		2					5	6	7	11		4					3				9	
	4				8		1	10		2		7			5	6		11									3			
	4					11	1	10	7							6				5					3	8	2		9	
	4						1	10	7	2					6			11		5					3	8				
		5	2	6		11			7			10							4		8	9	3					1		
	4						1					8		9		6		11		5	10	7	2		3					
			4			11	1		7					9		6				5	10		2		3	8				
	4					11	1	10	7	2				9	5	6							3			8				
	4			6		11					10	8		9	5								2		3	7		1		
	7	1	7	2	8	5	13	11	5	10	1	6	0	8	9	12	6	11	1	10	3	2	6	0	12	7	3	3	3	
					2			2			1	1		3	1	1	2	1				1								

arlow J	Brown C	Bugg JW	Burton JH	Burton O	Cameron J	Chalmers J	Clawley G	Copeland DC	Dryburgh W	Erentz HB	Fredericks GH	Gilhooley P	Haig-Brown AR	Houston R	Hughes E	Jones JL	Jones JT	Kirwan JF	Moles WJ	Morris T	Quinn D	Rainbird HA	Stephenson JW	Steven	Tait AG	Warner AC	Watson J	Williams CA	Woodward VJ	Own-goals
	4						1	10		2		7		9		6	8	11		5					3					
	4				7		1	10		2				9		6	8	11		5					3					
					8		1	10		2		7			5	6		11		4					3					
	4				9			10		2		7			5	6		11								8	3	1		
	4							10							5	6		11				7			3	8	2	1		
			4	6			1	10	7	2				9				11		5					3	8				
			5		8		1		7	2				9		6		11		4	10						3			
				6			1	10	7					9	5			11		4					3	8	2			
			6		9	11	1		7	2					5					4	10					8	3			
			4			11		10	7	2		8		9	6					5					3			1		
	4	0	4	2	5	2	7	8	5	8	0	4	0	6	6	6	2	8	0	8	2	1	0	0	7	5	5	3	0	
			1			2		2						2	2		3	1		2					1	2				

League Table

	P	W	D	L	F	A	Pts
Portsmouth	16	10	4	2	34	14	24
Bristol Rovers	16	9	2	5	36	22	20
Southampton	16	7	6	3	32	20	20
TOTTENHAM HOTSPUR	16	6	7	3	20	14	19
Millwall	16	6	3	7	23	29	15
Reading	16	7	0	9	20	21	14
Queen's Park Rangers	16	6	2	8	18	31	14
Brentford	16	3	4	9	16	34	10
West Ham United	16	2	4	10	15	29	8

LONDON LEAGUE	P	W	D	L	F	A	Pts
TOTTENHAM HOTSPUR	10	7	1	2	19	4	15
West Ham United	10	5	3	2	15	13	13
Woolwich Arsenal	10	6	0	4	14	10	12
Millwall	10	3	4	3	18	14	10
Queen's Park Rangers	10	2	3	5	9	15	7
Brentford	10	1	1	8	9	28	3

1903-04

SOUTHERN LEAGUE

Manager: John Cameron

Did you know that?

Spurs' match away to Bristol Rovers on 17 October 1903 was played at Bristol City's St John's Lane ground in Bedminster due to the inadequate accommodation at Eastville.

Match No.	Date		Opponents		Result		Scorers	Attendance
1	Sep	5	A	Fulham	D	0-0		10,00
2		12	H	Millwall	L	0-1		16,00
3		14	A	Brentford	D	0-0		4,00
4		19	A	Queen's Park Rangers	L	0-2		6,00
5		22	H	Plymouth Argyle	L	0-2		8,00
6	Oct	3	A	Reading	D	2-2	J.Jones, J.L.Jones	6,00
7		10	H	Wellingborough	W	1-0	J.Jones	9,00
8		17	A*	Bristol Rovers	L	0-1		8,00
9		24	H	Brighton & Hove Albion	D	2-2	Woodward, Chalmers	8,00
10	Nov	7	H	Northampton Town	W	2-1	Morris (pen), J.Jones	8,00
11		21	H	West Ham United	W	2-1	J.Jones, Kirwan	8,00
12	Dec	5	A	Luton Town	L	2-3	J.Jones (pen), Kirwan	6,00
13		19	A	Kettering Town	D	3-3	Woodward 2, Copeland	2,00
14		25	H	Portsmouth	D	1-1	J.Jones (pen)	20,00
15		26	A	Southampton	L	0-1		12,00
16	Jan	2	H	Fulham	W	1-0	Warner	10,00
17		9	A	Millwall	W	1-0	Woodward	10,00
18		16	H	Queen's Park Rangers	D	2-2	J.Jones 2	10,00
19		23	A	Plymouth Argyle	W	3-1	Brearley 2, Copeland	10,00
20		30	H	Reading	W	7-4	Warner, J.Jones (pen), Woodward 3, Copeland 2	8,00
21	Feb	13	H	Bristol Rovers	W	5-1	Warner, J.Jones (pen), Woodward 2, Kirwan	10,00
22		22	H	Swindon Town	W	1-0	Walton	7,00
23	Mar	12	H	Brentford	D	1-1	J.Jones	5,00
24		19	A	West Ham United	W	2-0	Walton 2	8,00
25		26	A	Swindon Town	D	0-0		3,00
26	Apr	1	H	Southampton	W	2-1	J.Jones, Woodward	21,30
27		2	H	Luton Town	D	1-1	Turner	10,00
28		4	A	Portsmouth	L	0-1		11,00
29		5	H	New Brompton	W	1-0	Morris	6,00
30		9	A	New Brompton	W	1-0	Kirwan	10,00
31		13	A	Brighton & Hove Albion	W	2-1	Walton, Kirwan	8,00
32		16	H	Kettering Town	W	5-1	Turner 4, Brearley	4,00
33		25	A	Northampton Town	W	1-0	Copeland	3,00
34		30	A	Wellingborough	D	3-3	J.Jones 3	3,00

*played at St Johns Lane (Bristol City)

Appearance

Goal

FA Cup

R1	Feb	6	A	Everton	W	2-1	Woodward, Balmer (og)	25,00
R2		20	H	Aston Villa	L*	0-1		32,00
R2r		26	A	Aston Villa	W	1-0	J.Jones	30,00
R3	Mar	5	H	Sheffield Wednesday	D	1-1	J.Jones	15,5C
R3r		10	A	Sheffield Wednesday	L*	0-2		32,00

*abandoned after 20 mins - crowd overflow

Appearance

Goal

Southern Charity Cup

R1	Sep	28	A	Millwall	L	1-3	Brearley	8,00

Appearance

Goal

Archer A	Badger HO	Berry WA	Brearley J	Brown C	Burton JH	Burton O	Cameron J	Chalmers J	Copeland DC	Erentz HB	Gilhooley P	Hughes E	Jones JL	Jones JT	Kirwan JF	Leach-Lewis AF	Mapley PJ	McConnachie J	McNaught JR	Mearns FC	Milton HA	Morris T	Pilch RG	Quinn D	Stephenson JW	Tait AG	Turner AD	Vaughan W	Walton J	Warner AC	Watson J	Williams CA	Woodward VJ	Own-goals
			9						10	2		4	6	8	11							5				3			7			1		
			9						10	2		4	6		11				5							3			7	8		1		
			9						10	2	8	4	6		11			7	5												3	1		
			9		4		8		10	2			6		11			7	5												3	1		
			8						10	2		4	6		11				5							3				7		1	9	
			9			6			10	2		4	5	8	11			7								3						1		
						6			10	2		4	5	8	11			7								3						1	9	
						6			10			4	5	8	11			7								3					2	1	9	
						6		11	10				5	8				7				4				3					2	1	9	
						5			10			2	6	8	11					1		4				3			7				9	
						6			10			2		8	11				5			4				3				7		1	9	
						6			10			2		8	11				5			4				3				7		1	9	
						6			10			2		8	11				5			4				3				7		1	9	
					6				10			2		8	11				5			4				3				7		1	9	
			9						10				6	8	11				5			4				3				7	2	1		
					6				10			5		8	11							4				3				7	2	1	9	
						6			10			5		8	11							4				3				7	2	1	9	
						6			10			5		8	11							4				3				7	2	1	9	
			9						10	2		5	6	8	11							4								7	3	1		
									10	2			6	8	11				5			4								7	3	1	9	
									10			5	6	8	11							4				3				7	2	1	9	
			9	4		6		11		2							3		5	1				10			7		8					
		9	5	4		6		11	10					8												3			7		2	1		
			4						10			5	6	8	11											3			7		2	1	9	
			4				9	11	10			5	6				3												7	8	2	1		
									10	2		5	6	8	11							4				3			7			1	9	
						6			10					8	11	5						4				3	7				2	1	9	
		9	4						10	2		5	6	8	11											3			7			1		
		9					10								11		3		5		6	4							7	8	2	1		
			9						10	2			6	8	11				5			4				3			7			1		
			9			6			10	2		5			11		3			1		4					7		8					
			9			6			10	2		5			11		3			1		4					7			8				
			9			6		11	10	2		5								1		4				3	7			8				
			9					11	10	2		5	6	8								4				3			7			1		
	0	3	18	2	3	16	3	6	32	17	1	25	20	24	28	1	5	6	13	5	1	22	0	1	0	25	5	0	13	17	16	29	17	
			3					1	5				1	15	5							2					5		4	3			10	

Archer A	Badger HO	Berry WA	Brearley J	Brown C	Burton JH	Burton O	Cameron J	Chalmers J	Copeland DC	Erentz HB	Gilhooley P	Hughes E	Jones JL	Jones JT	Kirwan JF	Leach-Lewis AF	Mapley PJ	McConnachie J	McNaught JR	Mearns FC	Milton HA	Morris T	Pilch RG	Quinn D	Stephenson JW	Tait AG	Turner AD	Vaughan W	Walton J	Warner AC	Watson J	Williams CA	Woodward VJ	Own-goals
									10			5	6	8	11							4				3				7	2	1	9	
									10			5	6	8	11							4				3				7	2	1	9	
									10			5	6	8	11							4				3				7	2	1	9	
			4						10			5	6	8	11											3				7	2	1	9	
			4						10			5	6	8	11											3				7	2	1	9	
	0	0	2	0	0	0	0	0	5	0	0	5	5	5	5	0	0	0	0	0	0	3	0	0	0	5	0	0	0	5	5	5	5	
														2																			1	1

Archer A	Badger HO	Berry WA	Brearley J	Brown C	Burton JH	Burton O	Cameron J	Chalmers J	Copeland DC	Erentz HB	Gilhooley P	Hughes E	Jones JL	Jones JT	Kirwan JF	Leach-Lewis AF	Mapley PJ	McConnachie J	McNaught JR	Mearns FC	Milton HA	Morris T	Pilch RG	Quinn D	Stephenson JW	Tait AG	Turner AD	Vaughan W	Walton J	Warner AC	Watson J	Williams CA	Woodward VJ	Own-goals
			9			6	10	11				4	5	8											2	3				7		1		
	0	0	1	0	0	1	1	1	0	0	0	1	1	1	0	0	0	0	0	0	0	0	0	0	1	1	0	0	0	1	0	1	0	
			1																															

League Table

	P	W	D	L	F	A	Pts
Southampton	34	22	6	6	75	30	50
TOTTENHAM HOTSPUR	34	16	11	7	54	37	43
Bristol Rovers	34	17	8	9	64	42	42
Portsmouth	34	17	8	9	41	38	42
Queen's Park Rangers	34	15	11	8	53	37	41
Reading	34	14	13	7	48	35	41
Millwall	34	16	8	10	64	42	40
Luton Town	34	14	12	8	38	33	40
Plymouth Argyle	34	13	10	11	44	34	36
Swindon Town	34	10	11	13	30	42	31
Fulham	34	9	12	13	34	36	30
West Ham United	34	10	7	17	39	44	27
Brentford	34	9	9	16	34	48	27
Wellingborough	34	11	5	18	44	63	27
Northampton Town	34	10	7	17	36	60	27
New Brompton	34	6	13	15	26	43	25
Brighton & Hove Albion	34	6	12	16	46	69	24
Kettering Town	34	6	7	21	39	76	19

1903-04 Cont.

Match No.	Date			Opponents	Result		Scorers	Attendance
Western League								
1	Sep	7	H	Reading	W	3-1	Brearley 3	6,00
2	Oct	5	H	Queen's Park Rangers	W	3-0	O.Burton, J.Jones, J.L.Jones	5,50
3		14	A	Reading	W	2-0	Cameron, Kirwan	
4		26	A	West Ham United	L*	0-1		50
5		31	A	Portsmouth	W	3-0	Woodward 2, Copeland	
6	Nov	2	H	Brentford	D	1-1	Copeland	5,00
7		9	A	Queen's Park Rangers	L	0-2		
8		30	H	Bristol Rovers	W	2-1	J.Jones, Badger	4,00
9	Dec	14	H	West Ham United	W	4-1	J.Jones 3, Copeland	3,00
10		28	H	Southampton	W	1-0	Kirwan	13,00
11	Feb	27	H	Portsmouth	D	1-1	Walton	12,00
12		29	H	Plymouth Argyle	W	5-1	Walter 2, Gilhholey, Berry, Chalmers (pen)	
13	Mar	28	A	Brentford	W	2-1	J.Jones, Copeland	
14	Apr	18	A	West Ham United	W	1-0	J.Jones	
15		20	A	Plymouth Argyle	D	0-0		4,00
16		23	A	Southampton	L	0-1		
17		27	A	Bristol Rovers	W	4-2	Warner 2, Copeland, Walton	

*abandoned at half-time - rain

Appearance
Goa

Match No.	Date			Opponents	Result		Scorers	Attendance
London League								
1	Sep	1	H	Woolwich Arsenal	L	0-1		8,00
2		21	H	Fulham	W	2-1	Cameron, Kirwan	3,00
3	Nov	14	A	Woolwich Arsenal	D	1-1	Kirwan	16,00
4		16	A	Brentford	W	2-0	J.Jones, Kirwan	
5		23	H	Millwall	L	2-3	Warner, Badger	3,00
6	Jan	11	H	Brentford	W	2-1	Walton, Brearley	3,00
7		18	A	West Ham United	W	2-0	J.Jones, Brearley	
8	Feb	15	A	Queen's Park Rangers	W	3-0	Walton 3	3,00
9	Mar	7	H	Queen's Park Rangers	L	1-3	Brown	2,50
10		14	A	Millwall	L	2-3	Turner, Chalmers	2,50
11		21	H	West Ham United	W	1-0	Warner	1,00
12	Apr	11	A	Fulham	W	5-1	Berry 2, Cameron, Badger, Copeland	1,00

Appearance
Goa

Badger HO	Berry WA	Brearley J	Brown C	Burton JH	Burton O	Cameron J	Chalmers J	Copeland DC	Erentz HB	Gilhooley P	Hughes E	Jones JL	Jones JT	Kirwan JF	Leach-Lewis AF	Mapley PJ	McConnachie J	McNaught JR	Mearns FC	Milton HA	Morris T	Pilch RG	Quinn D	Stephenson JW	Tait AG	Turner AD	Vaughan W	Walton J	Warner AC	Watson J	Williams CA	Woodward VJ	Own-goals
		9						10	2		4	6	8	11			5								3			7			1		
			4		6			10	2			5	8	11		7		1							3							9	
		9			6	8		10			4	5		11		7									3					2	1		
			4	5	6	10	11						8			7								2	3			9			1		
					6		11	10				5	8								4			2	3			7			1	9	
			4		6	8	11	10								7		1			5				3			9		2			
			4		6	9		10				5	8	11				1						2	3			7					
9					6			10			2		8	11			5				4				3				7		1		
9					6			10			2		8	11			5				4				3				7		1		
				6				10			5		8	11				1			4				3				7	2		9	
			4					10			5	6		11											3			8	7	2	1	9	
5	10	4			6		11		2	9						3		1								7		8					
		4			6		11	10	2		5		9												3	7			8		1		
		9						10	2				8	11		3	5			6	4							7			1		
9		4						10			5		8	11						6					3			7		2	1		
5					6			10	2					11							4				3	7			8		1	9	
						10	11	9	2			6					5				4							7	8	3	1		
5	1	6	5	2	11	5	6	15	7	1	8	7	11	11	0	2	4	5	5	2	8	0	0	3	14	3	0	10	7	6	12	5	
1	1	3			1	1	1	5		1		1	7	2														4	2			2	

Badger HO	Berry WA	Brearley J	Brown C	Burton JH	Burton O	Cameron J	Chalmers J	Copeland DC	Erentz HB	Gilhooley P	Hughes E	Jones JL	Jones JT	Kirwan JF	Leach-Lewis AF	Mapley PJ	McConnachie J	McNaught JR	Mearns FC	Milton HA	Morris T	Pilch RG	Quinn D	Stephenson JW	Tait AG	Turner AD	Vaughan W	Walton J	Warner AC	Watson J	Williams CA	Woodward VJ	Own-goals
		9						10	2		4	6	8	11							5				3			7			1		
		9		6	4	8		10	2	7		5		11																3	1		
					6			10			2		8	11			5				4				3			7			1	9	
					6			10		9	3		8	11			5					4							7		1		
9								10	2			5						1			4	6			3		11	7	8				
		9	4		6			10						11			5	1										8	7	2			
		9	4				11	10				6	8				5												7	2	1		
		9	4		6		11									2	5	1					10			7		8					
5			4		6		11			8						2		1					10			7		9					
5			4		6		11	10	3	9			8			2										7					1		
		4		10	6	9	11		2								5								3	7			8		1		
9	7	4			6	8		10	2					11			5													3	1		
4	1	7	5	2	9	3	5	9	6	4	3	4	5	6	0	3	0	7	4	0	3	2	2	0	4	4	1	6	5	4	8	1	
2	2	2	1			2	1	1					2	3												1		4	2				

League Table

	P	W	D	L	F	A	Pts
TOTTENHAM HOTSPUR	16	11	3	2	32	12	25
Southampton	16	9	3	4	30	18	21
Plymouth Argyle	16	8	4	4	22	18	20
Portsmouth	16	7	2	7	24	22	16
Brentford	16	6	4	6	19	23	16
Queen's Park Rangers	16	5	5	6	15	21	15
Reading	16	4	4	8	16	26	12
Bristol Rovers	16	4	3	9	29	29	11
West Ham United	16	2	4	10	13	31	8

LONDON LEAGUE	P	W	D	L	F	A	Pts
Millwall	12	11	1	0	38	8	23
TOTTENHAM HOTSPUR	12	7	1	4	23	14	15
Woolwich Arsenal	12	6	2	4	24	19	14
Queen's Park Rangers	12	5	2	5	18	23	12
Brentford	12	2	3	7	16	19	7
Fulham	12	3	1	8	10	29	7
West Ham United	12	2	2	8	14	31	6

1904-05

SOUTHERN LEAGUE

Manager: John Cameron

Did you know that?

At the end of the season Spurs undertook their first foreign tour. In two weeks they played seven games, three in Vienna and two each in Budapest and Prague. They lost only two games, one in Vienna, the other in Prague and both against Everton.

Match No.	Date			Opponents	Result		Scorers	Attendance
1	Sep	3	H	Fulham	L	0-1		17,0
2		10	A	Watford	W	1-0	Walton	7,0
3		17	H	Plymouth Argyle	W	2-0	Stansfield, Woodward	25,0
4		24	A	West Ham United	D	0-0		13,0
5	Oct	1	H	Reading	L	1-3	Copeland	13,0
6		8	A	Bristol Rovers	L	1-3	Hughes	11,0
7		15	H	Northampton Town	L	0-1		12,0
8		29	H	Brentford	D	1-1	Stansfield	9,8
9	Nov	5	A	Queen's Park Rangers	W	2-1	Morris, Brearley	12,0
10		12	H	Millwall	W	1-0	Warner	12,0
11		19	A	Brighton & Hove Albion	D	1-1	Bull	9,0
12		26	A	Luton Town	L	0-1		8,0
13	Dec	3	H	Swindon Town	W	6-3	Morris (pen), Walton 2, Glen, O'Hagan 2	10,0
14		10	A	New Brompton	D	1-1	Woodward	6,0
15		17	H	Wellingborough	W	8-0	Morris, Brearley, Walton 2, Woodward, Glen 3	5,0
16		26	A	Southampton	D	1-1	Kirwan	14,0
17		27	H	Portsmouth	D	1-1	Woodward	28,0
18		31	A	Fulham	L	0-1		9,0
19	Jan	7	H	Watford	W	2-0	Tait (pen), Woodward	8,0
20		21	H	West Ham United	W	1-0	Kirwan	13,0
21		28	A	Reading	L	2-3	Brearley, Glen	1,0
22	Feb	11	A	Northampton Town	W	3-0	Hughes, O'Hagan 2	8,0
23		25	A	Brentford	D	0-0		6,0
24	Mar	4	H	Queen's Park Rangers	W	5-1	Stansfield 2, Woodward, Glen 2	7,0
25		11	A	Millwall	W	2-0	Woodward, Glen	5,0
26		18	H	Brighton & Hove Albion	D	1-1	Chapman	7,0
27		25	H	Luton Town	W	1-0	O'Hagan	7,0
28	Apr	1	A	Swindon Town	L	1-2	Stansfield	7,0
29		5	A	Plymouth Argyle	L	1-2	Walton	8,0
30		8	H	New Brompton	W	2-0	Copeland, Glen	6,0
31		15	A	Wellingborough	W	1-0	Glen	3,0
32		21	H	Southampton	L	1-2	Kirwan	27,0
33		24	A	Portsmouth	L	2-3	Bull, O'Hagan	10,0
34		29	H	Bristol Rovers	W	1-0	George	10,0

Appearanc
Goa

FA Cup

R1	Feb	4	A	Middlesbrough	D	1-1	Glen	25,0
R1r		9	H	Middlesbrough	W	1-0	O'Hagan	18,0
R2		18	H	Newcastle United	D	1-1	Walton	19,0
R2r		22	A	Newcastle United	L	0-4		26,7

Appearance
Goa

Southern Charity Cup

R1	Oct	10	A	Woolwich Arsenal	W	3-1	Brearley, Woodward 2	8,0
SF	Jan	9	H	West Ham United	W	10-0	Tait (pen), Brearley 2, Woodward 5, O'Hagan 2	3,5
F	Apr	27	N*	Reading	D#	0-0		7,0

*played at Craven Cottage #trophy shared

Appearanc
Goa

Western League

1	Sep	7	A	Reading	W	1-0	Warner	3,0
2		19	H	Queen's Park Rangers	W	4-1	Morris (pen), Copeland 2, Glen	7,0
3		26	H	Bristol Rovers	W	1-0	Morris (pen)	6,0
4	Oct	3	A	Millwall	L	2-3	Copeland, Kirwan	4,0
5		13	A	Plymouth Argyle	L	0-5		9,0
6		22	A	Portsmouth	L	0-1		15,0
7		24	H	West Ham United	L	0-1		5,0
8	Nov	7	H	Reading	D	2-2	Berry	
9		14	A	Fulham	D	0-0		4,0
10		21	H	Plymouth Argyle	H	2-0	Brearley, Berry	5,0
11	Dec	24	H	Southampton	W*	2-1	Tait (pen), O'Hagan	
12	Jan	2	H	Fulham	L	0-5		
13	Feb	27	H	Millwall	W	4-1	Hughes, Swann, Stansfield, Glen	2,0
14	Mar	6	A	Bristol Rovers	L	1-2	Copeland	
15		20	A	Queen's Park Rangers	D	1-1	Copeland	2,0
16		27	A	West Ham United	D	1-1	Walton	2,0
17		29	H	Southampton	D	1-1	Tait (pen)	3,0
18	Apr	3	A	Brentford	L	0-2		
19		10	H	Brentford	D	0-0		1,0
20		17	H	Portsmouth	L	0-1		
21		22	A	Southampton	L	0-1		

*abandoned after 45 mins - rain

Appearance
Goa

Brearley J	Bull W	Burton O	Cameron J	Chapman H	Copeland DC	Eggett JH	Freeborough J	Gallacher JP	George JS	Glen A	Hughes E	Kirwan JF	McCurdy W	McNaught JR	Milton HA	Morgan C	Morris T	Murray WB	O'Hagan C	Pilch RG	Stansfield H	Swann A	Tait AG	Walton J	Warner AC	Watson J	Williams CA	Woodward VJ
6					10					8	5	11					4				9		3	7		2	1	
6					10					9	5	11					4						3	7	8	2	1	
6					10						5	11					4				8		3	7		2	1	9
6					10						5	11					4				8		3	7		2	1	9
6					10						5	11					4				8		3	7		2	1	9
	6				10					8	5	11					4				7		3			2	1	9
8	6										5	11	2				4		10		7		3				1	9
6					10	1					5						4	11			7		3		8	2		9
6	5				10	1						11					4					8	3		7	2		
6	5				10	1						11					4					8	3		7	2		
6	5				10	1						11					4						3	7		2		8
6	5					1						11					4		10				3	7		2		8
6	5					1				9		11	2				4		10				3	7				8
6	5	3				1			4	9		11	2						10					7				8
6		3				1				9		11	2	5			4		10					7				8
6	5					1						11	2				4		10				3	7	8			
					10	1			5			11	2				4						3	7	8	6		9
6	5				10	1						11	2				4				7		3		8			9
6	5					1				9		11					4		10		7		3			2		8
6	5				10	1				9	4	11	2								7					3		8
6	5					1				9		11	2				4		10		7					3		8
	5					1				9	6						4	11	10		7		3			2		
	5	3				1				10	6		2				4	11			8				7			
	5					1				10	6						4	11			8		3			2		9
	5				8	1				10	6			4				11			7		3			2		9
	5			9		1				10	6			4				11			8		3	7		2		
	5			8		1						11		6			4		10		9		3			2		
	5				8	1				9		11		6			4		10		7		3			2		
	5	6			8	1				10			2				4	11			7		3	9				
	5	3			8	1				10				6			4	11						7		2		9
	5	3		8		1	6			10		11					4				9			7		2		
	5	3				1					6	11					4		10		9			7	8	2		
	5	3				1						11		6			4		10		9			7	8	2		
	5	3			8	1			4			11	2	6					10		9			7				
19	26	9	0	3	18	27	1	0	3	18	15	26	12	8	0	0	29	8	14	0	23	2	24	19	10	25	7	19
3	2			1	2				1	10	2	3					3		6		5		1	6	1			7

Brearley J	Bull W	Burton O	Cameron J	Chapman H	Copeland DC	Eggett JH	Freeborough J	Gallacher JP	George JS	Glen A	Hughes E	Kirwan JF	McCurdy W	McNaught JR	Milton HA	Morgan C	Morris T	Murray WB	O'Hagan C	Pilch RG	Stansfield H	Swann A	Tait AG	Walton J	Warner AC	Watson J	Williams CA	Woodward VJ
6	5					1				9		11					4		10				3	7		2		8
6	5					1				9		11					4		10				3	7		2		8
6						1				9	5						4	11					3	7		2		8
6	5					1				9	2	11					4		10		7		3					8
4	3	0	0	0	0	4	0	0	0	4	2	3	0	0	0	0	4	1	3	0	1	0	4	3	0	3	0	4
										1									1					1				

Brearley J	Bull W	Burton O	Cameron J	Chapman H	Copeland DC	Eggett JH	Freeborough J	Gallacher JP	George JS	Glen A	Hughes E	Kirwan JF	McCurdy W	McNaught JR	Milton HA	Morgan C	Morris T	Murray WB	O'Hagan C	Pilch RG	Stansfield H	Swann A	Tait AG	Walton J	Warner AC	Watson J	Williams CA	Woodward VJ
8	6				10						5	11	2				4				7		3				1	9
6	5					1			4	9		11	2						10		7		3					8
	5	3	8			1					6						4	11	10					7		2		
2	3	1	1	0	1	2	0	0	1	1	2	2	2	0	0	0	2	1	2	0	2	0	2	1	0	1	1	2
3																			2				1					7

Brearley J	Bull W	Burton O	Cameron J	Chapman H	Copeland DC	Eggett JH	Freeborough J	Gallacher JP	George JS	Glen A	Hughes E	Kirwan JF	McCurdy W	McNaught JR	Milton HA	Morgan C	Morris T	Murray WB	O'Hagan C	Pilch RG	Stansfield H	Swann A	Tait AG	Walton J	Warner AC	Watson J	Williams CA	Woodward VJ
6					10					9	5	11					4						3	7	8	2	1	
8		6			10					9	5	11	2				4						3	7			1	
6					10					9	5	11					4				8		3	7		2	1	
	6				10					9	5	11					4		8		7		3			2	1	
4	6				10					8	5	11	2								7					3	1	
6					10	1						11	2	5			4				7				8	3		9
6					9	1						11	2	5			4		10		7				8	3		
6					10	1					5	11					4					8	3		7	2		
	5	6			10	1			4			11										8	3		7	2		
6					10	1	5					11	2				4						3	7				8
6	5					1				9		11	2				4		10				3	7				8
6	5				10	1						11				4			9		7		3		8	2		
6		3				1	2			10	5				4			11			9	8			7			
	5	6			10	1	3										4	11			8			7		2		
	5			9	10	1	6							4				11			8		3			2		
		6			8	1				10		11	2	5			4							9		3		
	5				8	1					6	11					4		10		9		3	7		2		
						1	5	7				11	2	6					10	4	8					3		
	5	3				1				10				6			4	11			9	8		7		2		
		3		8		1	6			10		11	2	5			4				9			7				
		3				1					4	11	2	5			6		10		9			7	8			
11	9	8	0	2	15	16	6	1	1	10	9	17	10	8	1	1	15	4	7	1	14	4	11	11	8	15	5	3
1					5					2	1	1					2		1		1	1	2	1	1			

League Table

	P	W	D	L	F	A	Pts
Bristol Rovers	34	20	8	6	74	36	48
Reading	34	18	7	9	57	38	43
Southampton	34	18	7	9	54	40	43
Plymouth Argyle	34	18	5	11	57	39	41
TOTTENHAM HOTSPUR	34	15	8	11	53	34	38
Fulham	34	14	10	10	46	34	38
Queen's Park Rangers	34	14	8	12	51	46	36
Portsmouth	34	16	4	14	61	56	36
New Brompton	34	11	11	12	40	40	33
Watford	34	15	3	16	44	45	33
West Ham United	34	12	8	14	48	42	32
Brighton & Hove Albion	34	13	6	15	44	45	32
Northampton Town	34	12	8	14	43	54	32
Brentford	34	10	9	15	33	38	29
Millwall	34	11	7	16	38	47	29
Swindon Town	34	12	5	17	41	59	29
Luton Town	34	12	3	19	45	54	27
Wellingborough	34	5	3	26	25	107	13

WESTERN LEAGUE	P	W	D	L	F	A	Pts
Plymouth Argyle	20	13	4	3	52	18	30
Brentford	20	11	6	3	30	22	28
Southampton	20	11	2	7	45	22	24
Portsmouth	20	10	3	7	29	30	23
West Ham United	20	8	4	8	37	42	20
Fulham	20	7	3	10	29	32	17
Millwall	20	7	3	10	32	40	17
TOTTENHAM HOTSPUR	20	5	6	9	20	28	16
Reading	20	6	3	11	27	37	15
Bristol Rovers	20	7	1	12	32	44	15
Queen's Park Rangers	20	6	3	11	27	45	15

1905-06

SOUTHERN LEAGUE

Manager: John Cameron

Did you know that?

Top scorer and centre-forward Peter Kyle and winger Chris Carrick were involved in such a serious breach of the club's training rules between Western League fixtures at Bristol Rovers and Plymouth Argyle in March that they were both suspended on the return to London. Neither was to play for Spurs again.

Match No.	Date			Opponents	Result		Scorers	Attendan
1	Sep	2	A	Reading	D	1-1	Kyle	12,0
2		9	H	Watford	W	1-0	Kyle	8,0
3		16	A	Brighton & Hove Albion	L	0-2		9,0
4		23	H	West Ham United	W	2-0	Chapman 2	14,0
5		30	A	Fulham	D	0-0		25,0
6	Oct	7	H	Queen's Park Rangers	W	2-1	Chapman, Kyle	13,0
7		14	A	Bristol Rovers	W	2-0	Tait (pen), Chapman	10,0
8		21	H	New Brompton	W	6-0	Walton 2, Chapman 2, Kyle, Glen	15,0
9	Nov	4	H	Swindon Town	W	2-1	Morris, Kyle	10,0
10		11	A	Millwall	L	1-2	Kyle	10,0
11		18	H	Luton Town	W	1-0	Woodward	22,0
12		25	H	Northampton Town	W	2-0	Bull, Carrick	13,0
13	Dec	2	A	Brentford	W	3-0	Walton, Chapman 2	10,0
14		16	A	Plymouth Argyle	L	1-2	Morris (pen)	10,0
15		25	H	Portsmouth	W	3-1	Chapman, Kyle, Carrick	33,0
16		26	A	Southampton	L	0-1		12,0
17		30	H	Reading	W	1-0	Glen (pen)	12,0
18	Jan	6	A	Watford	D	0-0		5,0
19		20	H	Brighton & Hove Albion	W	3-1	Bull, Walton, Woodward	10,0
20		27	A	West Ham United	W	1-0	Kyle	18,0
21	Feb	10	A	Queen's Park Rangers	D	0-0		10,0
22		12	H	Fulham	L	0-1		18,0
23		17	H	Bristol Rovers	D	2-2	Walton, Carrick	4,0
24	Mar	5	A	New Brompton	L	0-1		6,0
25		10	A	Swindon Town	L	0-2		3,0
26		17	H	Millwall	W	3-1	Shackleton, Brearley, Carrick	12,0
27		24	A	Luton Town	L	0-2		1,0
28		31	A	Northampton Town	D	0-0		6,0
29	Apr	7	H	Brentford	W	4-1	Berry, Chapman, Leach 2	8,0
30		13	H	Southampton	D	1-1	Chapman	22,0
31		14	A	Norwich City	L	1-4	Woodward	12,0
32		16	A	Portsmouth	L	0-1		12,0
33		17	H	Norwich City	W	3-0	Stansfield, Woodward 2	15,0
34		21	H	Plymouth Argyle	L	0-1		8,0
								Appearanc
								Goa

FA Cup

R1	Jan	13	H	Burnley	W	2-0	Woodward, Kyle	20,0
R2	Feb	3	H	Reading	W	3-2	Bull, Walton, Kyle	26,0
R3		24	H	Birmingham	D	1-1	Kyle	28,0
R3r		28	A	Birmingham	L*	0-2		34,0
								Appearanc
								Goa

*after extra-time

Southern Charity Cup

R1	Nov	8	H	Queen's Park Rangers	W	2-0	Kyle, Glen	6,0
SF	Apr	9	H	Woolwich Arsenal	D	0-0		8,0
SFr		28	A	Woolwich Arsenal	L	0-5		8,0
								Appearanc
								Goa

Blake JJ	Brearley J	Bull W	Burton O	Carrick C	Chaplin JF	Chapman H	Darnell J	Eggett JH	Freeborough J	Gaudson CE	George JS	Glen A	Hickling W	Hughes E	Kyle P	Leach G	McMullan F	McNaught JR	Milnes FH	Milton HA	Morris T	Murray WB	O'Hagan C	Page G	Shackleton J	Stansfield H	Tait AG	Walton J	Watson J	Whitbourne JG	Whyman A	Woodward VJ
	6	5				8		1							9						4	11	10				3	7	2			
	6	5				8		1							9						4	11	10			7	3		2			
	6	5				8		1													4	11	10				3	7	2			
		5				8	6	1							9						4	11	10			7	3		2			
		5				8	6	1							9						4	11	10				3	7	2			
		5				8	6	1							9						4	11	10				3	7	2			
		5				8	6	1				10			9						4	11					3	7	2			
		5				8	6	1				10			9						4	11					3	7	2			
		5				8	6	1				10			9						4	11					3	7	2			
		5				8	6	1				10			9						4	11					3	7	2			
		5						1				10		6	8						4	11					3	7	2			9
		5		11		8		1						6	9						4						3	7	2			10
		5		11		8		1						6	10						4						3	7	2			9
	6		3	11		8		1						5	10						4							7	2			9
		5	3	11		8		1						6	10						4							7	2			9
		5	3	11		8		1				10		6	9						4							7	2			
		5	3	11				1				8		6	10						4							7	2			9
		5	3	11		8		1						6	10						4							7	2			9
	6	5		11		8		1							10						4						3	7	2			9
	4	5		11		8		1				10		6	9												3	7	2			
		5		11		8		1				10		6	9						4						3	7	2			
		5		11		8		1				10		6	9						4						3	7	2			
	6			11		8		1				10		5	9						4						3	7	2			
		5		11		8		1				10		6	9						4						3		2			
	10	5		11				1			4			6	9						8				7		3		2			
	10	5		11		8		1						6	9						4				7		3		2			
	10	5				8		1				9		6							4						3		2		11	
	10	5				8		1						6							4				7		3		2		11	9
	10					8	6	1						5		9					4						3		2		11	
	10	5				8		1						6							4					7	3		2		11	9
	8	5	3				6	1								10					4	11				7			2			9
	8				2		4	1	5					6									10			7	3				11	
	8	5						1						6							4			10		7	3		2		11	9
		5			3	8		1				10		6							4					7			2		11	
0	16	30	6	15	2	28	10	34	1	0	1	14	0	22	25	2	0	0	0	0	32	12	7	1	3	7	27	21	33	0	7	12
	1	2		4		11						2			8	2					2				1	1	1	5				5

Blake JJ	Brearley J	Bull W	Burton O	Carrick C	Chaplin JF	Chapman H	Darnell J	Eggett JH	Freeborough J	Gaudson CE	George JS	Glen A	Hickling W	Hughes E	Kyle P	Leach G	McMullan F	McNaught JR	Milnes FH	Milton HA	Morris T	Murray WB	O'Hagan C	Page G	Shackleton J	Stansfield H	Tait AG	Walton J	Watson J	Whitbourne JG	Whyman A	Woodward VJ
		5		11				1				8		6	10						4						3	7	2			9
		5		11		8		1				10		6	9						4						3	7	2			
		5		11				1				10		6	9						4						3	7	2			8
		5		11				1				10		6	9						4						3	7	2			8
0	0	4	0	4	0	1	0	4	0	0	0	4	0	4	4	0	0	0	0	0	4	0	0	0	0	0	4	4	4	0	0	3
		1													3													1				1

Blake JJ	Brearley J	Bull W	Burton O	Carrick C	Chaplin JF	Chapman H	Darnell J	Eggett JH	Freeborough J	Gaudson CE	George JS	Glen A	Hickling W	Hughes E	Kyle P	Leach G	McMullan F	McNaught JR	Milnes FH	Milton HA	Morris T	Murray WB	O'Hagan C	Page G	Shackleton J	Stansfield H	Tait AG	Walton J	Watson J	Whitbourne JG	Whyman A	Woodward VJ
		5			2	8	6	1				10			9						4	11					3	7				
		5			2	8		1				10		6							4	11					3					9
	10				3	8	6	1						5							4					7			2		11	9
0	1	2	0	0	3	3	2	3	0	0	0	2	0	2	1	0	0	0	0	0	3	2	0	0	0	1	2	1	1	0	1	2
												1			1																	

League Table

	P	W	D	L	F	A	Pts
Fulham	34	19	12	3	44	15	50
Southampton	34	19	7	8	58	39	45
Portsmouth	34	17	9	8	61	35	43
Luton Town	34	17	7	10	64	40	41
TOTTENHAM HOTSPUR	34	16	7	11	46	29	39
Plymouth Argyle	34	16	7	11	52	33	39
Norwich City	34	13	10	11	46	38	36
Bristol Rovers	34	15	5	14	56	56	35
Brentford	34	14	7	13	43	52	35
Reading	34	12	9	13	53	46	33
West Ham United	34	14	5	15	42	39	33
Millwall	34	11	11	12	38	41	33
Queen's Park Rangers	34	12	7	15	58	44	31
Watford	34	8	10	16	38	57	26
Swindon Town	34	8	9	17	31	52	25
Brighton & Hove Albion	34	9	7	18	30	55	25
New Brompton	34	7	8	19	20	62	22
Northampton Town	34	8	5	21	32	79	21

1905-06 CONT.

Match No.	Date			Opponents	Result		Scorers	Attendan
Western League								
1	Sep	4	H	Reading	W	5-1	Chapman, Kyle, Berry	7,0
2		11	A	Queen's Park Rangers	D	1-1	Kyle	3,0
3		25	H	Bristol Rovers	L	0-1		4,0
4	Oct	2	H	Plymouth Aryle	L	0-2		6,0
5		11	A	Reading	D	0-0		
6		16	H	Fulham	W	1-0	Kyle	6,0
7		23	H	Millwall	W	5-0	Berry 4, Blake	6,0
8		28	A	Portsmouth	D	0-0		
9	Nov	6	A	West Ham United	L	1-4	Berry	4,0
10		13	H	Brentford	W	2-0	Freeborough, Stansfield	
11		20	A	Fulham	W	3-0	Stansfield, Kyle 2	2,0
12	Dec	23	H	Southampton	W	5-0	Walton 2 (1 pen), Glen, Woodward 2	9,0
13	Jan	29	H	Queen's Park Rangers	L	1-2	O'Hagan	3,0
14	Feb	19	A	Millwall	D	1-1	Brearley	1,5
15		26	A	Brentford	W	1-0	Leach	
16	Mar	3	H	Portsmouth	D	1-1	Kyle	6,0
17		19	A	Bristol Rovers	D	0-0		
18		21	A	Plymouth Aryle	D	0-0		
19		26	H	West Ham United	W	1-0	Whyman	1,0
20	Apr	25	A	Southampton	L	0-1		
								Appearanc
								Goa

Blake JJ	Brearley J	Bull W	Burton O	Carrick C	Chaplin JF	Chapman H	Darnell J	Eggett JH	Freeborough J	Gaudson CE	George JS	Glen A	Hickling W	Hughes E	Kyle P	Leach G	McMullan F	McNaught JR	Milnes FH	Milton HA	Morris T	Murray WB	O'Hagan C	Page G	Shackleton J	Stansfield H	Tait AG	Walton J	Watson J	Whitbourne JG	Whyman A	Woodward VJ
	6	5				8		1							9						4	11					3	7	2			
		5				8	6	1							9						4	11	10			7	3		2			
		5		11			6	1				10			9						4				8		3	7	2			
			6		2	8		1							9			5			4	11	10				3	7				
		5	3			8		1	6			10			9					4		11						7	2			
11		5			2	8	6	1						4	9	10											3	7				
11							6	1				10		5							4					8	3	7	2			
		5				8	6	1				10			9						4	11					3	7	2			
11			3					1	6	7	4			5									10			8			2			
	6			11	2				4					5									10			8	3	7		1		
	4	5			2			1				10		6	9							11				8		7	3			
	4	5	3	11			6	1				8			10													7	2			9
					2		6	1	4							9		5	3			11	10		7	8						
	10		3		2		6				4							5				11			7	8				1		
			3		2		6				4					9	8	5				11	10		7					1		
	6				2	8		1							9			5	3		4	11	10					7				
	10			11	2	8	6		5		4				9										7		3			1		
	10		6		3	8			5							9					4								2	1	11	
		5					6					10	3			9					4	7			8				2	1	11	

am untraced

Blake JJ	Brearley J	Bull W	Burton O	Carrick C	Chaplin JF	Chapman H	Darnell J	Eggett JH	Freeborough J	Gaudson CE	George JS	Glen A	Hickling W	Hughes E	Kyle P	Leach G	McMullan F	McNaught JR	Milnes FH	Milton HA	Morris T	Murray WB	O'Hagan C	Page G	Shackleton J	Stansfield H	Tait AG	Walton J	Watson J	Whitbourne JG	Whyman A	Woodward VJ
3	8	9	7	4	10	9	11	13	6	1	4	7	1	5	11	5	1	5	2	1	9	11	7	0	6	7	9	11	11	6	2	1
1	1					3			1			1			6	1							1		2				2		1	2

League Table

	P	W	D	L	F	A	Pts
Queen's Park Rangers	20	11	4	5	33	27	26
Southampton	20	10	5	5	41	35	25
Plymouth Argyle	20	8	8	4	34	23	24
TOTTENHAM HOTSPUR	20	7	7	6	28	17	21
Bristol Rovers	20	8	3	9	34	34	19
Millwall	20	7	5	8	28	29	19
West Ham United	20	7	5	8	32	35	19
Portsmouth	20	6	7	7	26	29	19
Reading	20	6	6	8	28	35	18
Fulham	20	5	5	10	23	32	15
Brentford	20	6	3	11	25	36	15

1906-07

SOUTHERN LEAGUE

Manager: John Cameron until March then Fred Kirkham

Did you know that?

Spurs chairman, Charles Roberts, was reputedly once a pitcher with Brooklyn Dodgers in New York and is often credited as the driving force behind efforts to popularise baseball in the UK. The first British Baseball Cup was competed for in the summer of 1906, Spurs beating Nondescripts 16 runs to three to win the trophy. They won the competition again two years later.

Match No.	Date		Opponents		Result		Scorers	Attendan
1	Sep	1	H	West Ham United	L	1-2	Dow	16,0
2		5	A	Watford	D	1-1	Hewitt	4,0
3		8	A	Bristol Rovers	W	3-2	Bull, Eames, Dow	10,0
4		15	A	Swindon Town	D	0-0		6,0
5		22	H	Norwich City	D	2-2	Walton, Hewitt	16,0
6		24	H	Fulham	W	5-1	Walton, Hewitt, Reid 2, Dow	13,0
7		29	A	Luton Town	W	2-0	Bull, Hewitt	10,0
8	Oct	6	H	Crystal Palace	W	3-0	Walton, Reid 2	20,0
9		13	A	Brentford	D	2-2	Reid 2 (1 pen)	8,0
10		27	A	Leyton	D	1-1	Woodward	15,0
11		29	A	Fulham	L	1-2	Stansfield	20,0
12	Nov	3	H	Portsmouth	D	1-1	Reid	20,0
13		10	A	New Brompton	W	1-0	Woodward	6,0
14		17	H	Plymouth Argyle	W	4-2	Hewitt 2, Reid 2	20,0
15		24	A	Brighton & Hove Albion	L	0-2		8,0
16	Dec	1	H	Reading	W	2-0	Hewitt, Reid	10,0
17		15	H	Northampton Town	W	6-0	Walton 2, Hewitt 2 (1 pen), Eames, Reid	7,0
18		22	A	Queen's Park Rangers	L	1-3	Morris	15,0
19		25	H	Millwall	W	3-1	Hewitt, Chapman, Reid	20,0
20		26	A	Southampton	L	1-2	Reid	8,0
21		29	A	West Ham United	L	2-4	Woodward, Reid	13,0
22	Jan	5	H	Bristol Rovers	W	4-0	Chapman, Woodward 2, Pickett	12,0
23		19	H	Swindon Town	W	3-0	Hewitt, Walton, Whyman	7,0
24		26	A	Norwich City	L	0-5		5,0
25	Feb	9	A	Crystal Palace	W	1-0	Pickett	8,0
26		16	H	Brentford	W	2-1	Chapma, Pickett	15,0
27	Mar	2	H	Leyton	D	0-0		14,0
28		9	A	Portsmouth	L	1-3	Woodward	12,0
29		16	H	New Brompton	W	2-0	Walton, Reid	6,0
30		23	A	Plymouth Argyle	D	0-0		5,0
31		25	H	Luton Town	L	1-2	Stansfield	9,0
32		29	H	Southampton	W	2-0	Woodward, Reid	20,0
33		30	H	Brighton & Hove Albion	W	3-0	Walton, Walker, Pickett	12,0
34	Apr	1	A	Millwall	L	0-2		12,0
35		6	A	Reading	L	0-2		8,0
36		13	H	Watford	D	0-0		9,0
37		20	A	Northampton Town	L	0-2		8,0
38		27	H	Queen's Park Rangers	W	2-0	Reid 2 (1 pen)	7,0

Appearanc
Goa

Western League

1	Sep	3	H	Plymouth Argyle	D	0-0		4,0
2		10	H	Southampton	L	2-3	Hughes, J.L.Jones, Cameron, Barlow	5,0
3	Oct	3	A	Southampton	L	0-2		2,0
4		8	A	West Ham United	L	0-5		4,0
5	Oct	20	H	Millwall	W	1-0	Stevenson (og)	4,0
6	Nov	7	A	Portsmouth	L	0-1		
7		24	H	Portsmouth	W	4-2	Brearley, Hewitt (pen), Walton 2	3,0
8	Dec	12	A	Plymouth Argyle	D	2-2	Reid, Orrell (og)	
9	Apr	8	H	West Ham United	W	4-0	Chapman, Whyman 3	
10		22	A	Millwall	D	0-0		1,5

Appearance
Goa

FA Cup

R1	Jan	12	H	Hull City	D	0-0		27,0
R1r		17	A	Hull City	D*	0-0		32,0
R1r		21	H#	Hull City	W	1-0	Chapman	20,0
R2	Feb	2	A	Blackburn Rovers	D	1-1	Walton	24,9
R2r		7	H	Blackburn Rovers	D^	1-1	Reid	29,9
R2r		11	N+	Blackburn Rovers	W	2-1	Walton, Reid	18,0
R3		23	A	Notts County	L	0-4		25,0

*abandoned after 10 mins of extra-time - bad light - result stood
#played at home by mutual consent ^after extra-time +played at Villa Park

Appearance
Goa

Southern Charity Cup

R1	Oct	22	H	West Ham United	W	2-0	Stansfield, Reid	8,0
SF	Mar	4	H	Queen's Park Rangers	W	4-0	Jones, Hewitt, Reid, Brearley	6,0
F	Apr	29	H	Southampton	W	2-0	Hewitt, Reid	10,0

Appearance
Goa

Berry WA	Brearley J	Bull W	Burton O	Chaplin JF	Chapman H	Darnell J	Dow W	Eames W	Eggett JH	Hewitt CW	Hughes E	Jones W	McDiarmid F	Morris T	Page G	Payne GC	Pickett AE	Reid J	Reilly MM	Stansfield H	Steel D	Tait AG	Walker RH	Walton J	Watson C	Watson J	Whitbourne JG	Whyman A	Wilkinson JW	Woodward VJ	Own-goals
		5					11	9	1	8			6	4								3	10	7		2					
9		5	2	3					1	8	6	4											10					11			
		5		3			11	9	1	8	6			4			10							7		2					
		5		3			11	9	1	8	6			4			10							7		2					
		5		3			11		1	8	6			4				10						7		2				9	
	6	5		2			11			8				4				10				3		7			1			9	
	6	5		2			11			8				4				10				3		7			1			9	
	6			2			11			8	5			4				10	1			3		7						9	
	6	5		2			11			8				4				10	1			3		7						9	
	5			2			11			8			6	4				10	1			3		7						9	
	6										5		11	4				10	1	8		3		7		2				9	
	11			2						8	5		6	4				10	1			3		7						9	
	11	5		2						8	6			4				10	1			3		7						9	
	11	5		2						8	6			4				10	1			3		7						9	
	11	5		2						8			6	4				10	1			3		7						9	
	11	5		2						8				4				10	1		6			7		3				9	
	11	5		2				9		8	6			4				10	1					7		3					
	11	5		2						8				4				10	1		6			7		3				9	
	11	5		2	9					8	6			4				10	1					7		3					
	11	5		2	9					8	6			4				10	1			3		7							
		5		2						8	6			4				10	1			3		7				11		9	
	11	5			8						6			4			10		1			3		7		2				9	
				2				9		8		5	6				10		1		4			7		3		11			
				2				9		8		5	6	4			10		1	11		3	7								
	11		3	2		6		9		7		5					10		1		4		8								
	11				9	6				8		5		4			10		1			3		7		2					
		5	3	2						8	6						10			11	4			7			1			9	
		5	3	2						8	6			4				10		11				7			1			9	
		5		2	8						6			4				10		11		3		7			1			9	
				2	9						6	5		4			11	10		8		3		7			1				
				2						9	6	5		4			11			10			8	7			1		3		
		5		2							6			4			11	10				3	8	7			1			9	
		5		2	9						6			4			11	10				3	8	7			1				
		5		2	9					7		6		4			11			10			8				1		3		
		5		2	9						6			4				10		11		3	8	7			1				
		5		2							6			4				10		11		3	8	7			1			9	
		5		2						8	6						11	10		9	4	3		7			1				
		5		2	9					8	6			4			11	10				3		7			1				
1	18	28	4	34	10	2	9	7	5	30	25	8	7	33	0	0	15	26	19	11	6	24	10	34	0	12	14	3	2	20	
		2			3		3	2		11				1			4	18		2			1	8				1		7	

Berry WA	Brearley J	Bull W	Burton O	Chaplin JF	Chapman H	Darnell J	Dow W	Eames W	Eggett JH	Hewitt CW	Hughes E	Jones W	McDiarmid F	Morris T	Page G	Payne GC	Pickett AE	Reid J	Reilly MM	Stansfield H	Steel D	Tait AG	Walker RH	Walton J	Watson C	Watson J	Whitbourne JG	Whyman A	Wilkinson JW	Woodward VJ	Own-goals
	5			3	8		11	9	1			4	6				10							7		2					
	5		2				11	9	1	8		4	6				10					3		7							
9	5			3			11			8	6			4					1				10	7		2					
	6						9			8	5							10	1	11	4				3	2					
	6			2	8		11				5			4	9			10	1					7		3					
	11	5		2						8	6			4				10	1	9				7		3					
	11	5						9		8			6			10			1		4	3		7		2					
	11	5						9		8	6			4				10	1			3		7		2					
	11		3	2	9	4				8			6								5			7			1	10			
	11	5	3	2	9	6				8								10			4			7			1				
1	10	4	3	6	4	2	5	4	2	8	5	2	4	4	1	1	2	5	6	2	4	3	1	9	1	7	2	1	0	0	
	2				1					1		1						1						2				3			2

Berry WA	Brearley J	Bull W	Burton O	Chaplin JF	Chapman H	Darnell J	Dow W	Eames W	Eggett JH	Hewitt CW	Hughes E	Jones W	McDiarmid F	Morris T	Page G	Payne GC	Pickett AE	Reid J	Reilly MM	Stansfield H	Steel D	Tait AG	Walker RH	Walton J	Watson C	Watson J	Whitbourne JG	Whyman A	Wilkinson JW	Woodward VJ	Own-goals
	11	5								8	6			4				10	1			3		7		2				9	
	11	5			8	6								4				10	1			3		7		2				9	
		5			9					8	6			4				10	1	11		3		7		2					
		5			9					8	6			4				10	1	11		3		7		2					
		5			9					8	6			4				10	1	11		3		7		2					
		5			9					8	6			4				10	1	11		3		7		2					
		5			8						6			4				10	1	11		3		7		2				9	
0	2	7	0	0	6	1	0	0	0	5	6	0	0	7	0	0	0	7	7	5	0	7	0	7	0	7	0	0	0	3	
					1													2						2							

Berry WA	Brearley J	Bull W	Burton O	Chaplin JF	Chapman H	Darnell J	Dow W	Eames W	Eggett JH	Hewitt CW	Hughes E	Jones W	McDiarmid F	Morris T	Page G	Payne GC	Pickett AE	Reid J	Reilly MM	Stansfield H	Steel D	Tait AG	Walker RH	Walton J	Watson C	Watson J	Whitbourne JG	Whyman A	Wilkinson JW	Woodward VJ	Own-goals
				2			11				5		6	4				10	1	8		3		7				9			
	11			2	9					8	6	5		4				10				3		7			1				
		5		2						8	6			4				10		11		3		7			1			9	
0	1	1	0	3	1	0	1	0	0	2	3	1	1	3	0	0	0	3	1	2	0	3	0	3	0	0	2	1	0	1	
	1									2		1						3		1											

League Table

	P	W	D	L	F	A	Pts
Fulham	38	20	13	5	58	32	53
Portsmouth	38	22	7	9	64	36	51
Brighton & Hove Albion	38	18	9	11	53	43	45
Luton Town	38	18	9	11	52	52	45
West Ham United	38	15	14	9	60	41	44
TOTTENHAM HOTSPUR	38	17	9	12	63	45	43
Millwall	38	18	6	14	71	50	42
Norwich City	38	15	12	11	57	48	42
Watford	38	13	16	9	46	43	42
Brentford	38	17	8	13	57	56	42
Southampton	38	13	9	16	49	56	35
Reading	38	14	6	18	57	47	34
Leyton	38	11	12	15	38	60	34
Bristol Rovers	38	12	9	17	55	54	33
Plymouth Argyle	38	10	13	15	43	50	33
New Brompton	38	12	9	17	47	59	33
Swindon Town	38	11	11	16	43	54	33
Queen's Park Rangers	38	11	10	17	47	55	32
Crystal Palace	38	8	9	21	46	66	25
Northampton Town	38	5	9	24	29	88	19

WESTERN LEAGUE	P	W	D	L	F	A	Pts
West Ham United	10	7	1	2	25	14	15
Plymouth Argyle	10	5	3	2	16	10	13
Portsmouth	10	4	2	4	16	19	10
TOTTENHAM HOTSPUR	10	3	3	4	13	15	9
Southampton	10	4	0	6	14	16	8
Millwall	10	1	3	6	5	15	5
Bristol Rovers	20	7	1	12	32	44	15
Queen's Park Rangers	20	6	3	11	27	45	15

1907-08

SOUTHERN LEAGUE

Manager: Fred Kirkham

Did you know that?

In 1908 the prolific composer Ezra Read penned one of his 'descriptive fantasias' for the pianoforte entitled *The Football Match*. Although Read had no apparent connection with Tottenham it was 'Dedicated to Tottenham Hotspur Football Club in admiration of their many gallant games.'

Match No.	Date			Opponents	Result		Scorers	Attendar
1	Sep	2	A	Queen's Park Rangers	D	3-3	Walton, Pass, McNair	6,0
2		7	A	West Ham United	D	1-1	McNair	10,0
3		14	H	Queen's Park Rangers	W	3-2	Bull, Darnell, Pass	20,0
4		21	H	New Brompton	W	2-1	McNair	16,0
5		28	A	Swindon Town	L	0-1		5,0
6	Oct	5	H	Crystal Palace	L	1-2	Stansfield	18,0
7		12	A	Luton Town	L	1-3	McNair	7,0
8		19	H	Brighton & Hove Albion	D	1-1	Morris (og)	12,0
9		26	A	Portsmouth	W	2-1	Seeburg 2	10,0
10	Nov	2	H	Bradford	D	0-0		4,5
11		9	A	Millwall	W	2-1	Woodward 2	8,0
12		16	H	Brentford	W	1-0	Reid	12,0
13		23	A	Bristol Rovers	D	0-0		8,0
14		30	H	Leyton	W	1-0	Woodward	12,0
15	Dec	7	A	Reading	L	1-3	Middlemiss	5,0
16		14	H	Watford	W	5-0	Steel, Woodward 2, Middlemiss, Hitch (og)	9,0
17		21	A	Norwich City	L	1-2	Middlemiss	5,0
18		25	H	Northampton Town	W	2-0	Woodward 2	25,0
19		26	A	Southampton	D	1-1	Walker	18,0
20		28	A	Northampton Town	L	1-2	Pass	9,0
21	Jan	4	H	West Ham United	W	3-2	Pass, Payne, Pickett	13,0
22		18	A	New Brompton	W	2-1	Woodward, Bull	5,0
23		20	H	Plymouth Argyle	L	0-1		10,0
24		25	H	Swindon Town	W	1-0	Reid	10,0
25	Feb	8	H	Luton Town	L	1-2	Walker	11,0
26		12	A	Crystal Palace	W	2-0	Pass, Pickett	8,0
27		15	A	Brighton & Hove Albion	L	0-2		3,0
28		29	A	Bradford	W	2-1	Seeburg, Middlemiss	7,0
29	Mar	7	H	Millwall	L	1-2	Minter	20,0
30		14	A	Brentford	L	0-3		6,0
31		21	H	Bristol Rovers	L	1-2	Woodward	11,0
32		28	A	Leyton	W	5-2	Woodruff 2, Woodward, Seeburg, Bidmead (og)	12,0
33	Apr	4	H	Reading	W	2-0	Minter 2	8,0
34		6	H	Portsmouth	W	2-0	Middlemiss, Phillips (og)	6,0
35		11	A	Watford	D	2-2	Woodruff, Minter	5,0
36		17	H	Southampton	W	3-0	Seeburg, Payne, Middlemiss	22,0
37		18	H	Norwich City	W	3-0	Payne, Middlemiss 2	10,0
38		20	A	Plymouth Argyle	L	0-1		8,0

Appearanc
Goa

Western League

1	Sep	9	H	Bristol Rovers	W	10-0	Morris, Walton, Pass 4, McNair, Reid 3	5
2		18	A	Bristol Rovers	L	1-2	Walton	
3		23	A	Millwall	L	0-2		4,0
4	Oct	2	A	Reading	W	2-1	Whyman, Seeburg	
5		7	H	West Ham United	W	2-1	Bull, Pickett	5,0
6		14	H	Reading	L	0-2		
7		23	A	Crystal Palace	L	0-2		5,0
8	Nov	4	A	West Ham United	W	3-1	Steel, Reid 2	
9		25	H	Millwall	L	0-3		3,0
10	Dec	2	H	Crystal Palace	W	1-0	Middlemiss	3,0
11		9	A	Luton Town	W	5-1	Walton, Pass 2, McNair, Payne	1,5
12	Dec	16	H	Luton Town	W	2-0	Seeburg, Payne	1,5

Appearance
Goa

FA Cup

R1	Jan	11	A	Everton	L	0-1		21,0

Appearance
Goal

Southern Charity Cup

R1	Sep	30	H	Millwall	D	1-1	Walton	7,0
R1r	Nov	19	A	Millwall	L	1-2	Whyman	70

Appearance
Goal

…ster	Bull W	Burton O	Chaplin JF	Coquet E	Cousins AC	Darnell J	Dixon A	Gipps TS	Gray JA	Hughes E	Lee J	Manning GS	Massey FJ	McNair WD	Middlemiss H	Minter WJ	Morris T	Pass JE	Payne GC	Pickett AE	Reid J	Seeburg MP	Stansfield H	Steel D	Tait AG	Walker RH	Walton J	Watson J	Whitbourne JG	Whyman A	Woodruff CL	Woodward VJ	Own-goals
	5		2				3			6				9			4	8			10						7		1	11			
	5		2			6	3							9			4	8			10						7		1	11			
	5		2			6	3							9			4	8				10					7		1	11			
	5		2			6	3					1		9			4	8		11		10					7						
	5	3	2			6						1		9			4	8		11	10						7						
	5		3			6						1		10			4	8					11				7	2				9	
	5		2			6	3					1		10			4	8					11				7					9	
		3	2			6						1		9			4				10		11	5			7					8	
	5	3	2						6			1					4	8				10	11				7					9	
	5	3	2						6			1					4	8				10	11				7					9	
		3							6			1					4				10			5		8	7	2		11		9	
		3	2						6			1			11		4				10			5		8	7					9	
		3	2						6			1			11		4				10			5		8	7					9	
		3	2						6			1			11		4				10			5		8	7					9	
		3	2						6			1			11		4				10			5		8	7			9			
					10				6			1			11		4							5	3	8	7	2				9	
		3	2		10				6			1		9	11		4							5		8	7						
		3	2			6						1			11		4		10					5		8	7					9	
		3	2			6						1			11		4	8			10			5		7						9	
		3	2						6			1					4	8	10	11				5		7						9	
		3	2						6			1					4	8	10	11				5		7						9	
	10	3	2						6			1		7	11		4							5		8						9	
	10	3	2						6			1		9	11		4							5		8							
	5	3	2						6			1		7	11		4	8			10	9											
	5	3	2						6			1		7	11		4			10						8						9	
	5	3	2			6						1		7	11			8		10		9		4									
	5	3	2			6						1		7	11			8		10		9		4									
	5	3	2			6						1			11			7		10		8		4						9			
	5	3		2		6						1			11	8		7		10				4								9	
	5	3		2		6						1			11	8		7		10				4						9			
		3	2			6									11	10	4						7	5					1	9		8	
		3		2		6						1			11		4			10		9		5							7	8	
		3		2		6						1			11	8	4			10		9		5							7		
	5	3	2			6									11	8				10		9		4					1		7		
		3		2		6						1			11	10	4					9		5							7	8	
		3	2			6						1			11	8	4		10			9		5							7		
	5	3	2			6						1			11	8	4		10			9	7										
	5			2		6	3					1			11	8			10			9	7	4									
	21	30	30	6	2	22	6	0	15	1	0	33	0	15	25	9	31	18	6	13	11	15	8	26	1	14	18	3	5	8	5	20	
	2					1								5	8	4		5	3	2	2	5	1	1		2	1				3	10	4

…ster	Bull W	Burton O	Chaplin JF	Coquet E	Cousins AC	Darnell J	Dixon A	Gipps TS	Gray JA	Hughes E	Lee J	Manning GS	Massey FJ	McNair WD	Middlemiss H	Minter WJ	Morris T	Pass JE	Payne GC	Pickett AE	Reid J	Seeburg MP	Stansfield H	Steel D	Tait AG	Walker RH	Walton J	Watson J	Whitbourne JG	Whyman A	Woodruff CL	Woodward VJ	Own-goals
	5		2			6								9			4	8			10				3		7		1	11			
	5						3		6	4				9				8				10					7	2	1	11			
		5	2			6	3					1					4	8	10			9					7			11			
			2			6	3					1	4					8				10	11	5			7			9			
	5					6	3					1		9						10		8	11	4			7	2					
		3									11	1	6	9			4					8		5			7	2				10	
									6			1					4	8		11		10		5	3	7		2		9			
			2			4			6			1		9				8			10		11	5	3		7						
					10		2		6	5		1			11		4					9			3	8	7						
			2			5		4		6		1		7	11			8			10				3					9			
		3				5	2			6		1		9			4	8	10								7			11			
	5					6						1	4	11				8	10			7			3			2		9			
0	4	3	5	0	1	8	6	1	4	4	1	10	3	8	2	0	6	9	3	2	3	8	3	5	6	2	9	5	2	8	0	1	
	1													2	1		1	6	2	1	5	2		1			3			1			

…ster	Bull W	Burton O	Chaplin JF	Coquet E	Cousins AC	Darnell J	Dixon A	Gipps TS	Gray JA	Hughes E	Lee J	Manning GS	Massey FJ	McNair WD	Middlemiss H	Minter WJ	Morris T	Pass JE	Payne GC	Pickett AE	Reid J	Seeburg MP	Stansfield H	Steel D	Tait AG	Walker RH	Walton J	Watson J	Whitbourne JG	Whyman A	Woodruff CL	Woodward VJ	Own-goals
	10	3	2						6			1		11			4	8						5		7						9	
0	1	1	1	0	0	0	0	0	1	0	0	1	0	1	0	0	1	1	0	0	0	0	0	1	0	1	0	0	0	0	0	1	

…ster	Bull W	Burton O	Chaplin JF	Coquet E	Cousins AC	Darnell J	Dixon A	Gipps TS	Gray JA	Hughes E	Lee J	Manning GS	Massey FJ	McNair WD	Middlemiss H	Minter WJ	Morris T	Pass JE	Payne GC	Pickett AE	Reid J	Seeburg MP	Stansfield H	Steel D	Tait AG	Walker RH	Walton J	Watson J	Whitbourne JG	Whyman A	Woodruff CL	Woodward VJ	Own-goals
		3	2						6			1		9			4	8				10	11	5			7						
		3	2						6			1		9			4				10			5		8	7			11			
0	0	2	2	0	0	0	0	0	2	0	0	2	0	2	0	0	2	1	0	0	1	1	1	2	0	1	2	0	0	1	0	0	
																											1			1			

League Table

	P	W	D	L	F	A	Pts
Queen's Park Rangers	38	21	9	8	82	57	51
Plymouth Argyle	38	19	11	8	50	31	49
Millwall	38	19	8	11	49	32	46
Crystal Palace	38	17	10	11	54	51	44
Swindon Town	38	16	10	12	55	40	42
Bristol Rovers	38	16	10	12	59	56	42
TOTTENHAM HOTSPUR	38	17	7	14	59	48	41
Northampton Town	38	15	11	12	50	41	41
Portsmouth	38	17	6	15	64	52	40
West Ham United	38	15	10	13	47	48	40
Southampton	38	16	6	16	51	60	38
Reading	38	15	6	17	55	50	36
Bradford	38	12	12	14	53	54	36
Watford	38	12	10	16	47	59	34
Norwich City	38	12	9	17	46	49	33
Brentford	38	14	5	19	49	53	33
Brighton & Hove Albion	38	12	8	18	46	59	32
Luton Town	38	12	6	20	33	56	30
Leyton	38	8	11	19	52	74	27
New Brompton	38	9	7	22	44	75	25

WESTERN LEAGUE	P	W	D	L	F	A	Pts
Millwall	12	9	2	1	31	13	20
Bristol Rovers	12	6	3	3	22	19	15
TOTTENHAM HOTSPUR	12	6	1	5	16	15	13
Luton Town	12	4	4	4	16	21	12
Reading	12	4	3	5	20	25	11
Crystal Palace	12	3	4	5	16	17	10

1908-09

DIVISION TWO

Manager: Directors

Did you know that?

The London Professional Football Charity Fund was instigated by Spurs after they decided their commitments as a Football League club would not allow them to participate in the Southern Charity Cup. Their first game against Clapton Orient on 2 November 1908 drew a crowd of 6,000 paying over £168.

LEAGUE DEBUTANTS

Sep 1	v Wolves	Ollie Burton
Sep 1	v Wolves	Ernie Coquet
Sep 1	v Wolves	Jabez Darnell
Sep 1	v Wolves	Bob Hewitson
Sep 1	v Wolves	Doug MacFarlane
Sep 1	v Wolves	Bert Middlemiss
Sep 1	v Wolves	Tom Morris
Sep 1	v Wolves	Danny Steel
Sep 1	v Wolves	Bobby Steel
Sep 1	v Wolves	Joe Walton
Sep 1	v Wolves	Vivian Woodward
Sep 5	v Leeds City	Billy Minter
Sep 26	v Hull City	Max Seeburg
Oct 10	v Blackpool	Tom Leslie
Nov 14	v Birmingham	Charlie Woodruff
Nov 28	v Grimsby Town	James Morton
Dec 28	v Wolves	Joe Brough
Feb 11	v Bolton Wanderers	Percy Humphreys
Mar 6	v Stockport County	Walter Bull
Mar 27	v Gainsborough Trinity	Fred Boreham
Mar 27	v Gainsborough Trinity	Fred Massey
Mar 27	v Gainsborough Trinity	Fred Wilkes
Apr 24	v Bradford Park Avenue	John Curtis

Match No.	Date			Opponents	Result		Scorers	Attendan
1	Sep	1	H	Wolverhampton Wanderers	W	3-0	Morris, Woodward 2	20,0
2		5	A	Leeds City	L	0-1		20,0
3		12	H	Barnsley	W	4-0	Walton, Woodward, Middlemiss 2	20,0
4		19	H	Bolton Wanderers	W	2-1	Minter, Middlemiss	25,0
5		26	A	Hull City	L	0-1		12,0
6	Oct	3	H	Derby County	D	0-0		25,0
7		10	A	Blackpool	D	1-1	R.Steel	6,0
8		17	H	Chesterfield	W	4-0	Walton, Minter 2, R.Steel	14,0
9		24	A	Glossop	D	1-1	Minter	3,0
10		31	H	Stockport County	D	0-0		16,0
11	Nov	7	A	West Bromwich Albion	L	0-3		20,0
12		14	H	Birmingham	W	4-0	Woodward 2, Middlemiss 2	25,0
13		21	A	Gainsborough Trinity	W	2-0	R.Steel, Middlemiss	6,0
14		28	H	Grimsby Town	W	2-0	Woodward 2	14,0
15	Dec	5	A	Fulham	W	3-2	Minter 2, R.Steel	35,0
16		12	H	Burnley	W	4-2	Minter, Woodward 2, R.Steel	10,0
17		19	A	Bradford Park Avenue	W	2-0	Minter, Woodward	5,0
18		25	A	Oldham Athletic	L	0-1		24,0
19		26	H	Oldham Athletic	W	3-0	Minter, Woodward, Middlemiss	40,0
20		28	A	Wolverhampton Wanderers	L	0-1		9,00
21	Jan	2	H	Leeds City	W	3-0	Minter 2, Middlemiss	16,0
22		9	A	Barnsley	D	1-1	Minter	7,00
23		23	A	Bolton Wanderers	W	1-0	R.Steel	24,00
24		30	H	Hull City	D	0-0		21,00
25	Feb	13	H	Blackpool	W	4-1	Minter, R.Steel, Middlemiss 2	15,00
26		27	H	Glossop	D	3-3	McFarlane, R.Steel 2	12,00
27	Mar	6	A	Stockport County	W	3-1	Minter, R.Steel, Middlemiss	5,00
28		8	A	Chesterfield	W	3-1	Woodward, Middlemiss 2	5,00
29		13	H	West Bromwich Albion	L	1-3	Woodruff	35,00
30		20	A	Birmingham	D	3-3	D.Steel, Woodward, R.Steel	8,00
31		27	H	Gainsborough Trinity	D	1-1	Woodward	15,00
32	Apr	03	A	Grimsby Town	W	2-1	Minter, McFarlane	5,00
33		9	H	Clapton Orient	L	0-1		33,00
34		10	H	Fulham	W	1-0	Woodward	22,00
35		12	A	Clapton Orient	D	0-0		20,00
36		17	A	Burnley	W	2-1	Woodward 2	8,00
37		24	H	Bradford Park Avenue	W	3-0	Curtis, Minter, Woodward	20,00
38		28	A	Derby County	D	1-1	R.Steel	9,00

Appearance
Goa

FA Cup

R1	Jan	16	A	Manchester City	W	4-3	Morris (pen), Minter 2, R. Steel	20,00
R2	Feb	6	H	Fulham	W	1-0	Walton, D.Steel	33,00
R3		20	H	Burnley	D	0-0		21,83
R3r		24	A	Burnley	L	1-3	Coquet (p)	30,00

Appearance
Goal

London FA Charity Cup

R1	Oct	5	H	Queen's Park Rangers	W	1-0	Minter	7,00
R2	Nov	30	A	West Ham United	W	2-0	Walton, D Steel	3,00
SF	Mar	2	N*	Millwall	L	0-2		5,00

*played at Upton Park

Appearance
Goal

London Professional Football Charity Fund

Nov	2	H	Clapton Orient	D	1-1	Minter	6,00

Appearances
Goals

Boreham F	Brough J	Bull W	Burton O	Coquet E	Curtis JJ	Darnell J	Hewitson R	Leslie TS	Massey FJ	McFarlane D	Middlemiss H	Minter WJ	Morris T	Morton JC	Seeburg MP	Steel D	Steel RL	Walton J	Wilkes F	Wood N	Woodruff CL	Woodward VJ
			3	2		6	1			9	11		4			5	10	7				8
			3	2		6	1			9	11	8	4			5	10	7				
			3	2		6	1				11	9	4			5	10	7				8
			3	2		6	1			9	11	8	4			5	10	7				
			3	2		6	1				11	9	4		8	5	10	7				
			3	2		6	1				11	9	4			5	10	7				8
			3	2			1	6		9	11	8	4			5	10	7				
			3	2		6	1			9	11	8	4			5	10	7				
			3	2		6	1			9	11	8	4			5	10	7				
			3	2		6	1			9	11		4			5	10	7				8
			3	2		6	1			7	11	9	4			5	10					8
			3	2		6	1				11	8	4			5	10				7	9
			3	2		6	1			9	11	8	4			5	10				7	
			3	2		6	1				11		4	9		5	10	7				8
			3	2		6	1				11	8	4			5	10	7				9
			3	2		6	1				11	8	4			5	10	7				9
			3	2		6	1				11	8	4			5	10	7				9
			3	2		6	1				11	8	4	9		5	10	7				
			3	2		6	1				11	8	4			5	10	7				9
	4		3	2		6	1				11	8				5	10	7				9
			3	2		6	1				11	8	4			5	10	7				9
			3	2		6	1				11	8	4			5	10	7				9
			3	2		6	1				11	8	4			5	10	7				9
			3	2		6	1				11	8	4			5	10	7				9
			3	2		6	1			9	11	8	4			5	10	7				
			3	2		6	1	4		9	11	8				5	10				7	
		4	3	2		6	1				11	8				5	10				7	9
		4	3	2		6	1				11	8				5	10				7	9
		4	3	2		6	1				11	8				5	10				7	9
		4	3	2		6	1				11	8				5	10				7	9
1		4	3			6			8	10	11					5			2		7	9
1		4	3	2		6				9	11	8				5	10	7				
1		4	3	2		6					11	8				5	10	7				9
1		4		2		6				7	11	8				5	10		3			9
1		4		2		6				7	11	8				5	10		3			9
1		4		2		6				7	11	8				5	10		3			9
1		4		2	7	6					11	8				5	10		3			9
1		4		2	7	6					11	8				5	10		3			9
8	1	12	33	37	2	37	30	2	1	16	38	34	24	2	1	38	37	24	6		8	27
					1					2	13	16	1			1	12	2			1	18

Boreham F	Brough J	Bull W	Burton O	Coquet E	Curtis JJ	Darnell J	Hewitson R	Leslie TS	Massey FJ	McFarlane D	Middlemiss H	Minter WJ	Morris T	Morton JC	Seeburg MP	Steel D	Steel RL	Walton J	Wilkes F	Wood N	Woodruff CL	Woodward VJ
			3	2		6	1				11	8	4			5	10	7				9
			3	2		6	1				11	8	4			5	10	7				9
			3	2		6	1				11	8	4			5	10	7				9
	4		3	2		6	1				11	8				5	10	7				9
0	1	0	4	4	0	4	4	0	0	0	4	4	3	0	0	4	4	4	0		0	4
				1								2	1				2					

Boreham F	Brough J	Bull W	Burton O	Coquet E	Curtis JJ	Darnell J	Hewitson R	Leslie TS	Massey FJ	McFarlane D	Middlemiss H	Minter WJ	Morris T	Morton JC	Seeburg MP	Steel D	Steel RL	Walton J	Wilkes F	Wood N	Woodruff CL	Woodward VJ
		2	3			6	1				11	9	4		8			7		10		
	4	2	3			6	1				11	8		9		5	10	7				
1		4	3	2		6			8	10	11			9		5					7	
1	1	3	3	1	0	3	2	0	1	1	3	2	1	2	1	2	1	2	0	1	1	0
												1				1		1				

Boreham F	Brough J	Bull W	Burton O	Coquet E	Curtis JJ	Darnell J	Hewitson R	Leslie TS	Massey FJ	McFarlane D	Middlemiss H	Minter WJ	Morris T	Morton JC	Seeburg MP	Steel D	Steel RL	Walton J	Wilkes F	Wood N	Woodruff CL	Woodward VJ
			3	2		6	1			7	11	8	4			5	10					9
0	0	0	1	1	0	1	1	0	0	1	1	1	1	0	0	1	1	0	0	0	0	1
												1										

League Table

	P	W	D	L	F	A	Pts
Bolton Wanderers	38	24	4	10	59	28	52
TOTTENHAM HOTSPUR	38	20	11	7	67	32	51
West Bromwich Albion	38	19	13	6	56	27	51
Hull City	38	19	6	13	63	39	44
Derby County	38	16	11	11	55	41	43
Oldham Athletic	38	17	6	15	55	43	40
Wolverhampton W	38	14	11	13	56	48	39
Glossop	38	15	8	15	57	53	38
Gainsborough Trinity	38	15	8	15	49	70	38
Fulham	38	13	11	14	58	48	37
Birmingham	38	14	9	15	58	61	37
Leeds City	38	14	7	17	43	53	35
Grimsby Town	38	14	7	17	41	54	35
Burnley	38	13	7	18	51	58	33
Clapton Orient	38	12	9	17	37	49	33
Bradford Park Avenue	38	13	6	19	51	59	32
Barnsley	38	11	10	17	48	57	32
Stockport County	38	14	3	21	39	71	31
Chesterfield	38	11	8	19	37	67	30
Blackpool	38	9	11	18	46	68	29

1909-10

DIVISION ONE

Manager: Directors

Did you know that?

Walter Tull was the first black player to appear for Spurs when he played against Sunderland on 1 September 1909. Preceded only by Arthur Wharton, a goalkeeper with Rotherham Town, as the first black player in the Football League, Tull went on to play for Northampton Town. During World War One he rose to the rank of 2nd Lieutenant, the first black officer in the British Army, before being killed at Favreuil, France, on 25 March 1918.

LEAGUE DEBUTANTS

Sep 1	v Sunderland Walter Tull
Sep 25	v Sheffield Wednesday Archie Lyle
Oct 30	v Notts County Frank Bentley
Oct 30	v Notts County Ivor Brown
Oct 30	v Notts County Frank Drabble
Nov 6	v Newcastle United William Harris
Nov 27	v Sheffield United John Joyce
Dec 11	v Bolton Wanderers Bert Elkin
Jan 29	v Bradford City Alex Steel
Mar 25	v Sunderland Jimmy Kennedy
Mar 26	v Liverpool David Brown
Apr 23	v Bolton Wanderers Tommy Lunn
Apr 23	v Bolton Wanderers Ernie Newman
Apr 30	v Chelsea Arthur Kerry

Match No.	Date			Opponents	Result		Scorers	Attendan
1	Sep	1	A	Sunderland	L	1-3	Morris	10,0
2		4	A	Everton	L	2-4	Minter, Middlemiss	20,0
3		11	H	Manchester United	D	2-2	R.Steel 2 (2 pens)	32,2
4		18	A	Bradford City	L	1-5	Tull	25,0
5		25	H	Sheffield Wednesday	W	3-0	D.Steel, Curtis, Minter	24,0
6	Oct	2	A	Bristol City	D	0-0		20,0
7		9	H	Bury	W	1-0	Middlemiss	30,0
8		16	H	Middlesbrough	L	1-3	Middlemiss	23,0
9		23	A	Preston North End	*	0-0		4,0
10		30	H	Notts County	L	1-3	Minter	23,0
11	Nov	6	A	Newcastle United	L	0-1		26,0
12		13	H	Liverpool	W	1-0	Middlemiss	22,0
13		20	A	Aston Villa	L	2-3	Minter, R.Steel	25,0
14		22	A	Preston North End	L	1-4	R.Steel	
15		27	H	Sheffield United	W	2-1	Minter, R.Steel (pen)	26,0
16	Dec	4	A	Woolwich Arsenal	L	0-1		18,0
17		11	H	Bolton Wanderers	D	1-1	Minter	20,0
18		18	A	Chelsea	L	1-2	Minter	50,0
19		25	H	Nottingham Forest	D	2-2	Humphreys 2	30,0
20		27	A	Nottingham Forest	D	2-2	R.Steel, Middlemiss	22,3
21	Jan	1	A	Blackburn Rovers	L	0-2		15,0
22		8	H	Everton	W	3-0	R.Steel, Middlemiss 2	24,0
23		22	A	Manchester United	L	0-5		8,0
24		29	H	Bradford City	D	0-0		22,0
25	Feb	12	H	Bristol City	W	3-2	Minter, Humphreys, Middlemiss	25,0
26		26	A	Middlesbrough	L	3-4	Minter 2, R.Steel	5,0
27	Mar	5	H	Preston North End	W	2-1	Minter, Humphreys	25,0
28		12	A	Notts County	L	0-3		15,0
29		14	A	Sheffield Wednesday	D	1-1	D.Steel	3,0
30		19	H	Newcastle United	L	0-4		25,0
31		25	H	Sunderland	W	5-1	Curtis, Humphreys 2, R.Steel, Middlemiss	35,0
32		26	A	Liverpool	L	0-2		15,0
33		29	H	Blackburn Rovers	W	4-0	Minter 3, Humphreys	23,0
34	Apr	2	H	Aston Villa	D	1-1	Humphreys	34,0
35		9	A	Sheffield United	D	1-1	Humphreys	10,0
36		16	H	Woolwich Arsenal	D	1-1	Curtis	39,8
37		20	A	Bury	L	1-3	Humphreys	4,0
38		23	A	Bolton Wanderers	W	2-0	Humphreys 2	3,0
39		30	H	Chelsea	W	2-1	Minter, Humphreys	35,0

*abandoned after 50 mins - rain

Appearanc

Go

FA Cup

R1	Jan	15	A	Plymouth Argyle	D	1-1	Humphreys	10,2
R1r		19	H	Plymouth Argyle	W	7-1	Minter, Humphreys 3, R.Steel (pen), Middlemiss 2	17,0
R2	Feb	5	A	Chelsea	W	1-0	Humphreys	31,7
R3		19	A	Swindon Town	L	2-3	Minter, R.Steel (pen)	11,8

Appearanc

Go

London FA Charity Cup

R1	Sep	20	A	Nunhead	W	9-0	Minter 2, R.Steel 4 (1 pen), Middlemiss 3	3,0
R2	Oct	11	H	Croydon Common	W	7-1	Minter 2, D.Brown, Middlemiss 3, Tull	
SF	Nov	8	N*	Queen's Park Rangers	D	0-0		12,0
SFr		15	N#	Queen's Park Rangers	W	4-1	Curtis, I.Brown, R.Steel (pen), Minter	10,0
F	Dec	8	N*	Fulham	L	1-4	Minter	17,0

*played at Stamford Bridge #played at Craven Cottage

Appearanc

Go

London Professional Football Charity Fund

	Nov	1	H	Woolwich Arsenal	W	3-0	Curtis 2, R.Steel	5,0

Appearanc

Go

Boreham F	Brown DC	Brown IRJ	Burton O	Coquet E	Curtis JJ	Darnell J	Drabble F	Elkin BHW	Gipps T	Harris W	Humphreys P	Joyce JW	Kennedy JJ	Kerry AHG	Leslie TS	Lunn TH	Lyle A	McFarlane D	Middlemiss H	Minter WJ	Morris T	Newman EH	Steel A	Steel D	Steel RL	Tull WDJ	Wilkes F	Woodruff CL
1				2	7	6													11	8	4			5	10	9	3	
1				2	7	6													11	8	4			5	10	9	3	
1				2	7	6													11	8	4			5	10	9	3	
1				2	7	6													11	8	4			5	10	9	3	
1				2	7	6											8	4	11	9				5	10		3	
1			3	2	7	6												4	11	9				5	10	8		
1			3	2	7	6												4	11	9				5	10	8		
1			3	2	7	6												4	11	8				5	10	9		
		9	3	2	7	6	1												11	8				5	10			
		9	3	2	7	6	1												11	8				5	10			
1		9			7					3									11	8	4			5	10		2	
1		9			7	6				3									11	8	4			5	10		2	
1		9			7	6				3									11	8	4			5	10		2	
1		9			7	6				3									11	8	4			5	10		2	
		9			7	6				3		1							11	8				5	10		2	
		9			7	6				3		1							11	8				5	10		2	
						6		3		2	9	1							11	8				5	10			7
				3	9	6		2				1							11	8				5	10			7
				3	7	6		2			9	1							11	8				5	10			
				3	7			2			9	1							11	8	4			5	10			
				3	7			2			9	1							11	8	4			5	10			
				3	7			2			9	1							11	8	4			5	10			
				3	7	6		2			9	1						4	11	8				5	10			
		9		3	7			2				1							11	8			4	5	10			
				3	7	6					9	1			2				11	8	4			5	10			
				3	7						9	1			2				11	8	4			5	10			
					7						9	1			2				11	8	4			5	10		3	
					7						9	1			2				11	8	4			5	10		3	
					7	6					9	1			2				11	8	4			5	10		3	
					7	6					9	1			2				11	8	4			5	10		3	
				2	7						9	1	5						11	8	4				10		3	
	9			3	7							1	5						11	8	4				10		2	
				2	7						9	1							11	8	4			5	10		3	
				3	7						9	1			2				11	8	4			5	10			
				3	7	6					9	1							11	8	4			5	10		2	
				2	7						9	1							11	8	4			5	10		3	
				2	7	6					9	1							11	8	4			5	10		3	
				2	7	6					9					1				8	4	11		5	10		3	
				2	7	6					9			11		1				8	4			5	10		3	
12	1	9	5	28	38	26	2	8	0	7	20	23	2	1	7	2	1	5	37	39	26	1	1	37	39	7	23	2
					3						13								9	15	1			2	9	1		

Boreham F	Brown DC	Brown IRJ	Burton O	Coquet E	Curtis JJ	Darnell J	Drabble F	Elkin BHW	Gipps T	Harris W	Humphreys P	Joyce JW	Kennedy JJ	Kerry AHG	Leslie TS	Lunn TH	Lyle A	McFarlane D	Middlemiss H	Minter WJ	Morris T	Newman EH	Steel A	Steel D	Steel RL	Tull WDJ	Wilkes F	Woodruff CL
				3	7			2			9	1							11	8	4			5	10			
				3	7			2			9	1							11	8	4			5	10			
				3	7	6					9	1			2				11	8	4			5	10			
				3	7	6					9	1			2				11	8	4			5	10			
0	0	0	0	4	4	2	0	2	0	0	4	4	0	0	2	0	0	0	4	4	4	0	0	4	4	0	0	0
											5								2	2					2			

Boreham F	Brown DC	Brown IRJ	Burton O	Coquet E	Curtis JJ	Darnell J	Drabble F	Elkin BHW	Gipps T	Harris W	Humphreys P	Joyce JW	Kennedy JJ	Kerry AHG	Leslie TS	Lunn TH	Lyle A	McFarlane D	Middlemiss H	Minter WJ	Morris T	Newman EH	Steel A	Steel D	Steel RL	Tull WDJ	Wilkes F	Woodruff CL
1			3	2	7				6									4	11	9				5	10	8		
1	9			2	7	6				3					4				11	8				5		10		
1		9								3									11	8	4			5	10		2	7
1		9			7	6				3					2				11	8	4			5	10			
1					8	6				3									11	9	5				10		2	7
5	1	2	1	2	4	3	0	0	1	4	0	0	0	0	2	0	0	1	5	5	3	0	0	4	4	2	2	2
	1	1			1														6	6					5	1		

Boreham F	Brown DC	Brown IRJ	Burton O	Coquet E	Curtis JJ	Darnell J	Drabble F	Elkin BHW	Gipps T	Harris W	Humphreys P	Joyce JW	Kennedy JJ	Kerry AHG	Leslie TS	Lunn TH	Lyle A	McFarlane D	Middlemiss H	Minter WJ	Morris T	Newman EH	Steel A	Steel D	Steel RL	Tull WDJ	Wilkes F	Woodruff CL
					8		1		6	3									11	9	4			5	10		2	7
0	0	0	0	0	1	0	1	0	1	1	0	0	0	0	0	0	0	0	1	1	1	0	0	1	1	0	1	1
					2																				1			

League Table

	P	W	D	L	F	A	Pts
Aston Villa	38	23	7	8	84	42	53
Liverpool	38	21	6	11	78	57	48
Blackburn Rovers	38	18	9	11	73	55	45
Newcastle United	38	19	7	12	70	56	45
Manchester United	38	19	7	12	69	61	45
Sheffield United	38	16	10	12	62	41	42
Bradford City	38	17	8	13	64	47	42
Sunderland	38	18	5	15	66	51	41
Notts County	38	15	10	13	67	59	40
Everton	38	16	8	14	51	56	40
Sheffield Wednesday	38	15	9	14	60	63	39
Preston North End	38	15	5	18	52	58	35
Bury	38	12	9	17	62	66	33
Nottingham Forest	38	11	11	16	54	72	33
TOTTENHAM HOTSPUR	38	11	10	17	53	69	32
Bristol City	38	12	8	18	45	60	32
Middlesbrough	38	11	9	18	56	73	31
Woolwich Arsenal	38	11	9	18	37	67	31
Chelsea	38	11	7	20	47	70	29
Bolton Wanderers	38	9	6	23	44	71	24

1910-11

DIVISION ONE

Manager: Directors

Did you know that?

Spurs were fined £10 for not playing a full team against Clapton Orient in the first round of the London FA Charity Cup on 19 September 1910.

LEAGUE DEBUTANTS

Oct 1	v Middlesbrough Eddie Birnie
Oct 1	v Middlesbrough Albert Gosnell
Oct 8	v Preston North End Bob McTavish
Oct 19	v Liverpool Ed Bulling
Nov 26	v Sunderland Tom Collins
Dec 17	v Blackburn Rovers Charlie Rance
Dec 31	v Sheffield Wednesday Ellis Crompton
Jan 21	v Newcastle United John McTavish
Feb 13	v Middlesbrough Tom Forman

Match No.	Date			Opponents	Result		Scorers	Attendan
1	Sep	1	A	Everton	L	0-2		22,0
2		3	H	Sheffield Wednesday	W	3-1	Darnell, R.Steel, Middlemiss	29,2
3		10	A	Bristol City	W	2-0	Middlemiss 2	20,0
4		17	H	Newcastle United	L	1-2	Minter	36,0
5		24	A	Oldham Athletic	L	0-2		14,0
6	Oct	1	A	Middlesbrough	L	0-2		20,0
7		8	H	Preston North End	D	1-1	Minter	24,0
8		15	A	Notts County	L	0-1		14,0
9		22	H	Manchester United	D	2-2	Minter, Humphreys	28,0
10		29	A	Liverpool	W	2-1	Minter, Humphreys	12,0
11	Nov	5	H	Bury	W	5-0	Curtis, Minter, Humphreys 2, Middlemiss	20,0
12		12	A	Sheffield United	L	0-3		10,0
13		19	H	Aston Villa	L	1-2	Humphreys	28,0
14		26	A	Sunderland	L	0-4		12,0
15	Dec	3	H	Woolwich Arsenal	W	3-1	Darnell, Minter, Humphreys	16,0
16		10	A	Bradford City	L	0-3		10,0
17		17	H	Blackburn Rovers	D	2-2	R.McTavish 2	16,0
18		24	A	Nottingham Forest	W	2-1	Minter, R.McTavish	10,0
19		26	H	Nottingham Forest	L	1-4	Minter	35,0
20		27	H	Manchester City	D	1-1	Tull	28,0
21		31	A	Sheffield Wednesday	L	1-2	Minter	25,0
22	Jan	3	A	Manchester City	L	1-2	Kennedy	10,0
23		7	H	Bristol City	W	3-2	Minter 3	18,0
24		21	A	Newcastle United	D	1-1	Minter	22,0
25		28	H	Oldham Athletic	*	1-1	Crompton	14,0
26	Feb	11	A	Preston North End	L	0-2		10,0
27		13	H	Middlesbrough	W	6-2	Minter, Humphreys, R.Steel 3, Forman	8,0
28		18	H	Notts County	W	3-0	Minter, Humphreys, R.Steel	26,0
29		25	A	Aston Villa	L	0-4		17,0
30	Mar	4	H	Liverpool	W	1-0	Minter	25,0
31		11	A	Bury	L	1-2	R.Steel	10,0
32		15	A	Manchester United	L	2-3	Birnie, Humphreys	13,0
33		18	H	Sheffield United	W	2-1	Humphreys, R.Steel	18,0
34		27	H	Oldham Athletic	W	2-0	Minter, R.Steel	7,0
35	Apr	1	H	Sunderland	D	1-1	Minter	26,0
36		8	A	Woolwich Arsenal	L	0-2		24,8
37		15	H	Bradford City	W	2-0	Minter, R.Steel	30,0
38		17	H	Everton	L	0-1		20,0
39		22	A	Blackburn Rovers	L	0-3		14,0

*abandoned after 45 mins - fog

Appearanc
Goa

FA Cup

R1	Jan	14	H	Millwall	W	2-1	Minter, Carmichael (og)	21,4
R2	Feb	4	A	Blackburn Rovers	D	0-0		25,0
R2r		9	H	Blackburn Rovers	L	0-2		26,9

Appearanc
Goa

London FA Charity Cup

R1	Sep	19	H	Clapton Orient	W	1-0	Rance	8,5
R2	Oct	10	H	Chelsea	W	3-0	Minter, Brown, R.Steel	8,9
SF	Nov	7	N*	Millwall	D	2-2	Minter, R.Steel	5,0
SFr		21	N#	Millwall	W	2-0	Minter, Middlemiss	7,8
F	Dec	5	N~	Fulham	W	2-1	Minter, Middlemiss	10,0

*played at Leyton #played at Homerton ~played at Stamford Bridge

Appearanc
Goa

London Professional Football Charity Fund

	Oct	3	A	Chelsea	W	3-0	Minter, Brown 2	9,0

Appearanc
Goa

ntley FW	Birnie EL	Brown IRJ	Bulling E	Collins T	Coquet E	Crompton GE	Curtis JJ	Darnell J	Elkin BHW	Forman T	Gosnell AA	Humphreys P	Joyce JW	Kennedy JJ	Leslie TS	Lunn TH	McTavish JK	McTavish R	Middlemiss H	Minter WJ	Morris T	Newman EH	Rance CS	Steel D	Steel RL	Tull WDJ	Wilkes F	Own-goals
							7	6	2			9				1			11	8	4			5	10		3	
							7	6	2			9				1			11	8	4			5	10		3	
							7	6	2			9				1			11	8	4			5	10		3	
		9					7	6	2							1			11	8	4			5	10		3	
		9					7	6	2							1			11	8	4			5	10		3	
	4				3		7	6	2		11					1			9	8		10		5				
					3		7	6	2				1				9		11	8	4			5	10			
					3		7	6	2			9	1						11	8	4			5	10			
					3		7	6	2			9	1	5					11	8				4	10			
			2		3		7	6				9	1	5					11	8	4				10			
					3		7	6	2			9		5		1			11	8				4	10			
					3		7	6	2			9		5		1			11	8				4	10			
			3				7	6	2			9				1			11	8				5	10			
				3	2		7	6				9				1			11	8				5	10			
				3	2		7	6				9				1		10	11	8				5				
		9		3	2		7	6								1		10	11	8				5				
				3	2		7	6								1		10	11	8		9	5					
				3			7	6	2		11					1		10		8	4		5			9		
				3			7	6	2		11	9				1		10		8	4			5				
				3			7	6	2							1			11	8			5	4	10	9		
				3		9	7	6	2							1			11	8			5	4	10			
				3		9	7	6	2					5		1		10	11	8				4				
				2		9	7	6			11			5		1		10		8				4			3	
				2		9	7	6								1		10		8				5	11		3	
				2	3	9	7	6								1	10			8				5	11			
		7		2	3	9		6						5	4	1		10	11	8								
				2				6		11		9				1	7			8				5	10		3	
				2				6		11		9				1	7			8				5	10		3	
				2				6			11	9				1	7			8				5	10		3	
				2				6				9				1	7		11	8				5	10		3	
				2				6				9				1	7		11	8				5	10		3	
	5			2				6				9				1	7		11	8					10		3	
				2			7	6				9				1			11	8			5		10		3	
				2			7	6				9				1			11	8			5		10		3	
				2			7	6				9				1			11	8			5		10		3	
				2			7	6								1			11	8			5		10	9	3	
	4			2			7	6				9				1			11	8			5		10		3	
	4			2			7	6	3			9				1			11	8			5		10			
				2				6				9				1	7	10		8	4		5		11		3	
7	4	4	2	26	13	6	31	39	18	2	5	24	4	7	1	35	9	10	30	39	11	2	11	27	30	3	19	
	1					1	1	2		1		10		1				3	4	19					9	1		

ntley FW	Birnie EL	Brown IRJ	Bulling E	Collins T	Coquet E	Crompton GE	Curtis JJ	Darnell J	Elkin BHW	Forman T	Gosnell AA	Humphreys P	Joyce JW	Kennedy JJ	Leslie TS	Lunn TH	McTavish JK	McTavish R	Middlemiss H	Minter WJ	Morris T	Newman EH	Rance CS	Steel D	Steel RL	Tull WDJ	Wilkes F	Own-goals
				2		9	7	6			11					1		10		8				5			3	
				2		9	7	6								1	10			8				5	11		3	
				2			7	6			11	9				1				8				5	10		3	
	0	0	0	3	0	2	3	3	0	0	2	1	0	0	0	3	1	1	0	3	0	0	0	3	2	0	3	
																				1								1

ntley FW	Birnie EL	Brown IRJ	Bulling E	Collins T	Coquet E	Crompton GE	Curtis JJ	Darnell J	Elkin BHW	Forman T	Gosnell AA	Humphreys P	Joyce JW	Kennedy JJ	Leslie TS	Lunn TH	McTavish JK	McTavish R	Middlemiss H	Minter WJ	Morris T	Newman EH	Rance CS	Steel D	Steel RL	Tull WDJ	Wilkes F	Own-goals
	4	9	3				7		2		11		1					10		8			5					
		9			3		7	6	2				1						11	8	4			5	10			
					3		7	6	2			9		5		1			11	8				4	10			
			3				7	6	2			9	1						11	8				5	10			
					3		7	6	2			9				1		10	11	8				5				
	1	2	2	0	3	0	5	4	5	0	1	3	3	1	0	2	0	2	4	5	1	0	1	4	3	0	0	
		1																	2	4			1		2			

ntley FW	Birnie EL	Brown IRJ	Bulling E	Collins T	Coquet E	Crompton GE	Curtis JJ	Darnell J	Elkin BHW	Forman T	Gosnell AA	Humphreys P	Joyce JW	Kennedy JJ	Leslie TS	Lunn TH	McTavish JK	McTavish R	Middlemiss H	Minter WJ	Morris T	Newman EH	Rance CS	Steel D	Steel RL	Tull WDJ	Wilkes F	Own-goals
		9			3		7	6	2		11		1	5				10		8	4							
	0	1	0	0	1	0	1	1	1	0	1	0	1	1	0	0	0	1	0	1	1	0	0	0	0	0	0	
		2																		1								

League Table

	P	W	D	L	F	A	Pts
Manchester United	38	22	8	8	72	40	52
Aston Villa	38	22	7	9	69	41	51
Sunderland	38	15	15	8	67	48	45
Everton	38	19	7	12	50	36	45
Bradford City	38	20	5	13	51	42	45
Sheffield Wednesday	38	17	8	13	47	48	42
Oldham Athletic	38	16	9	13	44	41	41
Newcastle United	38	15	10	13	61	43	40
Sheffield United	38	15	8	15	49	43	38
Woolwich Arsenal	38	13	12	13	41	49	38
Notts County	38	14	10	14	37	45	38
Blackburn Rovers	38	13	11	14	62	54	37
Liverpool	38	15	7	16	53	53	37
Preston North End	38	12	11	15	40	49	35
TOTTENHAM HOTSPUR	38	13	6	19	52	63	32
Middlesbrough	38	11	10	17	49	63	32
Manchester City	38	9	13	16	43	58	31
Bury	38	9	11	18	43	71	29
Bristol City	38	11	5	22	43	66	27
Nottingham Forest	38	9	7	22	55	75	25

1911-12

DIVISION ONE

Manager: Directors

Did you know that?

Alex Young did not take kindly to being dropped after three goals in five games. He demanded a transfer and in November 1911 was on his way to Manchester City. Just over four years later he was charged with the wilful murder of his brother. In June 1916 he was found guilty of manslaughter and sentenced to three years in prison after evidence was produced that during his playing career he had been subject to fits of temporary insanity.

LEAGUE DEBUTANTS

Sep 2	v Everton Alex Young
Oct 14	v Middlesbrough Ed Lightfoot
Oct 21	v Notts County Charlie Brittan
Dec 25	v Woolwich Arsenal Fred Webster
Jan 20	v Sunderland Jimmy Elliott
Jan 27	v Blackburn Rovers Ernie Bowering
Feb 17	v Middlesbrough Tom Mason
Apr 8	v Manchester City Bert Bliss
Apr 20	v Bolton Wanderers Arthur Grimsdell
Apr 20	v Bolton Wanderers Walter Tattersall

Match No.	Date			Opponents	Result		Scorers	Attendance
1	Sep	2	A	Everton	D	2-2	J.McTavish, Young	25,00
2		4	H	Sheffield Wednesday	W	3-1	Minter, Young 2	20,00
3		9	H	West Bromwich Albion	W	1-0	Minter	31,00
4		16	A	Sunderland	D	1-1	R.Steel	16,00
5		23	H	Blackburn Rovers	L	0-2		37,82
6		30	A	Sheffield Wednesday	L	0-4		15,00
7	Oct	7	H	Bury	W	2-1	Minter 2	18,00
8		14	A	Middlesbrough	L	0-2		15,00
9		21	H	Notts County	D	2-2	Minter, Middlemiss	25,00
10		28	H	Preston North End	W	6-2	Newman 3, Minter, Middlemiss 2	20,00
11	Nov	4	A	Manchester United	W	2-1	Minter, Middlemiss	26,0
12		11	H	Liverpool	W	2-0	Minter, Middlemiss	23,00
13		18	A	Aston Villa	D	2-2	R.Steel 2	30,00
14		25	H	Newcastle United	L	1-2	Newman	37,54
15	Dec	2	A	Sheffield United	W	2-1	R.Steel, Middlemiss	11,00
16		9	H	Oldham Athletic	W	4-0	J.McTavish, Minter, R.Steel, Middlemiss	20,0
17		16	A	Bolton Wanderers	L	0-1		20,00
18		23	H	Bradford City	L	2-3	R.Steel 2	30,00
19		25	H	Woolwich Arsenal	W	5-0	Darnell, J.McTavish, Minter 2, Middlemiss	47,10
20		26	A	Woolwich Arsenal	L	1-3	Minter	22,00
21		30	H	Everton	L	0-1		24,50
22	Jan	6	A	West Bromwich Albion	*	0-0		4,0
23		20	H	Sunderland	D	0-0		17,00
24		27	A	Blackburn Rovers	D	0-0		14,00
25	Feb	10	A	Bury	L	1-2	Elliott	6,00
26		17	H	Middlesbrough	W	2-1	Minter, R.Steel	22,00
27		24	A	Notts County	D	2-2	Minter 2	10,00
28	Mar	2	A	Preston North End	W	1-0	Minter	5,00
29		13	A	West Bromwich Albion	L	0-2		12,00
30		16	A	Liverpool	W	2-1	Newman, Mason	15,0
31		23	H	Aston Villa	W	2-1	Middlemiss 2	19,00
32		30	A	Newcastle United	L	0-2		21,00
33	Apr	5	A	Manchester City	L	1-2	Newman	39,8
34		6	H	Sheffield United	D	1-1	Middlemiss (pen)	26,00
35		8	H	Manchester City	L	0-2		20,00
36		9	H	Manchester United	D	1-1	Bliss	14,0
37		13	A	Oldham Athletic	L	1-2	Elliott	6,00
38		20	H	Bolton Wanderers	W	1-0	Minter	18,00
39		27	A	Bradford City	L	0-3		8,00

*abandoned after 57 mins - fog

Appearance
Goa

FA Cup

R1	Jan	13	A	West Bromwich Albion	L	0-3		22,00

Appearance
Goa

London FA Charity Cup

R1	Sep	18	A	Brentford	L	1-4	R.McTavish	3,00

Appearance
Goa

London Professional Football Charity Fund

	Oct	23	H	Fulham	W	3-0	Minter, R.Steel, Middlemiss	3,98

Appearance
Goa

Bliss H	Bowering EG	Brittan RC	Collins T	Crompton GE	Curtis JJ	Darnell J	Elliott JE	Forman T	Grimsdell A	Humphreys P	Joyce JW	Kennedy JJ	Lightfoot EJ	Lunn TH	Mason TL	McTavish JK	McTavish R	Middlemiss H	Minter WJ	Morris T	Newman EH	Rance CS	Steel D	Steel RL	Tattersall WS	Webster FJ	Wilkes F	Young AS
			2			6		11						1		7			8			5	4	10			3	9
			2			6		11						1		7			8			5	4	10			3	9
			2			6		11						1		7			8			5	4	10			3	9
			2			6		11		9				1		7			8			5	4	10			3	
			2			6		11						1		7			8			5	4	10			3	9
			2			6		11						1		7			8			5	4	10			3	9
			2	9		6								1		7		11	8			5	4	10			3	
			2	9		6							5	1		7		11	8				4	10			3	
		3	2	9		6								1		7		11	8			5	4	10				
		3	2			6							5	1		7		11	9		8		4	10				
			2			6							5	1		7		11	9	3	8		4	10				
		3	2			6							5	1		7		11	9		8		4	10				
		3	2			6							5	1		7		11	8		9		4	10				
		3	2			6							5	1		7		11	9		8		4	10				
		3	2			6							5	1		7		11	9		8		4	10				
		3	2			6							5	1		7		11	9		8		4	10				
		3	2			6							5	1		7		11	9		8		4	10				
		3	2			4								1		7		11	9		8	5	6	10				
			2			6								1		7		11	9		8	5	4	10		3		
			2			6								1		7		11	9		8	5	4	10		3		
		3				6								1		7		11	9		8	5	4	10		2		
		3	2			6								1		7		11	8		9	5	4	10				
			2		7	6	9						5	1				11	8				4	10		3		
	6	3	2		7		9						5	1		8		11					4	10				
	6	3	2		7		9						5	1				11	8				4	10				
	4	3	2		7								6	1	8			11	9			5		10				
	4	3	2		7								6	1	8			11	9			5		10				
		3	2		7	4							6	1	8			11	9			5		10				
	4	3	2		7	6							5	1	8			11	9					10				
		3	2			4							6	1	10	7		11	9		8		5					
		3	2			4							6	1		7		11	9		8		5	10				
		3	2			4							6	1		7		11	9		8		5	10				
		3	2			4					1		6			7		11	9		8		5	10				
	6	3				4					1				10	7		11	9		8	5					2	
10		3				4	9				1	6				7		11		2	8	5						
10		3			7	4					1	6				8		11	9							2		
10	6	3			7	4	9					5		1		8		11								2		
10		3	2			4			5			6		1				11	9		8				7			
10		3	2			4			5				6	1	8			11	9						7			
5	7	27	34	3	9	35	5	6	2	1	4	4	21	35	7	31	0	33	36	2	20	18	29	32	2	6	9	5
1						1	2								1	3		11	17		6			8				3

Bliss H	Bowering EG	Brittan RC	Collins T	Crompton GE	Curtis JJ	Darnell J	Elliott JE	Forman T	Grimsdell A	Humphreys P	Joyce JW	Kennedy JJ	Lightfoot EJ	Lunn TH	Mason TL	McTavish JK	McTavish R	Middlemiss H	Minter WJ	Morris T	Newman EH	Rance CS	Steel D	Steel RL	Tattersall WS	Webster FJ	Wilkes F	Young AS
		3	2			6								1		7		11	8		9	5	4	10				
0	0	1	1	0	0	1	0	0	0	0	0	0	0	1	0	1	0	1	1	0	1	1	1	1	0	0	0	0

Bliss H	Bowering EG	Brittan RC	Collins T	Crompton GE	Curtis JJ	Darnell J	Elliott JE	Forman T	Grimsdell A	Humphreys P	Joyce JW	Kennedy JJ	Lightfoot EJ	Lunn TH	Mason TL	McTavish JK	McTavish R	Middlemiss H	Minter WJ	Morris T	Newman EH	Rance CS	Steel D	Steel RL	Tattersall WS	Webster FJ	Wilkes F	Young AS
			2			6		11		9	1	5				7	10		8								3	
0	0	0	1	0	0	1	0	1	0	1	1	1	0	0	0	1	1	0	1	0	0	0	0	0	0	0	1	0
																	1											

Bliss H	Bowering EG	Brittan RC	Collins T	Crompton GE	Curtis JJ	Darnell J	Elliott JE	Forman T	Grimsdell A	Humphreys P	Joyce JW	Kennedy JJ	Lightfoot EJ	Lunn TH	Mason TL	McTavish JK	McTavish R	Middlemiss H	Minter WJ	Morris T	Newman EH	Rance CS	Steel D	Steel RL	Tattersall WS	Webster FJ	Wilkes F	Young AS
		3	2			6							5	1		7		11	9		8		4	10				
0	0	1	1	0	0	1	0	0	0	0	0	0	1	1	0	1	0	1	1	0	1	0	1	1	0	0	0	0
																		1	1					1				

League Table

	P	W	D	L	F	A	Pts
Blackburn Rovers	38	20	9	9	60	43	49
Everton	38	20	6	12	46	42	46
Newcastle United	38	18	8	12	64	50	44
Bolton Wanderers	38	20	3	15	54	43	43
Sheffield Wednesday	38	16	9	13	69	49	41
Aston Villa	38	17	7	14	76	63	41
Middlesbrough	38	16	8	14	56	45	40
Sunderland	38	14	11	13	58	51	39
West Bromwich Albion	38	15	9	14	43	47	39
Woolwich Arsenal	38	15	8	15	55	59	38
Bradford City	38	15	8	15	46	50	38
TOTTENHAM HOTSPUR	38	14	9	15	53	53	37
Manchester United	38	13	11	14	45	60	37
Sheffield United	38	13	10	15	63	56	36
Manchester City	38	13	9	16	56	58	35
Notts County	38	14	7	17	46	63	35
Liverpool	38	12	10	16	49	55	34
Oldham Athletic	38	12	10	16	46	54	34
Preston North End	38	13	7	18	40	57	33
Bury	38	6	9	23	32	59	21

1912-13

DIVISION ONE

Manager: Directors / Peter McWilliam

Did you know that?

In February 1913 goalkeeper Tommy Lunn acquired the license of the Chequers beer and wine house in the High Road, Lower Tottenham, despite having been warned by the Spurs directors that by doing so he would suspend himself. He did not play for Spurs again.

LEAGUE DEBUTANTS

Sep 2	v Everton Chris Young
Sep 9	v Sheffield Wednesday Gordon Jones
Sep 21	v Derby County Findlay Weir
Oct 19	v Manchester United Jimmy Cantrell
Nov 9	v Bolton Wanderers Soloman Upton
Apr 19	v Woolwich Arsenal John Tate
Apr 19	v Woolwich Arsenal Fanny Walden

Match No.	Date			Opponents	Result		Scorers	Attendanc
1	Sep	2	H	Everton	L	0-2		22,00
2		7	H	Sheffield Wednesday	L	2-4	Tattersall, Middlemiss	28,00
3		14	A	Blackburn Rovers	L	1-6	Minter	25,00
4		21	H	Derby County	L	1-2	Collins (pen)	25,00
5		28	A	Sunderland	D	2-2	Bliss, Middlemiss	8,00
6	Oct	5	A	Middlesbrough	D	1-1	Minter	18,00
7		12	H	Notts County	*	1-3	Rance	7,00
8		19	A	Manchester United	L	0-2		12,00
9		26	H	Aston Villa	D	3-3	Cantrell 2, Middlemiss	18,00
10	Nov	2	A	Liverpool	L	1-4	Minter	15,00
11		4	H	Notts County	L	0-3		11,00
12		9	H	Bolton Wanderers	L	0-1		23,00
13		16	A	Sheffield United	L	0-4		12,00
14		23	H	Newcastle United	W	1-0	Cantrell	26,00
15		30	A	Oldham Athletic	L	1-4	Middlemiss	12,00
16	Dec	7	H	Chelsea	W	1-0	Tattersall	36,77
17		14	A	Woolwich Arsenal	W	3-0	Cantrell 2, Steel	13,00
18		21	H	Bradford City	W	2-1	Cantrell, Middlemiss	20,00
19		25	A	Manchester City	D	2-2	Cantrell, Middlemiss	30,00
20		26	H	Manchester City	W	4-0	Minter, Cantrell 3	20,00
21		28	A	Sheffield Wednesday	L	1-2	Tattersall	15,00
22	Jan	1	A	Everton	W	2-1	Minter 2	30,00
23		4	H	Blackburn Rovers	L	0-1		33,00
24		18	A	Derby County	L	0-5		10,00
25		25	H	Sunderland	L	1-2	Minter	31,00
26	Feb	8	H	Middlesbrough	W	5-3	Minter 2, Elliott 2, Middlemiss	24,00
27		15	A	Notts County	W	1-0	Bliss	12,00
28		22	H	Sheffield United	W	1-0	Weir	25,00
29	Mar	1	A	Aston Villa	L	0-1		27,00
30		8	H	Liverpool	W	1-0	Middlemiss	20,00
31		15	A	Bolton Wanderers	L	0-2		25,00
32		21	H	West Bromwich Albion	W	3-1	Cantrell, Bliss 2	34,00
33		24	A	West Bromwich Albion	L	1-4	Middlemiss	20,00
34		29	A	Newcastle United	L	0-3		20,00
35		31	H	Manchester United	D	1-1	Minter	12,76
36	Apr	5	H	Oldham Athletic	W	1-0	Bliss	20,00
37		12	A	Chelsea	L	0-1		50,50
38		19	H	Woolwich Arsenal	D	1-1	Minter	20,00
39		26	A	Bradford City	L	1-3	Cantrell	10,00

*abandoned after 80 mins - fog

Appearance

Goal

FA Cup

R1	Jan	11	H	Blackpool	D	1-1	Rance	18,67
R1r		16	H*	Blackpool	W	6-1	Tattersall 2, Cantrell 2, Steel, Middlemiss	16,92
R2	Feb	1	A	Reading	L	0-1		17,79

*replay at home as Blackpool sold replay rights

Appearance

Goal

London FA Charity Cup

R1	Sep	23	H	Bromley	W	3-0	Minter 3	2,00
R2	Oct	21	H	Crystal Palace	*	2-0	Minter, Cantrell	4,44
R2r	Oct	28	H	Crystal Palace	D	3-3	Minter 2, Middlemiss	4,30
R2r	Nov	11	A	Crystal Palace	L	1-4	Middlemiss	2,00

*replay ordered as Cantrell was unregistered

Appearance

Goal

London Professional Football Charity Fund

	Oct	14	A	Fulham	L	0-1		9,00

Appearance

Goal

Bliss H	Brittan RC	Cantrell J	Collins T	Curtis JJ	Darnell J	Elliott JE	Grimsdell A	Jones G	Joyce JW	Lightfoot EJ	Lunn TH	Middlemiss H	Minter WJ	Morris T	Newman EH	Rance CS	Steel RL	Tate JA	Tattersall WS	Upton S	Walden FI	Webster FJ	Weir WF	Williams JLJ	Young C
10	3		2		4		5			6	1	11	8						7						9
	3		2					4		6	1	11	8			5	10		7						9
	3		2					4		6	1	11	8			5	10		7						9
	3		2					10		6	1	11	8			5			7				4		9
10			2					9		6	1	11	8			5			7			3	4		
10			2					9		6	1	11	8			5			7			3	4		
10	2							9		6	1	11	8			5			7			3	4		
	2	9						5		6	1	11	8		7		10					3	4		
		9	2							6	1	11	8			5	10		7			3	4		
		9	2							4	1	11	8			5	10		7			3	6		
			2				5			6	1	11	8		9		10		7			3	4		
		9	2		6					5	1	11	8				10			7		3	4		
		9	2		6			4			1	11	8				10			7		3	5		
		9	2							6	1	11	8			5	10		7			3	4		
		9	2				6			5	1	11	8				10		7			3	4		
		9	2						1	6		11	8			5	10		7			3	4		
		9	2						1	6		11	8			5	10		7			3	4		
		9	2				4		1			11	8			5	10		7			3	6		
		9	2				4		1			11	8			5	10		7			3	6		
		9	2				6		1			11	8			5	10		7			3	4		
		9	2				6		1			11	8			5	10		7			3	4		
10		9	2		4		6		1			11	8			5			7			3			
10		9	2				6		1			11	8			5			7			3	4		
		9	2				6		1			11	8			5	10		7			3	4		
		9	2				6				1	11	8			5	10		7			3	4		
10	2					9	6				1	11	8			5			7			3	4		
10	2					9	6		1			11	8			5			7			3	4		
10	2					9	6		1			11	8			5			7			3	4		
10	2					9	6		1			11	8			5			7			3	4		
10	2					9	6		1			11	8			5			7			3	4		
10	2					9	6		1			11			8	5			7			3	4		
10	2	9					6		1			11	8			5			7			3	4		
10	2	9					6		1			11	8			5			7			3	4		
10	2	9					6		1			11	8			5			7			3	4		
		9	2	7			6		1			11	8			5	10					3	4		
10		9	2	7			6		1			11	8			5						3	4		
10		9	2	7			6		1			11	8			5						3	4		
10		9	2				6					11	8			5		1			7	3	4		
10		9	2	7			6					11	8			5		1				3	4		
19	15	25	28	4	4	6	25	8	20	16	17	39	38	0	3	33	19	2	31	2	1	35	35	0	4
5		12	1			2						9	11			1	1		3				1		

Bliss H	Brittan RC	Cantrell J	Collins T	Curtis JJ	Darnell J	Elliott JE	Grimsdell A	Jones G	Joyce JW	Lightfoot EJ	Lunn TH	Middlemiss H	Minter WJ	Morris T	Newman EH	Rance CS	Steel RL	Tate JA	Tattersall WS	Upton S	Walden FI	Webster FJ	Weir WF	Williams JLJ	Young C
		9	2				6		1			11	8			5	10		7			3	4		
		9	2				6		1			11	8			5	10		7			3	4		
	2	9					6				1	11	8			5	10		7			3	4		
0	1	3	2	0	0	0	3	0	2	0	1	3	3	0	0	3	3	0	3	0	0	3	3	0	0
		2										1				1	1		2						

Bliss H	Brittan RC	Cantrell J	Collins T	Curtis JJ	Darnell J	Elliott JE	Grimsdell A	Jones G	Joyce JW	Lightfoot EJ	Lunn TH	Middlemiss H	Minter WJ	Morris T	Newman EH	Rance CS	Steel RL	Tate JA	Tattersall WS	Upton S	Walden FI	Webster FJ	Weir WF	Williams JLJ	Young C
	3		2					10		6	1	11	8			5			7				4		9
	2	9					5			6	1		8				10		7	11		3	4		
	2				6		5				1	11	8	4			10		7			3			9
	2				6			4			1	11	8			5	10			7		3		9	
0	4	1	1	0	2	0	2	2	0	2	4	3	4	1	0	2	3	0	3	2	0	3	2	1	2
		1										2	6												

Bliss H	Brittan RC	Cantrell J	Collins T	Curtis JJ	Darnell J	Elliott JE	Grimsdell A	Jones G	Joyce JW	Lightfoot EJ	Lunn TH	Middlemiss H	Minter WJ	Morris T	Newman EH	Rance CS	Steel RL	Tate JA	Tattersall WS	Upton S	Walden FI	Webster FJ	Weir WF	Williams JLJ	Young C
	2							9		6	1	11	8			5	10		7			3	4		
0	1	0	0	0	0	0	0	1	0	1	1	1	1	0	0	1	1	0	1	0	0	1	1	0	0

League Table

	P	W	D	L	F	A	Pts
Sunderland	38	25	4	9	86	43	54
Aston Villa	38	19	12	7	86	52	50
Sheffield Wednesday	38	21	7	10	75	55	49
Manchester United	38	19	8	11	69	43	46
Blackburn Rovers	38	16	13	9	79	43	45
Manchester City	38	18	8	12	53	37	44
Derby County	38	17	8	13	69	66	42
Bolton Wanderers	38	16	10	12	62	63	42
Oldham Athletic	38	14	14	10	50	55	42
West Bromwich Albion	38	13	12	13	57	50	38
Everton	38	15	7	16	48	54	37
Liverpool	38	16	5	17	61	71	37
Bradford City	38	12	11	15	50	60	35
Newcastle United	38	13	8	17	47	47	34
Sheffield United	38	14	6	18	56	70	34
Middlesbrough	38	11	10	17	55	69	32
TOTTENHAM HOTSPUR	38	12	6	20	45	72	30
Chelsea	38	11	6	21	51	73	28
Notts County	38	7	9	22	28	56	23
Woolwich Arsenal	38	3	12	23	26	74	18

1913-14

DIVISION ONE

Manager: Peter McWilliam

Did you know that?

In January 1914 Spurs gave a trial to H. Ekroth, a Swede. He did not prove good enough to be taken on but in July 1914 Spurs did sign Fred Streckfuss, a German aviator working at the German Embassy in London.

LEAGUE DEBUTANTS

Sep 1	v Sheffield United Jimmy Bauchop
Sep 1	v Sheffield United Arthur King
Oct 18	v Burnley Jim Fleming
Nov 15	v Newcastle United Bill Cartwright
Dec 13	v Aston Villa William Oliver
Jan 17	v Oldham Athletic Tommy Clay
Jan 17	v Oldham Athletic Harry Sparrow
Feb 7	v Manchester United Jimmy Banks
Feb 28	v Blackburn Rovers George Bowler
Apr 25	v Sheffield Wednesday Sid Crowl

Match No.	Date			Opponents	Result		Scorers	Attendance
1	Sep	1	A	Sheffield United	W	4-1	Walden, Minter, Bauchop 2	16,000
2		6	A	Chelsea	W	3-1	Grimsdell, Cantrell 2	65,000
3		8	H	Sheffield United	W	2-1	Cantrell 2	26,000
4		13	H	Derby County	D	1-1	Cantrell	40,000
5		20	A	Oldham Athletic	L	0-3		18,000
6		27	H	Manchester City	W	3-1	Minter 2, Cantrell	30,513
7	Oct	4	A	Manchester United	L	1-3	Middlemiss	39,000
8		11	H	Bradford City	D	0-0		30,000
9		18	A	Burnley	L	1-3	Cantrell	22,000
10		25	H	Blackburn Rovers	D	3-3	Minter, Cantrell, Middlemiss	46,128
11	Nov	1	A	Preston North End	W	2-1	Bauchop, Bliss	14,000
12		8	H	Sunderland	L	1-4	Cantrell	36,000
13		15	A	Newcastle United	L	0-2		23,000
14		22	H	Everton	W	4-1	Bauchop, Bliss 2, Middlemiss	22,000
15		29	A	Liverpool	L	1-2	Cantrell	21,000
16	Dec	6	H	West Bromwich Albion	W	3-0	Bauchop 2, Middlemiss	24,000
17		13	A	Aston Villa	D	3-3	Walden, Cantrell, Bliss	30,000
18		20	H	Sheffield Wednesday	D	1-1	Walden	22,000
19		26	H	Middlesbrough	L	0-1		37,055
20		27	H	Chelsea	L	1-2	Fleming	29,355
21	Jan	1	A	Bolton Wanderers	L	0-3		30,000
22		3	A	Derby County	L	0-4		10,000
23		17	H	Oldham Athletic	W	3-1	Lightfoot, Sparrow 2	25,000
24		24	A	Manchester City	L	1-2	Sparrow	30,000
25	Feb	7	H	Manchester United	W	2-1	Minter, Cantrell	28,000
26		14	A	Bradford City	L	1-2	Cantrell	18,000
27		23	H	Burnley	W	2-0	Walden (pen), Bliss	15,000
28		28	A	Blackburn Rovers	D	1-1	Walden	25,000
29	Mar	7	H	Preston North End	W	1-0	Cantrell	25,000
30		14	A	Sunderland	L	0-2		10,000
31		21	H	Newcastle United	D	0-0		20,000
32		28	A	Everton	D	1-1	Sparrow	15,000
33	Apr	4	H	Liverpool	D	0-0		19,800
34		10	H	Bolton Wanderers	W	3-0	Joyce, Cantrell, Bliss	39,020
35		11	A	West Bromwich Albion	D	1-1	Cantrell	15,000
36		13	A	Middlesbrough	L	0-6		22,000
37		18	H	Aston Villa	L	0-2		22,000
38		25	A	Sheffield Wednesday	L	0-2		12,000

Appearances
Goals

FA Cup

R1	Jan	10	A	Leicester City	D	5-5	Walden, Minter, Cantrell, Bliss 2	9,454
R1r		15	H	Leicester City	W	2-0	Walden, Bliss	20,252
R2		31	A	Manchester City	L	1-2	Bliss	36,256

Appearances
Goals

London FA Charity Cup

R1	Sep	22	H	Metrogas	W	11-2	Walden, Minter 2, Cantrell 3, Bauchop 4, Middlemiss	2,500
R2	Oct	14	A	Fulham	W	2-0	Middlemiss 2	6,500
SF	Nov	11	N*	Woolwich Arsenal	W	2-1	Fleming, Cantrell	7,800
F	Dec	8	N#	Crystal Palace	L	1-2	Walden	14,000

*played at Stamford Bridge #played at Highbury

Appearances
Goals

London Professional Football Charity Fund

Oct	27	H	Crystal Palace	L	1-2	Middlemiss	5,895

Appearances
Goals

Banks JA	Bauchop JR	Bliss H	Bowler GH	Brittan RC	Cantrell J	Cartwright W	Clay T	Collins T	Crowl SR	Darnell J	Elliott JE	Fleming JB	Gemmell G	Grimsdell A	Heggarty AE	Hobday A	Joyce JW	King A	Lightfoot EJ	Middlemiss H	Minter WJ	Newman EH	Oliver W	Sparrow H	Steel RL	Tate JA	Tattersall WS	Walden FI	Webster FJ	Weir WF
	10				9			2		6								1		11	8				5			7	3	4
	10				9			2						6				1		11	8				5			7	3	4
	10				9			2						6				1		11	8				5			7	3	4
	10				9			2						6				1		11	8				5			7	3	4
	10				9			2						6				1		11	8				5			7	3	4
	10				9			2						6				1		11	8				5			7	3	4
		10			9			2						6				1		11	8				5			7	3	4
		10			9			2						6				1		11	8				5			7	3	4
		10			9			2				7		6				1		11	8				5				3	4
		10			9			2						6				1		11	8				5			7	3	4
	9	10						2						6				1		11		8			5			7	3	4
		10			9			2						6				1		11	8				5			7	3	4
		10			9	3						8		6				1		11					5		7		2	4
	9	10				3						8		6				1		11					5			7	2	4
	11	10			9	3						8		6				1							5			7	2	4
	8	10			9	3			11					6				1							5			7	2	4
		10			9	3						8		6				1					11		5			7	2	4
		10			9	3						8		6				1					11		5			7	2	4
		10			9	3						8		6			1			11					5			7	2	4
		10			9			2				8		6			1			11					5			7	3	4
		10			9	3		2						6						11		8			5	1		7		4
		10			9	3		2						6				1		11		8			5			7		4
							2							6			1		4	11	8	10		9	5			7	3	
		10					2							6			1		4	11		8		9	5			7	3	
10					9	3	2							6			1			11	8				5			7		4
10					9	3	2							6			1			11	8				5			7		4
		10			9	3	2							6			1			11	8				5			7		4
8		10	4		9		2							6			1			11					5			7	3	
8		10	4		9		2							6			1			11					5			7	3	
8		10			9		2							6			1			11					5			7	3	4
8		10			9		2							6			1			11					5			7	3	4
8		10					2							6			1			11				9	5			7	3	4
8		10	4		9	2								6			1			11					5		7		3	
8		10			9		2							6			1			11					5		7		3	4
8		10			9		2				5			6			1			11							7		3	4
		10			9		2							6						11	8				5	1	7		3	4
8		10			9		2							6			1			11					5		7		3	4
8		10			9		2							6			1			11					5		7		3	4
12	10	29	3	0	33	13	15	15	1	1	1	8	0	37	0	0	17	19	2	34	16	5	2	3	37	2	7	30	33	33
6	6			16							1		1			1		1	4	5			4				5			

Banks JA	Bauchop JR	Bliss H	Bowler GH	Brittan RC	Cantrell J	Cartwright W	Clay T	Collins T	Crowl SR	Darnell J	Elliott JE	Fleming JB	Gemmell G	Grimsdell A	Heggarty AE	Hobday A	Joyce JW	King A	Lightfoot EJ	Middlemiss H	Minter WJ	Newman EH	Oliver W	Sparrow H	Steel RL	Tate JA	Tattersall WS	Walden FI	Webster FJ	Weir WF
		10			9	3		2						6				1	4	11	8				5			7		
		10				3		2					9	6			1		4	11	8				5			7		
		10			9			2						6			1		4	11		8			5			7	3	
0	0	3	0	0	2	2	0	3	0	0	0	0	1	3	0	0	2	1	3	3	2	1	0	0	3	0	0	3	1	0
		4			1																1							2		

Banks JA	Bauchop JR	Bliss H	Bowler GH	Brittan RC	Cantrell J	Cartwright W	Clay T	Collins T	Crowl SR	Darnell J	Elliott JE	Fleming JB	Gemmell G	Grimsdell A	Heggarty AE	Hobday A	Joyce JW	King A	Lightfoot EJ	Middlemiss H	Minter WJ	Newman EH	Oliver W	Sparrow H	Steel RL	Tate JA	Tattersall WS	Walden FI	Webster FJ	Weir WF
	10				9			2						6				1		11	8				5			7	3	4
		10		2	9									6				1		11	8				5			7	3	4
		10			9							8		6	11	2		1							5		7		3	4
	8	10			9	3						11		6				1							5			7	2	4
0	2	3	0	1	4	1	0	1	0	0	0	2	0	4	1	1	0	4	0	2	2	0	0	0	4	0	1	3	4	4
	4				4							1								3	2							2		

Banks JA	Bauchop JR	Bliss H	Bowler GH	Brittan RC	Cantrell J	Cartwright W	Clay T	Collins T	Crowl SR	Darnell J	Elliott JE	Fleming JB	Gemmell G	Grimsdell A	Heggarty AE	Hobday A	Joyce JW	King A	Lightfoot EJ	Middlemiss H	Minter WJ	Newman EH	Oliver W	Sparrow H	Steel RL	Tate JA	Tattersall WS	Walden FI	Webster FJ	Weir WF
	10		4	2	9	3								6				1		11	8				5		7			
0	1	0	1	1	1	1	0	0	0	0	0	0	0	1	0	0	0	1	0	1	1	0	0	0	1	0	1	0	0	0
																				1										

League Table

	P	W	D	L	F	A	Pts
Blackburn Rovers	38	20	11	7	78	42	51
Aston Villa	38	19	6	13	65	50	44
Middlesbrough	38	19	5	14	77	60	43
Oldham Athletic	38	17	9	12	55	45	43
West Bromwich Albion	38	15	13	10	46	42	43
Bolton Wanderers	38	16	10	12	65	52	42
Sunderland	38	17	6	15	63	52	40
Chelsea	38	16	7	15	46	55	39
Bradford City	38	12	14	12	40	40	38
Sheffield United	38	16	5	17	63	60	37
Newcastle United	38	13	11	14	39	48	37
Burnley	38	12	12	14	61	53	36
Manchester City	38	14	8	16	51	53	36
Manchester United	38	15	6	17	52	62	36
Everton	38	12	11	15	46	55	35
Liverpool	38	14	7	17	46	62	35
TOTTENHAM HOTSPUR	38	12	10	16	50	62	34
Sheffield Wednesday	38	13	8	17	53	70	34
Preston North End	38	12	6	20	52	69	30
Derby County	38	8	11	19	55	71	27

1914-15

DIVISION ONE

Manager: Peter McWilliam

Did you know that?

Finishing bottom of the table was bad enough for Spurs, but for some of their players' families greater disaster was to follow. During World War One Spurs players J. Fleming, J. Heddon, A. Hobday, J. Jarvie, E. Lightfoot, W. Lloyd, A. McGregor, F. Weir and N. Wood were to make the supreme sacrifice.

LEAGUE DEBUTANTS

Sep 2	v Everton Bill Jacques
Sep 12	v Bradford City John Pearson
Feb 13	v Middlesbrough John Eadon
Feb 13	v Middlesbrough Harry Lowe

Match No.	Date			Opponents	Result		Scorers	Attendance
1	Sep	2	H	Everton	L	1-3	Cantrell	9,000
2		5	H	Chelsea	D	1-1	Cantrell	26,000
3		12	A	Bradford City	D	2-2	Bliss 2	10,000
4		19	H	Burnley	L	1-3	Bliss	25,000
5		26	A	Manchester City	L	1-2	Sparrow	13,000
6		28	H	West Bromwich Albion	W	2-0	Clay (pen), Fleming	8,500
7	Oct	3	A	Newcastle United	L	0-4		12,000
8		10	H	Middlesbrough	D	3-3	Lightfoot, Walden, Cantrell	15,000
9		17	A	Sheffield United	D	1-1	Bliss	20,000
10		24	H	Aston Villa	L	0-2		25,000
11		31	A	Liverpool	L	2-7	Clay (pen), Bliss	12,000
12	Nov	7	H	Bradford	W	3-0	Cantrell, Bliss 2	14,000
13		14	A	Oldham Athletic	L	1-4	Bliss	10,000
14		21	H	Manchester United	W	2-0	Clay (pen), Cantrell	11,000
15		28	A	Bolton Wanderers	L	2-4	Clay (pen), Cantrell	8,000
16	Dec	5	H	Blackburn Rovers	L	0-4		14,000
17		12	A	Notts County	W	2-1	Cantrell, Bliss	8,000
18		19	H	Sunderland	L	0-6		5,000
19		25	A	Sheffield Wednesday	L	2-3	Minter, Bliss	26,000
20		26	H	Sheffield Wednesday	W	6-1	Steel, Sparrow, Bliss 4	8,000
21	Jan	1	A	Everton	D	1-1	Bliss	17,000
22		2	A	Chelsea	D	1-1	Middlemiss	31,000
23		16	H	Bradford City	D	0-0		12,000
24		23	A	Burnley	L	1-3	Cantrell	4,000
25	Feb	13	A	Middlesbrough	L	5-7	Cantrell 4, Bliss	8,000
26		20	H	Notts County	W	2-0	Weir, Iremonger (og)	12,000
27		27	A	Aston Villa	L	1-3	Bliss	16,000
28	Mar	10	H	Liverpool	D	1-1	Minter	12,000
29		13	A	Bradford	L	1-5	Minter	9,000
30		15	H	Manchester City	D	2-2	Minter, Sparrow	6,000
31		20	H	Oldham Athletic	W	1-0	Middlemiss	14,000
32		27	A	Manchester United	D	1-1	Minter	7,000
33	Apr	2	H	Newcastle United	D	0-0		18,000
34		3	H	Bolton Wanderers	W	4-2	Cantrell, Bliss 3	11,000
35		6	A	West Bromwich Albion	L	2-3	Steel, Cantrell	6,000
36		10	A	Blackburn Rovers	L	1-4	Bliss	10,000
37		19	H	Sheffield United	D	1-1	Fleming	7,500
38		24	A	Sunderland	L	0-5		10,000
								Appearances
								Goals

FA Cup

R1	Jan	9	H	Sunderland	W	2-1	Walden, Bliss	17,000
R2		30	A	Norwich City	L	2-3	Cantrell, Lansdale (og)	9,758
								Appearances
								Goals

London FA Charity Cup

R1	Sep	21	H	Nunhead	W	2-1	Bliss, Cantrell	
R2	Oct	19	A	Crystal Palace	L	1-3	Walden	2,000
								Appearances
								Goals

London Professional Football Charity Fund

	Oct	28	A	Crystal Palace	D	2-2	Minter, Sparrow	2,000
								Appearances
								Goals

	Banks JA	Bliss H	Cantrell J	Clay T	Collins T	Darnell J	Eadon JP	Fleming JB	Grimsdell A	Jacques W	Joyce JW	Lightfoot EJ	Lowe H	Middlemiss H	Minter WJ	Pearson J	Rance CS	Rutherford J	Sparrow H	Steel RL	Tattersall WS	Walden FI	Webster FJ	Weir WF	Own-goals
Match		10	9	2					6	1				11	8					5		7	3	4	
Match	8	10	9	2				4	6	1				11						5		7	3		
Match	8	10		2				4	6	1				11		3			9	5		7			
Match	8	10	9	2				4	6	1				11		3				5		7			
Match		8	10	2					6	1				11					9	5		7	3	4	
Match			10	2				8		1		6		11					9	5		7	3	4	
Match			10	2				8		1		6		11					9	5		7	3	4	
Match		10	9	2		4		8		1		6		11						5		7	3		
Match		10	9	2		4		8		1		6		11						5		7	3		
Match		10	9	2						1		6		11			5		8	4		7	3		
Match		10	9	2	3				4	1		6			8					5	11	7			
Match		10	9	2	3				4	1		6			8					5	11	7			
Match		10	9	2	3					1		6			8					5	11	7		4	
Match		10	9	2	3						1	6			8		5				11	7		4	
Match		10	9	2	3						1	6			8					5	11	7		4	
Match		10	9	2	3			4			1	6		11	8		5					7			
Match		10	9	2	3						1	6		11	8					5		7		4	
Match		10	9	2	3				6		1			11	8					5		7		4	
Match		10	9	2	3					1		6		11	8					5		7		4	
Match		10		2						1		6		11	8	3			9	5		7		4	
Match	8	10		2						1		6		11		3			9	5		7		4	
Match		10		2						1		6		11	8	3			9	5		7		4	
Match		10		2						1		6		11	8	3			9	5		7		4	
Match		10	9	2						1		6		11	8	3				5		7		4	
Match		10	9	2			1					6	8	11		3				5		7		4	
Match		10	9	2			1					6	8	11		3				5		7		4	
Match		10	9	2			1					6		11	8					5		7	3	4	
Match		10		2	3	6	1	9						11	8					5		7		4	
Match			10	2	3	6	1							11	8				9	5		7		4	
Match			10	2	3	6				1				11	8				9	5		7		4	
Match		10		2		6				1				11	8	3			9	5		7		4	
Match		10		2		6				1				11	8	3			9	5		7		4	
Match		10		2		6				1				11	8	3			9	5		7		4	
Match		10	9	2		6				1				11	8	3				5		7		4	
Match		10	9	2		6				1				11	8	3				5		7		4	
Match	8	10		2		6				1				11	9	3				5		7		4	
Match				2				10		1		6		11	8	3			9	5		7		4	
Match		10		2				9		1		6		11	8	3				5		7		4	
Appearances	5	33	26	38	12	11	5	11	8	28	5	23	2	33	26	17	3	0	15	36	5	38	9	29	
Goals		21	14	4				2				1		2	5				3	2		1		1	1

	Banks JA	Bliss H	Cantrell J	Clay T	Collins T	Darnell J	Eadon JP	Fleming JB	Grimsdell A	Jacques W	Joyce JW	Lightfoot EJ	Lowe H	Middlemiss H	Minter WJ	Pearson J	Rance CS	Rutherford J	Sparrow H	Steel RL	Tattersall WS	Walden FI	Webster FJ	Weir WF	Own-goals
Match		10		2						1		6		11	8	3			9	5		7		4	
Match		10	9	2						1		6		11	8	3				5		7		4	
Appearances	0	2	1	2	0	0	0	0	0	2	0	2	0	2	2	2	0	0	1	2	0	2	0	2	
Goals		1	1																			1			1

	Banks JA	Bliss H	Cantrell J	Clay T	Collins T	Darnell J	Eadon JP	Fleming JB	Grimsdell A	Jacques W	Joyce JW	Lightfoot EJ	Lowe H	Middlemiss H	Minter WJ	Pearson J	Rance CS	Rutherford J	Sparrow H	Steel RL	Tattersall WS	Walden FI	Webster FJ	Weir WF	Own-goals
Match		8	10	2				4	6	1				11					9	5		7	3		
Match			9		2	6				1			10	11				5	8			7	3	4	
Appearances	0	1	2	1	1	1	0	1	1	2	0	0	1	2	0	0	0	1	2	1	0	2	2	1	
Goals		1	1																			1			

	Banks JA	Bliss H	Cantrell J	Clay T	Collins T	Darnell J	Eadon JP	Fleming JB	Grimsdell A	Jacques W	Joyce JW	Lightfoot EJ	Lowe H	Middlemiss H	Minter WJ	Pearson J	Rance CS	Rutherford J	Sparrow H	Steel RL	Tattersall WS	Walden FI	Webster FJ	Weir WF	Own-goals
Match		10	11	2	3					1		6			8		5		9	4		7			
Appearances	0	1	1	1	1	0	0	0	0	1	0	1	0	0	1	0	1	0	1	1	0	1	0	0	
Goals															1				1						

League Table

	P	W	D	L	F	A	Pts
Everton	38	19	8	11	76	47	46
Oldham Athletic	38	17	11	10	70	56	45
Blackburn Rovers	38	18	7	13	83	61	43
Burnley	38	18	7	13	61	47	43
Manchester City	38	15	13	10	49	39	43
Sheffield United	38	15	13	10	49	41	43
Sheffield Wednesday	38	15	13	10	61	54	43
Sunderland	38	18	5	15	81	72	41
Bradford Park Avenue	38	17	7	14	69	65	41
West Bromwich Albion	38	15	10	13	49	43	40
Bradford City	38	13	14	11	55	49	40
Middlesbrough	38	13	12	13	62	74	38
Liverpool	38	14	9	15	65	75	37
Aston Villa	38	13	11	14	62	72	37
Newcastle United	38	11	10	17	46	48	32
Notts County	38	9	13	16	41	57	31
Bolton Wanderers	38	11	8	19	68	84	30
Manchester United	38	9	12	17	46	62	30
Chelsea	38	8	13	17	51	65	29
TOTTENHAM HOTSPUR	38	8	12	18	57	90	28

1915-16

LONDON FOOTBALL COMBINATION

Manager: Peter McWilliam

Did you know that?

GUEST PLAYERS

Percy Barton
Birmingham
Ted Bassett
Notts County
Alec Chaplin
Hibernians
J.J. Doyle
Bohemians
P. Glen
Gillingham
Fred Hopkin
Darlington
Tom Knighton
Glossop
Jimmy Morris
Merthyr Town
Andy Ralston
London Caledonians
Bill Thomas
Gillingham
George Travers
Manchester United
W. Watkins
Nunhead
Archie Wilson
Middlesbrough

Match No.	Date		Opponents		Result		Scorers	Attendance
1	Sep	4	A	Arsenal	L	0-2		14,879
2		11	H	Brentford	D	1-1	Glen	5,150
3		18	A	West Ham United	D	1-1	Rance	8,000
4		19	H	Chelsea	L	1-3	Bliss	8,683
5	Oct	2	H	Crystal Palace	L	2-4	Banks 2	1,800
6		9	A	Queen's Park Rangers	W	4-0	Bassett 2, Minter, Thomas	3,000
7		16	H	Fulham	W	3-1	Banks, Bliss 2	4,200
8		23	A	Clapton Orient	D	0-0		9,000
9		30	H	Watford	W	3-0	Bassett, Steel, Bliss	3,000
10	Nov	6	A	Millwall	L	2-3	Morris, Bliss	3,000
11		13	H	Arsenal	D	3-3	Travers, Bliss, Steel	7,000
12		20	A	Brentford	D	1-1	Bliss	3,000
13		27	H	West Ham United	W	3-0	Morris, Bliss 2	4,000
14	Dec	4	A	Chelsea	L	1-8	Rance	8,000
15		11	A	Crystal Palace	L	2-4	Steel, Bliss	300
16		18	H	Queen's Park Rangers	W	2-1	Knighton 2	2,000
17		25	H	Croydon Common	W	3-0	Clay (pen), Lloyd 2	4,000
18		27	A	Croydon Common	D	0-0		
19	Jan	1	A	Fulham	W	2-0	Bassett, Lloyd	2,000
20		8	H	Clapton Orient	D	1-1	Bassett	5,000
21		15	A	Watford	W	1-0	Lloyd	2,000
22		22	H	Millwall	D	2-2	Morris, Bassett	8,000
23	Feb	5	A	West Ham United	L	0-2		8,000
24		12	H	Croydon Common	W	2-0	Bassett, Bliss	3,000
25		19	A	Fulham	L	1-3	Steel	3,000
26		26	H	Luton Town	W	7-4	Clay (pen), Rance, Bassett, Banks, Bliss 3	3,000
27	Mar	4	A	Arsenal	W	3-0	Barton, Banks, Bliss	6,000
28		11	H	Queen's Park Rangers	D	0-0		3,000
29		18	A	Croydon Common	D	3-3	Clay (pen), Rance, Steel	1,500
30		25	H	Fulham	W	4-0	Lloyd 2, Bliss, Steel	6,000
31	Apr	1	A	Luton Town	W	2-1	Banks, Bliss	3,000
32		8	H	Arsenal	W	3-2	Clay (pen), Bassett, Bliss	7,000
33		15	A	Queen's Park Rangers	W	3-1	Banks 2, Hopkin	4,000
34		21	H	Crystal Palace	W	3-1	Bliss 3	10,000
35		22	A	Crystal Palace	L	0-4		10,000
36		29	H	West Ham United	D	1-1	Bliss	7,000
								Appearances
								Goals

Banks JA	Barton PH	Bassett EJ	Bliss H	Chaplin AB	Clay T	Darnell J	Doyle JJ	Elliott JE	Fricker FG	Glen P	Hopkin F	Jacques W	Joyce JW	Knighton T	Lloyd WH	Minter WJ	Morris J	Page RJ	Ralston AT	Rance CS	Steel R	Thomas WSL	Travers GEJ	Watkins W	Weir WF	Wilson A
9	6		10	3	2	4			7				1			8	11			5						
10	6				2	4		3		9			1			8	7	11		5						
8	6			3	2			4					1				7	11		5		10	9			
8	6		10	3	2			4					1				7			5		11	9			
9			8	3	2			4					1				7	11		5	6	10				
10		8	6					2					1			9	7			5	3	11			4	
8	3		10		2	6		4					1				7			5	9	11				
	3	8	10			6		4					1				7		2	5	9	11				
	3	8	10		2	6		4					1				7			5	9	11				
	3	8	10		2	6		4					1				7			5	9	11				
	6	8	10		2	4							1				7		3	5	11		9			
	6	8	10		2			4					1				7		3	5	9	11				
	6		10		2			4					1		8		7		3	5	9					11
	3	8	10		2	6		4					1				7			5	9					11
	3	8	10			4		2				1		9			7			5	6					11
	6	8	10		2			4				1		9			7			5	3					11
	6	8	10		2			4					1		9		7		3	5						11
	6	8	10		2			4				1					7		3	5	9					11
	6	8	10		2			4				1			9		7		3	5	11					
	6	8	10		2	4						1		9			7		3	5	11					
		8			2			4					1	10	9		7		3	5	6					11
		8	10		2			4				1			9		7		3	5	6					11
	6	8	10		2			4				1			9		7		3	5	11					
9	6	8	10			4		2					1				7		3	5	11					
9		8	10		2	6	3	4									7			5	11			1		
9		8	10		2	6		4				1					7			5	3					11
9	6	8	10		2			4				1					7			5	3					11
9	6	8	10		2			4				1					7		3	5	11					
9	6	7	10		2			4				1			8				3	5	11					
9	6		10		2			4				1			8		7		3	5	11					
9	6	8	10		2			4				1					7		3	5	11					
9	6	8	10		2			4			11	1					7			5	3					
9		8	10		2	6		4			11	1			3		7			5						
	6	8	10		2			4				1			9		7		3	5	11					
	6	8	10		2	11		4				1			9		7			5	3					
	6	8	10		2			4			11	1			9		7			5	3					
17	29	28	33	4	32	15	1	33	1	1	3	18	17	4	12	3	35	3	17	36	30	9	3	1	1	10
8	1	9	22		4					1	1			2	6	1	3			4	6	1	1			

League Table

1st COMPETITION	P	W	D	L	F	A	Pts
Chelsea	22	17	3	2	71	18	37
Millwall	22	12	6	4	46	24	30
Arsenal	22	10	5	7	43	46	25
West Ham United	22	10	4	8	47	35	24
Fulham	22	10	4	8	45	37	24
TOTTENHAM HOTSPUR	22	8	8	6	38	35	24
Brentford	22	6	8	8	36	40	20
Queen's Park Rangers	22	8	3	11	27	41	19
Crystal Palace	22	8	3	11	35	55	19
Watford	22	8	1	13	37	46	17
Clapton Orient	22	4	6	12	22	44	14
Croydon Common	22	3	5	14	24	50	11

2nd COMPETITION	P	W	D	L	F	A	Pts
Chelsea	14	10	1	3	50	15	21
West Ham United	14	9	2	3	32	16	20
TOTTENHAM HOTSPUR	14	8	3	3	32	22	19
Fulham	14	9	0	5	38	19	18
Millwall	14	8	2	4	30	22	18
Crystal Palace	14	8	2	4	41	29	18
Watford	14	5	3	6	22	20	13
Brentford	14	5	2	7	29	33	12
Croydon Common	14	4	3	7	28	27	11
Clapton Orient	14	3	4	7	17	27	10
Arsenal	14	3	4	7	19	31	10
Luton Town	14	4	1	9	31	44	9
Queen's Park Rangers	14	2	5	7	14	37	9
Reading	14	3	2	9	23	64	8

1916-17

LONDON FOOTBALL COMBINATION

Manager: Peter McWilliam

Did you know that?

GUEST PLAYERS

Percy Barton
Birmingham
Ted Bassett
Notts County
Tom Caldwell
Gillingham
S Clayton
Bradford
Charlie Crossley
Sunderland
Billy Grimes
Derby County
Charlie Hannaford
Tufnell Park
Sid Hoad
Manchester City
Kenneth Hunt
Oxford City
J McVey
Shelbourne
Jimmy Morris
Merthyr Town
Cec Potter
Norwich City
Herbert Powell
Boscombe
Andy Ralston
London Caledonians
H Slade
Reading
Bert Smith
Huddersfield Town
George Travers
Manchester United
W Watkins
Nunhead
Ernie Williamson
Arsenal

Match No.	Date			Opponents	Result		Scorers	Attendance
1	Sep	2	H	Chelsea	L	0-4		4,000
2		9	A	Arsenal	D	1-1	Bassett	6,000
3		16	H*	Luton Town	L	2-3	Morris, Travers	6,000
4		23	A	Reading	W	4-2	Barton, Bassett, Potter, Bliss	10,000
5		28	H*	West Ham United	L	1-2	Bliss	3,000
6		30	H^	Millwall	L	1-4	Bliss	6,000
7	Oct	7	A	Watford	W	2-0	Bassett, Banks	2,000
8		14	H^	Clapton Orient	W	4-2	Bassett, Banks 2, Bliss	4,000
9		21	A	Fulham	L	1-2	Banks	4,000
10		28	H^	Queen's Park Rangers	L	4-5	Walden 3, Grimes	4,000
11	Nov	4	A	West Ham United	L	1-4	Thwaites	8,000
12		11	A	Southampton	L	0-1		5,000
13		18	H*	Crystal Palace	W	3-1	Banks 2, Bliss	1,300
14		25	A	Chelsea	W	4-2	Clay (pen), Banks 2, Bliss	10,000
15	Dec	2	H*	Arsenal	W	4-1	Bassett, Banks 3	11,000
16		9	A	Luton Town	W	3-1	Walden, Banks 2	5,000
17		16	H*	Portsmouth	W#	1-0	Banks	2,000
18		23	A	Millwall	D	3-3	Walden, Bassett, Bliss	3,000
19		25	A	Brentford	W	5-1	Elliott, Bassett, Hannaford, Bliss 2	3,000
20		26	H^	Brentford	W	5-2	Elliott, Bassett 3, Crowl	3,000
21		30	H*	Watford	W	3-0	Barton, Bassett, Darnell	6,000
22	Jan	6	A	Clapton Orient	W	2-1	Bassett, Barton	3,000
23		13	H^	Fulham	W	1-0	Barton	4,000
24		20	A	Queen's Park Rangers	D	1-1	Bassett	3,000
25		27	H^	West Ham United	D	0-0		7,000
26	Feb	3	H*	Southampton	W	3-1	Potter, Banks, Bliss	5,000
27		10	A	Crystal Palace	W	1-0	Banks	2,000
28		17	A	Portsmouth	W	4-2	Bliss 4	5,000
29		24	H*	Crystal Palace	W	4-1	Bassett 2, Potter, Hawkins	1,500
30	Mar	3	H^	Luton Town	W	3-2	Clay 2 (pens), Bassett	5,000
31		10	A	Southampton	W	4-2	Bassett 2, Banks, Hawkins	4,000
32		17	H*	Clapton Orient	W	5-2	Walden, Bassett 4	3,000
33		24	A	West Ham United	L	0-3		12,000
34		31	H*	Portsmouth	W	10-0	Elliott, Bassett, Banks 5, Thwaites 2, Hulme (og)	10,000
35	Apr	6	H^	Arsenal	D	0-0		5,000
36		7	A	Crystal Palace	W	3-0	Banks 3	5,000
37		9	A	Arsenal	L	2-3	Rance, Banks	12,000
38		10	H*	Portsmouth	W	2-1	Walden, Middlemiss	2,000
39		14	A	Luton Town	L	4-5	Lloyd, Bliss 2, Barton	3,000
40		21	H^	Southampton	W	4-0	Bassett 2, Banks, Potter	2,000
41		28	A	Clapton Orient	W	8-0	Bassett, Banks 3, Bliss 4	4,000

*played at Highbury ^played at Homerton
#abandoned after 40 mins - fog

Appearances
Goals

Banks JA	Barton PH	Bassett EJ	Bearman A	Bliss H	Caldwell T	Clay T	Clayton SA	Croft T	Croft W	Crossley CA	Crowl SR	Darnell J	Elliott JE	Grimes WJ	Hannaford CW	Hawkins W	Hoad SJ	Hunt KRG	Jacques W	Lloyd WH	McGlashlan G	McVey J	Middlemiss H	Morris J	Potter CB	Powell H	Ralston AT	Rance CS	Slade HC	Smith B	Thwaites AW	Travers GEJ	Walden FI	Watkins W	Weir WF	Williamson EC	Own-goals
	6	7		10	11	2							4						1			8					3	5				9					
	6	8		10		2							5						1	11				7			3				4	9					
	6	8		10							11		4						1	2				7			3	5				9					
	6	8		10		2					11		5						1	4				7	9		3										
	6	8		10					2		11		5						1		4			7	9		3										
	6			10				2			11		5						1	9		7					3				4				8		
8	6	7		10		2					11		5						1						9		3				4						
9	6	8		10		2					11		4						1					7			3	5									
9	6	8				2					11		5	7					1								3		10		4						
4	6	8		10		2	3				11		5	9					1														7				
9	6			10		2							4						1	8							3	5			11		7				
0	6	8				2							4	11					1	5					9		3						7				
9	6	8		10		2						11	4						1								3	5					7				
9	3	8		10		2					11	6	5						1	4													7				
9	6	8		10		2							4						1								3	5		11			7				
9	6	8		10		2						4	5						1						11		3						7				
9	6	8				2						11	4					5	1	10							3						7				
	3	8		10							11	6	4						1	9							2	5					7				
	3	8		10							11	4	5		7				1	9							2				6						
	6	8		10				2			11	4	5						1	9							3						7				
9	6	8	10			2						11	5						1								3						7		4		
9	10	8				2							6				11		1	4							3	5					7				
9	10	8				2							6				11		1	4							3	5					7				
9	6	8				2							5				11			4					10		3						7	1			
9	6	8				2							4				11		1						10		3	5					7				
9	6			10		2					11		4						1						8		3	5					7				
9	6			10		2						11							1	8							3	5			4		7				
		8		10		2			5	9		6							1							11	3				4		7				
9	6	8				2										11			1	4					10		3	5					7				
9	6	8				2										11			1	4					10		3	5					7				
9	6	8				2							4			11			1	10							3	5					7				
9	6	8				2							4			11			1						10		3	5					7				
9	2	8											4			11			1	6					10		3	5					7				
9	6	8				2						4	5			11			1	7							3				10						
9	6	8		10		2							4			11			1								3	5					7				
9	3	8		10								6	4			11			1	2								5					7				
9	3	8		10								6	4						1				11				2	5					7				
9		8		10									4							2			11				3	5					7		6	1	
	10	8		9				2				6	5			11			1	4							3						7				
9	6	8		10		2							4						1						11		3	5					7				
9	6	8		10		2							4						1						11		3	5					7				
0	39	37	1	27	1	30	1	3	2	1	13	14	37	3	1	9	4	1	39	23	1	2	2	5	14	1	38	23	1	1	9	3	30	1	3	1	
0	5	26		20		3					1	1	3	1	1	2				1			1	1	4			1			3	1	7				1

League Table

	P	W	D	L	F	A	Pts
West Ham United	40	30	5	5	110	45	65
Millwall	40	26	6	8	85	48	58
Chelsea	40	24	5	11	93	48	53
TOTTENHAM HOTSPUR	40	24	5	11	112	64	53
Arsenal	40	19	10	11	62	47	48
Fulham	40	21	3	16	102	63	45
Luton Town	39	20	3	16	101	82	43
Crystal Palace	38	14	7	17	68	72	35
Southampton	39	13	8	18	57	80	34
Queen's Park Rangers	39	10	9	20	48	86	29
Watford	40	8	9	22	69	115	25
Brentford	40	9	7	24	56	99	25
Portsmouth^	40	9	4	27	58	117	22
Clapton Orient	40	6	7	27	49	104	19

* Not all clubs completed their fixtures

^Took over record of Reading after 7 games

1917-18

LONDON FOOTBALL COMBINATION

Manager: Peter McWilliam

Did you know that?

GUEST PLAYERS

Percy Barton
Birmingham
Ted Bassett
Notts County
Sam Beaton
Huddersfield Town
George Coomber
Brighton & Hove Albion
Warney Cresswell
North Shields Athletic
W. Hill
Cuckfield
Ernie Hoffman
South Shields
Archie Jack
Falkirk
Billy Lawrence
Merthyr Town
Alex Lindsay
Raith Rovers
Tommy Nuttall
Everton
Billy Peake
Bury
Cec Potter
Norwich City
Andy Ralston
London Caledonians
Saunders
Brentford
Alf Spencer
Clapton Orient
Bill Thomas
Gillingham
Eric Tomkins
Northampton Town

Match No.	Date			Opponents	Result		Scorers	Attendance
1	Sep	1	A	Crystal Palace	W	4-2	Rance, Bassett, Minter 2	2,000
2		8	H*	Chelsea	L	0-4		12,000
3		15	A	Brentford	L	2-5	Banks, Nuttall	3,000
4		22	H*	Arsenal	L	1-2	Potter	10,000
5		29	A	West Ham United	L	0-1		8,00
6	Oct	6	H*	Fulham	W	1-0	Banks (pen)	6,00
7		13	A	Queen's Park Rangers	W	3-2	Nuttall, Barnard	2,00
8		20	H^	Clapton Orient	W	2-1	A.Lindsay 2	3,00
9		27	H*	Crystal Palace	W	1-0	Banks	5,00
10	Nov	3	A	Chelsea	D	0-0		8,00
11		10	H*	Brentford	W	6-1	Walden 2, Banks, Nuttall, Lawrence, Hawkins	4,00
12		17	A^	Arsenal	W	1-0	Nuttall	10,00
13		24	H*	West Ham United	W	2-0	Banks 2	7,00
14	Dec	1	A	Fulham	L	3-4	Banks 2, Coomber	7,00
15		8	H^	Queen's Park Rangers	L	0-1		4,00
16		15	A	Clapton Orient	W	4-2	Banks 2, Nuttall, Spencer	4,00
17		22	A	Crystal Palace	W	3-2	Nuttal 2, Coomber	2,00
18		25	A	Millwall	W	6-0	Nuttall 2, Banks 3, Middlemiss	7,00
19		26	H^	Millwall	L	0-1		6,00
20		29	H*	Chelsea	W	2-0	Banks, Peake	8,00
21	Jan	5	A	Brentford	W	3-2	Banks, Hawkins 2	8,00
22		12	H*	Arsenal	W	4-1	Walden, Banks, Peake, Chipperfield (og)	9,00
23		19	A	West Ham United	D	2-2	Banks 2	3,00
24		26	H*	Fulham	L	0-1		15,00
25	Feb	2	A	Queen's Park Rangers	W	7-2	Rance, Walden, Nuttall, Peake 3, Hawkins	3,00
26		9	H^	Millwall	W	4-2	Rance, Walden, Banks 2	7,00
27		16	H*	Crystal Palace	W	8-0	Elliott, Banks 2 (1 pen), Peake, Potter 2, Hawkins 2	7,00
28		23	A	Chelsea	L	0-3		20,00
29	Mar	2	H*	Brentford	W	3-0	Banks, Minter, Hawkins	4,00
30		9	A	Arsenal	L	1-4	Minter	15,00
31		16	H*	West Ham United	L	0-5		10,00
32		23	A	Fulham	W	3-0	Walden, Potter, Jack	3,00
33		29	A	Clapton Orient	W	3-2	Walden, Jack, Middlemiss	7,00
34		30	H^	Queen's Park Rangers	L	1-2	Goldthorpe	5,00
35	Apr	1	H^	Clapton Orient	W	5-2	Goldthorpe 2, Jack 2, Middlemiss	3,00
36		6	A	Millwall	W	1-0	Goldthorpe	2,00
37>		13	A	Chelsea	D	1-1	Peake	5,00
38>		20	H*	Chelsea	L	0-1		5,00
39>		27	A	Fulham	L	0-3		5,00
40>	May	4	H+	Fulham	L	2-3	Thomas, Goldthorpe	2,00

*played at Highbury ^played at Homerton +played at Upton Park
>subsidiary fixtures

Appearance
Goal

Ayres	Baldwin A	Banks JA	Barnard J	Barton PH	Bassett EJ	Beaton S	Bird	Bliss H	Brown R	Clay T	Coomber GS	Cresswell W	Crowl SR	Darnell J	Elliott JE	Fleming W	Goldthorpe EH	Halle W	Hawkins W	Hill W	Hoffman EH	Jack A	Jacques W	Lawrence WH	Lightfoot E	Lindsay AF	Lindsay D	Lloyd WH	Middlemiss H	Minter WJ	Nuttall TAB	Peake WE	Potter CB	Ralston AT	Rance CS	Robinson	Saunders	Spencer A	Thomas WSL	Thwaites AW	Tomkins EF	Walden FI	Wren GC	Own-goals
		10			8						4			6	2								1							9				3	5				11			7		
		9			8					2	6		11		4								1											3	5				10			7		
		10			8						6	2			4				11				1								9			3	5							7		
					8					2	6				4				11				1			10							9	3	5							7		
					8					2	6				4				11				1			10					9			3	5							7		
		4			8									6	2				11				1			10					9			3	5							7		
		4	10								6				2				11				1			8					9			3	5							7		
		9								2				6	4				11				1	10		8								3	5							7		
		8									7			6	2				11				1	10							9			3	5					4				
		8								2				6	4				11				1	10	9									3	5							7		
		8										2		6	4				11				1	10							9			3	5							7		
		8								2				6	4				11				1		9						10			3	5							7		
		8									10	2			4				11				1								9			3	5						6	7		
		8								2	10			6	4				11		1										9			3	5							7		
		8									4				2				11				1	10							9			3	5						6	7		
		8								2	10				4								1								9			3	5			11			6	7		
		8								2	10				4				11				1								9			3	5						6	7		
		8		6								2			4	5			11				1						10		9			3								7		
		8		6								2			4				11				1						10				9	3	5							7		
		8								2					4				7				1						11		9	10		3	5						6			
		8					11			2				6	4				9				1											3	5		10					7		
		8								2				4	3				11				1								9	10			5						6	7		
		8		6								2			4			10	11				1					7			9			3	5									
		8						10						4	2				11				1									9		3	5						6	7		
		8				4		6		2									11				1								9	10		3	5							7		
		8												4	2				11				1								9	10		3	5						6	7		
		8							7	2					4				11				1									10	9	3	5						6			
		8								2					4				11				1									10	9	3	5						6	7		
		8										2		6	4				10			11	1							9				3	5							7		
		8		6						2									11				1							9		10		3	5						4	7		
	1	8							7			2		6	4				9			11										10		3	5									
												2			4				11			9					1					10	8	3	5						6	7		
												2		6	4		8		11			9					1		10					3	5							7		
1												2		6	4		8		3			9					1		10						5							7		
															2		8		3	4		9					1		10						5				11			7		
		9								2				6	3		8		11								1					10			5				4			7		
		9								2				6	4		8		11								1					10		3	5							7		
						2								6			8		11	7							1					10		3	5				9	4				
		9								2	8				5				11													10		3					4		6	7	1	
		9								2				6			8		11								1					10		3	5	4			7					
	1	33	1	4	6	2	1	2	2	20	13	11	1	20	36	1	7	1	37	2	1	6	29	5	2	5	8	1	6	3	18	15	5	36	38	1	1	1	7	2	13	33	1	
		23	2		1						2				1		5		7			4		1		2			3	4	10	7	4		3			1	1			7		1

League Table

	P	W	D	L	F	A	Pts
Chelsea	36	21	8	7	82	39	50
West Ham United	36	20	9	7	103	51	49
Fulham	36	20	7	9	75	60	47
TOTTENHAM HOTSPUR	36	22	2	12	86	56	46
Arsenal	36	16	5	15	76	57	37
Brentford	36	16	3	17	81	94	35
Crystal Palace	36	13	4	19	54	83	30
Queen's Park Rangers	36	14	2	20	48	73	30
Millwall	36	12	4	20	52	74	28
Clapton Orient	36	2	4	30	34	104	8

*Subsidiary fixtures not included in final standings

1918-19

LONDON FOOTBALL COMBINATION

Manager: Peter McWilliam

Did you know that?

GUEST PLAYERS

Percy Barton
Birmingham
Sam Beaton
Huddersfield Town
Bee
Sutton Town
Ken Bennett
Southend United
F. Blake
Ilford
A. Cain
Bohemians
Art Chester
Croydon Common
John Dockray
Exeter City
Scott Duncan
Rangers
Ernie Freeman
Northampton Town
Charlie Harbidge
Reading
Hoffman
Brentford
Archie Jack
Falkirk
Alex Lindsay
Raith Rovers
McCalmont
Linfield
Willie McIver
Stockport County
Billy Peake
Bury
Cec Potter
Norwich City
Andy Ralston
London Caledonians
Tommy Simons
Queen's Park Rangers
Bert Smith
Huddersfield Town
P. Smith
Rangers
Bill Thomas
Gillingham
Eric Tomkins
Northampton Town
Joey Walters
Oldham Athletic
Charlie Wilson
Coventry City
Ted Worrall
Sheffield Wednesday

Match No.	Date			Opponents	Result		Scorers	Attendance
1	Sep	7	A	Fulham	D	2-2	Barnard, Thomas	8,000
2		14	H^	Brentford	D	1-1	Thomas	3,000
3		21	A	West Ham United	W	1-0	Thomas	8,000
4		28	H^	Clapton Orient	W	2-0	Price 2	5,00
5	Oct	5	H*	Chelsea	W	2-1	Goldthorpe, Thomas	12,000
6		12	A	Arsenal	L	0-3		19,90
7		19	H*	Crystal Palace	W	2-0	Rance, A.Lindsay	2,00
8		26	A	Millwall	W	2-0	Price, Barnard	7,000
9	Nov	2	H^	Fulham	W	1-0	Simons	5,00
10		9	A	Brentford	L	1-7	Banks	6,000
11		16	H^	West Ham United	L	1-4	Rance	6,000
12		23	A	Clapton Orient	W	3-0	A.Lindsay 2, Simons	6,00
13		30	A	Chelsea	L	1-3	Peake	14,00
14	Dec	7	H*	Arsenal	W	1-0	McCalmomt	12,00
15		14	A	Crystal Palace	L	3-6	A.Lindsay, Goldthorpe	2,00
16		21	H^	Millwall	L	0-3		8,00
17		25	A	Queen's Park Rangers	D	1-1	Rance	8,00
18		26	H^	Queen's Park Rangers	D	0-0		6,00
19		28	A	Fulham	L	1-3	Banks	8,00
20	Jan	4	H^	Brentford	D	1-1	B.Smith	12,00
21		11	A	West Ham United	L	0-2		13,00
22		18	H^	Clapton Orient	L	2-4	Jack 2	7,00
23		25	H*	Chelsea	D	1-1	Goldthorpe	25,00
24	Feb	1	A	Arsenal	W	3-2	Bennett, Minter, Jack	16,00
25		8	H*	Crystal Palace	W	4-2	Minter 3, Banks	14,00
26		15	A	Queen's Park Rangers	L	1-7	Cain	10,00
27		22	H^	Fulham	L	0-2		10,00
28	Mar	1	A	Brentford	L	1-4	Walden	12,00
29		8	H^	West Ham United	L	0-1		17,19
30		15	A	Clapton Orient	W	2-1	Minter, Banks	16,00
31		22	A	Chelsea	W	2-1	Minter, Banks	25,00
32		29	H*	Arsenal	L	0-1		33,00
33	Apr	5	A	Crystal Palace	D	2-2	Minter, Elliott	10,00
34		12	H*	Queen's Park Rangers	L	2-3	Minter, Bliss	20,00
35		18	H^	Millwall	D	2-2	Minter, Middlemiss	18,00
36		21	A	Millwall	W	4-2	Wilson, Bliss, Middlemiss 2	18,00

*played at Highbury ^played at Homerton

Appearance
Goal

Victory Cup

R1	Mar	25	H*	West Ham United	W	3-1	Minter 2, Banks	9,00
SF	Apr	19	H^	Fulham	L	0-2		45,00

*played at Highbury ^played at Stamford Bridge

Appearance
Goal

Barnard J	Barton PH	Beaton S	Bee	Bennett JK	Blake FJC	Bliss H	Bowler GH	Brawn WF	Bully	Cain A	Cantrell J	Chester A	Clay T	Couchman HF	Darnell J	Dockray J	Duncan ASM	Eadon JP	Elliott JE	Frazer	Freeman E	Gee	Goldthorpe EH	Grimsdell A	Harbidge CW	Hawkins W	Hoffman	Jack A	Jacques W	Jennings S	Lindsay AF	Lindsay D	Lloyd WH	McCalmont	McIver W	Middlemiss H	Minter WJ	Parsons J	Pattinson	Peake WE	Potter CB	Price IH	Ralston AT	Rance CS	Simons HT	Smith B	Smith P	Thomas WSL	Tomkins EF	Walden FI	Walters J	Wilson C	Worrall JE
10															6	11			2							7					8	1											3	5				9	4				
		4													6	11			2							7				10	8	1											3	5				9					
		4													6	11			2				10			7					8	1											3	5				9					
		4													6	11			2				9			7					8	1										10		5			3						
	6												2			11							8									1										7	3	5				10	4				
					9										6	11										2					10	1										7	3	5				4					
		4											2										9			11					8	1										7		5			3		6				
10													2		6							3				11					8	1										7		5				4					
		4													6											11					8	1										7	3		10		2		5				
		4						7							6											2	11					1										8	3	5	10								
									10						6		7						9			11						1										8	3	5			2		4				
	6														4	11			3		9					7					8	1												5	10								2
													2		6				3		11					7					8	1	9							10				5					4				
													2			11			4				8									1		9						10				5					6				3
													2		6				4				9			7		11	1		8									10				5									3
	6																		2				9					11				1									10	7		5					4				3
	3		9				4								6				2							11		10							1									5		8							
	3														6				4							11		10							1						9			5		8							2
	6												2										9			11		10							1									5		8			4				3
10													2		6											11			1		8							4						5		9							3
10													2		6											11			1		8									9				5					4				3
10													2		6				4							11		9	1		8													5									3
											9		2										10		6	7		11	1														3	5					4				
				7									2		6				9									11	1								8							5					4				3
				7									2												6			11	1		8						9							5					4				3
				7						10			2		6				9							3		11	1															5					4				
	10												2											6				11			8	1							3					5					4	7			
	10												2	11										6				9	1														3	5					4	7			
	3											7	2											6				11	1		8													5				9	4		10		
	3											8	2			11								6					1								9							5					4	7			
	3										9		2											6					1							11	8							5					4	7			
	3			7									2			11			9					6					1								8							5					4				
	3												2		7	11			9	4				5					1								8												6				
	3					10							2											6					1							11	8							5					4			9	
7													2		6				3										1							11	8							5		4						9	
						10							2					1	3					6												11	8							5		4						9	
6	14	6	1	4	1	2	1	1	1	1	2	2	24	1	21	11	1	1	18	1	2	1	10	9	2	21	1	13	16	1	17	16	1	1	3	4	9	1	1	4	2	9	10	34	3	6	4	7	22	4	1	3	11
2				1		2				1									1				4					3			4			1		3	9			1		3		3	2	1		4		1		1	

Barnard J	Barton PH	Beaton S	Bee	Bennett JK	Blake FJC	Bliss H	Bowler GH	Brawn WF	Bully	Cain A	Cantrell J	Chester A	Clay T	Couchman HF	Darnell J	Dockray J	Duncan ASM	Eadon JP	Elliott JE	Frazer	Freeman E	Gee	Goldthorpe EH	Grimsdell A	Harbidge CW	Hawkins W	Hoffman	Jack A	Jacques W	Jennings S	Lindsay AF	Lindsay D	Lloyd WH	McCalmont	McIver W	Middlemiss H	Minter WJ	Parsons J	Pattinson	Peake WE	Potter CB	Price IH	Ralston AT	Rance CS	Simons HT	Smith B	Smith P	Thomas WSL	Tomkins EF	Walden FI	Walters J	Wilson C	Worrall JE
	3										9		2						4					6					1							11	8							5						7			
						10							2											5					1							11	8						3			4			6	7		9	
0	1	0	0	0	0	1	0	0	0	0	1	0	2	0	0	0	0	0	1	0	0	0	0	2	0	0	0	0	2	0	0	0	0	0	0	2	2	0	0	0	0	0	1	1	0	1	0	0	1	2	0	1	0
																																					2																

League Table

	P	W	D	L	F	A	Pts
Brentford	36	20	9	7	94	46	49
Arsenal	36	20	5	11	85	56	45
West Ham United	36	17	7	12	65	51	41
Fulham	36	17	6	13	70	55	40
Queen's Park Rangers	36	16	7	13	69	60	39
Chelsea	36	13	11	12	70	53	37
Crystal Palace	36	14	6	16	66	73	34
TOTTENHAM HOTSPUR	36	13	8	15	52	72	34
Millwall	36	10	9	17	50	67	29
Clapton Orient	36	3	6	27	35	123	12

1919-20

DIVISION TWO

Manager: Peter McWilliam

Did you know that?

When Spurs played two matches against Red Star Amical in Paris in May 1913 they were so impressed by the Parisians' 'keeper, Pierre Chayrigues, that they immediately tried to sign him but it was not until the summer of 1919 that they succeeded. He was not to make the breakthrough at Spurs but returned to Red Star and went on to become France's first choice, winning 21 caps.

LEAGUE DEBUTANTS

Aug 30	v Coventry City Jimmy Chipperfield
Aug 30	v Coventry City Alex Lindsay
Aug 30	v Coventry City Bert Smith
Sep 13	v South Shields Hugh Lorimer
Sep 20	v South Shields Charlie Wilson
Sep 27	v Lincoln City Bert Goodman
Oct 4	v Lincoln City Jimmy Dimmock
Oct 11	v Clapton Orient Jimmy Skinner
Dec 27	v Barnsley Bob Brown
Feb 28	v Bristol City Jimmy Archibald
Mar 20	v Rotherham County Billy Sage
Apr 5	v Wolves Jimmy Seed
Apr 10	v Stoke City Sid Castle
Apr 10	v Stoke City Charlie Walters
May 1	v Birmingham Bob MacDonald

Match No.	Date			Opponents	Result		Scorers	Attendanc
1	Aug	30	A	Coventry City	W	5-0	Grimsdell, Bliss 2, Chipperfield 2	15,00
2	Sep	1	H	Leicester City	W	4-0	Clay (pen), Cantrell 2, Bliss	21,06
3		6	H	Coventry City	W	4-1	Grimsdell, Cantrell, Bliss, Chipperfield	30,61
4		11	A	Leicester City	W	4-2	Clay (pen), Minter, Cantrell, Bliss	20,00
5		13	H	South Shields	W	2-0	Cantrell, Bliss	33,17
6		20	A	South Shields	W	3-0	Wilson 3	20,00
7		27	H	Lincoln City	W	6-1	Grimsdell, Minter, Wilson, Bliss 2, Chipperfield	35,00
8	Oct	4	A	Lincoln City	D	1-1	Goodman	7,00
9		11	H	Clapton Orient	W	2-1	Minter, Bliss	44,26
10		18	A	Clapton Orient	W	4-0	Minter, Bliss 3	32,64
11		27	A	Port Vale	W	1-0	Cantrell	17,00
12	Nov	1	H	Port Vale	W	2-0	Smith, Bliss	28,60
13		8	A	Bury	L	1-2	Wilson	12,00
14		15	H	Bury	W	2-1	Bliss, Chipperfield	32,00
15		22	A	Nottingham Forest	D	1-1	Chipperfield	18,00
16		29	H	Nottingham Forest	W	5-2	Walden, Cantrell, Bliss 2, Dimmock	28,00
17	Dec	6	A	Fulham	W	4-1	Grimsdell, Minter, Cantrell, Bliss	31,00
18		13	H	Fulham	W	4-0	Walden, Minter 2, Bliss	38,00
19		20	A	Barnsley	L	0-3		12,00
20		25	H	Hull City	W	4-0	Grimsdell (pen), Cantrell, Bliss 2	40,00
21		26	A	Hull City	W	3-1	Cantrell, Dimmock, Bell (og)	28,00
22		27	H	Barnsley	W	4-0	Grimsdell, Banks, Cantrell, Bliss	43,07
23	Jan	3	A	Stockport County	W	2-1	Bliss, Dimmock	15,00
24		17	H	Stockport County	W	2-0	Walden, Bliss	38,00
25		24	A	Huddersfield Town	D	1-1	Bliss	27,00
26	Feb	7	A	Blackpool	W	1-0	Walden	10,00
27		14	H	Blackpool	D	2-2	Banks, Wilson	40,00
28		16	H	Huddersfield Town	W	2-0	Grimsdell, Wilson	35,00
29		25	A	Bristol City	W	2-1	Bliss 2	12,00
30		28	H	Bristol City	W	2-0	Grimsdell, Cantrell	38,00
31	Mar	13	A	West Ham United	L	1-2	Grimsdell (pen)	25,69
32		20	H	Rotherham County	W	2-0	Smith, Cantrell	28,00
33		22	H	West Ham United	W	2-0	Cantrell, Dimmock	26,00
34		27	A	Rotherham County	D	1-1	Grimsdell (pen)	18,00
35	Apr	2	H	Wolverhampton Wanderers	W	4-2	Cantrell, Bliss 3	38,00
36		3	H	Stoke City	W	2-0	Grimsdell, Dimmock	36,00
37		5	A	Wolverhampton Wanderers	W	3-1	Grimsdell 2, Cantrell	25,00
38		10	A	Stoke City	W	3-1	Seed, Cantrell 2	12,0
39		17	H	Grimsby Town	W	3-1	Grimsdell, Bliss 2	32,00
40		24	A	Grimsby Town	L	0-2		10,00
41		26	H	Birmingham	D	0-0		30,00
42	May	1	A	Birmingham	W	1-0	Seed	39,00
								Appearance
								Goa

FA Cup

R1	Jan	10	A	Bristol Rovers	W	4-1	Cantrell 3, Bliss	17,00
R2		31	H	West Stanley	W	4-0	Banks, Wilson 2, Bliss	35,52
R3	Feb	21	H	West Ham United	W	3-0	Grimsdell, Wilson 2	47,64
R4	Mar	6	H	Aston Villa	L	0-1		52,17
								Appearance
								Goa

London FA Charity Cup

R1	Sep	22	H	Millwall	W	6-0	Banks 2, Wilson 4	7,90
R2	Oct	6	A	Crystal Palace	L	2-3	Clay 2 (2 pens)	4,00
								Appearance
								Goa

London Professional Football Charity Fund

	Sep	29	A	Arsenal	W	1-0	Minter	10,00
								Appearance
								Goa

FA Charity Shield

	May	15	H	West Bromwich Albion	L	0-2		36,00
								Appearance
								Goa

chibald JM

Banks JA	Bliss H	Brown RS	Cantrell J	Castle SE	Chipperfield JJ	Clay T	Dimmock JH	Elliott JE	French WG	Goodman AA	Grimsdell A	Jacques W	Lindsay AF	Lorimer HH	Lowe H	McDonald RJ	Middlemiss H	Minter WJ	Pearson J	Rance CS	Sage W	Seed JM	Skinner JF	Smith B	Walden FI	Walters C	Wilson C	Own-goals
	10		9		11	2					6	1	8					5	3					4	7			
	10		9		11	2					6	1	8					5	3					4	7			
	10		9		11	2					6	1	8					5	3					4	7			
	10		9		11	2					6	1						8	3	5				4	7			
	10		9		11	2					6	1		7				8	3	5				4				
	10				11	2					6	1		7				8	3	5				4			9	
	10				11					2	6	1		7				8	3	5				4			9	
8	10					2	11	6		9		1		7					3	5				4				
	10				11	2						1						8	3	5			6	4	7		9	
	10				11	2				9	6	1						8	3	5				4	7			
	10		9		11					2	6	1						8	3	5				4	7			
	10		9		11					2	6	1						8	3	5				4	7			
	10		11		6						2	1						8	3	5				4	7		9	
	10		9		11					2	6	1						8	3	5				4	7			
	10		9		11					2	6	1						8	3	5				4	7			
	10		9				11			2	6	1						8	3	5				4	7			
	10		9				11			2	6	1						8	3	5				4	7			
	10		9				11			2	6	1						8	3	5				4	7			
	10						11			2	6	1						8	3	5				4	7		9	
	10		9				11			2	6	1						8	3	5				4	7			
	10		9				11			2	6	1						8	3	5				4	7			
8	10	3	9				11			2	6	1								5				4	7			
8	10	3	9				11			2	6	1								5				4	7			
8	10	3				2	11				6	1								5				4	7		9	
8	10	3				2	11				6	1								5				4	7		9	
8	10	3				2	11				6	1								5				4	7		9	
8	10	3				2	11				6	1								5				4	7		9	
8	10					2	11			3	6	1								5				4	7		9	
8	10	3				2	11					1								5			6	4	7		9	
8	10	3	9			2	11				6	1												5	7			
8	10	3	9			2	11				5	1					7						6					
8	10	3	9			2	11					1									4			5	7			
8	10	3	9			2	11				6	1												5	7			
8	10	3	9			2	11				6	1					7							5				
8	10	3	9			2	11				6	1												5	7			
8	10	3	9			2	11				6	1												5	7			
	10	3	9			2	11				6	1					7					8		5				
	10	3	9	7		2	11					1			6							8				5		
	10	3	9	7		2	11				6	1										8		5				
	10	3				2	11				6	1					7					8		5			9	
8	10	3	9			2	11				6	1												5	7			
7	10	3	9		11						6	1				2						8		5				
18	42	20	29	2	15	27	27	1	0	16	37	42	3	4	1	1	4	20	21	26	1	5	3	40	31	1	12	
2	31		18		6	2	5			1	14							7				2		2	4		7	1

Banks JA	Bliss H	Brown RS	Cantrell J	Castle SE	Chipperfield JJ	Clay T	Dimmock JH	Elliott JE	French WG	Goodman AA	Grimsdell A	Jacques W	Lindsay AF	Lorimer HH	Lowe H	McDonald RJ	Middlemiss H	Minter WJ	Pearson J	Rance CS	Sage W	Seed JM	Skinner JF	Smith B	Walden FI	Walters C	Wilson C	Own-goals
8	10	3	9				11			2	6	1								5				4	7			
8	10	3				2	11				6	1								5				4	7		9	
8	10	3				2	11				6	1								5				4	7		9	
8	10	3	9			2	11				6	1												5	7			
4	4	4	2	0	0	3	4	0	0	1	4	4	0	0	0	0	0	0	0	3	0	0	0	4	4	0	2	
1	2		3								1																4	

Banks JA	Bliss H	Brown RS	Cantrell J	Castle SE	Chipperfield JJ	Clay T	Dimmock JH	Elliott JE	French WG	Goodman AA	Grimsdell A	Jacques W	Lindsay AF	Lorimer HH	Lowe H	McDonald RJ	Middlemiss H	Minter WJ	Pearson J	Rance CS	Sage W	Seed JM	Skinner JF	Smith B	Walden FI	Walters C	Wilson C	Own-goals
8	10				11					3	6	1		7		2				5				4			9	
8		3				2	10		1	9				7			11						5	4				
2	1	1	0	0	1	1	1	0	1	2	1	1	0	2	0	1	1	0	0	1	0	0	1	2	0	0	1	
2						2																					4	

Banks JA	Bliss H	Brown RS	Cantrell J	Castle SE	Chipperfield JJ	Clay T	Dimmock JH	Elliott JE	French WG	Goodman AA	Grimsdell A	Jacques W	Lindsay AF	Lorimer HH	Lowe H	McDonald RJ	Middlemiss H	Minter WJ	Pearson J	Rance CS	Sage W	Seed JM	Skinner JF	Smith B	Walden FI	Walters C	Wilson C	Own-goals
	10						11			2	6	1		7				8	3	5				4				
0	1	0	0	0	0	0	1	0	0	1	1	1	0	1	0	0	0	1	1	1	0	0	0	1	0	0	0	
																		1										

Banks JA	Bliss H	Brown RS	Cantrell J	Castle SE	Chipperfield JJ	Clay T	Dimmock JH	Elliott JE	French WG	Goodman AA	Grimsdell A	Jacques W	Lindsay AF	Lorimer HH	Lowe H	McDonald RJ	Middlemiss H	Minter WJ	Pearson J	Rance CS	Sage W	Seed JM	Skinner JF	Smith B	Walden FI	Walters C	Wilson C	Own-goals
7	10	3	9			2	11				6	1										8		5				
1	1	1	1	0	0	1	1	0	0	0	1	1	0	0	0	0	0	0	0	0	0	1	0	1	0	0	0	

League Table

	P	W	D	L	F	A	Pts
TOTTENHAM HOTSPUR	42	32	6	4	102	32	70
Huddersfield Town	42	28	8	6	97	38	64
Birmingham	42	24	8	10	85	34	56
Blackpool	42	21	10	11	65	47	52
Bury	42	20	8	14	60	44	48
Fulham	42	19	9	14	61	50	47
West Ham United	42	19	9	14	47	40	47
Bristol City	42	13	17	12	46	43	43
South Shields	42	15	12	15	58	48	42
Stoke	42	18	6	18	60	54	42
Hull City	42	18	6	18	78	72	42
Barnsley	42	15	10	17	61	55	40
Port Vale	42	16	8	18	59	62	40
Leicester City	42	15	10	17	41	61	40
Clapton Orient	42	16	6	20	51	59	38
Stockport County	42	14	9	19	52	61	37
Rotherham County	42	13	8	21	51	83	34
Nottingham Forest	42	11	9	22	43	73	31
Wolverhampton W	42	10	10	22	55	80	30
Coventry City	42	9	11	22	35	73	29
Lincoln City	42	9	9	24	44	101	27
Grimsby Town	42	10	5	27	34	75	25

1920-21

DIVISION ONE

Manager: Peter McWilliam

Did you know that?

After Spurs won the FA Cup in 1901 it was decorated with blue and white ribbons, starting a tradition that continues to this day. Following the celebration dinner in 1901 the ribbons were presented to Mrs Morton Cadman, wife of Spurs' vice-chairman. Twenty years later those same ribbons were produced by Mrs Cadman to adorn the FA Cup once again.

LEAGUE DEBUTANTS

Feb 26 v West Bromwich Albion
Matt Forster
Feb 26 v West Bromwich Albion
Alex Hunter
Mar 26 v Sunderland
Andy Thompson

Match No.	Date		Opponents		Result		Scorers	Attendanc
1	Aug	28	H	Blackburn Rovers	L	1-2	Bliss	47,3
2		30	A	Derby County	D	2-2	Clay (pen), Bliss	18,6
3	Sep	4	A	Blackburn Rovers	D	1-1	Seed	40,0
4		6	H	Derby County	W	2-0	Seed, Bliss	26,1
5		11	A	Aston Villa	L	2-4	Walden, Dimmock	55,0
6		18	H	Aston Villa	L	1-2	Bliss	42,0
7		25	A	Manchester United	W	1-0	Grimsdell	52,0
8	Oct	2	H	Manchester United	W	4-1	Walden 2, Seed 2	34,6
9		9	H	Chelsea	W	5-0	Wilson, Bliss 3, Dimmock	47,0
10		16	A	Chelsea	W	4-0	Wilson 2, Bliss, Dimmock	76,0
11		23	H	Burnley	L	1-2	Banks	39,6
12		30	A	Burnley	L	0-2		40,0
13	Nov	6	H	Oldham Athletic	W	5-1	Grimsdell 2, Seed 2, Bliss	27,8
14		13	A	Oldham Athletic	W	5-2	Seed 2, Wilson 2, Bliss	15,0
15		20	H	Preston North End	L	1-2	Walden	33,3
16		27	A	Preston North End	L	1-4	Smith	20,0
17	Dec	4	H	Sheffield United	W	4-1	Walden, Wilson 2, Dimmock	23,5
18		11	A	Sheffield United	D	1-1	Dimmok	25,0
19		18	H	Bolton Wanderers	W	5-2	Seed, Cantrell, Bliss 2, Dimmock	33,0
20		25	A	Newcastle United	D	1-1	Cantrell	30,0
21		27	H	Newcastle United	W	2-0	Bliss, Dimmock	54,5
22	Jan	1	A	Bolton Wanderers	L	0-1		45,0
23		15	H	Arsenal	W	2-1	Cantrell, Bliss	39,2
24		22	A	Arsenal	L	2-3	Smith, Cantrell	60,6
25	Feb	3	H	Bradford Park Avenue	W	2-0	Cantrell, Bliss	20,0
26		5	A	Bradford Park Avenue	D	1-1	Dimmock	18,0
27		12	H	Manchester City	W	2-0	Cantrell, Dimmock	32,0
28		23	A	West Bromwich Albion	L	1-3	Seed	16,0
29		26	H	West Bromwich Albion	W	1-0	Bliss	38,0
30	Mar	9	A	Manchester City	L	0-2		30,0
31		12	H	Everton	W	2-0	Archibald, Seed	30,0
32		25	A	Liverpool	D	1-1	Bliss	40,0
33		26	A	Sunderland	W	1-0	Seed	35,0
34		28	H	Liverpool	W	1-0	Smith	35,0
35	Apr	2	H	Sunderland	D	0-0		35,0
36		9	A	Bradford City	L	0-1		15,0
37		16	H	Bradford City	W	2-0	Wilson 2	30,0
38		25	A	Huddersfield Town	L	0-2		28,0
39		27	A	Everton	D	0-0		23,0
40		30	H	Huddersfield Town	W	1-0	Banks	35,0
41	May	2	A	Middlesbrough	L	0-1		10,0
42		7	H	Middlesbrough	D	2-2	Banks, Cantrell	25,0

Appearanc
Goa

FA Cup

R1	Jan	8	H	Bristol Rovers	W	6-2	Clay (pen), Smith, Walden, Seed, Cantrell, Bliss	35,1
R2		29	H	Bradford City	W	4-0	Banks, Seed 3	39,0
R3	Feb	19	A	Southend United	W	4-1	Banks, Seed, Cantrell, Bliss	11,6
R4	Mar	5	H	Aston Villa	W	1-0	Banks	51,9
SF		19	N*	Preston North End	W	2-1	Bliss 2	44,6
F		23	N#	Wolverhampton Wanderers	W	1-0	Dimmock	72,8

*played at Hillsborough #played at Stamford Bridge

Appearanc
Goa

London FA Charity Cup

R1	Oct	11	A	Barking	W	4-1	Wilson 2, Bliss, Dimmock	7,0
R2	Nov	1	H	Arsenal	W	3-1	Grimsdell, Walden, Banks	14,5
SF	Apr	11	N*	Clapton Orient	L	1-2	Castle	16,0

*played at Highbury

Appearanc
Goa

London Professional Football Charity Fund

	Oct	25	H	Arsenal	W	2-0	Wilson 2	17,4

Appearanc
Goa

FA Charity Shield

	May	16	H	Burnley	W	2-0	Cantrell, Bliss	18,0

Appearanc
Goa

chibald JM	Banks JA	Bliss H	Brown RS	Cantrell J	Castle SE	Chipperfield JJ	Clay T	Dimmock JH	Findlay A	Forster M	Grimsdell A	Hunter AC	Jacques W	Lindsay AF	Lorimer HH	Lowe H	McDonald RJ	Pearson J	Rance CS	Ross JR	Seed JM	Skinner JF	Smith B	Thompson A	Walden FI	Walters C	Wilson C
		10	3	9			2	11			6		1								8		4		7	5	
		10		9			2	11			6		1					3			8		4		7	5	
		10		9	7		2	11			6		1					3			8		4			5	
	7	10					2	11			6		1					3	5		8		4				9
		10		9				11			6		1				2	3	5		8		4		7		
		10		9				11			6		1				2	3	5		8		4		7		
		10					2	11			6		1				3		5		8		4		7		9
		10					2	11			6		1			5	3				8		4		7		9
		10					2	11			6		1				3		5		8		4		7		9
	8	10					2	11			6		1				3		5				4		7		9
	8	10					2	11					1				3		5			6	4		7		9
	10						2	11			6		1				3		5		8		4		7		9
		10					2	11			6		1				3		5		8		4		7		9
		10					2	11			6		1				3		5		8				7		9
		10					2	11			6		1				3		5		8		4		7		9
		10					2	11			6		1				3		5		8		4		7		9
		10					2	11			6		1				3		5		8		4		7		9
		10					2	11			6		1				3		5		8		4		7		9
		10		9			2	11			6		1				3				8		4		7	5	
		10		9			2	11			6		1				3				8		4		7	5	
		10		9			2	11			6		1				3				8		4		7	5	
		10		9			2	11			6		1				3				8		4		7	5	
		10		9			2	11			6		1				3				8		4		7	5	
		10		9			2	11			6		1				3				8		4		7	5	
	7	10		9			2	11			6		1				3				8		4			5	
	7	10		9			2	11			6		1				3				8		4			5	
	7	10		9			2	11			6		1				3				8		4			5	
	7						2	11					1	10		6	3				8					5	9
	7	10		9				11		2	6	1					3				8		4			5	
	7						2	11			6	1		10			3				8		4			5	9
	7	10						11		2	6	1					3				8					5	9
	7	10		9			2	11				1		8		6	3									5	
	7						1	11		2	6						3				8		4	10		5	9
	7	10		9			2	11			6		1				3				8		4			5	
	7	10		9			2	11			6		1				3				8		4			5	
	7			9			2					1				6	3				8	4		10		5	11
	7	10					2	11			6	1		8			3						4			5	9
					7			11		2	6	1				5	3				8		4	10			9
		10		9	7		2	11		3	6	1		8												5	
	7	10		9			2	11			6	1					3				8		4			5	
	7	10	3	9				11		2	6	1									8		4			5	
	7	10		9				11		2	6	1					3				8		4				
	20	36	2	23	3	0	35	41	0	7	38	11	30	5	0	5	36	5	14	0	37	2	36	3	22	25	20
	3	17		7			1	9			3										12		3		5		9

chibald JM	Banks JA	Bliss H	Brown RS	Cantrell J	Castle SE	Chipperfield JJ	Clay T	Dimmock JH	Findlay A	Forster M	Grimsdell A	Hunter AC	Jacques W	Lindsay AF	Lorimer HH	Lowe H	McDonald RJ	Pearson J	Rance CS	Ross JR	Seed JM	Skinner JF	Smith B	Thompson A	Walden FI	Walters C	Wilson C
		10		9			2	11			6		1				3				8		4		7	5	
	7	10		9			2	11			6		1				3				8		4			5	
	7	10		9			2	11			6		1				3				8		4			5	
	7	10		9			2	11			6	1					3				8		4			5	
	7	10		9			2	11			6	1					3				8		4			5	
	7	10		9			2	11			6	1					3				8		4			5	
	5	6	0	6	0	0	6	6	0	0	6	3	3	0	0	0	6	0	0	0	6	0	6	0	1	6	0
	3	4		2			1	1													5		1		1		

chibald JM	Banks JA	Bliss H	Brown RS	Cantrell J	Castle SE	Chipperfield JJ	Clay T	Dimmock JH	Findlay A	Forster M	Grimsdell A	Hunter AC	Jacques W	Lindsay AF	Lorimer HH	Lowe H	McDonald RJ	Pearson J	Rance CS	Ross JR	Seed JM	Skinner JF	Smith B	Thompson A	Walden FI	Walters C	Wilson C
	8	10					2	11			6		1		7		3		5				4				9
	10						2	11			6		1				3		5		8		4		7		9
			3		7	11				2			1	8		5				4		6		10			9
	2	1	1	0	1	1	2	2	0	1	2	0	3	1	1	1	2	0	2	1	1	1	2	1	1	0	3
	1	1			1			1			1														1		2

chibald JM	Banks JA	Bliss H	Brown RS	Cantrell J	Castle SE	Chipperfield JJ	Clay T	Dimmock JH	Findlay A	Forster M	Grimsdell A	Hunter AC	Jacques W	Lindsay AF	Lorimer HH	Lowe H	McDonald RJ	Pearson J	Rance CS	Ross JR	Seed JM	Skinner JF	Smith B	Thompson A	Walden FI	Walters C	Wilson C
	8						2	11	10		6		1				3		5				4		7		9
	1	0	0	0	0	0	1	1	1	0	1	0	1	0	0	0	1	0	1	0	0	0	1	0	1	0	1
																											2

chibald JM	Banks JA	Bliss H	Brown RS	Cantrell J	Castle SE	Chipperfield JJ	Clay T	Dimmock JH	Findlay A	Forster M	Grimsdell A	Hunter AC	Jacques W	Lindsay AF	Lorimer HH	Lowe H	McDonald RJ	Pearson J	Rance CS	Ross JR	Seed JM	Skinner JF	Smith B	Thompson A	Walden FI	Walters C	Wilson C
	7	10		9			2	11			6	1					3				8		4			5	
	1	1	0	1	0	0	1	1	0	0	1	1	0	0	0	0	1	0	0	0	1	0	1	0	0	1	0
		1		1																							

League Table

	P	W	D	L	F	A	Pts
Burnley	42	23	13	6	79	36	59
Manchester City	42	24	6	12	70	50	54
Bolton Wanderers	42	19	14	9	77	53	52
Liverpool	42	18	15	9	63	35	51
Newcastle United	42	20	10	12	66	45	50
TOTTENHAM HOTSPUR	42	19	9	14	70	48	47
Everton	42	17	13	12	66	55	47
Middlesbrough	42	17	12	13	53	53	46
Arsenal	42	15	14	13	59	63	44
Aston Villa	42	18	7	17	63	70	43
Blackburn Rovers	42	13	15	14	57	59	41
Sunderland	42	14	13	15	57	60	41
Manchester United	42	15	10	17	64	68	40
West Bromwich Albion	42	13	14	15	54	58	40
Bradford City	42	12	15	15	61	63	39
Preston North End	42	15	9	18	61	65	39
Huddersfield Town	42	15	9	18	42	49	39
Chelsea	42	13	13	16	48	58	39
Oldham Athletic	42	9	15	18	49	86	33
Sheffield United	42	6	18	18	42	68	30
Derby County	42	5	16	21	32	58	26
Bradford Park Avenue	42	8	8	26	43	76	24

1921-22

DIVISION ONE

Manager: Peter McWilliam

Did you know that?

In August 1921 Spurs purchased the Red House, the former hotel on the opposite corner of the main entrance to the ground, and, the White Hart that provided their headquarters for a time in the 1880s. A clock was mounted on the front of the building in 1934, and subsequently surmounted by a cockerel. To this day it is one of the most visible signs of the club's presence in Tottenham High Road.

LEAGUE DEBUTANTS

Mar 15 v Everton
Tich Handley

Apr 5 v Sunderland
Herbert Blake

Match No.	Date		Opponents		Result		Scorers	Attendanc
1	Aug	27	A	Cardiff City	W	1-0	Banks	50,0
2		29	H	Bolton Wanderers	L	1-2	Thompson	31,7
3	Sep	3	H	Cardiff City	W	4-1	Clay (pen), Thompson 2, Dimmock	35,0
4		5	A	Bolton Wanderers	L	0-1		40,0
5		10	H	Middlesbrough	L	2-4	Clay (pen), Bliss	34,8
6		17	A	Middlesbrough	D	0-0		20,0
7		24	H	Aston Villa	W	3-1	Clay (pen), Seed, Biss	47,0
8	Oct	1	A	Aston Villa	L	1-2	Dimmock	40,0
9		8	H	Manchester United	D	2-2	Wilson 2	36,1
10		15	A	Manchester United	L	1-2	Dimmok	40,0
11		22	H	Liverpool	L	0-1		31,5
12		29	A	Liverpool	D	1-1	Dimmock	25,0
13	Nov	5	H	Newcastle United	W	4-0	Grimsdell, Seed 3	34,4
14		12	A	Newcastle United	W	2-0	Seed, Lindsay	20,0
15		19	H	Burnley	D	1-1	Seed	45,0
16		26	A	Burnley	L	0-1		25,0
17	Dec	3	H	Sheffield United	W	2-1	Clay (pen), Skinner	27,3
18		10	A	Sheffield United	L	0-1		27,0
19		17	H	Chelsea	D	0-0		44,0
20		24	A	Chelsea	W	2-1	Bliss 2	54,0
21		26	H	Bradford City	W	1-0	Clay (pen)	34,4
22		27	A	Bradford City	W	4-0	Seed, Wilson 2, Thompson	25,0
23		31	H	Preston North End	W	5-0	Seed, Wilson 2, Thompson, Dimmock	28,0
24	Jan	14	A	Preston North End	W	2-1	Walden, Cantrell	20,0
25		21	A	West Bromwich Albion	L	0-3		20,0
26		30	H	West Bromwich Albion	W	2-0	Clay (pen), Wilson	30,0
27	Feb	4	A	Manchester City	D	3-3	Wilson, Bliss 2	20,0
28		11	H	Manchester City	W	3-1	Grimsdell, Bliss, Dimmock	43,0
29		25	H	Everton	W	2-0	Wilson, Dimmock	34,8
30	Mar	11	H	Sunderland	W	1-0	Thompson	41,0
31		15	A	Everton	D	0-0		30,0
32		18	H	Huddersfield Town	W	1-0	Skinner	36,1
33		27	A	Huddersfield Town	D	1-1	Lindsay	16,0
34	Apr	1	A	Birmingham	W	3-0	Clay (pen), Seed, Roulsen (og)	34,0
35		5	A	Sunderland	L	0-2		37,0
36		8	H	Birmingham	W	2-1	Lindsay, Jones (og)	19,6
37		14	H	Oldham Athletic	W	3-1	Clay (pen), Cantrell 2	34,8
38		15	H	Arsenal	W	2-0	Grimsdell, Seed	40,3
39		17	A	Oldham Athletic	L	0-1		31,3
40		22	A	Arsenal	L	0-1		42,0
41		29	H	Blackburn Rovers	W	2-1	Walden, Wilson	24,5
42	May	6	A	Blackburn Rovers	D	1-1	Wilson	25,0

Appearance
Goa

FA Cup

R1	Jan	7	A	Brentford	W	2-0	Seed, Cantrell	12,9
R2		28	H	Watford	W	1-0	Bliss	47,6
R3	Feb	18	H	Manchester City	W	2-1	Wilson, Bliss	53,8
R4	Mar	4	A	Cardiff City	D	1-1	Seed	55,0
R4r		9	H	Cardiff City	W	2-1	Wilson, Dimmock	53,6
SF		25	N*	Preston North End	L	1-2	Seed	50,0

*played at Hillsborough

Appearance
Goa

London FA Charity Cup

R1	Oct	17	H	London Caledonians	W	5-0	Walden 2, Seed, Whitton, Handley	5,0
R2		31	H	Brentford	D	1-1	Grimsdell	6,6
R2r	Nov	7	A	Brentford	W	3-2	Wilson, Thompson, Dimmock	12,0
SF		14	N*	Arsenal	D^	0-0		11,0
SFr		21	N#	Arsenal	L~	1-2	Clay (pen)	9,0

*played at Stamford Bridge #played at Homerton
^after 5 mins extra-time ~after extra-time

Appearance
Goa

London Professional Football Charity Fund

	Sep	12	A	West Ham United	L	0-1		11,0

Appearance
Goa

Banks JA	Blake HE	Bliss H	Cantrell J	Clay T	Dimmock JH	Forster M	French WG	Grimsdell A	Handley CHJ	Hunter AC	Jacques W	Lindsay AF	Lorimer HH	Lowe H	McDonald RJ	Pearson J	Seed JM	Skinner JF	Smith B	Thompson A	Walden FI	Walters C	Whitton WA	Wilson C	Own-goals
7		10	9	2	11			6		1					3		8		4			5			
7			9	2	11			6		1		8			3				4	10		5			
7			9	2	11			6		1		8			3				4	10		5			
7			9	2	11			6		1		8			3				4	10		5			
7		10	9	2	11			6		1					3		8					5			
				2	11			6		1					3		8			10	7	5		9	
7		10		2	11			6		1					3		8					5		9	
		10		2	11			6		1					3		8				7	5		9	
		10		2	11			6		1					3		8				7	5		9	
				2	11			6		1					3		8	4		10	7	5		9	
9					11	2		6		1					3		8	4		10	7	5			
				2	11			6			1	9	7		3		8	4		10		5			
		10		2	11			6			1	9			3		8	4			7	5			
		10		2	11			6			1	9			3		8	4			7	5			
		10		2	11			6			1	9			3		8	4			7	5			
		10		2	11			6			1	9		5	3		8	4			7				
		10		2	11			6			1	9		5	3		8	4			7				
		10		2	11			6			1	9		5	3		8	4			7				
		10	9	2	11			6			1					3	8		4		7	5			
		10	9	2	11			6			1				3		8		4		7	5			
		10	9	2	11			6			1			5	3		8		4		7				
7					11	2		6			1			5	3		8		4	10				9	
7				2	11			6			1			5	3		8		4	10				9	
		10	9	2	11			6			1			5	3		8		4		7				
7		10	9	2	11			6			1			5	3		8		4						
		10		2	11			6			1				3		8		4		7	5		9	
		10		2	11			6			1				3		8		4		7	5		9	
		10		2	11			6			1				3		8		4		7	5		9	
		10		2	11			6			1				3		8		4		7	5		9	
				2	11						1				3		8	6	4	10	7	5		9	
7					11			6	10		1	8		5	3	2		4						9	
		10		2	11			6		1		8			3			4			7	5		9	
		10		2	11						1	7		6	3		8		4			5		9	
				2	11						1			6	3		8		4	10	7	5		9	
	1				11	2								6	3		8		4	10	7	5		9	
	1				11	2		6				8				3			4	10	7	5		9	
	1		9	2	11			6				7			3		8		4	10		5			
	1		9	2	11			6							3		8		4	10	7	5			
	1	10		2	11										3		8	6	4		7	5		9	
	1		9	2	11			6							3		8	4		10	7	5			
	1			2	11										3		8	6	4	10	7	5		9	
	1			2	11							7			3		8	6	4	10		5		9	
11	8	23	13	37	42	4	0	35	1	12	22	16	1	12	40	3	36	16	25	18	28	33	0	21	
1		7	3	8	7			3				3					10	2		6	2			11	2

Banks JA	Blake HE	Bliss H	Cantrell J	Clay T	Dimmock JH	Forster M	French WG	Grimsdell A	Handley CHJ	Hunter AC	Jacques W	Lindsay AF	Lorimer HH	Lowe H	McDonald RJ	Pearson J	Seed JM	Skinner JF	Smith B	Thompson A	Walden FI	Walters C	Whitton WA	Wilson C	Own-goals
		10	9	2	11			6			1			5	3		8		4		7				
		10		2	11			6			1				3		8		4		7	5		9	
		10		2	11			6			1				3		8		4		7	5		9	
		10		2	11			6			1				3		8		4		7	5		9	
		10		2	11			6			1				3		8		4		7	5		9	
		10		2	11			6			1				3		8		4		7	5		9	
0	0	6	1	6	6	0	0	6	0	0	6	0	0	1	6	0	6	0	6	0	6	5	0	5	
		2	1		1												3							2	

Banks JA	Blake HE	Bliss H	Cantrell J	Clay T	Dimmock JH	Forster M	French WG	Grimsdell A	Handley CHJ	Hunter AC	Jacques W	Lindsay AF	Lorimer HH	Lowe H	McDonald RJ	Pearson J	Seed JM	Skinner JF	Smith B	Thompson A	Walden FI	Walters C	Whitton WA	Wilson C	Own-goals
				2	11			6	10	1					3		8	4			7	5	9		
				2	11			6			1	9	7		3		8	4		10		5			
				2	11						1		7	6	3		8	4		10		5		9	
7		10			11	2	1	6				9			3		8	4				5			
7		10		2	11					1		9			3			6		8		5			
2	0	2	0	4	5	1	1	3	1	2	2	3	2	1	5	0	4	5	0	3	1	5	1	1	
				1	1			1	1								1			1	2		1	1	

Banks JA	Blake HE	Bliss H	Cantrell J	Clay T	Dimmock JH	Forster M	French WG	Grimsdell A	Handley CHJ	Hunter AC	Jacques W	Lindsay AF	Lorimer HH	Lowe H	McDonald RJ	Pearson J	Seed JM	Skinner JF	Smith B	Thompson A	Walden FI	Walters C	Whitton WA	Wilson C	Own-goals
7				2	11	3		6		1							8			10		5		9	
1	0	0	0	1	1	1	0	1	0	1	0	0	0	0	0	0	1	0	0	1	0	1	0	1	

League Table

	P	W	D	L	F	A	Pts
Liverpool	42	22	13	7	63	36	57
TOTTENHAM HOTSPUR	42	21	9	12	65	39	51
Burnley	42	22	5	15	72	54	49
Cardiff City	42	19	10	13	61	53	48
Aston Villa	42	22	3	17	74	55	47
Bolton Wanderers	42	20	7	15	68	59	47
Newcastle United	42	18	10	14	59	45	46
Middlesbrough	42	16	14	12	79	69	46
Chelsea	42	17	12	13	40	43	46
Manchester City	42	18	9	15	65	70	45
Sheffield United	42	15	10	17	59	54	40
Sunderland	42	16	8	18	60	62	40
West Bromwich Albion	42	15	10	17	51	63	40
Huddersfield Town	42	15	9	18	53	54	39
Blackburn Rovers	42	13	12	17	54	57	38
Preston North End	42	13	12	17	42	65	38
Arsenal	42	15	7	20	47	56	37
Birmingham	42	15	7	20	48	60	37
Oldham Athletic	42	13	11	18	38	50	37
Everton	42	12	12	18	57	55	36
Bradford City	42	11	10	21	48	72	32
Manchester United	42	8	12	22	41	73	28

1922-23

DIVISION ONE

Manager: Peter McWilliam

Did you know that?

On 7 May 1923 the Duke of York became the first member of the royal family to visit White Hart Lane. He witnessed Spurs beat West Ham United 5–2 in a match for the benefit of the Docklands Settlement, a charity he was patron of.

LEAGUE DEBUTANTS

Sep 30	v Arsenal Sammy Brooks
Mar 14	v Manchester City Jimmy Ross
Mar 31	v Sunderland Buchanan Sharp
Apr 11	v Bolton Wanderers Fred Barnett
Apr 11	v Bolton Wanderers Geordie Maddison
Apr 14	v Birmingham Frank Hartley

Match No.	Date		Opponents		Result		Scorers	Attendanc
1	Aug	26	H	Cardiff City	D	1-1	Cantrell	43,16
2	Sep	2	A	Cardiff City	W	3-2	Smith, Seed, Bliss	50,00
3		4	H	Everton	W	2-0	Seed, Bliss	24,26
4		9	H	Burnley	L	1-3	Cantrell	39,43
5		16	A	Burnley	W	1-0	Bliss	20,00
6		23	H	Arsenal	L	1-2	Lindsay	40,5
7		30	A	Arsenal	W	2-0	Dimmock 2	55,0
8	Oct	7	A	Aston Villa	L	0-2		50,00
9		14	H	Aston Villa	L	1-2	Seed	43,2
10		21	H	West Bromwich Albion	W	3-1	Skinner, Walden, Brooks	26,18
11		28	A	West Bromwich Albion	L	1-5	Seed	23,00
12	Nov	4	H	Liverpool	L	2-4	Clay (pen), Grimsdell	35,00
13		11	A	Liverpool	D	0-0		29,00
14		18	H	Newcastle United	L	0-1		30,30
15		25	A	Newcastle United	D	1-1	Lindsay	25,0
16	Dec	2	H	Nottingham Forest	W	2-1	Seed, Dimmock	25,25
17		9	A	Nottingham Forest	W	1-0	Seed	15,00
18		16	A	Chelsea	D	0-0		50,0
19		23	H	Chelsea	W	3-1	Smith, Seed 2	33,06
20		25	H	Sheffield United	W	2-1	Cantrell, Handley	45,0
21		26	A	Sheffield United	L	0-2		42,0
22		30	A	Middlesbrough	L	0-2		8,00
23	Jan	1	A	Everton	L	1-3	Lindsay	20,0
24		6	H	Middlesbrough	W	2-0	Walden, Handley	35,00
25		20	A	Oldham Athletic	W	3-0	Grimsdell, Lindsay, Dimmock	9,00
26		27	H	Oldham Athletic	W	3-0	Clay 2 (2 pens), Lindsay	24,84
27	Feb	10	A	Blackburn Rovers	L	0-1		6,00
28		14	H	Blackburn Rovers	W	2-0	Lindsay 2	10,00
29		17	H	Bolton Wanderers	L	0-1		30,0
30	Mar	3	H	Manchester City	W	3-1	Walden, Seed, Handley	27,96
31		14	A	Manchester City	L	0-3		25,00
32		17	A	Stoke City	D	0-0		30,0
33		24	H	Stoke City	W	3-1	Lindsay, Handley, Dimmock	20,00
34		30	H	Preston North End	D	1-1	Handley	30,86
35		31	A	Sunderland	L	0-2		18,0
36	Apr	2	A	Preston North End	L	0-2		22,00
37		7	H	Sunderland	L	0-1		23,57
38		11	A	Bolton Wanderers	W	2-0	Cantrell, Dimmock	15,00
39		14	A	Birmingham	L	1-2	Lindsay	15,00
40		21	H	Birmingham	W	2-0	Lindsay 2	16,33
41		28	A	Huddersfield Town	L	0-1		15,00
42	May	5	H	Huddersfield Town	D	0-0		17,00

Appearance
Goa

FA Cup

R1	Jan	13	H*	Worksop Town	D	0-0		23,92
R1r	Jan	15	H	Worksop Town	W	9-0	Seed, Lindsay 4, Handley 3, Dimmock	23,12
R2	Feb	3	H	Manchester United	W	4-0	Lindsay, Handley 3	38,33
R3		24	A	Cardiff City	W	3-2	Seed, Lindsay, Handley	54,00
R4	Mar	10	H	Derby County	L	0-1		50,34

*played at home by mutual consent

Appearance
Goa

London FA Charity Cup

R1	Oct	23	A	Arsenal	A	2-3	Handley 2	12,00

Appearance
Goa

London Professional Football Charity Fund

Oct	2	H	West Ham United	W	2-1	Clay (pen), Wilson	7,00

Appearance
Goa

Barnett FW	Blake HE	Bliss H	Brooks S	Brown RS	Cantrell J	Clay T	Dimmock JH	Forster M	Grimsdell A	Handley CHJ	Hartley AF	Jacques W	Lindsay AF	Lowe H	Maddison G	McDonald RJ	Pearson J	Ross JR	Seed JM	Sharp B	Skinner JF	Smith B	Thompson A	Walden FI	Walters C	Wilson C
	1				9	2	11		6							3			8			4	10	7	5	
	1	10			9	2	11		6							3			8			4		7	5	
	1	10				2	11		6				9			3			8			4		7	5	
		10			9	2	11		6			1				3			8			4		7	5	
	1	10			9	2	11		6							3			8			4		7	5	
	1	10				2	11		6				9			3			8			4		7	5	
	1		11			2	10		6				7			3			8			4			5	9
	1		11			2	10		6				7			3			8			4			5	9
	1		11		9	2	10		6				7			3			8		4				5	
	1	10	11			2	9						8	6		3					4			7	5	
	1	10	11			2	9		6				7			3			8		4				5	
	1	10	11			2	9		6	7						3			8		4				5	
	1		7			2	11		9	10						3			8		6	4			5	
	1					2	11		9	10						3			8		6	4		7	5	
	1					2	11		6	10			9			3			8			4		7	5	
	1					2	11		6	10			9			3			8			4		7	5	
	1					2	11		6	10			9			3			8			4		7	5	
	1					2	11	3	6	10			9						8			4		7	5	
	1					2	11	3	6	10			9						8			4		7	5	
	1				9	2	11	3	6	10			8									4		7	5	
	1					2	11	3		10			9						8		6	4			5	
	1					2	11	3	6	10			9	5					8			4		7		
	1					2	11	3	6	10			9	5					8			4		7		
	1					2	11		6	10			9	5			3		8			4		7		
	1			3		2	11		6	10			9	5					8			4		7		
	1					2	11	3	6	10			9	5					8			4		7		
	1			3		2	11		6	10			9	5					8			4		7		
	1			3			11		2	10			9	5					8		6	4		7		
	1			3			11		2	10			9	5					8		6	4		7		
	1			3		2	11		6	10			9	5					8		4			7		
	1			3			11		6	10			9	5				2	8			4		7		
	1			3			11		6	10			9	5				2	8			4		7		
	1			3			11		6	10			9	5				2	8			4		7		
	1			3			11		6	10			9	5				2	8			4		7		
	1			3			11		6	7			9					2	8	10		4			5	
	1			3			11		6	7								2	8	10		4			5	
	1			3	9	2	11		6	10			7						8			4			5	
7					9	2	11	3	6	10			8		1						4				5	
7					9	2	11	3	6		10		8		1						4				5	
					9	2	11	3	6	10			8		1						4			7	5	
						2	11	3	6	10			9		1				8		4			7	5	
						2	11	3	6	10			9		1						4		8	7	5	
2	36	8	7	12	10	34	42	12	40	30	1	1	34	14	5	17	1	6	36	2	15	32	2	30	29	2
		3	1		4	3	6		2	5			11						9		1	2		3		

Barnett FW	Blake HE	Bliss H	Brooks S	Brown RS	Cantrell J	Clay T	Dimmock JH	Forster M	Grimsdell A	Handley CHJ	Hartley AF	Jacques W	Lindsay AF	Lowe H	Maddison G	McDonald RJ	Pearson J	Ross JR	Seed JM	Sharp B	Skinner JF	Smith B	Thompson A	Walden FI	Walters C	Wilson C
	1					2	11		6	10			9	5			3		8			4		7		
	1			3		2	11		6	10			9	5					8			4		7		
	1			3		2	11		6	10			9	5					8			4		7		
	1			3			11		2	10			9	5					8		6	4		7		
	1			3		2	11		6	10			9	5					8			4		7		
0	5	0	0	4	0	4	5	0	5	5	0	0	5	5	0	0	1	0	5	0	1	5	0	5	0	0
							1			7			6						2							

Barnett FW	Blake HE	Bliss H	Brooks S	Brown RS	Cantrell J	Clay T	Dimmock JH	Forster M	Grimsdell A	Handley CHJ	Hartley AF	Jacques W	Lindsay AF	Lowe H	Maddison G	McDonald RJ	Pearson J	Ross JR	Seed JM	Sharp B	Skinner JF	Smith B	Thompson A	Walden FI	Walters C	Wilson C
	1					2	9		6	11			7	5		3			8		4		10			
0	1	0	0	0	0	1	1	0	1	1	0	0	1	1	0	1	0	0	1	0	1	0	1	0	0	0
										2																

Barnett FW	Blake HE	Bliss H	Brooks S	Brown RS	Cantrell J	Clay T	Dimmock JH	Forster M	Grimsdell A	Handley CHJ	Hartley AF	Jacques W	Lindsay AF	Lowe H	Maddison G	McDonald RJ	Pearson J	Ross JR	Seed JM	Sharp B	Skinner JF	Smith B	Thompson A	Walden FI	Walters C	Wilson C
	1		11			2	10		6				7			3			8			4			5	9
0	1	0	1	0	0	1	1	0	1	0	0	0	1	0	0	1	0	0	1	0	0	1	0	0	1	1
						1																				1

League Table

	P	W	D	L	F	A	Pts
Liverpool	42	26	8	8	70	31	60
Sunderland	42	22	10	10	72	54	54
Huddersfield Town	42	21	11	10	60	32	53
Newcastle United	42	18	12	12	45	37	48
Everton	42	20	7	15	63	59	47
Aston Villa	42	18	10	14	64	51	46
West Bromwich Albion	42	17	11	14	58	49	45
Manchester City	42	17	11	14	50	49	45
Cardiff City	42	18	7	17	73	59	43
Sheffield United	42	16	10	16	68	64	42
Arsenal	42	16	10	16	61	62	42
TOTTENHAM HOTSPUR	42	17	7	18	50	50	41
Bolton Wanderers	42	14	12	16	50	58	40
Blackburn Rovers	42	14	12	16	47	62	40
Burnley	42	16	6	20	58	59	38
Preston North End	42	13	11	18	60	64	37
Birmingham	42	13	11	18	41	57	37
Middlesbrough	42	13	10	19	57	63	36
Chelsea	42	9	18	15	45	53	36
Nottingham Forest	42	13	8	21	41	70	34
Stoke	42	10	10	22	47	67	30
Oldham Athletic	42	10	10	22	35	65	30

1923-24

DIVISION ONE

Manager: Peter McWilliam

Did you know that?

In March 1924 Enfield Magistrates Court heard the story of how a man masquerading as Spurs' centre-half Charlie Walters had inveigled his way into a young woman's affections before deserting her when she fell pregnant.

LEAGUE DEBUTANTS

Jack Elkes, Sep 8 v Middlesbrough
Sid White, Nov 3 v Nottingham Forest
Dec 29 v Birmingham Cecil Poynton
Jan 19 v Newcastle United Frank Osborne
Feb 9 v West Ham United Harry Hargreaves

Match No.	Date		Opponents		Result		Scorers	Attendan
1	Aug	25	H	Preston North End	W	2-0	Lindsay, Handley	33,4
2		27	A	Chelsea	W	1-0	Lindsay	40,0
3	Sep	1	A	Preston North End	D	2-2	Handley, Dimmock	16,0
4		3	H	Chelsea	L	0-1		31,9
5		8	H	Middlesbrough	W	2-1	Lindsay 2	32,7
6		15	A	Middlesbrough	W	1-0	Lindsay	25,0
7		22	H	Bolton Wanderers	D	0-0		35,0
8		29	A	Bolton Wanderers	L	1-3	Lindsay	25,0
9	Oct	6	A	Notts County	D	0-0		19,0
10		13	H	Notts County	L	1-3	Elkes	28,5
11		20	A	Sunderland	L	0-1		20,0
12		27	H	Sunderland	D	1-1	Lindsay	24,8
13	Nov	3	A	Nottingham Forest	D	0-0		18,0
14		10	H	Nottingham Forest	W	3-0	Lindsay, Elkes, Handley	23,8
15		17	A	Arsenal	D	1-1	Seed	50,0
16		24	H	Arsenal	W	3-0	Lindsay 2, Elkes	31,6
17	Dec	1	H	West Bromwich Albion	D	0-0		23,0
18		8	A	West Bromwich Albion	L	1-4	Seed	23,0
19		15	H	Blackburn Rovers	W	2-1	Lindsay, Elkes	19,4
20		22	A	Blackburn Rovers	W	1-0	Lindsay	15,0
21		25	H	Huddersfield Town	W	1-0	Lindsay	44,2
22		26	A	Huddersfield Town	L	1-2	Handley	29,0
23		29	H	Birmingham	D	1-1	Lindsay	24,4
24	Jan	1	A	Manchester City	L	0-1		24,0
25		5	A	Birmingham	L	2-3	Thompson, Elkes	25,0
26		19	H	Newcastle United	W	2-0	Poynton, Elkes	25,6
27		26	A	Newcastle United	D	2-2	Clay (pen), Osborne	27,0
28	Feb	9	A	West Ham United	D	0-0		30,0
29		16	H	Cardiff City	D	1-1	Smith	32,4
30	Mar	1	H	Sheffield United	L	1-2	Dimmock	25,9
31		8	A	Sheffield United	L	2-6	Lindsay, Elkes	25,0
32		15	A	Aston Villa	D	0-0		30,0
33		22	H	Aston Villa	L	2-3	Lindsay, Elkes	28,7
34		29	A	Liverpool	L	0-1		22,0
35	Apr	5	H	Liverpool	D	1-1	Grimsdell	22,4
36		7	A	Cardiff City	L	1-2	Lindsay	25,0
37		12	H	Everton	L	2-5	Walden, Lindsay	14,6
38		19	A	Everton	L	2-4	Lindsay, Raitt (og)	20,0
39		21	H	Manchester City	W	4-1	Elkes, Lindsay, Hargreaves 2	11,7
40		22	H	West Ham United	L	0-1		18,1
41		26	A	Burnley	D	2-2	Elkes, Hargreaves	50,0
42	May	3	H	Burnley	W	1-0	Elkes	20,0

Appearance
Goa

FA Cup

R1	Jan	12	A	Crystal Palace	L	0-2		17,0

Appearance
Goa

London FA Charity Cup

R1	Oct	22	A	Crystal Palace	D	1-1	Clay (pen)	3,0
R1r		29	H	Crystal Palace	W	2-1	Sharp, Brooks	7,3
R2	Nov	5	A	Clapton Orient	L	0-2		7,0

Appearance
Goa

London Professional Football Charity Fund

	Oct	8	H	Clapton Orient	L	1-3	Dimmock (pen)	6,7

Appearance
Goa

nett FW	Blake HE	Brooks S	Brown RS	Clay T	Dimmock JH	Duffus JM	Elkes AJ	Forster M	Grimsdell A	Handley CHJ	Hargreaves H	Jennings AW	Knott VJ	Lindsay AF	Lowe H	Maddison G	McDonald RJ	Osborne FR	Poynton C	Ross JR	Sage W	Seed JM	Sharp B	Skinner JF	Smith B	Thompson A	Walden FI	Walters C	White SE	Own-goals
				2	11			3	6	10				9		1						8			4		7	5		
				2	11			3	6	10				9		1						8			4		7	5		
				2	11			3		10				9	6	1						8			4		7	5		
				2	11			3	6					9		1						8			4	10	7	5		
				2	11		10	3	6					9		1						8			4		7	5		
				2	11		10	3	6					9		1						8			4		7	5		
				2	11		10	3	6					9		1						8			4		7	5		
				2	11		10	3	6	8				9		1									4		7	5		
				2	11		10	3	6					9		1						8			4		7	5		
				2	11		10	3	6							1					9	8			4		7	5		
		11		2			10	3	6					9		1						8			4		7	5		
		11		2			10	3	6					9	5	1						8			4	7				
		11		2			10		3					9	5	1						8			4		7		6	
				2			10	3	6	11				9	5	1						8			4		7			
				2			10	3	6	11				9	5	1						8			4		7			
				2			10	3	6	11				9	5	1						8			4		7			
				2			10	3	6	11				9	5	1						8			4		7			
				2			10	3	6	11				9	5	1						8			4		7			
				2			10	3	6	11				9	5	1						8			4		7			
				2			10	3	6	11				9	5	1						8			4		7			
				2			10	3	6	11				9	5	1						8			4		7			
				2			10	3	6	11				9	5	1									4	8	7			
				2			10	3		11				9	5	1			6			8			4	7				
				2	11		10	3		7				9	5	1			6						4	8				
					11		10	3	6	7				9	5	1				2					4	8				
				2			10	3		11				9	5	1		8	6						4		7			
				2			10	3		11				9	5	1		8	6						4		7			
							10	3		11	9					1	2	8	4								7	5	6	
				2			10	3		11	9					1		8	6						4		7	5		
	1			2	11			3		10				9				8	6						4			5		
	1			2	11		10	3			9			8					6						4			5		
				2	11		10	3						8		1		9	6		5				4	7				
				2	11		10	3	6					9		1		8			5				4		7			
				2	11		10		6					9		1		8	3		5				4		7			
				2	11		10	3	6					9		1		8			5				4		7			
				2	11		10	3	6					9		1		8			5				4		7			
				2	11		10	3	6					9	5	1		8							4		7			
	1		3	2	11		10							9	5			8						6	4		7			
	1		3	2	11		8				10			9	5									6	4		7			
	1		3	2	11		8				10			9	5										4		7		6	
	1			2	11		8				10			9	5		3								4		7		6	
	1			2	11		8			7	10			9			3				5				4				6	
[illegible]	7	3	3	40	25	0	37	35	27	22	7	0	0	39	22	35	3	12	10	1	7	21	0	2	41	7	34	15	5	
				1	2		11		1	4	3			20				1	1			2			1	1	1			1

nett FW	Blake HE	Brooks S	Brown RS	Clay T	Dimmock JH	Duffus JM	Elkes AJ	Forster M	Grimsdell A	Handley CHJ	Hargreaves H	Jennings AW	Knott VJ	Lindsay AF	Lowe H	Maddison G	McDonald RJ	Osborne FR	Poynton C	Ross JR	Sage W	Seed JM	Sharp B	Skinner JF	Smith B	Thompson A	Walden FI	Walters C	White SE	Own-goals
				2			10	3	6	11				9	5	1									4	8	7			
0	0	0	0	1	0	0	1	1	1	1	0	0	0	1	1	1	0	0	0	0	0	0	0	0	1	1	1	0	0	

nett FW	Blake HE	Brooks S	Brown RS	Clay T	Dimmock JH	Duffus JM	Elkes AJ	Forster M	Grimsdell A	Handley CHJ	Hargreaves H	Jennings AW	Knott VJ	Lindsay AF	Lowe H	Maddison G	McDonald RJ	Osborne FR	Poynton C	Ross JR	Sage W	Seed JM	Sharp B	Skinner JF	Smith B	Thompson A	Walden FI	Walters C	White SE	Own-goals
		11		2			10	3	6	7						1					9	8			4			5		
		11		2		9		3	6				8		5	1							10		4	7				
		11		2					6			9			5	1	3					8	10		4		7			
0	0	3	0	3	0	1	1	2	3	1	0	1	1	0	2	3	1	0	0	0	1	2	2	0	3	1	1	1	0	
		1		1																			1							

nett FW	Blake HE	Brooks S	Brown RS	Clay T	Dimmock JH	Duffus JM	Elkes AJ	Forster M	Grimsdell A	Handley CHJ	Hargreaves H	Jennings AW	Knott VJ	Lindsay AF	Lowe H	Maddison G	McDonald RJ	Osborne FR	Poynton C	Ross JR	Sage W	Seed JM	Sharp B	Skinner JF	Smith B	Thompson A	Walden FI	Walters C	White SE	Own-goals
					11		9	3	6	10						1				2		8			4		7	5		
0	0	0	0	0	1	0	1	1	1	1	0	0	0	0	0	1	0	0	0	1	0	1	0	0	1	0	1	1	0	
					1																									

League Table

	P	W	D	L	F	A	Pts
Huddersfield Town	42	23	11	8	60	33	57
Cardiff City	42	22	13	7	61	34	57
Sunderland	42	22	9	11	71	54	53
Bolton Wanderers	42	18	14	10	68	34	50
Sheffield United	42	19	12	11	69	49	50
Aston Villa	42	18	13	11	52	37	49
Everton	42	18	13	11	62	53	49
Blackburn Rovers	42	17	11	14	54	50	45
Newcastle United	42	17	10	15	60	54	44
Notts County	42	14	14	14	44	49	42
Manchester City	42	15	12	15	54	71	42
Liverpool	42	15	11	16	49	48	41
West Ham United	42	13	15	14	40	43	41
Birmingham	42	13	13	16	41	49	39
TOTTENHAM HOTSPUR	42	12	14	16	50	56	38
West Bromwich Albion	42	12	14	16	51	62	38
Burnley	42	12	12	18	55	60	36
Preston North End	42	12	10	20	52	67	34
Arsenal	42	12	9	21	40	63	33
Nottingham Forest	42	10	12	20	42	64	32
Chelsea	42	9	14	19	31	53	32
Middlesbrough	42	7	8	27	37	60	22

1924-25

DIVISION ONE

Manager: Peter McWilliam

Did you know that?

In March 1925 Spurs were ordered to post warning notices that further misconduct could result in White Hart Lane being closed. It followed an incident in the Bolton Wanderers FA Cup tie on 31 January 1925 when what appeared to be an empty beer bottle was thrown on the pitch after a Spurs player had been badly fouled. Groundsman John Over was censured for not retaining the bottle and handing it to the referee after the match, even though it was the official who picked it up and pocketed it before giving it to an official!

LEAGUE DEBUTANTS

Aug 30	v Bolton Wanderers	Bill Hinton
Sep 6	v Notts County	Bill Lane
Nov 1	v Aston Villa	Harry Skitt

Match No.	Date			Opponents	Result		Scorers	Attendance
1	Aug	30	H	Bolton Wanderers	W	3-0	Clay (pen), Lindsay, Hargreaves	42,00
2	Sep	3	A	Birmingham	W	2-0	Seed, Dimmock	20,00
3		6	A	Notts County	D	0-0		20,03
4		8	A	West Bromwich Albion	L	0-2		17,00
5		13	H	Everton	D	0-0		35,03
6		20	A	Sunderland	L	1-4	Lindsay	30,00
7		22	H	West Bromwich Albion	L	0-1		16,28
8		27	H	Cardiff City	D	1-1	Elkes	38,32
9	Oct	4	A	Preston North End	W	3-0	Seed 2, Dimmock	20,00
10		11	H	Burnley	D	1-1	Handley	23,50
11		18	A	Leeds United	L	0-1		25,00
12		25	A	Arsenal	L	0-1		51,00
13	Nov	1	H	Aston Villa	L	1-3	Handley	19,05
14		8	A	Huddersfield Town	W	2-1	Thompson, Seed	18,00
15		10	H	Manchester City	D	1-1	Smith	10,78
16		15	H	Blackburn Rovers	W	5-0	Seed 2, Elkes 3	30,00
17		22	A	West Ham United	D	1-1	Elkes	30,00
18		29	H	Sheffield United	W	4-1	Seed, Hargreaves, Elkes, Handley	24,48
19	Dec	6	A	Newcastle United	D	1-1	Elkes	28,00
20		13	H	Liverpool	D	1-1	Hargreaves	25,60
21		20	A	Nottingham Forest	L	0-1		15,00
22		25	H	Bury	D	1-1	Elkes (pen)	35,71
23		27	A	Bolton Wanderers	L	0-3		18,00
24	Jan	1	A	Bury	L	2-5	Seed 2	18,00
25		3	H	Notts County	D	1-1	Elkes	23,93
26		17	A	Everton	L	0-1		30,00
27		24	H	Sunderland	W	1-0	Seed	26,69
28	Feb	7	H	Preston North End	W	2-0	Seed, Lane	35,00
29		14	A	Burnley	W	4-1	Clay (pen), Thompson, Seed, Lane	18,00
30		28	H	Arsenal	W	2-0	Elkes, Dimmock	29,45
31	Mar	7	A	Aston Villa	W	1-0	Lane	25,00
32		9	H	Leeds United	W	2-1	Seed, Lane	8,00
33		14	H	Huddersfield Town	L	1-2	Lane	35,00
34		18	A	Cardiff City	W	2-0	Seed 2	31,12
35		21	A	Blackburn Rovers	D	1-1	Thompson	15,00
36		28	H	West Ham United	D	1-1	Seed	29,32
37	Apr	4	A	Sheffield United	L	0-2		20,00
38		10	H	Birmingham	L	0-1		30,41
39		11	H	Newcastle United	W	3-0	Lane, Dimmock 2	23,14
40		18	A	Liverpool	L	0-1		12,00
41		25	H	Nottingham Forest	W	1-0	Seed	19,00
42	May	2	A	Manchester City	L	0-1		10,00

Appearance

Goa

FA Cup

R1	Jan	10	H	Northampton Town	W	3-0	Seed, Lindsay, Elkes	32,71
R2		31	H	Bolton Wanderers	D	1-1	Seed	52,63
R2r	Feb	4	A	Bolton Wanderers	W	1-0	Lane	51,77
R3		21	H	Blackburn Rovers	D	2-2	Lane, Dimmock	54,52
R3r		26	A	Blackburn Rovers	L	1-3	Dimmock	48,00

Appearance

Goal

London FA Charity Cup

R1	Oct	27	H	Fulham	H	5-1	Osborne, Hargreaves, Elkes 3	3,55
R2	Nov	17	H	Kingstonians	W	5-0	Skitt, Osborne, Seed, Hargreaves, Elkes	
SF		24	N*	Clapton Orient	L	1-2	Hargreaves	

*played at Highbury

Appearance

Goal

London Professional Football Charity Fund

	Nov	3	A	Clapton Orient	L*	1-2	Hargreaves (pen)	2,30

*abandoned after 20 mins of extra-time - bad light

Appearance

Goal

	Dimmock JH	Elkes AJ	Forster M	Grimsdell A	Handley CHJ	Hargreaves H	Hinton WFW	Lane WHC	Lindsay AF	Lowe H	McDonald RJ	Osborne FR	Poynton C	Sage W	Seed JM	Sharp B	Skinner JF	Skitt H	Smith B	Thompson A	Walters C	White SE
	11	5				10	1		9			7	3		8				4			6
	11	5				10	1		9			7	3		8				4			6
	11	5				10	1	9			3	7			8		6		4			
	11	5				10	1	9			3	7			8		6		4			
	11	5				10	1		9			7	3		8		6		4			
	11	5				10	1		9			7	3		8		6		4			
	11	5					1		9			7	3		8	10	6		4			
	11	10		6			1		9	5			3	7	8		4					
	11	10					1		9	5		7	3		8		6		4			
	11				10		1		9	5		7	3		8		6		4			
	11	10	2				1		9	5		7	3		8				4			6
	11	10	2				1		9	5		7	3		8				4			6
		10	2		11	9	1					7	3		8		6	5	4			
		10	2		11	9	1						3		8		6		4	7	5	
		10	2		11	9	1						3		8		6		4	7	5	
		10			11	9	1				2	7	3		8		6	5	4			
		10	2		11	9	1					7	3		8		6	5	4			
		10	2		11	9	1				3	7			8		6	5	4			
		10	2		11	9	1				3	7			8		6	5	4			
		10	2		11	9	1				3	7			8		6	5	4			
		10	3		11		1		9			7			8		6	5	4			
		10	2		11		1		9			7	3		8		6	5	4			
	11	10	2				1		9			7	3		8		6	5	4			
	11	10	2				1		9			7	3		8		6	5	4			
		10	2				1		9			7	3		8		6	5	4	11		
		10	2				1		9			7	3		8		6	5	4	11		
		10	2		7		1		9				3		8		6	5	4	11		
	11	10					1	9			3				8			5	4	7		6
	11	10		6			1	9			3				8		4	5		7		
	11	10	2				1	9			3				8		6	5	4	7		
	11	10		6			1	9			3				8			5	4	7		
	11	10	2	6			1	9		5	3				8				4	7		
	11		2	6	10		1	9			3				8			5	4	7		
	11			6	10		1	9					3		8		4	5		7		
	11	10		6			1	9					3		8		4	5		7		
	11	10		6			1	9					3		8		4	5		7		
	11			3		10	1	9	8								6	5	4	7		
	11			3		10	1	9							8		6	5	4	7		
	11		2	3		10	1	9							8		6	5	4	7		
	11			3		10	1	9							8		6	5	4	7		
	11			3		10	1	9							8		6	5	4	7		
	11		2	3		10	1	9							8		6	5	4	7		
Apps	29	33	21	14	14	20	42	17	18	6	12	23	24	1	41	1	34	27	37	20	2	5
Goals	5	10			3	3		6	2						17				1	3		

	Dimmock JH	Elkes AJ	Forster M	Grimsdell A	Handley CHJ	Hargreaves H	Hinton WFW	Lane WHC	Lindsay AF	Lowe H	McDonald RJ	Osborne FR	Poynton C	Sage W	Seed JM	Sharp B	Skinner JF	Skitt H	Smith B	Thompson A	Walters C	White SE
		10	2				1		9			7	3		8		6	5	4	11		
	11	10		6			1	9			3	7			8		4	5				
	11	10		6			1	9			3				8			5	4	7		
	11	10		6			1	9			3				8		4	5		7		
	11	10		6			1	9			3				8		4	5		7		
Apps	4	5	1	4	0	0	5	4	1	0	4	2	1	0	5	0	4	5	2	4	0	0
Goals	2	1						2	1						2							

	Dimmock JH	Elkes AJ	Forster M	Grimsdell A	Handley CHJ	Hargreaves H	Hinton WFW	Lane WHC	Lindsay AF	Lowe H	McDonald RJ	Osborne FR	Poynton C	Sage W	Seed JM	Sharp B	Skinner JF	Skitt H	Smith B	Thompson A	Walters C	White SE
		10	2		11	9	1					7	3		8		6	5	4			
		10			11	9	1				2	7	3		8		6	5	4			
			2		11	10	1		9			7	3				6	5	4	8		
Apps	0	2	2	0	3	3	3	0	1	0	1	3	3	0	2	0	3	3	3	1	0	0
Goals		4				3						2			1			1				

	Dimmock JH	Elkes AJ	Forster M	Grimsdell A	Handley CHJ	Hargreaves H	Hinton WFW	Lane WHC	Lindsay AF	Lowe H	McDonald RJ	Osborne FR	Poynton C	Sage W	Seed JM	Sharp B	Skinner JF	Skitt H	Smith B	Thompson A	Walters C	White SE
		10	2		11	9	1			5			3		8		6		4	7		
Apps	0	1	1	0	1	1	1	0	0	1	0	0	1	0	1	0	1	0	1	1	0	0
Goals						1																

League Table

	P	W	D	L	F	A	Pts
Huddersfield Town	42	21	16	5	69	28	58
West Bromwich Albion	42	23	10	9	58	34	56
Bolton Wanderers	42	22	11	9	76	34	55
Liverpool	42	20	10	12	63	55	50
Bury	42	17	15	10	54	51	49
Newcastle United	42	16	16	10	61	42	48
Sunderland	42	19	10	13	64	51	48
Birmingham	42	17	12	13	49	53	46
Notts County	42	16	13	13	42	31	45
Manchester City	42	17	9	16	76	68	43
Cardiff City	42	16	11	15	56	51	43
TOTTENHAM HOTSPUR	42	15	12	15	52	43	42
West Ham United	42	15	12	15	62	60	42
Sheffield United	42	13	13	16	55	63	39
Aston Villa	42	13	13	16	58	71	39
Blackburn Rovers	42	11	13	18	53	66	35
Everton	42	12	11	19	40	60	35
Leeds United	42	11	12	19	46	59	34
Burnley	42	11	12	19	46	75	34
Arsenal	42	14	5	23	46	58	33
Preston North End	42	10	6	26	37	74	26
Nottingham Forest	42	6	12	24	29	65	24

1925-26

DIVISION ONE

Manager: Peter McWilliam

Did you know that?

Frank Osborne's hat-trick of hat-tricks in the games against Liverpool, Leicester City and West Ham United in October–November 1925 remains a unique achievement in Spurs' history.

LEAGUE DEBUTANTS

Oct 10	v Bury Bill Kaine
Oct 31	v Leicester City Jimmy Smith
Mar 20	v West Ham United John Britton
Mar 25	v Newcastle United Bill Bann
Apr 3	v Bolton Wanderers Tommy Roe

Match No.	Date			Opponents	Result		Scorers	Attendance
1	Aug	29	A	Arsenal	W	1-0	Dimmock	53,18
2		31	A	Sheffield United	W	3-2	Osborne 2, Hargreaves	18,74
3	Sep	5	H	Manchester City	W	1-0	Seed	35,59
4		7	H	Sheffield United	W	3-2	Seed 2, Dimmock	21,97
5		12	A	Everton	D	1-1	Dimmock	37,50
6		14	H	Cardiff City	L	1-2	Elkes	26,71
7		19	H	Huddersfield Town	D	5-5	Clay (pen), Osborne, Elkes 2, Dimmock	20,88
8		21	A	Cardiff City	W	1-0	Dimmock	20,69
9		26	A	Sunderland	L	0-3		30,70
10	Oct	3	H	Blackburn Rovers	W	4-2	Thompson, Osborne 2, Dimmock	35,64
11		10	A	Bury	L	0-3		19,75
12		17	A	Manchester United	D	0-0		26,49
13		24	H	Liverpool	W	3-1	Osborne 3	29,95
14		31	A	Leicester City	L	3-5	Osborne 3	28,07
15	Nov	7	H	West Ham United	W	4-2	Osborne 3, Elkes	35,25
16		14	A	Newcastle United	L	1-3	Seed	23,39
17		21	H	Bolton Wanderers	L	2-3	Osborne, Elkes	26,79
18		28	A	Notts County	L	2--4	Elkes, Dimmock	12,19
19	Dec	5	H	Aston Villa	D	2-2	Osborne, Elkes	28,82
20		12	A	Burnley	W	2-1	Osborne, Dimmock	18,59
21		19	H	Leeds United	W	3-2	Thompson, Osborne, Elkes	19,20
22		25	A	Birmingham	L	1-3	Clay (pen)	29,58
23		26	H	Birmingham	W	2-1	Seed, Osborne	44,42
24	Jan	2	H	Arsenal	D	1-1	Thompson	43,22
25		16	A	Manchester City	D	0-0		25,24
26		23	H	Everton	D	1-1	Thompson	22,80
27	Feb	6	H	Sunderland	L	0-2		31,43
28		13	A	Blackburn Rovers	L	2-4	Osborne, Dimmock	21,58
29		20	H	Bury	W	4-2	Lindsay 2, Osborne 2	33,02
30		27	H	Manchester United	L	0-1		25,46
31	Mar	3	A	Huddersfield Town	L	1-2	Elkes	13,06
32		6	A	Liverpool	D	0-0		26,35
33		13	H	Leicester City	L	1-3	Osborne	23,91
34		20	A	West Ham United	L	1-3	Osborne	29,42
35		25	H	Newcastle United	W	1-0	Dimmock	11,77
36	Apr	2	H	West Bromwich Albion	W	3-2	Seed, Dimmock 2	27,91
37		3	A	Bolton Wanderers	D	1-1	Osborne	21,36
38		5	A	West Bromwich Albion	L	0-1		15,36
39		10	H	Notts County	W	4-0	Roe, Elkes, Dimmock 2	17,89
40		17	A	Aston Villa	L	0-3		11,77
41		24	H	Burnley	L	0-2		21,21
42	May	1	A	Leeds United	L	1-4	Elkes	16,15
								Appearances
								Goals

FA Cup

R1	Jan	9	H	West Ham United	W	5-0	Osborne 2, Dimmock 3	49,80
R2		30	H	Manchester United	D	2-2	Thompson, Lindsay	43,65
R2r	Feb	3	A	Manchester United	L	0-2		46,92
								Appearances
								Goals

London FA Charity Cup

R1	Sep	15	H	Brentford	L	1-2	Handley	1,98
								Appearances
								Goals

London Professional Football Charity Fund

	Nov	16	H	Queen's Park Rangers	W	1-0	Thompson	1,39
								Appearances
								Goals

Britton J	Clay T	Dimmock JH	Elkes AJ	Forster M	Grimsdell A	Handley CHJ	Hargreaves H	Hinton WFW	Kaine WEJC	Knott VJ	Lane WHC	Lindsay AF	Lowe H	Osborne FR	Poynton C	Roe TW	Sage W	Seed JM	Skinner JF	Skitt H	Smith B	Smith JHA	Thompson A	Walters C	White SE
	2	11		3	6	10		1				9						8	4	5			7		
	2	11		3	6		10	1				9		7				8	4	5					
	2	11	10	3	6			1				9		7				8		5	4				
	2	11	10	3	6			1				9		7				8	4					5	
	2	11	10	3	6			1				9	5	7				8			4				
	2	11	10	3	6			1				9	5	7				8			4				
	2	11	10	3	6			1				9		7				8	4		5				
	2	11	10	3	6			1			9			7			5				4		8		
	2	11	10	3	6			1			9			7				8	4	5					
	2	11	10	3	6			1						9					4	5	8		7		
	2	11	10	3					1					9			5	8	6		4		7		
	2	11	10	3	6				1					9			5	8			4		7		
	2	11	10	3	6			1						9				8		5	4		7		
	2	11	10	3	6									9				8		5	4	1	7		
	2	11	10	3										9				8	6	5	4	1	7		
	2	11	10	3										9				8	6	5	4	1	7		
	2	11	10	3										9				8	6	5	4	1	7		
	2	11	10	3					1					9				8	6	5	4		7		
	2	11	10	3					1					9				8	6	5	4		7		
	2	11	10	3					1					9				8	6	5	4		7		
	2	11	10	3					1					9				8	6	5	4		7		
	2	11		3					1			10		9			4	8		5	6		7		
	2			3			10		1			11		9				8	6	5	4		7		
	2	11	10	3					1			8		9					6	5	4		7		
	2	11	10	3					1			8		9						5	4		7		6
	2	11	10	3					1			9						8		5	4		7		6
	2	11		3			10	1				8		9						5	4		7		6
	2	11		3			10	1				8		9						5	4		7		6
	2	11		3			10	1				8		9						5	4		7		6
	2	11		3			10	1				8		9						5	4		7		6
	2		10	3			11							9				8		5	4	1	7		6
	2	11	10	3										9				8		5	4	1	7		6
	2	11	10	3										9				8		5	4	1	7		6
1	2	11	10	3							8			9						5	4		7		6
1		11	10	3								6		9				8		5	4		7		
1		11	10	3								6		9				8		5	4		7		
1		11		3								6		9		8		10		5	4		7		
1		11		3								6		9		8		10		5	4		7		
1		11	10	3								6		9		8				5	4		7		
1		11		3								6		9		8		10		5	4		7		
1		11	10	3								6		9				8		5	4		7		
1		11	8	3		10					9	6								5	4		7		
9	34	40	31	42	13	2	7	15	11	0	4	24	2	39	0	4	4	31	16	35	38	7	35	1	10
	2	14	11				1					2		25		1		6					4		

Britton J	Clay T	Dimmock JH	Elkes AJ	Forster M	Grimsdell A	Handley CHJ	Hargreaves H	Hinton WFW	Kaine WEJC	Knott VJ	Lane WHC	Lindsay AF	Lowe H	Osborne FR	Poynton C	Roe TW	Sage W	Seed JM	Skinner JF	Skitt H	Smith B	Smith JHA	Thompson A	Walters C	White SE
	2	11	10	3					1			8		9					6	5	4		7		
	2	11	10	3				1				9						8		5	4		7		6
	2	11	10	3				1				9						8		5	4		7		6
0	3	3	3	3	0	0	0	2	1	0	0	3	0	1	0	0	0	2	1	3	3	0	3	0	2
		3										1		2									1		

Britton J	Clay T	Dimmock JH	Elkes AJ	Forster M	Grimsdell A	Handley CHJ	Hargreaves H	Hinton WFW	Kaine WEJC	Knott VJ	Lane WHC	Lindsay AF	Lowe H	Osborne FR	Poynton C	Roe TW	Sage W	Seed JM	Skinner JF	Skitt H	Smith B	Smith JHA	Thompson A	Walters C	White SE
		11		3		10		1		8	9				5						4		7		6
0	0	1	0	1	0	1	0	1	0	1	1	0	0	0	1	0	0	0	0	0	1	0	1	0	1
						1																			

Britton J	Clay T	Dimmock JH	Elkes AJ	Forster M	Grimsdell A	Handley CHJ	Hargreaves H	Hinton WFW	Kaine WEJC	Knott VJ	Lane WHC	Lindsay AF	Lowe H	Osborne FR	Poynton C	Roe TW	Sage W	Seed JM	Skinner JF	Skitt H	Smith B	Smith JHA	Thompson A	Walters C	White SE
	2	11	10	3										9				8	6	5	4	1	7		
0	1	1	1	1	0	0	0	0	0	0	0	0	0	1	0	0	0	1	1	1	1	1	1	0	0
																							1		

League Table

	P	W	D	L	F	A	Pts
Huddersfield Town	42	21	16	5	69	28	58
West Bromwich Albion	42	23	10	9	58	34	56
Bolton Wanderers	42	22	11	9	76	34	55
Liverpool	42	20	10	12	63	55	50
Bury	42	17	15	10	54	51	49
Newcastle United	42	16	16	10	61	42	48
Sunderland	42	19	10	13	64	51	48
Birmingham	42	17	12	13	49	53	46
Notts County	42	16	13	13	42	31	45
Manchester City	42	17	9	16	76	68	43
Cardiff City	42	16	11	15	56	51	43
TOTTENHAM HOTSPUR	42	15	12	15	52	43	42
West Ham United	42	15	12	15	62	60	42
Sheffield United	42	13	13	16	55	63	39
Aston Villa	42	13	13	16	58	71	39
Blackburn Rovers	42	11	13	18	53	66	35
Everton	42	12	11	19	40	60	35
Leeds United	42	11	12	19	46	59	34
Burnley	42	11	12	19	46	75	34
Arsenal	42	14	5	23	46	58	33
Preston North End	42	10	6	26	37	74	26
Nottingham Forest	42	6	12	24	29	65	24

1926-27

DIVISION ONE

Manager: Peter McWilliam until February then Billy Minter

Did you know that?

Jimmy Blair became the first Spurs player to be sent off in a Football League game when he received his marching orders at Huddersfield Town on 29 January 1927.

LEAGUE DEBUTANTS

Aug 28 v Everton
John Blair
Jan 15 v Everton
Taffy O'Callaghan
Feb 19 v Bury
Arthur Sanders
Apr 16 v Newcastle United
Jock Richardson
Apr 30 v Liverpool
Walter Bellamy
Apr 30 v Liverpool
Joe Nicholls

Match No.	Date		Opponents		Result		Scorers	Attendanc
1	Aug	28	H	Everton	W	2-1	Blair, Osborne	28,32
2		30	H	Sheffield Wednesday	W	7-3	Elkes 2, Thompson, Blair, Osborne, Seed, Dimmock	19,72
3	Sep	4	A	Blackburn Rovers	L	0-1		21,96
4		6	H	Leicester City	D	2-2	Dimmock 2	19,46
5		11	H	Huddersfield Town	D	3-3	Thompson, Blair 2	29,51
6		13	A	Leicester City	D	2-2	Lane, Dimmock	24,92
7		18	A	Sunderland	L	2-3	Blair 2	17,45
8		25	H	West Bromwich Albion	W	3-0	Blair, Osborne, Seed	31,23
9	Oct	2	A	Bury	D	0-0		16,58
10		9	H	Birmingham	W	6-1	Blair 2, Roe 2, Seed, Dimmock	29,39
11		16	H	Sheffield United	W	3-1	Osborne 2, Seed	29,65
12		23	A	Derby County	L	1-4	Handley	20,32
13		30	H	Bolton Wanderers	W	1-0	Handley	29,99
14	Nov	6	A	Aston Villa	W	3-2	Seed 2, Dimmock	19,49
15		13	H	Cardiff City	W	4-1	Osborne 2, Handley, Dimmock	15,35
16		20	A	Burnley	L	0-5		17,95
17		27	H	Newcastle United	L	1-3	Dimmock	33,32
18	Dec	4	A	Leeds United	D	1-1	Dimmock	24,47
19		11	H	Liverpool	L	1-2	Blair	26,64
20		18	A	Arsenal	W	4-2	Seed, Osborne 2, Handley	49,42
21		25	H	Manchester United	D	1-1	Dimmock	37,28
22		27	A	Manchester United	L	1-2	Handley	50,66
23		28	A	Sheffield Wednesday	L	1-3	Dimmock	35,52
24	Jan	15	A	Everton	W	2-1	Blair, Dimmock	35,98
25		22	H	Blackburn Rovers	D	1-1	Handley	14,32
26		29	A	Huddersfield Town	L	0-2		15,14
27	Feb	5	H	Sunderland	L	0-2		32,50
28		12	A	West Bromwich Albion	L	0-5		15,38
29		19	H	Bury	W	1-0	Dimmock (pen)	19,75
30		26	A	Birmingham	L	0-1		21,14
31	Mar	5	A	Sheffield United	D	3-3	O'Callaghan 2, Sanders	21,73
32		12	H	Derby County	W	3-2	O'Callaghan, Roe, Dimmock	26,55
33		19	A	Bolton Wanderers	D	2-2	Sanders, Dimmock	17,76
34		26	H	Aston Villa	L	0-1		30,61
35	Apr	2	A	Cardiff City	W	2-1	O'Callaghan, Handley	13,38
36		9	H	Burnley	W	4-1	O'Callaghan, Sanders 2, Dimmock	15,48
37		15	H	West Ham United	L	1-3	Handley	42,01
38		16	A	Newcastle United	L	2-3	Sanders, Dimmock	32,15
39		18	A	West Ham United	W	2-1	Handley, Dimmock	21,35
40		23	H	Leeds United	W	4-1	Sanders 2, Handley, Dimmock (pen)	17,74
41		30	A	Liverpool	L	0-1		15,75
42	May	7	H	Arsenal	L	0-4		29,55

Appearance
Goa

FA Cup

R3	Jan	8	A	West Ham United	L	2-3	Handley, Dimmock	44,41

Appearance
Goa

London FA Charity Cup

R1	Sep	27	A	Millwall	L	2-5	Lane, Seed	2,83

Appearance
Goa

London Professional Football Charity Fund

	Nov	8	A	Clapton Orient	W	3-1	Thompson, Roe, Dimmock	86

Appearance
Goa

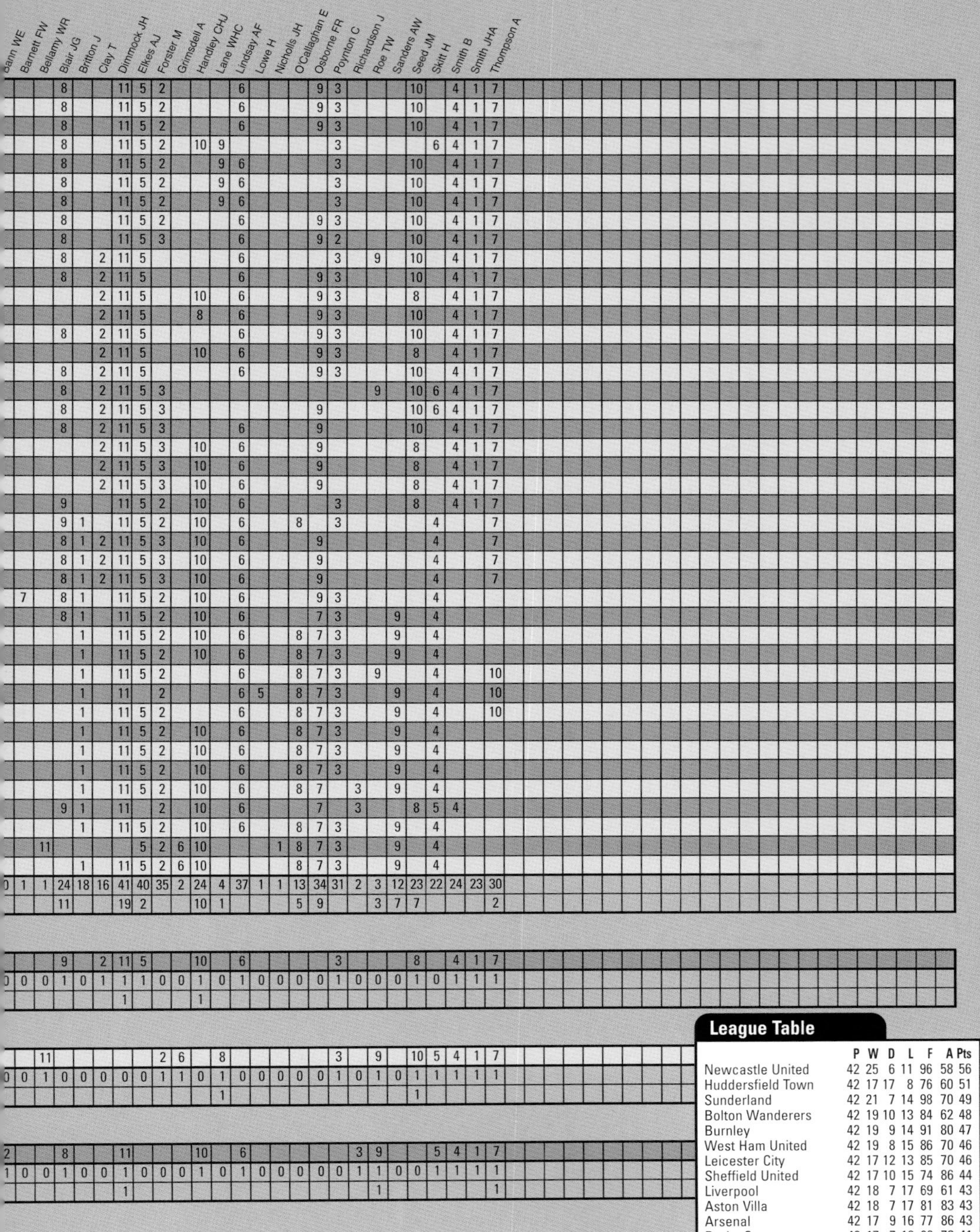

ann WE	Barnett FW	Bellamy WR	Blair JG	Britton J	Clay T	Dimmock JH	Elkes AJ	Forster M	Grimsdell A	Handley CHJ	Lane WHC	Lindsay AF	Lowe H	Nicholls JH	O'Callaghan E	Osborne FR	Poynton C	Richardson J	Roe TW	Sanders AW	Seed JM	Skitt H	Smith B	Smith JHA	Thompson A
			8			11	5	2				6				9	3				10		4	1	7
			8			11	5	2				6				9	3				10		4	1	7
			8			11	5	2				6				9	3				10		4	1	7
			8			11	5	2		10	9						3					6	4	1	7
			8			11	5	2			9	6					3				10		4	1	7
			8			11	5	2			9	6					3				10		4	1	7
			8			11	5	2			9	6					3				10		4	1	7
			8			11	5	2				6				9	3				10		4	1	7
			8			11	5	3				6				9	2				10		4	1	7
			8		2	11	5					6					3		9		10		4	1	7
			8		2	11	5					6				9	3				10		4	1	7
					2	11	5			10		6				9	3				8		4	1	7
					2	11	5			8		6				9	3				10		4	1	7
			8		2	11	5					6				9	3				10		4	1	7
					2	11	5			10		6				9	3				8		4	1	7
			8		2	11	5					6				9	3				10		4	1	7
			8		2	11	5	3											9		10	6	4	1	7
			8		2	11	5	3								9					10	6	4	1	7
			8		2	11	5	3				6				9					10		4	1	7
					2	11	5	3		10		6				9					8		4	1	7
					2	11	5	3		10		6				9					8		4	1	7
					2	11	5	3		10		6				9					8		4	1	7
			9			11	5	2		10		6					3				8		4	1	7
			9	1		11	5	2		10		6			8		3					4			7
			8	1	2	11	5	3		10		6				9						4			7
			8	1	2	11	5	3		10		6				9						4			7
			8	1	2	11	5	3		10		6				9						4			7
	7		8	1		11	5	2		10		6				9	3					4			
			8	1		11	5	2		10		6				7	3			9		4			
				1		11	5	2		10		6			8	7	3			9		4			
				1		11	5	2		10		6			8	7	3			9		4			
				1		11	5	2				6			8	7	3		9			4			10
				1		11		2				6	5		8	7	3			9		4			10
				1		11	5	2				6			8	7	3			9		4			10
				1		11	5	2		10		6			8	7	3			9		4			
				1		11	5	2		10		6			8	7	3			9		4			
				1		11	5	2		10		6			8	7	3			9		4			
				1		11	5	2		10		6			8	7		3		9		4			
			9	1		11		2		10		6				7		3			8	5	4		
				1		11	5	2		10		6			8	7	3			9		4			
		11					5	2	6	10				1	8	7	3			9		4			
				1		11	5	2	6	10					8	7	3			9		4			
0	1	1	24	18	16	41	40	35	2	24	4	37	1	1	13	34	31	2	3	12	23	22	24	23	30
			11			19	2			10	1				5	9			3	7	7				2

ann WE	Barnett FW	Bellamy WR	Blair JG	Britton J	Clay T	Dimmock JH	Elkes AJ	Forster M	Grimsdell A	Handley CHJ	Lane WHC	Lindsay AF	Lowe H	Nicholls JH	O'Callaghan E	Osborne FR	Poynton C	Richardson J	Roe TW	Sanders AW	Seed JM	Skitt H	Smith B	Smith JHA	Thompson A
			9		2	11	5			10		6					3				8		4	1	7
0	0	0	1	0	1	1	1	0	0	1	0	1	0	0	0	0	1	0	0	0	1	0	1	1	1
						1				1															

ann WE	Barnett FW	Bellamy WR	Blair JG	Britton J	Clay T	Dimmock JH	Elkes AJ	Forster M	Grimsdell A	Handley CHJ	Lane WHC	Lindsay AF	Lowe H	Nicholls JH	O'Callaghan E	Osborne FR	Poynton C	Richardson J	Roe TW	Sanders AW	Seed JM	Skitt H	Smith B	Smith JHA	Thompson A
		11						2	6		8						3		9		10	5	4	1	7
0	0	1	0	0	0	0	0	1	1	0	1	0	0	0	0	0	1	0	1	0	1	1	1	1	1
											1										1				

ann WE	Barnett FW	Bellamy WR	Blair JG	Britton J	Clay T	Dimmock JH	Elkes AJ	Forster M	Grimsdell A	Handley CHJ	Lane WHC	Lindsay AF	Lowe H	Nicholls JH	O'Callaghan E	Osborne FR	Poynton C	Richardson J	Roe TW	Sanders AW	Seed JM	Skitt H	Smith B	Smith JHA	Thompson A
2			8			11				10		6						3	9			5	4	1	7
1	0	0	1	0	0	1	0	0	0	1	0	1	0	0	0	0	0	1	1	0	0	1	1	1	1
						1													1						1

League Table

	P	W	D	L	F	A	Pts
Newcastle United	42	25	6	11	96	58	56
Huddersfield Town	42	17	17	8	76	60	51
Sunderland	42	21	7	14	98	70	49
Bolton Wanderers	42	19	10	13	84	62	48
Burnley	42	19	9	14	91	80	47
West Ham United	42	19	8	15	86	70	46
Leicester City	42	17	12	13	85	70	46
Sheffield United	42	17	10	15	74	86	44
Liverpool	42	18	7	17	69	61	43
Aston Villa	42	18	7	17	81	83	43
Arsenal	42	17	9	16	77	86	43
Derby County	42	17	7	18	86	73	41
TOTTENHAM HOTSPUR	42	16	9	17	76	78	41
Cardiff City	42	16	9	17	55	65	41
Manchester United	42	13	14	15	52	64	40
Sheffield Wednesday	42	15	9	18	75	92	39
Birmingham	42	17	4	21	64	73	38
Blackburn Rovers	42	15	8	19	77	96	38
Bury	42	12	12	18	68	77	36
Everton	42	12	10	20	64	90	34
Leeds United	42	11	8	23	69	88	30
West Bromwich Albion	42	11	8	23	65	86	30

1927-28

DIVISION ONE

Manager: Billy Minter

Did you know that?

When Peter McWilliam went to watch Mid-Rhondda against Ton Pentre in February 1920 it was said he had gone to run the rule over 'Darkie' Lowdell but returned with Jimmy Seed. In August 1927 Seed was transferred to Sheffield Wednesday with Lowdell moving to Spurs.

LEAGUE DEBUTANTS

Aug 27	v Birmingham	Albert Evans
Aug 27	v Birmingham	'Darkie' Lowdell
Sep 24	v Manchester United	Sid Helliwell
Oct 1	v Everton	Jimmy Townley
Dec 3	v Burnley	Cyril Spiers
Dec 31	v Birmingham	Jimmy Armstrong
Dec 31	v Birmingham	Percy Austin

Match No.	Date			Opponents	Result		Scorers	Attendance
1	Aug	27	H	Birmingham	W	1-0	O'Callaghan	37,40
2		31	A	Middlesbrough	L	1-3	Dimmock (pen)	29,11
3	Sep	3	A	Newcastle United	L	1-4	O'Callaghan	41,03
4		10	H	Huddersfield Town	D	2-2	Lindsay (pen), Dimmock	27,98
5		12	H	Middlesbrough	W	4-2	Blair 3, Dimmock (pen)	19,21
6		17	A	Portsmouth	L	0-3		26,11
7		22	H	Leicester City	W	2-1	Osborne, Blair	9,43
8		24	A	Manchester United	L	0-3		13,95
9	Oct	1	H	Everton	L	1-3	Townley	7,71
10		8	A	Cardiff City	L	1-2	Townley	21,81
11		15	H	Blackburn Rovers	D	1-1	Osborne	23,02
12		22	H	Sunderland	W	3-1	Osborne, Dimmock 2	19,03
13		29	A	Derby County	D	1-1	Grimsdell	15,96
14	Nov	5	H	West Ham United	W	5-3	Handley, O'Callaghan 2, Osborne, Elkes	35,09
15		12	A	Aston Villa	W	2-1	Osborne 2	30,75
16		19	H	Sheffield United	D	2-2	Osborn, Elkes	19,14
17	Dec	3	H	Burnley	W	5-0	Handley, O'Callaghan, Osborne 2, Dimmock	20,40
18		10	A	Bury	W	2-1	O'Callaghan 2	12,20
19		17	H	Liverpool	W	3-1	Osborne, Elkes 2	21,23
20		24	A	Leicester City	L	1-6	Handley	19,98
21		26	A	Bolton Wanderers	L	1-4	Elkes	25,22
22		31	A	Birmingham	L	2-3	O'Callaghan, Womack (og)	11,60
23	Jan	2	A	Arsenal	D	1-1	O'Callaghan	13,51
24		7	H	Newcastle United	W	5-2	Osborne 4, Dimmock	34,73
25		21	A	Huddersfield Town	L	2-4	O'Callaghan, Osborne	17,89
26	Feb	4	H	Manchester United	W	4-1	O'Callaghan, Armstrong 2, Dimmock	23,54
27		6	H	Bolton Wanderers	L	1-2	Armstrong	18,18
28		11	A	Everton	W	5-2	O'Callaghan 4, Dimmock	29,14
29		25	A	Blackburn Rovers	L	1-2	O'Callaghan	20,89
30	Mar	5	H	Cardiff City	W	1-0	Dimmock	15,55
31		10	H	Derby County	L	1-2	Armstrong	22,45
32		17	A	West Ham United	D	1-1	Osborne	33,90
33		19	H	Portsmouth	L	0-3		12,82
34		24	H	Aston Villa	W	2-1	Grimsdell (pen), Lindsay	21,53
35		28	A	Sunderland	D	0-0		9,24
36		31	A	Sheffield United	L	1-3	Handley	17,49
37	Apr	6	H	Sheffield Wednesday	L	1-3	Lindsay	26,43
38		7	H	Arsenal	W	2-0	O'Callaghan 2	39,19
39		10	A	Sheffield Wednesday	L	2-4	O'Callaghan, Osborne	15,90
40		14	A	Burnley	D	2-2	Osborne, Dimmock	10,90
41		21	H	Bury	L	1-4	Lindasy	15,61
42		28	A	Liverpool	L	0-2		31,78

Appearances

Goals

FA Cup

R3	Jan	14	A	Bristol City	W	2-1	O'Callaghan, Osborne	36,26
R4		28	H	Oldham Athletic	W	3-0	Handley, O'Callaghan, Dimmock	36,82
R5	Feb	18	A	Leicester City	W	3-0	O'Callaghan 2, Dimmock	47,29
R6	Mar	3	A	Huddersfield Town	L	1-6	O'Callaghan	52,39

Appearances

Goals

London FA Charity Cup

R1	Oct	17	A	Fulham	L	2-6	O'Callaghan, Dimmock (pen)

Appearances

Goals

London Professional Football Charity Fund

	Nov	17	H	Clapton Orient	W	4-3	O'Callaghan 3, Townley

Appearances

Goals

Armstrong JW	Austin PC	Barnett FW	Bellamy WR	Blair JG	Britton J	Clay T	Dimmock JH	Elkes AJ	Evans A	Forster M	Grimsdell A	Handley CHJ	Hartley AF	Helliwell S	Lindsay AF	Lowdell AE	Nicholls JH	O'Callaghan E	Osborne FR	Poynton C	Richardson J	Sanders AW	Skitt H	Smith B	Spiers CH	Thompson A	Townley JC	Own-goals
							11	10	9	2					6	4	1	8	7	3			5					
							11	10	9	2					6	4	1	8	7	3			5					
		7	11					10	9	2					6	4	1	8			3		5					
				9	1		11	10		2		7			6	4		8			3		5					
				9	1		11	10		2	6							8	7		3		5	4				
				9	1		11	10		2	6							8	7		3		5	4				
				9	1		11	10		2	6							8	7		3		5	4				
			11	9	1			10		2	6			5				8	7		3			4				
			11		1					2	6							8	7		3	9	5	4			10	
			11		1			9		2	6					4		8	7		3		5				10	
					1	2	11	9			6	10				4		8	7		3		5					
					1	2	11	10			6	7				4		8	9		3		5					
					1	2	11	10			6	7				4		8	9		3		5					
					1		11	10		2	6	7				4		8	9		3		5					
					1		11	10		2	6	7				4		8	9		3		5					
					1		11	10		2	6	7				4		8	9		3		5					
						2	11	10			6	7				4		8	9		3		5		1			
						2	11	10			6	7				4		8	9		3		5		1			
						2	11	10			6	7				4		8	9		3		5		1			
						2	11	10			6	7				4		8	9		3		5		1			
						2	11	10		3		7			6	4		8	9				5		1			
10	9					2	11			3		7			6	4		8					5		1			
10							11			2	6	7			9	4		8			3		5		1			
10							11			2	6	7				4		8	9		3		5		1			
						2	11	10		3	6					4		8	9				5		1	7		
10						2	11			3	6	7				4		8	9				5		1			
9						2	11	10				7			6	4		8			3		5		1			
10						2	11				6	7			9	4		8			3		5		1			
10						2	11				6	7				4		8	9		3		5		1			
10						2	11			3	6	7				4		8	9	5					1			
10						2	11			3	6	7				4		8	9	5					1			
							11			2	6		10		7	4		8	9	3			5		1			
9							11			2	6		10		7	4		8		3			5		1			
		7					11			2	6	10			9	4		8		3			5		1			
		7					11			2	6	10			9	4		8		3			5		1			
		7					11			2	6	10			9	4		8		3			5		1			
		7					11			2	6				9	4		8	10	3			5		1			
							11			2	6	7			10			8	9	3			5	4	1			
							11			2	6	7			10			8	9		3		5	4	1			
							11			2	6			5				8	9	3				4	1	7	10	
							11			2	6				10	4		8	9	3			5		1	7		
10							11			2	6				9	4		8		3			5		1	7		
11	1	5	4	5	13	16	38	22	3	32	35	26	2	2	19	34	3	42	31	14	24	1	38	8	26	4	3	
4				4			11	5			2	4			4			19	18								2	1

Armstrong JW	Austin PC	Barnett FW	Bellamy WR	Blair JG	Britton J	Clay T	Dimmock JH	Elkes AJ	Evans A	Forster M	Grimsdell A	Handley CHJ	Hartley AF	Helliwell S	Lindsay AF	Lowdell AE	Nicholls JH	O'Callaghan E	Osborne FR	Poynton C	Richardson J	Sanders AW	Skitt H	Smith B	Spiers CH	Thompson A	Townley JC	Own-goals
10							11			2	6	7				4		8	9		3		5		1			
10						2	11			3	6	7				4		8	9				5		1			
10						2	11				6	7			9	4		8			3		5		1			
10						2	11				6	7				4		8	9		3		5		1			
4	0	0	0	0	0	3	4	0	0	2	4	4	0	0	1	4	0	4	3	0	3	0	4	0	4	0	0	
							2					1						5	1									

Armstrong JW	Austin PC	Barnett FW	Bellamy WR	Blair JG	Britton J	Clay T	Dimmock JH	Elkes AJ	Evans A	Forster M	Grimsdell A	Handley CHJ	Hartley AF	Helliwell S	Lindsay AF	Lowdell AE	Nicholls JH	O'Callaghan E	Osborne FR	Poynton C	Richardson J	Sanders AW	Skitt H	Smith B	Spiers CH	Thompson A	Townley JC	Own-goals
					1	2	11	9	7		6	10						8			3		5	4				
0	0	0	0	0	1	1	1	1	1	0	1	1	0	0	0	0	0	1	0	0	1	0	1	1	0	0	0	
							1											1										

Armstrong JW	Austin PC	Barnett FW	Bellamy WR	Blair JG	Britton J	Clay T	Dimmock JH	Elkes AJ	Evans A	Forster M	Grimsdell A	Handley CHJ	Hartley AF	Helliwell S	Lindsay AF	Lowdell AE	Nicholls JH	O'Callaghan E	Osborne FR	Poynton C	Richardson J	Sanders AW	Skitt H	Smith B	Spiers CH	Thompson A	Townley JC	Own-goals
	9				1		11			2		7			6	4		8		5	3						10	
0	1	0	0	0	1	0	1	0	0	1	0	1	0	0	1	1	0	1	0	1	1	0	0	0	0	0	1	
																		3									1	

League Table

	P	W	D	L	F	A	Pts
Everton	42	20	13	9	102	66	53
Huddersfield Town	42	22	7	13	91	68	51
Leicester City	42	18	12	12	96	72	48
Derby County	42	17	10	15	96	83	44
Bury	42	20	4	18	80	80	44
Cardiff City	42	17	10	15	70	80	44
Bolton Wanderers	42	16	11	15	81	66	43
Aston Villa	42	17	9	16	78	73	43
Newcastle United	42	15	13	14	79	81	43
Arsenal	42	13	15	14	82	86	41
Birmingham	42	13	15	14	70	75	41
Blackburn Rovers	42	16	9	17	66	78	41
Sheffield United	42	15	10	17	79	86	40
Sheffield Wednesday	42	13	13	16	81	78	39
Sunderland	42	15	9	18	74	76	39
Liverpool	42	13	13	16	84	87	39
West Ham United	42	14	11	17	81	88	39
Manchester United	42	16	7	19	72	80	39
Burnley	42	16	7	19	82	98	39
Portsmouth	42	16	7	19	66	90	39
TOTTENHAM HOTSPUR	42	15	8	19	74	86	38
Middlesbrough	42	11	15	16	81	88	37

1928-29

DIVISION TWO

Manager: Billy Minter

Did you know that?

The crowd of 4,139 for the match with Hull City on 15 April 1929 is the smallest attendance for a Spurs League game since World War One.

LEAGUE DEBUTANTS

Aug 25	v Oldham Athletic Tom Roberts
Sep 1	v Southampton Randolph Galloway
Sep 8	v Wolves Joe Scott
Oct 6	v Hull City Tommy Cable
Nov 3	v Clapton Orient Harry Wilding
Nov 24	v Bristol City Arthur Crompton
Feb 9	v Port Vale Jimmy Smy
Feb 23	v Bradford John Knight
Mar 2	v Grimsby Town Edwin Herod
Mar 16	v Clapton Orient Ted Harper

Match No.	Date		Opponents		Result		Scorers	Attendance
1	Aug	25	H	Oldham Athletic	W	4-1	Elkes, Roberts 2, Osborne	33,173
2		27	H	Middlesbrough	L	2-5	Osborne, Dimmock	23,990
3	Sep	1	A	Southampton	D	1-1	Galloway	22,574
4		8	H	Wolverhampton Wanderers	W	3-2	Galloway, Hartley, Scott	26,018
5		15	A	Notts County	L	0-2		23,304
6		22	H	Millwall	W	2-1	Osborne 2	47,073
7		29	A	Port Vale	L	1-2	Osborne	12,502
8	Oct	6	H	Hull City	W	4-1	Scott, Osborne, Elkes 2	28,737
9		13	A	Bradford	L	1-4	Osborne	22,688
10		20	H	Grimsby Town	W	2-1	Scott, O'Callaghan	22,21[illegible]
11		27	A	Stoke City	L	0-2		15,333
12	Nov	3	H	Clapton Orient	W	2-1	Elkes 2	33,382
13		10	A	Swansea Town	L	0-4		6,936
14		17	H	Nottingham Forest	W	2-1	Wilding, Osborne	23,384
15		24	A	Bristol City	L	1-2	Crompton	13,937
16	Dec	1	H	Barnsley	W	2-0	Osborne, Elkes	18,951
17		8	A	Chelsea	D	1-1	Armstrong	45,840
18		15	H	Blackpool	L	1-2	Dimmock	15,729
19		22	A	West Bromwich Albion	L	2-3	Crompton, O'Callaghan	12,609
20		25	H	Reading	D	2-2	O'Callaghan, Dimmock	28,344
21		26	A	Reading	L	3-4	Osborne 2, Dimmock	23,730
22		29	A	Oldham Athletic	L	1-3	Osborne	12,833
23	Jan	1	A	Middlesbrough	L	0-3		25,145
24		5	H	Southampton	W	3-2	Poynton (pen), O'Callaghan, Osborne	15,962
25		19	A	Wolverhampton Wanderers	L	2-4	Osborne, Dimmock	11,956
26		26	H	Notts County	W	3-0	O'Callaghn, Elkes 2	16,946
27	Feb	2	A	Millwall	L	1-5	Thompson	18,974
28		9	H	Port Vale	W	4-2	Barnett, Osborne 2, Dimmock	21,342
29		23	H	Bradford	W	3-2	O'Callaghan, Dimmock 2	19,910
30	Mar	2	A	Grimsby Town	L	0-2		13,850
31		9	H	Stoke City	W	1-0	O'Callaghan	26,760
32		16	A	Clapton Orient	W	3-2	Harper, Dimmock 2	37,615
33		23	H	Swansea Town	D	1-1	Harper	25,109
34		29	A	Preston North End	D	2-2	Elkes, Dimmock	19,216
35		30	A	Nottingham Forest	D	2-2	Harper, Elkes	8,504
36	Apr	1	H	Preston North End	W	2-0	O'Callaghan, Elkes	23,125
37		6	H	Bristol City	D	1-1	Harper	22,396
38		13	A	Barnsley	L	1-4	Scott	8,449
39		15	A	Hull City	D	1-1	Harper	4,139
40		20	H	Chelsea	W	4-1	O'Callaghan, Harper 3	24,356
41		27	A	Blackpool	D	2-2	Harper, Dimmock	8,744
42	May	4	H	West Bromwich Albion	W	2-0	Harper 2	15,789

Appearances

Goals

FA Cup

R3	Jan	12	A	Reading	L	0-2		26,137

Appearances

Goals

London FA Charity Cup

R1	Oct	15	H	London Caledonians	W	2-1	Scott 2	2,000
R2		29	A	Queen's Park Rangers	D	1-1	Hartley	
R2r	Nov	5	H	Queen's Park Rangers	W	3-1	Helliwell, Hartley, Armstrong	3,371
SF		26	N*	Charlton Athletic	W	5-3	Compton, O'Callaghan, Armstrong 2, Hartley	4,000
F	May	6	N#	Millwall	W	5-1	O'Callaghan, Harper 3, Armstrong	5,000

*played at Upton Park, #played at Highbury

Appearances

Goals

London Professional Football Charity Fund

Dec	3	A	Clapton Orient	W	4-2	Skitt, O'callaghan, Armstrong, Bellamy	

Appearances

Goals

Armstrong JW	Bann WE	Barnett FW	Bellamy WR	Cable TH	Clay T	Crompton A	Dimmock JH	Elkes AJ	Evans A	Forster M	Galloway SR	Grimsdell A	Handley CHJ	Harper EC	Hartley AF	Helliwell S	Herod ERB	Knight JG	Lindsay AF	Lowdell AE	Nicholls JH	O'Callaghan E	Osborne FR	Poynton C	Reddish J	Richardson J	Roberts WT	Scott J	Skitt H	Smith B	Smy J	Spiers CH	Thompson A	Wilding HTO
							11	5		2		6								4		8	10	3			9					1	7	
							11	5		2		6								4		8	10			3	9					1	7	
							11			2	9	6			10					4	1	8				3			5				7	
										2	9	6			10					4	1	8				3		11	5				7	
	2							5			9	6			10					4	1	8				3		11					7	
	2							5	8			6							10	4	1		9			3		11					7	
	2							5				6	10							4	1	8	9			3		11					7	
			11	5				10		2		6								4	1	8	9	3				7						
			11	5				10		2		6								4	1	8	9	3				7						
			11					10		2		5								4	1	8	9	3				7	6					
			11					10	8	2						5				4	1		9	3				7	6					
			11					10		2										4	1		8	3			9	7	6					5
			11					10		2										4	1		8	3			9	7	6					5
							11	10		2										4		8	9			3			6			1	7	5
						7	11	10		2										4		8	9			3			6			1		5
						7	11	10		2										4		8	9			3			6			1		5
9						7	11			2										4		8	10			3			6			1		5
9						7	11			2										4		8	10			3			6			1		5
9						7	11			2										4		8	10	3					6			1		5
						7	11	10		2										4		8	9	3					6			1		5
0							11			2						5				4		8	9	3					6			1	7	
							11	10		2										4		8	9	3					6			1	7	5
							11	10		2									6	4		8	9	3								1	7	5
9							11			2						5			6			8	10	3					4			1	7	
						7	11	10		2						5			6	4		8	9	3								1		
		7					11	10		2						5				4		8	9	3						6		1		
		7					11	10		2						5				4			9	3						6		1	8	
		7					11			2		6								4		8	9	3							10	1		5
	2	7					11	9										5		4		8		6		3					10	1		
		7			2		11	9									3			4		8		6					5		10	1		
		7			2		11										3			4		8	9	6					5		10	1		
			7		2		11	10						9			3			4		8		6					5			1		
			7		2		11	10						9			3			4		8		6					5			1		
							11	10		2				9			3			4		8	7	6					5			1		
8							11	10		2				9			3			4			7						5	6		1		
			7				11	10		2				9			3			4		8							5	6		1		
0					2		11							9			3			4		8	7						5	6		1		
0										2				9			3			4		8	7					11	5	6		1		
0										2				9			3			4		8	7					11	5	6		1		
0							11			2				9			3			4		8	7						5	6		1		
0							11			2				9			3		4			8	7						5	6		1		
0						7	11			2				9			3		4			8							5	6		1		
2	4	6	9	2	5	8	30	27	2	33	3	11	1	11	3	6	13	1	6	39	11	36	33	23	0	12	4	12	29	10	4	31	13	12
1		1				2	12	11			2			11	1							9	16	1			2	4					1	1

Armstrong JW	Bann WE	Barnett FW	Bellamy WR	Cable TH	Clay T	Crompton A	Dimmock JH	Elkes AJ	Evans A	Forster M	Galloway SR	Grimsdell A	Handley CHJ	Harper EC	Hartley AF	Helliwell S	Herod ERB	Knight JG	Lindsay AF	Lowdell AE	Nicholls JH	O'Callaghan E	Osborne FR	Poynton C	Reddish J	Richardson J	Roberts WT	Scott J	Skitt H	Smith B	Smy J	Spiers CH	Thompson A	Wilding HTO
0							11			2						5			6			8	9	3					4			1	7	
1	0	0	0	0	0	0	1	0	0	1	0	0	0	0	0	1	0	0	1	0	0	1	1	1	0	0	0	0	1	0	0	1	1	0

Armstrong JW	Bann WE	Barnett FW	Bellamy WR	Cable TH	Clay T	Crompton A	Dimmock JH	Elkes AJ	Evans A	Forster M	Galloway SR	Grimsdell A	Handley CHJ	Harper EC	Hartley AF	Helliwell S	Herod ERB	Knight JG	Lindsay AF	Lowdell AE	Nicholls JH	O'Callaghan E	Osborne FR	Poynton C	Reddish J	Richardson J	Roberts WT	Scott J	Skitt H	Smith B	Smy J	Spiers CH	Thompson A	Wilding HTO
			11	5						2					10					4	1	8	9	3				7	6					
9			11						8	2					10	5				4	1			3				7	6					
9							11			2					8	5				4	1			3				7	6				10	
9						7	11			2					10	5				4		8			3				6			1		
10						7	11			2				9					4			8			3				5	6		1		
4	0	0	2	1	0	2	3	0	1	5	0	0	0	1	4	3	0	0	1	4	3	3	1	3	2	0	0	3	5	1	0	2	1	0
4						1								3	3	1						2						2						

Armstrong JW	Bann WE	Barnett FW	Bellamy WR	Cable TH	Clay T	Crompton A	Dimmock JH	Elkes AJ	Evans A	Forster M	Galloway SR	Grimsdell A	Handley CHJ	Harper EC	Hartley AF	Helliwell S	Herod ERB	Knight JG	Lindsay AF	Lowdell AE	Nicholls JH	O'Callaghan E	Osborne FR	Poynton C	Reddish J	Richardson J	Roberts WT	Scott J	Skitt H	Smith B	Smy J	Spiers CH	Thompson A	Wilding HTO
9			11			7				2					10	5				4	1	8				3			6					
1	0	0	1	0	0	1	0	0	0	1	0	0	0	0	1	1	0	0	0	1	1	1	0	0	0	1	0	0	1	0	0	0	0	0
1			1																			1							1					

League Table

	P	W	D	L	F	A	Pts
Middlesbrough	42	22	11	9	92	57	55
Grimsby Town	42	24	5	13	82	61	53
Bradford Park Avenue	42	22	4	16	88	70	48
Southampton	42	17	14	11	74	60	48
Notts County	42	19	9	14	78	65	47
Stoke City	42	17	12	13	74	51	46
West Bromwich Albion	42	19	8	15	80	79	46
Blackpool	42	19	7	16	92	76	45
Chelsea	42	17	10	15	64	65	44
TOTTENHAM HOTSPUR	42	17	9	16	75	81	43
Nottingham Forest	42	15	12	15	71	70	42
Hull City	42	13	14	15	58	63	40
Preston North End	42	15	9	18	78	79	39
Millwall	42	16	7	19	71	86	39
Reading	42	15	9	18	63	86	39
Barnsley	42	16	6	20	69	66	38
Wolverhampton W	42	15	7	20	77	81	37
Oldham Athletic	42	16	5	21	54	75	37
Swansea Town	42	13	10	19	62	75	36
Bristol City	42	13	10	19	58	72	36
Port Vale	42	15	4	23	71	86	34
Clapton Orient	42	12	8	22	45	72	32

1929-30

DIVISION TWO

Manager: Billy Minter until November then Percy Smith

Did you know that?

There were doubtless many brave men among the 23,071 spectators when Cardiff City visited Spurs on 9 November 1929 but none braver then the nine Welsh holders of the Victoria Cross, who accompanied City on their trip to London before attending a VC Reunion Dinner hosted by the Prince of Wales at the House of Lords that night.

LEAGUE DEBUTANTS

Aug 31	v Bradford Billy Cook
Aug 31	v Bradford Tom Meads
Dec 14	v Charlton Athletic John Illingworth
Dec 26	v Southampton Tom Evans
Feb 15	v Oldham Athletic Willie Davies
Feb 15	v Oldham Athletic Dick Rowley
Apr 21	v West Bromwich Albion Jack Reddish

Match No.	Date		Opponents		Result		Scorers	Attendance
1	Aug	31	A	Bradford	L	1-2	Dimmock	18,77
2	Sep	2	A	Millwall	W	5-2	Osborne, O'Callaghan, Cook, Dimmock 2	22,29
3		7	H	Barnsley	W	2-1	O'Callaghan, Cook	26,05
4		14	A	Blackpool	L	2-3	O'Callaghan, Smy	14,91
5		21	H	Bury	D	2-2	Crompton, Osborne	25,05
6		23	H	Millwall	D	1-1	O'Callaghan	16,62
7		28	A	Chelsea	L	0-3		46,77
8	Oct	5	H	Nottingham Forest	D	1-1	Cook	22,33
9		9	H	Stoke City	W	3-1	Osborne 3	8,54
10		12	A	Oldham Athletic	L	0-2		18,26
11		19	A	Wolverhampton Wanderers	L	0-3		26,59
12		26	H	Bradford City	D	1-1	Osborne	17,34
13	Nov	2	A	Swansea Town	W	1-0	Harper	8,96
14		9	H	Cardiff City	L	1-2	Meads	23,07
15		16	A	Preston North End	L	0-4		10,68
16		23	H	Bristol City	W	2-1	Harper, Dimmock	11,86
17		30	A	Notts County	W	1-0	Harper	10,29
18	Dec	7	H	Reading	D	0-0		11,52
19		14	A	Charlton Athletic	L	0-1		17,35
20		21	H	Hull City	D	2-2	Harper 2	9,10
21		25	H	Southampton	W	3-2	Osborne (pen), Harper 2	26,56
22		26	A	Southampton	L	0-1		25,20
23		28	H	Bradford	D	1-1	Dimmock	20,72
24	Jan	4	A	Barnsley	L	0-2		5,87
25		18	H	Blackpool	W	6-1	Meads, Harper 3, Cook, Dimmock	24,95
26		25	A	Bury	L	1-2	Cook	13,19
27	Feb	1	H	Chelsea	D	3-3	Thompson, Harper, Cook	33,62
28		8	A	Nottingham Forest	D	0-0		9,83
29		15	H	Oldham Athletic	W	2-1	Poynton (pen), Cook	35,51
30		22	H	Wolverhampton Wanderers	W	4-2	Thompson, Rowley 3	29,34
31	Mar	1	A	Bradford City	W	2-0	Cook, Bellamy	16,64
32		8	H	Swansea Town	W	3-0	Davies 2, Rowley	30,33
33		15	A	Cardiff City	L	0-1		15,40
34		22	H	Preston North End	W	1-0	Osborne	29,10
35		29	A	Bristol City	L	0-1		10,93
36	Apr	5	H	Notts County	W	2-0	Cook, Bellamy	17,84
37		12	A	Reading	L	0-3		11,18
38		18	H	West Bromwich Albion	L	0-2		25,22
39		19	H	Charlton Athletic	W	3-0	Harper 2, Smy	15,81
40		21	A	West Bromwich Albion	L	3-4	Osborne, Harper, Finch (og)	13,98
41		26	A	Hull City	L	0-2		6,39
42	May	3	A	Stoke City	L	0-1		6,56
								Appearances
								Goals

FA Cup

R3	Jan	11	H	Manchester City	D	2-2	Osborne, Cook	37,00
R3r		15	A	Manchester City	L	1-4	Thompson	37,71
								Appearances
								Goals

London FA Charity Cup

R1	Oct	14	A	Clapton Orient	L	1-2	Cook	3,00
								Appearances
								Goals

London Professional Football Charity Fund

	Nov	4	H	Crystal Palace	W	5-1	O'Callaghan, Garbutt 3, Cook	
								Appearances
								Goals

Armstrong JW	Bellamy WR	Cable TH	Cook GW	Crompton A	Davies W	Dimmock JH	Evans T	Forster M	Garbutt HP	Harper EC	Hartley AF	Herod ERB	Illingworth JW	Lindsay AF	Lowdell AE	Meads T	O'Callaghan E	Osborne FR	Poynton C	Reddish J	Rowley RWM	Scott J	Skitt H	Smy J	Spiers CH	Taylor A	Thompson A	Own-goals
9			10			11		2				3			4	6	8	7					5		1			
9			10			11		2				3			4	6	8	7					5		1			
9			10			11		2				3			4	6	8	7					5		1			
			9			11						2		6	4		8	7	3				5	10	1			
				7		11						2		6	4		8	9	3				5		1		10	
				7		11						2		6	4		8	9	3				5		1		10	
			9	7		11						2		6	4				3				5	10	1		8	
			10	7		11						2		6	4	9	8		3				5		1			
		5	10	7		11		2				3		9	4	6		8							1			
		5	10	7		11		2				3		9	4	6		8							1			
		5	10	7		11		2				3			4	6	9	8							1			
		5	8			11						2			4	6		9	3					10	1		7	
		5				11				9		2			4	6	8	10	3						1		7	
		5				11				9		2				8	10	3	6				4		1		7	
		5	10			11				9		2				6		8	3				4		1		7	
		5	10			11				9		2				6			3			7	4		1		8	
8		5	10			11				9		2				6			3			7	4		1			
8		5	10			11				9		2				6			3			7	4		1			
		5	10			11				9		3	2			6		8					4		1		7	
		5	10			11				9		3	2			6		8					4		1		7	
	7	5	10			11				9		3	2			6		8					4		1			
	7	5	9			11	6					3	2			10							4		1		8	
	7	5	10			11	6				8	3	2					9					4		1			
	7	5				11				9		3	2	6				8					4	10	1			
		5	10			11				9		3	2			6		7					4		1		8	
		5	10			11				9		3	2			6		7					4		1		8	
		5	10			11				9		3	2	6				7					4		1		8	
		5	10			11				9		2				6		7	3				4		1		8	
		5	10		7	11						2				6			3		9		4		1		8	
		5	10		7	11						2				6			3		9		4		1		8	
	11	5	10		7			2								6		8	3		9		4		1			
	11	5	10		7			2				3				6		8			9		4		1			
	11	5	10		7			2				3				6		8			9		4		1			
	11	5	10		7			2				3				6		8			9		4		1			
	11	5	10		7			2		9		3				6					8		4		1			
	11	5	10		7			2				3				6		9					4		1		8	
	11	5			7			2				3				6		10			9		4		1		8	
		5	10		7	11		2				3				6					9		4		1		8	
		5			7	11		2		9		3				6		8					4	10	1			
	11	5			7					9		2		6				8		3			4	10	1			
		5			7		6			9		2						8		3		11	4	10	1			
		5			7					9		2				6		8		3		11	4		1		10	
5	12	34	32	7	14	32	3	15	0	19	1	41	9	10	13	33	10	32	16	3	9	5	37	7	42	0	21	
	2		9	1	2	6				14						2	4	9	1		4			2			2	1

Armstrong JW	Bellamy WR	Cable TH	Cook GW	Crompton A	Davies W	Dimmock JH	Evans T	Forster M	Garbutt HP	Harper EC	Hartley AF	Herod ERB	Illingworth JW	Lindsay AF	Lowdell AE	Meads T	O'Callaghan E	Osborne FR	Poynton C	Reddish J	Rowley RWM	Scott J	Skitt H	Smy J	Spiers CH	Taylor A	Thompson A	Own-goals
		5	10			11				9		3	2	6				7					4		1		8	
		5	10			11				9		3	2	6				7					4		1		8	
0	0	2	2	0	0	2	0	0	0	2	0	2	2	2	0	0	0	2	0	0	0	0	2	0	2	0	2	
			1															1									1	

Armstrong JW	Bellamy WR	Cable TH	Cook GW	Crompton A	Davies W	Dimmock JH	Evans T	Forster M	Garbutt HP	Harper EC	Hartley AF	Herod ERB	Illingworth JW	Lindsay AF	Lowdell AE	Meads T	O'Callaghan E	Osborne FR	Poynton C	Reddish J	Rowley RWM	Scott J	Skitt H	Smy J	Spiers CH	Taylor A	Thompson A	Own-goals
		5	10	7		11		2				3			4	6	9	8								1		
0	0	1	1	1	0	1	0	1	0	0	0		1	0	0	1	1	1	1	0	0	0	0	0	0	0	1	0
			1																									

Armstrong JW	Bellamy WR	Cable TH	Cook GW	Crompton A	Davies W	Dimmock JH	Evans T	Forster M	Garbutt HP	Harper EC	Hartley AF	Herod ERB	Illingworth JW	Lindsay AF	Lowdell AE	Meads T	O'Callaghan E	Osborne FR	Poynton C	Reddish J	Rowley RWM	Scott J	Skitt H	Smy J	Spiers CH	Taylor A	Thompson A	Own-goals
		5	10			11	6		9			2					8		3				4		1		7	
0	0	1	1	0	0	1	1	0	1	0	0	1	0	0	0	0	1	0	1	0	0	0	1	0	1	0	1	
			1						3								1											

League Table

	P	W	D	L	F	A	Pts
Blackpool	42	27	4	11	98	67	58
Chelsea	42	22	11	9	74	46	55
Oldham Athletic	42	21	11	10	90	51	53
Bradford Park Avenue	42	19	12	11	91	70	50
Bury	42	22	5	15	78	67	49
West Bromwich Albion	42	21	5	16	105	73	47
Southampton	42	17	11	14	77	76	45
Cardiff City	42	18	8	16	61	59	44
Wolverhampton W	42	16	9	17	77	79	41
Nottingham Forest	42	13	15	14	55	69	41
Stoke City	42	16	8	18	74	72	40
TOTTENHAM HOTSPUR	42	15	9	18	59	61	39
Charlton Athletic	42	14	11	17	59	63	39
Millwall	42	12	15	15	57	73	39
Swansea Town	42	14	9	19	57	61	37
Preston North End	42	13	11	18	65	80	37
Barnsley	42	14	8	20	56	71	36
Bradford City	42	12	12	18	60	77	36
Reading	42	12	11	19	54	67	35
Bristol City	42	13	9	20	61	83	35
Hull City	42	14	7	21	51	78	35
Notts County	42	9	15	18	54	70	33

1930-31

DIVISION TWO

Manager: Percy Smith

Did you know that?

When Spurs met Port Vale on 29 November 1930 they played host to two Indian Princes. Col. His Highness Raj Rishi Shri Sewai Maharaj Dev of Alwar GCSI, GCIE and His Highness The Shri Maharaj of Jhalawar were in London for the Indian Round Table Conference trying to solve some of their country's problems. When they expressed a desire to see working life in Tottenham, Mr R.C. Morrison, MP for North Tottenham and secretary to Prime Minister Ramsey MacDonald, was quick to make the arrangements.

LEAGUE DEBUTANTS

Aug 30	v Reading	Bert Hodgkinson
Aug 30	v Reading	Bert Lyons
Aug 30	v Reading	Alf Messer
Sep 20	v Stoke City	George Hunt
Dec26	v Southampton	Les Howe
Dec 27	v Reading	Wally Alsford
Mar 14	v Bradford City	Jimmy Smailes

Match No.	Date			Opponents		Result	Scorers	Attendance
1	Aug	30	H	Reading	W	7-1	Harper 5, Cook, Dimmock	25,48
2	Sep	1	H	Burnley	W	8-1	Davies, O'Calaghan 2, Harper 2, Cook 3	23,51
3		6	A	Wolverhampton Wanderers	L	1-3	Cook	24,99
4		8	A	Preston North End	L	1-2	Harper	17,03
5		13	H	Bradford	W	3-2	Harper, Cook, Dimmock	18,82
6		15	H	Preston North End	D	0-0		18,79
7		20	A	Stoke City	L	1-2	Cook	10,25
8		27	H	Millwall	W	4-1	O'Callaghan, Harper, Smy, Dimmock	37,10
9	Oct	4	A	Oldham Athletic	W	2-1	Davies, Harper	15,55
10		11	H	Nottingham Forest	W	2-1	O'Callaghan, Harper	34,23
11		18	H	Bury	W	3-1	Harper, Cook, Dimmock	32,85
12		25	A	Everton	L	2-4	Smy 2	25,26
13	Nov	1	H	Charlton Athletic	W	5-0	O'Callaghan, Harper 3, Smy	24,54
14		8	A	Bradford City	L	0-2		13,71
15		15	H	Swansea Town	D	1-1	Lyons (pen)	20,21
16		22	A	West Bromwich Albion	W	2-0	Harper 2	17,92
17		29	H	Port Vale	W	5-0	Harper 4, Cook	23,60
18	Dec	6	A	Plymouth Argyle	L	0-2		24,54
19		13	H	Bristol City	W	4-1	Messer, Rowley 2, Cook	21,46
20		20	A	Barnsley	W	1-0	Bellamy	7,39
21		25	H	Southampton	L	1-3	O'Callaghan	36,65
22		26	A	Southampton	W	3-0	Davies, O'Callaghan, Rowley	22,40
23		27	A	Reading	W	2-1	Davies, O'Callaghan	16,57
24	Jan	3	H	Wolverhampton Wanderers	W	1-0	Cook	26,22
25		17	A	Bradford	L	1-4	Harper	15,22
26		26	H	Stoke City	W	3-0	Lyons (pen), Messer, Harper	10,92
27		31	A	Millwall	W	3-2	Harper, Bellamy 2	27,89
28	Feb	7	H	Oldham Athletic	W	4-0	Harper 3, Cook	27,70
29		14	A	Nottingham Forest	D	2-2	Harper 2	14,19
30		21	A	Bury	L	0-2		7,77
31	Mar	7	A	Charlton Athletic	L	0-1		18,06
32		14	H	Bradford City	W	3-1	Harper 2, Smailes	32,97
33		16	H	Everton	W	1-0	Harper	30,20
34		21	A	Swansea Town	W	2-1	Harper, Smailes	9,87
35		28	H	West Bromwich Albion	D	2-2	O'Callaghan, Smailes	49,92
36	Apr	3	H	Cardiff City	D	2-2	Hunt, Cook	41,54
37		4	A	Port Vale	L	0-3		14,29
38		6	A	Cardiff City	D	0-0		6,66
39		11	H	Plymouth Argyle	D	1-1	Hunt	33,54
40		18	A	Bristol City	L	1-2	Hunt	15,14
41		25	H	Barnsley	W	4-2	Harper 2, Hunt 2	20,76
42	May	2	A	Burnley	L	0-1		10,07
								Appearances
								Goals

FA Cup

R3	Jan	10	H	Preston North End	W	3-1	Harper, Cook, Dimmock	36,54
R4		24	A	West Bromwich Albion	L	0-1		40,85
								Appearances
								Goals

London FA Charity Cup

R1	Oct	13	H	Charlton Athletic	W	6-0	Davies 2, Harper 3, Cook	2,96
R2		27	A	Chelsea	W	2-1	Rowley, Hartley	5,00
SF	Nov	11	N*	Ilford	W	8-1	Howe 3, Davies, Thompson, Cook 3	
F	May	4	H	Arsenal	L	1-2	Lyons (pen)	10,16
								Appearances
								Goals

*played at Upton Park

London Professional Football Charity Fund

	Nov	3	A	Crystal Palace	D	2-2	Harper 2	
								Appearances
								Goals

Alsford WJ	Bellamy WR	Cable TH	Cook GW	Davies W	Dimmock JH	Evans T	Evans W	Harper EC	Hartley F	Herod ERB	Hodgkinson H	Howe LF	Hunt GS	Illingworth JW	Lyons AT	Meads T	Messer AT	Nicholls JH	O'Callaghan E	Osborne FR	Poynton C	Rowe AS	Rowley RWM	Scott J	Skitt H	Smailes J	Smy J	Spiers CH	Taylor A	Thompson A
			10	7	11			9			3				2	6	5		8						4			1		
			10	7	11			9			3				2	6	5		8						4			1		
			10	7	11			9			3				2	6	5		8						4			1		
			10	7	11			9		3					2	6	5		8						4			1		
		4	10	7	11			9		3					2	6	5		8									1		
			10	7	11			9		3					2	6	5			8					4			1		
			10	7							3		9		2	6	5		8					11	4			1		
				7	11			9			3				2	6	5		8						4		10	1		
				7	11			9			3				2	6	5		8						4		10	1		
				7	11			9			3				2	6	5		8						4		10	1		
			10	7	11			9			3				2	6	5		8						4			1		
	11			7				9			3				2	6	5		8						4		10	1		
	11	5		7				9			3				2	6			8						4		10	1		
	11	5		7				9			3				2	6			8						4		10	1		
	11	5		7				9			3				2	6			8	10					4			1		
			10	7	11			9			3				2	6	5		8						4			1		
			10	7	11			9			3				2	6	5		8						4			1		
	11		10	7				9			3				2	6	5		8						4			1		
	11		10	7							3				2	6	5		8				9		4			1		
	11		10	7							3				2	6	5		8				9		4			1		
	11		10	7							3				2	6	5		8				9		4			1		
	11		10	7							3	4			2	6	5		8				9					1		
4	11		10	7							3					6	5		8		2		9					1		
	11		10	7				9			3				2	6	5		8						4			1		
			10	7	11			9			3					6	5		8		2				4			1		
	11		10	7				9			3	4			2	6	5			8								1		
	11		10	7				9			3	4			2	6	5			8								1		
4	11		10	7				9			3				2	6	5		8									1		
4	11		10	7				9			3				2	6	5		8									1		
6	11		10	7				9			3				2		5		8				4					1		
4	11		10	7				9			3				2	6	5		8									1		
4			10	7				9			3				2	6	5		8							11		1		
4			10	7				9			3				2	6	5		8							11		1		
4				7				9			3		10		2	6	5		8							11		1		
4			10	7							3		9		2	6	5		8							11		1		
4			10	7							3		9		2	6	5		8							11		1		
			9	7							3				2	6	5			8			10		4	11		1		
4			9	7							3		10			6	5		8		2					11		1		
4				7							3		10		2	6	5		8	9						11		1		
			10	7							3		8		2	6	5						9		4	11		1		
4				7				9			3		10			6	5		8		2					11		1		
4				7				9			3		8			6	5		10		2					11		1		
4	17	4	31	42	13	0	0	30	0	3	39	3	9	0	37	41	39	0	37	6	5	0	8	1	24	11	6	42	0	0
	3		13	4	4			36					5		2		2		9				3			3	4			

Alsford WJ	Bellamy WR	Cable TH	Cook GW	Davies W	Dimmock JH	Evans T	Evans W	Harper EC	Hartley F	Herod ERB	Hodgkinson H	Howe LF	Hunt GS	Illingworth JW	Lyons AT	Meads T	Messer AT	Nicholls JH	O'Callaghan E	Osborne FR	Poynton C	Rowe AS	Rowley RWM	Scott J	Skitt H	Smailes J	Smy J	Spiers CH	Taylor A	Thompson A
			10	7	11			9			3				2	6	5		8						4			1		
			10	7	11			9			3				2	6	5								4			1		8
0	0	0	2	2	2	0	0	2	0	0	2	0	0	0	2	2	2	0	1	0	0	0	0	0	2	0	0	2	0	1
			1		1			1																						

Alsford WJ	Bellamy WR	Cable TH	Cook GW	Davies W	Dimmock JH	Evans T	Evans W	Harper EC	Hartley F	Herod ERB	Hodgkinson H	Howe LF	Hunt GS	Illingworth JW	Lyons AT	Meads T	Messer AT	Nicholls JH	O'Callaghan E	Osborne FR	Poynton C	Rowe AS	Rowley RWM	Scott J	Skitt H	Smailes J	Smy J	Spiers CH	Taylor A	Thompson A
	11		10	7				9			3				2	6	5	1							4					8
6	11								10	3		4	9	2								5	8						1	7
6	11		10	7							3	4			2		5	1					9							8
	7	5				6	11					9	8		2						3	4					10		1	
2	4	1	2	2	0	1	1	1	1	1	2	3	2	1	3	1	2	2	0	0	1	2	2	0	1	0	1	0	2	3
			4	3				3	1			3			1								1							1

Alsford WJ	Bellamy WR	Cable TH	Cook GW	Davies W	Dimmock JH	Evans T	Evans W	Harper EC	Hartley F	Herod ERB	Hodgkinson H	Howe LF	Hunt GS	Illingworth JW	Lyons AT	Meads T	Messer AT	Nicholls JH	O'Callaghan E	Osborne FR	Poynton C	Rowe AS	Rowley RWM	Scott J	Skitt H	Smailes J	Smy J	Spiers CH	Taylor A	Thompson A
4	11			7				9			3	5			2	6											10		1	8
1	1	0	0	1	0	0	0	1	0	0	1	1	0	0	1	1	0	0	0	0	0	0	0	0	0	0	1	0	1	1
								2																						

League Table

	P	W	D	L	F	A	Pts
Everton	42	28	5	9	121	66	61
West Bromwich Albion	42	22	10	10	83	49	54
TOTTENHAM HOTSPUR	42	22	7	13	88	55	51
Wolverhampton W	42	21	5	16	84	67	47
Port Vale	42	21	5	16	67	61	47
Bradford Park Avenue	42	18	10	14	97	66	46
Preston North End	42	17	11	14	83	64	45
Burnley	42	17	11	14	81	77	45
Southampton	42	19	6	17	74	62	44
Bradford City	42	17	10	15	61	63	44
Stoke City	42	17	10	15	64	71	44
Oldham Athletic	42	16	10	16	61	72	42
Bury	42	19	3	20	75	82	41
Millwall	42	16	7	19	71	80	39
Charlton Athletic	42	15	9	18	59	86	39
Bristol City	42	15	8	19	54	82	38
Nottingham Forest	42	14	9	19	80	85	37
Plymouth Argyle	42	14	8	20	76	84	36
Barnsley	42	13	9	20	59	79	35
Swansea Town	42	12	10	20	51	74	34
Reading	42	12	6	24	72	96	30
Cardiff City	42	8	9	25	47	87	25

1931-32

DIVISION TWO

Manager: Percy Smith

Did you know that?

In January 1932 Alex Steel died in St Albans. He had not made much of an impression at Spurs, playing in only one Football League match. That was against Bradford City on 29 January 1910, but it was still a notable occasion. With his brothers Bobby and Danny also playing it was the only time Spurs have fielded three brothers in the same League game.

LEAGUE DEBUTANTS

Aug 29	v Wolves	David Colquhoun
Aug 29	v Wolves	George Greenfield
Aug 31	v Preston North End	John Moran
Sep 12	v Manchester United	Jimmy Brain
Oct 10	v Burnley	Arthur Rowe
Oct 10	v Burnley	Allan Taylor
Nov 7	v Swansea Town	Willie Evans
Mar 19	v Swansea Town	Bill Felton
Mar 25	v Stoke City	Harry Marshall

Match No.	Date			Opponents	Result		Scorers	Attendance
1	Aug	29	A	Wolverhampton Wanderers	L	0-4		23,267
2		31	H	Preston North End	W	4-0	Davies, O'Callaghan, Hunt 2	22,104
3	Sep	5	H	Bradford	D	3-3	Meads, O'Callaghan, Rowley (pen)	27,108
4		7	A	Southampton	L	1-2	O'Callaghan	13,566
5		12	A	Manchester United	D	1-1	Rowley	9,557
6		14	H	Southampton	W	5-2	Meads 2, Brain, O'Callaghan, Bellamy	19,217
7		19	H	Barnsley	W	4-2	Brain, O'Callaghan 2, Bellamy	28,585
8		26	H	Nottingham Forest	L	1-3	Hunt	25,128
9	Oct	3	A	Chesterfield	L	2-4	Brain, Bellamy	15,192
10		10	H	Burnley	D	1-1	Harper	28,877
11		17	A	Notts County	L	1-3	Rowley	13,397
12		24	H	Plymouth Argyle	L	0-1		22,863
13		31	A	Bristol City	D	1-1	Hunt	9,129
14	Nov	7	H	Swansea Town	W	6-2	Davies 2, Hunt, O'Callaghan, W.Evans 2	20,834
15		14	A	Bury	D	1-1	OG (Mills)	7,628
16		21	H	Port Vale	W	9-3	Lyons (pen), Colquhoun, Davies 3, Brain 2, Hunt 2	22,226
17		28	A	Millwall	W	2-1	Hunt 2	28,424
18	Dec	5	H	Bradford City	L	1-5	W.Evans	26,622
19		12	A	Leeds United	L	0-1		15,689
20		19	H	Oldham Athletic	W	3-2	Hunt, O'Callaghan 2	10,339
21		25	H	Charlton Athletic	L	0-1		36,469
22		26	A	Charlton Athletic	W	5-2	Davies, Brain, Hunt 3	26,417
23	Jan	2	H	Wolverhampton Wanderers	D	3-3	Hunt 3	25,122
24		16	A	Bradford	L	1-2	O'Callaghan	12,596
25		23	H	Manchester United	W	4-1	Davies 2, Hunt, O'Callaghan	19,139
26		30	A	Barnsley	L	2-3	Hunt, O'Callaghan	5,852
27	Feb	6	A	Nottingham Forest	W	3-1	Brain 2, O'Callaghan	10,487
28		13	H	Chesterfield	D	3-3	Davies, Hunt, W.Evans	21,591
29		20	A	Burnley	L	0-2		7,517
30		27	H	Notts County	W	2-0	O'Callaghan 2	20,481
31	Mar	5	A	Plymouth Argyle	L	1-4	Davies	18,903
32		12	H	Bristol City	W	2-1	Davies, Greenfield	15,178
33		19	A	Swansea Town	D	1-1	T.Evans (pen)	11,357
34		25	H	Stoke City	D	3-3	T.Evans (pen), Hunt, O'Callaghan	26,503
35		26	H	Bury	D	0-0		20,822
36		28	A	Stoke City	D	2-2	Greenfield, W.Evans	15,042
37	Apr	2	A	Port Vale	W	3-1	Hunt, Greenfield 2	7,682
38		9	H	Millwall	W	1-0	T.Evans (pen)	22,495
39		16	A	Bradford City	L	0-2		12,740
40		23	H	Leeds United	W	3-1	O'Callaghan, Hunt, Greenfield	17,285
41		30	A	Oldham Athletic	W	2-1	Hunt 2	5,963
42	May	7	A	Preston North End	L	0-2		5,900
								Appearances
								Goals

FA Cup

Round	Date			Opponents	Result		Scorers	Attendance
R3	Jan	9	H	Sheffield Wednesday	D	2-2	Hunt, W.Evans	41,511
R3r		13	A	Sheffield Wednesday	L	1-3	Hunt (pen)	30,000
								Appearances
								Goals

Alsford WJ	Bellamy WR	Brain J	Cable TH	Colquhoun DW	Davies W	Evans T	Evans W	Felton W	Greenfield GW	Harper EC	Hodgkinson H	Hunt GS	Lyons AT	Marshall WH	Meads T	Messer AT	Moran J	Nicholls JH	O'Callaghan E	Poynton C	Reddish J	Rowe AS	Rowley RWM	Smailes J	Spiers CH	Taylor A	OG
				4	7				10	9	3				6	5			8	2				11	1		
	11			4	7						3	9			6	5	2		8				10		1		
	11			4	7						3	9			6	5	2		8				10		1		
	11			4	7						3	9			6	5	2		8				10		1		
	11	8		4	7						3				6	5	2		10				9		1		
	11	9		4	7						3	8			6	5	2		10						1		
	11	9		4	7						3	8			6	5	2		10						1		
	11	8		4	7						3	9			6	5	2		10						1		
	11	8	5	4	7							9			6		2		10	3					1		
				4	7				10	9			2		6					3		5	8	11		1	
				4	7					9			2		6	5			10	3			8	11		1	
6		9		4	7							10	2							3		5	8	11		1	
6		8		4	7				10			9	2							3		5		11		1	
6		8		4	7		11					9	2						10	3		5				1	
6		8		4	7		11				3	9	2						10			5				1	
6		8		4	7		11				3	9	2						10			5				1	
6		8		4	7		11				3	9	2						10			5				1	
6		8		4	7		11				3	9	2						10			5				1	
6	7	8		4			11				3	9	2						10			5				1	
6		8		4	7		11				3	9	2						10			5				1	
6		8		4	7		11				3	9	2						10			5				1	
		8		4	7	6	11				3	9	2						10			5				1	
		8		4	7	6	11				3	9	2						10			5				1	
		8		4	7		11					9			6		2		10	3		5			1		
		8		4	7		11					9			6		2		10	3		5			1		
		8		4	7		11					9			6		2		10	3		5			1		
		8		4	7		11					9			6				10	3	2	5			1		
		8		4	7		11					9			6		2		10	3		5			1		
		8		4	7		11					9	2		6				10	3		5			1		
		8		4	7		11					9	2		6	5			10	3					1		
		8		4	7		11					9	2		6	5			10	3					1		
	11	9	5	4	7				10						6				8	3	2					1	
	7	8		4		6	11	2				9							10	3		5				1	
	7			4		6	11	2				9		8					10	3		5				1	
		8			7	4	11	2	10			9			6						3	5				1	
		8			7	4	11	2	10			9			6					3		5				1	
		8			7	4	11	2	10			9			6					3		5				1	
		8			7	4	11	2	10			9			6					3		5				1	
		8			7	4	11	2	10			9			6					3		5				1	
					7	4	11	2	10			9			6				8	3		5				1	
				7		4	11	2	10			9			6			1	8	3		5					
				4	7	6	11	2	10			9						1	8	3		5					
10	12	32	2	36	38	12	28	10	12	3	17	37	17	1	27	11	12	2	34	25	3	29	7	5	17	23	
	3	8		1	12	3	5		5	1		24	1		3				17				3				1

Alsford WJ	Bellamy WR	Brain J	Cable TH	Colquhoun DW	Davies W	Evans T	Evans W	Felton W	Greenfield GW	Harper EC	Hodgkinson H	Hunt GS	Lyons AT	Marshall WH	Meads T	Messer AT	Moran J	Nicholls JH	O'Callaghan E	Poynton C	Reddish J	Rowe AS	Rowley RWM	Smailes J	Spiers CH	Taylor A	OG
		8		4	7	6	11					9	2						10	3		5			1		
		8		4	7	6	11					9							10	3	2	5			1		
0	0	2	0	2	2	2	2	0	0	0	0	2	1	0	0	0	0	0	2	2	1	2	0	0	2	0	
							1					2															

League Table

	P	W	D	L	F	A	Pts
Wolverhampton W	42	24	8	10	115	49	56
Leeds United	42	22	10	10	78	54	54
Stoke City	42	19	14	9	69	48	52
Plymouth Argyle	42	20	9	13	100	66	49
Bury	42	21	7	14	70	58	49
Bradford Park Avenue	42	21	7	14	72	63	49
Bradford City	42	16	13	13	80	61	45
TOTTENHAM HOTSPUR	42	16	11	15	87	78	43
Millwall	42	17	9	16	61	61	43
Charlton Athletic	42	17	9	16	61	66	43
Nottingham Forest	42	16	10	16	77	72	42
Manchester United	42	17	8	17	71	72	42
Preston North End	42	16	10	16	75	77	42
Southampton	42	17	7	18	66	77	41
Swansea Town	42	16	7	19	73	75	39
Notts County	42	13	12	17	75	75	38
Chesterfield	42	13	11	18	64	86	37
Oldham Athletic	42	13	10	19	62	84	36
Burnley	42	13	9	20	59	87	35
Port Vale	42	13	7	22	58	89	33
Barnsley	42	12	9	21	55	91	33
Bristol City	42	6	11	25	39	78	23

1932-33

DIVISION TWO

Manager: Percy Smith

Did you know that?

Arsenal's Herbert Chapman is often credited as the man behind the numbering of players' shirts. Certainly he had experimented with numbers in 1928, but Spurs had long been proponents of the idea. At the 1933 AGM of the Football League they managed to get the idea on the agenda but while they had some support, their proposal that clubs should be allowed to number shirts was rejected. Six years later numbering was made mandatory.

LEAGUE DEBUTANTS

Sep 5 v Nottingham Forest
Bill Whatley
Sep 10 v Manchester United
David Levene
Dec 20 v Notts County
Willie Hall
Mar 18 v Port Vale
Jimmy McCormick
Apr 1 v Chesterfield
Johnny Morrison
Apr 8 v Bradford City
Joe Allen

Match No.	Date		Opponents		Result		Scorers	Attendance
1	Aug	27	H	Charlton Athletic	W	4-1	Hunt 2, W.Evans 2	34,263
2		29	A	Nottingham Forest	L	1-3	Hunt	9,906
3	Sep	3	A	Stoke City	L	0-2		12,366
4		5	H	Nottingham Forest	D	0-0		13,757
5		10	H	Manchester United	W	6-1	Brain, Hunt 2, O'Callaghan, W.Evans 2 (1 pen)	23,333
6		17	A	Bury	L	0-1		11,602
7		24	A	Grimsby Town	L	2-3	Hunt 2	9,597
8	Oct	1	H	Oldham Athletic	D	1-1	Hunt	20,437
9		8	A	Preston North End	W	6-2	Colquhoun, O'Callaghan, Hunt, Greenfield, W.Evans 2	6,368
10		15	H	Burnley	W	4-1	Howe, Hunt, Greenfield, W.Evans	26,097
11		22	H	Southampton	W	5-0	O'Callaghan 3, Hunt, W.Evans	24,778
12		29	A	Millwall	W	4-1	Howe, O'Callaghan, Greefield, W.Evans	32,301
13	Nov	5	H	Port Vale	W	4-0	O'Callaghan 2, Hunt, W.Evans (pen)	33,071
14		12	A	Lincoln City	D	2-2	Howe, Greenfield	11,654
15		19	H	Chesterfield	W	4-1	O'Callaghan, W.Evans 3 (1 pen)	24,584
16		26	A	Bradford City	W	1-0	Hunt	18,351
17	Dec	3	H	Swansea Town	W	7-0	O'Callaghan, Hunt 2, Greenfield 2, W.Evans 2 (1 pen)	31,993
18		10	A	Fulham	D	2-2	Hunt 2	42,111
19		17	H	West Ham United	D	2-2	O'Callaghan, Hunt	45,129
20		24	A	Notts County	L	0-3		16,355
21		26	A	Bradford	D	3-3	Howe, O'Callaghan, W.Evans (pen)	25,318
22		27	H	Bradford	W	2-0	Hunt, W.Evans	48,478
23		31	A	Charlton Athletic	W	3-0	Hunt 2, W.Evans	26,666
24	Jan	7	H	Stoke City	W	3-2	Davies, Hunt 2	43,711
25		21	A	Manchester United	L	1-2	W.Evans	20,661
26	Feb	1	H	Bury	W	2-1	Hunt 2	19,836
27		4	H	Grimsby Town	W	4-3	O'Callaghan, Hunt, W.Evans 2	33,395
28		11	A	Oldham Athletic	W	5-1	O'Callaghan, Hunt 3, Hall	5,412
29		18	H	Preston North End	D	1-1	Hunt	41,209
30	Mar	4	A	Southampton	D	1-1	Hunt	11,806
31		11	H	Millwall	W	2-1	W.Evans 2 (1 pen)	50,299
32		18	A	Port Vale	D	1-1	W.Evans (pen)	14,588
33		25	H	Lincoln City	W	3-2	Brain, Hunt, W.Evans (pen)	33,930
34	Apr	1	A	Chesterfield	D	1-1	Morrison	10,631
35		8	H	Bradford City	D	1-1	Allen	32,202
36		14	H	Plymouth Argyle	D	0-0		44,483
37		15	A	Swansea Town	W	2-0	Howe, W.Evans	14,590
38		17	A	Plymouth Argyle	D	2-2	Howe 2	21,461
39		22	H	Fulham	D	0-0		44,312
40		24	A	Burnley	D	1-1	Hunt	11,353
41		29	A	West Ham United	L	0-1		31,706
42	May	6	H	Notts County	W	3-1	T.Evans, W.Evans 2 (1 pen)	28,015
								Appearances
								Goals

FA Cup

R3	Jan	14	A	Oldham Athletic	W	6-0	O'Callaghan, Hunt 3, W.Evans, Brunskill (og)	16,662
R4		28	A	Luton Town	L	0-2		17,213
								Appearances
								Goals

Allen J	Alsford WJ	Bellamy WR	Brain J	Colquhoun DW	Davies W	Evans T	Evans W	Felton W	Greenfield GW	Hall GW	Howe LF	Hunt GS	Levene DJ	McCormick J	Meads T	Morrison JA	Nicholls JH	O'Callaghan E	Poynton C	Rowe AS	Taylor A	Whatley WJ	Own-goals
				4	7	6	11	2	10			9					1	8	3	5			
				4	7	6	11	2	10			9					1	8	3	5			
				4	7	6	11	2	10			9					1	8	3	5			
			8	4	7		11	2				9			6		1	10		5		3	
		7	8	4			11	2				9	6				1	10		5		3	
		7	8	4			11	2				9	6				1	10		5		3	
			8	4	7		11	2				9	6				1	10		5		3	
			8	4	7		11	2				9	6				1	10		5		3	
				4			11	2	10		7	9			6		1	8		5		3	
				4			11	2	10		7	9			6		1	8		5		3	
				4			11	2	10		7	9			6		1	8		5		3	
				4			11	2	10		7	9			6		1	8		5		3	
				4			11	2	10		7	9			6		1	8		5		3	
				4			11	2	10		7	9			6		1	8		5		3	
				4			11	2	10		7	9			6		1	8		5		3	
				4			11	2	10		7	9			6		1	8		5		3	
				4			11	2	10		7	9			6		1	8		5		3	
				4			11	2	10		7	9			6		1	8		5		3	
	10			4			11	2			7	9			6		1	8		5		3	
				4			11	2		10	7	9			6		1	8		5		3	
				4			11			10	7	9			6		1	8	2	5		3	
	10			4	7		11	2				9			6		1	8		5		3	
				4	7		11	2		10		9			6		1	8		5		3	
				4	7		11	2		10		9			6		1	8		5		3	
				4	7		11	2		10		9	5		6		1	8				3	
				4	7		11	2		10		9			6		1	8		5		3	
				4	7		11	2		10		9			6		1	8		5		3	
				4	7		11	2		10		9			6		1	8		5		3	
				4	7		11	2		10		9			6		1	8		5		3	
			8			4	11	2		10		9			6		1	7		5		3	
						4	11	2		10	7	9			6		1	8		5		3	
			8			4	11	2		10		9		7	6		1			5		3	
			8			4	11	2		10		9		7	6		1			5		3	
			8			4	11	2		10				7	6	9	1			5		3	
0			8			4	11	2				9		7	6		1			5		3	
						4	11	2		10	8	9		7	6		1			5		3	
						4	11	2		10	8	9		7	6		1			5		3	
					7	4	11	2		10	8	9			6					5	1	3	
						4	11	2		10	8	9		7	6					5	1	3	
			8			4	11	2		10		9		7	6					5	1	3	
		7	8			4	11	2		10		9			6					5	1	3	
						4	11	2		10		9		7	6			8		5	1	3	
	2	3	12	29	15	16	42	41	13	21	18	41	5	9	35	1	37	32	4	41	5	39	
			2	1	1	1	28		6	1	7	33				1		14					

Allen J	Alsford WJ	Bellamy WR	Brain J	Colquhoun DW	Davies W	Evans T	Evans W	Felton W	Greenfield GW	Hall GW	Howe LF	Hunt GS	Levene DJ	McCormick J	Meads T	Morrison JA	Nicholls JH	O'Callaghan E	Poynton C	Rowe AS	Taylor A	Whatley WJ	Own-goals
				4	7		11	2		10		9	5		6		1	8	3				
				4	7		11	2		10		9	5		6		1	8				3	
0	0	0	0	2	2	0	2	2	0	2	0	2	2	0	2	0	2	2	1	0	0	1	
							1					3						1					1

League Table

	P	W	D	L	F	A	Pts
Stoke City	42	25	6	11	78	39	56
TOTTENHAM HOTSPUR	42	20	15	7	96	51	55
Fulham	42	20	10	12	78	65	50
Bury	42	20	9	13	84	59	49
Nottingham Forest	42	17	15	10	67	59	49
Manchester United	42	15	13	14	71	68	43
Millwall	42	16	11	15	59	57	43
Bradford Park Avenue	42	17	8	17	77	71	42
Preston North End	42	16	10	16	74	70	42
Swansea Town	42	19	4	19	50	54	42
Bradford City	42	14	13	15	65	61	41
Southampton	42	18	5	19	66	66	41
Grimsby Town	42	14	13	15	79	84	41
Plymouth Argyle	42	16	9	17	63	67	41
Notts County	42	15	10	17	67	78	40
Oldham Athletic	42	15	8	19	67	80	38
Port Vale	42	14	10	18	66	79	38
Lincoln City	42	12	13	17	72	87	37
Burnley	42	11	14	17	67	79	36
West Ham United	42	13	9	20	75	93	35
Chesterfield	42	12	10	20	61	84	34
Charlton Athletic	42	12	7	23	60	91	31

1933-34

DIVISION ONE

Manager: Percy Smith

Did you know that?

Alf Day had yet to make his League debut when called up to play for Wales against Northern Ireland on 4 November 1933.

LEAGUE DEBUTANTS

Oct 7	v Sunderland Fred Channell
Dec 26	v Huddersfield Town Len Bolan
Dec 26	v Huddersfield Town Alan Hall
Apr 14	v Manchester City Alf Day
Apr 28	v Sheffield Wednesday Foster Hedley

Match No.	Date		Opponents		Result		Scorers	Attendance
1	Aug	26	A	Sheffield United	D	0-0		16,58
2		28	H	Wolverhampton Wanderers	W	4-0	O'Callaghan 2, Hunt 2	20,95
3	Sep	2	H	Aston Villa	W	3-2	O'Callaghan, Hunt, W.Evans (pen)	44,97
4		4	A	Wolverhampton Wanderers	L	0-1		20,51
5		9	A	Leicester City	W	3-1	McCormick 3	26,11
6		16	H	Arsenal	D	1-1	Felton (pen)	56,61
7		23	H	Liverpool	L	0-3		33,08
8		30	A	Chelsea	W	4-0	O'Callaghan, Hunt 3	67,45
9	Oct	7	H	Sunderland	W	3-1	Hunt, G.W.Hall, W.Evans	44,23
10		14	A	Portsmouth	W	1-0	O'Callaghan	25,67
11		21	A	Everton	D	1-1	W.Evans	35,08
12		28	H	Middlesbrough	W	2-0	O'Callaghan, Hunt	35,80
13	Nov	4	A	West Bromwich Albion	W	2-1	Howe, W.Evans	32,29
14		11	H	Newcastle United	W	4-0	Hunt 2, W.Evans 2	41,37
15		18	A	Leeds United	D	0-0		19,68
16		25	H	Derby County	L	1-2	O'Callaghan	41,46
17	Dec	2	A	Manchester City	L	0-2		38,02
18		9	H	Birmingham	W	3-2	Howe, Hunt 2	26,14
19		16	A	Sheffield Wednesday	L	1-2	Howe	17,23
20		23	H	Blackburn Rovers	W	4-1	Howe, G.W.Hall, W.Evans 2	28,00
21		25	H	Huddersfield Town	L	1-3	G.W.Hall	53,95
22		26	A	Huddersfield Town	L	0-2		32,50
23		30	H	Sheffield United	W	4-1	Hunt 4	23,89
24	Jan	1	A	Blackburn Rovers	L	0-1		19,95
25		6	A	Aston Villa	W	5-1	Meads, McCormick 2, Howe, Hunt	35,29
26		20	H	Leicester City	L	0-1		31,39
27		31	A	Arsenal	W	3-1	Howe, W.Evans 2 (1 pen)	68,67
28	Feb	3	A	Liverpool	L	1-3	Hunt	30,80
29		10	H	Chelsea	W	2-1	Hunt, W.Evans (pen)	39,65
30		21	A	Sunderland	L	0-6		16,10
31		24	H	Portsmouth	D	0-0		26,92
32	Mar	3	H	Everton	W	3-0	Hunt 3	26,12
33		10	A	Middlesbrough	D	1-1	W.Evans	11,83
34		17	H	West Bromwich Albion	W	2-1	O'Callaghan, W.Evans (pen)	26,39
35		24	A	Newcastle United	W	3-1	Hunt 3	25,24
36		30	H	Stoke City	D	0-0		32,91
37		31	H	Leeds United	W	5-1	McCormick, Hunt 3, W.Evans	29,54
38	Apr	2	A	Stoke City	L	0-2		32,66
39		7	A	Derby County	L	3-4	McCormick, O'Callaghan, W.Evans (pen)	14,24
40		14	H	Manchester City	W	5-1	O'Callaghan 2, Hunt 2, W.Evans	26,07
41		21	A	Birmingham	L	0-2		24,57
42		28	H	Sheffield Wednesday	W	4-3	McCormick 2, Hunt 2	20,32
								Appearance
								Goal

FA Cup

R3	Jan	13	H	Everton	W	3-0	Howe, Hunt, W.Evans	45,63
R4		27	H	West Ham United	W	4-1	Hunt 2, W.Evans 2	51,74
R5	Feb	17	H	Aston Villa	L	0-1		44,36
								Appearance
								Goal

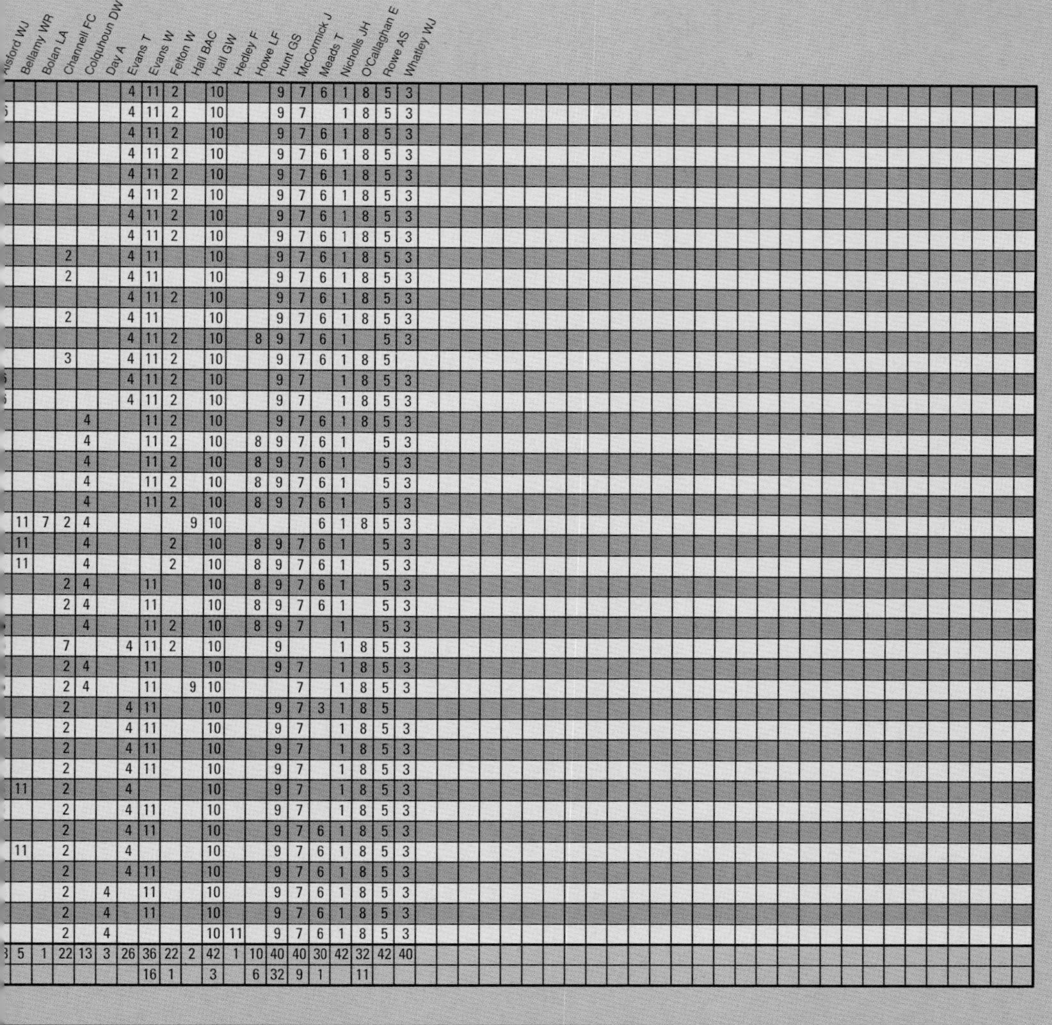

Alsford WJ	Bellamy WR	Bolan LA	Channell FC	Colquhoun DW	Day A	Evans T	Evans W	Felton W	Hall BAC	Hall GW	Hedley F	Howe LF	Hunt GS	McCormick J	Meads T	Nicholls JH	O'Callaghan E	Rowe AS	Whatley WJ
						4	11	2		10			9	7	6	1	8	5	3
[illegible]						4	11	2		10			9	7		1	8	5	3
						4	11	2		10			9	7	6	1	8	5	3
						4	11	2		10			9	7	6	1	8	5	3
						4	11	2		10			9	7	6	1	8	5	3
						4	11	2		10			9	7	6	1	8	5	3
						4	11	2		10			9	7	6	1	8	5	3
						4	11	2		10			9	7	6	1	8	5	3
			2			4	11			10			9	7	6	1	8	5	3
			2			4	11			10			9	7	6	1	8	5	3
						4	11	2		10			9	7	6	1	8	5	3
			2			4	11			10			9	7	6	1	8	5	3
						4	11	2		10		8	9	7	6	1		5	3
			3			4	11	2		10			9	7	6	1	8	5	
[illegible]						4	11	2		10			9	7		1	8	5	3
[illegible]						4	11	2		10			9	7		1	8	5	3
				4			11	2		10			9	7	6	1	8	5	3
				4			11	2		10		8	9	7	6	1		5	3
				4			11	2		10		8	9	7	6	1		5	3
				4			11	2		10		8	9	7	6	1		5	3
				4			11	2		10		8	9	7	6	1		5	3
	11	7	2	4					9	10					6	1	8	5	3
	11			4				2		10		8	9	7	6	1		5	3
	11			4				2		10		8	9	7	6	1		5	3
			2	4			11			10		8	9	7	6	1		5	3
			2	4			11			10		8	9	7	6	1		5	3
				4			11	2		10		8	9	7		1		5	3
			7			4	11	2		10			9			1	8	5	3
			2	4			11			10			9	7		1	8	5	3
			2	4			11		9	10				7		1	8	5	3
			2			4	11			10			9	7	3	1	8	5	
			2			4	11			10			9	7		1	8	5	3
			2			4	11			10			9	7		1	8	5	3
			2			4	11			10			9	7		1	8	5	3
	11		2			4				10			9	7		1	8	5	3
			2			4	11			10			9	7		1	8	5	3
			2			4	11			10			9	7	6	1	8	5	3
	11		2			4				10			9	7	6	1	8	5	3
			2			4	11			10			9	7	6	1	8	5	3
			2		4		11			10			9	7	6	1	8	5	3
			2		4		11			10			9	7	6	1	8	5	3
			2		4					10	11		9	7	6	1	8	5	3
3	5	1	22	13	3	26	36	22	2	42	1	10	40	40	30	42	32	42	40
							16	1		3		6	32	9	1		11		

Alsford WJ	Bellamy WR	Bolan LA	Channell FC	Colquhoun DW	Day A	Evans T	Evans W	Felton W	Hall BAC	Hall GW	Hedley F	Howe LF	Hunt GS	McCormick J	Meads T	Nicholls JH	O'Callaghan E	Rowe AS	Whatley WJ
			2	4			11			10		8	9	7	6	1		5	3
			2			4	11			10		8	9	7		1		5	3
			2	4			11			10		8	9	7		1		5	3
	0	0	3	2	0	1	3	0	0	3	0	3	3	3	1	3	0	3	3
							3					1	3						

League Table

	P	W	D	L	F	A	Pts
Arsenal	42	25	9	8	75	47	59
Huddersfield Town	42	23	10	9	90	61	56
TOTTENHAM HOTSPUR	42	21	7	14	79	56	49
Derby County	42	17	11	14	68	54	45
Manchester City	42	17	11	14	65	72	45
Sunderland	42	16	12	14	81	56	44
West Bromwich Albion	42	17	10	15	78	70	44
Blackburn Rovers	42	18	7	17	74	81	43
Leeds United	42	17	8	17	75	66	42
Portsmouth	42	15	12	15	52	55	42
Sheffield Wednesday	42	16	9	17	62	67	41
Stoke City	42	15	11	16	58	71	41
Aston Villa	42	14	12	16	78	75	40
Everton	42	12	16	14	62	63	40
Wolverhampton W	42	14	12	16	74	86	40
Middlesbrough	42	16	7	19	68	80	39
Leicester City	42	14	11	17	59	74	39
Liverpool	42	14	10	18	79	87	38
Chelsea	42	14	8	20	67	69	36
Birmingham	42	12	12	18	54	56	36
Newcastle United	42	10	14	18	68	77	34
Sheffield United	42	12	7	23	58	101	31

1934-35

DIVISION ONE

Manager: Percy Smith

Did you know that?

Having made a profit on the season of £8,776, Spurs were widely regarded as the richest football club in the country. Assets were £117,344, exceeding liabilities by £84,266, but the directors still wanted to increase their borrowing powers from £25,000 to £50,000. This was because the club had used £48,000 of liquid assets to pay for the erection of the new East Stand. There was still £7,000 to pay and the bank overdraft already stood at £23,000. They were given the requisite power at an EGM.

LEAGUE DEBUTANTS

Sep 22	v Aston Villa Edgar King
Sep 29	v Derby County George Goldsmith
Sep 29	v Derby County Fred Sargent
Dec 22	v Leeds United Charlie Jones
Dec 25	v Grimsby Town Doug Hunt
Dec 26	v Grimsby Town Almer Hall
Jan 1	v Blackburn Rovers James Fullwood
Feb 2	v Aston Villa Archie Burgon
Mar 6	v Arsenal Ernie Phypers
Mar 9	v Portsmouth Sam Bell
Mar 16	v Manchester City Andy Duncan
Apr 19	v Blackburn Rovers Percy Hooper

Match No.	Date			Opponents	Result		Scorers	Attendanc
1	Aug	25	H	Everton	D	1-1	G.W.Hall	50,58
2		27	H	Preston North End	L	1-2	W.Evans	24,96
3	Sep	1	A	Huddersfield Town	D	0-0		13,94
4		3	A	Preston North End	L	0-1		25,93
5		8	H	Wolverhampton Wanderers	W	3-1	McCormick, G.S.Hunt, G.W.Hall	37,11
6		15	A	Chelsea	W	3-1	O'Callaghan, G.S.Hunt, W.Evans	46,71
7		22	H	Aston Villa	L	0-2		42,08
8		29	A	Derby County	L	1-2	G.S.Hunt	15,45
9	Oct	6	H	Leicester City	D	2-2	Hedley, Frame (og)	37,40
10		13	A	Sunderland	W	2-1	G.S.Hunt, G.W.Hall	28,20
11		20	A	Arsenal	L	1-5	G.S.Hunt	70,54
12		27	H	Portsmouth	W	4-1	Bolan, Howe, G.S.Hunt 2	33,46
13	Nov	3	A	Manchester City	L	1-3	W.Evans	28,80
14		10	H	Middlesbrough	W	3-1	Howe, G.S.Hunt, W.Evans	25,76
15		17	A	West Bromwich Albion	L	0-4		20,41
16		24	H	Sheffield Wednesday	W	3-2	McCormick, W.Evans 2 (1 pen)	25,10
17	Dec	1	A	Birmingham	L	1-2	O'Callaghan	20,54
18		8	H	Stoke City	W	3-2	O'Callaghan, G.S.Hunt, Bellamy	31,08
19		15	A	Liverpool	L	1-4	O'Callaghan	24,68
20		22	H	Leeds United	D	1-1	W.Evans	23,66
21		25	A	Grimsby Town	L	0-3		19,70
22		26	H	Grimsby Town	W	2-1	A.G.Hall 2	45,51
23		29	A	Everton	L	2-5	McCormick, A.G.Hall	25,85
24	Jan	1	A	Blackburn Rovers	L	0-2		12,08
25		5	H	Huddersfield Town	D	0-0		35,52
26		19	A	Wolverhampton Wanderers	L	2-6	McCormick, W.Evans	28,20
27		30	H	Chelsea	L	1-3	D.A.Hunt	28,12
28	Feb	2	A	Aston Villa	L	0-1		36,97
29		9	H	Derby County	D	2-2	McCormick 2	42,94
30		23	H	Sunderland	D	1-1	Channell	44,88
31	Mar	6	H	Arsenal	L	0-6		47,71
32		9	A	Portsmouth	D	1-1	W.Evans (pen)	11,68
33		16	H	Manchester City	D	0-0		43,57
34		23	A	Middlesbrough	L	1-3	G.S.Hunt	14,62
35		28	A	Leicester City	L	0-6		13,06
36		30	H	West Bromwich Albion	L	0-1		29,16
37	Apr	6	A	Sheffield Wednesday	L	0-4		12,15
38		13	H	Birmingham	D	1-1	Bell	27,19
39		19	H	Blackburn Rovers	W	1-0	Bell	31,10
40		20	A	Stoke City	L	1-4	D.A.Hunt	11,57
41		27	H	Liverpool	W	5-1	Bolan, D.A.Hunt, W.Evans 3	15,61
42	May	4	A	Leeds United	L	3-4	Bolan, Morrison, D.A.Hunt	7,66
								Appearance
								Goal

FA Cup

R3	Jan	12	H	Manchester City	W	1-0	W.Evans	48,98
R4		26	H	Newcastle United	W	2-0	G.S.Hunt 2	61,19
R5	Feb	16	H	Bolton Wanderers	D	1-1	W.Evans	70,34
R5r		20	A	Bolton Wanderers	D	1-1	G.S.Hunt	47,45
R5r		25	N*	Bolton Wanderers	L	0-2		26,69
								Appearance
								Goal

*played at Villa Park

sford WJ	Bell S	Bellamy WR	Bolan LA	Brain J	Burgon FA	Channell FC	Colquhoun DW	Day A	Duncan A	Evans T	Evans W	Fullwood J	Goldsmith G	Greenfield GW	Hall AG	Hall GW	Hedley F	Hooper PGW	Howe LF	Hunt DA	Hunt GS	Illingworth JW	Jones C	King EF	Levene DJ	McCormick J	Meads T	Morrison JA	Nicholls JH	O'Callaghan E	Phypers E	Rowe AS	Sargent FA	Taylor A	Whatley WJ	Own-goals
						2				4	11					10					9					7			1	8		5			3	
						2		4			11					10					9					7	6		1	8		5			3	
						2		4			11					10			8		9					7	6		1			5			3	
						2		4		6	11			10		8					9					7			1			5			3	
						2	4			6	11					10					9					7			1	8		5			3	
						2	4			6	11					10					9					7			1	8		5			3	
				9		2		4		6	11					10								3		7			1	8		5				
						2		4		6			3			10	11		8		9								1			5	7			
						2				4						10	11		8		9					7	6		1			5			3	
						2				4	11					10			8		9					7	6		1			5			3	
						2	4			3	11					10			8		9					7	6		1			5				
			7			2				4	11					10			8		9						6		1			5			3	
			7			2				4	11					10			8		9						6		1			5			3	
			7			2				4	11								8		9						6		1	10		5			3	
						2				4	11								8		9					7	6		1	10		5			3	
						2				4	11								8		9					7	6		1	10		5			3	
						2				4	11								8		9					7	6		1	10		5			3	
		11				2				4				10					7		9						6		1	8		5			3	
		11				2				4				10					5		9					7	6			8				1	3	
						2				4	11			10							9		5			7	6			8				1	3	
						2				4	11			10					5	9						7	6			8				1	3	
		11				2				4					8				5	9						7	10							1	3	
		11				2				4					8					9			5			7	10							1	3	
		11				2				4		3		10	8				5	9						7								1		
						2				4	11				8						9				5	7				10				1	3	
		11				2				4	10				8				5	9						7								1	3	
		11				2				4	10				8				5	9						7								1	3	
					9	2				4	11				8										5	7				10				1	3	
					9	2				4	11				8				5							7				10				1	3	
						2					11				8				5	10					4	7		9						1	3	
					11	2									8				5	10	9					7					4			1	3	
	8					2		4			11								5		9					7	10							1	3	
	8		7			2		4	10								11		5		9													1	3	
	8		7			2		4	10		11								5		9													1	3	
						2			8	4	11	3				10			5		9					7								1		
	7					2		4	10		11				8				5		9								1						3	
	7					2			10		11								4	8	9		5						1		6				3	
	7					2			8		11					10			4		9		5											1	3	
	8		7			2					11					10		1	4		9		5												3	
			7		11										10			1	4	9	8	2	5												3	
	8		7			2					11					10		1	4	9			5												3	
			7			2					11					10			4	9			5				8	1						3	
	8	7	9	1	4	41	3	9	6	28	32	2	1	6	12	18	3	3	32	12	30	1	8	1	3	28	18	2	21	16	2	18	1	18	37	
	2	1	3			1					12				3	3	1		2	4	10					6		1		4						1

sford WJ	Bell S	Bellamy WR	Bolan LA	Brain J	Burgon FA	Channell FC	Colquhoun DW	Day A	Duncan A	Evans T	Evans W	Fullwood J	Goldsmith G	Greenfield GW	Hall AG	Hall GW	Hedley F	Hooper PGW	Howe LF	Hunt DA	Hunt GS	Illingworth JW	Jones C	King EF	Levene DJ	McCormick J	Meads T	Morrison JA	Nicholls JH	O'Callaghan E	Phypers E	Rowe AS	Sargent FA	Taylor A	Whatley WJ	Own-goals
		11				2				4	10				8				5	9						7								1	3	
		11				2				4	10				8				5		9					7								1	3	
		11				2				4	10				8				5		9					7								1	3	
						2				4	11				8				5		9					7		10						1	3	
						2		4							8		11		5	9						7				10				1	3	
	0	3	0	0	0	5	0	1	0	4	4	0	0	0	5	0	1	0	5	2	3	0	0	0	0	5	0	1	0	1	0	0	0	5	5	
											2										3															

League Table

	P	W	D	L	F	A	Pts
Arsenal	42	23	12	7	115	46	58
Sunderland	42	19	16	7	90	51	54
Sheffield Wednesday	42	18	13	11	70	64	49
Manchester City	42	20	8	14	82	67	48
Grimsby Town	42	17	11	14	78	60	45
Derby County	42	18	9	15	81	66	45
Liverpool	42	19	7	16	85	88	45
Everton	42	16	12	14	89	88	44
West Bromwich Albion	42	17	10	15	83	83	44
Stoke City	42	18	6	18	71	70	42
Preston North End	42	15	12	15	62	67	42
Chelsea	42	16	9	17	73	82	41
Aston Villa	42	14	13	15	74	88	41
Portsmouth	42	15	10	17	71	72	40
Blackburn Rovers	42	14	11	17	66	78	39
Huddersfield Town	42	14	10	18	76	71	38
Wolverhampton W	42	15	8	19	88	94	38
Leeds United	42	13	12	17	75	92	38
Birmingham	42	13	10	19	63	81	36
Middlesbrough	42	10	14	18	70	90	34
Leicester City	42	12	9	21	61	86	33
TOTTENHAM HOTSPUR	42	10	10	22	54	93	30

1935-36

DIVISION TWO

Manager: Jack Tresadern

Did you know that?

Although the match against Norwich City on 14 December 1935 kicked off at 2.15pm and half-time was curtailed, the light was so bad that 20 minutes from the end it was almost impossible to see the flight of the ball. Scores of paper flares were lit by spectators but even then few left the ground knowing Johnny Morrison had scored Spurs' winner seven minutes from time.

LEAGUE DEBUTANTS

Nov 16	v Bury Vic Buckingham
Nov 30	v Blackpool Bill Edrich
Mar 14	v West Ham United Ralph Ward
Mar 21	v Swansea Town Frank Grice
Mar 21	v Swansea Town Joe Meek
Apr 18	v Norwich City Albert Hall

Match No.	Date			Opponents	Result		Scorers	Attendanc
1	Aug	31	A	Bradford City	W	1-0	D.A.Hunt	14,35
2	Sep	2	H	Hull City	W	3-1	McCormick, Howe, D.A.Hunt	25,60
3		7	H	Newcastle United	L	1-2	Howe	47,44
4		9	A	Hull City	L	0-1		9,61
5		14	A	Sheffield United	D	1-1	Morrison	14,87
6		16	H	Barnsley	W	3-0	Duncan, Morrison 2	14,93
7		21	A	Manchester United	D	0-0		34,71
8		28	H	Port Vale	W	5-2	Howe 2, Morrison 3	32,87
9	Oct	5	A	Fulham	W	2-1	Duncan, W.Evans	37,29
10		12	H	Burnley	W	5-1	Howe, Morrison 2, G.W.Hall, W.Evans	34,48
11		19	H	Bradford	W	4-0	Morrison 2, G.W.Hall, W.Evans	37,79
12		26	A	Leicester City	L	1-4	Morrison	24,72
13	Nov	2	H	Swansea Town	W	7-2	Fullwood (pen), Morrison 2, G.W.Hall 3, W.Evans	36,12
14		9	A	West Ham United	D	2-2	Morrison 2	40,24
15		16	H	Bury	W	4-3	McCormick, Morrison, G.W.Hall, W.Evans	32,17
16		23	A	Southampton	L	0-2		21,33
17		30	H	Blackpool	W	3-1	Duncan, Morrison, Cardwell (og)	35,03
18	Dec	7	A	Nottingham Forest	L	1-4	Edrich	9,23
19		14	H	Norwich City	W	2-1	McCormick, Morrison	29,20
20		21	A	Doncaster Rovers	L	1-2	Morrison	20,13
21		25	H	Plymouth Argyle	L	1-2	Morrison	34,51
22		26	A	Plymouth Argyle	L	1-2	Bell	34,42
23		28	H	Bradford City	W	4-0	Howe (pen), Duncan, W.Evans 2	28,51
24	Jan	4	A	Newcastle United	W	4-1	Morrison, Bell, W.Evans 2	35,38
25		18	H	Sheffield United	D	1-1	W.Evans	35,53
26	Feb	1	A	Port Vale	W	5-1	Sargent, Morrison 3, W.Evans	10,77
27		5	H	Manchester United	D	0-0		20,08
28		8	H	Fulham	D	2-2	Sargent, W.Evans	45,27
29		22	A	Bradford	W	5-2	Sargent 2,Morrison, G.S.Hunt, W.Evans	6,98
30	Mar	4	H	Nottingham Forest	D	1-1	G.S.Hunt	14,70
31		7	A	Bury	D	1-1	Bell	6,01
32		14	H	West Ham United	L	1-3	G.S.Hunt	57,41
33		21	A	Swansea Town	D	1-1	Sargent	12,49
34		28	H	Southampton	W	8-0	Meek 3, G.S.Hunt 3 (1 pen), W.Evans 2	28,90
35	Apr	4	A	Blackpool	W	4-2	G.S.Hunt 3, Cardwell (og)	11,04
36		10	H	Charlton Athletic	D	1-1	Duncan	55,86
37		11	H	Leicester City	D	1-1	G.S.Hunt	35,28
38		13	A	Charlton Athletic	L	1-2	G.S.Hunt	46,71
39		18	A	Norwich City	L	0-1		23,95
40		20	A	Burnley	D	0-0		8,56
41		25	H	Doncaster Rovers	W	3-1	Meek 2, Duncan	15,09
42	May	2	A	Barnsley	D	0-0		9,27
								Appearance
								Goal

FA Cup

R3	Jan	11	H	Southend United	D	4-4	Sargent 2, Morrison 2	48,83
R3r		15	A	Southend United	W	2-1	Sargent, W.Evans	23,63
R4		25	H	Huddersfield Town	W	1-0	Howe	64,14
R5	Feb	15	A	Bradford	D	0-0		24,05
R5r		17	H	Bradford	W	2-1	G.S.Hunt 2	35,49
R6		29	A	Sheffield United	L	1-3	Morrison	22,29
								Appearance
								Goal

Bell S	Buckingham VF	Channell FC	Day A	Duncan A	Edrich WJ	Evans T	Evans W	Fullwood J	Grice F	Hall AE	Hall AG	Hall GW	Hooper PGW	Howe LF	Hunt DA	Hunt GS	Jones C	McCormick J	Meek J	Morrison JA	Nicholls JH	Phypers E	Rowe AS	Sargent FA	Taylor A	Ward RA	Whatley WJ	Own-goals
		2				4	11					10		8	9			7					5		1		3	
		2				4	11					10		8	9		5	7							1		3	
		2				4	11					10		8		9	5	7							1		3	
		2	4	10			11	3			8		1		9		5	7				6						
		2		8		4	11	3				10	1					7		9		6	5					
		2		8		4	11	3				10	1					7		9		6	5					
		2		8			11	3				10	1	4				7		9		6	5					
		2		8			11	3				10	1	4				7		9		6	5					
		2		8			11	3				10	1	4				7		9		6	5					
		2		8			11	3				10	1	4			5	7		9		6						
		2		8			11	3				10	1	4			5	7		9		6						
		2		8			11	3				10	1	4			5			9		6		7				
		2					11	3				10	1			9	5	7		8		6						
		2					11					10	1			8	5	7		9		6					3	
	5	2		8			11					10	1					7		9		6					3	
	4	2		8			11					10	1					7		9		6					3	
		2		8	11							10	1	4			5	7		9		6					3	
		2		8	11							10	1	5				7		9		6					3	
		2			11							10		8			5	7		9		6			1		3	
		2			11							10		8				7		9		6	5		1		3	
		2			11			3				10		8				7		9		6	5		1			
10	4	2		8			11	3												9	1	6	5	7				
10	3	2		8			11						1	4						9		6	5	7				
10	3	2		8			11						1	4						9		6	5	7				
		2		8			11					10		4						9		6	5	7	1		3	
		2					11				8	10		4						9		6	5	7	1		3	
		2			11						8	10		4						9		6	5	7	1		3	
8		2					11					10		4						9		6	5	7	1		3	
	3	2					11					10		4		9				8			5	7	1			
		2		8			11					10		4		9		7					5		1		3	
10	3	2					11							4		9				8		6	5	7	1			
		2					11					10		4		9				8			5	7	1	3		
	3						11		6			10		4					8	9	1		5	7		2		
	3			10			11		6					4		9			8		1		5	7		2		
	3			10			11		6					4		9			8		1		5	7		2		
	3			10			11		6					4		9			8		1		5	7		2		
	3			10			11		6			4		7	5	9			8		1					2		
							11		6			4		7		9			8	10	1		5			2	3	
	3						11		6	7		4	1			9			8	10			5			2		
	3				11	6						10	1	4		7			8	9			5				2	
	3			10	11	6							1	4		9			8				5	7			2	
	3			10	11	6					7		1	4					8	9			5				2	
5	16	32	1	24	9	8	33	12	7	1	4	32	21	33	4	15	10	21	10	32	7	26	28	16	14	8	19	
3				6	1		15	1				6		6	2	11		3	5	25				5				2

Bell S	Buckingham VF	Channell FC	Day A	Duncan A	Edrich WJ	Evans T	Evans W	Fullwood J	Grice F	Hall AE	Hall AG	Hall GW	Hooper PGW	Howe LF	Hunt DA	Hunt GS	Jones C	McCormick J	Meek J	Morrison JA	Nicholls JH	Phypers E	Rowe AS	Sargent FA	Taylor A	Ward RA	Whatley WJ	Own-goals
10	3	2		8			11						1	4						9		6	5	7				
		2		8			11					10		4						9		6	5	7	1		3	
		2		8			11					10		4						9		6	5	7	1		3	
		2					11					10		4		8				9			5	7	1		3	
		2					11	3				10		4		8				9			5	7	1			
	6	2					11					10		4		9				8			5	7	1		3	
1	2	6	0	3	0	0	6	1	0	0	0	5	1	6	0	3	0	0	0	6	0	3	6	6	5	0	4	
							1							1		2				3				3				

League Table

	P	W	D	L	F	A	Pts
Manchester United	42	22	12	8	85	43	56
Charlton Athletic	42	22	11	9	85	58	55
Sheffield United	42	20	12	10	79	50	52
West Ham United	42	22	8	12	90	68	52
TOTTENHAM HOTSPUR	42	18	13	11	91	55	49
Leicester City	42	19	10	13	79	57	48
Plymouth Argyle	42	20	8	14	71	57	48
Newcastle United	42	20	6	16	88	79	46
Fulham	42	15	14	13	76	52	44
Blackpool	42	18	7	17	93	72	43
Norwich City	42	17	9	16	72	65	43
Bradford City	42	15	13	14	55	65	43
Swansea Town	42	15	9	18	67	76	39
Bury	42	13	12	17	66	84	38
Burnley	42	12	13	17	50	59	37
Bradford Park Avenue	42	14	9	19	62	84	37
Southampton	42	14	9	19	47	65	37
Doncaster Rovers	42	14	9	19	51	71	37
Nottingham Forest	42	12	11	19	69	76	35
Barnsley	42	12	9	21	54	80	33
Port Vale	42	12	8	22	56	106	32
Hull City	42	5	10	27	47	111	20

1936-37

DIVISION TWO

Manager: Jack Tresadern

Did you know that?

Bill Edrich was a promising winger who had moved up from Norfolk to London principally to play cricket for Middlesex. After performing well for Lord Tennyson's team in India during 1937–38 he decided to give up football to concentrate on the summer game. While Spurs always harboured hopes Edrich would one day return to football and retained his League registration for several years, Edrich's first love was always cricket and he went on to become one of England's finest.

LEAGUE DEBUTANTS

Aug 29	v West Ham United	Stan Alexander
Aug 29	v West Ham United	John Hall
Aug 29	v West Ham United	George Ludford
Sep 12	v Newcastle United	Jim Blyth
Sep 12	v Newcastle United	Les Miller
Sep 19	v Bradford	Jimmy Brown
Jan 2	v Norwich City	Bert Ringrose
Jan 9	v Newcastle United	Albert Page

Match No.	Date		Opponents		Result		Scorers	Attendan
1	Aug	29	A	West Ham United	L	1-2	Morrison	31,9
2		31	A	Blackpool	D	0-0		23,8
3	Sep	5	H	Norwich City	L	2-3	G.S.Hunt, Edrich	32,7
4		12	A	Newcastle United	W	1-0	Morrison	28,3
5		14	H	Leicester City	W	4-2	Morrison 2, Bell, W.Evans	17,9
6		19	H	Bradford	W	5-1	Morrison 4, W.Evans	33,1
7		21	H	Blackpool	L	1-2	Morrison	16,3
8		26	A	Barnsley	L	0-1		12,0
9	Oct	3	H	Sheffield United	D	2-2	Morrison, Edrich	34,5
10		10	A	Burnley	L	1-3	Morrison	20,4
11		17	H	Southampton	W	4-0	McCormick, Morrison 2, G.W.Hall	26,3
12		24	A	Swansea Town	L	1-2	Meek	15,5
13		31	H	Bradford City	W	5-1	Ward, Meek, Morrison 3	16,6
14	Nov	7	A	Aston Villa	D	1-1	Morrison	37,2
15		14	H	Chesterfield	W	5-1	G.S.Hunt 3 (2 pens), Morrison, Miller	30,0
16		28	H	Plymouth Argyle	L	1-3	G.S.Hunt	32,3
17	Dec	5	A	Coventry City	L	0-1		27,3
18		12	H	Doncaster Rovers	W	2-0	McCormick, G.S.Hunt	16,8
19		19	A	Fulham	D	3-3	Ward (pen), Morrison, Miller	20,4
20		25	A	Blackburn Rovers	W	4-0	Meek, Morrison 2, Miller	26,7
21		26	H	West Ham United	L	2-3	Meek, Miller	34,1
22		28	H	Blackburn Rovers	W	5-1	McCormick, Miller 4	16,1
23	Jan	2	A	Norwich City	W	3-2	Morrison 3	13,1
24		9	H	Newcastle United	L	0-1		30,5
25		23	A	Bradford	L	2-3	Meek 2	7,4
26	Feb	3	H	Barnsley	W	3-0	Meek, Duncan, Edrich	11,0
27		6	A	Sheffield United	L	2-3	McCormick, Morrison	22,8
28		13	H	Burnley	W	3-0	McCormick, Morrison, Miller	30,2
29		24	A	Southampton	L	0-1		5,2
30		27	H	Swansea Town	W	3-1	Duncan 3	26,3
31	Mar	10	A	Bradford City	D	2-2	Meek, G.S.Hunt	6,0
32		13	H	Aston Villa	D	2-2	Meek, Miller	35,6
33		20	A	Chesterfield	W	3-1	McCormick 3	13,6
34		26	A	Bury	L	3-5	G.S.Hunt, Duncan, Miller	12,7
35		27	H	Nottingham Forest	W	2-1	G.S.Hunt 2	23,8
36		29	H	Bury	W	2-0	Duncan, Miller	27,6
37	Apr	3	A	Plymouth Argyle	D	2-2	Morrison, Duncan	19,1
38		10	H	Coventry City	W	3-1	Ward (pen), Duncan 2	18,5
39		17	A	Doncaster Rovers	D	1-1	Morrison	3,5
40		21	A	Nottingham Forest	L	0-3		14,6
41		24	H	Fulham	D	1-1	Alexander	21,1
42	May	1	A	Leicester City	L	1-4	Morrison	22,7
								Appearanc
								Goa

FA Cup

R3	Jan	16	A	Portsmouth	W	5-0	Morrison 3, Duncan, Miller	32,6
R4		30	H	Plymouth Argyle	W	1-0	McCormick	42,4
R5	Feb	20	A	Everton	D	1-1	McCormick	57,1
R5r		22	H	Everton	W	4-3	Meek, Morrison 3	46,9
R6	Mar	6	H	Preston North End	L	1-3	Duncan	71,9
								Appearanc
								Goa

Alsford WJ	Bell S	Blyth J	Brown J	Buckingham VF	Duncan A	Edrich WJ	Evans T	Evans W	Fullwood J	Grice F	Hall AE	Hall GW	Hall J	Hooper PGW	Howe LF	Hunt DA	Hunt GS	Ludford GA	McCormick J	Meek J	Miller LR	Morrison JA	Page AE	Phypers E	Ringrose AA	Rowe AS	Ward RA	Whatley WJ
				3				11		6			1		4			10	7			9				5	2	
6								11				10	1		4		9		7	8						5	2	3
6						11	4					10	1		5		9		7	8							2	3
	10	5			8				3			6	1		4				7		11	9					2	
	10	5			8			11	3			6	1		4							9					2	
		5	10		8			11	3			6	1		4							9					2	
		5			8			11	3		10	4	1		6							9					2	
			10			11						6	1		4	9						8				5	2	3
					10	11						6	1		4					8		9				5	2	3
					10	11				6				1	4				7	8		9				5	2	3
						11				6		10		1	4				7	8		9				5	2	3
			10			11				6			1		4				7	8		9				5	2	3
		5						11		6		10	1		4				7	8		9					2	3
		5	8					11		6		10	1		4				7			9					2	3
		5								6		10	1		4		8		7		11	9					2	3
		5								6		10	1		4		8		7		11	9					2	3
4		5								6		10	1				8		7		11	9					2	3
4		5								6		10	1		8		9		7		11						2	3
4		5		3	10					6			1						7	8	11	9					2	
4				3	10					6			1						7	8	11	9				5	2	
4				3	10					6			1						7	8	11	9				5	2	
				3	10							6	1		4		9		7	8	11					5		2
				6	10								1		4				7	8	11	9			2	5		3
				6	10				3				1		4				7		11	9	5		2			
				4	10					6			1						7	8	11	9	5				2	3
				4	10	11				6			1						7	8		9				5	2	3
				4	10	11				6			1						7	8		9				5	2	3
				4	10					6			1						7	8	11	9				5	2	3
				4								10		1	8		9				11		5	6	3		2	
				4	10					6			1						7	8	11	9				5	2	3
				4	10								1				9		7	8	11		5	6	2			3
				4	10					6			1				9		7	8	11		5		2			3
				4	10					6			1				9		7	8	11		5		2			3
				4	10					6			1				9		7	8	11		5		2			3
				4	10					6			1				9		7	8	11		5		2			3
				6	10								1		4				7	8	11	9	5		2			3
				6	10	11							1		4				7	8		9	5		2			3
				6	10								1		4				7	8	11	9	5				2	3
				6	10								1		4				7	8	11	9	5				2	3
				6	10	11							1		4				7	8		9	5				2	3
				6	8	11						10	1		4							9	5				2	3
				6	10							11	1		4				7	8		9	5				2	3
7	2	11	4	25	29	11	1	7	5	22	1	19	39	3	28	1	13	1	35	28	23	32	15	2	10	15	32	32
	1				9	3		2				1					10		8	9	12	29					3	

Alsford WJ	Bell S	Blyth J	Brown J	Buckingham VF	Duncan A	Edrich WJ	Evans T	Evans W	Fullwood J	Grice F	Hall AE	Hall GW	Hall J	Hooper PGW	Howe LF	Hunt DA	Hunt GS	Ludford GA	McCormick J	Meek J	Miller LR	Morrison JA	Page AE	Phypers E	Ringrose AA	Rowe AS	Ward RA	Whatley WJ
				4	10					6			1						7	8	11	9				5	2	3
				4	10					6			1						7	8	11	9				5	2	3
				4	10					6			1						7	8	11	9				5	2	3
				4	10					6			1						7	8	11	9				5	2	3
				4	10					6			1						7	8	11	9				5	2	3
0	0	0	0	5	5	0	0	0	0	5	0	0	5	0	0	0	0	0	5	5	5	5	0	0	0	5	5	5
					2														2	1	1	6						

League Table

	P	W	D	L	F	A	Pts
Leicester City	42	24	8	10	89	57	56
Blackpool	42	24	7	11	88	53	55
Bury	42	22	8	12	74	55	52
Newcastle United	42	22	5	15	80	56	49
Plymouth Argyle	42	18	13	11	71	53	49
West Ham United	42	19	11	12	73	55	49
Sheffield United	42	18	10	14	66	54	46
Coventry City	42	17	11	14	66	54	45
Aston Villa	42	16	12	14	82	70	44
TOTTENHAM HOTSPUR	42	17	9	16	88	66	43
Fulham	42	15	13	14	71	61	43
Blackburn Rovers	42	16	10	16	70	62	42
Burnley	42	16	10	16	57	61	42
Barnsley	42	16	9	17	50	64	41
Chesterfield	42	16	8	18	84	89	40
Swansea Town	42	15	7	20	50	65	37
Norwich City	42	14	8	20	63	71	36
Nottingham Forest	42	12	10	20	68	90	34
Southampton	42	11	12	19	53	77	34
Bradford Park Avenue	42	12	9	21	52	88	33
Bradford City	42	9	12	21	54	94	30
Doncaster Rovers	42	7	10	25	30	84	24

1937-38

DIVISION TWO

Manager: Jack Tresadern

Did you know that?

In January 1938 the Gresley B17 *Sandringham* class LNER steam locomotive No. 2830, previously named *Thoresby Park*, was renamed *Tottenham Hotspur*. It was the second such locomotive to carry Spurs' name, No. 2870 having done so between May and September 1937 before being renamed *City of London*.

LEAGUE DEBUTANTS

Aug 28	v Coventry City Isaac Spelman
Sep 16	v Sheffield Wednesday Jack Gibbons
Oct 9	v Manchester United Colin Lyman
Oct 23	v Plymouth Argyle Arthur Hitchins
Oct 23	v Plymouth Argyle George Jeffrey

Match No.	Date			Opponents	Result		Scorers	Attendan
1	Aug	28	H	Coventry City	D	0-0		32,5
2		30	H	Burnley	W	4-0	Ward (pen), Morrison 3	13,7
3	Sep	4	A	Nottingham Forest	L	1-3	Sargent	16,4
4		6	A	Burnley	L	1-2	Miller	11,2
5		11	H	Newcastle United	D	2-2	Sargent, Morrison	25,5
6		16	A	Sheffield Wednesday	W	3-0	Sargent, Morrison, Gibbons	13,2
7		18	A	Luton Town	W	4-2	Sargent, Morrison 2, Miller	23,7
8		25	H	Barnsley	W	3-0	G.W.Hall, Gibbons, Miller	26,4
9	Oct	2	A	Stockport County	L	2-3	G.W.Hall, Morrison	19,0
10		9	H	Manchester United	L	0-1		31,1
11		16	A	Fulham	L	1-3	Sargent	29,5
12		23	H	Plymouth Argyle	W	3-2	Sargent, Morrison, Jeffrey	22,7
13		30	A	Chesterfield	D	2-2	Ward (pen), Morrison	16,0
14	Nov	6	H	Swansea Town	W	2-0	Gibbons 2	22,3
15		13	A	Norwich City	L	1-2	Gibbons	19,0
16		20	H	West Ham United	W	2-0	Sargent, Gibbons	47,0
17		27	A	Bradford	L	1-3	Gibbons	10,7
18	Dec	4	H	Aston Villa	W	2-1	G.W.Hall, Morrison	37,2
19		11	A	Southampton	L	1-2	Gibbons	17,7
20		18	H	Blackburn Rovers	W	3-1	Grice, Lyman 2	20,2
21		25	A	Bury	W	2-1	Morrison, Gibbons	13,6
22		27	H	Bury	L	1-3	Gibbons	40,9
23	Jan	1	A	Coventry City	L	1-2	Duncan	24,3
24		15	H	Nottingham Forest	W	3-0	Sargent, G.W.Hall, Gibbons	21,2
25		29	H	Luton Town	W	3-0	Morrison, Lyman 2	29,8
26	Feb	2	A	Newcastle United	L	0-1		11,2
27		5	A	Barnsley	D	1-1	Sargent	13,3
28		19	A	Manchester United	W	1-0	Sargent	34,6
29		23	H	Stockport County	W	2-0	Howe 2	11,0
30		26	H	Fulham	D	1-1	Morrison	34,0
31	Mar	9	A	Plymouth Argyle	D	2-2	Morrison, Duncan	15,7
32		12	H	Chesterfield	W	2-0	Sargent, Miller	20,9
33		19	A	Swansea Town	L	2-3	Meek, Gibbons	10,6
34		26	H	Norwich City	W	4-0	Ward, Sargent, Morrison 2	18,4
35	Apr	2	A	West Ham United	W	3-1	Sargent, Gibbons, Miller	30,0
36		9	H	Bradford	W	2-1	Morrison 2	17,9
37		15	H	Sheffield United	L	1-2	Howe	23,1
38		16	A	Aston Villa	L	0-2		53,7
39		18	A	Sheffield United	L	0-1		45,3
40		23	H	Southampton	W	5-0	Ward (pen), Sargent, Morrison 3	15,9
41		30	A	Blackburn Rovers	L	1-2	Howe	7,0
42	May	7	H	Sheffield Wednesday	L	1-2	Sargent	13,3
								Appearanc
								Goa

FA Cup

R3	Jan	8	H	Blackburn Rovers	W	3-2	Sargent, Gibbons 2	35,5
R4		22	A	New Brighton	D	0-0		13,0
R4r		26	H	New Brighton	W	5-2	Morrison 2, Gibbons 2, Lyman	36,0
R5	Feb	12	A	Chesterfield	D	2-2	Gibbons, Miller	30,5
R5r		16	H	Chesterfield	W	2-1	Sargent, Morrison	36,9
R6	Mar	5	H	Sunderland	L	0-1		75,0
								Appearanc
								Goa

ingham VF

Duncan A	Fullwood J	Gibbons AH	Grice F	Hall AE	Hall GW	Hall J	Hitchins AW	Hooper PGW	Howe LF	Jeffrey G	Ludford GA	Lyman CC	McCormick J	Meek J	Miller LR	Morrison JA	Page AE	Rowe AS	Sargent FA	Spelman I	Ward RA	Whatley WJ
10					8	1							7			9	5		11	4	2	3
10					8	1			4				7			9	5		11		2	3
10					8	1			4				7			9	5		11		2	3
10	3		6		8	1			4						11	9	5		7		2	
10	3				8	1			4						11	9	5		7		2	
	3	10			8	1			4						11	9	5		7		2	
	3	10			8	1			4						11	9	5		7		2	
	3	10			8	1			4						11	9	5		7		2	
	3	10			8	1			4						11	9	5		7		2	
	3	10			8	1			4			11				9	5		7		2	
10	3				8	1			4			11				9		5	7		2	
	3		6	8		1	5		4	10		11				9			7		2	
	3	10	6		8		5	1	4			11				9			7		2	
		10	6		8		5	1	4			11				9			7		2	3
		10	6		8		5	1	4			11				9			7		2	3
		10	6		8			1	4			11				9	5		7		2	3
		10	6		8			1	4			11				9	5		7		2	3
		10	6		8			1	4			11				9	5		7		2	3
		10	6		8			1	4			11				9	5		7		2	3
		10	6		8			1	4			11				9	5		7		2	3
		10	6		8			1	4			11				9	5		7		2	3
		10	6	8				1	4			11				9	5		7		2	3
10			6				5	1				11		8		9			7		2	3
		10			8		5	1	4			11				9			7		2	3
10							5	1	4			11		8		9			7		2	3
10					8		5	1				11				9			7	4	2	3
		10	6		8			1				11				9		5	7		2	3
10	3				8		5	1			9				11				7	6	2	
					8		5	1	10						11	9			7	4	2	3
		10			8			1							11	9		5	7	6	2	3
10	3				8			1							11	9	5		7	6	2	
10			6					1	4					8	11	9		5	7		2	3
		9	6					1	4			10		8	11			5	7		2	
			6		8			1	4					10	11	9		5	7		2	
		10			8			1	4						11	9		5	7		2	3
		10						1	4					8	11	9		5	7		2	3
		10			8			1	4						11	9		5	7		2	3
		10						1				11		8		9	5		7	4	2	3
10		9		8				1				11					5		7	4	2	3
	3	10		8				1	4			11				9	5		7		2	
	3	10		8				1	4			11				9	5		7		2	
	3	10		8				1	4			11				9	5		7		2	
13	15	27	17	6	30	12	10	30	33	1	1	24	3	7	16	39	23	9	42	8	42	25
2		13	1		4				4	1		4		1	5	22			15		4	

Duncan A	Fullwood J	Gibbons AH	Grice F	Hall AE	Hall GW	Hall J	Hitchins AW	Hooper PGW	Howe LF	Jeffrey G	Ludford GA	Lyman CC	McCormick J	Meek J	Miller LR	Morrison JA	Page AE	Rowe AS	Sargent FA	Spelman I	Ward RA	Whatley WJ
		10			8		5	1	4			11				9			7		2	3
		10			8		5	1	4			11				9			7		2	3
		10			8		5	1	4			11				9			7		2	3
		10	6		8			1							11	9		5	7		2	3
		10	6		8			1							11	9		5	7		2	3
		10	6		8			1				11				9		5	7		2	3
0	0	6	3	0	6	0	3	6	3	0	0	4	0	0	2	6	0	3	6	0	6	6
		5										1			1	3			2			

League Table

	P	W	D	L	F	A	Pts
Aston Villa	42	25	7	10	73	35	57
Manchester United	42	22	9	11	82	50	53
Sheffield United	42	22	9	11	73	56	53
Coventry City	42	20	12	10	66	45	52
TOTTENHAM HOTSPUR	42	19	6	17	76	54	44
Burnley	42	17	10	15	54	54	44
Bradford Park Avenue	42	17	9	16	69	56	43
Fulham	42	16	11	15	61	57	43
West Ham United	42	14	14	14	53	52	42
Bury	42	18	5	19	63	60	41
Chesterfield	42	16	9	17	63	63	41
Luton Town	42	15	10	17	89	86	40
Plymouth Argyle	42	14	12	16	57	65	40
Norwich City	42	14	11	17	56	75	39
Southampton	42	15	9	18	55	77	39
Blackburn Rovers	42	14	10	18	71	80	38
Sheffield Wednesday	42	14	10	18	49	56	38
Swansea Town	42	13	12	17	45	73	38
Newcastle United	42	14	8	20	51	58	36
Nottingham Forest	42	14	8	20	47	60	36
Barnsley	42	11	14	17	50	64	36
Stockport County	42	11	9	22	43	70	31

1938-39

DIVISION TWO

Manager: Peter McWilliam

Did you know that?

When Spurs travelled to Manchester for their meeting with City on 5 November 1938, Bert Sproston was expected to occupy his usual right-back slot in Spurs' defence. He played at right-back that day but not for Spurs. Prior to the match his transfer to City was negotiated and completed.

LEAGUE DEBUTANTS

Aug 27	v Southampton Bert Sproston
Oct 22	v Blackburn Rovers Bill Nicholson
Nov 19	v Swansea City Freddie Cox
Feb 4	v Norwich City Ron Burgess
Feb 4	v Norwich City Albert Tomkin

Match No.	Date			Opponents	Result		Scorers	Attendan
1	Aug	27	A	Southampton	W	2-1	Sargent, G.W.Hall	22,6
2		29	H	Sheffield Wednesday	D	3-3	Howe, G.W.Hall 2	28,1
3	Sep	3	H	Coventry City	W	2-1	Morrison, Lyman	39,9
4		10	A	Nottingham Forest	L	1-2	G.W.Hall	18,5
5		12	H	Sheffield United	D	2-2	Morrison, A.E.Hall	21,3
6		17	H	Newcastle United	W	1-0	Whatley (pen)	39,6
7		24	A	West Bromwich Albion	L	3-4	G.W.Hall, Morrison, A.E.Hall	24,9
8	Oct	1	H	Norwich City	W	4-1	G.W.Hall, A.E.Hall 2, Lyman	30,0
9		8	A	Luton Town	D	0-0		21,0
10		15	H	Fulham	W	1-0	Lyman	46,6
11		22	A	Blackburn Rovers	L	1-3	Lyman	18,1
12		29	H	West Ham United	W	2-1	Lyman 2	51,1
13	Nov	5	A	Manchester City	L	0-2		47,9
14		12	H	Bradford	D	2-2	Spelman, Ludford	24,1
15		19	A	Swansea Town	D	1-1	Cox	13,1
16		26	H	Chesterfield	D	2-2	Whatley (pen), Ludford	24,4
17	Dec	3	A	Tranmere Rovers	W	2-0	A.E.Hall 2	12,0
18		10	H	Millwall	W	4-0	Ward (pen), Cox, G.W.Hall, A.E.Hall	47,2
19		17	A	Bury	L	1-3	A.E.Hall	5,7
20		24	H	Southampton	D	1-1	Ward (pen)	9,4
21		26	A	Burnley	L	0-1		15,6
22		27	H	Burnley	W	1-0	Duncan	30,2
23		31	A	Coventry City	L	0-4		19,4
24	Jan	14	H	Nottingham Forest	W	4-1	Sargent, A.E.Hall, Duncan Miller	19,0
25		28	H	West Bromwich Albion	D	2-2	Sargent, Morrison	38,1
26	Feb	4	A	Norwich City	W	2-1	Buckingham, Ludford	15,3
27		11	H	Luton Town	L	0-1		30,7
28		18	A	Fulham	L	0-1		26,4
29		25	H	Blackburn Rovers	W	4-3	Sargent, Morrison 2, Miller	22,7
30	Mar	1	A	Newcastle United	W	1-0	A.E.Hall	18,5
31		4	A	West Ham United	W	2-0	G.W.Hall, Duncan	20,8
32		11	H	Manchester City	L	2-3	Hitchins, G.W.Hall	27,4
33		18	A	Bradford	D	0-0		8,2
34		25	H	Swansea Town	W	3-0	Burgess, Morrison 2	17,4
35	Apr	1	A	Chesterfield	L	1-3	Spelman	15,2
36		7	H	Plymouth Argyle	W	1-0	Miller	33,6
37		8	H	Tranmere Rovers	W	3-1	Ward (pen), Morrison, Miller	19,2
38		10	A	Plymouth Argyle	W	1-0	Ludford	15,2
39		15	A	Millwall	L	0-2		33,4
40		22	H	Bury	W	4-3	Ludford 2, Duncan 2	16,2
41		29	A	Sheffield Wednesday	L	0-1		27,6
42	May	6	A	Sheffield United	L	1-6	Miller	38,4

Appearanc

Goa

FA Cup

R3	Jan	7	H	Watford	W	7-1	Ward (pen), Sargent, G.W.Hall 2, Duncan, Miller 2	34,8
R4		21	A	West Ham United	D	3-3	Sargent, Morrison, Duncan	42,7
R4r		30	H	West Ham United	D*	1-1	Sargent	50,7
R4r	Feb	2	N#	West Ham United	L	1-2	Morrison	50,4

*after extra-time #played at Highbury

Appearanc

Goa

…ingham VF	Duncan A	Fullwood J	Gibbons AH	Grice F	Hall AE	Hall GW	Hall J	Hitchins AW	Hooper PGW	Howe LF	Jeffrey G	Ludford GA	Lyman CC	McCormick J	Meek J	Miller LR	Morrison JA	Page AE	Rowe AS	Sargent FA	Spelman I	Ward RA	Whatley WJ
				10	8			1	4		11				9		5	7		2			3
				10	8			1	4		11				9		5	7		2			3
				10	8			1	4		11				9		5	7		2			3
				10	8			1	4		11				9		5	7		2			3
				10	8			1	4		11				9		5	7		2			3
				10	8			1	4		11				9		5	7		2			3
				10	8	1					11				9		5	7	4	2			3
				10	8			1		9	11						5	7	4			2	3
				10	8			1			11				9		5	7	4			2	3
				10	8			1			11				9		5	7	4	2			3
				10	8			1			11				9	3	5	7	4			2	
		10			8			1			11				9		5	7	4	2			3
		10			8			1			11				9		5	7	4			2	3
					10			1		9	11				8	3	5	7	4			2	
	7	10			8			1		9	11					3	5		4			2	
	7			10	8			1		9	11						5		4			2	3
	7			10	8		5	1							9			11	4			2	3
	7			10	8		5	1			11				9				4			2	3
	7			10	8		5	1			11				9				4			2	3
		10		9	8		5	1			11							7	4			2	3
	7	10		9	8		5	1						11					4			2	3
		10		9	8		5	1			11							7	4			2	3
		10		9	8		5	1						11				7	4			2	3
		10		9	8		5	1						11				7	4			2	3
					8		5	1	10		11				9			7	4			2	3
4		10			8			1		9						3	5	7			11	2	
4		10		9	8		5	1										7			11	2	3
4		10		8		1	5				11				9			7				2	3
4				10	8		5	1						11	9			7				2	3
4				10	8		5	1						11	9			7				2	3
4		10			8		5	1						11	9			7				2	3
4		10			8		5	1						11	9			7				2	3
4		10			8		5	1						11	9			7				2	3
4		10			8		5	1						11	9	3		7				2	
4					8		5	1				7		11	9	3			10			2	
4		10			8		5	1						11	9			7				2	3
4		10			8		5	1						11	9			7				2	3
10			6		8		5	1	4	9				11				7				2	3
4	8	9					5	1		10				11				7				2	3
4		10			8		5	1		9				11				7				2	3
4	7	10			8		5	1		9				11		3						2	
4	7	10			8		5	1		9				11		3						2	
17	9	21	1	24	40	2	25	40	8	10	22	1	0	17	27	8	17	34	20	9	2	33	34
1	2	5		10	9		1		1	6	6			5	9			4	2			3	2

…ingham VF	Duncan A	Fullwood J	Gibbons AH	Grice F	Hall AE	Hall GW	Hall J	Hitchins AW	Hooper PGW	Howe LF	Jeffrey G	Ludford GA	Lyman CC	McCormick J	Meek J	Miller LR	Morrison JA	Page AE	Rowe AS	Sargent FA	Spelman I	Ward RA	Whatley WJ
		10		9	8		5	1						11				7	4			2	3
		10			8		5	1						11	9			7	4			2	3
					10		5	1			11		8		9			7	4			2	3
				10	8		5	1			11				9			7	4			2	3
0	0	2	0	2	4	0	4	4	0	0	2	0	1	2	3	0	0	4	4	0	0	4	4
		2			2									2	2			3				1	

League Table

	P	W	D	L	F	A	Pts
Blackburn Rovers	42	25	5	12	94	60	55
Sheffield United	42	20	14	8	69	41	54
Sheffield Wednesday	42	21	11	10	88	59	53
Coventry City	42	21	8	13	62	45	50
Manchester City	42	21	7	14	96	72	49
Chesterfield	42	20	9	13	69	52	49
Luton Town	42	22	5	15	82	66	49
TOTTENHAM HOTSPUR	42	19	9	14	67	62	47
Newcastle United	42	18	10	14	61	48	46
West Bromwich Albion	42	18	9	15	89	72	45
West Ham United	42	17	10	15	70	52	44
Fulham	42	17	10	15	61	55	44
Millwall	42	14	14	14	64	53	42
Burnley	42	15	9	18	50	56	39
Plymouth Argyle	42	15	8	19	49	55	38
Bury	42	12	13	17	65	74	37
Bradford Park Avenue	42	12	11	19	61	82	35
Southampton	42	13	9	20	56	82	35
Swansea Town	42	11	12	19	50	83	34
Nottingham Forest	42	10	11	21	49	82	31
Norwich City	42	13	5	24	50	91	31
Tranmere Rovers	42	6	5	31	39	99	17

1939-40

DIVISION TWO

Manager: Peter McWilliam

Did you know that?

GUEST PLAYERS

George Burchell
Romford
Doug Hunt
Sheffield Wednesday
Syd Ottewell
Chesterfield
Vic Woodley
Chelsea

Match No.	Date			Opponents	Result		Scorers	Attendan
1	Aug	26	H	Birmingham	D	1-1	Sargent	28,3
2		31	A	Newport County	D	1-1	Burgess	19,7
3	Sep	2	A	West Bromwich Albion	W	4-3	Morrison 3, Dix	16,0
								Appearanc
								Goa

Football League South Group A

1	Oct	21	A	Southend United	W	2-1	Ludford 2	4,0
2		28	H	Millwall	W	3-0	Ludford, Medley 2	4,8
3	Nov	4	A	West Ham United	L	1-2	G.W.Hall	7,8
4		11	H	Watford	W	8-2	Bennett 3, Morrison 2, Medley 3	4,9
5		18	A*	Arsenal	L	1-2	Howe	15,0
6		25	H	Charlton Athletic	W	4-2	Sargent, Bennett 2, Howe	6,9
7	Dec	2	A	Clapton Orient	L	1-2	Howe	8,0
8		9	H	Crystal Palace	L	1-3	Morrison	4,2
9		16	A	Norwich City	L	2-5	Ludford 2	3,0
10		23	H	Southend United	L#	3-4	Bennett, A.E.Hall 2	1,0
11		25	A	Millwall	L	1-5	Morrison	7,2
12		26	H	West Ham United	L	0-1		4,2
13		30	A	Watford	L	1-6	A.E.Hall	2,0
14	Jan	13	A	Charlton Athletic	W	5-1	Howe, Sargent 2, Morrison, Medley	4,0
15		17	H	Southend United	L	2-4	Medley 2	1,0
16		20	H	Clapton Orient	L	2-3	Morrison 2	2,8
17		25	H	Arsenal	L	0-1		9,0
18	Feb	28	A	Crystal Palace	D	1-1	Stevens	2,0
19	May	27	H	Norwich City	D	2-2	G.W.Hall, Ludford	7
								Appearanc
								Goa

*played at White Hart Lane #abandoned after 60 mins - fog

Football League South Group C

1	Feb	10	A	West Ham United	L	0-2		7,5
2		17	H	Charlton Athletic	W	2-0	Burgess, Ludford	3,5
3		24	A	Chelsea	W	2-0	G.W.Hall, Dix	14,0
4	Mar	2	H	Southampton	W	4-1	Hunt, Dix 2, Medley	5,4
5		9	H	Brentford	D	1-1	G.W.Hall	9,8
6		16	A	Portsmouth	W	2-1	Duncan, Dix	7,0
7		22	H	Millwall	L	1-2	Lyman	15,0
8		23	A	Fulham	W	3-2	Morrison, Dix 2	8,0
9		25	A	Millwall	D	1-1	Ludford	14,6
10		30	H	Arsenal	H	1-1	Medley	15,0
11	Apr	6	H	West Ham United	L	2-6	Howe, Morrison	15,0
12		10	H	Fulham	W	3-1	Cox, Morrison 2	2,0
13		13	A	Charlton Athletic	W	4-2	Morrison 3, Medley	5,0
14		24	A*	Arsenal	W	4-2	Duncan, Morrison 2, Dix	4,4
15	May	4	A	Brentford	W	3-2	Morrison 3	3,0
16		11	H	Portsmouth	W	4-1	Morrison 3, Medley	5,3
17		18	A	Southampton	D	3-3	Morrison 3	3,0
18		25	H	Chelsea	W	3-2	Burgess, Duncan 2	4,8
								Appearance
								Goal

*played at White Hart Lane

Football League War Cup

R1	Apr	20	A	Crystal Palace	L	1-4	Cox	15,4
R1		27	H	Crystal Palace	W	2-1	Howe, Dix	12,3
								Appearance
								Goal

Buckingham VF	Burchell GS	Burgess WAR	Cox FJA	Ditchburn EG	Dix RW	Dorling GJ	Dowers AJ	Duncan A	Evans N	Hall AE	Hall GW	Hitchins AW	Hooper PGW	Howe LF	Hunt DA	Ludford GA	Lyman CC	McCormick J	McEwan FF	Medley LD	Morrison JA	Nicholson WE	Ottewell S	Page AE	Piper GH	Sargent FA	Spelman I	Stevens LWG	Tomkin AH	Ward RA	Whatley WJ	Wilbert GN	Woodley VR
6		4			10						8	5	1			9	11					3				7				2			
6		4			10						8	5	1			9						3				7			11	2			
6		4			10						8		1								9	3		5		7			11	2			
3	0	3	0	0	3	0	0	0	0	0	3	2	3	0	0	2	1	0	0	0	1	3	0	1	0	3	0	0	2	3	0	0	0
		1			1																3					1							

Buckingham VF	Burchell GS	Burgess WAR	Cox FJA	Ditchburn EG	Dix RW	Dorling GJ	Dowers AJ	Duncan A	Evans N	Hall AE	Hall GW	Hitchins AW	Hooper PGW	Howe LF	Hunt DA	Ludford GA	Lyman CC	McCormick J	McEwan FF	Medley LD	Morrison JA	Nicholson WE	Ottewell S	Page AE	Piper GH	Sargent FA	Spelman I	Stevens LWG	Tomkin AH	Ward RA	Whatley WJ	Wilbert GN	Woodley VR
6		4				2		10			8	5	1			9				11						7					3		
		4						10			8	5	1			9				11				2		7	6				3		
		4				2		10			8	5	1			9				11						7	6				3		
3						2		10				5	1	4						11	9					7	6						
						2		10			8	5	1	4						11	9					7	6				3		
		4				2					8	5	1	11							9					7	6				3		
4						2					8	5	1	7							9					11	6				3		
												5	1	4					10		9			2		7	6		11		3		
6						2							1	4		9			11		10			5		7					3		
6						2	7			10		5	1	4					11		9										3		
6						2				10			1	4		11					9			5		7					3		
6						2				10		5	1			11					9					7	4				3		
6	2						7			10		5	1			11					9						4				3		
6						2					8	5	1	4						11	9					7					3		
								10			8	5	1	4		6				11	9			2		7					3		
6								10			8	5	1	2						11	9					7	4				3		
		4			10						8	5	1	3			11	7			9						6			2			
			7								8		1	4						11	9			5	6			10		2	3		
		10		1					6		8	5		4		9										7				2	3	11	
10	1	6	1	1	1	11	2	7	1	4	12	16	18	14	0	9	1	1	3	9	15	0	0	6	1	15	11	1	1	3	17	1	0
										3	2			4		6				8	7					3		1					

Buckingham VF	Burchell GS	Burgess WAR	Cox FJA	Ditchburn EG	Dix RW	Dorling GJ	Dowers AJ	Duncan A	Evans N	Hall AE	Hall GW	Hitchins AW	Hooper PGW	Howe LF	Hunt DA	Ludford GA	Lyman CC	McCormick J	McEwan FF	Medley LD	Morrison JA	Nicholson WE	Ottewell S	Page AE	Piper GH	Sargent FA	Spelman I	Stevens LWG	Tomkin AH	Ward RA	Whatley WJ	Wilbert GN	Woodley VR
6											8		1	4	9			7		11	10			5						2	3		
		4			10						8	5	1	6		9		7		11										2	3		
6					10						8	5	1	4						11	9					7				2	3		
					10							5	1	4	9		7			11	8			6						2	3		
					10			8			4	5	1	6			7			11	9									2	3		
					10			8			4	5	1	6				7		11	9									2	3		
					10						4	5	1	6			7			11	9									2	3		
6					10						8	5	1	4			11	7			9									2	3		
6			7					10			8	5	1	4		9	11													2	3		
			7		10	3		8			4	5	1	6		9				11										2			
		4	7		10						8	5	1	6						11	9									2	3		
		4	7		10						8	5		6						11	9									2	3		1
		4	7		10			8				5	1	6						11	9									2	3		
		4	7		10			8				5	1	6						11	9									2	3		
		6	7		10						8	5	1	4						11	9									2	3		
		6	7					10			8	5	1	4						11	9									2	3		
					10			8			4	5	1	6				7		11	9									2	3		
		4	7	1				10			8	5		6							9		11							2	3		
4	0	8	9	1	14	1	0	9	0	0	15	17	16	18	2	3	5	5	0	15	15	0	1	2	0	1	0	0	0	18	17	0	1
		2	1		7			4			2			1	1	2	1			4	18												

Buckingham VF	Burchell GS	Burgess WAR	Cox FJA	Ditchburn EG	Dix RW	Dorling GJ	Dowers AJ	Duncan A	Evans N	Hall AE	Hall GW	Hitchins AW	Hooper PGW	Howe LF	Hunt DA	Ludford GA	Lyman CC	McCormick J	McEwan FF	Medley LD	Morrison JA	Nicholson WE	Ottewell S	Page AE	Piper GH	Sargent FA	Spelman I	Stevens LWG	Tomkin AH	Ward RA	Whatley WJ	Wilbert GN	Woodley VR
		4	7		10						8	5	1	6						11	9									2	3		
		4	7		10			8				5	1	6						11	9									2	3		
0	0	2	2	0	2	0	0	1	0	0	1	2	2	2	0	0	0	0	0	2	2	0	0	0	0	0	0	0	0	2	2	0	0
			1		1									1																			

League Table

	P	W	D	L	F	A	Pts
Luton Town	3	2	1	0	7	1	5
Birmingham	3	2	1	0	5	1	5
Coventry City	3	1	2	0	8	6	4
Plymouth Argyle	3	2	0	1	4	3	4
West Ham United	3	2	0	1	5	4	4
TOTTENHAM HOTSPUR	3	1	2	0	6	5	4
Leicester City	3	2	0	1	6	5	4
Nottingham Forest	3	2	0	1	5	5	4
Newport County	3	1	1	1	5	4	3
Millwall	3	1	1	1	5	4	3
Manchester City	3	1	1	1	6	5	3
West Bromwich Albion	3	1	1	1	8	8	3
Bury	3	1	1	1	4	5	3
Newcastle United	3	1	0	2	8	6	2
Chesterfield	2	1	0	1	2	2	2
Barnsley	3	1	0	2	7	8	2
Southampton	3	1	0	2	5	6	2
Sheffield Wednesday	3	1	0	2	3	5	2
Swansea Town	3	1	0	2	5	11	2
Fulham	3	0	1	2	3	6	1
Burnley	2	0	1	1	1	3	1
Bradford	3	0	1	2	2	7	1

Football League South Group A

	P	W	D	L	F	A	Pts
Arsenal	18	13	4	1	62	22	30
West Ham United	18	12	1	5	57	33	25
Millwall	18	8	5	5	46	38	21
Watford	18	9	3	6	44	38	21
Norwich City	18	7	6	5	41	36	20
Charlton Athletic	18	8	1	9	61	58	17
Crystal Palace	18	5	3	10	39	56	13
Clapton Orient	18	5	3	10	28	60	13
TOTTENHAM HOTSPUR	18	5	2	11	37	43	12
Southend United	18	4	0	14	30	61	8

Football League South Group C

	P	W	D	L	F	A	Pts
TOTTENHAM HOTSPUR	18	11	4	3	43	30	26
West Ham United	18	10	4	4	53	28	24
Arsenal	18	9	5	4	41	26	23
Brentford	18	8	4	6	42	34	20
Millwall	18	7	5	6	36	30	19
Charlton Athletic	18	7	4	7	39	36	18
Fulham	18	8	1	9	38	42	17
Southampton	18	5	3	10	28	55	13
Chelsea	18	4	3	11	33	53	11
Portsmouth	18	3	3	12	26	45	9

1940-41

FOOTBALL LEAGUE SOUTH

Manager: Peter McWilliam

Did you know that?

GUEST PLAYERS

W. Arnold
Leicester City
Ken Burditt
Colchester United
Doug Flack
Fulham
Les Henley
Margate
Taffy O'Callaghan
Fulham
Tom Paton
Bournemouth & Boscombe Athletic
Wilf Saunders
West Bromwich Albion

Match No.	Date		Opponents		Result		Scorers	Attendan
1	Aug	31	H	West Ham United	L	2-3	Burgess 2	2,0
2	Sep	7	A	West Ham United	W1	4-1	Burgess 3, Duncan	3,6
3	Sep	14	H	Chelsea	W2	3-2	Ward, Ludford 2	1,6
4		21	A	Chelsea	L	1-4	Duncan	1,7
5		28	H	Charlton Athletic	L	1-3	Medley	1,5
6	Oct	5	A	Queen's Park Rangers	D	1-1	Ludford	1,8
7		12	H	Arsenal	L3	2-3	Skinner, Medley	4,5
8		19	A	Charlton Athletic	L	0-4		5
9		26	H	Portsmouth	L	1-2	Howe	1,3
10	Nov	2	A	Luton Town	D	1-1	Ludford	1,1
11		16	A5	Arsenal	D	1-1	Burgess	1,9
12		23	H	Luton Town	W4	2-1	Duncan, Ludford	1,2
13		30	A6	Southend United	L	2-3	White, Ludford	1,0
14	Dec	7	H	Queen's Park Rangers	L	2-3	Sargent, Duncan	1,3
15		21	H	Clapton Orient	W	9-0	J.Sperrin 2, Gibbons 3, Duncan 2, Ludford 2	1,2
16		25	H	Millwall	D	3-3	Howe, Gibbons, Ludford	5,0
17		27	A5	Clapton Orient	W	7-0	J.Sperrin, O'Callaghan, Gibbons 3, W.Sperrin, Ludford	1,1
18	Mar	15	A5	Millwall	L	0-1		4,0
19	Apr	26	A	Aldershot	W	3-2	Hall, W.Sperrin, Gibbons	2,8
20	May	10	H	Crystal Palace	D	1-1	W.Sperrin	3,0
21		17	A	Leicester City	W	2-1	Burgess 2	3,0
22		24	H	Leicester City	W	3-0	Broadis, Gibbons, Ludford	3,0
23	Jun	7	H	Fulham	W	2-1	Ward (pen), Broadis	2,8

1 abandoned after 80 mins - air raid warning,
2 match halted after 15 mins - air raid warning - restarted 80 mins later
3 abandoned after 47 mins - air raid warning, 4 abandoned after 60 mins - air raid warning
5 played at White Hart Lane, 6 played at Chelmsford

Appearance
Goa

London War Cup

24	Jan	4	H	Clapton Orient	W	3-0	Gibbons 3	1,5
25		11	A	Clapton Orient	W	9-1	Hall, Broadis 2, Gibbons 3, Duncan, Ludford 2	1,0
26		18	A	Millwall	W	3-1	Broadis, Gibbons 2	6,0
27		25	H	Millwall	W	4-0	Ward (pen), Broadis, Ludford 2	2,2
28	Feb	1	H	West Ham United	L	1-2	Broadis	4,6
29		8	A	West Ham United	L	2-3	Hall, Gibbons	5,2
30	Apr	14	H	Reading	D	2-2	Wallis, Duncan	4,3
31		19	A	Reading	D	2-2	Duncan, Ludford	4,0
32	May	3	H	Arsenal	D	3-3	Ward (pen), K.Bennett, Gibbons	9,65
33		21	A*	Arsenal	W	3-0	Gibbons, Duncan 2	6,6
34		31	H	Brentford	L	0-2		6,4

*played at White Hart Lane

Appearance
Goa

Football League War Cup

R1	Feb	15	H	Bournemouth & Boscombe A	W	4-1	Buckingham, J.Sperrin, Ludford 2	3,4
R1		22	A	Bournemouth & Boscombe A	W	6-1	Ward (pen), Broadis 2, Gibbons 3	1,9
R2	Mar	1	H	Northampton Town	W	4-0	Broadis, Duncan 2, Bedford (og)	4,3
R2		8	A	Northampton Town	W	3-1	W.Sperrin, Broadis, Ludford	5,0
R3		22	H	Cardiff City	D	3-3	Broadis 3	5,2
R3		29	A	Cardiff City	W	3-2	Gibbons, Broadis, Ludford	22,00
R4	Apr	5	A*	Arsenal	L	1-2	Howe	22,10
R4		12	H	Arsenal	D	1-1	Ludford	25,25

*played at White Hart Lane

Appearance
Goa

ld W	Bennett KE	Bennett LD	Broadis IA	Browne J	Buckingham VF	Burditt FCK	Burgess WAR	Duncan A	Flack DW	Gibbons AH	Goodman A	Hall GW	Henley LD	Hitchins AW	Hooper PGW	Howe LF	Ludford GA	McCarthy AC	McCormick J	Medley LD	O'Callaghan E	Paton TG	Piper GH	Sainsbury R	Sargent FA	Saunders WW	Skinner GEH	Sperrin J	Sperrin WT	Wallis JC	Ward RA	Whatley WJ	White RBW	Own-goals
					6		9	10				8		5	1		11						4		7						2	3		
					6		9	10				4		5	1		11		7								8				2	3		
					6		4					8		5	1		11			10				9	7						2	3		
	8				6			10	1			4					9			11			5		7						2	3		
					6		9	10	1			4		5			11			8					7						2	3		
					6			10	1			8		5		4	9			11					7						2	3		
	7				6			10	1				4	5			9			11							8				2	3		
	7				6						10			5	1		9			11			4				8				2	3		
					6		9		1					5		4	11		7		10	8									2	3		
					6		4	10						5			9				11	8				1		7			2	3		
					6		9	10						5			11				8	7				1					2	3	4	
	7			9	6			10						5			11				8					1				2		3	4	
	6							11						5	1		9				8	7							10		2	3	4	
					6			11						5			9	1			8				7				10		2	3	4	
					3			10		9		6		5	1		11				8							7			2		4	
								10		9		8		5	1	6	11											7		2	3		4	
										9		6		5	1	3	11				8							7	10		2		4	
			8					10		9		6		5	1		11												7		2	3	4	
								10		9		6		5	1		11											7	8		2	3	4	
			8					10		9		6		5	1		11												7		2	3	4	
						10	9					6		5	1		8													7	2	3	4	
			8				9			10		6		5	1		11												7		2	3	4	
			8					10		9		6		5	1		11												7		2	3	4	
	5	0	4	1	14	1	9	17	5	8	1	15	1	22	14	4	23	1	2	6	8	4	3	1	6	3	3	5	8	3	22	20	13	
			2				8	6		9		1				2	11			2	1				1		1	3	3		2		1	

ld W	Bennett KE	Bennett LD	Broadis IA	Browne J	Buckingham VF	Burditt FCK	Burgess WAR	Duncan A	Flack DW	Gibbons AH	Goodman A	Hall GW	Henley LD	Hitchins AW	Hooper PGW	Howe LF	Ludford GA	McCarthy AC	McCormick J	Medley LD	O'Callaghan E	Paton TG	Piper GH	Sainsbury R	Sargent FA	Saunders WW	Skinner GEH	Sperrin J	Sperrin WT	Wallis JC	Ward RA	Whatley WJ	White RBW	Own-goals
			10					10		9		6		5	1		11				7										2	3	4	
			8					10		9		6		5	1		11											7			2	3	4	
			8					10		9		6		5	1		11											7			2	3	4	
			8					10		9		6		5	1		11											7			2	3	4	
		6	8							9		4		5	1		11										10	7		2	3			
			8		3			10		9		6		5	1		11											7			2		4	
					5			8		9		6			1		11												10	7	2	3	4	
					6			10		9		8		5	1		11												7		2	3	4	
	8							10		9		6		5	1	3	11												7		2		4	
			8					10		9		6		5	1		11												7		2	3	4	
			8					10		9		6		5	1		11												7		2	3	4	
	1	1	8	0	3	0	0	10	0	11	0	11	0	10	11	1	11	0	0	0	1	0	0	0	0	0	1	5	5	2	11	8	10	
	1		5					5		11		2					5													1	2			

ld W	Bennett KE	Bennett LD	Broadis IA	Browne J	Buckingham VF	Burditt FCK	Burgess WAR	Duncan A	Flack DW	Gibbons AH	Goodman A	Hall GW	Henley LD	Hitchins AW	Hooper PGW	Howe LF	Ludford GA	McCarthy AC	McCormick J	Medley LD	O'Callaghan E	Paton TG	Piper GH	Sainsbury R	Sargent FA	Saunders WW	Skinner GEH	Sperrin J	Sperrin WT	Wallis JC	Ward RA	Whatley WJ	White RBW	Own-goals
			8		6			11				10		5	1		9											7			2	3	4	
			8					10		9		6		5	1		11											7			2	3	4	
			8					10		9		6		5	1		11											7			2	3	4	
			8				9	10				6		5	1		11												7		2	3	4	
			10				8			9		6		5	1		11												7		2	3	4	
			10				6			9		8		5	1	7	11														2	3	4	
			10				6			9		8		5	1	7	11														2	3	4	
			10				6			9		8		5	1		11											7			2	3	4	
	0	0	8	0	1	0	5	4	0	6	0	8	0	8	8	2	8	0	0	0	0	0	0	0	0	0	0	4	2	0	8	8	8	
			8		1			2		4						1	5											1	1		1			1

League Table

	P	W	D	L	F	A	GA
Crystal Palace	27	16	4	7	86	44	1.954
West Ham United	25	14	6	5	70	39	1.794
Coventry City	10	5	3	2	28	16	1.750
Arsenal	19	10	5	4	66	38	1.736
Cardiff City	24	12	5	7	75	50	1.500
Reading	26	14	5	7	73	51	1.431
Norwich city	19	9	2	8	73	55	1.327
Watford	35	15	6	14	96	73	1.315
Portsmouth	31	16	2	13	92	71	1.296
TOTTENHAM HOTSPUR	23	9	5	9	53	41	1.293
Millwall	31	16	5	10	73	57	1.280
Walsall	32	14	7	11	100	80	1.250
West Bromwich Albion	28	13	5	10	83	69	1.202
Leicester City	33	17	5	11	87	73	1.191
Northampton Town	30	14	3	13	84	71	1.183
Bristol City	20	10	2	8	55	48	1.145
Mansfield	29	12	6	11	77	68	1.132
Charlton Athletic	19	7	4	8	37	34	1.088
Aldershot	24	14	2	8	73	68	1.073
Brentford	23	9	3	11	51	51	1.000
Chelsea	23	10	4	9	57	58	0.981
Birmingham	16	7	1	8	38	43	0.883
Fulham	30	10	7	13	62	73	0.849
Luton town	35	11	7	17	82	100	0.820
Stoke City	36	9	9	18	76	96	0.791
Queen's Park Rangers	23	8	3	12	47	60	0.783
Brighton & Hove Albion	25	8	7	10	51	75	0.680
Nottingham Forest	25	7	3	15	50	77	0.649
Bournemouth & Boscombe Athletic	27	9	3	15	59	92	0.641
Notts County	21	8	3	10	42	66	0.636
Southend United	29	12	4	13	64	101	0.633
Southampton	31	4	4	23	53	111	0.477
Swansea Town	10	2	1	7	12	33	0.363
Clapton Orient	15	1	3	11	19	66	0.287

* Final placings were decided on goal average

LONDON WAR CUP	P	W	D	L	F	A	Pts
Reading	10	6	4	0	29	8	16
TOTTENHAM HOTSPUR	10	5	3	2	32	14	13
West Ham United	10	6	1	3	23	19	13
Arsenal	10	5	2	3	38	18	12
Millwall	10	2	1	7	13	26	5
Clapton Orient	10	0	1	9	9	59	1

1941-42

FOOTBALL LEAGUE SOUTH

Manager: Peter McWilliam

Did you know that?

GUEST PLAYERS

Reg Edwards
Alloa Athletic
Jack Finch
Fulham
Alf Fitzgerald
Queens Park Rangers
Tom Kiernan
Albion Rovers
Wilf Mannion
Middlesbrough
McFarlane
St Bernards
David Noble
Clyde
Tommy Pearson
Newcastle United
Charlie Revell
Charlton Athletic
Joe Sibley
Southend United
Cyril Williams
Bristol City

Match No.	Date			Opponents	Result		Scorers	Attendan
1	Aug	30	H	Watford	W	5-0	Gibbons 2, Ludford 3	5,0
2	Sep	6	A	Aldershot	L	2-3	Gibbons 2	5,0
3		13	H	Millwall	W	3-0	L.Bennett, Gibbons, Ludford	6,6
4		20	A*	Arsenal	L	0-4		17,4
5		27	H	Queen's Park Rangers	W	3-1	Ludford 2, Noble	5,9
6	Oct	4	A	Reading	D	1-1	Gibbons	5,0
7		11	H	Brighton & Hove Albion	L	1-2	Broadis	4,5
8		18	A	Brentford	W	4-1	Ludford, Duncan 2, Noble	6,0
9		25	H	Crystal Palace	D	1-1	Ludford	4,8
10	Nov	1	A	Fulham	D	2-2	Gibbons, Noble	6,0
11		8	H	Clapton Orient	W	2-0	Broadis, Gibbons	5,6
12		15	A	Portsmouth	W	2-1	Ludford, Broadis	6,0
13		22	A	Chelsea	D	1-1	Duncan	6,7
14		29	A	Charlton Athletic	L	1-2	Ludford	4,2
15	Dec	6	H	West Ham United	D	1-1	Broadis	8,4
16		13	A	Watford	W	2-1	White, Hall	3,0
17		20	H	Aldershot	D	1-1	White	4,2
18		25	A	Millwall	W	2-1	Broadis 2	7,0
19		27	H	Arsenal	L	1-2	Ludford	16,7
20	Jan	3	A	Queen's Park Rangers	L	0-1		4,5
21		10	H	Reading	W	2-1	Broadis, Burgess	4,4
22		17	A	Brighton & Hove Albion	L	2-5	Sibley, Burgess	2,0
23		31	A	Crystal Palace	D	2-2	Gibbons, Ludford	5,3
24	Feb	14	A	Clapton Orient	W	3-2	Gibbons 3	4,5
25		21	H	Portsmouth	D	1-1	Gibbons	4,8
26		28	H	Chelsea	W	2-0	Ludford 2	6,5
27	Mar	7	H	Charlton Athletic	W	2-0	Gibbons, Revell	4,6
28		14	A	West Ham United	W	3-2	Broadis 2, Gibbons	7,9
29	Apr	25	H	Brentford	W	2-1	Howe, Broadis	5,1
30	May	2	H	Fulham	W	7-1	Broadis, Gibbons 2, Stevens 2, Ludford 2	3,7

*played at White Hart Lane

Appearanc
Goa

London War Cup

GR	Mar	21	A	Reading	W	2-1	Ward (pen), Howe	6,0
GR		28	H	Watford	W	5-2	Howe, Broadis, Gibbons 2, Ludford	4,6
GR	Apr	4	H	Reading	W	2-1	Duncan, Ludford	7,5
GR		6	A	Watford	D	0-0		4,5
GR		11	H	Charlton Athletic	L	0-3		9,5
GR		18	A	Charlton Athletic	L	0-4		7,6

Appearanc
Goa

Bennett LD	Broadis I	Buckingham VF	Burgess WAR	Cox FJA	Ditchburn EG	Duncan A	Edwards RC	Finch JA	Fitzgerald AM	Gibbons AH	Gilberg H	Hall GW	Hitchins AW	Hooper PGW	Howe LF	Jolliffe	Kiernan T	Ludford GA	Mannion WJ	McCormick J	McFarlane	Noble D	Pearson TU	Revell CH	Sainsbury R	Sainsbury WH	Sibley A	Sperrin J	Sperrin WT	Stevens LWG	Tickridge S	Trailor CH	Ward RA	Whatley WJ	White RBW	Williams CE	Woodward HJ
	8		6							9		10	5	1				11											7		2		3		4		
	8					10				9		6	5	1				11											7		2		3		4		
8	10									9		6	5	1	4			11											7		2		3				
	8		6							9		10	5	1				11											7		2		3		4		
	8					10						6	5	1				7				11									3		2		4		9
	8					10				9		6	5	1				7				11									3		2		4		
	8					10						6	5	1				9				11			7						3		2		4		
	8					10				9		5		1	6			7				11									3		2		4		
	8					10				9		5		1	6			7				11									3		2		4		
	8					10				9		5						7				11									3		2	6	4		
	7				1	10				9		8	5					11													3		2	6	4		
	8				1	10				9		6	5					7													3		2		4	11	
	8			7	1	10				9		4	5																		3		2	6		11	
	8					11						10	5					9										7			3		2	6	4		
	8				1	10				9		6	5																7		3		2		4	11	
	8					10				9	11	6	5					7													3		2		4		
	8					10				9	11	6	5	1																	3	7	2		4		
	8				1	10				9		6	5					11											7		3		2		4		
	8				1	10				9		5						11											7		3		2	6	4		
	8					10				11		6	5	1		9		7													3		2		4		
	8		9		1	10						6	5										11				7				3		2		4		
	8		9			10						6	5	1									11				7				3		2		4		
			4			10				9		6	5	1				11	8								7				3		2				
	10			7	1					9		6	5					11	8												3		2		4		
	8				1	10				9		6	5					11											7		3		2		4		
	10					11						6	5	1				9	8	7											3		2		4		
	10									9		4	5	1				7	8					11		6					3		2				
	8				1	10				9			5					11								6		7			3		2		4		
	8	6				10	9					4	5	1	7			11													3		2				
	8				1			7	6	9		4	5					11												10	3		2				
1	29	1	5	2	11	24	1	1	1	23	2	29	26	16	4	1	0	25	4	1	0	6	2	1	1	2	3	2	8	1	30	1	30	5	24	3	1
1	11		2			3				17		1			1			16				3		1			1			2					2		

Bennett LD	Broadis I	Buckingham VF	Burgess WAR	Cox FJA	Ditchburn EG	Duncan A	Edwards RC	Finch JA	Fitzgerald AM	Gibbons AH	Gilberg H	Hall GW	Hitchins AW	Hooper PGW	Howe LF	Jolliffe	Kiernan T	Ludford GA	Mannion WJ	McCormick J	McFarlane	Noble D	Pearson TU	Revell CH	Sainsbury R	Sainsbury WH	Sibley A	Sperrin J	Sperrin WT	Stevens LWG	Tickridge S	Trailor CH	Ward RA	Whatley WJ	White RBW	Williams CE	Woodward HJ
	8				1	11				9		6	5		10														7		3		2		4		
	8	6				10				9		4	5	1	7			11													3		2				
	8				1	10				9		6	5		7			11													3		2		4		
	8	6			1	10						5			11			9			7										3		2		4		
	10				1					9		6	5		7		8	11													3		2		4		
	10		6				11			9			5	1	4		8			7											3		2				
0	6	2	1	0	4	4	1	0	0	5	0	5	5	2	6	0	2	4	0	1	1	0	0	0	0	0	0	0	1	0	6	0	6	0	4	0	0
	1					1				2					2			2															1				

League Table

	P	W	D	L	F	A	Pts
Arsenal	30	23	2	5	108	43	48
Portsmouth	30	20	2	8	105	59	42
West Ham United	30	17	5	8	81	44	39
Aldershot	30	17	5	8	85	56	39
TOTTENHAM HOTSPUR	30	15	8	7	61	41	38
Crystal Palace	30	14	6	10	70	53	34
Reading	30	13	8	9	76	58	34
Charlton Athletic	30	14	5	11	72	64	33
Brentford	30	14	2	14	80	76	30
Queen's Park Rangers	30	11	3	16	52	59	25
Fulham	30	10	4	16	79	99	24
Brighton & Hove Albion	30	9	4	17	71	108	22
Chelsea	30	8	4	18	56	88	20
Millwall	30	7	5	18	53	82	19
Clapton Orient	30	5	7	18	42	94	17
Watford	30	6	4	20	47	114	16

LONDON WAR CUP	P	W	D	L	F	A	Pts
Charlton Athletic	6	4	1	1	17	6	9
TOTTENHAM HOTSPUR	6	3	1	2	9	11	7
Watford	6	2	1	3	10	12	5
Reading	6	1	1	4	9	16	3

1942-43

FOOTBALL LEAGUE SOUTH

Manager: Arthur Turner

Did you know that?

GUEST PLAYERS

Pat Beasley
  Huddersfield Town
Charlie Briggs
  Halifax Town
Bobby Browne
  Leeds United
Eddie Chapman
  West Ham United
Stan Eastham
  Liverpool
Reg Edwards
  Alloa Athletic
Harry Gurr
  Erith & Belvedere
Wilf Hares
  Newport County
Harry Jackson
  Burnley
Ernie Marshall
  Cardiff City
John Martin
  Aston Villa
Chic Muir
  Albion Rovers
David Nelson
  Arsenal
Tafffy O'Callaghan
  Fulham
Johnny Pattison
  Queen's Park Rangers
Jack Rowley
  Manchester United
Ron Staley
  Derby County

Match No.	Date			Opponents	Result		Scorers	Attendan
1	Aug	29	H	Crystal Palace	L	1-3	Ludford	5,6
2	Sep	5	A	Queen's Park Rangers	W	1-0	Sargent	4,3
3		12	H	Charlton Athletic	W	6-1	Martin, Ludford 3, Gibbons, Beasley	7,0
4		19	A	West Ham United	L	1-3	Ludford	10,1
5		26	H	Southampton	D	1-1	Gibbons	5,6
6	Oct	3	H	Aldershot	W	4-0	Gibbons 4	8,1
7		10	H	Millwall	W	2-1	Beasley, Martin	5,9
8		17	A	Reading	W	6-2	Beasley, O'Callaghan, Gibbons 3, Pattison	5,0
9		24	A	Portsmouth	L	0-1		8,5
10		31	H	Chelsea	D	1-1	Martin (pen)	12,6
11	Nov	7	H	Arsenal	W	1-0	Beasley	21,5
12		14	A	Luton Town	D	3-3	O'Callaghan, Gibbons, Martin	3,5
13		21	H	Watford	W	6-0	Ludford 2, Cox, Beasley, Gibbons, Head (og)	5,4
14		28	A	Crystal Palace	D	0-0		4,8
15	Dec	5	H	Queen's Park Rangers	W	6-0	Cox, Martin, Gibbons 2, Ludford, Redyard (og)	8,2
16		12	A	Charlton Athletic	W	3-0	Edwards, Ludford 2	7,0
17		19	H	West Ham United	W	2-0	Hall, Ludford	9,7
18		25	H	Brentford	D	1-1	Broadis	14,6
19		26	A	Brentford	L	1-2	Ludford	12,5
20	Jan	2	A	Southampton	L	1-2	Beasley	6,7
21		9	A	Aldershot	W	3-1	Beasley, Martin, Gibbons	4,0
22		16	A	Millwall	W	3-0	Broadis, Pattison 2	6,0
23		23	H	Reading	D	2-2	Beasley, Gibbons	7,3
24		30	H	Portsmouth	W	5-2	Beasley, Gibbons, Ludford 3	7,1
25	Feb	6	A	Chelsea	W	1-0	Gibbons	12,1
26		13	A*	Arsenal	L	0-1		30,6
27		20	H	Luton Town	W	4-1	Sperrin, Martin (pen), Ludford, Beasley	6,8
28		27	A	Watford	W	3-0	Ludford, Ward (pen), Sperrin	2,4

*played at White Hart Lane

Appearanc
Goa

Football League Cup

GR	Mar	6	H	Chelsea	W	2-0	Ludford 2	13,4
GR		13	A	Reading	D	1-1	Hall	6,0
GR		20	H	Millwall	W	5-0	Beasley, Martin 2 (1 pen), Nelson, O'Callaghan	8,1
GR		27	A	Chelsea	W	2-0	Ludford, Broadis	11,7
GR	Apr	3	H	Reading	L	1-2	Broadis	21,7
GR		10	A	Millwall	W	1-0	Beasley	6,0

Appearanc
Goa

arron G	Beasley AE	Bennett LD	Briggs CE	Broadis I	Browne RJ	Buckingham VF	Burgess WAR	Chapman E	Chisholm JR	Cox FJA	Ditchburn EG	Dix RW	Duncan A	Eastham S	Edwards RC	Finlay DO	Gibbons AH	Gurr HD	Hall GW	Hares W	Hooper PGW	Howe LF	Jackson H	Ludford GA	Marshall E	Martin JR	McCormick J	Muir A	Nelson D	Nicholson WE	O'Callaghan E	Pattison JRM	Rowley JF	Sainsbury WH	Sargent FA	Sperrin WT	Staley R	Ward RA	hatley WJ	White RGB	own-goals
							6		3		1		10			7	9		5					8										11				2		4	
					6				5		1								3	10				9							8				7		11	2		4	
	11				6				5		1					7	10		3					9		8												2		4	
					6				5								10		3		1	11		9		8										7		2		4	
	11								5		1					7	10		3			6		9		8												2		4	
	7		1						5								9		6					11		8					10							2	3	4	
	7		1						5								9		6					11		8					10							2	3	4	
	7								5								9		6					10				3			8	11						2		4	
	8								5		1								10				9		6		7			3		11						2		4	
	7								5								9		6		1		10			8						11						2	3	4	
	7						6		5		1						9		10							8						11						2	3	4	
									5					4			9		6		1			10		8					7	11						2	3		
	8								5	7							9				1	3		6							10	11						2		4	
	7							8	5						10				6		1			9								11						2	3	4	
				10					5	7							9		6		1	3		11		8												2		4	
		6		10					5						7		9		3		1			11		8												2		4	
				10					5						7		9		6		1	3		11		8												2		4	
	8			10					5		1						9		6			7		11														2	3	4	
	7						6		5		1						9		10			2		11		8													3	4	
	7			10					5		1						9		6			3		11		8												2		4	
	7			10					5								9				1	3		6		8						11						2		4	
	7			10					5								9		6		1	3				8						11						2		4	
	8								5	7							9	10	6		1	3										11						2		4	
	7						6		5								9		2		1	3		10		8						11								4	
	7			10					5								9		6		1	3		11		8												2		4	
	7			10					5								9				1	6		4		8						11						2	3		
	11								5			10							6		1	4		9		8										7		2	3		
	8								5										10		1	6		9			7									11		2	3	4	
	21	1	2	9	3	0	4	1	28	3	9	1	1	1	3	3	23	1	25	1	16	16	2	23	1	19	2	1	0	1	6	12	0	1	1	3	1	26	11	25	
	10			2						2					1		17		1					17		7					2	3			1	2		1			2

arron G	Beasley AE	Bennett LD	Briggs CE	Broadis I	Browne RJ	Buckingham VF	Burgess WAR	Chapman E	Chisholm JR	Cox FJA	Ditchburn EG	Dix RW	Duncan A	Eastham S	Edwards RC	Finlay DO	Gibbons AH	Gurr HD	Hall GW	Hares W	Hooper PGW	Howe LF	Jackson H	Ludford GA	Marshall E	Martin JR	McCormick J	Muir A	Nelson D	Nicholson WE	O'Callaghan E	Pattison JRM	Rowley JF	Sainsbury WH	Sargent FA	Sperrin WT	Staley R	Ward RA	hatley WJ	White RGB	own-goals
	7			8					5										10		1	6		9							11							2	3	4	
	7			8					5										10		1	6		9								11						2	3	4	
	7								5										6		1	4		9		8			10		11							2	3		
	7			10					5										6		1	4		9		8					11							2	3		
	7			10					5										6		1	4		11		8							9					2	3		
	8					6			5						7				10		1	4		11									9					2	3		
	6	0	0	4	0	1	0	0	6	0	0	0	0	0	1	0	0	0	6	0	6	6	0	6	0	3	0	0	1	0	3	1	2	0	0	0	0	6	6	2	
	2			2															1					3		2			1		1										

League Table

	P	W	D	L	F	A	Pts
Arsenal	28	21	1	6	102	40	43
TOTTENHAM HOTSPUR	28	16	6	6	68	28	38
Queen's Park Rangers	28	18	2	8	64	49	38
Portsmouth	28	16	3	9	66	52	35
Southampton	28	14	5	9	86	58	33
West Ham United	28	14	5	9	80	66	33
Chelsea	28	14	4	10	52	45	32
Aldershot	28	14	2	12	87	77	30
Brentford	28	12	5	11	64	63	29
Charlton Athletic	28	13	3	12	68	75	29
Clapton Orient	28	11	5	12	54	72	27
Brighton & Hove Albion	28	10	5	13	65	73	25
Reading	28	9	6	13	67	74	24
Fulham	28	10	2	16	69	78	22
Crystal Palace	28	7	5	16	49	75	19
Millwall	28	6	5	17	66	88	17
Watford	28	7	2	19	51	88	16
Luton Town	28	4	6	18	43	100	14

FOOTBALL LEAGUE CUP	P	W	D	L	F	A	Pts
Reading	6	5	1	0	24	5	11
TOTTENHAM HOTSPUR	6	4	1	1	12	3	9
Chelsea	6	2	0	4	9	18	4
Millwall	6	0	0	6	4	23	0

1943-44

FOOTBALL LEAGUE SOUTH

Manager: Arthur Turner

Did you know that?

GUEST PLAYERS

Pat Beasley
Huddersfield Town
Charlie Briggs
Halifax Town
Bernard Bryant
Walthamstow Avenue
Stan Clayton
Notts County
Jock Davie
Brighton & Hove Albion
Reg Edwards
Alloa Athletic
Jimmy Evans
Arsenal
Len Flack
Norwich City
H. Harris
Distillery
Doug Hunt
Sheffield Wednesday
Eric Jones
West Bromwich Albion
Tommy Manley
Brentford
John Martin
Aston Villa
Reg Mogford
Newport County
David Nelson
Arsenal
Tafffy O'Callaghan
Fulham
Frank O'Donnell
Aston Villa
Cliff Parker
Portsmouth
Jack Rowley
Manchester United
Reg Smith
Millwall
Trevor Smith
Crystal Palace
Joe Wilson
Brighton & Hove Albion
Albert Young
Arsenal

Match No.	Date			Opponents	Result		Scorers	Attendanc
1	Aug	28	H	Crystal Palace	D	1-1	Clayton	8,18
2	Sep	4	A	Queen's Park Rangers	L	0-1		10,77
3		11	H	Charlton Athletic	W	4-2	Beasley, Rowley 2, Mosley	9,95
4		18	A	West Ham United	D	3-3	O'Donnell 2, Rowley	12,14
5		25	H	Southampton	D	2-2	Bennett, O'Donnell	8,48
6	Oct	2	H	Aldershot	W	5-2	White, Martin, Rowley 2, Jones	13,15
7		9	H	Brighton & Hove Albion	W	2-0	Martin, Rowley	10,66
8		16	A	Reading	W	3-2	Burgess, Beasley, Jones	10,00
9		23	A	Luton Town	L	2-4	O'Donnell 2	3,00
10		30	H	Chelsea	W	5-1	Beasley, Rowley 2, T.Smith, Jones	10,37
11	Nov	6	A	Brentford	W	2-0	Rowley 2	9,56
12		13	A	Clapton Orient	W	4-0	Burgess 2, O'Donnell, Jones	4,00
13		20	H	Watford	W	4-2	Burgess 3, Jobling (og)	8,49
14		27	A	Crystal Palace	L	0-3		6,13
15	Dec	4	H	Queen's Park Rangers	D	2-2	Beasley, Jones	12,48
16		11	A	Charlton Athletic	W	2-0	Beasley, Rowley	3,50
17		18	H	Arsenal	W	2-1	Beasley, Rowley	23,68
18		25	H	Fulham	W	2-0	Walters, Jones	16,62
19		27	A	Fulham	W	2-0	Ludford, Jones	13,20
20	Jan	1	H	West Ham United	W	1-0	Cox	40,99
21		8	H	Brentford	W	1-0	Burgess	16,92
22		15	A	Southampton	W	3-2	Burgess, Beasley, O'Donnell	13,00
23		22	A	Aldershot	W	1-0	Howe	6,00
24		29	A	Brighton & Hove Albion	W	2-0	Ward, Walters	6,00
25	Feb	5	H	Reading	D	2-2	Walters 2	14,93
26		12	H	Luton Town	W	8-1	Beasley, Rowley 7	11,46
27	Apr	8	A	Chelsea	D	1-1	Russell (og)	25,00
28		22	A*	Arsenal	D	3-3	Burgess, Beasley, Martin	26,33
29		29	H	Clapton Orient	W	1-0	Whent	7,95
30	May	6	A	Watford	D	1-1	Bryant	2,65

*played at White Hart Lane

Appearance
Goal

Football League South Cup

GR	Feb	19	A*	Millwall	W	1-0	Beasley	4,00
GR		26	H	Portsmouth	W	1-0	Rowley	15,22
GR	Mar	4	A	Aldershot	L	1-2	Bryant	10,00
GR		11	H	Millwall	W	1-0	Cox	15,31
GR		18	A	Portsmouth	W	2-1	Rowley 2	15,00
GR		25	H	Aldershot	W	2-0	Burgess, Martin	39,26
SF	Apr	1	N#	Charlton Athletic	L	0-3		35,00

*played at Selhurst Park #played at Stamford Bridge

Appearance
Goal

Adams WH	Beasley AE	Bennett LD	Briggs CE	Browne J	Bryant BL	Buckingham VF	Burgess WAR	Chisholm JR	Clayton S	Cox FJA	Davie J	Ditchburn EG	Dix RW	Edwards RC	Evans JL	Flack WLW	Gibbins E	Gilberg H	Hall GW	Harris H	Hooper PGW	Howe LF	Hunt DA	Jones EN	Ludford GA	Manley TR	Martin JR	Mogford RWJ	Mosley WA	Nelson D	O'Callaghan E	O'Donnell FJ	Page AE	Parker HC	Rowley JF	Sainsbury WH	Sargent FA	Smith JCR	Smith JCT	Sperrin WT	Walters WE	Ward RA	Whatley WJ	Whent JR	White RBW	Willis A	Wilson JA	Young AE	Own-goals
	7					4		5	8				10								1	9			11																	2	3		6				
	8							5													1	7			10				4			9			11							2	3		6				
	7							5	10												1			11	6		8		4						9							2	3						
	7							5													1			11			8		4			9			10							2	3		6				
	7	8						5													1	6		11								9			10							2	3		4				
	7		1					5											6					11			8					9			10							2	3		4				
	7						6	5				1												11			8					9			10							2	3		4				
	7						6	5				1							10					11			8								9							2	3		4				
7						6	5				1												11	10		8					9										2	3		4					
					6	5				1												11			8								9				10			2	3		4						
	7					4		5				1							6					11			8								9				10			2	3						
	8						6	5		7		1							10					11								9										2	3		4				
	8						6	5		7		1							10					11											9							2	3		4				
	7					5	6					1	8						10						11										9							2	3		4				
	7					5				10		1												11	6		8								9							2	3		4				
	7						6	5		11		1										3			9		8								10	4						2							
	7						6	5				1												11	4		8					9			10							2	3						
	10						6	5				1												11	9		8														7	2			4			3	
	10						6	5				1												11	9						8										7	2			4			3	
	10						6	5		11		1													9						8										7	2	3		4				
3	10						6					1												11			8						5		9						7	2			4				
	8						6	5		11		1																				9			10						7	2	3		4				
	8			9				5								6					1	10			11	4															7	2				3			
				9		10	6	5		11		1																					4								7	2			8	3			
1							6	5			9	1				4												8							10						7	2				3			
	8						6	5		11		1																10							9						7	2	3			4			
1	7				9			5				1		10						8					6																	2	3		4				
	7					5	6					1						11									8					9										2	3		4		10		
1	7				9		6										5				1							10														2		8	4	3			
	4				7					11							5				1				6			10				9										2		8		3			
4	28	1	1	2	3	6	19	24	2	9	1	21	2	1	0	2	2	1	6	1	8	5	0	16	14	1	14	4	3	0	2	11	2	0	18	1	0	0	2	0	9	30	21	2	22	6	1	2	
	9	1			1		9		1	1												1		7	1		3		1			7			19				1		4	1		1	1				2

Adams WH	Beasley AE	Bennett LD	Briggs CE	Browne J	Bryant BL	Buckingham VF	Burgess WAR	Chisholm JR	Clayton S	Cox FJA	Davie J	Ditchburn EG	Dix RW	Edwards RC	Evans JL	Flack WLW	Gibbins E	Gilberg H	Hall GW	Harris H	Hooper PGW	Howe LF	Hunt DA	Jones EN	Ludford GA	Manley TR	Martin JR	Mogford RWJ	Mosley WA	Nelson D	O'Callaghan E	O'Donnell FJ	Page AE	Parker HC	Rowley JF	Sainsbury WH	Sargent FA	Smith JCR	Smith JCT	Sperrin WT	Walters WE	Ward RA	Whatley WJ	Whent JR	White RBW	Willis A	Wilson JA	Young AE	Own-goals
	8			9			10	5		11											1																				7	2	3		4	6			
	8						6	5		11		1						10				4													9						7	2	3						
	8				9		6	5		11		1																		10											7	2	3		4				
	8				9		5			11		1			4													10												7		2	3			6			
	7				9		6	5		11		1								8															10							2	3			4			
	7						6	5				1								10			9				8							11				4				2	3						
1	10				9			5		7											1	6															8					2	3		4				
1	7	0	0	1	4	0	6	6	0	6	0	5	0	0	1	0	0	1	0	2	2	2	1	0	0	0	1	1	0	1	0	0	0	1	2	0	1	1	0	1	3	7	7	0	3	3	0	0	
	1				1		1			1																	1								3														

League Table

	P	W	D	L	F	A	Pts
TOTTENHAM HOTSPUR	30	19	8	3	71	36	46
West Ham United	30	17	7	6	74	39	41
Queen's Park Rangers	30	14	12	4	69	54	40
Arsenal	30	14	10	6	72	42	38
Crystal Palace	30	16	5	9	75	53	37
Portsmouth	30	16	5	9	68	59	37
Brentford	30	14	7	9	71	51	35
Chelsea	30	16	2	12	79	55	34
Fulham	30	11	9	10	80	73	31
Millwall	30	13	4	13	70	66	30
Aldershot	30	12	6	12	64	73	30
Reading	30	12	3	15	73	62	27
Southampton	30	10	7	13	67	88	27
Charlton Athletic	30	9	7	14	57	73	25
Watford	30	6	8	16	58	80	20
Brighton & Hove Albion	30	9	2	19	55	82	20
Clapton Orient	30	4	3	23	32	87	11
Luton Town	30	3	5	22	42	104	11

FOOTBALL LEAGUE SOUTH CUP

	P	W	D	L	F	A	Pts
TOTTENHAM HOTSPUR	6	5	0	1	8	3	10
Aldershot	6	4	1	1	17	5	9
Millwall	6	1	1	4	7	15	3
Portsmouth	6	0	2	4	3	12	2

1944-45

FOOTBALL LEAGUE SOUTH

Manager: Arthur Turner

Did you know that?

GUEST PLAYERS

Alex Anderson
Heart of Midlothian
Pat Beasley
Huddersfield Town
Frank Boulton
Derby County
Harry Brown
Queen's Park Rangers
Charlie BurkeBournemouth &
Boscombe Athletic
Jonathan Burnett
Tooting & Mitcham
Harry Dukes
Norwich city
Dickie Dunn
West Ham United
Bobby Flavell
Airdrie
George Foreman
West Ham United
Fred Hall
Blackburn Rovers
Les Henley
Margate
Archie Hughes
Huddersfield Town
Jakey Jackson
Chelsea
John Martin
Aston Villa
Reg Mogford
Newport County
John Moodie
Airdrie
Matt Muir
Rochdale
John Oakes
Charlton Athletic
Frank O'Donnell
Aston Villa
Bob Pryde
Blackburn Rovers
Jack Rowley
Manchester United
Ken Smith
Bolton Wanderers
Ed Tunney
Wrexham
Alf Whittingham
Bradford City

Match No.	Date		Opponents		Result		Scorers	Attendance
1	Aug	26	H	West Ham United	D	2-2	O'Donnell, Stevens	14,37
2	Sep	2	H	Arsenal	W	4-0	Broadis 2, Ludford 2	13,62
3		9	A	Reading	D	0-0		9,06
4		16	H	Portsmouth	D	1-1	Walters	14,16
5		23	A	Southampton	W	3-1	Burgess, Stevens, Walters	12,600
6		30	H	Charlton Athletic	W	2-1	Stevens, Beasley	15,76
7	Oct	7	A	Crystal Palace	W	3-1	Ludford, Gilberg 2	9,00
8		14	H	Chelsea	L	1-5	Stevens	21,08
9		21	A	Luton Town	W	9-1	Walters 2, Howe, Foreman, Burgess 4, Ludford	7,00
10		28	H	Brentford	D	2-2	Gilberg 2	23,20
11	Nov	4	H	Aldershot	W	7-0	Walters, Beasley 3, Foreman 3	14,768
12		11	A	Millwall	W	4-3	Beasley, Foreman 2, Stevens	6,964
13		18	A	Clapton Orient	W	2-0	Foreman 2	7,500
14		25	H	Fulham	W	2-1	Walters, Beasley	14,300
15	Dec	2	A	West Ham United	W	1-0	Gilberg	23,00
16		9	A*	Arsenal	W	3-2	Gibbons 3	29,43
17		16	H	Reading	W	3-2	Burgess, Gibbons 2	9,93
18		23	A	Queen's Park Rangers	D	0-0		13,01
19		25	H	Queen's Park Rangers	W	4-2	Burgess, Gibbons, Gilberg, Mallett (og)	16,958
20		30	A	Portsmouth	D	0-0		15,00
21	Jan	6	H	Southampton	W	4-0	Ward (pen), Broadis, Gibbons 2	16,72
22		13	A	Charlton Athletic	W	2-1	Walters, Gibbons	13,000
23		20	H	Crystal Palace	W	3-1	Ward 2, Rowley	11,10
24		27	H	Chelsea	W	2-1	Walters, Rowley	20,540
25	Mar	24	A	Brentford	W	2-0	Burgess, Whittingham	16,750
26		31	A	Aldershot	W	2-1	Burgess, Henley	6,000
27	Apr	14	H	Millwall	W	4-0	Ward (pen), Beasley, Gibbons, A.E.Hall	13,59
28		21	H	Clapton Orient	W	4-0	Beasley, Burnett 2, Medley	10,31
29		28	A	Fulham	W	4-2	Ward (pen), Ludford, A.E.Hall, Freeman (og)	8,000
30	May	5	H	Luton Town	W	1-0	Beasley	5,984

*played at White Hart Lane

Appearances
Goals

Football League South Cup

GR	Feb	3	H	Queen's Park Rangers	D	1-1	Burgess	20,33
GR		10	A	West Ham United	L	0-1		21,000
GR		17	H	Aldershot	W	6-1	Walters 2, Gibbons 4	15,616
GR		24	A	Queen's Park Rangers	L	0-1		20,000
GR	Mar	3	H	West Ham United	W	4-1	Burgess, Martin, Gibbons 2	29,838
GR		10r	A	Aldershot	W	2-0	Flavell, Medley	6,000

Appearances
Goals

Adams WH	Anderson A	Beasley AE	Boulton FP	Broadis I	Brown HT	Burgess WAR	Burke C	Burnett J	Chisholm JR	Dix RW	Dukes HP	Dunn R	Flavell R	Foreman AG	Gibbons AH	Gilberg H	Goodman A	Hall AE	Hall FW	Henley LD	Hooper PGW	Howe LF	Hughes WA	Jackson J	Ludford GA	Lyman CC	Martin JR	Medley LD	Mogford RWJ	Moodie J	Muir MR	Oakes J	O'Donnell FJ	Page AE	Pryde RI	Rowley JF	Smith K	Stevens LWG	Swift WN	Tunney EL	Wallis JC	Walters WE	Ward RA	Whatley WJ	White RBW	Whittingham A	Willis A	Own-goals
		11				6																	1				8						9	5				10				7	2		4		3	
		10		8													11						1		9									6	5							7	2		4		3	
		11				6					1	10										4			9				8			5								3	7	2					
		11														8							1		6								9	5				10			3	7	2		4			
		11				6																	1		9												8	10	5		3	7	2				4	
		11				6	5						9											1					8									10			3	7	2				4	
						6	5						8			11								1	9					4							10				7	2				3	
			1			6													5			11			9				8									10				7	2		4		3	
						10	6							9					5			8	1		11																	7	2		4		3	
		8				9										10			5			6	1					11														7	2		4		3	
		8			1	6								9		10			5									11														7	2		4		3	
		8					6							9					5				1					11										10				7	2		4		3	
		8			1	6				10				9					5																			11				7	2		4		3	
		8			1									9					5			6						11										10				7	2		4		3	
		10				6							8		9	11			5				1																			7	2		4		3	
		10				6							8		9				5				1		11																	7	2		4		3	
		10				6							8		9	11			5				1																			7	2		4		3	
		8				6									9				5				1		11													10				7	2		4		3	
				10		6			5				8		9	11							1																			7	2		4		3	
11		8		10		6	5								9								1																			7	2		4		3	
11		10				6	5						8		9								1																			7	2		4		3	
11	1			10		6	4						8		9				5																							7	2				3	
6							5						8		9								1													10		11				7	2		4		3	
		11		8		6									9				5				1													10						7	2		4		3	
		10				6			5				8										1					11														7	2	3	4	9		
		10				6	5											9		8			1		11																	7	2		4		3	
		8				6			5						9	11		10					1																			7	2		4		3	
		8						9	4		1							10	5						6			11														7	2				3	
		8				6			5									10					1		9													11				7	2		4		3	
		8					9		5									10					1		6			11														7	2		4		3	
4	1	24	1	5	3	23	10	1	6	1	2	1	10	5	11	8	1	5	14	1	0	5	21	2	13	0	1	7	3	0	1	1	2	3	1	2	1	12	1	0	4	30	30	1	24	1	27	
		9		2		10		2					8	10	6			2		1		1			5			1					1			2		5				8	5			1		2

Adams WH	Anderson A	Beasley AE	Boulton FP	Broadis I	Brown HT	Burgess WAR	Burke C	Burnett J	Chisholm JR	Dix RW	Dukes HP	Dunn R	Flavell R	Foreman AG	Gibbons AH	Gilberg H	Goodman A	Hall AE	Hall FW	Henley LD	Hooper PGW	Howe LF	Hughes WA	Jackson J	Ludford GA	Lyman CC	Martin JR	Medley LD	Mogford RWJ	Moodie J	Muir MR	Oakes J	O'Donnell FJ	Page AE	Pryde RI	Rowley JF	Smith K	Stevens LWG	Swift WN	Tunney EL	Wallis JC	Walters WE	Ward RA	Whatley WJ	White RBW	Whittingham A	Willis A	Own-goals
		11				6							8		9				5											1						10						7	2		4		3	
		10		8		6									9				5				1					11														7	2		4		3	
						6							10		9				5		1						8	11														7	2		4		3	
		10				6	4		5		1				9												8	11														7	2				3	
						6			5				10		9								1		4	11	8															7	2				3	
						6	5						10									9	1				8	11											3		7	2		4			
0	0	3	0	1	0	6	2	0	2	0	1	0	4	0	5	0	0	0	3	0	1	1	3	0	1	1	4	4	0	1	0	0	0	0	0	1	0	0	0	1	0	6	6	0	4	0	5	
						2							1		6												1	1														2						

League Table

	P	W	D	L	F	A	Pts
TOTTENHAM HOTSPUR	30	23	6	1	81	30	52
West Ham United	30	22	3	5	96	47	47
Brentford	30	17	4	9	87	57	38
Chelsea	30	16	5	9	100	55	37
Southampton	30	17	3	10	96	69	37
Crystal Palace	30	15	5	10	74	70	35
Reading	30	14	6	10	78	68	34
Arsenal	30	14	3	13	77	67	31
Queen's Park Rangers	30	10	10	10	70	61	30
Watford	30	11	6	13	66	84	28
Fulham	30	11	4	15	79	83	26
Portsmouth	30	11	4	15	56	61	26
Charlton Athletic	30	12	2	16	72	81	26
Brighton & Hove Albion	30	10	2	18	66	95	22
Luton Town	30	6	7	17	56	104	19
Aldershot	30	7	4	19	44	85	18
Millwall	30	5	7	18	50	84	17
Clapton Orient	30	5	7	18	39	86	17

FOOTBALL LEAGUE SOUTH CUP

	P	W	D	L	F	A	Pts
West Ham United	6	4	1	1	14	6	9
Queen's Park Rangers	6	3	2	1	7	8	8
TOTTENHAM HOTSPUR	6	3	1	2	13	4	7
Aldershot	6	0	0	6	3	19	0

1945-46

FOOTBALL LEAGUE SOUTH

Manager: Arthur Turner until January then Joe Hulme

Did you know that?

GUEST PLAYERS

Jack Acquroff
Norwich City
Pat Beasley
Huddersfield Town
Jimmy Blair
Wood Green Town
Harry Ferrier
Barnsley
Fred Ford
Charlton Athletic
Tom Howshall
Clapton Orient
Jimmy Jinks
Millwall
Phil Joslin
Torquay United
George Smith
Charlton Athletic
Albert Young
Arsenal

Match No.	Date		Opponents		Result		Scorers	Attendance
1	Aug	25	H	Wolverhampton Wanderers	L	1-4	Broadis	33,852
2	Sep	1	A	Wolverhampton Wanderers	L	2-4	Ward (pen), Lyman	24,899
3		8	A	West Ham United	D	1-1	Burgess	26,437
4		12	H	Leicester City	W	6-2	Burgess 2, McCormick, A.E.Hall, Ludford 2	14,167
5		15	H	West Ham United	L	2-3	Gibbons 2	34,342
6		22	A	West Browmich Albion	L	0-5		24,433
7		29	H	West Bromwich Albion	W	4-2	Acquroff 2, Lyman 2	31,403
8	Oct	6	A	Birmingham City	L	0-8		21,608
9		13	H	Birmingham City	L	0-1		30,589
10		20	A	Swansea Town	L	2-4	Stevens, Gibbons	16,985
11		27	H	Swansea Town	W	3-1	A.E.Hall, Gibbons 2	20,407
12	Nov	3	H	Brentford	W	1-0	Gibbons	28,603
13		10	A	Brentford	W	3-1	A.E.Hall 2, Gibbons	19,270
14		17	A	Chelsea	W	2-1	Dix, Lyman	35,343
15		24	H	Chelsea	W	3-2	Broadis 2, Gibbons	43,717
16	Dec	1	H	Millwall	W	5-1	Ward (pen), Gibbons 3, Dix	34,807
17		8	A	Millwall	L	2-3	Burgess, Gibbons	24,143
18		15	A	Southampton	L	2-3	Ward (pen), Lyman	13,935
19		22	H	Southampton	W	4-3	Ward (pen), Gibbons 2, Lyman	17,932
20		25	H	Derby County	L	2-5	Broadis 2	33,700
21		26	A	Derby County	L	0-2		30,823
22		29	A	Leicester City	L	0-4		15,330
23	Jan	12	A	Luton Town	L	1-3	Skinner	9,528
24		19	H	Luton Town	L	2-3	Burgess, Lyman	13,108
25		26	H	Coventry City	W	2-0	Burgess, Whitchurch	17,632
26	Feb	2	A	Aston Villa	L	1-5	Burgess	30,736
27		9	A*	Arsenal	D	1-1	Blair	38,927
28		16	H	Arsenal	W	2-0	A.E.Hall, Whitchurch	44,510
29		20	H	Aston Villa	W	3-0	Jinks 2, Whitchurch	19,300
30		23	H	Charlton Athletic	W	2-1	Skinner, Dix	37,743
31	Mar	9	A	Fulham	D	1-1	Whitchurch	30,000
32		16	H	Fulham	L	1-3	Dix (pen)	23,211
33		23	H	Plymouth Argyle	W	2-0	Foreman 2	20,789
34		30	A	Plymouth Argyle	W	1-0	Foreman	25,000
35	Apr	6	A	Portsmouth	W	1-0	Medley	22,000
36		13	H	Portsmouth	W	2-0	Foreman 2	23,000
37		17	A	Charlton Athletic	L	0-1		10,000
38		19	H	Nottingham Forest	W	3-2	Ludford, Foreman, Medley	23,955
39		20	A	Newport County	W	4-1	Foreman 4	16,000
40		22	A	Nottingham Forest	W	2-0	Foreman, Medley	18,474
41		27	H	Newport County	W	1-0	Foreman	15,223
42	May	3	A	Coventry City	W	1-0	Foreman	11,446

*played at White Hart Lane

Appearances
Goals

FA Cup

R3	Jan	5	H	Brentford	D	2-2	Burgess, A.E.Hall	30,202
R3r		10	A	Brentford	L	0-2		21,050

Appearances
Goals

Acquroff J	Adams WH	Baily EF	Beasley AE	Bennett LD	Blair J	Broadis I	Buckingham VF	Burgess WAR	Chisholm JR	Cox FJA	Ditchburn EG	Dix RW	Duquemin LS	Ferrier H	Fletcher HD	Ford FGL	Foreman AG	Garwood LF	Gibbons AH	Gilberg H	Hall AE	Hall FW	Hall J	Howe LF	Howshall T	Hughes WA	Jinks JT	Joslin PJ	Ludford GA	Lyman CC	McCormick J	Medley LD	Morrison JA	Nicholson WE	Page AE	Rundle CR	Sargent FA	Skinner GEH	Smith GC	Stevens LWG	Walters WE	Ward RA	Whitchurch CH	White RBW	Willis A	Young AE
			7			8		6	5										9		10					1															11		2		4	3	
			7			8		6												9		10			4		1				11					5							2			3	
								6												10	11	8							1	4	9					5		7					2			3	
								6												10		8							1	9		7				5					11		2		4	3	
								6												10		8							1	9		7				5					11		2		4	3	
						7		6												10		8							1		9		11			5								2		4	3	
9								6								5			10				1							11		7								8		2		4		3
								6				10				5			9				1							11		7								8		2		4	3	
9								6				10				5			8							1															11	7	2		4	3	
																			10		9					1			6	11	7								5	8		2		4	3	
						7		6				10							9		8					1			4	11									5			2		3		
						7		6				10							9		8					1			4	11									5			2		3		
												10							9		8					1			4	11					5				6	7		2		3		
								6				10							9		8					1			4	11					5					7		2			3	
						7		6				10							9		8					1			4	11					5								2		3		
						7		6				10							9		8					1			4	11					5								2		3		
								6				10							9		8					1			4	11					5					7		2		3		
							7	6				10							9		8					1			4	11					5								2		3		
								6				10							9		8					1			4	11		7			5								2		3		
						8	7	6											9				1						4			11			5					10		2			3	
						8		6											10				1						4	9		11			5		7					2			3	
												10									8		1						4	11		7	9		5								2		6	3	
	3											10														1			6	9		11						8		7		5		4	2	
								6				10										5				1			9	11								8				2	7	4	3	
								9				10		3							7	5	1		6				4									8				2	11			
							5	6				10			9									1						4	7									8				2	11		3	
					9		3	6				10									7	5				1														8					11	4	2	
					9		3	6				10									7	5				1														8					11	4	2	
		10					3	6													7	5				1	9													8					11	4	2	
							3	6				10									7	5	1									9								8					11	4	2	
							3	6				10	9														1									5				8			7		11	4	2	
				9			3	6				10									7		1													5				8					11	4	2	
				8			3	6				10					9				7					1			4					5										11		2	
				8			3	6									9										1			4			7			5	10								11		2	
				8			3	6									9										1			4			11		5						10			7		2	
				8			3	6				10					9										1			4			11		5									7		2	
				8			3	6									9										1			4			11		5				10					7		2	
				8			3	6				10					9										1			4			11		5									7		2	
				8			3	6									9										1			4			11		5						10			7		2	
				8			3	6				10					9										1			4			11		5		7										2	
				8			3	6			1	10					9														4			11		5									7		2	
				8			3			7	1						9	4											6			11		5		10										2	
2	1	1	2	11	2	9	19	37	1	1	2	26	1	1	1	3	10	1	21	1	24	6	9	1	1	27	1	4	30	21	3	17	1	11	16	3	2	11	4	14	2	26	17	25	32	1
2					1	5		7				4					13		14		5						2		3	7	1	3						2		1		4	4			

Acquroff J	Adams WH	Baily EF	Beasley AE	Bennett LD	Blair J	Broadis I	Buckingham VF	Burgess WAR	Chisholm JR	Cox FJA	Ditchburn EG	Dix RW	Duquemin LS	Ferrier H	Fletcher HD	Ford FGL	Foreman AG	Garwood LF	Gibbons AH	Gilberg H	Hall AE	Hall FW	Hall J	Howe LF	Howshall T	Hughes WA	Jinks JT	Joslin PJ	Ludford GA	Lyman CC	McCormick J	Medley LD	Morrison JA	Nicholson WE	Page AE	Rundle CR	Sargent FA	Skinner GEH	Smith GC	Stevens LWG	Walters WE	Ward RA	Whitchurch CH	White RBW	Willis A	Young AE
								6				10										8					1			9	11		7			5								2		4	3	
	7						5	6				10										8					1			9	11													2		4	3	
0	1	0	0	0	0	0	1	2	0	0	0	2	0	0	0	0	0	0	0	0	2	0	0	0	0	2	0	0	2	2	0	1	0	0	1	0	0	0	0	0	0	2	0	2	2	0
								1														1																										

League Table

	P	W	D	L	F	A	Pts
Birmingham	42	28	5	9	96	45	61
Aston Villa	42	25	11	6	106	58	61
Charlton Athletic	42	25	10	7	92	45	60
Derby County	42	24	7	11	101	62	55
West Bromwich Albion	42	22	8	12	104	69	52
Wolverhampton W	42	20	11	11	75	48	51
West Ham United	42	20	11	11	94	76	51
Fulham	42	20	10	12	93	73	50
TOTTENHAM HOTSPUR	42	22	3	17	78	81	47
Chelsea	42	19	6	17	92	80	44
Arsenal	42	16	11	15	76	73	43
Millwall	42	17	8	17	79	105	42
Coventry City	42	15	10	17	70	69	40
Brentford	42	14	10	18	82	72	38
Nottingham Forest	42	12	13	17	72	73	37
Southampton	42	14	9	19	97	105	37
Swansea Town	42	15	7	20	90	112	37
Luton Town	42	13	7	22	60	92	33
Portsmouth	42	11	6	25	66	87	28
Leicester City	42	8	7	27	57	101	23
Newport County	42	9	2	31	52	125	20
Plymouth Argyle	42	3	8	31	39	120	14

1946-47

DIVISION TWO

Manager: Joe Hulme

Did you know that?

Spurs' flag flew at half mast and the players wore black armbands against Bradford on 21 December 1946 in memory of Mr Ralph Bullock, who died two days earlier. While not known to have played for Spurs, Bullock was connected to the club for over 50 years. At one time honorary secretary, he was one of the original directors when the limited company was formed and for many years honorary, or shareholders, auditor.

LEAGUE DEBUTANTS

Aug 31	v Birmingham City	Les Bennett
Aug 31	v Birmingham City	Ted Ditchburn
Aug 31	v Birmingham City	George Foreman
Aug 31	v Birmingham City	Les Medley
Aug 31	v Birmingham City	George Skinner
Aug 31	v Birmingham City	Arthur Willis
Sep 7	v West Bromwich Albion	Les Stevens
Sep 7	v West Bromwich Albion	Charlie Whitchurch
Sep 9	v Southampton	Charlie Rundle
Sep 9	v Southampton	Sid Tickridge
Sep 14	v Newcastle United	Ronnie Dix
Sep 19	v Newport County	Johnny Woodward
Jan 4	v West Bromwich Albion	Eddie Baily
Jan 4	v West Bromwich Albion	Sonny Walters
Jan 18	v Newcastle United	Harry Gilberg
Feb 18	v Burnley	Leon Joseph
Apr 7	v Nottingham Forest	Archie Hughes
May 10	v Southampton	Cyril Trailor
Jun 6	v Barnsley	Ernie Jones

Match No.	Date		Opponents		Result		Scorers	Attendance
1	Aug	31	H	Birmingham City	L	1-2	Foreman	51,256
2	Sep	7	A	West Bromwich Albion	L	2-3	Bennett, Medley	34,970
3		9	H	Southampton	W	2-1	Rundle, Bennett	22,153
4		14	H	Newcastle United	D	1-1	Bennett	52,213
5		19	A	Newport County	W	4-2	Ludford, Whitchurch, Bennett, Dix	18,169
6		21	A	Swansea Town	W	2-0	Bennett 2	22,934
7		28	H	Manchester City	D	0-0		55,253
8	Oct	5	H	Burnley	D	1-1	Medley	44,351
9		7	H	Newport County	W	3-1	Foreman 2, Medley	14,540
10		12	A	Barnsley	W	3-1	Burgess, Foreman, Medley	24,494
11		19	A	West Ham United	D	2-2	Bennett, Foreman	34,341
12		26	H	Sheffield Wednesday	W	2-0	Cox, Bennett	33,251
13	Nov	2	A	Fulham	D	1-1	Foreman	40,762
14		9	H	Bury	W	2-1	Burgess, Stevens	38,684
15		16	A	Luton Town	L	2-3	Bennett, Foreman	26,362
16		23	H	Plymouth Argyle	W	2-1	Bennett, Foreman	40,795
17		30	A	Leicester City	D	1-1	Foreman	34,543
18	Dec	7	H	Chesterfield	L	3-4	Ludford, Cox 2	38,654
19		14	A	Millwall	W	3-0	Rundle 2, Foreman	20,937
20		21	H	Bradford	D	3-3	Foreman 2, Dix (pen)	24,779
21		25	A	Coventry City	L	1-3	Burgess	23,307
22		26	H	Coventry City	D	0-0		44,311
23		28	A	Birmingham City	L	0-1		44,171
24	Jan	4	H	West Bromwich Albion	W	2-0	Burgess, Walters	40,537
25		18	A	Newcastle United	L	0-1		62,876
26		27	H	Swansea Town	W	3-1	Bennett, Dix, Whitchurch	6,292
27	Feb	1	A	Manchester City	L	0-1		41,645
28		18	A	Burnley	D	0-0		28,462
29	Mar	1	A	Sheffield Wednesday	L	1-5	Rundle	23,144
30		8	H	Fulham	D	1-1	Bennett	27,715
31		22	H	Luton Town	W	2-1	Cox, Dix	36,160
32		29	A	Plymouth Argyle	W	4-3	Bennett 2, Foreman 2	22,525
33	Apr	4	H	Nottingham Forest	W	2-0	Burgess, Rundle	29,176
34		5	H	Leicester City	W	2-1	Rundle 2	37,843
35		7	A	Nottingham Forest	D	1-1	Bennett	30,656
36		12	A	Chesterfield	D	0-0		14,802
37		19	H	Millwall	W	2-1	Rundle, Brolly (og)	34,311
38		26	A	Bradford	L	1-2	Rundle	11,371
39	May	3	A	Bury	W	2-1	Cox, Rundle	13,063
40		10	A	Southampton	L	0-1		12,884
41		17	H	West Ham United	D	0-0		37,503
42	Jun	7	H	Barnsley	D	1-1	Dix (pen)	17,575
								Appearances
								Goals

FA Cup

R3	Jan	11	H	Stoke City	D	2-2	Ludford, Bennett	65,681
R3r		15	A	Stoke City	L	0-1		38,361
								Appearances
								Goals

Baily EF	Bennett LD	Buckingham VF	Burgess WAR	Cox FJA	Ditchburn EG	Dix RW	Foreman AG	Gilberg H	Hall AE	Hughes WA	Jones WEA	Joseph L	Ludford GA	Medley LD	Nicholson WE	Rundle CR	Skinner GEH	Stevens LWG	Tickridge S	Trailor CH	Walters WE	Whitchurch CH	Willis A	Woodward HJ	Own-goals
	8	2	6	7	1		9						4	11	5		10						3		
	8	3	6		1		9						4	11	5			10				7	2		
	8	3	6		1		9						4	11	5	7		10	2						
	8		6		1	10	9						4	11	5	7			3				2		
	8		6		1	10	9						4	11					3			7	2	5	
	8		6		1	10	9						4	11					3			7	2	5	
	8		6		1	10	9						4	11					3			7	2	5	
	8	4	6		1	10	9		7					11	5				3				2		
	10		6		1	8	9						4	11	5				3			7	2		
	8		6	7	1	10	9						4	11	5				3				2		
	8			7	1	10	9						4		6			11	3				2	5	
	8		6	7	1	10	9						4		3			11					2	5	
	8		6	7	1	10	9						4		3			11					2	5	
	8		6	7	1	10	9						4		3			11					2	5	
	8		6	7	1	10	9						4		3			11					2	5	
	8		6	7	1	10	9						4		3			11					2	5	
	8		6	7	1	10	9						4		3			11					2	5	
	8		6	7	1	10	9						4		3			11					2	5	
		3	6	7	1	10	9						4		5	8		11					2		
	8	3	6	7	1	10	9						4		5			11					2		
	8	3	6	7	1	10	9						4		5			11					2		
		3	6		1	10	9		7				4		5	8		11	2						
		3	6		1	10	9		8				4		5			11	2			7			
10		3	6		1	8	9						4		5			11	2		7				
	8		6		1		9	11	7				4		5	10			3				2		
	8	3	6		1	10	9		7				4		5							11	2		
	8	3	6		1	10	9		7				4		5							11	2		
	8	3	6		1	10	9		7			11	4		5								2		
	8	3	6		1	10			7				4		5	9		11					2		
	8	3	6	7	1	10							4		5	9		11					2		
	8	3	6	7	1	10							4		5	9		11					2		
	8	2	6	7	1		10						4		5	9		11					3		
	8	3	6	7	1		10						4		5	9		11					2		
	8	3	6	7	1		10						4		5	9		11	2						
	8	3	6	7			10			1			4		5	9		11					2		
	8	3	6	7	1		10						4		5	9		11					2		
	8	3	6	7	1		10						4		5	9		11					2		
	8	3	6	7	1		10						4		5	9		11					2		
	8	3	6	7	1	10							4		5	9		11					2		
	8	3		7	1	10							4		5	9		11		6			2		
	8	3	6	7	1	10	9						4		5			11					2		
	8	3	6		1	10					7		4		5	9		11					2		
1	38	27	40	25	41	31	36	1	8	1	1	1	41	10	39	18	1	30	14	1	1	8	37	11	
	15		5	5		5	14						2	4		10		1			1	2			1

Baily EF	Bennett LD	Buckingham VF	Burgess WAR	Cox FJA	Ditchburn EG	Dix RW	Foreman AG	Gilberg H	Hall AE	Hughes WA	Jones WEA	Joseph L	Ludford GA	Medley LD	Nicholson WE	Rundle CR	Skinner GEH	Stevens LWG	Tickridge S	Trailor CH	Walters WE	Whitchurch CH	Willis A	Woodward HJ	Own-goals
	8	3	6		1	10	9						4		5			11			7		2		
	8	3	6		1	10	9						4		5			11			7		2		
0	2	2	2	0	2	2	2	0	0	0	0	0	2	0	2	0	0	2	0	0	2	0	2	0	
	1												1												

League Table

	P	W	D	L	F	A	Pts
Manchester City	42	26	10	6	78	35	62
Burnley	42	22	14	6	65	29	58
Birmingham City	42	25	5	12	74	33	55
Chesterfield	42	18	14	10	58	44	50
Newcastle United	42	19	10	13	95	62	48
TOTTENHAM HOTSPUR	42	17	14	11	65	53	48
West Bromwich Albion	42	20	8	14	88	75	48
Coventry City	42	16	13	13	66	59	45
Leicester City	42	18	7	17	69	64	43
Barnsley	42	17	8	17	84	86	42
Nottingham Forest	42	15	10	17	69	74	40
West Ham United	42	16	8	18	70	76	40
Luton Town	42	16	7	19	71	73	39
Southampton	42	15	9	18	69	76	39
Fulham	42	15	9	18	63	74	39
Bradford Park Avenue	42	14	11	17	65	77	39
Bury	42	12	12	18	80	78	36
Millwall	42	14	8	20	56	79	36
Plymouth Argyle	42	14	5	23	79	96	33
Sheffield Wednesday	42	12	8	22	67	88	32
Swansea Town	42	11	7	24	55	83	29
Newport County	42	10	3	29	61	133	23

1947-48

DIVISION TWO

Manager: Joe Hulme

Did you know that?

Legend has it that *MacNamara's Band* became Spurs' signature tune as a tribute to Danny Blanchflower, but it had been adopted by Spurs even before Blanchflower joined the club. It was in 1947 that the directors asked the Enfield Central Band to play the tune as the teams emerged because it was one the players would often sing on the way back from away games.

LEAGUE DEBUTANTS

Aug 23 v West Bromwich Albion
Jack Chisholm
Aug 30 v Sheffield Wednesday
Len Duquemin
Aug 30 v Sheffield Wednesday
Johnny Jordan
Mar 15 v Barnsley
Charlie Withers
Mar 26 v Millwall
Ken Flint

Match No.	Date		Opponents		Result		Scorers	Attendance
1	Aug	23	A	West Bromwich Albion	L	0-1		32,521
2		27	A	Bury	L	0-2		16,391
3		30	H	Sheffield Wednesday	W	5-1	Jordan 2, Duquemin, Bennett 2	36,751
4	Sep	1	H	Bury	D	2-2	Duquemin, Jones	29,635
5		6	A	Cardiff City	W	3-0	Duquemin 2, Bennett	48,894
6		8	A	West Ham United	D	1-1	Jordan	25,732
7		13	H	Bradford	W	3-1	Jordan, Duquemin 2	44,004
8		15	H	West Ham United	D	2-2	Jordan, Bennett	33,415
9		20	A	Nottingham Forest	L	0-1		26,202
10		27	H	Doncaster Rovers	W	2-0	Jordan 2	46,011
11	Oct	4	A	Southampton	D	1-1	Duquemin	23,860
12		11	A	Barnsley	L	1-2	Duquemin	24,715
13		18	H	Plymouth Argyle	W	2-0	Duquemin, Bennett	35,249
14		25	A	Luton Town	D	0-0		26,496
15	Nov	1	H	Brentford	W	4-0	Baily, Duquemin 3	42,362
16		8	A	Leicester City	W	3-0	Cox, Stevens 2	34,426
17		15	H	Leeds United	W	3-1	Burgess, Baily, Duquemin	41,563
18		22	A	Fulham	W	2-0	Duquemin, Stevens	36,147
19		29	H	Coventry City	W	2-1	Bennett, Stevens	41,843
20	Dec	6	A	Newcastle United	L	0-1		57,950
21		13	H	Birmingham City	L	1-2	Baily	53,730
22		20	H	West Bromwich Albion	D	1-1	Cox	40,219
23		25	H	Chesterfield	W	3-0	Baily, Duquemin, Bennett	44,863
24		27	A	Chesterfield	L	1-3	Burgess	19,495
25	Jan	3	A	Sheffield Wednesday	L	0-1		47,902
26		17	H	Cardiff City	W	2-1	Cox (pen), Jordan	57,386
27		31	A	Bradford	W	2-0	Cox, Jordan	20,807
28	Feb	14	A	Doncaster Rovers	D	1-1	Woodward	24,033
29		21	H	Southampton	D	0-0		29,784
30	Mar	6	A	Plymouth Argyle	D	1-1	Bennett	32,049
31		15	H	Barnsley	L	0-3		31,969
32		20	A	Brentford	L	0-2		31,297
33		26	A	Millwall	D	0-0		42,288
34		27	H	Leicester City	D	0-0		33,108
35		29	H	Millwall	W	3-2	Jordan (pen), Duquemin, Jones	31,339
36	Apr	3	A	Leeds United	W	3-1	Rundle, Baily, Flint	24,891
37		7	H	Luton Town	L	0-1		23,807
38		10	H	Fulham	L	0-2		32,490
39		12	H	Nottingham Forest	L	0-3		18,569
40		17	A	Coventry City	D	1-1	Barratt (og)	18,262
41		24	H	Newcastle United	D	1-1	Craig (og)	44,164
42	May	1	A	Birmingham City	D	0-0		35,569
								Appearances
								Goals

FA Cup

R3	Jan	10	A	Bolton Wanderers	W*	2-0	Duquemin 2	37,075
R4		24	H	West Bromwich Albion	W	3-1	Cox, Duquemin 2	71,853
R5	Feb	7	H	Leicester City	W	5-2	Duquemin 3, Cox 2 (1 pen)	69,049
R6		28	A	Southampton	W	1-0	Bennett	28,425
SF	Mar	13	N#	Blackpool	L*	1-3	Duquemin	70,687
								Appearances
								Goals

*after extra-time #played at Villa Park

Baily EF	Bennett LD	Buckingham VF	Burgess WAR	Chisolm JR	Cox FJA	Ditchburn EG	Dix RW	Duquemin LS	Flint K	Gilberg H	Hughes WA	Jones WEA	Jordan JW	Ludford GA	Medley LD	Nicholson WE	Rundle CR	Stevens LWG	Tickridge S	Trailor CH	Walters WE	Willis A	Withers CF	Woodward HJ	Own-goals
	8	3	6	5		1	10					7				4	9	11				2			
	8	3	6	5		1	10					7				4	9	11				2			
	10	3			7	1		9				11	8			4				6		2		5	
		3			7	1	10	9				11	8			4			2	6				5	
	10	3	6		7	1		9				11	8	4					2					5	
	10	3	6		7	1		9				11	8	4					2					5	
	10	3	6			1		9				7	8			4		11	2					5	
	10	3	6			1						7	8			4	9	11	2					5	
	10	3	6			1						7	8			4	9	11	2					5	
		3	6		7	1	10						8			4		11	2	9				5	
		3	6		7	1	10	9					8			4		11	2					5	
	10	3	6		7	1		9					8			4		11	2					5	
	10	3			7	1		9					8			4		11	2	6				5	
	10	3	6		7	1		9					8			4		11	2					5	
8	10	3	6		7	1		9						4		5		11	2						
8	10	3	6		7	1		9								4		11	2					5	
8	10	3	6		7	1		9								4		11	2					5	
8	10	3	6		7	1		9								4		11	2					5	
8	10	3	6		7	1		9								4		11	2					5	
8	10	3	6		7	1		9								4		11	2					5	
8	10	3	6		7	1		9								4		11	2					5	
8	10	3	6		7	1		9								4		11	2					5	
8	10	3	6		7	1		9								4		11	2					5	
8	10	3	6		7	1		9						4		5		11	2						
8	10	3	6		7	1		9						4		5		11	2						
8		3	6		7	1		9					10			4		11	2					5	
10		3	6		7	1		9				11	8			4			2					5	
10		3	6		7	1		9				11	8			4			2					5	
10		3			7	1		9				11	8	4		5			2	6					
10	8	3			7	1		9				11		4					2	6				5	
10	8		6			1		9							11	4			2		7		3	5	
10	8	3			7	1		9							11	4			2	6				5	
	10	3	6		7	1		9	11				8			4			2					5	
	10	3			7	1		9				11	8			4			2	6				5	
	10	3				1		9		7		11	8			4			2	6				5	
10	6	3			7	1			11				8			4	9		2					5	
10	6	3			7	1		9	11				8			4			2					5	
10	4	3	6		7	1		9	11								8		2					5	
10	8	3	6					9	11		1	7		4		5			2						
	10	3	6		7	1		9				11	8			4			2					5	
	10	3	6		7	1		9				11	8			4			2					5	
	10	3	6		7	1		9				11	8			4				2				5	
22	35	41	32	2	34	41	5	36	5	1	1	19	24	8	2	38	6	22	38	10	1	3	1	35	
5	8		2		4			16	1			2	10				1	4						1	2

Baily EF	Bennett LD	Buckingham VF	Burgess WAR	Chisolm JR	Cox FJA	Ditchburn EG	Dix RW	Duquemin LS	Flint K	Gilberg H	Hughes WA	Jones WEA	Jordan JW	Ludford GA	Medley LD	Nicholson WE	Rundle CR	Stevens LWG	Tickridge S	Trailor CH	Walters WE	Willis A	Withers CF	Woodward HJ	Own-goals
10		3	6		7	1		9					8			4		11	2					5	
10		3	6		7	1		9					8			4		11	2					5	
10		3	6		7	1		9					8			4		11	2					5	
8	10	3			7	1		9				11		4		5			2	6					
10	8	3	6		7	1		9						4	11	5			2						
5	2	5	4	0	5	5	0	5	0	0	0	1	3	2	1	5	0	3	5	1	0	0	0	3	
	1				3			8																	

League Table

	P	W	D	L	F	A	Pts
Birmingham City	42	22	15	5	55	24	59
Newcastle United	42	24	8	10	72	41	56
Southampton	42	21	10	11	71	53	52
Sheffield Wednesday	42	20	11	11	66	53	51
Cardiff City	42	18	11	13	61	58	47
West Ham United	42	16	14	12	55	53	46
West Bromwich Albion	42	18	9	15	63	58	45
TOTTENHAM HOTSPUR	42	15	14	13	56	43	44
Leicester City	42	16	11	15	60	57	43
Coventry City	42	14	13	15	59	52	41
Fulham	42	15	10	17	47	46	40
Barnsley	42	15	10	17	62	64	40
Luton Town	42	14	12	16	56	59	40
Bradford Park Avenue	42	16	8	18	68	72	40
Brentford	42	13	14	15	44	61	40
Chesterfield	42	16	7	19	54	55	39
Plymouth Argyle	42	9	20	13	40	58	38
Leeds United	42	14	8	20	62	72	36
Nottingham Forest	42	12	11	19	54	60	35
Bury	42	9	16	17	58	68	34
Doncaster Rovers	42	9	11	22	40	66	29
Millwall	42	9	11	22	44	74	29

1948-49

DIVISION TWO

Manager: Joe Hulme

Did you know that?

A minute's silence followed by the playing of the *Last Post* preceded the match against Plymouth Argyle at White Hart Lane in December 1948. A week earlier Morton F. Cadman, Spurs' life vice-president, had died aged 82. Cadman had first become associated with Spurs as a player in the 1880s, later serving as reserve-team captain, committee member, director and vice-chairman.

LEAGUE DEBUTANTS

Sep 11 v West Bromwich Albion
Cyril Toulouse
Oct 23 v Newcastle United
Len Garwood
Mar 19 v Luton Town
Harry Clarke

Match No.	Date		Opponents		Result		Scorers	Attendance
1	Aug	21	H	Sheffield Wednesday	W	3-2	Baily, Duquemin, Jones	51,265
2		23	A	Coventry City	L	0-2		21,110
3		28	A	Lincoln City	D	0-0		19,540
4		30	H	Coventry City	W	4-0	Cox, Duquemin 2, Jones	31,768
5	Sep	4	H	Chesterfield	W	4-0	Cox, Baily 2, Jones	46,804
6		8	A	Leeds United	D	0-0		33,793
7		11	A	West Bromwich Albion	D	2-2	Duquemin, Bennett	32,279
8		13	H	Leeds United	D	2-2	Cox, Jones	37,640
9		18	H	Bury	W	3-1	Duquemin, Bennett, Jones	60,442
10		25	A	West Ham United	L	0-1		38,132
11	Oct	2	H	Blackburn Rovers	W	4-0	Baily, Bennett 2, Jones	53,721
12		9	A	Cardiff City	W	1-0	Jones	56,018
13		16	H	Queen's Park Rangers	W	1-0	Baily	69,718
14		23	A	Luton Town	D	1-1	Baily	24,859
15		30	H	Bradford	W	5-1	Burgess 2, Duquemin, Bennett, Jones	47,955
16	Nov	6	A	Southampton	L	1-3	Jones	28,800
17		13	H	Barnsley	W	4-1	Bennett,, Duquemin, Baily 2	48,989
18		20	A	Grimsby Town	D	1-1	Cox	15,863
19		27	H	Nottingham Forest	*	0-0		31,989
20	Dec	4	A	Fulham	D	1-1	Nicholson	36,247
21		11	H	Plymouth Argyle	W	3-0	Baily, Duquemin, Boyd (og)	41,910
22		18	A	Sheffield Wednesday	L	1-3	Baily	40,256
23		25	A	Leicester City	W	2-1	Burgess, Bennett	30,949
24		27	H	Leicester City	D	1-1	Rundle	49,411
25	Jan	1	H	Lincoln City	L	1-2	Jones	33,218
26		15	A	Chesterfield	L	0-1		15,861
27		22	H	West Bromwich Albion	W	2-0	Baily, Jones	62,566
28	Feb	5	A	Bury	D	1-1	Bennett	17,679
29		12	H	Nottingham Forest	W	2-1	Duquemin, Bennett	37,599
30		19	H	West Ham United	D	1-1	Bennett	62,980
31		26	A	Blackburn Rovers	D	1-1	Jones	20,262
32	Mar	5	H	Cardiff City	L	0-1		51,183
33		12	A	Queen's Park Rangers	D	0-0		25,416
34		19	H	Luton Town	W	2-1	Bennett 2	41,839
35		26	A	Bradford	D	1-1	Duquemin	13,304
36	Apr	2	H	Southampton	L	0-1		69,265
37		9	A	Barnsley	L	1-4	Bennett	16,796
38		15	H	Brentford	W	2-0	Bennett, Medley	39,050
39		16	H	Grimsby Town	W	5-2	Bennett 2, Duquemin 2, Medley	29,808
40		18	A	Brentford	D	1-1	Walters	19,004
41		23	A	Nottingham Forest	D	2-2	Nicholson, Duquemin	27,126
42		30	H	Fulham	D	1-1	Duquemin	50,133
43	May	7	A	Plymouth Argyle	W	5-0	Duquemin, Bennett 3, Medley	23,927

*abandoned after 17 mins - fog

Appearances
Goals

FA Cup

R3	Jan	8	A	Arsenal	L	0-3		47,314

Appearances
Goals

Baily EF	Bennett LD	Buckingham VF	Burgess WAR	Clarke HA	Cox FJA	Ditchburn EG	Duquemin LS	Garwood LF	Gilberg H	Jones WEA	Ludford GA	Medley LD	Nicholson WE	Rundle CR	Stevens LWG	Tickridge S	Toulouse CH	Walters WE	Willis A	Withers CF	Woodward HJ	Own-goals
8	10	3	6		7	1	9			11			4			2					5	
8	10	3	6			1	9			7	4		5		11	2						
8	10	3	6		7	1	9			11			4			2					5	
8	10	3	6		7	1	9			11			4			2					5	
8	10	3	6		7	1	9			11			4			2					5	
8	10	3	6		7	1	9			11			4			2					5	
8	10	3	6		7	1	9			11			4			2	5					
8	10	3	6		7	1	9			11			4			2	5					
8	10	3	6		7	1	9			11	4		5			2						
8	10	3	6		7	1	9			11	4		5			2						
8	10	3	6		7	1	9			11	4		5			2						
8	10	5	6		7	1	9			11	4					2			3			
8	10	5	6		7	1	9			11			4			2			3			
8	10	5			7	1	9	6					4		11	2			3			
8	10	5	6		7	1	9			11			4			2			3			
8	10	5	6		7	1	9			11			4			2			3			
10	8	5	6		7	1	9			11			4			2			3			
8	10	5	6		7	1	9			11			4			2			3			
8	10	5	6			1	9			11			4			2		7	3			
8	10	5	6		7	1	9			11			4			2			3			
8	10	3	6		7	1	9			11			4						2		5	
8	10	3	6		7	1	9			11			4			2					5	
8	10	3	6		7	1	9			11			4			2					5	
8	10	3	6		7	1				11			4	9		2					5	
8	10	5	6		7	1				11			4	9		2			3			
8	10		6		7	1				11			4	9		2				3	5	
8	10		6			1	9			11			4			2		7		3	5	
8	10		6			1	9			11			4			2		7		3	5	
8	10		6			1	9			11			4			2		7		3	5	
8	10		6			1	9			11			4			2		7		3	5	
8	10		6		9	1				11			4			2		7		3	5	
8	10	3	6		9	1				11			4			2		7			5	
	10		6		7	1	9			11	3		4	8		2					5	
8	10		6	5	7	1	9			11	3		4			2						
8	10		6	5	7	1	9			11	3		4			2						
8	10		6	5	7	1	9			11	3		4			2						
0	8		6	5	7	1	9			11	3		4			2						
0	8		6	5		1	9					11	4			2		7		3		
0	8		6	5		1	9					11	4			2		7		3		
0	8		6	5		1	9					11	4			2		7		3		
0	8			5		1	9	6				11	4			2		7		3		
0	8		6	5		1	9					11	4			2		7		3		
8	10		6	5		1	9					11	4			2		7		3		
2	43	26	41	10	31	43	38	2	0	36	10	6	42	4	2	42	2	13	11	12	17	
1	19		3		4		15			12		3	2	1				1				1

Baily EF	Bennett LD	Buckingham VF	Burgess WAR	Clarke HA	Cox FJA	Ditchburn EG	Duquemin LS	Garwood LF	Gilberg H	Jones WEA	Ludford GA	Medley LD	Nicholson WE	Rundle CR	Stevens LWG	Tickridge S	Toulouse CH	Walters WE	Willis A	Withers CF	Woodward HJ	Own-goals
	10	3	6		7	1			8	11			4	9		2					5	
)	1	1	1	0	1	1	0	0	1	1	0	0	1	1	0	1	0	0	0	0	1	

League Table

	P	W	D	L	F	A	Pts
Fulham	42	24	9	9	77	37	57
West Bromwich Albion	42	24	8	10	69	39	56
Southampton	42	23	9	10	69	36	55
Cardiff City	42	19	13	10	62	47	51
TOTTENHAM HOTSPUR	42	17	16	9	72	44	50
Chesterfield	42	15	17	10	51	45	47
West Ham United	42	18	10	14	56	58	46
Sheffield Wednesday	42	15	13	14	63	56	43
Barnsley	42	14	12	16	62	61	40
Luton Town	42	14	12	16	55	57	40
Grimsby Town	42	15	10	17	72	76	40
Bury	42	17	6	19	67	76	40
Queen's Park Rangers	42	14	11	17	44	62	39
Blackburn Rovers	42	15	8	19	53	63	38
Leeds United	42	12	13	17	55	63	37
Coventry City	42	15	7	20	55	64	37
Bradford Park Avenue	42	13	11	18	65	78	37
Brentford	42	11	14	17	42	53	36
Leicester City	42	10	16	16	62	79	36

1949-50

DIVISION TWO

Manager: Arthur Rowe

Did you know that?

Unprecedented scenes were witnessed around White Hart Lane on Sunday 15 January 1950 when tickets for the forthcoming FA Cup tie with Sunderland went on sale. Queues began to form at 3pm the previous day and by the time tickets went on sale at 10am there were 30–40,000 people waiting. The 45,000 tickets available were sold by 1.30pm with over 3,000 people turned away.

LEAGUE DEBUTANTS

Aug 20	v Brentford Alf Ramsey
Nov 26	v Queen's Park Rangers Bobby Cook
Dec 17	v Brentford Jimmy Scarth
Dec 27	v Chesterfield Billy Rees
Apr 22	v Grimsby Town Tony Marchi

Match No.	Date			Opponents	Result		Scorers	Attendance
1	Aug	20	A	Brentford	W	4-1	Bennett, Duquemin, Medley 2	32,702
2		22	H	Plymouth Argyle	W	4-1	Ramsey (pen), Bennett, Baily, Medley	41,882
3		27	H	Blackburn Rovers	L	2-3	Walters 2	53,016
4		31	A	Plymouth Argyle	W	2-0	Bennett, Baily	24,828
5	Sep	3	A	Cardiff City	W	1-0	Medley	42,649
6		5	H	Sheffield Wednesday	W	1-0	Duquemin	37,697
7		10	H	Leeds United	W	2-0	Bennett, Baily	48,274
8		17	H	Bury	W	3-1	Nicholson, Duquemin, Baily	54,438
9		24	A	Leicester City	W	2-1	Walters, Duquemin	36,846
10	Oct	1	H	Bradford	W	5-0	Ramsey (pen), Walters, Bennett, Medley 2	54,905
11		8	A	Southampton	D	1-1	Walters	30,240
12		15	H	Coventry City	W	3-1	Bennett, Duquemin 2	54,375
13		22	A	Luton Town	D	1-1	Walters	27,319
14		29	H	Barnsley	W	2-0	Duquemin, Baily	54,856
15	Nov	5	A	West Ham United	W	1-0	Walters	31,374
16		12	H	Sheffield United	W	7-0	Walters 3, Duquemin 2, Medley 2	54,193
17		19	A	Grimsby Town	W	3-2	Ramsey. Bennett, Medley	22,482
18		26	H	Queen's Park Rangers	W	3-0	Nicholson, Bennett 2	62,783
19	Dec	3	A	Preston North End	W	3-1	Bennett, Duquemin, Medley	35,501
20		10	H	Swansea Town	W	3-1	Bennett, Duquemin 2	50,758
21		17	H	Brentford	D	1-1	Baily	49,297
22		24	A	Blackburn Rovers	W	2-1	Scarth, Medley	33,078
23		26	H	Chesterfield	W	1-0	Ramsey (pen)	61,879
24		27	A	Chesterfield	D	1-1	Scarth	26,341
25		31	H	Cardiff City	W	2-0	Rees, Baily	59,780
26	Jan	14	A	Leeds United	L	0-3		50,476
27		21	A	Bury	W	2-1	Walters, Bennett	27,386
28	Feb	4	H	Leicester City	L	0-2		60,595
29		18	A	Bradford	W	3-1	Duquemin 2, Rees	20,287
30		25	H	Southampton	W	4-0	Rees, Duquemin, Medley 2	70,302
31	Mar	4	A	Coventry City	W	1-0	Medley	36,320
32		11	H	Luton Town	D	0-0		53,145
33		18	A	Barnsley	L	0-2		22,346
34		25	H	West Ham United	W	4-1	Walters 2, Bennett, Medley	51,124
35	Apr	1	A	Queen's Park Rangers	W	2-0	Baily, Medley	29,771
36		7	H	Hull City	D	0-0		66,889
37		8	H	Preston North End	W	3-2	Walters, Bennett, Medley	49,170
38		10	A	Hull City	L	0-1		38,345
39		15	A	Sheffield United	L	1-2	Medley	41,419
40		22	H	Grimsby Town	L	1-2	Duquemin	46,423
41		29	A	Swansea Town	L	0-1		16,417
42	May	6	A	Sheffield Wednesday	D	0-0		50,777
								Appearances
								Goals

FA Cup

R3	Jan	7	A	Stoke City	W	1-0	Baily	47,000
R4		28	H	Sunderland	W	5-1	Walters 2, Bennett 2, Medley	66,246
R5	Feb	11	A	Everton	L	0-1		72,921
								Appearances
								Goals

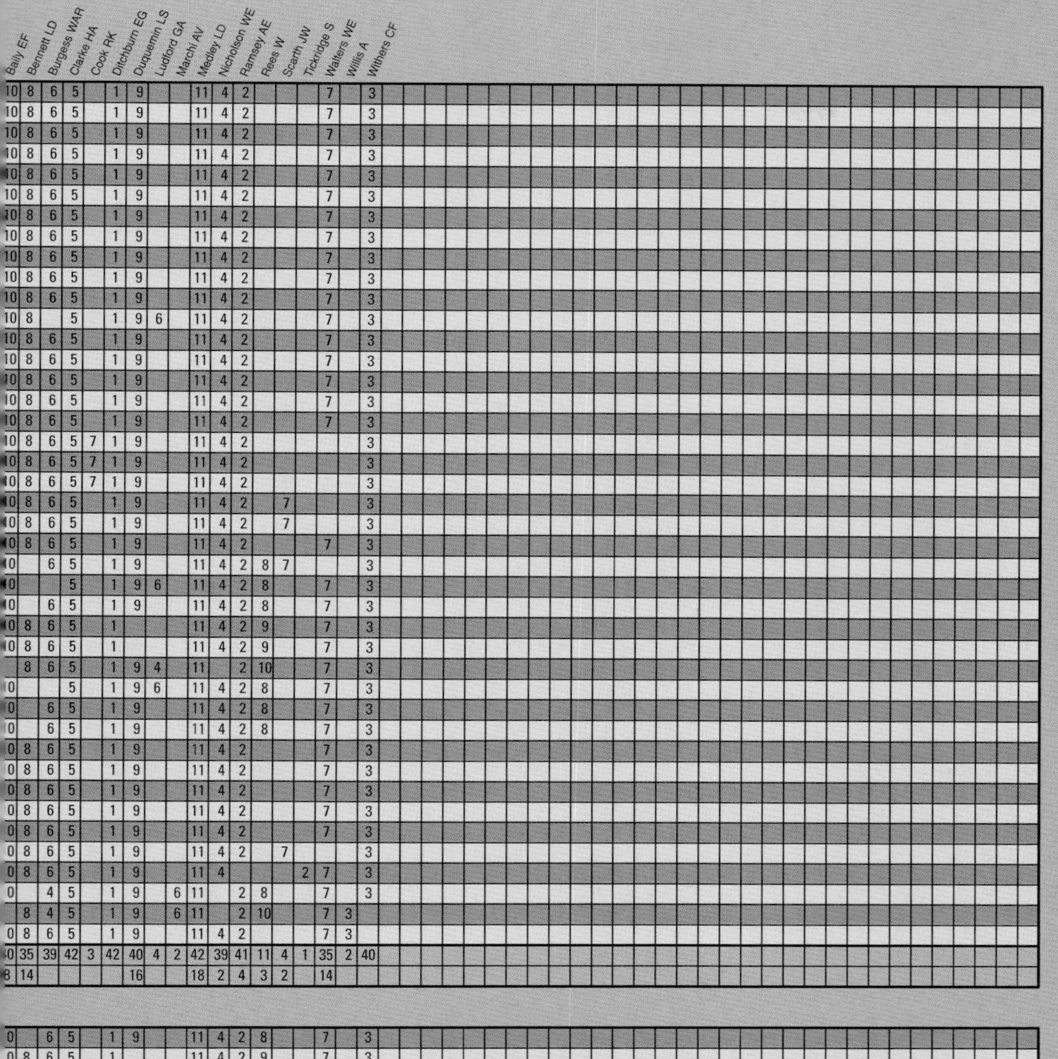

Baily EF	Bennett LD	Burgess WAR	Clarke HA	Cook RK	Ditchburn EG	Duquemin LS	Ludford GA	Marchi AV	Medley LD	Nicholson WE	Ramsey AE	Rees W	Scarth JW	Tickridge S	Walters WE	Willis A	Withers CF
10	8	6	5		1	9			11	4	2				7		3
10	8	6	5		1	9			11	4	2				7		3
10	8	6	5		1	9			11	4	2				7		3
10	8	6	5		1	9			11	4	2				7		3
10	8	6	5		1	9			11	4	2				7		3
10	8	6	5		1	9			11	4	2				7		3
10	8	6	5		1	9			11	4	2				7		3
10	8	6	5		1	9			11	4	2				7		3
10	8	6	5		1	9			11	4	2				7		3
10	8	6	5		1	9			11	4	2				7		3
10	8	6	5		1	9			11	4	2				7		3
10	8		5		1	9	6		11	4	2				7		3
10	8	6	5		1	9			11	4	2				7		3
10	8	6	5		1	9			11	4	2				7		3
10	8	6	5		1	9			11	4	2				7		3
10	8	6	5		1	9			11	4	2				7		3
10	8	6	5		1	9			11	4	2				7		3
10	8	6	5	7	1	9			11	4	2						3
10	8	6	5	7	1	9			11	4	2						3
10	8	6	5	7	1	9			11	4	2						3
10	8	6	5		1	9			11	4	2		7				3
10	8	6	5		1	9			11	4	2		7				3
10	8	6	5		1	9			11	4	2				7		3
10		6	5		1	9			11	4	2	8	7				3
10			5		1	9	6		11	4	2	8			7		3
10		6	5		1	9			11	4	2	8			7		3
10	8	6	5		1				11	4	2	9			7		3
10	8	6	5		1				11	4	2	9			7		3
	8	6	5		1	9	4		11		2	10			7		3
0			5		1	9	6		11	4	2	8			7		3
0		6	5		1	9			11	4	2	8			7		3
0		6	5		1	9			11	4	2	8			7		3
0	8	6	5		1	9			11	4	2				7		3
0	8	6	5		1	9			11	4	2				7		3
0	8	6	5		1	9			11	4	2				7		3
0	8	6	5		1	9			11	4	2				7		3
0	8	6	5		1	9			11	4	2				7		3
0	8	6	5		1	9			11	4	2		7				3
0	8	6	5		1	9			11	4				2	7		3
0		4	5		1	9		6	11		2	8			7		3
	8	4	5		1	9		6	11		2	10			7	3	
0	8	6	5		1	9			11	4	2				7	3	
40	35	39	42	3	42	40	4	2	42	39	41	11	4	1	35	2	40
8	14					16			18	2	4	3	2		14		

Baily EF	Bennett LD	Burgess WAR	Clarke HA	Cook RK	Ditchburn EG	Duquemin LS	Ludford GA	Marchi AV	Medley LD	Nicholson WE	Ramsey AE	Rees W	Scarth JW	Tickridge S	Walters WE	Willis A	Withers CF
0		6	5		1	9			11	4	2	8			7		3
0	8	6	5		1				11	4	2	9			7		3
0	8	6	5		1	9			11	4	2				7		3
3	2	3	3	0	3	2	0	0	3	3	3	2	0	0	3	0	3
1	2								1						2		

League Table

	P	W	D	L	F	A	Pts
TOTTENHAM HOTSPUR	42	27	7	8	81	35	61
Sheffield Wednesday	42	18	16	8	67	48	52
Sheffield United	42	19	14	9	68	49	52
Southampton	42	19	14	9	64	48	52
Leeds United	42	17	13	12	54	45	47
Preston North End	42	18	9	15	60	49	45
Hull City	42	17	11	14	64	72	45
Swansea Town	42	17	9	16	53	49	43
Brentford	42	15	13	14	44	49	43
Cardiff City	42	16	10	16	41	44	42
Grimsby Town	42	16	8	18	74	73	40
Coventry City	42	13	13	16	55	55	39
Barnsley	42	13	13	16	64	67	39
Chesterfield	42	15	9	18	43	47	39
Leicester City	42	12	15	15	55	65	39
Blackburn Rovers	42	14	10	18	55	60	38
Luton Town	42	10	18	14	41	51	38
Bury	42	14	9	19	60	65	37
West Ham United	42	12	12	18	53	61	36
Queen's Park Rangers	42	11	12	19	40	57	34
Plymouth Argyle	42	8	16	18	44	65	32
Bradford Park Avenue	42	10	11	21	51	77	31

1950-51

DIVISION ONE

Manager: Arthur Rowe

Did you know that?

With Arsenal heading the First Division table and Spurs in hot pursuit, there were rumours the meeting on 23 December 1950 would take place at Wembley. Spurs made it clear there was never any possibility of that happening but the fearful prophesies of the numbers expected actually kept many fans away.

LEAGUE DEBUTANTS

Aug 23 v Bolton Wanderers
Peter Murphy
Sep 23 v Sunderland
Sid McClellan
Sep 23 v Sunderland
Dennis Uphill
Oct 7 v Burnley
Colin Brittan
Mar 3 v Chelsea
Alex Wright

Match No.	Date		Opponents		Result		Scorers	Attendance
1	Aug	19	H	Blackpool	L	1-4	Baily	64,978
2		23	A	Bolton Wanderers	W	4-1	Walters, Murphy, Duquemin, Medley	21,745
3		26	A	Arsenal	D	2-2	Burgess, Walters	64,638
4		28	H	Bolton Wanderers	W	4-2	Duquemin 2, Baily, Howe (og)	44,246
5	Sep	2	A	Charlton Athletic	D	1-1	Ramsey (pen)	61,480
6		6	A	Liverpool	L	1-2	Medley	39,015
7		9	H	Manchester United	W	1-0	Walters	60,621
8		16	A	Wolverhampton Wanderers	L	1-2	Chatham (og)	55,364
9		23	H	Sunderland	D	1-1	Baily	59,190
10		30	A	Aston Villa	W	3-2	Murphy, Duquemin, Medley	36,538
11	Oct	7	H	Burnley	W	1-0	Medley	46,518
12		14	A	Chelsea	W	2-0	Walters, Duquemin	65,992
13		21	H	Stoke City	W	6-1	Walters, Bennett 2, Duquemin 2, Medley	54,124
14		28	A	West Bromwich Albion	W	2-1	Walters, Medley	44,543
15	Nov	4	H	Portsmouth	W	5-1	Walters, Duquemin, Baily 3	66,402
16		11	A	Everton	W	2-1	Baily, Medley	47,125
17		18	H	Newcastle United	W	7-0	Ramsey (pen), Walters, Bennett, Baily, Medley 3	70,336
18		25	A	Huddersfield Town	L	2-3	Nicholson, Walters	39,519
19	Dec	2	H	Middlesbrough	D	3-3	Ramsey (pen), Walters, Duquemin	61,148
20		9	A	Sheffield Wednesday	D	1-1	Bennett	44,367
21		16	A	Blackpool	W	1-0	Duquemin	22,203
22		23	H	Arsenal	W	1-0	Baily	54,898
23		25	A	Derby County	D	1-1	Murphy	32,301
24		26	H	Derby County	W	2-1	McClellan 2	59,885
25		30	H	Charlton Athletic	W	1-0	Walters	54,667
26	Jan	13	A	Manchester United	L	1-2	Baily	45,104
27		20	H	Wolverhampton Wanderers	W	2-1	Walters, McClellan	66,796
28	Feb	3	A	Sunderland	D	0-0		56,817
29		17	H	Aston Villa	W	3-2	Ramsey (pen), Baily, Medley	47,842
30		24	A	Burnley	L	0-2		33,047
31	Mar	3	H	Chelsea	W	2-1	Burgess, Wright	59,449
32		10	A	Stoke City	D	0-0		24,236
33		17	H	West Bromwich Albion	W	5-0	Bennett, Duquemin 3, Baily	45,353
34		23	A	Fulham	W	1-0	Murphy	47,391
35		24	A	Portsmouth	D	1-1	Uphill	49,716
36		26	H	Fulham	W	2-1	Bennett, Murphy	51,862
37		31	H	Everton	W	3-0	Walters, Bennett, Murphy	56,651
38	Apr	7	A	Newcastle United	W	1-0	Walters	41,241
39		14	H	Huddersfield Town	L	0-2		55,014
40		21	A	Middlesbrough	D	1-1	Murphy	36,689
41		28	H	Sheffield Wednesday	W	1-0	Duquemin	46,645
42	May	5	H	Liverpool	W	3-1	Walters, Murphy 2	49,072
								Appearances
								Goals

FA Cup

R3	Jan	6	A	Huddersfield Town	L	0-2		25,390
								Appearances
								Goals

Baily EF	Bennett LD	Brittan C	Burgess WAR	Clarke HA	Ditchburn EG	Duquemin LS	McClellan SB	Medley LD	Murphy P	Nicholson WE	Ramsey AE	Scarth JW	Tickridge S	Uphill DE	Walters WE	Willis A	Withers CF	Wright AM	Own-goals	
0	8		6	5	1	9		11		4	2				7		3			
0			6	5	1	9		11	8	4	2				7		3			
0			6	5	1	9		11	8	4	2				7	3				
0	8		6	5	1	9		11		4	2				7	3				
0	8		6	5	1	9		11		4	2				7	3				
0			6	5	1	9		11	8	4	2				7	3				
0	8		6	5	1	9			11	4	2				7	3				
0	8		6	5	1	9		11		4	2				7	3				
0			6	5	1		9	11		4	2			8	7	3				
0			6	5	1	9		11	8	4	2				7	3				
	10	6		5	1	9		11	8	4			2		7	3				
0	8		6	5	1	9		11		4	2				7	3				
0	8	6		5	1	9		11		4	2				7	3				
0	8		6	5	1	9		11		4	2				7	3				
0	8		6	5	1	9		11		4	2				7	3				
0	8		6	5	1	9		11		4	2				7	3				
0	8	6		5	1	9		11		4	2				7	3				
0	8	6		5	1	9		11		4	2				7	3				
0	8		6	5	1	9		11		4	2				7	3				
0	8		6	5	1	9		11		4	2				7	3				
0	8	6		5	1	9		11		4	2				7	3				
0	8		6	5	1	9		11		4	2				7	3				
	8	6		5	1	9		11	10	4	2				7	3				
0			6	5	1		9	11	8	4	2	7				3				
0	8		6	5	1	9		11		4	2				7	3				
0		4		5	1		9	11	8	6	2				7	3				
0			6	5	1		9	11	8	4	2				7	3				
0			6	5	1		9	11	8	4	2				7	3				
0		4	6	5	1		9	11	8		2				7	3				
0			6	5	1		9	11	8	4	2				7	3				
0			6	5	1			11	8	4	2				7	3		9		
0			6	5	1			11	8	4	2				7	3		9		
0	8		6	5	1	9			11	4	2				7	3				
0	8		6	5	1	9			11	4	2				7	3				
0			6	5	1	9			11	4	2			8	7	3				
0	8		6	5	1	9		7	11	4	2						3			
0	8		6	5	1	9			11	4	2				7	3				
0	8		6	5	1	9			11	4	2				7	3				
0	8		6	5	1	9			11	4					7	2	3			
0			6	5	1	9		11	8	4	2				7	3				
0			6	5	1	9		11	8	4	2				7	3				
0			6	5	1	9		11	8	4	2				7	3				
0	25	8	35	42	42	33	7	35	25	41	40	1	1	2	40	39	4	2		
2	7		2			14	3	11	9	1	4			1	15			1	2	

Baily EF	Bennett LD	Brittan C	Burgess WAR	Clarke HA	Ditchburn EG	Duquemin LS	McClellan SB	Medley LD	Murphy P	Nicholson WE	Ramsey AE	Scarth JW	Tickridge S	Uphill DE	Walters WE	Willis A	Withers CF	Wright AM	Own-goals	
0	8		6	5	1	9		11		4	2				7	3				R3
	1	0	1	1	1	1	0	1	0	1	1	0	0	0	1	1	0	0		

League Table

	P	W	D	L	F	A	Pts
TOTTENHAM HOTSPUR	42	25	10	7	82	44	60
Manchester United	42	24	8	10	74	40	56
Blackpool	42	20	10	12	79	53	50
Newcastle United	42	18	13	11	62	53	49
Arsenal	42	19	9	14	73	56	47
Middlesbrough	42	18	11	13	76	65	47
Portsmouth	42	16	15	11	71	68	47
Bolton Wanderers	42	19	7	16	64	61	45
Liverpool	42	16	11	15	53	59	43
Burnley	42	14	14	14	48	43	42
Derby County	42	16	8	18	81	75	40
Sunderland	42	12	16	14	63	73	40
Stoke City	42	13	14	15	50	59	40
Wolverhampton W	42	15	8	19	74	61	38
Aston Villa	42	12	13	17	66	68	37
West Bromwich Albion	42	13	11	18	53	61	37
Charlton Athletic	42	14	9	19	63	80	37
Fulham	42	13	11	18	52	68	37
Huddersfield Town	42	15	6	21	64	92	36
Chelsea	42	12	8	22	53	65	32
Sheffield Wednesday	42	12	8	22	64	83	32
Everton	42	12	8	22	48	86	32

1951-52

DIVISION ONE

Manager: Arthur Rowe

Did you know that?

Spurs scored a goal against Huddersfield Town on 2 April 1952 that was every bit as controversial as the one Pedro Mendes did not score against Manchester United over 50 years later. Eddie Baily's corner struck the back of the referee, and from the rebounded Baily crossed for Len Duquemin to get the only goal of the game. As the ball had not been played by another player after Baily had taken the initial corner the goal should not have stood, but the referee had his back to Baily and did not know he had played it twice. Huddersfield appealed as far as they could in an effort to get the game replayed but without success.

LEAGUE DEBUTANTS

Aug 18	v Middlesbrough	Brian Farley
Aug 20	v Fulham	Derek King
Aug 23	v West Bromwich Albion	Les Dicker
Sep 8	v Bolton Wanderers	Tommy Harmer
Oct 21	v Aston Villa	Ralph Wetton
Dec 1	v Liverpool	Harry Robshaw
Dec 25	v Charlton Athletic	George Robb
Mar 1	v Derby County	Chris Adams

Match No.	Date		Opponents		Result		Scorers	Attendance
1	Aug	18	A	Middlesbrough	L	1-2	Bennett	44,004
2		20	H	Fulham	W	1-0	Medley	48,766
3		25	H	West Bromwich Albion	W	3-1	Bennett 2, Medley	51,544
4		29	A	Fulham	W	2-1	Bennett, McClellan	33,920
5	Sep	1	A	Newcastle United	L	2-7	Scarth, Bennett	52,541
6		3	A	Burnley	D	1-1	Bennett	27,045
7		8	H	Bolton Wanderers	W	2-1	Bennett, Edwards (og)	61,838
8		10	H	Burnley	D	1-1	Ramsey (pen)	35,948
9		15	A	Stoke City	W	6-1	Ramsey (pen), Walters, Bennett, McClellan, Medley 2	27,154
10		22	H	Manchester United	W	2-0	Bennett, Medley	70,882
11		29	A	Arsenal	D	1-1	Murphy	68,164
12	Oct	6	H	Manchester City	L	1-2	Bennett	58,163
13		13	A	Derby County	L	2-4	Bennett, McClellan	27,495
14		20	H	Aston Villa	W	2-0	Bennett, Duquemin	49,247
15		27	A	Sunderland	W	1-0	Walters	50,513
16	Nov	3	H	Wolverhampton Wanderers	W	4-2	Ramsey (pen), Walters, Bennett, Duquemin	61,626
17		10	A	Huddersfield Town	D	1-1	Duquemin	30,259
18		17	H	Chelsea	W	3-2	Nicholson, Bennett, Duquemin	48,985
19		24	A	Portsmouth	L	0-2		46,815
20	Dec	1	H	Liverpool	L	2-3	Walters, Bennett	51,342
21		8	A	Blackpool	L	0-1		14,821
22		15	H	Middlesbrough	W	3-1	Bennett, Murphy 2	37,781
23		22	A	West Bromwich Albion	L	1-3	Murphy	29,962
24		25	A	Charlton Athletic	W	3-0	Medley, Bennett, Robb	37,711
25		26	H	Charlton Athletic	L	2-3	Walters, Murphy	49,350
26		29	H	Newcastle United	W	2-1	Walters, Medley	55,219
27	Jan	5	A	Bolton Wanderers	D	1-1	Harmer	46,354
28		19	H	Stoke City	W	2-0	Duquemin, Harmer	45,976
29		26	A	Manchester United	L	0-2		42,668
30	Feb	9	H	Arsenal	L	1-2	Walters	66,438
31		16	A	Manchester City	D	1-1	Walters	39,080
32		23	H	Preston North End	W	1-0	Harmer	49,193
33	Mar	1	H	Derby County	W	5-0	Walters, Bennett, Duquemin, Adams, Mozley (og)	44,388
34		8	A	Aston Villa	W	3-0	Walters, Duquemin 2	56,475
35		15	H	Sunderland	W	2-0	Bennett, Duquemin	51,745
36		22	A	Wolverhampton Wanderers	D	1-1	Baily	45,343
37	Apr	2	H	Huddersfield Town	W	1-0	Duquemin	22,396
38		12	H	Portsmouth	W	3-1	Duquemin, Baily 2	66,988
39		14	A	Preston North End	D	1-1	Ramsey (pen)	36,525
40		19	A	Liverpool	D	1-1	Duquemin	36,898
41		26	H	Blackpool	W	2-0	Ramsey, Baily	45,991
42		30	A	Chelsea	W	2-0	Bennett, Medley	46,574
								Appearances
								Goals

FA Cup

R3	Jan	12	A	Scunthorpe United	W	3-0	Baily, Duquemin 2	22,652
R4	Feb	2	H	Newcastle United	L	0-3		69,009
								Appearances
								Goals

FA Charity Shield

	Sep	24	H	Newcastle United	W	2-1	Bennett, Murphy	27,660
								Appearances
								Goals

dams CJ	Baily EF	Bennett LD	Brittan C	Burgess WAR	Clarke HA	Ditchburn EG	Duquemin LS	Farley BH	Harmer TC	King DA	McClellan SB	Medley LD	Murphy P	Nicholson WE	Ramsey AE	Robb GW	Robshaw HW	Scarth JW	Uphill DE	Walters WE	Wetton R	Willis A	Withers CF	Own-goals
	10	8		6		1	9	5				11	7	4	2							3		
	10	8		6		1	9			5		11	7	4	2							3		
		8		6		1	9			5		11	10	4	2					7		3		
		8	4	6		1					9	11	10	5	2			7				3		
		8	4	6		1					9	11	10	5	2			7				3		
		8	4	6		1					9	11	10	5	2					7		3		
		8	4	6		1			10		9	11		5	2					7		3		
		8	4	6		1	9					11	10	5	2					7		3		
		8	4	6		1			10		9	11		5	2					7		3		
		8		6	5	1			10		9	11		4	2					7		3		
				6	5	1			10		9	11	8	4	2					7		3		
	10	8		6	5	1					9	11		4	2					7		3		
	10	8		6	5	1					9	11		4	2					7		3		
		8			5	1	9		10				11	4						7	6	3	2	
	10	8		6	5	1	9					11		4	2					7			3	
	10	8			5	1	9					11		4	2					7	6		3	
	10	8		6	5	1	9					11		4	2					7			3	
	10	8		6	5	1	9					11		4	2					7			3	
	10	8		6	5	1	9					11		4	2					7			3	
	10	8		6	5	1	9					11			2		4			7			3	
	8			6	5	1	9					11	10		2					7	4		3	
	8	9		6	5	1						11	10	4	2					7			3	
	8	9		6	5	1						11	10	4	2					7			3	
	8	9		6	5	1			10			7			2	11					4		3	
	8	9		6	5	1						11	10		2					7	4		3	
	8			6	5	1	9		10			11			2					7	4		3	
	8			6	5	1	9		10			11		4	2					7			3	
	8			6	5	1	9		10			11		4	2					7			3	
	8			6	5	1	9		10			11		4	2					7			3	
	8			6	5	1	9		10			11		4	2					7			3	
		9		6	5	1			10			11		4	2				8	7			3	
		9		11	5	1			10					4	2				8	7	6		3	
1	10	8		6	5	1	9							4	2					7			3	
1	10	8		6	5	1	9							4	2					7			3	
1	10	8		6	5	1	9							4	2					7			3	
1	10	8		6	5	1	9							4						7		2	3	
1	10	8		6	5	1	9							4						7		2	3	
	10	8		6	5	1	9					11		4	2					7			3	
	10	8		6	5	1	9					11		4	2					7			3	
	10	8		6	5	1	9				11			4	2					7			3	
	10	8		6	5	1					9	11		4	2					7			3	
	10	8		6	5	1					9	11		4						7		2	3	
5	30	35	6	40	33	42	25	1	13	2	12	34	13	37	38	1	1	2	2	37	7	17	29	
	4	20					12		3		3	8	5	1	5	1		1		10				2

dams CJ	Baily EF	Bennett LD	Brittan C	Burgess WAR	Clarke HA	Ditchburn EG	Duquemin LS	Farley BH	Harmer TC	King DA	McClellan SB	Medley LD	Murphy P	Nicholson WE	Ramsey AE	Robb GW	Robshaw HW	Scarth JW	Uphill DE	Walters WE	Wetton R	Willis A	Withers CF	Own-goals
	8			6	5	1	9		10			11		4	2					7			3	
	8			6	5	1	9		10			11		4	2					7			3	
0	2	0	0	2	2	2	2	0	2	0	0	2	0	2	2	0	0	0	0	2	0	0	2	
	1						2																	

dams CJ	Baily EF	Bennett LD	Brittan C	Burgess WAR	Clarke HA	Ditchburn EG	Duquemin LS	Farley BH	Harmer TC	King DA	McClellan SB	Medley LD	Murphy P	Nicholson WE	Ramsey AE	Robb GW	Robshaw HW	Scarth JW	Uphill DE	Walters WE	Wetton R	Willis A	Withers CF	Own-goals
		8		6	5	1	9					11	10	4						7		3	2	
0	0	1	0	1	1	1	1	0	0	0	0	1	1	1	0	0	0	0	0	1	0	1	1	
		1											1											

League Table

	P	W	D	L	F	A	Pts
Manchester United	42	23	11	8	95	52	57
TOTTENHAM HOTSPUR	42	22	9	11	76	51	53
Arsenal	42	21	11	10	80	61	53
Portsmouth	42	20	8	14	68	58	48
Bolton Wanderers	42	19	10	13	65	61	48
Aston Villa	42	19	9	14	79	70	47
Preston North End	42	17	12	13	74	54	46
Newcastle United	42	18	9	15	98	73	45
Blackpool	42	18	9	15	64	64	45
Charlton Athletic	42	17	10	15	68	63	44
Liverpool	42	12	19	11	57	61	43
Sunderland	42	15	12	15	70	61	42
West Bromwich Albion	42	14	13	15	74	77	41
Burnley	42	15	10	17	56	63	40
Manchester City	42	13	13	16	58	61	39
Wolverhampton W	42	12	14	16	73	73	38
Derby County	42	15	7	20	63	80	37
Middlesbrough	42	15	6	21	64	88	36
Chelsea	42	14	8	20	52	72	36
Stoke City	42	12	7	23	49	88	31
Huddersfield Town	42	10	8	24	49	82	28
Fulham	42	8	11	23	58	77	27

1952-53

DIVISION ONE

Manager: Arthur Rowe

Did you know that?

For the FA Cup fourth-round meeting with Preston North End on 31 January 1953 Spurs were in difficulty when left-winger Les Medley had to drop out injured. Arthur Rowe sprung a major surprise by playing Charlie Withers, known only as a full-back, in the number-11 shirt. It proved a masterstroke, as Withers scored both Spurs' goals in a 2–2 draw. They were the only goals he scored in over 200 first-team appearances.

LEAGUE DEBUTANTS

Aug 23	v West Bromwich Albion Alan Grubb
Sep 15	v Liverpool Vic Groves
Oct 11	v Derby County Mel Hopkins
Jan 17	v Cardiff City Roy Hollis
Mar 7	v Blackpool Eddie Gibbins
Apr 4	v Bolton Wanderers Alfie Stokes
Apr 6	v Stoke City Johnny Brooks
Apr 18	v Sunderland Peter Baker

Match No.	Date			Opponents	Result		Scorers	Attendanc
1	Aug	23	H	West Bromwich Albion	L	3-4	Ramsey (pen), Bennett, Duquemin	56,55
2		27	A	Manchester City	W	1-0	Duquemin	33,62
3		30	A	Newcastle United	D	1-1	McClellan	59,62
4	Sep	1	H	Manchester City	D	3-3	Ramsey (pen), McClellan, Robb	41,11
5		6	H	Cardiff City	W	2-1	McClellan, Duquemin	62,15
6		10	A	Liverpool	L	1-2	Baily	49,86
7		13	A	Sheffield Wednesday	L	0-2		42,13
8		15	H	Liverpool	W	3-1	Groves 2, Harmer	37,31
9		20	H	Arsenal	L	1-3	Harmer	69,24
10		27	H	Burnley	W	2-1	Duquemin, Medley	43,03
11	Oct	4	A	Preston North End	L	0-1		28,10
12		11	A	Derby County	D	0-0		27,69
13		18	H	Blackpool	W	4-0	Ramsey (pen), Duquemin, Baily 2	53,92
14		25	A	Chelsea	L	1-2	Ramsey (pen)	62,68
15	Nov	1	H	Manchester United	L	1-2	Walters	44,28
16		8	A	Portsmouth	L	1-2	Uphill	40,46
17		15	H	Bolton Wanderers	D	1-1	Bennett	31,44
18		22	A	Aston Villa	W	3-0	Bennett, Duquemin, Dicker	32,26
19		29	H	Sunderland	D	2-2	Bennett, Duquemin	45,98
20	Dec	6	A	Wolverhampton Wanderers	D	0-0		37,06
21		13	H	Charlton Athletic	W	2-0	Walters, Bennett	35,68
22		20	A	West Bromwich Albion	L	1-2	Dicker	18,69
23		25	H	Middlesbrough	W	7-1	Bennett 4, Duquemin 2, Baily	36,10
24		27	A	Middlesbrough	W	4-0	Walters, Bennett, Duquemin, Bilcliff (og)	23,26
25	Jan	3	H	Newcastle United	W	3-2	Burgess 2, Duquemin	52,64
26		17	A	Cardiff City	D	0-0		36,42
27		24	H	Sheffield Wednesday	W	2-1	Walters, Baily	43,24
28	Feb	7	A	Arsenal	L	0-4		69,05
29		17	A	Burnley	L	2-3	Baily, Duquemin	13,77
30		21	H	Preston North End	D	4-4	Walters, Duquemin 3	50,07
31	Mar	7	A	Blackpool	L	0-2		26,79
32		12	H	Derby County	W	5-2	Bennett, Hollis, McClellan 2, Robb	13,93
33		14	H	Chelsea	L	2-3	Willis (pen), Bennett	47,90
34		25	A	Manchester United	L	2-3	Walters, McClellan	20,21
35		28	H	Portsmouth	D	3-3	Duquemin 2, Harmer	38,63
36	Apr	3	H	Stoke City	W	1-0	Harmer	35,60
37		4	A	Bolton Wanderers	W	3-2	McClellan, Stokes, Duquemin	40,18
38		6	A	Stoke City	L	0-2		25,34
39		11	H	Aston Villa	D	1-1	McClellan	39,21
40		18	A	Sunderland	D	1-1	Walters	24,95
41		25	H	Wolverhampton Wanderers	W	3-2	Ramsey (pen), Bennett 2	48,13
42		30	A	Charlton Athletic	L	2-3	Ramsey, Walters	9,26
								Appearance
								Goal

FA Cup

R3	Jan	10	A	Tranmere Rovers	D	1-1	Bennett	21,53
R3r		12	H	Tranmere Rovers	W	9-1	McClellan 3, Duquemin 2, Hollis 2, Baily 2	31,54
R4		31	A	Preston North End	D	2-2	Withers 2	34,95
R4r	Feb	4	H	Preston North End	W	1-0	Duquemin	55,60
R5		14	A	Halifax Town	W	3-0	Bennett 2, Duquemin	36,99
R6		28	A	Birmingham City	D	1-1	Bennett	52,34
R6r	Mar	4	H	Birmingham City	D*	2-2	Bennett, Duquemin	59,54
R6r		9	N#	Birmingham City	W	1-0	Walters	50,80
SF		21	N+	Blackpool	L	1-2	Duquemin	68,22
								Appearance
								Goal

*after extra-time #played at Molineux +played at Villa Park

Baily EF	Baker PRB	Bennett LD	Brittan C	Brooks J	Burgess WAR	Clarke HA	Dicker LR	Ditchburn EG	Duquemin LS	Gibbins E	Groves VG	Grubb AJ	Harmer TC	Hollis RW	Hopkins M	King DA	Marchi AV	McClellan SB	Medley LD	Nicholson WE	Ramsey AE	Robb GW	Stokes AE	Uphill DE	Walters WE	Wetton R	Willis A	Withers CF	Own-goals
10		8			6	5	11	1	9			7								4	2							3	
10		8			6	5		1	9			7									2	11				4	3		
10		8			6	5		1	9									11	7		2					4		3	
10		8			6	5		1	9									7			2	11				4		3	
10		8			6	5	11	1	9									7			2					4	3		
10		8			6	5	11	1	9									7			2					4	3		
10		8			6	5	11	1	9									7			2					4		3	
10						5		1	9		7		8							4	2	11				6	3		
10					6	5		1	9				8						7	4	2	11					3		
10		8				5		1	9										11	4	2				7	6		3	
		8			6	5		1	9				10							2					7	4		3	
10		8			6	5		1	9						3				11	4	2				7				
10		8				5		1	9										11	4	2				7	6	3		
10		8			6	5		1	9										11	4	2				7		3		
10					6	5		1	9										11	4	2			8	7		3		
10					6	5		1	9										11	4	2			8	7		3		
10		8			6	5	11	1										9		4	2				7		3		
		8			6	5	11	1	9				10							4	2				7		3		
		8			6	5	11	1	9				10							4	2				7		3		
		8			6	5	11	1	9				10							4	2				7		3		
		8	6			5	11	1	9				10							4	2				7		3		
		8	6			5	11	1	9				10							4	2				7		3		
10		8	6			5		1	9										11	4	2				7		3		
10		8	6			5		1	9										11	4	2				7		3		
10		8	6		7	5		1	9										11	4	2						3		
10			6			5		1	8					9				7	11	4							3	2	
10		8			6	5		1	9										11	4	2				7		3		
10		8	6			5		1	9										11	4	2				7		3		
8					6	5		1	9				10					11		4	2				7			3	
10		8			6	5		1	9										11	4	2				7		3		
8								1		5	7		10	9			4	11			2					6		3	
		8						1			7			9		5	4	10				11				6	3	2	
10		8	4		6			1	9							5		11							7		3	2	
10					6			1	9							5		8		4	2	11			7			3	
8					6			1	9				10			5			11	4	2				7			3	
8					6			1	9				10			5		7	11	4	2							3	
					6			1	9				10			5	4	7	11		2		8				3		
8		9	6	10		5		1									4	7	11		2						3		
					6			1	9				10			5		11		4	2		8		7			3	
	2	8			6			1	9				10			5			11	4					7		3		
		8			6			1	9				10			5	4		11	3	2				7				
		8			6			1	9				10		3	5		11		4	2				7				
30	1	30	9	1	30	31	10	42	38	1	3	2	17	3	2	10	5	17	21	31	37	6	2	2	26	12	27	15	
6		14			2		2		18		2		4	1				8	1		6	2	1	1	8		1		1

Baily EF	Baker PRB	Bennett LD	Brittan C	Brooks J	Burgess WAR	Clarke HA	Dicker LR	Ditchburn EG	Duquemin LS	Gibbins E	Groves VG	Grubb AJ	Harmer TC	Hollis RW	Hopkins M	King DA	Marchi AV	McClellan SB	Medley LD	Nicholson WE	Ramsey AE	Robb GW	Stokes AE	Uphill DE	Walters WE	Wetton R	Willis A	Withers CF	Own-goals
10		8			6	5		1	9										11	4	2				7		3		
10			6					1	8	5				9				7	11	4	2						3		
10		8			6	5		1	9											4	2				7		3	11	
10		8			6	5		1	9											4	2				7		3	11	
10		8	6			5		1	9										11	4	2				7		3		
10		8			6	5		1	9										11	4	2				7			3	
10		8	4		6			1	9	5									11		2				7			3	
10		8	4		6			1	9	5									11		2				7			3	
10		8			6	5		1	9									11		4	2				7			3	
9	0	8	4	0	7	6	0	9	9	3	0	0	0	1	0	0	0	2	6	7	9	0	0	0	8	0	5	6	
2		5							6					2				3							1			2	

League Table

	P	W	D	L	F	A	Pts
Arsenal	42	21	12	9	97	64	54
Preston North End	42	21	12	9	85	60	54
Wolverhampton W	42	19	13	10	86	63	51
West Bromwich Albion	42	21	8	13	66	60	50
Charlton Athletic	42	19	11	12	77	63	49
Burnley	42	18	12	12	67	52	48
Blackpool	42	19	9	14	71	70	47
Manchester United	42	18	10	14	69	72	46
Sunderland	42	15	13	14	68	82	43
TOTTENHAM HOTSPUR	42	15	11	16	78	69	41
Aston Villa	42	14	13	15	63	61	41
Cardiff City	42	14	12	16	54	46	40
Middlesbrough	42	14	11	17	70	77	39
Bolton Wanderers	42	15	9	18	61	69	39
Portsmouth	42	14	10	18	74	83	38
Newcastle United	42	14	9	19	59	70	37
Liverpool	42	14	8	20	61	82	36
Sheffield Wednesday	42	12	11	19	62	72	35
Chelsea	42	12	11	19	56	66	35
Manchester City	42	14	7	21	72	87	35
Stoke City	42	12	10	20	53	66	34
Derby County	42	11	10	21	59	74	32

1953-54

DIVISION ONE

Manager: Arthur Rowe

Did you know that?

After beating Arsenal in the semi-final, Spurs finished runners-up to Charlton Athletic in the first London five-a-side Football Championships held at the Empress Hall, Earls Court, on 5 May 1954. They were represented by Derek King, Colin Brittan, George Robb, Sid McClellan and Dickie Dowsett, with Eddie Gibbins and Brian Farley the reserves.

LEAGUE DEBUTANTS

Sep 26	v Manchester United George Hutchinson
Feb 27	v Arsenal Dave Dunmore
Mar 20	v Sunderland Ron Reynolds
May 19	v Preston North End Aled Owen

Match No.	Date			Opponents	Result		Scorers	Attendanc
1	Aug	19	H	Aston Villa	W	1-0	Parkes (og)	50,20
2		22	A	Sheffield Wednesday	L	1-2	Walters	38,11
3		26	H	Charlton Athletic	W	3-1	Baily, Robb 2	48,03
4		29	H	Middlesbrough	W	4-1	Walters, Bennett, Duquemin, Robb	44,91
5	Sep	3	A	Charlton Athletic	W	1-0	Groves	37,60
6		5	A	West Bromwich Albion	L	0-3		42,95
7		7	A	Burnley	L	2-4	Walters, Robb	34,28
8		12	H	Liverpool	W	2-1	Ramsey, Walters	47,53
9		16	H	Burnley	L	2-3	Duquemin 2	30,47
10		19	A	Newcastle United	W	3-1	Walters, Baily, Robb	53,05
11		26	H	Manchester United	D	1-1	Duquemin	52,83
12	Oct	3	A	Bolton Wanderers	L	0-2		39,84
13		10	H	Arsenal	L	1-4	Robb	69,82
14		17	A	Cardiff City	L	0-1		41,08
15		24	H	Manchester City	W	3-0	Duquemin, Robb 2	37,57
16		31	A	Sunderland	L	3-4	Walters, Duquemin, Robb	38,34
17	Nov	7	H	Chelsea	W	2-1	Walters, Baily	44,79
18		14	A	Blackpool	L	0-1		19,66
19		21	H	Huddersfield Town	W	1-0	Duquemin	42,50
20		28	A	Sheffield United	L	2-5	Walters, Bennett	31,33
21	Dec	5	H	Wolverhampton Wanderers	L	2-3	Bennett, Duquemin	48,16
22		12	A	Aston Villa	W	2-1	Walters, Baily	27,48
23		19	H	Sheffield Wednesday	W	3-1	Baker, Duquemin, Curtis (og)	25,95
24		25	H	Portsmouth	D	1-1	Brooks	36,50
25		26	A	Portsmouth	D	1-1	Walters	36,67
26	Jan	2	A	Middlesbrough	L	0-3		35,14
27		16	H	West Bromwich Albion	L	0-1		48,81
28		23	A	Liverpool	D	2-2	Walters, Lock (og)	43,59
29	Feb	6	H	Newcastle United	W	3-0	Walters, Robb 2	35,79
30		13	A	Manchester United	L	0-2		37,28
31		27	A	Arsenal	W	3-0	Walters, Robb 2	64,31
32	Mar	3	H	Bolton Wanderers	W	3-2	Walters, Stokes, Dunmore	16,72
33		6	H	Cardiff City	L	0-1		45,24
34		17	A	Manchester City	L	1-4	Marchi	9,98
35		20	H	Sunderland	L	0-3		39,39
36		27	A	Chelsea	L	0-1		49,31
37	Apr	3	H	Blackpool	D	2-2	Baily, Robb	43,87
38		10	A	Huddersfield Town	W	5-2	Hutchinson, Brooks, Harmer, Robb 2	26,23
39		16	A	Preston North End	L	1-2	Harmer	24,52
40		17	H	Sheffield United	W	2-1	Ramsey (pen), Brittan	35,10
41		19	H	Preston North End	L	2-6	Bennett, Dunmore	30,20
42		24	A	Wolverhampton Wanderers	L	0-2		44,05

Appearance

Goal

FA Cup

R3	Jan	9	A	Leeds United	D	3-3	Walters, Bennett 2	41,64
R3r		13	H	Leeds United	W	1-0	Bennett	35,02
R4		30	A	Manchester City	W	1-0	Bennett	51,18
R5	Feb	20	A	Hull City	D	1-1	Bennett	46,83
R5r		24	H	Hull City	W	2-0	Walters, Baily	52,93
R6	Mar	13	A	West Bromwich Albion	L	0-3		51,04

Appearance

Goal

ly EF	Baker PRB	Bennett LD	Brittan C	Brooks J	Burgess WAR	Clarke HA	Ditchburn EG	Dunmore DGI	Duquemin LS	Groves VG	Harmer TC	Hopkins M	Hutchinson GH	King DA	Marchi AV	McClellan SB	Nicholson WE	Owen AW	Ramsey AE	Reynolds RSM	Robb GW	Stokes AE	Walters WE	Wetton R	Willis A	Withers CF	Own-goals
0		8			6	5	1		9						4				2		11		7			3	
0		8			6	5	1								4	9			2		11		7			3	
0		8			6	5	1		9								4		2		11		7			3	
0		8			6	5	1		9								4		2		11		7			3	
0		8			6	5	1			9							4		2		11		7			3	
0				8	6	5	1		9								4		2		11		7			3	
0					6	5	1				8				9		4		2		11		7			3	
0		8			6	5	1		9										2		11		7	4		3	
0		8			6	5	1		9										2		11		7	4		3	
0		8	6			5	1		9					2							11		7	4		3	
0		8			6	5	1		9				7				4		2		11					3	
		8			6	5	1		9		10		7						2		11			4		3	
		8				5	1		9		10						4		2		11		7	6		3	
0				8	6	5	1		9								4		2		11		7			3	
0	2			8		5	1		9								4				11		7	6		3	
0				8	6	5	1		9								4		2		11		7			3	
0				8	6	5	1		9										2		11		7	4		3	
0				8	6	5	1		9								4		2		11		7			3	
0				8	6	5	1		9								4		2		11		7			3	
0		9		8	6	5	1										4		2		11		7			3	
0		8			6	5	1		9							11	4		2				7			3	
0		8	6			5	1		9								4		2		11		7			3	
0	2	8			6	5	1		9								4				11		7			3	
0				8		5	1		9								4		2		11		7	6		3	
				10		5	1		9			3					4		2		11	8	7	6			
		8		10		5	1		9			3			4				2		11		7	6			
0		8			6	5	1		9								4		2		11		7		3		
0		8			6	5	1		9								4		2		11		7		3		
0		8				5	1		9								4		2		11		7	6	3		
0		8				5	1		9								4		2		11		7	6	3		
0		8				5	1	9							4				2		11		7	6	3		
0					6	5	1	9							4				2		11	8	7		3		
0		8			6	5	1		9								4		2		11		7		3		
				8		5	1	9							10		4		2		11		7	6	3		
		8		10		5		9							4	7			2	1	11			6		3	
0		9		8		5										7	4		2	1	11			6		3	
0				8				9						5			4		2	1	11		7	6		3	
				8		5	1	9			10		7				4		2		11			6		3	
				8		5	1	9			10		7				4		2				11	6		3	
			4		6	5	1	9			10		11						2				7			3	
	2	8		10		5	1	9									4	11					7	6		3	
0	2	8				5	1	9								11	4						7	6	3		
3	4	26	3	18	24	41	39	10	27	1	6	2	5	2	8	5	30	1	37	3	37	2	37	21	9	31	
	1	4	1	2				2	9	1	2		1		1				2		16	1	14				3

ly EF	Baker PRB	Bennett LD	Brittan C	Brooks J	Burgess WAR	Clarke HA	Ditchburn EG	Dunmore DGI	Duquemin LS	Groves VG	Harmer TC	Hopkins M	Hutchinson GH	King DA	Marchi AV	McClellan SB	Nicholson WE	Owen AW	Ramsey AE	Reynolds RSM	Robb GW	Stokes AE	Walters WE	Wetton R	Willis A	Withers CF	Own-goals
0		8			6	5	1		9								4		2		11		7		3		
0		8			6	5	1		9								4		2		11		7		3		
0		8			6	5	1		9								4		2		11		7		3		
0		8			6	5	1		9								4		2		11		7		3		
0		8				5	1		9								4		2		11		7	6	3		
0		8			6	5	1		9								4		2		11		7		3		
	0	6	0	0	5	6	6	0	6	0	0	0	0	0	0	0	6	0	6	0	6	0	6	1	6	0	
		5																					2				

League Table

	P	W	D	L	F	A	Pts
Wolverhampton W	42	25	7	10	96	56	57
West Bromwich Albion	42	22	9	11	86	63	53
Huddersfield Town	42	20	11	11	78	61	51
Manchester United	42	18	12	12	73	58	48
Bolton Wanderers	42	18	12	12	75	60	48
Blackpool	42	19	10	13	80	69	48
Burnley	42	21	4	17	78	67	46
Chelsea	42	16	12	14	74	68	44
Charlton Athletic	42	19	6	17	75	77	44
Cardiff City	42	18	8	16	51	71	44
Preston North End	42	19	5	18	87	58	43
Arsenal	42	15	13	14	75	73	43
Aston Villa	42	16	9	17	70	68	41
Portsmouth	42	14	11	17	81	89	39
Newcastle United	42	14	10	18	72	77	38
TOTTENHAM HOTSPUR	42	16	5	21	65	76	37
Manchester City	42	14	9	19	62	77	37
Sunderland	42	14	8	20	81	89	36
Sheffield Wednesday	42	15	6	21	70	91	36
Sheffield United	42	11	11	20	69	90	33
Middlesbrough	42	10	10	22	60	91	30
Liverpool	42	9	10	23	68	97	28

1954-55

DIVISION ONE

Manager: Arthur Rowe

Did you know that?

Spurs only met the most famous ex-League club, Accrington Stanley, once. That was at Peel Park on 29 November 1954. A trial was given to Shelbourne full-back Bernard McNally but it was short-lived, as the game was abandoned after 52 minutes due to rain. McNally went on to play for Luton Town and the Republic of Ireland.

LEAGUE DEBUTANTS

Aug 21	v Aston Villa Dickie Dowsett
Sep 8	v Manchester United Alan Woods
Oct 16	v Newcastle United Johnny Gavin
Dec 11	v Manchester City Danny Blanchflower
Mar 19	v Sheffield United Terry Dyson
Apr 12	v Huddersfield Town Ron Henry

Match No.	Date			Opponents	Result		Scorers	Attendanc
1	Aug	21	A	Aston Villa	W	4-2	Dowsett, Bennett 2, Baily	44,19
2		25	H	Wolverhampton Wanderers	W	3-2	Dunmore 3	47,77
3		28	H	Sunderland	L	0-1		53,64
4		30	A	Wolverhampton Wanderers	L	2-4	Walters, Robb	37,38
5	Sep	4	A	Arsenal	L	0-2		53,97
6		8	H	Manchester United	L	0-2		35,16
7		11	A	Sheffield Wednesday	D	2-2	McClellan, Baily	34,04
8		15	A	Manchester United	L	1-2	McClellan	31,04
9		18	H	Portsmouth	D	1-1	McClellan	37,40
10		25	A	Blackpool	L	1-5	Ramsey (pen)	34,62
11	Oct	2	H	Charlton Athletic	L	1-4	Brooks	33,10
12		9	H	West Bromwich Albion	W	3-1	Ramsey (pen), McClellan 2	45,54
13		16	A	Newcastle United	D	4-4	Baily 2, McClellan 2	45,30
14		23	H	Preston North End	W	3-1	Ramsey (pen), McClellan, Dunmore	42,86
15		30	A	Sheffield United	L	1-4	Dunmore	24,08
16	Nov	6	H	Cardiff City	L	0-2		38,80
17		13	A	Chelsea	L	1-2	Gavin	52,96
18		20	H	Leicester City	W	5-1	Gavin 2, Baily, Robb 2	27,87
19		27	A	Burnley	W	2-1	Gavin, Baily	21,97
20	Dec	4	H	Everton	L	1-3	Baily	31,55
21		11	A	Manchester City	D	0-0		27,05
22		18	H	Aston Villa	D	1-1	Baily	28,13
23		25	A	Bolton Wanderers	W	2-1	Dunmore, Robb	25,97
24		26	H	Bolton Wanderers	W	2-0	Baily, Brooks	41,06
25	Jan	1	A	Sunderland	D	1-1	Dunmore	49,88
26		15	H	Arsenal	L	0-1		36,26
27		22	H	Sheffield Wednesday	W	7-2	Gavin 2, Brooks 2, Duquemin, Baily, Robb	26,31
28	Feb	5	A	Portsmouth	W	3-0	Gavin 2, Duquemin	27,53
29		12	H	Blackpool	W	3-2	Baily, Robb 2	47,38
30	Mar	5	H	Manchester City	D	2-2	Duquemin 2	35,35
31		12	A	Preston North End	L	0-1		24,34
32		19	H	Sheffield United	W	5-0	Gavin 4, Brooks	26,67
33		26	A	Cardiff City	W	2-1	Duquemin, Robb	14,46
34	Apr	2	H	Chelsea	L	2-4	Duquemin 2	53,15
35		9	A	Everton	L	0-1		42,21
36		11	H	Huddersfield Town	D	1-1	Brooks	23,33
37		12	A	Huddersfield Town	L	0-1		23,58
38		16	H	Burnley	L	0-3		23,55
39		23	A	Leicester City	L	0-2		23,90
40		27	A	West Bromwich Albion	W	2-1	Brooks, Baily	16,61
41		30	H	Newcastle United	W	2-1	Gavin, Stokoe (og)	37,26
42	May	5	A	Charlton Athletic	W	2-1	Walters, Duquemin	12,31
								Appearance
								Goal

FA Cup

R3	Jan	8	A	Gateshead	W	2-0	Brooks 2	18,84
R4		29	H	Port Vale	W	4-2	Gavin, Duquemin, Brooks 2	50,68
R5	Feb	19	A	York City	L	1-3	Robb	21,00
								Appearance
								Goal

Baker PRB	Bennett LD	Blanchflower RD	Brittan C	Brooks J	Clarke HA	Ditchburn EG	Dowsett GJ	Dunmore DGI	Duquemin LS	Dyson TK	Gavin JT	Harmer TC	Henry RP	Hopkins M	King DA	Marchi AV	McClellan SB	Nicholson WE	Ramsey AE	Reynolds RSM	Robb GW	Walters WE	Wetton R	Withers CF	Woods AE	Own-goals
	8		6		5	1	7	9											2		11		4	3		
	8		6		5	1		9											2		11	7	4	3		
	8		6		5	1		9											2		11	7	4	3		
	8		6		5	1		9											2		11	7	4	3		
	8		6		5	1		9											2		11	7	4	3		
			6		5	1		9				8		3					2		11	7			4	
			6			1			9			8		3	5		7		2		11				4	
			6			1			9			8		3	5		7		2		11				4	
			6			1			9			8		3	5		7		2		11				4	
	8		6			1		9						3	5		7		2		11				4	
				10		1		9						3	5	6	7	4	2		11					
				10	5	1		9								6	7	4	2		11			3		
				8	5	1		9			7					6	11	4	2					3		
				10	5	1		9			11			3		6	7	4	2							
				10	5	1		9			11			3		6	7	4	2							
				10	5	1					7			3		6	9	4	2		11					
				10	5			9			7					6		4	2	1	11			3		
				10	5			9			7			3		6		4	2	1	11					
				10	5			9			7			3		6		4	2	1	11					
				10	5			9			7			3		6		4	2	1	11					
		4		10	5			9			7			3		6			2	1	11					
		4		10	5			9			7			3		6			2	1	11					
		4		10	5			9			7			3		6			2	1	11					
		4		10	5			9			7			3		6			2	1	11					
		4		10	5			9			7			3		6			2	1	11					
		4		10	5			9			7			3		6			2	1	11					
		4		10	5				9		7			3		6			2	1	11					
		4		10	5				9		7			3		6			2	1	11					
		4		10	5				9		7			3		6			2	1	11					
		4		10	5				9		7			3		6			2	1	11					
		4		10	5				9		7	8		3		6			2	1	11					
2		4		8	5				9	11	7			3		6				1						
2		4		10	5				9		7			3		6				1	11					
2		4		10	5				9		7			3		6				1	11					
2		4		10	5				9		7			3		6				1	11					
2		4		10	5				9		7			3		6				1	11					
2		4		10					9		7		5	3		6				1	11					
		4			5				9		7			3		6	11		2	1					8	
		4		8	5				9		7			3		6			2	1		11				
		4		8	5				9		7			3		6				1	11			2		
2		4		8	5				9		7					6				1	11			3		
2		4		8	5				9							6				1	11	7		3		
8	6	22	10	31	36	16	1	22	19	1	29	5	1	32	5	32	11	10	33	26	36	7	5	11	6	
	2			7			1	7	8		13						8		3		8	2				1

Baker PRB	Bennett LD	Blanchflower RD	Brittan C	Brooks J	Clarke HA	Ditchburn EG	Dowsett GJ	Dunmore DGI	Duquemin LS	Dyson TK	Gavin JT	Harmer TC	Henry RP	Hopkins M	King DA	Marchi AV	McClellan SB	Nicholson WE	Ramsey AE	Reynolds RSM	Robb GW	Walters WE	Wetton R	Withers CF	Woods AE	Own-goals
		4		10	5			9			7			3		6			2	1	11					
		4		10	5				9		7			3		6			2	1	11					
		4		10	5				9					3		6			2	1	11	7				
0	0	3	0	3	3	0	0	1	2	0	2	0	0	3	0	3	0	0	3	3	3	1	0	0	0	
				4					1		1										1					

League Table

	P	W	D	L	F	A	Pts
Chelsea	42	20	12	10	81	57	52
Wolverhampton W	42	19	10	13	89	70	48
Portsmouth	42	18	12	12	74	62	48
Sunderland	42	15	18	9	64	54	48
Manchester United	42	20	7	15	84	74	47
Aston Villa	42	20	7	15	72	73	47
Manchester City	42	18	10	14	76	69	46
Newcastle United	42	17	9	16	89	77	43
Arsenal	42	17	9	16	69	63	43
Burnley	42	17	9	16	51	48	43
Everton	42	16	10	16	62	68	42
Huddersfield Town	42	14	13	15	63	68	41
Sheffield United	42	17	7	18	70	86	41
Preston North End	42	16	8	18	83	64	40
Charlton Athletic	42	15	10	17	76	75	40
TOTTENHAM HOTSPUR	42	16	8	18	72	73	40
West Bromwich Albion	42	16	8	18	76	96	40
Bolton Wanderers	42	13	13	16	62	69	39
Blackpool	42	14	10	18	60	64	38
Cardiff City	42	13	11	18	62	76	37
Leicester City	42	12	11	19	74	86	35
Sheffield Wednesday	42	8	10	24	63	100	26

1955-56

DIVISION ONE

Manager: Jimmy Anderson

Did you know that?

Spurs always had a close relationship with Pegasus, the joint Oxford and Cambridge Universities team. Vic Buckingham coached Oxford, Bill Nicholson Cambridge, and when Pegasus met Bishop Auckland in the 1951 Amateur Cup Final Arthur Rowe sent them a good luck telegram with a trademark message 'Make it Simple, Make it Quick.' As Rowe began to recover from the ill health that had forced him to retire as Spurs' manager, it was Pegasus who were first to offer him a role back in football and in September 1955 he took on the job of coaching them.

LEAGUE DEBUTANTS

Aug 31	v Manchester United Ernie Walley
Nov 5	v Cardiff City Maurice Norman
Dec 17	v Burnley Micky Dulin
Dec 24	v Luton Town Bobby Smith
Apr 2	v Preston North End John Ryden

Match No.	Date		Opponents		Result		Scorers	Attendan
1	Aug	20	H	Burnley	L	0-1		33,1
2		24	A	Manchester United	D	2-2	Gavin (pen), Stokes	28,7
3		27	A	Luton Town	L	1-2	Gavin	21,1
4		31	H	Manchester United	L	1-2	Clarke	27,4
5	Sep	3	H	Charlton Athletic	L	2-3	Clarke, Brooks	33,1
6		5	A	Sheffield United	L	0-2		19,6
7		10	H	Arsenal	W	3-1	Stokes 2, Baily	51,0
8		17	A	Everton	L	1-2	Walters	42,8
9		24	H	Newcastle United	W	3-1	Clarke, Stokes 2	41,0
10	Oct	1	A	Birmingham City	L	0-3		31,3
11		8	H	Bolton Wanderers	L	0-3		35,2
12		15	A	Chelsea	L	0-2		48,1
13		22	H	Sunderland	L	2-3	Brooks, Robb	36,3
14		29	A	Portsmouth	L	1-4	Robb	26,0
15	Nov	5	H	Cardiff City	D	1-1	Brooks (pen)	34,3
16		12	A	Manchester City	W	2-1	McClellan, Dunmore	24,0
17		19	H	Wolverhampton Wanderers	W	2-1	McClellan, Robb	51,3
18		26	A	Aston Villa	W	2-0	Clarke, McClellan	23,8
19	Dec	3	H	Blackpool	D	1-1	Brooks	51,3
20		10	A	Huddersfield Town	L	0-1		11,0
21		17	A	Burnley	L	0-2		20,3
22		24	H	Luton Town	W	2-1	Brooks, Duquemin	41,1
23		26	H	West Bromwich Albion	W	4-1	Norman, Brooks (pen), Duquemin 2	32,4
24		27	A	West Bromwich Albion	L	0-1		31,3
25		31	A	Charlton Athletic	W	2-1	Duquemin, Robb	37,8
26	Jan	14	A	Arsenal	W	1-0	Robb	60,6
27		21	H	Everton	D	1-1	Smith	37,1
28	Feb	4	A	Newcastle United	W	2-1	Robb, Duquemin	29,5
29		11	H	Birmingham City	L	0-1		26,1
30		25	H	Chelsea	W	4-0	Marchi, Brooks 2, Smith	46,7
31	Mar	10	H	Portsmouth	D	1-1	Smith	44,3
32		21	A	Bolton Wanderers	L	2-3	Smith, Robb	10,9
33		24	H	Manchester City	W	2-1	Brooks (pen), Smith	31,6
34		30	H	Preston North End	L	0-4		39,4
35		31	A	Sunderland	L	2-3	McClellan 2	22,3
36	Apr	2	A	Preston North End	D	3-3	Harmer 2 (1 pen), Ryden	26,6
37		7	H	Aston Villa	W	4-3	McClellan, Harmer, Smith, Brooks	36,2
38		14	A	Blackpool	W	2-0	McClellan, Smith	19,2
39		18	A	Wolverhampton Wanderers	L	1-5	Harmer (pen)	29,8
40		21	H	Huddersfield Town	L	1-2	Harmer (pen)	36,3
41		23	A	Cardiff City	D	0-0		19,6
42		28	H	Sheffield United	W	3-1	Smith 3	32,6

Appearanc

Goa

FA Cup

R3	Jan	7	H	Boston United	W	4-0	Duquemin, Smith 2, Robb	46,1
R4		28	H	Middlesbrough	W	3-1	Norman, Dunmore, Robb	41,8
R5	Feb	18	A	Doncaster Rovers	W	2-0	Brooks, Smith	30,4
R6	Mar	3	H	West Ham United	D	3-3	Harmer (pen), Duquemin, Robb	69,1
R6r		8	A	West Ham United	W	2-1	Harmer, Duquemin	34,9
SF		17	N*	Manchester City	L	0-1		69,7

*played at Villa Park

Appearanc

Goa

Baker PRB	Blanchflower RD	Brittan C	Brooks J	Clarke HA	Ditchburn EG	Dulin MC	Dunmore DGI	Duquemin LS	Dyson TK	Gavin JT	Harmer TC	Henry RP	Hopkins M	Marchi AV	McClellan SB	Norman M	Reynolds RSM	Robb GW	Ryden JJ	Smith RA	Stokes AE	Walley E	Walters WE	Withers CF
	4		8	5	1					7			3	6				11			9			2
	4		8	5	1					7			3	6				11			9			2
	4		8	5	1					7			3	6				11			9			2
	8			5	1			10					3	6				11			9	4	7	2
2	4		8	5	1								3	6				11			9		7	
2	4		8	5	1								3	6				11			9		7	
	4		8	5	1								3	6				11			9		7	2
	4		8	5	1								3	6				11			9		7	2
	4		8	5	1								3	6				11			9		7	2
	4		8	5	1						10		3	6				11			9		7	2
			8	5	1								3	6				11			9	4	7	2
2	4		8	5	1			9	11				3	6	10								7	
2	4		8	5	1		9						3	6				11					7	
2	4		8	5	1		9						3	6				11					7	
	4		8	5			9					3		6		2	1	11					7	
	4		8	5			9						3	6	7	2	1	11						
	4		8	5			9						3	6	7	2	1	11						
	4		8	5			9						3	6	7	2	1	11						
	4		8	5			9						3	6	7	2	1	11						
	4		8	5			9						3	6	7	2	1	11						
	4		8	5		7	9						3	6		2	1	11						
	4		8	5		7		9					3	6		2	1	11		10				
	4		8	5		7		9					3	6		2	1	11		10				
	4		8	5		7		9					3	6		2	1	11		10				
	4		8	5		7		9					3	6		2	1	11		10				
	4		8	5		7		9					3	6		2	1	11		10				
	4		8	5				9					3	6		2	1	11		10			7	
	4		8	5				9	11				3	6		2	1	7		10				
	4		8	5				9	11				3	6		2	1	7		10				
	4		8	5				9			7		3	6		2	1	11		10				
	4		8	5				9			7		3	6		2	1	11		10				
	4		8	5				9					3	6	7	2	1	11		10				
	4		8	5				9					3	6	7	2	1	11		10				
	4		8	5				9					3	6	7	2	1	11		10				
	4		8	5				9					3	6	7	2	1	11		10				
	4						9				8		3	6	7		1	11	5	10				2
	4		10								8		3	6	7	2	1	11	5	9				
	4		10	5							8		3	6	7	2	1	11		9				
	4		10	5							8		3	6	7	2	1	11		9				
	4		10	5							8		3	6	7	2	1	11		9				
		4		5				9			8		3	6		2	1	11		10			7	
	4		10								8		3	6	7	2	1	11	5	9				
5	40	1	39	39	14	6	10	17	3	3	10	1	41	42	16	27	28	41	3	21	11	2	14	10
			10	4			1	5		2	5			1	7	1		7	1	10	5		1	

Baker PRB	Blanchflower RD	Brittan C	Brooks J	Clarke HA	Ditchburn EG	Dulin MC	Dunmore DGI	Duquemin LS	Dyson TK	Gavin JT	Harmer TC	Henry RP	Hopkins M	Marchi AV	McClellan SB	Norman M	Reynolds RSM	Robb GW	Ryden JJ	Smith RA	Stokes AE	Walley E	Walters WE	Withers CF
	4		8	5		7		9					3	6		2	1	11		10				
	4		8	5			7	9					3	6		2	1	11		10				
	4		7	5				9			8		3	6		2	1	11		10				
	4		8	5				9			7		3	6		2	1	11		10				
	4		8	5				9			7		3	6		2	1	11		10				
	4		8	5			7	9					3	6		2	1	11		10				
0	6	0	6	6	0	1	2	6	0	0	3	0	6	6	0	6	6	6	0	6	0	0	0	0
			1				1	3			2					1		3		3				

League Table

	P	W	D	L	F	A	Pts
Manchester United	42	25	10	7	83	51	60
Blackpool	42	20	9	13	86	62	49
Wolverhampton W	42	20	9	13	89	65	49
Manchester City	42	18	10	14	82	69	46
Arsenal	42	18	10	14	60	61	46
Birmingham City	42	18	9	15	75	57	45
Burnley	42	18	8	16	64	54	44
Bolton Wanderers	42	18	7	17	71	58	43
Sunderland	42	17	9	16	80	95	43
Luton Town	42	17	8	17	66	64	42
Newcastle United	42	17	7	18	85	70	41
Portsmouth	42	16	9	17	78	85	41
West Bromwich Albion	42	18	5	19	58	70	41
Charlton Athletic	42	17	6	19	75	81	40
Everton	42	15	10	17	55	69	40
Chelsea	42	14	11	17	64	77	39
Cardiff City	42	15	9	18	55	69	39
TOTTENHAM HOTSPUR	42	15	7	20	61	71	37
Preston North End	42	14	8	20	73	72	36
Aston Villa	42	11	13	18	52	69	35
Huddersfield Town	42	14	7	21	54	83	35
Sheffield United	42	12	9	21	63	77	33

1956-57

DIVISION ONE

Manager: Jimmy Anderson

Did you know that?

With the development of floodlights, evening football was proving increasingly popular and Spurs were at the forefront of efforts to provide it on a regular and competitive basis. Although both the Football League and Scottish League refused to sanction it as a competition, Spurs were one of three English clubs who went ahead with a series of games against Scottish clubs. Manchester City and Newcastle United were the others.

LEAGUE DEBUTANTS

Aug 18 v Preston North End
Terry Medwin

Apr 29 v Nottingham Forest
Bert Wilkie

Match No.	Date		Opponents		Result		Scorers	Attendance
1	Aug	18	A	Preston North End	W	4-1	Medwin 2, Brooks 2	22,75
2		22	A	Manchester City	D	2-2	Medwin, Brooks	32,71
3		25	H	Leeds United	W	5-1	Blanchflower, Medwin, Smith, Brooks, Robb	51,21
4		29	H	Manchester City	W	3-2	Medwin, Harmer (pen), Smith	33,44
5	Sep	1	A	Bolton Wanderers	L	0-1		30,88
6		3	A	Blackpool	L	1-4	Brooks	28,46
7		8	H	Wolverhampton Wanderers	W	4-1	Smith 2, Brooks 2	62,59
8		15	A	Aston Villa	W	4-2	Harmer, Smith, Stokes, Robb	43,94
9		22	H	Luton Town	W	5-0	Harmer (pen), Stokes, Robb 2, Dunne (og)	58,96
10		29	A	Sunderland	W	2-0	Smith, Stokes	41,65
11	Oct	6	A	Chelsea	W	4-2	Stokes 3, Robb	55,78
12		13	H	Cardiff City	W	5-0	Stokes 2, Robb 3	52,49
13		20	A	Arsenal	L	1-3	Smith	60,58
14		27	H	Burnley	W	2-0	Medwin, Harmer (pen)	49,15
15	Nov	3	A	Portsmouth	W	3-2	Smith, Brooks, Wilson (og)	31,90
16		10	H	Newcastle United	W	3-1	Smith 2, Robb	51,72
17		17	A	Sheffield Wednesday	L	1-4	Harmer (pen)	32,11
18		24	H	Manchester United	D	2-2	Harmer (pen), Robb	57,72
19	Dec	1	A	Birmingham City	D	0-0		38,03
20		8	H	West Bromwich Albion	D	2-2	Harmer, Smith	36,09
21		15	H	Preston North End	D	1-1	Medwin	29,74
22		25	H	Everton	W	6-0	Medwin 2, Harmer (pen), Smith 2, Stokes	27,76
23		26	A	Everton	D	1-1	Robb	20,17
24		29	H	Bolton Wanderers	W	4-0	Dyson, Harmer (pen), Smith, Robb	42,03
25	Jan	12	A	Wolverhampton Wanderers	L	0-3		42,41
26		19	H	Aston Villa	W	3-0	Smith, Stokes 2	38,93
27	Feb	2	A	Luton Town	W	3-1	Duquemin, Stokes, Robb	22,58
28		9	H	Sunderland	W	5-2	Harmer (pen), Smith, Stokes 2, Anderson (og)	52,10
29		20	H	Chelsea	L	3-4	Medwin, Harmer (pen), Stokes	20,84
30	Mar	2	A	Leeds United	D	1-1	Stokes	33,89
31		9	A	West Bromwich Albion	D	1-1	Stokes	30,60
32		13	H	Arsenal	L	1-3	Medwin	64,55
33		16	H	Portsmouth	W	2-0	Smith, Mansell (og)	36,11
34		23	A	Newcastle United	D	2-2	Medwin, Stokes	37,95
35		30	H	Sheffield Wednesday	D	1-1	Harmer	34,48
36	Apr	6	A	Manchester United	D	0-0		60,58
37		13	H	Birmingham City	W	5-1	Medwin, Harmer (pen), Dunmore 2, Dyson	33,51
38		19	A	Charlton Athletic	D	1-1	Brooks	27,79
39		20	A	Cardiff City	W	3-0	Dunmore, Brooks, Dyson	25,18
40		22	H	Charlton Athletic	W	6-2	Medwin, Harmer 2, Smith, Brooks, Robb	25,57
41		27	H	Blackpool	W	2-1	Harmer 2 (1 pen)	49,87
42		29	A	Burnley	L	0-1		12,04
								Appearance
								Goal

FA Cup

R3	Jan	5	H	Leicester City	W	2-0	Blanchflower, Robb	56,49
R4		26	H	Chelsea	W	4-0	Medwin, Harmer, Smith, Stokes	66,39
R5	Feb	16	A	Bournemouth	L	1-3	Medwin	25,89
								Appearance
								Goa

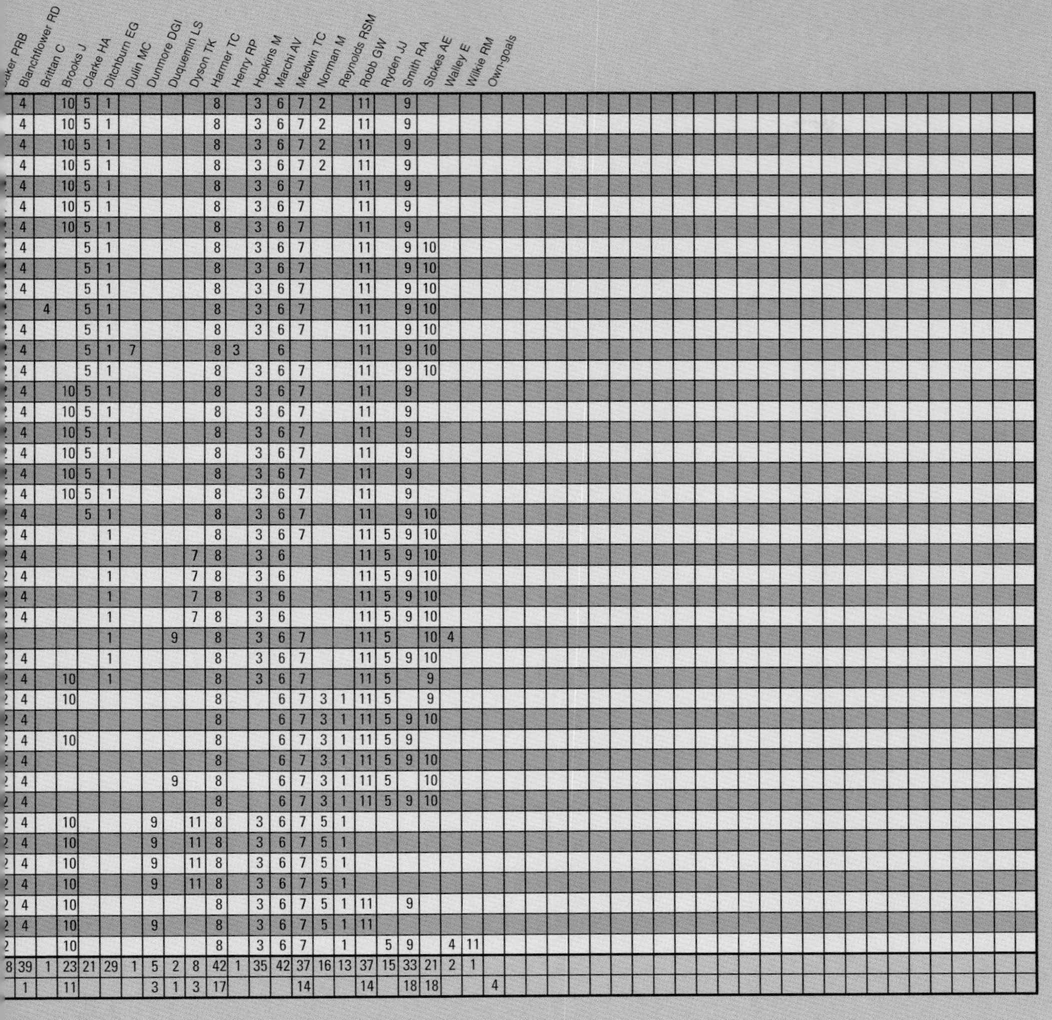

…aker PRB	Blanchflower RD	Brittan C	Brooks J	Clarke HA	Ditchburn EG	Dulin MC	Dunmore DGI	Duquemin LS	Dyson TK	Harmer TC	Henry RP	Hopkins M	Marchi AV	Medwin TC	Norman M	Reynolds RSM	Robb GW	Ryden JJ	Smith RA	Stokes AE	Walley E	Wilkie RM	Own-goals
	4		10	5	1					8		3	6	7	2		11		9				
	4		10	5	1					8		3	6	7	2		11		9				
	4		10	5	1					8		3	6	7	2		11		9				
	4		10	5	1					8		3	6	7	2		11		9				
2	4		10	5	1					8		3	6	7			11		9				
2	4		10	5	1					8		3	6	7			11		9				
2	4		10	5	1					8		3	6	7			11		9				
2	4			5	1					8		3	6	7			11		9	10			
2	4			5	1					8		3	6	7			11		9	10			
2	4			5	1					8		3	6	7			11		9	10			
2		4		5	1					8		3	6	7			11		9	10			
2	4			5	1					8		3	6	7			11		9	10			
2	4			5	1	7				8	3		6				11		9	10			
2	4			5	1					8		3	6	7			11		9	10			
2	4		10	5	1					8		3	6	7			11		9				
2	4		10	5	1					8		3	6	7			11		9				
2	4		10	5	1					8		3	6	7			11		9				
2	4		10	5	1					8		3	6	7			11		9				
2	4		10	5	1					8		3	6	7			11		9				
2	4		10	5	1					8		3	6	7			11		9				
2	4			5	1					8		3	6	7			11		9	10			
2	4				1					8		3	6	7			11	5	9	10			
2	4				1				7	8		3	6				11	5	9	10			
2	4				1				7	8		3	6				11	5	9	10			
2	4				1				7	8		3	6				11	5	9	10			
2	4				1				7	8		3	6				11	5	9	10			
2					1			9		8		3	6	7			11	5		10	4		
2	4				1					8		3	6	7			11	5	9	10			
2	4		10		1					8		3	6	7			11	5		9			
2	4		10							8			6	7	3	1	11	5		9			
2	4									8			6	7	3	1	11	5	9	10			
2	4		10							8			6	7	3	1	11	5	9				
2	4									8			6	7	3	1	11	5	9	10			
2	4							9		8			6	7	3	1	11	5		10			
2	4									8			6	7	3	1	11	5	9	10			
2	4		10				9		11	8		3	6	7	5	1							
2	4		10				9		11	8		3	6	7	5	1							
2	4		10				9		11	8		3	6	7	5	1							
2	4		10				9		11	8		3	6	7	5	1							
2	4		10							8		3	6	7	5	1	11		9				
2	4		10				9			8		3	6	7	5	1	11						
2			10							8		3	6	7		1		5	9		4	11	
8	39	1	23	21	29	1	5	2	8	42	1	35	42	37	16	13	37	15	33	21	2	1	
	1		11				3	1	3	17				14			14		18	18			4

…aker PRB	Blanchflower RD	Brittan C	Brooks J	Clarke HA	Ditchburn EG	Dulin MC	Dunmore DGI	Duquemin LS	Dyson TK	Harmer TC	Henry RP	Hopkins M	Marchi AV	Medwin TC	Norman M	Reynolds RSM	Robb GW	Ryden JJ	Smith RA	Stokes AE	Walley E	Wilkie RM	Own-goals
2	4				1				7	8		3	6				11	5	9	10			
2	4				1					8		3	6	7			11	5	9	10			
2	4				1					8		3	6	7			11	5	9	10			
3	3	0	0	0	3	0	0	0	1	3	0	3	3	2	0	0	3	3	3	3	0	0	
	1									1				2			1		1	1			

League Table

	P	W	D	L	F	A	Pts
Manchester United	42	28	8	6	103	54	64
TOTTENHAM HOTSPUR	42	22	12	8	104	56	56
Preston North End	42	23	10	9	84	56	56
Blackpool	42	22	9	11	93	65	53
Arsenal	42	21	8	13	85	69	50
Wolverhampton W	42	20	8	14	94	70	48
Burnley	42	18	10	14	56	50	46
Leeds United	42	15	14	13	72	63	44
Bolton Wanderers	42	16	12	14	65	65	44
Aston Villa	42	14	15	13	65	55	43
West Bromwich Albion	42	14	14	14	59	61	42
Chelsea	42	13	13	16	73	73	39
Birmingham City	42	15	9	18	69	69	39
Sheffield Wednesday	42	16	6	20	82	88	38
Everton	42	14	10	18	61	79	38
Luton Town	42	14	9	19	58	76	37
Newcastle United	42	14	8	20	67	87	36
Manchester City	42	13	9	20	78	88	35
Portsmouth	42	10	13	19	62	92	33
Sunderland	42	12	8	22	67	88	32
Cardiff City	42	10	9	23	53	88	29
Charlton Athletic	42	9	4	29	62	120	22

1957-58

DIVISION ONE

Manager: Jimmy Anderson

Did you know that?

Bobby Smith's 36 Football League goals equalled the club record set by Ted Harper in 1930–31. When FA Cup goals are added Smith's season's tally went one better than Harper. Harper still holds the record for the number of League goals in a season for Blackburn Rovers, 43 in 1925–26, and Preston North End, 37 in 1932–33.

LEAGUE DEBUTANTS

Aug 31	v Newcastle United	Jim Iley
Oct 19	v Bolton Wanderers	Tommy Bing
Dec 14	v Blackpool	Johnnie Hills
Feb 15	v Nottingham Forest	Jeff Ireland
Feb 22	v Arsenal	Cliff Jones
Apr 5	v Everton	Eddie Clayton

Match No.	Date			Opponents	Result		Scorers	Attendanc
1	Aug	24	H	Chelsea	D	1-1	Stokes	52,58
2		28	A	Portsmouth	L	1-5	Smith	33,47
3		31	A	Newcastle United	L	1-3	Smith	37,74
4	Sep	4	H	Portsmouth	L	3-5	Harmer (pen), Brooks, Dulin	35,81
5		7	H	Burnley	W	3-1	Dunmore 2, Dulin	40,10
6		11	A	Birmingham City	D	0-0		26,48
7		14	A	Preston North End	L	1-3	Stokes	23,36
8		18	H	Birmingham City	W	7-1	Harmer (pen), Stokes 5, Dyson	35,29
9		21	H	Sheffield Wednesday	W	4-2	Medwin, Smith 2, Dyson	39,95
10		28	A	Manchester City	L	1-5	Brannigan (og)	22,49
11	Oct	2	A	Wolverhampton Wanderers	L	0-4		36,02
12		5	H	Nottingham Forest	L	3-4	Medwin, Harmer, Brooks	51,42
13		12	H	Arsenal	W	3-1	Medwin 2, Smith	60,67
14		19	A	Bolton Wanderers	L	2-3	Smith, Robb	20,38
15		26	H	Leeds United	W	2-0	Medwin, Smith	33,86
16	Nov	2	A	Sunderland	D	1-1	Brooks	36,09
17		9	H	Everton	W	3-1	Brooks, Smith, Harmer (pen)	39,99
18		16	A	Aston Villa	D	1-1	Smith	28,39
19		23	H	Luton Town	W	3-1	Medwin 2, Brooks	41,24
20		30	A	Manchester United	W	4-3	Smith 3, Blanchflower (og)	43,30
21	Dec	7	H	Leicester City	L	1-4	Brooks	27,85
22		14	A	Blackpool	W	2-0	Smith 2	14,93
23		21	A	Chelsea	W	4-2	Medwin, Harmer, Smith 2	39,74
24		26	H	Wolverhampton Wanderers	W	1-0	Smith	58,39
25		28	H	Newcastle United	D	3-3	Norman, Harmer (pen), Stokes	51,64
26	Jan	11	A	Burnley	L	0-2		25,92
27		18	H	Preston North End	D	3-3	Medwin, Brooks (pen), Smith	43,94
28	Feb	1	A	Sheffield Wednesday	L	0-2		22,96
29		8	H	Manchester City	W	5-1	Smith 3, Brooks, Robb	37,53
30		15	A	Nottingham Forest	W	2-1	Brooks, Robb	32,33
31		22	A	Arsenal	D	4-4	Harmer 2 (1 pen), Smith 2	59,11
32	Mar	8	A	Leeds United	W	2-1	Smith 2	23,42
33		12	H	Bolton Wanderers	W	4-1	Brooks, Smith 3	22,97
34		15	H	Sunderland	L	0-1		40,75
35		22	A	Luton Town	D	0-0		22,38
36		29	H	Aston Villa	W	6-2	Medwin 2, Smith 4	34,10
37	Apr	4	H	West Bromwich Albion	D	0-0		56,16
38		5	A	Everton	W	4-3	Smith 2, Clayton 2	30,14
39		7	A	West Bromwich Albion	W	2-0	Medwin, Clayton	26,55
40		12	H	Manchester United	W	1-0	Harmer (pen)	59,83
41		19	A	Leicester City	W	3-1	Medwin, Smith, Jones	37,23
42		26	H	Blackpool	W	2-1	Medwin, Smtih	37,63
								Appearance
								Goal

FA Cup

R3	Jan	4	H	Leicester City	W	4-0	Medwin, Smith 2, Stokes	42,71
R4		25	H	Sheffield United	L	0-3		51,13
								Appearance
								Goal

ker PRB	Bing TE	Blanchflower RD	Brittan C	Brooks J	Clayton E	Ditchburn EG	Dulin MC	Dunmore DGI	Dyson TK	Harmer TC	Henry RP	Hills JR	Hopkins M	Iley J	Ireland JJC	Jones CW	Medwin TC	Norman M	Reynolds RSM	Robb GW	Ryden JJ	Smith RA	Stokes AE	Walley E	Own-goals
		4	6							8			3				7	2	1	11	5	9	10		
		4	6							8			3				7	2	1	11	5	9	10		
		4								8			3	6			7	2	1	11	5	9	10		
		4		10			11			8			3	6			7		1		5	9			
		4					11	9		8			3	6			7		1		5		10		
		4					11	9		8			3	6			7		1		5		10		
		4						9	11	8			3	6			7		1		5		10		
		4							11	8			3	6			7		1		5	9	10		
		4							11	8			3	6			7		1		5	9	10		
		4						9	11	8	3			6			7		1		5		10		
		4		11						8			3	6			7		1		5	9	10		
				11						8			3	6			7	5	1		4	9	10		
		4		11		1				8			3	6			7				5	9	10		
	7	4				1				8				6				3		11	5	9	10		
		4		8		1		9					3				7	5		11	6	10			
		4	6	8		1				10			3				7	5		11		9			
		4		8		1				10			3				7	5		11	6	9			
		4		8		1				10			3				7	5		11	6	9			
		4		8		1				10			3				7	5		11	6	9			
		4		8		1				10			3				7	5		11	6	9			
		4		8		1				10			3				7	5		11	6	9			
		4		8		1			11	10		2	3				7	5			6	9			
		4		10		1			11	8		2	3				7	5			6	9			
		4		10		1			11	8		2	3				7	5			6	9			
		4				1			11	8		2	3					5		7	6	9	10		
		4				1			11	10		2	3				7	5			6	9	8		
		4		8		1			11			2	3	10			7	5			6	9			
		4		10		1			11	8		2	3				7	5			6	9			
		4		10		1				8	3	2					7	5		11	6	9			
		4		10		1				8	3	2			7			5		11	6	9			
		4		10		1				8	3	2				11	7	5			6	9			
		4		8		1			11	10	3	2					7	5			6	9			
		4		8		1				10	3	2					7	5		11	6	9			
				8		1				10	3	2				11	7	5			6	9		4	
		4		8		1				10	3	2				11	7	5			6	9			
		4		8		1				10	3	2				11	7	5			6	9			
		4		8		1				10	3	2		6		11	7	5				9			
		4			10	1				8	3	2		6		11	7	5				9			
		4			10					8	3	2		6		11	7	5	1			9			
		4			10					8	3	2		6		11	7	5	1			9			
		4			8					10	3	2		6		11	7	5	1			9			
		4			10					8	3	2		6		11	7	5	1			9			
8	1	40	3	25	5	26	3	5	12	40	15	21	26	19	1	10	39	33	16	15	35	38	15	1	
				10	3		2	2	2	9						1	14	1		3		36	8		2

ker PRB	Bing TE	Blanchflower RD	Brittan C	Brooks J	Clayton E	Ditchburn EG	Dulin MC	Dunmore DGI	Dyson TK	Harmer TC	Henry RP	Hills JR	Hopkins M	Iley J	Ireland JJC	Jones CW	Medwin TC	Norman M	Reynolds RSM	Robb GW	Ryden JJ	Smith RA	Stokes AE	Walley E	Own-goals
		4				1			11	8		2	3				7	5			6	9	10		
		4		10		1			11	8		2	3				7	5			6	9			
[illegible]	0	2	0	1	0	2	0	0	2	2	0	2	2	0	0	0	2	2	0	0	2	2	1	0	
																	1					2	1		

League Table

	P	W	D	L	F	A	Pts
Wolverhampton W	42	28	8	6	103	47	64
Preston North End	42	26	7	9	100	51	59
TOTTENHAM HOTSPUR	42	21	9	12	93	77	51
West Bromwich Albion	42	18	14	10	92	70	50
Manchester City	42	22	5	15	104	100	49
Burnley	42	21	5	16	80	74	47
Blackpool	42	19	6	17	80	67	44
Luton Town	42	19	6	17	69	63	44
Manchester United	42	16	11	15	85	75	43
Nottingham Forest	42	16	10	16	69	63	42
Chelsea	42	15	12	15	83	79	42
Arsenal	42	16	7	19	73	85	39
Birmingham City	42	14	11	17	76	89	39
Aston Villa	42	16	7	19	73	86	39
Bolton Wanderers	42	14	10	18	65	87	38
Everton	42	13	11	18	65	75	37
Leeds United	42	14	9	19	51	63	37
Leicester City	42	14	5	23	91	112	33
Newcastle United	42	12	8	22	73	81	32
Portsmouth	42	12	8	22	73	88	32
Sunderland	42	10	12	20	54	97	32
Sheffield Wednesday	42	12	7	23	69	92	31

1958-59

DIVISION ONE

Manager: Jimmy Anderson until October then Bill Nicholson

Did you know that?

For many years it was traditional for Christmas and Boxing Day (unless one was a Sunday) fixtures to be against the same opponents. West Ham United's visit was the last time Spurs were called upon to play on Christmas Day; Sky TV have yet to change that.

LEAGUE DEBUTANTS

Aug 30 v Blackburn Rovers
John Hollowbread
Sep 17 v Nottingham Forest
Fred Sharpe
Jan 3 v Blackburn Rovers
Bill Dodge
Mar 21 v Manchester City
Dave Mackay

Match No.	Date			Opponents	Result		Scorers	Attendanc
1	Aug	23	H	Blackpool	L	2-3	Smith, Brooks	57,04
2		27	A	Chelsea	L	2-4	Medwin, Smith	59,20
3		30	A	Blackburn Rovers	L	0-5		41,83
4	Sep	3	H	Chelsea	W	4-0	Medwin 3, Robb	50,29
5		6	H	Newcastle United	L	1-3	Medwin	41,80
6		10	A	Nottingham Forest	D	1-1	Smith	26,09
7		13	A	Arsenal	L	1-3	Clayton	65,56
8		17	H	Nottingham Forest	W	1-0	Sharpe	39,43
9		20	A	Manchester United	D	2-2	Smith 2	62,27
10		27	H	Wolverhampton Wanderers	W	2-1	Smith, Clayton	48,56
11	Oct	4	A	Portsmouth	D	1-1	Stokes	26,40
12		11	H	Everton	W	10-4	Ryden, Medwin, Harmer, Smith 4, Stokes 2, Robb	37,79
13		18	A	Leicester City	W	4-3	Harmer (pen), Smith, Stokes 2	31,50
14		25	H	Leeds United	L	2-3	Iley, Smith	38,69
15	Nov	1	A	Manchester City	L	1-5	Smith	30,60
16		8	H	Bolton Wanderers	D	1-1	Smith	39,82
17		15	A	Luton Town	W	2-1	Dunmore, Medwin	23,59
18		22	H	Birmingham City	L	0-4		28,70
19		29	A	West Bromwich Albion	L	3-4	Dunmore, Smith 2	21,75
20	Dec	6	H	Preston North End	L	1-2	Smith	31,80
21		13	A	Burnley	L	1-3	Stokes	17,04
22		20	A	Blackpool	D	0-0		12,93
23		25	A	West Ham United	L	1-2	Smith	26,17
24		26	H	West Ham United	L	1-4	Stokes	43,81
25	Jan	3	H	Blackburn Rovers	W	3-1	Harmer (pen), Smith, Dunmore	39,55
26		17	A	Newcastle United	W	2-1	Dunmore 2	32,50
27		31	H	Arsenal	L	1-4	Smith	60,24
28	Feb	7	H	Manchester United	L	1-3	Norman	48,40
29		21	H	Portsmouth	D	4-4	Smith 2, Clayton, Jones (pen)	27,23
30		28	A	Everton	L	1-2	Jones	36,78
31	Mar	2	A	Wolverhampton Wanderers	D	1-1	Harmer	30,43
32		7	H	Leicester City	W	6-0	Blanchflower, Medwin 4, Dunmore	30,56
33		14	A	Leeds United	L	1-3	Norman	17,01
34		21	H	Manchester City	W	3-1	Medwin, Smith, Jones	34,49
35		27	H	Aston Villa	W	3-2	Medwin, Smith, Jones	45,05
36		28	A	Bolton Wanderers	L	1-4	Clayton	21,38
37		30	A	Aston Villa	D	1-1	Norman	34,35
38	Apr	4	H	Luton Town	W	3-0	Medwin, Smith, Brooks	37,09
39		8	H	Burnley	D	2-2	Smith 2	32,29
40		11	A	Birmingham City	L	1-5	Jones (pen)	20,55
41		18	H	West Bromwich Albion	W	5-0	Smith 4, Brooks	36,80
42		25	A	Preston North End	D	2-2	Smith, Brooks	20,32
								Appearance
								Goal

FA Cup

R3	Jan	10	H	West Ham United	W	2-0	Smith, Jones	56,25
R4		24	H	Newport County	W	4-1	Smith 2, Dunmore 2	50,56
R5	Feb	14	H	Norwich City	D	1-1	Jones	67,63
R5r		18	A	Norwich City	L	0-1		38,00
								Appearance
								Goal

Baker PRB	Blanchflower RD	Brooks J	Clayton E	Ditchburn EG	Dodge WC	Dunmore DGI	Dyson TK	Harmer TC	Henry RP	Hills JR	Hollowbread JF	Hopkins M	Iley J	Ireland JJC	Jones CW	Mackay DC	Medwin TC	Norman M	Robb GW	Ryden JJ	Sharpe FC	Smith RA	Stokes AE
	4	10		1			11	8	3	2			6				7	5				9	
	4	10		1			11	8	3	2			6				7	5				9	
2	4		8			9	11				1	3	6				7	5					10
2	4		10					8			1	3	6				7	5	11			9	
	4		10				11	8		2	1	3	6				7	5				9	
2	4		10					8			1	3	6				7	5	11			9	
2	4		10					8			1	3	6				7	5	11			9	
2		10									1	3	6				7		11	5	4	9	8
2	4		10								1	3	6				7		11	5		9	8
2	4		10								1	3	6				7		11	5		9	8
2			10							4	1	3	6	7					11	5		9	8
2	4							8			1	3	6				7		11	5		9	10
2	4							8	3		1		6	7					11	5		9	10
2	4						11	8			1	3	6				7			5		9	10
	4						11	8		2	1	3	6				7	5				9	10
2	4	7				9		8			1	3	6				11	5				10	
2	4	7				9		8			1	3	6				11	5				10	
2	4	7				9		8			1	3	6				11	5				10	
2	4	11				9		8			1	3	6				7	5				10	
	4	7				9		8	3	2	1		6		11			5				10	
	4							8	3	2	1		6		11		7	5				9	10
2	4							8	3		1		6		11		7	5				9	10
2	4							8	3		1		6		11		7	5				9	10
2	4	7						8	3		1		6		11			5				9	10
2		7			4	10		8			1	3	6		11			5				9	
2		7			4	10		8			1	3	6		11		9	5					
2		7			4	10		8			1	3	6		11			5				9	
2		7			4	10		8			1	3	6		11			5				9	
2	8		10		4						1	3	6		11		7	5				9	
2	4		10					8			1	3			11		7	5			6	9	
2	4	8				10		7			1	3			11		9	5		6			
2	4	8				10		7			1	3			11		9	5		6			
2	4	8				10		7			1	3			11		9	5		6			
2	4	10						8			1	3			11	6	7	5				9	
2	4	10						8			1	3	6		11		7	5				9	
2	4	10	7								1	3	6		11		9	5					8
2	4	10					11	8			1	3				6	7	5				9	
2	4	10						8			1	3	6		11		7	5				9	
2	4	10						8			1	3	6		11		7	5				9	
2	4	10						8			1	3	6		11		7	5				9	
2	4	10						8			1	3			11	6	7	5				9	
2	4	10						8			1	3			11	6	7	5				9	
36	36	25	11	2	5	13	7	35	8	7	40	34	34	2	22	4	35	35	9	10	2	36	14
	1	4	4			6		4					1		5		14	3	2	1	1	32	7

Baker PRB	Blanchflower RD	Brooks J	Clayton E	Ditchburn EG	Dodge WC	Dunmore DGI	Dyson TK	Harmer TC	Henry RP	Hills JR	Hollowbread JF	Hopkins M	Iley J	Ireland JJC	Jones CW	Mackay DC	Medwin TC	Norman M	Robb GW	Ryden JJ	Sharpe FC	Smith RA	Stokes AE
2		7			4	10		8			1	3	6		11			5				9	
2		7			4	10		8			1	3	6		11			5				9	
2		7			4	10		8			1	3	6		11			5				9	
2	8		10		4						1	3	6		11		7	5				9	
4	1	3	1	0	4	3	0	3	0	0	4	4	4	0	4	0	1	4	0	0	0	4	0
						2									2							3	

League Table

	P	W	D	L	F	A	Pts
Wolverhampton W	42	28	5	9	110	49	61
Manchester United	42	24	7	11	103	66	55
Arsenal	42	21	8	13	88	68	50
Bolton Wanderers	42	20	10	12	79	66	50
West Bromwich Albion	42	18	13	11	88	68	49
West Ham United	42	21	6	15	85	70	48
Burnley	42	19	10	13	81	70	48
Blackpool	42	18	11	13	66	49	47
Birmingham City	42	20	6	16	84	68	46
Blackburn Rovers	42	17	10	15	76	70	44
Newcastle United	42	17	7	18	80	80	41
Preston North End	42	17	7	18	70	77	41
Nottingham Forest	42	17	6	19	71	74	40
Chelsea	42	18	4	20	77	98	40
Leeds United	42	15	9	18	57	74	39
Everton	42	17	4	21	71	87	38
Luton Town	42	12	13	17	68	71	37
TOTTENHAM HOTSPUR	42	13	10	19	85	95	36
Leicester City	42	11	10	21	67	98	32
Manchester City	42	11	9	22	64	95	31
Aston Villa	42	11	8	23	58	87	30
Portsmouth	42	6	9	27	64	112	21

1959-60

DIVISION ONE

Manager: Bill Nicholson

Did you know that?

In the closing seconds of the first half against Manchester City on 16 April 1960, referee Pullin awarded Spurs a penalty for handball. Cliff Jones's kick was saved by Bert Trautmann but the ball rebounded for Jones to tap home, only for the 'goal' to be disallowed. The referee had extended the first half just long enough for the kick to be taken and blown the whistle immediately after Trautmann had made his save. It was an expensive decision. City scored the only goal of the game in the second half, effectively ending Spurs' hopes of taking the League title.

LEAGUE DEBUTANTS

Aug 22	v Newcastle United Bill Brown
Oct 17	v Sheffield Wednesday John White
Oct 17	v Sheffield Wednesday Len Worley
Dec 19	v Newcastle United Les Allen
Apr 9	v Everton John Smith

Match No.	Date		Opponents		Result		Scorers	Attendance
1	Aug	22	A	Newcastle United	W	5-1	Brooks 2, Jones 3	40,782
2		26	H	West Bromwich Albion	D	2-2	Medwin, R.Smith	54,114
3		29	H	Birmingham City	D	0-0		45,243
4	Sep	2	A	West Bromwich Albion	W	2-1	Harmer, R.Smith	35,924
5		5	A	Arsenal	D	1-1	Medwin	60,791
6		9	H	West Ham United	D	2-2	R.Smith, Jones	58,90
7		12	A	Manchester United	W	5-1	Mackay, Harmer, R.Smith 2, Dunmore	55,641
8		14	A	West Ham United	W	2-1	Marchi, R.Smith	36,831
9		19	H	Preston North End	W	5-1	Mackay, R.Smith, Dunmore, Jones 2	51,776
10		26	A	Leicester City	D	1-1	Jones (pen)	34,445
11	Oct	3	H	Burnley	D	1-1	Medwin	42,717
12		10	H	Wolverhampton Wanderers	W	5-1	R.Smith 4, Jones	59,344
13		17	A	Sheffield Wednesday	L	1-2	White	37,623
14		24	H	Nottingham Forest	W	2-1	R.Smith 2	52,002
15		31	A	Manchester City	W	2-1	Mackay, Jones	45,506
16	Nov	7	H	Bolton Wanderers	L	0-2		41,909
17		14	A	Luton Town	L	0-1		22,528
18		21	H	Everton	W	3-0	Jones (pen), Harris (og), King (og)	39,432
19		28	A	Blackpool	D	2-2	Mackay, R.Smith	17,085
20	Dec	5	H	Blackburn Rovers	W	2-1	Medwin, Bray (og)	37,130
21		12	A	Fulham	D	1-1	Jones (pen)	36,772
22		19	H	Newcastle United	W	4-0	Blanchflower, Norman, White, Jones	32,824
23		26	A	Leeds United	W	4-2	Harmer, R.Smith, Allen 2	36,037
24		28	H	Leeds United	L	1-4	Mackay	54,170
25	Jan	2	A	Birmingham City	W	1-0	Allen	27,558
26		16	H	Arsenal	W	3-0	R.Smith, Allen 2	58,962
27		23	H	Manchester United	W	2-1	R.Smith 2	62,602
28	Feb	6	A	Preston North End	D	1-1	Mackay	33,039
29		13	H	Leicester City	L	1-2	R.Smith	33,504
30		27	A	Blackburn Rovers	W	4-1	Mackay, R.Smith, Allen, Jones	29,228
31	Mar	1	A	Burnley	L	0-2		32,992
32		5	H	Sheffield Wednesday	W	4-1	White, Jones 3	53,822
33		12	A	Nottingham Forest	W	3-1	Mackay, White, Allen	35,291
34		19	H	Fulham	D	1-1	Mackay	52,189
35		26	A	Bolton Wanderers	L	1-2	Mackay	31,106
36	Apr	2	H	Luton Town	D	1-1	Jones	39,462
37		9	A	Everton	L	1-2	Jones	57,959
38		15	A	Chelsea	W	3-1	R.Smith 3	67,819
39		16	H	Manchester City	L	0-1		49,767
40		18	H	Chelsea	L	0-1		37,200
41		23	A	Wolverhampton Wanderers	W	3-1	Jones, R.Smith, Mackay	56,283
42		30	H	Blackpool	W	4-1	Blanchflower, Jones, White, R.Smith	49,823
								Appearances
								Goals

FA Cup

R3	Jan	9	A	Newport County	W	4-0	Blanchflower, R.Smith, Allen 2	22,655
R4		30	A	Crewe Alexandra	D	2-2	Allen, Jones	20,000
R4r	Feb	3	H	Crewe Alexandra	W	13-2	Harmer, R.Smith 4, Allen 5, Jones 3 (1 pen)	64,365
R5		20	H	Blackburn Rovers	L	1-3	Jones	54,745
								Appearances
								Goals

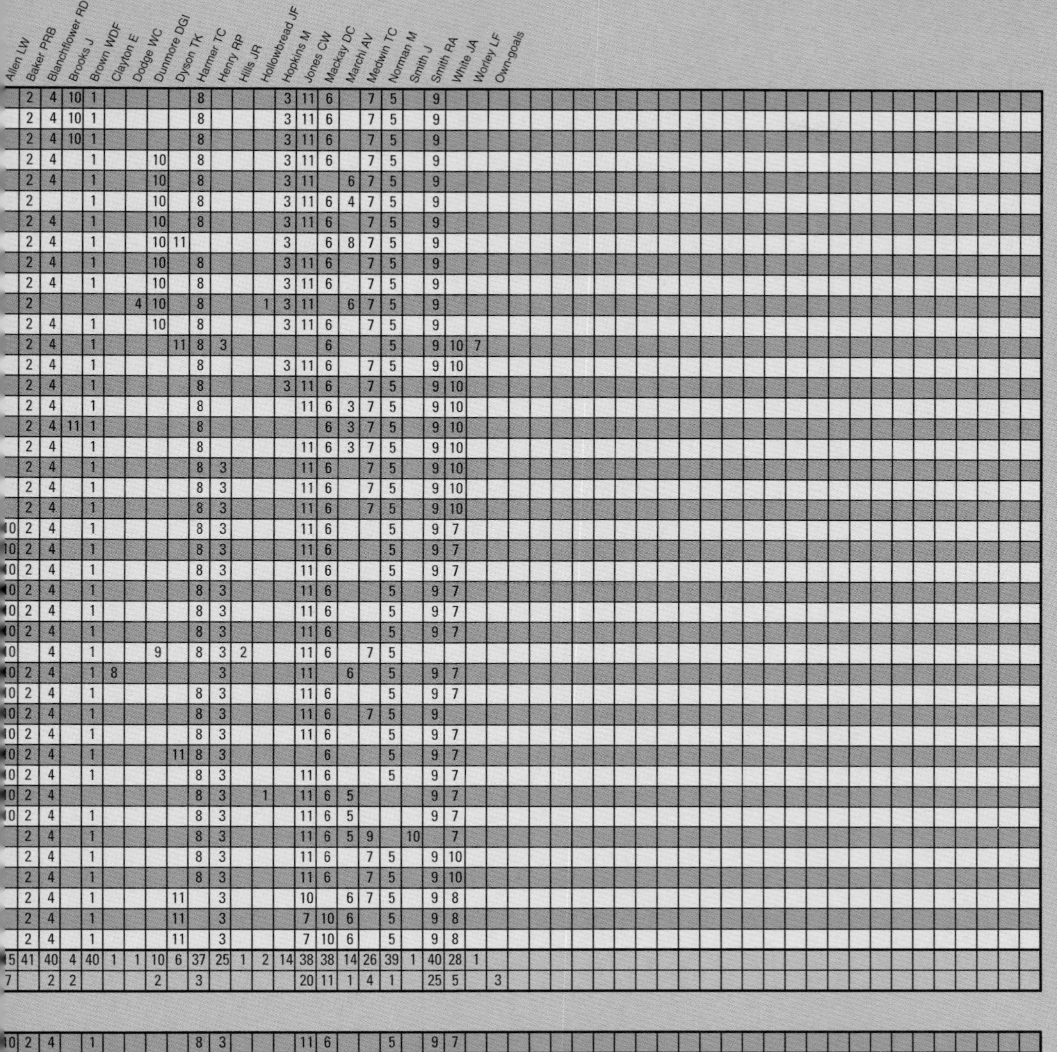

Allen LW	Baker PRB	Blanchflower RD	Brooks J	Brown WDF	Clayton E	Dodge WC	Dunmore DGI	Dyson TK	Harmer TC	Henry RP	Hills JR	Hollowbread JF	Hopkins M	Jones CW	Mackay DC	Marchi AV	Medwin TC	Norman M	Smith J	Smith RA	White JA	Worley LF	Own-goals
	2	4	10	1					8				3	11	6		7	5		9			
	2	4	10	1					8				3	11	6		7	5		9			
	2	4	10	1					8				3	11	6		7	5		9			
	2	4		1			10		8				3	11	6		7	5		9			
	2	4		1			10		8				3	11		6	7	5		9			
	2			1			10		8				3	11	6	4	7	5		9			
	2	4		1			10		8				3	11	6		7	5		9			
	2	4		1			10	11					3		6	8	7	5		9			
	2	4		1			10		8				3	11	6		7	5		9			
	2	4		1			10		8				3	11	6		7	5		9			
	2					4	10		8			1	3	11		6	7	5		9			
	2	4		1			10		8				3	11	6		7	5		9			
	2	4		1				11	8	3					6			5		9	10	7	
	2	4		1					8				3	11	6		7	5		9	10		
	2	4		1					8				3	11	6		7	5		9	10		
	2	4		1					8					11	6	3	7	5		9	10		
	2	4	11	1					8						6	3	7	5		9	10		
	2	4		1					8					11	6	3	7	5		9	10		
	2	4		1					8	3				11	6		7	5		9	10		
	2	4		1					8	3				11	6		7	5		9	10		
	2	4		1					8	3				11	6		7	5		9	10		
10	2	4		1					8	3				11	6			5		9	7		
10	2	4		1					8	3				11	6			5		9	7		
10	2	4		1					8	3				11	6			5		9	7		
10	2	4		1					8	3				11	6			5		9	7		
10	2	4		1					8	3				11	6			5		9	7		
10	2	4		1					8	3				11	6			5		9	7		
10		4		1			9		8	3	2			11	6		7	5					
10	2	4		1	8					3				11		6		5		9	7		
10	2	4		1					8	3				11	6			5		9	7		
10	2	4		1					8	3				11	6		7	5		9			
10	2	4		1					8	3				11	6			5		9	7		
10	2	4		1				11	8	3					6			5		9	7		
10	2	4		1					8	3				11	6			5		9	7		
10	2	4							8	3		1		11	6	5				9	7		
10	2	4		1					8	3				11	6	5				9	7		
	2	4		1					8	3				11	6	5	9		10		7		
	2	4		1					8	3				11	6		7	5		9	10		
	2	4		1					8	3				11	6		7	5		9	10		
	2	4		1				11		3				10		6	7	5		9	8		
	2	4		1				11		3				7	10	6		5		9	8		
	2	4		1				11		3				7	10	6		5		9	8		
5	41	40	4	40	1	1	10	6	37	25	1	2	14	38	38	14	26	39	1	40	28	1	
7		2	2				2		3					20	11	1	4	1		25	5		3

Allen LW	Baker PRB	Blanchflower RD	Brooks J	Brown WDF	Clayton E	Dodge WC	Dunmore DGI	Dyson TK	Harmer TC	Henry RP	Hills JR	Hollowbread JF	Hopkins M	Jones CW	Mackay DC	Marchi AV	Medwin TC	Norman M	Smith J	Smith RA	White JA	Worley LF	Own-goals
10	2	4		1					8	3				11	6			5		9	7		
10	2	4		1					8	3				11	6			5		9	7		
10		4		1					8	3	2			11	6			5		9	7		
10	2	4		1					8	3				11		6		5		9	7		
4	3	4	0	4	0	0	0	0	4	4	1	0	0	4	3	1	0	4	0	4	4	0	
8		1							1					5						5			

League Table

	P	W	D	L	F	A	Pts
Burnley	42	24	7	11	85	61	55
Wolverhampton W	42	24	6	12	106	67	54
TOTTENHAM HOTSPUR	42	21	11	10	86	50	53
West Bromwich Albion	42	19	11	12	83	57	49
Sheffield Wednesday	42	19	11	12	80	59	49
Bolton Wanderers	42	20	8	14	59	51	48
Manchester United	42	19	7	16	102	80	45
Newcastle United	42	18	8	16	82	78	44
Preston North End	42	16	12	14	79	76	44
Fulham	42	17	10	15	73	80	44
Blackpool	42	15	10	17	59	71	40
Leicester City	42	13	13	16	66	75	39
Arsenal	42	15	9	18	68	80	39
West Ham United	42	16	6	20	75	91	38
Everton	42	13	11	18	73	78	37
Manchester City	42	17	3	22	78	84	37
Blackburn Rovers	42	16	5	21	60	70	37
Chelsea	42	14	9	19	76	91	37
Birmingham City	42	13	10	19	63	80	36
Nottingham Forest	42	13	9	20	50	74	35
Leeds United	42	12	10	20	65	92	34
Luton Town	42	9	12	21	50	73	30

1960-61

DIVISION ONE

Manager: Bill Nicholson

Did you know that?

Records tumbled in the double season: 11 successive victories at the start of a season was the best in Football League history, unbeaten in the opening 16 games, 31 victories in 42 games, 16 away wins, only 17 players used, 50 points from only 29 games all First Division records, 66 points and 33 from away games equalled Arsenal's First Division record of 1930–31.

LEAGUE DEBUTANTS

Sep 7 v Bolton Wanderers
Frank Saul
Jan 16 v Manchester United
Ken Barton

Match No.	Date		Opponents		Result		Scorers	Attendance
1	Aug	20	H	Everton	W	2-0	R.Smith, Allen	50,393
2		22	A	Blackpool	W	3-1	Medwin, Dyson 2	27,656
3		27	A	Blackburn Rovers	W	4-1	R.Smith 2, Allen, Dyson	26,819
4		31	H	Blackpool	W	3-1	R.Smith 3	45,684
5	Sep	3	H	Manchester United	W	4-1	R.Smith 2, Allen 2	55,442
6		7	A	Bolton Wanderers	W	2-1	White, Allen	41,565
7		10	A	Arsenal	W	3-2	Saul, Allen, Dyson	59,868
8		14	H	Bolton Wanderers	W	3-1	Blanchflower (pen), R.Smith 2	43,559
9		17	A	Leicester City	W	2-1	R.Smith 2	30,129
10		24	H	Aston Villa	W	6-2	Mackay, White 2, R.Smith, Allen, Dyson	61,356
11	Oct	1	A	Wolverhampton Wanderers	W	4-0	Blachflower, Jones, Allen, Dyson	52,829
12		10	H	Manchester City	D	1-1	R.Smith	58,916
13		15	A	Nottingham Forest	W	4-0	Mackay, Jones 2, White	37,248
14		29	A	Newcastle United	W	4-3	Norman, Jones, White, R.Smith	51,369
15	Nov	2	H	Cardiff City	W	3-2	Blanchflower (pen), Medwin, Dyson	47,605
16		5	H	Fulham	W	5-1	Jones 2, White, Allen 2	56,270
17		12	A	Sheffield Wednesday	L	1-2	Norman	53,988
18		19	H	Birmingham City	W	6-0	Jones 2, White, R.Smith (pen), Dyson 2	46,010
19		26	A	West Bromwich Albion	W	3-1	R.Smith 2, Allen	39,017
20	Dec	3	H	Burnley	D	4-4	Norman, Mackay, Jones 2	58,737
21		10	A	Preston North End	W	1-0	White	21,657
22		17	A	Everton	W	3-1	Mackay, White, Allen	61,052
23		24	H	West Ham United	W	2-0	White, Dyson	54,930
24		26	A	West Ham United	W	3-0	White, Allen, Brown (og)	34,351
25		31	H	Blackburn Rovers	W	5-2	Blanchflower, R.Smith 2, Allen 2	48,742
26	Jan	16	A	Manchester United	L	0-2		65,535
27		21	H	Arsenal	W	4-2	Blanchflower (pen), R.Smith, Allen 2	65,251
28	Feb	4	H	Leicester City	L	2-3	Blanchflower (pen), Allen	53,627
29		11	A	Aston Villa	W	2-1	R.Smith, Dyson	50,786
30		22	H	Wolverhampton Wanderers	D	1-1	R.Smith	62,261
31		25	A	Manchester City	W	1-0	Medwin	40,278
32	Mar	11	A	Cardiff City	L	2-3	Allen, Dyson	45,463
33		22	H	Newcastle United	L	1-2	Allen	46,470
34		25	A	Fulham	D	0-0		38,536
35		31	H	Chelsea	W	4-2	Jones 2, Saul, Allen	65,032
36	Apr	1	H	Preston North End	W	5-0	Jones 3, White, Saul	46,325
37		3	A	Chelsea	W	3-2	Norman, R.Smith, Medwin	57,103
38		8	A	Birmingham City	W	3-2	White, R.Smith, Allen	40,961
39		17	H	Sheffield Wednesday	W	2-1	R.Smith, Allen	61,205
40		22	A	Burnley	L	2-4	Baker, R.Smith	28,991
41		26	H	Nottingham Forest	W	1-0	Medwin	35,743
42		29	H	West Bromwich Albion	L	1-2	R.Smith	52,054
								Appearances
								Goals

FA Cup

Match No.	Date		Opponents		Result		Scorers	Attendance
R3	Jan	7	H	Charlton Athletic	W	3-2	Allen 2, Dyson	54,969
R4		28	H	Crewe Alexandra	W	5-1	Mackay, Jones, R.Smith, Allen, Dyson	53,721
R5	Feb	18	A	Aston Villa	W	2-0	Jones, Neil (og)	65,474
R6	Mar	4	A	Sunderland	D	1-1	Jones	61,236
R6r		8	H	Sunderland	W	5-0	Mackay, R.Smith, Allen, Dyson 2	64,797
SF		18	N*	Burnley	W	3-0	Jones, R.Smith 2	69,968
F	May	6	N#	Leicester City	W	2-0	R.Smith, Dyson	100,000
								Appearances
								Goals

*played at Villa Park #played at Wembley Stadium

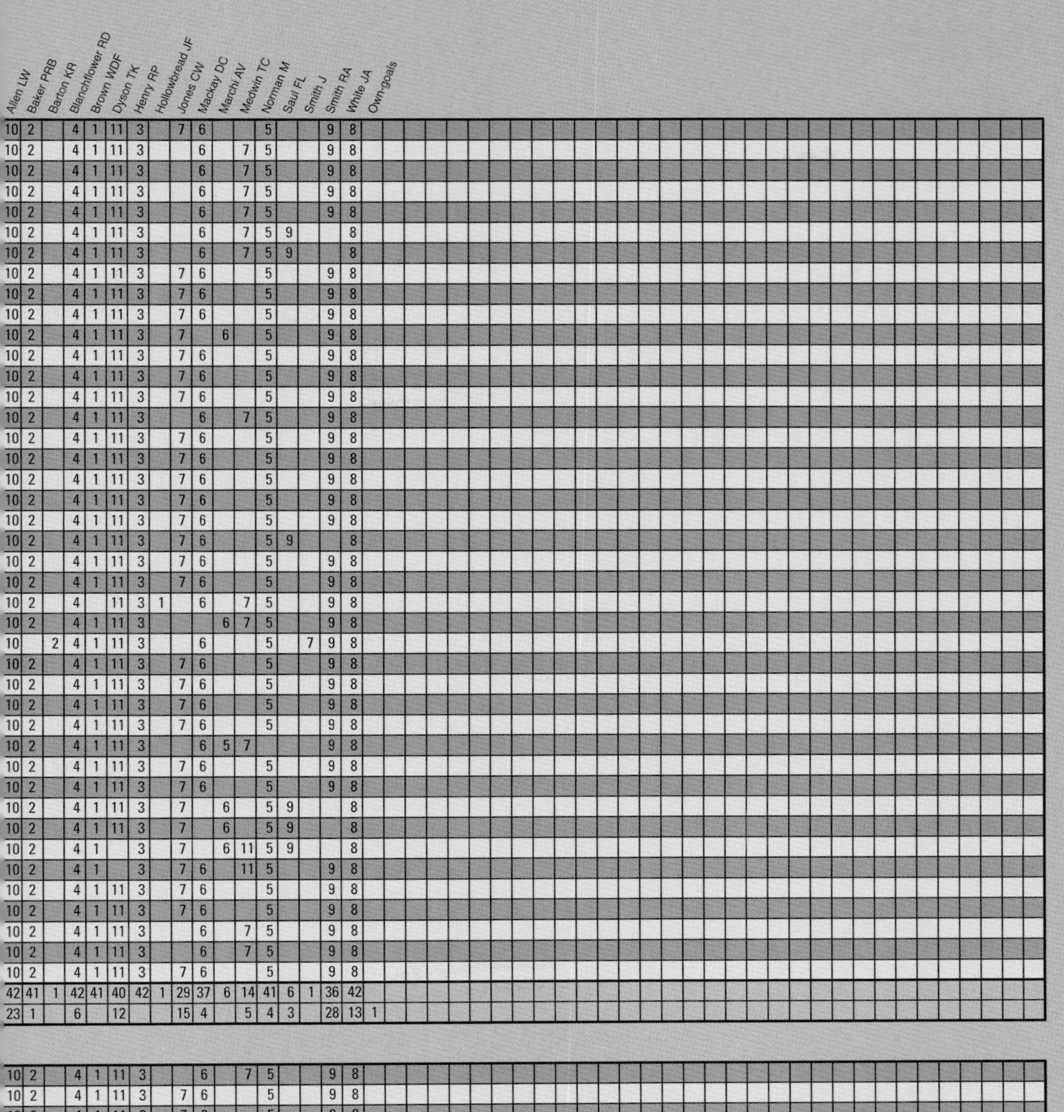

Allen LW	Baker PRB	Barton KR	Blanchflower RD	Brown WDF	Dyson TK	Henry RP	Hollowbread JF	Jones CW	Mackay DC	Marchi AV	Medwin TC	Norman M	Saul FL	Smith J	Smith RA	White JA	Own-goals
10	2		4	1	11	3		7	6			5			9	8	
10	2		4	1	11	3			6		7	5			9	8	
10	2		4	1	11	3			6		7	5			9	8	
10	2		4	1	11	3			6		7	5			9	8	
10	2		4	1	11	3			6		7	5			9	8	
10	2		4	1	11	3			6		7	5	9			8	
10	2		4	1	11	3			6		7	5	9			8	
10	2		4	1	11	3		7	6			5			9	8	
10	2		4	1	11	3		7	6			5			9	8	
10	2		4	1	11	3		7	6			5			9	8	
10	2		4	1	11	3		7		6		5			9	8	
10	2		4	1	11	3		7	6			5			9	8	
10	2		4	1	11	3		7	6			5			9	8	
10	2		4	1	11	3		7	6			5			9	8	
10	2		4	1	11	3			6		7	5			9	8	
10	2		4	1	11	3		7	6			5			9	8	
10	2		4	1	11	3		7	6			5			9	8	
10	2		4	1	11	3		7	6			5			9	8	
10	2		4	1	11	3		7	6			5			9	8	
10	2		4	1	11	3		7	6			5			9	8	
10	2		4	1	11	3		7	6			5	9			8	
10	2		4	1	11	3		7	6			5			9	8	
10	2		4	1	11	3		7	6			5			9	8	
10	2		4		11	3	1		6		7	5			9	8	
10	2		4	1	11	3				6	7	5			9	8	
10		2	4	1	11	3			6			5		7	9	8	
10	2		4	1	11	3		7	6			5			9	8	
10	2		4	1	11	3		7	6			5			9	8	
10	2		4	1	11	3		7	6			5			9	8	
10	2		4	1	11	3		7	6			5			9	8	
10	2		4	1	11	3			6	5	7				9	8	
10	2		4	1	11	3		7	6			5			9	8	
10	2		4	1	11	3		7	6			5			9	8	
10	2		4	1	11	3		7		6		5	9			8	
10	2		4	1	11	3		7		6		5	9			8	
10	2		4	1		3		7		6	11	5	9			8	
10	2		4	1		3		7	6		11	5			9	8	
10	2		4	1	11	3		7	6			5			9	8	
10	2		4	1	11	3		7	6			5			9	8	
10	2		4	1	11	3			6		7	5			9	8	
10	2		4	1	11	3			6		7	5			9	8	
10	2		4	1	11	3		7	6			5			9	8	
42	41	1	42	41	40	42	1	29	37	6	14	41	6	1	36	42	
23	1		6		12			15	4		5	4	3		28	13	1

Allen LW	Baker PRB	Barton KR	Blanchflower RD	Brown WDF	Dyson TK	Henry RP	Hollowbread JF	Jones CW	Mackay DC	Marchi AV	Medwin TC	Norman M	Saul FL	Smith J	Smith RA	White JA	Own-goals
10	2		4	1	11	3			6		7	5			9	8	
10	2		4	1	11	3		7	6			5			9	8	
10	2		4	1	11	3		7	6			5			9	8	
10	2		4	1	11	3		7	6			5			9	8	
10	2		4	1	11	3		7	6			5			9	8	
10	2		4	1	11	3		7	6			5			9	8	
10	2		4	1	11	3		7	6			5			9	8	
7	7	0	7	7	7	7	0	6	7	0	1	7	0	0	7	7	
4					5			4	2						5		1

League Table

	P	W	D	L	F	A	Pts
TOTTENHAM HOTSPUR	42	31	4	7	115	55	66
Sheffield Wednesday	42	23	12	7	78	47	58
Wolverhampton W	42	25	7	10	103	75	57
Burnley	42	22	7	13	102	77	51
Everton	42	22	6	14	87	69	50
Leicester City	42	18	9	15	87	70	45
Manchester United	42	18	9	15	88	76	45
Blackburn Rovers	42	15	13	14	77	76	43
Aston Villa	42	17	9	16	78	77	43
West Bromwich Albion	42	18	5	19	67	71	41
Arsenal	42	15	11	16	77	85	41
Chelsea	42	15	7	20	98	100	37
Manchester City	42	13	11	18	79	90	37
Nottingham Forest	42	14	9	19	62	78	37
Cardiff City	42	13	11	18	60	85	37
West Ham United	42	13	10	19	77	88	36
Fulham	42	14	8	20	72	95	36
Bolton Wanderers	42	12	11	19	58	73	35
Birmingham City	42	14	6	22	62	84	34
Blackpool	42	12	9	21	68	73	33
Newcastle United	42	11	10	21	86	109	32
Preston North End	42	10	10	22	43	71	30

1961-62

DIVISION ONE

Manager: Bill Nicholson

Did you know that?

Jimmy Greaves made his debut in Spurs' colours in a reserve match at Plymouth Argyle on 9 December 1961. The attendance was an astonishing 12,907.

LEAGUE DEBUTANTS

Aug 23 v West Ham United
Jimmy Collins
Dec 16 v Blackpool
Jimmy Greaves

Match No.	Date			Opponents	Result		Scorers	Attendance
1	Aug	19	A	Blackpool	W	2-1	Jones, R.Smith	29,023
2		23	H	West Ham United	D	2-2	Dyson 2	50,434
3		26	H	Arsenal	W	4-3	Allen, Dyson 3	59,371
4		28	A	West Ham United	L	1-2	Allen	36,274
5	Sep	2	H	Cardiff City	W	3-2	Blanchflower (pen), Jones, R.Smith	37,834
6		4	A	Sheffield United	D	1-1	White	32,902
7		9	A	Manchester United	L	0-1		57,135
8		16	H	Wolverhampton Wanderers	W	1-0	Mackay	45,334
9		23	A	Nottingham Forest	L	0-2		40,875
10		30	H	Aston Villa	W	1-0	Dyson	38,099
11	Oct	9	A	Bolton Wanderers	W	2-1	Allen, Clayton	24,726
12		14	H	Manchester City	W	2-0	Medwin, White	40,561
13		21	A	Ipswich Town	L	2-3	Jones 2	28,778
14		28	H	Burnley	W	4-2	Jones 2, Saul, Clayton	56,772
15	Nov	4	A	Everton	L	0-3		54,234
16		11	H	Fulham	W	4-2	Jones, White 2, Mackay	35,662
17		18	A	Sheffield Wednesday	D	0-0		43,085
18		25	H	Leicester City	L	1-2	White	41,745
19	Dec	2	A	West Bromwich Albion	W	4-2	Medwin, White, Allen, Howe (og)	28,701
20		9	H	Birmingham City	W	3-1	Allen 2, Mackay	32,509
21		16	H	Blackpool	W	5-2	Allen 2, Greaves 3	42,734
22		23	A	Arsenal	L	1-2	Mackay	63,440
23		26	A	Chelsea	W	2-0	Greaves, Jones	51,282
24		30	H	Chelsea	W	5-2	Mackay, Allen, Jones 3	44,630
25	Jan	13	A	Cardiff City	D	1-1	Mackay	33,606
26		20	H	Manchester United	D	2-2	Greaves 2	55,225
27	Feb	3	A	Wolverhampton Wanderers	L	1-3	White	45,687
28		10	H	Nottingham Forest	W	4-2	Medwin, R.Smith, Jones 2	42,710
29		21	A	Aston Villa	D	0-0		49,892
30		24	H	Bolton Wanderers	D	2-2	R.Smith, Greaves	36,470
31	Mar	3	A	Manchester City	L	2-6	Greaves 2	31,706
32		14	H	Ipswich Town	L	1-3	Greaves	51,098
33		17	A	Burnley	D	2-2	Greaves, Jones	46,810
34		24	H	Everton	W	3-1	Jones, White, Greaves	47,343
35	Apr	7	H	Sheffield Wednesday	W	4-0	Clayton, Saul, Greaves 2	40,846
36		9	H	Sheffield United	D	3-3	Blanchflower (pen), R.Smith, Greaves	49,030
37		17	A	Fulham	D	1-1	Greaves	43,355
38		20	H	Blackburn Rovers	W	4-1	Medwin, R.Smith, Greaves, Jones	55,183
39		21	H	West Bromwich Albion	L	1-2	Saul	53,512
40		23	A	Blackburn Rovers	W	1-0	Greaves	23,301
41		28	A	Birmingham City	W	3-2	Mackay, Greaves 2	29,614
42		30	A	Leicester City	W	3-2	Mackay, Medwin, Greaves	23,929

Appearances
Goals

FA Cup

R3	Jan	6	A	Birmingham City	D	3-3	Greaves 2, Jones	46,096
R3r		10	H	Birmingham City	W	4-2	Medwin 2, Allen, Greaves	62,917
R4		27	A	Plymouth Argyle	W	5-1	Medwin, White, Greaves 2, Jones	40,040
R5	Feb	17	A	West Bromwich Albion	W	4-2	R.Smith 2, Greaves 2	53,539
R6	Mar	10	H	Aston Villa	W	2-0	Blanchflower, Jones	64,000
SF		31	N*	Manchester United	W	3-1	Medwin, Greaves, Jones	65,000
F	May	5	N#	Burnley	W	3-1	Blanchflower (pen), R.Smith, Greaves	100,000

*played at Hillsborough #played at Wembley Stadium

Appearances
Goals

FA Charity Shield

Aug	12	H	FA XI	W	3-2	R.Smith, Allen 2	36,593

Appearances
Goals

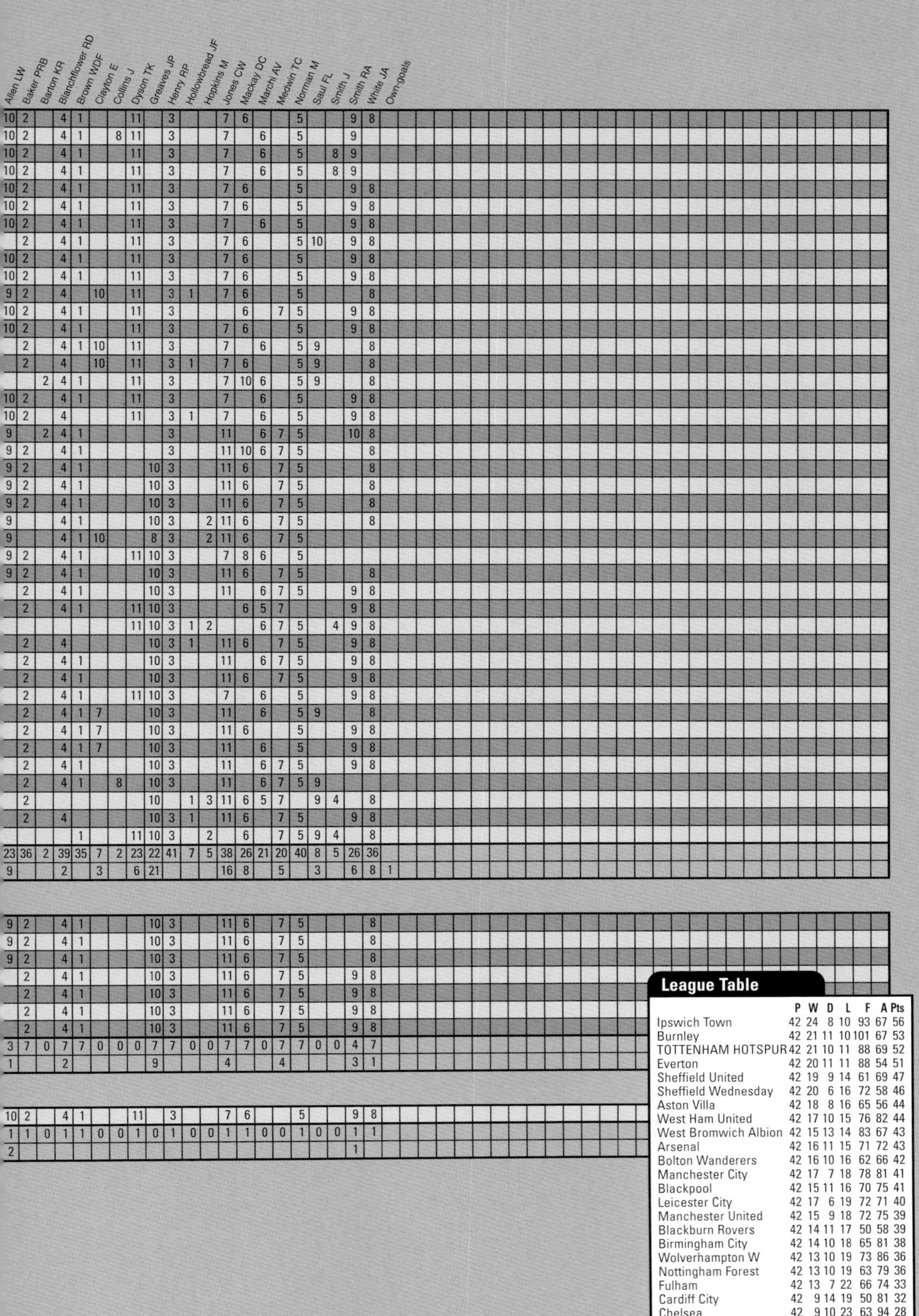

Allen LW	Baker PRB	Barton KR	Blanchflower RD	Brown WDF	Clayton E	Collins J	Dyson TK	Greaves JP	Henry RP	Hollowbread JF	Hopkins M	Jones CW	Mackay DC	Marchi AV	Medwin TC	Norman M	Saul FL	Smith J	Smith RA	White JA	Own-goals
10	2		4	1			11		3			7	6			5			9	8	
10	2		4	1		8	11		3			7		6		5			9		
10	2		4	1			11		3			7		6		5		8	9		
10	2		4	1			11		3			7		6		5		8	9		
10	2		4	1			11		3			7	6			5			9	8	
10	2		4	1			11		3			7	6			5			9	8	
10	2		4	1			11		3			7		6		5			9	8	
	2		4	1			11		3			7	6			5	10		9	8	
10	2		4	1			11		3			7	6			5			9	8	
10	2		4	1			11		3			7	6			5			9	8	
9	2		4		10		11		3	1		7	6			5				8	
10	2		4	1			11		3				6		7	5			9	8	
10	2		4	1			11		3			7	6			5			9	8	
	2		4	1	10		11		3			7		6		5	9			8	
	2		4		10		11		3	1		7	6			5	9			8	
		2	4	1			11		3			7	10	6		5	9			8	
10	2		4	1			11		3			7		6		5			9	8	
10	2		4				11		3	1		7		6		5			9	8	
9		2	4	1					3			11		6	7	5			10	8	
9	2		4	1					3			11	10	6	7	5				8	
9	2		4	1				10	3			11	6		7	5				8	
9	2		4	1				10	3			11	6		7	5				8	
9	2		4	1				10	3			11	6		7	5				8	
9			4	1				10	3		2	11	6		7	5				8	
9			4	1	10			8	3		2	11	6		7	5					
9	2		4	1			11	10	3			7	8	6		5					
9	2		4	1				10	3			11	6		7	5				8	
	2		4	1				10	3			11		6	7	5			9	8	
	2		4	1			11	10	3				6	5	7				9	8	
							11	10	3	1	2			6	7	5		4	9	8	
	2		4					10	3	1		11	6		7	5			9	8	
	2		4	1				10	3			11		6	7	5			9	8	
	2		4	1				10	3			11	6		7	5			9	8	
	2		4	1			11	10	3			7		6		5			9	8	
	2		4	1	7			10	3			11		6		5	9			8	
	2		4	1	7			10	3			11	6			5			9	8	
	2		4	1	7			10	3			11		6		5			9	8	
	2		4	1				10	3			11		6	7	5			9	8	
	2		4	1		8		10	3			11		6	7	5	9				
	2							10		1	3	11	6	5	7		9	4		8	
	2		4					10	3	1		11	6		7	5			9	8	
				1			11	10	3		2		6		7	5	9	4		8	
23	36	2	39	35	7	2	23	22	41	7	5	38	26	21	20	40	8	5	26	36	
9			2		3		6	21				16	8		5		3		6	8	1

Allen LW	Baker PRB	Barton KR	Blanchflower RD	Brown WDF	Clayton E	Collins J	Dyson TK	Greaves JP	Henry RP	Hollowbread JF	Hopkins M	Jones CW	Mackay DC	Marchi AV	Medwin TC	Norman M	Saul FL	Smith J	Smith RA	White JA	Own-goals
9	2		4	1				10	3			11	6		7	5				8	
9	2		4	1				10	3			11	6		7	5				8	
9	2		4	1				10	3			11	6		7	5				8	
	2		4	1				10	3			11	6		7	5			9	8	
	2		4	1				10	3			11	6		7	5			9	8	
	2		4	1				10	3			11	6		7	5			9	8	
	2		4	1				10	3			11	6		7	5			9	8	
3	7	0	7	7	0	0	0	7	7	0	0	7	7	0	7	7	0	0	4	7	
1			2					9				4			4				3	1	

Allen LW	Baker PRB	Barton KR	Blanchflower RD	Brown WDF	Clayton E	Collins J	Dyson TK	Greaves JP	Henry RP	Hollowbread JF	Hopkins M	Jones CW	Mackay DC	Marchi AV	Medwin TC	Norman M	Saul FL	Smith J	Smith RA	White JA	Own-goals
10	2		4	1			11		3			7	6			5			9	8	
1	1	0	1	1	0	0	1	0	1	0	0	1	1	0	0	1	0	0	1	1	
2																			1		

League Table

	P	W	D	L	F	A	Pts
Ipswich Town	42	24	8	10	93	67	56
Burnley	42	21	11	10	101	67	53
TOTTENHAM HOTSPUR	42	21	10	11	88	69	52
Everton	42	20	11	11	88	54	51
Sheffield United	42	19	9	14	61	69	47
Sheffield Wednesday	42	20	6	16	72	58	46
Aston Villa	42	18	8	16	65	56	44
West Ham United	42	17	10	15	76	82	44
West Bromwich Albion	42	15	13	14	83	67	43
Arsenal	42	16	11	15	71	72	43
Bolton Wanderers	42	16	10	16	62	66	42
Manchester City	42	17	7	18	78	81	41
Blackpool	42	15	11	16	70	75	41
Leicester City	42	17	6	19	72	71	40
Manchester United	42	15	9	18	72	75	39
Blackburn Rovers	42	14	11	17	50	58	39
Birmingham City	42	14	10	18	65	81	38
Wolverhampton W	42	13	10	19	73	86	36
Nottingham Forest	42	13	10	19	63	79	36
Fulham	42	13	7	22	66	74	33
Cardiff City	42	9	14	19	50	81	32
Chelsea	42	9	10	23	63	94	28

1962-63

DIVISION ONE

Manager: Bill Nicholson

Did you know that?

Jimmy Greaves was originally credited with one of Spurs' goals against Rangers on 31 October 1962. It was 25 years before close examination of film of the game indicated the goal should be awarded to John White.

LEAGUE DEBUTANTS

May 20 v Blackburn Rovers
Ron Piper

Match No.	Date			Opponents	Result		Scorers	Attendance
1	Aug	18	H	Birmingham City	W	3-0	Blanchflower (pen), Greaves, Jones	51,140
2		20	A	Aston Villa	L	1-2	Medwin	55,630
3		25	A	West Ham United	W	6-1	Medwin, White, Greaves 2, Jones, Lyall (og)	32,527
4		29	H	Aston Villa	W	4-2	White, Greaves 2, Jones	55,650
5	Sep	1	H	Manchester City	W	4-2	Blanchflower (pen), Medwin, Greaves, Jones	48,758
6		8	A	Blackpool	W	2-1	Norman, Allen	31,786
7		12	H	Wolverhampton Wanderers	L	1-2	White	61,412
8		15	H	Blackburn Rovers	W	4-1	Medwin, White, Alan, Taylor (og)	43,014
9		19	A	Wolverhampton Wanderers	D	2-2	Greaves 2	48,166
10		22	A	Sheffield United	L	1-3	Greaves	38,355
11		29	H	Nottingham Forest	W	9-2	Medwin, White, Allen (pen), Greaves 4, Jones 2	49,075
12	Oct	6	H	Arsenal	D	4-4	Mackay, White, Jones 2	61,749
13		13	A	West Bromwich Albion	W	2-1	Marchi, Jones	32,753
14		24	H	Manchester United	W	6-2	Medwin 2, Greaves 3, Jones	51,314
15		27	A	Leyton Orient	W	5-1	Medwin, White, Allen, Jones, Bishop (og)	30,967
16	Nov	3	H	Leicester City	W	4-0	Blanchflower (pen), Medwin, Greaves 2	52,361
17		10	A	Fulham	W	2-0	Mackay, Jones	39,961
18		17	H	Sheffield Wednesday	D	1-1	Mackay	42,390
19		24	A	Burnley	L	1-2	Greaves	44,478
20	Dec	1	H	Everton	D	0-0		60,626
21		8	A	Bolton Wanderers	L	0-1		20,737
22		15	A	Birmingham City	W	2-0	R.Smith, Greaves	36,623
23		22	H	West Ham United	D	4-4	J.Smith, Mackay 3	44,650
24		26	H	Ipswich Town	W	5-0	R.Smith, Greaves 3, Jones	34,822
25	Jan	19	H	Blackpool	W	2-0	Greaves 2	25,710
26	Feb	23	A	Arsenal	W	3-2	Marchi, R.Smith, Jones	59,980
27	Mar	2	H	West Bromwich Albion	W	2-1	R.Smith 2	41,193
28		9	A	Manchester United	W	2-0	Saul, Jones	53,416
29		16	A	Ipswich Town	W	4-2	Saul, Greaves 2 (1 pen), Jones	23,679
30		23	A	Leicester City	D	2-2	R.Smith, Greaves	41,622
31		27	H	Leyton Orient	W	2-0	R.Smith, Greaves (pen)	40,260
32		30	H	Burnley	D	1-1	Greaves	46,536
33	Apr	8	A	Sheffield Wednesday	L	1-3	McAnearney (og)	43,368
34		12	A	Liverpool	L	2-5	Jones, Dyson	54,463
35		13	H	Fulham	D	1-1	Greaves	45,951
36		15	H	Liverpool	W	7-2	Jones 2, Saul, Greaves 4 (1 pen)	53,727
37		20	A	Everton	L	0-1		67,650
38		27	H	Bolton Wanderers	W	4-1	Marchi, Greaves, White, R.Smith	40,965
39	May	4	H	Sheffield United	W	4-2	Jones, Saul, Greaves, Dyson	42,886
40		11	A	Manchester City	L	0-1		27,784
41		18	A	Nottingham Forest	D	1-1	Allen	27,995
42		20	A	Blackburn Rovers	L	0-3		22,867

Appearances
Goals

FA Cup

R3	Jan	16	H	Burnley	L	0-3		32,756

Appearances
Goals

FA Charity Shield

	Aug	11	A	Ipswich Town	W	5-1	Medwin, White, R.Smith, Greaves 2	20,179

Appearances
Goals

Allen LW	Baker PRB	Blanchflower RD	Brown WDF	Clayton E	Dyson TK	Greaves JP	Henry RP	Hollowbread JF	Hopkins M	Jones CW	Mackay DC	Marchi AV	Medwin TC	Norman M	Piper RD	Saul FL	Smith J	Smith RA	White JA	Own-goals
	2	4	1			10	3			11	6		7	5				9	8	
	2	4	1			10	3			11	6		7	5				9	8	
9	2	4	1			10	3			11	6		7	5					8	
9	2	4	1			10	3			11	6		7	5					8	
9	2	4	1			10	3			11	6		7	5					8	
9	2	4	1			10	3			11	6		7	5					8	
9	2	4	1			10	3			11	6		7	5					8	
9	2	4	1		11	10	3				6		7	5					8	
9	2	4	1		11	10	3				6		7	5					8	
9	2	4	1			10	3			11	6		7	5					8	
9	2	4	1			10	3			11	6		7	5					8	
9	2	4	1	10			3			11	6		7	5					8	
9	2		1			10	3			11	6	4	7	5					8	
9	2	4	1			10	3			11	6		7	5					8	
9	2	4	1			10	3			11		6	7	5					8	
9	2	4	1		11	10	3				6		7	5					8	
9	2	4	1			10	3			11	6		7	5					8	
9	2	4	1		11	10	3				6		7	5					8	
9	2	4	1			10	3			11	6		7	5					8	
9	2	4	1	7		10	3			11	8	6		5						
9	2	4	1	8		10	3			11	6		7	5						
	2		1			10	3			11	6	4	7	5				9	8	
	2		1			10	3			11	6	5	7				4	9	8	
	2		1			10	3			11	6		7	5			4	9	8	
	2		1			10	3			11	6	4	7	5				9	8	
	2		1			10	3			11	6	4	7	5				9	8	
	2		1			10	3			11	6	4	7	5				9	8	
			1			10	3		2	11	6	4		5		7		9	8	
9						10	3	1	2	11	6	4		5		7			8	
			1			10	3		2	11	6	4		5		7		9	8	
						10	3	1	2	11	6	4		5		7		9	8	
			1			10	3		2	11	6	4		5		7		9	8	
9			1			10	3		2	11	6	4		5		7			8	
9			1		11	10	3		2	7	6	4		5					8	
	2		1		11	10	3			7	6	5				9	4		8	
			1		11	10	3		2	7	6	5				9	4		8	
	2		1		11	10	3			7	6	5					4	9	8	
10	2	4	1		11	7	3					6		5				9	8	
	2	4	1		11	10	3			7	6			5		9			8	
	2	4	1		11	10	3			7		6		5			8	9		
9		4	1		11	10	3		2	7		6		5		8				
9	2		1		11	10	3			7		6		5	8		4			
25	33	24	40	3	13	41	42	2	9	37	37	22	26	38	1	10	7	15	37	
5		3			2	37				20	6	3	9	1		4	1	8	8	4

Allen LW	Baker PRB	Blanchflower RD	Brown WDF	Clayton E	Dyson TK	Greaves JP	Henry RP	Hollowbread JF	Hopkins M	Jones CW	Mackay DC	Marchi AV	Medwin TC	Norman M	Piper RD	Saul FL	Smith J	Smith RA	White JA	Own-goals
	2		1		11	10	3			7	6			5			4	9	8	
0	1	0	1	0	1	1	1	0	0	1	1	0	0	1	0	0	1	1	1	

Allen LW	Baker PRB	Blanchflower RD	Brown WDF	Clayton E	Dyson TK	Greaves JP	Henry RP	Hollowbread JF	Hopkins M	Jones CW	Mackay DC	Marchi AV	Medwin TC	Norman M	Piper RD	Saul FL	Smith J	Smith RA	White JA	Own-goals
	2	4	1			10	3			11	6		7	5				9	8	
0	1	1	1	0	0	1	1	0	0	1	1	0	1	1	0	0	0	1	1	
						2							1					1	1	

League Table

	P	W	D	L	F	A	Pts
Everton	42	25	11	6	84	42	61
TOTTENHAM HOTSPUR	42	23	9	10	111	62	55
Burnley	42	22	10	10	78	57	54
Leicester City	42	20	12	10	79	53	52
Wolverhampton W	42	20	10	12	93	65	50
Sheffield Wednesday	42	19	10	13	77	63	48
Arsenal	42	18	10	14	86	77	46
Liverpool	42	17	10	15	71	59	44
Nottingham Forest	42	17	10	15	67	69	44
Sheffield United	42	16	12	14	58	60	44
Blackburn Rovers	42	15	12	15	79	71	42
West Ham United	42	14	12	16	73	69	40
Blackpool	42	13	14	15	58	64	40
West Bromwich Albion	42	16	7	19	71	79	39
Aston Villa	42	15	8	19	62	68	38
Fulham	42	14	10	18	50	71	38
Ipswich Town	42	12	11	19	59	78	35
Bolton Wanderers	42	15	5	22	55	75	35
Manchester United	42	12	10	20	67	81	34
Birmingham City	42	10	13	19	63	90	33
Manchester City	42	10	11	21	58	102	31
Leyton Orient	42	6	9	27	37	81	21

1963-64

DIVISION ONE

Manager: Bill Nicholson

Did you know that?

After only a couple of months with Spurs, Alan Mullery was expected to collect his first full England cap on the 1964 summer tour of South America. Unfortunately he ricked his neck while shaving on the morning the squad flew out and had to withdraw. He had to wait until December 1964 before winning his first cap and went on to collect another 34.

LEAGUE DEBUTANTS

Sep 16	v Aston Villa Phil Beal
Jan 25	v Aston Villa Derek Possee
Feb 22	v Arsenal Laurie Brown
Mar 21	v Manchester United Alan Mullery
Mar 30	v Liverpool Jimmy Robertson

Match No.	Date		Opponents		Result		Scorers	Attendance
1	Aug	24	A	Stoke City	L	1-2	R.Smith	40,638
2		28	A	Wolverhampton Wanderers	W	4-1	R.Smith 2, Greaves 2 (1 pen)	41,488
3		31	H	Nottingham Forest	W	4-1	Jones, Greaves 3	49,407
4	Sep	4	H	Wolverhampton Wanderers	W	4-3	Norman, White, Dyson 2	51,851
5		7	A	Blackburn Rovers	L	2-7	Mackay, Greaves	20,949
6		14	H	Blackpool	W	6-1	Jones, White, R.Smith, Greaves 3	38,138
7		16	A	Aston Villa	W	4--2	Jones, Greaves 2, Dyson	36,643
8		21	A	Chelsea	W	3-0	Baker, R.Smith, Shellito (og)	57,401
9		28	H	West Ham United	W	3-0	Mackay, Jones, Brown (og)	51,667
10	Oct	2	H	Birmingham City	W	6-1	White, R.Smith, Greaves 3 (1 pen), Dyson	37,649
11		5	A	Sheffield United	D	3-3	R.Smith, Greaves, Dyson	33,606
12		15	A	Arsenal	D	4-4	Mackay, R.Smith 2, Greaves	67,857
13		19	H	Leicester City	D	1-1	Jones	50,251
14		26	A	Everton	L	0-1		65,386
15	Nov	2	H	Fulham	W	1-0	Greaves	42,023
16		9	A	Manchester United	L	1-4	Gregg (og)	57,513
17		16	H	Burnley	W	3-2	Norman, R.Smith 2	42,222
18		23	A	Ipswich Town	W	3-2	Marchi, Dyson 2	25,014
19		30	H	Sheffield Wednesday	D	1-1	R.Smith	39,378
20	Dec	7	A	Bolton Wanderers	W	3-1	Greaves, Dyson, Farrimond (og)	18,394
21		14	H	Stoke City	W	2-1	Greaves 2	36,776
22		21	A	Nottingham Forest	W	2-1	Jones, Greaves	23,888
23		26	A	West Bromwich Albion	D	4-4	Jones, R.Smith, Greaves 2	37,189
24		28	H	West Bromwich Albion	L	0-2		47,863
25	Jan	11	H	Blackburn Rovers	W	4-1	Greaves 3, Dyson	43,953
26		18	A	Blackpool	W	2-0	Greaves, Martin (og)	13,955
27		25	H	Aston Villa	W	3-1	Possee, Greaves, Dyson	36,394
28	Feb	1	H	Chelsea	L	1-2	Greaves	51,007
29		8	A	West Ham United	L	0-4		36,838
30		15	H	Sheffield United	D	0-0		30,833
31		22	H	Arsenal	W	3-1	Jones 2, Greaves (pen)	57,261
32		29	A	Birmingham City	W	2-1	Jones, Greaves (pen)	28,433
33	Mar	7	H	Everton	L	2-4	Allen, Dyson	41,926
34		21	H	Manchester United	L	2-3	L.Brown, Greaves (pen)	56,292
35		27	H	Liverpool	L	1-3	Norman	57,022
36		28	A	Fulham	D	1-1	Greaves	30,388
37		30	A	Liverpool	L	1-3	Mullery	52,904
38	Apr	4	H	Ipswich Town	W	6-3	Jones 3, White 2, Robertson	25,115
39		13	A	Sheffield Wednesday	L	0-2		26,628
40		18	H	Bolton Wanderers	W	1-0	Greaves	32,507
41		21	A	Burnley	L	2-7	Jones, Greaves	16,660
42		25	A	Leicester City	W	1-0	White	26,441
								Appearances
								Goals

FA Cup

R3	Jan	4	H	Chelsea	D	1-1	Dyson	49,382
R3r		8	A	Chelsea	L	0-2		70,123
								Appearances
								Goals

Allen LW	Baker PRB	Barton KR	Beal P	Blanchflower RD	Brown L	Brown WDF	Clayton E	Dyson TK	Greaves JP	Henry RP	Hollowbread JF	Hopkins M	Jones CW	Mackay DC	Marchi AV	Mullery AP	Norman M	Possee DJ	Robertson JG	Saul FL	Smith J	Smith RA	White JA	Own-goals
	2			4		1		11	10	3			7	6			5					9	8	
	2			4		1		11	10	3			7				5				6	9	8	
	2			4				11	10	3	1		7				5				6	9	8	
	2			4		1		11	10	3			7				5				6	9	8	
	2			4		1		11	10	3				6			5			7		9	8	
	2			4		1		11	10	3			7	6			5					9	8	
9	2		4			1		11	10	3			7	6			5						8	
	2			4		1		11	10	3			7	6			5					9	8	
				4		1		11	10	3		2	7	6			5					9	8	
				4				11	10	3	1	2	7	6			5					9	8	
				4		1		11	10	3		2	7	6			5					9	8	
	2			4		1		11	10	3			7	6			5					9	8	
	2			4		1		11	10	3			7	6			5					9	8	
	2			4		1		11	10	3			7	6			5					9	8	
	2			4		1		11	10	3			7	6			5					9	8	
	2			4		1		11	10	3			7	6			5					9	8	
	2					1		11	10	3			7	6	4		5					9	8	
9	2					1		11	10	3			7	6	4		5						8	
	2					1		11	10	3			7	6	4		5					9	8	
	2					1		11	10	3			7	6	4		5					9	8	
	2					1		11	10			3	7		4		5				6	9	8	
	2					1		11	10			3	7		4		5				6	9	8	
	2					1		11	10			3	7		4		5				6	9	8	
	2					1	8	11	10			3	7		4		5				6	9		
9	2		4					11	10		1	3	7		6		5						8	
9	2		4					11	10		1	3	7		6		5						8	
9	2		4					11	10		1	3			6		5	7					8	
9	2		4					11	10		1	3	7		6		5						8	
	2		4					11	10		1	3	7		6		5					9	8	
	2		4					11	10		1	3	7		6		5					9	8	
	2		4		9			11	10		1	3	7		6		5						8	
	2		4		9			11	10		1	3	7		6		5						8	
10	2		4		9			11	7		1	3			6		5						8	
	2				9			11	10	3	1		7		6	4	5						8	
	2				9			11	10	3	1		7		6	4	5						8	
			6		9	1		11	10	3		2	7			4	5						8	
10			6		9					3	1	2	7		4	8	5		11					
			6		9				10	3	1	2	7			4	5		11				8	
	2		6		9	1			10	3			7			4	5		11				8	
	2		6			1		11	10	3			7			4	5					9	8	
		2	6			1		11	10	3			7			4	5					9	8	
	2					1		11	10	3			7		6	4	5			9			8	
8	35	1	16	15	9	27	1	39	41	29	15	19	39	17	21	9	42	1	3	2	7	26	40	
1	1				1			11	35				14	3	1	1	3	1	1			13	6	5

Allen LW	Baker PRB	Barton KR	Beal P	Blanchflower RD	Brown L	Brown WDF	Clayton E	Dyson TK	Greaves JP	Henry RP	Hollowbread JF	Hopkins M	Jones CW	Mackay DC	Marchi AV	Mullery AP	Norman M	Possee DJ	Robertson JG	Saul FL	Smith J	Smith RA	White JA	Own-goals
	2		6				8	11	10		1	3	7				5				4	9		
9	2		4				8	11	10		1	3	7		6		5							
1	2	0	2	0	0	0	2	2	2	0	2	2	2	0	1	0	2	0	0	0	1	1	0	
								1																

League Table

	P	W	D	L	F	A	Pts
Liverpool	42	26	5	11	92	45	57
Manchester United	42	23	7	12	90	62	53
Everton	42	21	10	11	84	64	52
TOTTENHAM HOTSPUR	42	22	7	13	97	81	51
Chelsea	42	20	10	12	72	56	50
Sheffield Wednesday	42	19	11	12	84	67	49
Blackburn Rovers	42	18	10	14	89	65	46
Arsenal	42	17	11	14	90	82	45
Burnley	42	17	10	15	71	64	44
West Bromwich Albion	42	16	11	15	70	61	43
Leicester City	42	16	11	15	61	58	43
Sheffield United	42	16	11	15	61	64	43
Nottingham Forest	42	16	9	17	64	68	41
West Ham United	42	14	12	16	69	74	40
Fulham	42	13	13	16	58	65	39
Wolverhampton W	42	12	15	15	70	80	39
Stoke City	42	14	10	18	77	78	38
Blackpool	42	13	9	20	52	73	35
Aston Villa	42	11	12	19	62	71	34
Birmingham City	42	11	7	24	54	92	29
Bolton Wanderers	42	10	8	24	48	80	28
Ipswich Town	42	9	7	26	56	121	25

1964-65

DIVISION ONE

Manager: Bill Nicholson

Did you know that?

Public trial games used to be a regular feature of pre-season. On 14 August 1964 Spurs played their last Public Trial at White Lane, Les Allen scoring the only goal as the first team 'Whites' (Jennings, Knowles, Henry, Mullery, Norman, Beal, Jones, Greaves, Saul, Allen and Robertson), beat the reserve team 'Blues' (W.Brown, Baker, Dennis, L. Brown, A. Smith, Marchi, Possee, Gillingwater, Sainty, Mackay (Weller) and Dyson) before a crowd of 10,870.

LEAGUE DEBUTANTS

Aug 22 v Sheffield United
Pat Jennings
Aug 22 v Sheffield United
Cyril Knowles
Dec 5 v Sheffield Wednesday
Roy Low
Dec 19 v Everton
Alan Gilzean
Mar 27 v Wolves
Keith Weller

Match No.	Date		Opponents		Result		Scorers	Attendance
1	Aug	22	H	Sheffield United	W	2-0	Greaves, Saul	45,724
2		25	A	Burnley	D	2-2	Greaves, Saul	21,661
3		29	A	Everton	L	1-4	Jones	55,148
4	Sep	2	H	Burnley	W	4-1	Saul 3, Dyson	42,326
5		5	H	Birmingham City	W	4-1	Robertson, Greaves, Dyson, Foster (og)	34,809
6		9	A	Stoke City	L	0-2		36,329
7		12	A	West Ham United	L	2-3	Greaves 2, (1 pen)	36,730
8		16	H	Stoke City	W	2-1	Greaves, Saul	34,821
9		19	H	West Bromwich Albion	W	1-0	Greaves	36,993
10		26	A	Manchester United	L	1-4	Robertson	53,362
11		28	A	Blackpool	D	1-1	Jones	26,436
12	Oct	5	H	Fulham	W	3-0	Norman, Greaves, Saul	32,908
13		10	H	Arsenal	W	3-1	Robertson, Greaves, Saul	55,959
14		17	A	Leeds United	L	1-3	Greaves	41,464
15		24	H	Chelsea	D	1-1	Jones	52,927
16		31	A	Leicester City	L	2-4	Greaves, Allen	29,167
17	Nov	7	H	Sunderland	W	3-0	Robertson, Greaves, Jones	36,677
18		14	A	Wolverhampton Wanderers	L	1-3	L.Brown	28,728
19		21	H	Aston Villa	W	4-0	Mullery, Robertson, Greaves, Dyson	29,724
20		28	A	Liverpool	D	1-1	Greaves	41,198
21	Dec	5	H	Sheffield Wednesday	W	3-2	Greaves 2 (1 pen), Megson (og)	24,019
22		12	A	Sheffield United	D	3-3	Greaves, Saul 2	19,325
23		19	H	Everton	D	2-2	Greaves 2	41,994
24		26	A	Nottingham Forest	W	2-1	Gilzean, Jones	42,056
25		28	H	Nottingham Forest	W	4-0	Robertson, Greaves, Gilzean, Dyson	56,693
26	Jan	2	A	Birmingham City	L	0-1		33,833
27		16	H	West Ham United	W	3-2	Greaves 2, Dyson	50,054
28		23	A	West Bromwich Albion	L	0-2		23,718
29	Feb	6	H	Manchester United	W	1-0	Henry	58,639
30		13	A	Fulham	L	1-4	Greaves	27,708
31		23	A	Arsenal	L	1-3	Gilzean	48,367
32		27	H	Leeds United	D	0-0		42,350
33	Mar	10	A	Chelsea	L	1-3	Gilzean	51,390
34		13	H	Blackpool	W	4-1	Mullery, Robertson, Greaves, Jones	27,257
35		20	A	Sunderland	L	1-2	Greaves	44,394
36		27	H	Wolverhampton Wanderers	W	7-4	Clayton, Allen, Gilzean 2, Jones 3	25,974
37	Apr	3	A	Aston Villa	L	0-1		24,930
38		9	H	Liverpool	W	3-0	Saul, Low, Gilzean	28,441
39		16	H	Blackburn Rovers	W	5-2	Greaves 2, Gilzean 3	36,497
40		17	A	Sheffield Wednesday	L	0-1		21,843
41		19	A	Blackburn Rovers	L	1-3	Jones	14,026
42		24	H	Leicester City	W	6-2	Greaves 2 (1 pen), Gilzean, Jones 3	32,427
								Appearances
								Goals

FA Cup

Round	Date			Opponents	Result		Scorers	Attendance
R3	Jan	9	A	Torquay United	D	3-3	Norman, Gilzean 2	20,000
R3r		18	H	Torquay United	W	5-1	Robertson, Greaves 3, Gilzean	55,081
R4		30	H	Ipswich Town	W	5-0	Greaves 3 (1 pen), Gilzean 2	43,992
R5	Feb	20	A	Chelsea	L	0-1		63,205
								Appearances
								Goals

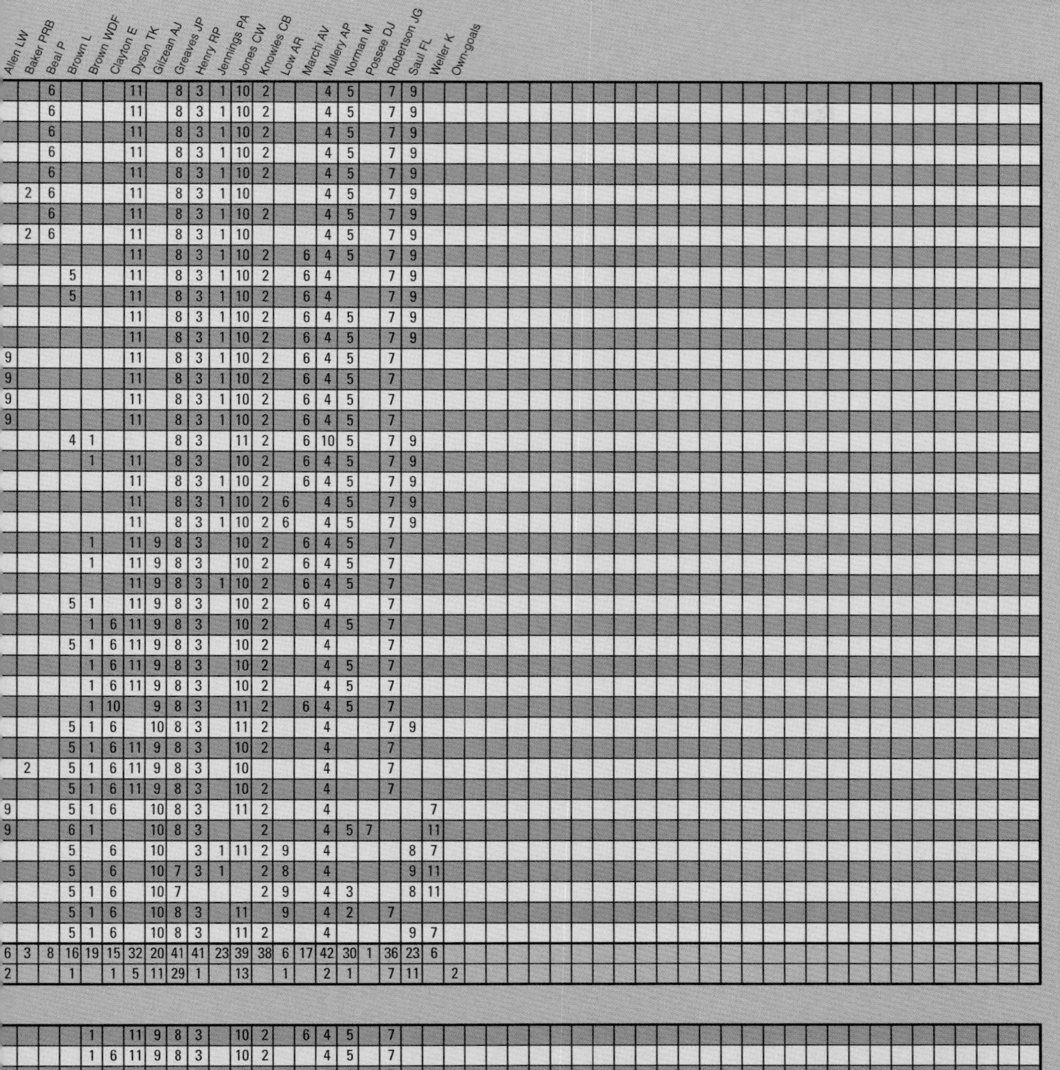

Allen LW	Baker PRB	Beal P	Brown L	Brown WDF	Clayton E	Dyson TK	Gilzean AJ	Greaves JP	Henry RP	Jennings PA	Jones CW	Knowles CB	Low AR	Marchi AV	Mullery AP	Norman M	Possee DJ	Robertson JG	Saul FL	Weller K	Own-goals
		6				11		8	3	1	10	2			4	5		7	9		
		6				11		8	3	1	10	2			4	5		7	9		
		6				11		8	3	1	10	2			4	5		7	9		
		6				11		8	3	1	10	2			4	5		7	9		
		6				11		8	3	1	10	2			4	5		7	9		
	2	6				11		8	3	1	10				4	5		7	9		
		6				11		8	3	1	10	2			4	5		7	9		
	2	6				11		8	3	1	10				4	5		7	9		
						11		8	3	1	10	2		6	4	5		7	9		
			5			11		8	3	1	10	2		6	4			7	9		
			5			11		8	3	1	10	2		6	4			7	9		
						11		8	3	1	10	2		6	4	5		7	9		
						11		8	3	1	10	2		6	4	5		7	9		
9						11		8	3	1	10	2		6	4	5		7			
9						11		8	3	1	10	2		6	4	5		7			
9						11		8	3	1	10	2		6	4	5		7			
9						11		8	3	1	10	2		6	4	5		7			
			4	1				8	3		11	2		6	10	5		7	9		
				1		11		8	3		10	2		6	4	5		7	9		
						11		8	3	1	10	2		6	4	5		7	9		
						11		8	3	1	10	2	6		4	5		7	9		
						11		8	3	1	10	2	6		4	5		7	9		
				1		11	9	8	3		10	2		6	4	5		7			
				1		11	9	8	3		10	2		6	4	5		7			
						11	9	8	3	1	10	2		6	4	5		7			
			5	1		11	9	8	3		10	2		6	4			7			
				1	6	11	9	8	3		10	2			4	5		7			
			5	1	6	11	9	8	3		10	2			4			7			
				1	6	11	9	8	3		10	2			4	5		7			
				1	6	11	9	8	3		10	2			4	5		7			
				1	10		9	8	3		11	2		6	4	5		7			
			5	1	6		10	8	3		11	2			4			7	9		
			5	1	6	11	9	8	3		10	2			4			7			
	2		5	1	6	11	9	8	3		10				4			7			
			5	1	6	11	9	8	3		10	2			4			7			
9			5	1	6		10	8	3		11	2			4					7	
9			6	1			10	8	3			2			4	5	7			11	
			5		6		10		3	1	11	2	9		4				8	7	
			5		6		10	7	3	1		2	8		4				9	11	
			5	1	6		10	7				2	9		4	3			8	11	
			5	1	6		10	8	3		11		9		4	2		7			
			5	1	6		10	8	3		11	2			4				9	7	
6	3	8	16	19	15	32	20	41	41	23	39	38	6	17	42	30	1	36	23	6	
2			1		1	5	11	29	1		13		1		2	1		7	11		2

Allen LW	Baker PRB	Beal P	Brown L	Brown WDF	Clayton E	Dyson TK	Gilzean AJ	Greaves JP	Henry RP	Jennings PA	Jones CW	Knowles CB	Low AR	Marchi AV	Mullery AP	Norman M	Possee DJ	Robertson JG	Saul FL	Weller K	Own-goals
				1		11	9	8	3		10	2		6	4	5		7			
				1	6	11	9	8	3		10	2			4	5		7			
				1	6	11	9	8	3		10	2			4	5		7			
				1	10		9	8	3		11	2		6	4	5		7			
0	0	0	0	4	3	3	4	4	4	0	4	4	0	2	4	4	0	4	0	0	
							5	6								1		1			

League Table

	P	W	D	L	F	A	Pts
Manchester United	42	26	9	7	89	39	61
Leeds United	42	26	9	7	83	52	61
Chelsea	42	24	8	10	89	54	56
Everton	42	17	15	10	69	60	49
Nottingham Forest	42	17	13	12	71	67	47
TOTTENHAM HOTSPUR	42	19	7	16	87	71	45
Liverpool	42	17	10	15	67	73	44
Sheffield Wednesday	42	16	11	15	57	55	43
West Ham United	42	19	4	19	82	71	42
Blackburn Rovers	42	16	10	16	83	79	42
Stoke City	42	16	10	16	67	66	42
Burnley	42	16	10	16	70	70	42
Arsenal	42	17	7	18	69	75	41
West Bromwich Albion	42	13	13	16	70	65	39
Sunderland	42	14	9	19	64	74	37
Aston Villa	42	16	5	21	57	82	37
Blackpool	42	12	11	19	67	78	35
Leicester City	42	11	13	18	69	85	35
Sheffield United	42	12	11	19	50	64	35
Fulham	42	11	12	19	60	78	34
Wolverhampton W	42	13	4	25	59	89	30
Birmingham City	42	8	11	23	64	96	27

1965-66

DIVISION ONE

Manager: Bill Nicholson

Did you know that?

Replacing Derek Possee against Arsenal on 11 September 1965, Roy Low became Spurs' first substitute in a Football League game.

LEAGUE DEBUTANTS

Aug 27 v Blackpool
Steve Pitt
Oct 6 v Sunderland
Neil Johnson
Mar 26 v Sunderland
John Collins
Mar 26 v Sunderland
Roger Hoy
Apr 8 v West Ham United
Joe Kinnear
May 5 v Blackburn Rovers
Terry Venables

Match No.	Date			Opponents	Result		Scorers	Attendance
1	Aug	25	H	Leicester City	W	4-2	Knowles, Possee, Greaves, Robertson	39,867
2		27	H	Blackpool	W	4-0	Clayton, Gilzean, Greaves 2	36,882
3	Sep	1	A	Leicester City	D	2-2	Possee, Greaves (pen)	28,463
4		4	A	Fulham	W	2-0	Mackay, Clayton	28,718
5		8	H	Leeds United	W	3-2	Mackay, Greaves 2	48,156
6		11	H	Arsenal	D	2-2	Gilzean, Saul	53,962
7		15	A	Leeds United	L	0-2		41,920
8		18	H	Liverpool	W	2-1	Clayton, Gilzean	46,925
9		25	A	Aston Villa	L	2-3	Norman, Robertson	29,856
10	Oct	6	H	Sunderland	W	3-0	Mackay, Clayton, Greaves	37,364
11		9	A	Everton	L	1-3	Mullery	40,022
12		16	H	Manchester United	W	5-1	Johnson, Clayton, Gilzean, Greaves, Robertson	58,051
13		23	A	Newcastle United	D	0-0		42,430
14		30	H	West Bromwich Albion	W	2-1	Greaves 2	43,658
15	Nov	6	A	Nottingham Forest	L	0-1		29,611
16		13	H	Sheffield Wednesday	L	2-3	Mackay (pen), Saul	30,422
17		20	A	Northampton Town	W	2-0	Mackay, Saul	17,611
18		27	H	Stoke City	D	2-2	Gilzean, Robertson	26,406
19	Dec	4	A	Burnley	D	1-1	Clayton	19,509
20		11	H	Chelsea	W	4-2	Gilzean 2, Jones 2	42,299
21		18	A	Manchester United	L	1-5	Jones	39,511
22		27	H	Sheffield United	W	1-0	Gilzean	45,766
23		28	A	Sheffield United	W	3-1	Saul, Jones 2	24,787
24	Jan	1	H	Everton	D	2-2	Knowles, Saul	34,953
25		8	A	Chelsea	L	1-2	Mackay (pen)	48,529
26		15	H	Newcastle United	D	2-2	Knowles, Weller	27,490
27		29	H	Blackburn Rovers	W	4-0	Saul, Gilzean 2, Greaves (pen)	34,573
28	Feb	5	A	Blackpool	D	0-0		13,103
29		19	H	Fulham	W	4-3	Saul, Jones 3	32,244
30	Mar	8	A	Arsenal	D	1-1	Possee	51,824
31		12	A	Liverpool	L	0-1		50,760
32		19	H	Aston Villa	D	5-5	L.Brown, Robertson, Greaves, Saul, Gilzean	28,371
33		26	A	Sunderland	L	0-2		27,828
34	Apr	2	H	Nottingham Forest	L	2-3	Robertson, Clayton	27,593
35		8	H	West Ham United	L	1-4	Gilzean	50,635
36		9	A	Sheffield Wednesday	D	1-1	Clayton	17,456
37		16	H	Northampton Town	D	1-1	Greaves (pen)	29,749
38		23	A	Stoke City	W	1-0	Greaves (pen)	19,112
39		25	A	West Ham United	L	0-2		32,232
40		30	H	Burnley	L	0-1		29,337
41	May	7	A	West Bromwich Albion	L	1-2	Clayton	22,586
42		9	A	Blackburn Rovers	W	1-0	Greaves	7,256
								Appearances
								Substitute
								Goals

FA Cup

Round	Date			Opponents	Result		Scorers	Attendance
R3	Jan	22	H	Middlesbrough	W	4-0	Mackay 2 (1 pen), Saul 2	37,349
R4	Feb	12	H	Burnley	W	4-3	Gilzean 3, Saul	50,611
R5	Mar	5	A	Preston North End	L	1-2	Greaves	36,792
								Appearances
								Substitute
								Goals

Beal P	Brown L	Brown WDF	Clayton E	Collins JL	Gilzean AJ	Greaves JP	Henry RP	Hoy RE	Jennings PA	Johnson NJ	Jones CW	Kinnear JP	Knowles CB	Low AR	Mackay DC	Mullery AP	Norman M	Pitt SW	Possee DJ	Robertson JG	Saul FL	Venables TF	Weller K
	5	1	8		9	10							3		6	4	2		7	11			
	5	1	8		9	10							3		6	4	2	11	7				
	5	1	8		9	10							3		6	4	2		7				11
	5	1	8		10	7							3		6	4	2		11		9		
	5	1	8		9	7							3		6	4	2			11	10		
	5	1	8		9	7							3	12	6	4	2		11		10		
	5	1	8		9	10							3		6	4	2			7			11
	5	1	8		9	10							3		6	4	2			7			11
	5	1	8		9	10							3		6	4	2			7			11
	5	1	8		9	10				7			3		6	4	2			11			
	5	1	8		9	10				7			3		6	4	2			11			
	5		8		9	10			1	7			3		6	4	2			11			
	5		8		9	10			1	7			3		6	4	2			11			
4	5		8		9	10			1	7			3		6		2			11			
	5	1	8		9					7			3		6	4	2			11	10		
	5		8		9				1	7			3		6	4	2			11	10		
2	5		8		10				1	11			3		6	4			7		9		
2	5		8		10				1				3		6	4			7	11	9		
2	5		8		10				1		11		3		6	4			7		9		
2	5		8		10				1		11		3		6	4				7	9		
2	5		8		10				1		11		3		6	4				7	9		
2	5		8		10				1		11		3		6	4				7	9		
2	5		8		10		3		1		11				6	4				7	9		
2	5		8		10				1		11		3		6	4				7	9		
2	5		8		10				1		11		3		6	4				7	9		
2	5		8		10				1				3		6	4			11	7			9
2	5		8		10	11			1	12			3		6	4				7	9		
2	5		4		10	11			1	6	8		3							7	9		
2	5				10	8			1		11		3		6	4				7	9		
	5		4		10	8			1				3		6	2			11	7	9		
	5		4		10	8			1				3		6	2			11	7	9		
	5		4		10	8			1				3		6	2			11	7	9		
			10	3	9	8		5	1				2		6	4				7	11		
		1	10	2	9	8		5					3		6	4				7	11		
		1			10	8		5				2	3		6	4			11	7	9		
6		1	8					5				2	3		10	4			11	7	9		
6	5	1	8		9	7						2	3		10	4				11			
6	5	1	8			7						2	3		10	4			11		9		
6	5		8		9	7			1			2	3		10	4			11				
6	5	1			8	7						2	3		10	4				11	9		
6	5	1	8		9	7						2	3		10	4			11				
6		1			9	7		5				2	3		10	4				11		8	
21	37	20	38	2	40	29	1	5	22	9	9	8	41	0	41	40	16	1	17	33	26	1	5
0	0	0	0	0	0	0	0	0	0	1	0	0	0	1	0	0	0	0	0	0	0	0	0
	1		9		12	15				1	8		3		6	1	1		3	6	8		1

Beal P	Brown L	Brown WDF	Clayton E	Collins JL	Gilzean AJ	Greaves JP	Henry RP	Hoy RE	Jennings PA	Johnson NJ	Jones CW	Kinnear JP	Knowles CB	Low AR	Mackay DC	Mullery AP	Norman M	Pitt SW	Possee DJ	Robertson JG	Saul FL	Venables TF	Weller K
2	5		8		10				1		11		3		6	4				7	9		
2	5		6		9	8			1		11		3			4				7	10		
2	5		8		10	11			1				3		6	4				7	9		
3	3	0	3	0	3	2	0	0	3	0	2	0	3	0	2	3	0	0	0	3	3	0	0
0	0	0	0	0	0	0	0	0	0	0	0	0	0	0	0	0	0	0	0	0	0	0	0
					3	1									2						3		

League Table

	P	W	D	L	F	A	Pts
Liverpool	42	26	9	7	79	34	61
Leeds United	42	23	9	10	79	38	55
Burnley	42	24	7	11	79	47	55
Manchester United	42	18	15	9	84	59	51
Chelsea	42	22	7	13	65	53	51
West Bromwich Albion	42	19	12	11	91	69	50
Leicester City	42	21	7	14	80	65	49
TOTTENHAM HOTSPUR	42	16	12	14	75	66	44
Sheffield United	42	16	11	15	56	59	43
Stoke City	42	15	12	15	65	64	42
Everton	42	15	11	16	56	62	41
West Ham United	42	15	9	18	70	83	39
Blackpool	42	14	9	19	55	65	37
Arsenal	42	12	13	17	62	75	37
Newcastle United	42	14	9	19	50	63	37
Aston Villa	42	15	6	21	69	80	36
Sheffield Wednesday	42	14	8	20	56	66	36
Nottingham Forest	42	14	8	20	56	72	36
Sunderland	42	14	8	20	51	72	36
Fulham	42	14	7	21	67	85	35
Northampton Town	42	10	13	19	55	92	33
Blackburn Rovers	42	8	4	30	57	88	20

1966-67

DIVISION ONE

Manager: Bill Nicholson

Did you know that?

Alan Gilzean went on to collect two winners' tankards in the Football League Cup but his first experience of the competition was not one he would want to remember. Spurs' first match in a competition they had previously scorned was at West Ham United on 14 September 1966. Gilzean was booked after an hour for arguing with referee Harry New and sent off five minutes later, although the referee would not tell even Bill Nicholson why.

LEAGUE DEBUTANTS

Aug 20	v Leeds United Mike England
Oct 15	v Blackpool Roy Brown
Apr 1	v Liverpool Dennis Bond

Match No.	Date		Opponents		Result		Scorers	Attendance
1	Aug	20	H	Leeds United	W	3-1	Mullery, Greaves, Gilzean	43,844
2		24	A	Stoke City	L	0-2		34,683
3		27	A	Newcastle United	W	2-0	Mackay, Robertson	35,780
4		31	H	Stoke City	W	2-0	Greaves (pen), Gilzean	37,908
5	Sep	3	H	Arsenal	W	3-1	Greaves 2, Jones	56,271
6		6	A	Sheffield United	L	1-2	Greaves (pen)	21,650
7		10	H	Manchester United	W	2-1	Greaves, Gilzean	56,295
8		17	A	Burnley	D	2-2	Greaves, Saul	25,184
9		24	H	Nottingham Forest	W	2-1	Mullery, Greaves	34,405
10	Oct	1	A	Fulham	W	4-3	Robertson, Greaves, Gilzean, Venables	28,628
11		8	A	Manchester City	W	2-1	Gilzean 2	32,551
12		15	H	Blackpool	L	1-3	Knowles	36,459
13		26	A	Chelsea	L	0-3		54,191
14		29	H	Aston Villa	L	0-1		31,014
15	Nov	5	A	Blackpool	D	2-2	Gilzean 2	16,524
16		12	H	West Ham United	L	3-4	Greaves (pen), Gilzean, Venables	57,157
17		19	A	Sheffield Wednesday	L	0-1		32,376
18		26	H	Southampton	W	5-3	Mullery, Mackay, Greaves (pen), Jones 2	35,736
19	Dec	3	A	Sunderland	W	1-0	Gilzean	32,733
20		10	H	Leicester City	W	2-0	Greaves, Rodrigues (og)	41,089
21		17	A	Leeds United	L	2-3	Greaves, Gilzean	29,852
22		26	A	West Bromwich Albion	L	0-3		37,969
23		27	H	West Bromwich Albion	D	0-0		39,129
24		31	H	Newcastle United	W	4-0	Mackay, Greaves 2, Venables	27,948
25	Jan	7	A	Arsenal	W	2-0	Robertson, Gilzean	49,851
26		14	A	Manchester United	L	0-1		57,365
27		21	H	Burnley	W	2-0	Greaves, Jones	42,187
28	Feb	4	A	Nottingham Forest	D	1-1	Greaves	41,822
29		11	H	Fulham	W	4-2	Greaves, Gilzean, Jones 2	43,961
30		25	H	Manchester City	D	1-1	Robertson	33,832
31	Mar	4	A	Aston Villa	D	3-3	Mullery, England, Gilzean	31,718
32		18	H	Chelsea	D	1-1	Greaves	49,553
33		22	A	Everton	W	1-0	Greaves	50,108
34		25	A	Leicester City	W	1-0	Robertson	27,711
35		27	H	Everton	W	2-0	Mullery, Gilzean	46,917
36	Apr	1	H	Liverpool	W	2-1	Greaves 2	53,135
37		15	H	Sheffield Wednesday	W	2-1	Saul 2	36,062
38		22	A	Southampton	W	1-0	Gilzean	30,258
39	May	3	H	Sunderland	W	1-0	Greaves (pen)	33,936
40		6	A	Liverpool	D	0-0		40,845
41		9	A	West Ham United	W	2-0	Greaves, Gilzean	35,758
42		13	H	Sheffield United	W	2-0	Greaves, Saul	44,912

Appearances
Substitute
Goals

FA Cup

R3	Jan	28	A	Millwall	D	0-0		41,260
R3r	Feb	1	H	Millwall	W	1-0	Gilzean	58,189
R4		18	H	Portsmouth	W	3-1	Greaves, Gilzean 2	57,910
R5	Mar	11	H	Bristol City	W	2-0	Greaves 2 (1 pen)	54,610
R6	Apr	8	A	Birmingham City	D	0-0		51,500
R6r		12	H	Birmingham City	W	6-0	Greaves 2, Gilzean, Venables 2, Saul	52,304
SF		29	N*	Nottingham Forest	W	2-1	Greaves, Saul	55,000
F	May	20	N#	Chelsea	W	2-1	Robertson, Saul	100,000

*played at Hillsborough #played at Wembley Stadium

Appearances
Substitute
Goals

Football League Cup

R2	Sep	14	A	West Ham United	L	0-1		34,068

Appearances
Substitute
Goals

…eal P	Bond DJT	Brown RE	Clayton E	England HM	Gilzean AJ	Greaves JP	Jennings PA	Jones CW	Kinnear JP	Knowles CB	Low AR	Mackay DC	Mullery AP	Robertson JG	Saul FL	Venables TF	Weller K	Own-goals
2				5	9	8	1	11		3		6	4	7		10		
2				5	9	8	1	11		3		6	4	7		10		
2				5	9	8	1	11		3		6	4	7		10		
4				5	9	8	1	11	2	3		6		7		10		
4				5	9	8	1	11	2	3		6		7		10		
4			11	5	9	8	1		2	3		**6**		7		10	12	
6			12	5	9	8	1		2	3			4	7		10	11	
				5	9	8	1		2	3		6	4	7	11	10		
				5	9	8	1	11	2	3		6	4	7		10		
				5	9	8	1		2	3		6	4	7	11	10		
2			12	5	9	8	1			3		6	4	7	11	10		
		1	2	5		8		11		3		6	4	7	9	10		
2				5	9	8	1	11		3		6	4		7	10		
2				5	9	8	1			3		6	4	7	11	10		
2				5	9	8	1	11		3		6	4	7		10		
2				5	9	8	1	11		3		6	4	7		10		
2				5	9	8	1	11		3		6	4	7		10		
2				5	9	8	1	11		3		6	4	7		10		
2				5	9	8	1	**11**		3	12	6	4	7		10		
2			**11**	5	9	8	1			3		6	4	7		10	12	
				5	9	8	1			3		6	4		11	10	7	
				5	9	8	1			3		6	4	7		10	11	
			12	5	9	8	1			3		**6**	4	7		10	11	
			6	5	**9**	8	1			3			4	7	12	10	11	
			6	5		8	1			3			4	7	9	10	11	
				5	9	8	1	11		3		6	4	7		10		
				5	9	8	1	**11**		3		6	4	7	12	10		
				5	9	8	1	11		3		6	4	7		10		
				5	9		1		12	3		6	4	7	8	10	11	
				5	9		1	11	2	3		6	4	7	10	8		
			10	5	9	8	1		2	3		6	4	7			11	
				5	9	8	1		2	3		6	4	7	11	10		
				5	9	8	1		2	3		6	4	7	11	10		
				5	9	8	1		2	3		6	4	7	11	10		
	12			5	9	8	1		2	3		**6**	4	7	11	10		
				5	9		1	11	2	3		6	4	7	8	10		
				5	9		1	11	2	3		6	4	7	8	10		
				5	9	8	1		2	3		6	4	7	11	10		
				5	9	8	1		2	3		6	4	7	11	10		
				5	9	8	1		2	3		6	4	7	11	10		
				5	9	8	1		2	3		6	4	7	11	10		
				5	9	8	1		2	3		6	4	7	11	10		
6	0	1	6	42	40	38	41	20	19	42	0	39	39	40	20	41	8	
	1	0	3	0	0	0	0	0	1	0	1	0	0	0	2	0	2	
				1	17	25		6		1		3	5	5	4	3		1

…eal P	Bond DJT	Brown RE	Clayton E	England HM	Gilzean AJ	Greaves JP	Jennings PA	Jones CW	Kinnear JP	Knowles CB	Low AR	Mackay DC	Mullery AP	Robertson JG	Saul FL	Venables TF	Weller K	Own-goals
				5	9	8	1	11	2	3		6	4	7		10		
				5	9	8	1	11	2	3		6	4	7		10		
				5	9	8	1	11		3		6	4	7		10		
				5	9	8	1	11	2	3		6	4	7		10		
				5	9	8	1		2	3		6	4	7	11	10		
				5	9	8	1		2	3		6	4	7	11	10		
				5	9	8	1	12	2	3		**6**	4	7	11	10		
				5	9	8	1		2	3		6	4	7	11	10		
	0	0	0	8	8	8	8	4	7	8	0	8	8	8	4	8	0	
	0	0	0	0	0	0	0	1	0	0	0	0	0	0	0	0	0	
					4	6								1	3	2		

…eal P	Bond DJT	Brown RE	Clayton E	England HM	Gilzean AJ	Greaves JP	Jennings PA	Jones CW	Kinnear JP	Knowles CB	Low AR	Mackay DC	Mullery AP	Robertson JG	Saul FL	Venables TF	Weller K	Own-goals
			6		9	8	1		2	3			4	7	11	10		
	0	0	1	0	1	1	1	0	1	1	0	0	1	1	1	1	0	
	0	0	0	0	0	0	0	0	0	0	0	0	0	0	0	0	0	

League Table

	P	W	D	L	F	A	Pts
Manchester United	42	24	12	6	84	45	60
Nottingham Forest	42	23	10	9	64	41	56
TOTTENHAM HOTSPUR	42	24	8	10	71	48	56
Leeds United	42	22	11	9	62	42	55
Liverpool	42	19	13	10	64	47	51
Everton	42	19	10	13	65	46	48
Arsenal	42	16	14	12	58	47	46
Leicester City	42	18	8	16	78	71	44
Chelsea	42	15	14	13	67	62	44
Sheffield United	42	16	10	16	52	59	42
Sheffield Wednesday	42	14	13	15	56	47	41
Stoke City	42	17	7	18	63	58	41
West Bromwich Albion	42	16	7	19	77	73	39
Burnley	42	15	9	18	66	76	39
Manchester City	42	12	15	15	43	52	39
West Ham United	42	14	8	20	80	84	36
Sunderland	42	14	8	20	58	72	36
Fulham	42	11	12	19	71	83	34
Southampton	42	14	6	22	74	92	34
Newcastle United	42	12	9	21	39	81	33
Aston Villa	42	11	7	24	54	85	29
Blackpool	42	6	9	27	41	76	21

1967-68

DIVISION ONE

Manager: Bill Nicholson

Did you know that?

Pat Jennings's goal against Manchester United in the FA Charity Shield on 12 August 1967 came from a long punt downfield that bounced on the edge of the United penalty area before soaring over United's Alex Stepney into the back of the net.

LEAGUE DEBUTANTS

Jan 17 v Sheffield Wednesday
Martin Chivers
Mar 1 v West Bromwich Albion
Tony Want

Match No.	Date			Opponents	Result		Scorers	Attendance
1	Aug	19	A	Leicester City	W	3-2	Kinnear, England, Saul	32,55
2		23	H	Everton	D	1-1	Gilzean	53,80
3		26	H	West Ham United	W	5-1	Mullery, Greaves 2 (1 pen), Saul, Jones	55,83
4		29	A	Everton	W	1-0	Saul	57,79
5	Sep	2	A	Burnley	L	1-5	Greaves	23,33
6		6	H	Wolverhampton Wanderers	W	2-1	Robertson, Greaves	44,40
7		9	H	Sheffield Wednesday	W	2-1	Gilzean, Saul	43,31
8		16	A	Arsenal	L	0-4		62,93
9		23	A	Manchester United	L	1-3	Gilzean	58,77
10		30	H	Sunderland	W	3-0	Greaves 2, Todd (og)	36,01
11	Oct	7	H	Sheffield United	D	1-1	Greaves	33,23
12		14	A	Coventry City	W	3-2	Greaves 2, Jones	38,00
13		25	H	Nottingham Forest	D	1-1	Greaves	40,92
14		28	A	Stoke City	L	1-2	Venables	27,14
15	Nov	4	H	Liverpool	D	1-1	Jones	47,68
16		11	A	Southampton	W	2-1	Robertson, Gilzean	29,90
17		18	H	Chelsea	W	2-0	Gilzean, Jones	53,98
18		25	A	West Bromwich Albion	L	0-2		29,03
19	Dec	2	H	Newcastle United	D	1-1	Gilzean	34,49
20		9	A	Manchester City	L	1-4	Greaves	35,79
21		16	H	Leicester City	L	0-1		26,03
22		23	A	West Ham United	L	1-2	Robertson	32,12
23		26	H	Fulham	D	2-2	Jones 2	36,27
24		30	A	Fulham	W	2-1	Robertson, Jones	30,05
25	Jan	17	A	Sheffield Wednesday	W	2-1	Chivers, Greaves	31,61
26		20	H	Arsenal	W	1-0	Gilzean	57,88
27	Feb	3	H	Manchester United	L	1-2	Chivers	57,69
28		10	A	Sunderland	W	1-0	Jones	31,73
29		26	A	Sheffield United	L	2-3	Greaves, Chivers	27,00
30	Mar	1	H	West Bromwich Albion	D	0-0		31,31
31		16	A	Nottingham Forest	D	0-0		37,70
32		23	H	Stoke City	W	3-0	England, Robertson, Jones	29,53
33		30	H	Burnley	W	5-0	England, Greaves 2, Venables, Jones	26,49
34	Apr	6	H	Southampton	W	6-1	Mullery, Greaves 2 (1 pen), Chivers, Jones, Hollywood (og)	41,83
35		12	H	Leeds United	W	2-1	Greaves, Chivers	56,58
36		13	A	Chelsea	L	0-2		53,04
37		17	A	Leeds United	L	0-1		48,93
38		20	H	Coventry City	W	4-2	Mackay, Greaves 2, Jones	36,17
39		27	A	Newcastle United	W	3-1	Gilzean, Chivers 2	30,28
40		29	A	Liverpool	D	1-1	Greaves	41,68
41	May	4	H	Manchester City	L	1-3	Greaves (pen)	51,24
42		11	A	Wolverhampton Wanderers	L	1-2	Greaves	40,92

Appearance
Substitut
Goal

FA Cup

Round	Date			Opponents	Result		Scorers	Attendance
R3	Jan	27	A	Manchester United	D	2-2	Chivers 2	63,50
R3r		31	H	Manchester United	W*	1-0	Robertson	57,20
R4	Feb	17	H	Preston North End	W	3-1	Greaves 2, Chivers	47,08
R5	Mar	9	H	Liverpool	D	1-1	Greaves	54,00
R5r		12	A	Liverpool	L	1-2	Jones	53,65

*after extra-time

Appearance
Substitut
Goa

FA Charity Shield

	Date			Opponents	Result		Scorers	Attendance
	Aug	12	A	Manchester United	D	3-3	Jennings, Robertson, Saul	54,10

Appearance
Substitut
Goal

Beal P	Bond DJT	Chivers MH	Clayton E	England HM	Gilzean AJ	Greaves JP	Hoy RE	Jennings PA	Jones CW	Kinnear JP	Knowles CB	Mackay DC	Mullery AP	Robertson JG	Saul FL	Venables TF	Want AG	Own-goals
				5	9	8		1		2	3	6		7	11	10		
				5	9	8		1		2	3	6	4	7	11	10		
2				5		8		1	11	2	3	**6**	4	7	9	10		
				5		8		1	11	2	3		4	7	9	10		
				5		8		1	11	2	3		4	7	9	10		
				5	9	8		1		2	3		4	7	11	10		
				5	9	8		1	12	2	3		4	7	11	10		
				5	9	8		1		2	3		4	7	11	10		
			10	5	9	8		1		2	3		4	7	11			
				5	9	8		1	11	2	3		4	7	12	10		
				5	9	8		1	**11**	2	3		4	7	12	10		
				5	9	8		1	11	2	3		4	7		10		
	12			5	9	8		1		2	3		4	7	**11**	10		
			12	5	9	**8**		1		2	3		4	7	11	10		
				5	9	8		1	11	2	3	6	4	7		10		
					9	8	5	1	11		3	6	4	7		10		
				5	9	8		1	11	2	3	6	4	7		10		
					9	8	5	1	11	2	3	6	4	7		10		
	10				9	8	5	1	11	2	3	6	4		7			
					9	8	5	1	11	2	3	6	4		7	10		
						8	5	1	11	2	3	6	4	7	9	10		
	10					**8**		1	11	2	3	6	4	7	9	12		
	10				8			1	11	2	3	6	4	7	9			
	10				8			1	11	2	3	6	4	7	9			
	8	9			10	11		1		2	3	6	4	7				
		9			8	11		1		2	3	6	4	7		10		
		9		5		8		1	11	2	3		4	7		10		
		9		5	8			1	7	2	3	6	4			10		
		9		5		7		1	11	2	3	6	4			10		
		9		5		8		1	11		2	6	4	7			3	
		9		5	10	8		1	12		2		4	**7**		6	3	
		9		5	12	8		1	11		2	6	4	7		10		
		9		5	7	8		1	11		3	6	4			10		
		9		5	7	8		1	11		3	6	4			10		
		9		5	7	8		1	11		3	**6**	4	12		10		
		9		5	7	8		1	11		3	6	4			10		
		9		5	7	8		1	11		3	6	4			10		
		9			12	8		1	11	5	3	6	4	7		10		
		9		5	7	8		1		12	**3**	6	4	11		10		
		9		5	11	8		1			3	6	4	7		10		
		9		5	11	8		1			3	6	4	7		10		
		9		5	11	8		1	12		3	**6**	4	7		10		
	5	18	1	31	32	39	5	42	27	29	42	29	41	33	17	35	2	
	1	0	1	0	2	0	0	0	3	1	0	0	0	1	2	1	0	
		7		3	8	23			12	1		1	2	5	4	2		2

Beal P	Bond DJT	Chivers MH	Clayton E	England HM	Gilzean AJ	Greaves JP	Hoy RE	Jennings PA	Jones CW	Kinnear JP	Knowles CB	Mackay DC	Mullery AP	Robertson JG	Saul FL	Venables TF	Want AG	Own-goals
		9		5	8			1	12	2	3	6	4	7		**10**		
		9		5	**8**	10		1		2	3	6	4	7		12		
		9		5	8	7		1	11	2	3	6	4			10		
		9		5	10	8		1	12		2	6	4	**7**			3	
		9		5	10	8		1	12		2	**6**	4			7	3	
	0	5	0	5	5	4	0	5	1	3	5	5	5	3	0	3	2	
	0	0	0	0	0	0	0	0	3	0	0	0	0	0	0	1	0	
		3				3			1					1				

Beal P	Bond DJT	Chivers MH	Clayton E	England HM	Gilzean AJ	Greaves JP	Hoy RE	Jennings PA	Jones CW	Kinnear JP	Knowles CB	Mackay DC	Mullery AP	Robertson JG	Saul FL	Venables TF	Want AG	Own-goals
				5	9	8		1		2	3	6	4	7	11	10		
	0	0	0	1	1	1	0	1	0	1	1	1	1	1	1	1	0	
	0	0	0	0	0	0	0	0	0	0	0	0	0	0	0	0	0	
								1						1	1			

League Table

	P	W	D	L	F	A	Pts
Manchester City	42	26	6	10	86	43	58
Manchester United	42	24	8	10	89	55	56
Liverpool	42	22	11	9	71	40	55
Leeds United	42	22	9	11	71	41	53
Everton	42	23	6	13	67	40	52
Chelsea	42	18	12	12	62	68	48
TOTTENHAM HOTSPUR	42	19	9	14	70	59	47
West Bromwich Albion	42	17	12	13	75	62	46
Arsenal	42	17	10	15	60	56	44
Newcastle United	42	13	15	14	54	67	41
Nottingham Forest	42	14	11	17	52	64	39
West Ham United	42	14	10	18	73	69	38
Leicester City	42	13	12	17	64	69	38
Burnley	42	14	10	18	64	71	38
Sunderland	42	13	11	18	51	61	37
Southampton	42	13	11	18	66	83	37
Wolverhampton W	42	14	8	20	66	75	36
Stoke City	42	14	7	21	50	73	35
Sheffield Wednesday	42	11	12	19	51	63	34
Coventry City	42	9	15	18	51	71	33
Sheffield United	42	11	10	21	49	70	32
Fulham	42	10	7	25	56	98	27

1968-69

DIVISION ONE

Manager: Bill Nicholson

Did you know that?

Against Leicester City on 5 October 1968, Jimmy Greaves scored possibly the finest individual goal seen at White Hart Lane. Taking a Pat Jennings clearance down out wide on the halfway line, he beat his marker as he got the ball under control then set off on a mesmeric dribble past three more defenders before slotting the ball home. For several matches the following season Spurs' programme cover featured a picture of Greaves slipping the ball past Peter Shilton as Leicester defenders could be seen in the background in varying stages of getting back to their feet.

LEAGUE DEBUTANTS

Aug 10	v Arsenal	Peter Collins
Aug 10	v Arsenal	Jimmy Pearce
Oct 19	v Liverpool	David Jenkins
Feb 15	v Queen's Park Rangers	Roger Morgan
Mar 24	v Arsenal	Ray Evans
Mar 24	v Arsenal	John Pratt

Match No.	Date			Opponents	Result		Scorers	Attendanc
1	Aug	10	H	Arsenal	L	1-2	Greaves	56,28
2		17	A	Everton	W	2-0	Greaves, Chivers	56,57
3		21	H	West Bromwich Albion	D	1-1	Gilzean	35,74
4		24	H	Sheffield Wednesday	L	1-2	England	30,54
5		28	A	Manchester United	L	1-3	Greaves	62,64
6		31	A	Chelsea	D	2-2	Jones, Greaves	48,41
7	Sep	7	H	Burnley	W	7-0	Jones 2, Robertson, Greaves 3 (1 pen), Chivers	30,16
8		14	A	West Ham United	D	2-2	Greaves, Gilzean	35,80
9		17	A	Coventry City	W	2-1	Chivers, Gilzean	40,95
10		21	H	Nottingham Forest	W	2-1	Jones, Greaves	37,38
11		28	A	Newcastle United	D	2-2	Mullery, Pearce	30,46
12	Oct	5	H	Leicester City	W	3-2	Greaves 3	36,62
13		9	H	Manchester United	D	2-2	Jones, Gilzean	56,20
14		12	A	Manchester City	L	0-4		38,01
15		19	H	Liverpool	W	2-1	Greaves 2	44,12
16		26	A	Ipswich Town	W	1-0	Gilzean	30,25
17	Nov	2	H	Stoke City	D	1-1	Greaves	33,30
18		9	A	Leeds United	D	0-0		38,99
19		16	H	Sunderland	W	5-1	Greaves 4, England	29,07
20		23	A	Southampton	L	1-2	Greaves	27,38
21	Dec	7	H	Wolverhampton Wanderers	L	0-2		30,84
22		14	H	Manchester City	D	1-1	England	28,46
23		21	A	Liverpool	L	0-1		43,84
24	Jan	11	A	Stoke City	D	1-1	Jenkins	21,72
25		18	H	Leeds United	D	0-0		42,39
26		29	H	Queen's Park Rangers	W	3-2	Beal, Gilzean, Jenkins	38,76
27	Feb	1	A	Sunderland	D	0-0		22,25
28		15	A	Queen's Park Rangers	D	1-1	Greaves	30,01
29		22	H	Wolverhampton Wanderers	D	1-1	Morgan	35,91
30	Mar	8	H	Everton	D	1-1	Morgan	44,88
31		18	H	Ipswich Town	D	2-2	Knowles, Greaves (pen)	21,60
32		22	H	Chelsea	W	1-0	Johnson	47,34
33		24	A	Arsenal	L	0-1		43,97
34		29	A	Burnley	D	2-2	Johnson, Pearce	14,54
35	Apr	2	H	Newcastle United	L	0-1		22,52
36		4	H	Coventry City	W	2-0	Johnson, Pearce	35,03
37		7	A	West Bromwich Albion	L	3-4	Knowles, Greaves 2 (1 pen)	24,17
38		12	A	Nottingham Forest	W	2-0	Greaves, Gilzean	22,92
39		19	H	West Ham United	W	1-0	Greaves	50,97
40		22	H	Southampton	W	2-1	Greaves, Morgan	29,20
41		29	A	Leicester City	L	0-1		35,83
42	May	12	A	Sheffield Wednesday	D	0-0		28,58
								Appearance
								Substitut
								Goa

FA Cup

R3	Jan	4	A	Walsall	W	1-0	Greaves	18,77
R4		25	H	Wolverhampton Wanderers	W	2-1	Johnson, Greaves	48,98
R5	Feb	12	H	Aston Villa	W	3-2	England, Greaves 2 (1 pen)	49,98
R6	Mar	1	A	Manchester City	L	0-1		48,87
								Appearance
								Substitut
								Goa

Football League Cup

R2	Sep	4	A	Aston Villa	W	4-1	Jones, Chivers 3	24,77
R3		25	H	Exeter City	W	6-3	Greaves 3, Pearce 2. Venables	25,79
R4	Oct	16	H	Peterborough United	W	1-0	Greaves	28,37
R5		30	H	Southampton	W	1-0	Collins	35,19
SF	Nov	20	A	Arsenal	L	0-1		55,23
SF	Dec	4	H	Arsenal	D	1-1	Greaves	55,92
								Appearance
								Substitut
								Goa

Beal P	Bond DJT	Chivers MH	Collins PJ	England HM	Evans RL	Gilzean AJ	Greaves JP	Jenkins DJ	Jennings PA	Johnson NJ	Jones CW	Kinnear JP	Knowles CB	Morgan RE	Mullery AP	Pearce JW	Pratt JA	Robertson JG	Venables TF	Want AG
2		9	6	5			8		1				3		4	11		7	10	
6		9		5		11	8		1			2	3		4			7	10	
6		9		5		11	**8**		1			2	3		4	12		7	10	
6		9		5		11	8		1			2	3		4			7	10	
6		9		5		**11**	8		1		12	2	3		4			7	10	
6		9		5		11	8		1		7	2	3		4			12	**10**	
6	10	9		5		11	8		1		**7**	2	3		4			12		
6		9		5		11	8		1			2	3		4			7	10	
6		9		5		11	8		1		7	2	3		4				10	
6		**9**		5		11	8		1		7	2	3		4			12	10	
6				5		11	8		1		7	2	3		4	9			10	
6				5		11	8		1			2			4	9		7	10	3
6				5		11	8		1		7	2			4	9			10	3
6				**5**		7	8		1			2	12		4	9		11	10	3
6			5			11	8	7	1			2	3		4	9			10	
6			5			11	8	7	1			2	3		4	9			10	
6	10		12	5		11	8	**7**	1			2	3		4	9				
6			7	5		11	8		1			2	3		4	9			10	
6			5	9		11	8		1			2	3		4	7			10	
6			**5**	9		11	8		1			2	3		4	7			10	12
6			5	9		11	8	7	1			2	**3**		4	12			10	
6			5	9		11	8	7	1			2	3		4				10	
6			5	9		11	8	7	1			2	3		4				10	
6				5		11	8	7	1			2	3		4	9			10	
6			12	5		11	8	7	1			**2**	3		4	9			10	
2			6	5		9	8	11	1	7			3		4				10	
2			6	5		9	8		1	7			3		4	11			10	
2			6	5			8	9	1				3	11	4	7			10	
2			6	5		9	8		1	12			3	11	4	**7**			10	
2			6	**5**		9	8		1	12			3	11	4	7			10	
2			6	5		9	8		1	12			3	11	4	7			**10**	
2			6	5		9	8		1	7			3		4	11			10	
			6		2	9	8	12	1	11					4	**7**	5		10	3
			6	5	2		8		1	7				11		9	4		10	3
			6	5	2		8		1	7				11	4	**9**	12		10	3
6				5	2		8		1	7			3	11	4	9	10			
				5	2	9	8		1	7			3	11	4				10	
2			5			9	8		1	7			3	**11**	4	12	6		10	
2			12	**5**		9	8		1	7			3	11	4	10	6			
2			5			9	8		1	7			3	11	4		6		10	
				5	12	9	8		1	7			3	11	4		6		10	
2			5			9	8		1	7			3	11	4		6			10
9	2	10	22	36	5	37	42	10	42	13	6	24	36	13	41	24	8	8	37	7
	0	0	3	0	1	0	0	1	0	3	1	0	1	0	0	3	1	3	0	1
		3		3		7	27	2		3	5		2	3	1	3		1		

Beal P	Bond DJT	Chivers MH	Collins PJ	England HM	Evans RL	Gilzean AJ	Greaves JP	Jenkins DJ	Jennings PA	Johnson NJ	Jones CW	Kinnear JP	Knowles CB	Morgan RE	Mullery AP	Pearce JW	Pratt JA	Robertson JG	Venables TF	Want AG
			5	9		11	8	7	1			2	3		4				10	
			6	5		9	8	11	1	7			3		4				10	
			6	5		**9**	8	12	1	7			3		4	11			10	
			6	5		9	8		1	7			3		4	11			10	
	0	0	4	4	0	4	4	2	4	3	0	1	4	0	4	2	0	0	4	0
	0	0	0	0	0	0	0	1	0	0	0	0	0	0	0	0	0	0	0	0
				1			4			1										

Beal P	Bond DJT	Chivers MH	Collins PJ	England HM	Evans RL	Gilzean AJ	Greaves JP	Jenkins DJ	Jennings PA	Johnson NJ	Jones CW	Kinnear JP	Knowles CB	Morgan RE	Mullery AP	Pearce JW	Pratt JA	Robertson JG	Venables TF	Want AG
	10	9		5		11	8		1		7	2	3		4					
				5		11	8		1		7	2	3		4	9			10	
	12		5			11	8		1			2			4	9		7	**10**	3
	7		12	5		11	8		1			2	3		4	9			10	
			5	9		11	8		1			2	3		4	7			10	
			5	9		11	8		1			2	3		4	7			10	
	2	1	3	5		6	6	0	6	0	2	6	5		6	5		1	5	1
	1	0	1	0	0	0	0	0	0	0	0	0	0	0	0	0	0	0	0	0
		3	1				5				1					2			1	

League Table

	P	W	D	L	F	A	Pts
Leeds United	42	27	13	2	66	26	67
Liverpool	42	25	11	6	63	24	61
Everton	42	21	15	6	77	36	57
Arsenal	42	22	12	8	56	27	56
Chelsea	42	20	10	12	73	53	50
TOTTENHAM HOTSPUR	42	14	17	11	61	51	45
Southampton	42	16	13	13	57	48	45
West Ham United	42	13	18	11	66	50	44
Newcastle United	42	15	14	13	61	55	44
West Bromwich Albion	42	16	11	15	64	67	43
Manchester United	42	15	12	15	57	53	42
Ipswich Town	42	15	11	16	59	60	41
Manchester City	42	15	10	17	64	55	40
Burnley	42	15	9	18	55	82	39
Sheffield Wednesday	42	10	16	16	41	54	36
Wolverhampton W	42	10	15	17	41	58	35
Sunderland	42	11	12	19	43	67	34
Nottingham Forest	42	10	13	19	45	57	33
Stoke City	42	9	15	18	40	63	33
Coventry City	42	10	11	21	46	64	31
Leicester City	42	9	12	21	39	68	30
Queen's Park Rangers	42	4	10	28	39	95	18

1969-70

DIVISION ONE

Manager: Bill Nicholson

Did you know that?

Although the FA Youth Cup started in 1952–53, it was not until 1969–70 that Spurs won it for the first time. After winning the first leg of the Final against Coventry City 1–0, Spurs lost the second leg at Highfield Road by the same margin. The first replay ended two-all but a solitary goal from Graeme Souness in the second replay secured the trophy. The winning team included Matt Dillon, Barry Daines and Steve Perryman, who all went on to make the grade with Spurs while Souness, Mike Flanagan and Ray Clarke all found success elsewhere. Spurs have won the trophy twice more, in 1973–74 and 1989–90.

LEAGUE DEBUTANTS

Sep 27	v Sunderland	Steve Perryman
Dec 7	v Ipswich	Roy Woolcott
Jan 17	v Sunderland	Ken Hancock
Mar 21	v Coventry City	Martin Peters
Mar 28	v West Bromwich Albion	Terry Naylor

Match No.	Date		Opponents		Result		Scorers	Attendance
1	Aug	9	A	Leeds United	L	1-3	Greaves	35,80
2		13	H	Burnley	W	4-0	Collins, Pearce, Greaves, Chivers	35,92
3		16	H	Liverpool	L	0-2		50,47
4		19	A	Burnley	W	2-0	Collins, Pearce	19,48
5		23	A	Crystal Palace	W	2-0	Pearce, Chivers	39,49
6		27	H	Chelsea	D	1-1	Pearce	47,66
7		30	H	Ipswich Town	W	3-2	Mullery, Greaves, Gilzean	33,33
8	Sep	6	A	West Ham United	W	1-0	Pearce	40,56
9		13	H	Manchester City	L	0-3		41,64
10		16	A	Arsenal	W	3-2	Chivers, Gilzean, Pratt	55,28
11		20	A	Derby County	L	0-5		41,82
12		27	H	Sunderland	L	0-1		30,52
13	Oct	4	A	Southampton	D	2-2	Greaves, Gilzean	23,90
14		7	A	Liverpool	D	0-0		46,51
15		11	H	Wolverhampton Wanderers	L	0-1		36,73
16		18	H	Newcastle United	W	2-1	Greaves 2	33,28
17		25	A	Stoke City	D	1-1	Gilzean	19,56
18	Nov	1	H	Sheffield Wednesday	W	1-0	Morgan	31,65
19		8	A	Nottingham Forest	D	2-2	Pearce, Greaves	24,03
20		15	H	West Bromwich Albion	W	2-0	Chivers, Morgan	28,34
21		22	A	Manchester United	L	1-3	Chivers	53,05
22	Dec	6	A	Coventry City	L	2-3	England, Gilzean	28,44
23		13	A	Manchester City	D	1-1	Johnson	29,21
24		17	H	Everton	*	0-0		28,49
25		20	H	West Ham United	L	0-2		28,37
26		26	H	Crystal Palace	W	2-0	Mullery, Perryman	32,84
27		27	A	Ipswich Town	L	0-2		24,65
28	Jan	10	H	Derby County	W	2-1	Greaves, Morgan	38,64
29		17	A	Sunderland	L	1-2	Morgan	13,99
30		31	H	Southampton	L	0-1		27,69
31	Feb	7	A	Wolverhampton Wanderers	D	2-2	Chivers 2	27,29
32		14	H	Leeds United	D	1-1	Cooper (og)	41,72
33		21	H	Stoke City	W	1-0	Mullery	29,97
34		28	A	Newcastle United	W	2-1	Pearce, Chivers	34,82
35	Mar	11	H	Everton	L	0-1		27,76
36		14	A	Everton	L	2-3	Gilzean, Bond (pen)	51,53
37		21	H	Coventry City	L	1-2	Peters	34,94
38		27	H	Nottingham Forest	W	4-1	Gilzean 2, Chivers 2	36,94
39		28	A	West Bromwich Albion	D	1-1	Peters	24,89
40		30	A	Sheffield Wednesday	W	1-0	Mullery	30,34
41	Apr	4	A	Chelsea	L	0-1		44,92
42		13	H	Manchester United	W	2-1	Gilzean, Chivers	41,80
43	May	2	H	Arsenal	W	1-0	Gilzean	46,96

*abandoned after 29 mins - floodlight failure

Appearance
Substitut
Goal

FA Cup

R3	Jan	3	A	Bradford City	D	2-2	Greaves, Morgan	23,00
R3r		7	H	Bradford City	W	5-0	Pearce 2, Greaves 2, Morgan	36,03
R4		24	H	Crystal Palace	D	0-0		43,94
R4r		28	A	Crystal Palace	L	0-1		45,98

Appearance
Substitut
Goal

Football League Cup

R2	Sep	3	A	Wolverhampton Wanderers	L	0-1		34,01

Appearance
Substitut
Goal

Beal P	Bond DJT	Chivers MH	Collins PJ	England HM	Evans RL	Gilzean AJ	Greaves JP	Hancock KP	Jenkins DJ	Jennings PA	Johnson NJ	Kinnear JP	Knowles CB	Morgan RE	Mullery AP	Naylor TP	Pearce JW	Perryman SJ	Peters MS	Pratt JA	Want AG	Woolcott RA	Own-goals
2		9	6	5		10	8			1			3	11	4						7		
		9	6	5		10	8			1			3	11	4		7				2		
		9	6	5		10	8			1			3	11	4		7				2		
		9	6	5		10	8			1			3	11	4		7				2		
2		9	6	5		10	8			1			3	11	4		**7**				2		
		9	6	5		10	8			1			3	11	4		7				2		
2		**9**	6	5		10	8			1			3	11	4		7				2		
2			6	5		9	8			1			3	11	**4**		7			10	12		
2		12	6	5		9	8			1			3	11	4		7			**10**			
2		**7**	6	5		9	8			1			3	11	4					10	12		
2			6	5		9	8			1			3	**11**	4		7			10	12		
2	10		6	5		9	8			1			3		4		7	11					
6	10			5		9	8			1			3	7	**4**		12	11			2		
6	10	9		5			8			1			3	7	4			11			2		
	10	9	6	5		7	8			1			3		4			11			2		
6		7		5		9	8			1			3	10	4			11			2		
6		**7**		5		9	8			1			3	10	4		12	11			2		
6				5		9	8			1			3	10	4		7	11			2		
6				5		9	8			1			3	10	4		7	11			2		
6		12		5		9	8			1			3	10	4		7	11			2		
		9		5		10	8			1			3	7	4		11	6			2		
		10	12	5		9	8			1	**7**		3		4			11		6	2		
		9		5	6	10	8			1	7	2	3		4		12	11					
			5		6		8		10	1	7	2	3		4		9	11					
5					6		8			1	7	2	3	10	4		9	11					
5					6	9	8			1	7	2	3	10	**4**		12	11					
5					6	11	8			1	7	2	3		4		12	10				**9**	
6				5		9	8			1		2	3	11	4		7	10					
6		12	5			9	8	1				2	3	11	4		**7**	10					
6	10	7		5	2					1				11	4		9			8	3		
6	10	7		5	2	12				1				11	4		9			**8**	3		
6	10	9		5	2					1				11	4		7			8	3		
6	10	9		5	2	12				1				11	**4**		7			8	3		
6	10	**9**		5	2				12	1				11	4		7			8	3		
6	**10**	9		5	2				12	1				11	4		7			8	3		
6	**10**		12	5	2	9				1				11			7	4		8	3		
6	10	12		5	2	9			**7**	1				11	4				8		3		
6		9	5		2	7				1				11	4			10	8		3		
		9	5			7				1		2	3	11	4	6	12	8	10				
		9		5	12	7				1		2	3	**11**	4	6		10	8				
6		9		5		7				1		2	3	11	4			8	10				
		9		5	2	7				1			3	11	4	6		8	10				
6		9		5	2	7				1			3	11	4		8		10				
29	12	27	17	36	16	34	29	1	2	42	6	10	34	37	42	3	26	24	7	12	26	1	
2	0	4	2	0	1	2	0	0	2	0	0	0	0	0	0	0	6	0	0	0	3	0	
	1	11	2	1		10	8				1			4	4		7	1	2	1			1

Beal P	Bond DJT	Chivers MH	Collins PJ	England HM	Evans RL	Gilzean AJ	Greaves JP	Hancock KP	Jenkins DJ	Jennings PA	Johnson NJ	Kinnear JP	Knowles CB	Morgan RE	Mullery AP	Naylor TP	Pearce JW	Perryman SJ	Peters MS	Pratt JA	Want AG	Woolcott RA	Own-goals
6				5		9	8			1	**7**	2	3	11	4		12	10					
6		12		**5**		9	8			1		2	3	11	4		7	10					
6		12		5		9	8			1		2	3	11	4		**7**	10					
6		7		5		9	8			1		2	3	11	4		12	**10**					
4	0	1	0	4	0	4	4	0	0	4	1	4	4	4	4	0	2	4	0	0	0	0	
0	0	2	0	0	0	0	0	0	0	0	0	0	0	0	0	0	2	0	0	0	0	0	
							3							2			2						

Beal P	Bond DJT	Chivers MH	Collins PJ	England HM	Evans RL	Gilzean AJ	Greaves JP	Hancock KP	Jenkins DJ	Jennings PA	Johnson NJ	Kinnear JP	Knowles CB	Morgan RE	Mullery AP	Naylor TP	Pearce JW	Perryman SJ	Peters MS	Pratt JA	Want AG	Woolcott RA	Own-goals
2		**9**	6	5			8			1			3	11	4		7			12	10		
1	0	1	1	1	0	0	1	0	0	1	0	0	1	1	1	0	1	0	0	0	1	0	
0	0	0	0	0	0	0	0	0	0	0	0	0	0	0	0	0	0	0	0	1	0	0	

League Table

	P	W	D	L	F	A	Pts
Everton	42	29	8	5	72	34	66
Leeds United	42	21	15	6	84	49	57
Chelsea	42	21	13	8	70	50	55
Derby County	42	22	9	11	64	37	53
Liverpool	42	20	11	11	65	42	51
Coventry City	42	19	11	12	58	48	49
Newcastle United	42	17	13	12	57	35	47
Manchester United	42	14	17	11	66	61	45
Stoke City	42	15	15	12	56	52	45
Manchester City	42	16	11	15	55	48	43
TOTTENHAM HOTSPUR	42	17	9	16	54	55	43
Arsenal	42	12	18	12	51	49	42
Wolverhampton W	42	12	16	14	55	57	40
Burnley	42	12	15	15	56	61	39
Nottingham Forest	42	10	18	14	50	71	38
West Bromwich Albion	42	14	9	19	58	66	37
West Ham United	42	12	12	18	51	60	36
Ipswich Town	42	10	11	21	40	63	31
Southampton	42	6	17	19	46	67	29
Crystal Palace	42	6	15	21	34	68	27
Sunderland	42	6	14	22	30	68	26
Sheffield Wednesday	42	8	9	25	40	71	25

1970-71

DIVISION ONE

Manager: Bill Nicholson

Did you know that?

Apart from Spurs and the two Scottish clubs they played, the first Texaco Cup competition featured Airdrie, Ards, Burnley, Derry City, Dundee, Heart of Midlothian, Limerick, Morton, Nottingham Forest, Shamrock Rovers, Stoke City, West Bromwich Albion and Wolverhampton Wanderers. Wolves beat Hearts in the two-leg Final.

LEAGUE DEBUTANTS

Oct 24 v Stoke City Jimmy Neighbour

Match No.	Date			Opponents	Result		Scorers	Attendance
1	Aug	15	H	West Ham United	D	2-2	Gilzean 2	53,640
2		19	H	Leeds United	L	0-2		39,927
3		22	A	Wolverhampton Wanderers	W	3-0	Mullery, Chivers, Morgan	23,896
4		25	A	Southampton	D	0-0		27,149
5		29	H	Coventry City	W	1-0	Chivers	27,103
6	Sep	1	A	Huddersfield Town	D	1-1	Chivers	26,701
7		5	A	Arsenal	L	0-2		48,931
8		12	H	Blackpool	W	3-0	Mullery (pen), Peters 2	19,894
9		19	A	Crystal Palace	W	3-0	Mullery, Chivers 2	41,308
10		26	H	Manchester City	W	2-0	Gilzean, Chivers	42,490
11	Oct	3	A	Derby County	D	1-1	Peters	36,007
12		10	H	Liverpool	W	1-0	Peters	44,547
13		17	A	West Ham United	D	2-2	Mullery, England	42,322
14		24	H	Stoke City	W	3-0	Gilzean, Chivers 2	36,238
15		31	A	Nottingham Forest	W	1-0	Chivers	25,301
16	Nov	7	H	Burnley	W	4-0	Gilzean, Perryman, Chivers 2	30,524
17		14	A	Chelsea	W	2-0	Mullery, Pearce	61,277
18		21	H	Newcastle United	L	1-2	Chivers	38,873
19		28	A	Everton	D	0-0		44,301
20	Dec	5	H	Manchester United	D	2-2	Gilzean, Peters	55,693
21		12	A	West Bromwich Albion	L	1-3	Chivers	26,584
22		19	H	Wolverhampton Wanderers	D	0-0		30,544
23	Jan	9	A	Leeds United	W	2-1	Chivers 2	43,867
24		16	H	Southampton	L	1-3	Chivers	39,486
25		30	H	Everton	W	2-1	Gilzean, Chivers	42,105
26	Feb	6	A	Manchester United	L	1-2	Peters	48,416
27		17	H	West Bromwich Albion	D	2-2	Mullery (pen), Gilzean	22,695
28		20	A	Newcastle United	L	0-1		31,718
29	Mar	10	H	Nottingham Forest	L	0-1		21,697
30		13	H	Chelsea	W	2-1	Chivers, Peters	49,292
31		20	A	Burnley	D	0-0		16,376
32		23	A	Ipswich Town	W	2-1	Gilzean, Peters	21,718
33	Apr	3	A	Coventry City	D	0-0		22,947
34		7	H	Derby County	W	2-1	Chivers, Pearce	25,627
35		10	H	Ipswich Town	W	2-0	Chivers, Morris (og)	28,708
36		12	A	Blackpool	D	0-0		16,541
37		17	A	Liverpool	D	0-0		46,363
38		24	H	Crystal Palace	W	2-0	Perryman, Blyth (og)	28,619
39		28	H	Huddersfield Town	D	1-1	Chivers	18,959
40	May	1	A	Manchester City	W	1-0	Perryman	19,761
41		3	H	Arsenal	L	0-1		51,992
42		5	A	Stoke City	W	1-0	Peters	14,019

Appearances
Substitute
Goals

FA Cup

R3	Jan	2	H	Sheffield Wednesday	W	4-1	Mullery, Gilzean 2, Peters	34,170
R4		23	A	Carlisle United	W	3-2	Gilzean, Peters, Neighbour	25,369
R5	Feb	13	H	Nottingham Forest	W	2-1	Gilzean, Chivers	46,366
R6	Mar	6	A	Liverpool	D	0-0		54,731
R6r		16	H	Liverpool	L	0-1		56,283

Appearances
Substitute
Goals

Football League Cup

R2	Sep	9	H	Swansea City	W	3-0	Perryman, Peters, Morgan	15,848
R3	Oct	7	H	Sheffield United	W	2-1	Chivers, Pearce	23,559
R4		28	H	West Bromwich Albion	W	5-0	Gilzean 2, Peters 3	31,598
R5	Nov	18	H	Coventry City	W	4-1	Gilzean, Chivers 3	31,864
SF	Dec	16	A	Bristol City	D	1-1	Gilzean	30,201
SF		23	H	Bristol City	W*	2-0	Chivers, Pearce	29,982
F	Feb	27	N#	Aston Villa	W	2-0	Chivers 2	100,000

* after extra-time #played at Wembley Stadium

Appearances
Substitute
Goals

Texaco Cup

R1	Sep	16	H	Dunfermline Athletic	W	4-0	England, Chivers 3	16,388
R1		29	A	Dunfermline Athletic	W	3-0	Chivers, Peters 2	9,000
R2	Oct	21	H	Motherwell	W	3-2	Chivers, Peters 2	19,670
R2	Nov	3	A	Motherwell	L	1-3	Pearce	22,688

Appearances
Substitute
Goals

Bond DJT	Chivers MH	Collins PJ	England HM	Evans RL	Gilzean AJ	Hancock KP	Jennings PA	Johnson NJ	Kinnear JP	Knowles CB	Morgan RE	Mullery AP	Naylor TP	Neighbour JE	Pearce JW	Perryman SJ	Peters MS	Pratt JA	Want AG	Own-goals
6	9		5	2	7		1			3		4			11	8	10			
	9	6	5	2	7		1			3		4			11	8	10			
	9	6	5		7		1		2	3	11	4				8	10			
12	9	6	5				1		2	3	11	4			**7**	8	10			
	9	6	5		7		1		2	3	**11**	4			12	8	10			
	9	**6**	5		7		1		2	3	11	4			12	8	10			
	9		5		7	1			2		11	4				8	10		3	
	9		5	2	7		1			3	11	4				8	10			
	9		5		7	1		12	2	3		4			**11**	8	10			
	9		5		7		1		2	3	**11**	4			12	8	10			
	9		5				1		2	3	11	4			7	8	10			
	9		5		7		1		2	3		4			11	8	10			
	9		5		7		1		2	3		4			11	8	10			
	9		5		**7**		1		2	3		4		12	11	8	10			
	9		5		7		1		2	3		4	12		11	**8**	10			
	9		5		7		1		2	3		4			11	8	10			
	9		5		7		1	12	2	3		4			11	**8**	10			
	9	6	5		7		1		2	3		4		12	**11**	8	10			
	9	6	5		7		1		2	3		4			11	8	10			
	9		5		7		1		2	3		4		12	11	**8**	10			
	9		5		7		1		2	3		4			11	8	10			
	9		5		7		1		2	3		4		12	**11**	8	10			
	9	5			7		1		2	3		4	6	**11**	12	8	10			
	9	**5**			7		1	12	2	3		4	6		11	8	10			
	9	5			7		1		2	3		4		11		8	10			
	9	5		2	7		1			3		4		11		8	10			
	9	5			7		1		2	3		4		11		8	10			
	9	5			7		1		2	3		4		**11**	12	8	10			
	9	5					1		2	3		4		11	7	8	10			
	9	5			**7**		1		2	3		4		12		8	10	11		
	9	**5**					1		2	3		4		11	12	8	10	7		
	9				7		1		2	**3**		4	5		11	8	10	12		
	9	5			7		1		2			4			11	8	10		3	
	9	5			7		1		2			4			11	8	10		3	
	9	5			7		1		2	3		4			11	8	10			
	9	5		2	**7**		1			3		4			11	8	10	12		
	9	5			7		1		**2**	3		4			12	8	10	11		
	9	5		2	7		1			**3**		4		11	12	8	10			
	9	5			7		1		2	3		4		11		8	10			
	9	5			7		1		2	3				11		8	10	4		
	9	5			**7**		1		2	3		4		11	12	8	10			
	9	5		2	**7**		1					4		11	12	8	10		3	
1	42	26	22	7	38	2	40	0	35	38	8	41	3	12	23	42	42	4	4	
1	0	0	0	0	0	0	0	3	0	0	0	0	1	5	10	0	0	2	0	
	21		1		9						1	6			2	3	9			2

Bond DJT	Chivers MH	Collins PJ	England HM	Evans RL	Gilzean AJ	Hancock KP	Jennings PA	Johnson NJ	Kinnear JP	Knowles CB	Morgan RE	Mullery AP	Naylor TP	Neighbour JE	Pearce JW	Perryman SJ	Peters MS	Pratt JA	Want AG	Own-goals
	9	5			7		1		2	3		4	6	11		8	10			
	9				7		1		2	3		4	5	11		8	10			
	9	5			7		1		2	3		4		11		8	10			
	9	5					1		2	3		4		11		8	10	7		
	9	5					1		2	3		4		11		8	10	7		
0	5	4	0	0	3	0	5	0	5	5	0	5	2	5	0	5	5	2	0	
0	0	0	0	0	0	0	0	0	0	0	0	0	0	0	0	0	0	0	0	
	1				4							1		1			2			

Bond DJT	Chivers MH	Collins PJ	England HM	Evans RL	Gilzean AJ	Hancock KP	Jennings PA	Johnson NJ	Kinnear JP	Knowles CB	Morgan RE	Mullery AP	Naylor TP	Neighbour JE	Pearce JW	Perryman SJ	Peters MS	Pratt JA	Want AG	Own-goals
	9		5		7	1			2		11	**4**			12	8	10		3	
	9		5		7		1		2	3	**11**	4			12	8	10			
	9		5		7		1		2	3		4			11	8	10			
	9		5		7		1		2	3		4		12	11		10	8		
	9		5		7		1		2	3		4			11	8	10			
	9		5		7		1		2	3		4		**11**	12	8	10			
	9	5			7		1		2	3		4		11		8	10			
0	7	1	6	0	7	1	6	0	7	6	2	7	0	2	3	6	7	1	1	
0	0	0	0	0	0	0	0	0	0	0	0	0	0	1	3	0	0	0	0	
	7				4						1				2	1	4			

Bond DJT	Chivers MH	Collins PJ	England HM	Evans RL	Gilzean AJ	Hancock KP	Jennings PA	Johnson NJ	Kinnear JP	Knowles CB	Morgan RE	Mullery AP	Naylor TP	Neighbour JE	Pearce JW	Perryman SJ	Peters MS	Pratt JA	Want AG	Own-goals
	9		5		7	1			2		**11**	4			12	8	10		3	
	9		5		**7**		1		2	3	11	4			12	8	10			
	9		5		7		1		2	3		4	6		11	8	10			
	9		5		7	1			2	3		4	**8**	12	11		10			
0	4	0	4	0	4	2	2	0	4	3	2	4	2	0	2	3	4	0	1	
0	0	0	0	0	0	0	0	0	0	0	0	0	0	1	2	0	0	0	0	
	5		1												1		4			

League Table

	P	W	D	L	F	A	Pts
Arsenal	42	29	7	6	71	29	65
Leeds United	42	27	10	5	72	30	64
TOTTENHAM HOTSPUR	42	19	14	9	54	33	52
Wolverhampton W	42	22	8	12	64	54	52
Liverpool	42	17	17	8	42	24	51
Chelsea	42	18	15	9	52	42	51
Southampton	42	17	12	13	56	44	46
Manchester United	42	16	11	15	65	66	43
Derby County	42	16	10	16	56	54	42
Coventry City	42	16	10	16	37	38	42
Manchester City	42	12	17	13	47	42	41
Newcastle United	42	14	13	15	44	46	41
Stoke City	42	12	13	17	44	48	37
Everton	42	12	13	17	54	60	37
Huddersfield Town	42	11	14	17	40	49	36
Nottingham Forest	42	14	8	20	42	61	36
West Bromwich Albion	42	10	15	17	58	75	35
Crystal Palace	42	12	11	19	39	57	35
Ipswich Town	42	12	10	20	42	48	34
West Ham United	42	10	14	18	47	60	34
Burnley	42	7	13	22	29	63	27
Blackpool	42	4	15	23	34	66	23

1971-72

DIVISION ONE

Manager: Bill Nicholson

Did you know that?

Spurs' match against Leeds United was played at Hull City's Boothferry Park on 25 August 1971 because Elland Road had been closed due to hooliganism.

LEAGUE DEBUTANTS

Aug 14 v Wolves
Ralph Coates
Nov 20 v West Bromwich Albion
Barry Daines
Dec 18 v Liverpool
Phil Holder

Match No.	Date		Venue	Opponents	Result		Scorers	Attendance
1	Aug	14	A	Wolverhampton Wanderers	D	2-2	Chivers, Gilzean	30,4
2		18	H	Newcastle United	D	0-0		42,7
3		21	H	Huddersfield Town	W	4-1	Chivers 2, Gilzean 2	33,2
4		25	A*	Leeds United	D	1-1	Gilzean	25,0
5		28	A	Manchester City	L	0-4		33,6
6	Sep	4	H	Liverpool	W	2-0	Chivers, Peters	50,1
7		11	A	Sheffield United	D	2-2	Peters, Gilzean	41,6
8		18	H	Crystal Palace	W	3-0	Mullery, Chivers, Peters (pen)	37,2
9		25	A	Coventry City	L	0-1		26,5
10	Oct	2	H	Ipswich Town	W	2-1	Chivers, Peters	33,5
11		9	A	Derby County	D	2-2	Pearce, Chivers	35,7
12		16	H	Wolverhampton Wanderers	W	4-1	Neighbour, Chivers 2, Gilzean	36,5
13		23	H	Nottingham Forest	W	6-1	Mullery, Chivers, Peters 2 (1 pen), Pearce 2	35,8
14		30	A	Stoke City	L	0-2		28,5
15	Nov	6	H	Everton	W	3-0	Pratt, Chivers 2	40,0
16		13	A	Manchester United	L	1-3	Chivers	54,0
17		20	H	West Bromwich Albion	W	3-2	England, Gilzean 2	31,8
18		24	H	Arsenal	D	1-1	Chivers	52,8
19		27	A	Chelsea	L	0-1		52,5
20	Dec	4	H	Southampton	W	1-0	Gilzean	31,3
21		11	A	Leicester City	W	1-0	Peters	30,7
22		18	A	Liverpool	D	0-0		43,4
23		27	H	West Ham United	L	0-1		53,8
24	Jan	1	A	Crystal Palace	D	1-1	Chivers	35,5
25		8	H	Manchester City	D	1-1	Peters	36,4
26		22	A	Newcastle United	L	1-3	Gilzean	30,1
27		29	H	Leeds United	W	1-0	Chivers	46,7
28	Feb	12	A	Nottingham Forest	W	1-0	Peters	20,2
29		19	H	Stoke City	W	2-0	Chivers 2	32,8
30	Mar	1	A	Everton	D	1-1	Peters	21,6
31		4	H	Manchester United	W	2-0	Perryman, Chivers	54,8
32		11	H	Derby County	L	0-1		36,3
33		25	H	Sheffield United	W	2-0	Gilzean, Chivers	30,9
34		28	A	Huddersfield Town	D	1-1	Pearce	16,1
35		31	H	Coventry City	W	1-0	Chivers	32,5
36	Apr	1	A	West Ham United	L	0-2		30,7
37		3	A	Ipswich Town	L	1-2	Chivers	24,3
38		8	A	West Bromwich Albion	D	1-1	Chivers	20,8
39		15	H	Chelsea	W	3-0	Chivers 2, Coates	45,7
40		22	A	Southampton	D	0-0		24,9
41		29	H	Leicester City	W	4-3	Knowles 2 (1 pen), England, Pearce	19,6
42	May	11	A	Arsenal	W	2-0	Mullery, Coates	42,0

*played at Boothferry Park, Hull

Appearance
Substitut
Goa

FA Cup

Round	Date		Venue	Opponents	Result		Scorers	Attendance
R3	Jan	15	H	Carlisle United	D	1-1	Gilzean	33,7
R3r		18	A	Carlisle United	W	3-1	Gilzean, Chivers 2	21,5
R4	Feb	5	H	Rotherham United	W	2-0	Gilzean, Peters	36,9
R5		26	A	Everton	W	2-0	Gilzean, Peters	50,5
R6	Mar	18	A	Leeds United	L	1-2	Pratt	43,9

Appearance
Substitu
Goa

Football League Cup

Round	Date		Venue	Opponents	Result		Scorers	Attendance
R2	Sep	8	A	West Bromwich Albion	W	1-0	Pearce	26,1
R3	Oct	6	A	Torquay United	W	4-1	Pearce, Chivers 2, Peters (pen)	20,2
R4		27	H	Preston North End	D	1-1	Chivers	30,3
R4r	Nov	8	A	Preston North End	W*	2-1	Perryman, Chivers	27,2
R5		17	H	Blackpool	W	2-0	Chivers, Peters	30,0
SF	Dec	22	A	Chelsea	L	2-3	Naylor, Chivers	43,3
SF	Jan	5	H	Chelsea	D	2-2	Chivers, Peters (pen)	52,7

*after extra-time

Appearance
Substitut
Goal

Anglo-Italian League Cup-Winners' Cup

Date		Venue	Opponents	Result		Scorers	Attendance
Sep	1	A	AC Torino	W	1-0	Chivers	28,0
	22	H	AC Torino	W	2-0	Chivers, Gilzean	34,10

Appearance
Substitut
Goa

eal P	Chivers MH	Coates R	Collins PJ	Daines BR	England HM	Evans RL	Gilzean AJ	Holder P	Jennings PA	Kinnear JP	Knowles CB	Morgan RE	Mullery AP	Naylor TP	Neighbour JE	Pearce JW	Perryman SJ	Peters MS	Pratt JA	Want AG
	9	7			5		11		1	2	3		4				8	10		
	9	7			5		11		1	2			4		12		8	10		3
	9	7			5		11		1	2			4	6			8		10	3
	9	7	12		5		11		1	2			4	6			8		10	3
	9	7			5		11		1	2			4	6			8	10		3
	9	7			5		11		1	2	3		4				8	10	12	
	9	7			5		11		1	2	3		4				8	10	12	
	9	7			5		11		1	2	3		4				8	10		
	9	7			5		11		1	2	3		4			12	8	10		
	9	7			5		11		1	2	3		4				8	10		
	9		5			2	11		1		3		4			7	8	10	12	
	9				5		11		1	2	3		4		7		8	10		
	9				5		11		1	2	3		4		7	12	8	10		
	9				5	2			1		3		4		11	7	8	10	12	
	9				5	2	11		1		3				7		8	10	4	
	9				5	2	7		1		3				11	12	8	10	4	
	9	4		1	5	2	11				3				7		8	10		
	9	4			5	2	11		1		3				7		8	10		
	9	4			5	2	11		1		3				7		8	10	12	
	9	4			5	2	11		1		3				7		8	10		
	9	4	5			2	11		1		3						8	10	7	
	9	4			5	2		12	1					8		11		10	7	3
	9	4			5	2	11		1		3				12		8	10	7	
	9	4			5	2	11		1		3						8	10	7	
	9	4			5	2	7		1						11	12	8	10		3
	9	4			5		7		1	2	3	12		11			8	10		
	9	4			5	2	7		1		3	11					8	10		
	9	4			5	2	7	8	1		3	11						10		
	9	4			5	2	7	12	1		3	11					8	10		
	9				5	2	7		1		3			6	11		8	10	4	
	9				5	2	7	4	1		3	11					8	10	12	
	9				5	2	7	4	1		3	11					8	10		
	9	4			5	2	7	10	1		3	11		6			8		12	
		4			5		7		1	2	3			6		9	8	10	11	
	9	4			5		7		1	2	3	11				12		10	8	
	9		5			2	7		1		3	12		6		11	8	10	4	
	9	4	5			2			1	12		11		6		7	8		10	3
	9	4			5		7		1	2	3		11	6			8	10		
	9	11	6		5		7		1	2	3		4			12	8	10		
	9	7	6		5				1	2			4	11		10	8		12	
		4			5		9		1	2	3				11	7	8		10	
		11			5		7		1	2	3		4			9	8		10	
2	39	32	6	1	38	22	38	4	41	20	34	8	18	12	12	9	39	35	15	7
0	0	0	1	0	0	0	0	2	0	1	0	2	0	0	2	6	0	0	8	0
	25	2			2		11				2		3		1	5	1	10	1	

eal P	Chivers MH	Coates R	Collins PJ	Daines BR	England HM	Evans RL	Gilzean AJ	Holder P	Jennings PA	Kinnear JP	Knowles CB	Morgan RE	Mullery AP	Naylor TP	Neighbour JE	Pearce JW	Perryman SJ	Peters MS	Pratt JA	Want AG
	9	4			5	2	7		1						11		8	10		3
	9	4	12		5		7		1	2	3			11			8	10		
	9	4			5	2	7		1		3				11	12	8	10		
	9				5	2	7		1		3	11					8	10	4	
	9	12			5	2	7		1		3	11					8	10	4	
5	5	3	0	0	5	4	5	0	5	1	4	2	0	1	2	0	5	5	2	1
0	0	1	1	0	0	0	0	0	0	0	0	0	0	0	0	1	0	0	0	0
	2						4											2	1	

eal P	Chivers MH	Coates R	Collins PJ	Daines BR	England HM	Evans RL	Gilzean AJ	Holder P	Jennings PA	Kinnear JP	Knowles CB	Morgan RE	Mullery AP	Naylor TP	Neighbour JE	Pearce JW	Perryman SJ	Peters MS	Pratt JA	Want AG
6	9	7			5				1	2	3		4			11	8	10		
6	9	7			5		11		1	2	3		4			12	8	10		
6	9				5	2			1		3		4		7	11	8	10		
6	9		12		5	2	7		1		3				11		8	10	4	
6	9	7			5	2	11		1		3				12		8	10	4	
6	9	4			5	2			1		3			8		11		10	7	
6	9	7			5	2	11		1		3					12	8	10	4	
7	7	5	0	0	7	5	4	0	7	2	7	0	3	1	2	3	6	7	4	0
0	0	0	1	0	0	0	0	0	0	0	0	0	0	0	1	2	0	0	0	0
	7													1		2	1	3		

eal P	Chivers MH	Coates R	Collins PJ	Daines BR	England HM	Evans RL	Gilzean AJ	Holder P	Jennings PA	Kinnear JP	Knowles CB	Morgan RE	Mullery AP	Naylor TP	Neighbour JE	Pearce JW	Perryman SJ	Peters MS	Pratt JA	Want AG
6	9	7			5		11		1	2			4				8	10		3
6	9	7			5		11		1	2	3		4				8	10		
2	2	2	0	0	2	0	2	0	2	2	1	0	2	0	0	0	2	2	0	1
0	0	0	0	0	0	0	0	0	0	0	0	0	0	0	0	0	0	0	0	0
	2						1													

League Table

	P	W	D	L	F	A	Pts
Derby County	42	24	10	8	69	33	58
Leeds United	42	24	9	9	73	31	57
Liverpool	42	24	9	9	64	30	57
Manchester City	42	23	11	8	77	45	57
Arsenal	42	22	8	12	58	40	52
TOTTENHAM HOTSPUR	42	19	13	10	63	42	51
Chelsea	42	18	12	12	58	49	48
Manchester United	42	19	10	13	69	61	48
Wolverhampton W	42	18	11	13	65	57	47
Sheffield United	42	17	12	13	61	60	46
Newcastle United	42	15	11	16	49	52	41
Leicester City	42	13	13	16	41	46	39
Ipswich Town	42	11	16	15	39	53	38
West Ham United	42	12	12	18	47	51	36
Everton	42	9	18	15	37	48	36
West Bromwich Albion	42	12	11	19	42	54	35
Stoke City	42	10	15	17	39	56	35
Coventry City	42	9	15	18	44	67	33
Southampton	42	12	7	23	52	80	31
Crystal Palace	42	8	13	21	39	65	29
Nottingham Forest	42	8	9	25	47	81	25
Huddersfield Town	42	6	13	23	27	59	25

1972-73

DIVISION ONE

Manager: Bill Nicholson

Did you know that?

The pressure all visitors to Anfield must face means Liverpool fans have witnessed some of football's finest goalkeeping displays, but on 31 March 1973 even they were stunned by Pat Jennings's performance. Jennings was superb and crowned his display with two penalty saves, the first from Kevin Keegan, the second, five minutes from time, from Tommy Smith that had Smith beating the ground in frustration and even referee Raby applauding.

LEAGUE DEBUTANTS

Oct 28 v Manchester United
Matt Dillon

Apr 21 v Leicester City
Ray Clarke

Match No.	Date			Opponents	Result		Scorers	Attendance
1	Aug	12	H	Coventry City	W	2-1	Peters 2	33,88
2		16	A	West Bromwich Albion	W	1-0	Peters	19,17
3		19	A	Wolverhampton Wanderers	L	2-3	Pratt, Peters	24,23
4		23	H	Birmingham City	W	2-0	Chivers, Coates	30,79
5		26	H	Leeds United	D	0-0		41,19
6		30	A	Newcastle United	W	1-0	Kinnear	27,91
7	Sep	2	A	Ipswich Town	D	1-1	Peters (pen)	23,14
8		9	H	Crystal Palace	W	2-1	England, Peters (pen)	28,54
9		16	A	Manchester City	L	1-2	Peters	31,75
10		23	H	West Ham United	W	1-0	Lampard (og)	51,29
11		30	A	Derby County	L	1-2	Perryman	32,13
12	Oct	7	H	Stoke City	W	4-3	Pratt 2, Gilzean, Coates	31,95
13		14	A	Norwich City	L	1-2	Chivers	34,44
14		21	H	Chelsea	L	0-1		47,42
15		28	A	Manchester United	W	4-1	Peters 4	52,49
16	Nov	4	A	Birmingham City	D	0-0		38,50
17		11	H	West Bromwich Albion	D	1-1	Chivers	25,87
18		18	A	Leicester City	W	1-0	Chivers	22,70
19		25	H	Liverpool	L	1-2	Chivers	45,49
20	Dec	2	A	Southampton	D	1-1	Chivers	16,48
21		9	H	Arsenal	L	1-2	Peters	47,51
22		16	A	Everton	L	1-3	Neighbour	31,12
23		23	H	Sheffield United	W	2-0	Perryman, Chivers	19,87
24		26	A	West Ham United	D	2-2	Peters, Pearce	37,39
25	Jan	6	A	Leeds United	L	1-2	Gilzean	32,40
26		20	H	Ipswich Town	L	0-1		33,01
27		27	A	Crystal Palace	D	0-0		44,53
28	Feb	10	H	Manchester City	L	2-3	Chivers 2	30,94
29		17	A	Coventry City	W	1-0	Pratt	26,85
30		24	H	Everton	W	3-0	Gilzean, Chivers, Pearce	27,42
31	Mar	10	H	Norwich City	W	3-0	Chivers 2 (1 pen), Pearce	25,08
32		14	A	Stoke City	D	1-1	Pearce	23,35
33		24	H	Manchester United	D	1-1	Chivers	50,01
34		31	A	Liverpool	D	1-1	Gilzean	48,47
35	Apr	3	A	Chelsea	W	1-0	Pratt	25,53
36		7	H	Southampton	L	1-2	Peters	23,69
37		14	A	Arsenal	D	1-1	Chivers	50,86
38		18	H	Derby County	W	1-0	McFarland (og)	22,65
39		21	H	Leicester City	D	1-1	Gilzean	23,31
40		28	H	Newcastle United	W	3-2	Chivers 2 (1 pen), Peters	21,72
41		30	H	Wolverhampton Wanderers	D	2-2	Coates, Collins	16,94
42	May	2	A	Sheffield United	L	2-3	Collins, Chivers (pen)	20,71

Appearances
Substitute
Goals

FA Cup

R3	Jan	13	A	Margate	W	6-0	Knowles, Pratt, Pearce, Chivers 2, Peters	8,50
R4	Feb	3	A	Derby County	D	1-1	Chivers	37,89
R4r		7	H	Derby County	L*	3-5	England (pen), Gilzean, Chivers	52,73

*after extra-time

Appearances
Substitute
Goals

Football League Cup

R2	Sep	6	H	Huddersfield Town	W	2-1	Gilzean, Chivers	21,422
R3	Oct	3	A	Middlesbrough	D	1-1	Pearce	23,822
R3r		11	H	Middlesbrough	D*	0-0		19,256
R3r		30	H	Middlesbrough	W*	2-1	Gilzean, Peters	19,287
R4	Nov	1	H	Millwall	W	2-0	Perryman, Peters	28,904
R5	Dec	4	A	Liverpool	D	1-1	Peters	48,677
R5r		6	H	Liverpool	W	3-1	Pratt, Chivers 2	34,565
SF		20	A	Wolverhampton Wanderers	W	2-1	Pratt, Peters	28,327
SF		30	H	Wolverhampton Wanderers	D*	2-2	Chivers, Peters	41,653
F	Mar	3	N#	Norwich City	W	1-0	Coates	100,000

*after extra-time #played at Wembley Stadium

Appearances
Substitute
Goals

eal P	Chivers MH	Clarke RC	Coates R	Collins PJ	Daines BR	Dillon ML	England HM	Evans RL	Gilzean AJ	Jennings PA	Kinnear JP	Knowles CB	Naylor TP	Neighbour JE	Pearce JW	Perryman SJ	Peters MS	Pratt JA	Own-goals
	9		11				5		7	1	2	3				8	10	4	
	9		11				5		7	1	2	3				8	10	4	
	9		11				5		7	1	2	3				8	10	4	
	9		11				5		7	1	**2**	3	12			8	10	4	
	9		**11**				5	2	7	1		3			12	8	10	4	
	9						5		**7**	1	2	3	12		11	8	10	4	
	9						5		7	1	2	3			11	8	10	4	
	9		11				5		7	1	**2**	3	6		12	8	10	4	
			11				5	2	7	1		3			9	8	10	4	
	9		12				5	2	7	1		3			11	8	**10**	4	
	9		11				5		**7**	1	2	3	10		12	8		4	
	9		11				5		7	1	2	3				8	10	4	
	9		11				5		7	1	2	3	4		12	8	**10**		
	9		11				5		7	1	2	3			12	8	10	**4**	
	9		**11**			6	5	2		1		3		12	7	8	10	4	
	9		**11**				5	2	7	1		3	6		4	8	10	12	
	9				1		5	2	7			3	6		11	8	10	4	
	9						5	2	7	1		3	6		11	8	10	4	
	9						5	2	7	1		3	6		11	8	10	4	
	9						5	2	7	1		3	6		11	8	10	4	
	9		12				5	2		1		3	6	**7**	11	8	10	4	
			6			5		2	7	1	3			9	11	8	10	4	
	9		11				5	2	7	1		3	6			8	10	4	
	9		7			5		2		1		3	6		11	8	10	4	
	9						5	2	7	1		3	6		11	8	10	4	
	9		11				5	2	7	1		3	6		8		10	4	
	9		11				5	2	7	1		3	**6**		12	8	10	4	
	9		12				5		7	1	2	3			11	8	10	**4**	
	9						5		7	1	2	3			11	8	10	4	
	9						5		7	1	2	3			11	8	10	4	
	9		4	5						1	2	3		7	11	8	10		
	9		4	5						1	2	3		7	11	8	10		
	9		4			5			7	1	2	3			11	8	10		
	9		4					5	**7**	1	2	3			12	8	10	11	
	9		4	5				3		1	2				11	8	10	7	
	9		4		1		5		7		**2**	3			12	8	10	11	
	9		**4**				5	12	7	1	2	3				8	10	11	
			4				5	3	7	1	2				9	8	10	11	
		12		5		6		3	**7**	1	2			11	9	8	10	4	
	9		4	5		6		3	7	1					11	8	10	2	
	9		4	5		6		3	7	1					11	8	10	2	
	9		4	5		6		2		1				7	11	8	10	3	
	38	0	29	7	2	8	31	23	35	40	24	35	14	6	27	41	41	37	
	0	1	3	0	0	0	0	1	0	0	0	0	2	1	8	0	0	1	
	17		3	2			1		5		1			1	4	2	15	5	2

eal P	Chivers MH	Clarke RC	Coates R	Collins PJ	Daines BR	Dillon ML	England HM	Evans RL	Gilzean AJ	Jennings PA	Kinnear JP	Knowles CB	Naylor TP	Neighbour JE	Pearce JW	Perryman SJ	Peters MS	Pratt JA	Own-goals
	9		11				5	2	7	1		3	6		12	**8**	10	4	
	9		11				5		**7**	1	2	3			12	8	10	4	
	9		**11**				5	2	7	1		3			12	8	10	4	
	3	0	3	0	0	0	3	2	3	3	1	3	1	0	0	3	3	3	
	0	0	0	0	0	0	0	0	0	0	0	0	0	0	3	0	0	0	
	4						1		1			1			1		1	1	

eal P	Chivers MH	Clarke RC	Coates R	Collins PJ	Daines BR	Dillon ML	England HM	Evans RL	Gilzean AJ	Jennings PA	Kinnear JP	Knowles CB	Naylor TP	Neighbour JE	Pearce JW	Perryman SJ	Peters MS	Pratt JA	Own-goals
	9		11				5		7	1	2	3	12		10	8		4	
	9		11				5			1	2	3	10		7	8		4	
	9		11				5		7	1	2	3	6		12	8	10	**4**	
	9		11			6	5	2	12	1		3			7	8	10	**4**	
	9		12				5	2	**7**	1		3	6		4	8	10	11	
	9						5	2	7	1		3	6		11	8	10	4	
	9						5	2	**7**	1		3	6	12	11	8	10	4	
	9						5	2	7	1		3	6		11	8	10	4	
	9		12				5	2	**7**	1		3	6		11	8	10	4	
	9		12				5		7	1	2	3			11	8	10	**4**	
	10	0	4	0	0	1	10	6	8	10	4	10	7	0	9	10	8	10	
	0	0	3	0	0	0	0	0	1	0	0	0	1	1	1	0	0	0	
	4		1						2						1	1	5	2	

League Table

	P	W	D	L	F	A	Pts
Liverpool	42	25	10	7	72	42	60
Arsenal	42	23	11	8	57	43	57
Leeds United	42	21	11	10	71	45	53
Ipswich Town	42	17	14	11	55	45	48
Wolverhampton W	42	18	11	13	66	54	47
West Ham United	42	17	12	13	67	53	46
Derby County	42	19	8	15	56	54	46
TOTTENHAM HOTSPUR	42	16	13	13	58	48	45
Newcastle United	42	16	13	13	60	51	45
Birmingham City	42	15	12	15	53	54	42
Manchester City	42	15	11	16	57	60	41
Chelsea	42	13	14	15	49	51	40
Southampton	42	11	18	13	47	52	40
Sheffield United	42	15	10	17	51	59	40
Stoke City	42	14	10	18	61	56	38
Leicester City	42	10	17	15	40	46	37
Everton	42	13	11	18	41	49	37
Manchester United	42	12	13	17	44	60	37
Coventry City	42	13	9	20	40	55	35
Norwich City	42	11	10	21	36	63	32
Crystal Palace	42	9	12	21	41	58	30
West Bromwich Albion	42	9	10	23	38	62	28

1973-74

DIVISION ONE

Manager: Bill Nicholson

Did you know that?

Alan Gilzean brought his long and distinguished career with Spurs to a close on the end-of-season trip to Mauritius. Having scored twice in each of Spurs' first two games against a Mauritius Select XI, he was welcomed onto the field for his final game on 16 June 1974 by the local band playing *For he's a jolly good fellow*. He signed off in the best possible manner, scoring a hat-trick before being carried around the ground by his teammates on a lap of honour.

LEAGUE DEBUTANTS

Oct 13	v Arsenal Chris McGrath
Apr 3	v Chelsea Neil McNab
May 11	v Newcastle United Terry Lee
May 11	v Newcastle United Keith Osgood

Match No.	Date			Opponents	Result		Scorers	Attendanc
1	Aug	25	A	Coventry City	L	0-1		25,09
2		28	A	Birmingham City	W	2-1	Peters 2	37,75
3	Sep	1	H	Leeds United	L	0-3		42,09
4		5	H	Burnley	L	2-3	Knowles, Chivers	25,54
5		8	A	West Ham United	W	1-0	Chivers	30,88
6		11	A	Burnley	D	2-2	Holder, Peters	25,15
7		15	H	Sheffield United	L	1-2	Chivers	26,35
8		22	A	Liverpool	L	2-3	Chivers, Peters	42,90
9		29	H	Derby County	W	1-0	Coates	31,40
10	Oct	6	A	Ipswich Town	D	0-0		23,90
11		13	H	Arsenal	W	2-0	Gilzean, Chivers	41,85
12		20	A	Norwich City	D	1-1	Gilzean	24,81
13		27	H	Newcastle United	L	0-2		31,25
14	Nov	3	A	Everton	D	1-1	Perryman	37,82
15		10	H	Manchester United	W	2-1	Knowles, Chivers	42,75
16		17	A	Southampton	D	1-1	Chivers	22,88
17		24	H	Wolverhampton Wanderers	L	1-3	Chivers (pen)	22,54
18	Dec	1	A	Leicester City	L	0-3		22,08
19		8	H	Stoke City	W	2-1	Evans, Pratt	14,03
20		15	H	Manchester City	L	0-2		17,06
21		22	A	Derby County	L	0-2		23,67
22		26	H	Queen's Park Rangers	D	0-0		30,76
23		29	H	West Ham United	W	2-0	Pratt, Chivers	33,17
24	Jan	1	A	Leeds United	D	1-1	McGrath	46,56
25		12	A	Sheffield United	D	2-2	McGrath, Coates	20,36
26		19	H	Coventry City	W	2-1	Peters 2	20,98
27	Feb	2	A	Manchester City	D	0-0		24,65
28		6	H	Birmingham City	W	4-2	Dillon, Chivers 3	14,34
29		16	A	Arsenal	W	1-0	McGrath	38,89
30		23	H	Ipswich Town	D	1-1	Pratt	26,28
31	Mar	2	A	Queen's Park Rangers	L	1-3	Chivers (pen)	25,77
32		16	H	Norwich City	D	0-0		18,47
33		23	A	Manchester United	W	1-0	Coates	36,27
34		30	H	Everton	L	0-2		19,83
35	Apr	3	H	Chelsea	L	1-2	Evans	23,64
36		6	A	Wolverhampton Wanderers	D	1-1	McGrath	24,07
37		13	H	Southampton	W	3-1	Pratt, Chivers 2	21,45
38		15	A	Chelsea	D	0-0		26,25
39		20	A	Stoke City	L	0-1		20,18
40		27	H	Leicester City	W	1-0	Chivers	20,11
41	May	8	H	Liverpool	D	1-1	McGrath	24,61
42		11	A	Newcastle United	W	2-0	Chivers, Gilzean	21,60

Appearance
Substitu
Goa

FA Cup

R3	Jan	5	A	Leicester City	L	0-1		28,28

Appearance
Substitu
Goa

Football League Cup

R2	Oct	8	A	Queen's Park Rangers	L	0-1		23,35

Appearance
Substitu
Goa

Chivers MH	Coates R	Daines BR	Dillon ML	England HM	Evans RL	Gilzean AJ	Holder P	Jennings PA	Kinnear JP	Knowles CB	Lee TWG	McGrath RC	McNab N	Naylor TP	Neighbour JE	Osgood K	Perryman SJ	Peters MS	Pratt JA
9	4		5		2	7	12	1		3					**11**		8	10	
9	11		5		2	4		1		3					7		8	10	
9	4		5		2	7		1		3					11		8	10	
9	11		5		2	7		1		3							8	10	4
9	4		5		2	**7**		1	12	3					11		8	10	
9	4		5		2		7	1	12	3					**11**		8	10	
9	4		5		2	7		1		3					11		8	10	
9				5	2	**7**	11	1	12	3							8	10	4
9	11	1		5	2	7				3							8	10	4
9	11	1		5	2	7				3							8	10	4
9		1		5	2	7				3		11					8	10	4
9	11	1		5	2	**7**				3		12		6			8	10	4
	11	1		5	2	7				3		**9**			12		8	10	4
	11			5	2	7		1		3				9			8	10	4
9				5	2	12		1		3		11		7			8	10	4
9	11			5	2			1		3		7					8	10	4
9	11			5	2	7		1		3		12					8	10	**4**
9	11			5	2			1		3				7			8	10	4
9	11			5	2			1		**3**		7		12	10		8		4
9	11			5	2	12		1				7		3			8	10	**4**
9	11			5	2	7		1						3			8	10	4
12	11			5	2	7		1				**9**		3			8	10	4
9	**11**			5	2	7		1				12		3			8	10	4
9			7	5	2			1				11		**3**	12		8	10	4
9	**11**		12	5	2			1				7		3			8	10	4
9	11			5	2			1				7		3	12		8	10	**4**
9	11			5	2			1				7		3			8	10	4
9	11		12	5	2			1				7		3			8	**10**	4
9	11			5	2	10		1				7		3			8		4
9	11			5	2			1				7		3			8	10	4
9	11		5		2	12		1				7		3			8	10	4
9	11		12	5	2			1				**7**		3			8	10	4
9	11			5	2			1				7		3			8	10	4
9	11			**5**	2	12		1				7		3			8	10	4
9	11		5		2	10		1	8			7	12	**3**					4
9	8			5	2			1	12			7		3	**11**			10	4
9				5	2	11	10	1						3	7		8		4
9			11	5	2		10	1						3	7		8		4
9	7		10	5			12	1	2					3	11		8		**4**
9	11			5			4	1	2			7		3			8	10	
9	11			5	2			1				7		3			8	10	4
9	7		3	5	2	11				8	1			10		12			4
39	36	5	13	33	40	21	5	36	3	20	1	22	0	27	11	0	39	35	35
1	0	0	3	0	0	4	2	0	4	0	0	3	1	1	3	1	0	0	0
17	3		1		2	3	1			2		5					1	6	4

Chivers MH	Coates R	Daines BR	Dillon ML	England HM	Evans RL	Gilzean AJ	Holder P	Jennings PA	Kinnear JP	Knowles CB	Lee TWG	McGrath RC	McNab N	Naylor TP	Neighbour JE	Osgood K	Perryman SJ	Peters MS	Pratt JA
9			3	5	2	7		1							11		8	10	4
1	0	0	1	1	1	1	0	1	0	0	0	0	0	0	1	0	1	1	1
0	0	0	0	0	0	0	0	0	0	0	0	0	0	0	0	0	0	0	0

Chivers MH	Coates R	Daines BR	Dillon ML	England HM	Evans RL	Gilzean AJ	Holder P	Jennings PA	Kinnear JP	Knowles CB	Lee TWG	McGrath RC	McNab N	Naylor TP	Neighbour JE	Osgood K	Perryman SJ	Peters MS	Pratt JA
9	**11**	1		5	2	7				3				4			8	10	12
1	1	1	0	1	1	1	0	0	0	1	0	0	0	1	0	0	1	1	0
0	0	0	0	0	0	0	0	0	0	0	0	0	0	0	0	0	0	0	1

League Table

	P	W	D	L	F	A	Pts
Leeds United	42	24	14	4	66	31	62
Liverpool	42	22	13	7	52	31	57
Derby County	42	17	14	11	52	42	48
Ipswich Town	42	18	11	13	67	58	47
Stoke City	42	15	16	11	54	42	46
Burnley	42	16	14	12	56	53	46
Everton	42	16	12	14	50	48	44
Queen's Park Rangers	42	13	17	12	56	52	43
Leicester City	42	13	16	13	51	41	42
Arsenal	42	14	14	14	49	51	42
TOTTENHAM HOTSPUR	42	14	14	14	45	50	42
Wolverhampton W	42	13	15	14	49	49	41
Sheffield United	42	14	12	16	44	49	40
Manchester City	42	14	12	16	39	46	40
Newcastle United	42	13	12	17	49	48	38
Coventry City	42	14	10	18	43	54	38
Chelsea	42	12	13	17	56	60	37
West Ham United	42	11	15	16	55	60	37
Birmingham City	42	12	13	17	52	64	37
Southampton	42	11	14	17	47	68	36
Manchester United	42	10	12	20	38	48	32
Norwich City	42	7	15	20	37	62	29

1974-75

DIVISION ONE

Manager: Bill Nicholson until September then Terry Neill

Did you know that?

In an effort to reduce congestion at the refreshment bars, October 1974 saw the introduction of kiosks in the upper sections of the East and West stands and the terraces below at White Hart Lane, solely for the sale of cigarettes, tobacco and cigars. From July 2006 the entire stadium, including the car park, became a smoke-free area.

LEAGUE DEBUTANTS

Aug 17	v Ipswich Town Chris Jones
Oct 26	v Luton Town John Duncan
Dec 7	v Newcastle United Alfie Conn
Feb 15	v Coventry City Don McAllister

Match No.	Date			Opponents	Result		Scorers	Attendanc
1	Aug	17	H	Ipswich Town	L	0-1		26,44
2		21	A	Manchester City	L	0-1		31,54
3		24	A	Carlisle United	L	0-1		18,42
4		28	H	Manchester City	L	1-2	Peters	20,07
5		31	H	Derby County	W	2-0	Neighbour 2	20,67
6	Sep	7	A	Liverpool	L	2-5	Perryman, Chivers	47,53
7		14	H	West Ham United	W	2-1	England, Chivers	27,95
8		21	A	Wolverhampton Wanderers	W	3-2	Chivers 2, Peters	20,64
9		28	H	Middlesbrough	L	1-2	Neighbour	23,28
10	Oct	5	H	Burnley	L	2-3	Pratt, England	18,44
11		12	A	Chelsea	L	0-1		32,66
12		16	H	Carlisle United	D	1-1	Chivers	12,81
13		19	H	Arsenal	W	2-0	Perryman, Chivers	36,29
14		26	A	Luton Town	D	1-1	Chivers	22,42
15	Nov	2	A	Stoke City	D	2-2	Duncan 2	24,66
16		9	H	Everton	D	1-1	Chivers	29,05
17		16	A	Leicester City	W	2-1	Coates, Peters	23,24
18		23	H	Birmingham City	D	0-0		27,76
19		30	A	Sheffield United	W	1-0	Duncan	20,28
20	Dec	4	A	Leeds United	L	1-2	Duncan	25,83
21		7	H	Newcastle United	W	3-0	Knowles 2, Chivers	23,42
22		14	A	Ipswich Town	L	0-4		20,81
23		21	H	Queen's Park Rangers	L	1-2	Duncan	21,15
24		26	A	West Ham United	D	1-1	Peters	37,68
25		28	H	Coventry City	D	1-1	Smith (og)	20,30
26	Jan	11	A	Newcastle United	W	5-2	Knowles, Conn 3, Duncan	39,67
27		18	H	Sheffield United	L	1-3	Duncan	15,81
28	Feb	1	A	Everton	L	0-1		40,91
29		8	H	Stoke City	L	0-2		22,94
30		15	A	Coventry City	D	1-1	Duncan	15,22
31		18	A	Birmingham City	L	0-1		24,24
32		22	H	Leicester City	L	0-3		20,93
33	Mar	1	A	Derby County	L	1-3	Jones	22,99
34		15	A	Middlesbrough	L	0-3		25,63
35		22	H	Liverpool	L	0-2		34,33
36		28	H	Wolverhampton Wanderers	W	3-0	Perryman 2, Duncan	27,23
37		29	A	Queen's Park Rangers	W	1-0	Duncan	25,46
38	Apr	5	H	Luton Town	W	2-1	Conn, Duncan	25,79
39		12	A	Burnley	L	2-3	Perryman, Duncan	17,86
40		19	H	Chelsea	W	2-0	Conn, Perryman	50,99
41		26	A	Arsenal	L	0-1		43,76
42		28	H	Leeds United	W	4-2	Knowles 2 (1 pen), Conn, Chivers	49,88

Appearance
Substitut
Goa

FA Cup

R3	Jan	4	A	Nottingham Forest	D	1-1	Chivers	23,35
R3r		8	H	Nottingham Forest	L	0-1		27,99

Appearance
Substitut
Goa

Football League Cup

R2	Sep	11	H	Middlesbrough	L	0-4		15,21

Appearance
Substitut
Goa

Beal P	Chivers MH	Coates R	Conn AJ	Daines BR	Duncan JP	England HM	Evans RL	Jennings PA	Jones CH	Kinnear JP	Knowles CB	McAllister D	McGrath RC	McNab N	Naylor TP	Neighbour JE	Osgood K	Perryman SJ	Peters MS	Pratt JA	Own-goals
		6				4	2	1	9				7		3	11	5	8	10		
6		4					2	1	9				7		3	11	5	8	10		
4		6				5	2	1	**9**				12		3	11		8	10	7	
6	9	4				5	2	1					7		3	11		8	10		
6	9	11				5	2	1							3	7		8	10	4	
6	9	11				**5**	2	1					12		3	7		8	10	4	
6	9	11				5	2	1			3					7		8	10	4	
6	9	11				5	2	1			3				12	7		8	**10**	4	
6	9	11				5	2	1			3					7		8	10	4	
6	9	11				5	2	1			3		10			7		8		4	
6	9					5	2	1	10		3				11	7		8		4	
	9	11				5	2	1	10		3				6	7		8		4	
	9	12				5	2	1	11		3				6	7		**8**	10	4	
	9	12			11	5	2	1			3				6	**7**		8	10	4	
3	9	7			11	5	2	1							6			8	10	4	
3	9	7			11	5	2	1							6	12		8	10	4	
3	9	7			11	5	2	1							6			8	10	4	
3	9	7			11	5	2	1					12		6			8	10	**4**	
	9	7			11	5	2	1			3				6			8	10	4	
	9	7			11	5	2	1			3				6			8	10	4	
2	**9**	7	12		11	5		1			3			4	6			8	10		
2		7			11	5		1			3		9	**4**	6			8	10	12	
2	9	7			11	5		1			3				6	12		8	10	4	
	9	7			11	5		1		2	3				6			8	10	4	
	9	7			11	5		1		2	3				6	12		8	10	4	
4			9		11	5	12	1		2	3				6	**7**		8	10		
4			9		11	5		1		2	3				6	7		8	10		
4	9		7		11	5		1		2					6			8	10	3	
4	9	12	7	1	11	5					3				6			8	**10**	2	
	9		7		11	5		1		2	3	4			6			8	10		
	9	12	7		11	5		1		2	3	4			**6**			8	10		
	9		7		11	5		1		2	3	4			**6**	12		8	10		
		10	7		11			1	9	2	3	4			6			8		5	
		10	7		11			1	9	2	3	4			6			8		5	
		10	7		11			1	9	2	**3**	4	12		6		5	8			
4			7		10			1	9	2	3				6	11	5	8			
4					10			1	9	**2**	3	12			6	11	5	8		7	
4	12		7		10			1	9	2	3					**11**	5	8		6	
4		10	7		11			1	9		3	2			6		5	8			
4			7		10			1	9	2	3				6	11	5	8			
4			7		10			1	9	2	3				6	**11**	5	8		12	
4	9		7					1	10	2	3				6		5	8		11	
28	27	26	16	1	28	31	20	41	16	17	31	7	5	2	37	21	10	42	29	27	
0	1	4	1	0	0	0	1	0	0	0	0	1	4	0	1	4	0	0	0	2	
	10	1	6		12	2			1		5					3		6	4	1	1

Beal P	Chivers MH	Coates R	Conn AJ	Daines BR	Duncan JP	England HM	Evans RL	Jennings PA	Jones CH	Kinnear JP	Knowles CB	McAllister D	McGrath RC	McNab N	Naylor TP	Neighbour JE	Osgood K	Perryman SJ	Peters MS	Pratt JA	Own-goals
	9	7			11	5		1		2	3				6			8	10	4	
		7	9		11	5		1		2	3				6	12		8	**10**	4	
0	1	2	1	0	2	2	0	2	0	2	2	0	0	0	2	0	0	2	2	2	
0	0	0	0	0	0	0	0	0	0	0	0	0	0	0	0	1	0	0	0	0	
	1																				

Beal P	Chivers MH	Coates R	Conn AJ	Daines BR	Duncan JP	England HM	Evans RL	Jennings PA	Jones CH	Kinnear JP	Knowles CB	McAllister D	McGrath RC	McNab N	Naylor TP	Neighbour JE	Osgood K	Perryman SJ	Peters MS	Pratt JA	Own-goals
6	9	11	12				2	1					10		3	7	**5**	8		4	
1	1	1	0	0	0	0	1	1	0	0	0	0	1	0	1	1	1	1	0	1	
0	0	0	1	0	0	0	0	0	0	0	0	0	0	0	0	0	0	0	0	0	

League Table

	P	W	D	L	F	A	Pts
Derby County	42	21	11	10	67	49	53
Liverpool	42	20	11	11	60	39	51
Ipswich Town	42	23	5	14	66	44	51
Everton	42	16	18	8	56	42	50
Stoke City	42	17	15	10	64	48	49
Sheffield United	42	18	13	11	58	51	49
Middlesbrough	42	18	12	12	54	40	48
Manchester City	42	18	10	14	54	54	46
Leeds United	42	16	13	13	57	49	45
Burnley	42	17	11	14	68	67	45
Queen's Park Rangers	42	16	10	16	54	54	42
Wolverhampton W	42	14	11	17	57	54	39
West Ham United	42	13	13	16	58	59	39
Coventry City	42	12	15	15	51	62	39
Newcastle United	42	15	9	18	59	72	39
Arsenal	42	13	11	18	47	49	37
Birmingham City	42	14	9	19	53	61	37
Leicester City	42	12	12	18	46	60	36
TOTTENHAM HOTSPUR	42	13	8	21	52	63	34
Luton Town	42	11	11	20	47	65	33
Chelsea	42	9	15	18	42	72	33
Carlisle United	42	12	5	25	43	59	29

1975-76

DIVISION ONE

Manager: Terry Neill

Did you know that?

Prior to the match against Manchester City on 18 October 1975, Pat Jennings was presented with a silver salver by Ted Ditchburn to mark Jennings overtaking Ditchburn's record of 418 Football League games for Spurs. Jennings went on to make 472 League appearances for Spurs, a total surpassed only by Steve Perryman's 655.

LEAGUE DEBUTANTS

Aug 30 v Norwich City
Ian Smith
Aug 30 v Norwich City
Glenn Hoddle
Sep 20 v Leeds United
Willie Young
Dec 13 v Liverpool
Steve Walford
Feb 21 v Stoke City
Micky Stead
Feb 28 v Leicester City
Martin Robinson
Mar 13 v Aston Villa
Noel Brotherston

Match No.	Date		Opponents		Result		Scorers	Attendance
1	Aug	16	H	Middlesbrough	W	1-0	Perryman	25,502
2		20	H	Ipswich Town	D	1-1	Duncan	28,351
3		23	A	Liverpool	L	2-3	Jones, Duncan	42,729
4		25	A	West Ham United	L	0-1		36,567
5		30	H	Norwich City	D	2-2	Pratt, Duncan	23,140
6	Sep	6	A	Manchester United	L	2-3	Chivers, Jones	51,641
7		13	H	Derby County	L	2-3	Chivers, Duncan	28,455
8		20	A	Leeds United	D	1-1	Pratt	27,372
9		27	H	Arsenal	D	0-0		37,064
10	Oct	4	A	Newcastle United	D	2-2	Pratt, Duncan	33,290
11		11	A	Aston Villa	D	1-1	Pratt	40,048
12		18	H	Manchester City	D	2-2	Jones 2	30,554
13		25	A	Leicester City	W	3-2	Coates, Perryman, Chivers	22,088
14	Nov	1	H	Wolverhampton Wanderers	W	2-1	Young, Neighbour	26,102
15		8	A	Queen's Park Rangers	D	0-0		28,434
16		15	H	Stoke City	D	1-1	Jones	25,698
17		22	A	Manchester City	L	1-2	Osgood	31,457
18		29	H	Burnley	W	2-1	Duncan 2	21,222
19	Dec	6	A	Sheffield United	W	2-1	Duncan 2	22,949
20		10	H	Everton	D	2-2	Pratt, Duncan	18,638
21		13	H	Liverpool	L	0-4		29,891
22		20	A	Middlesbrough	L	0-1		22,046
23		26	H	Birmingham City	L	1-3	Chivers (pen)	21,651
24		27	A	Coventry City	D	2-2	Duncan 2	21,125
25	Jan	10	A	Derby County	W	3-2	McAllister, Perryman, Neighbour	28,085
26		17	H	Manchester United	D	1-1	Duncan	49,189
27		31	A	Ipswich Town	W	2-1	Osgood (pen), Coates	24,049
28	Feb	7	H	West Ham United	D	1-1	Duncan	32,832
29		14	H	Queen's Park Rangers	L	0-3		28,190
30		21	A	Stoke City	W	2-1	Hoddle, Duncan	17,110
31		24	A	Everton	L	0-1		18,126
32		28	H	Leicester City	D	1-1	Chivers	21,427
33	Mar	6	A	Norwich City	L	1-3	Chivers	20,460
34		13	H	Aston Villa	W	5-2	McAllister, Perryman, Duncan, Robinson, Nicholl (og)	24,169
35		16	A	Wolverhampton Wanderers	W	1-0	Pratt	21,544
36		20	A	Burnley	W	2-1	Pratt, Duncan	15,490
37		27	H	Sheffield United	W	5-0	Young, Perryman 2, Chivers, Duncan	21,370
38	Apr	3	A	Arsenal	W	2-0	Pratt, Duncan	42,031
39		10	H	Leeds United	D	0-0		40,365
40		17	A	Birmingham City	L	1-3	Pratt	30,616
41		19	H	Coventry City	W	4-1	Pratt, Osgood, Duncan, Neighbour	21,107
42		24	H	Newcastle United	L	0-3		29,649
								Appearances
								Substitute
								Goals

FA Cup

R3	Jan	3	H	Stoke City	D	1-1	Duncan	26,715
R3r		24	A	Stoke City	L	1-2	Perryman	29,751
								Appearances
								Substitute
								Goals

Football League Cup

R2	Sep	9	A	Watford	W	1-0	Jones	14,997
R3	Oct	8	A	Crewe Alexandra	W	2-0	Pratt, Conn	10,561
R4	Nov	12	H	West Ham United	D	0-0		49,161
R4r		24	A	West Ham United	W*	2-0	Young, Duncan	38,443
R5	Dec	3	H	Doncaster Rovers	W	7-2	Pratt, Chivers 2, Duncan 3, Chappell (og)	25,702
SF	Jan	14	H	Newcastle United	W	1-0	Pratt	40,215
SF		21	A	Newcastle United	L	1-3	McAllister	49,657
								Appearances
								Substitute
								Goals

*after extra-time

Brotherston N	Chivers MH	Coates R	Conn AJ	Daines BR	Duncan JP	Hoddle G	Jennings PA	Jones CH	Kinnear JP	Knowles CB	McAllister D	McGrath RC	McNab N	Naylor TP	Neighbour JE	Osgood K	Perryman SJ	Pratt JA	Robinson MJ	Smith IR	Stead MJ	Walford SJ	Young WD	Own-goals
	9						1	10	2		6		7	3	11	5	8	4						
	9				12		1	10		3	6		7	**2**	11	5	8	4						
	9		7		11		1	10		3	6			2		5	8	4						
	9		7		**11**		1	10		3	6		12	2		5	8	4						
					11	12	1	10		**3**	6		7	8	9	5		4		2				
	12				11		1	10			6		7	3	9	5	8	4		**2**				
	4				9		1	10			6		7	3	11	5	8	2						
					9		1	10		3			7	2	11	6	8	4					5	
	12				**9**		1	10		3			7	2	11	6	8	4					5	
		12			9		1	10		**3**			7	2	11	6	8	4					5	
	10		7		**9**		1	12			3			2	11	6	8	4					5	
	9		7				1	10		3	2				11	6	8	4					5	
	9	3	7				1	10			2				11	6	8	4					5	
	9	4	**7**				1	10			3		12		11	6	8	2					5	
	9	7			12		1	10			3			2	11	6	8	4					5	
		7	11		9		1	10			**3**	12		2		6	8	4					5	
		7	12		**9**		1	10			3			2	11	6	8	4					5	
		7			9		1	10		3			12	2	**11**	6	8	4					5	
		7			9		1	10			3		8	2	11	6		4					5	
		7			9		1	10		3			12	2	11	6	8	4					5	
					9		1	**10**			3		7	2	11	6	8	4				12	5	
	9				10		1				3	7		2	11	6	8	4					5	
	9				10		1	12			3	**7**	11	2		6	8	4					5	
	9				10		1	12			3	**7**		2	11	6	8	4					5	
	9	7			10		1				3			2	11	6	8	4					5	
	9	7			10		1				3			2	11	6	8	4					5	
		7			9		1	10			3				11	6	8	4				2	5	
	12	7			9		1	10			3			2	**11**	6	8	4					5	
	12	**7**			9		1	10			3			2	11	6	8	4					5	
	10				**9**	7	1	12			3				11	6	8	4			2		5	
	10				9	7	1				3				11	6	8	4			2		5	
	9	12				7	1							2	11	6	8	**4**	10		3		5	
	9	7			10		1	12			3			**2**	11	6	8	4					5	
11	9	7			10	4	1				3			2		6	8		12				5	
	9	7			10	11	1				3			2		6	8	4					5	
	9	7		1	10	11					3			2		6	8	4					5	
	9	**7**		1	10			12			3			2	11	6	8	4					5	
	9				10		1	7			3			2	11	6	8	4					5	
	9	12			10		1	**7**			3			2	11	6	8	4					5	
	9	7			10		1	12			3			2	**11**	6	8	4					5	
	9	7			10		1	12			3			2	11	6	8	4					5	
	9	7			10		1	12						2	11	6	8	4			3		5	
1	28	21	7	2	35	6	40	25	1	10	35	3	11	36	35	42	40	41	1	2	4	1	35	
0	4	3	1	0	2	1	0	9	0	0	0	1	4	0	0	0	0	0	1	0	0	1	0	
	7	2			20	1		5			2				3	3	6	10	1				2	1

Brotherston N	Chivers MH	Coates R	Conn AJ	Daines BR	Duncan JP	Hoddle G	Jennings PA	Jones CH	Kinnear JP	Knowles CB	McAllister D	McGrath RC	McNab N	Naylor TP	Neighbour JE	Osgood K	Perryman SJ	Pratt JA	Robinson MJ	Smith IR	Stead MJ	Walford SJ	Young WD	Own-goals
	9	**7**			10		1	12			3			2	11	6	8	4					5	
		7			9		1	10			3			2	11	6	8	4					5	
0	1	2	0	0	2	0	2	1	0	0	2	0	0	2	2	2	2	2	0	0	0	0	2	
0	0	0	0	0	0	0	0	1	0	0	0	0	0	0	0	0	0	0	0	0	0	0	0	
					1												1							

Brotherston N	Chivers MH	Coates R	Conn AJ	Daines BR	Duncan JP	Hoddle G	Jennings PA	Jones CH	Kinnear JP	Knowles CB	McAllister D	McGrath RC	McNab N	Naylor TP	Neighbour JE	Osgood K	Perryman SJ	Pratt JA	Robinson MJ	Smith IR	Stead MJ	Walford SJ	Young WD	Own-goals
	4			1	9			10			6		11	3	7	5	8	2						
	10	8	7		9		1				3			2	11	6		4					5	
		7	12		**9**		1	10			3			2	11	6	8	4					5	
		7			9		1	10		12	**3**			2	11	6	8	4					5	
	9	7			10		1			3			12	2	11	6	8	**4**					5	
	9	7			10		1				3			2	11	6	8	4					5	
	9	7			10		1	12			3			2	11	**6**	8	4					5	
0	5	6	1	1	7	0	6	3	0	1	6	0	1	7	7	7	6	7	0	0	0	0	6	
0	0	0	1	0	0	0	0	1	0	1	0	0	1	0	0	0	0	0	0	0	0	0	0	
	2		1		4			1			1							3					1	1

League Table

	P	W	D	L	F	A	Pts
Liverpool	42	23	14	5	66	31	60
Queen's Park Rangers	42	24	11	7	67	33	59
Manchester United	42	23	10	9	68	42	56
Derby County	42	21	11	10	75	58	53
Leeds United	42	21	9	12	65	46	51
Ipswich Town	42	16	14	12	54	48	46
Leicester City	42	13	19	10	48	51	45
Manchester City	42	16	11	15	64	46	43
TOTTENHAM HOTSPUR	42	14	15	13	63	63	43
Norwich City	42	16	10	16	58	58	42
Everton	42	15	12	15	60	66	42
Stoke City	42	15	11	16	48	50	41
Middlesbrough	42	15	10	17	46	45	40
Coventry City	42	13	14	15	47	57	40
Newcastle United	42	15	9	18	71	62	39
Aston Villa	42	11	17	14	51	59	39
Arsenal	42	13	10	19	47	53	36
West Ham United	42	13	10	19	48	71	36
Birmingham City	42	13	7	22	57	75	33
Wolverhampton W	42	10	10	22	51	68	30
Burnley	42	9	10	23	43	66	28
Sheffield United	42	6	10	26	33	82	22

1976-77

DIVISION ONE

Manager: Keith Burkinshaw

Did you know that?

Double winner Ron Henry was in charge of the Spurs Juniors when he was suddenly called up in an emergency to play for the reserves against Reading on 5 March 1977. It was the first time Henry, 42, had played for eight years. A groin injury meant his reappearance only lasted 15 minutes.

LEAGUE DEBUTANTS

Aug 21 v Ipswich Town
Gerry Armstrong
Sep 4 v Manchester United
Ian Moores
Oct 2 v West Bromwich Albion
Peter Taylor
Oct 20 v Birmingham City
Andy Keeley
Nov 13 v Bristol City
John Gorman
Mar 12 v West Bromwich Albion
Jimmy Holmes

Match No.	Date		Opponents		Result		Scorers	Attendance
1	Aug	21	A	Ipswich Town	L	1-3	Jones	28,490
2		25	H	Newcastle United	L	0-2		24,022
3		28	H	Middlesbrough	D	0-0		21,721
4	Sep	4	A	Manchester United	W	3-2	Coates, Pratt, Moores	60,723
5		11	H	Leeds United	W	1-0	Jones	34,725
6		18	A	Liverpool	L	0-2		47,421
7		25	H	Norwich City	D	1-1	Hoddle	22,440
8	Oct	2	A	West Bromwich Albion	L	2-4	Jones, Taylor	23,461
9		16	A	Derby County	L	2-8	Osgood (pen), Perryman	24,216
10		20	H	Birmingham City	W	1-0	Osgood (pen)	20,193
11		23	H	Coventry City	L	0-1		21,877
12		30	H	Everton	D	3-3	McAllister, Osgood (pen), Pratt	26,047
13	Nov	6	A	West Ham United	L	3-5	Hoddle, Osgood (pen), Duncan	28,997
14		13	H	Bristol City	L	0-1		28,795
15		20	A	Sunderland	L	1-2	Moores	30,325
16		27	H	Stoke City	W	2-0	Osgood 2 (1 pen)	22,500
17	Dec	11	H	Manchester City	D	2-2	Taylor 2	24,608
18		18	A	Leicester City	L	1-2	Coates	16,397
19		27	H	Arsenal	D	2-2	Young, Duncan	47,751
20	Jan	1	H	West Ham United	W	2-1	Osgood (pen), Duncan	44,972
21		11	A	Queen's Park Rangers	L	1-2	Duncan	24,266
22		22	H	Ipswich Town	W	1-0	Taylor	35,126
23	Feb	5	A	Middlesbrough	L	0-2		21,231
24		12	H	Manchester United	L	1-3	Jones	49,946
25		19	A	Leeds United	L	1-2	Armstrong	26,858
26		26	A	Newcastle United	L	0-2		30,236
27	Mar	5	A	Norwich City	W	3-1	Pratt, Armstrong, Taylor	22,949
28		9	H	Liverpool	W	1-0	Coates	32,098
29		12	H	West Bromwich Albion	L	0-2		28,834
30		19	A	Birmingham City	W	2-1	Jones, Hoddle	23,398
31		23	H	Derby County	D	0-0		27,359
32		26	A	Everton	L	0-4		32,549
33	Apr	2	A	Coventry City	D	1-1	Taylor	16,210
34		9	H	Queen's Park Rangers	W	3-0	Jones 2, Taylor	32,680
35		11	A	Arsenal	L	0-1		47,432
36		12	A	Bristol City	L	0-1		27,568
37		16	H	Sunderland	D	1-1	Jones	34,155
38		20	A	Aston Villa	L	1-2	Armstrong	42,047
39		23	A	Stoke City	D	0-0		15,644
40		30	H	Aston Villa	W	3-1	Hoddle, Jones, Taylor	30,690
41	May	7	A	Manchester City	L	0-5		37,919
42		14	H	Leicester City	W	2-0	Pratt, Holmes	26,094
								Appearances
								Substitute
								Goals

FA Cup

R3	Jan	8	A	Cardiff City	L	0-1		27,868
								Appearances
								Substitute
								Goals

Football League Cup

R2	Aug	31	A	Middlesbrough	W	2-1	Moores, Neighbour	19,042
R3	Sep	22	H	Wrexham	L	2-3	Hoddle, Moores	19,156
								Appearances
								Substitute
								Goals

Armstrong GJ	Coates R	Conn AJ	Daines BR	Duncan JP	Gorman J	Hoddle G	Holmes JA	Jennings PA	Jones CH	Keeley AJ	McAllister D	McNab N	Moores IR	Naylor TP	Neighbour JE	Osgood K	Perryman SJ	Pratt JA	Stead MJ	Taylor PJ	Young WD
9	7		1						10		3			2	11	6	8	4			5
9	**7**	12	1						10		3			2	11	6	8	4			5
9	7		1			4			10		3			2	11	6	8				5
	7		1			4			10		3		9	2	11	6	8	12			5
	7		1			4			10		3		9	2	11	**6**	8	12			5
	7					4		1	10		3		9	2	11	6	8				5
		7				4		1	10				9	2	11	6	8	5	3		
	12	7				4		1	10				9	2		6	8	5	**3**	11	
		7				4		1	10				9	2		3	8	6		11	5
						4		1	10	2	3	12	9			6	8	**7**		11	5
	7					4		1	10	2	3	12	**9**			6	8			11	5
		10		**9**		4		1			3	12		2		6	8	7		11	5
	12	10	1	9		4					3			2		6	8	7		11	5
		7		9	3	4		1						2		6	8	10		11	5
		7			3	4		1					9	2		6	8	10		11	5
	10	7			3	4		1					9	2		6	8			11	5
	10	7			3	4		1					9	2		6	8			11	5
	10	**7**			3	4		1					9	2		6	8	12		11	5
	10	7		9	3	**4**		1						2		6	8	12		11	5
	10	7		9	3	4		1						2		6	8	5		11	
	10			9	3	4		1	7		12			2		6	8	5		11	
				9	3	4		1	7	5		10		2		6	8			11	
			1	9	3	4			7	5		10		2		6	8			11	
				9	3	4		1	7	5		10		2		6	8			11	
9	12				3	**4**		1	7			10		2		6	8	11			5
9	10		1		3				7			11		2		6	8	4			5
9	10		1		3	5			8					2		6	7	4		11	
9	10		1		**3**	6			7		12			2		5	8	4		11	
9	10		1			6	3		7			12		2		5	**8**	4		11	
9	10		1			8	3		7					2		5	6	4		11	
9	10		1			8	3		7					2		5	6	4		11	
9	10		1			8	3		7					2		5	6	4		11	
9	10		1			8	3		7					2		5	6	4		11	
9	10		1			8	3		7					2		5	6	4		11	
9	10		1			8	3		7					2		5	6	4		11	
9			1			8	**3**		7	12		10		2		5	6	4		11	
9	10		1			8			7					2		5	6	4	3	11	
12	10					8		1	7				9	2		5	6	4	3	**11**	
11	10					8	7	1					9	2		5	6	4	3		
11	10					8		1	7				**9**	2		5	6	4	3	12	
9	10					8		1	7				12	2		5	6	4	3	**11**	
11						8	10	1					9	2		5	6	4	3	7	
20	28	12	19	9	15	39	10	23	31	5	10	6	16	40	7	42	42	30	8	31	19
1	3	1	0	0	0	0	0	0	0	1	2	4	1	0	0	0	0	4	0	1	0
3	3			4		4	1		9		1		2			7	1	4		8	1

Armstrong GJ	Coates R	Conn AJ	Daines BR	Duncan JP	Gorman J	Hoddle G	Holmes JA	Jennings PA	Jones CH	Keeley AJ	McAllister D	McNab N	Moores IR	Naylor TP	Neighbour JE	Osgood K	Perryman SJ	Pratt JA	Stead MJ	Taylor PJ	Young WD
	10	7		9	3	4		1			12			2		6	8	5		11	
0	1	1	0	1	1	1	0	1	0	0	0	0	0	1	0	1	1	1	0	1	0
0	0	0	0	0	0	0	0	0	0	0	1	0	0	0	0	0	0	0	0	0	0

Armstrong GJ	Coates R	Conn AJ	Daines BR	Duncan JP	Gorman J	Hoddle G	Holmes JA	Jennings PA	Jones CH	Keeley AJ	McAllister D	McNab N	Moores IR	Naylor TP	Neighbour JE	Osgood K	Perryman SJ	Pratt JA	Stead MJ	Taylor PJ	Young WD
	7		1			4			10		3		9	2	11	6	**8**	12			5
	7					4		1	10		3		9	2	11	6	8	12			5
0	2	0	1	0	0	2	0	1	2	0	2	0	2	2	2	2	2	0	0	0	2
0	0	0	0	0	0	0	0	0	0	0	0	0	0	0	0	0	0	2	0	0	0
						1							2		1						

League Table

	P	W	D	L	F	A	Pts
Liverpool	42	23	11	8	62	33	57
Manchester City	42	21	14	7	60	34	56
Ipswich Town	42	22	8	12	66	39	52
Aston Villa	42	22	7	13	76	50	51
Newcastle United	42	18	13	11	64	49	49
Manchester United	42	18	11	13	71	62	47
West Bromwich Albion	42	16	13	13	62	56	45
Arsenal	42	16	11	15	64	59	43
Everton	42	14	14	14	62	64	42
Leeds United	42	15	12	15	48	51	42
Leicester City	42	12	18	12	47	60	42
Middlesbrough	42	14	13	15	40	45	41
Birmingham City	42	13	12	17	63	61	38
Queen's Park Rangers	42	13	12	17	47	52	38
Derby County	42	9	19	14	50	55	37
Norwich City	42	14	9	19	47	64	37
West Ham United	42	11	14	17	46	65	36
Bristol City	42	11	13	18	38	48	35
Coventry City	42	10	15	17	48	59	35
Sunderland	42	11	12	19	46	54	34
Stoke City	42	10	14	18	28	51	34
TOTTENHAM HOTSPUR	42	12	9	21	48	72	33

1977-78

DIVISION TWO

Manager: Keith Burkinshaw

Did you know that?

An average home Football League attendance of 33,417 made Spurs the best-supported club in the Second Division. In fact, it was a figure bettered by only six clubs in the First Division.

LEAGUE DEBUTANTS

Oct 22 v Bristol Rovers
Colin Lee

Match No.	Date			Opponents	Result		Scorers	Attendance
1	Aug	20	H	Sheffield United	W	4-2	Osgood 2 (2 pens), Duncan, Jones	27,673
2		24	A	Blackburn Rovers	D	0-0		9,540
3		27	H	Notts County	W	2-1	Duncan 2	25,839
4	Sep	3	A	Cardiff City	D	0-0		8,880
5		10	H	Fulham	W	1-0	Jones	31,939
6		17	A	Blackpool	W	2-0	Hoddle, Duncan	16,910
7		24	H	Luton Town	W	2-0	Osgood (pen), Jones	32,814
8	Oct	1	A	Orient	D	1-1	Taylor	24,131
9		4	A	Hull City	L	0-2		10,966
10		8	H	Oldham Athletic	W	5-1	Duncan 2, Robinson, Taylor 2	24,636
11		15	A	Charlton Athletic	L	1-4	Taylor	30,706
12		22	H	Bristol Rovers	W	9-0	Lee 4, Taylor, Moores 3, Hoddle	26,571
13		29	A	Stoke City	W	3-1	Pratt, Armstrong 2	21,012
14	Nov	5	H	Burnley	W	3-0	Hoddle, McNab, Taylor	30,634
15		12	A	Crystal Palace	W	2-1	Moores, Duncan	40,522
16		19	H	Brighton & Hove Albion	D	0-0		48,613
17		26	A	Bolton Wanderers	L	0-1		34,290
18	Dec	3	H	Southampton	D	0-0		37,873
19		10	A	Sunderland	W	2-1	Duncan 2	31,960
20		17	H	Crystal Palace	D	2-2	Hoddle 2	34,211
21		26	A	Millwall	W	3-1	Duncan, Lee, Taylor	14,644
22		27	H	Mansfield Town	D	1-1	Duncan	36,288
23		31	H	Blackburn Rovers	W	4-0	Hoddle, Pratt, Lee 2	30,520
24	Jan	2	A	Sheffield United	D	2-2	Duncan, Taylor	31,207
25		14	A	Notts County	D	3-3	Pratt 2, Lee	15,709
26		21	H	Cardiff City	W	2-1	Duncan 2	29,104
27	Feb	4	A	Fulham	D	1-1	Taylor	24,763
28		11	H	Blackpool	D	2-2	McAllister, Pratt	28,707
29		22	A	Luton Town	W	4-1	Hoddle 2, McAllister, Duncan	17,024
30		25	H	Orient	D	1-1	Lee	32,869
31	Mar	4	A	Oldham Athletic	D	1-1	McNab	14,122
32		11	H	Charlton Athletic	W	2-1	Hoddle (pen), Pratt	34,511
33		18	A	Bristol Rovers	W	3-2	Pratt, McNab, Jones	17,708
34		22	H	Stoke City	W	3-1	McAllister, Lee 2	30,646
35		25	A	Mansfield Town	D	3-3	Hoddle 2 (1 pen), Jones	12,144
36		27	H	Millwall	D	3-3	Hoddle, Jones 2	33,074
37	Apr	1	A	Burnley	L	1-2	Taylor	16,916
38		8	H	Bolton Wanderers	W	1-0	McAllister	50,097
39		15	A	Brighton & Hove Albion	L	1-3	Jones	32,647
40		22	H	Sunderland	L	2-3	Duncan, Taylor	38,220
41		26	H	Hull City	W	1-0	Perryman	36,913
42		29	A	Southampton	D	0-0		28,846

Appearances
Substitute
Goals

FA Cup

R3	Jan	7	H	Bolton Wanderers	D	2-2	Hoddle, Duncan	43,731
R3r		10	A	Bolton Wanderers	L*	1-2	Taylor (pen)	31,314

*after extra-time

Appearances
Substitute
Goals

Football League Cup

R2	Aug	31	H	Wimbledon	W	4-0	Osgood (pen), Duncan 3	22,807
R3	Oct	26	H	Coventry City	L	2-3	Pratt, Armstrong	35,099

Appearances
Substitute
Goals

Armstrong GJ	Coates R	Daines BR	Duncan JP	Hoddle G	Holmes JA	Jones CH	Lee C	McAllister D	McNab N	Moores IR	Naylor TP	Osgood K	Perryman SJ	Pratt JA	Robinson MJ	Stead MJ	Taylor PJ
		1	9	4	3	10			8		2	5	6	7			11
	4	1	9		3	10			8		2	5	6	7			11
		1	9	4	3	10			8		2	5	6	7			11
		1	9	4	3	10			8		2	5	6	7			11
		1	9	4	3	10			8		2	5	6	7			11
		1	9	4	3	10			8		2	5	6	7			11
12		1	**9**	4	3	10			8		2	5	6	7			11
9		1		4	3				8		2	5	6	7	10		11
9	12	1		4	3				8		2	5	6	**7**	10		11
	12	1	9	4	3				8		2	5	6	7	**10**		11
		1		4	3			5	8	9	2		6	7	**10**	12	11
		1		4	3		10	5	8	9	2		6	7			11
10		1		4	3			5	8	9	2		6	7			11
12		1		4	3		10	**5**	8	9	2		6	7			11
12		1	10	4	3				**8**	9	2	5	6	7			11
		1	**10**	4	3		12		8	9	2	5	6	7			11
		1	10	4	3				8	9	2	5	6	7			11
12		1	10	4			9	3	8		2	**5**	6	7			11
12		1	9	4	**3**		10		8		2	5	6	7			11
		1	9	4			10	3	8		2	5	6	7			11
		1	9	4			10	3	8		2	5	6	7			11
		1	9	4		10		3	8		2	5	6	7			11
12		1	**9**	4	3		10	5	8		2		6	7			11
12		1	9	4	3		10	**5**	8		2		6	7			11
11		1	9	4	3		10	5	8		2		6	7			
		1	9	4	3		10	5	8		2		6	7			11
		1	9	4	3		10	5	8		2		6	7			11
		1	9	4	3		10	5	8		2		6	7			11
		1	9	4	3		10	**5**	8	12	2		6	7			11
5		1	9	4	3		10		8		2		6	7			11
5		1		4	3	9	10		8		2		6	7			11
		1		4	3	9	10	5	8		2		6	7			11
		1		4	3	9	10	5	8	12	**2**		6	7			11
		1		4	3	9	10	5	8				6	7		2	11
		1		4	3	9	10	5	8				6	7		2	11
2		1		4	3	9	10	5	8				6	7			11
2		1		4	3	9	10	5	8				6	7			11
2		1		4	3	9	**10**	5	8	12			6	7			11
12		1		4	3	9	**10**	5	8		2		6	7			11
5		1	10	4	3	9	12		8		2		6	**7**			11
		1	10	4	3	9		5	8		2		6	7			11
12		1	**10**	4	3	9		5	8		2		6	7			11
10	1	42	27	41	38	20	23	25	42	7	37	18	42	42	4	2	41
9	2	0	0	0	0	0	2	0	0	3	0	0	0	0	0	1	0
2			16	12		8	11	4	3	4		3	1	7		1	11

Armstrong GJ	Coates R	Daines BR	Duncan JP	Hoddle G	Holmes JA	Jones CH	Lee C	McAllister D	McNab N	Moores IR	Naylor TP	Osgood K	Perryman SJ	Pratt JA	Robinson MJ	Stead MJ	Taylor PJ
12		1	9	4	3		10	5	8		2		6	**7**			11
12		1	9	4	3		10	5	**8**		2		6	7			11
0	0	2	2	2	2	0	2	2	2	0	2	0	2	2	0	0	2
2	0	0	0	0	0	0	0	0	0	0	0	0	0	0	0	0	0
			1	1													1

Armstrong GJ	Coates R	Daines BR	Duncan JP	Hoddle G	Holmes JA	Jones CH	Lee C	McAllister D	McNab N	Moores IR	Naylor TP	Osgood K	Perryman SJ	Pratt JA	Robinson MJ	Stead MJ	Taylor PJ
		1	9	4	3	10			8		2	5	6	7			11
10		1		4	3			5	8	9	2		6	7			11
1	0	2	1	2	2	1	0	1	2	1	2	1	2	2	0	0	2
0	0	0	0	0	0	0	0	0	0	0	0	0	0	0	0	0	0
1			3									1		1			

League Table

	P	W	D	L	F	A	Pts
Bolton Wanderers	42	24	10	8	63	33	58
Southampton	42	22	13	7	70	39	57
TOTTENHAM HOTSPUR	42	20	16	6	83	49	56
Brighton & Hove Albion	42	22	12	8	63	38	56
Blackburn Rovers	42	16	13	13	56	60	45
Sunderland	42	14	16	12	67	59	44
Stoke City	42	16	10	16	53	49	42
Oldham Athletic	42	13	16	13	54	58	42
Crystal Palace	42	13	15	14	50	47	41
Fulham	42	14	13	15	49	49	41
Burnley	42	15	10	17	56	64	40
Sheffield United	42	16	8	18	62	73	40
Luton Town	42	14	10	18	54	52	38
Orient	42	10	18	14	43	49	38
Notts County	42	11	16	15	54	62	38
Millwall	42	12	14	16	49	57	38
Charlton Athletic	42	13	12	17	55	68	38
Bristol Rovers	42	13	12	17	61	77	38
Cardiff City	42	13	12	17	51	71	38
Blackpool	42	12	13	17	59	60	37
Mansfield Town	42	10	11	21	49	69	31
Hull City	42	8	12	22	34	52	28

1978-79

DIVISION ONE

Manager: Keith Burkinshaw

Did you know that?

Spurs finished their summer tour with a game in Hamilton, Bermuda, against a Bermuda Select XI. With players having returned home early Spurs were so short of numbers that Milija Aleksic was pressed into service on the right wing, physiotherapist Mike Varney on the left wing and the club's assistant secretary Peter Day at left-back. In the second half Spurs called on four local players as substitutes, Aleksic, Varney and Day among those replaced.

LEAGUE DEBUTANTS

Aug 19	v Nottingham Forest Ossie Ardiles
Aug 19	v Nottingham Forest John Lacy
Aug 19	v Nottingham Forest Ricky Villa
Nov 4	v Norwich City Mark Kendall
Jan 20	v Leeds United Milija Aleksic
Feb 3	v Manchester City Stuart Beavon
Feb 3	v Manchester City Tony Galvin
Apr 10	v Arsenal Paul Miller
May 8	v Bolton Wanderers Mark Falco
May 8	v Bolton Wanderers Gordon Smith

Match No.	Date			Opponents	Result		Scorers	Attendance
1	Aug	19	A	Nottingham Forest	D	1-1	Villa	41,223
2		23	H	Aston Villa	L	1-4	Hoddle (pen)	47,892
3		26	H	Chelsea	D	2-2	Armstrong, Duncan	40,632
4	Sep	2	A	Liverpool	L	0-7		50,705
5		9	H	Bristol City	W	1-0	Rodgers (og)	34,035
6		16	A	Leeds United	W	2-1	Lee, Taylor	36,062
7		23	A	Manchester City	L	0-2		43,471
8		30	H	Coventry City	D	1-1	Hoddle	35,806
9	Oct	7	A	West Bromwich Albion	W	1-0	Taylor	33,068
10		14	H	Birmingham City	W	1-0	Ainscow (og)	41,230
11		21	A	Derby County	D	2-2	McAllister, Taylor	26,181
12		28	H	Bolton Wanderers	W	2-0	Pratt, Lee	37,337
13	Nov	4	A	Norwich City	D	2-2	Lee, Taylor	27,031
14		11	H	Nottingham Forest	L	1-3	Pratt	50,541
15		18	A	Chelsea	W	3-1	Lee 2, Hoddle	42,328
16		22	H	Liverpool	D	0-0		50,393
17		25	H	Wolverhampton Wanderers	W	1-0	Taylor	35,430
18	Dec	9	H	Ipswich Town	W	1-0	Pratt	33,882
19		16	A	Manchester United	L	0-2		52,026
20		23	H	Arsenal	L	0-5		42,273
21		26	A	Queen's Park Rangers	D	2-2	Lee, Taylor (pen)	24,845
22		30	A	Everton	D	1-1	Taylor	44,572
23	Jan	13	A	Bristol City	D	0-0		29,122
24		20	H	Leeds United	L	1-2	Hoddle	36,838
25	Feb	3	H	Manchester City	L	0-3		32,037
26		10	A	Coventry City	W	3-1	Lee, Taylor 2	25,071
27		24	A	Birmingham City	L	0-1		20,980
28	Mar	3	H	Derby County	W	2-0	Ardiles 2	28,089
29		17	H	Norwich City	D	0-0		24,982
30		24	A	Aston Villa	W	3-2	Jones, Hoddle 2	35,486
31		28	H	Southampton	D	0-0		23,570
32		31	A	Middlesbrough	L	0-1		19,172
33	Apr	3	A	Wolverhampton Wanderers	L	2-3	Jones 2	19,819
34		7	H	Middlesbrough	L	1-2	Taylor (pen)	21,580
35		10	A	Arsenal	L	0-1		53,896
36		14	H	Queen's Park Rangers	D	1-1	Perryman	28,854
37		16	A	Southampton	D	3-3	Pratt, Jones, Taylor	22,096
38		21	H	Manchester United	D	1-1	Jones	36,665
39		28	A	Ipswich Town	L	1-2	Hoddle (pen)	28,179
40	May	5	H	Everton	D	1-1	Ardiles	26,077
41		8	A	Bolton Wanderers	W	3-1	Holmes, Falco, Villa	17,879
42		14	H	West Bromwich Albion	W	1-0	Villa	24,789
								Appearances
								Substitute
								Goals

FA Cup

R3	Jan	10	H	Altrincham	D	1-1	Taylor (pen)	31,081
R3r		16	N#	Altrincham	W	3-0	Lee 3	27,878
R4	Feb	12	H	Wrexham	D	3-3	Hoddle, Jones, Roberts (og)	27,120
R4r		21	A	Wrexham	W*	3-2	Jones 3	16,050
R5		28	A	Oldham Athletic	W	1-0	Perryman	16,097
R6	Mar	10	H	Manchester United	D	1-1	Ardiles	51,800
R6r		14	A	Manchester United	L	0-2		54,510
								Appearances
								Substitute
								Goals

*after extra-time # played at Maine Road, Manchester

Football League Cup

R2	Aug	29	A	Swansea City	D	2-2	Hoddle (pen), Armstrong	24,335
R2r	Sep	6	H	Swansea City	L	1-3	Villa	33,672
								Appearances
								Substitute
								Goals

Aleksic MA	Ardiles OC	Armstrong GJ	Beavon MS	Daines BR	Duncan JP	Falco MP	Galvin A	Gorman J	Hoddle G	Holmes JA	Jones CH	Kendall M	Lacy J	Lee C	McAllister D	McNab N	Miller PR	Moores IR	Naylor TP	Perryman SJ	Pratt JA	Smith GM	Taylor PJ	Villa RJ	Own-goals
	8	9		1				3	4				5		2			10		6	12		**11**	7	
	8	9		1				3	4				5		2			10		6			11	7	
	8	9		1	10			3	4				5		2	11				6				7	
	8			1	10				4				5		2	11			3	6			9	7	
	8			1				3		4			5	9	2					6	10		11	7	
	8	12		1				3		4			5	9	2					6	10		11	**7**	
	8	12		1				3		4			5	9	2					**6**	10		11	7	
	8	**7**		1				3	12	4			5	9	2					6	10		11		
	8	5		1				3	7	4				9	2					6	10		11		
	8			1					10	4			5	9	3				2	6	7		11		
	8			1					10	4			5	9	3				2	6	7		11		
	8			1					**10**	4			5	9	3				2	6	7		11	12	
	8								10	4		1	5	9	3				2	6	7		11	12	
	8								10	4		1	5	9	3				2	6	7		11	12	
	8								10	4		1	5	9	3				2	6	7		11		
	8							3	**10**	4		1	5	9	2					6	7		11	12	
	8							3	**10**	4		1	5	9	2					6	7		11	12	
	8							3	10	4		1	5	9	2					6	7		11		
	8							3	10	**4**		1	5	9	2					6	7		11	12	
	8							3	10	4	12	1	5	9					2	6	**7**		11		
	8							3			10	1	5	9					2	6	7		11	4	
	8										10	1	5	9	3				2	6	7		11	4	
	8									2	10	1	5	9	3					6	7		11	4	
1	8								4	3	10		5	9	2					6	7		11		
	8	9	10				7		4	3		1	5		2					6			11		
	8	12						10	4	3		1	5	9					2	6	7		11		
		8							4	3	10	1	5						2	6	7		11	9	
	8								4	3	10	1	5		9				2	6	7			11	
	8								10	4		1	5	9	3				2	6	7		12	11	
	8								10	4	9	1	5		3				2	6	7			11	
	8								10	4	9	1	5		3				2	6	7			11	
	8								10	4	9	1	5	12	3				2	6	7			11	
									10	4	9	1	5		3				2	6	7		8	11	
	7								10	4	9	1			3				2	6	5		8	11	
				1					10	4	9				3		5		2	6	7		8	11	
				1					10	4	9				3		5		2	6	7		8	11	
	10									4	9	1			3		5		2	6	7		11	8	
	10								8		9	1	5		3		4			6	2		11	7	
1	8								10		9		5	2	3		4			6	7			11	
1	8								10	5	9			2	3		4			6	7			11	
1	8					9			10	5				2	**3**		4			6	7	12		11	
1	8								10		9		4	2	5					6	7	3		11	
5	38	7	1	14	2	1	1	15	34	33	18	23	35	26	38	2	7	2	22	42	37	1	32	26	
0	0	3	0	0	0	0	0	0	1	0	1	0	0	1	0	0	0	0	0	0	1	1	1	6	
	3	1			1	1			7	1	5			7	1					1	4		11	3	2

Aleksic MA	Ardiles OC	Armstrong GJ	Beavon MS	Daines BR	Duncan JP	Falco MP	Galvin A	Gorman J	Hoddle G	Holmes JA	Jones CH	Kendall M	Lacy J	Lee C	McAllister D	McNab N	Miller PR	Moores IR	Naylor TP	Perryman SJ	Pratt JA	Smith GM	Taylor PJ	Villa RJ	Own-goals
	8	12								3	10	1	5	**9**	2					6	7		11	4	
1	8									3	10		5	9	2				12	6	7		11	**4**	
		9						8	4	3	12	1	5	10					2	6	7		11		
		12							4	3	10	1	5	**9**					2	6	7		11	8	
	8								4	3	10	1	5	12	9				2	6	7		11		
	8								10	4	9	1	5		3				2	6	7		12	**11**	
	8								10	4	9	1	5		3				2	6	**7**		12	11	
1	5	1	0	0	0	0	0	1	5	7	6	6	7	4	5	0	0	0	5	7	7	0	5	5	
0	0	2	0	0	0	0	0	0	0	0	1	0	0	1	0	0	0	0	1	0	0	0	2	0	
	1								1		4			3						1			1		1

Aleksic MA	Ardiles OC	Armstrong GJ	Beavon MS	Daines BR	Duncan JP	Falco MP	Galvin A	Gorman J	Hoddle G	Holmes JA	Jones CH	Kendall M	Lacy J	Lee C	McAllister D	McNab N	Miller PR	Moores IR	Naylor TP	Perryman SJ	Pratt JA	Smith GM	Taylor PJ	Villa RJ	Own-goals
	7	12		1	9				4				5		2	10			3	6			11	8	
	8	5		1	9				4						3	10			2	6			11	7	
0	2	1	0	2	2	0	0	0	2	0	0	0	1	0	2	2	0	0	2	2	0	0	2	2	
0	0	1	0	0	0	0	0	0	0	0	0	0	0	0	0	0	0	0	0	0	0	0	0	0	
		1							1															1	

League Table

	P	W	D	L	F	A	Pts
Liverpool	42	30	8	4	85	16	68
Nottingham Forest	42	21	18	3	61	26	60
West Bromwich Albion	42	24	11	7	72	35	59
Everton	42	17	17	8	52	40	51
Leeds United	42	18	14	10	70	52	50
Ipswich Town	42	20	9	13	63	49	49
Arsenal	42	17	14	11	61	48	48
Aston Villa	42	15	16	11	59	49	46
Manchester United	42	15	15	12	60	63	45
Coventry City	42	14	16	12	58	68	44
TOTTENHAM HOTSPUR	42	13	15	14	48	61	41
Middlesbrough	42	15	10	17	57	50	40
Bristol City	42	15	10	17	47	51	40
Southampton	42	12	16	14	47	53	40
Manchester City	42	13	13	16	58	56	39
Norwich City	42	7	23	12	51	57	37
Bolton Wanderers	42	12	11	19	54	75	35
Wolverhampton W	42	13	8	21	44	68	34
Derby County	42	10	11	21	44	71	31
Queen's Park Rangers	42	6	13	23	45	73	25
Birmingham City	42	6	10	26	37	64	22
Chelsea	42	5	10	27	44	92	20

1979-80

DIVISION ONE

Manager: Keith Burkinshaw

Did you know that?

When Steve Perryman took to the field against Wolverhampton Wanderers on 30 April 1980 he overtook Pat Jennings's previous record of 472 Football League appearances for Spurs. Perryman went on to clock up 655 League appearances for Spurs. When Cup-ties, friendlies and tour games are added he becomes the only player to have appeared in more than 1,000 first-team games for the club.

LEAGUE DEBUTANTS

Aug 18 v Middlesbrough
Terry Yorath
Sep 1 v Manchester City
Chris Hughton
Sep 8 v Brighton and Hove Albion
Peter Southey
Dec 29 v Stoke City
Terry Gibson
Apr 19 v Everton
Mike Hazard

Match No.	Date			Opponents	Result		Scorers	Attendance
1	Aug	18	H	Middlesbrough	L	1-3	Hoddle	32,743
2		22	A	Norwich City	L	0-4		16,647
3		25	A	Stoke City	L	1-3	Perryman	22,832
4	Sep	1	H	Manchester City	W	2-1	Jones, Hoddle	30,901
5		8	H	Brighton & Hove Albion	W	2-1	Armstrong, Hoddle (pen)	34,107
6		15	A	Southampton	L	2-5	Jones, Hoddle	22,573
7		22	H	West Bromwich Albion	D	1-1	Hoddle (pen)	29,914
8		29	A	Coventry City	D	1-1	Jones	20,085
9	Oct	6	A	Crystal Palace	D	1-1	Villa	45,274
10		10	H	Norwich City	W	3-2	Hoddle 2, Villa	26,488
11		13	H	Derby County	W	1-0	Armstrong	33,269
12		20	A	Leeds United	W	2-1	Jones, Armstrong	25,203
13		27	H	Nottingham Forest	W	1-0	Hoddle	49,038
14	Nov	3	A	Middlesbrough	D	0-0		19,557
15		10	H	Bolton Wanderers	W	2-0	Yorath, Hoddle (pen)	33,155
16		17	A	Liverpool	L	1-2	Jones	51,092
17		24	A	Everton	D	1-1	Jones	31,079
18	Dec	1	H	Manchester United	L	1-2	Hoddle	51,389
19		8	A	Bristol City	W	3-1	Miller, Hoddle 2 (1 pen)	25,090
20		15	H	Aston Villa	L	1-2	Ardiles	30,555
21		21	A	Ipswich Town	L	1-3	McAllister	18,945
22		26	A	Arsenal	L	0-1		44,560
23		29	H	Stoke City	W	1-0	Pratt	28,810
24	Jan	12	A	Manchester City	D	1-1	Hoddle	34,837
25		19	A	Brighton & Hove Albion	W	2-0	Hughton, Villa	29,406
26	Feb	2	H	Southampton	D	0-0		37,155
27		9	A	West Bromwich Albion	L	1-2	Hoddle	26,319
28		23	A	Derby County	L	1-2	Galvin	21,183
29		27	H	Coventry City	W	4-3	Falco, Hoddle 3 (2 pens)	22,536
30	Mar	1	H	Leeds United	W	2-1	Falco, Hoddle	35,331
31		11	A	Nottingham Forest	L	0-4		25,633
32		15	H	Crystal Palace	D	0-0		28,419
33		22	A	Bolton Wanderers	L	1-2	Jones	14,474
34		29	H	Liverpool	W	2-0	Pratt, Hoddle (pen)	32,114
35	Apr	2	H	Ipswich Town	L	0-2		26,423
36		5	A	Wolverhampton Wanderers	W	2-1	Jones, Galvin	30,713
37		7	H	Arsenal	L	1-2	Jones	41,365
38		12	A	Manchester United	L	1-4	Ardiles	53,151
39		19	H	Everton	W	3-0	Miller, Ardiles, Galvin	25,245
40		23	H	Wolverhampton Wanderers	D	2-2	Armstrong, Galvin	19,843
41		26	A	Aston Villa	L	0-1		29,549
42	May	3	H	Bristol City	D	0-0		23,585
								Appearances
								Substitute
								Goals

FA Cup

Round	Date			Opponents	Result		Scorers	Attendance
R3	Jan	5	H	Manchester United	D	1-1	Ardiles	45,207
R3r		9	A	Manchester United	W*	1-0	Ardiles	53,762
R4		26	A	Swindon Town	D	0-0		26,000
R4r		30	H	Swindon Town	W	2-1	Armstrong 2	46,707
R5	Feb	16	H	Birmingham City	W	3-1	Armstrong, Hoddle 2 (1 pen)	49,936
R6	Mar	8	H	Liverpool	L	0-1		48,033
								Appearances
								Substitute
								Goals

*after-extra-time

Football League Cup

Round	Date			Opponents	Result		Scorers	Attendance
R2	Aug	29	H	Manchester United	W	2-1	Pratt, Hoddle	29,163
R2	Sep	5	A	Manchester United	L	1-3	Armstrong	48,292
								Appearances
								Substitute
								Goals

Aleksic MA	Ardiles OC	Armstrong GJ	Beavon MS	Daines BR	Falco MP	Galvin A	Gibson TB	Hazard M	Hoddle G	Hughton CWG	Jones CH	Kendall M	Lacy J	Lee C	McAllister D	Miller PR	Naylor TP	Perryman SJ	Pratt JA	Smith GM	Southey PC	Taylor PJ	Villa RJ	Yorath TC
	8			1	9				10		12		5	2				6	7	3			11	4
	8			1	7				10		9		5	2				6		3			11	4
	8			1	**9**				10		11		5	2	12			6	7	3				4
	8			1	12				10	3	9			11	2	5		6	7					4
		9	12	1					10	2	8			11		5		6	**7**		3			4
		9	11	1					10	2	8		5					6	7				3	4
	7	9		1					10	2	8				3	5		6					11	4
	7	9		1					10	2	8				3	5		6					11	4
	7	9		1					10	2	8				3	5		6	12				11	4
	7	9		1					10	2	8				3	5		6	12				11	**4**
	7	**9**		1					10	2	8			12	3	5		6	4				11	
	7	9		**1**					10	2	8				3	5		6	12				11	4
1	7	**9**							10	2	8			12	5			6		3			11	4
1	7	9							10	2	8				3			6		5			11	4
1	7	9							10	2	8				3			6		5			11	4
1	7	9							10	2	8				3			6		5			11	4
1	7	9							10	2	8				3			6		5			11	4
1	7	9							10	2	8				3			6	4	5			11	
	7			1					10	2	8			9		3		6	4	5			11	
	7			1					10	2	8			9		3		6	4	5			11	
	7			1					10	2	8			9	5	3		6					11	4
1	7	**9**				12			10	2	8				3			6	11	5				4
1	7					12	**9**		10	2	8				5			6	11	3				4
	7	9		1					10	2	**8**				3	5		6	12				11	4
	7	9		1					10	2					5	3		6	12			**8**	11	4
	7	9		1					10	2					5	3	6		8			11		4
	7	9		1					10	2	8				5	3	6						11	4
	7	9	**11**		8	12			10	2		1			5	3		6	4					
	7	9			8				10	2		1			5	3		6	4					11
	7	9		1	8				10	2					5	3		6					4	11
	7	9		1					10	2	8				5	3	12	6				11		**4**
	7	9		1					10	3	8				5		2	6		4		11		
	7	9		1					10	3	8				5	4	2	6				11		
	7	12		1					10	3	8				5		2	6	9			**11**		4
	7			1					10	3	8				5		2	6	9			11		4
	7			1		9			10	3	8				5	4		6	11					2
	7			1		11			10	3	8				5	2		6	9					4
	7	12		1		**11**			10	3	8				5	2		6	9					4
	7	9		1		11		**4**	10	3	8				5	2		6				12		
	7	9		1		11		10		3	**8**				5	2		6				12		4
	7	**11**		1	12	9			10	2	8				3	5		4						6
	7			1	9	11		4	10	3	8				5	2		6						
8	40	28	2	32	7	7	1	3	41	39	36	2	4	8	35	27	6	40	19	14	1	7	22	33
0	0	2	1	0	2	3	0	0	0	0	1	0	0	2	1	0	1	0	5	0	0	2	0	0
	3	4			2	4			19	1	9				1	2		1	2				3	1

Aleksic MA	Ardiles OC	Armstrong GJ	Beavon MS	Daines BR	Falco MP	Galvin A	Gibson TB	Hazard M	Hoddle G	Hughton CWG	Jones CH	Kendall M	Lacy J	Lee C	McAllister D	Miller PR	Naylor TP	Perryman SJ	Pratt JA	Smith GM	Southey PC	Taylor PJ	Villa RJ	Yorath TC
1	7						9		10	2	**8**				5	3		6	12				11	4
1	7	8					9		10	2					5	3		6	12				11	4
	7	9		1					10	2	8					3	5	6	12				**11**	4
	7	9		1					10	2	**8**				5	3		6	4			12	11	
	7	9		1	8				10	2					5	3		6	12				**11**	4
	7	9		1	8				10	2					5	3		6	12				**4**	11
2	6	5	0	4	2	0	2	0	6	6	3	0	0	0	5	6	1	6	1	0	0	0	6	5
0	0	0	0	0	0	0	0	0	0	0	0	0	0	0	0	0	0	0	5	0	0	1	0	0
	2	3							2															

Aleksic MA	Ardiles OC	Armstrong GJ	Beavon MS	Daines BR	Falco MP	Galvin A	Gibson TB	Hazard M	Hoddle G	Hughton CWG	Jones CH	Kendall M	Lacy J	Lee C	McAllister D	Miller PR	Naylor TP	Perryman SJ	Pratt JA	Smith GM	Southey PC	Taylor PJ	Villa RJ	Yorath TC
	8			1	12				10	3	9			11	2	5		6	**7**					4
		9	12	1					10	2			8	11		5		6	7	3				4
0	1	1	0	2	0	0	0	0	2	2	1	0	1	2	1	2	0	2	2	1	0	0	0	2
0	0	0	1	0	1	0	0	0	0	0	0	0	0	0	0	0	0	0	0	0	0	0	0	0
		1							1										1					

League Table

	P	W	D	L	F	A	Pts
Liverpool	42	25	10	7	81	30	60
Manchester United	42	24	10	8	65	35	58
Ipswich Town	42	22	9	11	68	39	53
Arsenal	42	18	16	8	52	36	52
Nottingham Forest	42	20	8	14	63	43	48
Wolverhampton W	42	19	9	14	58	47	47
Aston Villa	42	16	14	12	51	50	46
Southampton	42	18	9	15	65	53	45
Middlesbrough	42	16	12	14	50	44	44
West Bromwich Albion	42	11	19	12	54	50	41
Leeds United	42	13	14	15	46	50	40
Norwich City	42	13	14	15	58	66	40
Crystal Palace	42	12	16	14	41	50	40
TOTTENHAM HOTSPUR	42	15	10	17	52	62	40
Coventry City	42	16	7	19	56	66	39
Brighton & Hove Albion	42	11	15	16	47	57	37
Manchester City	42	12	13	17	43	66	37
Stoke City	42	13	10	19	44	58	36
Everton	42	9	17	16	43	51	35
Bristol City	42	9	13	20	37	66	31
Derby County	42	11	8	23	47	67	30
Bolton Wanderers	42	5	15	22	38	73	25

1980-81

DIVISION ONE

Manager: Keith Burkinshaw

Did you know that?

He may not have been a first-team regular, but Don McAllister was a valued member of the senior squad and there was no way Spurs wanted to let him leave when his contract expired at the end of the season. Spurs claimed to have written to him with the offer of a new contract but McAllister insisted he had not received their letter, thus entitling him to sign for another club without Spurs receiving a fee. Spurs took their case to the Football League but it decided in McAllister's favour.

LEAGUE DEBUTANTS

Aug 16	v Nottingham Forest	Steve Archibald
Aug 16	v Nottingham Forest	Garth Crooks
Oct 4	v Stoke City	Graham Roberts
Nov 29	v West Bromwich Albion	Garry Brooke
Dec 26	v Southampton	Gary O'Reilly
Jan 10	v Birmingham City	Georgio Mazzon

Match No.	Date			Opponents	Result		Scorers	Attendance
1	Aug	16	H	Nottingham Forest	W	2-0	Hoddle (pen), Crooks	43,398
2		19	A	Crystal Palace	W	4-3	Archibald, Hoddle, Crooks 2	27,481
3		23	H	Brighton & Hove Albion	D	2-2	Hoddle, Crooks	39,763
4		30	A	Arsenal	L	0-2		54,045
5	Sep	6	H	Manchester United	D	0-0		40,995
6		13	A	Leeds United	D	0-0		21,947
7		20	H	Sunderland	D	0-0		32,030
8		27	A	Leicester City	L	1-2	Villa	22,616
9	Oct	4	A	Stoke City	W	3-2	Hughton, Archibald, Taylor (pen)	18,614
10		11	H	Middlesbrough	W	3-2	Archibald, Villa, Crooks	27,380
11		18	A	Aston Villa	L	0-3		30,940
12		22	A	Manchester City	L	1-3	Hoddle	28,788
13		25	H	Coventry City	W	4-1	Archibald 2, Hoddle 2	25,484
14	Nov	1	A	Everton	D	2-2	Archibald 2	26,223
15		8	H	Wolverhampton Wanderers	D	2-2	Hoddle (pen), Crooks	29,244
16		12	H	Crystal Palace	W	4-2	Archibald, Crooks 3	25,777
17		15	A	Nottingham Forest	W	3-0	Ardiles, Archibald 2	25,400
18		22	A	Birmingham City	L	1-2	Ardiles	24,817
19		29	H	West Bromwich Albion	L	2-3	Lacy, Perryman	27,372
20	Dec	6	A	Liverpool	L	1-2	Archibald	39,545
21		13	H	Manchester City	W	2-1	Archibald, Hoddle	23,883
22		17	H	Ipswich Town	W	5-3	Perryman, Ardiles, Archibald, Hoddle, Crooks	22,741
23		20	A	Middlesbrough	L	1-4	Lacy	15,990
24		26	H	Southampton	D	4-4	Brooke 2, Archibald, Crooks	28,792
25		27	A	Norwich City	D	2-2	Archibald, Hoddle	23,145
26	Jan	10	H	Birmingham City	W	1-0	Crooks	24,909
27		17	H	Arsenal	W	2-0	Archibald 2	32,944
28		31	A	Brighton & Hove Albion	W	2-0	Ardiles, Crooks	23,610
29	Feb	7	H	Leeds United	D	1-1	Archibald	32,372
30		17	A	Manchester United	D	0-0		40,642
31		21	H	Leicester City	L	1-2	Archibald	27,326
32		28	A	Sunderland	D	1-1	Crooks	22,382
33	Mar	11	H	Stoke City	D	2-2	Ardiles, Brooke	28,742
34		14	A	Ipswich Town	L	0-3		32,044
35		21	H	Aston Villa	W	2-0	Archibald, Crooks	35,091
36		28	A	Coventry City	W	1-0	Roberts (og)	18,654
37	Apr	4	H	Everton	D	2-2	Galvin, Crooks	27,208
38		18	H	Norwich City	L	2-3	Miller, Hoddle (pen)	34,413
39		20	A	Southampton	D	1-1	Miller	23,735
40		25	H	Liverpool	D	1-1	Hoddle	35,334
41		30	A	Wolverhampton Wanderers	L	0-1		18,350
42	May	2	A	West Bromwich Albion	L	2-4	Smith, Falco	20,549
								Appearances
								Substitute
								Goals

FA Cup

R3	Jan	3	A	Queen's Park Rangers	D	0-0		28,892
R3r		7	H	Queen's Park Rangers	W	3-1	Galvin, Hoddle, Crooks	36,294
R4		24	H	Hull City	W	2-0	Archibald, Brooke	37,532
R5	Feb	14	H	Coventry City	W	3-1	Hughton, Ardiles, Archibald	36,688
R6	Mar	7	H	Exeter City	W	2-0	Miller, Roberts	40,629
SF	Apr	11	N*	Wolverhampton Wanderers	D#	2-2	Archibald, Hoddle	50,174
SFr		15	N^	Wolverhampton Wanderers	W	3-0	Villa, Crooks 2	52,539
F	May	9	N+	Manchester City	D#	1-1	Hutchinson (og)	100,000
Fr		14	N+	Manchester City	W	3-2	Villa 2, Crooks	96,000
								Appearances
								Substitute
								Goals

*played at Hillsborough ^played at Highbury +played at Wembley Stadium
#after extra-time

Football League Cup

R2	Aug	27	A	Leyton Orient	W	1-0	Lacy	20,087
R2	Sep	3	H	Leyton Orient	W	3-1	Archibald 2, Crooks	25,806
R3		24	H	Crystal Palace	D	0-0		29,654
R3r		30	A	Crystal Palace	W*	3-1	Villa, Hoddle, Crooks	26,885
R4	Nov	4	H	Arsenal	W	1-0	Ardiles	42,511
R5	Dec	2	A	West Ham United	L	0-1		36,003
								Appearances
								Substitute
								Goals

*after-extra-time

Aleksic MA	Archibald S	Ardiles OC	Armstrong GJ	Brooke GJ	Crooks GA	Daines BR	Falco MP	Galvin A	Hazard M	Hoddle G	Hughton CWG	Kendall M	Lacy J	Mazzon G	McAllister D	Miller PR	O'Reilly GM	Perryman SJ	Roberts GP	Smith GM	Taylor PJ	Villa RJ	Yorath TC	Own-goals
	8	**7**	12		11					10	3	1	5					6		2		9	4	
	8	7			11					10	3	1	5					6		2		9	4	
	8	7			11					10	3	1	5					6		2		9	4	
	8	7			11					10	3	1	5					6		**2**	12	9	4	
	8	**7**			11	1				10	3		5					6		2	12	9	4	
	8	7			11	1				10	3		5					6		2	4	9		
	8	7	12		11	1				10	3		5					6		2	**4**	9		
	8	7			11	1				10	3		5					6		2		9	4	
	8	7			**11**	1					3		5					6	12	2	10	9	4	
	8	**7**			11	1				10	3		5					6		2	12	9	4	
	8		12		11	1				10	3		5					6		2	7	9	**4**	
	8	7	12		**11**	1				10	3		5					6		2	4	9		
	8	7			11	1				10	3		5			4		6		2		9		
	8	7			11	1				10	3		5			4		6		2		9		
	8	7			11	1				10	**3**		5			4		6	12	2		9		
	8	7			11	1				10	3		5		**2**	4		6	12			9		
	8	7			11	1				10	3		5		2	4		6				9		
	8	7			11	1				10	3		5		2	4		6				9		
	8	**7**		12	11	1				10	3		5		2	4		6				9		
	8	7			11	1				10	3		5		2			6	4			9		
	8	**7**			11	1				10	3		5		2			6	4			9	12	
	8	7			11	1				10	3		5		2			6	4			**9**	12	
1	8	7			11					10	3		5		2			6	**4**			9	12	
1	8			7	11					10	**3**		5				12	6	4			9	2	
1	8			7	11					10			5			12	3	6	2			**9**	4	
	8			**7**	11	1		9		10			5	12	2	3		6	4					
	8			7	11	1		9		10			**5**		2	3		6	4				12	
	8	**7**		12	11	1		9		10			5		2	3		6	4					
	8	7		12	**11**	1		9		10			5		2	3		6	4					
	8	7			11	1		9		10	2		5			3		6	4					
	8	7		12	**11**	1		9		10	2		5			3		6	4					
	8	7			11	1		9		10	2			5		3		6	4	12				
	8	7		12	11	1		9		10	**2**				5	3		6	4					
	8	**7**		12	11	1		9		10	2				5	3		6	4					
1	8	7		5	11			9		10	2					3		6	4					
1	8	7		**5**	11			9		10	2					3		6	4	12				
1	8	7		**5**	11			9		10	2					3		6	4			12		
1	8	7		**5**	11			9	12	10	2					3		6	4					
1		7		12	**11**		8	9	10		2				5	4		3				6		
1	8	7		12	11			9		10					4	3		6		2		**5**		
	8	7		5		1	11	9	12						10	**3**		6	4	2				
1	12			7			11	9	8						4	3		6	**10**	2		5		
0	40	36	0	10	40	28	3	17	2	38	34	4	31	1	18	24	1	42	21	18	5	28	11	
0	1	0	4	8	0	0	0	0	2	0	0	0	0	1	0	1	1	0	3	2	3	1	4	
	20	5		3	16		1	1		12	1		2			2		2		1	1	2		1

Aleksic MA	Archibald S	Ardiles OC	Armstrong GJ	Brooke GJ	Crooks GA	Daines BR	Falco MP	Galvin A	Hazard M	Hoddle G	Hughton CWG	Kendall M	Lacy J	Mazzon G	McAllister D	Miller PR	O'Reilly GM	Perryman SJ	Roberts GP	Smith GM	Taylor PJ	Villa RJ	Yorath TC	Own-goals
	8			7	11	1		12		10			5			3		6	4			**9**	2	
	8			7	11	1		9		10			5		2	3		6	4					
	8	**7**		12	11	1		9		10					2	3		6	4				5	
	8	**7**		12	11	1		9		10	2		5			3		6	4					
	8	7			11	1		9		10	2			5		3		6	4					
1	8	7		12	11			9		10	2					3		5	4			**6**		
1	8	**7**		12	11			9		10	2					3		6	4			5		
1	8	7		12	11			9		10	2					3		5	4			**6**		
1	8	7			11			9		10	2					3		6	4			5		
4	9	7	0	2	9	5	0	8	0	9	6	0	3	1	2	9	0	9	9	0	0	5	2	
0	0	0	0	5	0	0	0	1	0	0	0	0	0	0	0	0	0	0	0	0	0	0	0	
	3	1		1	4			1		2	1					1			1			3		1

Aleksic MA	Archibald S	Ardiles OC	Armstrong GJ	Brooke GJ	Crooks GA	Daines BR	Falco MP	Galvin A	Hazard M	Hoddle G	Hughton CWG	Kendall M	Lacy J	Mazzon G	McAllister D	Miller PR	O'Reilly GM	Perryman SJ	Roberts GP	Smith GM	Taylor PJ	Villa RJ	Yorath TC	Own-goals
	8	7			11					10	3	1	5					6		2		9	4	
	8	**7**			11	1				10	3		5					6		2	12	9	4	
	8	7			11	1				10	3		5					6		2		9	4	
	8	**7**			11	1				10	3		5					6		2	12	9	4	
	8	**7**			11	1				10	3		5			4		6	12	2		9		
	8	7			11	1				10	3		5		2			6				9	4	
0	6	6	0	0	6	5	0	0	0	6	6	1	6	0	1	1	0	6	0	5	0	6	5	
0	0	0	0	0	0	0	0	0	0	0	0	0	0	0	0	0	0	0	1	0	2	0	0	
	2	1			2					1			1									1		

League Table

	P	W	D	L	F	A	Pts
Aston Villa	42	26	8	8	72	40	60
Ipswich Town	42	23	10	9	77	43	56
Arsenal	42	19	15	8	61	45	53
West Bromwich Albion	42	20	12	10	60	42	52
Liverpool	42	17	17	8	62	42	51
Southampton	42	20	10	12	76	56	50
Nottingham Forest	42	19	12	11	62	44	50
Manchester United	42	15	18	9	51	36	48
Leeds United	42	17	10	15	39	47	44
TOTTENHAM HOTSPUR	42	14	15	13	70	68	43
Stoke City	42	12	18	12	51	60	42
Manchester City	42	14	11	17	56	59	39
Birmingham City	42	13	12	17	50	61	38
Middlesbrough	42	16	5	21	53	61	37
Everton	42	13	10	19	55	58	36
Coventry City	42	13	10	19	48	68	36
Sunderland	42	14	7	21	52	53	35
Wolverhampton W	42	13	9	20	43	55	35
Brighton & Hove Albion	42	14	7	21	54	67	35
Norwich City	42	13	7	22	49	73	33
Leicester City	42	13	6	23	40	67	32
Crystal Palace	42	6	7	29	47	83	19

1981-82

DIVISION ONE

Manager: Keith Burkinshaw

Did you know that?

Ally Dick became Spurs' youngest ever League player when he played against Manchester City on 20 February 1982 aged 16 years and 301 days, beating the record of Neil McNab by just two days.

LEAGUE DEBUTANTS

Aug 29	v Middlesbrough Ray Clemence
Aug 29	v Middlesbrough Paul Price
Oct 31	v Southampton Pat Corbett
Feb 20	v Manchester City Ally Dick
May 1	v Coventry City Ian Crook
May 10	v West Ham United Tony Parks

Match No.	Date		Opponents		Result		Scorers	Attendance
1	Aug	29	A	Middlesbrough	W	3-1	Villa, Hoddle, Falco	20,490
2	Sep	2	H	West Ham United	L	0-4		41,200
3		5	H	Aston Villa	L	1-3	Villa	31,265
4		12	A	Wolverhampton Wanderers	W	1-0	Galvin	18,675
5		19	H	Everton	W	3-0	Hughton, Roberts, Hoddle (pen)	31,219
6		22	A	Swansea City	L	1-2	Hoddle (pen)	22,352
7		26	A	Manchester City	W	1-0	Falco	39,085
8	Oct	3	H	Nottingham Forest	W	3-0	Hazard, Falco 2	34,870
9		10	H	Stoke City	W	2-0	Ardiles, Crooks	30,520
10		17	A	Sunderland	W	2-0	Hazard, Archibald	25,317
11		24	H	Brighton & Hove Albion	L	0-1		37,294
12		31	A	Southampton	W	2-1	Roberts, Corbett	24,131
13	Nov	7	H	West Bromwich Albion	L	1-2	Crooks	32,436
14		21	H	Manchester United	W	3-1	Roberts, Hazard, Archibald	35,534
15		28	A	Notts County	D	2-2	Crooks 2	15,550
16	Dec	5	H	Coventry City	L	1-2	Hazard	27,972
17		12	A	Leeds United	D	0-0		28,780
18	Jan	27	H	Middlesbrough	W	1-0	Crooks	22,819
19		30	A	Everton	D	1-1	Villa	30,709
20	Feb	6	H	Wolverhampton Wanderers	W	6-1	Villa 3, Falco, Hoddle (pen), Crooks	29,960
21		17	A	Aston Villa	D	1-1	Crooks	23,877
22		20	H	Manchester City	W	2-0	Hoddle 2 (1 pen)	46,181
23		27	A	Stoke City	W	2-0	Crooks 2	20,592
24	Mar	9	A	Brighton & Hove Albion	W	3-1	Ardiles, Archibald, Crooks	27,082
25		20	H	Southampton	W	3-2	Roberts 3	46,827
26		23	A	Birmingham City	D	0-0		17,708
27		27	A	West Bromwich Albion	L	0-1		20,151
28		29	H	Arsenal	D	2-2	Hughton, Archibald	40,940
29	Apr	10	H	Ipswich Town	W	1-0	Hoddle	45,215
30		12	A	Arsenal	W	3-1	Hazard, Crooks 2	48,897
31		14	H	Sunderland	D	2-2	Galvin, Hoddle	39,898
32		17	A	Manchester United	L	0-2		50,724
33		24	H	Notts County	W	3-1	Villa, Archibald, Galvin	38,017
34		28	H	Birmingham City	D	1-1	Villa	25,470
35	May	1	A	Coventry City	D	0-0		15,408
36		3	H	Liverpool	D	2-2	Perryman, Archibald	38,091
37		5	H	Swansea City	W	2-1	Brooke 2 (1 pen)	26,348
38		8	H	Leeds United	W	2-1	Brooke, Burns (og)	35,020
39		10	A	West Ham United	D	2-2	Hoddle (pen), Brooke	27,667
40		12	A	Nottingham Forest	L	0-2		15,273
41		15	A	Liverpool	L	1-3	Hoddle	48,122
42		17	A	Ipswich Town	L	1-2	Crooks	21,202

Appearances
Substitute
Goals

FA Cup

R3	Jan	2	H	Arsenal	W	1-0	Crooks	38,421
R4		23	H	Leeds United	W	1-0	Crooks	46,126
R5	Feb	13	H	Aston Villa	W	1-0	Falco	43,419
R6	Mar	6	A	Chelsea	W	3-2	Hazard, Archibald, Hoddle	42,557
SF	Apr	3	N*	Leicester City	W	2-0	Crooks, Wilson (og)	46,606
F	May	22	N#	Queen's Park Rangers	D^	1-1	Hoddle	100,000
Fr		27	N#	Queen's Park Rangers	W	1-0	Hoddle (pen)	92,000

*played at Villa Park #played at Wembley Stadium ^after-extra-time

Appearances
Substitute
Goals

Football League (Milk) Cup

R2	Oct	7	H	Manchester United	W	1-0	Archibald	39,333
R2		28	A	Manchester United	W	1-0	Hazard	55,890
R3	Nov	11	H	Wrexham	W	2-0	Hughton, Hoddle	24,084
R4	Dec	2	H	Fulham	W	1-0	Hazard	30,214
R5	Jan	18	H	Nottingham Forest	W	1-0	Ardiles	31,192
SF	Feb	3	A	West Bromwich Albion	D	0-0		32,238
SF		10	H	West Bromwich Albion	W	1-0	Hazard	47,241
F	Mar	13	N*	Liverpool	L#	1-3	Archibald	100,000

*played at Wembley Stadium #after extra-time

Appearances
Substitute
Goals

FA Charity Shield

Aug	22	N*	Aston Villa	D	2-2	Falco 2	92,500

*played at Wembley Stadium

Appearances
Substitute
Goals

Aleksic MA	Archibald S	Ardiles OC	Brooke GJ	Clemence RN	Corbett PA	Crook IS	Crooks GA	Dick AJ	Falco MP	Galvin A	Gibson TB	Hazard M	Hoddle G	Hughton CWG	Jones CH	Lacy J	Mazzon G	Miller PR	O'Reilly GM	Parks A	Perryman SJ	Price PT	Roberts GP	Smith GM	Villa RJ	Own-goals
		7	8	1					11	9			10	2				3			6	4			5	
			8	1					11	9		7	10					3			6	**4**	2	12	5	
		7	8	1					11				10		9	12		**3**			6		2	4	5	
		7	**8**	1					11	9			10	2	12			3			6		4		5	
	8	7		1					11	9			10	2				3			6		4		5	
	8	7		1					11	9			10	2				3			6		4		5	
	8	7		1					11	9			10	2				3			6		4		5	
	8	7		1					11	9		5	10	2				3			6		4			
	8	7		1			11			9		12	10	2				3			6		4		**5**	
	8	7		1			11			9		**5**	10	2		12		3			6		4			
	8	7		1			11			9		5	10	2				3			6		4			
	8	7		1	12		**11**			9		5	10	2				3			6		4			
	8	**7**		1			11			9		5		2		12		3			6	10	4			
	8	7		1			11			9		5	10	2				3			6		4			
	8	7		1			11			9		5	10	2				3			6		4			
	8	7		1			11			9		5	10	**2**				3			6		4		12	
		7		1			11			9		**5**	10	2		12		3			6		4		8	
		7		1			11		8	9			10	2				3			6		4		5	
		7	12	1			11		**8**	9			10	2				3			6	4			5	
		7		1			**11**		8	9		12	10	2				3			6	4			5	
	12	7		1			11		8			5	10	2				3			6	9	**4**			
	8	7		1			11	**9**				5	10	2				3			6	4	12			
	8	**7**		1			11			9		5	10	2				3			6	4	12			
	8	7		1			11			9		5		2				3			6	4	10			
	8			1						9		5	10	2				3			6	4	7		11	
		7		1					10	9	**8**	5		2		12		3			6		4		11	
	8	7	12	1					**10**	9				2				3			6	5	4		11	
	8	7		1						9		11	10	2							6	4	3		5	
	8		12	1			11			9		5	10	2				3			6		4		7	
				1			11			9		5	10		8			3			6	4	2		7	
			12	1			11			**9**		5	10		8			3			6	4	2		7	
	8			1			11			9		5	10	2				**3**			6	12	4		7	
	8			1			11			9		5	10	2							6	3	4		7	
	8			1			11			9		10		2		5					6	3	4		7	
	8		11	1		12			10	**9**				2		5			3		6		4		7	
1	8		10			11			9					2	12	5		3	7		6		**4**			
1	8		10		3	**11**			9					2	12	5			7		6		4			
			4	1	3	**8**	11		9				10	2	12	5			7		6					
			8		**2**		11		9			7	10			5		3	12	1	6	4				
			7	1			11		8				10	2		5					6	3	4		9	
			7	1			**11**		8			5	10	2				3			6	12	4		9	
	8		7				11					5	**10**	2				3		1	6	12	4		9	
2	26	26	12	38	3	3	27	1	21	32	1	26	34	37	3	7	0	35	4	2	42	18	35	1	26	
0	1	0	4	0	1	1	0	0	0	0	0	2	0	0	4	5	0	0	1	0	0	3	2	1	1	
	6	2	4		1		13		5	3		5	10	2							1		6		8	1

Aleksic MA	Archibald S	Ardiles OC	Brooke GJ	Clemence RN	Corbett PA	Crook IS	Crooks GA	Dick AJ	Falco MP	Galvin A	Gibson TB	Hazard M	Hoddle G	Hughton CWG	Jones CH	Lacy J	Mazzon G	Miller PR	O'Reilly GM	Parks A	Perryman SJ	Price PT	Roberts GP	Smith GM	Villa RJ	Own-goals
		7		1			11		8	9			10	2				3			6		4		5	
		7		1			11		**8**	9		12	10	2				3			6		4		5	
	12	7		1			**11**		8	9			10	2				3			6	4	5			
	8	7		1			11			9		5	10	2				3			6	4				
	8	7		1			11			9		5	10	2				12			6	4	**3**			
	8		12	1			11			9		**5**	10	2				3			6	4	7			
	8		12	1			11			9		**5**	10	2				3			6	4	7			
0	4	5	0	7		0	7	0	3	7	0	4	7	7	0	0	0	6	0	0	7	5	6	0	2	
0	1	0	2	0		0	0	0	0	0	0	1	0	0	0	0	0	1	0	0	0	0	0	0	0	
	1						3		1			1	3													1

Aleksic MA	Archibald S	Ardiles OC	Brooke GJ	Clemence RN	Corbett PA	Crook IS	Crooks GA	Dick AJ	Falco MP	Galvin A	Gibson TB	Hazard M	Hoddle G	Hughton CWG	Jones CH	Lacy J	Mazzon G	Miller PR	O'Reilly GM	Parks A	Perryman SJ	Price PT	Roberts GP	Smith GM	Villa RJ	Own-goals
	8	7		1					**11**	9			10	2			12	3			6		4		5	
	8	7		1			11			9		5	10	2				3			6		4			
	8	7		1			11			9		5	10	2				3			6		4			
	8	7		1			11			9		5	10	2				3			6		4			
		7		1			11		**8**	9		12	10	2				3			6		4		5	
		7		1			11		8	9			10	2				3			6	4			5	
		7		1			11		8	9		5	10	2				3			6	4				
	8	7		1			11			9		**5**	10	2				3			6	4			12	
0	5	8	0	8		0	7	0	4	8	0	5	8	8	0	0	0	8	0	0	8	3	5	0	3	
0	0	0	0	0		0	0	0	0	0	0	1	0	0	0	0	1	0	0	0	0	0	0	0	1	
	2	1										3	1	1												

Aleksic MA	Archibald S	Ardiles OC	Brooke GJ	Clemence RN	Corbett PA	Crook IS	Crooks GA	Dick AJ	Falco MP	Galvin A	Gibson TB	Hazard M	Hoddle G	Hughton CWG	Jones CH	Lacy J	Mazzon G	Miller PR	O'Reilly GM	Parks A	Perryman SJ	Price PT	Roberts GP	Smith GM	Villa RJ	Own-goals
	8	7		1					11	9			10	2				3			6		4		5	
0	1	1	0	1	0	0	0	0	1	1	0	0	1	1	0	0	0	1	0	0	1	0	1	0	1	
0	0	0	0	0	0	0	0	0	0	0	0	0	0	0	0	0	0	0	0	0	0	0	0	0	0	
									2																	

League Table

	P	W	D	L	F	A	Pts
Liverpool	42	26	9	7	80	32	87
Ipswich Town	42	26	5	11	75	53	83
Manchester United	42	22	12	8	59	29	78
TOTTENHAM HOTSPUR	42	20	11	11	67	48	71
Arsenal	42	20	11	11	48	37	71
Swansea City	42	21	6	15	58	51	69
Southampton	42	19	9	14	72	67	66
Everton	42	17	13	12	56	50	64
West Ham United	42	14	16	12	66	57	58
Manchester City	42	15	13	14	49	50	58
Aston Villa	42	15	12	15	55	53	57
Nottingham Forest	42	15	12	15	42	48	57
Brighton & Hove Albion	42	13	13	16	43	52	52
Coventry City	42	13	11	18	56	62	50
Notts County	42	13	8	21	61	69	47
Birmingham City	42	10	14	18	53	61	44
West Bromwich Albion	42	11	11	20	46	57	44
Stoke City	42	12	8	22	44	63	44
Sunderland	42	11	11	20	38	58	44
Leeds United	42	10	12	20	39	61	42
Wolverhampton W	42	10	10	22	32	63	40
Middlesbrough	42	8	15	19	34	52	39

1982-83

DIVISION ONE

Manager: Keith Burkinshaw

Did you know that?

Martin Thomas, the Bristol Rovers and Wales Under-21 goalkeeper, was the first loan signing made by Spurs. He joined in December 1982 to provide cover for Ray Clemence because Tony Parks was out with injury. Thomas made eight appearances in the reserves but his only taste of first-team action was as a substitute against an Israeli Select XI three days before Christmas.

LEAGUE DEBUTANTS

Aug 28 v Luton Town
Gary Mabbutt
Jan 3 v Everton
Simon Webster
Mar 19 v Watford
Alan Brazil

Match No.	Date			Opponents	Result		Scorers	Attendance
1	Aug	28	H	Luton Town	D	2-2	Hazard, Mabbutt	35,195
2		31	A	Ipswich Town	W	2-1	Archibald, Crooks	23,224
3	Sep	4	A	Everton	L	1-3	Archibald	30,563
4		8	H	Southampton	W	6-0	Brooke (pen), Perryman, Galvin 2, Villa, Crooks	26,579
5		11	H	Manchester City	L	1-2	Mabbutt	32,483
6		18	A	Sunderland	W	1-0	Brooke	21,137
7		25	H	Nottingham Forest	W	4-1	Mabbutt 2, Crooks 2	30,662
8	Oct	2	A	Swansea City	L	0-2		16,381
9		9	H	Coventry City	W	4-0	Brooke 3 (1 pen), Crooks	25,188
10		16	A	Norwich City	D	0-0		21,668
11		23	H	Notts County	W	4-2	Brooke, Mabbutt, Crooks 2	26,183
12		30	A	Aston Villa	L	0-4		25,992
13	Nov	6	H	Watford	L	0-1		42,634
14		13	A	Manchester United	L	0-1		47,869
15		20	H	West Ham United	W	2-1	Archibald 2	41,960
16		27	A	Liverpool	L	0-3		40,691
17	Dec	4	H	West Bromwich Albion	D	1-1	Wile (og)	26,608
18		11	A	Stoke City	L	0-2		15,849
19		18	H	Birmingham City	W	2-1	Mabbutt 2	20,946
20		27	A	Arsenal	L	0-2		51,497
21		28	H	Brighton & Hove Albion	W	2-0	Villa, Hughton	23,994
22	Jan	1	A	West Ham United	L	0-3		33,383
23		3	H	Everton	W	2-1	Gibson 2	28,455
24		15	A	Luton Town	D	1-1	Hoddle	21,231
25		22	H	Sunderland	D	1-1	Gibson	25,250
26	Feb	5	A	Manchester City	D	2-2	Gibson, Brooke (pen)	26,357
27		12	H	Swansea City	W	1-0	Crooks	24,632
28		26	H	Norwich City	D	0-0		23,342
29	Mar	5	A	Notts County	L	0-3		11,841
30		12	A	Coventry City	D	1-1	Miller	11,027
31		19	A	Watford	W	1-0	Falco	27,373
32		23	H	Aston Villa	W	2-0	Falco 2	22,455
33	Apr	2	A	Brighton & Hove Albion	L	1-2	Roberts	20,341
34		4	H	Arsenal	W	5-0	Hughton 2, Brazil, Falco 2	43,642
35		9	A	Nottingham Forest	D	2-2	Mabbutt, Brazil	18,265
36		16	H	Ipswich Town	W	3-1	Mabbutt, Brazil 2	30,587
37		23	A	West Bromwich Albion	W	1-0	Archibald	14,879
38		30	H	Liverpool	W	2-0	Archibald 2	44,907
39	May	3	A	Southampton	W	2-1	Mabbutt, Brazil	21,602
40		7	A	Birmingham City	L	0-2		18,947
41		11	H	Manchester United	W	2-0	Roberts, Archibald	32,803
42		14	H	Stoke City	W	4-1	Brazil, Archibald 3	33,691

Appearances
Substitute
Goals

FA Cup

Round	Date			Opponents	Result		Scorers	Attendance
R3	Jan	8	H	Southampton	W	1-0	Hazard	38,040
R4		29	H	West Bromwich Albion	W	2-1	Gibson, Crooks	38,208
R5	Feb	19	A	Everton	L	0-2		42,995

Appearances
Substitute
Goals

Milk Cup

Round	Date			Opponents	Result		Scorers	Attendance
R2	Oct	6	H	Brighton & Hove Albion	D	1-1	Brooke (pen)	20,416
R2		26	A	Brighton & Hove Albion	W	1-0	Crooks	20,755
R3	Nov	9	A	Gillingham	W	4-2	Archibald 2, Crooks 2	14,366
R4	Dec	1	H	Luton Town	W	1-0	Villa	27,861
R5	Jan	19	H	Burnley	L	1-4	Gibson	30,771

Appearances
Substitute
Goals

FA Charity Shield

	Date			Opponents	Result		Scorers	Attendance
	Aug	21	N*	Liverpool	L	0-1		82,500

*played at Wembley Stadium

Appearances
Substitute
Goals

…chibald S	Ardiles OC	Brazil AB	Brooke GJ	Clemence RN	Corbett PA	Crook IS	Crooks GA	Dick AJ	Falco MP	Galvin A	Gibson TB	Hazard M	Hoddle G	Hughton CWG	Lacy J	Mabbutt GV	Mazzon G	Miller PR	O'Reilly GM	Parks A	Perryman SJ	Price PT	Roberts GP	Villa RJ	Webster SP	Own-goals
			12	1			11			9		**5**	10	2	4	7		3			6					
			5	1			11			9			10	2	4	7		3			6					
			5	1			11			9		12	10	2	4	7		**3**			6					
			5	1			11			9		7	**10**	2	4						6	3		12		
			5	1			11			9		**7**			4	2					6	3	12	10		
			5	1			11			9				2		7		4			6	3		10		
			5	1		12	11		9			**8**		2		7		4			6	3		10		
			5	1			11					9		2	3	7			12		6	4		10		
			5				11		12			9		2	3	7		4	6	1				10		
			5	1			11					9			3	7		4	6			2		10		
			7	1		12	11		8			6			5	9		4	3			2		**10**		
			7	1			11		8			6		3	5	9		4				2		10		
			4	1			11					12	10	2	5	7		3			6			**9**		
			9	1			11						10	2	5	7		3	4		6					
			12	1			11					5	10	2		7			4		**6**	3		9		
				1			11			9		**5**		2		10			4		6	3	12	7		
				1			11			9			10	2		7			4			3	6	5		
				1	12		**11**			9			10	2	4	7						3	6	5		
			12	1			11			9		8	10	2	3	7					6		4	**5**		
			12	1			11			**9**		5	10	2		7			3		6		4			
			7	1		12	11					5	10	2					3		6		**4**	9		
			9	1			11						10	2			3		7		6	4		5		
			7	1				11			9		10	2			4		3		6				5	
	7		5	1							**9**		12	2		11			3		6		4	10		
				1				7			9		10	2	3	11					6		4	5		
	7		10	1			11		12		9			2	3	8					6		4	5		
			10	1			11		12	7	9			**2**	3	8					6	4		5		
				1			11			7	9	**5**		2	3	8					6	4	12	10		
				1			11		10	7	9			2	3	8					6	4	12	**5**		
				1		**11**			10	7	9			2		8		5	3		6		4		12	
		10		1					9	8	11			2		7		5	3		6		4			
		8		1					9	11	12		**10**	2		7		5	3		6		4			
		10		1					9	11	**6**	12		2	5	7			3				4			
		10		1					11	9	6			2		7		5	3				4			
		10		1					11	9	6			2		7		5	**3**		12		4			
		10		1					11		9		12	2		7		5	**3**		6		4			
		11		1						9	12		10	2		7		5	3		6		4			
		11		1						9			10	2		7		5	3		6		4			
		11		1						9			10	2		7		5	3		6		4			
		11		1					12	9	**6**		10	2		7		5	3				4			
		11		1						9			10		2	7		5	3		6		4			
		11		1					12	9			10	2	4	7		5	**3**		6					
	2	12	19	41	0	1	26	2	11	26	14	15	22	38	22	38	2	23	25	1	32	16	20	22	1	
	0	0	4	0	1	3	0	0	5	0	2	3	2	0	0	0	0	0	1	0	1	0	4	1	1	
		6	7				8		5	2	4	1	1	3		10		1			1		2	2		1

…chibald S	Ardiles OC	Brazil AB	Brooke GJ	Clemence RN	Corbett PA	Crook IS	Crooks GA	Dick AJ	Falco MP	Galvin A	Gibson TB	Hazard M	Hoddle G	Hughton CWG	Lacy J	Mabbutt GV	Mazzon G	Miller PR	O'Reilly GM	Parks A	Perryman SJ	Price PT	Roberts GP	Villa RJ	Webster SP	Own-goals
			7	1				11			**9**	5		2		12			3		6		4	10		
	7		12	1			11	**10**			9			2	3	8					6		4	5		
				1			11			7	9	10	12	2	3	8					6	4		5		
	1	0	1	3		0	2	2	0	1	3	2	0	3	2	2	0	0	1	0	3	1	2	3	0	
	0	0	1	0		0	0	0	0	0	0	0	1	0	0	1	0	0	0	0	0	0	0	0	0	
							1				1	1														

…chibald S	Ardiles OC	Brazil AB	Brooke GJ	Clemence RN	Corbett PA	Crook IS	Crooks GA	Dick AJ	Falco MP	Galvin A	Gibson TB	Hazard M	Hoddle G	Hughton CWG	Lacy J	Mabbutt GV	Mazzon G	Miller PR	O'Reilly GM	Parks A	Perryman SJ	Price PT	Roberts GP	Villa RJ	Webster SP	Own-goals
			5	1			**11**		12			9		2	3	7			6			4		10		
			7	1			11		**8**			6			5	9	12	4	3			2		10		
			9	1			11					4	10	2	5	7		3			6					
				1			11			9			10	2		7			4			3	6	5		
	7		12	1							9		10	2		11			3		6		4	**5**		
	1	0	3	5		0	4	0	1	1	1	3	3	4	3	5	0	2	4	0	2	3	2	4	0	
	0	0	1	0		0	0	0	1	0	0	0	0	0	0	0	1	0	0	0	0	0	0	0	0	
			1				3				1													1		

…chibald S	Ardiles OC	Brazil AB	Brooke GJ	Clemence RN	Corbett PA	Crook IS	Crooks GA	Dick AJ	Falco MP	Galvin A	Gibson TB	Hazard M	Hoddle G	Hughton CWG	Lacy J	Mabbutt GV	Mazzon G	Miller PR	O'Reilly GM	Parks A	Perryman SJ	Price PT	Roberts GP	Villa RJ	Webster SP	Own-goals
				1			11		13	9		5	10	2	6	7		3	**4**		12					
	0	0	0	1	0	0	1	0	0	1	0	1	1	1	1	1	0	1	1	0	0	0	0	0	0	
	0	0	0	0	0	0	0	0	1	0	0	0	0	0	0	0	0	0	0	0	1	0	0	0	0	

League Table

	P	W	D	L	F	A	Pts
Liverpool	42	24	10	8	87	37	82
Watford	42	22	5	15	74	57	71
Manchester United	42	19	13	10	56	38	70
TOTTENHAM HOTSPUR	42	20	9	13	65	50	69
Nottingham Forest	42	20	9	13	62	50	69
Aston Villa	42	21	5	16	62	50	68
Everton	42	18	10	14	66	48	64
West Ham United	42	20	4	18	68	62	64
Ipswich Town	42	15	13	14	64	50	58
Arsenal	42	16	10	16	58	56	58
West Bromwich Albion	42	15	12	15	51	49	57
Southampton	42	15	12	15	54	58	57
Stoke City	42	16	9	17	53	64	57
Norwich City	42	14	12	16	52	58	54
Notts County	42	15	7	20	55	71	52
Sunderland	42	12	14	16	48	61	50
Birmingham City	42	12	14	16	40	55	50
Luton Town	42	12	13	17	65	84	49
Coventry City	42	13	9	20	48	59	48
Manchester City	42	13	8	21	47	70	47
Swansea City	42	10	11	21	51	69	41
Brighton & Hove Albion	42	9	13	20	38	68	40

1983-84

DIVISION ONE

Manager: Keith Burkinshaw

Did you know that?

On 17 November 1983 Channel Four broadcast for the first time *Those Glory, Glory Days*. Written by Julie Welch, produced by David Puttnam and part of the First Love series, the comedy-drama told the story of four teenage girls' passion for the double-winning team. Danny Blanchflower appeared in the film in which the leading character, Julia Herrick, imagined the Spurs skipper as 'God in a Spurs shirt'.

LEAGUE DEBUTANTS

Aug 27	v Ipswich Town	Gary Stevens
Aug 27	v Ipswich Town	Danny Thomas
Aug 29	v Coventry City	Mark Bowen
Nov 19	v Luton Town	Richard Cooke
Jan 2	v Watford	Allan Cockram
Feb 21	v Notts County	Ian Culverhouse
May 7	v Southampton	Robert Brace

Match No.	Date			Opponents	Result		Scorers	Attendance
1	Aug	27	A	Ipswich Town	L	1-3	Archibald	26,56
2		29	H	Coventry City	D	1-1	Hoddle (pen)	35,45
3	Sep	3	H	West Ham United	L	0-2		38,04
4		7	A	West Bromwich Albion	D	1-1	Roberts	14,83
5		10	A	Leicester City	W	3-0	Stevens, Mabbutt, Crooks	15,88
6		17	H	Everton	L	1-2	Falco	29,12
7		24	A	Watford	W	3-2	Hughton, Hoddle, Archibald	21,05
8	Oct	2	H	Nottingham Forest	W	2-1	Stevens, Archibald	30,59
9		15	A	Wolverhampton Wanderers	W	3-2	Archibald 2, Falco	12,52
10		22	A	Birmingham City	W	1-0	Archibald	18,93
11		29	H	Notts County	W	1-0	Archibald	29,19
12	Nov	5	A	Stoke City	D	1-1	Falco	14,72
13		12	H	Liverpool	D	2-2	Archibald, Hoddle (pen)	44,34
14		19	A	Luton Town	W	4-2	Dick, Archibald 2, Cooke	17,27
15		26	H	Queen's Park Rangers	W	3-2	Archibald, Falco 2	38,78
16	Dec	3	A	Norwich City	L	1-2	Dick	21,98
17		10	H	Southampton	D	0-0		29,71
18		16	A	Manchester United	L	2-4	Brazil, Falco	33,61
19		26	H	Arsenal	L	2-4	Roberts, Archibald	38,75
20		27	A	Aston Villa	D	0-0		30,12
21		31	A	West Ham United	L	1-4	Stevens	30,93
22	Jan	2	H	Watford	L	2-3	Hughton, Hoddle (pen)	32,49
23		14	H	Ipswich Town	W	2-0	Roberts, Falco	25,83
24		21	A	Everton	L	1-2	Archibald	17,99
25	Feb	4	A	Nottingham Forest	D	2-2	Hughton, Falco	21,48
26		8	H	Sunderland	W	3-0	Perryman, Archibald 2	19,32
27		11	H	Leicester City	W	3-2	Archibald, Falco, Galvin	28,41
28		21	A	Notts County	D	0-0		7,94
29		25	H	Birmingham City	L	0-1		23,56
30	Mar	3	H	Stoke City	W	1-0	Falco (pen)	18,27
31		10	A	Liverpool	L	1-3	Stevens	36,71
32		17	H	West Bromwich Albion	L	0-1		22,38
33		24	A	Coventry City	W	4-2	Roberts, Hazard, Brazil 2 (1 pen)	12,84
34		31	H	Wolverhampton Wanderers	W	1-0	Hazard	19,29
35	Apr	7	A	Sunderland	D	1-1	Falco	15,43
36		14	H	Luton Town	W	2-1	Roberts, Falco	25,39
37		18	H	Aston Villa	W	2-1	Roberts (pen), Mabbutt	18,66
38		21	A	Arsenal	L	2-3	Archibald 2	48,83
39		28	A	Queen's Park Rangers	L	1-2	Archibald	24,93
40	May	5	H	Norwich City	W	2-0	Archibald, Falco	18,87
41		7	A	Southampton	L	0-5		21,14
42		12	H	Manchester United	D	1-1	Archibald	39,79
								Appearance
								Substitut
								Goal

FA Cup

R3	Jan	7	A	Fulham	D	0-0		23,39
R3r		11	H	Fulham	W	2-0	Roberts, Archibald	32,89
R4		28	H	Norwich City	D	0-0		37,79
R4r	Feb	1	A	Norwich City	L	1-2	Falco	26,81
								Appearance
								Substitut
								Goal

Milk Cup

R2	Oct	5	H	Lincoln City	W	3-1	Galvin, Archibald, Houghton (og)	20,24
R2		26	A	Lincoln City	L	1-2	Falco	12,23
R3	Nov	9	H	Arsenal	L	1-2	Hoddle (pen)	48,20
								Appearance
								Substitut
								Goal

…chibald S	Ardiles OC	Bowen RM	Brace RL	Brazil AB	Brooke GJ	Clemence RN	Cockram AC	Cooke RE	Crook IS	Crooks GA	Culverhouse IB	Dick AJ	Falco MP	Galvin A	Hazard M	Hoddle G	Hughton CWG	Mabbutt GV	Miller PR	O'Reilly GM	Parks A	Perryman SJ	Price PT	Roberts GP	Stevens GA	Thomas DJ	Webster SP	Own-goals
				11		1							12	9	7	10		3				6		4	5	2		
		2		11		1							12	9		10		7				6		4	5	3		
						1				11			8	9		10	2	7	12			6		4	5	3		
					10	1				11			8	9			2	7		3		6		4	5			
		12			10	1				11			8	9			2	7		3		6		4	5			
				12	10	1				11			8	9			2	7		3		6	5	4				
				9	11	1							8	3		10	2	7				6		4	5			
				11	12	1							9	3		10	2	7				6		4	5			
					11	1							9	3		10	2	7				6	12	4	5			
						1			11				9	3		10	2	7		12		6		4	5			
					11	1				12			9	3		10	2	7				6		4	5			
						1							9	11		10	2	7		12		6		4	5	3		
				12		1						7	9	11		10	2					6		4	5	3		
						1		11				7	9			10	2					6		4	5	3		
						1		7				11	9			10	2					6		4	5	3		
						1		7				11	9			10	2			12		6		4	5	3		
				11	12	1		7					9			10				2		6		4	5	3		
	12			8		1						11	9	7		10				2		6		4	5	3		
	7			9		1		3				11	12			10	2					6		4	5			
				9		1							12	7		10	11			2		6		4	5	3		
	7	3				1						11	9							2		6			5	10	4	
		2			12	1	11						9			10	3			5		6			4	7		
		3						7		12			9	11		10			5		1	6		4	2			
		3											9	11		10		7	5		1	6		4	2			
	10												9	11			3	7	5		1	6		4	2	12		
	7												9	11		10	3		5		1	6		4	2			
	7											12	9	11		10	3		5		1	6		4	2			
	7			8							12		9	11		10	3		4		1	6			5	2		
				9				7				11			12	10	3		5		1	6			4	2		
	7			8	12							11	9		10		3		5		1	6		4	2			
				9		1				12		11			10		3		5			6		4	7	2		
	7			9		1									12		3	11	5			6		4	10	2		
				9		1								11	7		3		5			6		4	10	2		
				8									9	11	7		3		5		1	6		4	10	2		
				10	12								9	11	7		3		5		1	6		4	8	2		
													9	11	7		3	10	5		1	6		4	12	2		
													9	11	7		3	10	5		1	6		4	12	2		
									10	11				9			3	7	5		1	6		4	12	2		
													9	11	7		3	10	5		1	6			4	2		
								7		12			9	11			3	10	5		1	6			4	2		
		3	12	10	8	1	9	7	6	11	2								5	4								
													9	11			3	7	5		1	6		4	10	2		
	8	6	0	17	7	26	2	9	3	6	1	10	32	30	9	24	34	21	20	9	16	41	1	35	37	26	1	
	1	1	1	2	5	0	0	0	0	4	1	1	4	0	2	0	0	0	1	3	0	0	1	0	3	1	0	
				3				1		1		2	13	1	2	4	3	2				1		6	4			

…chibald S	Ardiles OC	Bowen RM	Brace RL	Brazil AB	Brooke GJ	Clemence RN	Cockram AC	Cooke RE	Crook IS	Crooks GA	Culverhouse IB	Dick AJ	Falco MP	Galvin A	Hazard M	Hoddle G	Hughton CWG	Mabbutt GV	Miller PR	O'Reilly GM	Parks A	Perryman SJ	Price PT	Roberts GP	Stevens GA	Thomas DJ	Webster SP	Own-goals
		3		8	7	1			12				9		11	10				5		6		4	2			
		3						7					9	11		10			5		1	6		4	2			
		3											9	11	12	10		7	5		1	6		4	2			
	10												9	11	12		3	7	5		1	6		4	2			
	1	3	0	1	1	1	0	1	0	0	0	0	4	3	1	3	1	2	3	1	3	4	0	4	4	0	0	
	0	0	0	0	0	0	0	0	1	0	0	0	0	0	2	0	0	0	0	0	0	0	0	0	0	0	0	
													1											1				

…chibald S	Ardiles OC	Bowen RM	Brace RL	Brazil AB	Brooke GJ	Clemence RN	Cockram AC	Cooke RE	Crook IS	Crooks GA	Culverhouse IB	Dick AJ	Falco MP	Galvin A	Hazard M	Hoddle G	Hughton CWG	Mabbutt GV	Miller PR	O'Reilly GM	Parks A	Perryman SJ	Price PT	Roberts GP	Stevens GA	Thomas DJ	Webster SP	Own-goals
					11	1							9	3	12	10	2	7				6		4	5			
						1			11	12			9	3		10	2	7				6		4	5			
				12		1							9	11		10	2					6	4	7	5	3		
	0	0	0	0	1	3	0	0	1	0	0	0	3	3	0	3	3	2	0	0	0	3	1	3	3	1	0	
	0	0	0	1	0	0	0	0	0	1	0	0	0	0	1	0	0	0	0	0	0	0	0	0	0	0	0	
													1	1		1												1

League Table

	P	W	D	L	F	A	Pts
Liverpool	42	22	14	6	73	32	80
Southampton	42	22	11	9	66	38	77
Nottingham Forest	42	22	8	12	76	45	74
Manchester United	42	20	14	8	71	41	74
Queen's Park Rangers	42	22	7	13	67	37	73
Arsenal	42	18	9	15	74	60	63
Everton	42	16	14	12	44	42	62
TOTTENHAM HOTSPUR	42	17	10	15	64	65	61
West Ham United	42	17	9	16	60	55	60
Aston Villa	42	17	9	16	59	61	60
Watford	42	16	9	17	68	77	57
Ipswich Town	42	15	8	19	55	57	53
Sunderland	42	13	13	16	42	53	52
Norwich City	42	12	15	15	48	49	51
Leicester City	42	13	12	17	65	68	51
Luton Town	42	14	9	19	53	66	51
West Bromwich Albion	42	14	9	19	48	62	51
Stoke City	42	13	11	18	44	63	50
Coventry City	42	13	11	18	57	77	50
Birmingham City	42	12	12	18	39	50	48
Notts County	42	10	11	21	50	72	41
Wolverhampton W	42	6	11	25	27	80	29

1984-85

DIVISION ONE

Manager: Peter Shreeves

Did you know that?

On 16 March 1985 a Garth Crooks goal gave Spurs victory at Liverpool. It was 73 years to the day since Spurs had last won at Anfield and at last banished the old joke that Spurs had not won there since the sinking of the *Titanic*.

LEAGUE DEBUTANTS

Aug 25 v Everton
Clive Allen
Aug 25 v Everton
John Chiedozie
Apr 15 v Arsenal
David Leworthy

Match No.	Date		Opponents		Result		Scorers	Attendanc
1	Aug	25	A	Everton	W	4-1	Falco, Allen 2, Chiedozie	35,63
2		27	H	Leicester City	D	2-2	Roberts 2 (1 pen)	30,04
3	Sep	1	H	Norwich City	W	3-1	Chiedozie, Falco, Galvin	24,94
4		4	A	Sunderland	L	0-1		18,89
5		8	A	Sheffield Wednesday	L	1-2	Falco	33,42
6		15	H	Queen's Park Rangers	W	5-0	Falco 2, Allen 2, Hazard	31,65
7		22	A	Aston Villa	W	1-0	Chiedozie	22,40
8		29	H	Luton Town	W	4-2	Roberts (pen), Perryman, Falco, Hazard	30,20
9	Oct	6	A	Southampton	L	0-1		21,82
10		12	H	Liverpool	W	1-0	Crooks	28,59
11		20	A	Manchester United	L	0-1		54,51
12		27	H	Stoke City	W	4-0	Roberts (pen), Chiedozie, Allen 2	23,47
13	Nov	3	H	West Bromwich Albion	L	2-3	Chiedozie, Hazard	24,49
14		10	A	Nottingham Forest	W	2-1	Hazard, Galvin	21,30
15		17	A	Ipswich Town	W	3-0	Mabbutt, Allen, Hoddle	21,89
16		24	H	Chelsea	D	1-1	Falco	31,19
17	Dec	1	A	Coventry City	D	1-1	Falco	14,51
18		8	H	Newcastle United	W	3-1	Roberts (pen), Falco 2	29,69
19		15	A	Watford	W	2-1	Falco, Crooks	24,22
20		22	A	Norwich City	W	2-1	Galvin, Crooks	17,68
21		26	H	West Ham United	D	2-2	Mabbutt, Crooks	37,18
22		29	H	Sunderland	W	2-0	Hoddle, Crooks	26,93
23	Jan	1	A	Arsenal	W	2-1	Falco, Crooks	48,71
24		12	A	Queen's Park Rangers	D	2-2	Falco, Crooks	27,40
25	Feb	2	A	Luton Town	D	2-2	Roberts, Falco	17,51
26		23	A	West Bromwich Albion	W	1-0	Falco	15,41
27	Mar	2	A	Stoke City	W	1-0	Crooks	12,55
28		12	H	Manchester United	L	1-2	Falco	42,91
29		16	A	Liverpool	W	1-0	Crooks	43,85
30		23	H	Southampton	W	5-1	Ardiles, Falco, Hoddle, Crooks, Brooke	33,77
31		30	H	Aston Villa	L	0-2		27,97
32	Apr	3	H	Everton	L	1-2	Roberts	48,10
33		6	A	West Ham United	D	1-1	Ardiles	24,45
34		13	A	Leicester City	W	2-1	Falco, Hoddle	15,60
35		17	H	Arsenal	L	0-2		40,39
36		20	H	Ipswich Town	L	2-3	Leworthy 2	20,34
37		27	A	Chelsea	D	1-1	Galvin	26,31
38	May	4	H	Coventry City	W	4-2	Falco 2, Hoddle, Hughton	16,71
39		6	A	Newcastle United	W	3-2	Leworthy, Hoddle, Crook	29,70
40		11	H	Watford	L	1-5	Hoddle (pen)	23,16
41		14	H	Sheffield Wednesday	W	2-0	Falco, Hoddle (pen)	15,66
42		17	H	Nottingham Forest	W	1-0	Falco	20,07

Appearance
Substitut
Goa

FA Cup

R3	Jan	5	H	Charlton Athletic	D	1-1	Crooks	29,02
R3r		23	A	Charlton Athletic	W	2-1	Falco, Galvin	21,40
R4		27	A	Liverpool	L	0-1		27,90

Appearance
Substitut
Goal

Milk Cup

R2	Sep	26	A	Halifax Town	W	5-1	Falco 2, Crooks 3	7,02
R2	Oct	9	H	Halifax Town	W	4-0	Hughton, Hazard 2, Crooks	14,80
R3		31	H	Liverpool	W	1-0	Allen	38,69
R4	Nov	21	A	Sunderland	D	0-0		27,42
R4r	Dec	5	H	Sunderland	L	1-2	Roberts (pen)	25,83

Appearance
Substitut
Goal

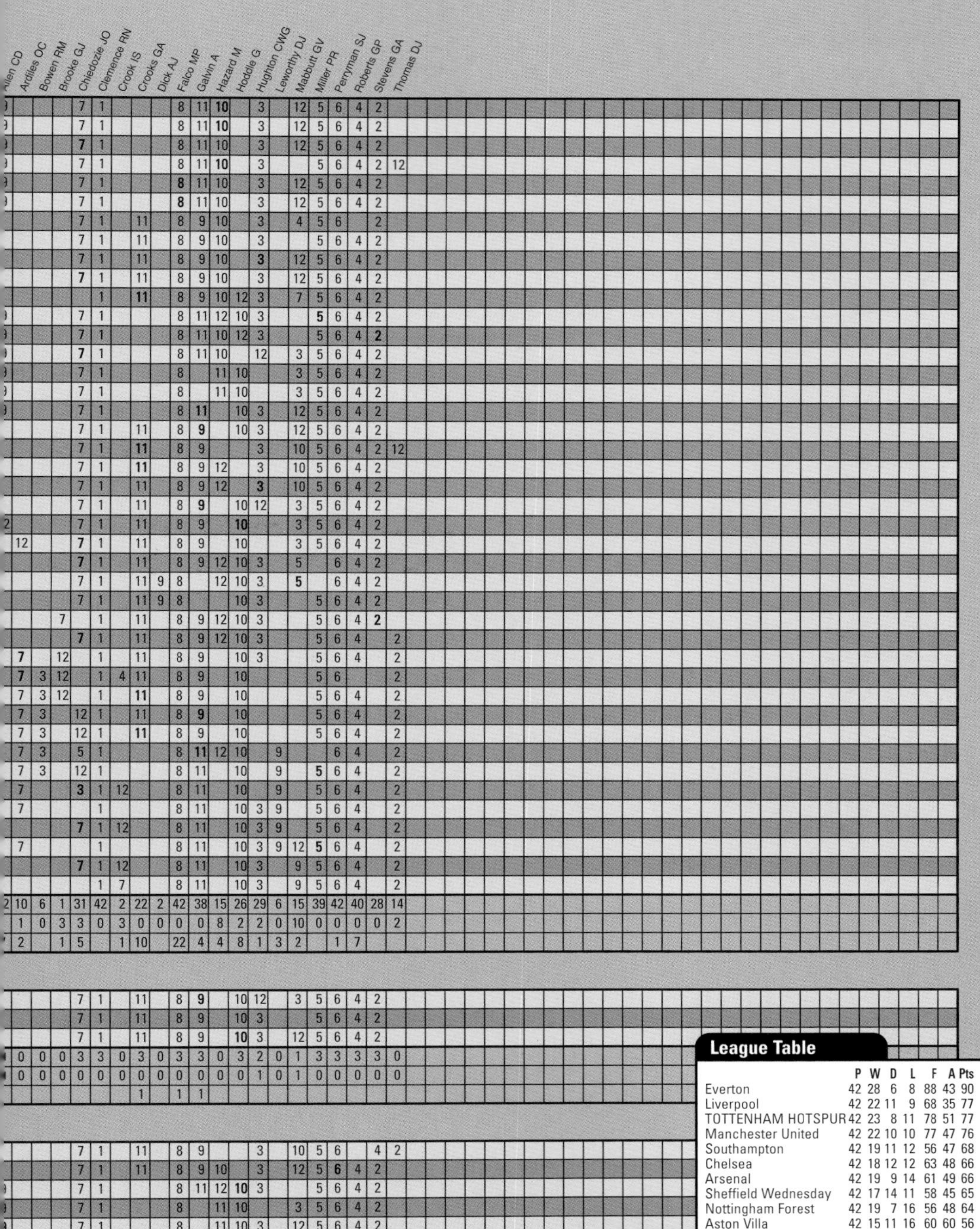

Allen CD	Ardiles OC	Bowen RM	Brooke GJ	Chiedozie JO	Clemence RN	Crook IS	Crooks GA	Dick AJ	Falco MP	Galvin A	Hazard M	Hoddle G	Hughton CWG	Leworthy DJ	Mabbutt GV	Miller PR	Perryman SJ	Roberts GP	Stevens GA	Thomas DJ
9				7	1				8	11	**10**		3		12	5	6	4	2	
9				7	1				8	11	**10**		3		12	5	6	4	2	
9				**7**	1				8	11	10		3		12	5	6	4	2	
9				7	1				8	11	**10**		3			5	6	4	2	12
9				7	1				**8**	11	10		3		12	5	6	4	2	
9				7	1				**8**	11	10		3		12	5	6	4	2	
				7	1		11		8	9	10		3		4	5	6		2	
				7	1		11		8	9	10		3			5	6	4	2	
				7	1		11		8	9	10		**3**		12	5	6	4	2	
				7	1		11		8	9	10		3		12	5	6	4	2	
					1		**11**		8	9	10	12	3		7	5	6	4	2	
9				7	1				8	11	12	10	3			**5**	6	4	2	
9				7	1				8	11	10	12	3			5	6	4	**2**	
9				**7**	1				8	11	10		12		3	5	6	4	2	
9				7	1				8		11	10			3	5	6	4	2	
9				7	1				8		11	10			3	5	6	4	2	
9				7	1				8	**11**		10	3		12	5	6	4	2	
				7	1		11		8	**9**		10	3		12	5	6	4	2	
				7	1		**11**		8	9			3		10	5	6	4	2	12
				7	1		**11**		8	9	12		3		10	5	6	4	2	
				7	1		11		8	9	12		**3**		10	5	6	4	2	
				7	1		11		8	**9**		10	12		3	5	6	4	2	
2				7	1		11		8	9		**10**			3	5	6	4	2	
	12			**7**	1		11		8	9		10			3	5	6	4	2	
				7	1		11		8	9	12	10	3		5		6	4	2	
				7	1		11	9	8		12	10	3		**5**		6	4	2	
				7	1		11	9	8			10	3			5	6	4	2	
			7		1		11		8	9	12	10	3			5	6	4	**2**	
				7	1		11		8	9	12	10	3			5	6	4		2
	7		12		1		11		8	9		10	3			5	6	4		2
	7	3	12		1	4	11		8	9		10				5	6			2
	7	3	12		1		**11**		8	9		10				5	6	4		2
	7	3		12	1		11		8	**9**		10				5	6	4		2
	7	3		12	1		**11**		8	9		10				5	6	4		2
	7	3		5	1				8	**11**	12	10		9			6	4		2
	7	3		12	1				8	11		10		9		**5**	6	4		2
	7			**3**	1	12			8	11		10		9		5	6	4		2
	7				1				8	11		10	3	9		5	6	4		2
				7	1	12			8	11		10	3	9		5	6	4		2
	7				1				8	11		10	3	9	12	**5**	6	4		2
				7	1	12			8	11		10	3		9	5	6	4		2
					1	7			8	11		10	3		9	5	6	4		2
2	10	6	1	31	42	2	22	2	42	38	15	26	29	6	15	39	42	40	28	14
	1	0	3	3	0	3	0	0	0	0	8	2	2	0	10	0	0	0	0	2
	2		1	5		1	10		22	4	4	8	1	3	2		1	7		

Allen CD	Ardiles OC	Bowen RM	Brooke GJ	Chiedozie JO	Clemence RN	Crook IS	Crooks GA	Dick AJ	Falco MP	Galvin A	Hazard M	Hoddle G	Hughton CWG	Leworthy DJ	Mabbutt GV	Miller PR	Perryman SJ	Roberts GP	Stevens GA	Thomas DJ
				7	1		11		8	**9**		10	12		3	5	6	4	2	
				7	1		11		8	9		10	3			5	6	4	2	
				7	1		11		8	9		**10**	3		12	5	6	4	2	
	0	0	0	3	3	0	3	0	3	3	0	3	2	0	1	3	3	3	3	0
	0	0	0	0	0	0	0	0	0	0	0	0	1	0	1	0	0	0	0	0
							1		1	1										

Allen CD	Ardiles OC	Bowen RM	Brooke GJ	Chiedozie JO	Clemence RN	Crook IS	Crooks GA	Dick AJ	Falco MP	Galvin A	Hazard M	Hoddle G	Hughton CWG	Leworthy DJ	Mabbutt GV	Miller PR	Perryman SJ	Roberts GP	Stevens GA	Thomas DJ
				7	1		11		8	9			3		10	5	6		4	2
				7	1		11		8	9	10		3		12	5	**6**	4	2	
9				7	1				8	11	12	**10**	3			5	6	4	2	
9				7	1				8		11	10			3	5	6	4	2	
9				7	1				8		11	10	3		12	5	6	4	2	
	0	0	0	5	5	0	2	0	5	3	3	3	4	0	2	5	5	4	5	1
	0	0	0	0	0	0	0	0	0	0	1	0	0	0	2	0	0	0	0	0
							4		2		2		1					1		

League Table

	P	W	D	L	F	A	Pts
Everton	42	28	6	8	88	43	90
Liverpool	42	22	11	9	68	35	77
TOTTENHAM HOTSPUR	42	23	8	11	78	51	77
Manchester United	42	22	10	10	77	47	76
Southampton	42	19	11	12	56	47	68
Chelsea	42	18	12	12	63	48	66
Arsenal	42	19	9	14	61	49	66
Sheffield Wednesday	42	17	14	11	58	45	65
Nottingham Forest	42	19	7	16	56	48	64
Aston Villa	42	15	11	16	60	60	56
Watford	42	14	13	15	81	71	55
West Bromwich Albion	42	16	7	19	58	62	55
Luton Town	42	15	9	18	57	61	54
Newcastle United	42	13	13	16	55	70	52
Leicester City	42	15	6	21	65	73	51
West Ham United	42	13	12	17	51	68	51
Ipswich Town	42	13	11	18	46	57	50
Coventry City	42	15	5	22	47	64	50
Queen's Park Rangers	42	13	11	18	53	72	50
Norwich City	42	13	10	19	46	64	49
Sunderland	42	10	10	22	40	62	40
Stoke City	42	3	8	31	24	91	17

1985-86

DIVISION ONE

Manager: Peter Shreeves

Did you know that?

When Pat Jennings made his final international appearance for Northern Ireland against Brazil on 12 June 1986 in the Mexico World Cup Finals, it was his 75th appearance for his country as a Spurs player. Even now no Spurs player has beaten that record. Jennings had made his first appearance for the Irish as a Spurs player against England in October 1964, his third cap having already won two with Watford. His final outing was his 119th cap, at the time a world record.

LEAGUE DEBUTANTS

Aug 17 v Watford
Paul Allen
Aug 17 v Watford
Chris Waddle
Feb 22 v Sheffield Wednesday
David Howells

Match No.	Date			Opponents	Result		Scorers	Attendanc
1	Aug	17	H	Watford	W	4-0	P.Allen, Falco, Waddle 2	29,88
2		21	A	Oxford United	D	1-1	Thomas	10,63
3		24	A	Ipswich Town	L	0-1		17,75
4		26	H	Everton	L	0-1		29,72
5		31	A	Manchester City	L	1-2	Miller	27,78
6	Sep	4	H	Chelsea	W	4-1	Roberts, Miller, Falco, Chiedozie	23,64
7		7	H	Newcastle United	W	5-1	Falco, Chiedozie 2, Hoddle, Hazard	23,88
8		14	A	Nottingham Forest	W	1-0	Hughton	17,55
9		21	H	Sheffield Wednesday	W	5-1	Falco 2, Hoddle, Waddle 2	23,60
10		28	A	Liverpool	L	1-4	Chiedozie	41,52
11	Oct	5	A	West Bromwich Albion	D	1-1	Waddle	12,04
12		20	A	Coventry City	W	3-2	Falco, Hoddle (pen), Chiedozie	13,54
13		26	H	Leicester City	L	1-3	Falco	17,94
14	Nov	2	A	Southampton	L	0-1		17,44
15		9	H	Luton Town	L	1-3	Cooke	19,16
16		16	A	Manchester United	D	0-0		54,57
17		23	H	Queen's Park Rangers	D	1-1	Mabbutt	20,34
18		30	A	Aston Villa	W	2-1	Mabbutt, Falco	14,09
19	Dec	7	H	Oxford United	W	5-1	Falco, C.Allen 2, Hoddle, Waddle	17,69
20		14	A	Watford	L	0-1		16,32
21		21	H	Ipswich Town	W	2-0	C.Allen, Hoddle	18,84
22		26	H	West Ham United	W	1-0	Perryman	33,83
23		28	A	Chelsea	L	0-2		37,11
24	Jan	1	A	Arsenal	D	0-0		45,10
25		11	H	Nottingham Forest	L	0-3		19,04
26		18	H	Manchester City	L	0-2		17,00
27	Feb	1	A	Everton	L	0-1		33,17
28		8	H	Coventry City	L	0-1		13,13
29		22	A	Sheffield Wednesday	W	2-1	Chiedozie, Howells	23,23
30	Mar	2	H	Liverpool	L	1-2	Waddle	16,43
31		8	H	West Bromwich Albion	W	5-0	Mabbutt, Falco 2, Galvin, Waddle	10,84
32		15	A	Birmingham City	W	2-1	Stevens, Waddle	9,39
33		22	A	Newcastle United	D	2-2	Hoddle, Waddle	30,61
34		29	H	Arsenal	W	1-0	Stevens	33,42
35		31	A	West Ham United	L	1-2	Ardiles	27,49
36	Apr	5	A	Leicester City	W	4-1	Bowen, Falco 3	9,57
37		12	A	Luton Town	D	1-1	C.Allen	13,14
38		16	H	Birmingham City	W	2-0	Chiedozie, Falco	9,35
39		19	H	Manchester United	D	0-0		32,35
40		26	A	Queen's Park Rangers	W	5-2	Falco 2, C.Allen 2, Hoddle	17,76
41	May	3	H	Aston Villa	W	4-2	Falco 2, C.Allen 2	14,85
42		5	H	Southampton	W	5-3	Galvin 3, C.Allen, Waddle	13,03
								Appearance
								Substitut
								Goal

FA Cup

R3	Jan	4	A	Oxford United	D	1-1	Chiedozie	10,63
R3r		8	H	Oxford United	W*	2-1	Waddle, C.Allen	19,13
R4		25	A	Notts County	D	1-1	C.Allen	17,54
R4r		29	H	Notts County	W	5-0	Chiedozie, Falco, C.Allen, Hoddle, Waddle	17,39
R5	Mar	4	H	Everton	L	1-2	Falco	23,33
								Appearance
								Substitut
								Goal

*after extra-time

Milk Cup

R2	Sep	23	A	Leyton Orient	L	0-2		13,82
R2	Oct	30	H	Leyton Orient	W	4-0	Roberts 2, Galvin, Waddle	21,04
R3	Nov	6	H	Wimbledon	W	2-0	Leworthy, Mabbutt	16,89
R4		20	H	Portsmouth	D	0-0		28,61
R4r		27	A	Portsmouth	D*	0-0		28,10
R4r	Dec	10	A	Portsmouth	L	0-1		26,30
								Appearance
								Substitut
								Goal

*after extra-time

Screensport Super Cup

GR	Oct	2	H	Southampton	W	2-1	Falco 2	11,54
GR	Dec	3	A	Liverpool	L	0-2		14,85
GR		17	A	Southampton	W	3-1	Falco, C.Allen, Leworthy	4,68
GR	Jan	14	H	Liverpool	L	0-3		10,07
SF	Feb	5	H	Everton	D	0-0		7,54
SF	Mar	19	A	Everton	L*	1-3	Falco	12,00
								Appearance
								Substitut
								Goal

*after extra-time

llen CD	Allen PK	Ardiles OC	Bowen RM	Chiedozie JO	Clemence RN	Cooke RE	Crook IS	Dick AJ	Falco MP	Galvin A	Hazard M	Hoddle G	Howells D	Hughton CWG	Jennings PA	Leworthy DJ	Mabbutt GV	Miller PR	Perryman SJ	Roberts GP	Stevens GA	Thomas DJ	Waddle CR
	4	7			1				8	11	10			3		12		5	6			2	9
	4	7			1				8	11	10			3				5	6			2	9
	6	7			1				8	11	10			3		12		5		4		2	9
	6	7			1		12		8	11		10		3				5		4		2	9
	6	7		12	1				8	11		10		3				5		4		2	9
	6	7		9	1				8			10		3		12		5		4		2	11
	6	7		9	1				8		12	10		3				5		4		2	11
	6	7		9	1				8			10		3				5	12	4		2	11
	6	7		9	1				8			10		3			12	5		4		2	11
	5	7		9	1				8			10		3			12		6	4		2	11
	9	7			1				8			10		3			12	5	6	4		2	11
		7		12	1				8	9		10		3				5	6	4	2		11
				7	1				8	9		10		3				5	6	4	2		11
		7			1		12		8	9				3		10	5		6	4	2		11
					1	12	7		8			10		3		9	5		6	4	2		11
	7				1				8	9		10		3			5		6	4	2		11
	7				1				8	9		10		3			5		6	4	2		11
	7				1				8			10		3			5		6	4	2		11
	12	7			1				8			10		3			5			4	2	6	11
	7	12			1				8	11				3			5		6	4	10	2	
	12	7			1				8			10		3			5		6		4	2	11
	12	7			1				8			10		3			5		6		4	2	11
	7	12			1				8			10		3			5		6		4	2	11
		7			1				8			10		3			5		6	4	2		11
2	8	7		9	1							10		3			5		6	4	2		11
	7				1		12		8					3			10	5	6	4	2		11
	12			7	1				8			10		3			4	5	6		2		11
	8			7	1	12		9				10					4	5	6	3	2		11
	2			7	1				8				9				4	5	6		10	3	11
	2			7	1				8			10					4	5	6		9	3	11
2	2				1				8	9		10					7	5		4	6	3	11
	2				1				8	9		10					7	5		4	6	3	11
	2	12			1				8	9		10					7	5		4	6	3	11
	2				1				8	9		10					7	5		4	6	3	11
2	2	10			1				8	9							7	5		4	6	3	11
	2	7	6	12	1				8	9				3			4	5					11
	2			7	1				8	9				3			4	5			6		11
	2		12	7	1				8	11				3			4	5		10	6		
				12	1				8	11		10		3			7	5		4	6	2	
				12	1				8	6		10					7	5		4	2	3	11
					1				8	6		10		3			7	5		4		2	11
					1				8	6		10		3			7	5		4	12	2	11
	29	20	1	13	42	0	1	1	40	23	3	31	1	33	0	2	29	29	22	32	28	27	39
	4	3	1	5	0	2	3	0	0	0	1	0	0	0	0	3	3	0	1	0	1	0	0
	1	1	1	7		1			19	4	1	7	1	1			3	2	1	1	2	1	11

llen CD	Allen PK	Ardiles OC	Bowen RM	Chiedozie JO	Clemence RN	Cooke RE	Crook IS	Dick AJ	Falco MP	Galvin A	Hazard M	Hoddle G	Howells D	Hughton CWG	Jennings PA	Leworthy DJ	Mabbutt GV	Miller PR	Perryman SJ	Roberts GP	Stevens GA	Thomas DJ	Waddle CR
	8	7		12	1							10		3			5		6	4	2		11
2	8	7		9	1							10		3			5		6	4	2		11
	7			12	1				9			10		3			4	5	6		2		11
	12			7	1				8			10		3			4	5	6		2		11
	2			12	1				8			10					7	5	6	4	9	3	11
	4	2	0	2	5	0	0	0	3	0	0	5	0	4	0	0	5	3	5	3	5	1	5
	1	0	0	3	0	0	0	0	0	0	0	0	0	0	0	0	0	0	0	0	0	0	0
				2					2			1											2

llen CD	Allen PK	Ardiles OC	Bowen RM	Chiedozie JO	Clemence RN	Cooke RE	Crook IS	Dick AJ	Falco MP	Galvin A	Hazard M	Hoddle G	Howells D	Hughton CWG	Jennings PA	Leworthy DJ	Mabbutt GV	Miller PR	Perryman SJ	Roberts GP	Stevens GA	Thomas DJ	Waddle CR
	6	7		9	1				8			10		3				5		4		2	11
		12		7	1				8	9		10		3			5		6	4	2		11
					1	7			8			10		3		12	9	5	6	4	2		11
	7				1	12			8	9		10		3			5		6	4	2		11
	7	10			1				8	9				3			5		6	4	2	12	11
	12	7			1				8			10		3			5			4	2	6	11
	3	3	0	2	6	1	0	0	6	3	0	5	0	6	0	0	5	2	4	6	5	2	6
	1	1	0	0	0	1	0	0	0	0	0	0	0	0	0	1	0	0	0	0	0	1	0
										1						1	1			2			1

llen CD	Allen PK	Ardiles OC	Bowen RM	Chiedozie JO	Clemence RN	Cooke RE	Crook IS	Dick AJ	Falco MP	Galvin A	Hazard M	Hoddle G	Howells D	Hughton CWG	Jennings PA	Leworthy DJ	Mabbutt GV	Miller PR	Perryman SJ	Roberts GP	Stevens GA	Thomas DJ	Waddle CR
	5	7		12	1				8			10		3			13		6	4		2	11
	7	13			1				8			10		3			5		6	4	2	12	11
	11	7			1	12			8					3		13	5		6	4	10	2	
	7			8		12				11				3	1		10	5	6	4	2		
	13			7	1		10		8					12			4	5	6	3	2		11
3	4		12	10	1				8	9				3			7	5			6	2	11
	5	2	0	3	5	0	1	0	5	2	0	2	0	5	1	0	5	3	5	5	5	3	4
	1	1	1	1	0	2	0	0	0	0	0	0	0	1	0	1	1	0	0	0	0	1	0
									4							1							

League Table

	P	W	D	L	F	A	Pts
Liverpool	42	26	10	6	89	37	88
Everton	42	26	8	8	87	41	86
West Ham United	42	26	6	10	74	40	84
Manchester United	42	22	10	10	70	36	76
Sheffield Wednesday	42	21	10	11	63	54	73
Chelsea	42	20	11	11	57	56	71
Arsenal	42	20	9	13	49	47	69
Nottingham Forest	42	19	11	12	69	53	68
Luton Town	42	18	12	12	61	44	66
TOTTENHAM HOTSPUR	42	19	8	15	74	52	65
Newcastle United	42	17	12	13	67	72	63
Watford	42	16	11	15	69	62	59
Queen's Park Rangers	42	15	7	20	53	64	52
Southampton	42	12	10	20	51	62	46
Manchester City	42	11	12	19	43	57	45
Aston Villa	42	10	14	18	51	67	44
Coventry City	42	11	10	21	48	71	43
Oxford United	42	10	12	20	62	80	42
Leicester City	42	10	12	20	54	76	42
Ipswich Town	42	11	8	23	32	55	41
Birmingham City	42	8	5	29	30	73	29
West Bromwich Albion	42	4	12	26	35	89	24

1986-87

DIVISION ONE

Manager: David Pleat

Did you know that?

Four players, Phil Gray, John Moncur, Paul Moran and Mark Stimson, made their Football League debuts at Everton on 11 May 1987 as David Pleat rested his senior men for the FA Cup Final five days later. Although nothing hinged on the result, Spurs were fined £10,000 by the FA for fielding a weakened team.

LEAGUE DEBUTANTS

Aug 23	v Aston Villa Richard Gough
Aug 23	v Aston Villa Mitchell Thomas
Oct 11	v Liverpool Nico Claesen
Nov 15	v Coventry City John Polston
Nov 29	v Nottingham Forest Shaun Close
Dec 26	v West Ham United Steve Hodge
Mar 18	v Charlton Athletic Neil Ruddock
Apr 7	v Sheffield Wednesday Tim O'Shea
May 2	v Nottingham Forest Vinny Samways
May 11	v Everton Phil Gray
May 11	v Everton John Moncur
May 11	v Everton Paul Moran
May 11	v Everton Mark Stimson

Match No.	Date			Opponents	Result		Scorers	Attendance
1	Aug	23	A	Aston Villa	W	3-0	C.Allen 3	24,71
2		25	H	Newcastle United	D	1-1	C.Allen	25,38
3		30	H	Manchester City	W	1-0	Roberts	23,16
4	Sep	2	A	Southampton	L	0-2		17,91
5		6	A	Arsenal	D	0-0		44,70
6		13	H	Chelsea	L	1-3	C.Allen (pen)	28,20
7		20	A	Leicester City	W	2-1	C.Allen 2	13,14
8		27	H	Everton	W	2-0	C.Allen 2	28,00
9	Oct	4	H	Luton Town	D	0-0		22,73
10		11	A	Liverpool	W	1-0	C.Allen	43,13
11		18	H	Sheffield Wednesday	D	1-1	C.Allen	26,87
12		25	A	Queen's Park Rangers	L	0-2		18,57
13	Nov	1	H	Wimbledon	L	1-2	M.Thomas	21,82
14		8	A	Norwich City	L	1-2	Claesen	22,01
15		15	H	Coventry City	W	1-0	C.Allen	20,25
16		22	A	Oxford United	W	4-2	C.Allen 2, Waddle 2	12,14
17		29	H	Nottingham Forest	L	2-3	C.Allen 2	30,04
18	Dec	7	A	Manchester United	D	3-3	Mabbutt, C.Allen, Moran (og)	35,26
19		13	H	Watford	W	2-1	Gough, Hoddle	23,13
20		20	A	Chelsea	W	2-0	C.Allen 2	21,57
21		26	H	West Ham United	W	4-0	Hodge, C.Allen 2, Waddle	39,01
22		27	A	Coventry City	L	3-4	C.Allen 2, Claesen	22,17
23	Jan	1	A	Charlton Athletic	W	2-0	Claesen, Galvin	19,74
24		4	H	Arsenal	L	1-2	M.Thomas	37,72
25		24	H	Aston Villa	W	3-0	Hodge 2, Claesen	19,12
26	Feb	14	H	Southampton	W	2-0	Hodge, Gough	22,06
27		25	H	Leicester City	W	5-0	C.Allen 2 (1 pen), P.Allen, Claesen 2	16,03
28	Mar	7	H	Queen's Park Rangers	W	1-0	C.Allen (pen)	21,07
29		22	H	Liverpool	W	1-0	Waddle	32,76
30		25	A	Newcastle United	D	1-1	Hoddle	30,83
31		28	A	Luton Town	L	1-3	Waddle	13,44
32	Apr	4	H	Norwich City	W	3-0	C.Allen 3	22,40
33		7	A	Sheffield Wednesday	W	1-0	C.Allen	19,48
34		15	A	Manchester City	D	1-1	Claesen	21,46
35		18	H	Charlton Athletic	W	1-0	C.Allen	26,92
36		20	A	West Ham United	L	1-2	C.Allen	23,97
37		22	A	Wimbledon	D	2-2	Claesen (pen), Bowen	7,91
38		25	H	Oxford United	W	3-1	P.Allen, Waddle, Hoddle	20,06
39	May	2	A	Nottingham Forest	L	0-2		19,83
40		4	H	Manchester United	W	4-0	M.Thomas 2, C.Allen (pen), P.Allen	36,69
41		9	A	Watford	L	0-1		20,02
42		11	A	Everton	L	0-1		28,28

Appearance
Substitut
Goal

FA Cup

R3	Jan	10	H	Scunthorpe United	W	3-2	Mabbutt, Waddle, Claesen	19,33
R4		31	H	Crystal Palace	W	4-0	Mabbutt, C.Allen (pen), Claesen, O'Reilly (og)	29,60
R5	Feb	21	H	Newcastle United	W	1-0	C.Allen (pen)	38,03
R6	Mar	15	A	Wimbledon	W	2-0	Waddle, Hoddle	15,63
SF	Apr	11	N*	Watford	W	4-0	Hodge 2, C.Allen, P.Allen	46,15
F	May	16	N#	Coventry City	L^	2-3	C.Allen, Mabbutt	98,00

*played at Villa Park #played at Wembley Stadium ^after extra-time

Appearance
Substitut
Goal

Littlewoods Challenge Cup

R2	Sep	23	A	Barnsley	W	3-2	Roberts, C.Allen, Waddle	10,07
R2	Oct	8	H	Barnsley	W	5-3	Close, Hoddle 2, Galvin, C.Allen	12,29
R3		29	H	Birmingham City	W	5-0	Roberts, C.Allen 2, Hoddle, Waddle	15,54
R4	Nov	26	A	Cambridge United	W	3-1	C.Allen, Close, Waddle	10,03
R5	Jan	27	A	West Ham United	D	1-1	C.Allen	28,64
R5r	Feb	2	H	West Ham United	W	5-0	C.Allen 3 (1 pen), Hoddle, Claesen	41,99
SF		8	A	Arsenal	W	1-0	C.Allen	41,25
SF	Mar	1	H	Arsenal	L*	1-2	C.Allen	37,09
SFr		4	H	Arsenal	L	1-2	C.Allen	41,00

*after extra-time

Appearances
Substitute
Goals

Allen PK	Ardiles OC	Bowen RM	Chiedozie JO	Claesen NPJ	Clemence RN	Close SC	Falco MP	Galvin A	Gough CR	Gray P	Hoddle G	Hodge SB	Howells DG	Hughton CWG	Mabbutt GV	Miller PR	Moncur JF	Moran P	O'Shea TJ	Parks A	Polston JD	Roberts GP	Ruddock N	Samways V	Stevens GA	Stimson M	Thomas DJ	Thomas MA	Waddle CR	Own-goals
12					1		8	11	5		**10**				6							4			2			3	9	
					1		8	11	5		10				6							4			2			3	9	
			8		1			11	5		10				6							4			2			3	9	
					1		8	11	5		10				6							**4**			2		12	3	9	
	12				1		**8**	11	5		10				6							4			2			3	9	
12					1		8	11	**5**		10				6							4			2			3	9	
11	12				1				5		10				6							4			**2**		8	3	9	
8					1		12	**11**	5		10				6							4					2	3	9	
8	12				1			11	5		10		7		6							4					2	3	9	
12				8	1			**11**	5		10				6							4			2			3	9	
11				8	1				5		10				6							4			2			3	9	
11	12			8	1				5		10				6							4			**2**			3	9	
11	12			8	1				5		10				6							4			**2**			3	9	
11				8	1				6		12			**2**	10	5						4						3	9	
11	12			8	1				5		10			**2**	6						4							3	9	
2	11			**8**	1				5		10				6						4						12	3	9	
2	**11**				1	8					10				6						5	4					12	3	9	
2	**11**				1			8	5		10				6							4					12	3	9	
8	12				1			**11**	5		10				6							4					2	3	9	
8	4							11	5		10				6					1							2	3	9	
8	12				1			11	5		10	4			6												2	**3**	9	
8	**3**			12	1			11	5		10	4			6												2		9	
8				11	1			12	5		10	**4**			6	3											2		9	
8	**4**			12	1			11	5		10				6												2	3	9	
8				**11**	1			12	5		10	4			6												2	3	9	
8	**11**			12	1				5		10	4			6												2	3	9	
8				11	1				5			4			6										10		2	3	9	
8				12	1			11	5			4			6										10		**2**	3	9	
8	11				1				5		10	4			6										2			3	9	
8	11				1				5		10	4			6										2			3	9	
8	12			11	1				5		10	**4**			6										2			3	9	
8	10			11	1			12	5			4		2	6													3	9	
8				**11**	1			10	5			4			6				12						2			3	9	
8		12		11	1				5		10	4			6										**2**			3	9	
8	**9**			11	1			12	5		10	4		2									6					3		
8				12	1			11	5		10	4		2							6							3	9	
8	4	10		**9**	1			11	5										7		2		6					3		
8	11			12	1				5		10	4		2	6													3	9	
8	11			10	1			**7**	5			4		2									6	12				3	9	
8	11			12	1				5		10	4		2	6													3	**9**	
8	**11**			12	1				5		10	4			6										2			3	9	
				9		12				8				2			10	**7**		1	5		6	11	4	3				
34	16	1	1	18	40	1	5	20	40	1	34	19	1	9	37	2	1	1	1	2	6	17	4	1	20	1	13	39	39	
3	9	1	0	8	0	1	1	4	0	0	1	0	0	0	0	0	0	0	1	0	0	0	0	1	0	0	4	0	0	
3		1		8				1	2		3	4			1							1						4	6	1

Allen PK	Ardiles OC	Bowen RM	Chiedozie JO	Claesen NPJ	Clemence RN	Close SC	Falco MP	Galvin A	Gough CR	Gray P	Hoddle G	Hodge SB	Howells DG	Hughton CWG	Mabbutt GV	Miller PR	Moncur JF	Moran P	O'Shea TJ	Parks A	Polston JD	Roberts GP	Ruddock N	Samways V	Stevens GA	Stimson M	Thomas DJ	Thomas MA	Waddle CR	Own-goals
8				11	1				5		10	4			6												2	3	9	
8				13	1			11	5		10	4			6										12		2	3	9	
8	11			13	1				5		10	**4**			6										12		2	3	9	
8	11			12	1				5		10	4			6								13		**2**			3	9	
8	11			12	1				5		10	4		2	6										13			3	9	
8	11			12	1				5		10	4		**2**	6										13			3	9	
6	4	0	0	1	6	0	0	1	6	0	6	6	0	2	6	0	0	0	0	0	0	0	0	0	1	0	3	6	6	
0	0	0	0	5	0	0	0	0	0	0	0	0	0	0	0	0	0	0	0	0	0	0	1	0	4	0	0	0	0	
1				2							1	2			3														2	1

Allen PK	Ardiles OC	Bowen RM	Chiedozie JO	Claesen NPJ	Clemence RN	Close SC	Falco MP	Galvin A	Gough CR	Gray P	Hoddle G	Hodge SB	Howells DG	Hughton CWG	Mabbutt GV	Miller PR	Moncur JF	Moran P	O'Shea TJ	Parks A	Polston JD	Roberts GP	Ruddock N	Samways V	Stevens GA	Stimson M	Thomas DJ	Thomas MA	Waddle CR	Own-goals
11					1		12		5		**10**				8	6						4					2	3	9	
12	7				1	8		11	**5**		10					6						4					2	3	9	
11				8	1				5		10				6	12						4			2			**3**	9	
2	11				1	8			**5**		10				6						12	4					13	3	9	
8	4				1			11	5		10				6												2	3	9	
8	4			11	1				5		10				6												2	3	9	
8	4			**11**	1			12	5		10				6												2	3	9	
8	**4**			11	1			13	5		10				6										12		2	3	9	
8	4			**11**	1			12	5						6										10		2	3	9	
8	7	0	0	5	9	2	0	2	9	0	8	0	0	0	8	2	0	0	0	0	0	4	0	0	2	0	7	9	9	
1	0	0	0	0	0	0	1	3	0	0	0	0	0	0	0	1	0	0	0	0	1	0	0	0	1	0	1	0	0	
				1		2		1			4											2							3	

League Table

	P	W	D	L	F	A	Pts
Everton	42	26	8	8	76	31	86
Liverpool	42	23	8	11	72	42	77
TOTTENHAM HOTSPUR	42	21	8	13	68	43	71
Arsenal	42	20	10	12	58	35	70
Norwich City	42	17	17	8	53	51	68
Wimbledon	42	19	9	14	57	50	66
Luton Town	42	18	12	12	47	45	66
Nottingham Forest	42	18	11	13	64	51	65
Watford	42	18	9	15	67	54	63
Coventry City	42	17	12	13	50	45	63
Manchester United	42	14	14	14	52	45	56
Southampton	42	14	10	18	69	68	52
Sheffield Wednesday	42	13	13	16	58	59	52
Chelsea	42	13	13	16	53	64	52
West Ham United	42	14	10	18	52	67	52
Queen's Park Rangers	42	13	11	18	48	64	50
Newcastle United	42	12	11	19	47	65	47
Oxford United	42	11	13	18	44	69	46
Charlton Athletic	42	11	11	20	45	55	44
Leicester City	42	11	9	22	54	76	42
Manchester City	42	8	15	19	36	57	39
Aston Villa	42	8	12	22	45	79	36

1987-88

DIVISION ONE

Manager: David Pleat until October then Terry Venables from December

Did you know that?

White Hart Lane staged a World Heavyweight Championship title eliminator between Joe Bugner and Frank Bruno on 24 October 1987, with Bruno stopping Bugner in the eighth round. It was the third boxing contest the club had staged. In June 1942 Freddie Mills knocked out Len Harvey in the second round to take Harvey's British light-heavyweight title and the British version of the World Championship and in July 1945 Bruce Woodcock knocked out Brian London in round six to become British heavyweight champion. Another contest was staged in September 1991 when Chris Eubank met Michael Watson for the WBO World Super-Middleweight title, with the referee stopping the fight in Eubank's favour in the 12th round. Watson suffered a blood clot on the brain but has since shown remarkable courage to rebuild his life.

LEAGUE DEBUTANTS

Aug 15	v Coventry City Chris Fairclough
Aug 15	v Coventry City Johnny Metgod
Dec 26	v Southampton Brian Statham
Jan 1	v Watford Terry Fenwick
Feb 23	v Manchester United Bobby Mimms
Feb 23	v Manchester United Paul Walsh

Match No.	Date		Opponents		Result		Scorers	Attendanc
1	Aug	15	A	Coventry City	L	1-2	Mabbutt	23,94
2		19	H	Newcastle United	W	3-1	C.Allen, Waddle, Hodge	26,26
3		22	H	Chelsea	W	1-0	Claesen	37,07
4		29	A	Watford	D	1-1	C.Allen (pen)	19,07
5	Sep	1	H	Oxford United	W	3-0	C.Allen, Claesen 2	21,81
6		5	A	Everton	D	0-0		32,38
7		12	H	Southampton	W	2-1	C.Allen (pen), Claesen	24,72
8		19	A	West Ham United	W	1-0	Fairclough	27,75
9		26	A	Manchester United	L	0-1		47,60
10	Oct	3	H	Sheffield Wednesday	W	2-0	P.Allen, Claesen	24,31
11		10	A	Norwich City	L	1-2	Claesen	18,66
12		18	H	Arsenal	L	1-2	Claesen	36,68
13		24	A	Nottingham Forest	L	0-3		23,54
14		31	H	Wimbledon	L	0-3		22,28
15	Nov	4	A	Portsmouth	D	0-0		15,30
16		14	H	Queen's Park Rangers	D	1-1	P.Allen	28,11
17		21	A	Luton Town	L	0-2		10,09
18		28	H	Liverpool	L	0-2		47,36
19	Dec	13	H	Charlton Athletic	L	0-1		20,39
20		20	A	Derby County	W	2-1	C.Allen, Claesen	17,59
21		26	A	Southampton	L	1-2	Fairclough	18,45
22		28	H	West Ham United	W	2-1	Fairclough, Waddle	39,45
23	Jan	1	H	Watford	W	2-1	C.Allen, Moran	25,23
24		2	A	Chelsea	D	0-0		29,31
25		16	H	Coventry City	D	2-2	C.Allen 2	25,65
26		23	A	Newcastle United	L	0-2		24,61
27	Feb	13	A	Oxford United	D	0-0		9,90
28		23	H	Manchester United	D	1-1	C.Allen	25,73
29		27	A	Sheffield Wednesday	W	3-0	C.Allen, P.Allen, Claesen	18,04
30	Mar	1	H	Derby County	D	0-0		15,98
31		6	A	Arsenal	L	1-2	C.Allen	37,14
32		9	H	Everton	W	2-1	Fairclough, Walsh	18,66
33		12	H	Norwich City	L	1-3	Claesen	19,32
34		19	A	Wimbledon	L	0-3		8,61
35		26	H	Nottingham Forest	D	1-1	Foster (og)	25,30
36	Apr	2	H	Portsmouth	L	0-1		18,61
37		4	A	Queen's Park Rangers	L	0-2		14,73
38		23	A	Liverpool	L	0-1		44,79
39	May	2	A	Charlton Athletic	D	1-1	Hodge	13,97
40		4	H	Luton Town	W	2-1	Mabbutt, Hodge	15,43
								Appearance
								Substitut
								Goal

FA Cup

R3	Jan	9	A	Oldham Athletic	W	4-2	Thomas, C.Allen 2, Waddle	16,93
R4		30	A	Port Vale	L	1-2	Ruddock	20,04
								Appearance
								Substitut
								Goal

Littlweoods Challenge Cup

R2	Sep	23	A	Torquay United	L	0-1		5,00
R2	Oct	7	H	Torquay United	W	3-0	Claesen 2, Cole (og)	20,97
R3		28	A	Aston Villa	L	1-2	Ardiles	29,11
								Appearance
								Substitut
								Goal

…llen CD	Allen PK	Ardiles OC	Claesen NPJ	Clemence RN	Close SC	Fairclough CH	Fenwick TW	Gough CR	Gray P	Hodge SB	Howells DG	Hughton CWG	Mabbutt GV	Metgod JAB	Mimms RA	Moncur JF	Moran P	O'Shea TJ	Parks A	Polston JD	Ruddock N	Samways V	Statham B	Stevens GA	Thomas MA	Waddle CR	Walsh PA	Own-goals
	8	13	11	1		5		4		10			6	12										2	3	9		
	8			1		5		4		10			6	11						12				**2**	3	9		
	8	2	12	1		5		4		10			6	**11**											3	9		
	8	2	11	1		5		4		10			6												3	9		
	8	2	11	1		5		4		10			6	13						12					**3**	9		
	8	2	11	1		5		4		**10**			6	12											3	9		
	8	9	11	1		5		4		10			6	12										**2**	3			
	8	9	11	1		5		4		10				12			**6**					13		2	3			
	8	9	11	1		5		4		10			6	13			**7**					12		2	3			
	8	9	11	1	12	5				10			6									4		2	3			
	8	**9**	11	1	7	5				10	12		6									4		2	3			
3	8	4	11		**7**	5				10			6						1			12		2	3	9		
	8	9	11		12	5						**2**	6			13			1			4		10	3			
	8	9	11		12	5						2	6						1		13	4		10	**3**			
2	8	9	11			5						3	6				**7**		1		4	10		2				
	8	9	**11**			5				10		3	6						1		4	12		2				
	8	9			13	5				10	11	3	6						1			4		**2**	12			
	8		12			5				10		**2**	6					13	1		4			11	3	9		
	8		11			5						2	6						1			4		10	3	9		
	8	10	11			5						12	**6**				13		1			4		2	3	9		
		10				5				8	13	2					11		1			**4**	12	6	3	9		
	8	10			13	5				4	11	2					7		1				12	**6**	3	9		
	8	10				5	2			4	12		6				**11**		1						3	9		
	8					5	4			10	12	2	6				11		1			13			3	9		
	8	**10**				5	4				13	2	6				11		1			12			3	9		
	8	10				5	4				13	**2**	6				11		1		12				3	9		
	8		11			5	4						6						1			10	2		3	9		
7	8	10				5	4						6		1								2		3	9	11	
7	8		12			5	4						6		1	9						10	2		3		**11**	
7	8	12				5	4						6		1	**9**						10	2		3		11	
7	8	9				5	4						6		1							10	2		3		11	
7	8	9				5	4						6		1	12						**10**	2		3		11	
7	8	9	12			5	4						6		1							**10**	2		3		11	
7	8	**9**				5	4			12			6		1							10	2		3		11	
	8		11			5	**4**			9	13		6		1		12					10	2		3		7	
	8		11			5	4			9	12		6		1	**3**	13					10	2				7	
	8					5	4			**9**	11		6	3	1		12					10	2			13	7	
2	8					5				11			6	**4**	1							10	2		3	9	7	
7	8		12			5	4			11			6	13	1							10	2		3	9		
7	8					5	**4**		13	11			6	10	1							12	2		3	9		
1	39	26	19	11	2	40	17	9	0	25	3	12	37	5	13	3	9	0	16	0	3	21	14	18	35	21	11	
3	0	2	5	0	5	0	0	0	1	1	8	1	0	7	0	2	4	1	0	2	2	5	4	0	1	1	0	
1	3		10			4				3			2				1									2	1	1

…llen CD	Allen PK	Ardiles OC	Claesen NPJ	Clemence RN	Close SC	Fairclough CH	Fenwick TW	Gough CR	Gray P	Hodge SB	Howells DG	Hughton CWG	Mabbutt GV	Metgod JAB	Mimms RA	Moncur JF	Moran P	O'Shea TJ	Parks A	Polston JD	Ruddock N	Samways V	Statham B	Stevens GA	Thomas MA	Waddle CR	Walsh PA	Own-goals
7		10				5	8			**4**	13	2	6				11		1				12		3	9		
7	8					5	10				12	2	6				11		1		4				3	9		
2	1	1	0	0	0	2	2	0	0	1	0	2	2	0	0	0	2	0	2	0	1	0	0	0	2	2	0	
0	0	0	0	0	0	0	0	0	0	0	2	0	0	0	0	0	0	0	0	0	0	0	1	0	0	0	0	
2																					1				1	1		

…llen CD	Allen PK	Ardiles OC	Claesen NPJ	Clemence RN	Close SC	Fairclough CH	Fenwick TW	Gough CR	Gray P	Hodge SB	Howells DG	Hughton CWG	Mabbutt GV	Metgod JAB	Mimms RA	Moncur JF	Moran P	O'Shea TJ	Parks A	Polston JD	Ruddock N	Samways V	Statham B	Stevens GA	Thomas MA	Waddle CR	Walsh PA	Own-goals
	8	2		1		5		4		10	7		6	**11**			12								3	9		
	8	9	11	1	7	5				10			6				12					**4**		2	3			
7	8	9	11			5						13	6	10			12		1			**4**		2	3			
1	3	3	2	2	1	3	0	1	0	2	1	0	3	2	0	0	0	0	1	0	0	2	0	2	3	1	0	
0	0	0	0	0	0	0	0	0	0	0	0	1	0	0	0	0	3	0	0	0	0	0	0	0	0	0	0	
		1	2																									1

League Table

	P	W	D	L	F	A	Pts
Liverpool	40	26	12	2	87	24	90
Manchester United	40	23	12	5	71	38	81
Nottingham Forest	40	20	13	7	67	39	73
Everton	40	19	13	8	53	27	70
Queen's Park Rangers	40	19	10	11	48	38	67
Arsenal	40	18	12	10	58	39	66
Wimbledon	40	14	15	11	58	47	57
Newcastle United	40	14	14	12	55	53	56
Luton Town	40	14	11	15	57	58	53
Coventry City	40	13	14	13	46	53	53
Sheffield Wednesday	40	15	8	17	52	66	53
Southampton	40	12	14	14	49	53	50
TOTTENHAM HOTSPUR	40	12	11	17	38	48	47
Norwich City	40	12	9	19	40	52	45
Derby County	40	10	13	17	35	45	43
West Ham United	40	9	15	16	40	52	42
Charlton Athletic	40	9	15	16	38	52	42
Chelsea	40	9	15	16	50	68	42
Portsmouth	40	7	14	19	36	66	35
Watford	40	7	11	22	27	51	32
Oxford United	40	6	13	21	44	80	31

1988-89

DIVISION ONE

Manager: Terry Venables

Did you know that?

The season got under way in the worst possible fashion, with the opening-day fixture against Coventry City at White Hart Lane being postponed. Work on refurbishment of the East Stand was not complete and when the Local Authority Safety Officer inspected the works on the morning of the match he decided the ground could not be made safe in time so Spurs had no option but to call the game off.

LEAGUE DEBUTANTS

Sep 3	v Newcastle United Paul Gascoigne
Oct 1	v Manchester United Paul Stewart
Nov 12	v Wimbledon Guy Butters
Dec 17	v West Ham United Mark Robson
Dec 26	v Luton Town Gudni Bergsson
Jan 15	v Nottingham Forest Erik Thorstvedt
Feb 21	v Norwich City Nayim

Match No.	Date			Opponents	Result		Scorers	Attendance
1	Sep	3	A	Newcastle United	D	2-2	Fenwick, Waddle	32,97
2		10	H	Arsenal	L	2-3	Gascoigne, Waddle	32,62
3		17	A	Liverpool	D	1-1	Fenwick	40,92
4		24	H	Middlesbrough	W	3-2	Fenwick (pen), Waddle, Howells	23,42
5	Oct	1	H	Manchester United	D	2-2	Walsh, Waddle	29,31
6		8	A	Charlton Athletic	D	2-2	Fenwick (pen), Allen	14,38
7		18	A	Norwich City	L	1-3	Fairclough	20,33
8		25	H	Southampton	L	1-2	Ray Wallace (og)	19,51
9		29	A	Aston Villa	L	1-2	Fenwick (pen)	26,23
10	Nov	5	H	Derby County	L	1-3	Stewart	22,86
11		12	H	Wimbledon	W	3-2	Butters, Fenwick (pen), Samways	23,58
12		20	A	Sheffield Wednesday	W	2-0	Stewart 2	15,38
13		23	H	Coventry City	D	1-1	Stewart	21,96
14		26	H	Queen's Park Rangers	D	2-2	Gascoigne, Waddle	26,69
15	Dec	3	A	Everton	L	0-1		17,37
16		10	H	Millwall	W	2-0	Gascoigne, Waddle	27,66
17		17	A	West Ham United	W	2-0	Thomas, Mabbutt	28,36
18		26	H	Luton Town	D	0-0		27,33
19		31	H	Newcastle United	W	2-0	Walsh, Waddle	27,73
20	Jan	2	A	Arsenal	L	0-2		45,12
21		15	H	Nottingham Forest	L	1-2	Waddle	16,90
22		21	A	Middlesbrough	D	2-2	Stewart 2	23,69
23	Feb	5	A	Manchester United	L	0-1		41,42
24		11	H	Charlton Athletic	D	1-1	Stewart	22,80
25		21	H	Norwich City	W	2-1	Gascoigne, Waddle	19,12
26		25	A	Southampton	W	2-0	Nayim, Waddle	16,70
27	Mar	1	H	Aston Villa	W	2-0	Waddle 2	19,09
28		11	A	Derby County	D	1-1	Gascoigne	18,20
29		18	A	Coventry City	D	1-1	Waddle	17,15
30		22	A	Nottingham Forest	W	2-1	Howells, Samways	23,09
31		26	H	Liverpool	L	1-2	Fenwick (pen)	30,01
32		28	A	Luton Town	W	3-1	Howells, Walsh, Gascoigne	11,14
33	Apr	1	H	West Ham United	W	3-0	Fenwick (pen), Nayim, Stewart	28,37
34		12	H	Sheffield Wednesday	D	0-0		17,27
35		15	A	Wimbledon	W	2-1	Waddle, Stewart	12,36
36		22	H	Everton	W	2-1	Walsh 2	28,56
37		29	A	Millwall	W	5-0	Walsh, Stewart 3, Samways	16,55
38	May	13	A	Queen's Park Rangers	L	0-1		21,87

Appearances
Substitutes
Goals

FA Cup

R3	Jan	7	A	Bradford City	L	0-1		15,91

Appearances
Substitutes
Goals

Littlewoods Challenge Cup

R2	Sep	27	A	Notts County	D	1-1	Samways	9,26
R2	Oct	11	H	Notts County	W	2-1	Fenwick (pen), Gascoigne	14,95
R3	Nov	1	H	Blackburn Rovers	D	0-0		18,814
R3r		9	A	Blackburn Rovers	W*	2-1	Thomas, Stewart	12,961
R4		29	A	Southampton	L	1-2	Osman (og)	17,35

*after extra-time

Appearances
Substitutes
Goals

Bergsson G	Butters G	Fairclough CH	Fenwick TW	Gascoigne PJ	Gray P	Howells DG	Hughton CWG	Mabbutt GV	Mimms RA	Moncur JF	Moran P	Nayim	Polston JD	Robson MA	Samways V	Statham B	Stevens GA	Stewart PA	Stimson M	Thomas MA	Thorstvedt E	Waddle CR	Walsh PA	Own-goals
		5	4	**8**		12	3	6	1		13					2				10		9	7	
		5	4	8		12		6	1		13				10	**2**				3		9	7	
		5	4	8		13	12	6	1						10	2				3		9	**7**	
		5	4	8		13		6	1		12				10	2				3		9	**7**	
			4	8		13	5	6	1						10	2		12		3		9	**7**	
			4	8		12		6	1						10	2		11		3		9	**7**	
		5		8		12		6	1			4			**10**		2	7		3		9		
		5		8				6	1			4					2	10		3		9	7	
		5	4	8		7		6	1	13							2	10	12	3		9		
		5	4	8		12		6	1		**7**				13		2	10		3		9		
	12	5	4	8				6	1		7				11		**2**	10		3		9		
	2	5	4	**8**		13		6	1		7				11			10		3		9		
	2	5	4	8				6	1		7				**11**			10		3		9	13	
	2	5	4	8	13			6	1						12			10		**3**		9	7	
	2	5	4	8				6	1						**7**			10		3		9	12	
	2	5	4	8				6	1									10		3		9	7	
	2	5	4	**8**				6	1				12	13				10		3		9	7	
5	2		4	**8**				6	1		13				12			10		3		9	7	
8	2	5	4			12		6	1									10		3		9	**7**	
8	2	5	4					6	1									10		3		9	7	
8	2	5	4	12		13	**3**	6										10			1	9	7	
5	2		4	8		**7**	3	6										10		13	1	9	12	
5	2		4	8		**7**	3	6										10		13	1	9	12	
5	2		4	8		**7**	3	6										10			1	9	12	
	2		4	8		12	3	6						**10**						5	1	9	7	
	2	5	4			12	3	6						**10**						8	1	9	7	
	2	5	4				3	6				8		10							1	9	7	
	2		4	8			3	6				**5**		13				10		12	1	9	7	
	2		4	**8**		12	3	6				5						10			1	9	7	
	2		4			8	3	6				**5**			12			10			1	9	7	
	2		4			8	3	6				**5**	12		13			10			1	9	7	
	2		4	8		5	3	6										10			1	9	7	
	2		4	8		12	3	6				**5**						10			1	9	7	
4	2			8		5	3	6							10						1	9	7	
	2		4	8		5	3	6										10			1	9	7	
	2		4	8		5	3	6				12			13			10			1	9	7	
	2		4	8		5	3	6				12			13			10			1	9	**7**	
	2			**8**		5	3	6				12	13		4			10			1	9	7	
8	27	20	34	31	0	12	20	38	20	0	4	8	0	3	12	6	5	29	0	22	18	38	28	
0	1	0	0	1	1	15	1	0	0	1	4	3	3	2	7	0	0	1	1	3	0	0	5	
	1	1	8	6		3		1				2			3			12		1		14	6	1

Bergsson G	Butters G	Fairclough CH	Fenwick TW	Gascoigne PJ	Gray P	Howells DG	Hughton CWG	Mabbutt GV	Mimms RA	Moncur JF	Moran P	Nayim	Polston JD	Robson MA	Samways V	Statham B	Stevens GA	Stewart PA	Stimson M	Thomas MA	Thorstvedt E	Waddle CR	Walsh PA	Own-goals
8	2	5	4				12	6	1		13							10		3		9	7	
1	1	1	1	0	0	0	0	1	1	0	0	0	0	0	0	0	0	1	0	1	0	1	1	
0	0	0	0	0	0	0	1	0	0	0	1	0	0	0	0	0	0	0	0	0	0	0	0	

Bergsson G	Butters G	Fairclough CH	Fenwick TW	Gascoigne PJ	Gray P	Howells DG	Hughton CWG	Mabbutt GV	Mimms RA	Moncur JF	Moran P	Nayim	Polston JD	Robson MA	Samways V	Statham B	Stevens GA	Stewart PA	Stimson M	Thomas MA	Thorstvedt E	Waddle CR	Walsh PA	Own-goals
		5	4	8				6	1						10	2				3		9	7	
			4	8		12		6	1						10	2		**11**		3		9	7	
		5	4	**8**				6	1		7				12		2	10		3		9		
	12	**5**	4	8				6	1						13		2	10		3		9	7	
	2	5	4	8				6	1		12				**7**			10		3		9		
0	1	4	5	5	0	0	0	5	5	0	1	0	0	0	3	2	2	4	0	5	0	5	3	
0	1	0	0	0	0	1	0	0	0	0	1	0	0	0	2	0	0	0	0	0	0	0	0	
			1	1											1			1		1				1

League Table

	P	W	D	L	F	A	Pts
Arsenal	38	22	10	6	73	36	76
Liverpool	38	22	10	6	65	28	76
Nottingham Forest	38	17	13	8	64	43	64
Norwich City	38	17	11	10	48	45	62
Derby County	38	17	7	14	40	38	58
TOTTENHAM HOTSPUR	38	15	12	11	60	46	57
Coventry City	38	14	13	11	47	42	55
Everton	38	14	12	12	50	45	54
Queen's Park Rangers	38	14	11	13	43	37	53
Millwall	38	14	11	13	47	52	53
Manchester United	38	13	12	13	45	35	51
Wimbledon	38	14	9	15	50	46	51
Southampton	38	10	15	13	52	66	45
Charlton Athletic	38	10	12	16	44	58	42
Sheffield Wednesday	38	10	12	16	34	51	42
Luton Town	38	10	11	17	42	52	41
Aston Villa	38	9	13	16	45	56	40
Middlesbrough	38	9	12	17	44	61	39
West Ham United	38	10	8	20	37	62	38
Newcastle United	38	7	10	21	32	63	31

1989-90

DIVISION ONE

Manager: Terry Venables

Did you know that?

Andy Polston replaced John Moncur in the match against Crystal Palace on 3 March 1990. With brother John in Spurs' starting line up, the Polstons became the first brothers to play together for Spurs in a League game since John and Bobby McTavish in April 1911.

LEAGUE DEBUTANTS

Aug 19	v Luton Town Gary Lineker
Aug 19	v Luton Town Steve Sedgley
Sep 9	v Aston Villa Pat van den Hauwe
Mar 3	v Crystal Palace Andy Polston

Match No.	Date		Opponents		Result		Scorers	Attendanc
1	Aug	19	H	Luton Town	W	2-1	Stewart, Allen	17,66
2		22	A	Everton	L	1-2	Allen	34,40
3		26	A	Manchester City	D	1-1	Gascoigne	32,00
4	Sep	9	A	Aston Villa	L	0-2		24,76
5		16	H	Chelsea	L	1-4	Gascoigne	16,26
6		23	A	Norwich City	D	2-2	Gascoigne, Lineker	20,09
7		30	H	Queen's Park Rangers	W	3-2	Lineker 3	23,78
8	Oct	14	A	Charlton Athletic	W	3-1	Thomas, Lineker, Gascoigne	17,69
9		18	H	Arsenal	W	2-1	Samways, Walsh	33,94
10		21	H	Sheffield Wednesday	W	3-0	Lineker 2, Moran	26,90
11		29	A	Liverpool	L	0-1		36,55
12	Nov	4	A	Southampton	D	1-1	Gascoigne	19,60
13		11	H	Wimbledon	L	0-1		26,87
14		18	A	Crystal Palace	W	3-2	Howells, Lineker (pen), Samways	26,36
15		25	H	Derby County	L	1-2	Stewart	28,07
16	Dec	2	A	Luton Town	D	0-0		12,62
17		9	H	Everton	W	2-1	Lineker, Stewart	29,37
18		16	A	Manchester United	W	1-0	Lineker	36,23
19		26	H	Millwall	W	3-1	Samways, Lineker, McCleary (og)	26,87
20		30	H	Nottingham Forest	L	2-3	Lineker 2	33,40
21	Jan	1	A	Coventry City	D	0-0		19,59
22		13	H	Manchester City	D	1-1	Howells	26,38
23		20	A	Arsenal	L	0-1		46,13
24	Feb	4	H	Norwich City	W	4-0	Lineker 3 (1 pen), Howells	19,59
25		10	A	Chelsea	W	2-1	Howells, Lineker	29,13
26		21	H	Aston Villa	L	0-2		32,47
27		24	A	Derby County	L	1-2	Moncur	19,67
28	Mar	3	H	Crystal Palace	L	0-1		26,18
29		10	H	Charlton Athletic	W	3-0	Polston, Lineker, Howells	21,10
30		17	A	Queen's Park Rangers	L	1-3	Walsh	16,69
31		21	H	Liverpool	W	1-0	Stewart	25,65
32		31	A	Sheffield Wednesday	W	4-2	Allen, Lineker 2, Stewart	26,58
33	Apr	7	A	Nottingham Forest	W	3-1	Stewart, Allen 2	21,66
34		14	H	Coventry City	W	3-2	Lineker 2, Stewart	23,31
35		16	A	Millwall	W	1-0	Lineker	10,57
36		21	H	Manchester United	W	2-1	Gascoigne, Lineker	33,31
37		28	A	Wimbledon	L	0-1		12,80
38	May	5	H	Southampton	W	2-1	Stewart, Allen	31,03
								Appearance
								Substitu
								Goa

FA Cup

R3	Jan	6	H	Southampton	L	1-3	Howells	33,13
								Appearance
								Substitu
								Goa

Littlewoods Challenge Cup

R2	Sep	20	H	Southend United	W	1-0	Fenwick	15,73
R2	Oct	4	A	Southend United	L	2-3	Allen, Nayim	10,40
R3		25	A	Manchester United	W	3-0	Lineker, Samways, Nayim	45,75
R4	Nov	22	A	Tranmere Rovers	D	2-2	Gascoigne, Higgins (og)	13,78
R4r		29	H	Tranmere Rovers	W	4-0	Howells, Stewart, Mabbutt, Allen	22,72
R5	Jan	6	A	Nottingham Forest	D	2-2	Lineker, Sedgley	30,04
R5r		24	H	Nottingham Forest	L	2-3	Nayim, Walsh	32,35
								Appearanc
								Substitu
								Goa

Allen PK	Bergsson G	Butters G	Fenwick TW	Gascoigne PJ	Howells DG	Hughton CWG	Lineker GW	Mabbutt GV	Mimms RA	Moncur JF	Moran P	Nayim	Polston A	Polston JD	Robson MA	Samways V	Sedgley SP	Stevens GA	Stewart PA	Thomas MA	Thorstvedt E	Van den Hauwe	Walsh PA	Own-goals
1	3	2	4	**8**	5		10	6								7	12		9		1		13	
1		2	4	**8**	5		10	6								12	7	3	9		1		13	
1		2	4	8	**5**		10	6								13	7	3	9		1		12	
1		**2**	4	8	5		10	6								7		12	9		1	3	13	
			4	8	5		10	6							13			3	**9**	12	1	2	7	
		2	4	8			10	6							12	**7**	11		9	5	1	3	13	
2		2	4	8			10	6				7					11		9	**5**	1	3		
		2	4	8			10	6				7				13	11		9	12	1	3		
			4	8	12		10	6								**9**	11			2	1	3	7	
			4	**8**	7		10	6			12					9	11			2	1	3		
	4				7		10	6			12	8				9	11			2	1	3	13	
	4			8	7		10	6								**9**	11			2	1	3	12	
3	4			8	5		10	6								9	11		12	2	1	3	**7**	
	4			8	5		**10**	6						11		7		3	9	2	1		12	
				8	**5**		10	6						13		7	4		9	2	1	3	12	
	3			8	5		**10**	6								7	11		9	2	1		12	
	12			8	5		10	6								**7**	11		9	2	1	3		
				8	5		10	6	1							7	11		9	2		3		
	3			8	5		10	6	1							7	11	12	9	**2**				
	2			8	5		10	6	1							7	11	12	9			3	13	
	2			**8**	5		10	6	1					12		7	11		9			3		
					5	6	10							8		7	11		9	2	1	3		
					5		10	6				13		8		7	11		9	2	1	**3**	12	
				8	5	2	**10**	6			12	9		4			11				1	3	7	
				8	5	2	10	6		13	12	9		4			11				1	3	**7**	
				8	5	2	10	6		12	13	9		4			11				1	3	7	
3					5	2	10	6		8		9		4			**11**			12	1	3	7	
				8	5	2	10	6		11		9	13	4	12						1	3	7	
				8	5	2	10	6				9		4							1	3	7	
				8	5	**2**	10	6		13		9		4					12		1	3	7	
	2			8	**5**		10	6				9					4		13	12	1	3	7	
	2			8	5		10	6				9					4		12	13	1	3	**7**	
	2			8	**5**		10	6				9					4		7	12	1	3	13	
	2			8			10	6				9					4		7	5	1	3		
	2			8	5		10	6				**9**					4		7	13	1	3	12	
	2			8	5		10	6				**9**				12	4		7	3	1			
	2			8	5		10					9		6		12	4		7	13	1	3		
	2			8	5		10	6				9					4		7	12	1	3		
	17	7	10	34	33	8	38	36	4	2	0	18	0	11	0	18	31	4	24	17	34	31	12	
	1	0	0	0	1	0	0	0	0	3	5	1	1	2	3	5	1	3	4	9	0	0	14	
				6	5		24			1	1			1		3			8	1			2	1

Allen PK	Bergsson G	Butters G	Fenwick TW	Gascoigne PJ	Howells DG	Hughton CWG	Lineker GW	Mabbutt GV	Mimms RA	Moncur JF	Moran P	Nayim	Polston A	Polston JD	Robson MA	Samways V	Sedgley SP	Stevens GA	Stewart PA	Thomas MA	Thorstvedt E	Van den Hauwe	Walsh PA	Own-goals
	3				5	8	10	6	1							**7**	11		9	2			12	
	1	0	0	0	1	1	1	1	1	0	0	0	0	0	0	1	1	0	1	1	0	0	0	
	0	0	0	0	0	0	0	0	0	0	0	0	0	0	0	0	0	0	0	0	0	0	1	
					1																			

Allen PK	Bergsson G	Butters G	Fenwick TW	Gascoigne PJ	Howells DG	Hughton CWG	Lineker GW	Mabbutt GV	Mimms RA	Moncur JF	Moran P	Nayim	Polston A	Polston JD	Robson MA	Samways V	Sedgley SP	Stevens GA	Stewart PA	Thomas MA	Thorstvedt E	Van den Hauwe	Walsh PA	Own-goals
		2	4	8				6							11	12	10		9	**5**	1	3	7	
			4	8	12		10	6				7					11		9	**2**	1	3	13	
			4		7		10	6			12	8				9	11			2	1	3		
	4			8	5		10	6						3		7		12	9	2	1		13	
				8	5		10	6								7	11		9	2	1	3		
					5		10	6				12		**8**		7	11		9	2	1	3		
					5	12	10	6				7		8			11		9	2	1	**3**	13	
	1	1	3	4	5	0	6	7	0	0	0	3	0	3	1	4	6	0	6	7	7	6	1	
	0	0	0	0	1	1	0	0	0	0	1	1	0	0	0	1	0	1	0	0	0	0	3	
			1	1	1		2	1				3				1	1		1				1	1

League Table

	P	W	D	L	F	A	Pts
Liverpool	38	23	10	5	78	37	79
Aston Villa	38	21	7	10	57	38	70
TOTTENHAM HOTSPUR	38	19	6	13	59	47	63
Arsenal	38	18	8	12	54	38	62
Chelsea	38	16	12	10	58	50	60
Everton	38	17	8	13	57	46	59
Southampton	38	15	10	13	71	63	55
Wimbledon	38	13	16	9	47	40	55
Nottingham Forest	38	15	9	14	55	47	54
Norwich City	38	13	14	11	44	42	53
Queen's Park Rangers	38	13	11	14	45	44	50
Coventry City	38	14	7	17	39	59	49
Manchester United	38	13	9	16	46	47	48
Manchester City	38	12	12	14	43	52	48
Crystal Palace	38	13	9	16	42	66	48
Derby County	38	13	7	18	43	40	46
Luton Town	38	10	13	15	43	57	43
Sheffield Wednesday	38	11	10	17	35	51	43
Charlton Athletic	38	7	9	22	31	57	30
Millwall	38	5	11	22	39	65	26

1990-91

DIVISION ONE

Manager: Terry Venables

Did you know that?

When Ian Walker made his Football League debut for Spurs at Norwich City on 10 April 1991, he was probably under closer scrutiny from the Norwich bench than he was from Spurs'. The Norwich coach was Ian's father, Mike Walker.

LEAGUE DEBUTANTS

Nov 10	v Wimbledon	Justin Edinburgh
Dec 1	v Chelsea	David Tuttle
Mar 16	v Aston Villa	Ian Hendon
Apr 10	v Norwich City	John Hendry
Apr 10	v Norwich City	Ian Walker
Apr 10	v Norwich City	Peter Garland

Match No.	Date			Opponents	Result		Scorers	Attendanc
1	Aug	25	H	Manchester City	W	3-1	Lineker 2, Gascoigne	33,50
2		28	A	Sunderland	D	0-0		30,21
3	Sep	1	A	Arsenal	D	0-0		40,00
4		8	H	Derby County	W	3-0	Gascoigne 3	29,61
5		15	A	Leeds United	W	2-0	Howells, Lineker	31,34
6		22	H	Crystal Palace	D	1-1	Gascoigne	34,85
7		29	H	Aston Villa	W	2-1	Lineker, Allen	34,93
8	Oct	6	A	Queen's Park Rangers	D	0-0		21,40
9		20	H	Sheffield United	W	4-0	Walsh 3, Nayim	34,61
10		27	A	Nottingham Forest	W	2-1	Howells 2	27,37
11	Nov	4	H	Liverpool	L	1-3	Lineker	35,00
12		10	H	Wimbledon	W	4-2	Stewart, Mabbutt, Walsh, Lineker (pen)	28,76
13		18	A	Everton	D	1-1	Howells	23,71
14		24	H	Norwich City	W	2-1	Lineker 2	33,94
15	Dec	1	A	Chelsea	L	2-3	Gascoigne, Lineker	33,47
16		8	H	Sunderland	D	3-3	Walsh 2, Lineker	30,43
17		15	A	Manchester City	L	1-2	Gascoigne	31,23
18		22	H	Luton Town	W	2-1	Stewart 2	27,00
19		26	A	Coventry City	L	0-2		22,73
20		29	A	Southampton	L	0-3		21,40
21	Jan	1	H	Manchester United	L	1-2	Lineker (pen)	29,39
22		12	H	Arsenal	D	0-0		34,75
23		20	A	Derby County	W	1-0	Lineker	17,74
24	Feb	2	H	Leeds United	D	0-0		32,25
25		23	A	Wimbledon	L	1-5	Bergsson	10,50
26	Mar	2	H	Chelsea	D	1-1	Lineker (pen)	26,16
27		16	A	Aston Villa	L	2-3	Samways, Allen	32,63
28		23	H	Queen's Park Rangers	D	0-0		30,86
29		30	H	Coventry City	D	2-2	Nayim 2	29,03
30	Apr	1	A	Luton Town	D	0-0		11,32
31		6	H	Southampton	W	2-0	Lineker 2	24,29
32		10	A	Norwich City	L	1-2	Hendry	19,01
33		17	A	Crystal Palace	L	0-1		26,28
34		20	A	Sheffield United	D	2-2	Edinburgh, Walsh	25,70
35		24	H	Everton	D	3-3	Allen, Mabbutt, Nayim	21,67
36	May	4	H	Nottingham Forest	D	1-1	Nayim	30,89
37		11	A	Liverpool	L	0-2		36,19
38		20	A	Manchester United	D	1-1	Hendry	46,79

Appearance
Substitu
Goa

FA Cup

R3	Jan	5	A	Blackpool	W	1-0	Stewart	9,5
R4		27	H	Oxford United	W	4-2	Mabbutt, Lineker, Gascoigne 2	31,66
R5	Feb	16	A	Portsmouth	W	2-1	Gascoigne 2	26,04
R6	Mar	10	H	Notts County	W	2-1	Nayim, Gascoigne	29,68
SF	Apr	14	N*	Arsenal	W	3-1	Gascoigne, Lineker 2	77,89
F	May	18	N*	Nottingham Forest	W	2-1	Stewart, Walker (og)	80,00

*played at Wembley Stadium

Appearance
Substitu
Goa

Rumbelows League Cup

R2	Sep	26	H	Hartlepool United	W	5-0	Lineker, Gascoigne 4 (1 pen)	19,7
R2	Oct	9	A	Hartlepool United	W	2-1	Stewart 2	9,63
R3		30	H	Bradford City	W	2-1	Gascoigne, Stewart	25,45
R4	Nov	27	A	Sheffield United	W	2-0	Stewart, Gascoigne	25,81
R5	Jan	16	A	Chelsea	D	0-0		34,17
R5r		23	H	Chelsea	L	0-3		33,86

Appearance
Substitu
Goa

Allen PK	Bergsson G	Dearden KC	Edinburgh JC	Fenwick TW	Garland PJ	Gascoigne PJ	Gray P	Hendon IM	Hendry JM	Howells DG	Lineker GW	Mabbutt GV	Moncur JF	Moran P	Nayim	Samways V	Sedgley SP	Stewart PA	Thomas MA	Thorstvedt E	Tuttle DP	Van den Hauwe	Walker IM	Walsh PA	Own-goals	
11	2					8				5	10	6			9	12	4	7		1		3				1
11	2					8				5	10	6			**9**	12	4	7		1		3		13		2
11	2					**8**				5	10	6			9		4	7	12	1		3				3
11	2					8				5	10	6			**9**	12	4	7		1		3		13		4
11	2					8				5	10	6			9		4	7		1		3				5
11	2					8				5	10	6			9		4	7		1		3				6
11	2					8				**5**	10	6			9		4	7	12	1		3		13		7
11						8				5	10	6			**9**	13	4	7	12	1		3		2		8
11						**8**				5		6	12		9		4	7	2	1		3		10		9
11						8				5	10	6			9		**4**	7	2	1		3		12		10
11	**2**					8				5	10	6			9		4	7	12	1		3		13		11
11			12			8				5	10	6			9		4	7	2	1		**3**		13		12
11						8				5	**10**	6			9		4	7	2	1		3		12		13
11						8				5	10	6			9		4	7	2	1		3				14
11			12			8				5	10	6			9			7	2	1	**4**	3		13		15
11			4			8				5	10	6			9	12		**7**	2	1		3		13		16
13						8				**5**	10	6			9	12	4	7	2	1		3		11		17
13						8				5	**10**	6			9	12	4	7	2	1		3		11		18
9						8				5	10	6			13	12	4	7	2	1		3		**11**		19
11	13									5	10	6			**9**	8	4	7	2	1		3		12		20
11						8				5	10	6		12	9		**4**	7	2	1		3				21
11			3	4		8				5	10	6						7	2	1				9		22
11			3	2						5	10				**6**	8	4	7	12	1		13		9		23
11				2							10	6			**5**	12	4	7	8	1		3		9		24
11	2		3				12				10	6	9		**5**	7	4		8	1						25
11			2			8	**9**				10	6	13		5		4	7	12	1		3				26
11			2				12	13			**10**	6	9			8	4	7	5	1		3				27
11			2				9				10	6	12		**5**	8	4	7	3	1				13		28
11			2				**9**					6	13		5	8	4	7	12	1		3		10		29
11												6	9		5	8		7	2	1	4	3		10		30
11			2				12				10	6	13			8	4	7	**5**	1		3		9		31
					13	8		12	10	2			11		7		4		5		6	**3**	1	9		32
11						8			13			6			5	9	4	7	2	1	12	**3**		10		33
11	12		2							5					8	**9**	4	7	3	1	6			10		34
11			2							5	10	6			4	9	13	7	3	1	12			**8**		35
11			2			8				5	10	6			7	9	4			1		**3**		12		36
11			2			8			13	**5**	10	6				9	4	**7**		1		3		12		37
	13		2	3					11	5	**10**	6				9	4	7	12	1				8		38
34	9		14	4	0	26	3	0	2	29	32	35	4	0	32	14	33	35	23	37	4	31	1	16		
2	3		2	0	1	0	3	2	2	0	0	0	5	1	1	9	1	0	8	0	2	1	0	13		
3	1		1			7			2	4	15	2			5	1		3						7		

Allen PK	Bergsson G	Dearden KC	Edinburgh JC	Fenwick TW	Garland PJ	Gascoigne PJ	Gray P	Hendon IM	Hendry JM	Howells DG	Lineker GW	Mabbutt GV	Moncur JF	Moran P	Nayim	Samways V	Sedgley SP	Stewart PA	Thomas MA	Thorstvedt E	Tuttle DP	Van den Hauwe	Walker IM	Walsh PA	Own-goals
11			3	2		8				5	10	6		9		4		7		1					
11				2		8				**5**	10	6			4		12	7		1		3		9	
11			2			8	12				10	6			5	**7**	4		9	1		3			
11			2			8					10	6			**5**	12	4	7	9	1		3		13	
11			2			**8**				5	10	6			12	9	4	7		1		3		13	
11			2			**8**				5	10	6			12	9	4	7		1		3		13	
6	0	0	5	2	0	6	0	0	0	4	6	6	0	1	3	4	4	5	2	6	0	5	0	1	
0	0	0	0	0	0	0	1	0	0	0	0	0	0	0	2	1	1	0	0	0	0	0	0	3	
						6					3	1			1			2							1

Allen PK	Bergsson G	Dearden KC	Edinburgh JC	Fenwick TW	Garland PJ	Gascoigne PJ	Gray P	Hendon IM	Hendry JM	Howells DG	Lineker GW	Mabbutt GV	Moncur JF	Moran P	Nayim	Samways V	Sedgley SP	Stewart PA	Thomas MA	Thorstvedt E	Tuttle DP	Van den Hauwe	Walker IM	Walsh PA	Own-goals
11			2			8				5	10	6			9		4	**7**	13	1		3		12	
11		1	3			12				**5**		6	8		13	10	4	7	2					9	
11						8				5	**10**	6	13		9		4	7	2	1		3		12	
11			3			8				5	10	6				9	**4**	7	2	1	12			13	
11			3	4						5	10	6			13	**8**	12	7	2	1				9	
11			3	**2**		8				5	10	6			13	4	12	7		1				9	
6	0	1	5	2	0	4	0	0	0	6	5	6	1	0	2	4	4	6	4	5	0	2	0	3	
0	0	0	0	0	0	1	0	0	0	0	0	0	1	0	3	0	2	0	1	0	1	0	0	3	
						6					1							4							

League Table

	P	W	D	L	F	A	Pts
Arsenal	38	24	13	1	74	18	83
Liverpool	38	23	7	8	77	40	76
Crystal Palace	38	20	9	9	50	41	69
Leeds United	38	19	7	12	65	47	64
Manchester City	38	17	11	10	64	53	62
Manchester United	38	16	12	10	58	45	59
Wimbledon	38	14	14	10	53	46	56
Nottingham Forest	38	14	12	12	65	50	54
Everton	38	13	12	13	50	46	51
TOTTENHAM HOTSPUR	38	11	16	11	51	50	49
Chelsea	38	13	10	15	58	69	49
Queen's Park Rangers	38	12	10	16	44	53	46
Sheffield United	38	13	7	18	36	55	46
Southampton	38	12	9	17	58	69	45
Norwich City	38	13	6	19	41	64	45
Coventry City	38	11	11	16	42	49	44
Aston Villa	38	9	14	15	46	58	41
Luton Town	38	10	7	21	42	61	37
Sunderland	38	8	10	20	38	60	34
Derby County	38	5	9	24	37	75	24

1991-92

DIVISION ONE

Manager: Peter Shreeves

Did you know that?

The financial straits Spurs found themselves in had resulted in shares in Tottenham Hotspur Plc being suspended on the London Stock Exchange in October 1990. It was not until the end of December 1991 that they were re-listed following a £7 million rights issue that put the company back on a firm financial footing.

LEAGUE DEBUTANTS

Aug 17	v Southampton Gordon Durie
Sep 28	v Manchester United Scott Houghton
Mar 7	v Leeds United Andy Gray
Mar 28	v Coventry City Jason Cundy
Apr 25	v Everton Jeff Minton

Match No.	Date			Opponents	Result		Scorers	Attendance
1	Aug	17	A	Southampton	W	3-2	Lineker 2, Durie	18,58
2		24	H	Chelsea	L	1-3	Lineker	34,64
3		28	A	Nottingham Forest	W	3-1	Lineker, Durie, Bergsson	24,01
4		31	A	Norwich City	W	1-0	Lineker	19,46
5	Sep	7	A	Aston Villa	D	0-0		33,09
6		14	H	Queen's Park Rangers	W	2-0	Lineker 2	30,05
7		21	A	Wimbledon	W	5-3	Lineker 4 (1 pen), Samways	11,92
8		28	H	Manchester United	L	1-2	Durie	35,08
9	Oct	5	A	Everton	L	1-3	Lineker	29,50
10		19	H	Manchester City	L	0-1		30,50
11		26	A	West Ham United	L	1-2	Lineker	23,94
12	Nov	2	A	Sheffield Wednesday	D	0-0		31,57
13		16	H	Luton Town	W	4-1	Houghton 2, Lineker 2	27,54
14		23	H	Sheffield United	L	0-1		28,16
15	Dec	1	A	Arsenal	L	0-2		38,89
16		7	H	Notts County	W	2-1	Walsh, Mabbutt	23,36
17		14	A	Leeds United	D	1-1	Howells	31,40
18		18	H	Liverpool	L	1-2	Walsh	27,43
19		22	A	Crystal Palace	W	2-1	Walsh, Lineker	22,49
20		26	H	Nottingham Forest	L	1-2	Stewart	31,07
21		28	H	Norwich City	W	3-0	Allen, Lineker, Nayim	27,96
22	Jan	1	A	Coventry City	W	2-1	Lineker, Stewart	19,63
23		11	A	Chelsea	L	0-2		28,62
24		18	H	Southampton	D	1-1	Mabbutt	23,19
25		25	H	Oldham Athletic	D	0-0		20,84
26	Feb	1	A	Manchester City	L	0-1		30,12
27		16	H	Crystal Palace	L	0-1		19,83
28		22	H	Arsenal	D	1-1	Stewart	33,12
29	Mar	7	H	Leeds United	L	1-3	Allen	27,62
30		11	A	Luton Town	D	0-0		11,49
31		14	H	Sheffield Wednesday	L	0-2		23,02
32		21	A	Liverpool	L	1-2	Stewart	36,96
33		28	H	Coventry City	W	4-3	Durie 3, Lineker	22,74
34	Apr	1	H	West Ham United	W	3-0	Lineker 3 1 (pen)	31,80
35		4	H	Aston Villa	L	2-5	Lineker, Teale (og)	26,37
36		7	A	Notts County	W	2-0	Lineker 2	9,20
37		11	A	Queen's Park Rangers	W	2-1	Gray, Durie	20,67
38		14	A	Sheffield United	L	0-2		21,52
39		18	H	Wimbledon	W	3-2	Lineker 2, Hendry	23,93
40		20	A	Oldham Athletic	L	0-1		15,44
41		25	H	Everton	D	3-3	Allen, Minton, Stewart	36,34
42	May	2	A	Manchester United	L	1-3	Lineker	44,59
								Appearances
								Substitute
								Goal

FA Cup

R3	Jan	5	A	Aston Villa	D	0-0		29,31
R3r		14	H	Aston Villa	L	0-1		25,46
								Appearance
								Substitute
								Goals

Rumbelows League Cup

R2	Sep	25	A	Swansea City	L	0-1		11,41
R2	Oct	9	H	Swansea City	W	5-1	Allen, Lineker (pen), Brazil (og), Stewart, Samways	20,19
R3		29	A	Grimsby Town	W	3-0	Howells, Lineker, Durie	17,01
R4	Dec	4	A	Coventry City	W	2-1	Allen, Durie	20,09
R5	Jan	8	H	Norwich City	W	2-1	Walsh, Lineker	29,47
SF	Feb	9	A	Nottingham Forest	D	1-1	Lineker (pen)	21,40
SF	Mar	1	H	Nottingham Forest	L*	1-2	Lineker	28,21
								Appearances
								Substitute
								Goals

*after extra-time

Tennents FA Charity Shield

Aug		10	N*	Arsenal	D	0-0		65,48
								Appearances
								Substitute
								Goals

*played at Wembley Stadium

Allen PK	Bergsson G	Cundy JV	Durie GS	Edinburgh JC	Fenwick TW	Gray AA	Hendon IM	Hendry JM	Houghton SA	Howells DG	Lineker GW	Mabbutt GV	Minton JST	Moncur JF	Nayim	Samways V	Sedgley SP	Stewart PA	Thorstvedt E	Tuttle DP	Van den Hauwe	Walker IM	Walsh PA	Own-goals
11	13		8		2					5	10	6			12	9	4	7	1		3			
11	12		8		2					5	10	6			4	9		7	1		3			
11	12		8		2			13		5	10	6			4	9		7			3	1		
	11		8		2					5	10	6			4	9		7			3	1		
	11		8		2					5	10	6			4	9		7			3	1		
12	11		8		2					5	10	6			4	9	13	7			3	1		
11	2		8				12				10	6			4	9	5	7			3	1		
11	2		8						13	12	10	6			4	9	3	7		5		1		
11	2		8				13			12	10	6			4	9	3	7	1	5				
11	5		8	2						12	10	6			4	9	7		1		3		13	
11	12		8	2					13		10	6			4	9	5	7	1		3			
11	12		8	2						5	10	6			9		4	7	1		3		13	
11	7			2					13	5	10	6			12	9	4		1		3		8	
	7		8	2					13	5	10	6			4	9	12		1		3		11	
11	4		8		2					5		6			12	9		7	1		3		10	
11	4		8		2					5		6			12	9	13	7	1		3		10	
11	4		8		2					5		6			12	9	13	7	1		3		10	
11	4				2					5	10	6			12	9		7	1		3		8	
11	4			3	2					5	10	6			12	9	13	7	1				8	
11	4				2					5	10	6			12	9	13	7	1		3		8	
11					2				12		10	6			5	9	4	7	1		3		8	
11				13	2				12	5	10	6				9	4	7	1		3		8	
11	13				2				12	5		6			10	9	4	7	1		3		8	
11	13		8	2					12		10	6				9	4	7			3	1	5	
11			8	2					12		10	6			5		4	7			3	1	9	
11	6		8	2	3					5	10				13	9	4	7				1	12	
11	13		8		2					5	10	6				9	4	7	1		3		12	
11			8		2					5	10	6			9		4	7	1		3		12	
11	13		8		2	9				5	10	6					4	7	1		3		12	
11	12		8	3	2	9				5		6					4	7	1				10	
11	12		8	3	2	9			13			6			5		4	7	1				10	
11			8	3	2	9				5		6					4	7	1		10		12	
11		5	8	3		4					10	6			9		13	7	1		2		12	
11		5	8	3		4					10	6			9		13	7			2	1	12	
11	2	5	8	3		4				7	10	6			9							1	12	
11		5		3		4		12		9	10	6					13	7			2	1	8	
11		5	8	3		4				9	10	6					13	7			2	1	12	
11		5		3	13	4		12		9	10					8	6	7			2	1		
11		5		3		4		12			10	6			9		13	7			2	1	8	
11		5		3		4		8			10	6			9	12	13	7			2	1		
11		5	8	3		4					10	6	9				13	7			2	1	12	
11		5	8	3		4				12	10	6	9					7			2	1		
38	17	10	31	22	22	14	0	1	0	27	35	40	2	0	22	26	21	38	24	2	35	18	17	
1	11	0	0	1	1	0	2	4	10	4	0	0	0	0	9	1	13	0	0	0	0	0	12	
3	1		7			1		1	2	1	28	2	1		1	1		5					3	1
11					2					5	10	6				9	4	7	1		3		8	
11	12		8		2						10	6			13	9	4	7	1		3		5	
2	0	0	1	0	2	0	0	0	0	1	2	2	0	0	0	2	2	2	2	0	2	0	2	
0	1	0	0	0	0	0	0	0	0	0	0	0	0	0	1	0	0	0	0	0	0	0	0	
11			8				2	13		10		6		12	4	9	5	7			3	1		
11	2		8						12		10	6			4	9	3	7	1	5				
11	12		8	2						4	10	6				9	5	7	1		3		13	
11	4		8		2					5		6			13	9	12	7	1		3		10	
11	13				2				12		10	6			5	9	4	7	1		3		8	
11	6		8	13	2					5	10				12	9	4	7	1		3			
11			8	12	2					5	10	6			9	13	4	7	1		3			
7	3	0	6	1	4	0	1	0	0	5	5	6	0	0	4	6	6	7	6	1	6	1	2	
0	2	0	0	2	0	0	0	1	2	0	0	0	0	1	2	1	1	0	0	0	0	0	1	
2			2							1	5					1		1					1	1
11					2					5	10	6			8	9	4	7	1		3			
1	0	0	0	0	1	0	0	0	0	1	1	1	0	0	1	1	1	1	1	0	1	0	0	
0	0	0	0	0	0	0	0	0	0	0	0	0	0	0	0	0	0	0	0	0	0	0	0	

League Table

	P	W	D	L	F	A	Pts
Leeds United	42	22	16	4	74	37	82
Manchester United	42	21	15	6	63	33	78
Sheffield Wednesday	42	21	12	9	62	49	75
Arsenal	42	19	15	8	81	46	72
Manchester City	42	20	10	12	61	48	70
Liverpool	42	16	16	10	47	40	64
Aston Villa	42	17	9	16	48	44	60
Nottingham Forest	42	16	11	15	60	58	59
Sheffield United	42	16	9	17	65	63	57
Crystal Palace	42	14	15	13	53	61	57
Queen's Park Rangers	42	12	18	12	48	47	54
Everton	42	13	14	15	52	51	53
Wimbledon	42	13	14	15	53	53	53
Chelsea	42	13	14	15	50	60	53
TOTTENHAM HOTSPUR	42	15	7	20	58	63	52
Southampton	42	14	10	18	39	55	52
Oldham Athletic	42	14	9	19	63	67	51
Norwich City	42	11	12	19	47	63	45
Coventry City	42	11	11	20	35	44	44
Luton Town	42	10	12	20	38	71	42
Notts County	42	10	10	22	40	62	40
West Ham United	42	9	11	22	37	59	38

1992-93

PREMIERSHIP

Managerial responsibilities: Terry Venables with first-team coach Doug Livermore

Did you know that?

Spurs' four goals against Southampton in February 1993 were scored in the space of four minutes 48 seconds.

LEAGUE DEBUTANTS

Aug 15 v Southampton Darren Anderton
Aug 15 v Southampton Andy Turner
Aug 22 v Crystal Palace Dean Austin
Aug 30 v Ipswich Town Teddy Sheringham
Sep 27 v Sheffield Wednesday Nick Barmby
Sep 27 v Sheffield Wednesday Kevin Watson
Dec 5 v Chelsea Sol Campbell
Mar 20 v Chelsea Stuart Nethercottl
Mar 20 v Chelsea Danny Hill
Apr 12 v Nottingham Forest Kevin Dearden
May 1 v Wimbledon Lee Hodges
May 5 v Liverpool David McDonald

Match No.	Date		Opponents		Result		Scorers	Attendance
1	Aug	15	A	Southampton	D	0-0		19,654
2		19	H	Coventry City	L	0-2		24,388
3		22	H	Crystal Palace	D	2-2	Durie, Sedgley	25,237
4		25	A	Leeds United	L	0-5		28,218
5		30	A	Ipswich Town	D	1-1	Cundy	20,100
6	Sep	2	H	Sheffield United	W	2-0	Sheringham, Durie	21,322
7		5	H	Everton	W	2-1	Allen, Turner	26,503
8		14	A	Coventry City	L	0-1		15,348
9		19	H	Manchester United	D	1-1	Durie	33,296
10		27	A	Sheffield Wednesday	L	0-2		24,895
11	Oct	3	A	Queen's Park Rangers	L	1-4	Sheringham	19,845
12		17	H	Middlesbrough	D	2-2	Sheringham (pen), Barmby	24,735
13		25	A	Wimbledon	D	1-1	Barmby	8,628
14		31	H	Liverpool	W	2-0	Nayim, Ruddock	32,917
15	Nov	7	A	Blackburn Rovers	W	2-0	Howells, Sheringham (pen)	17,305
16		21	H	Aston Villa	D	0-0		32,852
17		28	A	Manchester City	W	1-0	Phelan (og)	25,496
18	Dec	5	H	Chelsea	L	1-2	Campbell	31,540
19		12	H	Arsenal	W	1-0	Allen	33,707
20		19	A	Oldham Athletic	L	1-2	Sheringham	11,735
21		26	A	Norwich City	D	0-0		19,413
22		28	H	Nottingham Forest	W	2-1	Barmby, Mabbutt	32,118
23	Jan	9	A	Manchester United	L	1-4	Barmby	35,648
24		16	H	Sheffield Wednesday	L	0-2		25,702
25		27	H	Ipswich Town	L	0-2		25,738
26		30	A	Crystal Palace	W	3-1	Sheringham 2, Gray	20,937
27	Feb	7	H	Southampton	W	4-2	Sheringham 2, Barmby, Anderton	20,098
28		10	A	Everton	W	2-1	Mabbutt, Allen	16,164
29		20	H	Leeds United	W	4-0	Sheringham 3 (1 pen), Ruddock	32,040
30		27	H	Queen's Park Rangers	W	3-2	Sheringham 2, Anderton	32,341
31	Mar	2	A	Sheffield United	L	0-6		16,654
32		10	A	Aston Villa	D	0-0		37,727
33		20	A	Chelsea	D	1-1	Sheringham (pen)	25,157
34		24	H	Manchester City	W	3-1	Anderton, Nayim, Turner	27,247
35	Apr	9	H	Norwich City	W	5-1	Ruddock, Sheringham 2, Barmby, Nayim	31,425
36		12	A	Nottingham Forest	L	1-2	Sedgley	25,682
37		17	H	Oldham Athletic	W	4-1	Sheringham 2 (2 pens), Anderton, Turner	26,663
38		20	A	Middlesbrough	L	0-3		13,472
39	May	1	H	Wimbledon	D	1-1	Anderton	24,473
40		5	H	Blackburn Rovers	L	1-2	Anderton	23,097
41		8	A	Liverpool	L	2-6	Sheringham, Sedgley	43,385
42		11	A	Arsenal	W	3-1	Sheringham, Hendry 2	26,393
								Appearances
								Substitute
								Goals

FA Cup

R3	Jan	2	A*	Marlow	W	5-1	Sheringham, Barmby 2, Samways 2	26,636
R4		24	A	Norwich City	W	2-0	Sheringham 2	15,005
R5	Feb	14	H	Wimbledon	W	3-2	Anderton, Sheringham, Barmby	26,529
R6	Mar	7	A	Manchester City	W	4-2	Nayim 3, Sedgley	34,050
SF	Apr	4	N#	Arsenal	L	0-1		76,263
								Appearances
								Substitute
								Goals

*played at White Hart Lane #played at Wembley Stadium

Coca-Cola Cup

R2	Sep	21	H	Brentford	W	3-1	Sheringham, Watson, Durie	19,365
R2	Oct	7	A	Brentford	W	4-2	Anderton, Sheringham 2 (1 pen), Turner	11,445
R3		28	A	Manchester City	W	1-0	Samways	18,399
R4	Dec	2	A	Nottingham Forest	L	0-2		22,812
								Appearances
								Substitute
								Goals

Allen PK	Anderton DR	Austin DB	Barmby NJ	Bergsson G	Campbell SJ	Cundy JV	Dearden KC	Durie GS	Edinburgh JC	Fenwick TW	Gray AA	Hendry JM	Hill DRL	Hodges LL	Howells DG	Mabbutt GV	McDonald DH	Minton JST	Moran P	Nayim	Nethercott SD	Ruddock N	Samways V	Sedgley SP	Sheringham EP	Thorstvedt E	Turner AP	Tuttle DP	Van den Hauwe	Walker IM	Watson KE	Own-goals
11	10					5		8	3	2	12				4							6	9				**7**			1		
11	10					5		8	3	2	13				4							6	9			12	7			**1**		
11	10	12						8	3	**2**	13	7										6	9	4		1		5				
11	10	2				5		8	3						4							6	9	7		1						
11	7	2				5		8	3		12											6	9	4	10					1		
11	7	2				5		8			13											6	**9**	4	10		12		3	1		
11	**7**	2				5		8			4												9		10		12	6	3	1		
11	**7**	2				5		8			4											6	9	13	10		12		3	1		
11		2				5		8			**4**	12										6		7	10		9	13	3	1		
11	9	2	8			5			13															7	10		**4**	6	3	1	12	
11	9		8			5			**2**	12												6	4	7	10		13		3	1		
11	**9**		13					8	2											12		6	4	7	10			5	3	1		
11		3	13					8	2							5				9		6	4	7	10	12				**1**		
11		3	**4**					8	2						13	5				9		6		7	10	1	12					
11		3						8	2						7	5				9		6	4		10	1						
11		3	12			13		**8**	2						7	5				9		6	4		10	1						
		3	8			12			2						**7**	5			13	9		6	4		10	1					11	
	13	3	8		12	7			2							5				9		6	4		10	1					**11**	
11		2	12					**8**	3						7	5				9		6	4		10	1						
11		2	12					8	3						7	5				**9**		6	4		10	1						
11	9	2	**8**						3						7	5			12			6	4		10	1						
11	**9**	2	8	13					3						7	5			12			6	4		10	1						
11	13	**2**	8	12					3						7	5				9		6	4		10	1						
11	9	2	8	13					**3**			12			7	5						6	4		10	1						
11	9	2	7					**8**	3						12	5						6	4		10	1			13			
11	9	2							3		**8**				7	5						6	4		10	1			12			
11	9	2	8						3		12				**7**	5						6	4		10	1			13			
11	9	2							3		**8**				7	5				12		6	4		10	1			13			
11	9	2	8						3		12				**7**	5						6	4		10	1			13			
11	9	2	**8**			6			3		7					5				12			4		10	1						
11	9	2				6					7	12				5				**8**			4	13	10	1			3			
	9	2							3		**11**					5				8		6	4	7	10	1	12					
	9	2		13					3		4		12							8	5	6			10	1	**11**				7	
11	**9**	2		13												5				8		6	4	7	10	1	12		3			
11	9	2	**4**						3							5				8	12	6		7	10	1	13					
11	9	2	4				12		3							5				8		6		7	10	**1**	13					
11	9	2	8						3							5						6	**4**	7	10		12			1		
11	9	**2**	8						3	12						5						6	4	7	10		13			1		
11	9										12			13		5					2	6	4	7	10		8		3	1		
11	9												12	13		5					**2**	6	4	7	10		8		3	1		
11	9												4	13		5	2				12	6		7	10				**3**	1	8	
11	9											**8**	4	12		5	2					6		7	10				3	1		
38	32	33	17	0	0	13	0	17	31	3	9	2	2	0	16	29	2	0	0	15	3	38	34	20	38	25	7	4	13	17	4	
0	2	1	5	5	1	2	1	0	1	2	8	3	2	4	2	0	0	0	3	3	2	0	0	2	0	2	11	1	5	0	1	
3	6		6		1	1		3			1	2			1	2				3		3		3	21		3					1

Allen PK	Anderton DR	Austin DB	Barmby NJ	Bergsson G	Campbell SJ	Cundy JV	Dearden KC	Durie GS	Edinburgh JC	Fenwick TW	Gray AA	Hendry JM	Hill DRL	Hodges LL	Howells DG	Mabbutt GV	McDonald DH	Minton JST	Moran P	Nayim	Nethercott SD	Ruddock N	Samways V	Sedgley SP	Sheringham EP	Thorstvedt E	Turner AP	Tuttle DP	Van den Hauwe	Walker IM	Watson KE	Own-goals
11	13	2	8						3						7	5				9		6	**4**		10	1					12	
11	9	2	7					**8**	3						12	5						6	4		10	1						
11	9	2	8						3						7	5						6	4		10	1						
11	**9**	2							3							5				8		6	4	7	10	1	12					
11	9	2	12	13					3							5				8		6	**4**	7	10	1						
5	4	5	3	0	0	0	0	1	5	0	0	0	0	0	2	5	0	0	0	3	0	5	5	2	5	5	0	0	0	0	0	
0	1	0	1	1	0	0	0	0	0	0	0	0	0	0	1	0	0	0	0	0	0	0	0	0	0	0	1	0	0	0	1	
	1		3																	3			2	1	4							

Allen PK	Anderton DR	Austin DB	Barmby NJ	Bergsson G	Campbell SJ	Cundy JV	Dearden KC	Durie GS	Edinburgh JC	Fenwick TW	Gray AA	Hendry JM	Hill DRL	Hodges LL	Howells DG	Mabbutt GV	McDonald DH	Minton JST	Moran P	Nayim	Nethercott SD	Ruddock N	Samways V	Sedgley SP	Sheringham EP	Thorstvedt E	Turner AP	Tuttle DP	Van den Hauwe	Walker IM	Watson KE	Own-goals
11	9					5		8	12									13				6		7	10			2	3	1	**4**	
11	9	12	8						2													6	**4**	7	10		13	5	3	1		
11		3	8						2						13	5				9		6	**4**	7	10	1	12					
11		3	12			7		**8**	2							5				9		6	4		10	1					13	
4	2	2	2	0	0	2	0	2	3	0	0	0	0	0	0	2	0	0	0	2	0	4	3	3	4	2	0	2	2	2	1	
0	0	1	1	0	0	0	0	0	1	0	0	0	0	0	1	0	0	1	0	0	0	0	0	0	0	0	2	0	0	0	1	
	1							1															1		3		1				1	

League Table

	P	W	D	L	F	A	Pts
Manchester United	42	24	12	6	67	31	84
Aston Villa	42	21	11	10	57	40	74
Norwich City	42	21	9	12	61	65	72
Blackburn Rovers	42	20	11	11	68	46	71
Queen's Park Rangers	42	17	12	13	63	55	63
Liverpool	42	16	11	15	62	55	59
Sheffield Wednesday	42	15	14	13	55	51	59
TOTTENHAM HOTSPUR	42	16	11	15	60	66	59
Manchester City	42	15	12	15	56	51	57
Arsenal	42	15	11	16	40	38	56
Chelsea	42	14	14	14	51	54	56
Wimbledon	42	14	12	16	56	55	54
Everton	42	15	8	19	53	55	53
Sheffield United	42	14	10	18	54	53	52
Coventry City	42	13	13	16	52	57	52
Ipswich Town	42	12	16	14	50	55	52
Leeds United	42	12	15	15	57	62	51
Southampton	42	13	11	18	54	61	50
Oldham Athletic	42	13	10	19	63	74	49
Crystal Palace	42	11	16	15	48	61	49
Middlesbrough	42	11	11	20	54	75	44
Nottingham Forest	42	10	10	22	41	62	40

1993-94

PREMIERSHIP

Manager: Ossie Ardiles

Did you know that?

Spurs were the only club to go the whole Premiership season without being involved in a goalless draw. It was the seventh season since joining the League Spurs had not featured in a League nil–nil. The previous occasions were 1910–11, 1912–13, 1928–29, 1951–52, 1953–54 and 1984–85.

LEAGUE DEBUTANTS

Aug 14	v Newcastle United Colin Calderwood
Aug 14	v Newcastle United Jason Dozzell
Aug 16	v Arsenal Darren Caskey
Sep 26	v Ipswich Town Steve Carr
Oct 3	v Everton David Kerslake
Oct 30	v Blackburn Rovers Steve Robinson
Jan 22	v Swindon Town Paul Mahorn
Feb 5	v Sheffield Wednesday Ronny Rosenthal
Feb 5	v Sheffield Wednesday Kevin Scott

Match No.	Date			Opponents	Result		Scorers	Attendance
1	Aug	14	A	Newcastle United	W	1-0	Sheringham	35,216
2		16	H	Arsenal	L	0-1		28,355
3		21	H	Manchester City	W	1-0	Sedgley	24,535
4		25	A	Liverpool	W	2-1	Sheringham 2 (1 pen)	42,456
5		28	A	Aston Villa	L	0-1		32,498
6	Sep	1	H	Chelsea	D	1-1	Sheringham (pen)	27,567
7		11	A	Sheffield United	D	2-2	Sheringham 2	21,345
8		18	H	Oldham Athletic	W	5-0	Sheringham, Sedgley 2, Durie, Dozzell	24,614
9		26	A	Ipswich Town	D	2-2	Sheringham, Dozzell	19,411
10	Oct	3	H	Everton	W	3-2	Sheringham, Anderton, Caskey	27,487
11		16	A	Manchester United	L	1-2	Caskey	44,655
12		23	H	Swindon Town	D	1-1	Dozzell	31,394
13		30	A	Blackburn Rovers	L	0-1		16,849
14	Nov	6	A	Southampton	L	0-1		16,017
15		20	H	Leeds United	D	1-1	Anderton	31,275
16		24	H	Wimbledon	D	1-1	Barmby	17,744
17		27	A	Queen's Park Rangers	D	1-1	Anderton	17,694
18	Dec	4	H	Newcastle United	L	1-2	Barmby (pen)	30,780
19		6	A	Arsenal	D	1-1	Anderton	35,669
20		11	A	Manchester City	W	2-0	Dozzell 2	21,566
21		18	H	Liverpool	D	3-3	Samways, Hazard (pen), Caskey	31,394
22		27	H	Norwich City	L	1-3	Barmby	31,130
23		28	A	West Ham United	W	3-1	Dozzell, Hazard, Anderton	20,787
24	Jan	1	H	Coventry City	L	1-2	Caskey	26,015
25		3	A	Sheffield Wednesday	L	0-1		32,513
26		15	H	Manchester United	L	0-1		31,343
27		22	A	Swindon Town	L	1-2	Barmby	16,563
28	Feb	5	H	Sheffield Wednesday	L	1-3	Rosenthal	23,078
29		12	H	Blackburn Rovers	L	0-2		30,236
30		27	A	Chelsea	L	3-4	Sedgley, Dozzell, Gray (pen)	19,807
31	Mar	2	H	Aston Villa	D	1-1	Rosenthal	17,452
32		5	H	Sheffield United	D	2-2	Scott, Dozzell	25,741
33		19	H	Ipswich Town	D	1-1	Barmby	26,653
34		26	A	Everton	W	1-0	Sedgley	23,580
35	Apr	2	A	Norwich City	W	2-1	Sheringham, Woodthorpe (og)	21,181
36		4	H	West Ham United	L	1-4	Sheringham (pen)	31,502
37		9	A	Coventry City	L	0-1		14,491
38		17	A	Leeds United	L	0-2		33,658
39		23	H	Southampton	W	3-0	Sedgley, Samways, Anderton	25,959
40		30	A	Wimbledon	L	1-2	Sheringham (pen)	20,875
41	May	5	A	Oldham Athletic	W	2-0	Samways, Howells	14,283
42		7	H	Queen's Park Rangers	L	1-2	Sheringham	26,105
								Appearances
								Substitute
								Goals

FA Cup

R3	Jan	8	A	Peterborough United	D	1-1	Dozzell	19,169
R3r		19	H	Peterborough United	D*	1-1	Barmby	24,893
R4		29	A	Ipswich Town	L	0-3		22,539
								Appearances
								Substitute
								Goals

*after extra-time - Spurs won 5-4 on pens

Coca-Cola Cup

R2	Sep	22	A	Burnley	D	0-0		16,844
R2	Oct	6	H	Burnley	W	3-1	Sheringham 2, Howells	20,614
R3		27	A	Derby County	W	1-0	Barmby	19,885
R4	Dec	1	H	Blackburn Rovers	W	1-0	Campbell	22,295
R5	Jan	11	H	Aston Villa	L	1-2	Caskey	31,408
								Appearances
								Substitute
								Goals

Allen PK	Anderton DR	Austin DB	Barmby NJ	Calderwood C	Campbell SJ	Carr S	Caskey DM	Dozzell JAW	Durie GS	Edinburgh JC	Gray AA	Hazard M	Hendry JM	Hill DRL	Howells DG	Kerslake D	Mabbutt GV	Mahorn PG	Moran P	Nethercott S	Robinson S	Rosenthal R	Samways V	Scott KW	Sedgley SP	Sheringham EP	Thorstvedt E	Turner AP	Walker IM	Own-goals
		2		5	3			9	**8**						11		6						4		7	10	1	12		
		2		5	3		12	9	8						**11**		6						4		7	10	1			
	13	2		5	3		12	9	8						**11**		6						4		7	10	1			
		2		5	3		12	9	8						**11**		6						4		7	10	1			
	13	2		5	3		12	9	8						**11**		6						4		7	10	1			
	9	2		5	**3**			11	8						12		6						4		7	10	1			
12	9	2		5	**3**			11	8								6						4		7	10	1			
	9	**2**		5	3		12	11	8								6		13				4		7	10	1			
	9			5	3	**2**	12	11	8								6						4		7	10	1			
	9			5	**3**		8	11						12		2	6		13				4		7	10	1			
			7		3		11	9		13					5	2	6		12				4		8	**10**	1			
	9		**7**	5	3			11						13	10	2	6		12				4		8		1			
	9		7	5	2			4		3			13		11		6		12		10				8		1			
	9		7	5	2		12	**10**		3		11					6						4		8		1			
	9		**7**	5	2				8	3		11			12		6						4		10		1			
	9		7	5	2		12			3		10			11		**6**						4		8		1			
	9		7	5	2		8			3		10			**11**					13	12		4		6		1			
	9	13	7	5	**11**		10	12		3		8				2							4		6		1			
	9	12		5	11		10	7		3		8	13			2							**4**		6		1			
	9			5	11		10	7		3		8				2							4		6		1			
	9		7	5			10	11		3		8				2							4		6		1			
	9		7	5			10	11		3		8				2							4		6		1			
	9		**7**	5	12		10	11		3		8				2							4		6		1			
	9		7	5	12		10	11		3		**8**				2							4		6		1			
	9		**7**	5	12		10	11		3		8				2							4		6		1			
	9	12	7	5	11		10			**3**		8	13			2							4		6				1	
	9	2	7	5	12		10			3								11		6			4		8		1		13	
	9	2	7				**10**			3	12									5		11	4	8	6				1	
	9	2	7				10			3										5		11	4	8	6				1	
	9	2			12			10		**3**	13						6			5		11	4	8	7				1	
	9	2	7		3			10									6					11	4	8	5				1	
	9	**2**	7		3		12	10									6					11	4	8	5				1	
	9	**2**	7		3		4	10								12	6					11		8	5				1	
	9		7		12			13		**3**						2	6			5		11	4	8	10				1	
	9		7		3			10								2	6					**11**	4	8	5	12			1	
	9		7		3			10							13	2	6					**11**	4	8	5	12			1	
	9		7		**3**			13							11	2	6					12	4	8	5	10	1			
	9	2			12			4		3		13			7		6					11		8	5	10	1			
	9	2	7							3		13			8		6			5		12	**4**		11	10	1			
	9	2	7							3		13			8		6			5		12	**4**		11	10	1			
		2						12		3					9		6			5		**11**	4	8	7	10	1			
	9	2	**7**							3		13		8			6			5		12	4		11	10	1			
0	35	20	27	26	27	1	16	28	10	24	0	13	0	1	15	16	29	1	0	9	1	11	39	12	42	17	32	0	10	
1	2	3	0	0	7	0	9	4	0	1	2	4	3	2	3	1	0	0	5	1	1	4	0	0	0	2	0	1	1	
	6		5				4	8	1		1	2			1							2	3	1	6	13				1

Allen PK	Anderton DR	Austin DB	Barmby NJ	Calderwood C	Campbell SJ	Carr S	Caskey DM	Dozzell JAW	Durie GS	Edinburgh JC	Gray AA	Hazard M	Hendry JM	Hill DRL	Howells DG	Kerslake D	Mabbutt GV	Mahorn PG	Moran P	Nethercott S	Robinson S	Rosenthal R	Samways V	Scott KW	Sedgley SP	Sheringham EP	Thorstvedt E	Turner AP	Walker IM	Own-goals
	9		**7**	5	12		10	11		3		8				2							4		6		1			
	9	2	7	5	11		10			3		**8**	13			12							4		6				1	
	9	2	7	5	12		10	**11**		3										6			4		8				1	
0	3	2	3	3	1	0	3	2	0	3	0	2	0	0	0	1	0		0	1		0	3	0	3	0	1	0	2	
0	0	0	0	0	2	0	0	0	0	0	0	0	1	0	0	1	0		0	0		0	0	0	0	0	0	0	0	
			1					1																						

Allen PK	Anderton DR	Austin DB	Barmby NJ	Calderwood C	Campbell SJ	Carr S	Caskey DM	Dozzell JAW	Durie GS	Edinburgh JC	Gray AA	Hazard M	Hendry JM	Hill DRL	Howells DG	Kerslake D	Mabbutt GV	Mahorn PG	Moran P	Nethercott S	Robinson S	Rosenthal R	Samways V	Scott KW	Sedgley SP	Sheringham EP	Thorstvedt E	Turner AP	Walker IM	Own-goals
	9			5	3	**2**	12	11	8								6						4		7	10			1	
	9			5	3		11		**8**						12	2	6		13				4		7	10	1			
	9		7	5	2			11		3					10		6						4		8		1			
	9	12	7	5	11		10	8		3						**2**							4		6		1			
	9		7	5	**11**		10	8		3			12			2							4		6		1			
0	5	0	3	5	5	1	3	4	2	3	0	0	0	0	1	3	3		0	0		0	5	0	5	2	4	0	1	
0	0	1	0	0	0	0	1	0	0	0	0	0	1	0	1	0	0		1	0		0	0	0	0	0	0	0	0	
			1		1		1								1											2				

League Table

	P	W	D	L	F	A	Pts
Manchester United	42	27	11	4	80	38	92
Blackburn Rovers	42	25	9	8	63	36	84
Newcastle United	42	23	8	11	82	41	77
Arsenal	42	18	17	7	53	28	71
Leeds United	42	18	16	8	65	39	70
Wimbledon	42	18	11	13	56	53	65
Sheffield Wednesday	42	16	16	10	76	54	64
Liverpool	42	17	9	16	59	55	60
Queen's Park Rangers	42	16	12	14	62	61	60
Aston Villa	42	15	12	15	46	50	57
Coventry City	42	14	14	14	43	45	56
Norwich City	42	12	17	13	65	61	53
West Ham United	42	13	13	16	47	58	52
Chelsea	42	13	12	17	49	53	51
TOTTENHAM HOTSPUR	42	11	12	19	54	59	45
Manchester City	42	9	18	15	38	49	45
Everton	42	12	8	22	42	63	44
Southampton	42	12	7	23	49	66	43
Ipswich Town	42	9	16	17	35	58	43
Sheffield United	42	8	18	16	42	60	42
Oldham Athletic	42	9	13	20	42	68	40
Swindon Town	42	5	15	22	47	100	30

1994-95

PREMIERSHIP

Manager: Ossie Ardiles until November then Gerry Francis

Did you know that?

At Southampton in the FA Cup fifth-round replay on 1 March 1995 Spurs were two down and seemingly out of the competition. In two second-half minutes substitute Ronny Rosenthal scored with two screamers. He completed his hat-trick in extra-time as Spurs completed an incredible recovery to win 6–2.

LEAGUE DEBUTANTS

Aug 20	v Sheffield Wednesday Ilie Dumitrescu
Aug 20	v Sheffield Wednesday Jurgen Klinsmann
Sep 24	v Nottingham Forest Gica Popescu
May 9	v Coventry City Gerry McMahon

Match No.	Date		Opponents		Result		Scorers	Attendance
1	Aug	20	A	Sheffield Wednesday	W	4-3	Sheringham, Anderton, Barmby, Klinsmann	34,051
2		24	H	Everton	W	2-1	Klinsmann 2	24,553
3		27	H	Manchester United	L	0-1		24,502
4		30	A	Ipswich Town	W	3-1	Klinsmann 2, Dumitrescu	22,559
5	Sep	12	H	Southampton	L	1-2	Klinsmann	22,387
6		17	A	Leicester City	L	1-3	Klinsmann	21,300
7		24	H	Nottingham Forest	L	1-4	Dumitrescu	24,558
8	Oct	1	A	Wimbledon	W	2-1	Sheringham, Popescu	16,802
9		8	H	Queen's Park Rangers	D	1-1	Barmby	25,799
10		15	A	Leeds United	D	1-1	Sheringham	39,224
11		22	A	Manchester City	L	2-5	Dumitrescu 2 (1 pen)	25,473
12		29	H	West Ham United	W	3-1	Klinsmann, Sheringham, Barmby	26,271
13	Nov	5	A	Blackburn Rovers	L	0-2		26,933
14		19	H	Aston Villa	L	3-4	Sheringham, Klinsmann (pen), Bosnich (og)	26,899
15		23	H	Chelsea	D	0-0		27,037
16		26	A	Liverpool	D	1-1	Ruddock 9og)	35,007
17	Dec	3	H	Newcastle United	W	4-2	Sheringham 3, Popescu	28,002
18		10	H	Sheffield Wednesday	W	3-1	Barmby, Klinsmann, Calderwood	25,912
19		17	A	Everton	D	0-0		32,809
20		26	A	Norwich City	W	2-0	Barmby, Sheringham	21,814
21		27	H	Crystal Palace	D	0-0		27,730
22		31	A	Coventry City	W	4-0	Barmby, Anderton, Sheringham, Darby (og)	19,951
23	Jan	2	H	Arsenal	W	1-0	Popescu	28,747
24		14	A	West Ham United	W	2-1	Sheringham, Klinsmann	24,573
25		25	A	Aston Villa	L	0-1		40,017
26	Feb	5	H	Blackburn Rovers	W	3-1	Klinsmann, Anderton, Barmby	28,124
27		11	A	Chelsea	D	1-1	Sheringham	30,812
28		25	H	Wimbledon	L	1-2	Klinsmann	27,258
29	Mar	4	A	Nottingham Forest	D	2-2	Sheringham, Calderwood	28,711
30		8	H	Ipswich Town	W	3-0	Klinsmann, Barmby, Youds (og)	24,930
31		15	A	Manchester United	D	0-0		43,802
32		18	H	Leicester City	W	1-0	Klinsmann	30,851
33		22	H	Liverpool	D	0-0		31,988
34	Apr	2	A	Southampton	L	3-4	Sheringham 2, Klinsmann	15,105
35		11	H	Manchester City	W	2-1	Howells, Klinsmann	27,410
36		14	A	Crystal Palace	D	1-1	Klinsmann	18,149
37		17	H	Norwich City	W	1-0	Sheringham	32,304
38		29	A	Arsenal	D	1-1	Klinsmann	38,377
39	May	3	A	Newcastle United	D	3-3	Barmby, Klinsmann, Anderton	35,603
40		6	A	Queen's Park Rangers	L	1-2	Sheringham	18,637
41		9	H	Coventry City	L	1-3	Anderton	24,134
42		14	H	Leeds United	D	1-1	Sheringham	33,040
								Appearances
								Substitute
								Goals

FA Cup

R3	Jan	7	H	Altrincham	W	3-0	Sheringham, Rosenthal, Nethercott	25,057
R4		29	A	Sunderland	W	4-1	Klinsmann 2 (1 pen), Sheringham, Mabbutt	21,135
R5	Feb	18	H	Southampton	D	1-1	Klinsmann	28,091
R5r	Mar	1	A	Southampton	W*	6-2	Rosenthal 3, Sheringham, Barmby, Anderton	15,172
R6		11	A	Liverpool	W	2-1	Sheringham, Klinsmann	39,592
SF	Apr	9	N#	Everton	L	1-4	Klinsmann (pen)	38,226
								Appearances
								Substitute
								Goals

*after extra-time #at Elland Road

Coca-Cola Cup

R2	Sep	21	A	Watford	W	63	Anderton, Klinsmann 3, Sheringham, Dumitrescu	13,659
R2	Oct	4	H	Watford	L	2-3	Barmby, Klinsmann	17,798
R3		25	A	Notts County	L	0-3		16,952
								Appearances
								Substitute
								Goals

Anderton DR	Austin DB	Barmby NJ	Calderwood C	Campbell SJ	Caskey DM	Dozzell JAW	Dumitrescu I	Edinburgh JC	Hazard M	Hill DRL	Howells DG	Kerslake D	Klinsmann J	Mabbutt GV	McMahon GJ	Nethercott S	Popescu G	Rosenthal R	Scott KW	Sheringham EP	Thorstvedt E	Turner AP	Walker IM	Own-goals
9		7	5	6			**8**	3	12			2	11	13		4				10			1	
9		7	5	6			**8**	3	12			2	11	13		4				10			1	
9		7	**5**	6			8	3	12			2	11			4				10			1	
9		7	5	6			8	3				2	11	12		**4**				10			1	
9		**7**	5	6			8	3	12			2	11			4				10			1	
9		7	**5**	6			8	3	12			2	11			4				10			1	
9				5			8	3	**7**	12		2	11	6			4			10			1	
9	2					7	**8**		12			3	11	6			4		5	10			1	
		7	5	6		**8**		3	12	9		2	11					13	4	10			1	
		7	12	**6**		9	8	3				2	11				4		5	10			1	
		7		6		**9**	8	3	12			2	11				4		5	10			1	
		7		5		9	8	**3**	10	13		2	11	6			4			12	1			
		7		5		9		3	12		8	2	11	**6**			4	13		10			1	
9		12	5	3	**7**						8	2	11	6		13	4			10			1	
9	2	**7**	5	3			12				8		11	6			4			10			1	
9	2	7	5	3			12				8		11	6			4			10			1	
9	2	7	5	3				12			8		11	6			4			10			1	
9	2	7	5	3							4		8	6				11		10			1	
9	2	7	5	3							8			6			4	11		10			1	
9	2	7	5	3							**8**		11	6		12	4			10			1	
9	2	7	5	3							**8**		11	6		12	4	13		10			1	
9	2	**7**	5	3							8		11	6		13	4	12		10			1	
9	2		5	3							8		7	6		12	**4**	11		10			1	
9	2	7	5	**3**				12			8		11	6			4			10			1	
9	2	7	5	8	12			3					**11**	6			4			10			1	
9		**7**	5	2				3			8		11	6		12	4			10			1	
9		7	5	2				3			8		11	6			4			10			1	
9	12	7	5	**2**				3			8		11	6			4	13		10			1	
9	2	7	5					3			4		8	6				11		10			1	
9	2	7	5		12			3			**4**		8	6				11		10			1	
9	2	7	5					3			4		8	6				11		10			1	
9	2	7	5					3			4		8	6				11		10			1	
9	2	7						3			4	12	8	6		**5**		11		10			1	
9	2	7	5								4	3	8	6				11		10			1	
9	2	**7**	5					3			8		11	6		12	4	13		10			1	
9	2	7	5					3					8	6			4	11		10			1	
9	2	**7**	5		12			3					8	6			4	11		10			1	
9	2	7	5					3			4		8	6				11		10			1	
9	2	**7**	5	12				3			4		8	6				11		10			1	
9		7	5	2				3			4	12	8	6		13		**11**		10			1	
9		7	5	**2**				3			4		8	6	11	12				10			1	
9			5			12		3				2	8	6	**11**	4				10		7	1	
37	23	37	35	29	1	6	11	29	2	1	26	16	41	33	2	8	23	14	4	41	1	1	41	
0	1	1	1	1	3	1	2	2	9	2	0	2	0	3	0	9	0	6	0	1	0	0	0	
5		9	2				4				1		20				3			18				4

Anderton DR	Austin DB	Barmby NJ	Calderwood C	Campbell SJ	Caskey DM	Dozzell JAW	Dumitrescu I	Edinburgh JC	Hazard M	Hill DRL	Howells DG	Kerslake D	Klinsmann J	Mabbutt GV	McMahon GJ	Nethercott S	Popescu G	Rosenthal R	Scott KW	Sheringham EP	Thorstvedt E	Turner AP	Walker IM	Own-goals
9	2	7	5	3							4		8	6		12		**11**		10			1	
9		7	5	2				3			**8**		11	6		12	4			10			1	
9	12	7	5	2				3			8		**11**	6			4			10			1	
9	2	7	5		13			3			8		11	6		**4**		12		10			1	
9	2	7	5					3			4		8	6				11		10			1	
9	2	7	5								8		11	6		**3**	4	12		10			1	
6	4	6	6	3	0	0	0	4	0	0	6	0	6	6	0	2	3	2	0	6	0	0	6	
0	1	0	0	0	1	0	0	0	0	0	0	0	0	0	0	2	0	2	0	0	0	0	0	
1		1											5	1		1		4		4				

Anderton DR	Austin DB	Barmby NJ	Calderwood C	Campbell SJ	Caskey DM	Dozzell JAW	Dumitrescu I	Edinburgh JC	Hazard M	Hill DRL	Howells DG	Kerslake D	Klinsmann J	Mabbutt GV	McMahon GJ	Nethercott S	Popescu G	Rosenthal R	Scott KW	Sheringham EP	Thorstvedt E	Turner AP	Walker IM	Own-goals
9				5			8	**3**	7	13	12	2	11	6			4			10			1	
9	2	7		5		8				12	4	3	10	6				11					1	
	2	7	**5**	6		9	8	3	12				11				4			10	1			
2	2	2	1	3	0	2	2	2	1	0	1	2	3	2	0	0	2	1	0	2	1	0	2	
0	0	0	0	0	0	0	0	0	1	2	1	0	0	0	0	0	0	0	0	0	0	0	0	
1		1					1						4							1				

League Table

	P	W	D	L	F	A	Pts
Blackburn Rovers	42	27	8	7	80	39	89
Manchester United	42	26	10	6	77	28	88
Nottingham Forest	42	22	11	9	72	43	77
Liverpool	42	21	11	10	65	37	74
Leeds United	42	20	13	9	59	38	73
Newcastle United	42	20	12	10	67	47	72
TOTTENHAM HOTSPUR	42	16	14	12	66	58	62
Queen's Park Rangers	42	17	9	16	61	59	60
Wimbledon	42	15	11	16	48	65	56
Southampton	42	12	18	12	61	63	54
Chelsea	42	13	15	14	50	55	54
Arsenal	42	13	12	17	52	49	51
Sheffield Wednesday	42	13	12	17	49	57	51
West Ham United	42	13	11	18	44	48	50
Everton	42	11	17	14	44	51	50
Coventry City	42	12	14	16	44	62	50
Manchester City	42	12	13	17	53	64	49
Aston Villa	42	11	15	16	51	56	48
Crystal Palace	42	11	12	19	34	49	45
Norwich City	42	10	13	19	37	54	43
Leicester City	42	6	11	25	45	80	29
Ipswich Town	42	7	6	29	36	93	27

1995-96

PREMIERSHIP

Manager: Gerry Francis

Did you know that?

Spurs' new 'Jumbotron' giant screen over the South Stand was officially initiated for the opening home game of the season against Aston Villa. The screen provided pre-match entertainment and live away-match screenings, the first being the match with Middlesbrough on 21 November 1995.

LEAGUE DEBUTANTS

Aug 19	v Manchester City Chris Armstrong
Aug 26	v Liverpool Clive Wilson
Oct 14	v Nottingham Forest Ruel Fox
Dec 16	v Wimbledon Steve Slade
Feb 23	v Liverpool Andy Sinton

Match No.	Date			Opponents	Result		Scorers	Attendance
1	Aug	19	A	Manchester City	D	1-1	Sheringham	30,827
2		23	H	Aston Villa	L	0-1		26,726
3		26	H	Liverpool	L	1-3	Barnes (og)	31,254
4		30	A	West Ham United	D	1-1	Rosenthal	23,516
5	Sep	9	H	Leeds United	W	2-1	Howells, Sheringham	30,034
6		16	A	Sheffield Wednesday	W	3-1	Sheringham 2 (1 pen), Walker (og)	26,565
7		25	A	Queen's Park Rangers	W	3-2	Sheringham 2 (1 pen), Dozzell	15,659
8		30	H	Wimbledon	W	3-1	Sheringham 2, Elkins (og)	25,321
9	Oct	14	H	Nottingham Forest	L	0-1		32,876
10		22	A	Everton	D	1-1	Armstrong	33,629
11		29	H	Newcastle United	D	1-1	Armstrong	32,279
12	Nov	4	A	Coventry City	W	3-2	Fox, Sheringham, Howells	17,545
13		18	H	Arsenal	W	2-1	Sheringham, Armstrong	32,894
14		21	A	Middlesbrough	W	1-0	Armstrong	29,487
15		25	A	Chelsea	D	0-0		31,059
16	Dec	2	H	Everton	D	0-0		32,894
17		9	H	Queen's Park Rangers	W	1-0	Sheringham	28,851
18		16	A	Wimbledon	W	1-0	Fox	16,193
19		23	H	Bolton Wanderers	D	2-2	Sheringham, Armstrong	30,702
20		26	A	Southampton	D	0-0		15,238
21		30	A	Blackburn Rovers	L	1-2	Sheringham	30,004
22	Jan	1	H	Manchester United	W	4-1	Sheringham, Campbell, Armstrong 2	32,852
23		13	H	Manchester City	W	1-0	Armstrong	31,438
24		21	A	Aston Villa	L	1-2	Fox	35,666
25	Feb	3	A	Liverpool	D	0-0		40,628
26		12	H	West Ham United	L	0-1		29,781
27		24	H	Sheffield Wednesday	W	1-0	Armstrong	32,047
28	Mar	2	H	Southampton	W	1-0	Dozzell	26,320
29		16	H	Blackburn Rovers	L	2-3	Sheringham, Armstrong	31,803
30		21	A	Bolton Wanderers	W	3-2	Howells, Fox, Armstrong	17,829
31		24	A	Manchester United	L	0-1		50,157
32		30	H	Coventry City	W	3-1	Sheringham, Fox 2	26,808
33	Apr	6	A	Nottingham Forest	L	1-2	Armstrong	27,053
34		8	H	Middlesbrough	D	1-1	Armstrong	32,036
35		15	A	Arsenal	D	0-0		38,273
36		27	H	Chelsea	D	1-1	Armstrong	32,918
37	May	2	A	Leeds United	W	3-1	Armstrong, Anderton 2	30,061
38		5	A	Newcastle United	D	1-1	Dozzell	36,589
								Appearances
								Substitute
								Goals

FA Cup

R3	Jan	6	A	Hereford United	D	1-1	Rosenthal	8,806
R3r		17	H	Hereford United	W	5-1	Sheringham 3, Armstrong 2	31,534
R4		27	H	Wolverhampton Wanderers	D	1-1	Wilson	32,812
R4r	Feb	7	A	Wolverhampton Wanderers	W	2-0	Rosenthal, Sheringham	27,846
R5		19	A	Nottingham Forest	*	0-0		17,009
R5		28	A	Nottingham Forest	D	2-2	Armstrong 2	18,600
R5r	Mar	9	H	Nottingham Forest	L#	1-1	Sheringham	31,055
								Appearances
								Substitute
								Goals

*abandoned after 14 mins - snow
#after extra-time - lost 1-3 on pens

Coca-Cola Cup

R2	Sep	20	H	Chester City	W	4-0	Armstrong 2, Sheringham, Rosenthal	17,645
R2	Oct	4	A	Chester City	W	3-1	Sheringham 2, Howells	5,372
R3		25	A	Coventry City	L	2-3	Armstrong, Busst (og)	18,227
								Appearances
								Substitute
								Goals

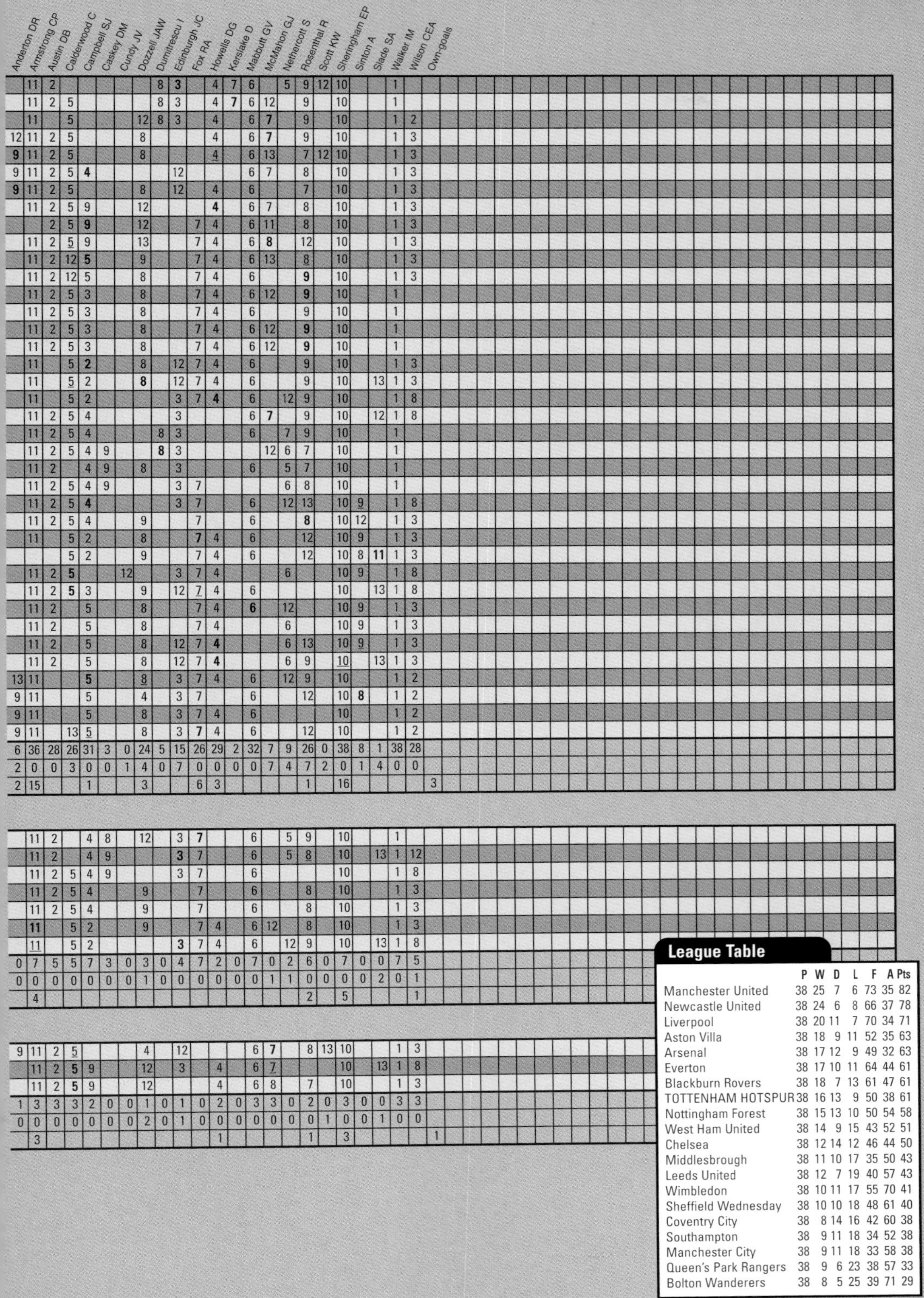

Anderton DR	Armstrong CP	Austin DB	Calderwood C	Campbell SJ	Caskey DM	Cundy JV	Dozzell JAW	Dumitrescu I	Edinburgh JC	Fox RA	Howells DG	Kerslake D	Mabbutt GV	McMahon GJ	Nethercott S	Rosenthal R	Scott KW	Sheringham EP	Sinton A	Slade SA	Walker IM	Wilson CEA	Own-goals
	11	2						8	**3**		4	7	6		5	9	12	10			1		
	11	2	5					8	3		4	**7**	6	12		9		10			1		
	11		5				12	8	3		4		6	**7**		9		10			1	2	
12	11	2	5				8				4		6	**7**		9		10			1	3	
9	11	2	5				8				4		6	13		7	12	10			1	3	
9	11	2	5	**4**					12				6	7		8		10			1	3	
9	11	2	5				8		12		4		6			7		10			1	3	
	11	2	5	9			12				**4**		6	7		8		10			1	3	
		2	5	**9**			12			7	4		6	11		8		10			1	3	
	11	2	5	9			13			7	4		6	**8**		12		10			1	3	
	11	2	12	**5**			9			7	4		6	13		8		10			1	3	
	11	2	12	5			8			7	4		6			**9**		10			1	3	
	11	2	5	3			8			7	4		6	12		**9**		10			1		
	11	2	5	3			8			7	4		6			9		10			1		
	11	2	5	3			8			**7**	4		6	12		**9**		10			1		
	11	2	5	3			8			7	4		6	12		**9**		10			1		
	11		5	**2**			8		12	7	4		6			9		10			1	3	
	11		5	2			**8**		12	7	4		6			9		10		13	1	3	
	11		5	2					3	7	**4**		6		12	9		10			1	8	
	11	2	5	4					3				6	**7**		9		10		12	1	8	
	11	2	5	4				8	3				6		7	9		10			1		
	11	2	5	4	9			**8**	3					12	6	7		10			1		
	11	2		4	9		8		3				6		5	7		10			1		
	11	2	5	4	9				3	7					6	8		10			1		
	11	2	5	**4**					3	7			6		12	13		10	9		1	8	
	11	2	5	4			9			7			6			**8**		10	12		1	3	
	11		5	2			8			**7**	4		6			12		10	9		1	3	
			5	2			9			7	4		6			12		10	8	**11**	1	3	
	11	2	**5**			12			3	7	4				6			10	9		1	8	
	11	2	**5**	3			9		12	7	4		6					10		13	1	8	
	11	2		5			8			7	4		**6**		12			10	9		1	3	
	11	2		5			8			7	4				6			10	9		1	3	
	11	2		5			8		12	7	**4**				6	13		10	9		1	3	
	11	2		5			8		12	7	**4**				6	9		10		13	1	3	
13	11			**5**			8		3	7	4		6		12	9		10			1	2	
9	11			5			4		3	7			6			12		10	**8**		1	2	
9	11			5			8		3	7	4		6					10			1	2	
9	11		13	5			8		3	**7**	4		6			12		10			1	2	
6	36	28	26	31	3	0	24	5	15	26	29	2	32	7	9	26	0	38	8	1	38	28	
2	0	0	3	0	0	1	4	0	7	0	0	0	0	7	4	7	2	0	1	4	0	0	
2	15			1			3			6	3					1		16					3

Anderton DR	Armstrong CP	Austin DB	Calderwood C	Campbell SJ	Caskey DM	Cundy JV	Dozzell JAW	Dumitrescu I	Edinburgh JC	Fox RA	Howells DG	Kerslake D	Mabbutt GV	McMahon GJ	Nethercott S	Rosenthal R	Scott KW	Sheringham EP	Sinton A	Slade SA	Walker IM	Wilson CEA	Own-goals
	11	2		4	8		12		3	**7**			6		5	9		10			1		
	11	2		4	9				**3**	7			6		5	8		10		13	1	12	
	11	2	5	4	9				3	7			6					10			1	8	
	11	2	5	4			9			7			6			8		10			1	3	
	11	2	5	4			9			7			6			8		10			1	3	
	11		5	2			9			7	4		6	12		8		10			1	3	
	11		5	2					**3**	7	4		6		12	9		10		13	1	8	
0	7	5	5	7	3	0	3	0	4	7	2	0	7	0	2	6	0	7	0	0	7	5	
0	0	0	0	0	0	0	1	0	0	0	0	0	0	1	1	0	0	0	0	2	0	1	
	4															2		5				1	

Anderton DR	Armstrong CP	Austin DB	Calderwood C	Campbell SJ	Caskey DM	Cundy JV	Dozzell JAW	Dumitrescu I	Edinburgh JC	Fox RA	Howells DG	Kerslake D	Mabbutt GV	McMahon GJ	Nethercott S	Rosenthal R	Scott KW	Sheringham EP	Sinton A	Slade SA	Walker IM	Wilson CEA	Own-goals
9	11	2	5				4		12				6	**7**		8	13	10			1	3	
	11	2	**5**	9			12		3		4		6	7				10		13	1	8	
	11	2	**5**	9			12				4		6	8		7		10			1	3	
1	3	3	3	2	0	0	1	0	1	0	2	0	3	3	0	2	0	3	0	0	3	3	
0	0	0	0	0	0	0	2	0	1	0	0	0	0	0	0	0	1	0	0	1	0	0	
	3										1					1		3					1

League Table

	P	W	D	L	F	A	Pts
Manchester United	38	25	7	6	73	35	82
Newcastle United	38	24	6	8	66	37	78
Liverpool	38	20	11	7	70	34	71
Aston Villa	38	18	9	11	52	35	63
Arsenal	38	17	12	9	49	32	63
Everton	38	17	10	11	64	44	61
Blackburn Rovers	38	18	7	13	61	47	61
TOTTENHAM HOTSPUR	38	16	13	9	50	38	61
Nottingham Forest	38	15	13	10	50	54	58
West Ham United	38	14	9	15	43	52	51
Chelsea	38	12	14	12	46	44	50
Middlesbrough	38	11	10	17	35	50	43
Leeds United	38	12	7	19	40	57	43
Wimbledon	38	10	11	17	55	70	41
Sheffield Wednesday	38	10	10	18	48	61	40
Coventry City	38	8	14	16	42	60	38
Southampton	38	9	11	18	34	52	38
Manchester City	38	9	11	18	33	58	38
Queen's Park Rangers	38	9	6	23	38	57	33
Bolton Wanderers	38	8	5	25	39	71	29

1996-97

PREMIERSHIP

Manager: Gerry Francis

Did you know that?

Spurs received many plaudits for their 1996 Christmas card. Based on the cover of the Beatles *Sgt. Pepper's Lonely Hearts Club Band* album, many of the club's most famous names from the past joined manager Gerry Francis and the entire first-team squad in various disguises.

LEAGUE DEBUTANTS

Sep 4 v Wimbledon
Allan Nielsen
Sep 4 v Wimbledon
Rory Allen
Dec 7 v Coventry City
Steffen Iversen
Dec 21 v Sheffield Wednesday
John Scales
Jan 12 v Manchester United
Ramon Vega
Apr 9 v Sheffield Wednesday
Neale Fenn
Apr 19 v Aston Villa
Paul McVeigh
May 3 v Liverpool
Espen Baardsen
May 11 v Coventry City
Jamie Clapham

Match No.	Date			Opponents	Result		Scorers	Attendance
1	Aug	17	A	Blackburn Rovers	W	2-0	Armstrong 2	26,960
2		21	H	Derby County	D	1-1	Sheringham	28,219
3		24	H	Everton	D	0-0		29,696
4	Sep	4	A	Wimbledon	L	0-1		17,506
5		7	H	Newcastle United	L	1-2	Allen	32,535
6		14	A	Southampton	W	1-0	Armstrong (pen)	15,251
7		22	H	Leicester City	L	1-2	Wilson (pen)	24,159
8		29	A	Manchester United	L	0-2		54,943
9	Oct	12	H	Aston Villa	W	1-0	Nielsen	32,847
10		19	A	Middlesbrough	W	3-0	Sheringham 2, Fox	30,215
11		26	A	Chelsea	L	1-3	Armstrong	28,373
12	Nov	2	H	West Ham United	W	1-0	Armstrong	32,999
13		16	H	Sunderland	W	2-0	Sinton, Sheringham	31,867
14		24	A	Arsenal	L	1-3	Sinton	38,264
15	Dec	2	H	Liverpool	L	0-2		32,899
16		7	A	Coventry City	W	2-1	Sheringham, Sinton	19,675
17		14	A	Leeds United	D	0-0		33,783
18		21	H	Sheffield Wednesday	D	1-1	Nielsen	30,996
19		26	H	Southampton	W	3-1	Iversen 2, Nielsen	30,549
20		28	A	Newcastle United	L	1-7	Nielsen	36,308
21	Jan	12	H	Manchester United	L	1-2	Allen	33,026
22		19	A	Nottingham Forest	L	1-2	Sinton	27,303
23		29	H	Blackburn Rovers	W	2-1	Iversen, Sinton	22,943
24	Feb	1	H	Chelsea	L	1-2	Howells	33,027
25		15	H	Arsenal	D	0-0		33,039
26		24	A	West Ham United	L	3-4	Sheringham, Anderton, Howells	23,998
27	Mar	1	H	Nottingham Forest	L	0-1		32,805
28		4	A	Sunderland	W	4-0	Iversen 3, Nielsen	20,785
29		15	H	Leeds United	W	1-0	Anderton	33,040
30		19	A	Leicester City	D	1-1	Sheringham	20,593
31		22	A	Derby County	L	2-4	Rosenthal, Dozzell	18,083
32	Apr	5	H	Wimbledon	W	1-0	Dozzell	32,654
33		9	A	Sheffield Wednesday	L	1-2	Nielsen	22,667
34		12	A	Everton	L	0-1		36,380
35		19	A	Aston Villa	D	1-1	Vega	39,339
36		24	H	Middlesbrough	W	1-0	Sinton	29,940
37	May	3	A	Liverpool	L	1-2	Anderton	40,003
38		11	H	Coventry City	L	1-2	McVeigh	33,029
								Appearances
								Substitute
								Goals

FA Cup

R3	Jan	5	A	Manchester United	L	0-2		52,495
								Appearances
								Substitute
								Goals

Coca-Cola Cup

R2	Sep	17	A	Preston North End	D	1-1	Anderton	16,258
R2		25	H	Preston North End	W	3-0	Anderton, Allen 2	20,080
R3	Oct	23	H	Sunderland	W	2-1	Armstrong, Campbell	24,867
R4	Nov	27	A	Bolton Wanderers	L	1-6	Sheringham	18,621
								Appearances
								Substitute
								Goals

Allen RW	Anderton DR	Armstrong CP	Austin DB	Baardsen PE	Calderwood C	Campbell SJ	Carr S	Clapham JR	Dozzell JAW	Edinburgh JC	Fenn NMC	Fox RA	Howells DG	Iversen S	Mabbutt GV	McVeigh PF	Nethercott S	Nielsen A	Rosenthal R	Scales JR	Sheringham EP	Sinton A	Vega R	Walker IM	Wilson CEA
	9	11			5	2			14	3		7	4		**6**		12				10	8		1	13
	9	11			5	6			12	3		7	4						13		10	8		1	2
		11			5	6			9	3		7	4						12		10	8		1	2
14	**9**				5	6			10	3		7	4				12	*8*	13			11		1	2
10	**9**	11			5	6				3		12	4					8	13			7		1	2
10	9	11			5	6				3		12	4				14	*8*	13			**7**		1	2
10	9				5	6				**3**		7	4				2	8	13			12		1	11
11					5	6	2			12		7	**4**					8	13		10	9		1	3
		11			5	6	2			12		7	4				13	8			10	**9**		1	3
		11			5	6	2			3		7	4					8			10			1	9
13		11			5	6	2		12	3		**7**	4					8			10			1	9
7		11			5	6	2			3			4					8	12		10			1	9
	9	11			5	6	2						4					8	12		10	7		1	3
	9	11			5	6	2						4					8			10	7		1	3
13		11			5	6	2			12		7	4					8			10	**9**		1	3
					5	6	2		12			7	4	11				**8**			10	9		1	3
					5	6	2					7	4	11				8			10	9		1	3
					5	**6**	2					7	4	11				8		12	10	9		1	3
					5	6	2					**7**	4	11				8		12	10	9		1	3
					5	6	2		12			7	4	11				8	13		10	**9**		1	3
9			13		5	6	**7**			3		12	4	11								10	2	1	8
9					5	6	7			3			**4**	11			12	8	13			10	2	1	14
9	12					6	2			3		**7**	4	11			13	8				10	5	1	
9	12		2			6	**7**			*3*		14	4	11			5	8				10		1	13
	9		2		5	6	7			3			4	10					11			8		1	
	9		2		5	6	7						4	11				12	13		10	**8**		1	3
			2		5	6			13				4	11				8	12	7	10	9		1	3
	9		2		5	6	12						4	11				8		7	10			1	3
	9		2		5	6	3		8					**11**					12	4	10	7		1	
			2		5	6	3		12				**4**	11				8	13	7	10	9		1	
			2		5	6	3		4					11				8	12	7	10	**9**		1	
			2			6			4	3		7						8	11	5	10	9		1	
	9		2		12	**6**	13			3	14	7						8	11	5	10	4		1	
			13		5	6	**7**		9	3	14	12						8	11	*4*	10		2	1	
			2		5	6			9	3	13		**4**			11	12				10	8	7	1	
			2		5	6			11	3			4					8			10	9	7	1	
	9		2	14	5	6			8			12	4			13				3	10	11	7	*1*	
				1		6	2	13	8	3	12	7				**9**				4	10	11	5		
9	14	12	13	1	33	38	24	0	10	21	0	19	32	16	1	2	2	28	4	10	29	32	8	37	23
3	2	0	2	1	1	0	2	1	7	3	4	6	0	0	0	1	7	1	16	2	0	1	0	0	3
2	3	5							2			1	2	6		1		6	1		7	6	1		1

Allen RW	Anderton DR	Armstrong CP	Austin DB	Baardsen PE	Calderwood C	Campbell SJ	Carr S	Clapham JR	Dozzell JAW	Edinburgh JC	Fenn NMC	Fox RA	Howells DG	Iversen S	Mabbutt GV	McVeigh PF	Nethercott S	Nielsen A	Rosenthal R	Scales JR	Sheringham EP	Sinton A	Vega R	Walker IM	Wilson CEA
9			2		5	6	7			3	11		4					8				10		1	
1	0	0	1	0	1	1	1	0	0	1	1	0	1	0	0	0	0	1	0	0	0	1	0	1	0
0	0	0	0	0	0	0	0	0	0	0	0	0	0	0	0	0	0	0	0	0	0	0	0	0	0

Allen RW	Anderton DR	Armstrong CP	Austin DB	Baardsen PE	Calderwood C	Campbell SJ	Carr S	Clapham JR	Dozzell JAW	Edinburgh JC	Fenn NMC	Fox RA	Howells DG	Iversen S	Mabbutt GV	McVeigh PF	Nethercott S	Nielsen A	Rosenthal R	Scales JR	Sheringham EP	Sinton A	Vega R	Walker IM	Wilson CEA
10	9	11			5	6				3		7	4					8						1	2
11	**9**				5	6	2					7	4					12			10	8		1	3
12		11			5	6	2			3		7	4					**8**			10			1	9
	9	11			5	6	2		**8**			12	4								10	7		1	3
2	3	3	0	0	4	4	3	0	1	2	0	3	4	0	0	0	0	2	0	0	3	2	0	4	4
1	0	0	0	0	0	0	0	0	0	0	0	1	0	0	0	0	0	1	0	0	0	0	0	0	0
2	2	1				1															1				

League Table

	P	W	D	L	F	A	Pts
Manchester United	38	21	12	5	76	44	75
Newcastle United	38	19	11	8	73	40	68
Arsenal	38	19	11	8	62	32	68
Liverpool	38	19	11	8	62	37	68
Aston Villa	38	17	10	11	47	34	61
Chelsea	38	16	11	11	58	55	59
Sheffield Wednesday	38	14	15	9	50	51	57
Wimbledon	38	15	11	12	49	46	56
Leicester City	38	12	11	15	46	54	47
TOTTENHAM HOTSPUR	38	13	7	18	44	51	46
Leeds United	38	11	13	14	28	38	46
Derby County	38	11	13	14	45	58	46
Blackburn Rovers	38	9	15	14	42	43	42
West Ham United	38	10	12	16	39	48	42
Everton	38	10	12	16	44	57	42
Southampton	38	10	11	17	50	56	41
Coventry City	38	9	14	15	38	54	41
Sunderland	38	10	10	18	35	53	40
Middlesbrough	38	10	12	16	51	60	39
Nottingham Forest	38	6	16	16	31	59	34

1997-98

PREMIERSHIP

Manager: Gerry Francis until November then Christian Gross as head coach

Did you know that?

When Sol Campbell led England out against Belgium on 29 May 1998 he became the seventh Spurs player to captain England, following in the footsteps of Vivian Woodward, Arthur Grimsdell, Alf Ramsey, Alan Mullery, Martin Peters and Gary Lineker.

LEAGUE DEBUTANTS

Aug 10	v Manchester United Stephen Clemence
Aug 10	v Manchester United Les Ferdinand
Aug 10	v Manchester United David Ginola
Aug 23	v Derby County Jose Dominguez
Jan 10	v Manchester United Nicola Berti
Jan 10	v Manchester United Gary Brady
Mar 1	v Bolton Wanderers Moussa Saib

Match No.	Date		Opponents		Result		Scorers	Attendance
1	Aug	10	H	Manchester United	L	0-2		26,359
2		13	A	West Ham United	L	1-2	Ferdinand	25,354
3		23	H	Derby County	W	1-0	Calderwood	25,886
4		27	H	Aston Villa	W	3-2	Ferdinand 2, Fox	26,317
5		30	A	Arsenal	D	0-0		38,102
6	Sep	12	A	Leicester City	L	0-3		20,683
7		20	H	Blackburn Rovers	D	0-0		26,573
8		23	A	Bolton Wanderers	D	1-1	Armstrong	23,433
9		27	H	Wimbledon	D	0-0		26,261
10	Oct	4	A	Newcastle United	L	0-1		36,709
11		19	H	Sheffield Wednesday	W	3-2	Dominguez, Armstrong, Ginola	25,097
12		25	A	Southampton	L	2-3	Dominguez, Ginola	15,255
13	Nov	1	H	Leeds United	L	0-1		26,441
14		8	A	Liverpool	L	0-4		38,006
15		24	H	Crystal Palace	L	0-1		25,634
16		29	A	Everton	W	2-0	Vega, Ginola	36,670
17	Dec	6	H	Chelsea	L	1-6	Vega	28,476
18		13	A	Coventry City	L	0-4		19,499
19		20	H	Barnsley	W	3-0	Nielsen, Ginola 2	28,232
20		26	A	Aston Villa	L	1-4	Calderwood	38,644
21		28	H	Arsenal	D	1-1	Nielsen	29,610
22	Jan	10	A	Manchester United	L	0-2		55,281
23		17	H	West Ham United	W	1-0	Klinsmann	30,284
24		31	A	Derby County	L	1-2	Fox	30,187
25	Feb	7	A	Blackburn Rovers	W	3-0	Berti, Armstrong, Fox	30,388
26		14	H	Leicester City	D	1-1	Calderwood	28,355
27		21	A	Sheffield Wednesday	L	0-1		29,871
28	Mar	1	H	Bolton Wanderers	W	1-0	Nielsen	29,032
29		4	A	Leeds United	L	0-1		31,394
30		14	H	Liverpool	D	3-3	Klinsmann, Ginola, Vega	30,245
31		28	A	Crystal Palace	W	3-1	Berti, Armstrong, Klinsmann	26,116
32	Apr	4	H	Everton	D	1-1	Armstrong	35,646
33		11	A	Chelsea	L	0-2		34,149
34		13	H	Coventry City	D	1-1	Berti	33,463
35		18	A	Barnsley	D	1-1	Calderwood	18,692
36		25	H	Newcastle United	W	2-0	Klinsmann, Ferdinand	35,847
37	May	2	A	Wimbledon	W	6-2	Ferdinand, Klinsmann 4, Saib	25,820
38		10	H	Southampton	D	1-1	Klinsmann	35,995

Appearances
Substitute
Goals

FA Cup

R3	Jan	5	H	Fulham	W	3-1	Clemence, Calderwood, Taylor (og)	27,909
R4		24	H	Barnsley	D	1-1	Campbell	28,722
R4r	Feb	4	A	Barnsley	L	1-3	Ginola	18,220

Appearances
Substitute
Goals

Coca-Cola Cup

R2	Sep	17	H	Carlisle United	W	3-2	Fenn, Fox, Mahorn	19,255
R2		30	A	Carlisle United	W	2-0	Ginola (pen), Armstrong	13,571
R3	Oct	15	A	Derby County	L	1-2	Ginola	20,390

Appearances
Substitute
Goals

Allen RW	Anderton DR	Armstrong CP	Baardsen PE	Berti N	Brady G	Calderwood C	Campbell SJ	Carr S	Clemence SN	Dominguez JMM	Edinburgh JC	Fenn NMC	Ferdinand L	Fox RA	Ginola DDM	Howells DG	Iversen S	Klinsmann J	Mabbutt GV	Mahorn PG	Nielsen A	Saib M	Scales JR	Sinton A	Vega R	Walker IM	Wilson CEA	Own-goals
							6	2	**11**		3		10		7	4	9				8			12	5	1		
							6	2	13		3		10		7	4	9				**8**		11	12	5	1		
						5		2	11	13	3		10		7	4	9				12		6	**8**		1		
						5		2	11		**3**	13	10	7		4	9		12				6	8		1		
							6	2	**8**	13	3		10	*7*		4	9		14		12		5	11		1		
		12					5	2	11	9			**10**		7	4			6		8		3			1		
							5	2	8	10	3			7	11	4			6	**9**					12	1		
		13				5	4	2	8	10	**3**			7	11				6	9					12	1		
		11					5	2	3	9			10	**7**	8				6		12				4	1		
		11				5	8	2	**3**	13			10	7	9				6					12	4	1		
	14	11				12	6	**2**		10	3	*13*		7	9	4								8	5	1		
	12	11				*13*	6	2		10	3	14		**7**	9	4								8	5	1		
	14	11					5	12		10	3			7	9	*4*	13		**6**				2	8		1		
11	*9*	12				5	6	2		14	3				7	4	10						8	13		1		
14	9						6	2	4		**3**		10		7		*11*				13		5	8	12	1		
	14					5	**6**	2					10	7	9		13				8		12	11	4	1	3	
14	13					5		2			12		10	7	9						8		*6*	**11**	4	1	3	
	9					5		2	13		12		10	7	11		14		6		8			4		1	**3**	
	9					5	6	2	12	14			10	7	**11**		13				8			4		1	3	
14	13					5	4	2	12					7	9		10		*6*		8			**11**		1	3	
						5	6	2	10	13				7	**11**		12	9			8				4	1	3	
			1	10	13	5	6	2	**8**	11				7				9						12	4		3	
			1	8	14	**5**	6	2		13				7	11	12		9						10	4		3	
			1	8			6	2		13			10	7	11	12		9						**4**	5		3	
		13	1	9	14		6	2	12				10	7	11	4					**8**				5		*3*	
		11	1	9	13	5	6	2			12			7	10						8				4		**3**	
		11	1	9	13	5	6	2		12	**3**			7	10	4					8							
		11	1	4	13	5	6	2						7	*10*	12		9			8	14					3	
			1	10	13		6	2				12		7	11	4		9			8	14			5		**3**	
		11	1	4	13		6	2						7	*10*	12		9			8				5		3	
		11		8	14	5	6	**2**		13				7		12		9				10			4	1	3	
		11		*4*		13	6	**2**						7	10	12		9			8	14			5	1	3	
	14	**11**		*4*		13	6	2					12	7	10			9			8	3			5	1		
		11		4		13	6	2					12	7	10			9			8	3			5	1		
	12	13		3		5	6	2					**10**	7	11			9			8				4	1		
	9			3		5	6	2					10	7	11			8				12			4	1		
	9	12		3		5	6	2					**10**	7	4			11			8	13				1		
	9			3		**5**	6	2					10	7	4			11	12		8	13				1		
1	7	13	9	17	0	21	34	37	12	8	13	0	19	32	34	14	8	15	8	2	21	3	9	14	22	29	16	
3	8	6	0	0	9	5	0	1	5	10	3	4	2	0	0	6	5	0	3	0	4	6	1	5	3	0	0	
		5		3		4				2			5	3	6			9			3	1			3			

Allen RW	Anderton DR	Armstrong CP	Baardsen PE	Berti N	Brady G	Calderwood C	Campbell SJ	Carr S	Clemence SN	Dominguez JMM	Edinburgh JC	Fenn NMC	Ferdinand L	Fox RA	Ginola DDM	Howells DG	Iversen S	Klinsmann J	Mabbutt GV	Mahorn PG	Nielsen A	Saib M	Scales JR	Sinton A	Vega R	Walker IM	Wilson CEA	Own-goals
			12		8	5	6	2	10	7					11			9		13					4	**1**	3	
			1	8		12	6	2					**10**	7	11			9						5	4		3	
		12	1	**8**	14		6	2	4				10	7	11	13		9							5		3	
0	0	0	2	2	1	1	3	3	2	1	0	0	2	2	3	0	0	3	0	0	0	0	0	1	3	1	3	
0	0	1	1	0	1	1	0	0	0	0	0	0	0	0	0	1	0	0	0	1	0	0	0	0	0	0	0	
						1	1		1						1													1

Allen RW	Anderton DR	Armstrong CP	Baardsen PE	Berti N	Brady G	Calderwood C	Campbell SJ	Carr S	Clemence SN	Dominguez JMM	Edinburgh JC	Fenn NMC	Ferdinand L	Fox RA	Ginola DDM	Howells DG	Iversen S	Klinsmann J	Mabbutt GV	Mahorn PG	Nielsen A	Saib M	Scales JR	Sinton A	Vega R	Walker IM	Wilson CEA	Own-goals
							5		4	10	3	**9**		7	11				6	12	8		2			1		
		11				5	6	2	3	12			10	7	**9**								8		4	1		
		11				12	6	2		10	3			7	9	4								8	**5**	1		
0	0	2	0	0	0	1	3	2	2	2	2	1	1	3	3	1	0	0	1	0	1	0	2	1	2	3	0	
0	0	0	0	0	0	1	0	0	0	1	0	0	0	0	0	0	0	0	0	1	0	0	0	0	0	0	0	
		1										1		1	2					1								

League Table

	P	W	D	L	F	A	Pts
Arsenal	38	23	9	6	68	33	78
Manchester United	38	23	8	7	73	26	77
Liverpool	38	18	11	9	68	42	65
Chelsea	38	20	3	15	71	43	63
Leeds United	38	17	8	13	57	46	59
Blackburn Rovers	38	16	10	12	57	52	58
Aston Villa	38	17	6	15	49	48	57
West Ham United	38	16	8	14	56	57	56
Derby County	38	16	7	15	52	49	55
Leicester City	38	13	14	11	51	41	53
Coventry City	38	12	16	10	46	44	52
Southampton	38	14	6	18	50	55	48
Newcastle United	38	11	11	16	35	44	44
TOTTENHAM HOTSPUR	38	11	11	16	44	56	44
Wimbledon	38	10	14	14	34	46	44
Sheffield Wednesday	38	12	8	18	52	67	44
Everton	38	9	13	16	41	56	40
Bolton Wanderers	38	9	13	16	41	61	40
Barnsley	38	10	5	23	37	82	35
Crystal Palace	38	8	9	21	37	71	33

1998-99

PREMIERSHIP

Manager: Christian Gross until September then George Graham from October

Did you know that?

When he was voted both Footballer of the Year by the Football Writers' Association and Player of the Year by the Professional Footballers' Association in 1999, David Ginola equalled the feat of Clive Allen who won both awards in 1987. Pat Jennings in 1976 is the only other Spurs player to win the PFA award, but the FWA award has gone to Danny Blanchflower (1958 and 1961), Pat Jennings (1973), Steve Perryman (1982), Gary Lineker (1992) and Jurgen Klinsmann (1995).

LEAGUE DEBUTANTS

Aug 15	v Wimbledon	Paolo Tramezzani
Sep 19	v Southampton	Hans Segers
Nov 28	v West Ham United	Luke Young
Jan 9	v Sheffield Wednesday	Steffen Freund
Jan 16	v Wimbledon	Mauricio Taricco
Feb 6	v Coventry City	Tim Sherwood
Apr 5	v Newcastle United	Roger Nilsen
May 1	v Liverpool	Ledley King

Match No.	Date			Opponents	Result		Scorers	Attendance
1	Aug	15	A	Wimbledon	L	1-3	Fox	23,031
2		22	H	Sheffield Wednesday	L	0-3		32,129
3		29	A	Everton	W	1-0	Ferdinand	39,378
4	Sep	9	H	Blackburn Rovers	W	2-1	Ferdinand, Nielsen	28,338
5		13	H	Middlesbrough	L	0-3		30,437
6		19	A	Southampton	D	1-1	Fox	15,204
7		26	H	Leeds United	D	3-3	Vega, Iversen, Campbell	35,535
8	Oct	3	A	Derby County	W	1-0	Campbell	30,083
9		19	A	Leicester City	L	1-2	Ferdinand	20,787
10		24	H	Newcastle United	W	2-0	Iversen 2	36,047
11	Nov	2	H	Charlton Athletic	D	2-2	Nielsen, Armstrong	32,202
12		7	A	Aston Villa	L	2-3	Anderton (pen), Vega	39,241
13		14	A	Arsenal	D	0-0		38,278
14		21	H	Nottingham Forest	W	2-0	Armstrong, Nielsen	35,832
15		28	A	West Ham United	L	1-2	Armstrong	26,044
16	Dec	5	H	Liverpool	W	2-1	Fox, Carragher (og)	36,125
17		12	H	Manchester United	D	2-2	Campbell 2	36,079
18		19	A	Chelsea	L	0-2		34,831
19		26	A	Coventry City	D	1-1	Campbell	23,098
20		28	H	Everton	W	4-1	Ferdinand, Armstrong 3	36,053
21	Jan	9	A	Sheffield Wednesday	D	0-0		28,204
22		16	H	Wimbledon	D	0-0		32,422
23		30	A	Blackburn Rovers	D	1-1	Iversen	29,643
24	Feb	6	H	Coventry City	D	0-0		34,376
25		20	A	Middlesbrough	D	0-0		34,687
26		27	H	Derby County	D	1-1	Sherwood	35,392
27	Mar	2	H	Southampton	W	3-0	Armstrong, Iversen, Dominguez	28,580
28		10	A	Leeds United	L	0-2		34,521
29		13	H	Aston Villa	W	1-0	Sherwood	35,963
30	Apr	3	H	Leicester City	L	0-2		35,415
31		5	A	Newcastle United	D	1-1	Anderton (pen)	36,655
32		17	A	Nottingham Forest	W	1-0	Iversen	25,181
33		20	A	Charlton Athletic	W	4-1	Iversen, Campbell, Dominguez, Ginola	20,043
34		24	H	West Ham United	L	1-2	Ginola	36,089
35	May	1	A	Liverpool	L	2-3	Carragher (og), Iversen	44,007
36		5	H	Arsenal	L	1-3	Anderton	36,019
37		10	H	Chelsea	D	2-2	Iversen, Ginola	35,878
38		16	A	Manchester United	L	1-2	Ferdinand	55,189
								Appearances
								Substitute
								Goals

FA Cup

R3	Jan	2	H	Watford	W	5-2	Iversen 2, Anderton (pen), Nielsen, Fox	36,022
R4		23	A	Wimbledon	D	1-1	Ginola	22,229
R4r	Feb	2	H	Wimbledon	W	3-0	Sinton, Nielsen 2	24,049
R5		13	A	Leeds United	D	1-1	Sherwood	39,696
R5r		24	H	Leeds United	W	2-0	Anderton, Ginola	32,307
R6	Mar	16	A	Barnsley	W	1-0	Ginola	18,793
SF	Apr	13	N*	Newcastle United	L#	0-2		53,609
								Appearances
								Substitute
								Goals

*played at Old Trafford #after extra-time

Worthington Cup

R2	Sep	15	A	Brentford	W	3-2	Carr, Dominguez, Vega	11,831
R2		23	H	Brentford	W	3-2	Nielsen, Campbell, Armstrong	22,980
R3	Oct	27	A	Northampton Town	W	3-1	Armstrong 2, Campbell	7,422
R4	Nov	10	A	Liverpool	W	3-1	Iversen, Scales, Nielsen	20,772
R5	Dec	2	H	Manchester United	W	3-1	Armstrong 2, Ginola	35,702
SF	Jan	27	H	Wimbledon	D	0-0		35,997
SF	Feb	16	A	Wimbledon	W	1-0	Iversen	25,204
F	Mar	21	N*	Leicester City	W	1-0	Nielsen	77,892
								Appearances
								Substitute
								Goals

*played at Wembley Stadium

Allen RW	Anderton DR	Armstrong CP	Baardsen PE	Berti N	Calderwood C	Campbell SJ	Carr S	Clemence SN	Dominguez JMM	Edinburgh JC	Ferdinand L	Fox RA	Freund S	Ginola DDM	Gower M	Iversen S	King LB	Nielsen A	Nilsen R	Saib M	Scales JR	Segers HJCA	Sherwood TA	Sinton A	Taricco MR	Tramezzani P	Vega R	Walker IM	Wilson CEA	Young LP	Own-goals
	9	11		**4**		6	2				10	7		8				12		13						3	5	1			
	9	11				5	2		13		10	7		8				6		12						3	**4**	1			
	9	12	1		5	8	2				**10**	7		11				6								3	4				
			1	4	5		2	**9**			10	7		11				6		12				13		3	8				
		12	1	4	8	5	2	**9**			10	*7*		11				6		13				14		3					
				4	5	6	2	9	12		10	7		11								1				3	8				
	9	11	1		14	5	2	8	13	3	**10**	7				12		6									4				
	9	12	1		5	4	2	13		3	10	*7*		**11**				6									8				
	9	12	1		5	6	*2*	8	13	3	10	7		**11**													4				
	9	11	1		5	4	2	13		3	**10**			*7*		12		6			8										
12	9	11	1		5	4	2	13		3		**7**						6			8			10							
14	9		1			5	2	10		**3**		*7*		11		8		6			4			13			12				
	9	11	1		**5**	4	2			3						7		6			10			12			8				
14	9	*11*	1		5	4	2	13		**3**				7		10		6			8			12							
	9	11	1			5	2	**8**				12		7		10		6						3						4	
	9	11				5	2				12	7		8		**10**		6						3				1		4	
12	9	11				5	2				10	**7**		8				6						3				1		4	
14	9	11				5	2	12		13	10	*7*		**8**				6						3				1		4	
	9	11				5	2	12			10	7		**8**		13		6						3				1		4	
	9	11				5	2	12			10	7		8		13		**6**						3				1		4	
	9	12				5	2	13		14	**10**		4	7		11		6						3				1		8	
		11			*5*	6	2	10		3		12	4	7		9								**8**	13		14	1			
	9	12				8	2			3	10		4			11		6						**7**			5	1			
	9	12				5	2				10		4			**11**		6					13	7	3			1		8	
	9	12				6	2				**10**		4	7		11							8		3		5	1			
	9	**11**				6			12	3			4	7		10							8		2		5	1			
		11				5	2		13				4	*7*		9		6					8		3		12	1		**10**	
	9	11				6	2			3	14		4	*7*		*10*		12					8	13				1		5	
	9	11				5	2		13		10			7		14		6					8	12	**3**		4	1			
		12				5	2			3	10	**7**	4	9		11		6						13				1		8	
	9	11				6	2						4			10			5				8	7	3			1			
	12	11				5	2				**10**		4			9		6					8		3			1		7	
	9	11				6	2		13				**4**	7		10		12	5				8		3			1			
	9	13				6	2		10				4	7		11		12					8		3			1		5	
	9	11				6	2	**8**	7			14	4			10	12		5				13		3			1			
	9	11				6	2		13				**4**	*7*		10							8	12	**3**			1		5	
	9	11				6	2	12	13				**4**	*7*		10					5		8		3			1			
	9					6	2		*12*	3	10		4	**7**		11					5		8	14				1		13	
0	31	24	12	4	11	37	37	9	2	14	22	17	17	30	0	22	0	24	3	0	7	1	12	12	12	6	13	25	0	14	
5	1	10	0	0	1	0	0	9	11	2	2	3	0	0	0	5	1	4	0	4	0	0	2	10	1	0	3	0	0	1	
	3	7				6			2		5	3		3		9		3					2				2				2

Allen RW	Anderton DR	Armstrong CP	Baardsen PE	Berti N	Calderwood C	Campbell SJ	Carr S	Clemence SN	Dominguez JMM	Edinburgh JC	Ferdinand L	Fox RA	Freund S	Ginola DDM	Gower M	Iversen S	King LB	Nielsen A	Nilsen R	Saib M	Scales JR	Segers HJCA	Sherwood TA	Sinton A	Taricco MR	Tramezzani P	Vega R	Walker IM	Wilson CEA	Young LP	Own-goals
	9					5	2	12		13	10	7		8		11		6						3				1		4	
	9	11				6	2			3	12	**7**	4	8		10											5	1			
	9	12				5	2			3	10		*4*			11		6						7	13		8	1		14	
	9					6	2			3	10		4	*7*		11		12					8	13				1		5	
	9	12				6	2			3	**10**		4	7		11							8	14			5	1		13	
	9	11				6	2				**10**		4	*7*		12							8	13	3		5	1			
	9	11				6	2				10		4	*7*		13		14					8	*12*	3			1		5	
0	7	3	0	0	0	7	7	0	0	4	6	2	6	6	0	5	0	2	0	0	0	0	4	2	2	0	4	7	0	3	
0	0	2	0	0	0	0	0	1	0	1	1	0	0	0	0	2	0	2	0	0	0	0	0	4	1	0	0	0	0	2	
	2											1		3		2		3					1	1							

Allen RW	Anderton DR	Armstrong CP	Baardsen PE	Berti N	Calderwood C	Campbell SJ	Carr S	Clemence SN	Dominguez JMM	Edinburgh JC	Ferdinand L	Fox RA	Freund S	Ginola DDM	Gower M	Iversen S	King LB	Nielsen A	Nilsen R	Saib M	Scales JR	Segers HJCA	Sherwood TA	Sinton A	Taricco MR	Tramezzani P	Vega R	Walker IM	Wilson CEA	Young LP	Own-goals
9		11	1		5	6	2	7	12					8	13									10		3	4				
	9	11			5	4	2	10	12	3		7		**8**	13			6				1									
13	9	11	1		5	4	2	12		3				**7**		10		6			8										
12	9		1		5	4	2					14		**11**		10		6			8			*7*			3		13		
	9	11			**5**	4	2				13	12		7		10		6						3				1		8	
	9	11				5	2			3	13		4	**7**		8		6						12			10	1			
	9					5	2			**3**	10		4	*7*		11		6						12			8	1		13	
	9					5	2			3	10		4	**7**		11		6						12			8	1			
1	7	5	3	0	5	8	8	2	0	5	2	1	3	8	0	6	0	7	0	0	2	1	0	3	0	1	5	4	0	1	
2	0	0	0	0	0	0	0	1	2	0	2	2	0	0	2	0	0	0	0	0	0	0	0	3	0	0	0	0	1	1	
		5				2	1		1					1		2		3			1						1				

League Table

	P	W	D	L	F	A	Pts
Manchester United	38	22	13	3	80	37	79
Arsenal	38	22	12	4	59	17	78
Chelsea	38	20	15	3	57	30	75
Leeds United	38	18	13	7	62	34	67
West Ham United	38	16	9	13	46	53	57
Aston Villa	38	15	10	13	51	46	55
Liverpool	38	15	9	14	68	49	54
Derby County	38	13	13	12	40	45	52
Middlesbrough	38	12	15	11	48	54	51
Leicester City	38	12	13	13	40	46	49
TOTTENHAM HOTSPUR	38	11	14	13	47	50	47
Sheffield Wednesday	38	13	7	18	41	42	46
Newcastle United	38	11	13	14	48	54	46
Everton	38	11	10	17	42	47	43
Coventry City	38	11	9	18	39	51	42
Wimbledon	38	10	12	16	40	63	42
Southampton	38	11	8	19	37	64	41
Charlton Athletic	38	8	12	18	41	56	36
Blackburn Rovers	38	7	14	17	38	52	35
Nottingham Forest	38	7	9	22	35	69	30

1999-2000

PREMIERSHIP

Manager: George Graham

Did you know that?

When John Piercy replaced Chris Armstrong against Derby County on 16 October 2000 he became the 500th player to appear for Spurs in Football/Premier League games.

LEAGUE DEBUTANTS

Aug 7	v West Ham United Chris Perry
Aug 7	v West Ham United Oyvind Leonhardsen
Oct 16	v Derby County John Piercy
Jan 22	v Sheffield Wednesday Willem Korsten
Apr 9	v Liverpool Simon Davies
Apr 9	v Liverpool Matthew Etherington
Apr 29	v Derby County Dave McEwen
May 6	v Manchester United Gary Doherty

Match No.	Date		Opponents		Result		Scorers	Attendance
1	Aug	7	A	West Ham United	L	0-1		26,010
2		9	H	Newcastle United	W	3-1	Iversen, Ferdinand, Sherwood	28,701
3		14	H	Everton	W	3-2	Sherwood, Leonhardsen, Iversen	34,539
4		21	A	Sheffield Wednesday	W	2-1	Ferdinand, Leonhardsen	24,027
5		28	H	Leeds United	L	1-2	Sherwood	36,012
6	Sep	12	A	Bradford City	D	1-1	Perry	18,143
7		19	H	Coventry City	W	3-2	Iversen, Armstrong, Leonhardsen	35,224
8		26	A	Wimbledon	D	1-1	Carr	17,368
9	Oct	3	H	Leicester City	L	2-3	Iversen 2	35,591
10		16	A	Derby County	W	1-0	Armstrong	29,815
11		23	H	Manchester United	W	3-1	Iversen, Carr, Scholes (og)	36,072
12		31	A	Sunderland	L	1-2	Iversen	41,904
13	Nov	7	H	Arsenal	W	2-1	Iversen, Sherwood	36,085
14		20	A	Southampton	W	1-0	Leonhardsen	15,248
15		28	A	Newcastle United	L	1-2	Armstrong	36,460
16	Dec	6	H	West Ham United	D	0-0		36,233
17		18	A	Middlesbrough	L	1-2	Vega	33,129
18		26	H	Watford	W	4-0	Ginola, Iversen, Sherwood 2	36,089
19		29	A	Aston Villa	D	1-1	Sherwood	39,217
20	Jan	3	H	Liverpool	W	1-0	Armstrong	36,044
21		12	A	Chelsea	L	0-1		34,989
22		15	A	Everton	D	2-2	Armstrong, Ginola	36,144
23		22	H	Sheffield Wednesday	L	0-1		35,897
24	Feb	5	H	Chelsea	L	0-1		36,041
25		12	A	Leeds United	L	0-1		40,127
26		26	A	Coventry City	W	1-0	Armstrong	23,077
27	Mar	4	H	Bradford City	D	1-1	Iversen	35,472
28		11	H	Southampton	W	7-2	Anderton, Armstrong 2, Iversen 3, Richards (og)	36,024
29		19	A	Arsenal	L	1-2	Armstrong	38,131
30		25	A	Watford	D	1-1	Armstrong	20,050
31	Apr	3	H	Middlesbrough	L	2-3	Armstrong, Ginola	31,796
32		9	A	Liverpool	L	0-2		44,536
33		15	H	Aston Villa	L	2-4	Iversen, Armstrong	35,304
34		19	A	Leicester City	W	1-0	Ginola	19,764
35		22	H	Wimbledon	W	2-0	Armstrong, Anderton	33,086
36		29	H	Derby County	D	1-1	Clemence	33,044
37	May	6	A	Manchester United	L	1-3	Armstrong	61,629
38		14	H	Sunderland	W	3-1	Anderton (pen), Sherwood, Carr	36,070
								Appearances
								Substitute
								Goals

FA Cup

R3	Dec	12	H	Newcastle United	D	1-1	Iversen	33,116
R3r		22	A	Newcastle United	L	1-6	Ginola	35,415
								Appearances
								Substitute
								Goals

Worthington Cup

R3	Oct	12	H	Crewe Alexandra	W	3-1	Leonhardsen, Ginola, Sherwood	25,486
R4	Dec	1	A	Fulham	L	1-3	Iversen	18,134
								Appearances
								Substitute
								Goals

Anderton DR	Armstrong CP	Campbell SJ	Carr S	Clemence SN	Davies S	Doherty GMT	Dominguez JMM	Edinburgh JC	Etherington M	Ferdinand L	Fox RA	Freund S	Ginola DDM	Iversen S	King LB	Korsten W	Leonhardsen O	McEwen D	Nielsen A	Perry CJ	Piercy JW	Scales JR	Sherwood TA	Taricco MR	Vega R	Walker IM	Young LP	Own-goals
7		**5**	2				9	3		13		4	*11*	10			14			6		12	8			1		
7			2				12			**9**		13	11	10			4			6		5	8	*3*		1	14	
7			2							9		12	11	10			4			6		5	8	3		1		
7			2							9		12	**11**	10			4			6			8	3		1	5	
			2				12			**9**		4	11	10			7		13	6			8	3		1	5	
	13		2							9		4	**11**	10			7		12	6			8	3		1	5	
	9		2				12					4	**11**	10			7		13	6			8	3		1	5	
	9		2				12					4		10			7		11	6			8	3		1	5	
	9		2									4	**11**	10			7		12	6			8	3	13	1	5	
	9	5	2										**11**	10	4		7		8	6	14		12	3	13	1		
		5	2								9	4	11	10			7				13		8	3	12	1	**6**	
		5	2	8			13					4	11	10			7			12	**9**		14	3	6	1		
	9	5	2	4			12	3			13		**11**	10			7			6			8			1		
	9	5					12	2				4	**11**	10			7			6			8	3		1		
	9	5		13			12	2				4	11	10			**7**			6			8	3		1		
	12	5					**9**					4	11	10			7		13	6			8	3		1	2	
	9	5						12			14	4	**7**	10					11	6			13	3	8	1	2	
	9	5	2	4			12						**11**	10					7	6			8	3		1		
	9	5	2	4									11	10					**7**	6			8	3		1	12	
	9	5	2	4									11	10						6			8	3		1	7	
7	9	5	2	4				3					11	10						6			8			1		
7	9	5	2	4				**3**					11	10					13	6			8			1	12	
7	9	5	2	4				**3**					11	10		14			13	6			8			1	12	
7	9	5	2	4									11	10		13			12	6			8	3		1		
7	9	5	2	4			12						**10**			11			13	6			8	3		1		
7	9	5	2	13								4	11				10			6			8	**3**		1	12	
7	9	5	2							12		4	11	10			**8**			6				3		1	13	
7	9	5	2									4	11	10			8			**6**				3		1	12	
7	9	**5**	2							13		4	*11*	10		14	8			6				3		1	12	
7	9		2	13						12		4	11	**10**			8			6		5		3		1		
7	9	5	2	12								4	8	10		**11**				6				3		1		
7	9	5	2	8	13				12			4	**11**	10						6				3		1		
7	9	5	2	8								4	11	10						6				3		1		
7	9	5	2	8					14			4	11	*10*		13				6				**3**		1	12	
7	9	5	2	3					12			4	**8**	10		11				6						1		
7	9	5	2	4	12				13				8	*10*		**11**		14		6						1	3	
7	9	5	2	3	8	14			**11**			4		10	12	13				6						1		
7	9	5	2			13						4	11	10	3		**8**			6			12			1		
22	29	29	34	16	1	0	2	7	1	5	1	24	36	36	2	4	21	0	5	36	1	3	23	29	2	38	11	
0	2	0	0	4	2	2	10	1	4	4	2	3	0	0	1	5	1	1	9	1	2	1	4	0	3	0	9	
3	14		3	1						2			4	14			4			1			8		1			2

Anderton DR	Armstrong CP	Campbell SJ	Carr S	Clemence SN	Davies S	Doherty GMT	Dominguez JMM	Edinburgh JC	Etherington M	Ferdinand L	Fox RA	Freund S	Ginola DDM	Iversen S	King LB	Korsten W	Leonhardsen O	McEwen D	Nielsen A	Perry CJ	Piercy JW	Scales JR	Sherwood TA	Taricco MR	Vega R	Walker IM	Young LP	Own-goals
	13	5					**9**	3			7	4	11	10					8	6					12	1	2	
	14	5		9			13				*12*		11	10					**7**	6			8	3	4	1	**2**	
0	0	2	0	1	0	0	1	1	0	0	1	1	2	2	0	0	0	0	2	2	0	0	1	1	1	2	2	
0	2	0	0	0	0	0	1	0	0	0	1	0	0	0	0	0	0	0	0	0	0	0	0	0	1	0	0	
													1	1														

Anderton DR	Armstrong CP	Campbell SJ	Carr S	Clemence SN	Davies S	Doherty GMT	Dominguez JMM	Edinburgh JC	Etherington M	Ferdinand L	Fox RA	Freund S	Ginola DDM	Iversen S	King LB	Korsten W	Leonhardsen O	McEwen D	Nielsen A	Perry CJ	Piercy JW	Scales JR	Sherwood TA	Taricco MR	Vega R	Walker IM	Young LP	Own-goals
	9	5	2									4	11	12			7			6	**10**		8	3		1		
	9	5					14	**2**				4	11	10			7			6			8	3	13	1	12	
0	2	2	1	0	0	0	0	1	0	0	0	2	2	1	0	0	2	0	0	2	1	0	2	2	0	2	0	
0	0	0	0	0	0	0	1	0	0	0	0	0	0	1	0	0	0	0	0	0	0	0	0	0	1	0	1	
													1	1			1						1					

League Table

	P	W	D	L	F	A	Pts
Manchester United	38	28	7	3	97	45	91
Arsenal	38	22	7	9	73	43	73
Leeds United	38	21	6	11	58	43	69
Liverpool	38	19	10	9	51	30	67
Chelsea	38	18	11	9	53	34	65
Aston Villa	38	15	13	10	46	35	58
Sunderland	38	16	10	12	57	56	58
Leicester City	38	16	7	15	55	55	55
West Ham United	38	15	10	13	52	53	55
TOTTENHAM HOTSPUR	38	15	8	15	57	49	53
Newcastle United	38	14	10	14	63	54	52
Middlesbrough	38	14	10	14	46	52	52
Everton	38	12	14	12	59	49	50
Coventry City	38	12	8	18	47	54	44
Southampton	38	12	8	18	45	62	44
Derby County	38	9	11	18	44	57	38
Bradford City	38	9	9	20	38	68	36
Wimbledon	38	7	12	19	46	74	33
Sheffield Wednesday	38	8	7	23	38	70	31
Watford	38	6	6	26	35	77	24

2000-01

PREMIERSHIP

Manager: George Graham until March then Glenn Hoddle

Did you know that?

Ledley King's goal at Bradford City on 9 December 2000 was timed at 9.7 seconds. It remains the fastest goal ever scored in the Premiership.

LEAGUE DEBUTANTS

Aug 19 v Ipswich Town Sergei Rebrov
Aug 19 v Ipswich Town Neil Sullivan
Aug 19 v Ipswich Town Ben Thatcher
Nov 19 v Liverpool Alton Thelwell
Jan 31 v West Ham United Andy Booth
Mar 3 v Derby County Anthony Gardner

Match No.	Date			Opponents	Result		Scorers	Attendance
1	Aug	19	H	Ipswich Town	W	3-1	Anderton (pen), Carr, Ferdinand	36,148
2		22	A	Middlesbrough	D	1-1	Leonhardsen	31,254
3		26	A	Newcastle United	L	0-2		51,573
4	Sep	5	H	Everton	W	3-2	Rebrov 2 (1 pen), Ferdinand	36,010
5		11	H	West Ham United	W	1-0	Campbell	33,282
6		16	A	Charlton Athletic	L	0-1		20,043
7		23	H	Manchester City	D	0-0		36,069
8		30	A	Leeds United	L	3-4	Rebrov 2, Perry	37,562
9	Oct	14	A	Coventry City	L	1-2	Rebrov	21,435
10		21	H	Derby County	W	3-1	Leonhardsen 2, Carr	34,483
11		28	A	Chelsea	L	0-3		34,966
12	Nov	4	H	Sunderland	W	2-1	Sherwood, Armstrong	36,016
13		11	A	Aston Villa	L	0-2		33,608
14		19	H	Liverpool	W	2-1	Ferdinand, Sherwood	36,036
15		25	H	Leicester City	W	3-0	Ferdinand 3	35,636
16	Dec	2	A	Manchester United	L	0-2		67,583
17		9	A	Bradford City	D	3-3	King, Campbell, Armstrong	17,225
18		18	H	Arsenal	D	1-1	Rebrov	36,062
19		23	H	Middlesbrough	D	0-0		35,638
20		27	A	Southampton	L	0-2		15,237
21		30	A	Ipswich Town	L	0-3		22,234
22	Jan	2	H	Newcastle United	W	4-2	Doherty, Anderton (pen), Rebrov, Ferdinand	34,324
23		13	A	Everton	D	0-0		32,290
24		20	H	Southampton	D	0-0		36,095
25		31	A	West Ham United	D	0-0		26,048
26	Feb	3	H	Charlton Athletic	D	0-0		35,368
27		10	A	Manchester City	W	1-0	Rebrov	34,399
28		24	H	Leeds United	L	1-2	Ferdinand	36,070
29	Mar	3	A	Derby County	L	1-2	West (og)	29,410
30		17	H	Coventry City	W	3-0	Iversen, Ferdinand, Rebrov	35,606
31		31	A	Arsenal	L	0-2		38,121
32	Apr	10	H	Bradford City	W	2-1	Iversen, Davies	28,306
33		14	A	Sunderland	W	3-2	Clemence, Doherty 2	48,029
34		17	H	Chelsea	L	0-3		36,074
35		22	A	Liverpool	L	1-3	Korsten	43,547
36		28	H	Aston Villa	D	0-0		36,096
37	May	5	A	Leicester City	L	2-4	Davies, Carr	21,056
38		19	H	Manchester United	W	3-1	Korsten 2, Ferdinand	36,072

Appearances
Substitute
Goals

FA Cup

Round	Date			Opponents	Result		Scorers	Attendance
R3	Jan	6	A	Leyton Orient	W	1-0	Doherty	12,336
R4	Feb	7	A	Charlton Athletic	W	4-2	Anderton, Leonhardsen, Rebrov, Rufus (og)	18,101
R5		17	H	Stockport County	W	4-0	King, Davies 2, Flynn (og)	36,040
R6	Mar	11	A	West Ham United	W	3-2	Rebrov 2, Doherty	26,048
SF	Apr	8	N*	Arsenal	L	1-2	Doherty	63,541

*played at Old Trafford

Appearances
Substitute
Goals

Worthington Cup

Round	Date			Opponents	Result		Scorers	Attendance
R2	Sep	19	A	Brentford	D	0-0		8,580
R2r		26	H	Brentford	W	2-0	Leonhardsen, Iversen	26,909
R3	Oct	31	H	Birmingham City	L	1-3	Anderton (pen)	27,096

Appearances
Substitute
Goals

Anderton DR	Armstrong CP	Booth AD	Campbell SJ	Carr S	Clemence SN	Davies S	Doherty GMT	Dominguez JMM	Etherington M	Ferdinand L	Freund S	Gardner A	Iversen S	King LB	Korsten W	Leonhardsen O	McEwen D	Perry CJ	Piercy JW	Rebrov S	Sherwood TA	Sullivan N	Taricco MR	Thatcher BD	Thelwell AA	Vega R	Walker IM	Young LP	Own-goals
7			5	2						12	4		**10**			9		6		11	8	1	13	3					
7			5	2						12	4		10			9		6		**11**	8	1		3					
7			5	2						12	4		**10**			9		6		11	8	1	13	3				14	
7			5	2	12					*9*	4		14			10		6		11	8	1	13	3					
			5	2						9	4		10			7				11	8	1	3	13		12		**6**	
			5	2	12					9	4		10			7		13		11	**8**	1	3			6			
				2			12			**9**	4		10			7		6		11	8	1		3		5		13	
12				2						**9**	4		10			7		6		11	8	1		3		5			
7				2				13		9	**4**		12			10		6		11	8			3		5	1		
7				2	4	14		12		9					13	**10**		6		11	8	1		3		5			
7				2	10	12	13			9	**4**				11			6			8	1				5		3	
7	12			2	10					9								6		**11**	8	1		3		5		4	
7	12			2	10		13			**9**								6		11	8	1		3		5		4	
7	12			2	10					9	13			4				6		**11**	8	1			5			3	
7	14		5	2	10					9	13			4				**6**		*11*	8	1		12	3				
7	**10**		5	2	11					9				4	12			6			8	1			3				
	10		5	2	7					9	4			11	13			6			**8**	1			3	12			
7	12		5	2	10					9				4				6		**11**	8	1			3				
7	12		5	2	10					**9**				4		13		6		11	8	1			3				
7	*9*		5	**2**	10		13							4	14	8		6		11	12	1			3				
7			5		10	12	9							4	11	2		6		13	**8**	1			3				
7			5		3		2			9				4		**10**		6		11	8	1					12	13	
7					3	12	2							4	9	**10**	13	6		11	8	1						5	
7			5		8		2			**9**	4			10		13	12	6		11							1	3	
7		9	5		3		2				4			10		8	12	6		**11**							1	13	
7		9	5		3		2		13		4			**10**		8		6		11	12	1							
7		12	5	13			9				4			10		2		**6**		11	8	1						3	
			5		3	**7**	6		14	*9*	4		13	10						11	8	1			12			2	
		10	5		3		6			9	4	12	13	7							8	1			**11**			2	
			5		3		2			9	4		10	8				6		11		1						7	
						8	2		13	9	4	5	10		**11**			6	12			1			3			7	
				2	3	9	4						**10**		13	7		6		11	8	1			12			5	
				2	3	7	9					12		5	13	10		6	14	11	8	1						4	
				2	*10*	4	9		14			12			7			6	13	11	8	1			5			3	
				2	10	**4**	9					5			11	7			12		8	1			6			3	
				2	10	**4**	5		13	9		6			11	7					8	1			12			3	
				2	10	4	11			9		5				7					8	1			6			3	
				2	10	4	5		11	9		**6**			8	7		12	13			1						3	
22	3	3	21	27	27	9	18	0	1	25	19	5	10	18	8	23	0	30	0	28	31	35	2	10	13	8	3	19	
1	6	1	0	1	2	4	4	2	5	3	2	3	4	0	6	2	3	2	5	1	2	0	3	2	3	2	1	4	
2	2		2	3	1	2	3			10			2	1	3	3		1		9	2								1

Anderton DR	Armstrong CP	Booth AD	Campbell SJ	Carr S	Clemence SN	Davies S	Doherty GMT	Dominguez JMM	Etherington M	Ferdinand L	Freund S	Gardner A	Iversen S	King LB	Korsten W	Leonhardsen O	McEwen D	Perry CJ	Piercy JW	Rebrov S	Sherwood TA	Sullivan N	Taricco MR	Thatcher BD	Thelwell AA	Vega R	Walker IM	Young LP	Own-goals
7			5		3		2			**9**				4	12	10		6		11	8	1							
7			5	12			9				4			10		2		**6**		11	8	1						3	
			5		3	12	6			9	4			10	14	**7**				*11*	8	1			13			2	
			5		3		2			**9**	4		10	8	12			6		11		1						7	
			5	2	**3**		4			*9*			10	13		14		6		11	8	1			12			7	
2	0	0	5	1	4	0	5	0	0	4	3	0	2	4	0	3	0	4	0	5	4	5	0	0	0	0	0	4	
0	0	0	0	1	0	1	0	0	0	0	0	0	0	1	3	1	0	0	0	0	0	0	0	0	2	0	0	0	
1						2	3							1		1				3									2

Anderton DR	Armstrong CP	Booth AD	Campbell SJ	Carr S	Clemence SN	Davies S	Doherty GMT	Dominguez JMM	Etherington M	Ferdinand L	Freund S	Gardner A	Iversen S	King LB	Korsten W	Leonhardsen O	McEwen D	Perry CJ	Piercy JW	Rebrov S	Sherwood TA	Sullivan N	Taricco MR	Thatcher BD	Thelwell AA	Vega R	Walker IM	Young LP	Own-goals
			5	2	8				9	14	4		10			7		6		*11*		1		3		12	13		
				2				12		**9**	4		10			7		6		11	8	1		3		5			
7				2	10	12		14		9	**4**				*11*			6			8	1		3		5		13	
1	0	0	1	3	2	0	0	0	1	2	3	0	2	0	1	2	0	3	0	2	2	3	0	3	0	2	0	0	
0	0	0	0	0	0	1	0	2	0	1	0	0	0	0	0	0	0	0	0	0	0	0	0	0	0	1	1	1	
1													1			1													

League Table

	P	W	D	L	F	A	Pts
Manchester United	38	24	8	6	79	31	80
Arsenal	38	20	10	8	63	38	70
Liverpool	38	20	9	9	71	39	69
Leeds United	38	20	8	10	64	43	68
Ipswich Town	38	20	6	12	57	42	66
Chelsea	38	17	10	11	68	45	61
Sunderland	38	15	12	11	46	41	57
Aston Villa	38	13	15	10	46	43	54
Charlton Athletic	38	14	10	14	50	57	52
Southampton	38	14	10	14	40	48	52
Newcastle United	38	14	9	15	44	50	51
TOTTENHAM HOTSPUR	38	13	10	15	47	54	49
Leicester City	38	14	6	18	39	51	48
Middlesbrough	38	9	15	14	44	44	42
West Ham United	38	10	12	16	45	50	42
Everton	38	11	9	18	45	59	42
Derby County	38	10	12	16	37	59	42
Manchester City	38	8	10	20	41	65	34
Coventry City	38	8	10	20	36	63	34
Bradford City	38	5	11	22	30	70	26

2001-02

PREMIERSHIP

Manager: Glenn Hoddle

Did you know that?

In September 2001 Spurs bought Dave Mackay's double winners' medals at Sotheby's Football Memorabilia auction in London. A hammer price of £18,000 was paid, over £21,000 with buyer's premium, with the medals intended to form the centrepiece of the club's proposed museum. The museum remains on the drawing board.

LEAGUE DEBUTANTS

Aug 18 v Aston Villa Goran Bunjevcevic
Aug 18 v Aston Villa Gus Poyet
Aug 18 v Aston Villa Christian Ziege
Sep 29 v Manchester United Dean Richards
Dec 29 v Aston Villa Kasey Keller

Match No.	Date		Opponents		Result		Scorers	Attendance
1	Aug	18	H	Aston Villa	D	0-0		36,059
2		20	A	Everton	D	1-1	Anderton	29,503
3		25	A	Blackburn Rovers	L	1-2	Ziege	24,992
4	Sep	9	H	Southampton	W	2-0	Ziege, Davies	33,668
5		16	H	Chelsea	L	2-3	Sheringham 2	36,037
6		19	A	Sunderland	W	2-1	Ziege, Sheringham	47,310
7		22	A	Liverpool	L	0-1		44,116
8		29	H	Manchester United	L	3-5	Richards, Ferdinand, Ziege	36,038
9	Oct	15	H	Derby County	W	3-1	Ferdinand, Ziege, Poyet	30,148
10		21	A	Newcastle United	W	2-0	Poyet, Speed (og)	50,593
11		27	H	Middlesbrough	W	2-1	Sheringham (pen), Ferdinand	36,062
12	Nov	4	A	Leeds United	L	1-2	Poyet	40,203
13		17	H	Arsenal	D	1-1	Poyet	36,049
14		29	A	West Ham United	W	1-0	Ferdinand	32,780
15	Dec	3	H	Bolton Wanderers	W	3-2	Poyet, Ferdinand, Sheringham	32,971
16		8	A	Charlton Athletic	L	1-3	Poyet	25,125
17		15	H	Fulham	W	4-0	Ferdinand, Anderton, Davies, Rebrov	36,054
18		22	H	Ipswich Town	L	1-2	Davies	36,043
19		26	A	Southampton	L	0-1		31,719
20		29	A	Aston Villa	D	1-1	Ferdinand	41,134
21	Jan	1	H	Blackburn Rovers	W	1-0	Richards	35,131
22		12	A	Ipswich Town	L	1-2	Poyet	25,007
23		19	H	Everton	D	1-1	Ferdinand	36,056
24		30	H	Newcastle United	L	1-3	Iversen	35,798
25	Feb	2	A	Derby County	L	0-1		27,721
26		9	H	Leicester City	W	2-1	Anderton, Davies	35,973
27	Mar	2	H	Sunderland	W	2-1	Poyet, Ferdinand	36,062
28		6	A	Manchester United	L	0-4		67,599
29		13	A	Chelsea	L	0-4		39,652
30		18	H	Charlton Athletic	L	0-1		29,602
31		24	A	Fulham	W	2-0	Sheringham, Poyet	15,885
32		30	A	Middlesbrough	D	1-1	Iversen	31,258
33	Apr	1	H	Leeds United	W	2-1	Iversen, Sheringham	35,167
34		6	A	Arsenal	L	1-2	Sheringham (pen)	38,186
35		13	H	West Ham United	D	1-1	Sheringham	36,083
36		20	A	Bolton Wanderers	D	1-1	Iversen	25,817
37		27	H	Liverpool	W	1-0	Poyet	36,017
38	May	11	A	Leicester City	L	1-2	Sheringham (pen)	21,716
								Appearances
								Substitute
								Goals

FA Cup

R3	Jan	16	A	Coventry City	W	2-0	Poyet, Ferdinand	20,758
R4	Feb	5	H	Bolton Wanderers	W	4-0	Anderton (pen), Iversen, Etherington, Barness (og)	27,093
R5		17	H	Tranmere Rovers	W	4-0	Ziege, Poyet 2, Sheringham	30,696
R6	Mar	9	H	Chelsea	L	0-4		32,896
								Appearances
								Substitute
								Goals

Worthington Cup

R2	Sep	13	H	Torquay United	W	2-0	King, Ferdinand	20,347
R3	Oct	9	A	Tranmere Rovers	W	4-0	Sheringham (pen), Anderton, Poyet, Rebrov	12,386
R4	Nov	29	A	Fulham	W	2-1	Rebrov, Davies	17,006
R5	Dec	11	H	Bolton Wanderers	W	6-0	Davies, Ferdinand 3, Iversen, Barness (og)	28,430
SF	Jan	9	A	Chelsea	L	1-2	Ferdinand	37,264
SF		23	H	Chelsea	W	5-1	Iversen, Sherwood, Sheringham, Davies, Rebrov	34,799
F	Feb	24	N*	Blackburn Rovers	L	1-2	Ziege	72,500
								Appearances
								Substitute
								Goals

*played at Millennium Stadium

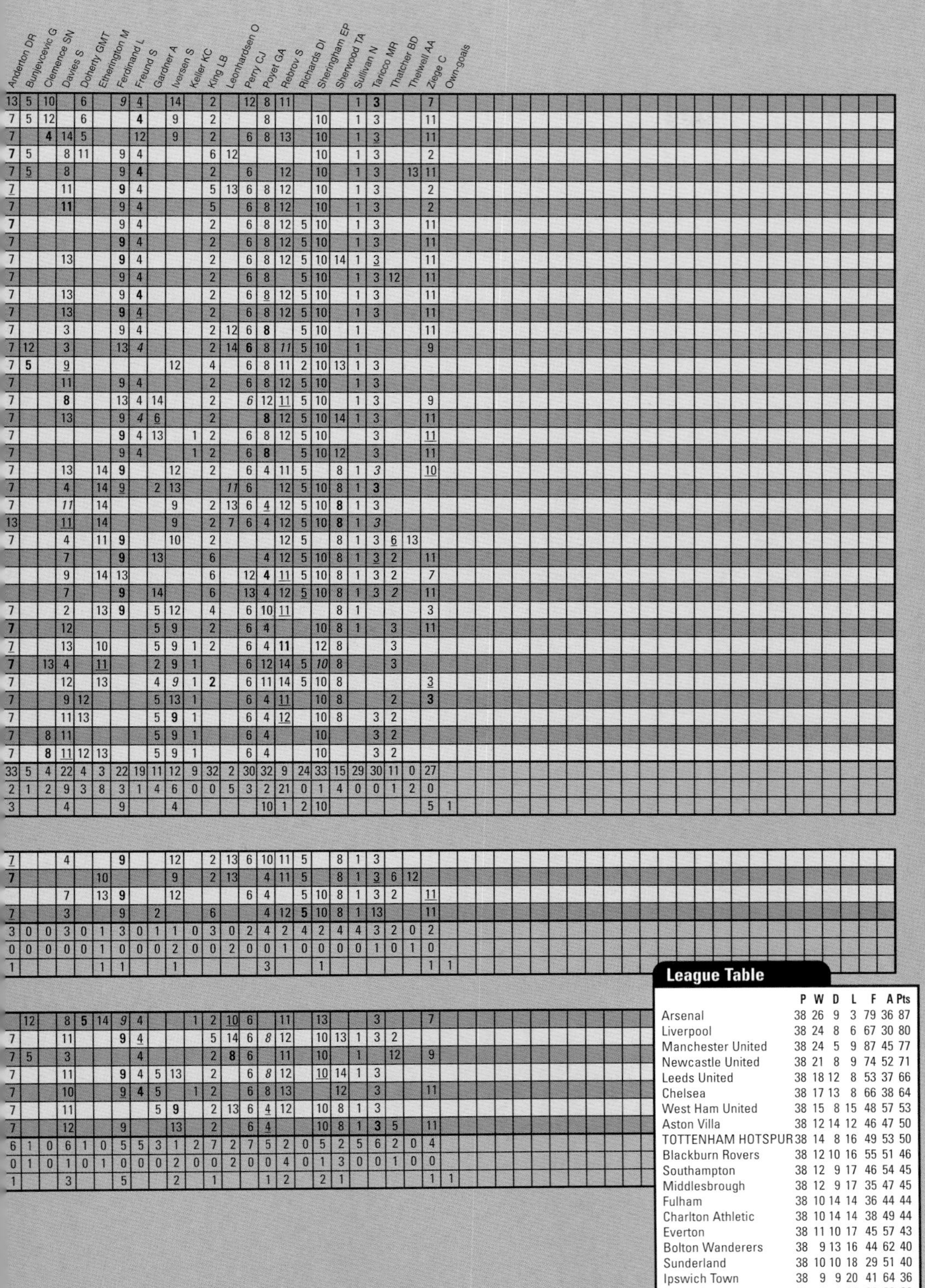

Anderton DR	Bunjevcevic G	Clemence SN	Davies S	Doherty GMT	Etherington M	Ferdinand L	Freund S	Gardner A	Iversen S	Keller KC	King LB	Leonhardsen O	Perry CJ	Poyet GA	Rebrov S	Richards DI	Sheringham EP	Sherwood TA	Sullivan N	Taricco MR	Thatcher BD	Thelwall AA	Ziege C	Own-goals
13	5	10		6		*9*	4		14		2		12	8	11				1	**3**			7	
7	5	12		6			**4**		9		2			8			10		1	3			11	
7		**4**	14	5			12		9		2		6	8	13		10		1	3			11	
7	5		8	11		9	4				6	12					10		1	3			2	
7	5		8			9	**4**				2		6		12		10		1	3		13	11	
7			11			**9**	4				5	13	6	8	12		10		1	3			2	
7			**11**			9	4				5		6	8	12		10		1	3			2	
7						9	4				2		6	8	12	5	10		1	3			11	
7						**9**	4				2		6	8	12	5	10		1	3			11	
7			13			**9**	4				2		6	8	12	5	10	14	1	3			11	
7						9	4				2		6	8		5	10		1	3	12		11	
7			13			9	**4**				2		6	8	12	5	10		1	3			11	
7			13			**9**	4				2		6	8	12	5	10		1	3			11	
7			3			9	4				2	12	6	**8**		5	10		1				11	
7	12		3			13	*4*				2	14	**6**	8	*11*	5	10		1				9	
7	**5**		9						12		4		6	8	11	2	10	13	1	3				
7			11			9	4				2		6	8	12	5	10		1	3				
7			**8**			13	4	14			2		*6*	12	11	5	10		1	3			9	
7			13			9	*4*	6			2			**8**	12	5	10	14	1	3			11	
7						**9**	4	13		1	2		6	8	12	5	10			3			11	
7						9	4			1	2		6	**8**		5	10	12		3			11	
7			13		14	**9**			12		2		6	4	11	5		8	1	*3*			10	
7			4		14	9		2	13			*11*	6		12	5	10	8	1	**3**				
7			*11*		14				9		2	13	6	4	12	5	10	**8**	1	3				
13			11		14				9		2	7	6	4	12	5	10	**8**	1	*3*				
7			4		11	**9**			10		2				12	5		8	1	3	6	13		
			7			**9**		13			6			4	12	5	10	8	1	3	2		11	
			9		14	13					6		12	**4**	11	5	10	8	1	3	2		7	
			7			**9**		14			6		13	4	12	5	10	8	1	3	*2*		11	
7			2		13	**9**		5	12		4		6	10	11			8	1				3	
7			12					5	9		2		6	4			10	8	1		3		11	
7			13		10			5	9	1	2		6	4	**11**		12	8			3			
7		13	4		11			2	9	1			6	12	14	5	*10*	8			3			
7			12		13			4	*9*	1	**2**		6	11	14	5	10	8					3	
7			9	12				5	13	1			6	4	11		10	8			2		**3**	
7			11	13				5	**9**	1			6	4	12		10	8		3	2			
7		8	11					5	9	1			6	4			10			3	2			
7		**8**	11	12	13			5	9	1			6	4			10			3	2			
33	5	4	22	4	3	22	19	11	12	9	32	2	30	32	9	24	33	15	29	30	11	0	27	
2	1	2	9	3	8	3	1	4	6	0	0	5	3	2	21	0	1	4	0	0	1	2	0	
3			4			9			4					10	1	2	10						5	1

Anderton DR	Bunjevcevic G	Clemence SN	Davies S	Doherty GMT	Etherington M	Ferdinand L	Freund S	Gardner A	Iversen S	Keller KC	King LB	Leonhardsen O	Perry CJ	Poyet GA	Rebrov S	Richards DI	Sheringham EP	Sherwood TA	Sullivan N	Taricco MR	Thatcher BD	Thelwall AA	Ziege C	Own-goals
7			4			**9**			12		2	13	6	10	11	5		8	1	3				
7					10				9		2	13		4	11	5		8	1	3	6	12		
			7		13	**9**			12				6	4		5	10	8	1	3	2		11	
7			3			9		2			6			4	12	**5**	10	8	1	13			11	
3	0	0	3	0	1	3	0	1	1	0	3	0	2	4	2	4	2	4	4	3	2	0	2	
0	0	0	0	0	1	0	0	0	2	0	0	2	0	0	1	0	0	0	0	1	0	1	0	
1					1	1			1					3			1						1	1

Anderton DR	Bunjevcevic G	Clemence SN	Davies S	Doherty GMT	Etherington M	Ferdinand L	Freund S	Gardner A	Iversen S	Keller KC	King LB	Leonhardsen O	Perry CJ	Poyet GA	Rebrov S	Richards DI	Sheringham EP	Sherwood TA	Sullivan N	Taricco MR	Thatcher BD	Thelwall AA	Ziege C	Own-goals
	12		8	**5**	14	*9*	4			1	2	10	6		11		13			3			7	
7			11			**9**	4				5	14	6	*8*	12		10	13	1	3	2			
7	5		3				4				2	**8**	6		11		10		1		12		9	
7			11			**9**	4	5	13		2		6	*8*	12		10	14	1	3				
7			10			9	**4**	5		1	2		6	8	13			12		3			11	
7			11					5	**9**		2	13	6	4	12		10	8	1	3				
7			12			9			13		2		6	4			10	8	1	**3**	5		11	
6	1	0	6	1	0	5	5	3	1	2	7	2	7	5	2	0	5	2	5	6	2	0	4	
0	1	0	1	0	1	0	0	0	2	0	0	2	0	0	4	0	1	3	0	0	1	0	0	
1			3			5			2		1			1	2		2	1					1	1

League Table

	P	W	D	L	F	A	Pts
Arsenal	38	26	9	3	79	36	87
Liverpool	38	24	8	6	67	30	80
Manchester United	38	24	5	9	87	45	77
Newcastle United	38	21	8	9	74	52	71
Leeds United	38	18	12	8	53	37	66
Chelsea	38	17	13	8	66	38	64
West Ham United	38	15	8	15	48	57	53
Aston Villa	38	12	14	12	46	47	50
TOTTENHAM HOTSPUR	38	14	8	16	49	53	50
Blackburn Rovers	38	12	10	16	55	51	46
Southampton	38	12	9	17	46	54	45
Middlesbrough	38	12	9	17	35	47	45
Fulham	38	10	14	14	36	44	44
Charlton Athletic	38	10	14	14	38	49	44
Everton	38	11	10	17	45	57	43
Bolton Wanderers	38	9	13	16	44	62	40
Sunderland	38	10	10	18	29	51	40
Ipswich Town	38	9	9	20	41	64	36
Derby County	38	8	6	24	33	63	30
Leicester City	38	5	13	20	30	64	28

2002-03

PREMIERSHIP

Manager: Glenn Hoddle

Did you know that?

On 17 October 2002 a Spurs team featuring former legends Paul Gascoigne, Jurgen Klinsmann, David Ginola, Colin Calderwood, Chris Waddle and Clive and Paul Allen met DC United to raise funds for the Tottenham Tribute Trust. The Trust was formed to help former players of the club who had fallen on hard times following their retirement and has since quietly and effectively done just that.

LEAGUE DEBUTANTS

Aug 17	v Everton Milenko Acimovic
Aug 17	v Everton Jamie Redknapp
Aug 31	v Southampton Jonathan Blondel
Sep 15	v West Ham United Robbie Keane
Mar 16	v Liverpool Jamie Slabber
Apr 18	v Manchester City Kazu Toda

Match No.	Date		Opponents		Result		Scorers	Attendance
1	Aug	17	A	Everton	D	2-2	Etherington, Ferdinand	40,120
2		24	H	Aston Villa	W	1-0	Redknapp	35,384
3		27	A	Charlton Athletic	W	1-0	Davies	26,392
4		31	H	Southampton	W	2-1	Ferdinand, Sheringham (pen)	35,573
5	Sep	11	A	Fulham	L	2-3	Richards, Sheringham	16,757
6		15	H	West Ham United	W	3-2	Davies, Sheringham (pen), Gardner	36,005
7		21	A	Manchester United	L	0-1		67,611
8		28	H	Middlesbrough	L	0-3		36,082
9	Oct	6	A	Blackburn Rovers	W	2-1	Keane, Redknapp	26,203
10		20	H	Bolton Wanderers	W	3-1	Keane 2, Davies	35,909
11		26	A	Liverpool	L	1-2	Richards	44,084
12	Nov	3	H	Chelsea	D	0-0		36,049
13		10	A	Sunderland	L	0-2		40,024
14		16	A	Arsenal	L	0-3		38,152
15		24	H	Leeds United	W	2-0	Sheringham, Keane	35,842
16		30	A	Birmingham City	D	1-1	Sheringham	29,505
17	Dec	8	H	West Bromwich Albion	W	3-1	Ziege, Keane, Poyet	35,958
18		15	H	Arsenal	D	1-1	Ziege	36,076
19		23	A	Manchester City	W	3-2	Perry, Davies, Poyet	34,563
20		26	H	Charlton Athletic	D	2-2	Keane, Iversen	36,043
21		30	A	Newcastle United	L	1-2	Dabizas (og)	52,145
22	Jan	1	A	Southampton	L	0-1		31,890
23		12	H	Everton	W	4-3	Poyet, Keane 3	36,070
24		18	A	Aston Villa	W	1-0	Sheringham	38,576
25		29	H	Newcastle United	L	0-1		36,084
26	Feb	1	A	Chelsea	D	1-1	Sheringham	41,384
27		8	H	Sunderland	W	4-1	Poyet, Doherty, Davies, Sheringham	36,075
28		24	H	Fulham	D	1-1	Sheringham (pen)	34,704
29	Mar	1	A	West Ham United	L	0-2		35,049
30		16	H	Liverpool	L	2-3	Taricco, Sheringham	36,077
31		24	A	Bolton Wanderers	L	0-1		23,084
32	Apr	5	H	Birmingham City	W	2-1	Keane, Poyet	36,058
33		12	A	Leeds United	D	2-2	Sheringham, Keane	39,560
34		18	H	Manchester City	L	0-2		36,075
35		21	A	West Bromwich Albion	W	3-2	Keane 2, Sheringham	26,899
36		27	H	Manchester United	L	0-2		36,073
37	May	3	A	Middlesbrough	L	1-5	Redknapp	30,230
38		11	H	Blackburn Rovers	L	0-4		36,036
								Appearances
								Substitute
								Goals

FA Cup

R3	Jan	4	A	Southampton	L	0-4		25,589
								Appearances
								Substitute
								Goals

Worthington Cup

R2	Oct	1	H	Cardiff City	W	1-0	Sheringham	23,732
R3	Nov	6	A	Burnley	L	1-2	Poyet	13,512
								Appearances
								Substitute
								Goals

Acimovic M	Anderton DR	Blondel J	Bunjevcevic G	Carr S	Clemence SN	Davies S	Doherty GMT	Etherington M	Ferdinand L	Freund S	Gardner A	Iversen S	Keane RD	Keller KC	King LB	Perry CJ	Poyet GA	Redknapp JF	Richards DI	Sheringham EP	Slabber J	Taricco MR	Thatcher BD	Toda K	Ziege C	Own-goals
14			5	**2**		7		11	13		6	*9*		1				8	4	10		3	12			
8			12			7	14	**11**	*9*		5			1				4	6	10		3	13		2	
			5			7	**9**	11	12		4			1				8	6	10		3			2	
8		14	13			7	5	11	**9**			12		1				4	6	10		3	2			
8			5			7	13	*11*	9		4	14		1		**6**			3	10			2		12	
			5			8	12	*11*			2	14	9	1		**6**		4		10		3	13		7	
13			5			7	6	11	12			**8**	9	1				4	3	10			2			
14			5			7	12	11	9			*10*	8	1				4	6	13			2		**3**	
11			5			7				4		13	9	1		12		8	6	10		**3**	2			
			5	2		7		**11**		4			9	1		6	12	8	3	10						
13			5	2		7		14	12	4			9	1		6	11	*8*	3	**10**						
12			5	2		7			13	4			9	1		6	**11**	8	3	10						
13	7		12	2		8				4		14	9	1		6	**11**		3	10			*5*			
	14		5	2		7		**11**		4		13	9	1	6		12	*8*	3	10						
	7		5	2		12				4		14	9	1	6		*8*	13	3	10					**11**	
14	7		5	2						4		12	**9**	1	6		*8*	13	3	10					11	
	7			2		11						12	9	1	**4**	6	13	8	5	10					3	
	7		5	2		12				4			9	1	3		8		6	10					11	
	7			2		8				4		**9**	10	1	3	6	12		5						11	
	7		5	2		12			13	*4*		14	9	1	3	6	8			10					11	
14			5	2		11			13	4		9	*10*	1	7	6	**8**			12		3				
14	13		**5**	2						4		*9*	11	1	7	6	12		8	10		3				
12	7		5	2		11	4					**9**	10	1	3	6	8									
	7		5	2		11				12			9	1	4		**8**		6	10		3				
	7		5	2		11	12				6		**9**	1	3		8		4	10						
	7		5	2		11	12	13			**6**	9		1	4		8			10		3				
	7		5	2		11	12	13		14			**9**	1	4		8		6	10		3				
12	7		5	2		11	9	13						1	4		**8**		6	10		3				
14	7		**5**	2		11	9	*8*		13				1	4				6	10		3	12			
			5	2		11	*9*	7		12				1	6		8			10	13	**3**	4			
	7		5	2		11	12	13					9	1	6		8			10		3	**4**			
	7		5	2		11		12					9	1	4	6	8			10		**3**				
	7		5	2		11		12			6		9	1	4		**8**			10		3				
14	7		**5**	2		11					6		9	1	4	13	*8*			10		3		12		
			5	2		11		7			3		9	1	4	13	12		*6*	10				**8**		
			13	2		11		7			12	14	9	1	6		8		**5**	10		3		*4*		
			5	2		11		13			4		9	1	7	6	**8**	12		10		3				
				2		11		7					9	1	5	6	8	4		10		**3**		13	12	
4	18	0	31	30	0	33	7	15	4	13	11	8	29	38	25	15	22	14	26	34	0	21	8	2	10	
13	2	1	4	0	0	3	8	8	7	4	1	11	0	0	0	3	6	3	0	2	1	0	4	2	2	
						5	1	1	2		1	1	13			1	5	3	2	12		1			2	1

Acimovic M	Anderton DR	Blondel J	Bunjevcevic G	Carr S	Clemence SN	Davies S	Doherty GMT	Etherington M	Ferdinand L	Freund S	Gardner A	Iversen S	Keane RD	Keller KC	King LB	Perry CJ	Poyet GA	Redknapp JF	Richards DI	Sheringham EP	Slabber J	Taricco MR	Thatcher BD	Toda K	Ziege C	Own-goals
	12			2		*11*	14			4		13	9	1	5	**6**	8			10		3	7			
0	0	0	0	1	0	1	0	0	0	1	0	0	1	1	1	1	1	0	0	1	0	1	1	0	0	
0	1	0	0	0	0	0	1	0	0	0	0	1	0	0	0	0	0	0	0	0	0	0	0	0	0	

Acimovic M	Anderton DR	Blondel J	Bunjevcevic G	Carr S	Clemence SN	Davies S	Doherty GMT	Etherington M	Ferdinand L	Freund S	Gardner A	Iversen S	Keane RD	Keller KC	King LB	Perry CJ	Poyet GA	Redknapp JF	Richards DI	Sheringham EP	Slabber J	Taricco MR	Thatcher BD	Toda K	Ziege C	Own-goals
8			5			7	12	11	14	4		13	*9*	1					6	10		**3**	2			
	13		5	2	3	7	14	11	**9**		4	*10*	12	1		6	8									
1	0	0	2	1	1	2	0	2	1	1	1	1	1	2	0	1	1	0	1	1	0	1	1	0	0	
0	1	0	0	0	0	0	2	0	1	0	0	1	1	0	0	0	0	0	0	0	0	0	0	0	0	
																	1			1						

League Table

	P	W	D	L	F	A	Pts
Manchester United	38	25	8	5	74	34	83
Arsenal	38	23	9	6	85	42	78
Newcastle United	38	21	6	11	63	48	69
Chelsea	38	19	10	9	68	38	67
Liverpool	38	18	10	10	61	41	64
Blackburn Rovers	38	16	12	10	52	43	60
Everton	38	17	8	13	48	49	59
Southampton	38	13	13	12	43	46	52
Manchester City	38	15	6	17	47	54	51
TOTTENHAM HOTSPUR	38	14	8	16	51	62	50
Middlesbrough	38	13	10	15	48	44	49
Charlton Athletic	38	14	7	17	45	56	49
Birmingham City	38	13	9	16	41	49	48
Fulham	38	13	9	16	41	50	48
Leeds United	38	14	5	19	58	57	47
Aston Villa	38	12	9	17	42	47	45
Bolton Wanderers	38	10	14	14	41	51	44
West Ham United	38	10	12	16	42	59	42
West Bromwich Albion	38	6	8	24	29	65	26
Sunderland	38	4	7	27	21	65	19

2003-04

PREMIERSHIP

Manager: Glenn Hoddle until September then David Pleat as caretaker manager

Did you know that?

Spurs played two games in South Africa in July 2003 as part of the country's bid to host the 2010 World Cup. Many of the touring party returned with souvenirs of the trip but Director of Football David Pleat went a step further. He was so impressed with the Orlando Pirates centre-half, Mbulelo Mabizela, that he brought the South African captain back with him.

LEAGUE DEBUTANTS

Aug 16	v Birmingham City Rohan Ricketts
Aug 16	v Birmingham City Helder Postiga
Aug 16	v Birmingham City Bobby Zamora
Aug 16	v Birmingham City Dean Marney
Aug 23	v Leeds United Frederic Kanoute
Sep 13	v Chelsea Stephan Dalmat
Sep 13	v Chelsea Paul Konchesky
Oct 19	v Leicester City Mbulelo Mabizela
Dec 26	v Portsmouth Johnnie Jackson
Dec 28	v Charlton Athletic Stephen Kelly
Jan 17	v Liverpool Michael Brown
Feb 7	v Portsmouth Jermain Defoe
May 15	v Wolves Mark Yeates

Match No.	Date			Opponents	Result		Scorers	Attendance
1	Aug	16	A	Birmingham City	L	0-1		29,358
2		23	H	Leeds United	W	2-1	Taricco, Kanoute	34,354
3		27	A	Liverpool	D	0-0		43,778
4		30	H	Fulham	L	0-3		33,421
5	Sep	13	A	Chelsea	L	2-4	Kanoute 2	41,165
6		20	H	Southampton	L	1-3	Kanoute	35,784
7		28	A	Manchester City	D	0-0		46,842
8	Oct	4	H	Everton	W	3-0	Kanoute, Poyet, Keane	36,137
9		20	A	Leicester City	W	2-1	Mabizela, Kanoute	31,521
10		26	H	Middlesbrough	D	0-0		32,643
11	Nov	1	H	Bolton Wanderers	L	0-1		35,191
12		8	A	Arsenal	L	1-2	Anderton	38,101
13		23	H	Aston Villa	W	2-1	Ricketts, Keane	33,140
14		29	A	Blackburn Rovers	L	0-1		22,802
15	Dec	6	H	Wolverhampton Wanderers	W	5-2	Keane 3, Kanoute, Dalmat	34,825
16		13	A	Newcastle United	L	0-4		52,139
17		21	H	Manchester United	L	1-2	Poyet	35,910
18		26	A	Portsmouth	L	0-2		20,078
19		28	H	Charlton Athletic	L	0-1		34,534
20	Jan	7	H	Birmingham City	W	4-1	Dalmat 2, Davies, Keane	30,016
21		10	A	Leeds United	W	1-0	Keane	35,365
22		17	H	Liverpool	W	2-1	Keane (pen), Postiga	36,104
23		31	A	Fulham	L	1-2	Keane (pen)	17,024
24	Feb	7	H	Portsmouth	W	4-3	Defoe, Keane 2, Poyet	36,107
25		11	A	Charlton Athletic	W	4-2	Davies, Defoe, King, Jackson	26,645
26		22	H	Leicester City	D	4-4	Brown, Defoe 2, Keane	35,218
27	Mar	9	A	Middlesbrough	L	0-1		31,789
28		14	H	Newcastle United	W	1-0	O'Brien (og)	36,083
29		20	A	Manchester United	L	0-3		67,644
30		27	A	Southampton	L	0-1		31,973
31	Apr	3	H	Chelsea	L	0-1		36,101
32		9	A	Everton	L	1-3	Carr	38,086
33		12	H	Manchester City	D	1-1	Defoe	35,282
34		17	A	Bolton Wanderers	L	0-2		26,440
35		25	H	Arsenal	D	2-2	Redknapp, Keane (pen)	36,097
36	May	2	A	Aston Villa	L	0-1		42,573
37		8	H	Blackburn Rovers	W	1-0	Defoe	35,698
38		15	A	Wolverhampton Wanderers	W	2-0	Keane, Defoe	29,389
								Appearances
								Substitute
								Goals

FA Cup

R3	Jan	3	H	Crystal Palace	W	3-0	Kanoute 3	32,340
R4		25	A	Manchester City	D	1-1	Doherty	28,840
R4r	Feb	4	H	Manchester City	L	3-4	King, Keane, Ziege	30,400
								Appearances
								Substitute
								Goals

Carling Cup

R2	Sep	24	A	Coventry City	W	3-0	Kanoute, Keane, Ricketts	15,474
R3	Oct	29	H	West Ham United	W*	1-0	Zamora	36,053
R4	Dec	3	H	Manchester City	W	3-1	Anderton, Postiga, Kanoute	31,727
R5		17	H	Middlesbrough	L#	1-1	Anderton	25,307
								Appearances
								Substitute
								Goals

*after extra-time # lost 4-5 on pens after extra-time

Anderton DR	Blondel J	Brown MR	Bunjevcevic G	Carr S	Dalmat S	Davies S	Defoe JC	Doherty GMT	Gardner A	Jackson J	Kanoute F	Keane RD	Keller KC	Kelly S	King LB	Konchesky PM	Mabizela M	Marney D	Postiga HMM	Poyet GA	Redknapp JF	Richards DI	Ricketts R	Taricco MR	Yeates M	Zamora RL	Ziege C	Own-goals
			5	2		9		4	6			10	1					12	8		7		11	**3**		13		
				2		7			6		13		1		4			12	8		10	5	11	**3**		9		
12				2		7			6		13		1		4				**8**		10	5	11	3		9		
13				2		7			6		9		1		**4**				8		10	5	11	3		12		
7			13	2	14				6		9		1		4	12					8	5	11	**3**		10		
14			**5**	2	*11*				4		9	13	1						12		8	6	7	3		10		
7			**5**	2	13				4		9	10	1			11				8		6	12	3				
7				2	12				6		9	10	1			4			13	8		5	11	**3**				
7				2	12			5			9	10	1			*11*	13			8		6	**4**	3		14		
7				2	11				6			10	1		13	**4**			14	8		5	12	3		*9*		
7	12			2				6				10	1		4	11	13		14	*8*		5		**3**		9		
7				2	*11*				6			10	1		4	9	13		**8**			5	14	3		12		
7				2	11				6			10	1		4	9			**8**			5	13	3		12		
7				2	*11*				6			10	1		4	9	14		**8**			5	13	3		12		
7				2	13				6		9	10	1		4	12				**8**		5	11	3				
7				2	14				6		9	10	1		4	*11*	12		13	**8**		5		3				
7				2	*11*				6		9	10	1		4	8			14	13		5	12	**3**				
				2	*11*				6	7	9	10	1		**4**				12	8		5	14	3		13		
									6	7	9	10	1	2	4		12		13	8		5	*11*	**3**		14		
7				2	11	8		5		3	9	*10*	1	12	6				13	4			14					
7				2	11	8		5	6		9	10	1		4					12				3				
7		6		2	11	9		4	5	13		10	1						**8**					3		12		
		6		2	11	9		4	5			10	1		7				**8**							12	3	
		6		2	11	8	**9**		5	3		10	1		7					12		4	13					
		6		2		8	**9**	4		11		10	1		7					12		5		3				
13		**6**		2		8	9	4		11	12	10	1		7							5		3				
7		**6**		2	14		9		5	11		10	1		8				13	12		4		3				
		6		2	13		8	4	5		**9**	10	1		7						12			3			11	
		6		2	12		*9*	5	4		14	10	1		8			7			13			**3**			11	
		6		2	13		7	4	5	**3**	9	10	1	14	8						12						*11*	
		6		2			9	4	5	13	14	10	1	12	8						7			**3**			*11*	
		6	13	2		**7**	9	4	5		14	10	1	3							8		12				*11*	
		6	13	**2**		7	10	4	5		9	14	1	12						*11*	8			3				
		6				**7**	10	4	5		9	13	1	2	3					*11*	8		12	14				
		6	13			7	14		5	*11*	9	10	1	**2**	4					12	8			3				
		6				7	11	13	5		9	10	1	**2**							8	4	12	3				
		6				7	9		5		14	10	1	2	4					13	8		*11*	**3**			12	
		6					9		5		13	**10**	1	2	4					12	8		11		7		3	
16	0	17	3	32	12	17	14	16	33	9	19	31	38	7	28	10	0	1	9	12	14	23	12	31	1	6	7	
4	1	0	4	0	10	0	1	1	0	2	8	3	0	4	1	2	6	2	10	8	3	0	12	1	0	10	1	
1		1		1	3	2	7			1	7	14			1		1		1	3	1		1	1				1

Anderton DR	Blondel J	Brown MR	Bunjevcevic G	Carr S	Dalmat S	Davies S	Defoe JC	Doherty GMT	Gardner A	Jackson J	Kanoute F	Keane RD	Keller KC	Kelly S	King LB	Konchesky PM	Mabizela M	Marney D	Postiga HMM	Poyet GA	Redknapp JF	Richards DI	Ricketts R	Taricco MR	Yeates M	Zamora RL	Ziege C	Own-goals
				2	11	12		5	6	7	9	10	1		**4**					8				3		13		
7		6		2	13	9		5	4	12		10	1		11				8					**3**				
		6		2	11	9			5	12		10	1		7				8	13		4					**3**	
1	0	2	0	3	2	2	0	2	3	1	1	3	3	0	3	0	0		2	1	0	1	0	2	0	0	1	
0	0	0	0	0	1	1	0	0	0	2	0	0	0	0	0	0	0		0	1	0	0	0	0	0	1	0	
								1			3	1			1												1	

Anderton DR	Blondel J	Brown MR	Bunjevcevic G	Carr S	Dalmat S	Davies S	Defoe JC	Doherty GMT	Gardner A	Jackson J	Kanoute F	Keane RD	Keller KC	Kelly S	King LB	Konchesky PM	Mabizela M	Marney D	Postiga HMM	Poyet GA	Redknapp JF	Richards DI	Ricketts R	Taricco MR	Yeates M	Zamora RL	Ziege C	Own-goals
7	11		5	2					4		9	**10**	1						12	8		6	13	3				
	12			2	*11*			5	6			10	1		4	8	14		13				7			9	**3**	
7				2	13			5	6		12	10	1		4	14			**8**	9			*11*	3				
7				2	14			12	6		9	10	1		4	8				13		**5**	*11*	3				
3	1	0	1	4	1	0	0	2	4	0	2	4	4	0	3	2	0		1	2	0	2	3	3	0	1	1	
0	1	0	0	0	2	0	0	1	0	0	1	0	0	0	0	1	1		2	1	0	0	1	0	0	0	0	
2											2	1							1				1			1		

League Table

	P	W	D	L	F	A	Pts
Arsenal	38	26	12	0	73	26	90
Chelsea	38	24	7	7	67	30	79
Manchester United	38	23	6	9	64	35	75
Liverpool	38	16	12	10	55	37	60
Newcastle United	38	13	17	8	52	40	56
Aston Villa	38	15	11	12	48	44	56
Charlton Athletic	38	14	11	13	51	51	53
Bolton Wanderers	38	14	11	13	48	56	53
Fulham	38	14	10	14	52	46	52
Birmingham City	38	12	14	12	43	48	50
Middlesbrough	38	13	9	16	44	52	48
Southampton	38	12	11	15	44	45	47
Portsmouth	38	12	9	17	47	54	45
TOTTENHAM HOTSPUR	38	13	6	19	47	57	45
Blackburn Rovers	38	12	8	18	51	59	44
Manchester City	38	9	14	15	55	54	41
Everton	38	9	12	17	45	57	39
Leicester City	38	6	15	17	48	65	33
Leeds United	38	8	9	21	40	79	33
Wolverhampton W	38	7	12	19	38	77	33

2004-05

PREMIERSHIP

Head coach: Jacques Santini until November then Martin Jol

Did you know that?

At Old Trafford on 4 January 2005 Pedro Mendes scored one of the finest, and most notorious, 'goals that never were'. With the game scoreless and only seconds remaining, he hit a speculative lob from just inside the Manchester United half. United 'keeper Roy Carroll misjudged the flight of the ball and spilled it over his shoulder, the ball a good yard over the line before he scooped it out. Nearly 70,000 spectators, and millions watching on TV, clearly saw the ball cross the line. Sadly, the referee and his assistant did not.

LEAGUE DEBUTANTS

Aug 14	v Liverpool	Sean Davis
Aug 14	v Liverpool	Erik Edman
Aug 14	v Liverpool	Phil Ifil
Aug 14	v Liverpool	Pedro Mendes
Aug 14	v Liverpool	Noureddine Naybet
Aug 14	v Liverpool	Paul Robinson
Aug 14	v Liverpool	Thimothee Atouba
Aug 25	v West Bromwich Albion	Noe Pamarot
Oct 2	v Everton	Reto Ziegler
Oct 18	v Portsmouth	Michael Carrick
Nov 22	v Aston Villa	Calum Davenport
Feb 5	v Portsmouth	Andy Reid
Feb 5	v Portsmouth	Mido
Apr 16	v Liverpool	Michael Dawson
May 1	v Aston Villa	Radek Cerny

Match No.	Date		Opponents		Result		Scorers	Attendance
1	Aug	14	H	Liverpool	D	1-1	Defoe	35,101
2		21	A	Newcastle United	W	1-0	Atouba	52,185
3		25	A	West Bromwich Albion	D	1-1	Defoe	27,191
4		28	H	Birmingham City	W	1-0	Defoe	35,290
5	Sep	12	H	Norwich City	D	0-0		36,095
6		19	A	Chelsea	D	0-0		42,246
7		25	H	Manchester United	L	0-1		36,103
8	Oct	2	A	Everton	W	1-0	Pamarot	38,264
9		18	A	Portsmouth	L	0-1		20,121
10		23	H	Bolton Wanderers	L	1-2	Keane	36,025
11		30	A	Fulham	L	0-2		21,317
12	Nov	6	H	Charlton Athletic	L	2-3	Keane (pen), Defoe	35,423
13		13	H	Arsenal	L	4-5	Naybet, Defoe, King, Kanoute	36,095
14		22	A	Aston Villa	L	0-1		35,702
15		28	H	Middlesbrough	W	2-0	Defoe, Kanoute	35,772
16	Dec	4	A	Blackburn Rovers	W	1-0	Keane	22,182
17		11	A	Manchester City	W	1-0	Kanoute	45,805
18		18	H	Southampton	W	5-1	Defoe 3, Kanoute, Keane	36,054
19		26	A	Norwich City	W	2-0	Keane, Brown	24,508
20		28	H	Crystal Palace	D	1-1	Defoe	36,100
21	Jan	1	H	Everton	W	5-2	Marney 2, Ziegler, Mendes, Keane	36,102
22		4	A	Manchester United	D	0-0		67,962
23		15	H	Chelsea	L	0-2		36,105
24		22	A	Crystal Palace	L	0-3		23,723
25	Feb	1	A	Bolton Wanderers	L	1-3	Defoe	24,780
26		5	H	Portsmouth	W	3-1	Mido 2, Keane	36,105
27		26	H	Fulham	W	2-0	Kanoute, Keane	35,885
28	Mar	5	A	Southampton	L	0-1		31,903
29		16	A	Charlton Athletic	L	0-2		26,832
30		19	H	Manchester City	W	2-1	Defoe, Keane	35,861
31	Apr	2	A	Birmingham City	D	1-1	Kelly	29,304
32		10	H	Newcastle United	W	1-0	Defoe	35,885
33		16	A	Liverpool	D	2-2	Edman, Keane	44,029
34		20	H	West Bromwich Albion	D	1-1	Keane	35,885
35		25	A	Arsenal	L	0-1		38,147
36	May	1	H	Aston Villa	W	5-1	Kanoute 2, King, Reid, Kelly	36,078
37		7	A	Middlesbrough	L	0-1		34,766
38		15	H	Blackburn Rovers	D	0-0		35,797

Appearances
Substitute
Goals

FA Cup

R3	Jan	8	H	Brighton & Hove Albion	W	2-1	King, Keane	36,094
R4		29	A	West Bromwich Albion	D	1-1	Defoe (pen)	22,441
R4r	Feb	12	H	West Bromwich Albion	W	3-1	Keane (pen), Defoe 2	27,860
R5		20	H	Nottingham Forest	D	1-1	Defoe	35,640
R5r	Mar	2	A	Nottingham Forest	W	3-0	Pamarot, Keane, Mido	28,062
R6		13	A	Newcastle United	L	0-1		51,307

Appearances
Substitute
Goals

Football League Cup

R2	Sep	23	A	Oldham Athletic	W	6-0	Kanoute 2, Keane, Defoe, Bunjevcevic, Gardner	8,548
R3	Oct	27	H	Bolton Wanderers	W*	4-3	Defoe 2, Bunjevcevic, Brown	18,037
R4	Nov	9	A	Burnley	W	3-0	Keane 2, Defoe	10,639
R5	Dec	1	H	Liverpool	L#	1-1	Defoe	36,100

*after extra-time #lost 3-4 on pens after extra-time

Appearances
Substitute
Goals

Atouba TE	Brown MR	Bunjevcevic G	Carrick M	Cerny R	Davenport CRP	Davies S	Davis S	Dawson MR	Defoe JC	Doherty GMT	Edman EK	Gardner A	Ifil P	Jackson J	Kanoute F	Keane RD	Keller KC	Kelly S	King LB	Mabizela M	Marney D	Mendes PM	Mido HA	Naybet N	Pamarot N	Redknapp JF	Reid A	Ricketts R	Robinson PW	Yeates M	Ziegler R
14	13						4		10	12	3		6	11	9				5			8		2		7			1		
11	12						4		10		3	13	6	14	9				5			8		2		7			1		
11	12						4		10		3			14	9	13			5			8		2	6	7			1		
	11						4		9		3	12		7	14	10			5			8		2	6	13			1		
7	11					14			10		3			12	9	13			5			8		2	6	4			1		
11	13					7			9		3				12	10			5			8		2	6	4			1		
						13			11		3			12	9	10			5	7		8		2	6	4			1		
11						7			9		3	12				10			5			8		2	6	4			1		13
6	11		14			7			9			3		13	12	10			5			8		2	4				1		
						7	12		14			3		11	9	10			5			8		2	6	4			1		13
	11	5	12			14	4		9						13	10			6			8		2	3				1		7
		5	12			7			11						9	10			6			8		2	3	4			1		13
	11		4			12			9		3	13			14	10			6			8		2	5				1		7
7	11		4		13				10		3				9	14			6			8		2	5				1		12
3			4						9						12	10			6			8		2	5			7	1		11
5	11		4						9			14			13	10		3	6			8		2		12			1		7
3	11		4									12			9	10		14	6			8		2	5	13		7	1		
3	11		4						10			5			9	13			6			12			2			7	1		8
7	11		4						13		3				9	10			6			8		2	5	14			1		12
	11		4						10		3	5			9	13			6			12			2			7	1		8
			4								3				9	10			6		11	8		2	5	12		13	1		7
			4								3	12				10			6		11	8		2	5			9	1		7
	11		4						9		3	13				10			6		12	8		2	5				1	14	7
13			4						9		3					10		14	6		11	8		2	5				1	12	7
8	11		4			7			12		3	5			9	10		2	6										1		
3	11	12	4			7			10							13		5	6				9	2			8		1		
	11		4			7			10		3				13	12		5	6				9	2			8		1		
	11		4			7			10		3	5			14	13		2	6				9				8		1		12
	11		4				13		14		3	5			9	10		12	6						2		7		1		8
3	11		4			7			10			12			14	13		5	6				9	2			8		1		
	11		4				14		10		3				9			13	6				12	2	5		7		1		8
	11		4			7	14		10		3	5			9	13		2	6								8		1		12
			8			7	4	5	12		3				9	10		2	6								11		1		13
12			8			7	4	5	9		3					10		2	6				13				11		1		14
			8			7	4	5	10		3				9	14		2	6				13				11		1		12
			8	12		7	4	5	14		3				9	10		2	6				13				11		1		
			8	1		7	4	5	10		3				9	13		2	6				14				11				12
			8	1		7	4		13		3				9	10		5	6		12			2			11				
15	20	2	26	2	0	17	11	5	28	0	28	8	2	3	22	23	0	13	38	1	3	22	4	27	23	9	13	5	36	0	12
3	4	1	3	1	1	4	4	0	7	1	0	9	0	5	10	12	0	4	0	0	2	2	5	0	0	5	0	1	0	2	11
1	1								13		1				7	11		2	2		2	1	2	1	1		1				1

Atouba TE	Brown MR	Bunjevcevic G	Carrick M	Cerny R	Davenport CRP	Davies S	Davis S	Dawson MR	Defoe JC	Doherty GMT	Edman EK	Gardner A	Ifil P	Jackson J	Kanoute F	Keane RD	Keller KC	Kelly S	King LB	Mabizela M	Marney D	Mendes PM	Mido HA	Naybet N	Pamarot N	Redknapp JF	Reid A	Ricketts R	Robinson PW	Yeates M	Ziegler R
	11		4						9		3	5				10		2	6		12	8							1	13	7
8	11		4			7			10		3	5			9	13		2	6		12								1		
3	11		4			12			8			5			9	10		2	6										1		7
3	11		4			7			10						9	12		5	6				13	2					1		8
3	11		13			7					12	5			9	10		6				8	14		2				1		4
3	11		4			7			10			12			9	13			6		14			2	5				1		8
5	6	0	5	0	0	4	0	0	5	0	2	4	0	0	5	3	0	5	5	0	0	2	0	2	2	0	0	0	6	0	5
0	0	0	1	0	0	1	0	0	0	0	1	1	0	0	0	3	0	0	0	0	3	0	2	0	0	0	0	0	0	1	0
									4							3			1				1		1						

Atouba TE	Brown MR	Bunjevcevic G	Carrick M	Cerny R	Davenport CRP	Davies S	Davis S	Dawson MR	Defoe JC	Doherty GMT	Edman EK	Gardner A	Ifil P	Jackson J	Kanoute F	Keane RD	Keller KC	Kelly S	King LB	Mabizela M	Marney D	Mendes PM	Mido HA	Naybet N	Pamarot N	Redknapp JF	Reid A	Ricketts R	Robinson PW	Yeates M	Ziegler R
	11	5				7			14			4		3	9	10	1		6	2		13				8		12			
	13	5	12			7	4		10						9	14	1		6			8		2	3						11
	11		4			13			9				12		14	10		3	6			8		2	5				1		7
3	11		4						12			5			9	10			6			13			2			7	1		8
1	3	2	2	0	0	2	1	0	2	0	0	2	0	1	3	3	2	1	4	1	0	2	0	2	3	1	0	1	2	0	3
0	1	0	1	0	0	1	0	0	2	0	0	0	1	0	1	1	0	0	0	0	0	2	0	0	0	0	0	1	0	0	0
	1	2							5			1			2	3															

League Table

	P	W	D	L	F	A	Pts
Chelsea	38	29	8	1	72	15	95
Arsenal	38	25	8	5	87	36	83
Manchester United	38	22	11	5	58	26	77
Everton	38	18	7	13	45	46	61
Liverpool	38	17	7	14	52	41	58
Bolton Wanderers	38	16	10	12	49	44	58
Middlesbrough	38	14	13	11	53	46	55
Manchester City	38	13	13	12	47	39	52
TOTTENHAM HOTSPUR	38	14	10	14	47	41	52
Aston Villa	38	12	11	15	45	52	47
Charlton Athletic	38	12	10	16	42	58	46
Birmingham City	38	11	12	15	40	46	45
Fulham	38	12	8	18	52	60	44
Newcastle United	38	10	14	14	47	57	44
Blackburn Rovers	38	9	15	14	32	43	42
Portsmouth	38	10	9	19	43	59	39
West Bromwich Albion	38	6	16	16	36	61	34
Crystal Palace	38	7	12	19	41	62	33
Norwich City	38	7	12	19	42	77	33
Southampton	38	6	14	18	45	66	32

2005-06

PREMIERSHIP

Head coach: Martin Jol

Did you know that?

During the January transfer window Spurs were involved in a triple transfer deal with Portsmouth, Sean Davis, Pedro Mendes and Noe Pamarot all joining the south-coast club in a deal valued at about £7.5 million.

LEAGUE DEBUTANTS

Aug 13	v Portsmouth	Wayne Routledge
Aug 13	v Portsmouth	Paul Stalteri
Aug 13	v Portsmouth	Teemu Tainio
Aug 20	v Middlesbrough	Edgar Davids
Aug 27	v Chelsea	Aaron Lennon
Sep 10	v Liverpool	Lee Young-Pyo
Sep 10	v Liverpool	Jermaine Jenas
Sep 10	v Liverpool	Gregorz Rasiak
Jan 31	v Fulham	Tom Huddlestone
Feb 12	v Sunderland	Danny Murphy
Apr 17	v Manchester United	Lee Barnard

Match No.	Date			Opponents	Result		Scorers	Attendance
1	Aug	13	A	Portsmouth	W	2-0	Griffin (og), Defoe	20,215
2		20	H	Middlesbrough	W	2-0	Defoe, Mido	35,844
3		24	A	Blackburn Rovers	D	0-0		22,375
4		27	H	Chelsea	L	0-2		36,077
5	Sep	10	H	Liverpool	D	0-0		36,148
6		17	A	Aston Villa	D	1-1	Keane	33,686
7		26	H	Fulham	W	1-0	Defoe	35,427
8	Oct	1	A	Charlton Athletic	W	3-2	King, Mido, Keane	27,111
9		15	H	Everton	W	2-0	Mido, Jenas	36,247
10		22	A	Manchester United	D	1-1	Jenas	67,856
11		29	H	Arsenal	D	1-1	King	36,154
12	Nov	7	A	Bolton Wanderers	L	0-1		26,634
13		20	H	West Ham United	D	1-1	Mido	36,154
14		26	A	Wigan Athletic	W	2-1	Keane, Davids	22,611
15	Dec	3	H	Sunderland	W	3-2	Mido, Keane, Carrick	36,244
16		12	H	Portsmouth	W	3-1	King, Mido (pen), Defoe	36,141
17		18	A	Middlesbrough	D	3-3	Keane, Jenas, Mido	27,614
18		26	H	Birmingham City	W	2-0	Keane (pen), Defoe	36,045
19		28	A	West Bromwich Albion	L	0-2		27,510
20		31	H	Newcastle United	W	2-0	Tainio, Mido	36,246
21	Jan	4	A	Manchester City	W	2-0	Mido, Keane	40,808
22		14	A	Liverpool	L	0-1		44,983
23		21	H	Aston Villa	D	0-0		36,243
24		31	A	Fulham	L	0-1		21,081
25	Feb	5	H	Charlton Athletic	W	3-1	Defoe 2, Jenas	36,034
26		12	A	Sunderland	D	1-1	Keane	34,700
27		19	H	Wigan Athletic	D	2-2	Mido, Defoe	35,676
28	Mar	5	H	Blackburn Rovers	W	3-2	Keane 2, Mido	36,080
29		11	A	Chelsea	L	1-2	Jenas	42,243
30		18	A	Birmingham City	W	2-0	Lennon, Keane	26,398
31		27	H	West Bromwich Albion	W	2-1	Keane 2 (1 pen)	36,152
32	Apr	1	A	Newcastle United	L	1-3	Keane	52,301
33		8	H	Manchester City	W	2-1	Stalteri, Carrick	36,167
34		15	A	Everton	W	1-0	Keane (pen)	39,856
35		17	H	Manchester United	L	1-2	Jenas	36,141
36		22	A	Arsenal	D	1-1	Keane	38,326
37		30	H	Bolton Wanderers	W	1-0	Lennon	36,179
38	May	7	A	West Ham United	L	1-2	Defoe	34,970
								Appearances
								Substitute
								Goals

FA Cup

R3	Jan	8	A	Leicester City	L	2-3	Jenas, Stalteri	19,844
								Appearances
								Substitute
								Goals

Football League Cup

R2	Sep	20	A	Grimsby Town	L	0-1		8,206
								Appearances
								Substitute
								Goals

Barnard L	Brown MR	Carrick M	Davenport CRP	Davids ES	Davis S	Dawson MR	Defoe JC	Edman EK	Gardner A	Huddlestone T	Jackson J	Jenas JA	Kanoute F	Keane RD	Kelly S	King LB	Lee YP	Lennon AJ	Mendes PM	Mido HA	Murphy DB	Naybet N	Pamarot N	Rasiak G	Reid A	Robinson PW	Routledge W	Stalteri P	Tainio T	Own-goals
		4				5	9	3	6				13						12	10					11	1	**7**	2	8	
		4		8		5	**9**	3	6					12						10					11	1		2	7	
	4			12		5	13	3	6					10					8	**9**					11	1		2	7	
		4		8		5	9		6						3			12		10					11	1		2	**7**	
	13	4		8			9		6			11		12		5	3	7						**10**		1		2		
		4					9		**6**			7		13		5	3					12		10	11	1		2	8	
				8			9					11		13		5	3	**7**	4	*10*		6		14	12	1		2		
				11		14	9					8		13	3	5		7	**4**	*10*		6				1		2	12	
		4		11		6	9					8		13		5	3	**7**		10					12	1		2		
		4		11		6	9					8		12		5	3	**7**	13	10						1		2		
		4				6	*9*					8		14		5	3	**7**	13	10					12	1		2	11	
	13	4		8		6	9					7		12		5	**3**			10						1		2	11	
		4		8		6	13					7		10		5	3	12		9						1		2	**11**	
		4		8		6						7		10		5	3			9						1		2	11	
		4		8		6	13					**7**		10		5	3	12		9						1		2	11	
		4		8		6	13					7		10		5	3			9					14	1	*12*	2	**11**	
	14	4		8		6	*12*					7		10		5	3			9				13	**11**	1		2		
	14	4		8		6	12					11		*10*		5	3	**7**		9			13			1		2		
	14	4		8		6	9		5			7		12			3			13				10		1	**11**	2		
	12	4		8		6	13		5			7		10			3			9						1		2	**11**	
	11	4				6	13		5			8		10			**3**	7		*9*			12	14		1		2		
		4		8	-	6	12					7		10		5	3	13		9						1		2	**11**	
	13	4		8	-	6	*9*					**7**		10	2	5	3	12						14		1			11	
		4				6	14		13	12		8		10	3	5		7						*9*	**11**	1		2		
		4					9		6	12	13	8		10	3	5		7								1		2	**11**	
		4		**8**		6	9			14		7		10		5	3	*11*		13	12					1		2		
		4		8	-	6	9			13				12		5	3	7		10	**11**					1		2		
		4		**8**		6						7		10		5	3	12		9	13					1		2	11	
		4		8		6	12					7		**10**		5	3			9						1		2	11	
		4		11		6	9					8		**10**	2	5	3	7			12					1				
		4		11	-	6	9					8		10	**2**	5	3	7		12	13					1			14	
		4		11	-	6	12		5			8		10	2		3	**7**		9	13					1				
		4		13			12		6			8		10		5	3	**7**		9						1		2	11	
		4	13	14			9		6			8		10		*5*	3	7			12					1		2	**11**	
13		4	5	**11**		6	9					8		10			3	7			12					1		2		
		4		11		6	9		5					10			3	**7**			12					1		2	8	
12		4	14			6	9		5					**10**			3	7			*11*				13	1		2	8	
13		**4**	14	8		6	9		5					10	2		3	7							12	1			*11*	
0	2	35	1	28	0	31	23	3	16	0	0	30	0	25	9	26	31	21	3	24	2	2	0	4	7	38	2	33	22	
3	7	0	3	3	0	1	13	0	1	4	1	0	1	11	0	0	0	6	3	3	8	1	2	4	6	0	1	0	2	
		2		1			9					6		16		3		2		11								1	1	1

Barnard L	Brown MR	Carrick M	Davenport CRP	Davids ES	Davis S	Dawson MR	Defoe JC	Edman EK	Gardner A	Huddlestone T	Jackson J	Jenas JA	Kanoute F	Keane RD	Kelly S	King LB	Lee YP	Lennon AJ	Mendes PM	Mido HA	Murphy DB	Naybet N	Pamarot N	Rasiak G	Reid A	Robinson PW	Routledge W	Stalteri P	Tainio T	Own-goals
	11	4				6	12		5			8		10	3			7						9		1		2	13	
0	1	1	0	0	0	1	0	0	1	0	0	1	0	1	1	0	0	1	0	0	0	0	0	1	0	1	0	1	0	
0	0	0	0	0	0	0	1	0	0	0	0	0	0	0	0	0	0	0	0	0	0	0	0	0	0	0	0	0	1	
												1																1		

Barnard L	Brown MR	Carrick M	Davenport CRP	Davids ES	Davis S	Dawson MR	Defoe JC	Edman EK	Gardner A	Huddlestone T	Jackson J	Jenas JA	Kanoute F	Keane RD	Kelly S	King LB	Lee YP	Lennon AJ	Mendes PM	Mido HA	Murphy DB	Naybet N	Pamarot N	Rasiak G	Reid A	Robinson PW	Routledge W	Stalteri P	Tainio T	Own-goals
	8	4			13		9					7		10		5	3	12					6		**11**	1		2		
0	1	1	0	0	0	0	1	0	0	0	0	1	0	1	0	1	1	0	0	0	0	1	0	0	1	1	0	1	0	
0	0	0	0	0	1	0	0	0	0	0	0	0	0	0	0	0	0	1	0	0	0	0	0	0	0	0	0	0	0	

League Table

	P	W	D	L	F	A	Pts
Chelsea	38	29	4	5	72	22	91
Manchester United	38	25	8	5	72	34	83
Liverpool	38	25	7	6	57	25	82
Arsenal	38	20	7	11	68	31	67
TOTTENHAM HOTSPUR	38	18	11	9	53	38	65
Blackburn Rovers	38	19	6	13	51	42	63
Newcastle United	38	17	7	14	47	42	58
Bolton Wanderers	38	15	11	12	49	41	56
West Ham United	38	16	7	15	52	55	55
Wigan Athletic	38	15	6	17	45	52	51
Everton	38	14	8	16	34	49	50
Fulham	38	14	6	18	48	58	48
Charlton Athletic	38	13	8	17	41	55	47
Middlesbrough	38	12	9	17	48	58	45
Manchester City	38	13	4	21	43	48	43
Aston Villa	38	10	12	16	42	55	42
Portsmouth	38	10	8	20	37	62	38
Birmingham City	38	8	10	20	28	50	34
West Bromwich Albion	38	7	9	22	31	58	30

2006-07

PREMIERSHIP

Head coach: Martin Jol

Did you know that?

Paul Robinson became the first Spurs goalkeeper to score from open play in the Football/Premier League when his free-kick from inside his own half bounced over Watford 'keeper Ben Foster on 17 March. The only previous 'keeper to score for Spurs in a League game was 'Tiny' Joyce, who converted a penalty against Bolton Wanderers in April 1914.

LEAGUE DEBUTANTS

Aug 19 v Bolton Wanderers
Didier Zokora
Aug 19 v Bolton Wanderers
Dimitar Berbatov
Aug 19 v Bolton Wanderers
Beniot Assou-Ekotto
Sep 9 v Manchester United
Pascal Chimbonda
Sep 9 v Manchester United
Hossam Ghaly
Nov 19 v Blackburn Rovers
Steed Malbranque
Feb 10 v Sheffield United
Ricardo Rocha
Mar 4 v West Ham United
Adel Taarabt

Match No.	Date		Opponents		Result		Scorers	Attendance
1	Aug	19	A	Bolton Wanderers	L	0-2		22,899
2		22	H	Sheffield United	W	2-0	Berbatov, Jenas	35,287
3		26	H	Everton	L	0-2		35,540
4	Sep	9	A	Manchester United	L	0-1		75,453
5		17	H	Fulham	D	0-0		36,131
6		23	A	Liverpool	L	0-3		44,330
7	Oct	1	H	Portsmouth	W	2-1	Murphy, Defoe (pen)	36,063
8		14	A	Aston Villa	D	1-1	Angel (og)	42,551
9		22	H	West Ham United	W	1-0	Mido	36,162
10		28	A	Watford	D	0-0		19,660
11	Nov	5	H	Chelsea	W	2-1	Dawson, Lennon	36,070
12		12	A	Reading	L	1-3	Keane (pen)	24,110
13		19	A	Blackburn Rovers	D	1-1	Defoe (pen)	18,083
14		26	H	Wigan Athletic	W	3-1	Defoe, Lennon, Berbatov	35,205
17	Dec	2	A	Arsenal	L	0-3		60,115
16		5	H	Middlesbrough	W	2-1	Berbatov, Keane	34,154
17		9	H	Charlton Athletic	W	5-1	Malbranque, Defoe, Tainio, Berbatov 2	35,565
18		17	H	Manchester City	W	2-1	Davenport, Huddlestone	39,825
19		23	A	Newcastle United	L	1-3	Taylor (og)	52,079
20		26	H	Aston Villa	W	2-1	Defoe 2	35,295
21		30	H	Liverpool	L	0-1		36,170
22	Jan	1	A	Portsmouth	D	1-1	Malbranque	20,194
23		14	H	Newcastle United	L	2-3	Defoe, Berbatov	35,942
24		20	A	Fulham	D	1-1	Chimbonda	23,580
25	Feb	4	H	Manchester United	L	0-4		36,146
26		10	A	Sheffield United	L	1-2	Jenas	32,144
27		21	A	Everton	W	2-1	Jenas, Berbatov	34,121
28		25	H	Bolton Wanderers	W	4-1	Jenas, Lennon, Keane 2	35,747
29	Mar	4	A	West Ham United	W	4-3	Tainio, Defoe (pen), Berbatov, Stalteri	34,966
30		17	H	Watford	W	3-1	Robinson, Ghaly, Jenas	36,051
31	Apr	1	H	Reading	W	1-0	Keane (pen)	36,067
32		7	A	Chelsea	L	0-1		41,864
33		15	A	Wigan Athletic	D	3-3	Berbatov, Kean 2 (1 pen)	16,506
34		21	H	Arsenal	D	2-2	Keane, Jenas	36,050
35		28	A	Middlesbrough	W	3-2	Berbatov, Keane 2	27,861
36	May	7	A	Charlton Athletic	W	2-0	Berbatov, Defoe	26,399
37		10	H	Blackburn Rovers	D	1-1	Defoe	35,974
38		13	H	Manchester City	W	2-1	Keane, Berbatov	35,426

Appearances
Substitute
Goals

FA Cup

R3	Jan	7	A	Cardiff City	D	0-0		
R3r		17	H	Cardiff City	W	4-0	Keane, Lennon, Defoe, Malbranque	27,641
R4		27	H	Southend United	W	3-1	Jenas, Keane, Mido	33,406
R5	Feb	18	A	Fulham	W	4-0	Keane 2, Berbatov 2	18,655
R6	Mar	11	A	Chelsea	D	3-3	Ghaly, Berbatov, Essien (og)	41,517
R6r		19	H	Chelsea	L	1-2	Keane (pen)	35,519

Appearances
Substitute
Goals

Coca-Cola Cup

R3	Oct	25	A	Milton Keynes Dons	W	5-0	Defoe 2, Mido 2, Keane	8,306
R4	Nov	8	H	Port Vale	W*	3-1	Huddlestone 2, Defoe	34,560
R5	Dec	20	H	Southend United	W	1-0	Defoe	35,811
SF1	Jan	24	H	Arsenal	D	2-2	Berbatov, Baptista (og)	35,485
SF2		31	A	Arsenal	L	1-3	Mido	59,872

*After extra-time

Appearances
Substitute
Goals

Assou-Ekotto BPD	Barcham A	Barnard LJ	Berbatov DI	Cerny R	Chimbonda P	Davenport CRP	Davids ES	Dawson MR	Defoe JC	Dervite D	Gardner AD	Ghaly H	Huddlestone TA	Ifil PN	Jenas JA	Keane RD	King LB	Lee YP	Lennon AJ	Malbranque S	Mido HA	Murphy DB	O'Hara J	Robinson PW	Rocha RS	Stalteri PA	Taarabt A	Tainio T	Ziegler RP	Zokora AD	Own-goals
2			9			6	8	5	10				12		7	13		3	11					1						4	
2			9			6	4	5	13						7	10		3	11					1				8		12	
2			9			6	4	5	12						7	10		3	11					1				8		13	
3					2		8	5	14			11			7	10	6				9	12		1					13	4	
3					2		12	5	13						8	10	6				9	7		1				11		4	
3					2		13	5	9						8	10	6				12	7		1				11		4	
3			9		2	13		5	10			11	12		8	14	6					7		1						4	
3			9		2	6	13	5	10			11			8				14			7		1		12				4	
3					2		4	5	10			13	7		8	12	6		11		9			1							
3			9		2			5	12			11	4		8	10	6		7			13		1							
3			9		2			5	12			11			8	10	6		7					1						4	
3			9					5	12			11	13		8	10	6	2	7					1						4	
3			13				8	5	10			11	7				6	2		12	9			1						4	
3			9		2			5	10				8			12	6		11	7				1						4	
3			9		2			5	14						13	10	6	12	11	7				1				8		4	
			9		2			5	10				8			12	6	3	11	7		14		1				13		4	
			9		2			5	10				4				6	3	11	7	14	13		1		12		8			
			9		2	5			10			11	4				6	3		7	12			1				8			
			9		2			5				11	8				6	3		7	12	10		1						4	
			9		2	12		5	10			11	8				6	3		7		13		1						4	
			13		2	6		5	10			11	8					3		7	9	12		1						4	
			9		2	6		5	10		12	11	4					3		7		13		1				8			
			9		2	6		5	10			12	4			13		3	11	7				1				8		14	
			9		2			5	10		6	11	4			13		3	14	7				1				8		12	
			9		2			5	10		6	12	8			13		3	11	7				1						4	
3			9		2			5	13						8	10				7	12			1	6			11		4	
			9		2			5			6				8	10		3	11	12				1				7		4	
			9		2			5							8	10		3	11	13				1	6	12		7		4	
			9		2			5	10		6	7	13		8			3	11					1		14	12	4			
					2			5	10			11	4		8			3	13	7	9			1	6	12					
			9		2			5	13				12		8	10		3	11	7				1	6					4	
			14		2			5	10			11			8					7	9			1	6	3	12	4		13	
			9		2			5	13					3	7	10			11	12				1	6			8		4	
			9		2			5	12				14		7	10	6		11	13				1	3			8		4	
			9		2			5				11			8	10	6		12	7				1	3					4	
			9		2			5	13		12				7	10	6		11	14				1	3			8		4	
			9		2			5	10		3	12				13	6		11	7				1				8		4	
			9		2			5	13		3				7	10	6		11	12				1				8		4	
16	0	0	30	0	33	8	6	37	20	0	6	17	15	1	24	18	21	20	22	18	7	5	0	38	9	1	0	20	0	26	
0	0	0	3	0	0	2	3	0	14	0	2	4	6	0	1	9	0	1	4	7	5	7	0	0	0	5	2	1	1	5	
			12		1	1		1	10			1	1		6	11			3	2	1	1		1		1		2			2

Assou-Ekotto BPD	Barcham A	Barnard LJ	Berbatov DI	Cerny R	Chimbonda P	Davenport CRP	Davids ES	Dawson MR	Defoe JC	Dervite D	Gardner AD	Ghaly H	Huddlestone TA	Ifil PN	Jenas JA	Keane RD	King LB	Lee YP	Lennon AJ	Malbranque S	Mido HA	Murphy DB	O'Hara J	Robinson PW	Rocha RS	Stalteri PA	Taarabt A	Tainio T	Ziegler RP	Zokora AD	Own-goals
			9		2	6		5	10		12		4			13		3	14	7		11		1				8			
3			9		2			5	14		6	13	8			10			11	7				1				12		4	
				1				5	14			7	13		8	10		3	11	12	9				6	2				4	
			12		2			5			6	13				10		3	11	7	9			1				8		4	
			9	1				5	10		12	7						3	11	14	13				6	2		8		4	
			9		2			5	13						8	10		3	11	7				1	6	12				4	
1	0	0	4	2	4	1	0	6	2	0	2	2	2	0	2	4	0	5	5	4	2	1	0	4	3	2	0	3	0	5	
0	0	0	1	0	0	0	0	0	3	0	2	2	1	0	0	1	0	0	1	2	1	0	0	0	0	1	0	1	0	0	
			3						1			1			1	5			1	1	1										1

Assou-Ekotto BPD	Barcham A	Barnard LJ	Berbatov DI	Cerny R	Chimbonda P	Davenport CRP	Davids ES	Dawson MR	Defoe JC	Dervite D	Gardner AD	Ghaly H	Huddlestone TA	Ifil PN	Jenas JA	Keane RD	King LB	Lee YP	Lennon AJ	Malbranque S	Mido HA	Murphy DB	O'Hara J	Robinson PW	Rocha RS	Stalteri PA	Taarabt A	Tainio T	Ziegler RP	Zokora AD	Own-goals
				1		5	4	12	10		6	11	7			14			13		9	8				2			3		
	9		13	1			4	5	10	6		12	7	2				3	14	11		8									
3			13			6	12	5	10				4							7	9	11		1		2		8			
3			9		2			5	10		6		8			12			11	7	13			1						4	
3					2			5	9		6	11	14		8	10				7	13			1	12					4	
3	1	0	1	2	2	2	2	4	5	1	3	2	4	1	1	1	0	1	1	4	2	3	0	3	0	2	0	1	1	2	
0	0	0	2	0	0	0	1	1	0	0	0	1	1	0	0	2	0	0	2	0	2	0	0	0	1	0	0	0	0	0	
			1						4				2			1					3										1

League Table

	P	W	D	L	F	A	Pts
Manchester United	38	28	5	5	83	27	89
Chelsea	38	24	11	3	64	24	83
Liverpool	38	20	8	10	57	27	68
Arsenal	38	19	11	8	63	35	68
TOTTENHAM HOTSPUR	38	17	9	12	57	54	60
Everton	38	15	13	10	52	36	58
Bolton Wanderers	38	16	8	14	47	52	56
Reading	38	16	7	15	52	47	55
Portsmouth	38	14	12	12	45	42	54
Blackburn Rovers	38	15	7	16	52	54	52
Aston Villa	38	11	17	10	43	41	50
Middlesbrough	38	12	10	16	44	49	46
Newcastle United	38	11	10	17	38	47	43
Manchester City	38	11	9	18	29	44	42
West Ham United	38	12	5	21	35	59	41
Fulham	38	8	15	15	38	60	39
Wigan Athletic	38	10	8	20	37	59	38
Sheffield United	38	10	8	20	32	55	38
Charlton Athletic	38	8	10	20	34	60	34

2007-08

PREMIERSHIP

Head coach: Martin Jol until October then Juande Ramos

Did you know that?

PA Sports statistics recorded Spurs hitting the frame of the goal on no less than 18 occasions during the season, more than any other club in the Premier League.

LEAGUE DEBUTANTS

Aug 11 v Sunderland
Younes Kaboul
Aug 11 v Sunderland
Darren Bent
Aug 26 v Manchester United
Gareth Bale
Nov 3 v Middlesbrough
Kevin Prince Boateng
Dec 15 v Portsmouth
Jamie O'Hara
Jan 30 v Everton
Chris Gunter
Jan 30 v Everton
Jonathan Woodgate
Feb 2 v Manchester United
Alan Hutton
Mar 9 v West Ham United
Gilberto

Match No.	Date		Opponents		Result		Scorers	Attendance
1	Aug	11	A	Sunderland	L	0-1		43,967
2		14	H	Everton	L	1-3	Gardner	35,716
3		18	H	Derby County	W	4-0	Malbranque 2, Jenas, Bent	35,600
4		26	A	Manchester United	L	0-1		75,696
5	Sep	1	A	Fulham	D	3-3	Kaboul, Berbatov, Bale	24,007
6		15	H	Arsenal	L	1-3	Bale	36,053
7		23	A	Bolton Wanderers	D	1-1	Keane	20,308
8	Oct	1	H	Aston Villa	D	4-4	Berbatov, Chimbonda, Keane (pen), Kaboul	36,094
9		7	A	Liverpool	D	2-2	Keane 2	43,986
10		22	A	Newcastle United	L	1-3	Keane	51,411
11		28	H	Blackburn Rovers	L	1-2	Keane (pen)	36,086
12	Nov	3	A	Middlesbrough	D	1-1	Bent	25,625
13		11	H	Wigan Athletic	W	4-0	Jenas 2, Lennon, Bent	35,504
14		25	A	West Ham United	D	1-1	Dawson	34,966
15	Dec	2	H	Birmingham City	L	2-3	Keane 2 (1 pen)	35,635
16		9	H	ManchesterCity	W	2-1	Chimbonda, Defoe	35,646
17		15	A	Portsmouth	W	1-0	Berbatov	20,520
18		22	A	Arsenal	L	1-2	Berbatov	60,087
19		26	H	Fulham	W	5-1	Keane 2, Huddlestone 2, Defoe	36,077
20		29	H	Reading	W	6-4	Berbatov 4, Malbranque, Defoe	36,178
21	Jan	1	A	Aston Villa	L	1-2	Defoe	41,609
22		12	A	Chelsea	L	0-2		41,777
23		19	H	Sunderland	W	2-0	Lennon, Keane	36,070
24		30	A	Everton	D	0-0		35,840
25	Feb	2	H	Manchester United	D	1-1	Berbatov	36,075
26		9	A	Derby County	W	3-0	Keane, Kaboul, Berbatov (pen)	33,058
27	Mar	1	A	Birmingham City	L	1-4	Jenas	26,055
28		9	H	West Ham United	W	4-0	Berbatov 2, Gilberto, Bent	36,062
29		16	A	Manchester City	L	1-2	Keane	40,180
30		19	H	Chelsea	D	4-4	Woodgate, Berbatov, Huddlestone, Keane	36,178
31		22	H	Portsmouth	W	2-0	Bent, O'Hara	35,998
32		30	H	Newcastle United	L	1-4	Bent	36,067
33	Apr	5	A	Blackburn Rovers	D	1-1	Berbatov	24,592
34		12	H	Middlesbrough	D	1-1	OG (Grounds)	36,092
35		19	A	Wigan Athletic	D	1-1	Berbatov	18,673
36		26	H	Bolton Wanderers	D	1-1	Malbranque	36,176
37	May	3	A	Reading	W	1-0	Keane	24,125
38		11	H	Liverpool	L	0-2		36,063

Appearances
Substitute
Goals

FA Cup

R3	Jan	5	H	Reading	D	2-2	Berbatov 2 (1 pen)	35,243
R3r		15	A	Reading	W	1-0	Keane	22,130
R4		27	A	ManchesterUnited	L	1-3	Keane	75,369

Appearances
Substitute
Goals

Carling Cup

R2	Sep	26	H	Middlesbrough	W	2-0	Bale, Huddlestone	30,084
R3	Oct	31	H	Blackpool	W	2-0	Keane, Chimbonda	32,196
R4	Dec	18	A	Manchester City	W	2-0	Defoe, Malbranque	38,564
SF1	Jan	9	A	Arsenal	D	1-1	Jenas	53,163
SF2		22	H	Arsenal	W	5-1	Jenas, OG (Bendtner), Keane, Lennon, Malbranque	35,979
F	Feb	24	N*	Chelsea	W#	2-1	Berbatov (pen), Woodgate	87,660

*At Wembley #After extra-time

Appearances
Substitute
Goals

Assou-Ekotto BPD	Bale GF	Bent DA	Berbatov DI	Boateng KP	Cerny R	Chimbonda P	Dawson MR	Defoe JC	Gardner AD	Gilberto	Gunter CR	Huddlestone TA	Hutton A	Jenas JA	Kaboul Y	Keane RD	King LB	Lee YP	Lennon AJ	Malbranque S	O'Hara JD	Robinson PW	Rocha RS	Routledge WNA	Stalteri PA	Taarabt A	Tainio TM	Woodgate JS	Zokora AD	OG
		13	9			2		14	3			12		8	5	10				11		1			7		6		**4**	
		11	9			2		14	3					8	**5**	10				6		1	12	13	7				4	
		9				**2**		14	6			4		8		10		3		11		1	5	7		13			12	
	7		9			2		14	6			4		8		10		**3**		11		1	*5*			12			13	
	11		9			2	12	13				4		8	5	*10*		3		**7**		1	6							
	11	12	9			2	5					4		8	6	10		3	13	**7**		1								
3		12	***9***			2	5							8		10			13	7		1	6				*11*		4	
	3	13	*9*			2	5	14				8			6	10			**7**	12		1					11		4	
	7		9			2	11							8	5	10		3		12		1					**6**		4	
	7	*9*	12		1	2	6							8	5	10		3	13	**11**							14		4	
		12	*9*		1	2	6	13				8			5	10		3	11	**7**									4	
		9	13	**4**		2	6	10						8	5	14		3	11	7		1							12	
		13	9			2	6	14						8	5	*10*		3	11	**7**		1					12		4	
	3	12	9			2	6	13						8	**5**	*10*			11	7		1							4	
	3	8	9			2	6	14				13			*5*	10		12	11	7		1							4	
		10	**9**	14		2	6	13						8	5			3	11	7		1					12		4	
		10	9	**6**		2		13						8	5			3	11	7	12	1					14		4	
			9	*4*		2		14				13			5	10		**3**	11	7	8	1				12	6			
			9	13		2		14				4			5	10	**6**	3	11	7	8	1				12				
			9	14		2		12				4		8	5	*10*	**6**	3	11	7		1					13			
			9	*6*			2	10				13		8	**5**	14		3	11	7	12	1							4	
			9	8	1	2	5	12							14	10	6	3	11	7	**4**					13				
			9	6	1	13	5	10				2		8		14		3	11		**4**				*7*		12			
			9	12	1	2					**3**	6		8		10			11	7	4							5		
			9	13	1	2	5					4	3	8		**10**			*11*	7	12							6		
		9	14	**4**	1	2	*5*					6	3	8	13	10			11	7	12									
		10	9			2					12	8	3	13	5	14				7	11	1					*6*		**4**	
		14	9			2	5			13		8	3			10			11	*7*		1					12	**6**	4	
		13	9			2	5					14	3	8		*10*			11	**7**	12	1						6	4	
		12	9			2						13	3	*8*		10	**6**		11	7		1						5	4	
		12	9			2	**5**					8	3			*10*			11	7	14	1					13	6	4	
		11	9				5					8	2			10			13	7	3	1				14	12	6	**4**	
		13	9		1	**2**	5			12		14	3	8		*10*			11	7								6	4	
		14	9		1	**2**	5			12		13	3	8		10			11	7								6	4	
		12	9		1		5					6	2	8		**10**			11	7	3								4	
		13	9		1		*5*			3		12	**2**	8		10			11	7	14							6	4	
		9		12	1		5			3		*11*	2	8		**10**				7	13							6	4	
		12	9		1		**5**			3		14	2	8		10			11	7							13	6	4	
1	8	11	33	7	13	31	26	3	4	3	1	18	14	28	19	32	4	17	25	35	9	25	4	1	3	0	6	12	25	
0	0	16	3	6	0	1	1	16	0	3	1	10	0	1	2	4	0	1	4	2	8	0	1	1	0	6	10	0	3	
	2	6	15			2	1	4	1	1		3		4	3	15			2	4	1							1		1

Assou-Ekotto BPD	Bale GF	Bent DA	Berbatov DI	Boateng KP	Cerny R	Chimbonda P	Dawson MR	Defoe JC	Gardner AD	Gilberto	Gunter CR	Huddlestone TA	Hutton A	Jenas JA	Kaboul Y	Keane RD	King LB	Lee YP	Lennon AJ	Malbranque S	O'Hara JD	Robinson PW	Rocha RS	Routledge WNA	Stalteri PA	Taarabt A	Tainio TM	Woodgate JS	Zokora AD	OG
			9			2	5					12		8		*10*	6	**3**	11	**7**		1				13			4	
				11	1	2	4	9			3			8	**5**	10			14	7	13				12		*6*			
			9	14	1		5	13			12	4		8		10		**3**	11	7	2						*6*			
0	0	0	2	1	2	2	3	1	0	0	1	1	0	3	1	3	1	2	2	3	1	1	0	0	0	0	2	0	1	
0	0	0	0	1	0	0	0	1	0	0	1	1	0	0	0	0	0	0	1	0	1	0	0	0	1	1	0	0	0	
			2													2														

Assou-Ekotto BPD	Bale GF	Bent DA	Berbatov DI	Boateng KP	Cerny R	Chimbonda P	Dawson MR	Defoe JC	Gardner AD	Gilberto	Gunter CR	Huddlestone TA	Hutton A	Jenas JA	Kaboul Y	Keane RD	King LB	Lee YP	Lennon AJ	Malbranque S	O'Hara JD	Robinson PW	Rocha RS	Routledge WNA	Stalteri PA	Taarabt A	Tainio TM	Woodgate JS	Zokora AD	OG
	3		9			2	5	*10*				4		**8**	6	13			7			1					11		12	
		13	*9*			2	6	14						8	5	10		3	11	7		1					12		4	
			9	6		2		*10*				12		8	5			3	11	**7**	14	1					13		4	
			9	12	1	2	5	13						8		*10*	6	3	11	**7**	4									
			9	13	1	2	5	12				14		8		*10*	4	3	11	7							6			
			9			**2**						12	3	8	13	*10*	6		11	7		1					14	5	4	
0	1	0	6	1	2	6	4	2	0	0	0	1	1	6	3	4	3	4	6	5	1	4	0	0	0	0	2	1	3	
0	0	1	0	2	0	0	0	3	0	0	0	3	0	0	1	1	0	0	0	0	1	0	0	0	0	0	3	0	1	
	1		1			1		1				1		2		2			1	2								1		1

League Table

	P	W	D	L	F	A	Pts
Manchester United	38	27	6	5	80	22	87
Chelsea	38	25	10	3	65	26	85
Arsenal	38	24	11	3	74	31	83
Liverpool	38	21	13	4	67	28	76
Everton	38	19	8	11	55	33	65
Aston Villa	38	16	12	10	71	51	60
Blackburn Rovers	38	15	13	10	50	48	58
Portsmouth	38	16	9	13	48	40	57
Manchester City	38	15	10	13	45	53	55
West Ham United	38	13	10	15	42	50	49
Tottenham Hotspur	38	11	13	14	66	61	46
Newcastle United	38	11	10	17	45	65	43
Middlesbrough	38	10	12	16	43	53	42
Wigan Athletic	38	10	10	18	34	51	40
Sunderland	38	11	6	21	36	59	39
Bolton	38	9	10	19	36	54	37
Fulham	38	8	12	18	38	60	36
Reading	38	10	6	22	41	66	36
Birmingham City	38	8	11	19	46	62	35
Derby County	38	1	8	29	20	89	11

2008-09

PREMIERSHIP

Head coach: Juande Ramos until October then manager Harry Redknapp

Did you know that?

John Bostock became the youngest player to appear for Spurs in a competitive match when he went on as a 79th-minute substitute against Dinamo Zagreb on 6 November 2008. He was 16 years and 295 days old.

LEAGUE DEBUTANTS

Aug 16 v Middlesbrough Heurelho Gomes
Aug 16 v Middlesbrough Giovani
Aug 16 v Middlesbrough Luka Modric
Aug 16 v Middlesbrough David Bentley
Sept 15 v Aston Villa Vedran Corluka
Sept 15 v Aston Villa Roman Pavlyuchenko
Sept 21 v Wigan Athletic Fraizer Campbell
Jan 27 v Stoke City Carlo Cudicini
Jan 30 v Bolton Wanderers Wilson Palacios

Match No.	Date			Opponents	Result		Scorers	Attendance
1	Aug	16	A	Middlesbrough	L	1-2	OG (Huth)	32,623
2		23	H	Sunderland	L	1-2	Jenas	36,034
3		31	A	Chelsea	D	1-1	Bent	41,790
4	Sep	15	H	Aston Villa	L	1-2	Bent	36,075
5		21	H	Wigan Athletic	D	0-0		35,808
6		28	A	Portsmouth	L	0-2		20,352
7	Oct	5	H	Hull City	L	0-1		36,062
8		19	A	Stoke City	L	1-2	Bent	27,500
9		26	H	Bolton Wanderers	W	2-0	Pavlyuchenko, Bent (pen)	35,507
10		29	A	Arsenal	D	4-4	Bentley, Bent, Jenas, Lennon	60,043
11	Nov	1	H	Liverpool	W	2-1	OG (Carragher), Pavlyuchenko	36,183
12		9	A	Manchester City	W	2-1	Bent 2	41,893
13		15	A	Fulham	L	1-2	Campbell	25,139
14		23	H	Blackburn Rovers	W	1-0	Pavlyuchenko	35,903
17		30	H	Everton	L	0-1		35,742
16	Dec	8	A	West Ham United	W	2-0	King, O'Hara	34,277
17		13	H	Manchester United	D	0-0		35,882
18		21	A	Newcastle United	L	1-2	Modric	47,982
19		26	H	Fulham	D	0-0		35,866
20		28	A	West Bromwich Albion	L	0-2		26,344
21	Jan	11	A	Wigan Athletic	L	0-1		17,500
22		18	H	Portsmouth	D	1-1	Defoe	36,011
23		27	H	Stoke City	W	3-1	Lennon, Defoe, Dawson	36,072
24		31	A	Bolton Wanderers	L	2-3	Bent 2	21,575
25	Feb	8	H	Arsenal	D	0-0		36,021
26		23	A	Hull City	W	2-1	Lennon, Woodgate	24,742
27	Mar	4	H	Middlesbrough	W	4-0	Keane, Pavlyuchenko, Lennon 2	35,761
28		7	A	Sunderland	D	1-1	Keane	37,894
29		15	A	Aston Villa	W	2-1	Jenas, Bent	41,205
30		21	H	Chelsea	W	1-0	Modric	36,034
31	Apr	4	A	Blackburn Rovers	L	1-2	Keane (pen)	21,891
32		11	H	West Ham United	W	1-0	Pavlyuchenko	35,969
33		19	H	Newcastle United	W	1-0	Bent	35,850
34		25	A	Manchester United	L	2-5	Bent, Modric	75,458
35	May	2	H	West Bromwich Albion	W	1-0	Jenas	35,836
36		9	A	Everton	D	0-0		36,646
37		16	H	Manchester City	W	2-1	Defoe, Keane (pen)	36,000
38		24	A	Liverpool	L	1-3	Keane	43,937

Appearances
Substitute
Goals

FA Cup

R3	Jan	2	H	Wigan Athletic	W	3-1	Pavlyuchenko 2 (1 pen), Modric	34,040
R4		24	A	Manchester United	L	1-2	Pavlyuchenko	75,014

Appearances
Substitute
Goals

Carling Cup

R2	Sep	23	A	Newcastle United	W	2-1	Pavlyuchenko, O'Hara	20,577
R3	Nov	12	H	Liverpool	W	4-2	Pavlyuchenko 2, Campbell 2	33,242
R4	Dec	3	A	Watford	W	2-1	Pavlyuchenko (pen), Bent	16,501
SF1	Jan	6	H	Burnley	D	4-1	Dawson, O'Hara, Pavlyuchenko, OG (Duff)	31,377
SF2		21	A	Burnley	L#	2-3	Pavlyuchenko, Defoe	19,533
F	Mar	1	N*	Manchester United	L#^	0-0		88,217

*At Wembley #After extra-time ^1-4 on penalties

Appearances
Substitute
Goals

Alnwick BR	Assou-Ekotto BPD	Bale GF	Bent DA	Bentley DM	Berbatov DI	Boateng KP	Campbell FL	Chimbonda P	Corluka V	Cudicini C	Dawson MR	Defoe JC	Gilberto	Giovani	Gomes HS	Gunter CR	Huddlestone TA	Hutton A	Jenas JA	Keane RD	King LB	Lennon AJ	Modric L	O'Hara JD	Palacios WRS	Pavlyuchenko RA	Sanchez CD	Taarabt A	Woodgate JS	Zokora AD	OG
	3	13	10	5	14						6			9	1				8			7	11	12					2	4	
	9	3	10	5										12	1		13		8		6	**7**	11						2	4	
		3	10	*5*										9	1	**2**	12		8		6	14	11	13					7	4	
		3	10	12					2		*5*			13	1		6		14			7	8			9			11	**4**	
	2	**3**	10	*5*			14		11						1		12		8			13		7		9			6	4	
	3		13	5					2		7		11	12	1				8			14		10		*9*			6	**4**	
		3	14	12			10		5					13	1	**2**			8			7	11			9			6	4	
		3	10	**5**					*9*		13				1			2	8			7	11			12			6	4	
	3		12	5					11						1		6	2	8		4	13	7	*10*		**9**					
	11	*3*	14	5					10						1	12	6	**2**	8			13	7			9			4		
	3		10	5					2						1		6	12			8	13	7	9		14			11	4	
	3		10	5					2						1		6		8		9	12	**7**						11	4	
		3	10	5			14		2						1		**6**		8		7	13	*9*			12			11	4	
	3		10	**5**			13		2						1		6		8		4	7		12		*9*			11		
	3	12	10	5		13	14		2						1		*6*				11	7				9			8	4	
	3		13	**5**					2						1				8		6	7	10	12		*9*			11	4	
	3		14	5					2		11				1		12		*8*			7	10	13		9			**6**	4	
	3			5			12		2		11				1		6				10	7	8			**9**				4	
	3		10	**5**			12		2		9				1		*6*		13		11	7	8			14				4	
	3	14	10	*5*			12		2		9				1				8			7	11	13					6	**4**	
		3	14						2		**5**	10			1				12		11	13	*8*	7		9			6	4	
		3	14	12					2		13	10			1						*6*	7	8	11		9			5	4	
	3			5			13		2	1	11	10					12					**7**	8			*9*			6	4	
	3		14	5				12	**2**	1	10								13			7	8		11	9			6	*4*	
	3		14					12	**2**	1	5								8	10		7	11		4	9		13	6		
	3		10						2	1	12								8	9	5	7	11		4	14			**6**	13	
	3		13								5				1		12		**8**	10		7	11	14	2	*9*			6	4	
			10	13				3	**2**						1		14		8	9	6	7	11		*4*	12			5		
	3		10						12						1				8	9	6	7	*11*	13	2				5	**4**	
	3		10						2						1				8	9	6	**7**	*11*	13	4				5	12	
	3		10						2						1				8	9	6	**7**	11		4				5	12	
	3		*10*						2						1		6		**8**	9	4	7	11			13			5	12	
	3		*10*						2		**5**	13			1		6	12		9		7	11		8				4		
	3	13	10						2						1		12		8	**9**	6	7	*11*		4				5		
	3								2			12			1				8	10	6	7	11		4	**9**			5		
		3							7			9			1		6	2	8	10	4		**11**			12			5		
	3						14		2			7			1		6	12	*8*	10	4		11			9			**5**	13	
	11	**3**	12	13					5			9			1			2	*8*	10	6		7			14				4	
0	29	12	21	20	0	0	1	1	33	4	13	6	1	2	34	2	14	5	28	14	24	26	34	6	11	19	0	0	34	24	
0	0	4	12	5	1	1	9	2	1	0	3	2	0	4	0	1	8	3	4	0	0	9	0	9	0	9	0	1	0	5	
			12	1			1				1	3							4	5	1	5	3	1		5			1		2

Alnwick BR	Assou-Ekotto BPD	Bale GF	Bent DA	Bentley DM	Berbatov DI	Boateng KP	Campbell FL	Chimbonda P	Corluka V	Cudicini C	Dawson MR	Defoe JC	Gilberto	Giovani	Gomes HS	Gunter CR	Huddlestone TA	Hutton A	Jenas JA	Keane RD	King LB	Lennon AJ	Modric L	O'Hara JD	Palacios WRS	Pavlyuchenko RA	Sanchez CD	Taarabt A	Woodgate JS	Zokora AD	OG
		3	**10**	5			12		2		8				1							13	*11*	7		9			6	4	
1	11	**3**		*5*					10		8	13		14		2	6						7			9		12		4	
1	1	2	1	2	0	0	0	0	2	0	2	0	0	0	1	1	1	0	0	0	0	0	2	1	0	2	0	0	1	2	
0	0	0	0	0	0	0	1	0	0	0	0	1	0	1	0	0	0	0	0	0	0	1	0	0	0	0	0	1	0	0	
																							1			3					

Alnwick BR	Assou-Ekotto BPD	Bale GF	Bent DA	Bentley DM	Berbatov DI	Boateng KP	Campbell FL	Chimbonda P	Corluka V	Cudicini C	Dawson MR	Defoe JC	Gilberto	Giovani	Gomes HS	Gunter CR	Huddlestone TA	Hutton A	Jenas JA	Keane RD	King LB	Lennon AJ	Modric L	O'Hara JD	Palacios WRS	Pavlyuchenko RA	Sanchez CD	Taarabt A	Woodgate JS	Zokora AD	OG
	11	**3**					13		2					12	1				8		6	7	14	10		9			5	4	
		3	14			13	10		8		5				**1**		6	2				7		11		*9*	12			4	
	3		12				**10**		2		5				1				8			7		11		9			6	4	
		3		**5**			10		2		6				1							7	8	12		9			11	4	
1	3	14		5							8	9				**2**	6						7	11		13		12	10	4	
	3	13	10	12					2		5				1				*8*		6	**7**	11	14		9				4	
1	4	3	1	2	0	0	3	0	5	0	5	1	0	0	5	1	2	1	3	0	2	5	3	4	0	5	0	0	4	6	
0	0	2	2	1	0	1	1	0	0	0	0	0	0	1	0	0	0	0	0	0	0	0	1	2	0	1	1	1	0	0	
			1				2				1	1												2		6					1

League Table

	P	W	D	L	F	A	Pts
Manchester United	38	28	6	4	68	24	90
Liverpool	38	25	11	2	77	27	86
Chelsea	38	25	8	5	68	24	83
Arsenal	38	20	12	6	68	37	72
Everton	38	17	12	9	55	37	63
Aston Villa	38	17	11	10	54	48	62
Fulham	38	14	11	13	39	34	53
Tottenham Hotspur	38	14	9	15	45	45	51
West Ham United	38	14	9	15	42	45	51
Manchester City	38	15	5	18	58	50	50
Wigan Athletic	38	12	9	17	34	45	45
Stoke City	38	12	9	17	38	55	45
Bolton	38	11	8	19	41	53	41
Portsmouth	38	10	11	17	38	57	41
Blackburn Rovers	38	10	11	17	40	60	41
Sunderland	38	9	9	20	34	54	36
Hull City	38	8	11	19	39	64	35
Newcastle United	38	7	13	18	40	59	34
Middlesbrough	38	7	11	20	28	57	32
West Bromwich Albion	38	8	8	22	36	67	32

2009-10

PREMIERSHIP

Manager: Harry Redknapp

Did you know that?

Spurs did not use a substitute in the match with Aston Villa on 6 February 2010. It was the first time in the Premier League Spurs had not called a player from the bench into action since the game with Wigan Athletic on 26 November 2005.

LEAGUE DEBUTANTS

Aug 16 v Liverpool
Sebastien Bassong
Aug 16 v Liverpool
Peter Crouch
Aug 23 v West Ham United
Kyle Naughton
Sept 12 v Manchester United
Niko Kranjcar
Feb 11 v Wolverhampton Wanderers
Eidur Gudjohnsen
Mar 20 v Stoke City
Jake Livermore
Mar 27 v Portsmouth
Kyle Walker
Apr 14 v Arsenal
Danny Rose
May 9 v Burnley
Ben Alnwick

Match No.	Date			Opponents	Result		Scorers	Attendance
1	Aug	16	H	Liverpool	W	2-1	Assou-Ekotto, Bassong	35,935
2		19	A	Hull City	W	5-1	Defoe 3, Palacios, Keane	24,735
3		23	A	West Ham United	W	2-1	Defoe, Lennon	33,095
4		29	H	Birmingham City	W	2-1	Crouch, Lennon	35,318
5	Sep	12	H	Manchester United	L	1-3	Defoe	35,785
6		20	A	Chelsea	L	0-3		41,623
7		26	H	Burnley	W	5-0	Keane 4 (1 pen), Jenas	35,462
8	Oct	3	A	Bolton Wanderers	D	2-2	Kranjcar, Corluka	21,305
9		17	A	Portsmouth	W	2-1	King, Defoe	20,821
10		24	H	Stoke City	L	0-1		36,031
11		31	A	Arsenal	L	0-3		60,103
12	Nov	7	H	Sunderland	W	2-0	Keane, Huddlestone	35,955
13		22	H	Wigan Athletic	W	9-1	Defoe 5, Crouch, Lennon, Bentley, Kranjcar	35,650
14		28	A	Aston Villa	D	1-1	Dawson	39,866
17	Dec	6	A	Everton	D	2-2	Defoe, Dawson	34,003
16		12	H	Wolverhampton Wanderers	L	0-1		36,012
17		16	H	Manchester City	W	3-0	Kranjcar 2, Defoe	35,891
18		19	A	Blackburn Rovers	W	2-0	Crouch 2	26,490
19		26	A	Fulham	D	0-0		25,679
20		28	H	West Ham United	W	2-0	Modric, Defoe	35,994
21	Jan	16	H	Hull City	D	0-0		35,729
22		20	A	Liverpool	L	0-2		42,016
23		26	H	Fulham	W	2-0	Crouch, Bentley	35,467
24		30	A	Birmingham City	D	1-1	Defoe	27,238
25	Feb	6	H	Aston Villa	D	0-0		35,899
26		10	A	Wolverhampton Wanderers	L	0-1		27,992
27		21	A	Wigan Athletic	W	3-0	Defoe, Pavlyuchenko 2	16,165
28		28	H	Everton	W	2-1	Pavlyuchenko, Modric	35,912
29	Mar	13	H	Blackburn Rovers	W	3-1	Defoe, Pavlyuchenko 2	35,474
30		20	A	Stoke City	W	2-1	Gudjohnsen, Kranjcar	27,575
31		27	H	Portsmouth	W	2-0	Crouch, Kranjcar	35,870
32	Apr	3	A	Sunderland	L	1-3	Crouch	43,184
33		10	H	Arsenal	W	2-1	Rose, Bale	36,041
34		17	H	Chelsea	W	2-1	Defoe (pen), Bale	35,814
35		25	A	Manchester United	L	1-3	King, Defoe	75,268
36	May	1	H	Bolton Wanderers	W	1-0	Huddlestone	35,852
37		5	A	Manchester City	W	1-0	Crouch	47,370
38		9	A	Burnley	L	2-4	Bale, Modric	21,161

Appearances
Substitute
Goals

FA Cup

Round	Date			Opponents	Result		Scorers	Attendance
R3	Jan	2	H	Peterborough United	W	4-0	Kranjcar 2, Defoe, Keane (pen)	35,862
R4		23	H	Leeds United	D	2-2	Pavlyuchenko, Crouch	35,750
R4r	Feb	3	A	Leeds United	W	3-1	Defoe 3	37,704
R5		14	A	Bolton Wanderers	D	1-1	Defoe	13,596
R5r		24	H	Bolton Wanderers	W	4-0	Pavlyuchenko 2, OG (Jaaskelainen), OG (O'Brien)	31,436
R6	Mar	6	A	Fulham	D	0-0		24,533
R6r		24	H	Fulham	W	3-1	Bentley, Pavlyuchenko, Gudjohnsen	35,432
SF	Apr	11	N*	Portsmouth	L#	0-2		84,602

* played at Wembley

Appearances
Substitute
Goals

Carling Cup

Round	Date			Opponents	Result		Scorers	Attendance
R2	Aug	26	A	Doncaster Rovers	W	5-1	Huddlestone, O'Hara, Crouch, Bentley, Pavlyuchenko	12,923
R3	Sep	23	A	Preston North End	W	5-1	Crouch 3, Defoe, Keane	16,533
R4	Oct	27	H	Everton	W	2-0	Huddlestone, Keane	35,843
R5	Dec	1	A	Manchester United	L	0-2		57,212

Appearances
Substitute
Goals

Almwick BR	Assou-Ekotto BPD	Bale GF	Bassong SAN	Bentley DM	Boateng KP	Button DRE	Corluka V	Crouch PJ	Cudicini C	Dawson MR	Defoe JC	Giovani	Gomes HS	Gudjohnsen ES	Huddlestone TA	Hutton A	Jenas JA	Kaboul Y	Keane RD	King LB	Kranjcar N	Lennon AJ	Livermore JDL	Modric L	Naughton K	O'Hara JD	Palacios WRS	Pavlyuchenko RA	Rose DL	Walker K	Woodgate JS	OG
	3		5				2	13			9		1		6				10	4		7		11		14	8	12				
	3		5	14			4	13	12		9		1		6	2			10			7		11			8					
	3		5				2	13	1		9				6				10	4		7		11	12	14	8					
	3		5				2	14	1		9				6	12			10	4		7		11			8	13				
	3		5				2	9	1		11				6	12	13		10	4	14	7					8					
	3		5				2	14	1		9				6	12	8		10	4	13	7					11					
	3	13	5				2	14	1	12	9				6		8		10		11	7					4					
	3		5				2	9	1		12				6		8		10		11	7					4					
	3		5				2	13		12	9		1		6		8		10	4	11	7					14					
	3		5				2	9		12			1		6		14		10		11	7					8	13			4	
	3	13	11	5			2	9					1		6	12	8		10	4							7	14				
	3						2	9		12	11		1		6		8		10	4	13						7				5	
	3		12	13			2	9		4	10		1		6		14				11	7					8				5	
	3		4				2	9		5	10		1		6				12		11	7					8					
	3	12	4				2	9		5	10		1		6	13	14				11	7					8					
	3		4				2	13		5	9	14	1		6				11		11	7		12			8					
	3	12	4				2	9		5	10		1		6		13				11	7					8					
	3		4				2	9		5	10		1		6	12	13		14		11	7					8					
	3		4				2	9		5	12		1				8		10		11	7		13			6					
	3	12					2	9		5	10		1		6		13			4	14	7		11			8					
		3	4				2	13		5	9		1		6		12		10		7			11			8					
		3	13				2	9		5	10		1			12	8		14	6	7			11			4					
		3		5			2	9		4	10		1		6				12	8				11			7					
		3		5			2	9		4	10		1		6		12		13	8				11			7					
		3		5			2	9		4	10		1		6					8				11			7					
		3	2	5				13		7	10		1	9	6		8	4			11			14			12					
		3	12	5			2	9		4	10		1		6					8	11			14			7	13				
		3	4				2	13		5	10		1		6			12			11			8			7	9				
	6	3	4				2	13		5	10		1	12							11			8			7	9				
	11	3	6				2	10		5			1	13				4			7		12	8				9				
	14	3	8	5				9		4			1	10	6			12			11			7				13		2		
	7	3	6	5				14			12		1	10				4			13			11			8	9		2		
	2	3		14				12		5	10		1	13	6			4		8				7				9	11			
	2	3	8	5				12		7	10		1	13	6			4						11				9				
	2	3		5				13		8	10		1	14	6					4		12		11			7	9				
	2	3		5				14		8	10		1	13	6			4		11		12		7				9				
	2	3		12				9		5	10		1		6			4		8		7		11			14	13				
1	2	3						9		5	10			13	6			4		8		7		11			12	14				
1	29	18	25	11	0	0	29	21	6	25	31	0	31	3	33	1	9	8	15	19	19	20	0	21	0	0	29	8	1	2	3	
0	1	5	3	4	0	0	0	17	1	4	3	1	0	7	0	7	9	2	5	0	5	2	1	4	1	2	4	8	0	0	0	
	1	3	1	2			1	8		2	18			1	2		1		6	2	6	3		3			1	5	1			

Almwick BR	Assou-Ekotto BPD	Bale GF	Bassong SAN	Bentley DM	Boateng KP	Button DRE	Corluka V	Crouch PJ	Cudicini C	Dawson MR	Defoe JC	Giovani	Gomes HS	Gudjohnsen ES	Huddlestone TA	Hutton A	Jenas JA	Kaboul Y	Keane RD	King LB	Kranjcar N	Lennon AJ	Livermore JDL	Modric L	Naughton K	O'Hara JD	Palacios WRS	Pavlyuchenko RA	Rose DL	Walker K	Woodgate JS	OG
		3	4							5	9		1		6	2			10		7			11	12		8	14	13			
		3	6					9		5	10		1			2	8		12		7			4			14	13	11			
		3	11	5			2	9		4	10		1		6		8				7											
		3		5			2	9		8	10		1		6					4	12			11			7					
	11	3		5			2			4	10		1	14	6						13			8			7	9	12			
	6	3	4				2	10		5	12		1								11			8			7	9				
	7	3	5	14			2	9		6			1	10	13						11			8			4	12				
		3	8	5			2	9		4	10		1	13	6						12			11			7	14				
0	3	8	6	4	0	0	6	6	0	8	6	0	8	1	5	2	2	0	1	1	5	0	0	7	0	0	6	2	1	0	0	
0	0	0	0	1	0	0	0	0	0	0	1	0	0	2	1	0	0	0	1	0	3	0	0	0	1	0	1	4	2	0	0	
				1				1			5			1					1		2							4				2

Almwick BR	Assou-Ekotto BPD	Bale GF	Bassong SAN	Bentley DM	Boateng KP	Button DRE	Corluka V	Crouch PJ	Cudicini C	Dawson MR	Defoe JC	Giovani	Gomes HS	Gudjohnsen ES	Huddlestone TA	Hutton A	Jenas JA	Kaboul Y	Keane RD	King LB	Kranjcar N	Lennon AJ	Livermore JDL	Modric L	Naughton K	O'Hara JD	Palacios WRS	Pavlyuchenko RA	Rose DL	Walker K	Woodgate JS	OG
			4	5	13	12	11	10	1			7			6	2									3	8		9	14			
		3		5			12	9		4	10	7	1		6	2	8		13			13					11					
	11	3	8	5						4			1		6	2			10								7	9				
		3	4	5				12		6	9		1		13	2	8		10			7					11					
0	1	3	3	4	0	0	1	2	1	3	2	2	3	0	3	4	2	0	2	0	0	1	0	0	1	1	3	2	0	0	0	
0	0	0	0	0	1	1	1	1	0	0	0	0	0	0	1	0	0	0	1	0	0	1	0	0	0	0	0	0	1	0	0	
				1				4			1				2				2							1		1				

League Table

	P	W	D	L	F	A	Pts
Chelsea	38	27	5	6	103	32	86
Manchester United	38	27	4	7	86	28	85
Arsenal	38	23	6	9	83	41	75
Tottenham Hotspur	38	21	7	10	67	41	70
Manchester City	38	18	13	7	73	45	67
Aston Villa	38	17	13	8	52	39	64
Liverpool	38	18	9	11	61	35	63
Everton	38	16	13	9	60	49	61
Birmingham City	38	13	11	14	38	47	50
Blackburn Rovers	38	13	11	14	41	55	50
Stoke City	38	11	14	13	34	48	47
Fulham	38	12	10	16	39	46	46
Sunderland	38	11	11	16	48	56	44
Bolton	38	10	9	19	42	67	39
Wolverhampton	38	9	11	18	32	56	38
Wigan Athletic	38	9	9	20	37	79	36
West Ham United	38	8	11	19	47	66	35
Burnley	38	8	6	24	42	82	30
Hull City	38	6	12	20	34	75	30
Portsmouth	38	7	7	24	34	66	18

2010-11

PREMIERSHIP

Manager: Harry Redknapp

Did you know that?

When South African international Steven Pienaar made his Spurs' debut at Newcastle on 22 January 2011 he became the 600th player to appear for Spurs in Football/Premier League competition.

LEAGUE DEBUTANTS

Sept 11	v West Bromwich Albion William Gallas
Sept 11	v West Bromwich Albion Rafael Van der Vaart
Oct 2	v Aston Villa Sandro
Jan 22	v Newcastle United Steven Pienaar

Match No.	Date			Opponents	Result		Scorers	Attendance
1	Aug	14	H	Manchester City	D	0-0		35,928
2		21	A	Stoke City	W	2-1	Bale 2	27,243
3		28	H	Wigan Athletic	L	0-1		35,101
4	Sep	11	A	West Bromwich Albion	D	1-1	Modric	23,642
5		18	H	Wolverhampton Wanderers	W	3-1	Van der Vaart (pen), Pavlyuchenko, Hutton	35,940
6		25	A	West Ham United	L	0-1		34,190
7	Oct	2	H	Aston Villa	W	2-1	Van der Vaart 2	35,871
8		16	A	Fulham	W	2-1	Pavlyuchenko, Huddlestone	25,615
9		23	H	Everton	D	1-1	Van der Vaart	35,967
10		30	A	Manchester United	L	0-2		75,223
11	Nov	6	A	Bolton Wanderers	L	2-4	Hutton, Pavlyuchenko	20,225
12		9	H	Sunderland	D	1-1	Van der Vaart	35,843
13		13	H	Blackburn Rovers	W	4-2	Bale 2, Pavlyuchenko, Crouch	35,700
14		20	A	Arsenal	W	3-2	Bale, Van der Vaart (pen), Kaboul	60,102
17		28	H	Liverpool	W	2-1	OG (Skrtel), Lennon	35,692
16	Dec	4	A	Birmingham City	D	1-1	Bassong	25,770
17		12	H	Chelsea	D	1-1	Pavlyuchenko	35,787
18		26	A	Aston Villa	W	2-1	Van der Vaart 2	39,411
19		28	H	Newcastle United	W	2-0	Lennon, Bale	35,927
20	Jan	1	H	Fulham	W	1-0	Bale	35,603
21		5	A	Everton	L	1-2	Van der Vaart	34,124
22		16	H	Manchester United	D	0-0		35,828
23		22	A	Newcastle United	D	1-1	Lennon	51,010
24	Feb	2	A	Blackburn Rovers	W	1-0	Crouch	23,253
25		5	H	Bolton Wanderers	W	2-1	Van der Vaart (pen), Kranjcar	36,197
26		12	A	Sunderland	W	2-1	Dawson, Kranjcar	40,986
27		22	A	Blackpool	L	1-3	Pavlyuchenko	16,069
28	Mar	6	A	Wolverhampton Wanderers	D	3-3	Defoe 2, Pavlyuchenko	28,669
29		19	H	West Ham United	D	0-0		36,010
30	Apr	2	A	Wigan Athletic	D	0-0		18,578
31		9	H	Stoke City	W	3-2	Crouch 2, Modric	32,702
32		20	H	Arsenal	D	3-3	Van der Vaart (1 pen) 2, Huddlestone	36,138
33		23	H	West Bromwich Albion	D	2-2	Pavlyuchenko, Defoe	36,160
34		30	A	Chelsea	L	1-2	Sandro	41,681
35	May	7	H	Blackpool	D	1-1	Defoe	35,585
36		10	A	Manchester City	L	0-1		47,069
37		15	A	Liverpool	W	2-0	Van der Vaart, Modric (pen)	44,893
38		22	H	BirminghamCity	W	2-1	Pavlyuchenko 2	36,119
								Appearances
								Substitute
								Goals

FA Cup

R3	Jan	9	H	Charlton Athletic	W	3-0	Townsend, Defoe 2	35,698
R4		30	A	Fulham	L	0-4		21,829
								Appearances
								Substitute
								Goals

Carling Cup

R2	Sep	26	H	Arsenal	L	1-4	Keane	35,883
								Appearances
								Substitute
								Goals

Assou-Ekotto BPD	Bale GF	Bassong SAN	Bentley DM	Caulker SR	Corluka V	Crouch PJ	Cudicini C	Dawson MR	Defoe JC	Gallas WE	Giovani	Gomes H	Huddlestone TA	Hutton A	Jenas JA	Kaboul Y	Keane RD	King LB	Kranjcar N	Lennon AJ	Livermore JCL	Modric L	Naughton K	Palacios WRS	Pavlyuchenko RA	Pienaar SJ	Pletikosa S	Rose D	Sandro	Townsend AD	Van der Vaart RF	Walker KA	OG
11	3				2	*9*		5	10		12	1	6				13	4		**7**		8			14								
11	3				2	9		5				1	6		8	4				**7**				10								12	
11	3					*9*	1	5	10		12		6			4		2	14	**7**				8	13								
	3				2	12	1			5			6			4	13		14	**7**		10		8	*9*						11		
2	3					9	1			7			6	12	8	**4**	*10*	5		14					13						11		
	3	5			4	*9*	1				14		6	2	8		12			**7**		10			13						11		
4	3	5				10						1	6	2	8					13		**7**		12	*9*				14		11		
7	3	12				14				4		1	6	2				**5**		13		10			9				*8*		11		
6	3					9				5		1		2		4				**7**		10		*8*	12				13		11		
6	3					14				5		1		2	**8**	4	*10*			7		9		12	13						11		
11	3		13			9				5		1	12	2		4			*7*			10		8	14				**6**				
10	3		5			12				7		1	6	2		4						8			**9**						11		
6	3					10				5		1		2	8	4						7		13	**9**				12		*11*		
6	3					13			12	5		1		2	8	4				**7**		10		14	*9*						11		
6	3	12				9			13	5		1		2		**4**				7		10		8					14		*11*		
11	3	6				9			**10**	5		1		2						7		8		4	12								
11	3	6				14		5	10			1		2			13			7		8		**4**	*9*				12				
6	3				14	13		5	9			1		2	12	4				**7**		8		10							*11*		
6	3	12				14		5				1		2	13	4				7		8		*10*	**9**						11		
6	3				12	13		5		4		1		**2**	14					7		8		10	*9*						11		
6	**3**					9		5		4		1		2	8		13		12	7		10									11		
6	3					9		5	12	4		1		2						7		10		**8**							11		
	3	12				13	1	5	9	6				2	*8*				14	7		4				10					11		
3		5			2	9			**10**	6		1			8					7				4					12		11		
3					2	*9*		5	10	6		1			8				12	7				**4**	13	14					11		
3					2			5	**10**	6		1			8				7	13				12	9	*11*			4				
3		*6*				13		5	10	2		1			12				14	7		8		4	9	11							
3	12							5	10	6		1		2	8				13	14		7			9	**11**			4				
10	3				*2*			5	9	6		1		13						7		8			12				4		**11**		
3		6			2	13		5	*10*			1			8				12	14		**7**			9				4		11		
8	3				2	10		5		12		1	6			4						7			9						11		
8	*3*				**2**	10		5		4		1	6			12				13		7			9				14		11		
8	3					14		5	10	2		1	**6**			4				12		7			9				13		11		
	3				**2**			5	13	6		1			14	4				7		10			*9*	12			8		11		
	3					12		5	10	2		1				4			13	14		7			9			*6*	8		11		
					2	9	1	5	14	*6*						13				7		10		**4**		12		3	8		11		
		12				9	1	5	14							4		2	13	7		8				*10*		3	**6**		11		
						9	1	5	10				*6*			4		2	13	7		8			12			3	11				
30	29	7	1	0	13	20	8	24	16	26	0	30	13	19	14	19	2	6	2	25	0	32	0	16	18	5	0	4	11	0	28	0	
0	1	5	1	0	2	14	0	0	6	1	3	0	1	2	5	2	5	0	11	9	0	0	0	5	11	3	0	0	8	0	0	1	
	7	1				4		1	4				2	2		1			2	3		3			8				1		13		1

Assou-Ekotto BPD	Bale GF	Bassong SAN	Bentley DM	Caulker SR	Corluka V	Crouch PJ	Cudicini C	Dawson MR	Defoe JC	Gallas WE	Giovani	Gomes H	Huddlestone TA	Hutton A	Jenas JA	Kaboul Y	Keane RD	King LB	Kranjcar N	Lennon AJ	Livermore JCL	Modric L	Naughton K	Palacios WRS	Pavlyuchenko RA	Pienaar SJ	Pletikosa S	Rose D	Sandro	Townsend AD	Van der Vaart RF	Walker KA	OG
3		6			2		1	5	10										11			12		**8**	9				4	7			
3		6				13		5	*9*	12		1		2	14					7		8				10			**4**		11		
2	0	2	0	0	1	0	1	2	2	0	0	1	0	1	0	0	0	0	1	1	0	1	0	1	1	1	0	0	2	1	1	0	
0	0	0	0	0	0	1	0	0	0	1	0	0	0	0	1	0	0	0	0	0	0	1	0	0	0	0	0	0	0	0	0	0	
									2																					1			

Assou-Ekotto BPD	Bale GF	Bassong SAN	Bentley DM	Caulker SR	Corluka V	Crouch PJ	Cudicini C	Dawson MR	Defoe JC	Gallas WE	Giovani	Gomes H	Huddlestone TA	Hutton A	Jenas JA	Kaboul Y	Keane RD	King LB	Kranjcar N	Lennon AJ	Livermore JCL	Modric L	Naughton K	Palacios WRS	Pavlyuchenko RA	Pienaar SJ	Pletikosa S	Rose D	Sandro	Townsend AD	Van der Vaart RF	Walker KA	OG
3		4	5	6							*10*						13		14	12	**7**		2	8	9		1		11				
1	0	1	1	1	0	0	0	0	0	0	1	0	0	0	0	0	0	0	0	0	1	0	1	1	1	0	1	0	1	0	0	0	
0	0	0	0	0	0	0	0	0	0	0	0	0	0	0	0	0	1	0	1	1	0	0	0	0	0	0	0	0	0	0	0	0	
																	1																

League Table

	P	W	D	L	F	A	Pts
Manchester United	38	23	11	4	78	37	80
Chelsea	38	21	8	9	69	33	71
Manchester City	38	21	8	9	60	33	71
Arsenal	38	19	11	8	72	43	68
Tottenham Hotspur	38	16	14	8	55	46	62
Liverpool	38	17	7	14	59	44	58
Everton	38	13	15	10	51	45	54
Fulham	38	11	16	11	49	43	49
Aston Villa	38	12	12	14	48	59	48
Sunderland	38	12	11	15	45	56	47
West Bromwich Albion	38	12	11	15	56	71	47
Newcastle United	38	11	13	14	56	57	46
Stoke City	38	13	7	18	46	48	46
Bolton	38	12	10	16	52	56	46
Blackburn Rovers	38	11	10	17	46	59	43
Wigan Athletic	38	9	15	14	40	61	42
Wolverhampton	38	11	7	20	46	66	40
Birmingham City	38	8	15	15	37	58	39
Blackpool	38	10	9	19	55	78	39
West Ham United	38	7	12	19	43	70	33

RECORDS AGAINST OTHER CLUBS

The list below details Spurs record against all clubs they have played in the Football/Premier League. It does not include the three expunged matches from 1939–40 or any abandoned matches. Opponents are identified by their current name.

OPPONENTS	P	W	D	L	F	A
Arsenal	148	47	41	60	205	228
Aston Villa	136	54	33	49	220	205
Barnsley	28	14	5	9	51	35
Birmingham City	81	39	16	26	130	91
Blackburn Rovers	94	44	18	32	161	131
Blackpool	52	26	14	12	105	67
Bolton Wanderers	86	38	14	34	133	119
Bradford City	32	12	10	10	46	44
Bradford Park Avenue	32	16	8	8	75	50
Brentford	6	3	2	1	12	5
Brighton & Hove Albion	10	5	2	3	15	10
Bristol City	20	10	5	5	28	18
Bristol Rovers	2	2	0	0	12	2
Burnley	90	33	22	35	166	142
Bury	40	18	8	14	67	66
Cardiff City	40	20	10	10	60	37
Carlisle United	2	0	1	1	1	2
Charlton Athletic	50	25	9	16	95	62
Chelsea	126	43	30	53	181	184
Chesterfield	20	9	6	5	45	28
Coventry City	82	37	22	23	135	103
Crystal Palace	28	13	10	5	44	28
Derby County	64	23	17	24	94	100
Doncaster Rovers	6	3	2	1	10	5
Everton	148	54	47	47	227	199
Fulham	64	30	24	10	106	69
Gainsborough Trinity	2	1	1	0	3	1
Glossop	2	0	2	0	4	4
Grimsby Town	14	8	1	5	27	24
Huddersfield Town	36	9	13	14	44	50
Hull City	18	7	5	6	25	16
Ipswich town	50	22	8	20	81	75
Leeds City	2	1	0	1	3	1

OPPONENTS	*P*	*W*	*D*	*L*	*F*	*A*
Leicester City	88	41	17	30	166	149
Leyton Orient	10	6	3	1	20	8
Lincoln City	6	2	3	1	13	8
Liverpool	136	39	34	63	154	215
Luton Town	46	21	17	8	75	46
Manchester City	124	47	31	46	165	178
Manchester United	148	35	39	74	186	242
Mansfield Town	2	0	2	0	4	4
Middlesbrough	80	27	20	33	124	137
Millwall	22	17	3	2	54	25
Newcastle United	132	56	29	47	215	191
Newport County	2	2	0	0	7	3
Northampton Town	2	1	1	0	3	1
Norwich City	48	22	12	14	82	59
Nottingham Forest	104	49	24	31	175	138
Notts County	34	16	8	10	52	45
Oldham Athletic	36	22	3	11	78	41
Oxford United	6	4	2	0	16	5
Plymouth Argyle	22	10	6	6	39	29
Portsmouth	40	16	13	11	64	58
Port Vale	12	9	1	2	40	15
Preston North End	52	22	13	17	96	79
Queen's Park Rangers	42	16	14	12	61	53
Reading	10	5	2	3	23	18
Rotherham United	2	1	1	0	3	1
Sheffield United	82	32	24	26	151	137
Sheffield Wednesday	96	41	17	38	160	143
Southampton	98	41	25	32	171	120
South Shields	2	2	0	0	5	0
Stockport County	6	4	1	1	11	5
Stoke City	72	39	15	18	120	79
Sunderland	96	35	26	35	129	132
Swansea City	26	15	5	6	56	28
Swindon Town	2	0	1	1	2	3
Tranmere Rovers	2	2	0	0	5	1
Watford	16	8	3	5	26	19
West Bromwich Albion	116	42	26	48	182	183
West Ham United	118	48	30	40	184	164
Wigan Athletic	12	5	5	2	27	11
Wimbledon	28	11	7	10	43	43
Wolverhampton W.	80	39	15	26	159	133
	3757	**1548**	**930**	**1279**	**6080**	**5269**

SPURS IN EUROPE

1961–62

European Champions Cup

13 September preliminary round first leg v Gornik Zabreze (a) 2–4
Jones, Dyson
Brown, Baker, Henry, Blanchflower, Norman, Mackay, Jones, White, R.Smith, Allen, Dyson
70,000

20 September preliminary round second leg v Gornik Zabreze (h) 8–1
Blanchflower, Jones 3, White, R.Smith 2, Dyson
Brown, Baker, Henry, Blanchflower, Norman, Mackay, Jones, White, R.Smith, Allen, Dyson
56,737

1 November first round first leg v Feyenoord (a) 3–1
Saul 2, Dyson
Brown, Baker, Henry, Blanchflower, Norman, Marchi, Jones, White, Saul, Clayton, Dyson
61,719

15 November first round second leg v Feyenoord (h) 1–1
Dyson
Brown, Baker, Henry, Blanchflower, Norman, Marchi, Jones, White, Saul, Mackay, Dyson
62,144

14 February second round first leg v Dukla Prague (a) 0–1
Brown, Baker, Henry, Marchi, Norman, Mackay, Medwin, White, R.Smith, Blanchflower, Jones
64,000

26 February second round second leg v Dukla Prague (h) 4–1
Mackay 2, R.Smith 2
Brown, Baker, Henry, Blanchflower, Norman, Marchi, Medwin, White, R.Smith, Mackay, Jones
55,388

21 March semi-final first leg v Benfica (a) 1–3
R.Smith
Brown, Baker, Henry, Marchi, Norman, Mackay, Greaves, White, R.Smith, Blanchflower, Jones
86,000

5 April semi-final second leg v Benfica (h) 2–1
Blanchflower (pen), R.Smith
Brown, Baker, Henry, Blanchflower, Norman, Mackay, Medwin, White, R.Smith, Greaves, Jones
64,448

1962–63

European Cup-winners' Cup

31 October first round first leg v Glasgow Rangers (h) 5–2
Norman, White 2, Allen, Shearer (og)
Brown, Baker, Henry, Blanchflower, Norman, Mackay, Medwin, White, Allen, Greaves, Jones
58,859

12 November first round second leg v Glasgow Rangers (a) 3–2
R.Smith R, Greaves
Brown, Baker, Henry, Blanchflower, Norman, Mackay, Medwin, White, R.Smith, Greaves, Jones
80,000

5 March second round first leg v Slovan Bratislava (a) 0–2
Brown, Baker, Henry, Marchi, Norman, Mackay, Saul, White, R.Smith, Greaves, Jones
32,000

14 March second round second leg v Slovan Bratislava (h) 6–0
Mackay, White, R.Smith, Greaves 2, Jones
Brown, Hopkins, Henry, Marchi, Norman, Mackay, Saul, White, R.Smith, Greaves, Jones
61,504

24 April semi-final first leg v OFK Belgrade (a) 2–1
White, Dyson
Brown, Baker, Henry, Marchi, Norman, Mackay, Greaves, J.Smith, R.Smith, White, Dyson
45,000

1 May semi-final second leg v OFK Belgrade (h) 3–1
Mackay, Jones, R.Smith
Brown, Baker, Henry, Blanchflower, Norman, Marchi, Jones, White, R.Smith, Mackay, Dyson
59,736

15 May Final v Atletico Madrid (Rotterdam) 5–1
White, Greaves 2, Dyson 2
Brown, Baker, Henry, Blanchflower, Norman, Marchi, Jones, White, R.Smith, Greaves, Dyson
40,000

1963–64

European Cup-winners' Cup

3 December first round first leg v Manchester United (h) 2–0
Mackay, Dyson
W.Brown, Baker, Henry, Marchi, Norman, Mackay, Jones, White, R.Smith, Greaves, Dyson
57,447

10 December first round second leg v Manchester United (a) 1–4
Greaves
W.Brown, Baker, Henry, Marchi, Norman, Mackay, Jones, White, R.Smith, Greaves, Dyson
48,639

1967–68
European Cup-winners' Cup

20 September first round first leg v Hadjuk Split (a) 2–0
Robertson, Greaves
Jennings, Kinnear, Knowles, Mullery, England, Beal, Robertson, Greaves, Gilzean, Venables, Saul
25,000

27 September first round second leg v Hadjuk Split (h) 4–3
Robertson 2, Gilzean, Venables
Jennings, Kinnear, Knowles, Mullery, England, Beal, Robertson, Greaves, Gilzean, Venables, Jones
38,623

29 November second round first leg v Olympique Lyonnais (a) 0–1
Jennings, Kinnear, Knowles, Mullery, Hoy, Mackay, Robertson, Greaves, Gilzean, Venables, Jones
10,997

13 December second round second leg v Olympique Lyonnais (h) 4–3
Greaves 2 (1 pen), Gilzean, Jones
Jennings, Kinnear, Knowles, Bond, Hoy, Mackay, Robertson, Greaves, Gilzean, Venables, Jones
41,895
(Spurs lost on away goals)

1971–72
UEFA Cup

14 September first round first leg v Keflavik (a) 6–1
Mullery 2, Coates, Gilzean 3
Jennings, Kinnear, Knowles, Mullery (Souness), England, Beal, Coates (Pearce), Perryman, Chivers, Peters, Gilzean
18,000

28 September second round second leg v Keflavik (h) 9–0
Knowles, Coates, Perryman, Chivers 3, Holder, Gilzean 2
Jennings, Evans, Knowles, Mullery (Pearce), England, Beal, Coates, Perryman, Chivers, Peters (Holder), Gilzean
23,818

20 October second round first leg v FC Nantes (a) 0–0
Jennings, Kinnear, Knowles, Mullery, England, Beal, Neighbour, Perryman, Chivers, Peters, Gilzean (Morgan)
20,033

2 November second round second leg v FC Nantes (h) 1–0
Peters
Jennings, Evans, Knowles, Pratt, England, Beal, Neighbour, Perryman, Chivers, Peters, Gilzean (Pearce)
32,630

8 December third round first leg v Rapid Bucharest (h) 3–0
Chivers 2, Peters
Jennings, Evans, Knowles, Coates (Pearce), England, Beal, Gilzean, Perryman, Chivers, Peters, Neighbour
30,702

15 December third round second leg v Rapid Bucharest (a) 2–0
Chivers, Pearce
Jennings, Evans, Knowles, Coates, Collins, Beal, Pratt, Perryman (Naylor), Chivers, Peters, Gilzean (Pearce)
12,000

7 March fourth round first leg v Unizale Textile Arad (a) 2–0
England, Morgan
Jennings, Evans, Knowles, Pratt, England, Beal, Gilzean (Collins), Perryman, Chivers, Peters, Morgan
20,000

21 March fourth round second leg v Unizale Textile Arad (h) 1–1
Gilzean
Jennings, Evans, Knowles, Coates, England, Naylor, Gilzean, Perryman, Pratt, Peters, Morgan
30,253

5 April semi-final first leg v AC Milan (h) 2–1
Perryman 2
Jennings, Kinnear, Knowles, Coates (Neighbour), England, Naylor, Gilzean, Perryman, Chivers, Peters, Mullery
42,064

19 April semi-final second leg v AC Milan (a) 1–1
Mullery
Jennings, Kinnear, Knowles, Mullery, England, Beal, Coates, Perryman, Chivers, Peters, Pratt (Naylor)
68,482

3 May Final first leg v Wolverhampton Wanderers (a) 2–1
Chivers 2
Jennings, Kinnear, Knowles, Mullery, England, Beal, Gilzean, Perryman, Chivers, Peters, Coates (Pratt)
38,362

17 May Final second leg v Wolverhampton Wanderers (h) 1–1
Mullery
Jennings, Kinnear, Knowles, Mullery, England, Beal, Gilzean, Perryman, Chivers, Peters, Coates
54,303

1972–73

UEFA Cup

13 September first round first leg v Lyn Oslo (a) 6–3
Pratt, Gilzean 2, Chivers 2, Peters
Jennings, Evans, Knowles, Pratt, England, Naylor, Gilzean, Perryman, Chivers, Peters, Pearce
10,770

27 September first round second leg v Lyn Oslo (h) 6–0
Chivers 3, Pearce, Coates 2
Jennings, Kinnear, Knowles, Pratt (Holder), England, Beal (Naylor), Gilzean, Perryman, Chivers, Pearce, Coates
21,109

25 October second round first leg v Olympiakos Piraeus (h) 4–0
Pearce 2, Chivers, Coates
Jennings, Evans, Knowles, Pearce, England, Beal (Naylor), Gilzean (Neighbour), Perryman, Chivers, Peters, Coates
27,815

8 November second round second leg v Olympiakos Piraeus (a) 0–1
Jennings, Evans, Knowles, Pearce, England, Dillon, Gilzean, Perryman, Chivers, Naylor, Pratt
35,000

29 November third round first leg v Red Star Belgrade (h) 2–0
Gilzean, Chivers
Jennings, Evans, Knowles, Pratt, England, Naylor, Gilzean, Perryman, Chivers, Peters, Pearce
23,958

13 December third round second leg v Red Star Belgrade (a) 0–1
Jennings, Evans, Knowles, Pratt, England, Kinnear, Coates, Perryman, Chivers, Peters, Pearce
70,000

7 March fourth round first leg v Vitoria Setubal (h) 1–0
Evans
Jennings, Kinnear, Knowles, Coates, England, Beal, Gilzean (Evans), Perryman, Chivers, Peters, Pearce
30,469

21 March fourth round second leg v Vitoria Setubal (a) 1–2
Chivers
Jennings, Kinnear, Knowles, Coates, England, Beal, Gilzean (Naylor), Perryman, Chivers, Peters, Pearce
30,000
(Spurs won on away goals)

10 April semi-final first leg v Liverpool (a) 0–1

Jennings, Kinnear, Knowles, Coates (Pearce), England, Beal, Gilzean, Perryman, Chivers (Evans), Peters, Pratt
42,174

25 April semi-final second leg v Liverpool (h) 2–1

Peters 2
Jennings, Kinnear (Evans), Knowles (Pearce), Coates, England, Beal, Gilzean, Perryman, Chivers, Peters, Pratt
46,919
(Spurs lost on away goals)

1973–74

UEFA Cup

19 September first round first leg v Grasshopper Zurich (a) 5–1

Evans, Chivers 2, Gilzean 2
Jennings, Evans, Knowles, Coates (Holder), England, Beal, Pratt, Perryman, Chivers, Peters, Neighbour (Gilzean)
11,200

3 October first round second leg v Grasshopper Zurich (h) 4–1

England, Peters 2, Lador (og)
Daines, Evans, Knowles, Pratt, England, Beal, Gilzean, Perryman, Chivers, Peters, Coates
18,105

24 October second round first leg v Aberdeen (a) 1–1

Coates
Daines, Evans, Kinnear (Naylor), Pratt, England, Beal, Gilzean, Perryman, McGrath, Peters, Coates (Neighbour)
30,000

7 November second round second leg v Aberdeen (h) 4–1

Peters, Neighbour, McGrath 2
Jennings, Evans, Knowles, Pratt, England, Beal, Gilzean, Perryman, Chivers, Peters, Neighbour (McGrath)
21,785

28 November third round first leg v Dinamo Tbilisi (a) 1–1

Coates
Jennings, Evans, Knowles, Pratt, England, Beal, Naylor, Perryman, Chivers, Peters, Coates
45,000

12 December third round second leg v Dinamo Tbilisi (h) 5–1

McGrath, Chivers 2, Peters 2
Jennings, Evans, Naylor, Pratt, England, Beal, McGrath, Perryman, Chivers, Peters, Coates
18,602

6 March fourth round first leg v 1FC Cologne (a) 2–1
McGrath, Peters
Jennings, Evans, Naylor, Pratt, England, Beal, McGrath, Perryman, Chivers, Peters, Dillon
28,000

20 March fourth round second leg v 1FC Cologne (h) 3–0
Chivers, Peters, Coates
Jennings, Evans, Naylor, Pratt, England, Beal, McGrath, Perryman, Chivers, Peters, Coates
40,968

10 April semi-final first leg v 1FC Lokomotive Leipzig (a) 2–1
Peters, Coates
Jennings, Evans, Naylor, Pratt, England, Beal, Neighbour, Perryman, Chivers, Peters, Coates (Holder)
74,000

24 April semi-final second leg v 1FC Lokomotive Leipzig (h) 2–0
McGrath, Chivers
Jennings, Kinnear, Naylor, Pratt (Holder), England, Beal, McGrath, Perryman, Chivers, Peters, Coates
41,280

21 May Final first leg v Feyenoord (h) 2–2
England, Van Deele (og)
Jennings, Evans, Naylor, Pratt, England, Beal (Dillon), McGrath, Perryman, Chivers, Peters, Coates
46,281

29 May Final second leg v Feyenoord (a) 0–2
Jennings, Evans, Naylor, Pratt (Holder), England, Beal, McGrath, Perryman, Chivers, Peters, Coates
62,988

1981–82

European Cup-winners' Cup

16 September first round first leg v Ajax (a) 3–1
Villa, Falco 2
Clemence, Hughton, Miller, Roberts, Villa, Perryman, Ardiles, Archibald, Galvin, Hoddle, Falco
21,742

29 September first round second leg v Ajax (h) 3–0
Ardiles, Galvin, Falco
Clemence, Hughton, Miller, Roberts (Lacy), Villa, Perryman, Ardiles, Archibald, Galvin, Hoddle, Falco
34,606

21 October second round first leg v Dundalk (a) 1–1
Crooks
Clemence, Hughton, Miller, Roberts, Hazard, Perryman, Ardiles, Archibald, Galvin (Smith), Hoddle, Crooks
17,500

4 November second round second leg v Dundalk (h) 1–0
Crooks
Clemence, Hughton, Miller, Roberts, Hazard, Perryman, Ardiles, Archibald, Galvin, Hoddle, Crooks
33,455

3 March third round first leg v Eintracht Frankfurt (h) 2–0
Miller, Hazard
Clemence, Hughton, Miller, Price, Hazard, Perryman, Ardiles, Archibald, Galvin, Hoddle, Crooks (Falco)
38,172

17 March third round second leg v Eintracht Frankfurt (a) 1–2
Hoddle
Clemence, Hughton, Miller, Price, Hazard, Perryman, Ardiles (Roberts), Archibald, Galvin, Hoddle, Falco (Villa)
45,000

7 April semi-final first leg v Barcelona (h) 1–1
Roberts
Clemence, Hughton, Miller (Jones), Price, Hazard, Perryman, Roberts, Villa, Galvin, Hoddle, Crooks
41,545

21 April semi-final second leg v Barcelona (a) 0–1
Clemence, Hughton, Price (Falco), Roberts, Hazard, Perryman, Villa, Archibald, Galvin, Hoddle, Crooks
80,000

1982–83

European Cup-winners' Cup

15 September first round first leg v Coleraine (a) 3–0
Archibald, Crooks 2
Clemence, Hughton, Price, Lacy, Brooke, Perryman, Mabbutt (Hazard), Archibald, Galvin, Villa, Crooks
12,000

28 September first round second leg v Coleraine (h) 4–0
Brooke, Mabbutt, Crooks, Gibson
Clemence (Parks), Hughton, Price, Lacy, Brooke, Perryman, Mabbutt, Archibald, Hazard, Villa, Crooks (Gibson)
20,925

20 October second round first leg v Bayern Munich (h) 1–1
Archibald
Clemence, Price, O'Reilly (Gibson), Miller, Lacy, Hazard, Brooke, Archibald (Falco), Mabbutt, Villa, Crooks
36,488

3 November second round second leg v Bayern Munich (a) 1–4
Hughton
Clemence, Price, Hughton, Miller (Perryman), Lacy, Hazard, Mabbutt, Archibald, Brooke (Hoddle), Villa, Crooks
55,000

1983–84

UEFA Cup

14 September first round first leg v Drogheda United (a) 6–0
Mabbutt 2, Falco 2, Galvin, Crooks
Clemence, Hughton, O'Reilly, Roberts, Price, Perryman, Mabbutt, Falco, Galvin, Brooke, Crooks
7,000

28 September first round second leg v Drogheda United (h) 8–0
Hughton, Roberts 2, Archibald, Falco 2, Brazil 2
Clemence, Hughton (O'Reilly), Galvin, Roberts, Price, Perryman, Mabbutt, Archibald, Falco, Hoddle, Brazil
19,831

19 October second round first leg v Feyenoord (h) 4–2
Galvin 2, Archibald 2
Clemence, Hughton, Galvin, Roberts, Stevens, Perryman, Mabbutt, Archibald, Falco, Hoddle, Brooke (Crook)
35,404

2 November second round second leg v Feyenoord (a) 2–0
Hughton, Galvin
Clemence, Hughton, Thomas, Roberts, Stevens, Perryman, Mabbutt, Archibald, Falco (Brazil), Hoddle, Galvin
49,241

23 November third round first leg v Bayern Munich (a) 0–1
Clemence, Hughton, Thomas, Roberts, Stevens, Perryman, Hazard (Brooke), Archibald, Falco, Hoddle, Dick (Brazil)
20,000

7 December third round second leg v Bayern Munich (h) 2–0
Archibald, Falco
Clemence, Hughton (O'Reilly), Thomas, Roberts, Stevens, Perryman, Cooke, Archibald, Falco, Hoddle, Dick (Brooke)
41,977

7 March fourth round first leg v FK Austria Vienna (h) 2–0
Archibald, Brazil
Parks, Stevens, Hughton, Roberts, Miller, Perryman, Ardiles, Archibald, Brazil, Hazard (Hoddle), Dick
34,069

21 March fourth round second leg v FK Austria Vienna (a) 2–2
Ardiles, Brazil
Clemence, Stevens, Hughton, Roberts (Thomas), Miller, Perryman, Ardiles, Archibald, Brazil (Falco), Mabbutt, Galvin
21,000

11 April semi-final first leg v Hadjuk Split (a) 1–2
Falco
Parks, Thomas, Hughton, Roberts, Miller, Perryman, Hazard, Archibald, Falco, Mabbutt (Crook), Galvin
40,000

25 April semi-final second leg v Hadjuk Split (h) 1–0
Hazard
Parks, Thomas, Hughton, Roberts, Miller, Perryman, Hazard, Archibald, Falco, Stevens (Mabbutt), Galvin
43,969
(Spurs won on away goals)

9 May Final first leg v Anderlecht (a) 1–1
Miller
Parks, Thomas, Hughton, Roberts, Miller, Perryman, Hazard, Archibald, Falco, Stevens (Mabbutt), Galvin
38,000

23 May Final second leg v Anderlecht (h) 1–1
Roberts
Parks, Thomas, Hughton, Roberts, Miller (Ardiles), Mabbutt (Dick), Hazard, Archibald, Falco, Stevens, Galvin
46,258
(After extra-time, Spurs won 4–3 on penalties)

1984–85

UEFA Cup

19 September first round first leg v SC Braga (a) 3–0
Falco 2, Galvin
Clemence, Mabbutt, Hughton, Roberts, Miller, Perryman, Chiedozie, Falco, Allen (Crooks), Hazard (Thomas), Galvin
30,000

3 October first round second leg v SC Braga (h) 6–0
Stevens, Hughton, Falco, Crooks 3
Clemence, Stevens, Hughton, Roberts, Miller (Hoddle), Perryman, Chiedozie, Falco (Cooke), Galvin, Hazard, Crooks
22,478

24 October second round first leg v Club Brugge KV (a) 1–2

Allen

Clemence, Stevens, Hughton, Roberts, Miller, Perryman, Chiedozie, Falco, Galvin, Hazard (Hoddle), Crooks (Allen)

27,000

7 November second round second leg v Club Brugge KV (h) 3–0

Roberts, Allen, Hazard

Clemence, Stevens, Mabbutt, Roberts, Miller, Perryman, Chiedozie (Brooke), Falco (Thomas), Allen, Hazard, Galvin

34,356

28 November third round first leg v Bohemians Prague (h) 2–0

Stevens, Ondra (og)

Clemence, Stevens, Mabbutt (Hughton), Roberts, Miller, Perryman, Chiedozie, Falco, Allen, Hoddle, Hazard (Cooke)

27,971

12 December third round second leg v Bohemians Prague (a) 1–1

Falco

Clemence, Stevens, Hughton, Roberts, Miller, Perryman, Chiedozie, Falco, Galvin, Hoddle (Mabbutt), Crooks (Thomas)

17,500

6 March fourth round first leg v Real Madrid (h) 0–1

Clemence, Stevens, Hughton, Hazard, Miller (Dick), Perryman, Chiedozie (Brooke), Falco, Galvin, Hoddle, Crooks

39,914

20 March fourth round second leg v Real Madrid (a) 0–0

Clemence, Thomas, Hughton, Roberts, Miller, Perryman, Hazard, Falco, Galvin (Dick), Hoddle, Crooks (Brooke)

95,000

1991–92

European Cup-winners' Cup

21 August preliminary round first leg v Sparkasse Stockerau (Vienna) 1–0

Durie

Thorstvedt, Fenwick, Van den Hauwe, Nayim, Howells, Mabbutt, Stewart, Durie, Samways (Hendon), Lineker, Allen

17,700

September preliminary round second leg v Sparkasse Stockerau (h) 1–0

Mabbutt

Walker, Fenwick, Van den Hauwe, Nayim, Howells (Sedgley), Mabbutt, Stewart, Durie, Samways, Lineker (Moran), Bergsson

28,072

17 September first round first leg v Hadjuk Split (Linz) 0–1
Walker, Fenwick, Van den Hauwe, Nayim, Howells (Allen), Mabbutt, Stewart, Durie, Samways, Lineker (Sedgley), Bergsson
7,000

2 October first round second leg v Hadjuk Split (h) 2–0
Tuttle, Durie
Thorstvedt, Bergsson, Sedgley, Nayim, Tuttle, Mabbutt, Stewart, Durie, Samways, Lineker (Hendon), Allen
24,297

23 October second round first leg v Porto (h) 3–1
Durie, Lineker 2
Thorstvedt, Edinburgh, Van den Hauwe, Sedgley, Walsh (Houghton), Mabbutt, Stewart, Durie, Samways (Bergsson), Lineker, Allen
23,621

7 November second round second leg v Porto (a) 0–0
Thorstvedt, Edinburgh, Van den Hauwe, Bergsson, Howells, Mabbutt, Stewart, Durie (Sedgley), Samways, Lineker (Walsh), Allen
55,000

4 March third round first leg v Feyenoord (a) 0–1
Thorstvedt, Fenwick, Van den Hauwe, Sedgley, Howells (Samways), Mabbutt, Stewart, Durie, Nayim, Lineker (Walsh), Allen
38,385

18 March third round second leg v Feyenoord (h) 0–0
Thorstvedt, Bergsson, Edinburgh, Sedgley, Howells (Houghton), Mabbutt, Stewart, Durie, Nayim (Walsh), Lineker, Allen
29,834

1999–2000

UEFA Cup

16 September first round first leg v Zimbru Chisinau (h) 3–0
Leonhardsen, Perry, Sherwood
Walker, Carr, Taricco (Edinburgh), Freund, Young, Perry, Leonhardsen, Sherwood, Armstrong (Dominguez), Iversen, Ginola
32,660

30 September first round second leg v Zimbru Chisinau (a) 0–0
Walker, Carr, Taricco (Edinburgh), Freund, Young, Perry, Leonhardsen, Clemence, Armstrong (Dominguez), Iversen, Nielsen
6,000

28 October second round first leg v 1FC Kaiserslautern (h) 1–0
Iversen (pen)
Walker, Carr, Taricco, Freund, Campbell, Perry, Leonhardsen, Sherwood, Fox (Clemence), Iversen, Ginola
35,177

4 November second round second leg v 1FC Kaiserslautern (a) 0–2
Walker, Carr, Edinburgh (Young), Freund, Campbell, Perry, Leonhardsen, Sherwood, Armstrong (Ginola), Iversen, Clemence
29,044

2006–07
UEFA Cup

14 September first round first leg v Slavia Prague (a) 1–0
Jenas
Robinson, Assou-Ekotto, Chimbonda, Dawson, King, Huddlestone (Davids), Jenas, Tainio, Zokora, Defoe (Keane), Mido
14,869

28 September first round second leg v Slavia Prague (h) 1–0
Keane
Robinson, Chimbonda, Davenport, Dawson, Lee, Jenas, Murphy (Ghaly), Ziegler (Tainio), Zokora, Keane, Mido
35,191

Group B
19 October v Besiktas (a) 2–0
Ghaly, Berbatov
Robinson, Assou-Ekotto, Chimbonda, Dawson, King, Ghaly (Lennon), Huddlestone, Jenas, Murphy (Ziegler), Berbatov (Defoe), Keane
42,000

2 November v Club Brugge (h) 3–1
Berbatov 2, Keane
Robinson, Assou-Ekotto, Chimbonda, Dawson, King, Ghaly, Jenas, Lennon (Murphy), Zokora, Berbatov (Mido), Keane
35,716

23 November v Bayer Leverkusen (a) 1–0
Berbatov
Robinson, Assou-Ekotto, Chimbonda, Dawson, King, Lennon, Malbranque (Huddlestone), Tainio, Zokora, Berbatov (Mido), Keane
22,500

14 December v Dinamo Bucharest (h) 3–1
Berbatov, Defoe 2
Robinson, Assou-Ekotto, Chimbonda (Stalteri), Dawson, King (Davenport), Ghaly, Huddlestone (Malbranque), Lennon, Zokora, Berbatov, Defoe
34,004

Round three - bye

8 March fourth round first leg v Sporting Braga (a) 2–3
Keane 2, Malbranque
Robinson, Chimbonda, Dawson, Gardner, Lee, Lennon, Malbranque, Tainio (Huddlestone), Zokora, Berbatov, Keane
15,000

15 March fourth round first leg v Sporting Braga (h) 3–2
Berbatov 2, Malbranque
Cerny, Chimbonda, Dawson, Lee, Stalteri, Huddlestone, Lennon (Ghaly), Malbranque, Zokora, Berbatov, Keane (Defoe)
33,761

5 April quarter-final first leg v Sevilla (a) 1–2
Keane
Robinson, Chimbonda, Dawson, Lee, Stalteri, Jenas, Lennon (Malbranque), Tainio (Ghaly), Zokora, Berbatov, Keane
32,000

12 April quarter-final second leg v Sevilla (h) 2–2
Defoe, Lennon
Robinson, Chimbonda, Dawson, King, Jenas, Lennon, Malbranque, Tainio, Zokora (Defoe), Berbatov, Keane
35,284

2007–08

UEFA CUP

20 September first round first leg v Anorthosis Famagusta (h) 6–1
Defoe 2, Dawson, Kaboul, Keane, Bent
Cerny, Chimbonda, Assou-Ekotto (Bale), Zokora, Kaboul, Dawson, Lennon, Huddlestone, Bent, Keane (Defoe), Malbranque (Taarabt)
35,780

4 October first round second leg v Anorthosis Famagusta (a) 1–1
Keane
Robinson, Boateng (Bale), Lee (Keane), Zokora, Dawson, Gardner, Stalteri, Huddlestone, Bent (Taarabt), Defoe, Malbranque
6,606

Group G
25 October v Getafe (h) 1–2
Defoe
Cerny, Chimbonda, Lee, Zokora (Tainio), Kaboul, Gardner (Dawson), Malbranque (Keane), Huddlestone, Berbatov, Defoe, Lennon
26,122

8 November v Hapoel Tel Aviv (a) 2–0
Keane, Berbatov
Robinson, Chimbonda, Lee, Zokora, Dawson, Malbranque (Defoe), Stalteri, Jenas (Boateng), Berbatov, Keane (Bent), Lennon
10,000

29 November v Aalborg BK (h) 3–2
Bent, Malbranque, Berbatov
Robinson, Chimbonda, Lee (Bent), Zokora, Dawson, Bale, Malbranque, Jenas (Huddlestone), Berbatov (Boateng), Keane, Lennon
29,758

6 December v Anderlecht (a) 1–1
Berbatov (pen)
Robinson, Chimbonda, Lee (Stalteri), Zokora, Dawson, Huddlestone, Malbranque, Jenas, Bent (Defoe), Keane (Berbatov), Lennon
22,500

14 February Round of 32 first leg v Slavia Prague (a) 2–1
Berbato, Keane
Cerny, Chimbonda, Huddlestone, Zokora, Woodgate, Tainio (O'Hara), Malbranque, Jenas, Berbatov, Keane (Bent), Lennon
11,134

21 February Round of 32 second leg v Slavia Prague (h) 1–1
O'Hara
Robinson, Chimbonda (Malbranque), Woodgate, Zokora, Kaboul, Tainio, O'Hara, Huddlestone, Berbatov (Keane), Bent, Lennon (Jenas)
34,224

6 March Round of 16 first leg v PSV Eindhoven (h) 0–1
Robinson, Chimbonda, Gilberto (O'Hara), Zokora, Woodgate, King (Taarabt), Malbranque, Jenas, Huddlestone, Berbatov, Keane, Lennon
33,259

12 March Round of 16 second leg v PSV Eindhoven (a) 1–0
Berbatov
Robinson, Chimbonda, Lee (Bent), Zokora, Woodgate, King (Lennon), Malbranque, Jenas, Berbatov, Keane (O'Hara), Huddlestone
33,000
(After extra–time, Spurs lost 5–6 on penalties)

2008–09

UEFA CUP

18 September first round first leg v Wisla Krakow (h) 2–1
Bentley, Bent
Gomes, Gunter (O'Hara), Bale, Zokora, Bentley, King, Lennon (Campbell), Jenas, Giovani (Assou–Ekotto), Bent, Woodgate
35,751

1 October first round second leg v Wisla Krakow (a) 1–1
OG (Glowacki)
Gomes, Gunter, Bale, Zokora, Woodgate, King, Lennon (Dawson), Jenas, Campbell (O'Hara), Bent, Modric (Huddlestone)
15,000

Group D
23 October v Udinese (a) 0–2
Gomes, Hutton, Bale, Zokora, Woodgate (Giovani), King, Lennon, Jenas, O'Hara, Bent, Assou–Ekotto (Modric)
22,000

6 November v Dinamo Zagreb (h) 4–0
Bent 3, Huddlestone
Gomes, Hutton, Bale, Zokora, Bentley (Bostock), Huddlestone, Lennon, Modric (Campbell), Dawson, Bent, Woodgate (Gunter)
32,788

27 November v NEC Nijmegen (a) 1–0
O'Hara
Gomes, Gunter, Bale, Zokora, Bentley (Mason), Huddlestone, Dawson, Woodgate, Campbell (Obika), Bent (Lennon), O'Hara
12,000

18 December v Spartak Moscow (h) 2–2
Modric, Huddlestone
Gomes, Gunter, Bale, Zokora, Bentley, Huddlestone, Modric, O'Hara, Campbell, Dawson, Gilberto (Lennon)
28,906

19 February Round of 32 first leg v Shakhtar Donetsk (a) 0–2
Gomes, Gunter, Chimbonda, Zokora, Bentley, Huddlestone, Parrett (Bostock), Jenas, Campbell, Giovani (Bent), Dawson
25,000

26 February Round of 32 second leg v Shakhtar Donetsk (h) 1–1
Giovani
Gomes, Gunter, Bale, Palacios, Chimbonda, Huddlestone, O'Hara (Parrett), Giovani, Campbell, Obika, Gilberto (Bostock)
30,595

2010–11

UEFA CHAMPIONS LEAGUE

17 August Play-off first leg v Young Boys (a) 2–3
Bassong, Pavlyuchenko
Gomes, Corluka, Bale, Palacios, Dawson, Bassong, Giovani, Modric (Kranjcar), Pavlyuchenko, Defoe (Keane), Assou-Ekotto (Huddlestone)
30,166

25 August Play-off second leg v Young Boys (h) 4–0
Crouch 3 (1 pen),Defoe
Gomes (Cudicini), Corluka, Bale (Kranjcar), King, Dawson, Huddlestone, Lennon, Palacios, Crouch, Defoe (Pavlyuchenko), Assou-Ekotto
34,709

Group A
14 September v Werder Bremen (a) 2–2
Crouch, OG (Pasanen)
Cudicini, Corluka, Bale, Kaboul, King, Huddlestone, Lennon (Palacios), Jenas, Crouch, Assou-Ekotto, Van der Vaart (Keane)
30,344

29 September v FC Twente (h) 4–1
Pavlyuchenko 2 (2 pens), Van der Vaart, Bale
Gomes, Hutton, Bale, King, Bassong, Huddlestone, Modric (Lennon), Assou–Ekotto, Pavlyuchenko (Keane), Crouch (Jenas),Van der Vaart
32,318

20 October v Internazionale (a) 3–4
Bale 3
Gomes, Hutton, Bale, Gallas, Bassong, Huddlestone (Palacios), Lennon, Jenas, Crouch (Keane), Modric (Cudicini), Assou–Ekotto
49,551

2 November v Internazionale (h) 3–1
Van der Vaart, Crouch, Pavlyuchenko
Cudicini, Hutton, Bale, Kaboul, Gallas, Huddlestone, Lennon (Palacios), Modric, Crouch (Pavlyuchenko), Assou–Ekotto, Van der Vaart (Jenas)
36,310

24 November v Werder Bremen (h) 3–0
Kaboul, Modric, Crouch
Gomes, Hutton, Bale (Kranjcar), Kaboul, Gallas, Assou–Ekotto, Lennon, Jenas (Palacios), Pavlyuchenko (Defoe), Crouch, Modric
33,546

7 December v FC Twente (a) 3–3
OG (Wisgerhof), Defoe 2
Gomes, Corluka, Bale, Palacios, Gallas, Bassong, Kranjcar (Crouch), Jenas (Lennon), Pavlyuchenko (Keane), Defoe, Assou–Ekotto
24,000

15 February Round of 16 first leg v AC Milan (a) 1–0
Crouch
Gomes, Corluka (Woodgate), Assou–Ekotto, Palacios, Dawson, Gallas, Lennon, Sandro, Crouch, Pienaar (Kranjcar), Van der Vaart (Modric).
75,652

9 March Round of 16 second leg v AC Milan (h) 0–0
Gomes, Corluka, Assou–Ekotto, Sandro, Dawson, Gallas, Lennon, Modric, Crouch (Pavlyuchenko), Pienaar (Jenas), Van der Vaart (Bale).
34,320

5 April Quarter-final first leg v Real Madrid (a) 0–4
Gomes, Corluka (Bassong), Bale, Sandro, Dawson, Gallas, Modric, Jenas, Crouch, Assou–Ekotto, Van der Vaart (Defoe).
71,657

13 April Quarter-final second leg v Real Madrid (h) 0–1
Gomes, Corluka, Bale, Gallas, Dawson, Huddlestone (Sandro), Lennon (Defoe), Modric (Kranjcar), Pavlyuchenko, Assou–Ekotto, Van der Vaart.
34,311

SPURS IN PRE-LEAGUE DAYS

With the exception of the 1892–93 season, when they competed in the short-lived Southern Alliance, Spurs fixtures prior to joining the Southern League in 1896–97 consisted of friendly or Cup matches. In the early days of the club's existence it was down to the club secretary to send match reports to the local newspaper, but even when he did space was limited and match information was only given in the barest detail. It was only as the club's reputation grew that more than passing interest was shown in them by the local press and their matches came to be reported in any detail. All the information that has been traced for seasons prior to 1896–97 is set out in this section.

1882–83

Friendlies

30 September v Radicals (Unknown) 0–2
Team unknown

6 January v Latymer (a) 1–8
Team unknown

1883–84

Friendlies

6 October v Brownlow Rovers (h) 9–0
Scorers unknown
Leaman, Tyrell, Dexter, Casey, Lovis, Lomas, Cottrell, Watson, Fisher, Harston, Buckle
(Jull mentioned in match report but not in team line up recalled years later by a former player)

13 October v Evelyn (h) 6–1
Team unknown
(One Spurs goal disputed)

20 October v Grange Park (h) 1–3
Buckle,
Team unknown but included Buckle

27 October v Leyton Rovers (h) 1–0
Buckle
Team unknown but included Buckle

10 November v Brownlow Rovers (a) 1–0
Jull
Team unknown but included Jull
(Abandoned after 80 mins – ball burst)

24 November v Sekforde Rovers (h) 2–0
Team unknown but included Baillie, Watson and Buckle

1 December v Sekforde Rovers (a) 1–0
Team unknown but included Tyrell

8 December v Leyton Rovers (a) 1–3
Buckle
Team unknown but Spurs fielded only 10 players including Buckle

15 December v Claremont (h) 2–0
Team unknown
(60 min game)

22 December v Latymer (h) 2–0
Buckle and unknown
Team unknown but included Buckle

12 January v Woodgrange (a) 0–1
Team unknown but included Jull, Harston and Buckle

19 January v Grafton (a) 1–0
Team unknown

26 January v Albion (h) 0–1
Team unknown
(50 min game)

2 February v Clarence (a) 1–0
Team unknown

9 February v Albion (a) 3–0
Jull 3
Team unknown but included Jull and Thompson

16 February v Hanover United third XI (h) 1–2
Jull
Team unknown but included Jull
(80 min game)

23 February v Grange Park (h) 1–0
Buckle
Team unknown but included Buckle
(60 min game)

8 March v Hanover United second XI (a) 2–0
Team unknown

15 March v Latymer (a) 2–0
Watson, Randall
Team unknown but included Jull, Randall, Watson, Tyrell and Baillie

22 March v Remington (h) 2–0
Jull, Watson
Team unknown but included Jull, Tyrell, Watson, Baillie and Buckle
(80 min game)

1884–85

Friendlies

4 October v Remington (h) 4–0
Amos 2, Buckle 2
Team unknown but included Jull, Amos, Bull and Buckle

11 October v Abbey (h) 1–0
Amos
Team unknown but included Jull, Amos, Bull, Tyrell, Harston and Buckle

18 October v Woodgrange (h) 4–5
Mason, Unknown 3
Team unknown but included Jull, Amos, Bull, Mason, Tyrell and Buckle

25 October v Grange Park (h) 4–0
Team unknown but included Jull, Randall and Tyrell
(60 min game)

1 November v Sekforde Rovers (a) 4–0
Team unknown but included Jull, Cawkill, Tyrell, Amos and Buckle

8 November v Marlborough Rovers (h) 1–0
Team unknown

15 November v Latymer (a) 2–1
Team unknown

22 November v St Peters second XI (h) 3–2
Team unknown

29 November v Hadley (h) 0–1
Team unknown
(60 min game)

6 December v Tottenham (h) 4–0
Team unknown

13 December v Woodgrange (a) 0–0
Team unknown but Spurs fielded only 10 men
(40 min game)

20 December v Sekforde Rovers (h) 5–0
Team unknown

26 December v Grove (h) result unknown
Team unknown

27 December v Enfield (h) 3–0
Team unknown

3 January v Hadley (a) result unknown
Team unknown

10 January v Abbey (a) 1–1
Team unknown but Spurs fielded only nine men
(Both goals disputed)

17 January v Grange Park (a) 0–1
Team unknown but included Bumberry, Cawkill, Lomas and Mason

24 January v Victoria Wanderers (h) 5–0
Team unknown
(60 min game)

31 January v St Martins (h) 1–0
Team unknown

7 February v Fillebrook (h) 3–0
Buckle, Unknown 2
Team unknown but Spurs fielded only 10 men including Jull, Bull, Buckle, Mason and Harston

14 February v Latymer (h) 0–0
Team unknown
(75 min game)

21 February v St Peters (h) 1–1
Team unknown

28 February v Bedford Rovers (a) 1–1
Team unknown but Spurs fielded only 10 men

7 March v Marlborough Rovers (a) 1–0
Team unknown

14 March v Victoria Wanderers (a) Result unknown
Team unknown

21 March v Remington (a) Result unknown
Team unknown

28 March v St Martins (a) Result unknown
Team unknown

4 April v Mars (h) Result unknown
Team unknown

11 April v Grove (a) Result unknown
Team unknown

1885–86

London Association Cup
17 October first round v St Albans (h) 5–2
Harston, Mason 2, Amos 2
Bumberry, Jull, Tyrell, Bull, Lovis, Casey, Buckle, Harston, Mason, Amos, Cottrell
400

7 November second round v Casuals (h) 0–8
Bumberry, Jull, Tyrell, Bull, Conu, Casey, Buckle, Harston, Mason, Amos, Cottrell

Friendlies
3 October v Silesia College (a) 4–3
Team unknown

10 October v Grange Park (a) 0–3
Team unknown

24 October v Westminster Rovers (h) 3–1
Team unknown

14 November v Fairfield (a) 0–1
Team unknown but Spurs fielded only 10 men including Jull, Adlington, Bull and Harston

21 November v South Hackney (a) 3–1
Team unknown

28 November v Dalston Rovers (h) 3–0
Team unknown

26 December v Edmonton Independent (a) 2–1
Team unknown

2 January v St Martins (h) 3–0
Team unknown

9 January v Dalston Rovers (a) win but score unknown
Team unknown

16 January v Woodgrange (a) 0–3
Team unknown but Spurs fielded only 10 men

6 February v Edmonton Independent (h) 4–1
Team unknown

13 February v Grange Park second XI (h) 0–3
Team unknown

20 February v South Hackney (h) 8–0
Team unknown

27 February v Silesia College (h) 1–2
Team unknown

6 March v Ilford (h) 6–1
Team unknown

13 March v Rutland (h) 5–0
Randall 4, Mason
Team unknown but included Mason and Randall

20 March v Upton Excelsior (h) win but score unknown
Team unknown

27 March v Enfield Lock (h) 7–0
Team unknown
(One Spurs goal disputed)

10 April v Park (h) 8–0
Scorers unknown
Anderson, Jull, Tyrell, Bull, Casey, Lovis, Buckle, Harston, Mason, Cottrell, Randall

17 April v Hermitage (h) 3–0
Team unknown

1886–87

London Association Cup
16 October first round v Upton Park (a) 0–6
Lomas, Jull, Tyrell, H.Bull, Casey, Lovis, Cottrell, Randall, Buckle, Harston, Mason

East End Cup
18 December first round v Phoenix (h) 6–0
Buckle 2, Mason 2, Harston 2
Anderson, Jull, Tyrell, H.Bull, Casey, Lovis, Buckle, Mason, Cottrell, Harston, Randall

15 January second round v Park (h) 2–0
Mason, Unknown
Anderson, Jull, Tyrell, H.Bull, Casey, Lovis, Buckle, Cottrell, Mason, Harston, Randall

19 February third round v St Lukes (h) 2–1
Buckle, Mason
Anderson, Jull, Tyrell, H.Bull, Casey, Lovis, Buckle, Harston, Mason, Cottrell, Randall

26 March semi-final v London Caledonians (h) 1–0
Team unknown
(London Caledonians failed to attend. Spurs kicked off, scored and claimed result but replay ordered)

16 April semi-final replay v London Caledonians (h) 0–1
Anderson, Jull, Tyrell, H.Bull, Casey, Lovis, Buckle, Harston, Mason, Cottrell, Randall

Friendlies
2 October v South Hackney (h) 13–1
Team unknown

9 October v Woodford Bridge (h) 2–0
Team unknown

30 October v Old St Pauls (h) 1–1
Team unknown

13 November v Silesia (a) 2–3
Buckle, Mason
Bumberry, Jull, Tyrell, H.Bull, E.Bull, Casey, Lovis, Cottrell, Mason, Randall, Buckle

27 November v Fillebrook (a) 1–4
Buckle
Team unknown but included Jull, Mason and Buckle

4 December v Iona (a) 5–0
Cottrell, Harston, Randall, Purdie 2
Team unknown but included Randall, Cottrell, Purdie and Harston

27 December v Dreadnought (h) 6–0
Team unknown

22 January v Foxes (h) 2–1
Team unknown
(80 min game)

5 February v Park (h) 4–1
Team unknown but Spurs fielded only 10 men

12 February v Fillebrook (h) 3–0
Team unknown

19 February v St Lukes (h) 2–1
Buckle, Mason
Anderson, Jull, Tyrell, H.Bull, Casey, Lovis, Buckle, Harston, Mason, Cottrell, Randall

5 March v Edmonton Association (a) 3–1
Team unknown
(One Spurs' goal disputed)

19 March v London Caledonians (North Greenwich) 0–2
Anderson, Jull, Tyrell, Lovis, Casey, H.Bull, Randall, Harston, Mason, Cottrell, Buckle
(Due to be semi-final of East End Cup but as pitch in a poor state clubs agreed to play friendly)

23 April v Enfield Lock (h) 7–1
Team unknown
(One Spurs goal disputed)

1887–88

London Senior Cup

8 October first round v Hendon (a) 0–6
Anderson, Jull, Tyrell, Bull, Lovis, Baldock, Buckle, Harston, Mason, Cottrell, Bird

Friendlies

1 October v Buckhurst Hill (h) 6–1
Team unknown

12 November v Nondescripts (h) 6–1
Team unknown

19 November v Royal Arsenal (h) 2–1
Team unknown
(Abandoned after 75 mins – bad light)

3 December v Luton Town (a) 2–1
Mason, Harston
Team unknown but included Mason, Cottrell and Harston

10 December v Priory (a) 3–0
Team unknown but Spurs fielded only 10 men

24 December v Balmoral (h) 1–1
Team unknown

31 December v St Matrins (h) 3–0
Team unknown

7 January v St Brides (h) 3–2
Buckle, Cottrell, Mason
Team unknown but included Cottrell, Mason and Buckle

14 January v Bowes Park (a) 2–2
Team unknown but included Jull, Tyrell, Bull, Lovis, Casey, Hudson, Baldock, Mason, Harston and Adlington

21 January v Old St Pauls (a) 2–1
Team unknown

4 February v Royal Arsenal (a) 2–6
Team unknown but Spurs fielded only nine men

18 February v Olympic (a) 5–1
Team unknown

17 March v St Brides (a) 3–0
Buckle, Unknown 2
Team unknown but included Buckle

2 April v Clapton (a) 1–6
Team unknown

1888–89

London Senior Cup

13 October first round v Old Etonians (h) 2–8
Buckle, Purdie
Baldock, Jull, Crossley, Bull, Casey, Tyrell, Buckle, Harston, Purdie, Mason, Cottrell

Middlesex Senior Cup

10 January first round v Civil Engineers (h) 0–0
Team unknown

19 January first round replay v Civil Engineers (a) 1–4
Team unknown but included Jull, Casey, Buckle and Harston

Friendlies

22 September v Royal Arsenal (a) 1–0
Team unknown but included Baldock, Jull and Casey

29 September v St Albans (a) 1–2
Scorer unknown
Baldock, Jull, Crossley, Hudson, Tyrell, Casey, Cottrell, Williams, Mason, Harston, Buckle

20 October v Clapton (h) 2–5
Team unknown

17 November v Millwall Rovers (h) 1–1
Team unknown
(60 min game)

24 November v Plaistow (h) 4–0
Team unknown but included Jull

1 December v Old St Marks (h) 5–1
Team unknown but Spurs fielded only 10 men

8 December v Upton Excelsior (h) 3–3
Team unknown

15 December v Plaistow (a) 2–1
Payne, Buckle
Team unknown but Spurs fielded only 10 men including Payne and Buckle

22 December v Bowes Park (a) 4–0
Jull 2, Buckle, Cottrell
Team unknown but included Jull, Bull, Cottrell and Buckle

26 December v Orion Gymnasium (h) 6–1
Team unknown but included Mason

16 January v Windsor Phoenix (a) 1–2
Buckle
Adlington, Jull, Crossley, Casey, Simpson, Latymer, Buckle, Harston, Parker, Mason, Goddard

2 March v Windsor Phoenix (a) 1–2
Buckle
Team unknown but included Buckle.

9 March v Royal Arsenal (h) 0–1
Team unknown

16 March v Edmonton (h) 1–1
Harston
Team unknown but included Harston

13 April v Orion Gymnasium (h) 6–1
Team unknown

1889–90

London Senior Cup

2 November second round v Old St Marks (a) 0–4
Walford, Jull, Littleford, Casey, Davies, Baldock, Buckle, Harston, Marpole, Cottrell, Lovis

Middlesex Senior Cup

18 January first round v Old St Stephens (a) 4–2
Lovis, Harston, Humber 2
Team unknown but included Jull, Littleford, Lovis, Casey, Humber and Harston

11 February second round v Clapton (h) 2–4
Team unknown

Friendlies

21 September v Royal Arsenal (a) 1–10
Parker
Anderson, Griffith, Jull, Baldock, Pracey, Ayres, Cottrell, Cadman, Tyrell, Buckle, Parker
1,500

28 September v Westminster (h) 13–0
Buckle, Harston, Cottrell, Tyrell, Unknown 9
Team unknown but included Cadman, Lovis, Tyrell, Cottrell, Harston and Buckle

5 October v Vulcan (h) 5–1
Lovis, Jull, Unknown 3
Walford, Marpole, Jull, Casey, Baldock, Leaman, Buckle, Harston, Mason, Cottrell, Lovis

12 October v Iona (h) 10–0
Jull 5, Unknown 5
Team unknown but included Littleford, Lovis, Davies and Jull

19 October v Edmonton (a) 2–3
Team unknown

9 November v Clapton (h) 5–3
Team unknown

16 November v Finchley (a) 1–1
Team unknown

23 November v Hampstead (h) 1–0
Team unknown

30 November v Foxes (h) 1–0
Team unknown

4 January v Foxes (h) 1–1
Cottrell
Team unknown but included Walford, Jull, Cottrell and Buckle

11 January v Romford (a) 0–0
Team unknown
(40 min game)

1 February v Robin Hood (h) 1–0
Team unknown

8 February v Vulcan (h) 2–1
Buckle, Bassett
Team unknown but included Casey, Bassett and Buckle

1 March v Swindon Town (a) 1–2
Cottrell
Walford, Jull, Littleford, Casey, Simpson, Bassett, Buckle, Perry, Humber, Cottrell, Harston
(One Swindon goal disputed)

8 March v Edmonton (h) 1–4
Unknown
Walford, Littleford, Jull, Casey, Cadman, Bassett, Lovis, Cottrell, Humber, Harston, Buckle

15 March v Unity (h) 3–1
Team unknown but included Jull and Bassett

4 April v Dreadnought (h) 0–1
Team unknown

5 April v Uxbridge (a) 2–2
Team unknown

7 April v Maidenhead (a) 3–2
Team unknown

Matches were arranged against Acton, Luton Town, Old St Stephens, Olympic, Wolverton and Woodford, but no details are known. Spurs also drew a match against Foxes 2–2 at home on an unknown date with Bumbery scoring one of the goals.

1890–91

London Senior Cup
1 November second preliminary round v Queen's Park Rangers (a) 1–1
Cottrell
Team unknown but included Walford, Jull, Simpson, Cottrell, Baxter and Buckle

8 November second prel round replay v Queen's Park Rangers (h) 2–1
Buckle, Harston
Team unknown but included Baxter, Harston and Buckle
350

22 November third prel round v Barking (h) 2–0
Baxter, Buckle
Team unknown but included Walford, Jull, Casey, Baxter, Harston and Buckle
400

24 January first round v Barnes (a) 1–0
Cottrell
Team unknown but included Simpson and Cottrell

31 January second round v Millwall Athletic (a) 1–5
Harston
Walford, Jull, Bassett, Simpson, Cadman, Drysdale, Baxter, Cottrell, Perry, Harston, Buckle
200

Middlesex Senior Cup
7 February first round v Orion Gymnasium (h) 7–1
Team and scorers unknown

14 February second round v Clapton (h) lost but score unknown
Team unknown

Friendlies
27 September v Hampstead (h) 6–3
Team and scorers unknown

4 October v Grove House (h) result unknown
Team unknown

11 October v Edmonton (a) 4–6
Team unknown

18 October v Luton Town (a) 1–4
Baxter
Team unknown but included Baxter

25 October v Northumberland Fusiliers (h) 1–0
Team unknown

15 November v City Ramblers (h) 1–0
Buckle
Team unknown but included Cottrell and Buckle

6 December v Unity (a) 1–1
Pilbrow
Team unknown but Spurs fielded only nine men including Jull and Pilbrow

21 February v Vulcan (h) 6–0
Team unknown

28 February v Old St Stephens (h) 3–0
Buckle 2, Unknown
Team unknown but included Jull and Buckle

7 March v 1st Scots Guards (h) result unknown
Team unknown

1891–92

London Senior Cup

10 October first round v Caledonian Athletic (h) 5–3
Cottrell, Bassett 2, H.Leese, Millard
Team unknown but included J.Jull, Bassett, Cadman, Cottrell, Lovis, H.Leese and Millard

31 October second round v Hampstead (a) 3–2
Lovis, Cottrell, Buckle
Anderson, J.Jull, Bassett, Casey, Monk, Simpson, Lovis, Harston, Cottrell, Buckle, H.Leese

21 November third round v City Ramblers (a) 1–4
Leese H (pen)
Monk, J.Jull, Bassett, Casey, Bull, Simpson, Lovis, Harston, Cottrell, Buckle, H.Leese

Middlesex Senior Cup

5 December second round v Minerva (a) 0–2
Team unknown but included Monk, J.Jull, Bassett, Lovis, Miller and H.Leese

Luton Charity Cup

7 November first round v Coldstream Guards (h) 3–3
Harston, Cottrell, Opponent (og)
Team unknown but included Anderson, Dingwell, Fox, H.Leese, Cottrell and Harston

14 November first round replay v Coldstream Guards (h) 7–2
Cottrell 5, Millard, Weston
Team unknown but included Monk, Dingwell, Millard, Cottrell, Weston, Lovis and H.Leese (played at home by mutual consent)

19 December v second round 1st Scots Guards (a) 0–4
Team unknown but included Monk

Friendlies

26 September v Hampstead (h) 6–2
Scorers unknown
Team unknown but included J.Jull, Bull and F.Leese

3 October v Grange Park (h) 4–2
Team unknown but Spurs fielded only 10 men

24 October v Clapton (h) 1–2
Millard
Team unknown but included Anderson, J.Jull, Simpson, Fox, Lovis, Bassett, Cottrell, H.Leese and Millard

28 November v Old St Stephens (h) 0–0
Monk, J.Jull, Dingwell, Bull, Casey, Bassett, Lovis, Fox, Cottrell, Buckle (ten men only)

12 December v Forest Swifts (h) 1–1
Scorer unknown
Monk, J.Jull, Casey, Shillingworth, Miller, H.Leese, Harkins, Lovis, Weston, Shepherd (10 men only)
(Abandoned after 60 mins – bad light)

2 January v Uxbridge (h) 3–0
Weston, Tyler, H.Leese
Monk, J.Jull, Coulson, Bassett, F.Leese, Casey, Sykes, Weston, Tyler, Miller, H.Leese

9 January v Queen's Park Rangers (h) 1–2
Tyler
Monk, J.Jull, F.Leese, Casey, Crossley, Bull, Cottrell, Weston, Tyler, Joel, H.Leese

23 January v Westminster Criterion (h) 2–2
Sykes, Tyler
Monk, J.Jull, Casey, Bull, Briggs, Miller, Sykes, Weston, Tyler, Brigden, Ellis

30 January v Old St Lukes (h) 3–1
Team and scorers unknown

6 February v St Albans (a) 1–2
Tyler
Monk, J.Jull, Baldock, H.Leese, Briggs, Casey, Buckle, Hurry, Tyler, Hepburn, Sykes
1,000

13 February v Clapton (a) 2–0
Miller, Weston
Monk, J.Jull, Harston, Hurry, Briggs, Tyler, Buckle, Miller, Weston, Hepburn, Sykes

20 February v City Ramblers (h) result unknown
Team unknown

26 February v Hampstead (h) 6–2
Team unknown but included J.Jull, Bull and F.Leese

27 February v Grenadier Guards (h) 9–0
Barnes, Tyler, Barber, Sykes 2, Unknown 4
Team unknown but included Briggs, Tyler, Barber, Barnes, Weston and Sykes

3 March v Grange Park (h) 4–2
Team unknown

12 March v Casuals (h) 3–1
Lovis 2, Hepburn
Monk, J.Jull, Coulson, Casey, Briggs, Bull, Lovis, Harston, Tyler, Hepburn, H.Leese

26 March v Luton Town (a) 1–3
Scorer unknown
Monk, Coulson, J.Jull, Casey, Briggs, H.Jull, Sykes, Harston, Tyler, Hepburn, Williams

18 April v St Albans (a) 2–0
Briggs, Unknown
Monk, Renals, J.Jull, Edwards, Shillingworth, Casey, Shepherd, Brigden, Briggs, Hopkins, Sykes

Matches were arranged against Carpenters Institute, Gresham, Maidenhead, Orion Gymnasium and Shalford St Peters but details are not known.

1892–93

Southern Alliance
24 September v Polytechnic (a) 2–1
Brigden, Sykes
Team unknown but included Monk, Jull, Moody, Welham, Cottrell, Cubberley, Brigden and Sykes

15 October v Old St Stephens (a) 0–3
Monk, Moody, Welham, Jull, Simpson, Briggs, Brigden, Ellis, Cottrell, Harston, Sykes

5 November v Windsor and Eton (a) 2–1
Weston, Unknown
Monk, Moody, Welham, Jull, Briggs, Simpson, Weston, Cottrell, Brigden, Ellis, Sykes

19 November v Erith (h) 3–2
Briggs, Jull 2
Monk, Moody, Welham, Casey, Briggs, Simpson, Sykes, Cottrell, Jull, Brigden, Ellis

14 January v Erith (a) 1–2
Sykes
Team unknown but included Monk, Jull, Welham, Casey, Brigden and Sykes

21 January v Slough (a) 3–3
H.Lovis, Bell 2
Monk, Moody, Jull, Baldock, Casey, J.Lovis, Sykes, Bell, S.Lovis, Ellis, H.Lovis

4 February v Slough (h) 5–2
Bell 2, Jull 2, Opponent (og)
Monk, Moody, Welham, P.Lovis, Briggs, Bull, Sykes, Baxter, Jull, S.Lovis, Bell

11 February v Polytechnic (h) 2–2
Sykes 2
Monk, Moody, Welham, Casey, Briggs, Jull, Sykes, Bell, Cottrell, Brigden, Ellis

25 February v Upton Park (h) 1–0
Bell
Hart, Moody, Jull, Casey, Briggs, Bull, Cubberley, Sykes, Bell, Brigden, Ellis
1,000

4 March v Windsor and Eton (h) 5–2
Baxter 2, Gilderson, Fortnam, Cattell
Hart, Moody, F.Markham, W.Markham, Jull, E.Markham, Sykes, Baxter, Gilderson, Fortnam, Cattell

25 March v Old St Stephens (h) 1–2
Brigden
Monk, Rose, Welham, Jull, Gamble, Bull, Sykes, Cubberley, Cattell, Brigden, Ellis
2,500

8 April v Upton Park (a) 4–1
Team unknown but included Briggs and Sykes

London Senior Cup
3 December third round v Polytechnic (a) 2–2
Scorers unknown
Monk, Jull, Welham, Casey, Briggs, Simpson, Sykes, Bull, Cottrell, Brigden, Ellis

17 December third round replay v Polytechnic (h) 3–0
Jull 3
Team unknown but included Moody, Welham and Jull

28 January fourth round v Casuals (h) 0–1
Monk, Moody, Welham, Casey, Briggs, Simpson, Sykes, Cottrell, Jull, Brigden, P.Lovis
3,000

Wolverton & District Charity Cup
15 April semi-final v Smethwick 0–2
Hart, Jull, Moody, Gamble, Briggs, Thornley, Sykes, Meggs, Cattell, Brigden, Ellis
1,500
(Played at Wolverton)

Friendlies
17 September v Paddington (h) 10–0
Team unknown but included Monk, Jull, Moody, Welham, Cottrell, Sykes, Brigden and Lomas

1 October v Royal Arsenal Athletic (h) 3–0
Jull, Harston 2
Monk, Moody, Welham, Jull, Briggs, Simpson, Sykes, Lomas, Cottrell, Harston, Ellis
600

8 October v second Coldstream Guards (h) 6–0
Team unknown

22 October v 1st Coldstream Guards (h) 3–2
Baxter, Cottrell 2
Monk, Moody, Welham, Jull, Briggs, Simpson, Sykes, Cottrell, Baxter, Brigden, Ellis

29 October v second Scots Guards (h) 2–4
Baxter 2
Team unknown but included Monk, Moody, Briggs, Cottrell, Baxter and Brigden
700

12 November v Clapton (h) 1–2
Team unknown
(70 min game)

26 November v Caledonian Athletic (h) 5–0
Team unknown

10 December v Hampstead (h) 1–1
Team unknown

24 December v Coldstream Guards (h) result unknown
Team unknown

26 December v Edmonton (h) result unknown
Team unknown

27 December v Maidstone (a) 0–0
Team unknown

18 February v London Welsh (h) 2–2
Briggs, Fortnam
Team unknown but included Hart, Jull, Briggs, Fortnam and Sykes

11 March v Queen's Park Rangers (h) 1–0
Brigden
Team unknown but included Hart, Jull, Bull, Briggs, Cubberley, Brigden and Ellis

1 April v City Ramblers (h) 1–0
Palmer
Monk, Moody, Jull, Baldock, Tyrell, Bull, Meggs, Fortnam, Palmer, Brigden, Ellis

22 April v London Welsh (h) 4–1
Sykes 2, Cottrell 2
Moody, Rose, Jull, F.Markham, Briggs, Bull, Sykes, Baxter, Cottrell, Brigden, Ellis

1893–94

FA Amateur Cup
11 November first round v Vampires (h) 3–1
Briggs, Mills, Taylor
Monk, Moody, Welham, Shepherd, Briggs, Jull, Sykes, Cubberley, Mills, Taylor, Ellis

London Senior Cup
21 October first round v Old St Marks (h) 0–0
Monk, Jull, Welham, Shepherd, Briggs, Newby, Sykes, Cubberley, Tyler, Hepburn, Burton
2,000

28 October first round replay v Old St Marks (h) 1–6
Briggs
Monk, Jull, Welham, Shepherd, Briggs, Newby, Sykes, Cubberley, Bowyer, Brigden, Ellis
(played at home by mutual consent)

Middlesex Senior Cup
13 January first round v third Grenadier Guards (h) 1–1
Cubberley
Monk, Rose, Welham, Shepherd, Briggs, Jull, Sykes, Cubberley, Shaw, Coleman, Renals

20 January first round replay v third Grenadier Guards (h) 0–2
Monk, Jull, Rose, Shepherd, Casey, Newby, Sykes, Cubberley, Briggs, Renals, Shearing
(played at home by mutual consent)

London Charity Cup
9 December first round v Crusaders (h) 2–5
Sykes, Taylor
Monk, Moody, Welham, Shepherd, Briggs, Jull, Sykes, Cubberley, Mills, Taylor, Renals
2,000

Wolverton & District Charity Cup
27 January first round v Chesham (h) 2–2
Sykes, Jull
Monk, Moody, Welham, Shepherd, Briggs, Newby, Sykes, Cubberley, Milne, MacDonald, Jull

24 February first round replay v Chesham (a) 3–1
Cubberley, MacLachlan, Payne
Monk, Jull, Welham, Shepherd, Briggs, Newby, Sykes, Cubberley, Milne, MacLachlan, Payne
500

10 March semi-final v Smethwick (Wolverton) 0–1
Monk, Jull, Welham, Shepherd, Briggs, Newby, Shaw, Cubberley, Milne, MacLachlan, Payne

Friendlies
16 September v Enfield (a) 1–5
Hepburn
Team unknown but included Monk, Moody, Welham, Newby, Hepburn, Baker, Ellis and Sykes

23 September v Romford (h) 2–2
Sykes, Meggs
Monk, Jull, Welham, Kingan, Newby, Briggs, Sykes, Griffiths, Meggs, Brigden, Ellis
1,000

30 September v Casuals (h) 0–1
Monk, Jull, Welham, Shepherd, Briggs, Newby, Sykes, Meggs, Cottrell, Hepburn, Ellis
2,000

7 October v City Ramblers (h) 2–0
Briggs, Hepburn
Monk, Jull, Welham, Shepherd, Briggs, Newby, Sykes, Baxter, Tyler, Hepburn, Ellis
1,000

14 October v London Welsh (h) 1–0
Cubberley
Monk, Jull, Welham, Shepherd, Briggs, Newby, Sykes, Cubberley, Tyler, Brigden, Ellis

4 November v 1st Scots Guards (h) 1–2
Mills
Monk, Moody, Welham, Shepherd, Briggs, Jull, Cubberley, Renals, Mills, Taylor, Ellis
1,000

18 November v London Welsh (h) 2–1
Sykes, Cubberley
Monk, Rose, Welham, Jull, Casey, Shepherd, Sykes, Cubberley, Mills, Taylor, Renals
200

16 December v Erith (h) 0–1
Monk, Moody, Welham, Shepherd, Casey, Jull, Sykes, Cubberley, Mills, MacLachlan, Renals
1,000

19 December v Friars (h) 2–1
Hepburn 2
Perrin, Rose, Welham, Tarbolton, Casey, Jull, Sykes, Bannerman, Hepburn, Newbury, Renals

23 December v Wolverton (h) 2–2
Briggs, Renals
Monk, Rose, Moody, Shepherd, Briggs, Jull, Sykes, Cubberley, Mills, Taylor, Renals
1,000

26 December v Southampton St Marys (a) 0–1
Monk, Moody, Welham, Shepherd, Briggs, Jull, Casey, Cubberley, Mills, Jones, Renals
6,000

30 December v Uxbridge (a) 0–1
Monk, Jull, Rose, Shepherd, Briggs, Casey, Sykes, Cubberley, Mills, Coleman, Renals

3 February v City Ramblers (h) 0–0
Monk, Jull, Welham, Shepherd, Briggs, Newby, Sykes, Cubberley, Milne, MacLachlan, Aitken

8 February v London Hospital (h) 1–1
Nesbit
Wood, McGahey, Briggs, Mordin, Mills, E.Markham, Baxter, Nesbit, King, MacLachlan, Jull
300

10 February v Polytechnic (h) 5–0
Milne, Payne 4
Monk, Jull, Welham, Shepherd, Briggs, Newby, Shaw, Cubberley, Milne, MacLachlan, Payne

17 February v Highland Light Infantry (h) 2–2
Briggs, Milne
Monk, Jull, Welham, Shepherd, Briggs, Newby, Sykes, Cubberley, Milne, MacLachlan, Payne
400

3 March v Uxbridge (h) 1–1
Shaw
Monk, Jull, Welham, Shepherd, Briggs, Newby, Shaw, Cubberley, Milne, MacLachlan, Payne
2,000

23 March v second Scots Guards (h) 3–1
Simmonds 2, Payne
Monk, Jull, Shepherd, Jackson, Fincham, Milne, Cubberley, Bannerman, Simmonds, Payne, MacLachlan
3,000

24 March v Slough (h) 2–0
Bannerman, Payne
Monk, Jull, Shepherd, Fincham, Milne, Newby, Sykes, Cubberley, Bannerman, MacLachlan, Payne
2,500

26 March v New Brompton (a) 3–3
Newby, Fincham, Payne
Monk, Shepherd, Jull, Newby, Milne, Fincham, Sykes, Cubberley, Gilderson, Payne, MacLachlan
2,500

31 March v Polytechnic (h) 0–0
Monk, Shepherd, Jull, Newby, Lovis, Milne, Sykes, Cubberley, Bannerman, MacLachlan, Ellis

7 April v Old St Stephens (h) 1–1
Simmonds
Monk, Gorman, Welham, Shepherd, Milne, Fincham, Sykes, Cubberley, Simmonds, MacLachlan, Jull
1,000

14 April v Ilford (h) 0–1
Monk, Gorman, Welham, Shepherd, Briggs, Jull, Sykes, Cubberley, Simmonds, MacLachlan, Payne

21 April v Crouch End (a) 2–2
Cubberley, MacLachlan
Monk, Gorman, Welham, Shepherd, Briggs, Jull, Sykes, Cubberley, Edwards, MacLachlan, Payne
3,000

1894–95

FA Cup

13 October first qualifying round v West Herts (h) 3–2
Hunter, Goodall 2
Monk, Jull, Welham, Shepherd, Briggs, Julian, Cubberley, Goodall, Hunter, Eccles, E.Payne
2,000

3 November second qualifying round v Wolverton (h) 5–3
Goodall, Hunter 2, E.Payne 2
Ambler, Burrows, Jull, Shepherd, Briggs, Julian, Cubberley, Goodall, Hunter, Eccles, E.Payne
1,000

24 November third qualifying round v Clapton (a) 4–0
Eccles 2, Hunter, Goodall
Ambler, Jull, Burrows, Shepherd, Briggs, Julian, E.Payne, Eccles, Hunter, Goodall, Cubberley
5,000

15 December fourth qualifying round v Luton Town (h) 2–2
Eccles, Cubberley
Ambler, Jull, Burrows, Welham, Julian, Shepherd, E.Payne, Eccles, Hunter, Goodall, Cubberley
5,000

19 December fourth qualifying round replay v Luton Town (a) 0–4
Ambler, Jull, Burrows, Welham, Julian, Shepherd, E.Payne, Eccles, Hunter, Coleman, Cubberley
4,000

FA Amateur Cup

20 October first qualifying round v Old Harrovians (h) 7–0
Julian, R.Simpson, Edwards, Hunter 2, Goodall, Cubberley
Monk, Sullivan, Welham, Shepherd, Julian, R.Simpson, Eccles, Edwards, Hunter, Goodall, Cubberley

10 November second qualifying round v City Ramblers (h) 6–1
Shepherd, Goodall, Hunter 2, E.Payne 2
Ambler, Burrows, Jull, Shepherd, Briggs, Julian, Cubberley, Goodall, Hunter, Eccles, E.Payne
1,000

1 December third qualifying round v Romford (a) 8–0
E.Payne 2, Eccles, Hunter 3, Goodall 2
Ambler, Jull, Burrows, Shepherd, Briggs, Julian, E.Payne, Eccles, Hunter, Goodall, Cubberley

22 December qualifying round divisional final v London Welsh (h) 1–1
E.Payne
Ambler, Jull, Burrows, Welham, Julian, Shepherd, E.Payne, Eccles, Hunter, Goodall, Cubberley
1,500

5 January qualifying round divisional final replay v London Welsh (h) 3–3
Shaw, Hunter, Eccles
Ambler, Burrows, Jull, Shepherd, H.Simpson, Welham, Shaw, Goodall, Hunter, Eccles, E.Payne
1,000

19 January v qualifying round divisional final second replay London Welsh (Spotted Dog) 4–2
Jull, Welham, E.Payne, Hunter
Ambler, Burrows, Jull, Julian, Welham, Shepherd, E.Payne, Eccles, Hunter, Rose, Nixon
1,000

23 February first round v Beeston (h) 2–0
Julian, Hunter
Ambler, Burrows, Welham, Shepherd, Collins, Julian, Cubberley, Goodall, Hunter, Eccles, E.Payne
2,500

16 March second round v Old Carthusians (h) 0–5
Ambler, Burrows, Markham, Julian, Collins, Shepherd, Clements, Rose, Hunter, Eccles, E.Payne
4,000

London Senior Cup
26 January first round v London Welsh (h) 5–0
Hunter, Eccles, E.Payne 3
Ambler, Burrows, Jull, Shepherd, Welham, Julian, Baily, Collins, Hunter, Eccles, E.Payne
1,500

2 March second round v Old Westminsters (a) 3–3
Rose, Goodall 2
Ambler, Burrows, Hay, Julian, Collins, Shepherd, E.Payne, Rose, Hunter, Goodall, Baily

9 March second round replay v Old Westminsters (h) 4–5
Baily, Hunter, Reynolds, E.Payne
Ambler, Burrows, Jull, Shepherd, Collins, Julian, Baily, Hunter, Reynolds, Clements, E.Payne
2,500

London Charity Cup
8 December first round v Crusaders (h) 4–2
Goodall 2, Welham, Eccles
Ambler, Jull, Burrows, Shepherd, Welham, Julian, E.Payne, Eccles, Hunter, Goodall, Cubberley
2,000

21 March semi-final v Old Carthusians (a) 0–3
Ambler, Burrows, Barker, Smith, Collins, Julian, Reynolds, Hunter, Eccles, E.Payne, Clements
1,200

Friendlies
15 September v Uxbridge (a) 0–2
Monk, Jull, Welham, Shepherd, Briggs, Dickie, Cubberley, Eccles, Hunter, Goodall, E.Payne

22 September v Casuals (h) 3–1
Hunter 2, E.Payne
Monk, Jull, Welham, Shepherd, Briggs, Dickie, Cubberley, Goodall, Hunter, Eccles, E.Payne

29 September v London Caledonians (a) 1–3
Hunter
Monk, Jull, Welham, Julian, Briggs, Dickie, E.Payne, Eccles, Hunter, Cubberley, Shepherd
3,000

6 October v third Grenadier Guards (h) 1–1
E.Payne
Monk, Burrows, Welham, Julian, Briggs, Shepherd, Elliott, Cubberley, Goodall, Eccles, E.Payne

27 October v Crouch End (a) 2–2
Julian, Goodall
Fenn, Burrows, Caldecott, Julian, Newby, Shepherd, Eccles, Cubberley, Hunter, Goodall, E.Payne
1,000

17 November v Highland Light Infantry (h) 1–1
Hunter
Ambler, Burrows, Jull, Shepherd, Briggs, Julian, Cubberley, Goodall, Hunter, Eccles, E.Payne
1,500

25 December v Sheffield & District League (h) 7–1
Goodall 2, Hunter 3, Jones, E.Payne
Ambler, Burrows, Jull, Shepherd, Smith, McKenzie, Cubberley, Goodall, Hunter, Jones, E.Payne
1,500

26 December v West Liverpool (h) 3–0
Hunter, E.Payne, H.Payne
Ambler, Burrows, Jull, Shepherd, Oliver, McKenzie, Sykes, Goodall, Hunter, H.Payne, E.Payne
1,500

29 December v Vampires (h) 4–1
Goodall 2, Hunter, Jones
Ambler, Burrows, Jull, Shepherd, Simmonds, Oliver, Shaw, Goodall, Hunter, Jones, E.Payne

23 March v London Caldeonians (h) 5–1
Julian, Collins, Goodall, Hunter 2
Ambler, Burrows, Jull, Stirling, Collins, Julian, Clements, Goodall, Hunter, Eccles, E.Payne

30 March v City Ramblers (h) 2–0
Hunter, Carver
Ambler, Burrows, Jull, Shepherd, Collins, Julian, Sykes, Brennan, Hunter, Carver, Clements

6 April v Casuals (h) 1–2
Clements
Ambler, Burrows, Jull, Shepherd, Collins, Julian, Clements, Cottrell, Hunter, Newman, E.Payne
(70 min game)

12 April v Liverpool Casuals (h) 6–0
Wilkinson, Laycock, Hunter 2, McElheney 2
Ambler, Burrows, Barker, Stirling, Collins, Julian, Wilkinson, Laycock, Hunter, McElheney, E.Payne

13 April v second Scots Guards (h) 1–1
Shepherd
Ambler, Burrows, Jull, Shepherd, Collins, Julian, Clements, Sykes, Hunter, Simmonds, Pryor

15 April v Southampton St Marys (a) 0–0
Ambler, Burrows, Jull, Stirling, Collins, Julian, Pryor, Ward-Leaver, Hunter, McElheney, E.Payne

16 April v Bristol South End (a) 7–0
Pryor, Clements, Hunter 2, McElheney, E.Payne 2
Ambler, Burrows, Jull, Shepherd, Stirling, Julian, Pryor, Clements, Hunter, McElheney, E.Payne
2,000

25 April (W Stirling Benefit) v London Caledonians (a) 2–0
Pryor 2
Ambler, Burrows, Jull, Stirling, Collins, Julian, Pryor, Mayor, Hunter, McElheney, E.Payne
(70 min game)

1895–96

FA Cup

12 October first qualifying round v Luton Town (a) 2–1
Hunter, Owen
Ambler, Briggs, Burrows, McKenzie, Collins, Shepherd, Payne, Clements, Hunter, Owen, Pryor
2,000

2 November second qualifying round v Vampires (a) 2–4
Pryor, Clements
Ambler, Shepherd, Williams, Burne, Briggs, Collins, Pryor, Cattell, Hunter, Clements, Payne
(Replay ordered as pitch incorrectly marked)

16 November second qualifying round replay v Vampires (h) 2–1
Pryor, Hunter
Monk, Burrows, Jull, Collins, Almond, Briggs, Pryor, Gilmore, Hunter, Clements, Payne
2,500

23 November third qualifying round v Ilford (a) 5–1
Almond, Pryor 2, Payne 2
Ambler, Burrows, Jull, Collins, Almond, Briggs, Pryor, Gilmore, Hunter, Clements, Payne
500

14 December fourth qualifying round v Old St Stephens (h) 2–1
Clements, Sullivan (og)
Ambler, Collins, Jull, Shepherd, Almond, Briggs, Pryor, Eccles, Hunter, Clements, Payne
3,000

1 February first round v Stoke (a) 0–5
Ambler, Hay, Montgomery, Collins, Almond, Briggs, Pryor, Lanham, Hunter, Clements, Payne
6,000

London Charity Cup
9 November first round v Old Westminsters (a) 2–1
Pryor, Payne
Ambler, Burrows, McGahey, Collins, Almond, Briggs, Pryor, S.Brown, Hunter, Clements, Payne
2,000

Friendlies
7 September v Royal Engineers (a) 3–0
Pryor, Eccles, Payne
Ambler, Burrows, Jull, F.Markham, Briggs, McKenzie, Pryor, Clements, Hunter, Eccles, Payne

14 September v 1st Royal Scots Greys (h) 3–2
Clements, Payne 2
Ambler, Burrows, Jull, F.Markham, Briggs, McKenzie, Pryor, Clements, Hunter, Eccles, Payne
2,000

21 September v Casuals (h) 3–2
Pryor, Clements, Payne
Ambler, Burrows, Jull, Collins, Briggs, McKenzie, Pryor, Eccles, Hunter, Clements, Payne
2,000

28 September v Royal Ordnance (h) 2–0
Hunter, Burne
Ambler, Burrows, Jull, Clements, Collins, McKenzie, Pryor, Eccles, Hunter, Burne, Payne
2,000

5 October v Clapton (a) 4–5
Clements 3, Payne
Ambler, Burrows, Jull, Collins, Briggs, McKenzie, Pryor, Goodall, Hunter, Clements, Payne

19 October v Ilford (a) 2–0
Hunter 2
Ambler, Burrows, Williams, McKenzie, Briggs, Collins, Pryor, Butler, Hunter, Clements, Payne

26 October v Royal Artillery (h) 1–2
Burton
Ambler, Burrows, Williams, Shepherd, Briggs, Collins, Pryor, Burton, Hunter, Clements, Payne
2,000

7 November v Luton Town (h) 0–2
Ambler, Burrows, Marjoram, Collins, Briggs, Julian, Pryor, Burne, Hunter, Clements, Payne
1,000

30 November v London Welsh (a) 3–2
Hunter 2, Payne
Ross, J.Dawson, Jull, Collins, Almond, Briggs, Pryor, Gilmore, Hunter, Clements, Payne

7 December v London Caledonians (h) 0–3
Ambler, Jull, Marjoram, Shepherd, Almond, Collins, Sykes, Gilmore, Hunter, Clements, Payne
3,000

21 December v Casuals (h) 3–1
Hunter, Clements, Payne
Ambler, McGahey, Marjoram, Shepherd, Almond, Collins, Pryor, Lindsay, Hunter, Clements, Payne
1,000

25 December v Millwall Athletic (a) 3–5
Hunter 2, Clements
Ambler, E.Markham, McGahey, Regan, Collins, McKenzie, Pryor, Lindsay, Hunter, Clements, Payne
2,000

26 December v Accrington (h) 3–0
Briggs, Clements 2
Ambler, Jull, J.Dawson, Briggs, Collins, F.Markham, Pryor, Lindsay, Hunter, Clements, Payne
2,000

28 December v Freemantle (h) 2–2
Clements, Hunter (pen)
Ambler, Jull, Collins, Shepherd, Almond, Briggs, Payne, Clements, Hunter, Lindsay, Pryor
2,000

4 January v Reading (h) 2–1
Lanham, Payne
Ambler, Burrows, Montgomery, Collins, Almond, Briggs, Pryor, Logan, Lanham, Clements, Payne
3,000

11 January v Millwall Athletic (h) 1–1
Lanham
Ambler, McGahey, Jull, Collins, Almond, Briggs, Pryor, Logan, Lanham, Clements, Payne
6,000

18 January v Ilford (h) 2–1
Russell, Payne
Ambler, E.Dawson, Montgomery, Collins, Almond, Briggs, Pryor, Lanham, Russell, Clements, Payne

25 January v Notts County (h) 1–5
Clements
Ambler, Slark, Montgomery, Collins, Almond, Briggs, Pryor, Lanham, Hunter, Clements, Payne
1,200

8 February v 1st Royal Scots Greys (h) 2–1
Logan 2
Ambler, McGahey, Montgomery, Collins, Almond, Briggs, Pryor, Logan, Lanham, Clements, Payne
1,500

10 February v Luton Town (a) 0–9
Ambler, Beveridge, Montgomery, Collins, Buchan, Briggs, Lanham, McInroy, Hunter, Clements, Payne
1,000

15 February v Royal Ordnance (a) 1–2
Hunter
Ambler, McGahey, Montgomery, Collins, Almond, Hughes, Pryor, Lanham, Hunter, Clements, Payne
1,500

22 February v Clapton (h) 4–0
Lanham, Clements 2, Payne
Ambler, McGahey, Montgomery, Collins, Almond, Briggs, Logan, Lanham, Hunter, Clements, Payne
2,000

29 February v Burslem Port Vale (h) 4–0
Logan 2, Lanham, Clements
Ambler, McGahey, Montgomery, Collins, Almond, Briggs, Lanham, Logan, Hunter, Clements, Payne
1,500

4 March v Gravesend United (a) 1–1
Unknown
Monk, Buist, Montgomery, Collins, Almond, Julian, Lanham, Logan, Hunter, Clements, Pryor

7 March v 1st Scots Guards (h) 8–0
Lanham 4, Logan 4
Ambler, Burrows, Montgomery, Shepherd, Almond, Collins, Lanham, Logan, W.Brown, Clements, Payne
1,000

9 March v Royal Ordnance (a) 1–3
Logan
Ambler, McGahey, Montgomery, E.Markham, Johnson, Julian, Lanham, Logan, W.Brown, Clements, Payne
600

14 March v Uxbridge (h) 4–0
Burrows, Almond, Brown, Clements
Ambler, Burrows, Montgomery, Collins, Almond, Shepherd, Lanham, Logan, W.Brown, Clements, Payne
1,000

16 March v Woolwich Arsenal (a) 3–1
Hunter, W.Brown, OG (Gilmer)
Ambler, McGahey, Montgomery, Collins, Briggs, F.Markham, Lanham, Hunter, W.Brown, Clements, Logan
1,000

19 March v Royal Ordnance (h) 2–2
Clements 2
Jull, E.Markham, Montgomery, Collins, Julian, F.Markham, Pryor, Lanham, W.Brown, Clements, Payne
400

21 March v Manchester Regiment (h) 8–1
Almond, Logan, Hunter 2 (1 pen), Clements 2, Payne 2
Ambler, Jull, Montgomery, Shepherd, Almond, Collins, Logan, Hunter, W.Brown, Clements, Payne
1,500

26 March v Woolwich Arsenal (h) 1–3
Clements
Ambler, Hay, Montgomery, Collins, Almond, F.Markham, Logan, Hunter, W.Brown, Clements, Payne
2,500

28 March v London Caledonians (a) 5–0
Hunter 2, W.Brown, Clements, Payne,
Ambler, McGahey, Collins, Shepherd, Almond, Smith, Logan, Hunter, W.Brown, Clements, Payne
3,000

3 April v Reading (a) 3–2
Lanham, Hunter, Payne
Ambler, McGahey, Montgomery, Smith, Almond, Collins, Lanham, Hunter, W.Brown, Clements, Payne
4,000

4 April v Oswaldtwistle Rovers (h) 4–0
Logan, W.Brown 3
Ambler, McGahey, Owen, F.Markham, Almond, Collins, Logan, Hunter, W.Brown, Clements, Payne
2,000

6 April v Middlesbrough (h) 5–0
W.Brown 2, Clements 2, Payne
Ambler, Montgomery, McGahey, Smith, Almond, Collins, Logan, Hunter, W.Brown, Clements, Payne
3,000

7 April v Swindon Town (h) 2–3
Clements 2
Ambler, Montgomery, E.Markham, Shepherd (McGahey), Collins, F.Markham, Lanham, Hunter, W.Brown, Clements, Logan

11 April v Aston Villa (h) 1–3
Logan
Ambler, Owen, Montgomery, Collins, Almond, F.Markham, Logan, Hunter, W.Brown, Clements, Payne
6,000

15 April v Swindon Town (a) 2–0
Clements, Payne
Ambler, McGahey, Montgomery, Collins, Buist, Welch, Pryor, Logan, W.Brown, Clements, Payne
1,500

18 April v Southampton St Marys (a) 1–4
Lanham
Ambler, Owen, Montgomery, Collins, Almond, Smith, Lanham, Hunter, W.Brown, Clements, Payne
1,500

22 April v Gravesend United (a) 1–1
Clements
Flowers, Montgomery, Buist, Welch, Cherrie, Crump, Lanham, Logan, W.Brown, Clements, Pryor

25 April v Wellingborough (h) 3–1
Almond, Lanham, W.Brown
Ambler, Collins, Montgomery, Cherrie, Almond, Crump, Lanham, Hunter, W.Brown, Clements, Pryor
1,500

30 April v Woolwich Arsenal (h) 3–2
Almond, Clements, Payne
Ambler, McGahey, Montgomery, Collins (Shepherd), Almond, Crump, Lanham, Logan, W.Brown, Clements, Payne
1,500

PRE-LEAGUE PLAYER STATS

The details below are for all players who have been identified as playing for Spurs prior to the club joining the Football League in 1908. All known appearances and goals are included. Matches that were abandoned or later ignored, for instance where a club left the League are also included.

		SOUTHERN		OTHER LEAGUES		FA CUP		OTHERS			TOTAL		
NAME	SEASON	APPS	GOALS	APPS	GOALS	APPS	GOALS	APPS	SUBS	GOALS	APPS	SUBS	GOALS
Edward Adlington	1885–89		0		0		0	3		0	3		
W Aitken	1893–94							1			1		
Jimmy Allen	1896–97	4		9	1			10		2	23		3
W (Billie) Almond	1895–97	16	2	5		7		32		8	60		10
Charlie J Ambler	1894–00	22		19		12		79	1		132	1	
Robert H Amos	1884–86		0		0		0	6		5	6		5
John C Anderson	1885–92		0		0		0	11		0	11		
W (Bill) C Anson	1900–01	4		1				1			6		
Arthur Archer	1903–04			5							5		
Tom H Atherton	1898–99	2		11	4						13		4
J Ayres	1889–90							1			1		
George H Badenoch	1906–07	1		1				1			3		
H (Bert) O Badger	1903–04			9	3			1		2	10		5
Baillie	1883–84							3			3		
W Baily	1894–95							3		1	3		1
Baker	1893–94							1			1		
George R Baldock	1887–93		0	1		0		10		1	11		1
Alec C Bannerman	1893–94							4		1	4		1
Barber	1891–92							1		1	1		1
G Barker	1894–95							2			2		
John Barlow	1901–03	7		14	8		0	5		1	26		9
FW Barnes	1891–92							1		1	1		1
G Bassett	1889–92		0		0		0	12		3	12		3
JM Baxter	1890–94		0	2	2		0	10		5	12		7
Bell	1892–93			4	5						4		5
Frank Berry	1900–01	1		1				1			3		
William A Berry	1903–07	19	1	17	12	1		3		0	40		13
Beveridge	1895–96							1			1		
J Bird	1887–88							1			1		
David G Black	1897–98	20	8	15	6	2	2	20		9	57		25
Joe Blake	1905–06			3	1						3		1
Bowyer	1893–94							1			1		
Tom H Bradshaw	1898–99	24	5	33	8	9	5	3		1	69		19
John Brearley	1903–07	71	7	42	9	8		10		8	131		24
A Brennan	1894–95							1			1		
Brewster	1907–08	1									1		
J (Motor) Brigden	1891–94		0	8	2		0	14		1	22		3
Stanley S Briggs	1891–98	7	1	13	2	10		82		8	112		11
Alex Brown	1900–02	46	30	28	22	11	15	28		29	113		96
Charles Brown	1902–04	14		21	1		0	3		0	38		1
RP Brown	1896–97							3		1	3		1
S Brown	1895–97		0		0		0	3		0	3		
William Brown	1895–96							18		8	18		8
Buchan	1895–96							1			1		
William F Buckingham	1900–01	6		3							9		
R (Bobby) Buckle	1883–92		0		0		0	54		28	54		28
James W Bugg	1902–03			1							1		
R (Bobby) Buist	1895–96							3			3		
E Bull	1886–87							1			1		
Hedley T Bull	1884–93		0	3		0		30		0	33		

		SOUTHERN		OTHER LEAGUES		FA CUP		OTHERS			TOTAL		
NAME	SEASON	APPS	GOALS	APPS	GOALS	APPS	GOALS	APPS	SUBS	GOALS	APPS	SUBS	GOALS
Walter Bull	1904–08	105	8	26	1	15	1	21		4	167		14
Tom W Bumberry	1884–90		0		0		0	5		1	5		1
R Burne	1895–96					1		2		1	3		1
Ly Burrows	1894–98	27	1	21	1	12		58		1	118		3
A Burton	1893–96		0		0		0	2		1	2		1
John H Burton	1900–04	21	3	25	1		0	4		1	50		5
Ollie Burton	1902–08	65		45	1	1		14		0	125		1
E Butler	1895–96							1			1		
Morton F Cadman	1889–92		0		0		0	5		0	5		
R (Bob) Cain	1898–99	24		32	1	10		3			69		1
W Caldecott	1894–95							1			1		
John Cameron	1899–05	117	43	93	46	25	7	54		43	289		139
Chris Carrick	1905–06	15	4	4		4		1		1	24		5
Carver	1894–95							1		1	1		1
Ham D Casey	1883–94		0	5		0		43		0	48		
C Cattell	1891–96		0	2	1	1		1		0	4		1
Cawkill	1884–85							2			2		
James Chalmers	1902–04	10	1	18	4		0	4		1	32		6
John F Chaplin	1905–08	66		21		1		12		0	100		
Herbert Chapman	1904–07	41	15	15	4	7	1	4		0	67		20
T Cherrie	1895–96							2			2		
George Clawley	1899–03	83		50		12		40		0	185		
J Clements	1896–97							3		1	3		1
R (Bob) W Clements	1894–98	21	14	16	6	9	4	82		47	128		71
Coe	1896–97							1			1		
Alf Coleman	1893–95		0		0	1		2		0	3		
James S Collins	1894–97	2		2		6		58		1	68		1
J Conu	1885–86							1			1		
HJ Cook	1896–97							1			1		
David C Copeland	1899–05	144	50	97	30	20	3	39		23	300		106
Ernie Coquet	1907–08	6						1			7		
Frank S Cottrell	1883–95		0	5		0		46		19	51		19
W Coulson	1891–92							3			3		
Albert C Cousins	1907–08	2		1							3		
Craig	1896–97							1			1		
AJ Crossley	1889–92		0		0		0	4		0	4		
W (Harry) Crump	1895–00	31	2	25	3	4	3	47		5	107		13
Archie W Cubberley	1892–95		0	3		5	1	41		6	49		7
Joe Cullen	1897–98	43		45		12		25		0	125		
Jabez Darnell	1905–08	34	1	21		1		6		0	62		1
Jimmy W Davidson	1897–98	17	5	13	1			16		9	46		15
RO Davies	1889–90							2			2		
E Dawson	1895–96							1			1		
J Dawson	1895–96							2			2		
James Devlin	1896–97	21	1	12	3	3		23		1	59		5
Fred W Dexter	1883–84							1			1		
JS Dickie	1894–95							3			3		
W Dingwell	1891–92							3			3		
Arthur Dixon	1907–08	6		6				1			13		
William Dow	1906–07	9	3	5				1			15		3
Ed Downie	1897–99	11		14		0		12		0	37		
William Dryburgh	1902–03	16	2	10		4	1	1			31		3
RT Drysdale	1890–91							1			1		
Wally Eames	1906–07	7	2	4							11		2
Jimmy W Eccles	1894–96		0		0	6	3	22		5	28		8
Edwards	1891–92							1			1		
Albie Edwards	1896–97							3			3		
Harry C Edwards	1893–95		0		0		0	2		1	2		1
Jack H Eggett	1904–07	66		31		8		11		0	116		

NAME	SEASON	SOUTHERN APPS	SOUTHERN GOALS	OTHER LEAGUES APPS	OTHER LEAGUES GOALS	FA CUP APPS	FA CUP GOALS	OTHERS APPS	OTHERS SUBS	OTHERS GOALS	TOTAL APPS	TOTAL SUBS	TOTAL GOALS
Arthur Elliott	1894–95							1			1		
H Ellis	1891–94		0	7		0		17		0	24		
Harry B Erentz	1898–04	134		102	1	21		47	1	1	304	1	2
F Fenn	1894–95							1			1		
P Finch	1900–01			1							1		
EJ Fincham	1893–94							4		1	4		1
John T Fisher	1883–84							1			1		
Tom T Fitchie	1901–02	1						1		1	2		1
W (Billy) Fleming	1896–97	2	1					3		2	5		3
J Flowers	1895–96							1			1		
WM Fortnam	1892–93			1	1			2		1	3		2
W Fortnum	1900–01	2	1								2		1
C Fox	1891–92							3			3		
George H Fredericks	1902–03	1		1	1						2		1
James Freeborough	1904–06	2		12	1		0	1		0	15		1
Gair	1896–97							1			1		
J (Pat) Gallacher	1904–05			1				2			3		
S Gamble	1892–93			1				1			2		
Gardiner	1896–97							5			5		
CE Gaudson	1905–06			1							1		
John S George	1904–06	4	1	5		0		2		0	11		1
E Gilderson	1892–94		0	1	1		0	1		0	2		1
Patrick Gilhooley	1901–04	17	2	29	5	3		9		0	58		7
J Gilmore	1895–96					2		2			4		
Tommy S Gipps	1907–08			1							1		
Alex Glen	1904–06	32	12	17	3	8	1	10		9	67		25
G Harry Goddard	1888–89							1			1		
Donald Goodall	1894–96		0		0	4	4	18		14	22		18
Goodman	1896–97							1			1		
W (Kempsie) Gorman	1893–94							3			3		
James A Gray	1907–08	15		4		1		3			23		
H Griffith	1889–90							1			1		
Fred J Griffiths	1901–02	9		9		3		2			23		
W Griffiths	1893–94							1			1		
David Haddow	1899–01	26		15		1		16		0	58		
Alan R Haig-Brown	1901–03	4		0		0		3		0	7		
Alex R Hall	1897–99	24		23		2	1	23		0	72		1
Ellis Hargreaves	1897–98			1				1			2		
H Harkins	1891–92							1			1		
W (Billy) R Harston	1883–93		0	1		0		39		13	40		13
W Hart	1892–93			2				3			5		
James M Hartley	1897–99	18	9	24	11	3	1	19		14	64		35
Tom Hatfield	1896–97	1		1				9			11		
Alf Hawley	1900–01	3	2	2				1		1	6		3
William Hay	1894–97		0		0	1		3		0	4		
AE Hepburn	1891–94		0		0		0	9		5	9		5
Charlie W Hewitt	1906–07	30	11	8	1	5		4		2	47		14
William Hickling	1905–06			1							1		
Hickson	1898–99			3				1		1	4		1
Hobson	1896–97			1	1			2			3		1
A Hopkins	1891–92							1			1		
R (Bob) Houston	1902–03	9	3	14	5			3		3	26		11
JC Hubble	1902–03							1			1		
Hudson	1888–89							1			1		
Hudson	1898–99			1							1		
EG Hudson	1900–01	1									1		
W Hudson	1887–88							1			1		
E (Ted) Hughes	1899–08	151	9	81	7	31	2	49	1	2	312	1	20
Matt R Hughes	1895–96							1			1		

		SOUTHERN		OTHER LEAGUES		FA CUP		OTHERS			TOTAL		
NAME	SEASON	APPS	GOALS	APPS	GOALS	APPS	GOALS	APPS	SUBS	GOALS	APPS	SUBS	GOALS
C Humber	1889–90							3		2	3		2
Peter J Hunter	1894–97		0	1		11	6	63		45	75		51
J Hurry	1891–92							2			2		
Leon J Hyde	1899–02	18	5	15	1		0	15		3	48		9
Herbert Jackson	1893–94							1			1		
W (Bill) H Janes	1896–97							1			1		
W Jenkins	1907–08							1			1		
Joel	1891–92							1			1		
A Johnson	1895–96							1			1		
Arthur E Jones	1900–01	8	1	10	5			7		2	25		8
Jimmy Jones	1899–00			1							1		
Jack L Jones	1897–04	135	7	103	5	31	1	68		3	337		16
John T Jones	1902–04	32	19	24	14	5	2	4		1	65		36
Richard L Jones	1893–94							1			1		
R Jones	1894–95							2		2	2		2
W (Billy) Jones	1906–07	8		2	1			1		1	11		2
W (Bill) Joyce	1897–99	40	34	43	29	12	7	23		23	118		93
J W (Bill) Julian	1894–96		0		0	5		28		4	33		4
H Jull	1891–92							1			1		
Jack C Jull	1883–97		0	13	4	8		140		20	161		24
Tommy E Jull	1896–97			1				2			3		
Keith	1896–97							1			1		
Kerry	1898–99			1							1		
AH King	1893–94							1			1		
Kingan	1893–94							1			1		
John F Kirwan	1899–05	157	41	96	27	24	2	64	1	28	341	1	98
Joe Knowles	1897–98	19		14		1		16	1		50	1	
Peter Kyle	1905–06	25	8	11	6	4	3	2		2	42		19
Charlie H Lanham	1895–97	2		3	1	1		31		17	37		18
Fred Latham	1896–97			2				1			3		
T Latymer	1888–89							1			1		
Laycock	1894–95							1		1	1		1
George Leach	1905–06	2	2	5	1						7		3
Allan F Leach-Lewis	1903–05	1		0		0		1		0	2		
Stuart Leaman	1883–90		0		0		0	2		0	2		
J Lee	1907–08			1							1		
W (Billy) Leech	1898–99	4	2	8	4			1			13		6
FJ Leese	1891–92							3			3		
H Leese	1891–92							12		4	12		4
AK Leigh	1900–01			1							1		
Ernest W Levy	1899–00							1			1		
Jimmy Lindsay	1895–96							4			4		
A Littleford	1889–90							5			5		
A Logan	1895–96							20		12	20		12
J Lomas	1892–93							2			2		
William Lomas	1883–87		0		0		0	3		0	3		
Frank B Lovis	1883–94		0		0		0	28		5	28		5
Herbert Lovis	1892–93			1	1						1		1
John S Lovis	1892–93			1							1		
Percy Lovis	1892–93			1				1			2		
S Lovis	1892–93			2							2		
A MacDonald	1893–94							1			1		
CF MacLachlan	1893–94							15		2	15		2
John Madden	1897–98	2		4				2			8		
James Mair	1896–97	2		7				10			19		
Gordon S Manning	1907–08	33		10		1		5		0	49		
Percy J Mapley	1903–04	5		5							10		
Arthur E Marjoram	1895–97		0		0		0	4		0	4		
E (Bunks) S Markham	1892–99	3		7		0		9		0	19		

NAME	SEASON	SOUTHERN APPS	SOUTHERN GOALS	OTHER LEAGUES APPS	OTHER LEAGUES GOALS	FA CUP APPS	FA CUP GOALS	OTHERS APPS	OTHERS SUBS	OTHERS GOALS	TOTAL APPS	TOTAL SUBS	TOTAL GOALS
F (Dick) Markham	1892–97		0	1		0		11		0	12		
W (Wal) Markham	1892–97		0	1		0		1		0	2		
DW Marpole	1889–90							2			2		
W (Billy) Mason	1884–90		0		0		0	24		11	24		11
Fred J Massey	1907–08			3							3		
J Mayor	1894–95							1			1		
John McConnachie	1903–04	6		4							10		
W (Bill) McCurdy	1904–05	12		10				7			29		
John McDermott	1896–97							2			2		
Frank McDiarmid	1906–07	7		4				1			12		
Ralph McElhaney	1896–97	19	6	11		3	1	20		11	53		18
J McElheney	1894–95							4		3	4		3
Charlie P McGahey	1893–99		0		0		0	18	1		18	1	
Davie McInroy	1895–96							1			1		
Kenny McKay	1898–99	18	5	22	14	9	1	4		5	53		25
Lewis H McKenzie	1894–96		0		0	1		9		0	10		
Frank McMullan	1905–06			1							1		
Willie D McNair	1907–08	15	5	8	2	1		3			27		7
James R McNaught	1898–06	105		82	5	13	1	49		3	249		9
Tom G Meade	1897–99	15	5	2	1	2	3	13		7	32		16
Fred C Mearns	1903–04	5		9				1			15		
W (Bill) P Meates	1899–00							1			1		
Jimmy W Meggs	1892–94		0		0		0	4		1	4		1
Jimmy Melia	1898–01	38	1	29		3		20		2	90		3
H Bert Middlemiss	1907–08	25	8	2	1			2			29		9
Milarvie	1896–97							1			1		
Millard	1891–92							3		2	3		2
W Miller	1891–92							5		1	5		1
Alex Milligan	1896–97							2			2		
Jimmy Milliken	1896–97	19	6	11	3	3		19		4	52		13
J (Scottie) Mills	1893–94							9		2	9		2
S Milne	1893–94							12		2	12		2
Fred H Milnes	1905–06			2							2		
Harry A Milton	1903–06	1		4		0		0		0	5		
W (Billy) J Minter	1907–08	9	4					1			10		4
Joe Moffatt	1900–01	6	3	3				5			14		3
Walter J Moles	1900–03	3		3		0		3		0	9		
Cuthbert V Monk	1891–96		0	9		2		59		0	70		
Steve M Monk	1897–98							2			2		
Gerald Montgomery	1901–02			1				3			4		
Jock Montgomery	1895–98	36		19		5		70		1	130		1
R Moody	1892–94		0	9		0		17		0	26		
WB Mordin	1893–94							1			1		
Charles Morgan	1904–05			1				1			2		
Tom Morris	1899–08	243	21	109	15	32		59		8	443		44
Willie B Murray	1904–06	20		15		1		5		1	41		1
Nesbit	1893–94							1		1	1		1
Willie M Newbigging	1896–97	10	2	11	4	3	3	23		13	47		22
BE Newbury	1893–94							1			1		
W Newby	1893–95		0		0		0	19		1	19		1
Newman	1894–95							1			1		
AC Nixon	1894–95							1			1		
Oates	1896–97							1			1		
O'Donnell	1904–05							1			1		
Charlie O'Hagan	1904–06	21	6	14	2	3	1	9		11	47		20
Jack Oliver	1894–95							2	1		2	1	
ML Owen	1895–96					1	1	3			4		1
George Page	1905–07	1		1		0		0		0	2		
Palmer	1892–93							1		1	1		1

NAME	SEASON	SOUTHERN APPS	SOUTHERN GOALS	OTHER LEAGUES APPS	OTHER LEAGUES GOALS	FA CUP APPS	FA CUP GOALS	OTHERS APPS	OTHERS SUBS	OTHERS GOALS	TOTAL APPS	TOTAL SUBS	TOTAL GOALS
Tom Pangbourne	1900–01	2						6		1	8		1
GA Parker	1888–90		0		0		0	2		1	2		1
Jimmy E Pass	1907–08	18	5	9	6	1		3			31		11
Payne	1888–89							1		1	1		1
Ernie G Payne	1893–99	20	5	11	1	14	6	92		52	137		64
George C Payne	1906–08	6	3	4	2		0	2		2	12		7
H Payne	1894–95							1		1	1		1
Percy A Perrin	1893–94							1			1		
H Perry	1889–91		0		0		0	2		1	2		1
Arthur E Pickett	1906–08	28	6	4	1		0	2		0	34		7
W Pilbrow	1890–91							1		1	1		1
Robert G Pilch	1903–05		0	3		0		0		0	3		
Albert J Pracy	1889–90							1			1		
Tom P Pratt	1899–00	30	24	12	8	1		17		21	60		53
Harry Pryor	1894–96		0		0	6	4	29		6	35		10
Tom Purdie	1886–89		0		0		0	2		3	2		3
David Quinn	1902–04	1		7		0		2		1	10		1
W (Joe) Raby	1899–00	2		3				7		8	12		8
HA Rainbird	1902–03			3	1			1			4		1
J (Billy) G Randall	1883–87		0		0		0	12		6	12		6
Charles D Regan	1895–97		0	1		0		4		0	5		
James Reid	1906–08	37	20	8	6	7	2	7		4	59		32
Matt M Reilly	1906–07	19		6		7		3			35		
JH Renals	1891–94		0		0		0	11		1	11		1
W Reynolds	1894–95							2		1	2		1
J (Willie) Roberts	1899–00			2	2			1			3		2
Alex Robertson	1896–97	1	1					4		2	5		3
L Rose	1892–95		0	1		0		10		1	11		1
George Ross	1895–96							1			1		
Art G Rule	1898–00	7	1	3		0		2		3	12		4
J Russell	1895–96							1		1	1		1
Sands	1900–01			1							1		
WJ Scott	1896–97							3			3		
Max P Seeburg	1907–08	15	5	8	2		0	4		4	27		11
John Shackleton	1905–06	3	1	6							9		1
W Burt Shaw	1893–95		0		0		0	6		2	6		2
William K Shearing	1893–94							1			1		
W Jack Shepherd	1891–97		0	1		8		66	1	2	75	1	2
M Shillingworth	1891–92							2			2		
H Simmonds	1893–95		0		0		0	5		3	5		3
Harry Simpson	1888–95		0	3		0		13		0	16		
R (Bob) W Simpson	1894–95							1		1	1		1
SG Slark	1895–96							1			1		
FE Smith	1894–96		0		0		0	6		0	6		
Tom Smith	1898–02	94	25	67	14	20	2	43		13	224		54
Tom Soulsby	1901–02			1				1			2		
Harry Stansfield	1904–08	49	9	26	3	6		12		3	93		15
Danny Steel	1906–08	32	1	9	1	1		3		0	45		2
John W Stephenson	1901–04	1		15		0		6		0	22		
Steven	1902–03							1			1		
R (Bob) C Stevens	1899–02	3		2		0		3		0	8		
J Stirling	1894–95							5			5		
R (Bob) Stormont	1897–01	93	8	71	10	14	1	54		5	232		24
Jack Sullivan	1894–95							1			1		
Herbert S Sunderland	1896–97							2			2		
Andrew Swann	1904–05	2		4	1						6		1
J (Louis) Sykes	1891–96		0	12	4		0	45		9	57		13
Alexander Tait	1899–08	205	3	109	3	36		66		4	416		10
R (Bob) Tannahill	1897–98	11	3	5	3	2		11		3	29		9

NAME	SEASON	SOUTHERN APPS	SOUTHERN GOALS	OTHER LEAGUES APPS	OTHER LEAGUES GOALS	FA CUP APPS	FA CUP GOALS	OTHERS APPS	OTHERS SUBS	OTHERS GOALS	TOTAL APPS	TOTAL SUBS	TOTAL GOALS
Tarbolton	1893–94							1			1		
SG Taylor	1893–94							5		2	5		2
John H Thompson	1883–84							1			1		
Thorburn	1896–97							2			2		
JW Thornley	1892–93							1			1		
Archie D Turner	1903–04	5	5	7	1						12		6
W Tyler	1891–94		0		0		0	11		5	11		5
W (Billy) CTyrrell	1883–93		0		0		0	25		1	25		1
W Vaughan	1903–04			1							1		
Frank S Walford	1889–91		0		0		0	8		0	8		
R (Bob) H Walker	1906–08	24	3	3		1		3		0	31		3
Wilfred H Waller	1898–00	4		1		0		0		0	5		
Joe Walton	1903–08	105	24	56	16	14	4	15		6	190		50
J Ward–Leaver	1894–95							1			1		
Alf C Warner	1902–05	47	12	32	7	5		6		4	90		23
Alec Watson	1883–84							4		2	4		2
Claude Watson	1906–07			1							1		
John Watson	1902–08	103		56		23		11		0	193		
A Welch	1895–96							2			2		
Jack W Welham	1892–95		0	8		3		42		2	53		2
S Weston	1891–93		0	1	1		0	7		3	8		4
Jack G Whitbourne	1905–08	19		10		0		3		0	32		
Alf Whyman	1905–08	18	1	11	5		0	5		3	34		9
Wilkinson	1894–95							1		1	1		1
John W Wilkinson	1906–07	2									2		
Williams	1888–89							1			1		
Charlie A Williams	1902–05	37		31		5		7		0	80		
FG Williams	1891–92							1			1		
T Williams	1895–96					1		2			3		
Frank Wilson	1896–97	5	3	3	1			2		1	10		5
F Wood	1893–94							1			1		
Charlie L Woodruff	1907–08	5	3								5		3
Vivian J Woodward	1900–08	104	45	16	7	20	5	21		21	161		78
Yates	1904–05							1			1		
Own Goals	1891–08		8		8		2		0	6		0	24

SPURS ON TOUR

Prior to modern times it was easy to define a 'tour match' as one played outside the country, outside the normal League season and where Spurs moved around from place to place. With international travel now being so easy, pre-season and end-of-season games are the rule rather than the exception, such a simple definition is no longer appropriate.

Included in this section are matches played by Spurs that all would recognise as 'tour matches' but it also includes games played during pre-season and at the end of the season where the club has travelled abroad and played more than one game. (There's one exception to that: 1972 when Spurs went to Israel for a match. As that was in the middle of summer it is included here as it would be difficult to classify it as either a 1971–72 or 1972–73 season match.

One-off matches outside the country are included in the 'Friendlies' section.

1905 AUSTRO-HUNGARY

4 May v Vienna (Vienna) 6–0

McNaught, Glen 3, O'Hagan 2

Eggett, Watson, Tait, Bull, McNaught, Hughes, Glen, O'Hagan, Woodward, Copeland, Kirwan

7 May v Everton (Vienna) 0–2

Team unknown but included Woodward

10 May v Vienna Athletic Club (Vienna) 4–1

Morris, Murray, Woodward 2

Team unknown but included Morris, Murray and Woodward

12 May v Buda Pesth Thorna (Budapest) 7–1

Morris 2, Walton, Stansfield, Cameron 3

Team unknown but included Morris, Walton, Stansfield and Cameron

14 May v Testgyakorborora (Budapest) 12–1

Bull, Stansfield, Cameron, Woodward 4, Glen 2, O'Hagan 3

Team unknown but included Bull, Stansfield, Cameron, Woodward, Glen and O'Hagan

16 May v Everton (Prague) 0–1

Team unknown

17 May v Slavia Prague (a) 8–1

Bull 2, Walton 2, Cameron 2, Glen, O'Hagan,

Team unknown but included Bull, Walton, Glen, Cameron and O'Hagan

1907 BELGIUM

19 May v Union Saint Gilloise (Ostend) 8–1

Seeburg 3, Woodward 2, Payne 2, Whyman

Manning, Burton, Watson, Walker, Morris, Bull, Darnell, Seeburg, Woodward, Payne, Whyman

20 May v Fulham (Ostend) 2–1

Whyman, Bull

Team unknown but included Bull, Darnell, Woodward and Whyman

1909 ARGENTINA AND URUGUAY

5 June v Everton (Palermo) 2–2

Tull, Middlemiss

Boreham, Coquet, Wilkes, Bull, Steel, MacFarlane, Curtis, Minter, Tull, Clark, Middlemiss

8,000

10 June v Uruguay League (Montevideo) 8–0

Curtis 2, Minter 2, McConnon, Clark 3

Boreham, Coquet, Wilkes, Morris, Steel, Bull, Curtis, Minter, McConnon, Clark, Middlemiss

1,500

13 June v Argentinos (Palermo) 1–0

McConnon

Boreham, Coquet, Wilkes, Morris, Steel, MacFarlane, Curtis, Minter, McConnon, Clark, Middlemiss

14,000

16 June v Liga Argentina (Palermo) 4–1

Bull, Minter, Clark, MacFarlane

Boreham, Coquet, Wilkes, Bull, Steel, MacFarlane, Curtis, Minter, Tull, Clark, Middlemiss

4,000

19 June v Everton (Palermo) 0–4
Boreham, Coquet, Wilkes, Bull, Steel, Morris, Curtis, Minter, Tull, Clark, Middlemiss
4,000

20 June v Rosario (Rosario) 9–0
Team and scorers unknown
6,000

24 June v Alumini (Alumini) 5–0
Morris, Curtis, Minter 2, MacFarlane
Boreham, Coquet, Wilkes, Morris, Steel, Bull, Curtis, MacFarlane, Minter, Tull, Middlemiss
8,000

1911 GERMANY

7 May v North German Combined XI (Hamburg) 4–1
Team and scorers unknown

13 May v Preussen (Berlin) 7–0
Team and scorers unknown

14 May v Hertha FC (Berlin) 4–1
Team and scorers unknown

20 May v Wacker FC (Leipzig) 8–1
Team and scorers unknown

21 May Eintracht FC (Brunswick) 4–1
Team and scorers unknown

25 May v Kickers-Victoria FC (Frankfurt) 6–0
Team and scorers unknown

1912 BELGIUM, GERMANY AND AUSTRO-HUNGARY

12 May (Decker Cup) v Hull City (Brussels) 0–2
Lunn, Norris, Gliddon, Darnell, D.Steel, Lightfoot, Curtis, Minter, Elliott, R.Steel (Bliss), Middlemiss
4,000

16 May v Bewegungs Spiele (Leipzig) 3–1
Grimsdell, Tattersall, Bliss
Lunn, Bowering, Gliddon, Lightfoot, D.Steel, Grimsdell, Middlemiss, Minter, Elliott, Bliss, Tattersall

20 May v Sports Athletic Club (Vienna) 5–2
Team and scorers unknown

24 May v Woolwich Arsenal (Vienna) 0–4
Team unknown

27 May v Ferencvarosi Torna (Budapest) 4–1
Scorers unknown
Team unknown but included Lunn, Darnell, Minter, Bliss and Middlemiss

28 May v Olympic Players (Budapest) 2–2
Scorers unknown
Team unknown but included Bliss and Middlemiss

30 May v Olympic Players (Budapest) 4–3
Scorers unknown
Team unknown but included Bliss

2 June v Olympic Players (Vienna) 0–3
Team unknown

1913 FRANCE

1 May v Red Star Amical (Paris) 2–1
Minter, Bliss
Team unknown but included Tate, R.Steel, Walden, Minter and Bliss
4,000

4 May v Red Star Amical (Paris) 9–0
Grimsdell 3, Fleming 3, Minter 2, Bliss
Team unknown but included Tate, R.Steel, Grimsdell, Walden, Minter, Fleming and Bliss

1914 GERMANY, ITALY AND SWITZERLAND

3 May v Hanover FC (a) 6–3
Banks, Elliott, Bliss, Middlemiss 3
Joyce, Clay, Cartwright, Weir, Steel, Grimsdell, Tattersall, Banks, Elliott, Bliss, Middlemiss
10,000

6 May v 1st Club of Nuremberg (a) 1–1
Sparrow
Team unknown but included Joyce, Sparrow and Middlemiss
5,000

9 May v Bayern Munich (a) 6–0
Joyce (pen), Banks 2, Sparrow 3
Joyce, Clay, Cartwright, Fleming, Elliott, Lightfoot, Tattersall, Banks, Sparrow, Bliss, Middlemiss

10 May v Furth FC (a) 2–2
Bliss 2 (1 pen)
Joyce, Clay, Cartwright, Weir, Steel, Grimsdell, Tattersall, Banks, Sparrow, Bliss, Middlemiss
10,000

13 May v Milan (a) 5–0
Fleming, Elliott 2, Bliss 2
Joyce, Clay, Pearson, Fleming, Steel, Lightfoot, Tattersall, Banks, Elliott, Bliss, Middlemiss
10,000

17 May v Zurich (a) 6–0
Tattersall 2, Elliott, Bliss 3
Joyce, Clay, Cartwright, Fleming, Weir, Lightfoot, Tattersall, Banks, Elliott, Bliss, Middlemiss
5,000

21 May v St Gallen (a) 3–0
Scorers unknown
Team unknown but included Steel

23 May v Pforzheim (a) 4–0
Scorers unknown
Team unknown but included Joyce, Pearson, Steel, Tattersall and Fleming

24 May v Stuttgart (a) 1–0
Team and scorer unknown

1925 SWITZERLAND

9 May v Basel Old Boys (a) 3–0
Thompson, Lane, Dimmock
Team unknown but included Thompson, Lane and Dimmock

10 May v Zurich Young Fellows (a) 2–0
Seed, Handley
Team unknown but included Lindsay, Smith, Seed and Handley

17 May v Wintherthur (a) 4–0
Seed 2, Lane, Dimmock
Team unknown but included Seed, Lane and Dimmock

18 May v Lausanne (a) 6–1
Handley 3, Dimmock 3 (1 pen)
Hinton, Clay, Grimsdell, Smith, Skitt, White, Thompson, Seed, Lane, Handley, Dimmock

20 May v La Chaux de Fonds (a) 8–1
Richardson, Smith, White, Lindsay, Handley3, Dimmock
Team unknown but included Richardson, Smith, White, Handley, Lindsay and Dimmock

21 May v Berne (a) 5–0
Clay, Lindsay 3, Dimmock
Team unknown but included Clay, Lindsay and Dimmock

24 May v Basel (a) 1–0
Lindsay
Team unknown but included Lindsay

1928 HOLLAND

6 May v Olympic A Team (Amsterdam) 5–2
Grimsdell, Thompson, O'Callaghan 2, Dimmock
Spiers, Forster, Poynton, Lowdell, Skitt, Grimsdell, Thompson, O'Callaghan, Lindsay, Armstrong, Dimmock

9 May v Den Haag (The Hague) 6–2
Skitt 2, Thompson, Dimmock 3
Team unknown but included Skitt, Thompson and Dimmock

13 May v All Holland (Almelo) 3–0
Thompson, Townley, Dimmock
Team unknown but included Spiers, Poynton, Thompson, O'Callaghan, Lindsay, Townley and Dimmock

16 May v Rotterdam (Rotterdam) 3–0
Thompson, O'Callaghan, Dimmock
Team unknown but included Thompson, O'Callaghan and Dimmock

1929 MALTA

11 May v Sliema Wanderers (a) 7–1
Harper 3, Armstrong 2, Crompton, Lindsay
Spiers, Forster (Illingworth), Herod, Lindsay, Skitt, Smith, Crompton, O'Callaghan, Harper, Armstrong, Dimmock

12 May v Valetta United (a) 2–1
Harper, Crompton
Spiers, Illingworth, Herod, Lindsay, Skitt, Smith, Crompton, O'Callaghan, Harper, Armstrong, Dimmock

16 May v British Army (Valetta) 5–0
Thompson, Armstrong, Garbutt, Crompton 2
Spiers, Illingworth, Herod, Lindsay, Skitt, Smith, Crompton, O'Callaghan, Garbutt, Thompson, Armstrong

18 May v Royal Navy (Valetta) 1–0
Harper (pen)
Spiers, Illingworth, Herod, Lindsay, Skitt, Smith, O'Callaghan, Crompton, Harper, Thompson, Garbutt

19 May v Floriana (a) 2–1
Harper 2
Spiers, Illingworth, Herod, Lindsay, Skitt, Smith, Crompton, O'Callaghan, Harper, Armstrong, Dimmock

21 May (Valetta Cup) v Pick of Malta (Valetta) 5–1
Garbutt 3, Harper 2
Spiers, Illingworth, Herod, Lindsay, Skitt, Smith, Thompson, O'Callaghan, Harper, Armstrong, Garbutt

1932 CHANNEL ISLANDS

12 May v Guernsey (a) 2–1
Greenfield 2
Spiers, Felton, Poynton, Colquhoun, Rowe, T.Evans, Davies, O'Callaghan, Hunt, Greenfield, W.Evans
5,000

16 May v Jersey (a) 9–0
Colquhoun, Davies, O'Callaghan, Hunt 6
Spiers, T.Evans, Poynton, Colquhoun, Rowe, Day, Davies, O'Callaghan, Hunt, Greenfield, W.Evans
6,000

1933 CHANNEL ISLANDS

11 May v Channel Islands (Guernsey) 6–0
T.Evans, Hall 2, W.Evans 2 (1 pen), Opponent (og)
Taylor, Felton, Whatley, T.Evans, Rowe, Alsford, McCormick, O'Callaghan, Brain, Hall, W.Evans

13 May v Guernsey (a) 8–0
McCormick, O'Callaghan, Hall 2, W.Evans 4
Taylor, T.Evans, Whatley, Colquhoun, Rowe, Alsford, McCormick, O'Callaghan, Brain, Hall, W.Evans

18 May v Jersey (a) 5–1
Alsford, Colquhoun 2, W.Evans
Taylor, Felton, Whatley, T.Evans, Rowe, Alsford, McCormick, O'Callaghan, Colquhoun, Hall, W.Evans

1935 CHANNEL ISLANDS

16 May v Channel Islands (Guernsey) 5–0
Alsford, A.G.Hall, D.A.Hunt, G.W.Hall
Nicholls, Channell, Fullwood, Howe, Jones, Alsford, Bolan, A.G.Hall, D.A.Hunt, G.W.Hall Hedley

18 May v Guernsey (a) 5–0
A.G.Hall, D.A.Hunt 4
Nicholls, Channell, Fullwood, Phypers, Howe, Alsford, Bolan, A.G.Hall, D.A.Hunt, G.W.Hall, Hedley

1947 FRANCE

13 June v Olympique de Marseilles (a) 1–2
Gilberg
Ditchburn, Willis, Buckingham, Ludford, Nicholson, Burgess, Jones, Bennett, Rundle, Stevens, Gilberg

15 June v Toulouse (a) 1–2
Rundle
Ditchburn, Tickridge, Buckingham, Ludford, Woodward, Nicholson, Jones, Bennett, Rundle, Dix, Stevens

19 June v Olympique de Montpellier (a) 1–0
Duquemin
Ditchburn, Willis, Tickridge, Trailor, Woodward, Burgess, Jones, Bennett, Duquemin, Foreman, Stevens

21 June v Saint-Etienne (a) 2–0
Rundle, Bennett
Ditchburn, Tickridge, Buckingham, Ludford, Woodward, Burgess, Rundle, Bennett, Duquemin, Dix, Stevens

1948 CHANNEL ISLANDS

8 May v Jersey (a) 3–0
Baily, Duquemin, Bennett
Ditchburn, Tickridge, Buckingham, Ludford, Woodward, Burgess, Cox, Baily, Duquemin, Bennett, Jones

11 May v Guernsey (a) 7–0
Duquemin 3 (1 pen), Cox 2, Bennett 2
Ditchburn, Tickridge, Withers, Gilberg, Woodward, Burgess, Cox, Jordan, Duquemin, Bennett, Jones

1950 GERMANY AND BELGIUM

14 May v Hanover Arminia (a) 3–0
Willis (pen), Harmer, Scarth
Ditchburn, Tickridge, Willis, Gilberg, Clarke, Burgess, Walters, Bennett, Duquemin, Harmer, Scarth
20,000

18 May v Tennis-Borussia (Berlin) 2–0
Gilberg, Walters
Ditchburn, Willis, Withers, Gilberg, Clarke, Burgess, Walters, Bennett, Duquemin, Scarth, Adams
70,000

21 May v Wacker Club (Berlin) 5–2
Bennett, Duquemin, Baily 2, Opponent (og)
Ditchburn, Ramsey, Withers, Nicholson, Farley, Burgess, Walters, Bennett, Duquemin, Baily, Scarth
25,000

24 May v Borussia Dortmund (a) 4–0
Walters, Duquemin, Baily, Gilberg
Ditchburn, Ramsey, Withers, Nicholson, Clarke, Burgess, Walters, Bennett, Duquemin, Baily, Gilberg

27 May v Royal Beerschott (Antwerp) 1–2
Duquemin
Ditchburn, Ramsey, Willis, Nicholson, Clarke, Burgess, Walters, Bennett, Duquemin, Baily, Gilberg

1951 DENMARK

29 May v Combined Copenhagen XI (a) 4–2
Walters, Bennett, Duquemin 2
Reynolds, Ramsey, Willis, Nicholson, Clarke, Burgess, Walters, Bennett, Duquemin, Baily, Murphy

30 May v Combined Copenhagen XI (a) 2–2
Walters, McClellan
Reynolds, Withers, Willis, Nicholson, Clarke, Brittan, Walters, Bennett, McClellan, Murphy, Medley

31 May v Combined Copenhagen XI (a) 2–0
Nicholson, Duquemin
Reynolds, Ramsey, Withers, Nicholson, Clarke, Burgess, Walters, Murphy, Duquemin, Baily, Medley

1952 NORTH AMERICA

22 May v Toronto & District FA (Toronto) 7–0
Walters 2, Bennett, Duquemin 2, Harmer 2
Ditchburn, Willis, Withers, Wetton, Clarke, Burgess, Walters, Bennett, Duquemin, Harmer, Medley

28 May v Saskatchewan FA (Saskatoon) 18–1
McClellan 9, Bennett 3, Duquemin 2, Uphill, Adams 3
Team unknown but included Ditchburn (Hayes), Uphill, Bennett (Harmer), Duquemin, McClellan and Adams
5,000

31 May v British Columbia FA (Vancouver) 9–2
Ramsey (pen), Walters 2, Bennett 4, Duquemin 2
Team unknown but included Ditchburn, Ramsey, Clarke, Walters, Bennett, Duquemin, Harmer and Medley
10,000

2 June v Victoria & District FA (Victoria) 7–0
Walters, Adams, Baily 4, Medley
Team unknown but included Walters, Adams, Baily and Medley
6,000

4 June v British Columbia FA (Vancouver) 8–2
Walters 2, Duquemin, Baily 2, Bennett 3
Team unnkown but included Ditchburn, Clarke, Burgess, Walters, Bennett, Duquemin, Baily and Medley

7 June v Alberta FA (Calgary) 11–0
Wetton, McClellan 2, Baily, Duquemin 2, Harmer 3, Uphill2
Team unknown but included Ditchburn, Wetton, McClellan, Baily, Duquemin, Harmer and Uphill

9 June v Manitoba FA (Winnipeg) 5–0
Walters, Bennett 3, Duquemin
Ditchburn, Ramsey, Willis, Nicholson, Clarke, Wetton, Walters, Bennett, Duquemin, Baily, Medley
24,321

14 June v Manchester United (Toronto) 5–0
Walters, Bennett, Duquemin, Baily, Medley,
Ditchburn, Ramsey, Willis, Nicholson, Clarke, Wetton, Walters, Bennett, Duquemin, Baily, Medley

15 June v Manchester United (New York) 7–1
McClellan, Bennett 2, Duquemin 4
Ditchburn, Ramsey, Withers, Wetton, Clarke, Burgess, McClellan, Bennett, Duquemin, Baily, Medley

18 June v Quebec FA (Montreal) 8–0
Wetton, McClellan 3, Bennett 3, Medley
Ditchburn, Ramsey, Willis, Wetton, Clarke, Burgess, Walters, Bennett, Duquemin (McClellan), Baily, Medley

1954 AUSTRIA AND WEST GERMANY

28 April v Austrian State XI (Vienna) 0–2
Ditchburn, Withers, Willis, Nicholson, Clarke, Burgess, Walters, Bennett, Dunmore, Baily, Robb
15,000

1 May v Vfb Stuttgart (a) 1–3
Duquemin
Reynolds, Ramsey, Willis, Burgess, Marchi, Wetton, Walters, Brooks, Duquemin, Harmer, Baily (Withers)
12,000

5 May v Eintracht Brunswick (a) 0–1
Reynolds, Baker, Withers, Marchi, Clarke, Wetton, Walters, Brooks, Duquemin, Harmer, Dunmore
10,000

8 May v SV Hamburg (a) 2–2
Walters, Bennett
Reynolds, Ramsey (Withers), Willis, Nicholson, Marchi, Wetton, Walters, Bennett, Duquemin, Baily, Dunmore
15,000

1955 AUSTRIA, HUNGARY AND FRANCE

11 May v FC Austria (Vienna) 2–6
Duquemin 2
Reynolds, Baker, Hopkins, Blanchflower, Clarke, Marchi, Gavin, Brooks, Duquemin, Baily, Robb
17,000

15 May v FC Kinizsi (Budapest) 1–4
Brooks
Reynolds, Baker, Hopkins, Blanchflower, Clarke, Marchi, Walters, Brooks, Duquemin, Baily, Robb
70,000

18 May v FC Vasas (Budapest) 2–4
Brooks 2
Reynolds, Withers, Hopkins (Baker), Blanchflower, Clarke, Marchi, Walters, Brooks, Duquemin, Baily, Gavin
52,000

20 May v Pecs Dozsa (Pecs) 1–0
Gavin
Reynolds, Nicholson, Withers, Blanchflower, Clarke, Marchi, Walters, Brooks, Duquemin, Baily, Gavin
22,000

25 May v Racing Club de Paris (a) 0–0
Reynolds, Baker, Withers, Blanchflower, Clarke, Marchi, Walters, Brooks, Duquemin, Harmer, Gavin
8,000

1957 NORTH AMERICA

19 May v Celtic (New York) 4–3
Dulin, Smith 3
Reynolds, Baker, Henry, Blanchflower, Ryden, Marchi, Dulin, Harmer, Smith, Brooks, Dyson
12,342

22 May v Essex County All Stars (Windsor) 8–1
Walley, Harmer 2 (2 pens), Smith 4, Wilkie
Reynolds, Hills, Henry, Blanchflower (Walley), Ryden, Marchi, Dulin (Bing), Harmer, Smith, Stokes, Wilkie
4,200

25 May v Ontario All Stars (Ontario) 7–0
Harmer, Smith 5, Stokes
Reynolds, Baker, Henry, Blanchflower, Ryden, Marchi, Dulin, Harmer, Smith, Stokes, Dyson (Wilkie)
10,000

29 May v Alberta All Stars (Calgary) 6–1
Blanchflower, Dulin, Smith, Dunmore, Stokes 2
Reynolds, Baker, Henry, Blanchflower, Ryden, Marchi, Dulin, Harmer, Smith (Dunmore), Stokes, Brooks
5,000

1 June v Celtic (Vancouver) 6–3
Blanchflower, Smith 2, Stokes 2, Brooks,
Reynolds, Baker, Henry, Blanchflower, Ryden, Marchi, Dulin, Harmer, Smith, Stokes, Brooks
21,121

3 June v British Columbia All Stars (Vancouver) 0–2
Reynolds, Baker, Henry, Blanchflower, Ryden, Marchi, Dulin, Harmer, Smith, Stokes, Brooks
9,164

5 June v Manitoba All Stars (Winnipeg) 12–0
Dulin 2, Harmer, Dunmore, Stokes 5, Dyson 3
Reynolds, Hills, Henry, Blanchflower (Baker), Ryden, Walley, Dulin (Bing), Harmer, Dunmore, Stokes, Dyson
4,500

8 June v Celtic (Toronto) 3–1
Smith 3
Reynolds, Hills, Henry, Blanchflower, Ryden, Walley, Dulin, Harmer, Smith, Brooks, Dyson
24,198

9 June v Celtic (Montreal) 0–2
Reynolds, Baker, Henry, Walley (Blanchflower), Ryden, Marchi, Dulin, Harmer, Smith (Dunmore), Stokes, Brooks
8,000

1959 USSR

27 May v Torpedo Moscow (a) 1–0
Medwin
Hollowbread, Baker, Hopkins, Blanchflower, Norman, Mackay, Medwin, Harmer (Clayton), Smith, Brooks, Jones
50,000

1 June v Dynamo Kiev (a) 2–1
Brooks 2
Reynolds, Baker, Henry, Blanchflower, Norman, Mackay, Medwin (Clayton), Harmer, Dunmore (Smith), Brooks, Jones
60,000

4 June v CCCP Select XI (Leningrad) 1–3
Brooks
Reynolds, Baker, Henry, Blanchflower (Mackay), Norman, Iley, Harmer, Brooks (Dunmore), Smith, Clayton, Jones
100,000

1961 HOLLAND

15 May v Feyenoord (a) 2–1
Medwin, Allen
Brown, Baker, Henry, Blanchflower, Norman, Mackay, Medwin, White, Saul, Allen, Dyson
40,940

17 May v Amsterdam Select XI (a) 3–0
White, Allen, Dyson
Brown, Baker, Henry, Blanchflower, Norman, Marchi, Medwin, White, Saul, Allen, Dyson
30,000

1962 ISRAEL

26 May v Tel Aviv Select XI (a) 2–1
Mackay, Clayton
Brown, Baker, Henry, Blanchflower, Marchi, Mackay, Medwin, White, R.Smith, Clayton, Dyson
35,000

30 May v Haifa Select XI (a) 5–0
Mackay, White, Saul, Allen, Clayton
Brown, Baker, Henry, Blanchflower (J.Smith), Marchi, Mackay, Medwin (Dyson), White, Saul, Allen, Clayton
12,000

1963 SOUTH AFRICA

31 May v NSAFL Invitation XI (Cape Town) 5–1

Saul, Allen 3, Jones

Brown, Baker, Hopkins, Blanchflower, Marchi, J.Smith, Medwin (Dyson), White, Saul, Allen, Jones

21,000

8 June v NFL Select XI (Durban) 5–2

Jones 2, Greaves 2, Dyson

Brown, Baker, Henry, J.Smith, Norman, Marchi, Jones, White, R.Smith, Greaves, Dyson

25,000

12 June v South African XI (Johannesburg) 3–1

Clayton, R.Smith, Greaves

Hollowbread, Hopkins, Henry, Blanchflower, Norman, Marchi, Clayton, White, R.Smith, Greaves, Dyson

1965 HOLLAND

18 May v DWS Club (a) 0–1

Jennings, Norman, Henry, Mullery, Brown, Clayton, Robertson, Saul, Mackay (Low), Gilzean, Jones

22 May v Telstar Club (a) 3–2

Saul, Jones 2

Jennings, Knowles, Henry, Mullery, Norman, Beal, Weller, Clayton, Saul, Mackay, Jones

10,000

ISRAEL

21 June v Hakoah (a) 3–1

Greaves 2 (1 pen), Jones

Jennings, Knowles, Henry, Mullery, Norman, Mackay, Weller, Greaves, Saul, Gilzean, Jones

15,000

24 June (John White Cup) v Maccabi Tel Aviv (a) 3–2

Mullery, Mackay, Gilzean1

W.Brown, Norman, Knowles, Mullery, L.Brown, Mackay, Pitt, Greaves, Saul (Clayton), Gilzean, Jones (Weller)

SPAIN

14 August (Costa Del Sol Tournament semi-final) v Valencia (Malaga) 2–1

Clayton, Jones

W.Brown, Norman, Knowles, Mullery, L.Brown, Mackay, Possee, Clayton, Gilzean, Greaves, Jones (Robertson)

30,000

15 August (Costa Del Sol Tournament final) v Standard Liege (Malaga) 1–0

Mullery

W.Brown, Norman, Knowles, Mullery, L.Brown, Mackay, Possee, Clayton (Saul), Gilzean, Greaves, Robertson (Beal)

15,000

1966 BERMUDA, NORTH AMERICA AND MEXICO

19 May v Bermuda Select XI (Hamilton) 3–2

Gilzean 2, Venables

W.Brown (Jennings), Kinnear, Knowles (Henry), Mullery, Hoy (L.Brown), Beal, Possee (Clayton), Mackay, Gilzean (Saul), Venables, Robertson

21 May v Celtic (Toronto) 0–1

W.Brown, Kinnear, Knowles, Mullery, Hoy, Mackay, Possee, Gilzean, Venables, Saul, Robertson

25,000

25 May v Hartford Select XI (Hartford) 3–0

Weller 2, Saul

Jennings, Beal, Knowles, Mullery, L.Brown, Clayton, Weller, Gilzean, Venables, Saul, Possee

29 May v Bologna (Jersey) City 0–1

Jennings, Kinnear, Knowles, Mullery, L.Brown, Mackay, Possee (Weller), Gilzean, Venables, Saul, Robertson

1 June v Celtic (San Francisco) 1–2

Mackay (pen)

W.Brown, Kinnear (Henry), Knowles, Mullery, L.Brown, Mackay, Possee, Gilzean, Venables, Saul, Robertson

12,000

4 June v Celtic (Vancouver) 1–1
Venables
Jennings, Beal, Knowles, Mullery, L.Brown, Mackay, Possee, Clayton, Weller, Venables, Robertson (Gilzean)

8 June v British Columbia XI (Vancouver) 3–0
Mullery, Mackay, Saul
W.Brown, Beal, Henry, Mullery, L.Brown, Mackay, Possee, Gilzean, Venables, Saul, Weller

12 June v Mexican National XI (Mexico City) 1–0
Gilzean
Jennings, Beal, Knowles, Mullery, L.Brown, Mackay, Weller (Gilzean), Clayton (Henry), Saul, Venables, Robertson (Possee)
100,000

15 June v America Club of Mexico (Mexico City) 2–0
Weller, Gilzean
Jennings, Beal, Henry, Mullery, L.Brown, Mackay, Weller (Possee), Clayton, Saul (Gilzean), Venables, Robertson

17 June v Bayern Munich (Detroit) 3–0
Weller, Saul, Venables
W.Brown, Beal, Knowles, Mullery, L.Brown, Henry, Weller, Clayton, Saul, Venables, Robertson
11,250

19 June v Bayern Munich (Chicago) 1–1
Henry
Jennings, Beal, Knowles, Mullery, L.Brown, Henry, Weller (Possee), Clayton, Saul (Gilzean), Venables, Robertson

SPAIN

14 August (Costa Del Sol Tournament) v Malaga CD (Malaga) 2–1
Mullery, Gilzean
Jennings, Kinnear, Knowles, Mullery, Henry, Mackay, Robertson, Greaves, Gilzean, Venables, Jones

15 August (Costa Del Sol Tournament) v Benfica (Malaga) 2–1
Robertson, Greaves
Jennings, Kinnear, Knowles, Mullery, Henry, Mackay, Robertson (Weller), Beal, Gilzean, Venables, Greaves
30,000

1967 SWITZERLAND

30 May v FC Zurich (a) 2–0
Robertson 2
Jennings, Kinnear, Want, Mullery, England, Mackay, Robertson, Greaves, Gilzean, Venables, Saul, Used subs: Johnson, Jones
5,000

1 June v BSC Young Boys (a) 3–2
Greaves 2, Bond
Jennings, Kinnear, Want, Clayton, England, Mackay, Robertson, Greaves, Gilzean, Bond, Jones. Used subs: Johnson, Saul
6,000

7 June FC Servette (a) 4–1
Greaves 2, Venables, Saul
Jennings, Kinnear, Want, Mullery, England, Mackay, Robertson, Greaves, Gilzean, Venables, Saul. Used subs: Johnson, Jones
10,000

1968 GREECE AND CYPRUS

15 May v Panathinakos (a) 2–2
Gilzean 2
Jennings, Beal, Want, Mullery, England, Mackay, Jones (Robertson), Greaves, Chivers, Venables, Gilzean

19 May v Anorthosis (a) 5–0
Robertson 3, Greaves 2
Jennings, Kinnear, Want, Collins, Beal, Venables, Robertson, Pearce, Bond, Greaves, Gilzean

22 May v AEL (a) 7–1
Jones 2, Bond, Robertson, Gilzean 3,
Jennings, Kinnear, Want, Collins, England, Pearce, Jones, Venables, Bond, Greaves (Robertson), Gilzean

25 May v Cyprus International XI (Nicosia) 3–0
Robertson 2, Gilzean
Jennings, Kinnear, Want, Collins, England, Mackay, Jones (Pratt), Bond, Beal, Robertson, Gilzean

29 May v Apoel (a) 3–0
Robertson, Pearce, Jones
Jennings, Kinnear, Want, Beal, Collins, Mackay, Robertson, Bond (Pearce), Gilzean (Pratt), Venables, Jones (Johnson)

1969 NORTH AMERICA

15 May v West Ham United (Baltimore) 4–3
Greaves 2, Pearce, Morgan
Jennings, Want, Knowles, Perryman, Collins, Beal, Johnson, Greaves, Pearce, Venables, Morgan
4,700

17 May v Aston Villa (Atlanta) 2–2
Greaves 2
Hancock, Want, Knowles, Perryman (Pratt), Evans, Beal, Jenkins (Johnson), Greaves, Pearce, Venables, Morgan
4,000

28 May (Toronto Cup) v Fiorentina (Toronto) 0–3
Jennings, Want (Evans), Knowles, Perryman, Collins, Beal, Pearce, Greaves, Gilzean (Johnson), Venables, Morgan
20,152

1 June (Toronto Cup) v Rangers (Toronto) 4–3
Greaves 3 (2 pens), Morgan
Hancock, Want, Knowles, Perryman, Evans, Beal, Johnson (Venables), Greaves, Pearce, Pratt, Morgan
10,506

1970 MALTA

13 May v Valetta (a) 3–0
Gilzean, Pratt, Morgan
Jennings, Evans, Want, Pearce, England, Beal, Gilzean, Bond, Chivers, Pratt, Morgan

16 May v Sliema Wanderers (a) 2–1
Pearce, Chivers
Jennings, Evans, Knowles, Pearce (Johnson), England, Beal, Gilzean, Bond, Chivers, Perryman, Morgan (Pratt)

17 May v Maltese Select XI (a) 0–1
Jennings, Evans, Want, Perryman, Collins, Beal, Gilzean, Bond, Chivers (Pearce), Pratt, Johnson

1970 SPAIN

7 August (Palma de Mallorca Tournament) v FC Cologne (Palma) 0–1
Jennings, Evans, Knowles, Mullery, England, Beal, Gilzean, Perryman, Chivers, Peters, Pearce (Collins)

8 August (Palma de Mallorca Tournament) v Athletico Madrid (Palma) 0–1
Jennings, Kinnear, Knowles, Mullery (Bond), Collins, Beal, Gilzean, Perryman, Chivers, Peters, Pearce

1971 JAPAN

27 May v All Japan XI (Kobe) 6–0
Kinnear, Collins, Gilzean, Chivers 2, Pratt
Jennings, Kinnear, Knowles (Want), Mullery, Collins, Beal, Gilzean, Perryman, Chivers, Pratt, Neighbour (Morgan)

3 June v All Japan XI (Tokyo) 7–2
Mullery, Gilzean 2, Chivers 2, Pratt 2,
Jennings, Kinnear, Knowles, Mullery, Collins, Beal, Gilzean, Perryman, Chivers, Pratt, Neighbour (Morgan)
35,000

9 June v All Japan XI (Tokyo) 3–0
Mullery 2 (1 pen), Chivers
Jennings, Want, Knowles, Mullery, Collins, Beal, Gilzean, Perryman, Chivers, Pratt, Morgan (Pearce)
50,000

1972 ISRAEL

7 June v Maccabi Tel Aviv (a) 3–2
Pearce, Gilzean, Peters
Jennings, Evans, Knowles, Mullery, England, Beal, Pearce (Naylor), Pratt, Gilzean, Peters, Coates (Neighbour)
18,000

1974 MAURITIUS

8 June v Mauritius Select XI (Curepipe) 5–0
Chivers 3, Gilzean 2
Jennings, Evans, Knowles (Naylor), Beal, Dillon, Pratt, Coates, Perryman, Chivers, Gilzean, McGrath
18,000

13 June v Mauritius Select XI (Curepipe) 6–3
Knowles (pen), Gilzean 2, Perryman 2, Peters
Jennings, Kinnear (Pratt), Knowles, Naylor, Beal, Holder, Neighbour (McGrath), McNab (Coates), Gilzean, Perryman, Peters
5,000

16 June v Mauritius Select XI (Curepipe) 6–0
Coates, Perryman, Gilzean 3, Peters,
Jennings, Evans, Knowles, Beal, Naylor, Pratt, Coates, Perryman, Gilzean, Peters, McGrath
10,000

1975 WEST GERMANY AND HOLLAND

23 July v Rot-Weiss Essen (a) 1–1
Jones
Jennings, Kinnear, Pratt, Coates, Osgood, McAllister, Conn, Perryman, Chivers, Jones, McNab

25 July v Karlsruher SC (a) 1–2
Kinnear (pen)
Jennings, Kinnear, McAllister (McNab), Pratt, Osgood, Naylor, McGrath (Conn), Perryman, Chivers, Duncan (Jones), Neighbour

29 July v Hanover 96 (a) 1–1
Jones
Jennings, Kinnear, McAllister, Pratt, Osgood, Naylor, Coates, Perryman, Chivers, Jones, Neighbour

3 August v NAC Breda (a) 1–0
Kinnear (pen)
Jennings, Osgood, Knowles, Pratt, McAllister, Naylor, Coates (McNab [Kinnear]), Perryman, Chivers, Jones, McGrath

1976 CANADA, FIJI AND AUSTRALASIA

27 April v Toronto Metros-Croatia (Toronto) 1–0
Coates
Jennings (Daines), Naylor, Stead, Hoddle (Pratt), Young, Osgood, Jones (Armstrong), Perryman, Chivers, Coates, Neighbour
5,000

1 May v Fijian Select XI (Lautoka) 4–0
Chivers, Duncan, Armstrong, Jones
Daines (Kendall), Stead, Naylor, Pratt, Young (Walford), Osgood, Hoddle, Coates, Chivers (Duncan), Armstrong, Jones
6,000

3 May v Auckland FA XI (Auckland) 5–3
Pratt, Osgood (pen), Neighbour, Duncan 2,
Daines, Stead, Walford, Pratt, Young, Osgood, Neighbour, Armstrong, Duncan, Perryman, Coates
10,000

5 May v Wellington FA XI (Wellington) 3–2
Pratt, Armstrong, Duncan
Daines, Stead, McAllister (Coates), Pratt, Young, Osgood, Neighbour, Naylor, Armstrong, Duncan, Hoddle
8,500

9 May v Victoria (Melbourne) 3–1
Pratt, Perryman, Jones
Daines (Kendall), Osgood, Naylor (Stead), Pratt (Hoddle), Young, Walford, Neighbour, Perryman, Jones, Armstrong (Duncan), Coates
15,000

12 May v Northern New South Wales (Newcastle) 5–1
Young, Hoddle, Chivers, Osgood (pen), Smythe (og)
Kendall, Naylor (Neill), Stead, Pratt (Neighbour), Young, Walford, Hoddle, Perryman (Armstrong), Jones, Chivers, Osgood
7,000

16 May v Australian National XI (Sydney) 3–2
Neighbour, Jones, Coates
Daines, Naylor, Stead, Pratt, Young, Osgood, Neighbour, Perryman, Chivers, Jones, Coates
26,561

17 May v Southern Australia (Adelaide) 5–2
Osgood 2, Jones, Chivers, Coates
Kendall, Naylor (Armstrong), Stead, Pratt, Young, Walford, Neighbour, Osgood, Jones, Chivers, Coates
15,200

23 May v Western Australia (Perth) 4–0
Chivers 3, Jones
Daines (Kendall), Naylor, Stead (Armstrong), Pratt (Hoddle), Young, Osgood (Walford), Neighbour, Perryman, Chivers, Jones, Coates
18,000

1976 WEST GERMANY

24 July v Vfl Osnabrück (a) 3–1
Armstrong, Jones 2
Jennings, Naylor, McAllister, Pratt, Young, Osgood, Coates, Perryman (Hoddle), Armstrong (Conn), Jones, Neighbour

28 July v Eintracht Frankfurt (a) 1–4
Young
Jennings, Naylor, McAllister, Pratt, Young, Osgood, Coates, Perryman, Armstrong (Conn), Jones, Neighbour

31 July v 1FC Cologne (a) 1–3
Jones
Daines, Naylor, Stead, Pratt, Young, Osgood, Coates, Perryman, Hoddle, Jones, Neighbour

4 August KSV Baunatal (a) 2–1
Jones 2
Daines, Stead (Naylor), McAllister, Pratt, Young, Walford (Osgood), Coates, Perryman, Hoddle (Robinson), Jones, Conn

6 August v FV Bad Honnef (a) 2–0
Conn, Armstrong
Jennings (Daines), Naylor, McAllister, Pratt, Young, Walford (Stead), Robinson (Conn), Perryman, Armstrong, Osgood, Neighbour

1977 NORWAY

17 May v Stord (a) 5–0
Osgood, Armstrong, Jones, Moores, Taylor
Jennings (Daines), Naylor, Stead, Pratt, Osgood, Perryman, Holmes, Hoddle, Armstrong (Jones), Moores, Taylor

19 May v Sogndal (a) 6–0
Pratt, Perryman, Armstrong 2, Jones, Taylor
Jennings (Daines), Naylor (Jennings), Stead, Pratt (Coates), Osgood, Perryman, Jones, Hoddle (Armstrong), Moores, Holmes, Taylor

1977 SWEDEN

7 August (Nolia Cup semi-final) v Royal Union (Umea) 2–0
Duncan, Moores
Daines, Naylor (Stead), Holmes, Hoddle, Armstrong, Perryman, Coates, McNab (Gorman), Duncan (Moores), Jones, Pratt

10 August (Nolia Cup final) v Leicester City (Umea) 2–1
Moores, Opponent (og)
Daines, Naylor, Holmes, Hoddle, Armstrong, Perryman, Coates, McNab, Duncan, Moores, Pratt

12 August v Norsjo IF (a) 3–2
Armstrong, Duncan, Jones
Kendall, Stead, Holmes, Naylor, Armstrong, Perryman, Coates, McNab, Moores (Duncan [Moores]), Jones, Pratt

1978 SYRIA

8 May v Aleppo (a) 1–0
Jones
Daines (Kendall), Naylor, Holmes (Stead), Hoddle, McAllister, Perryman, Pratt, McNab, Jones, Duncan (Moores [Falco]), Taylor
25,000

10 May v Syrian Police (Damascus) 4–0
Holmes, Falco, Taylor 2
Daines (Kendall), Naylor, Holmes, Hoddle, McAllister, Perryman, Pratt, McNab, Duncan (Falco), Stead, Taylor
12,000

1978 NORWAY AND SWEDEN

15 May v Hamar (a) 0–3
Daines (Kendall), Naylor, Holmes, Sloan (McNab), McAllister, Perryman (Gorman), Pratt (Stead), McNab (Hoddle), Jones (Moores), Duncan (Perryman), Taylor
2,500

17 May v Kvik Halden (a) 2–0
McNab, Taylor (pen)
Daines (Kendall), Naylor, Stead (Gorman), Sloan (Hoddle), McAllister, Holmes, Pratt, McNab, Jones, Duncan (Moores), Taylor
1,500

18 May v Karlstad (a) 4–1
Pratt, Moores, Duncan 2
Daines (Kendall), Naylor, Holmes (Gorman), Hoddle, McAllister, Perryman, Pratt, McNab, Moores (Stead), Duncan, Taylor
2,000

1979 KUWAIT, MALAYSIA, JAPAN AND BERMUDA

16 May v Kuwait Army XI (a) 2–1

Falco, Villa

Aleksic, Lee, Smith, McAllister (Naylor), Lacy, Perryman, Pratt (Beavon), Ardiles (Galvin), Jones (Falco), Hoddle, Villa

4,000

23 May v Malaysian Select XI (Kuala Lumpar) 4–0

Lee, Falco 3 (1 pen)

Aleksic, Lee, Smith (McAllister), Miller, Lacy, Perryman (Beavon), Pratt, Naylor, Falco, Galvin, Villa

30,000

27 May (Japan Cup) v Indonesia (Yokohama) 6–0

Lee 2, McAllister, Galvin, Villa 2

Aleksic, Lee, McAllister, Miller, Lacy, Perryman, Pratt, Beavon, Galvin, Falco (Jones), Villa

2,000

29 May (Japan Cup) v Japan A (Tokyo) 2–0

Jones, Ardiles

Aleksic, Lee, Smith, Miller, McAllister, Perryman, Pratt (Beavon), Naylor, Jones, Ardiles, Villa

12,000

31 May (Japan Cup) v Fiorentina (Nishigaoka) 1–1

Lee

Daines, Lee, Smith, McAllister, Lacy, Beavon, Pratt, Naylor, Jones, Galvin, Villa

12,000

2 June (Japan Cup) v San Lorenzo (Tokyo) 3–3

Lee, Pratt, Galvin

Aleksic, Lee, Smith, Miller, Lacy, Perryman, Pratt, Ardiles (Falco), Galvin, Jones, Villa

12,000

(Spurs won 5–2 on penalties)

4 June (Japan Cup Final) v Dundee United (Tokyo) 2–0

Smith, Ardiles

Aleksic, Lee, Smith, McAllister, Lacy, Perryman, Pratt, Naylor, Jones (Falco), Ardiles, Villa

14,000

6 June v Bermuda Select XI (Hamilton) 3–1

Lee, Bean, Jones

Daines, Lee, Day (Marshall), McAllister, Lacy, Pratt, Aleksic (Bean), Naylor, Jones, Smith, Varney (Astwood)

1,200

1980 AUSTRIA

11 May v Rapid/FC Austria XI (Vienna) 0–3

Daines, Miller, Hughton, Naylor, McAllister, Perryman, Ardiles, Jones, Falco (Roberts), Taylor, Galvin

4,000

13 May v Gais/Sturm Select XI (Graz) 0–2

Kendall, Lacy, Hughton, Naylor, McAllister, Perryman, Roberts (Falco), Jones, Hazard, Taylor, Galvin

3,000

1981 BAHRAIN AND KUWAIT

24 May v Bahrain Select XI (Isa Town) 3–0

Miller, Galvin, Brooke

Aleksic, McAllister, Miller (Cooper), Roberts, Villa, Perryman (Mazzon), Ardiles, Hazard (Crook), Galvin, Brooke, Crooks (Falco)

26 May v Kuwait Army XI (a) 2–1

Brooke, Crooks

Daines, McAllister, Miller, Roberts, Villa, Perryman, Ardiles, Hazard (Crook), Galvin, Brooke (Mazzon), Crooks (Falco)

28 May v Bahrain Select XI (Isa Town) 5–3

Miller, Galvin, Falco 2, Crooks,

Daines, McAllister, Miller (Mazzon), Roberts, Villa (Cooper [Crook]), Perryman, Ardiles, Hazard, Galvin, Falco, Crooks

1981 TURKEY

10 June v Trabzonspor (a) 4–0

Villa, Ardiles, Falco, Crooks,

Aleksic, Hughton, Miller, Roberts, Villa, Perryman, Ardiles, Falco (Smith), Galvin, Hoddle (Mazzon), Crooks (Hazard)

22,000

13 June v Fenerbahce (a) 5–1

Villa, Falco, Galvin, Hoddle, Crooks

Daines, Smith, Miller (Mazzon), Roberts, Villa (Falco), Perryman, Ardiles (Hazard), Archibald, Galvin, Hoddle, Crooks

40,000

1982 HOLLAND

13 August (Amsterdam 707 Tournament) v Ajax (a) 2–3

Roberts 2

Clemence, Hughton, Miller, Roberts (Brooke), Hazard, Mabbutt, Archibald, Galvin, Hoddle, Crooks, Lacy

40,000

15 August (Amsterdam 707 Tournament) v 1FC Cologne (Amsterdam) 0–0

Clemence, Hughton, Miller, Hazard, Mabbutt, O'Reilly, Archibald, Falco, Lacy, Gibson, Brooke

35,000

(Spurs lost 1–3 on penalties)

ISRAEL

20 December v Borussia Mönchengladbach (Tel Aviv) 0–2

Clemence, Hughton, Lacy (Price), Roberts, Villa, Perryman, Mabbutt, Brooke (Cooke), Galvin, Falco, Crooks

3,000

22 December v Israel Select XI (Tel Aviv) 2–2

Brooke, Mazzon

Clemence (Thomas), Hughton, Price, Lacy (Culverhouse), Villa (Mazzon), Perryman, Mabbutt, Hazard, Galvin (Cooke), Brooke, Crook

7,000

1983 TRINIDAD AND TOBAGO

17 May v Trinidad & Tobago (Port of Spain) 2–2

Archibald, Crooks

Clemence (Parks), Hughton, Price, Roberts, Hazard (Brazil), Perryman, Mabbutt, Archibald, Galvin, Hoddle, Crooks

10,000

20 May v ASL Trinidad (a) 2–1

Gibson, Brazil

Clemence, Hughton, Lacy, Mabbutt (Crook), Miller, Perryman, Gibson (Crooks), Falco, Galvin, Hoddle (Parks), Brazil

5,000

1983 SWAZILAND

4 June (Royal Swazi Hotel Tournament) v Manchester United (Lobamba) 1–2

Archibald

Clemence, Hughton, O'Reilly, Roberts, Miller, Perryman (Hazard), Mabbutt, Archibald (Falco), Galvin, Hoddle, Brazil (Crooks)

6,000

11 June (Royal Swazi Hotel Tournament) v Manchester United (Lobamba) 2–0

Perryman, Mabbutt

Clemence, Hughton, Price, Roberts, Miller, Perryman, Mabbutt, Falco (Crooks), Galvin, Hoddle (Hazard), Brazil

5,000

(Spurs won tournament 3–2 on penalties)

1984 SWAZILAND

2 June (Royal Swazi Sun Challenge) v Liverpool (Lobamba) 2–5

Thomas, Falco

Parks, Thomas, Hughton, Galvin, Miller, Perryman, Ardiles, Hazard (Brooke), Falco, Brazil (Crook), Crooks

8,000

9 June (Royal Swazi Sun Challenge) v Liverpool (Lobamba) 1–1

Brazil

Clemence, Thomas, Hughton, O'Reilly, Miller, Perryman (Crook), Ardiles (Bowen), Hazard, Falco (Crooks), Brazil, Galvin

6,000

1984 SWEDEN AND NORWAY

27 July v Stjordal Blink (a) 9–0

Falco, Galvin, Ardiles, Hoddle, Crooks, Kempes 3, Opponent (og)

Clemence, Thomas (Mabbutt), Hughton, Roberts, Stevens, Perryman, Ardiles, Kempes (Miller), Falco (Crooks), Hazard (Hoddle), Galvin

5,000

29 July v Ostersund (a) 4–0

Galvin, Stevens, Crooks, Hoddle (pen)

Parks, Thomas, Hughton, Roberts (Hoddle), Miller, Perryman, Ardiles, Kempes, Falco (Crooks), Stevens, Galvin

4,000

30 July v Viking (a) 1–0
Crooks
Clemence, Thomas, Hughton, Roberts, Stevens, Perryman, Ardiles (Hoddle), Kempes, Falco (Crooks), Hazard (Miller), Galvin
4,900

1985 HONG KONG AND AUSTRALIA

23 May v Seiko (Hong Kong) 4–0
Mabbutt 2, Falco, Dick
Clemence, Thomas, Hughton, Roberts (Culverhouse), Miller, Mabbutt, Ardiles, Falco, Crook (Dick), Hazard (Leworthy), Galvin
20,000

29 May ($200,000 Tournament) v Australia Soccer Federation (Melbourne) 0–1
Clemence, Thomas, Bowen, Roberts, Miller (Culverhouse), Mabbutt, Ardiles, Falco, Leworthy, Hazard (Crook), Dick
20,503

1 June ($200,000 Tournament) v Udinese (Sydney) 0–2
Clemence, Thomas (Culverhouse), Bowen, Roberts, Miller, Mabbutt, Ardiles, Falco, Crook (Leworthy), Hazard, Dick

5 June ($200,000 Tournament) v Vasco da Gama (Adelaide) 1–1
Falco
Clemence, Thomas, Hughton, Roberts, Miller (Culverhouse), Mabbutt, Ardiles, Falco, Dick, Hazard (Leworthy), Galvin (Crook)

9 June ($200,000 Tournament third/fourth place play-off) v Udinese (Melbourne) 4–1
Miller, Falco, Leworthy, Opponent (og)
Clemence, Thomas, Hughton, Roberts, Miller, Mabbutt, Ardiles (Crook), Falco, Leworthy, Chiedozie (Hazard), Galvin (Dick)

1986 SPAIN

19 August (Juan Gamper Tournament) v PSV Eindhoven (Barcelona) 1–1
Falco
Clemence, Stevens, Thomas M, Roberts (Ardiles), Miller (Gough), Mabbutt, Waddle, Falco, C.Allen (P.Allen), Hoddle, Galvin
80,000

20 August (Juan Gamper Tournament) v AC Milan (Barcelona) 2–1
Falco, Mabbutt
Clemence, D.Thomas, Hughton, P.Allen, Gough, Miller, Ardiles (Stevens), Waddle (Falco), Chiedozie, Hoddle (Mabbutt), Cooke
100,000

1987 SWEDEN AND FINLAND

30 July v Orebro SK (a) 1–3
Mabbutt
Parks, Polston (Fairclough), Mabbutt, Gough, Ruddock (Stevens), Metgod (Ardiles), C.Allen (Thomas), P.Allen, Waddle, Hodge (Galvin), Samways (Claesen)
4,800

1 August v Lansi Uudenmaan District (Karjaa) 7–2
Fairclough, C.Allen 2, Close 4
Clemence, Polston (Ruddock), Thomas, Gough, Fairclough, Mabbutt, Robson (C.Allen), Close, Waddle, Ardiles (Metgod), Galvin
2,700

3 August v IFK/VSK Vasteras Select XI (a) 4–2
Waddle, C.Allen, Close 2
Clemence, Thomas, Ruddock (Samways), Ardiles, Fairclough, Mabbutt, C.Allen, P.Allen, Waddle, Hodge (Galvin), Metgod (Close)
3,381

5 August v Marsta IK (a) 5–0
Claesen 2, Metgod, Mabbutt, Stevens
Clemence, Stevens, Thomas (Samways), Gough, Fairclough, Mabbutt, Claesen, P.Allen (C.Allen), Galvin (P.Allen), Ardiles (Metgod), Samways (Hodge)
1,800

6 August v Swedish Div 1 North Select XI (Gavle) 0–1
Parks, Stevens (Metgod), Polston, Metgod (Samways), Fairclough, Ruddock, Robson (Mabbutt), Close (Ardiles), Claesen, Hodge, Galvin (Close)
1,762

1988 SWEDEN

26 July v Vederslav/Danningelanda IF (a) 4–1

Walsh 3, Stewart (pen)
Mimms (Guthrie), Statham, Thomas (Stimson), Fenwick, Fairclough, Mabbutt, Walsh (Gray), Gascoigne (Howells), Waddle (Robson), Samways, Stewart (Moran)
1,850

28 July v Trelleborgs FF (a) 3–0

Fenwick 2 (1 pen), Moran
Mimms, Stimson, Fenwick, Fairclough, Mabbutt, Allen, Walsh (Moran), Gascoigne (Howells), Waddle, Stewart (Gray), Samways (Robson)
3,226

31 July v GAIS (a) 1–1

Walsh
Mimms (Guthrie), Mabbutt, Stimson, Fenwick, Fairclough, Allen (Howells [Robson]), Walsh (Gray), Gascoigne, Waddle, Stewart, Samways
2,350

2 August v Jonkopings Sodra IF (a) 1–1

Waddle
Guthrie, Statham, Stimson (Fairclough), Fenwick, Mabbutt, Robson (Howells), Walsh (Gray), Gascoigne, Waddle, Stewart (Allen), Samways (Moran)
2,131

1989 IRELAND, SCOTLAND NORWAY AND SPAIN

23 July v Bohemians (a) 2–0

Stewart, Walsh
Thorstvedt, Butters, Hughton, Sedgley (Thomas), Bergsson (Polston), Mabbutt, Samways (Robson), Gascoigne (Howells), Stewart (Hendon), Lineker (Walsh), Nayim
10,000

25 July v Cork City (a) 3–0

Mabbutt, Gascoigne, Lineker
Thorstvedt, Butters (Stevens), Hughton (Hendon), Sedgley, Bergsson (Polston), Mabbutt, Samways (Robson), Gascoigne (Thomas), Stewart (Walsh), Lineker, Nayim (Howells)
7,000

6 August v Rangers (a) 0–1

Thorstvedt, Butters, Hughton (Bergsson), Fenwick, Nayim (Allen), Mabbutt, Sedgley, Gascoigne, Stewart (Moran), Lineker (Walsh), Samways (Howells)
41,214

8 August v Viking (a) 5–1

Stewart, Fenwick (pen), Gascoigne, Lineker 2,
Thorstvedt, Butters, Bergsson, Fenwick, Allen, Mabbutt, Sedgley (Robson), Samways (Gascoigne), Stewart, Lineker, Howells
8,000

10 August v Brann (a) 2–0

Lineker 2
Thorstvedt, Butters (Mabbutt), Polston, Fenwick (Hendon), Stevens (Bergsson), Allen, Howells (Gascoigne), Samways (Sedgley), Walsh, Lineker (Moran), Robson
7,118

11 August v (XVII Trofeo de Madrid) Dinamo Bucharest (Madrid) 1–3

Howells
Thorstvedt, Butters, Bergsson, Fenwick, Allen (Robson), Mabbutt, Sedgley, Gascoigne (Moran), Stewart, Walsh, Howells (Hendon)
2,500

13 August (XVII Trofeo de Madrid) v Athletico Madrid (a) 0–1

Thorstvedt, Butters, Bergsson (Polston), Fenwick, Howells, Mabbutt, Robson (Sedgley), Gascoigne, Walsh, Lineker, Allen
10,000

1990 IRELAND, NORWAY AND SCOTLAND

1 August v Shelbourne (a) 3–0

Gascoigne 2, Lineker
Thorstvedt (Mimms), Bergsson, Van den Hauwe (Edinburgh), Sedgley (Butters), Howells (Moncur), Mabbutt, Stewart (Lineker), Thomas (Gascoigne), Nayim, Walsh (Moran), Allen
10,000

3 August v Derry City (a) 3–0

Stewart 2, Lineker
Thorstvedt (Mimms), Bergsson (Thomas), Edinburgh (Butters), Sedgley, Howells, Mabbutt, Stewart (Walsh), Gascoigne (Moncur), Nayim, Lineker (Moran), Allen
12,000

7 August v Brann (a) 1–0
Howells
Thorstvedt (Mimms), Bergsson, Edinburgh, Sedgley, Howells, Mabbutt, Stewart (Moran), Gascoigne (Thomas), Nayim, Lineker (Walsh), Allen
3,791

9 August v Viking (a) 1–1
Walsh
Thorstvedt, Polston (Bergsson), Edinburgh (Sedgley), Thomas, Butters, Mabbutt, Walsh, Gascoigne (Nayim), Moncur, Lineker (Moran), Allen (Howells)
7,151

11 August v Sogndal (a) 1–0
Moran
Mimms (Thorstvedt), Bergsson (Butters), Edinburgh, Sedgley, Howells, Mabbutt (Polston), Walsh (Stewart), Gascoigne (Lineker), Moncur, Moran, Allen (Nayim)
2,804

13 August v Heart of Midlothian (a) 1–1
Howells
Thorstvedt, Bergsson, Edinburgh, Sedgley, Howells, Mabbutt, Stewart (Walsh), Gascoigne (Moncur), Nayim, Lineker (Moran), Allen
18,068

1991 JAPAN

2 June (Kirin Cup) v Vasco da Gama (Kobe) 0–0
Walker, Edinburgh, Thomas, Sedgley, Howells, Tuttle, Stewart, Walsh, Samways, Hendry, Allen
15,000

5 June (Kirin Cup) v Thailand (Nagoya) 2–1
Hendry, Edwards
Walker, Edinburgh (Edwards), Thomas, Sedgley, Hendon, Tuttle, Stewart, Walsh, Samways, Houghton (Hendry), Allen
25,000

9 June (Kirin Cup) v Japan (Tokyo) 0–4
Walker, Edinburgh, Thomas (Edwards), Sedgley, Howells (Garland), Tuttle, Stewart, Hendry, Samways, Lineker, Allen
45,000

IRELAND, NORWAY, SCOTLAND AND ITALY

23 July (Glencar Spring Water Challenge) v Sligo Rovers (a) 4–0
Mabbutt, Stewart (pen), Samways, Thomas
Thorstvedt (Walker), Edinburgh, Van den Hauwe (Bergsson), Sedgley, Nayim, Mabbutt, Stewart, Walsh, Samways (Moncur), Lineker (Thomas [Tuttle]), Allen (Fenwick)
6,000

25 July v Drogheda United (a) 2–0
Mabbutt, Lineker
Thorstvedt, Edinburgh (Edwards), Fenwick, Sedgley, Nayim, Mabbutt, Stewart, Moncur, Samways (Walsh), Lineker (Gray), Bergsson
3,000

27 July v Shelbourne (a) 3–1
Samways, Walsh, Gray
Thorstvedt, Edinburgh, Fenwick, Sedgley (Moncur), Nayim, Mabbutt, Stewart (Gray), Edwards, Samways (Tuttle), Lineker (Walsh), Bergsson
6,000

30 July v Brann (a) 1–1
Stewart
Thorstvedt, Edinburgh (Hendon), Fenwick (Bergsson), Sedgley, Nayim (Edwards), Mabbutt (Moncur), Stewart, Walsh, Samways, Lineker (Gray), Allen
4,043

1 August v Bryne (a) 0–4
Thorstvedt, Edinburgh (Hendon), Fenwick (Bergsson), Sedgley, Nayim (Edwards), Mabbutt (Moncur), Stewart, Walsh, Samways, Lineker (Gray), Allen
2,342

4 August v Celtic (a) 0–1
Thorstvedt, Fenwick, Van den Hauwe (Edinburgh), Sedgley (Bergsson), Howells (Hendon), Mabbutt, Stewart, Nayim, Samways, Lineker (Walsh), Allen (Moncur)
23,000

11 August (Nicola Ceravolo Memorial Tournament) v Messina (Catanzaro) 0–2
Thorstvedt, Edinburgh, Statham (Sedgley), Hendon, Tuttle, Bergsson, Garland, Walsh (Robson), Hendry, Gray, Moncur (Edwards)
10,00

13 August (Nicola Cerovolo Memorial Tournament) v Catanzaro (Catanzaro) 1–0
Bergsson
Thorstvedt (Walker), Bergsson, Van den Hauwe, Sedgley (Tuttle), Hendon, Mabbutt, Stewart (Hendry), Nayim, Samways, Lineker (Gray), Allen
28,000

1993 IRELAND AND NORWAY

16 July v Shelbourne XI (a) 4–2
Barmby, Sheringham, Turner, Flood (og)
Walker (Dearden), Austin (Bergsson [P.Gray]), Edinburgh (Hendon), Samways, Cundy, Mabbutt (Howells), Sedgley, Barmby, Anderton, Sheringham (Hodges), Turner
4,000

18 July v Drogheda United (a) 3–1
Anderton, Sheringham 2
Walker (Dearden), Austin, Sedgley, Samways (Hendon), Cundy, Mabbutt, Howells (P.Gray), Barmby, Anderton, Sheringham, Turner (Hodges)
3,000

23 July v Team Nord-Trodelag (Steinkjer) 1–0
Sheringham
Walker (Thorstvedt), Austin (Culverhouse), Hendon (Hill), Samways, Calderwood, Mabbutt (Cundy), Barmby, Sedgley, Anderton (Moran), Sheringham, Turner (Durie)
3,000

25 July v Lyn Oslo (a) 0–0
Thorstvedt (Walker), Austin, Cundy, Hendon, Calderwood, Mabbutt, Hill, Sedgley, Anderton (Moran), Sheringham, Turner (Durie)
3,873

27 July v Team Porsgrunn (a) 5–4
Moran, Sheringham 3, R.Numme (og)
Thorstvedt (Walker), Culverhouse (Durie), Cundy, Samways, Calderwood, Mabbutt, Hill, Sedgley, Moran (Hodges), Sheringham, Turner
3,000

1995 HONG KONG, CHINA AND SINGAPORE

21 May (Euro-Asia Challenge) v Eastern/Kitchee Select (Hong Kong) 7–2
Anderton, Klinsmann 2, Barmby 2, Kerslake, Dozzell
Walker, Kerslake, Scott, Dozzell, Nethercott, Mabbutt, Barmby, Klinsmann, Anderton, Sheringham, Caskey
10,514

24 May v Guangzhou (a) 2–1
Sheringham 2
Walker, Kerslake, Edinburgh, Dozzell, Nethercott (Cundy), Mabbutt, Barmby, Watson (Hendry), Anderton, Sheringham, Turner (Hill)
7,500

26 May v Singapore Lions (a) 1–1
Anderton
Walker, Kerslake, Edinburgh, Dozzell (Cundy), Nethercott, Mabbutt, Barmby, Howells (Watson), Anderton, Sheringham, Hill (Turner)
20,000

DENMARK AND SWEDEN

22 July v Silkeborg (Bjerringbro) 1–3
Cundy
Walker, Austin (Nethercott), Edinburgh (Campbell), Caskey (Dozzell), Calderwood (Cundy), Mabbutt (Scott), McMahon (Hill), Howells (Kerslake), Armstrong, Barmby (Dumitrescu), Rosenthal (Barmby)
3,500

23 July v Halmstad (Vimberg) 1–2
Nethercott
Walker (Thorstvedt), Campbell (Scott), Edinburgh (Austin), Caskey (Dozzell), Calderwood, Mabbutt (Nethercott), McMahon, Howells (Kerslake), Armstrong (Dumitrescu), Dumitrescu (Barmby), Rosenthal (Hill)
2,500

24 July v IFK Gothenburg (Varberg) 2–0
Dozzell, Rosenthal
Walker, Campbell, Edinburgh, Caskey, Calderwood, Mabbutt, McMahon, Dozzell (Nethercott), Barmby, Rosenthal, Armstrong
4,378

26 July v Hassleholm (a) 1–3
Dozzell
Thorstvedt, Austin, Campbell, Kerslake, Scott (Calderwood), Nethercott (Mabbutt), McMahon (Hill), Dumitrescu, Rosenthal (Barmby), Dozzell (Caskey), Armstrong (Edinburgh)
1,782

1996 NORWAY

23 July v Ham-Kam (Hamar Stadion) 2–0
Anderton, Armstrong
Baardsen, Carr, Edinburgh (Clapham), Sinton (Rosenthal), Calderwood (Campbell), Mabbutt (Nethercott), Fox (Sinton), Dozzell, Anderton (Allen), Allen (Mahorn), Armstrong
2,736

25 July v Odd Grenland (a) 1–2
Rosenthal
Walker, Carr, Edinburgh (Clapham), Wilson, Calderwood, Mabbutt (Nethercott), Fox, Dozzell (Campbell), Allen (Mahorn), Sinton (Rosenthal), Armstrong (Mabbutt)
2,407

26 July v Raufoss (a) 0–0
Walker (Baardsen), Carr (Calderwood), Clapham, Howells, Nethercott (Wilson), Mabbutt, Rosenthal, Campbell, Anderton, Mahorn (Fox), Armstrong
750

1997 NORWAY

15 July v Ski (a) 2–3
Vega, Nielsen
Walker, Carr, Edinburgh (Clapham), Howells (Mabbutt), Vega, Scales (Austin), Fox, Nielsen (Whalley), McVeigh (Mahorn), Fenn (Armstrong), Sinton (Clemence)
2,150

17 July v Faaberg (a) 2–0
Fenn, McVeigh
Walker, Carr (Brady), Clapham (Edinburgh), Howells (Maher), Arber, Mabbutt, Maher (Vega), Nielsen (Whalley), McVeigh, Mahorn (Fenn), Sinton (Fox)
2,082

18 July v Fredrikstad (a) 0–0
Walker, Carr, Edinburgh (Clapham), Howells (Mabbutt), Vega, Arber, Fox (Ginola), Maher, Fenn (Brady), Mahorn (McVeigh), Whalley (Sinton)
2,226

21 July v Rosenborg (a) 0–2
Walker, Carr (Maher), Edinburgh, Howells, Vega, Mabbutt (Campbell), Fox (Ginola), Arber (Brady), Mahorn (McVeigh), Fenn, Clemence
4,239

1998 HOLLAND

5 August v De Tubanters (a) 6–1
Sinton, Ferdinand, Berti, Armstrong, Allen, Calderwood
Baardsen (Segers), Carr, Tramezzani (Wilson), Berti (Vega), Edinburgh, Calderwood, Fox (Dominguez), Sinton, Anderton (Clemence), Ferdinand (Armstrong), Allen
850

8 August v Feyenoord (a) 1–1
Armstrong
Walker, Carr, Tramezzani, Berti, Calderwood, Campbell (Vega), Fox, Saib (Clemence), Ginola, Ferdinand (Allen), Armstrong (Sinton)
30,767

1999 SWEDEN

15 July v Elfsborg (Varberg) 1–1
Nielsen
Walker (Baardsen), Edinburgh (Scales), Taricco (Carr), Freund (Sherwood), Young (Campbell), Perry, Anderton, Ginola, Dominguez (Fox), Iversen, Nielsen
3,065

17 July v Lysekil (a) 7–1
Campbell, Iversen 3, Dominguez 2, Carr,
Walker (Baardsen), Carr, Edinburgh (Taricco), Freund, Campbell (Young), Perry (Scales), Fox (Anderton), Ginola, Dominguez, Iversen, Nielsen (Sherwood)
2,143

20 July v GAIS (a) 3–0
Iversen 3
Walker, Carr, Taricco (Edinburgh), Ginola (Fox), Campbell, Perry, Anderton, Sherwood (Young), Dominguez (Ferdinand), Iversen, Nielsen
4,644

2000 SWEDEN AND FINLAND

19 July v AIK Skelleftea (Byske) 4–0

Armstrong, Iversen 2, Ferdinand
Walker (Sullivan), Young (Campbell), Thatcher, Freund, Vega (Gardner), Perry (Carr), Anderton (Leonhardsen), Sherwood (Clemence), Armstrong (Ferdinand), Ginola (Etherington), Rebrov (Iversen)
2,980

22 July v Tervarit (a) 4–0

Ferdinand, Armstrong, Rebrov, Iversen,
Sullivan (Walker), Young (Carr), Thatcher (Taricco), Clemence (Freund), Vega (Gardner), Perry (Campbell), Anderton (Leonhardsen), Sherwood, Ferdinand (Iversen), Armstrong (Rebrov), Ginola (Etherington)
4,829

24 July v Bodens (a) 6–0

Rebrov, Iversen 2, Sherwood, Armstrong 2 (1 pen)
Sullivan (Walker), Carr (Young), Taricco (Thatcher), Freund (Sherwood), Campbell (Perry), Gardner (Vega), Leonhardsen (Anderton), Clemence, Ginola (Etherington), Iversen (Armstrong), Rebrov (Ferdinand)
6,322

2003 SOUTH AFRICA

26 July (SA 2010 Bid) v Orlando Pirates (Durban) 1–2

Musasa (og)
Burch, Carr, Taricco (Galbraith), Toda, Gardner, Perry, Davies, Postiga, Redknapp (Anderton), Poyet (Keane), Etherington

29 July (SA 2010 Bid) v Kaizer Chiefs (Cape Town) 2–0

Keane, Etherington
Burch, Carr, Taricco (Kelly), Redknapp (Ricketts), Bunjevcevic, Gardner, Anderton, Postiga (Poyet), Acimovic (Davies), Keane, Etherington

2004 SWEDEN

13 July v Falkenbergs (a) 1–1

Barnard
Burch, Kelly (Ifil), McKie (O'Hara), Hughes, O'Donoghue, Bunjevcevic (Doherty), Marney, Jackson, Barnard (Malcolm), Yeates (Price), Ricketts (Slabber)
1,654

15 July v FC Copenhagen (Gothenberg) 2–2

Richards, Defoe
Keller, Carr, Taricco, Davis, Bunjevcevic, Richards, Davies (Marney), Brown, Defoe, Keane, Jackson (Ricketts)
15,104

17 July v Trollhattan (a) 0–1

Fulop, Kelly (Carr), McKie, Davis (Mendes), Doherty, Mabizela, Marney (Keane), Hughes (O'Hara), Barnard (Slabber [Malcolm]), Yeates, Ricketts
2,127

SPAIN

3 August (Kappa Cup) v Feyenoord (Seville) 1–2

Kanoute
Keller, S.Carr (Edman), Taricco, Redknapp (Mendes), Bunjevcevic, Doherty, Marney (Jackson), Brown (Gardner), Kanoute (Defoe), Bakari, Ricketts (Hughes)
1000

5 August (Kappa Cup) v Partizan Belgrade (Seville) 1–1

Defoe
Robinson, Ifil, Edman (Taricco), Davis (Jackson), Gardner, King, Ricketts, Hughes, Silva, Defoe (Bakari), Brown (Marney)
500

2005 SOUTH KOREA

16 July (Peace Cup) v Boca Juniors (Suwon) 2–2

Defoe, Mido
Cerney, Marney, Bunjevcevic, Carrick, Dawson (Gardner), King (Huddlestone), Tainio, Mendes, Mido (Keane), Defoe (Routledge), Reid (El Hamdaoui)
118,909

18 July (Peace Cup) v Sundowns (Suwon) 3–1

Keane 2, Kanoute
Cerny, Kelly, Edman, Huddlestone (Marney), Davenport, Gardner, Routledge, Mendes (Tainio), Kanoute, Keane, Reid (Lennon)
22,832

21 July (Peaqce Cup) v Real Sociedad (Ulsan) 1–1

Mido
Fulop, Kelly, Edman, Carrick, Davenport, Gardner, Routledge (Lennon), Mendes (Reid), Mido (Keane), Defoe (El Hamadaoui), Tainio (Marney)
24,435

24 July (Peace Cup Final) v Olympique Lyonnais (Seoul) 3–1
Keane 2, Berthod (og)
Cerny, Kelly, Edman (Bunjevcevic), Carrick, Gardner, King, Routledge, Tainio (Mendes [Marney]), Mido (Kanoute), Keane (Defoe), Reid
48,734

2006 FRANCE

13 July Girondins de Bordeaux (Albertville) 2–1
Defoe, McKenna
Cerny, Ifil (McKenna), Assou-Ekotto, Davids, Dawson, Gardner, Routledge (Ziegler), Murphy (C.Lee), Berbatov (Barnard), Defoe (O'Hara), Reid
2,000

14 July OGC Nice (Evian) 1–0
Barnard
Fulop, Stalteri (Ifil), Ziegler, Huddlestone, King, Davenport (Murphy), Routledge (Defoe), Ghaly, Barnard (McKenna), Tainio, O'Hara
400

18 July Celta Vigo (Annecy) 2–0
Defoe 2
Cerny, Ghaly (C.Lee), Assou-Ekotto, Davids (Tainio), Davenport (Dawson), King (Huddlestone), Routledge (Ifil), Murphy (Defoe), Barnard (Berbatov), Keane (McKenna), Ziegler (O'Hara)
750

2007 SOUTH AFRICA

21 July (Vodacom Challenge) v Kaizer Chiefs (Durban) 2–1
Keane, Berbatov
Robinson, Ifil (Daniels), Rocha, Zokora, Kaboul (Gardner), Dawson, Malbranque, Jenas, Berbatov (Taarabt), Keane, Routledge (Bent)
42,155

24 July (Vodacom Challenge) v Orlando Pirates (Cape Town) 2–1
Bent, Routledge
Cerny, Chimbonda, Taarabt (O'Hara), Huddlestone, Kaboul, Gardner, Stalteri, Jenas (Malbranque), Bent, Defoe, Routledge
24,917

28 July (Vodacom Challenge) v Orlando Pirates (Pretoria) 3–0
Bent 2, Berbatov
Robinson, Chimbonda, Rocha, Zokora (Routledge), Dawson, Huddlestone (Keane), Stalteri, Taarabt (Jenas), Berbatov (Tainio), Bent (Defore), Malbranque (Maghoma)
34,666

2009 CHINA AND HONG KONG

29 July (Barclays Asia Trophy) v West Ham United (Beijing) 1–0
Defoe
Cudicini, Hutton, Assou–Ekotto, O'Hara, Corluka, Huddlestone, Naughton (Lennon), Palacios (Livermore), Pavlyuchenko (Keane), Defoe, Modric
30,000

31 July (Barclays Asia Trophy) v Hull City (Beijing) 3–0
Keane 2 (I pen), Lennon
Gomes, Chimbonda (Hutton), Assou–Ekotto, Palacios (Livermore), Corluka, Huddlestone, Lennon, Jenas (Naughton), Keane, Defoe, Modric
25,000

2 August (Panasonic Invitation Cup) v South China (Hong Kong) 0–2
Cudicini (Gomes), Hutton (Defoe), Rose, O'Hara, Chimbonda, Livermore, Naughton, Jenas (Keane), Pavlyuchenko (Modric), Obika (Lennon), Bostock
23,025

2010 UNITED STATES OF AMERICA

17 July v San Jose Earthquakes (a) 0–0
Cudicini, Hutton (Modric), Bale, Kaboul, Huddlestone (Butcher), Jenas, Keane (Mason), Naughton (Kranjcar), Walker (Smith), Townsend, Obika (Pavlyuchenko).
10,712

23 July (Barclays New York Challenge) v New York Red Bulls (a) 2–1
Keane, Bale
Cudicini, Hutton, Bale, Huddlestone, Jenas, Keane, Modric (Mason), Naughton (Townsend), Kranjcar (Rose), Corluka (Taarabt), Walker
20,312

25 July (Barclays New York Challenge) v Sporting Lisbon (New York) 2–2
Keane, Obika
Cudicini (Button), Hutton, Bale, Huddlestone, Jenas, Keane, Taarabt (Obika), Naughton (Rose), Kranjcar (Townsend), Corluka, Walker
23,228

FRIENDLIES

1896–97

3 September v Rossendale (h) 7–0
Crump, McElhaney, Newbigging 2, R.Clements 2, Payne
Ambler, Burrows, Montgomery, Briggs, Devlin, Crump, McElhaney, McDermott, Newbigging, R.Clements, Payne

10 September v London Caledonians (h) 3–3
Devlin, R.Clements 2
Sunderland, Burrows, Montgomery, Briggs, Devlin, Crump, McDermott, Milliken, Newbigging, R.Clements, Payne
550

17 September v Casuals (h) 4–0
McElhaney, Newbigging 3
Sunderland, Burrows, Montgomery, Crump, Briggs, Devlin, McElhaney, Milliken, Newbigging, R.Clements, Payne
650

24 September v Luton Town (h) 0–0
Collins (Ambler), Burrows, Montgomery, Devlin, Briggs, Crump, Thorburn, McElhaney, Newbigging, R.Clements, Milliken
2,000
Abandoned after 75 mins – rain

26 September v Casuals (a) 4–1
McElhaney, Newbigging 2, R.Clements
Ambler, Burrows, Montgomery, Devlin, Briggs, Collins, McElhaney, Milliken, Newbigging, R.Clements, Payne
2,000

1 October v 1st Coldstream Guards (h) 4–0
Milliken, R.Clements, Payne 2 (1 pen)
Hatfield, Collins, Montgomery, Devlin, Briggs, Crump, Thorburn, Milliken, Newbigging, R.Clements, Payne
600

8 October v Royal Scots Greys (h) 5–0
Newbigging 2, R.Clements 2, Payne
Hatfield, Collins, Scott, Devlin, Briggs, Crump, McElhaney, Milliken, Newbigging, R.Clements, Payne
600

29 October v Southampton St Marys (h) 3–1
R.Brown, Newbigging, Crump,
Hatfield, Hay, Montgomery, Devlin, Briggs, Collins, Lanham, R.Brown, Newbigging, R.Clements, Crump
4,000

16 November v Luton Town (a) 0–3
Hatfield, Goodman, Milarvie, Devlin, Collins, Crump, McElhaney, Milliken, Fleming, R.Clements, Newbigging
1,000

21 November v Blackpool (h) 0–2
Ambler, Burrows, Montgomery, Briggs, Almond, Mair, McElhaney, Milliken, Fleming, Newbigging, Payne
2,500

19 December v Clapton (a) 2–1
Hunter, Payne
Ambler, Burrows, Montgomery, Devlin, Almond, Mair, McElhaney, Milliken, Hunter, Payne, Crump
2,000
80-minute game

26 December v Vampires (h) 4–0
Montgomery, J.Clements, R.Clements, Payne
Hatfield, Burrows, T.Jull, Regan, Mair, Oates, Milliken, J.Clements, Montgomery, R.Clements, Payne
500

26 December v third Grenadier Guards (h) 2–3
R.Clements, Payne
Ambler, Mair, Montgomery, Regan, Almond, Crump, McElhaney, Devlin, Milliken, R.Clements, Payne
2,000

29 December v Northfleet (h) 4–0
McElhaney 2, Milliken, Allen
Gardiner, Mair, Montgomery, Devlin, Keith, Crump, McElhaney, Milliken, Allen, R.Clements, Newbigging

11 January v Chatham (a) 1–2
Newbigging
Gardiner, Scott, Montgomery, Devlin, Regan, Crump, McElhaney, Allen, Newbigging, R.Clements, Craig

23 January v Aston Villa (h) 2–2
Lanham 2
Ambler, Burrows, Montgomery, Devlin, Almond, Crump, McElhaney, Lanham, Newbigging, R.Clements, Payne
3,000

28 January v Chatham (h) 2–2
Lanham, R.Clements
Gardiner, Mair, Montgomery, Devlin, Coe, Crump, McElhaney, Lanham, Allen, R.Clements, Hobson
700

6 February v third Grenadier Guards (h) 9–3
Almond 2, McElhaney, Milliken 2, Robertson, R.Clements, Payne 2
Gardiner, Burrows, Montgomery, Devlin, Almond, Crump, McElhaney, Milliken, Robertson, R.Clements, Payne
2,000

10 February v Gravesend United (a) 3–1
Robertson, McElhaney 2
Gardiner, Scott, Montgomery, Devlin, Newbigging, Crump, McElhaney, Lanham, Robertson, Milliken, R.Clements
1,200

15 February v Southampton St Marys (a) 0–2
Ambler, Montgomery, Marjoram, Crump, Mair, Devlin, Lanham, Newbigging, Robertson, Milliken, McElhaney

9 March v Eastbourne (a) 1–0
Allen
Hatfield, Burrows, Montgomery, Devlin, Newbigging, E.Markham, Lanham, R.Brown, Allen, R.Clements, Crump
60-minute match

22 March v Gravesend United (h) 3–2
McElhaney Wilson, Crump
Hatfield, E.Markham, Montgomery, Devlin, Allen, Briggs, McElhaney, Milliken, Wilson, R.Clements, Crump
800

16 April v Nottingham Forest (h) 1–1
Crump
Latham, Montgomery, Mair, R.Clements, Allen, Crump, Lanham, Payne, Newbigging, J.Clements, Edwards
4,000

20 April v Blackburn Rovers (h) 1–2
Lanham
Ambler, Allen, Montgomery, Mair, W.Markham, E.Markham, Lanham, J.Clements, Newbigging, R.Clements, Edwards
2,000

22 April v Everton (h) 2–1
Lanham, Newbigging
Ambler, Milligan, Montgomery, Shepherd, Allen, Crump, Lanham, S.Brown, Newbigging, R.Clements, Edwards
1,500

26 April v London Caledonians (a) 1–1
Newbigging
Hatfield, T.Jull, Montgomery, F.Markham, Allen, Crump, Janes, R.Brown, Newbigging, Gair, Hobson
700
Abandoned after 45 mins – opponent broke leg

1897–98

1 September v Glossop North End (h) 3–2
Hartley, Joyce, Black,
Cullen, Knowles, Montgomery, Hall, Jones, Stormont, Tannahill, Meade, Hartley, Joyce, Black
2,000

9 September v Royal Scots Fusilliers (h) 12–0
Tannahill, Davidson 4, Joyce 3, Meade 3, Black
Cullen, Knowles, Montgomery, Hall, Jones, Stormont, Tannahill, Davidson, Joyce, Meade, Black
800

11 September v Chorley (h) 3–1
Jones, Joyce, Meade
Cullen, Burrows, Montgomery, Hall, Jones, Stormont, Tannahill, Davidson, Joyce, Meade, Black
3,000

23 September v second Scots Guards (h) 4–1
Davidson, Meade, Joyce, Black
Cullen, Burrows, Montgomery, Hall, Jones, Stormont, Tannahill, Davidson, Meade, Joyce, Black
600

7 October v third Grenadier Guards (h) 4–0
Davidson, Hartley 2, Joyce
Cullen, Knowles, Crump, Hall, Jones, Stormont, Tannahill, Davidson, Hartley, Joyce, Hargreaves
500

20 October v Reading (h) 2–1
Hartley, Black
Cullen, Knowles, Montgomery, Hall, Jones, Crump, Hartley, Davidson, Joyce, Meade, Black
800

2 November v Eastbourne (a) 2–0
Joyce 2
Cullen, Burrows, Montgomery, Hall, Briggs, Jones, Tannahill, Meade, Joyce, Stormont, Black

9 November v New Brompton (h) 3–0
Tannahill, Hartley, Joyce
Cullen, Knowles, Montgomery, Hall, Briggs, Crump, Tannahill, Hartley, Joyce, Stormont, Black
1,000

1 December v Gravesend United (a) 0–3
Ambler, Knowles, Montgomery, Hall, Jones, Crump, Tannahill, Davidson, Joyce, Clements, Black

11 December v Kettering (h) 1–0
Black
Ambler, Downie, Knowles, Hall, Crump, Clements, Meade, Davidson, Joyce, Stormont, Black
1,000

27 December v Ilkeston Town (h) 4–2
Joyce 2, Black 2
Cullen, Burrows, Downie, Hall, Jones (Knowles), Crump, Payne, Meade, Joyce, Stormont, Black
5,000

28 December v Stockton (h) 3–0
Joyce 2, Clements
Ambler, Knowles, Montgomery, Hartley, Crump, Stormont, Payne, Davidson, Joyce, Clements, Black
3,000

27 January v Gravesend United (h) 1–2
Davidson
Cullen, Montgomery, Knowles, Hall, Jones, Stormont, Tannahill, Davidson, Joyce, Hartley, Crump
600

9 February v Sussex (Hove) 2–1
Meade, Hartley
Cullen, Knowles, Montgomery, Hall, Jones, Downie, Hartley, Davidson, Meade, Stormont, Black
1,000

12 February v Sheffield United (h) 1–1
Davidson
Cullen, Knowles, Montgomery, Hall, Jones, Crump, Hartley, Davidson, Joyce, Stormont, Black
10,000

15 February v St Barnards (h) 4–0
Hartley 3, Black
Cullen, Knowles, Montgomery, Hall, Jones, Crump, Hartley, Davidson, Joyce, Stormont, Black
500

28 February v Chesham (a) 4–2
Jones, Hartley, Joyce, Clements
Cullen, Montgomery, Monk, Hall, Jones, Downie, Hartley, Madden, Joyce, Clements, Black

9 March v Tunbridge Wells (a) 5–0
Davidson, Stormont, Joyce 3
Cullen, Knowles, Montgomery, Hall, Downie, Crump, Hartley, Davidson, Meade, Stormont, Joyce
800

26 March v Sunderland (h) 0–2
Cullen, Burrows, Knowles, Hall, Jones, Downie, Hartley, Madden, Joyce, Stormont, Black
2,000
70-minute game

12 April v Lincoln City (h) 2–1
Tannahill, Clements
Cullen, Knowles, Montgomery, Crump, Jones, Downie, Tannahill, Davidson, Hartley, Clements, Black
3,000

18 April v Reading (a) 3–3
Clements, Hartley 2
Cullen, Knowles, Jones, Downie, Stormont, Crump, Tannahill, Davidson, Hartley, Clements, Black

25 April v Aston Villa (h) 2–3
Hartley, Black
Cullen, Burrows, Downie, Hall, Jones, Crump, Hartley, Meade, Joyce, Stormont, Black
3,000
80 minute game

28 April v Woolwich Arsenal (a) 0–3
Cullen, Burrows, Montgomery, Hall, Jones, Downie, Hartley, Davidson, Joyce, Stormont, Crump
2,000

30 April v Bolton Wanderers (h) 2–2
Joyce, Crump
Cullen, Burrows, Monk, Hall, Downie, Crump, Hartley, Meade, Joyce, Stormont, Black
4,000

1898–99

1 September v Gainsborough Trinity (h) 6–2
Smith, McKay 3, Joyce 2 (1 pen)
Cullen, Melia, Cain, Jones, McNaught, Stormont, Smith, McKay, Joyce, Cameron, Bradshaw
250

12 September v Surrey Wanderers (h) 5–0
McKay, Joyce 2, Cameron, Bradshaw
Cullen, Erentz, Cain, Jones, Hall, Stormont, Smith, McKay, Joyce, Cameron, Bradshaw
600

1 October v Burton Wanderers (h) 5–2
Hartley, McKay, Meade, Payne, Taft (og)
Cullen, McGahey, Cain, Jones, Downie, Stormont, Hartley, McKay, Meade, Payne, Bradshaw
5,000

27 December v Ilkeston Town (h) 1–0
Hickson
Cullen, Melia, Erentz, Jones, Hall, Stormont, Hartley, McKay, Cameron, Hickson, Leech
2,000
60-minute game

1899–1900

4 September v Notts County (h) 4–1
Pratt, Copeland 3
Clawley, Erentz, Tait, J.L.Jones, McNaught, Morris, Smith, Pratt, Copeland, Cameron, Kirwan
5,000

13 September v Richmond (a) 3–1
Copeland, Pratt, Raby
Clawley, Erentz, Tait, Hughes, McNaught, Morris, Smith, Pratt, Copeland, Kirwan, Raby
1,500

27 September v Clapton (a) 4–1
Hyde 2, Pratt, Raby
Clawley, Erentz, Tait, Morris, McNaught, Stormont, Smith, Pratt, Raby, Hyde, Kirwan

30 September v Southampton (a) 1–2
Smith
Clawley, Erentz, Tait, Morris, McNaught, J.L.Jones, Smith, Pratt, Copeland, Cameron, Kirwan
5,000

28 October v Southampton (h) 4–3
Stormont, Cameron, Copeland, Kirwan
Meates, Melia, Tait, J.L.Jones, Morris, Stormont, Smith, Cameron, Pratt, Copeland, Kirwan
5,000

11 November v Ilkeston Town (h) 7–0
Melia, Smith, Rule 2, Copeland 2, Pratt
Haddow, Melia, Tait, J.L.Jones, Morris, Stormont, Smith, Rule, Pratt, Copeland, Kirwan

18 November v Bolton Wanderers (h) 4–0
Rule, Pratt, Cameron 2
Haddow, Melia, Tait, Hughes, Morris, Stormont, Smith, Rule, Pratt, Cameron, Kirwan
5,000

25 November v Corinthians (h) 5–1
Cameron 2, Copeland, Kirwan 2
Haddow, Melia, Tait, J.L.Jones, Morris, Stormont, Smith, Cameron, Pratt, Copeland, Kirwan
8,500

27 November v The Kaffirs (h) 6–4
Kirwan 2, Melia, Raby 2, Stormont
Haddow, Melia, Tait, Hughes, McNaught, Stormont, Kirwan, Raby, Erentz, Copeland, Hyde
3,500
70 minute match

18 December (Reservists' Fund Benefit) v HR Burke's XI (h) 12–2
Cameron 2, Copeland 4, Kirwan 4, Pratt, Smith
Haddow, Erentz, Crump, Hughes, McNaught, Stormont, Smith, Cameron, Pratt, Copeland, Kirwan
400

1 January v Middlesbrough (a) 2–2
Raby, Pratt
Haddow, Erentz, Stevens, Crump, McNaught, Hughes, Smith, Raby, Pratt, Kirwan, Hyde
4,000

2 January v Sunderland (a) 3–1
Hughes, Pratt 2
Haddow, Erentz, Tait, JL.Jones, McNaught, Hughes, Smith, Cameron, Pratt, Kirwan, Hyde

5 February v Oxford University (h) 6–0
Smith 2, Cameron, Pratt 3
Haddow, Erentz, Tait, Morris, McNaught, Stormont, Smith, Cameron, Pratt, Copeland, Kirwan
1,500

12 February v Chesterfield (h) 7–2
Raby 2, Pratt 4 (1 pen), Copeland
Haddow, Erentz, Tait, Morris, McNaught, J.L.Jones, Smith, Raby, Pratt, Copeland, Kirwan

21 February v Gravesend United (a) 1–3
Smith
Haddow, Erentz, Hughes, J.L.Jones, McNaught, Stormont, Smith, Levy, Kirwan, Copeland, Hyde
1,000

5 March v Stoke (h) 6–0
Cameron, Pratt 4, Kirwan
Haddow, Melia, Tait, J.L.Jones, McNaught, Hughes, Raby, Cameron, Pratt, Copeland, Kirwan
2,000

17 March v Corinthians (a) 3–1
Cameron 2, Kirwan
Haddow, Melia, Tait, Morris, McNaught, J.L.Jones, Smith, Cameron, Pratt, Stormont, Kirwan
4,000

21 April v Aston Villa (a) 3–4
Cameron, Copeland 2
Clawley, Erentz, Tait, J.L.Jones, McNaught, Stormont, Smith, Cameron, Pratt, Copeland, Kirwan

1900–01

3 September v Bristol Rovers (a) 0–1
Haddow, Melia, Tait, Morris, McNaught, Stormont, Smith, Moffatt, Brown, Pangbourne, Kirwan
2,000

8 September v Southampton (a) 3–1
Brown 3
Clawley, Melia, Tait, Morris, McNaught, J.L.Jones, Smith, Cameron, Brown, Stormont, Kirwan
4,000

10 September v Reading (h) 3–3
McNaught, Smith, Cameron,
Clawley, Melia, Tait, Morris, McNaught, J.L.Jones, Smith, Cameron, Brown, Stormont, Kirwan
3,000

17 September (Arthur Millar Benefit) v Millwall (a) 2–1
Cameron 2
Clawley, Melia, Hughes, Erentz, AE.Jones, J.L.Jones, Smith, Cameron, Brown, Stormont, Kirwan
4,000

24 September v Richmond Association (h) 8–0
Smith, Pangbourne, Brown 4, Stormont, Kirwan
Clawley, Melia, Hughes, Erentz, McNaught, J.L.Jones, Smith, Pangbourne, Brown, Stormont, Kirwan

27 September (David Calderwood Benefit) v Notts County (a) 1–4
Brown
Clawley, Melia, Tait, Erentz, Stevens, J.L.Jones, Smith, Cameron, Brown, Hyde, Kirwan

3 October v Reading (h) 1–1
Smith
Clawley, Melia, Tait, Erentz, McNaught, J.L.Jones, Smith, Cameron, Brown, Stormont, Kirwan
3,000

8 October v Notts County (h) 1–1
Brown
Clawley, Tait, Melia, Morris, McNaught, Hughes, Smith, Moffatt, Brown, Stormont, Kirwan
3,000

13 October v Corinthians (h) 2–2
Smith, Brown
Clawley, Melia, Tait, J.L.Jones, McNaught, Stormont, Smith, Pangbourne, Brown, Cameron, Kirwan
5,000

22 October v Luton Town (h) 1–3
Brown
Clawley, Erentz, Tait, J.L.Jones, McNaught, Stormont, Berry, Pangbourne, Brown, Cameron, Hyde
2,000

31 October v Queen's Park Rangers (h) 7–0
A.E.Jones, Cameron 2, Brown 2, J.L.Jones, Kirwan
Clawley, Erentz, Tait, Hughes, McNaught, Stormont, A.E.Jones, Cameron, Brown, J.L.Jones, Kirwan
1,500

3 November v Portsmouth (a) 3–1
Cameron, Brown, Kirwan
Clawley, Erentz, Tait, Hughes, McNaught, Stormont, A.E.Jones, Cameron, Brown, J.L.Jones, Kirwan
6,000

5 November v Cambridge University (h) 3–1
Hughes, Brown, AE.Jones
Clawley, Erentz, Tait, Hughes, McNaught, Stormont, A.E.Jones, Cameron, Brown, J.L.Jones, Kirwan
1,500

12 November v Luton Town (a) 0–1
Clawley, Erentz, Hughes, Moles, McNaught, Stormont, Smith, A.E.Jones, Brown, Pangbourne, Hyde

17 December v Preston North End (h) 1–1
Morris
Clawley, Erentz, Tait, Hughes, McNaught, Stormont, A.E.Jones, Morris, Brown, J.L.Jones, Kirwan

29 December v Newark (h) 3–0
Morris 2, Kirwan
Haddow, Erentz, Hughes, A.E.Jones, McNaught, Stormont, Moffatt, Morris, Brown, Kirwan, Hyde
2,500

5 January v Clapton (h) 3–0
Brown 3
Clawley, Erentz, Tait, Anson, Hughes, Stormont, Hyde, Morris, Brown, J.L.Jones, Kirwan
2,500

8 January v German Association (h) 9–6
Tait 3, Hyde, Morris 2 (1 pen), Brown 2, Kirwan
Haddow, Melia, Tait, JL.Jones, McNaught, Stormont, Hyde, Morris, Brown, Moffatt, Kirwan
800

4 February v Oxford University (h) 5–2
Erentz, Smith, Brown 2, Copeland
Clawley, Erentz, Tait, Morris, McNaught, Stormont, Smith, Cameron, Brown, Copeland, Kirwan

1901–02

1 September v Heart of Midlothian (h) 0–0
Clawley, Erentz, Tait, Morris, Hughes, Jones, Smith, Cameron, Brown, Copeland, Kirwan
12,000

23 September v Sheffield United (a) 1–3
Cameron
Clawley, Tait, Erentz, Jones, Hughes, Morris, Hyde, Copeland, Cameron, Gilhooley, Smith
3,500

16 October v Rest of Southern League (h) 2–0
Cameron 2 (1 pen)
Clawley, Stephenson, Tait, Montgomery, Hughes, Burton, Gilhooley, Barlow, Woodward, Cameron, Kirwan
1,500

13 November v West Norwood (a) 3–1
Brown 3
Clawley, Erentz, Tait, Montgomery, McNaught, Jones, Smith, Cameron, Brown, Copeland, Kirwan

25 November v Cambridge University (h) 3–1
Brown, Kirwan 2
Clawley, Stevens, Tait, Montgomery, McNaught, Jones, Soulsby, Cameron, Brown, Barlow (Kirwan), Hyde
2,000

30 November v Corinthians (h) 2–1
Cameron, Brown
Clawley, Erentz, Tait, Morris, McNaught, Jones, Smith, Cameron, Brown, Copeland, Kirwan
10,000

2 December (Drill Hall Benefit) v Army Association (h) 2–1
Cameron, Brown
Clawley, Stephenson, Tait, Hughes, McNaught, Jones, Haig-Brown, Cameron, Brown, Copeland, Kirwan
3,000

14 December v Corinthians (a) 0–3
Clawley, Erentz, Tait, Morris, Hughes, Jones, Smith, Barlow, Cameron, Copeland, Kirwan
4,000

1 January v Everton (a) 1–3
Smith
Griffiths, Erentz, Tait, Morris, Hughes, Jones, Smith, Copeland, Cameron, Kirwan, Woodward
10,000

2 January v Heart of Midlothian (a) 1–3
Unknown
Griffiths, Erentz, Tait, Morris, McNaught, Jones, Smith, Gilhooley, Brown, Copeland, Kirwan
4,000

1 March (Dewar Shield) v Corinthians (h) 5–2
Cameron 3, Brown, Kirwan
Clawley, Erentz, Tait, Hughes, Morris, Jones, Smith, Cameron, Brown, Copeland, Kirwan
9,000

1 April v Sheffield United (h) 3–2
Fitchie, Kirwan 2
Moles, Erentz, Tait, Burton, McNaught, Jones, Smith, Cameron, Copeland, Fitchie, Kirwan
8,000

30 April (Frank Bedlingfield Benefit) v Portsmouth (a) 2–0
Barlow, Cameron
Clawley, Erentz, Stephenson, Morris, McNaught, Hughes, Gilhooley, Barlow, Cameron, Copeland, Kirwan
2,000

1902–03

15 November v Corinthians (a) 3–1
Copeland 2, Kirwan
Clawley, Erentz, Tait, C.Brown, Morris, J.L.Jones, Gilhooley, Cameron, Woodward, Copeland, Kirwan
4,000

13 December v Corinthians (h) 2–2
Houston, Chalmers
Williams, Watson, Tait, Morris, Hughes, J.L.Jones, Haig-Brown, Warner, Houston, Copeland, Chalmers
6,000

6 April v Queens Park (h) 1–0
J.Burton
Williams, Stephenson, Tait, J.Burton, Morris, O.Burton, Haig-Brown, Gilhooley, Cameron, Hubble, Kirwan
2,000

30 April v Nottingham Forest (h) 2–1
Woodward 2
Clawley, Erentz, Tait, Hughes, Morris, O.Burton, Dryburgh, Gilhooley, Woodward, Copeland, Kirwan
2,000

1903–04

7 December v Burnley (h) 4–0
Warner, Badger 2, Cameron
Mearns, Watson, Erentz, Brown, McNaught, O.Burton, Warner, Quinn, Badger, Cameron, Chalmers

12 December v Corinthians (h) 5–1
Warner, J.Jones, Woodward 2, Copeland
Williams, Tait, Hughes, Morris, McNaught, JL.Jones, Warner, J.Jones, Woodward, Copeland, Kirwan
5,000

1904–05

2 November (Cottage Hospital Benefit) v Littlehampton & District (a) 7–0

Cameron 2, Copeland 2, McNaught, Warner 2
Williams, McCurdy, Tait, Morris, Hughes, McNaught, Stansfield, Warner, Cameron, Copeland, Kirwan
2,000

28 November v Cambridge University (h) 2–2

O'Hagan, Potter (og)
Eggett, McCurdy, Burton, Hughes, Leach-Lewis, McNaught, Gallacher, Warner, Glen, O'Hagan, Kirwan

15 December (Essex Cricket Club Benefit) v Corinthians (Leyton) 6–2

Walton, Glen, O'Hagan 2, Woodward
Eggett, McCurdy, Burton, Morris, Bull, Brearley, Walton, Woodward, Glen, O'Hagan, Kirwan
3,000

14 January v Corinthians (h) 0–2

Eggett, McCurdy, Gallacher, George, Bull, Hughes, Walton, Stansfield, Glen, O'Hagan, Kirwan
8,000

25 April v Sheffield United (h) 0–0

Yates, Watson, Burton, Morgan, Bull, Freeborough, Walton, Cameron, Stansfield, O'Donnell, Murray
4,000

1905–06

9 December v Corinthians (h) 3–1

Walton, Kyle, Carrick
Eggett, Watson, Burton, Morris, Bull, Brearley, Walton, Berry, Woodward, Kyle, Carrick
11,000

1906–07

14 November v Corinthians (a) 1–6

Brearley
Reilly, Chaplin, Tait, Morris, Bull, Hughes, Badenoch, Hewitt, Stansfield, Reid, Brearley

8 December v Corinthians (h) 5–0

Woodward, Reid, Brearley 2, Timmis (og)
Reilly, Chaplin, J.Watson, Morris, Bull, Hughes, Walton, Hewitt, Woodward, Reid, Brearley
5,000

1907–08

1 February v Woolwich Arsenal (h) 0–1

Manning, Chaplin, Burton, Morris, Bull, Gray, McNair, Pass, Woodward, Reid, Middlemiss
11,000

22 February v Chelsea (a) 1–1

Seeburg
Whitbourne, Chaplin, Burton, Steel, Bull, Darnell, Walker, Pass, Seeburg, Pickett, Middlemiss
10,000

30 April v Clapton Orient (a) 0–2

Manning, Coquet, Dixon, Morris, Bull, Darnell, Pickett, Minter, Seeburg, Payne, Jenkins
2,000

1908–09

29 April v Clapton Orient (a) 3–2

Tull 2, Curtis
Boreham, Leslie, Wilkes, Bentley, D.Steel, Darnell, Curtis, Minter, Tull, R.Steel, Middlemiss

1909–10

29 September v Reading (a) 3–2

Tull 2, Minter
Drabble, Coquet, Wilkes, Bentley, D.Steel, Leslie, Curtis, McConnon, Minter, Tull, Middlemiss
2,000

1911–12

3 February v Clapton Orient (h) 3–2

Minter, Elliott 2
Joyce, Webster, Brittan, Bentley, Lightfoot, Bowering, Curtis, Minter, Elliott, Mason, Middlemiss
8,000

18 April (Ernie Freeman Benefit) v Northampton Town (a) 0–2

Lunn, Webster, Brittan, Darnell, Kennedy, Bowering, Curtis, J.McTavish, Elliott, Bliss, Middlemiss
7,000

29 April (Daily Telegraph Titanic Fund) v Woolwich Arsenal (Park Royal) 0–3

Lunn, Webster, Collins, Lightfoot, D.Steel, Darnell, Curtis, Bliss, Minter, R.Steel, Middlemiss
5,000

1912–13

9 April v Watford (a) 0–0

Joyce, Collins, Webster, Weir, Elliott, Grimsdell, Tattersall, Minter, Cantrell, Bliss, Middlemiss
2,000

1913–14

21 February v Chelsea (h) 3–7

Sparrow, Banks, Bliss
McCleneghan, Collins, Pearson, Weir, Rance, Lightfoot, Tattersall, Banks, Sparrow, Bliss, Middlemiss
3,500

5 March (Variety Artistes Benevolent Fund/Prince of Wales Hospital) v Music Hall Artists (h) 3–2

Banks, Cantrell, Bliss
Joyce, Clay, Webster, Bowler, Steel, Grimsdell, Walden, Banks, Cantrell, Bliss, Middlemiss
1,200
30-minute match

1914–15

22 August (War Relief Fund) v Arsenal (h) 1–5

Minter
Jacques, Clay, Webster, Fleming, Steel, Grimsdell, Walden, Minter, Cantrell, Woodger, Crowl
13,500

15 October v Chelsea (a) 1–1

Sparrow
Watkins, Collins, Cartwright, Steel, Rance, Lightfoot, Tattersall, Banks, Sparrow, Lowe, Middlemiss
7,000

6 February v Fulham (h) 2–2

Steel, Cantrell
Eadon, Clay, Pearson, Weir, Steel, Lightfoot, Fleming, Lowe, Cantrell, Woodger, Middlemiss
3,000

1915–16

29 January (Footballers' Battalion Comfort Fund) v Clapton Orient (h) 0–1

Joyce, Clay, Ralston, Darnell, Rance, Barton, Morris, Lloyd, Bassett, Bliss, Steel
3,000

24 April v Norwich City (a) 1–1

McGregor
Watkins, Clay, Butcher, Elliott, Rance, Darnell, Morris, Lloyd, McGregor, Steel, Ramsay
5,000

6 May v Clapton Orient (a) 2–3

Bassett, Bliss
Jacques, Clay, Steel, Elliott, Rance, Barton, Morris, Bassett, Lloyd, Bliss, Hopkin
1,000

1916–17

5 May v West Ham United (a) 3–3

Potter, Banks, Barnard
Jacques, Clay, Feeburg, Elliott, Barton, Darnell, Potter, Bassett, Banks, Barnard, Casey

1918–19

31 August v Corporal H Price's XI (St Albans) 1–1

A.Lindsay
Brandham, Thomas, Elliott, Beaton, Darnell, McCracken, Brooks, A.Lindsay, Barnard, Robson, Dockray
3,000

11 December v RAF (Reading) (a) 2–1

Thwaites, Clay, Ralston, Elliott, Rance, Darnell, Hawkins, Thomas, McCalmont, Jack, Dimmock
1,000

26 April v Clapton Orient (a) 1–6

Roper
Jacques, Draper, Ferris, Darnell, Rance, Robson, Rees, Minter, Roper, Simons, Middlemiss
15,000

26 April v Crystal Palace (a) 0–3

French, Clay, Craig, Thomas, Elliott, Tomkins, 'Slender' (Chester), Upex, Wilson, Banks, Dockray
2,000

10 May (National War Fund) v Fulham (h) 2–2

Grimsdell 2
Hatfield, Wilson, Elliott, Tomkins, Rance, Grimsdell, Furr, Minter, Bay, Bliss, Dimmock
5,000

24 May v Arsenal (a) 0–0
Jacques, Pearson, Clay, Tomkins, Rutherford, Barton, Dimmock, Innes, Minter, Powell, Furr
6,000

1919–20

15 December v Corinthians (h) 4–1
Cantrell 2, Wilson 2
Jacques, Pearson, McDonald, Smith, Rance, Skinner, Lorimer, Minter, Cantrell, Wilson, Dimmock
6,000

8 May (Norfolk & Norwich Hospital Cup) v Norwich City (a) 4–0
Banks 2, Bliss 2
Jacques, Clay, Brown, Archibald, Smith, Grimsdell, Banks, Seed, Cantrell, Bliss, Dimmock
11,902

1920–21

22 September (Tom Coulson Dependant's Benefit) v Watford (a) 2–4
Seed, Banks
Hunter, Clay, R.McDonald, Smith, D.R.McDonald, Grimsdell, Walden, Seed, Banks, O'Donnell, Dimmock
4,500

14 May (Royal Military College Fete and Gala) v Fulham (Camberley) 4–0
Grimsdell, Banks, Wilson, Bliss
Hunter, Clay, McDonald, Smith, Walters, Grimsdell, Banks, Seed, Wilson, Bliss, Dimmock

1921–22

19 September v Partick Thistle (a) 1–3
Wilson
Hunter, Clay, McDonald, Archibald, Walters, Grimsdell, Banks, Seed, Wilson, Thompson, Dimmock
20,000

22 September v Inverness (a) 3–6
Grimsdell, Lindsay, Thompson
Hunter, Clay, McDonald, Archibald, Lowe, Grimsdell, Walden, Lindsay, Seed, Thompson, Dimmock

6 October (Docklands Settlement/Malvern Mission) v Corinthians (h) 2–1
Smith, Banks
French, Clay, McDonald, Smith, Lowe, Grimsdell, Lorimer, Seed, Banks, Bliss, Handley
10,694

13 May (Royal Military College Fete and Gala) v Chelsea (Camberley) 1–1
Seed
Hampton, Clay, McDonald, Smith, Walters, Skinner, Lindsay, Seed, Wilson, Thompson, Dimmock
5,000

1922–23

11 September v Corinthians (a) 2–1
Brooks, Hunter (og)
Jacques, Clay, McDonald, Skinner, Walters, Grimsdell, Walden, Handley, Lindsay, Dimmock, Brooks
10,000

16 October v Llanelly (a) 1–2
Whitton
Blake, Forster, McDonald, Poynton, Grimsdell, Lowe, Sage, Seed, Whitton, Dimmock, Handley
12,000

7 May (Dockland Settlement) v West Ham United (h) 5–2
Lindsay, Handley 3, Dimmock
Maddison, Clay, Forster, Smith, Walters, Grimsdell, Barnett, Thompson, Lindsay, Handley, Dimmock
5,000

1923–24

2 February v Chelsea (a) 0–0
Maddison, Bann, Forster, Smith, Walters, Duffus, Handley, Thompson, Osborne, Elkes, Brooks
15,000

23 February v West Ham United (a) 1–1
Thompson
Blake, Clay, Forster, Smith, Walters, Poynton, McCudden, Thompson, Minter, Elkes, Handley
15,000

17 March (Dockland Settlement) v West Ham United (a) 1–1
Lindsay
Maddison, Clay, Forster, Smith, Sage, Poynton, Thompson, Lindsay, Osborne, Elkes, Handley

16 April v Inter-Varsities (h) 7–1
Osborne, Lindsay, Elkes 2, Dimmock 3
Blake, Clay, Poynton, Smith, Lowe, Skinner, Thompson, Osborne, Lindsay, Elkes, Dimmock
3,000

1925–26

27 March v Hull City (a) 0–5
Britton, Bann, McDonald, Seed, Skitt, Grimsdell, Vanner, Lane, Minter, Handley, Dimmock
5,000

3 May (Docklands Settlement) v West Ham United (a) 1–1
Blair
J.Smith, Bann, Richardson, B.Smith, Elkes, Lindsay, Thompson, Blair, Lane, Seed, Handley

1927–28

25 April v Ebbw Vale (a) 7–3
O'Callaghan 2, Lindsay, Armstrong, Dimmock 3
Spiers, Forster, Poynton, Lowdell, Skitt, Grimsdell, Thompson, O'Callaghan, Lindsay, Armstrong, Dimmock

1929–30

1 May v Yeovil & Petters (a) 6–4
Osborne 2, Harper 2, O'Callaghan, Dimmock
Spiers, Herod, Reddish, Skitt, Cable, Meads, Davies, Osborne, Harper, O'Callaghan, Dimmock

1930–31

8 December West Ham United (a) 2–1
Davies, Bellamy
Spiers, Lyons, Hodgkinson, Skitt, Messer, Meads, Davies, O'Callaghan, Harper, Cook, Bellamy

28 February v Huddersfield Town (h) 2–4
Harper, Goodall (og)
Spiers, Lyons, Hodgkinson, Skitt, Messer, Alsford, Davies, O'Callaghan, Harper, Cook, Bellamy
13,225

1933–34

30 April v Luton Town (a) 2–2
O'Callaghan, Hedley
Nicholls, Channell, Whatley, Day, Rowe, Meads, McCormick, O'Callaghan, Hunt, G.W.Hall, Hedley

2 May (Dewar Shield) v Corinthians (h) 7–4
O'Callaghan 2, Hunt 3, W.Evans 2,
Nicholls, Channell, Whatley, Day, Rowe, Meads, McCormick, O'Callaghan, Hunt, G.W.Hall, W.Evans
5,117

1934–35

24 April v Burton Town (a) 2–2
Bell, G.S.Hunt
Hooper, Illingworth, Fullwood, Howe, Alsford, Phypers, Bolan, Bell, G.S.Hunt, Duncan, W.Evans

1938–39

20 August (Jubilee Trust Fund) v Arsenal (a) 2–0
Morrison, Lyman
Hooper, Sproston, Whatley, Howe, Page, Buckingham, Sargent, G.W.Hall, Morrison, A.E.Hall, Lyman
41,997

17 April v Arsenal (Colchester) 1–2
Duncan
Hooper, Ward, Whatley, Burgess, Hitchins, Buckingham, Cox, G.W.Hall, Ludford, Duncan, Medley

1939–40

19 August (Jubilee Trust Fund) v Arsenal (h) 0–1
Hooper, Ward, Nicholson, Burgess, Hitchins, Buckingham, Sargent, G.W.Hall, Ludford, Dix, Lyman
32,702

23 September v Chelmsford City (a) 2–4
G.W.Hall, Ludford
Hooper, Howe, Whatley, Burgess, Hitchins, Buckingham, Cox, G.W.Hall, Ludford, Sargent, Tomkin
5,000

30 September v Chelsea (a) 2–4
Ludford, Medley
Hooper, Dorling, Whatley, Burgess, Hitchins, Howe, Sargent, G.W.Hall, Ludford, Duncan, Medley
6,388

7 October v West Ham United (h) 0–2
Hooper, Dorling, Whatley, Burgess, Hitchins, Spelman, Sargent, G.W.Hall, Ludford, Duncan, Medley
5,201

1941–42

25 May v Crystal Palace (a) 5–3
Chisholm, W.Sainsbury, Gibbons, Edwards, Gregory (og)
Hooper, Ward, Tickridge, Chisholm, Hitchins, Hall, W.Sainsbury, Broadis, Gibbons, Edwards, Ludford
4,000

1942–43

17 April v Queen's Park Rangers (a) 1–1
Ludford
Hooper, Ward, Whatley, Palmer, Howe, Buckingham, Beasley, Milton, Ludford, O'Callaghan, Trigg

24 April v Charlton Athletic (h) 2–1
Martin, E.Jones
Hooper, Ward, Whatley, Willis, Chisholm, Buckingham, Beasley, Martin, Rowley, Hall, E.Jones
5,267

26 April v Fulham (h) 3–0
Rowley 2, Ludford
Hooper, Ward, Whatley, Howe, Chisholm, Buckingham, Beasley, Martin, Rowley, Hall, Ludford
2,968

1 May v Clapton Orient (h) 4–3
Ludford, Holley 2, M.E.Sturgess
L.Sturgess, Ward, Whatley, Howe, Chisholm, Hall, Ludford, Bennett, Holley, M.E.Sturgess, O'Callaghan
3,194

8 May v Arsenal (h) 1–2
Ludford
Hooper, Ward, Howe, L.Jones, Chisholm, Buckingham, Beasley, Hall, Ludford, Clayton, Burley
8,560

1943–44

10 April v Millwall (a) 0–0
Ditchburn, Ward, Whatley, Durston, Gibbins, R.Evans, Downer, Whent, Ludford, Beasley, Adams
4,000

1944–45

19 August (Lady Rootes Charity Cup) v Coventry City (a) 1–3
Howe
Hughes, Ward, Willis, White, Page, Burgess, Walters, Martin, Ludford, Howe, Beasley
10,000

7 April v Crystal Palace (a) 1–3
Opponent (og)
Hughes, Ward, Willis, White, Burke, Burgess, Walters, Walker, Woodward, Gurr, A.E.Hall

19 May v Arsenal (h) 4–0
Walters, Flavell, Dix, Howe
Roberts, Ward, Willis, Ludford, Burke, Burgess, Walters, Flavell, Lyman, Dix, Howe
10,450

26 May v Fulham (h) 2–2
Ludford, Burgess
Roberts, Ward, Willis, Ludford, Burke, Burgess, Walters, Broadis, Lyman, A.E.Hall, Beasley
3,037

1945–46

2 March v Chelsea (h) 4–2
Foreman 2, Dix, Whitchurch
Hughes, Willis, Buckingham, White, Nicholson, Ludford, Griffiths, Rundle, Foreman, Dix, Whitchurch
12,749

1946–47

25 January v Arsenal (h) 2–0
Woodward, Hall
Hughes, Tickridge, Whatley, Woodward, Chisholm, Trailor, Hall, Bennett, Duquemin, Dix, Whitchurch
16,537

12 May (Norwich Hospital Charity Cup) v Norwich City (a) 2–0
Bennett 2
Ditchburn, Willis, Buckingham, Ludford, Nicholson, Trailor, Cox, Bennett, Rundle, Dix, Stevens
18,687

1948–49

29 January v Middlesbrough (h) 4–1

Burgess, Baily, Bennett, Jones

Ditchburn, Tickridge, Buckingham, Nicholson, Woodward, Burgess, Walters, Baily, Duquemin, Bennett, Jones

20,000

25 April v Hibernian (h) 2–5

Bennett, Duquemin

Ditchburn, Tickridge, Withers, Garwood, Clarke, Trailor, Walters, Bennett, Duquemin, Baily, Medley

24,190

9 May v Cornwall County XI Penzance 2–0

Rundle, Medley

Ditchburn, Tickridge, Withers, Nicholson, Clarke, Burgess, Walters, Bennett, Westwood, Rundle, Medley

1949–50

24 April (Les Pyle Benefit) v Chelmsford City (a) 4–1

Bennett 3, Duquemin

Ditchburn, Ramsey, Willis, Gilberg, Farley, Marchi, Walters, Bennett, Duquemin, Rees, Medley

6,000

1 May v Hibernian (h) 0–1

Ditchburn, Ramsey, Willis, Gilberg, Clarke, Marchi, Walters, Bennett, Duquemin, Harmer, Medley

33,558

8 May (Norwich Hospital Charity Cup) v Norwich City (a) 2–2

Duquemin, Scarth

Ditchburn, Tickridge, Willis, Gilberg, Clarke, Burgess, Walters, Bennett, Duquemin, Rundle, Scarth

13,929

1950–51

18 September v Lovells Athletic (h) 8–0

Burgess, Scarth 2, Duquemin 3, Harmer, Medley

Ditchburn, Henty, Willis, Nicholson, Clarke, Burgess, Walters, Scarth, Duquemin, Harmer, Medley

3,124

27 January v Cardiff City (a) 3–2

McClellan, Baily, Adams

Ditchburn, Ramsey, Willis, Garwood, Clarke, Burgess, Walters, Murphy, McClellan, Baily, Adams

11,000

6 February v Combined Liege XI (a) 4–1

Walters, Murphy 2, McClellan

Ditchburn, Ramsey, Willis, Nicholson, Clarke, Burgess, Walters, Murphy, McClellan, Baily, Medley

15,000

23 April v Hibernian (a) 0–0

Ditchburn, Ramsey, Willis, Nicholson, Clarke, Burgess, Walters, Murphy, Duquemin, Baily, Medley

39,000

30 April (Denny Foreman Benefit) v Chelmsford City (a) 7–3

Bennett, McClellan 4, Murphy 2

Reynolds, Willis, Withers, Brittan, Farley, Burgess, Walters, Bennett, McClellan, Murphy, Medley

7 May (Festival of Britain) v FC Austria (h) 0–1

Ditchburn, Withers, Willis, Nicholson, Clarke, Burgess, Walters, Murphy, Duquemin, Baily, Medley

30,000

12 May (Festival of Britain) v Borussia Dortmund (h) 2–1

Baily, Murphy

Ditchburn (Withers), Ramsey, Willis, Brittan, Clarke, Marchi, Walters, Bennett, McClellan, Baily, Murphy

2,900

16 May v Racing Club de Paris (a) 4–2

Baily, Duquemin, McClellan, Medley

Reynolds, Withers, Willis, Bennett, Clarke, Brittan, Walters, Baily, Duquemin (McClellan), Murphy, Medley

1951–52

10 October v Copenhagen Combined XI (h) 2–1

Walters, Medley

Ditchburn, Ramsey, Willis, Nicholson, Clarke, Burgess, Walters, Bennett, McClellan, Baily, Medley

26 March (Le Soir Cup) v FC Austria (Brussels) 2–2
Bennett, Duquemin
Ditchburn, Ramsey, Willis, Nicholson, Clarke, Burgess, Walters, Bennett, Duquemin, Baily, Adams
45,000

23 April v Hibernian (h) 1–2
Ramsey (pen)
Ditchburn, Ramsey, Withers, Nicholson, Clarke, Burgess, Walters, Bennett, Duquemin, Baily, McClellan
28,000

3 May v Racing Club de Paris (a) 2–1
Ramsey, Bennett
Ditchburn, Ramsey, Withers, Nicholson (Robshaw), Clarke, Burgess, Walters, Bennett, Duquemin, Baily, Medley
20,000

5 May (Ipswich Hospital Charity Cup) v Ipswich Town (a) 2–2
Bennett, Meadows
Ditchburn, Ramsey, Withers, Robshaw, Clarke, Burgess, Walters, Bennett, Meadows, Baily, Medley
13,974

8 May (Braintree, Witham & Dist Tuberculosis After-Care) v Crittall Athletic (a) 8–1
Walters, Uphill, Baily, Duquemin 2, Harmer, McClellan, Opponent (og)
Ditchburn, Willis, Gibbins, Bennett, Clarke, Wetton, Walters (Uphill), Baily (Dowsett), Duquemin, Harmer (Adams), McClellan

1952–53

27 October v Gloucester City (a) 1–2
Baily
Ditchburn, Ramsey, Withers, Robshaw, Farley, Wetton, Walters, Bennett, Duquemin, Baily, Harmer

16 April v West Ham United (a) 1–2
Walters
Ditchburn, Baker, Withers, Nicholson, Clarke, Brittan, Walters, Bennett, Laybourne, Baily, Medley
25,000

20 April (Stan Wicks Testimonial) v Reading (a) 4–0
Duquemin 2, Baily, McClellan
Ditchburn, Ramsey, Willis, Marchi, Clarke, Farley, Brooks, Bennett, Duquemin, Baily, McClellan
9,000

4 May (Lord Mayor of London's National Flood and Tempest Distress Fund) v Arsenal (a) 2–0
Bennett, Duquemin
Ditchburn, Baker, Hopkins, Wetton, King, Burgess, Walters, Bennett, Duquemin, Baily, McClellan
21,778

11 May (Coronation Cup semi-final) v Hibernian (Ibrox Park) 1–1
Walters
Reynolds, Baker, Nicholson, Marchi, King, Brittan, Walters, Bennett, Duquemin, Baily, McClellan
43,000

12 May (Coronation Cup semi-final rep) v Hibernian (Hampden Park) 1–2
McClellan
Reynolds, Baker, Nicholson, Marchi, King, Brittan, Walters, Bennett, Duquemin, Baily, McClellan
13,000

15 May v Heart of Midlothian (a) 0–2
Reynolds, Nicholson, Withers, Marchi, King, Brittan, Brooks, Baily, Bennett, Harmer, McClellan
15,000

30 May v Racing Club de Paris (a) 1–1
Duquemin
Reynolds, Withers, Hopkins, Wetton, King, Burgess, Walters, Bennett, Duquemin, Baily, Brooks (McClellan)
10,000

1953–54

21 September v Hibernian (a) 1–0
Wetton
Ditchburn, Baker, Withers, Bennett, Clarke, Wetton, McClellan, Brooks, Duquemin, Baily, Owen

29 September v Racing Club de Paris (h) 5–3
Burgess, Hutchinson, Bennett 2, Duquemin
Ditchburn, Ramsey, Withers, Wetton, Farley, Burgess, Hutchinson, Bennett, Duquemin, Harmer, Robb
28,070

19 October v Millwall (a) 2–0
Walters, Bennett
Reynolds, Baker, Withers, Nicholson, Clarke, Wetton, Walters, Brooks, Bennett, Baily, Robb
18,000

28 October v FC Austria (h) 3–2
Walters, Duquemin, Harmer
Ditchburn, Ramsey, Withers, Nicholson, Clarke, Burgess, Walters, Brooks, Duquemin, Harmer, Robb
37,184

5 April v Hibernian (h) 3–2
Burgess, Duquemin, Robb
Ditchburn, Baker, Withers, Brittan, Clarke, Burgess, Hutchinson, Bennett, Duquemin, Harmer, Robb

1954–55

14 August v Lille Olympique (a) 1–1
Duquemin
Ditchburn, Ramsey, Withers, Wetton, Clarke, Brittan (Walley), Dulin, Bennett, Duquemin, Baily (McClellan), Robb
50,000

11 October v Queen's Park Rangers (a) 1–2
Ramsey
Ditchburn, Ramsey, Withers, Hills, Adams, Nicholson, Dulin, Baily, Duquemin, Brooks, Spivey

18 October v Sportklub Wacker (h) 1–2
McClellan
Ditchburn, Ramsey, Hopkins, Nicholson, King, Marchi, McClellan, Harmer, Dunmore, Brooks, Gavin
22,303

2 November v Rot-Weiss Essen (h) 4–2
Ramsey 2 (1 pen), Brooks 2
Ditchburn, Ramsey, Withers, Nicholson, Adams, Marchi, McClellan, Brooks, Dunmore, Baily, Gavin
21,000

15 November v Finchley (h) 2–2
Walters, Baily
Reynolds, Ramsey, Withers, Wetton, Price, Bennett, Walters, Baily, Duquemin, Harmer, Robb

29 November v Accrington Stanley (a) 0–0
Reynolds, Baker, McNally, Wetton, Clarke, Marchi, Walters, Baily, Dunmore, Brooks, Dyson
6,286
(Abandoned after 52 mins – rain)

2 March v Arsenal (h) 1–4
Robb
Reynolds, Ramsey, Hopkins, Blanchflower, Clarke, Marchi, Gavin, Baily, Duquemin, Brooks, Robb
14,350

9 March v Racing Club de Paris (h) 6–0
Blanchflower, Marchi, Dulin, Duquemin, Brooks 2
Reynolds, Baker, Hopkins, Blanchflower, Price, Marchi, Dulin, Harmer, Duquemin, Brooks, Robb
8,100

14 March v Hibernian (a) 1–1
McClellan
Reynolds, Baker, Hopkins, Blanchflower, Clarke, Marchi, Gavin, McClellan, Duquemin, Brooks, Robb

30 March v FC Servette (h) 5–1
Gavin 2, Brooks, Duquemin, McClellan
Reynolds, Baker, Henry, Blanchflower, King, Marchi (Woods), Gavin, Brooks, Duquemin, McClellan, Robb
6,542

1955–56

25 September v Aarhus Gymnastikforening (a) 4–3
Brooks 2, Stokes, Robb
Ditchburn, Withers, Hopkins, Blanchflower, Clarke, Marchi, Walters, Brooks, Stokes, Baily, Robb

12 October v FC Vasas (h) 1–2
McClellan
Ditchburn, Baker, Hopkins, Blanchflower, Clarke, Marchi, Walters, Brooks, Duquemin, McClellan, Robb (Dyson)

24 October v Plymouth Argyle (a) 0–0
Ditchburn, Baker, Hopkins, Barton, Clarke, Marchi, Walters, Brooks, Duquemin, Baily, Robb

14 November v Partick Thistle (a) 0–1
Reynolds, Norman, Hopkins, Blanchflower, Ryden, Marchi, McClellan, Brooks, Stokes, Baily, Dyson
12,500

6 December v Swansea Town (h) 4–1
Dulin, Brooks, Duquemin, Baily
Reynolds, Norman, Hopkins, Blanchflower, Clarke, Marchi, Dulin, Brooks, Duquemin, Baily, Robb
15,000

1956–57

11 September v Racing Club de Paris (h) 2–0
Marchi, Medwin
Ditchburn, Baker, Hopkins, Blanchflower, Clarke, Marchi, Medwin, Harmer, Smith, Stokes, Dyson
25,000

17 September (Anglo-Scottish Floodlit Tournament) v Hibernian (a) 5–1
Blanchflower, Harmer, Smith 2, Dyson
Ditchburn, Baker, Hopkins, Blanchflower, Clarke, Marchi, Medwin, Harmer, Smith, Stokes, Dyson
15,000

26 September (Anglo-Scottish Floodlit Tournament) v Partick Thistle (h) 4–1
Medwin, Smith, Stokes 2
Ditchburn, Baker, Hopkins, Blanchflower, Clarke, Marchi, Medwin, Harmer, Smith, Stokes, Robb
26,210

15 October (Anglo-Scottish Floodlit Tournament) v Heart of Midlothian (a) 2–3
Harmer (pen), Dyson
Ditchburn, Baker, Hopkins, Blanchflower, Clarke, Marchi, Medwin, Harmer, Smith, Stokes, Dyson
17,000

31 October (Anglo-Scottish Floodlit Tournament) v Hibernian (h) 3–3
Hopkins, Medwin, Brooks
Ditchburn, Baker, Hopkins, Blanchflower, Clarke, Marchi, Medwin, Harmer, Smith, Brooks, Robb
16,561

12 November (Anglo-Scottish Floodlit Tournament) v Heart of Midlothian (h) 4–2
Smith 3, Stokes
Hollowbread, Baker, Norman, Blanchflower, Ryden, Marchi, Dyson, Harmer, Smith, Stokes, Robb
17,542

26 November (Anglo-Scottish Floodlit Tournament) v Partick Thistle (a) 0–2
Reynolds, Norman, Hopkins, Blanchflower, Ryden, Marchi, Medwin, Harmer, Smith, Stokes, Dyson
9,000

3 December v Red Banner (MTK) (h) 7–1
Blanchflower, Medwin, Duquemin, Stokes 3, Robb
Reynolds, Norman, Hopkins, Blanchflower, Clarke, Walley, Medwin, Harmer, Duquemin, Stokes, Robb
31,860

19 March v Combined Antwerp XI (a) 2–1
Medwin, Smith
Reynolds, Baker, Norman, Blanchflower, Ryden, Marchi, Medwin, Harmer, Smith, Stokes, Dyson
20,000

1957–58

3 August v Vfb Stuttgart (a) 2–2
Smith 2
Reynolds, Norman, Hopkins, Blanchflower, Ryden, Walley, Medwin, Harmer, Smith, Stokes, Dulin
17,000

14 October v Hibernain (a) 2–5
Smith 2
Hollowbread, Baker, Hopkins, Blanchflower, Ryden, Iley, Bing, Harmer, Smith, Walley, Dyson
26,000

23 October v Swiss National XI (Basel) 5–4
Smith 4, Dunmore
Ditchburn, Baker, Hopkins, Blanchflower, Ryden, Iley, Bing, Smith, Dunmore, Brooks, Medwin

6 November v Bristol City (a) 3–4
Brooks 2, Harmer
Ditchburn, Baker, Hopkins, Ryden, Norman, Iley, Medwin, Brooks, Smith, Harmer, Dyson
13,089

11 November v Vfb Stuttgart (h) 3–2
Ryden, Smith, Robb
Ditchburn, Baker, Henry, Blanchflower, Norman, Ryden, Ireland, Brooks, Smith, Harmer, Robb
13,425

1 March v Partick Thistle (h) 4–1
Medwin 2, Brooks, Smith
Ditchburn, Hills, Henry, Blanchflower, Norman, Ryden, Medwin, Brooks, Smith, Harmer, Jones (Dyson)
25,748

27 March v Rotterdam Select XI (a) 4–1
Medwin, Brooks, Smith, Harmer
Ditchburn, Hills, Henry, Blanchflower, Laurel, Ryden, Medwin, Brooks, Smith, Harmer, Dyson
43,000

14 April v Hibernian (h) 4–0
Ireland, Dunmore 2, Robb
Reynolds, Hills, Henry, Walley, Norman, Iley, Ireland, Harmer, Dunmore, Clayton, Robb
15,919

24 April v Canto Do Rio (h) 4–1
Blanchflower, Smith, Clayton 2
Reynolds, Hills, Henry, Blanchflower, Norman, Iley, Medwin, Harmer, Smith, Clayton, Dyson
22,268

1958–59

14 October v Bela Vista (h) 3–1
Stokes 2, Robb
Hollowbread, Baker, Hopkins, Dodge, Ryden, Iley, Medwin, Harmer, Smith, Stokes, Robb
15,576

10 November v Hibernian (h) 5–2
Dunmore 3, Medwin 2
Hollowbread, Baker, Hopkins, Blanchflower, Norman, Iley, Brooks, Harmer, Dunmore, Smith, Medwin
11,180

8 December v Bucharest Select XI (h) 4–2
Medwin, Harmer (pen), Stokes, Jones
Hollowbread, Hills, Henry, Dodge, Norman, Iley, Medwin, Harmer, Smith, Stokes, Jones
10,359

1959–60

21 October (Campbell, Meeson & Reeves Testimonial) v Reading (a) 5–2
Brooks, R.Smith, Jones 3
Hollowbread, Baker, Hopkins, Marchi, Smith A, Mackay, Medwin, Brooks, R.Smith (Saul), Dunmore, Jones
10,000

16 November v Moscow Torpedo (h) 3–2
Mackay, White, R.Smith
Brown, Baker, Marchi, Blanchflower (Henry), Norman, Mackay, Medwin, White, R.Smith, Dunmore, Jones
44,984

2 May v Crystal Palace (a) 2–2
Saul, R.Smith
Hollowbread, Barton, Henry, Blanchflower, Norman, J.Smith, Jones, Harmer, Saul, R.Smith, Dyson

25 May v Juventus (a) 0–2
Brown, Baker, Henry, Blanchflower, Norman, Marchi, Medwin, White (Harmer), R.Smith (Saul), Mackay, Jones
40,000

1960–61

24 October v Army XI (h) 3–5
Opponent (og), Allen, Aitchison
Brown, Baker, Henry, Dodge, Norman, Marchi, Aitchison, Collins, Saul, Allen, Dyson
5,947

14 November v Dinamo Tbilisi (h) 5–2
Mackay 2, Medwin 2, Dyson
Brown, Baker, Henry, Blanchflower, Norman, Mackay, Medwin, White, R.Smith, Allen, Dyson
38,649

1962–63

14 November v Zamalek (a) 7–3
Medwin, White, Greaves 2, Jones, Dyson 2
Brown, Baker, Henry, Blanchflower, Norman, Mackay, Medwin, White, Allen, Greaves, Jones (Dyson)
60,000

26 January v Arsenal (h) 3–1
Greaves 2, Jones
Brown, Baker (Dennis), Henry, Marchi, Norman, Mackay, Medwin, Clayton, R.Smith, Greaves, Jones
19,883

2 February v Portsmouth (a) 3–2
Mackay, Medwin, Greaves
Brown, Baker, Henry, Marchi, Norman, Mackay, Medwin, Clayton, R.Smith, Greaves, Jones
12,000

1963–64

28 April v Coventry City (a) 6–5
White, Saul 2, Allen 3
W.Brown, Baker, Henry, Mullery, L.Brown, Marchi, Jones, White, Saul, Allen, Dyson
15,638

1964–65

5 August (Glasgow Charity Cup) v Glasgow XI (Hampden Park) 2–4
Saul, Robertson
W.Brown, Knowles, Henry, Mullery, Norman, Beal, Jones, Greaves, Saul, Mackay, Robertson
58,768

8 August v Feyenoord (a) 3–4
Greaves, Mackay, Dyson
Jennings, Knowles, Henry, Mullery, Norman, Beal, Jones, Greaves, Saul, Mackay, Dyson
37,714

23 September v Copenhagen Select XI (a) 1–2
Saul
W.Brown, Knowles, Henry, Mullery, L.Brown, Marchi, Robertson, Greaves, Saul, Jones, Possee

8 December v Leytonstone (a) 5–0
Allen 2, Dyson 2, Saul
Jennings, Baker, Dennis, Beal, Smith, Low, Weller, Clayton, Saul, Allen, Dyson

27 April v Anderlecht (a) 2–4
Greaves, Gilzean
W.Brown, Norman, Henry, Mullery, Brown L, Clayton, Weller, Greaves, Saul, Gilzean, Jones
10,000

29 April v Coventry City (a) 3–0
Mullery, Saul, Low
Jennings, Norman, Henry, Mullery, Brown L, Clayton, Robertson, Saul, Low, Gilzean, Dyson
13,660

1965–66

22 September v Walton & Hersham (a) 8–1
Mullery, Gilzean 4, Greaves 3
Jennings, Norman, Knowles, Mullery, L.Brown, Low, Robertson, Clayton, Gilzean, Greaves, Jones (Johnson)
4,000

18 November v Hungarian Select XI (h) 4–0
Mackay (pen), Gilzean 3
Jennings, Norman, Knowles, Mullery, L.Brown, Mackay, Possee, Clayton, Saul, Gilzean, Robertson
22,635

3 May v WKS Legia (a) 0–2
W.Brown, Kinnear, Knowles, Mullery, L.Brown, Beal, Robertson (Johnson), Clayton (Mackay), Saul, Gilzean, Possee
70,000

15 May v Sarpsborg (a) 3–0
Gilzean 2, Weller
Jennings, Embery, Henry, Beal, Hoy, Mackay, Possee, Gillingwater (Johnson), Gilzean, Smith, Weller

1966–67

10 October v Dundee (a) 3–2
Mackay, Greaves 2
Brown W, Clayton, Henry, Mullery, England, Mackay, Robertson, Greaves, Saul, Venables, Jones (Weller)
15,000

23 November v Polish Select XI (h) 2–1
Greaves, Jones
Jennings, Beal, Knowles, Mullery, England, Mackay, Weller, Greaves, Gilzean (Saul), Venables (Clayton), Jones
13,058

1967–68

5 August v Celtic (Hampden Park) 3–3

Greaves 2, Gilzean
Jennings, Kinnear, Knowles, Mullery, England, Mackay, Robertson, Greaves, Gilzean, Venables, Saul
91,708

1968–69

31 July v Rangers (h) 3–1

Mullery, Collins 2
Jennings, Beal, Knowles, Mullery, England, Collins, Robertson, Greaves, Chivers, Venables, Gilzean
25,000

3 August v FK Austria (a) 2–2

Pearce, Greaves
Jennings, Kinnear, Knowles, Mullery, England, Beal, Robertson (Pearce), Greaves, Chivers, Venables, Jones
20,000

1969–70

2 August v Heart of Midlothian (a) 1–1

Morgan
Jennings, Beal (Want), Knowles, Mullery, England, Collins, Johnson (Gilzean), Greaves, Chivers, Pearce, Morgan
20,000

4 August v Rangers (a) 1–0

Pearce
Jennings, Want, Knowles, Mullery, England, Beal, Gilzean, Greaves, Chivers, Pearce (Pratt), Morgan
55,000

1970–71

3 August v Rangers (h) 2–0

Gilzean, Morgan
Jennings, Evans, Knowles, Mullery, England, Beal, Gilzean, Perryman, Chivers, Peters, Morgan
26,168

1971–72

7 August v Heart of Midlothian (a) 1–2

Chivers
Jennings, Kinnear, Knowles, Mullery, England, Beal, Coates, Perryman, Chivers, Peters, Gilzean
12,000

9 August v Rangers (a) 0–1

Jennings, Kinnear (Evans), Knowles, Mullery, England, Beal, Coates, Perryman, Chivers, Peters, Gilzean
55,000

1972–73

29 July v Bournemouth & Boscombe Athletic (a) 4–2

Kinnear, Perryman, Peters (pen), Pearce
Jennings, Kinnear, Knowles, Naylor, England, Beal, Gilzean, Perryman, Coates, Peters, Pearce
13,050

2 August v Aston Villa (a) 0–0

Jennings, Kinnear, Evans, Naylor (Coates), England, Beal, Gilzean, Perryman, Chivers, Peters, Pearce (Morgan)
23,538

7 August v Celtic (a) 0–1

Jennings, Kinnear, Knowles, Coates, England, Beal, Gilzean, Perryman, Chivers, Peters, Pratt
36,000

1973–74

8 August (Sjaak Swart Testimonial) v Ajax (a) 1–4

Peters
Jennings, Evans, Knowles, Pratt, Collins, Beal, Gilzean, Perryman, Chivers (Holder), Peters, Coates
65,000

11 August v Cardiff City (a) 3–1

Perryman, Gilzean, Peters
Jennings, Evans (Kinnear), Knowles, Pratt, Dillon, Beal, Neighbour (Holder), Perryman, Gilzean, Peters, Coates
9,418

18 August v Sunderland (a) 1–0

Neighbour
Jennings, Evans, Knowles, Pratt, Dillon, Beal (Holder), Neighbour, Perryman, Chivers, Peters, Coates
22,509

1974–75

3 August v Heart of Midlothian (a) 1–1

Pratt
Jennings, Evans, Naylor (Pratt), Beal, England, Conn (McNab), Pearce (McGrath), Perryman (Holder), Jones, Peters, Coates
13,326

7 August v Portsmouth (a) 2–0
Jones, Neighbour
Jennings, Evans, Naylor, Beal, Osgood, Holder (McNab), McGrath, Perryman, Jones, Peters, Coates (Neighbour)
6,259

10 August v Fulham (a) 1–0
Peters
Jennings, Evans, Naylor, Beal, England (Osgood), Holder, McGrath, Perryman, Jones, Peters (Chivers), Coates
7,989

24 January v Watford (a) 3–2
McNab, Conn, Duncan
Jennings, Kinnear, Pratt, Beal, England (Osgood), Naylor, Coates (McNab), Perryman, Chivers, Conn, Duncan (Neighbour)
7,475

27 January (Starlight Room Inauguration) v Enfield (a) 2–1
Chivers 2 (1 pen)
Daines (Lee), Kinnear, Pratt, Beal, Osgood, Naylor, Neighbour (McGrath), Conn, Chivers, Peters, McNab (Coates)

26 February v Red Star Belgrade (a) 1–0
Jones
Jennings, Kinnear, Knowles, McAllister, England, Naylor, Coates (Neighbour), Perryman, Duncan, Jones, Conn
25,000

1975–76

8 August v Bristol Rovers (a) 4–1
Coates, Chivers 2, Jones
Jennings, Kinnear (Smith), Naylor, Pratt, Osgood, McAllister, Coates, McNab, Chivers, Jones, Neighbour (McGrath)

29 September v Le Stade Rennais (a) 1–1
Young
Daines, Smith, McAllister, Pratt, Young (Walford), Osgood, McNab, Coates, Duncan (Robinson), Jones, McGrath (Naylor)

27 October (Barry Kitchener Testimonial) v Millwall (a) 1–3
McNab
Daines, McAllister, Duncan, Pratt, Young, Osgood, McNab, Perryman (Walford), Coates, Chivers, Neighbour (Brotherston)
7,006

21 April (Ray Dingwall Testimonial) v North Herts XI (Stevenage) 1–2
Armstrong
Daines (Kendall), Stead, McAllister (Smith), McNab, Young, Walford, Coates, Hoddle, Chivers (McGrath), Armstrong, Jones

1976–77

10 August v Swindon Town (a) 1–3
Perryman
Jennings, Naylor, McAllister, Pratt, Young (Hoddle), Osgood, Coates, Perryman, McGrath (K.Stead), Conn, Neighbour
4,535

16 August v Royal Antwerp (h) 1–1
Armstrong
Daines, Naylor, McAllister, Pratt (Conn), Young, Osgood, Coates, Perryman, Armstrong, Jones, Neighbour
9,880

9 October (Peter Simpson Testimonial) v Arsenal (a) 2–1
Conn, Duncan
Daines, Naylor, Young, Hoddle, Pratt, Osgood (Keeley), Conn, Perryman, Moores, Duncan (Jones), Coates
19,456

12 October v Napredac Krusevac (a) 0–4
Daines, Naylor (Keeley), Osgood, Hoddle, Young, Pratt, Conn (McNab), Perryman, Duncan (Moores), Jones, Coates
20,000

1977–78

22 November (Pat Rice Testimonial) v Arsenal (a) 3–1
Heffernan, Coates, Duncan
Daines, Naylor, Holmes (Heffernan), Coates, Osgood, Perryman, Pratt, McNab, Lee (Armstrong), Duncan (Moores), Taylor
17,154

3 May (Opening of Ground) v Truro City (a) 8–2
Stead 2, Armstrong 2, Pratt, Duncan, Falco, Taylor
Daines, Naylor, Holmes, Stead, McAllister, Perryman, Pratt, McNab, Duncan (Falco), Armstrong, Taylor
5,000

5 May (Angell & Blower Testimonial) v Orient (a) 3–1
Jones, Duncan, Taylor
Daines (Kendall), Naylor (Stead), Holmes, Hoddle, McAllister, Armstrong, Moores, McNab (Pratt), Jones, Duncan, Taylor
3,672

1978–79

5 August v Aberdeen (a) 1–3
Taylor
Daines, Naylor, Holmes, Hoddle, Lacy, Perryman, Pratt, McNab, Duncan (Armstrong), Lee (Jones), Taylor
18,000

8 August v Royal Antwerp (a) 3–1
Hoddle (pen), Moores 2
Daines, McAllister, Gorman, Hoddle, Lacy, Perryman (Holmes), Villa, Ardiles (McNab), Armstrong, Moores, Taylor (Duncan)
3,700

10 August v VVV Venlo (a) 0–1
Daines, Naylor, Holmes, Pratt, Lacy, Perryman, Villa (McNab), Ardiles, Duncan (Lee), Jones (Armstrong), Taylor
7,000

12 August v Bohemians (a) 4–0
Hoddle, Armstrong, Moores, Taylor
Daines, McAllister, Gorman, Hoddle, Lacy, Perryman (Holmes), Villa, Ardiles, Armstrong (Jones), Moores, Taylor
11,400

19 September (John Anderson Testimonial) v Aldershot (a) 1–1
Villa
Daines (Kendall), McAllister (Jones), Gorman, Naylor, Lacy, Perryman (Beavon), Villa, McNab, Lee, Pratt, Taylor (Moores)
7,834

26 September v 1FK Gothenburg (a) 0–1
Kendall, Hughton, Pratt, Hoddle, Lacy, Holmes, Villa (Armstrong), Ardiles (Beavon), Lee, Taylor, Jones
9,900

9 October v Saudi Arabian XI (Jeddah) 4–2
Lacy, Armstrong, Lee, Taylor
Daines (Kendall), Naylor, McAllister, Holmes, Lacy, McNab, Armstrong, Ardiles (Beavon), Lee, Pratt, Taylor (Galvin)
17,000

16 October (John Mcalle Testimonial) v Wolverhampton Wanderers (a) 1–2
Jones
Daines (Kendall), Naylor, Holmes, Lacy (Bowgett), McAllister, Armstrong (Hoddle), Villa, Ardiles, Jones, McNab, Pratt (Lee)
4,684

4 December (Billy Bonds Testimonial) v West Ham United (a) 2–4
Holmes, Pratt
Kendall (Daines), Gorman, McAllister, Holmes, Lacy, Perryman, Pratt, Villa, Lee (Armstrong), Hoddle (Ardiles), Taylor
21,081

18 December v El Nasr (a) 7–0
Hoddle 2, Galvin, Ardiles, Beavon
Aleksic (Kendall), Naylor, Gorman, Hoddle, Lacy, Perryman, Pratt (Galvin), Ardiles (Beavon), Lee, Villa, Taylor
5,000

24 April (Ian Gillard Testimonial) v Queen's Park Rangers (a) 3–1
Villa 3
Aleksic, Lee, McAllister, Miller (Holmes), Lacy, Perryman, Hoddle, Ardiles, Jones (Armstrong), Villa, Pratt (Beavon)
3,937

11 May (Graham Knight Testimonial) v Gillingham (a) 3–2
Falco, Hoddle, Villa
Daines (Aleksic), Lee, McAllister, Holmes, Miller, Perryman (Gibson), Pratt, Ardiles, Falco (Jones), Hoddle, Villa
8,655

1979–80

2 August v Gillingham (a) 1–1
Hoddle
Aleksic, Lee, Lacy, McAllister (Miller), Smith, Hoddle, Perryman (Beavon), Pratt, Galvin, Villa, Jones (Falco)
4,900

4 August v Oxford United (a) 1–2
Beavon
Aleksic, Southey, Smith, Mazzon, Miller, Perryman, Pratt (Hoddle), Galvin, Jones (Falco), Beavon, Villa
4,449

7 August v Dundee United (a) 2–3
Falco, Villa
Aleksic, Lee, Smith, McAllister, Lacy, Perryman, Pratt, Ardiles, Falco, Hoddle, Villa
10,000

8 August v Aberdeen (a) 0–2
Aleksic, Southey (Jones), Lacy, McAllister, Miller, Perryman, Pratt, Ardiles (Galvin), Falco, Hoddle, Villa (Beavon)
11,000

11 August v Orient (a) 1–1
Hoddle
Aleksic, Lee, Smith, Miller, Lacy, Perryman, Pratt (Beavon), Ardiles (Jones), Falco, Hoddle (Galvin), Villa
6,845

6 November v Widad (a) 4–2
Jones 2, Beavon, Hoddle
Aleksic, Hughton (Yorath), Smith, Pratt, McAllister (Lacy), Perryman, Ardiles (Galvin), Jones, Armstrong (Beavon), Hoddle, Villa

15 April (Martin Hinshelwood Testimonial) v Crystal Palace (a) 3–2
McAllister, Armstrong, Taylor
Daines (Kendall), Hughton, McAllister, Naylor (Armstrong), Miller, Perryman, Ardiles, Jones, Hazard, Galvin (Taylor), Pratt
7,040

5 May (Keith Miller Testimonial) v Bournemouth (a) 2–1
Gibson 2
Daines (Parks), O'Reilly, Hughton, Naylor, McAllister, Perryman (Mazzon), Hazard (Gibson), Jones (Falco), Taylor, Hoddle (Roberts), Galvin
6,623

7 May (Opening of Lights) v Hertford Town (a) 4–0
Roberts, Falco 3
Kendall (Daines), Hughton, Miller, Yorath, McAllister (O'Reilly), Perryman (Mazzon), Roberts, Taylor, Falco, Hoddle, Galvin

1980–81

28 July v Southend United (a) 1–1
Archibald
Kendall (Daines), Smith, Hughton (Holmes), Roberts, Miller, Perryman, Ardiles, Archibald, Crooks, Hazard, Taylor
7,080

30 July v Portsmouth (a) 2–1
Hughton, Falco
Daines, Perryman, Hughton, Yorath, Miller, Holmes, Ardiles (Roberts), Crooks (Gibson), Falco, Hoddle, Hazard
9,934

2 August v PSV Eindhoven (Beilen) 2–4
Ardiles, Taylor
Daines, Perryman, Hughton, Yorath, Miller, Holmes, Ardiles, Crooks, Armstrong, Hoddle, Taylor (Hazard)
7,400

4 August v Rangers (a) 1–2
Lacy
Daines, Smith, Hughton, Yorath, Lacy, Perryman, Ardiles, Archibald, Crooks, Hoddle, Villa
31,000

5 August v Dundee United (a) 1–4
Crooks
Daines, Smith, Hughton, Yorath, Miller, Perryman, Ardiles (Taylor), Archibald, Villa, Hoddle, Crooks
5,416

8 August v Swansea City (a) 0–1
Kendall, Smith, Hughton, Yorath, Miller (Hoddle), Perryman, Ardiles (Roberts), Crooks, Armstrong, Hoddle (Hazard), Villa
11,000

17 November v Weymouth (a) 6–1
Ardiles 2, Villa 2, Gibson, Dyer (og)
Daines, McAllister (Southey), Holmes, Smith, O'Reilly, Perryman (Crook), Ardiles (McAllister), Crooks (Gibson), Falco, Villa, Brooke
4,850

2 February v Jersey Select XI (a) 5–0
Ardiles, Archibald 3, Brooke
Aleksic (Daines), Perryman, Hughton, McAllister, Miller (Lacy), Roberts (Hazard), Ardiles, Archibald, Galvin, Hoddle, Brooke
4,000

1981–82

8 August v Glentoran (a) 3–3
Ardiles, Hoddle (pen), Falco
Aleksic, Hughton (Miller), Price, Roberts (Cooper), Villa, Perryman, Ardiles, Archibald, Galvin, Hoddle, Falco (Brooke)
12,000

10 August v Limerick (a) 6–2
Archibald, Hoddle 4, Falco
Aleksic (Parks), Miller, Price, Roberts (Cooper), Villa, Perryman, Ardiles (Hughton), Archibald, Galvin, Hoddle, Brooke (Falco)
12,000

12 August v Norwich City (a) 2–2
Brooke, Falco
Aleksic, Perryman, Price, Roberts, Miller, Villa (Cooper), Ardiles (Crook), Brooke (Dick), Galvin, Hoddle, Falco
8,000

16 August (Willie Miller Testimonial) v Aberdeen (a) 1–0
Brooke (pen)
Aleksic, Hughton, Miller (Lacy), Roberts, Price, Perryman, Brooke, Archibald (Hazard), Falco (Dick), Hoddle, Galvin
11,000

12 October (Paul Price Testimonial) v Luton Town (a) 2–2
Hoddle, Crooks
Clemence (Aleksic), Perryman, Price (Mazzon), Roberts, Lacy (Corbett), Galvin, Hazard, Ardiles, Gibson, Hoddle, Crooks (McCabe)
7,562

14 November v Israel Select XI Jaffa 3–2
Hazard 3 (1 pen)
Parks, Perryman (Southey), Miller, Roberts (Smith), Hughton, Lacy, Ardiles (Dick), Galvin, Hazard, Gibson, Crooks
4,000

22 December v Plymouth Argyle (a) 1–1
Hoddle
Clemence (Parks), Perryman, Hughton, Roberts (Lacy), Miller (Price), Hoddle, Ardiles (Hazard), Galvin, Villa, Falco, Crooks (Brooke)
6,151

29 December v Sporting Lisbon (a) 2–3
Roberts, Villa
Clemence, Hughton, Price, Roberts, Villa, Perryman, Ardiles (Hazard), Falco, Galvin, Hoddle, Crooks

22 February v Jersey Select XI (a) 8–3
Hughton (pen), Hazard, Perryman, Falco 2, Gibson 2, Crooks
Parks, Hughton, Miller (O'Reilly), Price, Hazard, Perryman (Smith), Ardiles, Falco, Galvin (Gibson), Roberts, Crooks
2,500

1982–83

3 August v Scunthorpe United (a) 5–0
Falco 2, Gibson 2, Roberts
Clemence (Parks), Miller, Mabbutt, Roberts, Lacy, O'Reilly, Gibson, Brooke (Dick), Falco, Hoddle (Crook), Crooks (Cooke)
5,589

6 August v FC Lausanne (a) 0–3
Clemence, Hughton, Miller, Roberts, Lacy, Mabbutt, Brooke (Crook), Archibald, Falco (Gibson), Hoddle, Crooks
5,800

8 August v Rangers (a) 1–0
Mabbutt
Clemence, Hughton, Miller, Roberts, Lacy, Mabbutt, Brooke (Falco), Archibald (Gibson), O'Reilly, Hoddle (Crook), Crooks
24,800

20 September (Steve Brinkman Benefit) v Barnet (a) 1–2
Hazard
Parks (Webster), Mazzon, Dixon (Southey), Miller, Brooke, Perryman, Hazard, Crook, Falco, Villa, Crooks (Gibson)
3,251

26 March v Northerners Athletic (Jersey) 6–1
Hazard, Archibald 3, Brazil 2
Clemence, Perryman (O'Reilly), Hughton, Lacy (Ardiles), Roberts, Hoddle, Hazard, Gibson (Falco), Archibald, Brazil, Galvin
3,000

19 April (Centenary) v Bristol Rovers (a) 3–2
O'Reilly, Perryman, Crooks
Clemence, Hughton (Ardiles), O'Reilly, Roberts, Miller (Webster), Perryman, Mabbutt, Brazil (Villa), Galvin, Hoddle, Crooks
11,541

23 May (Colin Powell Testimonial) v Charlton Athletic (a) 4–4
Falco 4
Clemence (Parks), Price, Hughton, Perryman, Miller (O'Reilly), Roberts, Mabbutt (Crook), Brooke, Galvin (Hazard), Falco, Crooks
4,460

30 May v Aalesund (a) 3–2
Crooks 3
Parks, Hughton (Southey), O'Reilly, Hazard, Miller, Perryman, Gibson (Crook), Brooke (Culverhouse), Galvin, Falco, Crooks
5,000

1983–84

2 August v Hertford Town (a) 2–1
Archibald, Crooks
Clemence, Hughton (Crook), O'Reilly, Stevens, Miller, Brooke, Ardiles, Archibald, Galvin, Hoddle, Crooks
2,200

4 August v Enfield (a) 4–1
Roberts, Hoddle, Crooks 2
Clemence, Bowen, O'Reilly, Roberts, Stevens, Perryman, Ardiles, Archibald, Galvin, Hoddle, Crooks
3,056

6 August v Brentford (a) 4–2
Roberts, Brazil, Crooks, Whitehead (og)
Parks, Thomas, Bowen, Roberts, Stevens, Perryman, Ardiles, Brazil (Crooks), Falco, Hazard (Archibald), Galvin
6,405

9 August v Portsmouth (a) 3–1
Roberts, Galvin, Mabbutt
Clemence, Hughton, Thomas (Bowen), Roberts, Stevens, Perryman, Ardiles (Mabbutt), Brazil, Falco (Gibson), Hoddle, Galvin
11,631

12 August v Brighton & Hove Albion (a) 0–0
Clemence, Hughton, Thomas (Ardiles), Roberts, Stevens, Perryman, Mabbutt, Brazil (Falco), Galvin, Hoddle, Crooks
4,988

16 August v Celtic (a) 1–1
Falco
Clemence, Hughton, Thomas, Roberts, Stevens, Perryman, Ardiles, Brazil, Galvin, Hoddle, Crooks (Falco)
25,300

17 August (Hamish McAlpine Testimonial) v Dundee United (a) 1–1
Galvin
Clemence, O'Reilly, Galvin, Price, Miller, Hazard, Ardiles, Archibald, Falco (Brazil), Hoddle (Thomas [Roberts]), Mabbutt
10,738

8 October v Vale Recreation (a) 7–2
Hazard, Archibald 4, Brazil, Falco
Parks, Hughton (Bowen), Galvin (Crook), O'Reilly, Price, Perryman, Hazard, Archibald, Brazil, Falco, Brooke
1,700

26 March (Dave Basssett Testimonial) v Wimbledon (a) 5–0
Hazard, Falco 2, Crooks 2
Parks (Andrews), Thomas (Culverhouse), Hughton, Roberts, Miller, Perryman (Crook), Brooke, Hazard, Falco, Crooks, Dick
3,344

18 May (Pat Holland Testimonial) v West Ham United (a) 1–4
Archibald
Parks (Corder), Culverhouse (Perryman), Hughton (Bowen), Roberts, Miller, Hazard, Ardiles, Archibald, Falco (Crooks), Mabbutt, Brazil
6,241

1984–85

4 August v Enfield (a) 7–0

Stevens, Brooke, Hazard, Crooks 4
Clemence (Parks), Stevens (Brooke), Hughton, Roberts, Miller, Perryman (Thomas), Ardiles (Bowen), Kempes, Galvin, Hazard, Crooks
2,411

6 August v OGC Nice (a) 2–2

Miller 2
Clemence (Parks), Thomas, Hughton, Roberts, Miller, Mabbutt, Hazard (Bowen), Kempes, Galvin, Hoddle (Perryman), Crooks
5,100

11 August v Brentford (a) 3–0

Allen 2, Galvin
Clemence, Stevens (Mabbutt), Hughton (Bowen), Roberts, Miller, Perryman (Thomas), Ardiles, Falco (Allen), Galvin, Hazard, Crooks (Falco)
3,612

16 August v Manchester City (a) 2–0

Roberts (pen), Galvin
Clemence, Stevens (Chiedozie), Hughton, Roberts, Miller, Perryman (Thomas), Ardiles (Mabbutt), Falco (Crooks), Allen, Hazard, Galvin
8,288

18 August v Sheffield United (a) 3–0

Allen 2, Falco
Clemence, Thomas, Hughton (Bowen), Roberts, Miller, Stevens, Chiedozie, Falco (Crooks), Allen, Mabbutt, Galvin
8,000

12 September (Gregorio Benito Testimonial) v Real Madrid (a) 0–1

Clemence, Mabbutt, Thomas, Crook (Bowen), Stevens (Miller), Perryman, Brooke, Falco, Allen (Crooks), Hazard (Cooke), Chiedozie
35,000

14 October v Malta National XI (a) 1–0

Dick
Parks, Thomas, Perryman, Crook, Miller, Roberts, Brooke, Mabbutt, Falco (Culverhouse), Crooks (Cooke), Dick

13 November (Larry Pritchard Testimonial) v Sutton United (a) 5–3

Crooks 3, Crook, Falco
Parks, Culverhouse, Miller (Brooke), Crook, Bowen, Perryman, Ardiles, Hoddle, Chiedozie, Falco (Baker), Crooks

8 March v Kuwait National XI Amman 1–0

Crooks
Clemence, Stevens, Hughton, Roberts, Miller, Perryman, Chiedozie, Falco (Thomas), Galvin, Hoddle, Crooks (Hazard)
9,000

8 April v Guernsey FA XI (a) 5–0

Clemence (pen), Falco 2, Crooks, Ardiles
Clemence, Thomas, Bowen, Culverhouse, Miller (Crooks), Crook, Ardiles, Falco, Leworthy, Hoddle, Chiedozie
2,000

29 April (Bristol Brain Cancer Research Fund) v Bristol Rovers (a) 6–2

Cooke, Leworthy 3, Dick 2
Parks, Thomas (Samways), Culverhouse, Roberts, Miller, Perryman (Mabbutt), Ardiles (Cooke), Falco, Leworthy, Chiedozie, Dick
5,500

8 May (Pat Jennings Testimonial) v Arsenal (a) 3–2

Crook, Falco 2
Clemence (Parks), Thomas, Mabbutt, Roberts, Miller (Galvin), Perryman, Crook, Falco, Leworthy, Hoddle, Dick
25,252

1985–86

18 July v Wycombe Wanderers (Bisham Abbey) 4–1

Thomas, Leworthy, Waddle, Galvin
Clemence, Thomas, Roberts, Hoddle (Cooke), Miller, Mabbutt, Ardiles, P.Allen, C.Allen (Leworthy), Waddle, Galvin

24 July v Chesterfield (a) 4–2

Roberts, Waddle 2, Chiedozie
Clemence, Thomas, Hughton, Roberts (Perryman), Miller, P.Allen, Ardiles, Falco, Waddle, Chiedozie, Galvin (Leworthy)
5,000

27 July v AFC Bournemouth (a) 3–0
Miller, Falco, Galvin
Clemence, Thomas (Chiedozie), Hughton, Roberts, Miller, P.Allen, Ardiles, Falco, Waddle (Leworthy), Hoddle, Galvin

31 July v Plymouth Argyle (a) 0–1
Clemence, Thomas, Hughton, Roberts, Miller, P.Allen, Ardiles, Falco, Waddle, Chiedozie, Galvin (Leworthy)
8,345

3 August v Exeter City (a) 2–2
Falco, Hazard
Clemence, Thomas, Hughton, Roberts, Miller, P.Allen (Hazard), Ardiles, Falco (Samways), Waddle (Leworthy), Chiedozie, Galvin (Dick)
3,798

10 August v Norwich City (a) 1–1
Leworthy
Clemence, Thomas, Hughton, P.Allen (Chiedozie), Miller, Perryman, Ardiles, Falco, Leworthy (Roberts), Hazard (Leworthy), Galvin (Dick)
5,137

10 September v Fareham Town (a) 6–3
Chiedozie, Leworthy 3, Cooke, Samways
Parks, Mabbutt, Thomas, Roberts, Miller (Galvin), Ardiles, Chiedozie, Leworthy, Falco (Cooke), Hazard, Samways

14 October (Brian Thompson Testimonial) v Maidstone United (a) 2–1
Falco, Galvin
Clemence, Stevens, Mabbutt, Roberts, Miller, Perryman (Grenfell), Ardiles (Moncur), Falco, Chiedozie, Cooke, Galvin
3,315

10 February v Jersey Select XI St Helier 7–0
C.Allen 2 (1 pen), Thomas, Hoddle, Waddle, P.Allen, Mabbutt
Clemence (Jennings), Thomas, Hughton, Mabbutt, Miller, Ardiles (Crook), P.Allen, Chiedozie, C.Allen, Hoddle (Ardiles), Waddle
2,750

6 April v Rangers (a) 2–0
Chiedozie, P.Allen
Clemence (Parks), Thomas, Hughton, Mabbutt, Miller (Ruddock), Bowen, Chiedozie (Samways), P.Allen, Falco, Waddle, Galvin (Dick)
12,665

22 April (Colin Johnson Testimonial) v Chelmsford City (a) 8–2
Falco 5, C.Allen 2, Chiedozie
Clemence (Parks), Thomas, Ruddock, Roberts, Miller, Mabbutt, Pratt (Bowen), Crook, Falco, C.Allen (Close), Chiedozie
1,189

9 May (Danis Salman Testimonial) v Brentford (a) 3–4
Chiedozie, C.Allen 2
Clemence, P.Allen, Hughton, Roberts, Mabbutt, Perryman, Chiedozie (Dick), Crook (Moncur), Galvin, C.Allen, Thomas
2,129

12 May (Gerhardt Ampofo Testimonial) v West Ham United (a) 1–5
C.Allen
Parks (Banks), P.Allen, Thomas, Roberts (Moncur), Hughton, Mabbutt (Polston), Chiedozie (Dick), Cooke, C.Allen, Crook, Galvin
4,127

1986–87

4 August v Aldershot (a) 3–2
C.Allen 2, Galvin
Parks, Stevens, Hughton (M.Thomas), Roberts (Hughton), Miller, Ruddock, Mabbutt, Galvin (Cooke), C.Allen (Falco), Hoddle (Bowen), Waddle
2,693

8 August (Gerry Ryan Testimonial) v Brighton & Hove Albion (a) 4–0
Falco 2, Waddle 2 (1 pen)
Clemence, D.Thomas (Ardiles), Hughton, Roberts, Miller, Mabbutt, Waddle, Falco (Howells), C.Allen, Stevens, Galvin
10,759

12 August (Mark Weatherly Testimonial) v Gillingham (a) 1–1
Falco
Clemence, D.Thomas, Hughton, Roberts, Miller, Mabbutt, Waddle, Falco, C.Allen (Howells), Stevens, Galvin
4,071

4 November v SV Hamburg (h) 5–1
Mabbutt, C.Allen 3, Claesen
Clemence, D.Thomas, Hughton, Ardiles (Polston), Gough, Mabbutt, C.Allen, Claesen, Waddle, Hoddle (Moran), P.Allen
5,095

16 December v Bermuda National XI (Hamilton) 3–1

C.Allen, Hoddle, Waddle (pen)
Clemence, D.Thomas (Polston), M.Thomas, Roberts (Howells), Gough, Mabbutt, C.Allen (Close), P.Allen (Bowen), Waddle, Hoddle, Galvin (Ardiles)
4,000

20 January (Roy Coyle Testimonial) v Linfield (a) 3–2

C.Allen (pen), D.Thomas, Opponent (og)
Clemence, D.Thomas, Stevens (Ruddock), Hodge (Galvin), Gough, Mabbutt, C.Allen, P.Allen, Waddle, Hoddle (Ardiles), Claesen

28 May v Millonarios (Miami) 0–1

Team unknown but included: Dearden, O'Shea, M.Thomas, Hodge, C.Allen, P.Allen, Howells
8,219

1987–88

23 July v Exeter City (a) 1–0

Metgod
Clemence, Polston, Thomas (Metgod), Gough, Fairclough, Mabbutt, C.Allen, P.Allen (Waddle), Claesen (Galvin), Samways (Ardiles), Galvin (Hodge)
3,512

25 July v AFC Bournemouth (a) 4–4

Waddle, Hodge, C.Allen 2
Clemence, Ardiles (Galvin), Thomas, Gough, Fairclough (Ruddock), Mabbutt (Polston), Metgod (Samways), P.Allen, Waddle, Hodge, Claesen (C.Allen)
6,189

10 November v St Alban's City (a) 6–0

Samways, Close 2, Howells, Stevens
Parks, Stevens, Thomas (Stimson), Ruddock, Statham, P.Allen (O'Shea), Samways (Moran), Ardiles, Howells (Samways), Close, Hodge (Moncur)
1,198

5 December v Brentford (a) 0–0

Parks, Stevens, Hughton, Samways (Cook), Fairclough, Mabbutt, C.Allen (Johnston), P.Allen, Waddle, Moncur, Claesen
4,327

15 February v AS Monaco (h) 0–4

Parks, Statham, Ruddock, Moncur, Fairclough, Mabbutt, Moran (Stimson), P.Allen, Walsh (Howells), Samways (Metgod), Claesen
21,644

19 February (Mick Brown Benefit) v West Bromwich Albion (a) 1–4

Walsh
Parks, Statham, Hughton (Thomas), Fairclough, Fenwick, Mabbutt, C.Allen (Claesen), P.Allen (Hodge [P.Allen]), Waddle (Moran), Ardiles (Metgod [C.Allen]), Walsh
3,169

15 April (Jeff Radcliffe Testimonial) v Hull City (a) 1–2

Walsh
Mimms, Statham, Thomas, Metgod, Fairclough, Mabbutt (Ruddock), Walsh, P.Allen (Hodge), Waddle, Samways (Howells), Claesen (C.Allen)
2,077

26 April (Jim Cannon Testimonial) v Crystal Palace (a) 3–3

Hodge, Walsh, Claesen
Mimms, Statham, Thomas (Manuel), Fenwick, Ruddock, Hodge, Walsh, P.Allen, Howells (Moran), Samways, Claesen (Gray)
5,534

6 May (Kevin Millett Testimonial) v Barnet (a) 2–1

Waddle (pen), Walsh
Mimms, Statham, Thomas (Manuel), Metgod (Howells), Fairclough (Ruddock), Mabbutt, Walsh (Gray), P.Allen, Waddle, Moran, Hodge
1,804

10 May v Euskadi (Bilbao) 0–4

Mimms (Parks), Statham, Thomas (Stimson), Fenwick, Metgod (Ruddock), Mabbutt, Walsh, P.Allen (Claesen), Waddle, Samways, Hodge (Howells [Moran])
18,000

1988–89

7 August (David Narey Testimonial) v Dundee United (a) 1–1

Walsh

Mimms, Allen, Stimson (Hughton), Fenwick, Fairclough, Mabbutt, Walsh, Gascoigne (Statham), Waddle (Howells), Stewart (Gray), Samways

9,548

10 August (Martin Hicks Testimonial) v Reading (a) 1–2

Gascoigne

Mimms (Guthrie), Allen, Stimson, Fenwick (Butters), Fairclough, Mabbutt (Statham), Walsh (Howells), Gascoigne (Moncur), Waddle (Robson), Stewart (Gray), Samways

4,598

13 August (Makita International Tournament) v Arsenal (Wembley) 0–4

Mimms, Allen, Stimson, Fenwick, Fairclough, Mabbutt, Walsh, Gascoigne, Waddle, Stewart (Gray), Samways (Howells)

30,104

14 August (Makita International Tournament) v AC Milan (Wembley) 1–2

Fenwick

Mimms, Thomas, Hughton, Fenwick, Fairclough, Mabbutt, Walsh (Moran), Gascoigne, Waddle, Stewart, Allen

27,369

16 August (Colin Pates Testimonial) v Chelsea (a) 0–0

Mimms, Thomas (Moncur), Hughton (Stimson), Fenwick, Fairclough, Mabbutt, Walsh (Gray), Gascoigne, Waddle (Stewart), Moran (Howells), Allen (Statham)

8,379

21 August (Alvin Martin Testimonial) v West Ham United (a) 0–2

Mimms, Statham, Hughton, Fenwick, Fairclough, Mabbutt, Walsh, Gascoigne (Gray), Waddle (Moran), Samways, Allen (Howells)

12,650

6 September (Michael Hughes Benefit) v Swansea City (a) 3–0

Gascoigne, Howells, Gray

Mimms (Guthrie), Statham, Hughton, Fenwick, Fairclough, Mabbutt, Walsh, Gascoigne (Gray), Moran, Thomas (Howells), Allen (Moncur)

4,091

18 October v Home Farm (a) 4–0

Fenwick (pen), Howells, Stewart, Brazil (og)

Mimms, Stevens, Thomas, Fenwick, Fairclough (A.Polston), Mabbutt (Butters), Moran (Robson), Moncur, Stewart, Howells, Allen

3,000

17 January v AC Monaco (h) 1–3

Moncur (pen)

Thorstvedt, Butters, Hughton, Bergsson (Moncur), Fairclough (Thomas), Mabbutt, Howells, Gascoigne (Samways), Waddle (Walsh), Stewart (Robson), Allen (Nayim)

9,964

4 March v Bordeaux (h) 1–2

Mabbutt

Thorstvedt, Butters, Bergsson (A.Polston), Fenwick, Moncur (Fairclough), Mabbutt, Walsh (Gray), Nayim, Samways (Moran), Stewart, Allen (Gilzean)

2,847

4 April (Steve Gritt Testimonial) v Charlton Athletic (a) 3–4

Walsh, Stewart 2

Thorstvedt, Butters, Hughton, Bergsson, Nayim, Mabbutt, Walsh (Johnston), Howells (Stevens), Statham (Theodosiou), Stewart, Allen (Cook)

1,762

1989–90

31 October v Caen (Cherbourg) 2–1

Stewart, Howells

Mimms, Thomas (Gormley), Van den Hauwe (Hendon), Bergsson (Tuttle), Allen (Garland), Butters, Walsh (Statham), J.Polston, Samways (Howells), Stewart, Sedgley

6 November (Paul Ramsey Testimonial) v Leicester City (a) 5–2
Gascoigne 2, Stewart 2, Sedgley
Thorstvedt (Mimms), J.Polston, Van den Hauwe (Hendon), Bergsson (Stevens), Allen (Garland), Howells (Butters), Walsh, Gascoigne, Stewart, Lineker (Robson), Sedgley (Gray)
7,024

26 January (Geoff Crudgington Testimonial) v Plymouth Argyle (a) 3–0
Mabbutt, Gascoigne, Morrison (og)
Thorstvedt, Thomas, Hughton, Allen, J.Polston, Mabbutt, Walsh, Gascoigne (Moran), Stewart, Lineker (Nayim), Moncur

3 April (Graham Moseley Testimonial) v Brighton 1983 (a) 3–0
Gascoigne 2, Stewart
Thorstvedt, Bergsson (A.Polston), Van den Hauwe (Hughton), Sedgley (J.Polston), Howells (Thomas), Mabbutt, Walsh (Gray), Gascoigne, Stewart, Lineker (Samways), Allen (Moncur)
6,410

23 April v Valerengens IF (a) 1–1
Howells
Thorstvedt, Bergsson, J.Polston (Butters), Sedgley (A.Polston), Howells, Mabbutt (Gray), Stewart (Moran), Samways, Nayim, Walsh, Allen (Garland)
3,357

1990–91

20 August v Southend United (a) 4–1
Walsh, Stewart, Samways, Benjamin (og)
Mimms, Bergsson (Hendon), Van den Hauwe (Edinburgh), Sedgley (Tuttle), Samways (Thomas), Mabbutt, Stewart, Gascoigne, Nayim (Garland), Walsh (Lineker), Allen
7,345

13 October (Graham Rix Testimonial) v Arsenal (a) 5–2
Stewart 3, Samways, Walsh
Mimms, Bergsson (Edinburgh), Van den Hauwe (Statham), Sedgley, Thomas, Tuttle, Stewart, Moncur, Nayim, Samways, Walsh (Van den Hauwe)
14,806

12 November (Billy Bonds Testimonial) v West Ham United (a) 3–4
Stewart 2, Houghton
Mimms, Bergsson (Polston), Edinburgh, Sedgley, Edwards, Thomas (Tuttle), Stewart (Hendon), Moran (Houghton), Walsh (Smith), Samways, Allen
10,443

1991–92

5 May (Harry Parsons Testimonial) v Cardiff City (a) 2–0
Gray, Hendry
Walker, Allen, Sedgley, Gray (Houghton), Cundy (Tuttle), Mabbutt, Stewart, Radosavijevic (McDonald), Hendry (Gilzean), Howells, Nayim
11,070

8 May (Garreth Roberts Testimonial) v Hull City XI (a) 6–2
Samways, Hendry 2, Barmby 2, Turner
Walker, Allen, McDonald (Caskey), Gray, Cundy (Nethercott), Sedgley, Samways, Minton (Campbell), Hendry (Hodges), Barmby, Turner
9,994

1992–93

24 July v Heart of Midlothian (a) 2–1
Durie 2
Walker (Thorstvedt), Fenwick (Austin), Van den Hauwe (Edinburgh), Gray (Anderton), Cundy (Tuttle), Ruddock (Sedgley), Nayim, Howells, Samways (Cundy), Hendry (Durie [Ruddock]), Allen (Gray)
7,018

29 July v Brighton & Hove Albion (a) 1–1
Samways
Walker, Edinburgh, Van den Hauwe (Tuttle), Howells (Gray), Cundy, Ruddock, Nayim (Hodges), Durie (Barmby), Samways (Beadle), Anderton, Allen
4,877

1 August v Glenavon (a) 1–0
Samways
Walker, Tuttle, Edinburgh (Austin), Gray, Cundy (Howells), Ruddock (Cundy), Nayim, Durie, Samways (Allen), McMahon (Anderton), Fenwick
4,500

3 August v West Bromwich Albion (a) 2–0
Hendry, Nayim
Thorstvedt, Austin, Edinburgh, Gray (Watson), Fenwick, Ruddock (Cundy), Turner (Nayim), Durie (Anderton), Hendry (Barmby), Howells, Allen (Samways)
8,078

5 August (City Celebration) v Sunderland (a) 3–0
Anderton 3 (1 pen)
Walker, Fenwick (Austin), Edinburgh, Howells, Cundy, Ruddock, Anderton, Durie (Turner), Samways (Watson), Hendry (Barmby), Allen
22,672

8 August v Watford (a) 1–0
Ruddock
Thorstvedt, Austin, Edinburgh (Landon), Howells (Watson), Cundy, Ruddock, Nayim (Turner), Hendry (Barmby), Samways (Gray), Anderton, Allen
5,567

10 August v Portsmouth (a) 2–4
Samways 2
Thorstvedt (Walker), Landon, Sedgley (Nethercott), Howells, Cundy, Ruddock, Gray, Turner (Hendry), Samways (Watson), Anderton (Houghton), Allen (Barmby)
10,929

23 September (Capital Cup) v Lazio (a) 0–3
Walker, Tuttle (Mabbutt), Edinburgh, Hendon, Cundy (Nethercott), Ruddock (Fenwick), Sedgley (Watson), Barmby (Hendry), Anderton, Sheringham (Mahorn), Turner (Minton)
20,000

20 October (Capital Cup) v Lazio (h) 0–2
Walker, Edinburgh, Van den Hauwe (Austin), Samways (Howells), Mabbutt, Ruddock, Sedgley (Watson), Durie (Turner), Barmby, Nayim, Allen (Anderton)
11,112

10 November (Harold Woolacott Testimonial) v Swansea City (a) 3–3
Cundy, Sheringham, Legg (og)
Thorstvedt (Dearden), Austin (Nethercott), Edinburgh, Samways (Barmby), Mabbutt, Ruddock, Cundy, Durie (Hodges), Nayim (Watson), Sheringham (Mahorn), Allen (McMahon)
3,527

28 March (Malcolm Allison Testimonial) v Crystal Palace (a) 3–3
Nayim, Ruddock, Barmby
Dearden, Austin (Bergsson), Edinburgh, Samways, Mabbutt, Ruddock, Sedgley, Nayim, Moran (Gray), Barmby, Allen
1,607

23 April v Real Zaragoza (a) 0–2
Walker, Bergsson, Edinburgh, Samways (Gray), Nethercott (Allen), Ruddock, Sedgley (Turner), Barmby (Hodges), Anderton (Watson), Nayim, Allen (Fenwick)
30,000

27 April (Fiorucci Cup) v Real Madrid (h) 0–1
Walker, Bergsson (Fenwick), Edinburgh, Samways, Mabbutt, Ruddock, Sedgley, Nayim, Watson (Hodges), Moran, Allen
7,651
(45-min match)

27 April (Fiorucci Cup) v Internazionale (h) 0–0
Dearden, Fenwick, Van den Hauwe, Gray, Nethercott, Ruddock, Sedgley, Nayim, Hodges, Hill, Allen (McMahon)
7,651
(45-min match – Spurs lost 5–6 on penalties)

1993–94

31 July (Makita International Tournament) v Lazio (h) 3–2
Calderwood, Anderton, Sheringham
Thorstvedt, Austin, Campbell (Hendon), Samways, Calderwood, Mabbutt, Barmby, Sedgley, Anderton, Sheringham, Allen (Caskey)
13,554

1 August (Makita International Tournament) v Chelsea (h) 0–4
Walker, Austin, Cundy (Hill), Hendon (Allen), Calderwood, Mabbutt, Barmby, Sedgley, Anderton, Sheringham, Caskey
12,780

6 August (Keith Millen Testimonial) v Brentford (a) 0–0
Thorstvedt, Austin, Campbell (Caskey), Samways, Calderwood, Mabbutt, Sedgley, Durie (Turner), Dozzell, Sheringham, Howells (Hill)
4,500

9 August v Peterborough United (a) 2–1
Campbell, Sheringham
Walker, Austin, Campbell, Samways, Calderwood, Mabbutt, Sedgley, Durie, Howells (Hill), Sheringham, Caskey
6,250

11 October v Brann (a) 0–2
Thorstvedt (Walker), Kerslake, Edinburgh, Samways, Nethercott, Mabbutt, Barmby, Sedgley, Hodges (Robinson), Hill, Caskey (McMahon)
3,912

15 February v Atletico Madrid (Jerez) 2–1
Sedgley, Gray (pen)
Walker, Kerslake, Edinburgh (Campbell), Scott, Calderwood, Mabbutt, Sedgley, Gray, Anderton (Hill), Mahorn (Turner), Rosenthal
500

1994–95

22 July (Richard Cooke Testimonial) v Bournemouth (a) 5–0
Calderwood, Howells, Hill, Caskey
Walker (Day), Austin (Carr), Kerslake, Calderwood (Mabbutt), Cundy (Campbell), Nethercott (Scott), Barmby, Howells (Caskey), Anderton (Hendry), Hill, Rosenthal (Turner)
5,126

26 July v Cambridge United (a) 3–0
Rosenthal, Scott, Robinson
Walker (Day), Austin, Kerslake, Calderwood (Mabbutt), Campbell, Nethercott (Scott), Barmby (Robinson), Howells (Caskey), Anderton, Hill, Rosenthal
5,251

29 July v Bristol City (a) 3–1
Howells, Rosenthal, Anderton
Walker (Day), Austin (Carr), Kerslake, Calderwood, Campbell (Mabbutt), Nethercott (Scott), Barmby, Howells (Burke), Anderton, Hill (Caskey), Rosenthal (Mahorn)
6,700

2 August v Brighton and Hove Albion (a) 3–0
Kerslake, Anderton, Barmby
Walker (Day), Austin (Carr), Kerslake (Scott), Calderwood (Dozzell), Nethercott (Mabbutt), Campbell, Barmby, Howells (Caskey), Anderton, Mahorn (Hill), Rosenthal
11,860

6 August v Watford (a) 1–1
Sheringham
Walker, Austin, Kerslake (Carr), Calderwood (Hill), Nethercott (Mabbutt), Campbell, Barmby, Howells, Anderton (Rosenthal), Sheringham, Klinsmann
14,021

9 August v Shelbourne (a) 1–0
Klinsmann
Walker, Carr (Austin), Kerslake, Calderwood, Campbell, Mabbutt, Hill, Dozzell (Barmby), Anderton (Rosenthal), Sheringham, Klinsmann
12,000

11 November v Reading (a) 1–1
Nash
Walker (Day), Austin (Kerslake), Scott (Edinburgh), Howells (Brady), Nethercott (Calderwood), Mabbutt, Caskey, Campbell, Slade (Watson), Dozzell (Nash), Turner
5,305

1995–96

29 July (Ibrox International Tournament) v Sampdoria (Ibrox Park) 0–2
Walker, Campbell, Edinburgh, Howells (Caskey), Calderwood, Mabbutt, Barmby, Dumitrescu (Turner), Anderton, McMahon (Kerslake), Rosenthal
18,225

30 July (Ibrox International Tournament) v Steaua Bucharest (Ibrox Park) 2–3
Caskey, Turner
Thorstvedt, Austin, Campbell (Mabbutt), Kerslake, Calderwood, Nethercott, Barmby (Rosenthal), Dumitrescu, Caskey, McMahon (Edinburgh), Turner
19,493

2 August v Derby County (a) 0–1
Walker, Austin, Edinburgh (Wilson), Howells, Calderwood, Mabbutt, Barmby, Kerslake, Anderton, Slade (Dumitrescu), Rosenthal
8,198

5 August v Watford (a) 2–0
Anderton, Dumitrescu
Walker, Austin, Cundy (Scott), Howells (Dozzell), Calderwood (Nethercott), Mabbutt, Dumitrescu, Kerslake, Anderton (Hill), Slade (Calderwood), Caskey (Slade)
7,354

1996–97

31 July v Brentford (a) 3–0

Campbell, Armstrong, Sheringham
Walker, Carr, Campbell, Howells (Dozzell), Calderwood (Nethercott), Mabbutt, Fox (McMahon), Rosenthal, Anderton (Clapham), Sheringham (Allen), Armstrong
3,175

3 August v Reading (a) 1–0

McMahon
Walker (Baardsen), Campbell (Carr), Edinburgh, Howells, Calderwood (Nethercott), Mabbutt, Fox (McMahon), Dozzell, Rosenthal (Sinton), Sheringham, Armstrong
8,293

7 August (CTA International Trophy) v Southend United (a) 3–1

Dozzell, Sheringham, Armstrong
Walker, Campbell, Edinburgh, Howells (Dozzell), Calderwood, Mabbutt (Carr), Fox, Dozzell (Anderton), Sinton (Rosenthal), Sheringham, Armstrong
9,414

10 August (Colin Walsh Testimonial) v Charlton Athletic (a) 3–1

Fox, Sinton, Armstrong
Walker (Baardsen), Campbell, Wilson (Carr), Howells, Calderwood (Edinburgh), Mabbutt (Nethercott), Fox, Dozzell, Sinton (McMahon), Sheringham, Armstrong (Allen)
10,655

1997–98

23 July v Leyton Orient (a) 1–0

Clemence
Baardsen, Scales (Maher), Clapham, Howells (Mabbutt), Vega, Campbell, Ginola, Clemence, Mahorn (Fox), Fenn, Brady
11,770

26 July v Swindon Town (a) 2–2

Fenn, Howells
Baardsen, Scales (Carr), Edinburgh, Howells (Mabbutt), Vega (Calderwood), Campbell, Fox, Clemence, Mahorn (McVeigh), Fenn, Sinton
7,020

29 July (Oxfordshire 'Bill Halsey' Memorial Trophy) v Oxford United (a) 3–2

Vega, Clemence, Sinton
Walker, Carr, Edinburgh, Howells, Calderwood, Campbell (Vega), Fox (Brady), Clemence, Mahorn, Fenn (McVeigh), Sinton
8,024

1998–99

10 July v Grasshoppers (a) 1–3

Vega
Walker, Carr, Tramezzani (Saib), Berti (Telesnikov), Vega, Scales (Edinburgh), Fox, Clemence, Allen (Armstrong), Sinton (Dominguez), Ginola
7,600

15 July v Peterborough United (a) 6–0

Tramezzani, Ginola, Allen, Saib, Sinton, Fenn
Walker, Carr, Tramezzani (Edinburgh), Berti (Sinton), Vega, Darcy, Fox, Saib, Allen, Armstrong (Clemence), Ginola (Fenn)
6,037

19 July v Brondby (a) 0–3

Walker, Carr, Tramezzani, Berti (Sinton), Vega, Darcy (Edinburgh), Fox, Saib, Allen (Fenn), Clemence, Ginola
10,180

22 July v Birmingham City (a) 2–4

Allen, Vega
Visi, Carr, Edinburgh, Berti, Vega, Tramezzani, Fox (Gower), Saib, Ginola (Dominguez), Clemence (Allen), Armstrong (Gain)
6,070

25 July v Celtic (a) 1–2

Armstrong
Baardsen, Carr, Tramezzani, Ginola, Vega, Scales (Edinburgh), Fox (Gower), Saib, Allen (Calderwood), Clemence, Armstrong (Dominguez)
53,872

29 July v Norwich City (a) 3–1

Saib, Armstrong, Vega
Walker, Carr, Tramezzani, Berti, Vega, Calderwood (Edinburgh [Calderwood]), Fox (Clemence), Saib, Allen, Armstrong (Dominguez), Ginola
16,053

1 August v Queen's Park Rangers (a) 0–0
Walker, Carr, Tramezzani (Wilson), Ginola (Berti), Vega, Calderwood, Fox (Sinton), Saib (Dominguez), Camara, Clemence, Armstrong (Allen)
9,500

11 August v St Albans City (a) 6–2
Ferdinand 3, Carr, Ginola (pen), Fox
Baardsen, Carr (Calderwood), Tramezzani (Wilson), Ginola (Clemence), Vega, Campbell, Dominguez (Edinburgh), Nielsen (Berti), Anderton (Fox), Ferdinand, Allen (Armstrong)
4,406

1999–2000

24 July v Heart of Midlothian (a) 2–2
Iversen, Murray (og)
Walker, Carr, Taricco (Edinburgh), Gower (Fox), Campbell (King), Perry, Anderton, Young, Dominguez, Iversen, Ginola
9,710

28 July v Queen's Park Rangers (a) 2–2
Iversen 2
Walker, Carr, Edinburgh (Taricco), Young, Campbell, Perry, Anderton, Sherwood, Dominguez (Gower), Iversen, Ginola (Korsten)
10,514

31 July v Wolverhampton Wanderers (a) 1–1
Iversen
Walker, Carr, Taricco (Edinburgh), Gower, Campbell, Perry, Anderton, Sherwood, Ginola (Korsten), Iversen, Nielsen (Fox)
11,418

3 September v (Opening of Ground) Bishop's Stortford (a) 6–0
Dominguez 2, Clemence, Armstrong, Fox 2
Segers, Edinburgh, Taricco (Hillier), Freund (Gower), Thelwell, Perry (Lee), Clemence, Fox, Armstrong (Crouch), Dominguez, Ginola (Piercy)
3,109

2000–01

29 July v Birmingham City (a) 1–0
Iversen
Walker, Carr, Thatcher, Freund, Campbell, Perry, Anderton, Sherwood (Clemence), Leonhardsen (Young), Iversen (Ferdinand), Rebrov
5,566

2 August (Simon Morgan Testimonial) v Fulham (a) 0–0
Sullivan, Carr, Thatcher (Taricco), Clemence, Campbell, Perry, Anderton, Sherwood (Etherington), Ferdinand (Iversen), Leonhardsen (Armstrong), Rebrov
12,928

5 August (Danny Maddix Testimonial) v Queen's Park Rangers (a) 2–0
Ferdinand, Sherwood
Sullivan, Carr, Taricco (Thatcher), Clemence, Campbell, Vega (Perry), Anderton, Sherwood (Young), Ferdinand (Rebrov), Iversen (Armstrong), Leonhardsen (Davies)
12,042

8 August v Peterborough United (a) 2–1
Rebrov, Sherwood
Walker, Carr, Thatcher (Taricco), Freund, Campbell, Perry (Young), Anderton, Sherwood (Davies), Ferdinand (Iversen), Clemence, Rebrov (Armstrong)
8,137

12 August v Vitesse Arnhem (a) 2–0
Iversen, Anderton
Sullivan, Carr, Thatcher (Taricco), Freund, Campbell, Perry, Anderton (Davies), Sherwood (Young), Ferdinand (Iversen), Clemence, Rebrov
9,800

2001–02

13 July v Stevenage Borough (a) 8–1
Poyet 3, Ferguson 2, Kamanan 2, Freund
Sullivan (Kelly), Piercy (Anderton), Etherington (Jackson), Toner (Taricco), Thelwell (Hillier), Bunjevcevic (Perry), Davies (Sherwood), Poyet (Consorti [Barnard]), Ferdinand (Iversen), Clemence (Freund), Ferguson (Kamanan)
5,914

17 July v Swindon Town (a) 3–1
Piercy, Iversen, Kamanan
Sullivan, Carr (Piercy), Jackson (Clemence), Bunjevcevic (Perry), Thelwell (Hillier), Young (Taricco), Anderton (Leonhardsen), Sherwood (Freund), Ferdinand (Iversen), Davies (Poyet), Ferguson (Kamanan)
8,595

19 July (Steve Castle Testimonial) v Leyton Orient (a) 2–1
Davies, Rebrov
Kelly, Carr, Jackson (Taricco), Doherty, Bunjevcevic (Perry), Young, Leonhardsen, Sherwood (Freund), Davies (Poyet), Iversen, Rebrov
6,635

21 July v Wycombe Wanderers (a) 2–1
Iversen, Sheringham
Sullivan, Carr, Taricco (Ziege), King, Bunjevcevic, Perry, Anderton (Sherwood), Poyet, Ferdinand (Iversen), Sheringham (Rebrov), Clemence
8,018

25 July v Portsmouth (a) 5–2
Iversen, Sheringham, Clemence, Rebrov 2
Sullivan, Carr (Leonhardsen), Doherty (Bunjevcevic), Freund (Clemence), Bunjevcevic (Perry), King, Anderton (Poyet), Ziege (Taricco), Iversen (Ferdinand), Sheringham (Rebrov), Davies (Sherwood)
15,144

1 August v Reading (a) 2–0
Poyet, Rebrov
Sullivan, Carr, Doherty, Freund, Bunjevcevic, King, Anderton, Poyet, Ferdinand, Ziege, Rebrov
21,874

4 August (Keith Stevens Benefit) v Millwall (a) 2–1
Rebrov, Ferdinand
Sullivan, Perry, Taricco, King, Bunjevcevic, Clemence, Leonhardsen, Sherwood, Davies, Iversen, Rebrov (Ferdinand)
16,250

7 August v Luton Town (a) 1–1
Rebrov (pen)
Kelly, Thelwell, Piercy, Freund, Doherty (Bunjevcevic), Perry (King), Leonhardsen (Clemence), Poyet (Davies), Etherington (Rebrov), Iversen (Kamanan), Ziege (Taricco)
9,175

12 August v AEK Athens (a) 1–2
Poyet
Sullivan, Taricco, King (Thelwell), Freund, Bunjevcevic, Doherty (Perry), Clemence, Ziege, Poyet (Davies), Iversen (Ferdinand), Rebrov
3,000

2002–03

21 July v Stevenage Borough (a) 4–0
Anderton 2, Jackson, Rebrov
Sullivan (Hirschfeld), Carr (Leonhardsen), Jackson (Etherington), Henry, Bunjevcevic (Perry), Richards (Thatcher), Anderton (Davies), Poyet (Redknapp), Doherty (Barnard), Acimovic (Rebrov), Ricketts (Bortolozzo)
4,964

23 July (Richard Wilkins Testimonial) v Colchester United (a) 3–1
Barnard, Doherty, Leonhardsen
Sullivan (Hirschfeld), Taricco (Leonhardsen), Thatcher (Richards), Ricketts (Etherington), Perry (Bunjevcevic), Henry (O'Donoghue), Anderton (Bortolozzo), Davies (Rebrov), Doherty (Barnard), Acimovic (Poyet), Jackson
6,003

25 July v AFC Bournemouth (a) 1–0
Rebrov
Sullivan, Doherty (Henry), Thatcher, Redknapp (Leonhardsen), Perry, Marney (Jackson), Davies, Rebrov (Snee), Iversen (Barnard), Acimovic, Etherington
6,640

27 July v Gillingham (a) 2–1
Poyet 2
Hirschfeld, Carr (Leonhardsen), Taricco (Jackson), Doherty (O'Donoghue), Bunjevcevic, Richards, Anderton, Bortolozzo (Ricketts), Iversen (Sutton), Poyet (Etherington), Barnard
9,060

28 July v Queen's Park Rangers (a) 2–3
Etherington, Henry
Sullivan, Carr (Leonhardsen), Thatcher, Redknapp (Jackson), Perry, O'Donoghue (Henry), Davies, Iversen, Doherty, Acimovic, Etherington
7,035

31 July (Simon Rodger Testimonial) v Crystal Palace (a) 4–0
Iversen 2, Davies, Anderton (pen)
Hirschfeld, Carr, Taricco, Bunjevcevic, Doherty (Perry), Richards (Gardner), Anderton (Blondel), Davies, Iversen, Acimovic (Redknapp), Rebrov (Bo)
13,131

3 August (Nigel Gibbs Testimonial) v Watford (a) 1–0
Sherwood
Sullivan, Henry (O'Donoghue), Thatcher (Jackson), Ricketts (Sheringham), Doherty, Bortolozzo (Ziege), Leonhardsen, Redknapp (Sherwood), Bo, Etherington, Rebrov
10,547

4 August v Feyenoord (a) 2–2
Sheringham, Iversen
Keller, Carr, Taricco, Blondel (Sherwood), Perry, Bunjevcevic, Anderton, Davies, Iversen, Sheringham (Doherty), Ziege (Etherington)
40,000

7 August v Celtic (h) 1–1
Iversen
Keller, Carr, Bunjevcevic, Davies, Perry, Richards, Anderton, Acimovic (Doherty), Iversen, Sheringham, Ziege (Taricco)
22,365

11 August v Lazio (h) 2–2
Richards, Redknapp
Keller, Carr, Taricco, Bunjevcevic, Perry (Gardner), Richards, Redknapp (Blondel), Acimovic (Bortolozzo), Rebrov, Sheringham (Iversen), Etherington
21,184

17 October (Tottenham Tribute Trust) v DC United (h) 0–1
Keller (Hirschfeld), Doherty (Calderwood [Kelly]), Marney (P.Allen), Freund (Clemence), Bunjevcevic (Carr), Perry (Henry), Poyet (Waddle), Gascoigne (Blondel), Klinsmann (C.Allen), Sheringham (Rebrov), Ginola (Etherington)
30,480

4 March v Bohemians (a) 1–3
Doherty
Sullivan, Carr (Marney), Taricco (Jackson), Toda, Thatcher, King (Thelwell), Anderton, Etherington (Freund), Doherty, Sheringham (Ricketts), Acimovic
7,450

14 May v DC United (a) 0–1
Keller, Carr (Marney), King, Toda, Bunjevcevic (Taricco), Perry, Acimovic (Davies), Redknapp (Poyet), Keane (Acimovic), Sheringham (Barnard), Ziege (Bunjevcevic)
14,028

2003–04

16 July v Stevenage Borough (a) 2–0
Acimovic, Postiga
Sullivan, Marney (Ricketts), Bunjevcevic (Taricco), King (Toda), Gardner (Kelly), Ziege (Perry), Anderton (Davies), Redknapp (Postiga), Slabber (Poyet), Acimovic (Jackson), Blondel (Etherington)
6,449

19 July (Dave Jones Testimonial) v Wycombe Wanderers (a) 3–2
Postiga, Davies, Beasant (og)
Sullivan, Kelly, Bunjevcevic, Toda, Gardner, Ziege (Galbraith), Davies, Postiga (Slabber), Acimovic (Yeates), Redknapp, Ricketts
5,389

20 July v Oxford United (a) 3–0
Zamora 2, Keane
Burch, Hughes (Carr), Taricco, Jackson (Galbraith), Henry, Perry, Anderton, Poyet, Zamora (Keane), Blondel, Etherington (Yeates)
6,277

22 July v Norwich City (a) 3–0
Anderton, Davies, Zamora
Hirschfeld (Burch), Carr (Marney), Taricco (Perry), Toda, Bunjevcevic (Kelly), Gardner, Anderton (Ricketts), Postiga (Zamora), Davies (Acimovic), Keane (Poyet), Galbraith (Etherington)
15,646

3 August v PSV Eindhoven (h) 0–2
Keller, Carr, Taricco, Gardner, Redknapp (Marney), Perry, Anderton (Bunjevcevic), Postiga, Davies (Ricketts), Keane, Acimovic (Poyet)
22,861

10 August v Sporting Clube de Portugal (h) 0–0
Keller, Carr, Taricco, Mabizela (Doherty), Bunjevcevic, Gardner, Ricketts (Poyet), Postiga (Zamora), Davies (Marney), Keane, Redknapp
19,557

2004–05

20 July v Stevenage Borough (a) 2–1
Keane (pen), Defoe
Keller, Kelly (Ifil), Taricco (McKie), Mendes (Hughes), O'Donoghue (Doherty), Bunjevcevic (Mabizela), Yeates (McKenna), Marney (O'Hara), Malcolm, Keane (Defoe), Jackson (Ricketts)
7,044

24 July v Hull City (a) 2–2
Defoe 2
Robinson, Carr, Bunjevcevic (McKie), Davis (Mbulelo), Doherty, Gardner (King), Ricketts, Mendes, Defoe (Malcolm), Keane (Yeates), Jackson (Marney)
13,316

25 July v Sheffield United (a) 1–2
Keane
Keller, Kelly (Carr), Bunjevcevic (McKie), Davis, King (Gardner), Richards, Mabizela, Redknapp (Hughes), Yeates, Keane (Malcolm), Jackson (Ricketts)
8,788

28 July v Rangers (a) 0–2
Robinson, S.Carr, Bunjevcevic, Davis (Doherty), Gardner (McKie), King, Ricketts, Mendes (Mabizela), Defoe, Keane (Marney [Hughes]), Jackson
35,750

31 July v Nottingham Forest (a) 2–0
Kanoute, Keane (pen)
Keller, S.Carr, Taricco, Redknapp (Hughes), Doherty, King, Davis (Marney), Mendes, Defoe (Silva), Kanoute (Bakari), Jackson (Yeates)
18,845

7 August v Cagliari (h) 1–2
Kanoute
Robinson, Taricco (Ifil), Edman, Davis (Brown), Doherty, King (Bunjevcevic), Redknapp (Ricketts), Mendes, Kanoute (Bakari), Defoe, Jackson
21,441

10 August v Celtic (a) 0–2
Keller, Mabizela, Bunjevcevic, Hughes, Doherty, Richards (Defendi), Brown (McKenna), O'Hara, Yeates, Silva, Ricketts
30,000

20 May v Club M (Mauritius) 2–0
Keane, Barnard
Cerny (Fulop), Kelly, Jackson, Carrick, Bunjevcevic, King, Marney (McKenna), Reid, Defoe, Keane, Yeates (Barnard)
11,000

2005–06

9 July v Stevenage Borough (a) 3–0
Kanoute, Mido, Defoe
Cerny (Fulop), Marney (Kelly), Jackson (Edman), Carrick (El Hamdaoui), Davenport (Dawson), Huddlestone (Bunjevcevic), Lennon (Routledge), Tainio (Mendes), Kanoute (Mido), Keane (Defoe), Yeates (Reid)
4,000

30 July Reading (a) 2–0
Mido, Defoe
Cerny (Burch), Kelly, Ziegler (Bunjevcevic), Mendes, Gardner, King, Routledge, Tainio, Mido, Defoe, Reid (El Hamdaoui)
18,281

6 August v Porto (h) 2–0
Defoe 2
Robinson (Cerny), Staltieri, Edman, Carrick, Dawson, Gardner, Routledge (Keane), Tainio, Mido (Kanoute), Defoe, Reid (Davids)
36,112

2006–07

22 July Birmingham City (a) 2–0
Berbatov 2
Fulop, Routledge (Ifil), Assou-Ekotto, Huddlestone, Dawson, King (Davenport), Ghaly (Ziegler), Tainio, Berbatov (Barnard), Keane (Murphy), Defoe (O'Hara)
8,946

25 July Stevenage Borough (a) 3–0
Defoe 2 (1 pen), Berbatov (pen)
Cerny, Tainio, Assou-Ekotto, Huddlestone, Dawson, King (O'Hara), Ghaly (Routledge), David, Berbatov (Barnard), Keane (Ifil), Defoe
4,000

30 July Internazionale (h) 2–1
Tainio 2
Cerny (Fulop), Routledge, Assou-Ekotto, Huddlestone (Ghaly), Dawson, Davenport, Tainio, Davids, Berbatov, Keane (Murphy), Defoe (Ziegler)
36,252

5 August Borussia Dortmund (a) 1–1
Berbatov
Robinson, Lee (Staltieri), Assou-Ekotto, Zokora (Huddlestone), Dawson, Davenport, Lennon (Defoe), Jenas (Ghaly), Berbatov (Routledge), Keane, Murphy (Ziegler)
38,500

12 August Real Sociedad (h) 2–1
Defoe, Dawson
Robinson, Lee, Assou-Ekotto, Zakora, Dawson, Davenport, Lennon (Ghaly), Jenas (Huddlestone), Berbatov, Defoe (Murphy), Davids (Ziegler)
25,914

2007–08

7 July v Stevenage Borough (a) 3–1
Keane (pen), Bent, Taarabt
Cerny, Ifil (Riley), Daniels (Hughton), Murphy (Livermore), Rocha (Mills), Gardner, Malbranque, Taarabt, Bent (Barcham), Keane, O'Hara (Maghoma)
7000

12 July v St Patrick's Athletic (a) 1–0
Keane
Cerny, Rocha, Bale (Ifil), Zokora, Kaboul, Gardner (Dawson), Malbranque, Murphy (O'Hara), Bent (Barnard), Keane, Taarabt (Maghoma)
4,600

1 August v Leyton Orient (a) 4–2
Keane 2 (1 pen), Bent, Defoe
Robinson (Cerny), Ifil, Stalteri, Huddlestone, Dawson (Rocha), Kaboul, Jenas (O'Hara), Bent, Berbatov (Defoe), Keane (Taarabt), Malbranque (Routledge)
9,126

4 August v Torino (h) 2–0
Keane, Berbatov
Robinson, Chimbonda, Rocha (Stalteri), Zokora (Bent), Kaboul, Dawson, Tainio (Huddlestone), Jenas, Berbatov (Defoe), Keane (Taarabt), Malbranque (Routledge)
30,823

2008–09

24 July v Hercules (a) 1–1
Bent
Gomes, Gunter, Assou–Ekotto (O'Hara), Dawson, Woodgate (Zokora), Lennon (Bostock), Jenas (Townsend), Huddlestone, Giovani, Bent, Berbatov
6,000

28 July v Norwich City (a) 5–1
Bent 4, OG (Stepanovic)
Gomes, Gunter, O'Hara, Dawson, Zokora, King (Assou–Ekotto), Dawson (Huddlestone), Giovani (Taarabt), Jenas, Bent, Modric (Lennon), Gilberto (Bale)
25243

30 July v Leyton Orient (a) 5–1
Bent 3, Lennon, Modric
Jansson, Gunter (Jenas), Bale (Townsend), Zokora (Smith), Dawson, Huddlestone, Lennon (Taarabt), Giovani, Bent, Modric (O'Hara), Gilberto (Assou–Ekotto)
8,920

1 August (Feyenoord Jubileum Toernooi) v Celtic (Rotterdam) 2–0
Bent, Bentley
Gomes, Woodgate (Bale), Assou–Ekotto, Zokora (Gunter), Dawson, Huddlestone (King), Lennon (Bentley), Jenas, Berbatov, Bent, Modric (O'Hara)
25,000

3 August (Feyenoord Jubileum Toernooi) v Borussia Dortmund (Rotterdam) 3–0
Bent, Bentley
Gomes, Dawson, Bale (Lennon), Zokora, Bentley (Gunter), Huddlestone, O'Hara, Jenas (Smith), Giovani, Bent (Berbatov), Gilberto
15,000

10 August v Roma (h) 5–0
Bent 2, Bentley 2, Lennon
Gomes (Jansson), Woodgate, Assou–Ekotto (Bale), Zokora (Gunter), Bentley (Gilberto), Dawson (King), Giovani, Jenas (O'Hara), Berbatov (Lennon), Bent, Modric (Huddlestone)
35,841

2009–10

15 July v Exeter City (a) 3–0
O'Hara, Bent, Lennon
Cudicini (Button), Hutton (Gunter), Chimbonda (Assou–Ekotto), Dervite (Livermore), Bentley (Modric), Huddlestone (Boateng), Rose (Lennon), O'Hara (Palacios), Keane (Bent), Defoe (Pavlyuchenko), Corluka (Dawson)
8,636

17 July v AFC Bournemouth (a) 3–0
Keane, Defoe, Palacios
Cudicini, Chimbonda (Hutton), Dervite (Assou-Ekotto), Dawson (Corluka), Bentley (Livermore), Huddlestone, Rose (Lennon), Boateng (O'Hara), Keane (Defoe), Bent (Pavlyuchenko), Modric (Palacios)
9,074

21 July v Peterborough United (a) 4–0
Bent, Defoe, Modric, Pavlyuchenko
Cudicini (Jansson), Chimbonda, Assou-Ekotto, Palacaios, Corluka (Huddlestone), Dervite, Lennon, Jenas (Boateng [Livermore]), Pavlyuchenko, Bent (Defoe), O'Hara (Modric)
7,688

24 July Wembley Cup v Barcelona (Wembley) 1–1
Livermore
Cudicini (Gomes), Hutton (Naughton), Assou-Ekotto, O'Hara (Chimbonda), Corluka (Dervite), Huddlestone (Bostock), Lennon, Jenas (Keane), Defoe, Palacios (Livermore), Modric (Rose)
57,992

26 July Wembley Cup v Celtic (Wembley) 0–2
Gomes (Cudicini), Hutton (Naughton), Assou-Ekotto (Rose), Chimbonda, Dervite (Corluka), Huddlestone (Bostock), Lennon (Modric), Palacios (Livermore), Keane (Defoe), Bent (Pavlyuchenko), O'Hara (Obika)
64,562

9 August v Olympiakos (h) 3–0
Pavlyuchenko, Corluka, Defoe
Gomes (Cudicini), Naughton (Chimbonda), Assou-Ekotto, King (Corluka), Bentley (Boateng), Huddlestone (Bostock), Bassong, O'Hara (Modric{Livermore]), Crouch (Pavlyuchenko), Keane (Defoe), Rose (Lennon)
26,462

2010–11

10 July v AFC Bournemouth (a) 4–0
Obika, Rose, Pavlyuchenko 2
Cudicini (Alnwick), Hutton (Smith), Bale (Rose), Bentley (Townsend), Keane (Modric), Parrett (Naughton), Mason (Jenas), Bostock (Taarabt), Obika (Pavlyuchenko), Butcher (Kaboul), Caulker (Livermore)
5,995

29 July v Villarreal (h) 1–4
Giovani
Gomes (Button), Hutton (Walker), Huddlestone (Parrett), Lennon (Bale), Jenas (Rose), Keane (Crouch), Naughton (Assou-Ekotto), Defoe (Giovani), Dawson (Bassong), Kranjcar (Taarabt), Corluka
17,917

3 August (Eusebio Cup) v Benfica (a) 1–0
Bale
Gomes (Cudicini), Walker (Naughton), Bale (Rose), Corluka, Dawson, Huddlestone, Lennon, Jenas, Crouch (Defoe), Giovani (Townsend), Modric (Kranjcar)
30,215

7 August v Fiorentina (h) 3–2
Pavlyuchenko, Keane 2
Gomes (Cudicini), Bassong, Assou-Ekotto (Naughton), Kaboul, King (Walker), Palacios (Livermore), Lennon (Kranjcar), Jenas (Huddlestone), Pavlyuchenko (Rose), Crouch (Keane), Giovani
28,228

TESTIMONIALS BENEFITS AND MEMORIALS

Most of the matches detailed in this section were played as a reward for long and distinguished service to Tottenham Hotspur, although, in some instances, they were tributes to players whose careers or lives had been brought to a tragic early end, notably John Jones, John White and Peter Southey. In the case of Cyril Knowles it was both. Most of the matches were a reward for what the beneficiaries had done during their time as Spurs players but matches have also been staged for people like Bill Nicholson and Keith Burkinshaw, who brought success to Spurs as managers. In one case, that of Jack Oliver, it was actually to show that what he had achieved as president and chairman of the club had not been forgotten when he fell on hard times.

For may years it was not Spurs' practice to grant players testimonials, although they often provided the opposition for players of other clubs. The policy was only changed in the 1970s, the first player so honoured being Jimmy Greaves.

Many former Spurs players have been supported by testimonial matches organised by other clubs or private individuals, but as Spurs did not participate in those games they are not recorded here.

It should be noted that service to Spurs is the criteria for inclusion in this section. Spurs have played matches for former players who have been honoured for their service to other clubs, such as Richard Cooke, Danny Maddix and Pat Jennings, and details of those games appear in the Friendly section of this book.

1899-1900

J.L. Jones & R.Stormont Benefit
11 December v Players of the South (h) 4–1
Stormont, Pratt, Cameron, Copeland
Haddow, Erentz, Tait, J.L. Jones, McNaught, Stormont, Smith, Cameron, Pratt, Copeland, Hyde
1,357

T.H. Bradshaw Benefit Match
2 April v Thames Ironworks (a) 3–0
Raby, Cameron 2
Clawley, Melia, Tait, Morris, McNaught, JL.Jones, Raby, Cameron, Copeland, Roberts, Hyde
1,000

1900-01

T. Smith & J McNaught Benefit
15 October v Millwall (h) 2–1
Hawley, Kirwan
Clawley, Erentz, Tait, J.L. Jones, McNaught, Hughes, Smith, Pangbourne, Moffatt, Hawley, Kirwan
5,000

Jack Oliver Benefit
14 January v C Wreford-Brown's XI (h) 4–2
Cameron 2, Kirwan 2
Clawley, Erentz, Tait, McNaught, Morris, Hughes, Smith, Cameron, Brown, Copeland, Kirwan
2,500

1904-05

J. Jones Dependants' Benefit
5 December v George Robey's XI (h) 2–1
Cameron, Glen
Eggett, McCurdy, Tait, Morris, Bull, Brearley, Walton, Cameron, Glen, O'Hagan, Kirwan
7,000

1945-46

G.W. (Willie) Hall Benefit
7 May v FA XI (h) 4–1
Cox, Foreman 2, Medley
Ditchburn, Willis, Buckingham, Ludford, Nicholson, Burgess, Cox, Bennett, Foreman, Gibbons, Medley
30,220

1948-49

Fred Sargent Memorial
20 September v Chelmsford City (a) 5–1
Walters, Bennett, Duquemin 2, Jones
Markham, Tickridge, Withers, Ludford, Nicholson, Trailor, Walters, Baily, Duquemin, Bennett, Jones
7,659

1964-65

John White Memorial
11 November v Scotland XI (h) 2–6
Marchi, White
W.Brown, Baker, Henry, Mullery, L.Brown, Marchi, Robertson, Greaves, White, Jones, Dyson
29,375

1972-73

Jimmy Greaves Testimonial

17 October v Feyenoord (h) 2–1
Evans, Greaves
Daines, Evans, Knowles, Coates (Holder), England (Naylor), Beal, Gilzean (Pearce), Perryman, Chivers, Greaves, Peters
45,799

1973-74

Phil Beal Testimonial

3 December v Bayern Munich (h) 2–2
Pratt, Gilzean
Jennings, Evans, Knowles, Pratt, England, Beal, Gilzean (Neighbour), Perryman, Chivers, Peters (McGrath), Coates
19,150

1974-75

Alan Gilzean Testimonial

27 November v Red Star Belgrade (h) 2–0
Knowles, Gilzean
Jennings (Daines), Evans (Kinnear), Knowles (Pratt), McNab, England (Dillon), Naylor, Gilzean, Perryman (McGrath), Jones, Peters (Neighbour), Conn (Coates)
22,239

1975-76

Cyril Knowles Testimonial

22 October v Arsenal (h) 2–2
McAllister, C.Knowles
Jennings (Daines), McAllister (Smith), C.Knowles, Conn, Young, Osgood, McNab, Coates, Chivers, Jones (P.Knowles), Neighbour
17,343

Joe Kinnear Testimonial

23 March v Brighton & Hove Albion (a) 6–1
Pratt, Stead, Osgood, Armstrong, Chivers, Jones
Daines, Naylor, McAllister, Pratt (Stead), Young (Keeley), Osgood, Coates (Armstrong), Brotherston, Chivers, Jones, Robinson
7,124

1976-77

Pat Jennings Testimonial

23 November v Arsenal (h) 3–2
Taylor, Greaves 2
Jennings (Daines), Osgood, Knowles (Gorman), McNab, Young (McAllister), Naylor, Taylor, Perryman (Pratt), Moores, Greaves, Coates
28,924

1977-78

John Pratt Testimonial

12 May v Arsenal (h) 3–5
Perryman, Moores 2
Daines (Kendall), Naylor (Stead), Holmes, Hoddle, McAllister, Perryman, Pratt, McNab (Coates), Moores, Greaves, C.W. Jones (Taylor)
23,044

1978-79

Steve Perryman Testimonial

30 April v West Ham United (h) 2–2
Villa, Ardiles
Aleksic (Kendall), Naylor, Smith, Miller (McAllister), Lacy, Perryman (Villa), Pratt (Lee), Ardiles, Jones, Hoddle, Greaves
17,702

1979-80

Terry Naylor Testimonial

29 April v Crystal Palace (h) 0–2
Daines (Kendall), Naylor, Holmes (Lacy), Yorath, Miller, Beal (Hazard), Ardiles, Jones (Taylor), Chivers, Hoddle, Kinnear (Galvin)
6,363

1980-81

Barry Daines Testimonial

11 May v West Ham United (h) 2–3
Hazard, Gibson
Daines (Aleksic), Perryman (Corbett), Mazzon, McAllister, Miller (Coates), Taylor (Gibson), Ardiles (Currie), Archibald, Villa, Hazard, Crooks (Falco)
7,172

1983-84

Bill Nicholson Testimonial

21 August v West Ham United (h) 1–1
Brazil
Clemence, Hughton (Mabbutt), Thomas, Roberts, Stevens, Perryman, Ardiles (Hazard), Brazil, Galvin (Archibald), Hoddle (Price), Falco
20,101

Keith Burkinshaw Testimonial

29 May v England XI (h) 2–2
Hughton, Brady
Jennings (Parks), Thomas, Hughton, Roberts (Stevens), Miller, Perryman (Hazard), Ardiles (Taylor), Crooks, Falco, Brady, Galvin
20,518

1984-85

Peter Southey Memorial

20 August v Fulham (h) 3–1

Crooks, Allen 2

Clemence (Parks), Thomas, Hughton, Roberts (Bowen), Miller, Stevens (Crook), Chiedozie (Brooke), Falco (Crooks), Allen, Mabbutt, Galvin

5,579

1985-86

Glenn Hoddle Testimonial

4 August v Arsenal (h) 1–1

Leworthy

Clemence, Thomas, Hughton, Roberts, Culverhouse, P. Allen, Ardiles (Crook), Hazard (Chiedozie), Leworthy, Hoddle (Samways), Waddle

13,567

Ossie Ardiles Benefit

1 May v Inter Milan (h) 2–1

Falco, C. Allen

Clemence (Jennings), Roberts (Thomas), Hughton, Mabbutt, Miller, Galvin (Samways), Ardiles (Waddle), Falco, C.Allen, Maradona, Hoddle

30,536

1986-87

Paul Miller Testimonial

2 August v Rangers (h) 1–1

C. Allen

Clemence, D. Thomas (Stevens), M. Thomas (Hughton), Roberts, Miller (Ruddock), Mabbutt, Cooke (Waddle), Falco, C. Allen, Ardiles (Hoddle), Galvin

16,365

1987-88

Chris Hughton Testimonial

10 August v Arsenal (h) 3–1

Thomas, C. Allen, Claesen

Clemence (Parks), Stevens (Polston), Thomas, Gough, Fairclough, Mabbutt, C. Allen, P. Allen, Waddle (Galvin), Hodge, Claesen

17,826

Tony Galvin Testimonial

20 October v West Ham United (h) 2–2

P. Allen, Archibald

Parks, Stevens (Polston [Hodge {Close}]), Hughton, P. Allen (Ardiles), Ruddock, Mabbutt, C. Allen, Archibald (Gray), Villa, Samways (Moncur), Galvin

7,258

Danny Thomas Benefit

28 March v Manchester United (h) 2–3

Archibald, Hodge

Parks, Hughton (Moncur), Thomas, Roberts (Ruddock), P. Allen, Mabbutt, C. Allen (Moran), Archibald, Dalglish (Howells), Hodge, Barnes (Chiedozie)

20,190

1989-90

Danny Blanchflower Benefit

1 May v Northern Ireland XI (h) 2–1

Howells, Gascoigne (pen)

Thorstvedt (Mimms), A. Polston (Perryman), Thomas, Sedgley, Howells (Garland), J. Polston (Butters), Stewart (Gormley), Gascoigne (A. Polston), Nayim (Ardiles), Lineker (Walsh), Allen (Taylor)

6,769

1990-91

Ray Clemence Benefit

17 August v West Ham United (h) 4–1

Lineker (1 pen) 2, Gascoigne, Nayim

Clemence (Thorstvedt), Ardiles (Nayim), Edinburgh, Sedgley (Butters), Howells (Samways), Mabbutt, Stewart, Gascoigne (Moncur), Dalglish (Hendon), Lineker (Walsh), Allen

17,456

1991-92

Cyril Knowles Memorial

10 November v Spurs '81-82 (h) 2–2

Samways, OG (Clemence)

Dearden, Edinburgh, Van den Hauwe, Sedgley, Howells (Houghton), Polston (Hendon), Nayim, Hendry (Morah), Samways (Campbell), Walsh, Allen (Robson)

12,732

1992-93

Eddie Baily Testimonial

14 May v Enfield (a) 5–1

Sheringham 2, Anderton, Gray, OG (Heald)

Walker (Dearden), McDonald (Campbell), Tuttle, Samways (Watson), Nethercott, Ruddock (Hodges), Sedgley (Gray), Hill (Turner [Caskey]), Anderton (McMahon), Sheringham (Mahorn), Hendry

2,700

1993-94

Cyril Knowles Memorial
19 October v Hartlepool United (a) 3–1
Sedgley, Dozzell, Howells
Walker, Campbell (Moran), Edinburgh, Samways, Calderwood, Mabbutt (Nethercott), Barmby, Sedgley (Robinson), Howells, Dozzell, Hill
1,593

1995-96

Gary Mabbutt Testimonial
12 August v Newcastle United (h) 0–2
Walker, Austin, Edinburgh (Wilson), Howells (Kerslake), Campbell (Nethercott), Mabbutt, Caskey (Dozzell), Dumitrescu, Turner (Hill), Sheringham (Rosenthal), Armstrong (Slade)
17,288

1997-98

David Howells Testimonial
2 August v Fiorentina (h) 0–2
Walker (Baardsen), Carr, Edinburgh (Calderwood), Howells (Mabbutt), Vega, Campbell, Ginola, Nielsen, Mahorn (Clemence), Ferdinand, Sinton (Fox [Iversen])
14,605

1999-2000

Justin Edinburgh Testimonial
9 May v Portsmouth (a) 2–4
Iversen, Anderton
Walker (Baardsen), Carr (Clemence), King, Freund (Korsten), Campbell (Gardner), Perry (Scales), Anderton (Leonhardsen), Sherwood (Davies), Doherty (McEwen), Iversen (Etherington), Ginola (Gower)
6,775

2001-02

Bill Nicholson Testimonial
8 August v Fiorentina (h) 3–0
Iversen, Ferdinand, Poyet
Sullivan, Taricco (Piercy), King, Freund (Davies), Doherty (Perry), Bunjevcevic, Clemence, Ziege, Ferdinand (Iversen), Poyet, Rebrov (Etherington)
35,877

INTERNATIONALS

Details up to 26 May 2011.

FULL INTERNATIONALS

ALGERIA

Moussa Saib: 28 February 1999 Liberia, 9 April 1999 Liberia, 6 June 1999 Tunisia, 20 June 1999 Uganda, [while on loan to Al Nasr – 24 January 2000 Congo, 29 January 2000 Gabon, 2 February 2000 South Africa, 6 February 2000 Cameroon, 26 May 2000 Burkina Faso] (9 appearances)

ARGENTINA

Ossie Ardiles: 22 May 1979 Holland, 25 June 1979 Rest of the World, 1 January 1981 West Germany, 4 January 1981 Brazil, 14 January 1982 USSR, 5 May 1982 Bulgaria, 12 May 1982 Rumania, 13 June 1982 Belgium, 18 June 1982 Hungary (1), 23 June 1982 El Salvador, 29 June 1982 Italy, 2 July 1982 Brazil (12 appearances 1 goal)

BELGIUM

Jonathan Blondel: 21 August 2002 Poland (sub) (1 appearance)

Nico Claesen: 14 October 1986 Luxembourg (3), 19 November 1986 Bulgaria, 4 February 1987 Portugal, 1 April 1987 Scotland (3), 29 April 1987 Republic of Ireland, 9 September 1987 Holland, 23 September 1987 Bulgaria, 14 October 1987 Scotland, 11 November 1987 Luxembourg (9 appearances 6 goals)

BRAZIL

Gilberto: 31 May 2008 Canada, 6 June 2008 Venezuela, 15 June 2008 Paraguay, 18 June 2008 Argentina, 7 September 2008 Chile (5 appearances)

Heurelho Gomes: 2 June 2010 Zimbabwe (sub), 7 June 2010 Tanzania (2 appearances)

Sandro: 7 October 2010 Iran (sub), 11 October 2010 Ukraine (sub), 9 February 2011 France (sub), 27 March 2011 Scotland (sub) (4 appearances)

BULGARIA

Dimitar Berbatov: 15 August 2006 Wales, 2 September 2006 Rumania, 7 October 2006 Holland, 11 October 2006 Luxembourg, 15 November 2006 Slovakia, 7 February 2007 Cyprus (2), 28 March 2007 Albania, 2 June 2007 Belarus (2), 6 June 2007 Belarus, 8 September 2007 Netherlands, 12 September 2007 Luxembourg (2), 17 October 2007 Albania, 17 November 2007 Rumania, 21 November 2007 Slovenia (1), 6 February 2008 Northern Ireland, 26 March 2008 Finland, 20 August 2008 Bosnia-Herzegovina (2) (17 apps, 10 goals)

CAMEROON

Benoit Assou-Ekotto: 11 February 09 Guinea, 28 March 2009 Togo, 5 September 2009 Gabon, 9 September 2009 Gabon, 14 November 2009 Morocco, 3 March 2010 Italy, 29 May 2010 Slovakia,1 June 2010 Portugal, 5 June 2010 Serbia, 14 June 2010 Japan, 19 June 2010 Denmark, 24 June 2010 Holland, 11 August 2010 Poland, 4 September 2010 Mauritius, 9 October 2010 DR Congo, 26 March 2011 Senegal (16 appearances)

Thimothee Atouba: 5 September 2004 Egypt, 9 October 2004 Sudan,17 November 2004 Germany, 9 February 2005 Senegal, 27 March 2005 Sudan, (5 appearances)
Sebastien Bassong: 12 August 2009 Austria, 5 September 2009 Gabon, 14 October 2009 Angola, 3 March 2010 Italy, 29 May 2010 Slovakia5 June 2010 Serbia, 14 June 2010 Japan, 20 June 2010 Denmark, 11 August 2010 Poland, 4 September 2010 Mauritius, 9 October 2010 DR Congo, 9 February 2011 Macedonia (12 appearances)

CANADA

Lars Hirschfeld: 15 October 2002 Scotland, 18 January 2003 USA, 12 February 2003 Libya, 12 July 2003 Costa Rica, 14 July 2003 Cuba, 11 October 2003 Finland (sub), 15 November 2003 Czech Republic, 18 November 2003 Republic of Ireland (8 appearances)
Paul Stalteri: 4 September 2006 Jamaica, 8 October 2006 Jamaica, 27 March 2007 Bermuda (1), 1 June 2007 Venezuela, 6 June 2007 Costa Rica, 9 June 2007 Guadeloupe, 11 June 2007 Haiti, 16 June 2007 Guatemala, 21 June 2007 USA, 22 August 07 Iceland, 12 September 2007 Costa Rica, 20 November 2007 South Africa, 31 May 2008 Brazil, 4 June 2008 Panama, 15 June 2008 St Vincent & Grenadines, 20 June 2008 St Vincent & Grenadines, 20 August 2008 Jamaica, 6 September 2008 Honduras, 10 September 2008 Mexico, 11 October 2008 Honduras, 15 October 2008 Mexico, 19 November 2008 Jamaica (22 appearances 1 goal)

CROATIA

Vedran Corluka: 6 September 2008 Kazakhstan, 10 September 2008 England, 11 October 2008 Ukraine, 15 October 228 Andorra, 11 February 09 Rumania, 1 April 2009 Andorra, 6 June 2009 Ukraine, 12 August 2009 Belarus, 5 September 2009 Belarus, 8 October 2009 Qatar (1), 14 October 2009 Kazakhstan, 3 March 2010 Belgium, 11 August 2010 Slovakia, 3 September 2010 Latvia, 7 September 2010 Greece, 9 October 2010 Israel, 17 November 2010 Malta, 9 February 2011 Czech Republic, 26 March 2011 Georgia, 29 March 2011 France (20 appearances 1 goal)
Niko Kranjcar: 5 September 2009 Belarus, 9 September 2009 England, 8 October 2009 Qatar, 14 October 2009 Kazakhstan (1), 14 November 2009 Liechtenstein, 3 March 2010 Belgium (1), 11 August 2010 Slovakia, 3 September 2010 Latvia, 7 September 2010 Greece, 9 October 2010 Israel (2), 12 October 2010 Norway (1), 17 November 2010 Malta (2), 9 February 2011 Czech Republic, 26 March 2011 Georgia, 29 March 2011 France (15 appearances 7 goals)
Luka Modric: 6 September 2008 Kazakhstan (1), 10 September 2008 England, 11 October 2008 Ukraine, 15 October 2008 Andorra (1), 11 February 09 Rumania, 6 June 2009 Ukraine (1), 12 August 2009 Belarus, 3 March 2010 Belgium, 19 May 2010 Austria, 23 May 2010 Wales, 11 August 2010 Slovakia, 7 September 2010 Greece, 9 October 2010 Israel, 12 October 2010 Norway, 17 November 2010 Malta, 26 March 2011 Georgia, 29 March 2011 France (17 appearances 3 goals)
Stipe Pletikosa: [while on loan from Spartak Moscow – 12 October 2010 Norway, 29 March 2011 France (sub)] (2 appearances)

DENMARK

Allan Nielsen: 1 September 1996 Slovenia (1), 9 October 1996 Greece, 9 November 1996 France, 29 March 1997 Croatia, 30 April 1997 Slovenia (2), 8 June 1997 Bosnia-Herzegovina, 20 August 1997 Bosnia-Herzegovina, 10 September 1997 Croatia, 11 October 1997 Greece, 25 March 1998 Scotland, 22 April 1998 Norway, 28 May 1998 Sweden, 5 June 1998 Cameroon (sub), 12 June 1998 Saudi Arabia (sub), 18 June 1998 South Africa (1), 24 June 1998 France, 28 June 1998 Nigeria, 3 July 1998 Brazil, 19 August 1998 Czech Republic, 5 September 1998 Belarus, 10 February 1999 Croatia, 27 March 1999 Italy, 6 June 1999 Belarus, 9 June 1999 Wales, 4 September 1999 Switzerland (1), 8 September 1999 Italy, 10 October 1999 Iran, 3 June 2000 Belgium, 11 June 2000 France, 16 June 00 Holland (30 appearances 5 goals)

EGYPT

Hossam Ghaly: 7 October 2006 Botswana, 15 November 2006 South Africa, 25 March 2007 Mauritania (1), 3 June 2007 Mauritania, 13 November 2007 UAE, 16 November 2007 Sudan, 21 November 2007 Libya, 25 November 2007 Saudi Arabia (1), 5 January 2008 Namibia, 1 June 2008 DR Congo, 22 June 2008 Malawi (11 appearances 2 goals)
Ahmed Hossam (Mido): [While on loan from Roma 27 March 2005 Libya (1) 19 June 2005 Ivory Coast (sub), 17 August 2005 Portugal, 4 September 2005 Benin (1), 16 November 2005 Tunisia (1), 20 January 2006 Libya (1), 24 January 2006 Morocco, 28 January 2006 Ivory Coast, 7 February 2006 Senegal], 2 September 2006 Burundi, 7 October 2006 Botswana, 7 February 2007 Sweden, (12 appearances 4 goals)

ENGLAND

Clive Allen: 29 April 1987 Turkey, 17 February 1988 Israel (2 appearances)
Wally Alsford: 6 April 1935 Scotland (1 appearance)
Darren Anderton: 9 March 1994 Denmark, 17 May 1994 Greece (1), 22 May 1994 Norway, 7 September 1994 USA, 15 February 1995 Republic of Ireland (aban), 29 March 1995 Uruguay, 3 June 1995 Japan (1), 8 June 1995 Sweden (1), 11 June 1995 Brazil, 17 May 1996 Hungary (2), 23 May 1996 China, 8 June 1996 Switzerland, 15 June 1996 Scotland, 18 June 1996 Holland, 22 June 1996 Spain, 26 June 1996 Germany, 23 May 1998 Saudi Arabia, 27 May 1998 Morocco, 15 June 1998 Tunisia, 22 June 1998 Rumania, 26 June 1998 Columbia (1), 30 June 1998 Argentina, 5 September 1998 Sweden, 10 October 1998 Bulgaria, 14 October 1998 Luxembourg, 18 November 1998 Czech Republic (1), 10 February 1999 France, 2 September 2000 France, 15 November 2000 Italy (sub), 10 November 2001 Sweden (sub) (30 appearances 7 goals)
Eddie Baily: 2 July 1950 Spain, 7 October 1950 Northern Ireland (2), 15 November 1950 Wales (2), 22 November 1950 Yugoslavia, 20 October 1951 Wales (1), 28 November 1951 Austria, 25 May 1952 Austria, 28 May 1952 Switzerland, 4 October 1952 Northern Ireland (9 appearances 5 goals)
Nicky Barmby: 29 March 1995 Uruguay (sub), 8 June 1995 Sweden (sub) (2 appearances)
Darren Bent: 21 November 2007 Croatia (sub), 19 November 2008 Germany (sub) (2 appearances)
David Bentley: 20 August 2008 Czech Republic (sub) (1 appearance)
Bert Bliss: 9 April 1921 Scotland (1 appearance)
Johnny Brooks: 14 November Wales (1), 28 November 1956 Yugoslavia (1), 5 December 1956 Denmark (3 appearances 2 goals)
Sol Campbell: 17 May 1996 Hungary (sub), 15 June 1996 Scotland (sub), 9 November 1996 Georgia, 12 February 1997 Italy, 30 April 1997 Georgia, 24 May 1997 South Africa (sub), 31 May 1997 Poland, 7 June 1997 France, 10 June 1997 Brazil, 10 September 1997 Moldova, 11 October 1997 Italy, 15 November 1997 Cameroon, 11 February 1998 Chile, 22 April 1998 Portugal, 27 May 1998 Morocco, 29 May 1998 Belgium, 15 June 1998 Tunisia, 19 June 1998 Rumania, 26 June 1998 Columbia, 30 June 1998 Argentina, 5 September 1998 Sweden, 10 October 1998 Bulgaria, 14 October 1998 Luxembourg, 18 November 1998 Czech Republic, 27 March 1999 Poland, 5 June 1999 Sweden, 9 June 1999 Bulgaria, 13 November 1999 Scotland, 17 November 1999 Scotland, 23 February 2000 Argentina, 27 May 2000 Brazil, 31 May 2000 Ukraine, 3 June 2000 Malta, 12 June 2000 Portugal, 17 June 2000 Germany, 20 June 2000 Rumania, 2 September 2000 France, 28 February 2001 Spain, 24 March 2001 Finland, 28 March 2001 Albania (40 appearances)
Michael Carrick: 28 May 2005 USA, 31 May 2005 Columbia, 1 March 2006 Uruguay, 3 June 2006 Jamaica (sub), 25 June 2006 Ecuador (5 appearances)
Martin Chivers: 3 February 1971 Malta, 21 April 1971 Greece (1), 12 May 1971 Malta (2),

15 May 1971 Northern Ireland, 22 May 1971 Scotland (2), 13 October 1971 Switzerland (1), 10 November 1971 Switzerland (sub), 1 December 1971 Greece (1), 29 April 1972 West Germany, 13 May 1972 West Germany, 23 May 1972 Northern Ireland (sub), 27 May 1972 Scotland, 15 November 1972 Wales, 24 January 1973 Wales, 14 February 1973 Scotland (1), 12 May 1973 Northern Ireland (2), 15 May 1973 Wales (1), 19 May 1973 Scotland, 27 May 1973 Czechoslovakia, 6 June 1973 Poland, 10 June 1973 USSR (1), 14 June 1973 Italy, 26 September 1973 Austria (1), 17 October 1973 Poland (24 appearances 13 goals)

Harry Clarke: 3 April 1954 Scotland (1 appearance)

Tommy Clay: 15 March 1920 Wales, 22 October 1921 Northern Ireland, 13 March 1922 Wales, 8 April 1922 Scotland (4 appearances)

Ray Clemence: 9 September 1981 Norway, 23 February 1982 Northern Ireland, 3 June 1982 Finland, 15 December 1982 Luxembourg, 16 November 1983 Luxembourg (5 appearances)

Ralph Coates: 12 May 1971 Malta, 19 May 1971 Wales (2 appearances)

Peter Crouch: 14 October 2009 Belarus (1), 14 November 2009 Brazil (sub), 3 March 2010 Egypt (sub) (2), 24 May 2010 Mexico (1), 12 June 2010 USA (sub), 18 June 2010 Algeria (sub), 12 October 2010 Montenegro, 17 November 2010 France (sub) (1) (8 appearances 5 goals)

Michael Dawson: 11 August 2010 Hungary (sub), 3 September 2010 Bulgaria, 9 February 2011 Denmark, 26 March 2011 Wales (4 appearances)

Jermain Defoe: 31 March 2004 Sweden (sub), 5 June 2004 Iceland (sub), 18 August 2004 Ukraine (sub), 4 September 2004 Austria (sub), 8 September 2004 Poland (1), 9 October 2004 Wales, 13 October 2004 Azerbaijan, 17 November 2004 Spain (sub), 26 March 2005 Northern Ireland (sub), 30 March 2005 Azerbaijan (sub), 28 May 2005 USA (sub), 31 May 2005 Columbia (sub), 17 August 2005 Denmark, 3 September 2005 Wales (sub), 7 September 2005 Northern Ireland (sub), 1 March 2006 Uruguay (sub), 16 August 2006 Greece, 2 September 2006 Andorra (2), 6 September 2006 Macedonia, 7 October 2006 Macedonia (sub), 11 October 2006 Croatia (sub), 7 February 2007 Spain (sub), 24 March 2007 Israel (sub), 28 March 2007 Andorra (sub), 16 November 2007 Austria (sub), 21 November 2007 Croatia (sub), 10 June 2009 Andorra (sub) (2), 12 August 2009 Holland (sub) (2), 5 September 2009 Slovenia (sub) (1), 9 September 2009 Croatia (sub), 14 November 2009 Brazil (sub), 3 March 2010 Egypt 24 May 2010 Mexico (sub), 18 June 2010 Algeria (sub), 23 June 2010 Slovenia (1), 27 June 2010 Germany, 3 September 2010 Bulgaria (3), 7 September 2010 Switzerland, 29 March 2011 Ghana (sub) (39 appearances 12 goals)

Jimmy Dimmock: 9 April 1921 Scotland, 1 March 1926 Wales, 24 May 1926 Belgium (3 appearances)

Ted Ditchburn: 2 December 1948 Switzerland, 13 May 1949 Sweden, 8 June 1953 USA, 14 November 1956 Wales, 28 November 1956 Yugoslavia, 5 December 1956 Denmark (6 appearances)

Terry Fenwick: 11 February 1988 Israel (sub) (1 appearance)

Les Ferdinand: 10 September 1997 Moldova, 23 May 1998 Saudi Arabia (sub), 27 May 1998 Morocco (sub), 29 May 1998 Belgium (4 appearances)

Anthony Gardner: 31 March 2004 Sweden (sub) (1 appearance)

Paul Gascoigne: 14 September 1988 Denmark (sub), 16 November 1988 Saudi Arabia (sub), 26 April 1989 Albania (sub) (1), 23 May 1989 Chile, 27 May 1989 Scotland (sub), 6 September 1989 Sweden (sub), 28 March 1990 Brazil (sub), 25 April 1990 Czechoslovakia (1), 15 May 1990 Denmark, 22 May 1990 Uruguay, 2 June 1990 Tunisia, 11 June 1990 Republic of Ireland, 16 June 1990 Holland, 21 June 1990 Egypt, 26 June 1990 Belgium, 1 July 1990 Cameroon, 4 July 1990 West Germany, 12 September 1990 Hungary, 17 October 1990 Poland, 6 February 1991 Cameroon (20 appearances 2 goals)

Jimmy Greaves: 14 April 1962 Scotland, 9 May 1962 Switzerland, 20 May 1962 Peru (3), 31 May 1962 Hungary, 2 June 1962 Argentina (1), 7 June 1962 Bulgaria, 10 June 1962 Brazil, 3 October

1962 France, 20 October 1962 Northern Ireland (1), 22 November 1962 Wales (1), 27 February 1963 France, 6 April 1963 Scotland, 8 May 1963 Brazil, 20 May 1963 Czechoslovakia (2), 5 June 1963 Switzerland, 17 October 1963 Wales (1), 23 October 1963 Rest of World (1), 20 November 1963 Northern Ireland (4), 6 May 1964 Uruguay, 17 May 1964 Portugal, 24 May 1964 Republic of Ireland (1), 30 May 1964 Brazil (1), 4 June 1964 Portugal, 6 June 1964 Argentina, 3 October 1964 Northern Ireland (3), 21 October 1964 Belgium, 9 December 1964 Holland (1), 10 April 1965 Scotland (1), 5 May 1965 Hungary (1), 9 May 1965 Yugoslavia, 2 October 1965 Wales, 20 October 1965 Austria, 4 May 1966 Yugoslavia (1), 29 June 1966 Norway (4), 3 July 1966 Denmark, 5 July 1966 Poland, 11 July 1966 Uruguay, 16 July 1966 Mexico, 20 July 1966 France, 15 April 1967 Scotland, 24 May 1967 Spain (1), 27 May 1967 Austria (42 appearances 28 goals)
Arthur Grimsdell: 15 March 1920 Wales, 10 April 1920 Scotland, 23 October 1920 Northern Ireland, 9 April 1921 Scotland, 21 October 1922 Northern Ireland, 5 March 1923 Wales (6 appearances)
Willie Hall: 6 December 1933 France, 23 October 1937 Northern Ireland (1), 17 November 1937 Wales (1), 1 December 1937 Czechoslovakia, 9 April 1938 Scotland, 26 October 1938 Rest of Europe (1), 10 November 1938 Northern Ireland (5), 15 April 1939 Scotland, 13 May 1939 Italy (1), 18 May 1939 Yugoslavia (10 appearances 9 goals)
Ron Henry: 27 February 1963 France (1 appearance)
Glenn Hoddle: 22 November 1979 Bulgaria (1), 17 May 1980 Wales, 31 May 1980 Australia (1), 18 June 1980 Spain, 25 March 1981 Spain (1), 20 May 1981 Wales, 23 May 1981 Scotland, 9 September 1981 Norway, 23 February 1982 Northern Ireland (1), 27 April 1982 Wales, 2 June 1982 Iceland, 20 June 1982 Czechoslovakia (sub), 25 June 1982 Kuwait, 15 December 1982 Luxembourg (sub) (1), 28 May 1983 Northern Ireland, 1 June 1983 Scotland, 12 October 1983 Hungary (1), 16 November 1983 Luxembourg, 29 February 1984 France, 26 March 1985 Republic of Ireland (sub), 25 May 1985 Scotland, 6 June 1985 Italy (sub), 9 June 1985 Mexico, 12 June 1985 West Germany, 16 June 1985 USA, 11 September 1985 Rumania (1), 16 October 1985 Turkey, 13 November 1985 Northern Ireland, 26 February 1986 Israel, 26 March 1986 USSR, 23 April 1986 Scotland (1), 17 May 1986 Mexico, 24 May 1986 Canada, 3 June 1986 Portugal, 6 June 1986 Morocco, 11 June 1986 Poland, 18 June 1986 Paraguay, 22 June 1986 Argentina, 10 September 1986 Sweden, 15 October 1986 Northern Ireland, 12 November 1986 Yugoslavia, 10 February 1987 Spain, 29 April 1987 Turkey, 23 May 1987 Scotland (44 appearances 8 goals)
Steve Hodge: 10 February 1987 Spain, 1 April 1987 Northern Ireland, 29 April 1987 Turkey, 23 May 1987 Scotland (4 appearances)
Tom Huddlestone: 14 November 2009 Brazil (sub), 24 May 2010 Mexico (sub), 30 May 2010 Japan (3 appearances)
George Hunt: 13 March 1933 Italy, 1 April 1933 Scotland (1), 20 May 1933 Switzerland (3 appearances 1 goal)
Jermaine Jenas: 12 October 2005 Poland (sub), 1 March 2006 Uruguay (sub), 1 June 2007 Brazil (sub), 6 June 2007 Estonia (sub), 6 February 2008 Switzerland (1), 20 August 2008 Czech Republic (sub), 10 September 2008 Croatia (sub), 14 November 2009 Brazil (8 appearances 1 goal)
Ledley King: 27 March 2002 Italy (sub), 12 February 2003 Australia (sub), 18 February 2004 Portugal (1), 1 June 2004 Japan (sub), 5 June 2004 Iceland (sub), 13 June 2004 France, 21 June 2004 Croatia (sub), 18 August 2004 Ukraine, 4 September 2004 Austria, 8 September 2004 Poland, 9 October 2004 Wales (sub), 30 March 2005 Azerbaijan (sub), 8 October 2005 Austria (sub), 12 October 2005 Poland, 12 November 2005 Argentina 1 March 2006, Uruguay (sub), 7 October 2206 Macedonia, 1 June 2007 Brazil, 6 June 2007 Estonia, 24 May 201 Mexico (1), 12 June 2010 USA (21 appearances 2 goals)
Cyril Knowles: 6 December 1967 USSR, 3 April 1968 Spain, 22 May 1968 Sweden, 1 June 1968 West Germany (4 appearances)

Aaron Lennon: 3 June 2006 Jamaica (sub), 15 June 2006 Trinidad & Tobago (sub), 25 June 2006 Ecuador (sub), 1 July 2006 Portugal (sub), 16 August 2006 Greece (sub), 2 September 2006 Andorra (sub), 6 September 2006 Macedonia (sub), 24 March 2007 Israel, 28 March 2007 Andorra, 28 March 2009 Slovakia, 1 April 2009 Ukraine, 5 September 2009 Slovenia (sub), 9 September 2009 Croatia, 10 October 2009 Ukraine, 14 October 2009 Belarus, 24 May 2010 Mexico (sub), 30 May 2010 Japan, 12 June 2010 USA, 18 June 2010 Algeria (19 appearances)
Gary Lineker: 6 September 1989 Sweden, 11 October 1989 Poland, 15 November 1989 Italy, 13 December 1989 Yugoslavia, 28 March 1990 Brazil (1), 25 April 1990 Czechoslovakia, 15 May 1990 Denmark (1), 22 May 1990 Uruguay, 2 June 1990 Tunisia, 11 June 1990 Republic of Ireland (1), 16 June 1990 Holland, 21 June 1990 Egypt, 26 June 1990 Belgium, 1 July 1990 Cameroon (2), 4 July 1990 West Germany (1), 7 July 1990 Italy, 12 September 1990 Hungary (1), 17 October 1990 Poland (1), 13 November 1990 Republic of Ireland, 6 February 1991 Cameroon (2), 27 March 1991 Republic of Ireland, 1 May 1991 Turkey, 25 May 1991 Argentina (1), 1 June 1991 Australia, 3 June 1991 New Zealand (1), 12 June 1991 Malaysia (4), 11 September 1991 Germany, 16 October 1991 Turkey, 13 November 1991 Poland (1), 19 February 1992 France (sub) (1), 25 March 1992 Czechoslovakia (sub), 29 April 1992 CIS (1), 12 May 1992 Hungary, 17 May 1992 Brazil, 3 June 1992 Finland, 11 June 1992 Denmark, 14 June 1992 France, 17 June 1992 Sweden (38 appearances 19 goals)
Gary Mabbutt: 13 October 1982 West Germany, 17 November 1982 Greece, 15 December 1982 Luxembourg, 23 February 1983 Wales, 30 March 1983 Greece, 27 April 1983 Hungary, 28 May 1983 Northern Ireland, 1 June 1983 Scotland (sub), 12 October 1983 Hungary, 12 November 1986 Yugoslavia (1), 1 April 1987 Northern Ireland, 29 April 1987 Turkey, 9 September 1987 West Germany, 16 October 1991 Turkey, 13 November 1991 Poland, 25 March 1992 Czechoslovakia (16 appearances 1 goal)
Les Medley: 15 November 1950 Wales, 22 November 1950 Yugoslavia, 3 October 1951 France (1), 20 October 1951 Wales, 14 November 1951 Northern Ireland, 28 November 1951 Austria (6 appearances 1 goal)
Alan Mullery: 9 December 1964 Holland, 24 May 1967 Spain, 27 May 1967 Austria, 21 October 1967 Wales, 22 November 1967 Northern Ireland, 6 December 1967 USSR, 24 February 1968 Scotland, 3 April 1968 Spain, 8 May 1968 Spain, 22 May 1968 Sweden, 5 June 1968 Yugoslavia, 6 November 1968 Rumania, 11 December 1968 Bulgaria, 12 March 1969 France, 3 May 1969 Northern Ireland, 10 May 1969 Scotland, 1 June 1969 Mexico, 8 June 1969 Uruguay, 12 June 1969 Brazil, 5 November 1969 Holland, 10 December 1969 Portugal, 14 January 1970 Holland (sub), 18 April 1970 Wales, 21 April 1970 Northern Ireland, 25 April 1970 Scotland (sub), 20 May 1970 Columbia, 24 May 1970 Ecuador, 2 June 1970 Rumania, 7 June 1970 Brazil, 11 June 1970 Czechoslovakia, 14 June 1970 West Germany (1), 25 November 1970 East Germany, 3 February 1971 Malta, 21 April 1971 Greece, 13 October 1971 Switzerland (35 appearances 1 goal)
Bill Nicholson: 19 May 1951 Portugal (1) (1 appearance 1 goal)
Maurice Norman: 20 May 1962 Peru, 31 May 1962 Hungary, 2 June 1962 Argentina, 7 June 1962 Bulgaria, 10 June 1962 Brazil, 3 October 1962 France, 6 April 1963 Scotland, 8 May 1963 Brazil, 20 May 1963 Czechoslovakia, 2 June 1963 East Germany, 12 October 1963 Wales, 23 October 1963 Rest of World, 20 November 1963 Northern Ireland, 11 April 1964 Scotland, 6 May 1964 Uruguay, 17 May 1964 Portugal, 27 May 1964 USA, 30 May 1964 Brazil, 4 June 1964 Portugal, 6 June 1964 Argentina, 3 October 1964 Northern Ireland, 21 October 1964 Belgium, 9 December 1964 Holland (23 appearances)
Frank Osbourne: 8 December 1924 Belgium, 24 May 1926 Belgium (3) (2 appearances 3 goals)
Steve Perryman: 2 June 1982 Iceland (sub) (1 appearance)
Martin Peters: 18 April 1970 Wales, 21 April 1970 Northern Ireland (1), 25 April 1970 Scotland, 20 May 1970 Columbia (2), 24 May 1970 Ecuador, 2 June 1970 Rumania, 7 June 1970 Brazil, 11 June 1970 Czechoslovakia, 14 June 1970 West Germany (1), 25 November 1970 East Germany

(1), 3 February 1971 Malta (1), 21 April 1971 Greece, 12 May 1971 Malta, 15 May 1971 Northern Ireland, 19 May 1971 Wales, 22 May 1971 Scotland (1), 13 October 1971 Switzerland, 1 December 1971 Greece, 29 April 1972 West Germany, 13 May 1972 West Germany (sub), 23 May 1972 Northern Ireland (sub), 14 February 1973 Scotland, 12 May 1973 Northern Ireland, 15 May 1973 Wales (1), 19 May 1973 Scotland (1), 27 May 1973 Czechoslovakia, 6 June 1973 Poland, 10 June 1973 USSR, 14 June 1973 Italy, 26 September 1973 Austria, 17 October 1973 Poland, 14 November 1973 Italy, 3 April 1974 Portugal, 18 May 1974 Scotland (34 appearances 9 goals)

Alf Ramsey: 30 November 1949 Italy, 15 April 1950 Scotland, 14 May 1950 Portugal, 18 May 1950 Belgium, 15 June 1950 Chile, 29 June 1950 USA, 2 July 1950 Spain, 7 October 1950 Northern Ireland, 15 November 1950 Wales, 22 November 1950 Yugoslavia, 14 April 1951 Scotland, 9 May 1951 Argentina, 19 May 1951 Portugal, 3 October 1951 France, 20 October 1951 Wales, 14 November 1951 Northern Ireland, 28 November 1951 Austria (1), 5 April 1952 Scotland, 18 May 1952 Italy, 25 May 1952 Austria, 28 May 1952 Switzerland, 4 October 1952 Northern Ireland, 12 November 1952 Wales, 26 November 1952 Belgium, 18 April 1953 Scotland, 17 May 1953 Argentina, 24 May 1953 Chile, 31 May 1953 Uruguay, 8 June 1953 USA, 21 October 1953 Rest of Europe (1), 25 November 1953 Hungary (1) (31 appearances 3 goals)

George Robb: 25 November 1953 Hungary (1 appearance)

Graham Roberts: 29 May 1983 Northern Ireland, 1 June 1983 Scotland, 29 February 1984 France, 4 April 1984 Northern Ireland, 26 May 1984 Scotland, 2 June 1984 USSR (6 appearances)

Paul Robinson: 5 June 2004 Iceland, 8 September 2004 Poland, 9 October 2004 Wales, 13 October 2004 Azerbaijan, 17 November 2004 Spain, 9 February 2005 Holland, 26 March 2005 Northern Ireland, 30 March 2005 Azerbaijan, 17 August 2005 Denmark, 3 September 2005 Wales, 7 September 2005 Northern Ireland, 8 October 2005 Austria, 12 October 2005 Poland, 12 November 2005 Argentina, 1 March 2006 Uruguay, 30.05.2006 Hungary, 3 June 2006 Jamaica, 10 June 2006 Paraguay, 15 June 2006 Trinidad & Tobago, 20 June 2006 Sweden, 25 June 2006 Ecuador, 1 July 2006 Portugal, 16 August 2006 Greece, 2 September 2006 Andorra, 6 September 2006 Macedonia, 7 October 2006 Macedonia, 11 October 2006 Croatia, 15 November 2006 Holland, 24 March 2007 Israel, 28 March 2005 Andorra, 1 June 2007 Brazil, 6 June 2007 Estonia, 22 August 2007 Germany, 8 September 2007 Israel, 12 September 2007 Russia, 13 October 2007 Estonia, 17 October 2007 Russia (37 appearances)

Arthur Rowe: 6 December 1933 France (1 appearance)

Jimmy Seed: 21 May 1921 Belgium, 21 October 1922 Northern Ireland, 5 March 1923 Wales, 19 March 1923 Belgium (1), 4 April 1925 Scotland (5 appearances 1 goal)

Teddy Sheringham: 29 May 1993 Poland, 2 June 1993 Norway, 7 September 1994 USA, 12 October 1994 Rumania (sub), 16 November 1994 Nigeria (sub), 29 March 1995 Uruguay, 3 June 1995 Japan (sub), 8 June 1995 Sweden (1), 11 June 1995 Brazil, 6 September 1995 Colombia (sub), 11 October 1995 Norway (sub), 15 November 1995 Switzerland (1), 27 March 1996 Bulgaria, 24 April 1996 Croatia, 18 May 1996 Hungary, 8 June 1996 Switzerland, 15 June 1996 Scotland, 18 June 1996 Holland (2), 22 June 1996 Spain, 26 June 1996 Germany, 9 November 1996 Georgia (1), 29 March 1997 Mexico (1), 30 April 1997 Georgia (1), 24 May 1997 South Africa, 31 May 1997 Poland (1), 4 June 1997 Italy, 7 June 1997 France (sub), 10 June 1997 Brazil, 6 October 2001 Greece (sub) (1), 10 November 2001 Sweden (sub), 27 March 2002 Italy (sub), 17 April 2002 Paraguay (sub), 21 May 2002 South Korea (sub), 26 May 200 Cameroon (sub), 7 June 2002 Argentina (sub), 12 June 2002 Nigeria (sub), 15 June 2002 Denmark (sub), 21 June 2002 Brazil (sub) (38 appearances 9 goals)

Tim Sherwood: 27 March 1999 Poland, 27 April 1999 Hungary, 5 June 1999 Sweden (3 appearances)

Bert Smith: 9 April 1921 Scotland, 13 March 1922 Wales (2 appearances)

Bobby Smith: 8 October 1960 Northern Ireland (1), 19 October 1960 Luxembourg (2), 26 October 1960 Spain (2), 23 November 1960 Wales (1), 15 April 1961 Scotland (2), 21 May

1961 Portugal, 14 April 1962 Scotland, 27 February 1963 France (1), 6 April 1963 Scotland, 8 May 1963 Brazil, 20 May 1963 Czechoslovakia (1), 2 June 1963 East Germany, 12 October 1963 Wales (2), 23 October 1963 Rest of World, 20 November 1963 Northern Ireland (1) (15 appearances 13 goals)

Bert Sproston: 22 October 1938 Wales, 26 October 1938 Rest of Europe (2 appearances)

Gary Stevens: 17 October 1984 Finland (sub), 14 November 1984 Turkey (sub), 27 February 1985 Northern Ireland, 23 April 1986 Scotland (sub), 17 May 1986 Mexico (sub), 3 June 1986 Morocco (sub), 18 June 1986 Paraguay (sub) (7 appearances)

Paul Stewart: 11 September 1991 Germany (sub), 25 March 1992 Czechoslovakia (sub), 29 April 1992 CIS (sub) (3 appearances)

Chris Waddle: 11 September 1985 Rumania, 16 October 1985 Turkey (1), 13 November 1985 Northern Ireland, 26 February 1986 Israel, 26 March 1986 USSR (1), 23 April 1986 Scotland, 17 May 1986 Mexico, 24 May 1986 Canada, 3 June 1986 Portugal, 6 June 1986 Morocco, 11 June 1986 Poland (sub), 22 June 1986 Argentina (sub), 10 September 1986 Sweden (sub), 15 October 1986 Northern Ireland (1), 12 November 1986 Yugoslavia, 10 February 1987 Spain, 1 April 1987 Northern Ireland (1), 29 April 1987 Turkey, 19 May 1987 Brazil, 23 May 1987 Scotland, 9 September 1987 West Germany, 11 February 1988 Israel, 27 April 1988 Hungary, 21 May 1988 Scotland (sub), 24 May 1988 Colombia, 28 May 1988 Switzerland (sub), 12 June 1988 Republic of Ireland, 15 June 1988 Holland, 19 October 1988 Sweden, 16 November 1988 Saudi Arabia, 8 March 1989 Albania, 26 April 1989 Albania (1), 23 May 1989 Chile, 27 May 1989 Scotland (1), 3 June 1989 Poland, 7 June 1989 Denmark (36 appearances 6 goals)

Fanny Walden: 4 April 1914 Scotland, 13 March 1922 Wales (2 appearances)

Ian Walker: 18 May 1996 Hungary (sub), 23 May 1996 China (sub), 12 February 1997 Italy (3 appearances)

Arthur Willis: 3 October 1951 France (1 appearance)

Jonathan Woodgate: 1 June .2008 Trinidad & Tobago, 20 August 2008 Czech Republic (sub) (2 appearances)

Vivian Woodward: 14 February 1903 Ireland (2), 2 March 1903 Wales (1), 4 April 1903 Scotland (1), 12 March 1904 Ireland, 9 April 1904 Scotland, 25 February 1905 Ireland, 27 March 1905 Wales (2), 1 April 1905 Scotland, 6 April 1907 Scotland, 15 February 1908 Ireland (1), 16 March 1908 Wales (3), 4 April 1908 Scotland, 6 June 1908 Austria (1), 8 June 1908 Austria (4), 10 June 1908 Hungary (1), 12 June 1908 Bohemia, 13 February 1909 Ireland (2), 15 March 1909 Wales, 29 May 1909 Hungary (2), 31 May 1909 Hungary (4), 1 June 1909 Austria (3) (21 appearances 27 goals)

FINLAND

Teemu Tainio: 17 August 2005 Macedonia, 3 September 2005 Andorra, 7 September 2005 Macedonia, 8 October 2005 Rumania, 12 October 2005 Czech Republic, 2 September 2006 Poland, 6 September 2006 Portugal, 2 June 2007 Serbia, 22 August 2007 Kazakhstan (1), 8 September 2007 Serbia, 12 September 2007 Poland, 17 November 2007 Azerbaijan, 21 November 2007 Portugal, 26 March 2008 Bulgaria, 2 June 2008 Belarus (15 appearances 1 gl)

GERMANY

Jurgen Klinsmann: 7 September 1994 Russia, 12 October 1994 Hungary, 16 November 1994 Albania (1), 14 December 1994 Moldova (1), 18 December 1994 Albania (1), 22 February 1995 Spain, 29 March 1995 Georgia (2), 26 April 1995 Wales, 7 June 1995 Bulgaria (1), 25 March 1998 Brazil, 30 May 1998 Columbia (sub), 5 June 1998 Luxembourg (1), 15 June 1998 USA (1), 21 June 1998 Yugoslavia, 25 June 1998 Iran (1), 29 June 1998 Mexico (1), 4 July 1998 Croatia (17 appearances 10 goals)

Christian Ziege: 15 August 2001 Hungary, 6 October 2001 Finland, 10 November 2001 Ukraine, 14 November 2001 Ukraine, 27 March 2002 USA (1), 14 May 2002 Wales, 18 May 2002 Austria, 1 June 2002 Saudi Arabia, 5 June 2002 Republic of Ireland, 11 June 2002 Cameroon, 21 June 2002 USA, 30 June 2002 Brazil (sub), 27 May 2004 Malta (sub). (13 appearances 1 goal)

HOLLAND

Edgar Davids: 12 October 2005 Macedonia (sub) (1 appearance)
Rafael van der Vaart: 3 September 2010 San Marino (sub), 7 September 2010 Finland, 8 October 2010 Moldova, 12 October 2010 Sweden, 17 November 2010 Turkey, 25 March 2011 Hungary (1), 29 March 2011 Hungary (7 appearances 1goal)

HONDURAS

Wilson Palacios: 28 March 2009 Trinidad & Tobago, 1 April 2009 Mexico, 6 June 2009 USA, 10 June 2009 El Salvador, 12 August 2009 Costa Rica, 9 September 2009 Mexico, 10 October 2009 USA, 14 October 2009 El Salvador, 14 November 2009 Latvia, 18 November 2009 Peru, 3 March 2010 Turkey, 2 June 2010 Azerbaijan, 5 June 2010 Rumania, 16 June 2010 Chile, 21 June 2010 Spain, 25 June 2010 Switzerland, 9 February 2011 Ecuador (20 appearances)

HUNGARY

Marton Fulop: 31 May 2005 France (sub), 16 August 2006 Austria (sub) (2 appearances)

ICELAND

Gudni Bergsson: 19 May 1989 England "B", 31 May 1989 USSR, 14 June 1989 Austria, 23 August 1989 Austria, 6 September 1989 East Germany, 20 September 1989 Turkey, 28 March 1990 Luxembourg, 30 May 1990 Albania, 5 September 1990 France, 26 September 1990 Czechoslovakia, 10 October 1990 Spain, 27 April 1991 England "B", 1 May 1991 Wales, 26 May 1991 Albania, 5 June 1991 Czechoslovakia, 17 July 1991 Turkey, 25 September 1991 Spain, 20 November 1991 France, 8 April 1992 Israel, 13 May 1992 Greece, 3 June 1992 Hungary, 8 August 1992 Israel, 7 October 1992 Greece, 14 October 1992 Russia, 17 April 1993 USA, 20 May 1993 Luxembourg, 2 June 1993 Russia, 16 June 1993 Hungary, 8 September 1993 Luxembourg, 17 October 1993 Tunisia (30 appearances)
Emil Hallfredsson: 30 March 2005 Italy (sub), [while on loan to Malmo - 28 February 2006 Trinidad & Tobago, 7 October 2006 Latvia (sub), 11 October 2006 Sweden], 28 March 2007 Spain, 2 June 2007 Liechtenstein, 6 June 2007 Sweden (7 appearances)

IRELAND

John Kirwan: 24 February 1900 Wales, 22 February 1902 Wales, 22 March 1902 England, 14 February 1903 England, 21 March 1903 Scotland (1), 28 March 1903 Wales, 12 March 1904 England (1), 21 March 1904 Wales, 26 March 1904 Scotland, 25 February 1905 England, 18 March 1905 Scotland, 8 April 1905 Wales (12 appearances 2 goals)
Charlie O'Hagan: 18 March 1905 Scotland, 8 April 1905 Wales (1), 17 February 1906 England, 17 March 1906 Scotland, 2 April 1906 Wales (5 appearances 1 goal)

ISRAEL

Ronny Rosenthal: 31 May 1994 Argentina, 17 August 1994 Croatia, 4 September 1994 Poland, 12 October 1994 Slovakia, 16 November 1994 Azerbaijan (1), 29 November 1994 Cyprus (1), 14 December 1994 Rumania (1), 29 March 1995 France, 25 April 1995 Poland (1), 6 September

1995 Slovakia (sub), 11 October 1995 Azerbaijan, 15 November 1995 France, 1 September 1996 Bulgaria. 9 October 1996 Russia (sub), 10 November 1996 Cyprus, 26 February 1997 Germany, 12 March 1997 Sweden, 31 March 1997 Luxembourg, 8 June 1997 Russia (19 appearances 4 goals)

IVORY COAST

Didier Zokora: 16 August 2006 Senegal, 8 October 2006 Gabon, 15 November 2006 Sweden (sub), 6 February 2007 Guinea, 3 June 2007 Madagascar, 22 August 2007 Egypt, 8 September 2007 Gabon, 17 October 2007 Austria, 17 November 2007 Angola, 12 January 2008 Kuwait, 21 January 2008 Nigeria, 25 January 2008 Benin, 3 February 2008 Guinea, 7 February 2008 Egypt, 9 February 2008 Ghana, 26 March 2008 Tunisia, 22 May 2008 Paraguay, 24 May 2008 Japan, 1 June 2008 Mozambique, 8 June 2008 Madagascar, 14 June 2008 Botswana, 22 June 2008 Botswana (1), 20 August 2008 Guinea, 7 September 2008 Mozambique, 11 October 2008 Madagascar, 19 November 2008 Israel, 11 February 09 Turkey, 29 March 2009 Malawi, 7 June 2009 Guinea, 13 June 2009 Cameroon (sub), 20 June 2009 Burkina Faso (31 appearances 1 goal)

MALI

Freddi Kanoute: 15 January 2004 Algeria, 26 January 2004 Kenya (2), 30 January 2004 Burkina Faso (1), 7 February 2004 Guinea (1), 11 February 2004 Morocco, 13 February 2004 Nigeria, 28 April 2004 Tunisia, 6 June 2004 Liberia, 19 June 2004 Zambia (1), 4 July 2004 DR Congo, 18 August 2004 DR Congo (1), 5 September 2004 Senegal (1) 9 February 2005 Guinea, 27 March 2005 Togo, 5 June 2005 Liberia, 18 June 2005 Zambia (16 appearances 7 goals)

MEXICO

Giovani dos Santos: 20 August 2008 Honduras, 6 September 2008 Jamaica, 10 September 2008 Canada, 11 October 2008 Jamaica, 15 October 2008 Canada, 11 February 200 USA, 10 June 2009 Trinidad & Tobago (sub), 24 June 2009 Venezuela (2), 5 July 2009 Nicaragua , 9 July 2009 Panama, 12 July 2009 Guadeloupe, 19 July 2009 Haiti (1), 23 July 2009 Costa Rica, 26 July 2009 USA (1), 12 August 2009 USA, 5 September 2009 Costa Rica (1), 9 September 2009 Honduras, [while on loan to Galatasaray – 3 March 2010 New Zealand], 24 May 2010 England, 3 June 2010 Italy, 11 June 2010 South Africa, 17 June 2010 France, 22.6 February 010 Uruguay, 27 June 2010 Argentina, 11 August 2010 Spain , 4 September 2010 Ecuador, 7 September 2010 Columbia, 12 October 2010 Venezuela (1) [while on loan to Racing Santander 9 February 2011 Bosnia & Herzegovina, 26 March 2011 Paraguay (sub), 29 March 2011 Venezuela] (31 appearances 6 goals)

MOROCCO

Noureddine Naybet: 5 September 2004 Tunisia, 10 October 2004 Guinea, 9 February 2005 Kenya, 26 March 2005 Guinea, 4 June 2005 Malawi, 18 June 2005 Kenya, 10 January 2006 DR Congo, 14 January 2006 Zimbabwe, 17 January 2006 Angola, 21 January 2006 Ivory Coast, 24 January 2006 Egypt, 28 January 2006 Libya (12 appearances)

Adel Taarabt: 11 February 2009 Czech Republic (sub) [while on loan to Queens Park Rangers – 28 March 2009 Gabon (sub), 31 March 2009 Angola (1), 12 August 2009 DR Congo (sub), 6 September 2009 Togo (sub) (1), 10 October 2009 Gabon (1), 14 November 2009 Cameroon] (7 appearances 3 goals)

NIGERIA

John Chiedozie: 20 October 1984 Liberia, 6 July 1985 Tunisia, 20 July 1985 Tunisia (3 appearances)

NORTHERN IRELAND

Gerry Armstrong: 27 April 1977 West Germany, 28 May 1977 England, 3 June 1977 Wales (sub), 11 June 1977 Iceland (sub), 16 November 1977 Belgium (2), 13 May 1978 Scotland, 16 May 1978 England, 19 May 1978 Wales, 20 September 1978 Republic of Ireland, 25 October 1978 Denmark, 29 November 1978 Bulgaria (1), 7 February 1979 England, 2 May 1979 Bulgaria (1), 19 May 1979 England, 22 May 1979 Scotland. 25 May 1979 Wales, 6 June 1979 Denmark, 17 October 1979 England, 21 November 1979 Republic of Ireland (1), 26 March 1980 Israel, 16 May 1980 Scotland, 20 May 1980 England, 23 May 1980 Wales, 11 June 1980 Australia, 15 June 1980 Australia, 18 June 1980 Australia, 22 June 1980 Western Australia (1), 15 October 1980 Sweden (28 appearances 6 goals)

Danny Blanchflower: 20 April 1955 Wales, 8 October 1955 Scotland, 2 November 1955 England, 11 April 1956 Wales, 6 October 1956 England, 7 November 1956 Scotland, 16 January 1957 Portugal, 10 April 1957 Wales, 25 April 1957 Italy, 1 May 1957 Portugal, 5 October 1957 Scotland, 6 November 1957 England, 4 December 1957 Italy, 15 January 1958 Italy, 16 April 1958 Wales, 8 June 1958 Czechoslovakia, 11 June 1958 Argentina, 15 June 1958 West Germany, 17 June 1958 Czechoslovakia, 19 June 1958 France, 4 October 1958 England, 15 October 1958 Spain, 5 November 1958 Scotland, 22 April 1959 Wales, 3 October 1959 Scotland, 18 November 1959 England, 6 April 1960 Wales (1), 8 October 1960 England, 26 October 1960 West Germany. 9 November 1960 Scotland (1), 12 April 1961 Wales, 10 May 1961 West Germany, 7 October 1961 Scotland, 17 October 1961 Greece, 22 November 1961 England, 11 April 1962 Wales, 9 May 1962 Holland, 10 October 1962 Poland, 20 October 1962 England, 7 November 1962 Scotland, 28 November 1962 Poland (41 appearances 2 goals)

Pat Jennings: 3 October 1964 England, 14 October 1964 Switzerland, 14 November 1964 Switzerland, 25 November 1964 Scotland, 7 April 1965 Holland, 7 May 1965 Albania, 2 October 1965 Scotland, 10 November 1965 England, 24 November 1965 Albania, 30 March 1966 Wales, 7 May 1966 West Germany, 22 October 1966 England, 16 November 1966 Scotland, 21 October 1967 Scotland, 22 November 1967 England, 2 February 1968 Wales, 10 September 1968 Israel, 23 October 1968 Turkey, 11 December 1968 Turkey, 3 May 1969 England, 6 May 1969 Scotland, 10 May 1969 Wales, 10 September 1969 USSR, 22 October 1969 USSR, 18 April 1970 Scotland, 21 April 1970 England, 3 February 1971 Cyprus, 21 April 1971 Cyprus, 15 May 1971 England, 18 May 1971 Scotland, 22 May 1971 Wales, 13 October 1971 USSR, 16 February 1972 Spain, 20 May 1972 Scotland, 23 May 1972 England, 27 May 1972 Wales, 18 October 1972 Bulgaria, 14 February 1973 Cyprus, 28 March 1973 Portugal, 12 May 1973 England, 16 May 1973 Scotland, 19 May 1973 Wales, 14 November 1973 Portugal, 11 May 1974 Scotland, 15 May 1974 England, 18 May 1974 Wales, 4 September 1974 Norway, 30 October 1974 Sweden, 16 March 1975 Yugoslavia, 17 May 1975 England, 20 May 1975 Scotland, 23 May 1975 Wales, 3 September 1975 Sweden, 23 October 1975 Norway, 19 November 1975 Yugoslavia, 24 March 1976 Israel, 8 May 1976 Scotland, 11 May 1976 England, 14 May 1976 Wales, 13 October 1976 Holland, 10 November 1976 Belgium, 27 April 1977 West Germany, 28 May 1977 England, 1 June 1977 Scotland, 3 June 1977 Wales, 11 June 1977 Iceland, 11 September 1985 Turkey, 16 October 1985 Rumania, 13 November 1985 England, 26 February 1986 France, 26 March 1986 Denmark, 23 April 1986 Morocco, 3 June 1986 Algeria, 7 June 1986 Spain, 12 June 1986 Brazil (75 appearances)

Chris McGrath: 1 May 1974 Scotland, 15 May 1974 England, 18 May 1974 Wales, 4 September 1974 Norway, 24 March 1976 Israel (sub), 13 October 1976 Holland (1) (6 appearances 1 gl)

Gerard McMahon: 22 May 1995 Canada (sub), 26 May 1995 Chile, 7 June 1995 Latvia, 10 October 1995 Liechtenstein (1), 27 March 1996 Norway (sub), 24 April 1996 Sweden (1), 29 May 1996 Germany (7 appearances 2 goals)

Paul McVeigh: 27 April 1999 Canada (sub) (1) (1 appearance 1 goal)

Dick Rowley: 22 April 1931 Wales (1), 19 September 1931 Scotland (2 appearances 1 gl)

NORWAY

Espen Baardsen: 6 September 1998 Latvia, 20 January 1999 Israel, 18 August 99 Lithuania (sub), 31 January 2000 Iceland (4 appearances)

Frode Grodas: 25 February 1998 France, 22 April 1998 Denmark, 20 May 1998 Mexico, 27 May 1998 Saudi Arabia, 10 June 1998 Morocco, 16 June 1998 Scotland, 23 June 1998 Brazil, 27 June 1998 Italy (8 appearances)

Steffen Iversen: 14 October 1998 Albania (sub), 18 November 1998 Egypt, 27 March 1999 Greece, 28 April 1999 Georgia (1), 20 May 1999 Jamaica (1), 30 May 1999 Georgia (1), 5 June 1999 Albania (1), 18 August 1999 Lithuania, 4 September 1999 Greece, 8 September 99 Slovenia (1), 9 October 1999 Latvia, 14 November 1999 Germany, 29 March 2000 Switzerland, 26 April 2000 Belgium, 27 May 2000 Slovakia (sub) (1), 13 June 2000 Spain (1), 18 June 2000 Yugoslavia, 21 June 2000 Slovenia, 16 August 2000 Finland, 2 September 2000 Armenia, 7 October 2000 Wales, 11 October 2000 Ukraine, 24 March 2001 Poland (sub), 28 March 2001 Belarus, 15 August 2001 Turkey, 1 September 2001 Poland, 5 September 2001 Wales, 13 February 2002 Belgium, 17 April 2002 Sweden, 14 May 200 Japan, 22 May 2002 Iceland, 7 September 2002, Denmark, 12 October 2002 Rumania (1), 16 October 2002 Bosnia-Herzegovina, 20 November 2002 Austria, 30 April 2003 Republic of Ireland, 22 May 2003 Finland, 7 June 2003 Denmark, 11 June 2003 Rumania (sub) (39 appearances 8 goals)

Oyvind Leonhardsen: 18 August 1999 Lithuania, 4 September 1999 Greece (1), 8 September 1999 Slovenia (1), 9 October 1999 Latvia, 14 November 1999 Germany, 2 September 2000 Armenia, 7 October 2000 Wales, 11 October 2000 Ukraine, 25 April 2001 Bulgaria (2), 2 June 2001 Ukraine, 6 June 2001 Belarus, 1 September 2001 Poland, 5 September 2001 Wales, 13 February 2002 Belgium, 17 April 2002 Sweden, 14 May 2002 Japan, 22 May 2002 Iceland, 21 August 2002 Holland (sub) (18 appearances 4 goals)

Erik Thorstvedt: 2 May 1989 Poland, 21 May 1989 Cyprus, 23 August 1989 Greece, 5 September 1989 France, 11 October 1989 Yugoslavia, 15 November 1989 Scotland, 7 February 1990 Malta, 27 March 1990 Northern Ireland, 22 August 1990 Sweden, 12 September 1990 USSR, 10 October 1990 Hungary, 31 October 1990 Cameroon, 14 November 1990 Cyprus, 1 May 1991 Cyprus, 23 May 1991 Rumania, 5 June 1991 Italy, 28 August 1991 USSR, 25 September 1991 Czechoslovakia, 13 November 1991 Italy, 9 September 1992 San Marino, 23 September 1992 Holland, 7 October 1992 San Marino, 14 October 1992 England, 30 March 1993 v Qatar, 2 June 1993 England, 9 June 1993 Holland, 8 September 1993 USA, 22 September 1993 Poland, 10 November 1993 Turkey, 19 January 1994 Costa Rica, 22 May 1994 England, 1 June 1994 Denmark, 5 June 1994 Sweden, 19 June 1994 Mexico, 23 June 1994 Italy, 28 June 1994 Republic of Ireland, 12 October 1994 Holland, 6 February 1995 Estonia, 29 March 1995 Luxembourg, 25 May 1995 Ghana, 7 June 1995 Malta, 22 July 1995 France, 16 August 1995 Czech Republic, 6 September 1995 Czech Republic, 10 October 1995 England, 27 March 1996 Northern Ireland (sub) (46 appearances)

POLAND

Gregorz Rasiak: 3 September 2005 Austria, 7 September 2005 Wales, 7 October 2205 Iceland, 12 October 2005 England, 13 November 2005 Ecuador (sub) [while on loan to Southampton 1 March 2006 USA] (6 appearances)

PORTUGAL

Helder Postiga: 20 August 03 Kazakhstan (sub), 31 March 2004 Italy (sub), 28 April 2004 Sweden (sub), 29 May 2004 Luxembourg (sub), 5 June 200 Lithuania (sub) (1), 24 June 2004 England (sub) (1) (6 apps 2 goals)

REPUBLIC OF IRELAND

Steve Carr: 28 April 1999 Sweden, 29 May 1999 Northern Ireland, 9 June 1999 Macedonia, 1 September 1999 Yugoslavia (sub), 4 September 1999 Croatia, 8 September 1999 Malta, 13 November 1999 Turkey, 17 November 1999 Turkey, 30 May 2000 Scotland, 4 June 2000 Mexico, 6 June 2000 USA, 11 June 2000 South Africa, 2 September 2000 Holland, 7 October 2000 Portugal, 11 October 2000 Estonia, 25 April 2001 Andorra (sub), 2 June 2001 Portugal, 6 June 2001 Estonia, 12 February 2003 Scotland, 29 March 2003 Georgia, 2 April 2003 Albania, 30 April 2003 Norway, 7 June 2003 Albania, 16 June 2003 Georgia, 19 August 2003 Australia, 6 September 2003 Russia, 9 September 2003 Turkey (sub), 11 October 2003 Switzerland, 18 November 2003 Canada, 18 February 2004 Brazil (30 appearances)

Gary Doherty: 6 June 2000 USA, 11 June 2000 South Africa (sub), 24 March 2001 Cyprus (sub), 28 March 2001 Andorra (sub), 25 April 2001 Andorra, 2 June 2001 Portugal (sub), 6 June 2001 Estonia (sub), 17 April 2002 USA (sub) (1), 21 August 2002 Finland (sub), 7 September 2002 Russia (sub) (1), 16 October 2002 Switzerland (sub), 20 November 2002 Greece, 12 February 2003 Scotland, 12 February 2003 Scotland, 29 March 2003 Georgia (1), 2 April 2003 Albania (sub), 7 June 2003 Albania (sub) 16 June 2003 Georgia (1), 19 August 2003 Australia, 6 September 2003 Russia (sub), 9 September 2003 Turkey, 18 November 2003 Canada, 31 March 2004 Czech Republic, 28 April 2004 Poland, 29 May 2004 Nigeria, 2 June 2004 Jamaica, 18 August 2004 Bulgaria (27 appearances 4 goals)

Tony Galvin: 22 September 1982 Holland, 30 March 1983 Malta, 12 October 1983 Holland (sub), 4 April 1984 Israel (sub), 8 August 1984 Mexico, 12 September 1984 USSR, 17 October 1984 Norway, 14 November 1984 Denmark, 5 February 1985 Italy, 1 May 1985 Norway, 26 May 1985 Spain, 23 April 1986 Uruguay, 25 May 1986 Iceland, 27 May 1986 Czechoslovakia, 10 September 1986 Belgium, 18 February 1987 Scotland, 1 April 1987 Bulgaria, 29 April 1987 Belgium, 28 May 1987 Luxembourg (1) (19 appearances 1 goal)

Johnny Gavin: 1 May 1955 Holland, 28 May 1955 West Germany (2 appearances)

Jimmy Holmes: 30 March 1977 France, 24 April 1977 Poland, 1 June 1977 Bulgaria, 12 October 1977 Bulgaria, 5 April 1978 Turkey, 12 April 1978 Poland, 21 May 1978 Norway, 24 May 1978 Denmark, 20 September 1978 Northern Ireland, 25 October 1978 England, 2 May 1979 Denmark, 19 May 1979 Bulgaria (12 appearances)

Chris Hughton: 29 October 1979 USA, 6 February 1980 England, 30 April 1980 Switzerland, 16 May 1980 Argentina, 10 September 1980 Holland, 15 October 1980 Belgium, 28 October 1980 France, 19 November 1980 Cyprus (1), 24 February 1981 Wales, 25 March 1981 Belgium, 23 May 1981 Poland, 14 October 1981 France, 22 September 1982 Holland, 17 November 1982 Spain, 30 March 1983 Malta, 27 April 1983 Spain, 21 September 1983 Iceland, 12 October 1983 Holland, 16 November 1983 Malta, 8 August 1984 Mexico (sub), 12 September 1984 USSR, 17 October 1984 Norway, 5 February 1985 Italy, 27 February 1985 Israel, 26 March 1985 England, 26 May 1985 Spain, 11 September 1985 Switzerland, 16 October 1985 USSR, 23 April 1986 Uruguay, 25 May 1986 Iceland, 10 September 1986 Belgium, 1 April 1987 Bulgaria, 10 November 1987 Israel, 27 April 1988 Yugoslavia, 27 May 1988 Poland, 1 June 1988 Norway, 12 June 1988 England, 15 June 1988 USSR, 18 June 1988 Holland, 14 September 1988 Northern Ireland, 7 February 1989 France, 8 March 1989 Hungary, 26 April 1989 Spain, 28 May 1989 Malta, 4 June 1989 Hungary, 28 March 1990 Wales (sub), 25 April 1990 USSR (sub), 16 May 1990 Finland, 27 May 1990 Turkey (sub), 2 June 1990 Malta, 17 October 1990 Turkey (51 appearances 1 goal)

Robbie Keane: 7 September 2002 Russia, 16 October 2002 Switzerland, 2 April 2003 Albania, 30 April 2003 Norway, 7 June 2003 Albania (1), 16 June 2003 Georgia (1), 19 August 2003 Australia, 11 October 2003 Switzerland, 18 November 2003 Canada (2), 18 February 2004 Brazil, 31 March 2004 Czech Republic (1), 27 May 2004 Rumania, 29 May 2004 Nigeria, 5 June 2004 Holland (1), 4 September 2004 Cyprus (1), 8 September 2004 Switzerland, 9 October 2004 France, 13 October 2004 Faroe Islands (2), 16 11.2004 Croatia (1), 9 February 2005 Portugal,

26 March 2005 Israel, 29 March 2005 China, 4 June 2005 Israel (1), 7 September 2005 France, 8 October 2005 Cyprus, 12 October 2005 Switzerland, 1 March 2006 Sweden (1), 24 May 2006 Chile, 2 September 2006 Germany, 7 October 2006 Cyprus, 11 October 2006 Czech Republic, 15 November 2006 San Marino (3), 7 February 2007 San Marino, 24 March 2007 Wales, 22 August 2007 Denmark (2), 8 September 2007 Slovakia, 12 September 2007 Czech Republic, 13 October 2007 Germany, 17 October 2007, 17 November 2007 Wales (1), 6 February 2008 Brazil, 24 May 2008 Serbia, 29 May 2008 Columbia (1), 11 February 09 Georgia (2), 28 March 2009 Bulgaria, 1 April 2009 Italy (1), 29 May 2009 Nigeria (1), 6 June 2009 Bulgaria, 12 August 2009 Australia, 5 September 2009 Cyprus (1), 10 October 2009 Italy, 14 October 2009 Montenegro, 14 November 2009 France, 18 November 2009 France (1) [while on loan to Celtic – 2 March 2010 Brazil], 25 May 2010 Paraguay, 28 May 2010 Algeria (2), 11 August 2010 Argentina, 3 September 2010 Armenia, 7 September 2010 Andorra (1) , 8 October 2010 Russia (1), 12 October 2010 Slovakia, [while on loan to West Ham United 26 March 20 Macedonia (1)], 24 May 2011 Northern Ireland (2) (63 appearances 33 goals)
Stephen Kelly: 25 May 2006 Chile (1 appearance)
Joe Kinnear: 22 February 1967 Turkey, 22 November 1967 Czechoslovakia, 15 May 1968 Poland, 10 November 1968 Austria, 7 October 1969 Czechoslovakia, 15 October 1969 Denmark, 5 November 1969 Hungary, 6 May 1970 Poland, 28 October 1970 Sweden (sub), 10 May 1971 Italy, 18 June 1972 Iran, 19 June 1972 Ecuador, 21 June 1972 Chile, 25 June 1972 Portugal, 18 October 1972 USSR, 15 November 1972 France, 21 October 1973 Poland, 5 May 1974 Brazil, 8 May 1974 Uruguay, 12 May 1974 Chile, 30 October 1974 USSR, 20 November 1974 Turkey, 11 March 1975 West Germany "B", 11 May 1975 Switzerland, 18 May 1975 USSR (25 appearances)
Andy Reid: 9 February 2005 Portugal, 29 March 2005 China, 4 June 2005 Israel, 8 June 2005 Faroe Islands, 17 August 2005 Italy (1), 7 September 2005 France, 12 October 2005 Switzerland, 24 May 2006 Chile (sub) (8 appearances 1 goal))

RUMANIA

Ilie Dumitrescu: 7 September 1994 Azerbaijan, 8 October 1994 France, 12 October 1994 England (1), 12 November 1994 Slovakia, 14 December 1994 Israel, 29 March 1995 Poland, 26 April 1995 Azerbaijan (1), 7 June 1995 Israel, 10 October 1995 France, 15 November 1995 Slovakia (sub) (10 appearances 2 goals)
Gica Popescu: 8 October 1994 France, 12 October 1994 England, 12 November 1994 Slovakia (1), 14 December 1994 Israel, 29 March 1995 Poland, 26 April 1995 Azerbaijan (6 appearances 1 goal)

RUSSIA

Roman Pavlyuchenko: 10 September 2009 Wales (1), 28 March 2009 Azerbaijan (1), 1 April 2009 Liechtenstein, 10 June 2009 Finland (sub), 12 August 2009 Argentina (sub) (1), 5 September 2009 Liechtenstein (2), 9 September 2009 Wales (1), 10 October 2009 Germany (sub), 14 November 2009 Slovenia, 18 November 2009 Slovenia, 3 March 2010Hungary (sub) (1), 11 August 2010 Bulgaria (sub), 3 September 2010 Andorra (sub), 7 September 2010 Slovakia (sub), 9 February 2011 Iran, (sub) 29 March 2011 Qater (1) (16 appearances 8 goals)

SCOTLAND

Steve Archibald: 16 May 1980 Northern Ireland, 28 May 1980 Poland, 31 May 1980 Hungary (1), 10 September 1980 Sweden (sub), 25 February 1981 Israel, 25 March 1981 Northern Ireland, 28 April 1981 Israel, 19 May 1981 Northern Ireland (1), 23 May 1981 England, 14 October 1981 Northern Ireland, 18 November 1981 Portugal, 24 February 1982 Spain (sub), 23 March 1982

Holland, 15 June 1982 New Zealand (sub) (1), 18 June 1982 Brazil, 23 June 1982 Russia, 13 October 1982 East Germany, 17 November 1982 Switzerland (sub), 15 December 1982 Belgium, 16 November 1983 East Germany, 26 May 1984 England, 1 June 1984 France (22 appearances 3 goals)

Alan Brazil: 28 May 1983 Wales (1), 1 June 1983 England (sub) (2 appearances 1gl)

Sandy Brown: 5 April 1902 England (later declared unofficial due to Ibrox disaster) (1 appearance)

Bill Brown: 3 October 1959 Wales, 14 November 1959 Northern Ireland, 4 May 1960 Poland, 29 May 1960 Austria, 5 June 1960 Hungary, 8 June 1960 Turkey, 26 September 1961 Czechoslovakia, 7 October 1961 Northern Ireland, 8 November 1961 Wales, 14 April 1962 England, 20 October 1962 Wales, 7 November 1962 Northern Ireland, 6 April 1963 England, 8 May 1963 Austria, 12 October 1963 Northern Ireland, 7 November 1963 Wales, 20 November 1963 Norway, 10 April 1965 England, 8 May 1965 Spain, 23 May 1965 Poland, 27 May 1965 Finland, 2 October 1965 Northern Ireland, 13 October 1965 Poland, 9 November 1965 Italy (24 appearances)

Colin Calderwood: 29 March 1995 Russia, 26 April 1995 San Marino (1), 21 May 1995 Japan, 24 May 1995 Ecuador, 7 June 1995 Faroe Islands, 16 August 1995 Greece, 6 September 1995 Finland, 10 October 1995 Sweden, 15 November 1995 San Marino, 26 May 1996 USA, 30 May 1996 Colombia, 10 June 1996 Holland, 15 June 1996 England, 18 June 1996 Switzerland, 31 August 1996 Austria, 5 October 1996 Latvia, 9.101996 Estonia (aban), 10 November 1996 Sweden, 11 February 1997 Estonia, 29 March 1997 Estonia, 2 April 1997 Austria, 30 April 1997 Sweden, 7 September 1997 Belarus, 11 October 1997 Latvia, 12 November 1997 France, 25 March 1998 Denmark, 22 April 1998 Finland, 23 May 1998 Colombia, 30 May 1998 USA, 10 June 1998 Brazil, 16 June 1998 Norway, 5 September 1998 Lithuania, 10 October 1998 Estonia (33 appearances 1 goal)

Alfie Conn: 20 May 1975 Northern Ireland (sub), 24 May 1975 England (2 appearances)

Gordon Durie: 11 September 1991 Switzerland (1), 16 October 1991 Rumania, 13 November 1991 San Marino (1), 19 February 1992 Northern Ireland (sub), 25 March 1992 Finland, 21 May 1992 Canada, 3 June 1992 Norway (sub), 12 June 1992 Holland, 15 June 1992 Germany, 9 September 1992 Switzerland, 18 November 1992 Italy, 8 September 1993 Switzerland, 13 October 1993 Italy (13 appearances 2 goals)

Alan Gilzean: 8 May 1965 Spain, 2 October 1965 Northern Ireland (2), 13 October 1965 Poland, 9 November 1965 Italy, 24 November 1965 Wales, 22 November 1967 Wales (2), 6 November 1968 Austria (sub), 11 December 1968 Cyprus (2), 16 April 1969 West Germany, 3 May 1969 Wales (1), 10 May 1969 England, 17 May 1969 Cyprus, 22 October 1969 West Germany (1), 5 November 1969 Austria, 18 April 1970 Northern Ireland, 25 April 1970 England (sub), 21 April 1971 Portugal (17 appearances 8 goals)

Richard Gough: 10 September 1986 Bulgaria, 15 October 1986 Republic of Ireland, 12 November 1986 Luxembourg, 18 February 1987 Republic of Ireland, 1 April 1987 Belgium, 23 May 1987 England, 26 May 1987 Brazil, 9 September 1987 Hungary (8 appearances)

Alan Hutton: 26 March 2008 Croatia, 19 November 2008 Argentina, 28 March 2009 Holland (sub), 1 April 2009 Iceland, 12 August 2009 Norway, 5 September 2009 Macedonia, 9 September 2009 Holland, 14 November 2009 Wales, [while on loan to Sunderland - 3 March 2010 Czech Republic], 3 September 2010 Lithuania, 7 September 2010 Liechtenstein, 8 October 2010 Czech Republic, 9 February 2011 Northern Ireland, 27 March 2011 Brazil (14 appearances)

Dave Mackay: 11 April 1959 England, 6 May 1959 West Germany, 3 October 1959 Northern Ireland, 14 November 1959 Wales, 4 May 1960 Poland, 29 May 1960 Austria (1), 5 June 1960 Hungary, 8 June 1960 Turkey, 22 October 1960 Wales, 9 November 1960 Northern Ireland, 15 April 1961 England (1), 6 April 1963 England, 8 May 1963 Austria, 4 June 1963 Norway, 12 October 1963 Northern Ireland, 7 November 1963 Norway (2), 20 November 1963 Wales, 2 October 1965 Northern Ireland (18 appearances 4 goals)

Jimmy Robertson: 3 October 1964 Wales (1 appearance)
Neil Sullivan: 2 September 2000 Latvia, 7 October 2000 San Marino, 11 October 2000 Croatia, 24 March 2001 Belgium, 28 March 2001 San Marino, 25 April 2001 Poland, 1 September 2001 Croatia, 5 September 2001 Belgium, 6 October 2001 Latvia, 27 March 2002 France, 16 May 2002 South Korea, 12 February 2003 Republic of Ireland (12 appearances)
John White: 14 November 1959 Wales, 4 May 1960 Poland, 29 May 1960 Austria, 8 June 1960 Turkey, 22 October 1960 Wales, 26 September 1961 Czechoslovakia, 7 October 1961 Northern Ireland, 8 November 1961 Wales, 29 November 1961 Czechoslovakia, 14 April 1962 England, 20 October 1962 Wales, 7 November 1962 Northern Ireland, 6 April 1963 England, 12 October 1963 Northern Ireland, 7 November 1963 Norway, 20 November 1963 Wales (1), 11 April 1964 England, 12 May 1964 West Germany (18 appearances 1 goal)

SERBIA-MONTENEGRO (formerly Yugoslavia)

Goran Bunjevcevic: 12 February 2003 Azerbaijan, 11 October 2003 Wales (2 appearances)

SLOVENIA

Milenko Acimovic: 17 May 2002 Ghana, 2 June 2002 Spain (sub), 8 June 2002 South Africa, 12 June 2002 Paraguay (1), 21 August 2002 Italy (sub), 7 September 2002 Malta, 12 February 2003 Switzerland, 7 June 2003 Israel, 20 August 03 Hungary, 6 September 2003 Israel, 10 September 2003 France, 11 October 2003 Cyprus, 15 November 2003 Croatia, 19 November 2003 Croatia, [while on loan to Lille 18 February 2004 Poland, 31 March 2004 Latvia] (16 appearances 1 goal)

SOUTH AFRICA

Bongani Khumalo: 9 February 2011 Kenya, [while on loan to Preston North End 26 March 2011 Egypt] (2 appearances)
Mbulelo Mabizela: 11 October 2003 Costa Rica, 15 November 2003 Egypt, 19 November 2003 Tunisia, 17 January 2004 Senegal. 27 January 2004 Benin, 31 January 2004 Nigeria, 4 February 2004 Morocco, 30 March 2004 Australia, 5 June 2004 Cape Verde Islands (2), 20 June 2004 Ghana, 3 July 2004 Burkina Faso, 18 August 2004 Tunisia, 5 September 2004 DR Congo (13 apps 2 goals)
Steven Pienaar: 9 February 2011 Kenya (1), 26 March 2011 Egypt (2 appearances 1 goal)

SOUTH KOREA

Lee Young-Pyo: 12 November 2005 Sweden, 16 November 2005 Serbia & Montenegro, 1 March 2006 Angola, 26 May 2006 Bosnia & Herzegovina, 1 June 2006 Norway, 4 June 2006 Ghana, 13 June 2006 Togo, 18 June 2006 France, 23 June 2006 Switzerland, 2 September 2006 Iran, 6 September 2006 Chinese Taipei, 11 October 2006 Syria, 6 February 2007 Greece, 24 March 2007 Uruguay, 6 February 2008 Turkmenistan, 26 March 2008 PR Korea, 31 May 2008 Jordan, 7 June 2008 Jordan (18 appearances)

SWEDEN

Erik Edman: 18 August 2004 Holland, 4 September 2004 Malta, 8 September 2004 Croatia, 9 February 2005 France, 26 March 2005 Bulgaria (1), 4 June 2005 Malta, 17 August 2005 Czech Republic (7 appearances 1 goal)

SWITZERLAND

Ramon Vega: 30 April 1997 Hungary, 11 October 1997 Azerbaijan, 25 March 1998 England (1), 22 April 1998 Northern Ireland, 2 September 1998 Yugoslavia (sub), 10 October 1998 Italy (6 apps 1 goal)
Reto Ziegler: 26 March 2005 France, 30 March 2005 Cyprus, 4 June 2005 Faroe Islands (sub) (3 appearances)

UKRAINE

Sergei Rebrov: 2 September 2000 Poland, 7 October 2000 Armenia, 11 October 2000 Norway, 24 March 2001 Belarus, 28 March 2001 Wales, 2 June 2001 Norway, 6 June 2001 Wales, 1 September 2001 Belarus, 5 September 2001 Armenia, 10 November 2001 Germany, 14 November 2001 Germany (sub), 27 March 2002 Rumania, 17 April 2002 Georgia (1), 17 May 2002 Yugoslavia, 20 May 2002 Belarus, 21 August 2002 Iran, 12 October 2002 Greece (sub), 16 October 2002 Northern Ireland (sub) [Whilst on loan to Fenerbahce –12 February 2003 Turkey, 30 April 2003 Denmark, 7 June 2003 Armenia, 11 June 2003 Greece, 20 August 2003 Rumania (sub), 6 September 2003 Northern Ireland, 11 October 2003 Macedonia (sub), 18,2,2004 Libya, 31 March 2004 Macedonia (sub), 28 April 2004 Slovakia (sub), 6 June 2004 France (sub)] (29 appearances 1 gl)

UNITED STATES OF AMERICA

Kasey Keller: 19 January 2002 Korea Republic, 21 January 2002 Cuba, 27 January 2002 El Salvador, 30 January 2002 Canada, 2 February 2002 Costa Rica, 2 March 2002 Honduras, 27 March 2002 Germany, 17 April 2002 Republic of Ireland (sub), 16 May 2002 Jamaica, 19 May 2002 Holland (sub), 29 March 2003 Venezuela, 6 July 2003 Paraguay, 12 July 2003 El Salvador, 14 July 2003 Martinique, 19 July 03 Cuba, 23 July 2003 Brazil, 26 July 2003 Costa Rica, 18 February 2004 Holland, 13 June 2004 Grenada, 20 June 2004 Grenada. 18 August 2004 Jamaica, 8 September 2004 Panama, 9 October 2004 El Salvador, 13 October 2004 Panama [while on loan to Southampton – 17 November 2004 Jamaica] (25 apps)

WALES

Gareth Bale: 22 August 2007 Bulgaria, 8 September 2007 Germany, 12 September 2007 Slovakia, 13 October 2007 Cyprus, 17 October 2007 San Marino, 6 September 2008 Azerbaijan, 10 September 2008 Russia, 11 October 2008 Liechtenstein, 15 October 2008 Germany, 19 November 2008 Denmark, 11 February 09 Poland, 28 March 2009 Finland, 1 April 2009 Germany, 29 May 2009 Estonia, 10 October 2009 Finland, 14 October 2009 Liechtenstein, 14 November 2009 Scotland, 3 March 2010 Sweden, 3 September 2010 Montenegro, 8 October 2010 Bulgaria, 12 October 2010 Switzerland (1) (21 appearances 1 goal)

Mark Bowen: 10 May 1986 Canada (sub), 20 May 1986 Canada (sub) (2 appearances)

Ron Burgess: 19 October 1946 Scotland, 13 November 1946 England, 16 April 1947 Northern Ireland, 18 October 1947 England, 12 November 1947 Scotland, 23.101948 Scotland, 10 November 1948 England, 9 March 1949 Northern Ireland, 15 May 1949 Portugal, 23 May 1949 Belgium, 26 May 1949 Switzerland, 15 October 1949 England, 9 November 1949 Scotland, 23 November 1949 Belgium, 8 March 1950 Northern Ireland, 21 October 1950 Scotland, 7 March 1951 Northern Ireland, 12 May 1951 Portugal, 16 May 1951 Switzerland (1), 20 October 1951 England, 20 November 1951 Scotland, 5 December 1951 Rest of the UK, 19 March 1952 Northern Ireland, 18 October 1952 Scotland, 12 November 1952 England, 15 April 1953 Northern Ireland, 14 May 1953 France, 21 May 1953 Yugoslavia, 10 October 1953 England, 4 November 1953 Scotland, 31 March 1954 Northern Ireland, 9 May 1954 Austria (32 apps 1 goal)

Simon Davies: 28 March 2001 Ukraine (sub), 6 June 2001 Ukraine, 1 September 2001 Armenia, 5 September 2001 Norway, 6 October 2001 Belarus, 13 February 2002 Argentina, 27 March 2002 Czech Republic, 14 May 2002 Germany, 21 August 2002 Croatia (1), 7 September 2002 Finland (1), 16 October 2002 Italy (1), 20 November 2002 Azerbaijan, 12 February 2003 Bosnia-Herzegovenia, 29 March 2003 Azerbaijan, 25 May 2003 USA, 20 August 03 Serbia-Montenegro, 6 September 2003 Italy, 10 September 2003 Finland (1), 18 February 2004 Scotland, 9 October 2004 England, 13 October 2004 Poland (21 apps 4 goals)

Alf Day: 4 November 1933 Northern Ireland (1 appearance)
Mike England: 22 October 1966 Scotland, 16 November 1966 England, 21 October 1967 England, 28 February 1968 Northern Ireland, 8 May 1968 West Germany, 16 April 1969 East Germany, 28 July 1969 Rest of U.K., 22 October 1969 East Germany, 4 November 1969 Italy (1), 18 April 1970 England, 22 April 1970 Scotland, 25 April 1970 Northern Ireland, 11 November 1970 Rumania, 13 October 1971 Finland, 20 May 1972 England, 24 May 1972 Scotland, 27 May 1972 Northern Ireland, 15 November 1972 England, 24 January 1973 England, 12 May 1973 Scotland, 15 May 1973 England, 26 September 1973 Poland, 30 October 1974 Hungary, 20 November 1974 Luxembourg (1) (24 appearances 2 goals)
Willie Evans: 7 December 1932 Northern Ireland, 4 October 1933 Scotland (1), 15 November 1933 England, 29 September 1934 England, 5 February 1936 England, 11 March 1936 Northern Ireland (6 appearances 1 goal)
Chris Gunter: 6 February 2008 Norway, 28 May 2008 Iceland, 1 June 2008 Holland, 6 September 2008 Azerbaijan, 10 September 2008 Russia, 11 October 2008 Liechtenstein, 15 October 2008 Germany, 19 November 2008 Denmark, 11 February 09 Poland, [while on loan to Nottingham forest – 28 March 2009 Finland, 1 April 2009 Germany (sub)], 29 May 2009 Estonia, 6 June 2009 Azerbaijan (13 appearances)
Mel Hopkins: 11 April 1956 Northern Ireland, 20 October 1956 Scotland, 14 November 1956 England, 10 April 1957 Northern Ireland, 1 May 1957 Czechoslovakia, 19 May 1957 East Germany, 26 May 1957 Czechoslovakia, 25 September 1957 East Germany, 19 October 1957 England, 13 November 1957 Scotland, 15 January 1958 Israel, 5 February 1958 Israel, 10 April 1958 Northern Ireland, 8 June 1958 Hungary, 11 June 1958 Mexico, 15 June 1958 Sweden, 17 June 1958 Hungary, 19 June 1958 Brazil, 18 October 1958 Scotland, 26 November 1958 England, 22 April 1959 Northern Ireland, 17 October 1959 England, 4 November 1959 Scotland, 12 April 1961 Northern Ireland, 19 April 1961 Spain, 18 May 1961 Spain, 26 May 1961 Hungary, 11 April 1962 Northern Ireland, 12 May 1962 Brazil, 16 May 1962 Brazil, 22 May 1962 Mexico, 20 October 1962 Scotland, 7 November 1962 Hungary, 3 April 1963 Northern Ireland (34 appearances)
Ted Hughes: 2 March 1901 Scotland, 18 March 1901 England, 22 February 1902 Ireland, 29 February 1904 England, 12 March 1904 Scotland, 21 March 1904 Ireland, 6 March 1905 Scotland, 27 March 1905 England, 8 April 1905 Ireland, 3 March 1906 Scotland, 2 April 1906 Ireland, 18 March 1907 England (12 appearances)
Cliff Jones: 16 April 1958 Northern Ireland, 8 June 1958 Hungary, 11 June 1958 Mexico, 15 June 1958 Sweden, 17 June 1958 Hungary, 19 June 1958 Brazil, 22 April 1959 Northern Ireland, 17 October 1959 England, 4 November 1959 Scotland, 6 April 1960 Northern Ireland, 28 September 1960 Republic of Ireland (2), 22 October 1960 Scotland (1), 23 November 1960 England, 12 April 1961 Northern Ireland (2), 18 May 1961 Spain, 28 May 1961 Hungary (1), 14 October 1961 England, 8 November 1961 Scotland, 11 April 1962 Northern Ireland, 12 May 1962 Brazil, 16 May 1962 Brazil, 22 May 1962 Mexico, 20 October 1962 Scotland, 20 March 1963 Hungary (1), 3 April 1963 Northern Ireland (3), 12 October 1963 England, 20 November 1963 Scotland, 15 April 1964 Northern Ireland, 3 October 1964 Scotland, 21 October 1964 Denmark, 18 November 1964 England (1), 9 December 1964 Greece, 17 March 1965 Greece, 31 March 1965 Northern Ireland (1), 1 May 1965 Italy, 30 May 1965 USSR, 22 October 1966 Scotland, 16 November 1966 England, 21 October 1967 England, 22 November 1967 Scotland, 8 May 1968 West Germany (41 appearances 12 goals)
John L Jones: 19 February 1898 Ireland, 19 March 1898 Scotland, 28 March 1898 England, 4 March 1899 Ireland, 18 March 1899 Scotland, 3 February 1900 Scotland, 22 February 1902 Ireland, 3 March 1902 England, 15 March 1902 Scotland, 29 February 1904 England, 12 March 1904 Scotland, 21 March 1904 Ireland (12 appearances)
Ernie Jones: 23 October 1948 Scotland, 10 November 1948 England (2 appearances)

Terry Medwin: 28 October 1956 Scotland (1), 14 November 1956 England, 10 April 1957 Northern Ireland, 1 May 1957 Czechoslovakia, 19 May 1957 East Germany, 26 May 1957 Czechoslovakia, 19 October 1957 England, 13 November 1957 Scotland (1), 15 January 1958 Israel, 5 February 1958 Israel, 16 April 1958 Northern Ireland, 8 June 1958 Hungary, 11 June 1958 Mexico, 17 June 1958 Hungary (1), 19 June 1958 Brazil, 18 October 1958 Scotland, 26 November 1958 England, 22 April 1959 Northern Ireland, 17 October 1959 England, 4 November 1959 Scotland, 6 April 1960 Northern Ireland (2), 28 September 1960 Republic of Ireland, 22 October 1960 Scotland, 23 November 1960 England, 19 April 1961 Spain, 7 November 1962 Hungary (1), 21 November 1962 England (27 appearances 6 goals)
Taffy O'Callaghan: 2 February 1929 Northern Ireland, 26 October 1929 Scotland (1), 31 October 1931 Scotland, 18 November 1931 England, 26 October 1932 Scotland (2), 16 November 1932 England, 7 December 1932 Northern Ireland, 4 October 1933 Scotland, 4 November 1933 Northern Ireland, 15 November 1933 England, 29 September 1934 England (11 appearances 3 goals)
Paul Price: 18 November 1981 USSR, 24 March 1982 Spain, 2 June 1982 France, 22 September 1982 Norway, 15 December 1982 Yugoslavia, 23 February 1983 England, 27 April 1983 Bulgaria, 28 May 1983 Scotland, 31 May 1983 Northern Ireland, 21 September 1983 Norway, 12 October 1983 Rumania, 16 November 1983 Bulgaria, 14 December 1983 Yugoslavia, 28 February 1984 Scotland (sub) (14 appearances)
Billy Rees: 8 March 1950 Northern Ireland (1 appearance)
Bill Whatley: 22 October 1938 England, 9 November 1938 Scotland (2 appearances)
Terry Yorath: 11 September 1979 Republic of Ireland, 21 November 1979 Turkey, 17 May 1980 England, 21 May 1980 Scotland, 23 May 1980 Northern Ireland, 2 June 1980 Iceland, 15 October 1980 Turkey, 19 November 1980 Czechoslovakia (8 appearances)

YUGOSLAVIA

Goran Bunjevcevic: 6 September 2002 Czech Republic (1 appearance)

INTERNATIONAL TRIALS

ENGLAND

Wally Alsford: 27 March 1935 Rest v. England (1 appearance)
Bert Bliss: 9 February 1920 South v. England, 7 February 1921 South v. England (2 appearances)
Tom Bradshaw: 1 February 1899 South v. North (1 appearance)
John Brearley: 16 January 1905 Professionals of the South v. Amateurs of the South (1 appearance)
Walter Bull: 13 February 1905 South v. North, 8 January 1906 Professionals of South v. Amateurs of South, 22 January 1906 South v. North (3 appearances)
Fred Channell: 27 March 1935 Rest v. England (1 appearance)
George Clawley: 21 January 1903 South v. North (1 appearance)
Tommy Clay: 14 April 1919 South v. North, 22 February 1922 England v. South, 12 February 1923 South v. England (3 appearances)
John Curtis: 31 January 1910 Whites v. Stripes (1 appearance)
Jimmy Dimmock: 7 February 1921 South v. England, 28 February 1921 England v. North (1), 10 February 1926 Rest v. England (3 appearances 1 goal)
Jack Elkes: 21 January 1924 South v. North, 11 February 1924 Rest v. England, 19 January 1925 South v. North, 18 January 1926 Rest v. England (4 appearances)
Matt Forster: 7 February 1927 Rest v. England (1 appearance)

Arthur Grimsdell: 24 November 1913 South v. England, 14 April 1919 South v. North, 9 February 1920 England v. South, 25 February 1920 England v. North (1), 7 February 1921 England v. South, 28 February 1921 England v. North, 6 January 1922 England v. North, 22 February 1922 England v. South, 12 February 1923 South v. England (9 appearances 1 goal)
Willie Hall: 13 October 1937 Probables v. Possibles (1 appearance)
George Hunt: 22 March 1933 Rest v. England (2) (1 appearance 2 goals)
Bert Middlemiss: 25 January 1909 South v. North, 22 January 1912 Stripes v. Whites, 25 November 1912 South v. England, 24 November 1913 South v. England (4 appearances)
Tom Morris: 7 March 1900 South v. North, 26 January 1903 South v. North (2 appearances)
Joe Nicholls: 21 March 1934 Rest v. England (1 appearance)
Frank Osbourne: 19 January 1925 South v. North (2), 18 January 1926 England v. Rest (2 appearances 2 goals)
Jimmy Seed: 22 February 1922 South v. England, 12 February 1923 South v. England, 19 January 1925 South v. North (1), 9 February 1925 England v. Rest (4 appearances 1 goal)
Bert Smith: 9 February 1920 South v. England, 7 February 1921 England v. South, 22 February 1922 South v. England, 21 January 1924 South v. North (4 appearances 1 goal)
Cyril Spiers: 4 March 1931 Rest v. England (1 appearance)
Fanny Walden: 21 January 1914 England v. North, 22 February 1922 South v. England, 12 February 1923 South v. England (3 appearances)
Joe Walton: 16 January 1905 Southern Professionals v. Southern Amateurs, 13 February 1905 South v. North (1), 8 January 1906 Southern Professionals v. Southern Amateurs (3 appearances 1 goal)
Vivian Woodward: 26 January 1903 South v. North (1), 25 January 1904 South v. North, 13 February 1905 South v. North, 3 January 1906 Amateurs v. Professionals, 8 January 1906 Southern Amateurs v. Southern Professionals, 22 January 1906 South v. North (1), 27 January 1908 South v. North, 25 January 1909 South v. North (8 appearances 2 goals)

SCOTLAND

Sandy Brown: 24 March 1902 Anglo-Scots v. Home Scots (1 appearance)
Tom Collins: 20 March 1911 Anglo-Scots v. Home Scots, 11 March 1912 Anglo-Scots v. Home Scots (2 appearances)
David Copeland: 23 March 1903 Anglo-Scots v. Home Scots (1 appearance)
Alex Lindsay: 20 March 1923 Anglo-Scots v. Home Scots (1 appearance)
James McNaught: 28 March 1899 Anglo-Scots v. Home Scots (1 appearance)
Danny Steel: 22 March 1908 Anglo-Scots v. Home Scots, 21 March 1910 Anglo-Scots v. Home Scots, 11 March 1912 Anglo-Scots v. Home Scots (3 appearances)
Bobby Steel: 22 March 1909 Anglo-Scots v. Home Scots (1 appearance)
Sandy Tait: 23 March 1903 Anglo-Scots v. Home Scots (1 appearance)

B INTERNATIONALS

ENGLAND

Darren Anderton: 21 April 1998 Russia (1 appearance)
Eddie Baily: 18 January 1950 Switzerland, 11 May 1950 Italy, 17 May 1950 Holland (3 appearances)
Nicky Barmby: 13 December 1994 Republic of Ireland (sub) (1 appearance)
Sol Campbell: 13 December 1994 Republic of Ireland (1 appearance)
Michael Carrick: 25 May 2006 Belarus (1 appearance)
Harry Clarke: 24 March 1954 West Germany (1 appearance)

Michael Dawson: 25 May 2006 Belarus (sub), 2 May 2007 Albania (2 appearances)
Jermain Defoe: 25 May 2006 Belarus (sub), 24 May 2007 Albania (sub) (2 appearances)
Ted Ditchburn: 18 May 1949 Holland, 18 January 1950 Switzerland (2 appearances)
Chris Fairclough: 14 October 1987 Malta (1 appearance)
Les Ferdinand: 21 April 1998 Russia (1) (1 appearance 1 goal)
Paul Gascoigne: 16 May 1989 Switzerland (1), 19 May 1989 Iceland, 14 November 1989 Italy, 12 December 1989 Yugoslavia (4 appearances 1 goal)
Tommy Harmer: 26 March 1952 Holland (1 appearance)
Glenn Hoddle: 12 June 1979 Austria (abandoned), 15 October 1979 New Zealand (1) (2 appearances 1 goal)
Jermaine Jenas: 25 May 2006 Belarus (1), 24 May 2007 Albania (2 appearances 1 goal)
Ledley King: 24 May 2007 Albania (1 appearance)
Aaron Lennon: 25 May 2006 Belarus, 24 May 2007 Albania (2 appearances)
Gary Mabbutt: 13 November 1984 New Zealand (1),16 May 1989 Switzerland, 19 May 1989 Iceland, 22 May 1989 Norway, 11 December 1990 Algeria, 5 February 1991 Wales, 27 April 1991 Iceland, 18 February 1992 France, 28 April 1992 CIS (9 appearances)
Tony Marchi: 6 February 1957 Scotland (1 appearance)
Bill Nicholson: 19 May 1948 Switzerland, 18 January 1950 Switzerland, 11 May 1950 Italy, 17 May 1950 Holland (4 appearances)
George Robb: 24 March 1954 West Germany, 16 May 1954 Yugoslavia, 22 May 1954 Switzerland (3 appearances)
Graham Roberts: 13 November 1984 New Zealand (1 appearance)
Paul Stewart: 16 May 1989 Switzerland (sub), 19 May 1989 Iceland, 22 May 1989 Norway, 27 April 1991 Iceland, 18 February 1992 France (1) (5 appearances 1 goal)
Alfie Stokes: 6 February 1957 Scotland (1 appearance)
Mitchell Thomas: 14 October 1987 Malta (1 appearance)
Ian Walker: 21 April 1998 Russia (1 appearance)
Sonny Walters: 22 February 1950 Holland (1 appearance)
Charlie Withers: 26 March 1952 Holland (1 appearance)

NORTHERN IRELAND

Gerard McMahon: 10 May 1994 England (sub), 21 February 1995 Scotland (sub) (2 appearances)
Steve Robinson: 10 May 1994 England (sub) (1 appearance)

REPUBLIC OF IRELAND

Ross Darcy: 17 March 1997 FAI National League (1 appearance)
Neale Fenn: 11 March 1998 Northern Ireland, 9 February 1999 FAI National League (2) (2 appearances 2 goals)
Peter Gain: 17 March 1997 FAI National League (1 appearance)
David McDonald: 12 February 1992 Denmark (1 appearance)
Kevin Maher: 17 March 1997 FAI National League (sub) (1 appearance)

UNDER-23 INTERNATIONALS

ENGLAND

Les Allen: 8 February 1961 Wales (1 appearance)
Martin Chivers: 7 February 1968 Scotland (1), 1 May 1968 Hungary (1), 26 May 1968 Italy, 30 May 1968 Hungary, 2 June 1968 West Germany (5 appearances 2 goals)

Jimmy Greaves: 28 February 1962 Scotland (2) (1 appearance 2 goals)
Jim Iley: 23 April 1958 Wales (1 appearance)
Cyril Knowles: 4 November 1964 Wales, 12 October 1966 Wales (1), 1 March 1967 Scotland, 31 May 1967 Greece, 4 June 1967 Bulgaria, 7 June 1967 Turkey (6 appearances 1 goal)
Roger Morgan: 8 April 1970 Bulgaria (2) (1 appearance 2 goals)
Maurice Norman: 8 February 1956 Scotland, 24 May 1957 Rumania, 31 May 1957 Czechoslovakia (3 appearances)
Steve Perryman: 1 June 1972 East Germany, 4 June 1972 Poland, 7 June 1972 USSR, 13 February 1973 Scotland, 24 May 1973 Denmark, 29 May 1973 Holland, 1 June 1973 Czechoslovakia, 16 October 1973 Poland, 13 November 1973 Denmark, 16 January 1974 Wales, 13 March 1974 Scotland, 11 May 1974 Turkey, 15 May 1974 Yugoslavia, 28 October 1974 Czechoslovakia, 19 November 1974 Portugal, 18 December 1974 Scotland, 21 January 1975 Wales (17 appearances)
Alfie Stokes: 28 September 1955 Denmark (2) (1 appearance 2 goals)

NORTHERN IRELAND

Phil Gray: 15 May 1990 Republic of Ireland (1 appearance)
Mark Hughes: 27 April 2004 Serbia-Montenegro (sub) (1 appearance)
Richard Johnston: 11 April 1989 Republic of Ireland (sub) (1 appearance)

SCOTLAND

Alfie Conn: 31 May 1975 Rumania, 28 October 1975 Denmark, 16 December 1975 Rumania (3 appearances)
Jimmy Robertson: 17 May 1964 France (2), 2 December 1964 Wales, 7 February 1968 England (3 appearances 2 goals)
John White: 25 November 1959 Wales (1 appearance)

WALES

John Collins: 12 October 1966 England, 22 February 1967 Northern Ireland (abandoned), 1 November 1967 England, 20 March 1968 Northern Ireland, 2 October 1968 England (5 appearances)
Mel Hopkins: 23 April 1958 England (1 appearance)
Cliff Jones: 23 April 1958 England (1 appearance)

UNDER-21 INTERNATIONALS

BELGIUM

Jonathan Blondel: 6 September 2002 Bulgaria (1), 15 October 2002 Estonia, 19 November 2002 Scotland, 28 March 2003 Croatia, 29 April 2003 Poland, 6 June 2003 Bulgaria (sub), 10 October 2003 Estonia (1), 4 November 2003 England Non-League (8 appearances 2 goals)

CZECH REPUBLIC

Tomas Pekhart: 21 August 2007 Scotland, 8 September 2007 Armenia (sub) (1), 11 September 2007 Liechtenstein (2), 14 October 2007 Liechtenstein (1), 17 October 2007 Armenia (1), 17 November 2007 Turkey.26 March 2008 France (1), 19 August 2008 Portugal, 6 September 2008 Turkey (sub), [while on loan to Southampton 18 November 2008 England], [while on loan to Slavia Prague – 27 March 2009 Egypt, 29 March 2009 South Korea (sub), 9 June 2009 San Marino (3)] (13 appearances 9 goals)

ENGLAND

Paul Allen: 10 September 1985 Rumania (1 appearance)

Rory Allen: 14 May 1998 France (sub), 16 May 98 South Africa, 18 May 98 Argentina (sub). (3 appearances)

Ben Alnwick: 21 August 2007 Rumania (sub) (1 app)

Darren Anderton: 8 September 1992 Spain (1), 16 February 1993 San Marino (1), 27 April 1993 Holland (1), 28 May 1993 Poland (1), 1 June 1993 Norway, 7 June 1993 Portugal, 9 June 1993 Czechoslovakia, 11 June 1993 Brazil, 13 June 1993 Scotland, 15 June 1993 France, 7 September 1993 Poland, 17 November 1993 San Marino (1) (12 appearances 5 goals)

Nicky Barmby: 8 March 1994 Denmark, 6 September 1994 Portugal, 11 October 1994 Austria (sub) (3 appearances)

Guy Butters: 5 June 1989 Bulgaria, 7 June 1989 Senegal, 9 June 1989 Republic of Ireland (sub) (3 appearances)

Sol Campbell: 8 March 1994 Denmark, 29 May 1994 Russia, 31 May 1994 France, 2 June 1994 USA, 5 June 1994 Belgium (1), 7 June 1994 Portugal, 6 September 1994 Portugal, 11 October 1994 Austria, 15 November 1994 Republic of Ireland, 10 October 1995 Norway (1), 14 November 1995 Austria (11 appearances 2 goals)

Fraizer Campbell: [On loan from Manchester United – 5 September 2008 Portugal (sub), 10 October 2008 Wales, 14 October 2008 Wales, 18 November 2008 Czech Republic (1), 10 February 2009 Ecuador (1), 27 March 2009 Norway (1), 31 March 2009 France (sub), 8 June 2009 Azerbaijan, 15 June 2009 Finland (sub), 18 June 2008 Spain (sub) (1), 22 June 2009 Germany] (11 appearances 3goals)

Steve Caulker: [while on loan to Bristol City - 16 November 2010 Germany (sub)] (1 appearance)

Stephen Clemence: 4 September 1998 Sweden (sub) (1 appearance)

Richard Cooke: 12 March 1986 Denmark (sub) (1 appearance)

Calum Davenport: 3 September 2004 Austria, 7 September 2004 Poland, [while on loan to West Ham United 8 October 2004 Wales, 12 October 2004 Azerbaijan, 16 November 2004 Spain (sub)], [while on loan to Southampton - 25 March 2005 Germany, 29 March 2005 Azerbaijan], 16 August 2005 Denmark (8 appearances)

Michael Dawson: 16 August 2005 Denmark, 2 September 2005 Wales (1), 6 September 2005 Germany, 7 October 2005 Austria, 11 November 2005 France, 15 November 2005 France (6 appearances 1 goal)

Chris Day: 23 April 1996 Croatia, 24 May 1996 Belgium, 1 June 1996 Brazil (3 appearances)

Matthew Etherington: 12 February 02 Slovenia (sub), 26 March 2002 Italy, 6 September 2002 Yugoslavia (sub) (3 appearances)

Chris Fairclough: 10 November 1987 Yugoslavia, 27 April 1988 France (2 appearances)

Anthony Gardner: 26 March 2002 Italy (sub) (1 appearance)

Ian Hendon: 12 May 1992 Hungary, 24 May 1992 Mexico, 26 May 1992 Czechoslovakia, 28 May 1992 France, 8 September 1992 Spain, 13 October 1992 Norway, 17 November 1992 Turkey (7 appearances)

Danny Hill: 6 June 1995 Brazil, 8 June 1995 Malaysia, 10 June 1995 Angola, 12 June 95 France (4 appearances)

Glenn Hoddle: 15 December 1976 Wales (sub), 12 October 1977 Finland (sub), 8 March 1978 Italy, 5 April 1978 Italy, 19 April 1978 Yugoslavia, 19 September 1978 Denmark (1), 6 February 1979 Wales (1), 5 June 1979 Bulgaria, 12 February 1980 Scotland, 4 March 1980 Scotland, 16 April 1980 East Germany, 23 April 1980 East Germany (12 appearances 2 goals)

Tom Huddlestone: 7 October 2005 Austria, 11 October 2005 Poland, [on loan to Wolverhampton Wanderers 11 November 2005 France, 15 November 2005 France], 28 February 2006 Norway], 15 August 2006 Moldova, 6 September 2006 Switzerland, 6 October 2006 Germany, 10.10 2006

Germany, 14 November 2006 Holland, 6 February 2007 Spain, 24 March 2007 Italy (sub), 5 June 2007 Slovakia (1), 11 June 2007 Czech Republic, 17 June 2007 Serbia (sub) 21 August 2007 Rumania (sub), 11 September 2007 Bulgaria (1), 12 October 2007 Montenegro, 16 October 2007 Republic of Ireland, 16 November 2007 Bulgaria , 20 November 2007 Portugal, 5 February 2008 Republic of Ireland, 15 May 2008 Wales (1), 19 August 2008 Slovenia, 5 September 2008 Portugal, 10 October 2008 Wales, 14 October 2008 Wales, 10 February 09 Ecuador, 27 March 2009 Norway (1), 31 March 2009 France (30 appearances 5 goals)

Chris Jones: 1 May 1978 Yugoslavia (sub) (1 appearance)

Ledley King: 3 September 1999 Luxembourg (sub), 27 May 200 Italy, 29 May 2000 Turkey (1), 1 June 2000 Slovakia, 14 November 2000 Italy (abandoned), 27 February 2001 Spain (sub), 23 March 2001 Finland, 31 August 2001 Germany, 4 September 2001 Albania, 5 October 2001 Greece, 10 November 2001 Holland, 13 November 2001 Holland (12 appearances 1 goal)

Paul Konchesky [while on loan from Charlton Athletic: 5 September 2003 Macedonia, 9 September 2003 Portugal] (2 appearances)

Aaron Lennon: 7 October 2005 Austria, 11 October 2005 Poland, 5 February 2008 Republic of Ireland, 19 August 2008 Slovenia, 18 November 2008 Czech Republic (5 apps)

Gary Mabbutt: 21 September 1982 Denmark (2), 28 March 1984 France, 12 March 1986 Denmark, 9 April 1986 Italy (4 appearances 2 goals)

Dean Marney: 8 February 2005 v Holland (sub) (1 appearance)

Kyle Naughton: 11 August 2009 Holland (sub), 4 September 2009 Macedonia, 8 September 2009 Greece, 14 November 2009 Portugal (sub), [while on loan to Leicester City 8 February 2011 Italy, 24 March 2011 Denmark, 28 March 2011 Iceland] (7 appearances)

Stuart Nethercott: 8 March 1994 Denmark, 29 May 1994 Russia, 31 May 1994 France, 2 June 1994 USA, 5 June 1994 Belgium, 7 June 1994 Portugal, 25 April 1995 Latvia, 7 June 1995 Latvia (8 appearances)

Jamie O'Hara: 25 March 2008 Poland, 15 May 2008 Wales (sub), 10 October 2008 Wales, 14 October 2008 Wales, 18 November 2008 Czech Republic, 27 March 2009 Norway, 31 March 2009 France (sub) (7 appearances)

Danny Rose: 8 June 2009 Azerbaijan (sub), 22 June 2009 Germany, 11 August 2009 Holland, 4 September 2009 Macedonia, 8 September 2009 Greece, [while on loan to Peterborough United 9 October 2009 Macedonia, 14 November 2009 Portugal (1), 10 November 2009 Lithuania], 10 August 2010 Uzbekistan (1), 3 September 201 Portugal, 7 September 2010 Lithuania [while on loan to Bristol City 8 October 2010 Romania, 12 October 2010 Romania, 16 November 2010 Germany, 24 March 2011 Denmark (sub), 28 March 2011 Iceland] (16 appearances 2 goals)

Wayne Routledge: [while on loan to Portsmouth – 28 February 2006 Norway], 15 August 2006 Moldova, [while on loan to Fulham 6 September 2006 Switzerland, 6 October 2006 Germany, 14 November 2006 Holland, 24 March 2007 Italy (1)], 5 June 2007 Slovakia (sub), 11 June 2007 Czech Republic (sub), 17 June 2007 Serbia (sub) (10 appearances 1goal)

Vinny Samways: 28 May 1988 Switzerland (sub), 7 June 1988 USSR (1), 12 June 1988 France, 13 September 1988 Denmark, 18 October 1988 Sweden (5 appearances 1 goal)

Steve Sedgley: 5 September 1989 Sweden (1 appearance)

Steve Slade: 24 May 1996 Belgium (1), 28 May 1996 Angola, 30 May 1996 Portugal (1), 1 June 1996 Brazil (4 appearances 2 goals)

Brian Statham: 28 May 1988 Switzerland, 13 September 1988 Denmark (sub), 18 November 1988 Sweden (3 appearances)

Gary Stevens: 11 October 1983 Hungary, 28 February 1984 France, 28 March 1984 France (sub), 2 May 1984 Italy (sub), 17 May 1984 Spain, 24 May 1984 Spain (sub), 9 April 1986 Italy (7 appearances)

Alton Thelwell: 27 February 2001 Spain (sub) (1 appearance)

Danny Thomas: 2 May 1984 Italy, 17 May 1984 Spain (2 appearances)

Ian Walker: 5 December 1990 Wales, 12 May 1992 Hungary, 26 May 1992 Czechoslovakia, 28 May 1992 France, 8 September 1992 Spain, 13 October 1992 Norway, 17 November 1992 Turkey, 16 February 1993 San Marino, 7 September 1993 Poland (9 appearances)
Kyle Walker: 3 March 2010 Greece, 10 August 2010 Uzbekistan, 3 September 2010 Portugal, 7 September 2010 Lithuania (4 apps)
Luke Young: 27 April 1999 Hungary, 8 October 2002 Denmark (sub), 22 February 2000 Argentina (sub), 29 May 2000 Turkey, 1 June 2000 Slovakia, 31 August 2000 Georgia (1), 23 March 2001 Finland, 27 March 2001 Albania, 24 May 2001 Mexico, 5 June 2001 Greece (10 appearances 1goal)

FRANCE

Dorian Dervite: [while on loan to Southend United – 27 March 2009 Estonia, 31 March 2009 England], 4 June 2009 Qatar, 6 June 2009 Portugal, 10 June 2009 Argentina, 12 August 2009 Poland (sub) (1), 5 September 2009 Slovenia (7 appearances 1 goal)
Younes Kaboul: 7 September 2007 Wales, 12 September 2007 Malta, 16 October 2007 Romania, 15 November 2007 Armenia, 20 November 2007 Wales, 5 February 2008 Spain, 26 March 2008 Czech Republic, 25 May 2008 Holland, 28 May 2008 Portugal, 31 May 2008 Sweden (10 appearances)

GERMANY

Kevin-Prince Boateng: [while on loan to Borussia Dortmund – 10 February 2009 Republic of Ireland] (1 appearance)

HUNGARY

Marton Fulop: 18 August 2004 Scotland, 3 September 2004 Croatia, 7 September 2004 Iceland, 16 November 2004 Malta, 9 February 2005 Cyprus, 3 June 2005 Iceland, 29 March 2005 Bulgaria, [on loan to Coventry City 2 September 2005 Malta, 7 September 2005 Sweden, 7 October 2005 Bulgaria, 11 October 2005 Croatia, 11 November 2005 Italy, 15 November 2005 Italy] (11 appearances)

ICELAND

Emil Hallfredsson: 25 March 2005 Croatia, 3 June 2005 Hungary, 7 June 2005 Malta, 2 September 2005 Croatia (1), 6 September 2005 Bulgaria (1), 11 October 2005 Sweden, [while on loan to Malmo – 1 June 2006 Andorra (1), 16,8,2006 Austria, 1 September 2006 Italy] (9 appearances 3 goals)

NORTHERN IRELAND

Jonathan Black: 15 October 2002 Ukraine (sub) (1 appearance)
Phil Gray: 3 April 1990 Israel (1) (1 appearance 1 goal)
Mark Hughes: 11 October 2002 Spain (sub), 15 October 2002 Ukraine (sub), 11 February 2003 Finland, 28 March 2003 Armenia, 1 April 2003 Greece, 10 June 2003 Spain, 5 September 2003 Ukraine, 9 September 2003 Armenia, 10 October 2003 Greece (sub), 18 August 2004 Switzerland, [while on loan to Oldham Athletic - 8 February 2005 Scotland] (11 appearances)
Kieran McKenna: 14 November 2006 Germany, 6 February 2007 Wales, 24 March 2007 Rumania, 21 August 2007 v Finland, 7 September 2007 Germany, 12 September 2007 Luxembourg (6 apps)
Gerard McMahon: 22 March 1994 Rumania (sub) (1 appearance)
Paul McVeigh: 20 May 1998 Scotland (sub), 22 May 1998 Republic of Ireland, 4 September 1998 Turkey, 17 November 1998 Moldova, 26 March 1999 Germany, 30 March 1999 Moldova, 2 June

1999 Republic of Ireland, 17 August 1999 France, 3 September 1999 Turkey (sub), 7 September 1999 Germany (sub), 8 October 1999 Finland (11 appearances)
Steve Robinson: 22 March 1994 Rumania (1 appearance)
Ciaran Toner: 28 March 2000 Malta (sub), 29 May 2000 Scotland (sub), 2 June 2000 Wales, 6 October 2000 Denmark, 10 October 2000 Iceland, 23 March 2001 Czech Republic, 27 March 2001 Bulgaria, 1 June 2001 Bulgaria, 5 June 2001 Czech Republic, 31 August 2001 Denmark, 4 September 2001 Iceland, 5 October 2001 Malta (12 appearances)

NORWAY

Espen Baardsen: 31 July 1996 Poland, 31 August 1996 France, 8 October 1996 Hungary, 31 October 1996 Sweden, 9 November 1996 Switzerland, 13 February 1997 South Korea, 3 April 1997 Lebanon, 29 April 1997 Finland, 20 July 1997 Iceland, 19 August 1997 Finland, 9 September 1997 Switzerland, 8 October 1997 South Africa, 29 October 1997 France, 11 March 1998 Greece, 24 March 1998 Belgium B, 21 April 1998 Scotland B, 24 May 1998 Sweden, 27 May 1998 Spain, 31 May 1998 Holland, 9 October 1998 Slovenia, 13 October 98 Albania, 28 April 1999 Georgia, 3 September 1999 Greece, 7 September 99 Slovenia, 8 October 1999 Latvia, 13 November 1999 Spain, 16 November 1999 Spain (27 appearances)
Steffen Iversen: 19 August 1997 Finland, 9 September 1997 Switzerland (1), 21 April 1998 Scotland B (sub), 24 May 1998 Sweden (1), 27 May 1998 Spain, 31 May 98 Holland (2) (6 appearances 4 goals)

PORTUGAL

Helder Postiga: 5 September 2003 Turkey, 9 September 2003 England (1), 10 October 2003 Slovakia (2), 15 November 2003 France, 18 November 2003 France (5 appearances 3 goals)

REPUBLIC OF IRELAND

Steve Carr: 15 November 1994 England, 27 March 1995 England, 25 April 1995 Portugal, 10 June 1995 Austria, 5 September 1995 Austria, 10 October 1995 Latvia, 26 March 1996 Russia, 30 May 1996 Norway, 8 October 1996 Macedonia (1), 9 November 1996 Iceland, 1 April 1997 Macedonia, 5 September 1997 Iceland, (12 appearances 1 goal)
Owen Coll: 14 November 1995 Portugal, 26 March 1996 Russia (sub) (2 appearances)
Ross Darcy: 8 October 1996 Macedonia, 9 November 1996 Iceland, 9 September 1997 Lithuania, 24 March 1998 Czech Republic, 4 September 98 Croatia (sub), 18 November 1998 Yugoslavia (sub) (6 appearances)
Terry Dixon: 1 September 2006 Belgium (sub) (1 appearance)
Gary Doherty: 25 May 2000 Colombia, 27 May 2000 Ghana, 1 September 2000 Netherlands, 6 October 2000 Portugal, 10 October 2000 Estonia (5 appearances)
Neale Fenn: 29 April 97 Rumania, 19 August 1997 Lithuania (2), 5 September 1997 Iceland, 22 May 1998 Northern Ireland, 27 April 1999 Sweden, 31 May 1999 Scotland, 8 June 1999 Macedonia, 3 September 1999 Croatia, 7 September 99 Malta (1) (11 appearances 3 goals)
Peter Gain: 9 September 1997 Lithuania (1) (1 appearance 1 goal)
Eddie Gormley: 5 June 1989 Senegal (sub), 7 June 1989 Bulgaria, 10 June 1989 France (sub) (3 appearances)
Stephen Kelly: 2 June 2003 Germany, 6.6 2003 Albania, 10 June 2003 Georgia, 19 August 2003 Poland, 5 September 2003 Russia, 10 October 2003 Switzerland, 23 February 2004 Portugal, 25 February 2004 Italy, 27 February 2004 Madeira Islands, 27 April 2004 Poland, 25 May 2004 Scotland, 3 September 2004 Cyprus, 7 September 2004 Switzerland, 8 October 2004 France, 8 February 2005 Portugal,16 August 2005 Northern Ireland, 6 September 2005 France (17 appearances)
David McDonald: 30 April 1991 Poland, 15 October 1991 Poland, 12 November 1991 Turkey (3 appearances)

Kevin Maher: 26 March 1996 Russia, 1 April 1997 Macedonia, 29 April 1997 Rumania, 19 August 1997 Lithuania, 9 September 98 Lithuania (5 appearances)
Andy Turner: 27 April 1993 Denmark, 12 October 1993 Spain, 15 November 1994 England, 27 March 1995 England, 5 September 1995 Austria, 14 November 1995 Portugal (sub), 26 March 1996 Russia (7 appearances)
Mark Yeates: 23 February 2004 Portugal, 27 February 2004 Madeira Islands, 8 February 2005 Portugal, [while on loan to Colchester United - 28 February 2006 Sweden] (4 appearances)

SCOTLAND

Steve Archibald: 18 November 1980 Denmark (1 appearance)
John Hendry: 18 February 1992 Denmark (sub) (1 appearance)
Neil McNab: 8 February 1978 Wales (1 appearance)

SWEDEN

Oscar Jansson: 31 March 2009 Belgium, 7 October 2010 Austria, 9 February 2011 Portugal (3 appearances)

SWITZERLAND

Reto Ziegler: 7 September 2004 Republic of Ireland, 8 October 2004 Israel, 17 November 2004 Belarus, [on loan to SV Hamburg 2 September 2005 Israel, 6 September 2005 Cyprus, 7 October 2005 France, 11 October 2005 Republic of Ireland, 13 November 2005 Portugal, 16 November 2005 Portugal], [while on loan to Wigan Athletic 26 April 2006 Rumania (1), 18 May 2006 Belgium], 16 August 2006 Denmark, 1 September 2006 Moldova, 6 September 2006 England, 15 November 2006 Slovenia, [while on loan to Sampdoria 7 February 2007 France, 24 March 2007 Turkey, 27 March 2007 Bosnia-Herzegovina, 5 June 2007 Sweden] (18 appearances 1 goal)

WALES

Gareth Bale: 20 August 2008 Romania (1 appearance)
Mark Bowen: 22 September 1982 Norway, 15 November 1984 Bulgaria, 13 December 1984 Yugoslavia (3 appearances)
Simon Davies: 31 May 2000 Scotland, 1 September 2000 Belarus, 6 October 2000 Norway, 10 October 2000 Poland, 23 March 2001 Armenia (5 appearances)
Chris Gunter: 25 March 2008 Bosnia-Herzegovina, 15 May 2008 England, 20 August 2008 Romania (3 apps)
Ian Hillier: 27 March 2001 Ukraine (sub), 1 June 2001 Poland (sub), 5 June 2001 Ukraine, [while on loan to Luton Town 31 August 2001 Armenia, 4 September 2001 Norway] (5 appearances)
Mark Kendall: 8 February 1978 Scotland (1 appearance)
Gareth Knott: 1 June 1996 San Marino (1 appearance)

WAR-TIME INTERNATIONALS

ENGLAND

Vic Buckingham: 26 April 1941 Wales, 7 June 1941 Wales (2 appearances)
Ted Ditchburn: 19 February 1944 Scotland, 6 May 1944 Wales (2 appearances)
Jack Gibbons: 24 October 1942 Wales (1 appearance)
Willie Hall: 11 November 1939 Wales, 13 April 1940 Wales, 9 May 1942 Wales (3 appearances)

WALES

Ron Burgess: 11 November 1939 England, 18 November 1939 England, 26 April 1941 England, 25 September 1943 England, 6 May 1944 England, 16 September 1944 England, 5 May 1945 England, 20 October 1945 England, 10 November 1945 Scotland, 4 May 1946 Northern Ireland (10 appearances)
Bill Whatley: 11 November 1939 England (1 appearance)

VICTORY INTERNATIONALS

ENGLAND

Arthur Grimsdell: 26 April 1919 Scotland, 3 May 1919 Scotland (2) (2 appearances 2 goals)

FOOTBALL LEAGUE

Clive Allen: 8 August 1987 Rest of the World (1 appearance)
Les Allen: 29 November 1962 Italian League (1) (1 appearance 1 goal)
Ossie Ardiles: 8 August 1987 Rest of the World (sub), 8 September 1987 Irish League (2 appearances)
Eddie Baily: 15 February 1950 League of Ireland (1), 22 March 1950 Scottish League, 18 October 1950 Irish League, 4 April 1951 League of Ireland, 24 September 1952 Irish League, 20 October 1954 Irish League (6 appearances 1 goal)
Danny Blanchflower: 12 October 1960 Irish League (1) (1 appearance 1 goal)
Ron Burgess: 12 March 1947 Scottish League (1 appearance)
Tommy Clay: 4 October 1922 Irish League (1 appearance)
Ted Ditchburn: 12 March 1947 Scottish League, 30 April 1947 League of Ireland, 17 March 1948 Scottish League, 14 April 1948 League of Ireland, 20 September 1948 Irish League, 29 November 1950 Scottish League (6 appearances)
Jack Elkes: 11 October 1924 Irish League, 14 March 1925 Scottish League, 19 March 1927 Scottish League (1) (3 appearances 1 goal)
Richard Gough: 8 August 1987 Rest of World (1 appearance)
Jimmy Greaves: 29 November 1962 Italian League (1), 18 March 1964 Scottish League (1), 17 March 1965 Scottish League, 16 March 1966 Scottish League (1), 15 March 1967 Scottish League, 8 November 1967 League of Ireland (1) (6 appearances 4 goals)
Arthur Grimsdell: 20 March 1920 Scottish League (1 appearance)
Willie Hall: 31 October 1934 Scottish League, 6 October 1937 Irish League (1), 2 November 1938 Scottish League (3 appearances 1 goal)
David Howells: 13 November 1990 Irish League (1 appearance)
Jim Iley: 8 October 1958 Scottish League (1 appearance)
Cliff Jones: 23 March 1960 Scottish League, 12 October 1960 Irish League, 1 November 1960 Italian League (3 appearances)
Cyril Knowles: 20 March 1968 Scottish League (1 appearance)
Tommy Lunn: 14 November 1910 Southern League (1 appearance)
Gary Mabbutt: 13 November 1990 Irish League (1 appearance)
Dave Mackay: 23 March 1960 Scottish League, 12 October 1960 Irish League (2 appearances)
Les Medley: 31 October 1951 Scottish League (1 appearance)
Johnny Metgod: 8 September 1987 Irish League (1 appearance)

Bert Middlemiss: 11 April 1910 Southern League (1 appearance)
Alan Mullery: 9 May 1964 Italian League, 28 October 1964 Irish League (2 appearances)
Bill Nicholson: 15 February 1950 League of Ireland (1 appearance)
Maurice Norman: 9 May 1964 Italian League (1 appearance)
Martin Peters: 18 March 1970 Scottish League (sub), 23 September 1970 Irish League (1) (2 appearances 1 goal)
Alf Ramsey: 22 March 1950 Scottish League, 4 April 1951 League of Ireland, 31 October 1951 Scottish League, 24 September 1952 Irish League (1), 5 May 1953 Danish Combination (5 appearances 1 goal)
George Robb: 23 September 1953 Irish League (1 appearance)
Bert Smith: 18 February 1922 Scottish League (1 appearance)
Cyril Spiers: 5 November 1930 Scottish League (1 appearance)
Bert Sproston: 21 September 1938 Irish League, 2 November 1938 Scottish League (2 appearances)
Alfie Stokes: 13 March 1957 Scottish League (1 appearance)
Chris Waddle: 8 August 1987 Rest of World (1 appearance)
Fanny Walden: 26 October 1914 Southern League (1 appearance)
John White: 12 October 1960 Irish League (1 appearance)
Vivian Woodward: 10 October 1908 Irish League (2) (1 appearance 2 goals)

PLAYERS RECORDS

Detailed below are the career appearances and goals scored records of all players who have appeared for Spurs since the club joined the Football League in 1908. Abandoned matches and those later expunged from the records, such as the three games at the start of the 1939–40 season are included.

		LEAGUE			FA CUP			FL CUP			EURO			OTHERS			TOTAL		
NAME	SEASON	APPS	SUBS	GOALS	APPS	SUBS	GOALS	APPS	SUBS	GOALS	APPS	SUBS	GOALS	APPS	SUBS	GOALS	APPS	SUBS	GOALS
Milenko Acimovic	2002–04	4	13	0	0	0	0	1	0	0	0	0	0	13	2	1	18	15	1
Jack Acquroff	1945–46	0	0	0	0	0	0	0	0	0	0	0	0	2	0	2	2	0	2
Chris J Adams	1950–53	6	0	1	0	0	0	0	0	0	0	0	0	5	1	5	11	1	6
Dexter W Adams	1954–55	0	0	0	0	0	0	0	0	0	0	0	0	2	0	0	2	0	0
W (Bill) H Adams	1943–46	0	0	0	1	0	0	0	0	0	0	0	0	11	0	0	12	0	0
Barrie G Aitchison	1960–61	0	0	0	0	0	0	0	0	0	0	0	0	1	0	1	1	0	1
Milija A Aleksic	1978–82	25	0	0	7	0	0	0	0	0	0	0	0	23	3	0	55	3	0
Stan Alexander	1936–37	9	0	1	0	0	0	0	0	0	0	0	0	0	0	0	9	0	1
Clive D Allen	1984–03	97	8	60	11	1	9	13	1	13	3	1	2	32	7	29	156	18	113
Joe Allen	1932–33	1	0	1	0	0	0	0	0	0	0	0	0	0	0		1	0	1
Les W Allen	1959–65	119	0	47	15	0	13	0	0	0	3	0	1	10	0	14	147	0	75
Paul K Allen	1985–03	276	16	23	26	1	1	42	2	4	6	1	0	94	7	3	444	27	31
Rory W Allen	1996–99	10	11	2	1	0	0	3	3	2	0	0	0	9	5	3	23	19	7
Ben R Alnwick	2008–11	1	0	0	1	0	0	1	0	0	0	0	0	0	1	0	3	1	0
Wally J Alsford	1930–37	81	0	0	9	0	0	0	0	0	0	0	0	10	0	2	100	0	2
Alex Anderson	1944–45	0	0	0	0	0	0	0	0	0	0	0	0	1	0	0	1	0	0
Darren R Anderton	1992–04	273	26	34	26	2	6	30	1	8	0	0	0	60	9	18	389	38	66
Danny M Andrews	1983–84	0	0	0	0	0	0	0	0	0	0	0	0	0	1	0	0	1	0
Mark A Arber	1997 Tour	0	0	0	0	0	0	0	0	0	0	0	0	3	0	0	3	0	0
Jimmy Archibald	1919–22	24	0	1	1	0	0	0	0	0	0	0	0	8	0	0	33	0	1
Steve Archibald	1980–88	128	3	58	17	1	5	18	0	7	22	0	7	25	2	18	210	6	95
Ossie C Ardiles	1978–91	222	16	16	32	0	4	31	1	3	8	1	2	92	15	12	385	33	37
Chris P Armstrong	1995–01	117	24	48	10	5	4	15	0	10	3	0	0	21	8	13	166	37	75
Gerry J Armstrong	1975–81	65	19	10	6	4	3	3	1	3	0	0	0	22	13	16	96	37	32
Jimmy W Armstrong	1927–30	28	0	5	5	0	0	0	0	0	0	0	0	12	0	9	45	0	14
W Arnold	1940–41	0	0	0	0	0	0	0	0	0	0	0	0	1	0	0	1	0	0
Benoit PD Assou-Ekotto	2006–11	105	1	1	7	0	0	9	0	0	19	1	0	17	5	0	157	7	1
Astwood	1979 Tour	0	0	0	0	0	0	0	0	0	0	0	0	0	1	0	0	1	0
Thimothee E Atouba	2004–05	15	3	1	5	0	0	1	0	0	0	0	0	0	0	0	21	3	1

NAME	SEASON	LEAGUE APPS	LEAGUE SUBS	LEAGUE GOALS	FA CUP APPS	FA CUP SUBS	FA CUP GOALS	FL CUP APPS	FL CUP SUBS	FL CUP GOALS	EURO APPS	EURO SUBS	EURO GOALS	OTHERS APPS	OTHERS SUBS	OTHERS GOALS	TOTAL APPS	TOTAL SUBS	TOTAL GOALS
Dean B Austin	1992–97	117	7	0	17	1	0	7	2	0	0	0	0	24	7	0	165	17	0
Percy C Austin	1927–28	1	0	0	0	0	0	0	0	0	0	0	0	1	0	0	2	0	0
Ayres	1917–18	0	0	0	0	0	0	0	0	0	0	0	0	2	0	0	2	0	0
P Espen Baardsen	1996–00	22	1	0	2	1	0	3	0	0	0	0	0	6	7	0	33	9	0
Eddie F Baily	1945–56	297	0	64	29	0	5	0	0	0	0	0	0	56	0	21	382	0	90
Dagul Bakari	2004–05	0	0	0	0	0	0	0	0	0	0	0	0	1	3	0	1	3	0
Peter RB Baker	1952–65	299	0	3	27	0	0	0	0	0	16	0	0	58	2	0	400	2	3
Sean Baker	1984–85	0	0	0	0	0	0	0	0	0	0	0	0	0	1	0	0	1	0
A Baldwin	1917–18	0	0	0	0	0	0	0	0	0	0	0	0	1	0	0	1	0	0
Gareth Bale	2007–11	67	10	12	10	0	0	7	2	1	18	3	4	8	4	2	110	19	19
Jimmy A Banks	1913–23	68	0	6	9	0	4	0	0	0	0	0	0	133	0	81	210	0	91
Kingsley P Banks	1985–86	0	0	0	0	0	0	0	0	0	0	0	0	0	1	0	0	1	0
W (Bill) E Bann	1923–29	12	0	0	0	0	0	0	0	0	0	0	0	5	0	0	17	0	0
Nicky J Barmby	1991–96	81	6	20	12	1	5	7	1	2	0	0	0	25	9	8	125	17	35
Andy Barcham	2006–08	0	0	0	0	0	0	1	0	0	0	0	0	0	1	0	1	1	0
J Barnard	1916–19	0	0	0	0	0	0	0	0	0	0	0	0	9	0	5	9	0	5
Lee J Barnard	2001–08	0	3	0	0	0	0	0	0	0	0	0	0	5	9	3	5	12	3
John CB Barnes	1987–88	0	0	0	0	0	0	0	0	0	0	0	0	1	0	0	1	0	0
Fred W Barnett	1922–29	16	0	1	0	0	0	0	0	0	0	0	0	1	0	0	17	0	1
George Barron	1942–43	0	0	0	0	0	0	0	0	0	0	0	0	1	0	0	1	0	0
Ken R Barton	1955–64	4	0	0	0	0	0	0	0	0	0	0	0	2	0	0	6	0	0
Percy H Barton	1915–19	0	0	0	0	0	0	0	0	0	0	0	0	91	0	6	91	0	6
E (Ted) J Bassett	1915–18	0	0	0	0	0	0	0	0	0	0	0	0	74	0	37	74	0	37
Sebastien Bassong N	2009–11	32	8	2	8	0	0	4	0	0	4	1	1	2	1	0	50	10	3
Jimmy R Bauchop	1913–14	10	0	6	0	0	0	0	0	0	0	0	0	3	0	4	13	0	10
Bay	1918–19	0	0	0	0	0	0	0	0	0	0	0	0	1	0	0	1	0	0
Peter CWJ Beadle	1992–93	0	0	0	0	0	0	0	0	0	0	0	0	0	1	0	0	1	0
Phi)l Beal	1963–80	330	3	1	30	0	0	27	0	0	30	0	0	62	1	0	479	4	1
Ralph Bean	1979 Tour	0	0	0	0	0	0	0	0	0	0	0	0	0	1	1	0	1	1
A Bearman	1916–17	0	0	0	0	0	0	0	0	0	0	0	0	1	0	0	1	0	0
A (Pat) Beasley	1942–46	0	0	0	0	0	0	0	0	0	0	0	0	98	0	31	98	0	31
Sam Beaton	1917–19	0	0	0	0	0	0	0	0	0	0	0	0	9	0	0	9	0	0
M Stuart Beavon	1978–80	3	1	0	0	0	0	0	1	0	0	0	0	3	12	3	6	14	3
Bee	1918–19	0	0	0	0	0	0	0	0	0	0	0	0	1	0	0	1	0	0
Sammy Bell	1934–37	15	0	6	1	0	0	0	0	0	0	0	0	1	0	1	17	0	7
Walter R Bellamy	1926–35	70	0	9	3	0	0	0	0	0	0	0	0	11	0	2	84	0	11
FJ Bennett	1942–42	0	0	0	0	0	0	0	0	0	0	0	0	3	0	0	3	0	0
J Ken Bennett	1918–19	0	0	0	0	0	0	0	0	0	0	0	0	4	0	1	4	0	1

NAME	SEASON	LEAGUE APPS	LEAGUE SUBS	LEAGUE GOALS	FA CUP APPS	FA CUP SUBS	FA CUP GOALS	FL CUP APPS	FL CUP SUBS	FL CUP GOALS	EURO APPS	EURO SUBS	EURO GOALS	OTHERS APPS	OTHERS SUBS	OTHERS GOALS	TOTAL APPS	TOTAL SUBS	TOTAL GOALS
Ken E Bennett	1940–41	0	0	0	0	0	0	0	0	0	0	0	0	6	0	1	6	0	1
Les D Bennett	1939–55	273	0	103	22	0	14	0	0	0	0	0	0	84	0	52	379	0	169
Darren Bent	2007–10	32	28	18	1	0	0	1	3	1	9	5	6	14	3	18	57	39	43
David M Bentley	2008–11	32	10	3	6	1	1	7	1	1	5	0	1	6	1	3	56	13	9
Frank W Bentley	1908–12	38	0	0	5	0	0	0	0	0	0	0	0	10	0	0	53	0	0
Dimitar I Berbatov	2006–09	63	7	27	6	1	5	7	2	2	15	1	11	13	2	7	104	13	52
Gudni Bergsson	1988–93	51	20	2	2	2	0	4	2	0	5	1	0	26	9	1	88	34	3
Nicola Berti	1997–99	21	0	3	2	0	0	0	0	0	0	0	0	7	2	1	30	2	4
Tommy E Bing	1957–58	1	0	0	0	0	0	0	0	0	0	0	0	2	2	0	3	2	0
Bird	1917–18	0	0	0	0	0	0	0	0	0	0	0	0	1	0	0	1	0	0
E (Ted) L Birnie	1910–11	4	0	1	0	0	0	0	0	0	0	0	0	1	0	0	5	0	1
Jimmy Blair	1945–46	0	0	0	0	0	0	0	0	0	0	0	0	2	0	1	2	0	1
John G Blair	1925–28	29	0	15	1	0	0	0	0	0	0	0	0	2	0	1	32	0	16
FJC Blake	1918–19	0	0	0	0	0	0	0	0	0	0	0	0	1	0	0	1	0	0
H (Bert) E Blake	1921–24	51	0	0	5	0	0	0	0	0	0	0	0	5	0	0	61	0	0
R Danny Blanchflower	1954–64	337	0	15	33	0	4	0	0	0	12	0	2	54	1	6	436	1	27
H (Bert) Bliss	1911–23	195	0	91	21	0	13	0	0	0	0	0	0	99	0	64	315	0	168
Jonathan Blondel	2002–04	0	2	0	0	0	0	1	1	0	0	0	0	3	3	0	4	6	0
Jim Blyth	1936–37	11	0	0	0	0	0	0	0	0	0	0	0	0	0	0	11	0	0
Qu Bo	2002–03	0	0	0	0	0	0	0	0	0	0	0	0	1	1	0	1	1	0
Kevin–Prince Boateng	2007–10	7	7	0	1	1	0	1	4	0	1	2	0	1	3	0	11	17	0
Len A Bolan	1933–35	10	0	3	0	0	0	0	0	0	0	0	0	3	0	0	13	0	3
Dennis JT Bond	1966=71	20	3	1	0	0	0	2	1	0	1	0	0	8	1	2	31	5	3
Andy D Booth	2000–01	3	1	0	0	0	0	0	0	0	0	0	0	0	0	0	3	1	0
Gaspar Borbas	1912 Tour	0	0	0	0	0	0	0	0	0	0	0	0	1	0	0	1	0	0
Fred Boreham	1908–10	20	0	0	0	0	0	0	0	0	0	0	0	13	0	0	33	0	0
Diego Bortolozzo	2002–03	0	0	0	0	0	0	0	0	0	0	0	0	2	3	0	2	3	0
John J Bostock	2008–11	0	0	0	0	0	0	0	0	0	0	3	0	2	4	0	2	7	0
Frank P Boulton	1944–45	0	0	0	0	0	0	0	0	0	0	0	0	1	0	0	1	0	0
Mark R Bowen	1983–87	14	3	2	3	0	0	0	0	0	0	0	0	7	14	0	24	17	2
Ernie G Bowering	1911–12	7	0	0	0	0	0	0	0	0	0	0	0	3	0	0	10	0	0
Paul Bowgett	1978–79	0	0	0	0	0	0	0	0	0	0	0	0	0	1	0	0	1	0
George H Bowler	1913–19	3	0	0	0	0	0	0	0	0	0	0	0	3	0	0	6	0	0
Robert L Brace	1983–84	0	1	0	0	0	0	0	0	0	0	0	0	0	0	0	0	1	0
Garry Brady	1994–98	0	9	0	1	1	0	0	0	0	0	0	0	1	5	0	2	15	0
W Liam Brady	1983–84	0	0	0	0	0	0	0	0	0	0	0	0	1	0	1	1	0	1
Jimmy Brain	1931–35	45	0	10	2	0	0	0	0	0	0	0	0	2	0	0	49	0	10
Jimmy Brandham	1918–19	0	0	0	0	0	0	0	0	0	0	0	0	1	0	0	1	0	0

NAME	SEASON	LEAGUE APPS	LEAGUE SUBS	LEAGUE GOALS	FA CUP APPS	FA CUP SUBS	FA CUP GOALS	FL CUP APPS	FL CUP SUBS	FL CUP GOALS	EURO APPS	EURO SUBS	EURO GOALS	OTHERS APPS	OTHERS SUBS	OTHERS GOALS	TOTAL APPS	TOTAL SUBS	TOTAL GOALS
W (Billy) F Brawn	1918–19	0	0	0	0	0	0	0	0	0	0	0	0	1	0	0	1	0	0
Alan B Brazil	1982–84	29	2	9	1	0	0	0	1	0	3	2	4	14	2	7	47	7	20
Charlie E Briggs	1942–44	0	0	0	0	0	0	0	0	0	0	0	0	3	0	0	3	0	0
R Charlie Brittain	1911–14	42	0	0	2	0	0	0	0	0	0	0	0	10	0	0	54	0	0
Colin Brittan	1950–58	41	0	1	4	0	0	0	0	0	0	0	0	10	0	0	55	0	1
Jock Britton	1925–28	40	0	0	0	0	0	0	0	0	0	0	0	3	0	0	43	0	0
Ivor A Broadis	1940–46	0	0	0	0	0	0	0	0	0	0	0	0	85	0	38	85	0	38
Gary J Brooke	1980–85	49	24	15	4	8	1	4	1	1	6	5	1	21	7	7	84	45	25
Brooks	1918–19	0	0	0	0	0	0	0	0	0	0	0	0	1	0	0	1	0	0
Johnny Brooks	1952–60	166	0	46	13	0	5	0	0	0	0	0	0	43	0	21	222	0	72
Noel Brotherston	1975–76	1	0	0	0	0	0	0	0	0	0	0	0	1	1	0	2	1	0
Joe Brough	1908–09	1	0	0	1	0	0	0	0	0	0	0	0	1	0	0	3	0	0
David C Brown	1909–10	1	0	0	0	0	0	0	0	0	0	0	0	1	0	1	2	0	1
Harry T Brown	1944–45	0	0	0	0	0	0	0	0	0	0	0	0	3	0	0	3	0	0
Ivor RJ Brown	1909–11	13	0	0	0	0	0	0	0	0	0	0	0	5	0	4	18	0	4
Jimmy Brown	1936–37	4	0	0	0	0	0	0	0	0	0	0	0	0	0	0	4	0	0
Laurie Brown	1963–66	62	0	3	3	0	0	0	0	0	0	0	0	21	1	0	86	1	3
Michael R Brown	2003–06	39	11	2	9	0	0	4	1	1	0	0	0	4	2	1	56	14	4
"R Brown"	1917–18	0	0	0	0	0	0	0	0	0	0	0	0	2	0	0	2	0	0
Roy EE Brown	1966–67	1	0	0	0	0	0	0	0	0	0	0	0	0	0	0	1	0	0
R (Bob) S Brown	1919–24	37	0	0	8	0	0	0	0	0	0	0	0	4	0	0	49	0	0
W (Bill) DF Brown	1959–67	222	0	0	23	0	0	0	0	0	17	0	0	30	0	0	292	0	0
Jack Browne	1940–44	0	0	0	0	0	0	0	0	0	0	0	0	4	0	0	4	0	0
R (Bobby) J Browne	1942–43	0	0	0	0	0	0	0	0	0	0	0	0	3	0	0	3	0	0
Bernard L Bryant	1943–44	0	0	0	0	0	0	0	0	0	0	0	0	7	0	2	7	0	2
Vic F Buckingham	1935–49	208	0	1	26	0	0	0	0	0	0	0	0	77	0	1	311	0	2
Walter Bull	1908–09	12	0	0	0	0	0	0	0	0	0	0	0	7	0	1	19	0	1
Ed Bulling	1910–11	2	0	0	0	0	0	0	0	0	0	0	0	2	0	0	4	0	0
Bully	1918–19	0	0	0	0	0	0	0	0	0	0	0	0	1	0	0	1	0	0
Goran P Bunjevcevic	2001–06	41	10	0	0	0	0	6	1	2	0	0	0	32	9	2	79	20	4
Rob Burch	2003–06	0	0	0	0	0	0	0	0	0	0	0	0	4	2	0	4	2	0
George S Burchell	1939–40	0	0	0	0	0	0	0	0	0	0	0	0	1	0	0	1	0	0
FC Ken Burditt	1940–41		0	0	0	0	0	0	0	0	0	0	0	1	0	0	1	0	0
WA Ron Burgess	1938–54	301	0	16	27	0	1	0	0	0	0	0	0	178	0	46	506	0	63
F Archie Burgon	1934–35	4	0	0	0	0	0	0	0	0	0	0	0	0	0	0	4	0	0
Charlie Burke	1944–45	0	0	0	0	0	0	0	0	0	0	0	0	15	0	0	15	0	0
Mark S Burke	1994–95	0	0	0	0	0	0	0	0	0	0	0	0	0	1	0	0	1	0
Ben Burley	1942–43	0	0	0	0	0	0	0	0	0	0	0	0	1	0	0	1	0	0

NAME	SEASON	LEAGUE			FA CUP			FL CUP			EURO			OTHERS			TOTAL		
		APPS	SUBS	GOALS	APPS	SUBS	GOALS	APPS	SUBS	GOALS	APPS	SUBS	GOALS	APPS	SUBS	GOALS	APPS	SUBS	GOALS
Jonathan Burnett	1944–45		0	0	0	0	0	0	0	0	0	0	0	1	0	2	1	0	2
Ollie Burton	1908–10	38	0	0	4	0	0	0	0	0	0	0	0	5	0	0	47	0	0
Calum J Butcher	2010–11	0	0	0	0	0	0	0	0	0	0	0	0	1	1	0	1	1	0
G Butcher	1915–16	0	0	0	0	0	0	0	0	0	0	0	0	1	0	0	1	0	0
Guy Butters	1988–91	34	1	1	1	0	0	2	1	0	0	0	0	12	9	0	49	11	1
David Button	2009–11	0	0	0	0	0	0	0	1	0	0	0	0	0	3	0	0	4	0
Tommy H Cable	1928–32	42	0	0	2	0	0	0	0	0	0	0	0	5	0	0	49	0	0
A Cain	1918–19	0	0	0	0	0	0	0	0	0	0	0	0	1	0	1	1	0	1
Colin Calderwood	1993–03	152	11	6	16	1	1	19	1	0	0	0	0	33	9	3	220	22	10
Tom Caldwell	1916–17	0	0	0	0	0	0	0	0	0	0	0	0	1	0	0	1	0	0
AS (Titi) Camara	1998–99	0	0	0	0	0	0	0	0	0	0	0	0	1	0	0	1	0	0
Frazier L Campbell	2008–09	1	9	1	0	1	0	3	1	2	5	2	0	0	0	0	9	13	3
Sol J Campbell	1991–01	246	9	10	29	2	1	28	0	4	2	0	0	39	12	3	344	23	18
Jimmy Cantrell	1912–23	159	0	74	15	0	10	0	0	0	0	0	0	20	0	11	194	0	95
Steve B Carr	1993–05	222	4	7	16	1	0	23	0	1	4	0	0	57	15	2	322	20	10
Michael A Carrick	2004–06	61	3	2	6	1	0	3	1	0	0	0	0	6	1	0	76	6	2
W (Bill) Cartwright	1913–15	13	0	0	2	0	0	0	0	0	0	0	0	7	0	0	22	0	0
Jack Casey	1916–17	0	0	0	0	0	0	0	0	0	0	0	0	1	0	0	1	0	0
Darren M Caskey	1991–96	20	12	4	6	1	0	3	1	1	0	0	0	11	10	2	40	24	7
Sid ER Castle	1919–21	5	0	0	0	0	0	0	0	0	0	0	0	1	0	1	6	0	1
Steve R Caulker	2010–11	0	0	0	0	0	0	1	0	0	0	0	0	1	0	0	2	0	0
Radek Cerny	2004–08	15	1	0	4	0	0	4	0	0	4	0	0	13	2	0	40	3	0
Fred C Channell	1933–36	95	0	1	14	0	0	0	0	0	0	0	0	4	0	0	113	0	1
Alex B Chaplin	1915–16	0	0	0	0	0	0	0	0	0	0	0	0	4	0	0	4	0	0
Eddie Chapman	1942–43	0	0	0	0	0	0	0	0	0	0	0	0	1	0	0	1	0	0
Art Chester	1918–19	0	0	0	0	0	0	0	0	0	0	0	0	2	1	0	2	1	0
John O Chiedozie	1984–88	45	8	12	5	3	2	7	0	0	7	0	0	22	6	5	86	17	19
Pascal Chimbonda	2006–10	65	3	3	6	0	0	8	0	1	21	0	0	9	2	0	109	5	4
Jimmy J Chipperfield	1919–21	15	0	6	0	0	0	0	0	0	0	0	0	2	0	0	17	0	6
Jack R Chisholm	1941–48	2	0	0	0	0	0	0	0	0	0	0	0	79	0	1	81	0	1
Martin H Chivers	1967–80	268	10	118	22	2	11	33	0	23	32	0	22	47	1	28	402	13	202
Nico PJ Claesen	1986–88	37	13	18	1	5	2	7	0	3	0	0	0	11	3	5	56	21	28
Jamie R Clapham	1995–98	0	1	0	0	0	0	0	0	0	0	0	0	3	5	0	3	6	0
David H Clarke	1909 Tour	0	0	0	0	0	0	0	0	0	0	0	0	5	0	4	5	0	4
Harry A Clarke	1948–57	295	0	4	27	0	0	0	0	0	0	0	0	59	0	0	381	0	4
Ray C Clarke	1972–73	0	1	0	0	0	0	0	0	0	0	0	0	0	0	0	0	1	0
Tommy Clay	1913–29	318	0	23	33	0	1	0	0	0	0	0	0	157	0	13	508	0	37
Eddie Clayton	1957–68	88	4	20	9	0	0	1	0	0	1	0	0	26	4	6	125	8	26

NAME	SEASON	LEAGUE APPS	LEAGUE SUBS	LEAGUE GOALS	FA CUP APPS	FA CUP SUBS	FA CUP GOALS	FL CUP APPS	FL CUP SUBS	FL CUP GOALS	EURO APPS	EURO SUBS	EURO GOALS	OTHERS APPS	OTHERS SUBS	OTHERS GOALS	TOTAL APPS	TOTAL SUBS	TOTAL GOALS
SA Clayton	1916–17	0	0	0	0	0	0	0	0	0	0	0	0	1	0	0	1	0	0
Stan Clayton	1942–44	0	0	0	0	0	0	0	0	0	0	0	0	3	0	1	3	0	1
Ray N Clemence	1981–91	240	0	0	25	0	0	38	0	0	27	0	0	77	0	1	407	0	1
Stephen N Clemence	1997–03	68	22	2	7	1	1	7	1	0	2	1	0	21	14	4	105	39	7
Shaun C Close	1985–88	3	6	0	0	0	0	3	0	2	0	0	0	3	5	8	9	11	10
Ralph Coates	1971–81	173	15	14	11	1	0	19	3	1	26	0	9	48	9	6	277	28	30
Alan Cockram	1983–84	2	0	0	0	0	0	0	0	0	0	0	0	0	0	0	2	0	0
Jimmy Collins	1960–62	2	0	0	0	0	0	0	0	0	0	0	0	1	0	0	3	0	0
John L Collins	1965–66	2	0	0	0	0	0	0	0	0	0	0	0	0	0	0	2	0	0
Peter J Collins	1968–74	78	6	4	8	1	0	5	2	1	1	1	0	14	2	3	106	12	8
Tom Collins	1910–15	115	0	1	9	0	0	0	0	0	0	0	0	10	0	0	134	0	1
David W Colquhoun	1931–35	81	0	2	6	0	0	0	0	0	0	0	0	4	0	3	91	0	5
Alfie J Conn	1974–77	35	3	6	2	0	0	1	2	1	0	0	0	11	5	3	49	10	10
Maurizio Consorti	2001–02	0	0	0	0	0	0	0	0	0	0	0	0	0	1	0	0	1	0
G W (Billy) Cook	1929–31	63	0	22	4	0	2	0	0	0	0	0	0	6	0	6	73	0	30
Jason P Cook	1987–89	0	0	0	0	0	0	0	0	0	0	0	0	0	2	0	0	2	0
R (Bobby) K Cook	1949–50	3	0	0	0	0	0	0	0	0	0	0	0	0	0	0	3	0	0
Richard E Cooke	1982–87	9	2	2	1	0	0	1	1	0	1	2	0	4	11	2	16	16	4
George S Coomber	1917–18	0	0	0	0	0	0	0	0	0	0	0	0	13	0	2	13	0	2
John A Cooper	1981–82	0	0	0	0	0	0	0	0	0	0	0	0	0	6	0	0	6	0
Ernie Coquet	1908–11	78	0	0	8	0	1	0	0	0	0	0	0	16	0	0	102	0	1
Pat A Corbett	1980–83	3	2	1	0	0	0	0	0	0	0	0	0	0	2	0	3	4	1
Peter Corder	1983–84	0	0	0	0	0	0	0	0	0	0	0	0	0	1	0	0	1	0
Vedran Corluka	2008–11	75	3	1	9	0	0	6	1	0	8	0	0	9	3	1	107	7	2
HF Couchman	1918–19	0	0	0	0	0	0	0	0	0	0	0	0	1	0	0	1	0	0
Freddie JA Cox	1938–49	99	0	15	6	0	3	0	0	0	0	0	0	39	0	9	144	0	27
Craig	1918–19	0	0	0	0	0	0	0	0	0	0	0	0	1	0	0	1	0	0
Warney Cresswell	1917–18	0	0	0	0	0	0	0	0	0	0	0	0	11	0	0	11	0	0
T Croft	1916–17	0	0	0	0	0	0	0	0	0	0	0	0	3	0	0	3	0	0
W Croft	1916–17	0	0	0	0	0	0	0	0	0	0	0	0	2	0	0	2	0	0
Arthur Crompton	1928–30	15	0	3	0	0	0	0	0	0	0	0	0	9	0	5	24	0	8
G Ellis Crompton	1910–12	9	0	1	2	0	0	0	0	0	0	0	0	0	0	0	11	0	1
Ian S Crook	1980–86	10	10	1	0	1	0	1	0	0	0	2	0	13	22	2	24	35	3
Garth A Crooks	1980–85	121	4	48	21	0	9	19	1	9	15	1	9	42	14	31	218	20	106
Charlie A Crossley	1916–17	Dec	0	0	0	0	0	0	0	0	0	0	0	1	0	0	1	0	0
Peter J Crouch	1999–11	41	31	12	6	1	1	2	1	4	9	1	7	3	2	0	61	36	24
Sid R Crowl	1913–18	1	0	0	0	0	0	0	0	0	0	0	0	15	0	1	16	0	1
Carlo Cudicini	2008–11	18	1	0	1	0	0	1	0	0	2	2	0	10	4	0	32	7	0

NAME	SEASON	LEAGUE APPS	LEAGUE SUBS	LEAGUE GOALS	FA CUP APPS	FA CUP SUBS	FA CUP GOALS	FL CUP APPS	FL CUP SUBS	FL CUP GOALS	EURO APPS	EURO SUBS	EURO GOALS	OTHERS APPS	OTHERS SUBS	OTHERS GOALS	TOTAL APPS	TOTAL SUBS	TOTAL GOALS
David P Culverhouse	1993 Tour	0	0	0	0	0	0	0	0	0	0	0	0	1	1	0	1	1	0
Ian B Culverhouse	1982–86	1	1	0	0	0	0	0	0	0	0	0	0	5	8	0	6	9	0
Jason V Cundy	1991–96	23	3	1	0	0	0	2	0	0	0	0	0	17	7	2	42	10	3
A (Tony) W Currie	1980–81	0	0	0	0	0	0	0	0	0	0	0	0	0	1	0	0	1	0
John J Curtis	1908–13	84	0	5	7	0	0	0	0	0	0	0	0	24	0	7	115	0	12
Barry R Daines	1971–81	146	0	0	11	0	0	14	0	0	2	0	0	51	11	0	224	11	0
Kenny M Dalglish	1987–91	0	0	0	0	0	0	0	0	0	0	0	0	2	0	0	2	0	0
Stephane Dalmat	2003–04	12	10	3	2	1	0	1	2	0	0	0	0	0	0	0	15	13	3
Charlie Daniels	2007–08	0	0	0	0	0	0	0	0	0	0	0	0	1	1	0	1	1	0
Ross Darcy	1998–99	0	0	0	0	0	0	0	0	0	0	0	0	2	0	0	2	0	0
Jabez Darnell	1908–19	153	0	3	10	0	0	0	0	0	0	0	0	98	0	1	261	0	4
Calum RP Davenport	2004–07	9	6	1	1	0	0	2	0	0	1	1	0	8	1	0	21	8	1
Edgar S Davids	2005–07	34	6	1	0	0	0	2	1	0	0	1	0	5	1	0	41	9	1
Jock Davie	1943–44	0	0	0	0	0	0	0	0	0	0	0	0	1	0	0	1	0	0
Simon Davies	1999–05	99	22	13	10	3	2	10	3	3	0	0	0	17	12	4	136	40	22
Willie Davies	1929–33	109	0	19	6	0	0	0	0	0	0	0	0	8	0	5	123	0	24
Sean Davis	2004–06	11	4	0	0	0	0	1	1	0	0	0	0	8	0	0	20	5	0
Michael R Dawson	2004–11	161	9	6	22	0	0	16	1	1	25	2	1	21	4	1	245	16	9
Alf Day	1932–36	13	0	0	1	0	0	0	0	0	0	0	0	3	0	0	17	0	0
Chris N Day	1994–95	0	0	0	0	0	0	0	0	0	0	0	0	0	5	0	0	5	0
Peter Day	1979 Tour	0	0	0	0	0	0	0	0	0	0	0	0	1	0	0	1	0	0
Kevin C Dearden	1986–93	0	1	0	0	0	0	1	0	0	0	0	0	4	4	0	5	5	0
Rodrigo Defendi	2004–05	0	0	0	0	0	0	0	0	0	0	0	0	0	1	0	0	1	0
Jermain C Defoe	2003–11	141	62	68	18	6	12	17	5	12	11	10	9	28	18	26	215	101	127
Alan Dennis	1962–65	0	0	0	0	0	0	0	0	0	0	0	0	1	1	0	1	1	0
Dorian Dervite	2006–10	0	0	0	0	0	0	1	0	0	0	0	0	4	1	0	5	1	0
Ally J Dick	1981–86	16	1	2	2	0	0	0	0	0	3	3	0	7	11	4	28	15	6
Leslie R Dicker	1952–53	10	0	2	0	0	0	0	0	0	0	0	0	0	0	0	10	0	2
M (Matt) L Dillon	1972–75	21	3	1	1	0	0	1	0	0	2	1	0	3	1	0	28	5	1
Jimmy H Dimmock	1918–31	400	0	100	38	0	12	0	0	0	0	0	0	55	0	26	493	0	138
E (Ted) G Ditchburn	1939–59	419	0	0	34	0	0	0	0	0	0	0	0	121	0	0	574	0	0
Ronnie W Dix	1939–48	39	0	6	4	0	0	0	0	0	0	0	0	54	0	14	97	0	20
Kenny Dixon	1982–83	0	0	0	0	0	0	0	0	0	0	0	0	1	0	0	1	0	0
John Dockray	1918–19	0	0	0	0	0	0	0	0	0	0	0	0	13	0	0	13	0	0
W (Bill) C Dodge	1958–61	6	0	0	4	0	0	0	0	0	0	0	0	3	0	0	13	0	0
Gary MT Doherty	1999–05	45	19	4	7	1	4	3	3	0	0	0	0	22	6	2	77	29	10
Jose MM Dominguez	1997–01	12	33	4	2	1	0	2	6	1	0	2	0	7	6	4	23	48	9
George J Dorling	1939–40	0	0	0	0	0	0	0	0	0	0	0	0	14	0	0	14	0	0

NAME	SEASON	LEAGUE			FA CUP			FL CUP			EURO			OTHERS			TOTAL		
		APPS	SUBS	GOALS	APPS	SUBS	GOALS	APPS	SUBS	GOALS	APPS	SUBS	GOALS	APPS	SUBS	GOALS	APPS	SUBS	GOALS
A Johnny Dowers	1939–40	0	0	0	0	0	0	0	0	0	0	0	0	2	0	0	2	0	0
Fred Downer	1943–44	0	0	0	0	0	0	0	0	0	0	0	0	1	0	0	1	0	0
G (Dickie) J Dowsett	1951–55	1	0	1	0	0	0	0	0	0	0	0	0	0	1	0	1	1	1
JJ Doyle	1915–16	0	0	0	0	0	0	0	0	0	0	0	0	1	0	0	1	0	0
Jason AW Dozzell	1993–97	68	16	13	5	1	1	8	2	0	0	0	0	14	6	5	95	25	19
Frank Drabble	1909–10	2	0	0	0	0	0	0	0	0	0	0	0	2	0	0	4	0	0
Draper	1918–19	0	0	0	0	0	0	0	0	0	0	0	0	1	0	0	1	0	0
Jack M Duffus	1923–24	0	0	0	0	0	0	0	0	0	0	0	0	2	0	0	2	0	0
Harry P Dukes	1944–45	0	0	0	0	0	0	0	0	0	0	0	0	3	0	0	3	0	0
Micky Dulin	1954–58	10	0	2	1	0	0	0	0	0	0	0	0	14	0	6	25	0	8
Ilie Dumitrescu	1994–96	16	2	4	0	0	0	2	0	1	0	0	0	6	2	1	24	4	6
A Scott M Duncan	1918–19	0	0	0	0	0	0	0	0	0	0	0	0	1	0	0	1	0	0
Andy Duncan	1934–43	93	0	22	10	0	4	0	0	0	0	0	0	81	0	22	184	0	48
John P Duncan	1974–79	101	2	53	7	0	2	10	0	7	0	0	0	21	4	13	139	6	75
Dave Gl Dunmore	1953–60	75	0	23	6	0	3	0	0	0	0	0	0	13	3	8	94	3	34
R (Dickie) Dunn	1944–45	0	0	0	0	0	0	0	0	0	0	0	0	1	0	0	1	0	0
Len S Duquemin	1945–57	275	0	114	33	0	20	0	0	0	0	0	0	66	0	53	374	0	187
Gordon S Durie	1991–94	58	0	11	2	0	0	10	0	3	8	0	3	8	4	2	86	4	19
Durston	1943–44	0	0	0	0	0	0	0	0	0	0	0	0	1	0	0	1	0	0
Terry K Dyson	1954–65	184	0	41	16	0	6	0	0	0	9	0	8	30	5	13	239	5	68
John P Eadon	1914–19	5	0	0	0	0	0	0	0	0	0	0	0	2	0	0	7	0	0
Stan Eastham	1942–43	0	0	0	0	0	0	0	0	0	0	0	0	1	0	0	1	0	0
Justin C Edinburgh	1990–00	190	23	1	27	1	0	25	4	0	4	2	0	56	19	0	302	49	1
Erik K Edman	2004–06	31	0	1	2	1	0	0	0	0	0	0	0	6	2	0	39	3	1
W (Bill) J Edrich	1935–37	20	0	4	0	0	0	0	0	0	0	0	0	0	0	0	20	0	4
Matt D Edwards	1990–91	0	0	0	0	0	0	0	0	0	0	0	0	2	6	1	2	6	1
Reg C Edwards	1941–44	0	0	0	0	0	0	0	0	0	0	0	0	8	0	2	8	0	2
Mounir El Hamdaoui	2005–06	0	0	0	0	0	0	0	0	0	0	0	0	0	4	0	0	4	0
A Jack Elkes	1923–29	190	0	50	10	0	1	0	0	0	0	0	0	12	0	6	212	0	57
Bert HW Elkin	1909–11	26	0	0	2	0	0	0	0	0	0	0	0	6	0	0	34	0	0
Jimmy E Elliott	1911–20	13	0	4	0	0	0	0	0	0	0	0	0	141	0	11	154	0	15
Ben J Embery	1965–66	0	0	0	0	0	0	0	0	0	0	0	0	1	0	0	1	0	0
H Mike England	1966–75	300	0	14	32	0	2	30	0	0	35	0	3	37	0	1	434	0	20
Matt Etherington	1999–04	20	25	1	1	1	1	3	1	0	0	0	0	10	13	2	34	40	4
Albert Evans	1927–29	5	0	0	0	0	0	0	0	0	0	0	0	2	0	0	7	0	0
Jimmy L Evans	1943–44	0	0	0	0	0	0	0	0	0	0	0	0	1	0	0	1	0	0
Norman Evans	1939–40	0	0	0	0	0	0	0	0	0	0	0	0	1	0	0	1	0	0
R Evans	1943–44	0	0	0	0	0	0	0	0	0	0	0	0	1	0	0	1	0	0

NAME	SEASON	LEAGUE			FA CUP			FL CUP			EURO			OTHERS			TOTAL		
		APPS	SUBS	GOALS	APPS	SUBS	GOALS	APPS	SUBS	GOALS	APPS	SUBS	GOALS	APPS	SUBS	GOALS	APPS	SUBS	GOALS
Ray L Evans	1968–75	133	4	2	7	0	0	13	0	0	22	3	2	20	2	1	195	9	5
Tom Evans	1929–37	94	0	4	7	0	0	0	0	0	0	0	0	7	0	1	108	0	5
Willie Evans	1930–37	178	0	78	17	0	8	0	0	0	0	0	0	8	0	10	203	0	96
C (Chris) H Fairclough	1987–89	60	0	5	3	0	0	7	0	0	0	0	0	24	3	1	94	3	6
Mark P Falco	1977–87	162	12	68	15	0	5	19	3	3	21	4	13	76	23	62	293	42	151
Brian H Farley	1949–54	1	0	0	0	0	0	0	0	0	0	0	0	6	0	0	7	0	0
Jack Feebury	1916–17	0	0	0	0	0	0	0	0	0	0	0	0	1	0	0	1	0	0
W (Bill) Felton	1931–34	73	0	1	2	0	0	0	0	0	0	0	0	3	0	0	78	0	1
Neale MC Fenn	1996–99	0	8	0	1	0	0	1	0	1	0	0	0	6	3	3	8	11	4
Terry W Fenwick	1987–92	90	3	8	7	0	0	14	0	2	4	0	0	32	4	5	147	7	15
Les Ferdinand	1997–03	97	21	33	15	1	1	11	4	5	0	0	0	14	7	9	137	33	48
Steve Ferguson	2001–02	0	0	0	0	0	0	0	0	0	0	0	0	2	0	2	2	0	2
Harry Ferrier	1945–46	0	0	0	0	0	0	0	0	0	0	0	0	1	0	0	1	0	0
Ferris	1918–19	0	0	0	0	0	0	0	0	0	0	0	0	1	0	0	1	0	0
Jack A Finch	1941–42	0	0	0	0	0	0	0	0	0	0	0	0	1	0	0	1	0	0
Andy Findlay	1920–21	0	0	0	0	0	0	0	0	0	0	0	0	1	0	0	1	0	0
Donald O Finlay	1942–43	0	0	0	0	0	0	0	0	0	0	0	0	3	0	0	3	0	0
Alf M Fitzgerald	1941–42	0	0	0	0	0	0	0	0	0	0	0	0	1	0	0	1	0	0
Doug W Flack	1940–41	0	0	0	0	0	0	0	0	0	0	0	0	5	0	0	5	0	0
W Len W Flack	1943–44	0	0	0	0	0	0	0	0	0	0	0	0	2	0	0	2	0	0
R (Bobby) Flavell	1944–45	0	0	0	0	0	0	0	0	0	0	0	0	15	0	2	15	0	2
Jim BM Fleming	1913–15	19	0	3	0	0	0	0	0	0	0	0	0	10	0	5	29	0	8
W (Bill) Fleming	1917–18	0	0	0	0	0	0	0	0	0	0	0	0	1	0	0	1	0	0
Harry D Fletcher	1945–46	0	0	0	0	0	0	0	0	0	0	0	0	1	0	0	1	0	0
Ken Flint	1947–48	5	0	1	0	0	0	0	0	0	0	0	0	0	0	0	5	0	1
Fred GL Ford	1945–46	0	0	0	0	0	0	0	0	0	0	0		3	0	0	3	0	0
A George Foreman	1944–47	36	0	14	2	0	0	0	0	0	0	0	0	18	0	25	56	0	39
Tom Forman	1910–12	8	0	1	0	0	0	0	0	0	0	0	0	1	0	0	9	0	1
Matt Forster	1920–30	236	0	0	8	0	0	0	0	0	0	0	0	28	0	0	272	0	0
Ruel A Fox	1995–00	95	11	13	12	1	1	7	3	1	1	0	0	22	9	4	137	24	19
Frazer	1918–19	0	0	0	0	0	0	0	0	0	0	0	0	1	0	0	1	0	0
Ernie Freeman	1918–19	0	0	0	0	0	0	0	0	0	0	0	0	2	0	0	2	0	0
W (Bill) G French	1918–22	0	0	0	0	0	0	0	0	0	0	0	0	4	0	0	4	0	0
Steffen Freund	1998–03	92	10	0	11	0	0	14	0	0	4	0	0	15	5	1	136	15	1
Frank G Fricker	1915–16	0	0	0	0	0	0	0	0	0	0	0	0	1	0	0	1	0	0
Jimmy Fullwood	1934–38	34	0	1	1	0	0	0	0	0	0	0	0	3	0	0	38	0	1
Marton Fulop	2004–07	0	0	0	0	0	0	0	0	0	0	0	0	4	3	0	4	3	0
W (Billy) Furr	1918–19	0	0	0	0	0	0	0	0	0	0	0	0	2	0	0	2	0	0

NAME	SEASON	LEAGUE			FA CUP			FL CUP			EURO			OTHERS			TOTAL		
		APPS	SUBS	GOALS	APPS	SUBS	GOALS	APPS	SUBS	GOALS	APPS	SUBS	GOALS	APPS	SUBS	GOALS	APPS	SUBS	GOALS
Peter Gain	1998–99	0	0	0	0	0	0	0	0	0	0	0	0	0	1	0	0	1	0
David Galbraith	2003–04	0	0	0	0	0	0	0	0	0	0	0	0	1	3	0	1	3	0
William E Gallas	2010–11	26	1	0	0	1	0	0	0	0	8	0	0	8	0	0	42	2	0
S Randolph Galloway	1928–29	3	0	2	0	0	0	0	0	0	0	0	0	0	0		3	0	2
A (Tony) Galvin	1978–88	194	7	20	23	1	2	20	3	3	25	0	6	88	14	16	350	25	47
Harry P Garbutt	1929–30	0	0	0	0	0	0	0	0	0	0	0	0	4	0	7	4	0	7
Anthony D Gardner	1999–08	94	20	2	11	3	0	13	0	1	3	0	0	20	9	1	141	32	4
Peter J Garland	1989–91	0	1	0	0	0	0	0	0	0	0	0	0	1	6	0	1	7	0
Len F Garwood	1945–51	2	0	0	0	0	0	0	0	0	0	0	0	4	0	0	6	0	0
Paul J Gascoigne	1988–03	91	1	19	6	0	6	13	1	8	0	0	0	29	3	13	139	5	46
Johnny T Gavin	1954–56	32	0	15	2	0	1	0	0	0	0	0	0	9	0	3	43	0	19
Gee	1918–19	0	0	0	0	0	0	0	0	0	0	0	0	1	0	0	1	0	0
George Gemmell	1913–14	0	0	0	1	0	0	0	0	0	0	0	0	0	0	0	1	0	0
Hossam Ghaly	2006–07	17	4	1	2	2	1	2	1	0	3	3	1	4	3	0	28	13	3
Eddie Gibbins	1943–53	1	0	0	3	0	0	0	0	0	0	0	0	4	0	0	8	0	0
A (Jack) H Gibbons	1937–46	27	0	13	6	0	5	0	0	0	0	0	0	115	0	91	148	0	109
Terry B Gibson	1978–84	16	2	4	5	0	1	1	0	1	0	2	1	7	10	9	29	14	16
Harry Gilberg	1941–50	2	0	0	1	0	0	0	0	0	0	0	0	22	0	9	25	0	9
Gilberto	2007–09	4	3	1	0	0	0	0	0	0	3	0	0	3	1	0	10	4	1
David Gillingwater	1965–66	0	0	0	0	0	0	0	0	0	0	0	0	1	0	0	1	0	0
Alan J Gilzean	1964–75	335	8	93	40	0	21	27	1	6	27	1	13	62	5	40	491	15	173
Ian R Gilzean	1988–92	0	0	0	0	0	0	0	0	0	0	0	0	0	2	0	0	2	0
David DM Ginola	1997–03	100	0	13	11	0	5	13	0	4	2	1	0	23	2	2	149	3	24
Giovani (dos Santos)	2008–11	2	8	0	0	1	0	3	1	0	4	1	1	6	2	2	15	13	3
Tommy S Gipps	1909–10	0	0	0	0	0	0	0	0	0	0	0	0	2	0	0	2	0	0
P Glen	1915–16	0	0	0	0	0	0	0	0	0	0	0	0	1	0	1	1	0	1
George Gliddon	1912 Tour	0	0	0	0	0	0	0	0	0	0	0	0	2	0	0	2	0	0
George Goldsmith	1934–35	1	0	0	0	0	0	0	0	0	0	0	0	0	0	0	1	0	0
Ernie H Goldthorpe	1917–19	0	0	0	0	0	0	0	0	0	0	0	0	17	0	9	17	0	9
Heurelho DS Gomes	2008–11	95	0	0	10	0	0	8	0	0	18	0	0	11	2	0	142	2	0
A (Bert) A Goodman	1919–20	16	0	1	1	0	0	0	0	0	0	0	0	3	0	0	20	0	1
Albert Goodman	1940–45	0	0	0	0	0	0	0	0	0	0	0	0	2	0	0	2	0	0
John Gorman	1976–79	30	0	0	2	0	0	0	0	0	0	0	0	5	5	0	37	5	0
Eddie J Gormley	1989–90	0	0	0	0	0	0	0	0	0	0	0	0	0	2	0	0	2	0
Albert A Gosnell	1910–11	5	0	0	2	0	0	0	0	0	0	0	0	2	0	0	9	0	0
C Richard Gough	1986–88	49	0	2	6	0	0	10	0	0	0	0	0	10	1	0	75	1	2
Mark Gower	1998–00	0	0	0	0	0	0	0	2	0	0	0	0	2	5	0	2	7	0
Andy A Gray	1991–94	23	10	3	0	0	0	0	0	0	0	0	0	8	7	3	31	17	6

NAME	SEASON	LEAGUE			FA CUP			FL CUP			EURO			OTHERS			TOTAL		
		APPS	SUBS	GOALS	APPS	SUBS	GOALS	APPS	SUBS	GOALS	APPS	SUBS	GOALS	APPS	SUBS	GOALS	APPS	SUBS	GOALS
Phil Gray	1986–91	4	5	0	0	1	0	0	0	0	0	0	0	1	22	2	5	28	2
Jimmy P Greaves	1961–79	322	0	220	36	0	32	8	0	5	14	0	9	40	0	40	420	0	306
George W Greenfield	1931–35	31	0	11	0	0	0	0	0	0	0	0	0	2	0	2	33	0	13
Steve J Grenfell	1985–86	0	0	0	0	0	0	0	0	0	0	0	0	0	1	0	0	1	0
Frank Grice	1935–39	47	0	1	8	0	0	0	0	0	0	0	0	0	0	0	55	0	1
J Griffiths	1945–46	0	0	0	0	0	0	0	0	0	0	0	0	1	0	0	1	0	0
W (Billy) J Grimes	1916–17	0	0	0	0	0	0	0	0	0	0	0	0	3	0	1	3	0	1
Arthur Grimsdell	1911–29	324	0	26	36	0	1	0	0	0	0	0	0	59	0	11	419	0	38
Vic G Groves	1952–54	4	0	3	0	0	0	0	0	0	0	0	0	0	0	0	4	0	3
Alan J Grubb	1952–53	2	0	0	0	0	0	0	0	0	0	0	0	0	0	0	2	0	0
Eidur Gudjohnsen	2009–10	3	7	1	1	2	1	0	0	0	0	0	0	0	0	0	4	9	2
Chris Gunter	2007–10	3	2	0	2	1	0	1	0	0	6	1	0	3	4	0	15	8	0
Harry D Gurr	1942–45	0	0	0	0	0	0	0	0	0	0	0	0	2	0	0	2	0	0
Peter J Guthrie	1988–89	0	0	0	0	0	0	0	0	0	0	0	0	1	4	0	1	4	0
Albert EB Hall	1935–47	40	0	10	4	0	1	0	0	0	0	0	0	37	0	11	81	0	22
Almer G Hall	1934–36	16	0	3	5	0	0	0	0	0	0	0	0	2	0	2	23	0	5
B Alan C Hall	1933–34	2	0	0	0	0	0	0	0	0	0	0	0	0	0	0	2	0	0
Fred W Hall	1944–46	0	0	0	0	0	0	0	0	0	0	0	0	23	0	0	23	0	0
G Willie Hall	1932–44	205	0	27	20	0	2	0	0	0	0	0	0	151	0	16	376	0	45
Jack Hall	1936–46	53	0	0	5	0	0	0	0	0	0	0	0	9	0	0	67	0	0
W Halle	1917–18	0	0	0	0	0	0	0	0	0	0	0	0	1	0	0	1	0	0
Colin MK Hampton	1921–22	0	0	0	0	0	0	0	0	0	0	0	0	1	0	0	1	0	0
Ken P Hancock	1969–71	3	0	0	0	0	0	1	0	0	0	0	0	4	0	0	8	0	0
Charlie HL Handley	1921–29	120	0	26	11	0	9	0	0	0	0	0	0	24	0	14	155	0	49
Charlie W Hannaford	1916–17	0	0	0	0	0	0	0	0	0	0	0	0	1	0	1	1	0	1
Charlie W Harbidge	1918–19	0	0	0	0	0	0	0	0	0	0	0	0	2	0	0	2	0	0
Wilf Hares	1942–43	0	0	0	0	0	0	0	0	0	0	0	0	1	0	0	1	0	0
Harry Hargreaves	1923–26	34	0	7	0	0	0	0	0	0	0	0	0	4	0	4	38	0	11
Tommy C Harmer	1949–60	205	0	47	17	0	4	0	0	0	0	0	0	51	2	18	273	2	69
E (Ted) C Harper	1928–32	63	0	62	4	0	1	0	0	0	0	0	0	11	0	20	78	0	83
H Harris	1943–44	0	0	0	0	0	0	0	0	0	0	0	0	3	0	0	3	0	0
W (Bill) Harris	1909–10	7	0	0	0	0	0	0	0	0	0	0	0	5	0	0	12	0	0
Frank Hartley	1922–31	7	0	1	0	0	0	0	0	0	0	0	0	6	0	4	13	0	5
Hatfied	1918–19	0	0	0	0	0	0	0	0	0	0	0	0	1	0	0	1	0	0
W (Billy) Hawkins	1916–19	0	0	0	0	0	0	0	0	0	0	0	0	68	0	9	68	0	9
Hayes	1952 Tour	0	0	0	0	0	0	0	0	0	0	0	0	0	1	0	0	1	0
Stan Hayhurst	1948–49	0	0	0	0	0	0	0	0	0	0	0	0	1	0	0	1	0	0
Mickey Hazard	1979–95	88	31	15	9	3	2	12	4	5	22	1	3	41	17	11	172	56	36

NAME	SEASON	LEAGUE APPS	LEAGUE SUBS	LEAGUE GOALS	FA CUP APPS	FA CUP SUBS	FA CUP GOALS	FL CUP APPS	FL CUP SUBS	FL CUP GOALS	EURO APPS	EURO SUBS	EURO GOALS	OTHERS APPS	OTHERS SUBS	OTHERS GOALS	TOTAL APPS	TOTAL SUBS	TOTAL GOALS
Foster Hedley	1933–35	4	0	1	1	0	0	0	0	0	0	0	0	3	0	1	8	0	2
Tom P Heffernan	1977–78	0	0	0	0	0	0	0	0	0	0	0	0	0	1	1	0	1	1
Archie E Heggarty	1913–14	0	0	0	0	0	0	0	0	0	0	0	0	1	0	0	1	0	0
Sid Helliwell	1927–29	8	0	0	1	0	0	0	0	0	0	0	0	4	0	1	13	0	1
Ian M Hendon	1989–94	0	4	0	0	0	0	1	0	0	0	2	0	7	16	0	8	22	0
John M Hendry	1990–95	5	12	5	0	1	0	0	2	0	0	0	0	11	6	5	16	21	10
Les D Henley	1940–45	0	0	0	0	0	0	0	0	0	0	0	0	2	0	1	2	0	1
Ron P Henry	1954–67	247	0	1	23	0	0	0	0	0	17	0	0	51	4	1	338	4	2
Ronnie S Henry	2002–04	0	0	0	0	0	0	0	0	0	0	0	0	4	3	1	4	3	1
R (Tex) Henty	1950–51	0	0	0	0	0	0	0	0	0	0	0	0	1	0	0	1	0	0
ER (Baden) Herod	1928–31	57	0	0	2	0	0	0	0	0	0	0	0	10	0	0	69	0	0
R (Bob) Hewitson	1908–09	30	0	0	4	0	0	0	0	0	0	0	0	3	0	0	37	0	0
Danny RL Hill	1992–96	4	6	0	0	0	0	0	2	0	0	0	0	11	13	1	15	21	1
W Hill	1917–18	0	0	0	0	0	0	0	0	0	0	0	0	2	0	0	2	0	0
Ian M Hillier	1999–02	0	0	0	0	0	0	0	0	0	0	0	0	0	3	0	0	3	0
Johnnie R Hills	1954–60	29	0	0	3	0	0	0	0	0	0	0	0	9	0	0	41	0	0
W (Bill) FW Hinton	1924–26	57	0	0	7	0	0	0	0	0	0	0	0	6	0	0	70	0	0
Lars Hirschfeld	2003–04	0	0	0	0	0	0	0	0	0	0	0	0	3	3	0	3	3	0
Arthur Hitchins	1937–42	37	0	1	7	0	0	0	0	0	0	0	0	112	0	0	156	0	1
Sid J Hoad	1916–17	0	0	0	0	0	0	0	0	0	0	0	0	4	0	0	4	0	0
Alf Hobday	1913–14	0	0	0	0	0	0	0	0	0	0	0	0	1	0	0	1	0	0
Glenn Hoddle	1975–87	370	7	88	47	1	11	44	0	10	17	4	1	88	12	22	566	24	132
Steve B Hodge	1986–88	44	1	7	7	0	2	2	0	0	0	0	0	12	5	3	65	6	12
Lee L Hodges	1991–94	0	4	0	0	0	0	0	0	0	0	0	0	2	9	0	2	13	0
H (Bert) Hodgkinson	1930–32	56	0	0	2	0	0	0	0	0	0	0	0	5	0	0	63	0	0
Ernie H Hoffman	1917–18	0	0	0	0	0	0	0	0	0	0	0	0	1	0	0	1	0	0
Hoffman	1918–19	0	0	0	0	0	0	0	0	0	0	0	0	1	0	0	1	0	0
Phil Holder	1971–75	9	4	1	0	0	0	0	0	0	0	6	1	3	5	0	12	15	2
Tom Holley	1942–43	0	0	0	0	0	0	0	0	0	0	0	0	1	0	2	1	0	2
Roy W Hollis	1952–53	3	0	1	1	0	2	0	0	0	0	0	0	0	0	0	4	0	3
John F Hollowbread	1956–64	67	0	0	6	0	0	0	0	0	0	0	0	9	0	0	82	0	0
Jimmy P Holmes	1976–81	81	0	2	9	0	0	2	0	0	0	0	0	25	4	2	117	4	4
Percy GW Hooper	1934–45	100	0	0	11	0	0	0	0	0	0	0	0	132	0	0	243	0	0
Fred Hopkin	1915–16	0	0	0	0	0	0	0	0	0	0	0	0	4	0	1	4	0	1
Mel Hopkins	1952–64	219	0	0	20	0	0	0	0	0	1	0	0	31	0	1	271	0	1
Scott A Houghton	1990–93	0	10	2	0	0	0	0	2	0	0	2	0	1	4	1	1	18	3
Les F Howe	1930–46	165	0	26	17	0	2	0	0	0	0	0	0	103	0	19	285	0	47
David G Howells	1985–98	238	39	22	17	4	1	26	5	4	6	0	0	62	26	13	349	74	40

NAME	SEASON	LEAGUE APPS	LEAGUE SUBS	LEAGUE GOALS	FA CUP APPS	FA CUP SUBS	FA CUP GOALS	FL CUP APPS	FL CUP SUBS	FL CUP GOALS	EURO APPS	EURO SUBS	EURO GOALS	OTHERS APPS	OTHERS SUBS	OTHERS GOALS	TOTAL APPS	TOTAL SUBS	TOTAL GOALS
Tom Howshall	1945–46	0	0	0	0	0	0	0	0	0	0	0	0	1	0	0	1	0	0
Roger E Hoy	1965–68	10	0	0	0	0	0	0	0	0	2	0	0	3	0	0	15	0	0
Tom A Huddlestone	2005–11	93	29	8	9	3	0	10	5	5	22	6	2	25	9	0	159	52	15
Mark Hughes	2003–05	0	0	0	0	0	0	0	0	0	0	0	0	5	4	0	5	4	0
W Archie Hughes	1944–48	2	0	0	2	0	0	0	0	0	0	0	0	55	0	0	59	0	0
Chris WG Hughton	1978–90	293	4	12	34	2	1	33	2	2	29	1	4	96	5	3	485	14	22
Cian Hughton	2007–08	0	0	0	0	0	0	0	0	0	0	0	0	0	1	0	0	1	0
Percy Humphreys	1909–12	45	0	23	5	0	5	0	0	0	0	0	0	4	0	0	54	0	28
Doug A Hunt	1934–44	17	0	6	2	0	0	0	0	0	0	0	0	5	0	7	24	0	13
George S Hunt	1930–37	185	0	125	13	0	13	0	0	0	0	0	0	7	0	10	205	0	148
Kenneth RG Hunt	1916–17	0	0	0	0	0	0	0	0	0	0	0	0	1	0	0	1	0	0
Alex C Hunter	1920–22	23	0	0	3	0	0	0	0	0	0	0	0	8	0	0	34	0	0
George H Hutchinson	1953–54	5	0	1	0	0	0	0	0	0	0	0	0	2	0	1	7	0	2
Alan Hutton	2007–11	39	12	2	3	0	0	6	0	0	6	0	0	10	2	0	64	14	2
Phil N Ifil	2004–08	3	0	0	0	0	0	1	1	0	0	0	0	5	9	0	9	10	0
Jim Iley	1057–59	53	0	1	4	0	0	0	0	0	0	0	0	9	0	0	66	0	1
John W Illingworth	1929–35	10	0	0	2	0	0	0	0	0	0	0	0	7	1	0	19	1	0
A Innes	1918–19	0	0	0	0	0	0	0	0	0	0	0	0	1	0	0	1	0	0
Jeff CC Ireland	1957–59	3	0	0	0	0	0	0	0	0	0	0	0	2	0	1	5	0	1
Steffen Iversen	1996–03	112	31	36	10	5	4	11	4	6	4	0	1	21	11	26	158	51	73
Archie Jack	1917–19	0	0	0	0	0	0	0	0	0	0	0	0	20	0	7	20	0	7
Harry Jackson	1942–43	0	0	0	0	0	0	0	0	0	0	0	0	2	0	0	2	0	0
Jakey Jackson	1944–45	0	0	0	0	0	0	0	0	0	0	0	0	2	0	0	2	0	0
Johnny Jackson	2001–06	12	8	1	1	2	0	1	0	0	0	0	0	15	9	1	29	19	2
W (Bill) Jacques	1914–23	123	0	0	15	0	0	0	0	0	0	0	0	124	0	0	262	0	0
Oscar Jansson	2008–10	0	0	0	0	0	0	0	0	0	0	0	0	1	2	0	1	2	0
George Jeffrey	1937–38	1	0	1	0	0	0	0	0	0	0	0	0	0	0	0	1	0	1
Jermaine A Jenas	2005–11	133	20	21	8	1	2	13	0	2	21	4	1	21	3	0	196	28	26
David J Jenkins	1968–70	12	3	2	2	1	0	0	0	0	0	0	0	1	0	0	15	4	2
Alf W Jennings	1923–24	0	0	0	0	0	0	0	0	0	0	0	0	1	0	0	1	0	0
Pat A Jennings	1964–86	473	0	0	43	0	0	39	0	0	36	0	0	82	3	1	673	3	1
Sam Jennings	1918–19	0	0	0	0	0	0	0	0	0	0	0	0	1	0	0	1	0	0
Jimmy T Jinks	1945–46	0	0	0	0	0	0	0	0	0	0	0	0	1	0	2	1	0	2
Neil J Johnson	1965–71	28	7	5	4	0	1	0	0	0	0	0	0	4	10	0	36	17	6
Richard W Johnston	1987–89	0	0	0	0	0	0	0	0	0	0	0	0	0	2	0	0	2	0
Joliffe	1941–42	0	0	0	0	0	0	0	0	0	0	0	0	1	0	0	1	0	0
Charlie Jones	1934–36	18	0	0	0	0	0	0	0	0	0	0	0	1	0	0	19	0	0
Chris Jones	1974–82	149	15	37	10	2	4	7	1	1	0	1	0	52	10	25	218	29	67

NAME	SEASON	LEAGUE			FA CUP			FL CUP			EURO			OTHERS			TOTAL		
		APPS	SUBS	GOALS	APPS	SUBS	GOALS	APPS	SUBS	GOALS	APPS	SUBS	GOALS	APPS	SUBS	GOALS	APPS	SUBS	GOALS
Cliff W Jones	1957–78	314	4	135	35	4	16	2	0	1	19	0	7	38	2	15	408	10	174
Eric N Jones	1942–44	0	0	0	0	0	0	0	0	0	0	0	0	17	0	7	17	0	7
Gordon Jones	1912–13	8	0	0	0	0	0	0	0	0	0	0	0	3	0	0	11	0	0
Len Jones	1942–43	0	0	0	0	0	0	0	0	0	0	0	0	1	0	1	1	0	1
W Ernie A Jones	1946–49	56	0	14	2	0	0	0	0	0	0	0	0	7	0	2	65	0	16
Johnny W Jordan	1947–48	24	0	10	3	0	0	0	0	0	0	0	0	1	0	0	28	0	10
Leon Joseph	1946–47	1	0	0	0	0	0	0	0	0	0	0	0	0	0	0	1	0	0
Phil J Joslin	1945–46	0	0	0	0	0	0	0	0	0	0	0	0	4	0	0	4	0	0
JW (John) Joyce	1909–16	73	0	1	8	0	0	0	0	0	0	0	0	33	0	1	114	0	2
Younes Kaboul	2007–11	46	6	4	1	0	0	3	1	0	6	0	2	7	1	0	63	8	6
W (Bill) EJC Kaine	1925–26	11	0	0	1	0	0	0	0	0	0	0	0	0	0	0	12	0	0
Yannick Kamanan	2001–02	0	0	0	0	0	0	0	0	0	0	0	0	0	3	3	0	3	3
Fredi O Kanoute	2003–06	41	19	14	6	0	3	5	2	4	0	0	0	5	3	7	57	24	28
Robbie D Keane	2002–11	189	49	91	16	5	12	16	7	10	15	9	8	34	12	26	270	82	147
Andy J Keeley	1975–77	5	1	0	0	0	0	0	0	0	0	0	0	0	3	0	5	4	0
Kasey C Keller	2001–05	85	0	0	4	0	0	10	0	0	0	0	0	13	0	0	112	0	0
Gavin Kelly	2001–02	0	0	0	0	0	0	0	0	0	0	0	0	2	1	0	2	1	0
Stephen MD Kelly	2002–06	29	8	2	6	0	0	1	0	0	0	0	0	10	5	0	46	13	2
Mario A Kempes	1984–85	0	0	0	0	0	0	0	0	0	0	0	0	5	0	3	5	0	3
Mark Kendall	1975–81	29	0	0	6	0	0	1	0	0	0	0	0	9	18	0	45	18	0
Jimmy J Kennedy	1909–12	13	0	1	0	0	0	0	0	0	0	0	0	4	0	0	17	0	1
Arthur HG Kerry	1909–10	1	0	0	0	0	0	0	0	0	0	0	0	0	0	0	1	0	0
David Kerslake	1993–96	34	3	0	1	1	0	5	0	0	0	0	0	15	5	2	55	9	2
Tom Kiernan	1941–42	0	0	0	0	0	0	0	0	0	0	0	0	2	0	0	2	0	0
Arthur King	1913–14	19	0	0	1	0	0	0	0	0	0	0	0	5	0	0	25	0	0
Derek A King	1951–55	19	0	0	0	0	0	0	0	0	0	0	0	7	0	0	26	0	0
Eddie F King	1934–35	1	0	0	0	0	0	0	0	0	0	0	0	0	0	0	1	0	0
Ledley B King	1998–11	243	3	10	18	1	3	20	0	1	14	0	0	26	5	0	321	9	14
Joe P Kinnear	1965–80	190	7	2	24	0	0	20	0	0	18	0	0	40	3	4	292	10	6
Jurgen Klinsmann	1994–03	56	0	29	9	0	5	3	0	4	0	0	0	4	0	3	72	0	41
John G Knight	1928–29	1	0	0	0	0	0	0	0	0	0	0	0	0	0	0	1	0	0
Tom Knighton	1915–16	0	0	0	0	0	0	0	0	0	0	0	0	4	0	2	4	0	2
Vic J Knott	1923–26	0	0	0	0	0	0	0	0	0	0	0	0	2	0	0	2	0	0
Cyril B Knowles	1964–77	401	1	15	42	0	1	32	1	0	30	0	1	62	0	3	597	2	20
Peter Knowles	1975–76	0	0	0	0	0	0	0	0	0	0	0	0	0	1	0	0	1	0
Paul M Konchesky	2003–04	10	2	0	0	0	0	2	1	0	0	0	0	0	0	0	12	3	0
Willem Korsten	1999–01	12	11	3	0	3	0	1	0	0	0	0	0	0	3	0	13	17	3
Niko Kranjcar	2009–11	21	16	8	6	3	2	0	1	0	1	5	0	3	3	0	31	28	10

NAME	SEASON	LEAGUE APPS	LEAGUE SUBS	LEAGUE GOALS	FA CUP APPS	FA CUP SUBS	FA CUP GOALS	FL CUP APPS	FL CUP SUBS	FL CUP GOALS	EURO APPS	EURO SUBS	EURO GOALS	OTHERS APPS	OTHERS SUBS	OTHERS GOALS	TOTAL APPS	TOTAL SUBS	TOTAL GOALS
John Lacy	1978–83	99	5	2	12	0	0	11	0	1	4	1	0	37	5	2	167	11	5
Chris S Landon	1992–93	0	0	0	0	0	0	0	0	0	0	0	0	1	1	0	1	1	0
W (Bill) HC Lane	1924–27	25	0	7	4	0	2	0	0	0	0	0	0	7	0	3	36	0	12
John A Laurel	1957–58	0	0	0	0	0	0	0	0	0	0	0	0	1	0	0	1	0	0
W (Billy) H Lawrence	1917–18	0	0	0	0	0	0	0	0	0	0	0	0	5	0	1	5	0	1
Jack S Laybourne	1952–53	0	0	0	0	0	0	0	0	0	0	0	0	1	0	0	1	0	0
Charlie Lee	2006 Tour	0	0	0	0	0	0	0	0	0	0	0	0	0	2	0	0	2	0
Colin Lee	1977–80	57	5	18	6	1	3	2	0	0	0	0	0	20	3	9	85	9	30
David JF Lee	1999–00	0	0	0	0	0	0	0	0	0	0	0	0	0	1	0	0	1	0
Terry WG Lee	1973–75	1	0	0	0	0	0	0	0	0	0	0	0	0	1	0	1	1	0
Lee Young–Pyo	2005–08	68	2	0	7	0	0	6	0	0	10	0	0	2	0	0	93	2	0
Aaron J Lennon	2005–11	139	34	18	9	3	1	13	5	1	27	6	1	13	12	4	201	60	25
Oyvind Leonhardsen	1999–03	46	8	7	3	3	1	6	2	2	4	0	1	8	10	1	67	23	12
Tom S Leslie	1908–11	10	0	0	2	0	0	0	0	0	0	0	0	4	0	0	16	0	0
David J Levene	1932–35	8	0	0	2	0	0	0	0	0	0	0	0	0	0	0	10	0	0
David J Leworthy	1984–86	8	3	3	0	0	0	0	1	1	0	0	0	8	9	11	16	13	15
Ed J Lightfoot	1911–18	62	0	2	5	0	0	0	0	0	0	0	0	18	0	0	85	0	2
Alex F Lindsay	1917–30	211	0	42	15	0	8	0	0	0	0	0	0	53	0	18	279	0	68
D Lindsay	1917–19	0	0	0	0	0	0	0	0	0	0	0	0	24	0	0	24	0	0
Gary W Lineker	1989–92	105	0	67	9	0	3	16	0	8	8	0	2	24	3	10	162	3	90
Jake Livermore	2007–11	0	1	0	0	0	0	1	0	0	0	0	0	1	11	1	2	12	1
W Harry Lloyd	1915–19	0	0	0	0	0	0	0	0	0	0	0	0	40	0	7	40	0	7
Hugh H Lorimer	1919–22	5	0	0	0	0	0	0	0	0	0	0	0	8	0	0	13	0	0
A Roy Low	1964–67	6	2	1	0	0	0	0	0	0	0	0	0	3	1	1	9	3	2
A (Darkie) E Lowdell	1927–30	86	0	0	4	0	0	0	0	0	0	0	0	9	0	0	99	0	0
Harry Lowe	1914–27	65	0	0	7	0	0	0	0	0	0	0	0	13	0	0	85	0	0
George A Ludford	1936–50	77	0	8	6	0	1	0	0	0	0	0	0	192	0	83	275	0	92
Tommy H Lunn	1909–13	89	0	0	5	0	0	0	0	0	0	0	0	13	0	0	107	0	0
Archie Lyle	1909–10	1	0	0	0	0	0	0	0	0	0	0	0	0	0	0	1	0	0
Colin C Lyman	1937–46	47	0	10	8	0	1	0	0	0	0	0	0	32	0	9	87	0	20
AlBert T Lyons	1930–32	54	0	3	3	0	0	0	0	0	0	0	0	6	0	1	63	0	4
Gary V Mabbutt	1982–98	458	19	27	46	2	5	60	2	2	22	3	4	143	23	15	729	49	53
Mbulelo Mabizela	2003–05	1	6	1	0	0	0	1	1	0	0	0	0	4	2	0	6	9	1
Doug MacFarlane	1908–10	21	0	2	0	0	0	0	0	0	0	0	0	7	0	2	28	0	4
Dave C Mackay	1958–68	268	0	42	33	0	4	0	0	0	17	0	5	44	2	12	362	2	63
George Maddison	1922–24	40	0	0	1	0	0	0	0	0	0	0	0	7	0	0	48	0	0
Jacques Maghoma	2007–08	0	0	0	0	0	0	0	0	0	0	0	0	0	3	0	0	3	0
Kevin A Maher	1997–98	0	0	0	0	0	0	0	0	0	0	0	0	2	3	0	2	3	0

NAME	SEASON	LEAGUE APPS	LEAGUE SUBS	LEAGUE GOALS	FA CUP APPS	FA CUP SUBS	FA CUP GOALS	FL CUP APPS	FL CUP SUBS	FL CUP GOALS	EURO APPS	EURO SUBS	EURO GOALS	OTHERS APPS	OTHERS SUBS	OTHERS GOALS	TOTAL APPS	TOTAL SUBS	TOTAL GOALS
Paul G Mahorn	1992–98	3	0	0	0	1	0	0	1	1	0	0	0	10	7	0	13	9	1
Steed Malbranque	2006–08	53	9	6	7	2	1	9	0	2	13	3	3	6	1	0	88	15	12
Michael Malcolm	2004–05	0	0	0	0	0	0	0	0	0	0	0	0	1	3	0	1	3	0
Tommy R Manley	1943–44	0	0	0	0	0	0	0	0	0	0	0	0	1	0	0	1	0	0
Wilf J Mannion	1941–42	0	0	0	0	0	0	0	0	0	0	0	0	4	0	0	4	0	0
W (Billy) AJ Manuel	1987–88	0	0	0	0	0	0	0	0	0	0	0	0	0	2	0	0	2	0
Diego A Maradona	1985–86	0	0	0	0	0	0	0	0	0	0	0	0	1	0	0	1	0	0
A (Tony) V Marchi	1949–65	232	0	7	16	0	0	0	0	0	12	0	0	57	0	3	317	0	10
Stan H Markham	1948–49	0	0	0	0	0	0	0	0	0	0	0	0	1	0	0	1	0	0
Dean Marney	2002–06	4	4	2	0	3	0	0	0	0	0	0	0	10	13	0	14	20	2
Alan Marshall	1979 Tour	0	0	0	0	0	0	0	0	0	0	0	0	0	1	0	0	1	0
Ernie Marshall	1942–43	0	0	0	0	0	0	0	0	0	0	0	0	1	0	0	1	0	0
WH Harry Marshall	1931–32	1	0	0	0	0	0	0	0	0	0	0	0	0	0	0	1	0	0
John R Martin	1942–45	0	0	0	0	0	0	0	0	0	0	0	0	45	0	15	45	0	15
Ryan G Mason	2008–10	0	0	0	0	0	0	0	0	0	0	1	0	1	2	0	1	3	0
Tom L Mason	1911–12	7	0	1	0	0	0	0	0	0	0	0	0	1	0	0	8	0	1
Fred J Massey	1908–09	1	0	0	0	0	0	0	0	0	0	0	0	1	0	0	2	0	0
George Mazzon	1979–83	3	1	0	1	0	0	0	2	0	0	0	0	3	9	1	7	12	1
Don McAllister	1974–81	168	4	9	16	1	0	13	0	1	0	0	0	55	3	3	252	8	13
Mike McCabe	1981–82	0	0	0	0	0	0	0	0	0	0	0	0	0	1	0	0	1	0
McCalmont	1918–19	0	0	0	0	0	0	0	0	0	0	0	0	2	0	1	2	0	1
Albert A McCarthy	1940–41	0	0	0	0	0	0	0	0	0	0	0	0	1	0	0	1	0	0
Sid B McClellan	1950–56	68	0	29	2	0	3	0	0	0	0	0	0	23	4	30	93	4	62
Harry McCleneghan	1913–14	0	0	0	0	0	0	0	0	0	0	0	0	1	0	0	1	0	0
Patrick McConnon	1909–10	0	0	0	0	0	0	0	0	0	0	0	0	3	0	2	3	0	2
Jimmy McCormick	1932–46	137	0	26	13	0	2	0	0	0	0	0	0	20	0	2	170	0	30
McCracken	1918–19	0	0	0	0	0	0	0	0	0	0	0	0	1	0	0	1	0	0
J Frank McCudden	1923–24	0	0	0	0	0	0	0	0	0	0	0	0	1	0	0	1	0	0
David H McDonald	1991–93	2	0	0	0	0	0	0	0	0	0	0	0	2	1	0	4	1	0
D Roy McDonald	1920–21	0	0	0	0	0	0	0	0	0	0	0	0	1	0	0	1	0	0
R (Bob) J McDonald	1919–26	109	0	0	16	0	0	0	0	0	0	0	0	24	0	0	149	0	0
Frank F McEwan	1939–40	0	0	0	0	0	0	0	0	0	0	0	0	3	0	0	3	0	0
Dave McEwen	1999–01	0	4	0	0	0	0	0	0	0	0	0	0	0	1	0	0	5	0
McFarlane	1941–42	0	0	0	0	0	0	0	0	0	0	0	0	1	0	0	1	0	0
G McGlashlan	1916–17	0	0	0	0	0	0	0	0	0	0	0	0	1	0	0	1	0	0
R Chris McGrath	1973–77	30	8	5	0	0	0	1	0	0	7	1	5	8	7	0	46	16	10
T McGregor	1915–16	0	0	0	0	0	0	0	0	0	0	0	0	1	0	1	1	0	1
Willie McIver	1918–19	0	0	0	0	0	0	0	0	0	0	0	0	3	0	0	3	0	0

NAME	SEASON	LEAGUE APPS	LEAGUE SUBS	LEAGUE GOALS	FA CUP APPS	FA CUP SUBS	FA CUP GOALS	FL CUP APPS	FL CUP SUBS	FL CUP GOALS	EURO APPS	EURO SUBS	EURO GOALS	OTHERS APPS	OTHERS SUBS	OTHERS GOALS	TOTAL APPS	TOTAL SUBS	TOTAL GOALS
Kieran McKenna	2004–06	0	0	0	0	0	0	0	0	0	0	0	0	0	6	1	0	6	1
Marcel McKie	2004–05	0	0	0	0	0	0	0	0	0	0	0	0	2	4	0	2	4	0
Gerry J McMahon	1992–97	9	7	0	0	1	0	3	0	0	0	0	0	7	7	1	19	15	1
Neil McNab	1973–79	63	9	3	2	0	0	5	1	0	0	0	0	26	8	3	96	18	6
Brendan J McNally	1954–55	0	0	0	0	0	0	0	0	0	0	0	0	1	0	0	1	0	0
John K McTavish	1910–12	40	0	3	2	0	0	0	0	0	0	0	0	3	0	0	45	0	3
R (Bob) McTavish	1910–12	10	0	3	1	0	0	0	0	0	0	0	0	4	0	1	15	0	4
Paul F McVeigh	1996–98	2	1	1	0	0	0	0	0	0	0	0	0	2	4	1	4	5	2
J McVey	1916–17	0	0	0	0	0	0	0	0	0	0	0	0	2	0	0	2	0	0
Horace Meadows	1951–52	0	0	0	0	0	0	0	0	0	0	0	0	1	0	1	1	0	1
Tommy Meads	1929–35	184	0	6	5	0	0	0	0	0	0	0	0	7	0	0	196	0	6
Les D Medley	1938–53	150	0	45	14	0	1	0	0	0	0	0	0	89	0	28	253	0	74
Terry C Medwin	1956–63	197	0	65	13	0	7	0	0	0	5	0	0	32	0	18	247	0	90
Joe Meek	1935–39	45	0	15	6	0	1	0	0	0	0	0	0	0	0	0	51	0	16
Pedro MS Mendes	2004–06	25	5	1	2	0	0	2	2	0	0	0	0	9	6	0	38	13	1
Alf T Messer	1930–32	50	0	2	2	0	0	0	0	0	0	0	0	4	0	0	56	0	2
Johnny AB Metgod	1987–88	5	7	0	0	0	0	2	0	0	0	0	0	7	5	2	14	12	2
H Bert Middlemiss	1908–20	248	0	52	17	0	3	0	0	0	0	0	0	66	0	26	331	0	81
AHH Abdelhamid (Mido)	2004–07	35	13	14	2	3	2	2	2	3	2	2	0	5	1	4	46	21	23
Les Miller	1936–39	56	0	22	9	0	4	0	0	0	0	0	0	0	0	0	65	0	26
Paul Miller	1978–87	206	2	7	30	1	1	22	1	0	23	0	2	92	6	6	373	10	16
Leigh Mills	2007–08	0	0	0	0	0	0	0	0	0	0	0	0	0	1	0	0	1	0
G Milton	1942–43	0	0	0	0	0	0	0	0	0	0	0	0	1	0	0	1	0	0
R (Bobby) A Mimms	1987–91	37	0	0	2	0	0	5	0	0	0	0	0	20	5	0	64	5	0
W (Billy) J Minter	1908–26	248	0	95	19	0	6	0	0	0	0	0	0	67	0	51	334	0	152
Jeff ST Minton	1991–93	2	0	1	0	0	0	0	1	0	0	0	0	1	1	0	3	2	1
Luka Modric	2008–11	87	4	9	10	1	1	3	1	0	11	2	2	10	7	2	121	15	14
Reg WJ Mogford	1943–45	0	0	0	0	0	0	0	0	0	0	0	0	8	0	1	8	0	1
John F Moncur	1985–92	10	11	1	0	0	0	1	2	0	0	0	0	10	20	1	21	33	2
Jock Moodie	1944–45	0	0	0	0	0	0	0	0	0	0	0	0	1	0	0	1	0	0
Ian R Moores	1976–79	25	4	6	0	0	0	3	0	2	0	0	0	11	7	9	39	11	17
Ollie Morah	1991–92	0	0	0	0	0	0	0	0	0	0	0	0	0	1	0	0	1	0
Jack Moran	1931–32	12	0	0	0	0	0	0	0	0	0	0	0	0	0	0	12	0	0
Paul Moran	1986–94	14	22	2	3	1	0	1	6	0	0	1	0	10	25	3	28	55	5
Roger E Morgan	1968–73	66	2	8	6	0	2	3	0	1	2	1	1	12	3	5	89	6	17
Jimmy Morris	1915–17	0	0	0	0	0	0	0	0	0	0	0	0	43	0	4	43	0	4
Tom H Morris	1908–13	63	0	2	7	0	1	0	0	0	0	0	0	13	0	1	83	0	4
Johnny A Morrison	1932–46	134	0	90	21	0	14	0	0	0	0	0	0	34	0	26	189	0	130

NAME	SEASON	LEAGUE APPS	LEAGUE SUBS	LEAGUE GOALS	FA CUP APPS	FA CUP SUBS	FA CUP GOALS	FL CUP APPS	FL CUP SUBS	FL CUP GOALS	EURO APPS	EURO SUBS	EURO GOALS	OTHERS APPS	OTHERS SUBS	OTHERS GOALS	TOTAL APPS	TOTAL SUBS	TOTAL GOALS
Jimmy C Morton	1908–09	2	0	0	0	0	0	0	0	0	0	0	0	2	0	0	4	0	0
W (Bill) Moseley	1943–44	0	0	0	0	0	0	0	0	0	0	0	0	3	0	1	3	0	1
A (Chic) Muir	1942–43	0	0	0	0	0	0	0	0	0	0	0	0	1	0	0	1	0	0
Matt R Muir	1944–45	0	0	0	0	0	0	0	0	0	0	0	0	1	0	0	1	0	0
Alan P Mullery	1963–72	313	0	25	33	0	1	18	0	0	10	0	4	55	0	9	429	0	39
Danny B Murphy	2005–08	7	15	1	1	0	0	3	0	0	2	1	0	5	4	0	18	20	1
Peter Murphy	1950–52	38	0	14	0	0	0	0	0	0	0	0	0	11	0	6	49	0	20
Martin Nash	1994–95	0	0	0	0	0	0	0	0	0	0	0	0	0	1	1	0	1	1
Kyle Naughton	2009–11	0	1	0	0	1	0	2	0	0	0	0	0	7	6	0	9	8	0
Noureddine Naybet	2004–06	29	1	1	2	0	0	3	0	0	0	0	0	0	0	0	34	1	1
MA Amar (Nayim)	1998–93	95	17	11	6	3	4	11	6	3	6	0	0	33	6	3	151	32	21
Terry MP Naylor	1969–80	237	6	0	17	1	0	23	1	1	13	6	0	66	8	0	356	22	1
Jimmy E Neighbour	1970–77	104	15	8	10	1	1	14	3	1	6	3	1	24	10	4	158	32	15
WJ Terry Neill	1976 Tours	0	0	0	0	0	0	0	0	0	0	0	0	0	1	0	0	1	0
David Nelson	1942–44	0	0	0	0	0	0	0	0	0	0	0	0	2	0	1	2	0	1
Stuart D Nethercott	1991–97	31	23	0	5	3	1	0	0	0	0	0	0	16	15	1	52	41	2
Ernie H Newman	1909–14	31	0	6	2	0	0	0	0	0	0	0	0	1	0	0	34	0	6
Joe H Nicholls	1926–36	124	0	0	5	0	0	0	0	0	0	0	0	10	0	0	139	0	0
W (Bill) E Nicholson	1938–55	318	0	6	27	0	0	0	0	0	0	0	0	49	0	1	394	0	7
Allan Nielsen	1996–00	78	18	12	5	2	3	10	1	3	1	0	0	8	0	2	102	21	20
Roger Nilsen	1998–99	3	0	0	0	0	0	0	0	0	0	0	0	0	0	0	3	0	0
David Noble	1941–42	0	0	0	0	0	0	0	0	0	0	0	0	6	0	3	6	0	3
Maurice Norman	1955–66	357	0	16	37	0	2	0	0	0	17	0	1	43	0	0	454	0	19
Norris	1912 Tour	0	0	0	0	0	0	0	0	0	0	0	0	1	0	0	1	0	0
Tommy AB Nuttall	1917–18	0	0	0	0	0	0	0	0	0	0	0	0	18	0	10	18	0	10
John Oakes	1944–45	0	0	0	0	0	0	0	0	0	0	0	0	1	0	0	1	0	0
Jon C Obika	2008–11	0	0	0	0	0	0	0	0	0	1	1	0	3	2	2	4	3	2
E (Taffy) O'Callaghan	1926–44	252	0	92	11	0	6	0	0	0	0	0	0	50	0	23	313	0	121
Frank J O'Donnell	1943–45	0	0	0	0	0	0	0	0	0	0	0	0	13	0	8	13	0	8
James O'Donnell	1920–21	0	0	0	0	0	0	0	0	0	0	0	0	1	0	0	1	0	0
Paul O'Donoghue	2002–05	0	0	0	0	0	0	0	0	0	0	0	0	3	3	0	3	3	0
Jamie O'Hara	2004–10	15	19	2	2	1	0	6	3	3	5	5	2	12	15	2	40	43	9
W (Bill) Oliver	1913–14	2	0	0	0	0	0	0	0	0	0	0	0	0	0	0	2	0	0
Gary M O'Reilly	1979–84	39	6	0	2	0	0	4	0	0	2	2	0	14	4	1	61	12	1
Frank R Osborne	1923–31	210	0	78	9	0	4	0	0	0	0	0	0	10	0	5	229	0	87
Keith Osgood	1973–78	112	1	13	3	0	0	11	0	1	0	0	0	32	3	6	158	4	20
Tim J O'Shea	1986–88	1	2	0	0	0	0	0	0	0	0	0	0	1	1	0	2	3	0
Syd Ottewell	1939–40	0	0	0	0	0	0	0	0	0	0	0	0	1	0	0	1	0	0

NAME	SEASON	LEAGUE			FA CUP			FL CUP			EURO			OTHERS			TOTAL		
		APPS	SUBS	GOALS	APPS	SUBS	GOALS	APPS	SUBS	GOALS	APPS	SUBS	GOALS	APPS	SUBS	GOALS	APPS	SUBS	GOALS
Aled W Owen	1953–54	1	0	0	0	0	0	0	0	0	0	0	0	1	0	0	2	0	0
A (Bert) E Page	1936–46	56	0	0	1	0	0	0	0	0	0	0	0	31	0	0	88	0	0
RJ Page	1915–16	0	0	0	0	0	0	0	0	0	0	0	0	3	0	0	3	0	0
Wilson R Palacios S	2008–11	56	9	1	7	1	0	4	0	0	5	4	0	6	2	1	78	16	2
Palmer	1942–43	0	0	0	0	0	0	0	0	0	0	0	0	1	0	0	1	0	0
L Noe Pamarot	2004–06	23	2	1	2	0	1	3	0	0	0	0	0	0	0	0	28	2	2
H Cliff Parker	1943–44	0	0	0	0	0	0	0	0	0	0	0	0	1	0	0	1	0	0
A (Tony) Parks	1979–88	37	0	0	5	0	0	1	0	0	5	1	0	24	16	0	72	17	0
Dean G Parrett	2008–11	0	0	0	0	0	0	0	0	0	1	1	0	1	1	0	2	2	0
J Parsons	1918–19	0	0	0	0	0	0	0	0	0	0	0	0	1	0	0	1	0	0
Tom G Paton	1940–41	0	0	0	0	0	0	0	0	0	0	0	0	4	0	0	4	0	0
Pattinson	1918–19	0	0	0	0	0	0	0	0	0	0	0	0	1	0	0	1	0	0
Johnny RM Pattison	1942–43	0	0	0	0	0	0	0	0	0	0	0	0	13	0	3	13	0	3
Roman A Pavlyuchenko	2008–11	45	28	18	5	4	7	8	1	7	5	3	4	4	6	5	67	42	41
W (Billy) E Peake	1917–19	0	0	0	0	0	0	0	0	0	0	0	0	19	0	8	19	0	8
Jimmy W Pearce	1968–75	109	33	21	4	6	3	21	6	7	8	7	4	18	7	8	160	59	43
John Pearson	1913–23	47	0	0	3	0	0	0	0	0	0	0	0	7	0	0	57	0	0
Tommy U Pearson	1941–42	0	0	0	0	0	0	0	0	0	0	0	0	2	0	0	2	0	0
Chris J Perry	1999–04	111	9	3	9	0	0	13	0	0	4	0	1	28	12	0	165	21	4
Steve J Perryman	1969–90	654	2	31	69	0	2	66	0	3	63	1	3	162	5	12	1014	8	51
Martin S Peters	1969–75	189	0	46	16	0	5	23	0	12	32	0	13	27	0	11	287	0	87
Ernie Phypers	1934–37	30	0	0	3	0	0	0	0	0	0	0	0	2	0	0	35	0	0
Steven J Pienaar	2010–11	5	3	0	1	0	0	0	0	0	2	0	0	0	0	0	8	3	0
John W Piercy	1999–01	1	7	0	0	0	0	1	0	0	0	0	0	2	3	1	4	10	1
Gilbert H Piper	1939–41	0	0	0	0	0	0	0	0	0	0	0	0	4	0	0	4	0	0
Ron D Piper	1962–63	1	0	0	0	0	0	0	0	0	0	0	0	0	0	0	1	0	0
Steve W Pitt	1965–66	1	0	0	0	0	0	0	0	0	0	0	0	1	0	0	2	0	0
Stipe Pletikosa	2010–11	0	0	0	0	0	0	1	0	0	0	0	0	0	0	0	1	0	0
Andy A Polston	1988–92	0	1	0	0	0	0	0	0	0	0	0	0	4	9	0	4	10	0
John W Polston	1985–90	17	7	1	0	0	0	3	1	0	0	0	0	9	7	0	29	15	1
G (Gica) Popescu	1994–95	23	0	3	3	0	0	2	0	0	0	0	0	0	0	0	28	0	3
Derek J Possee	1963–66	19	0	4	0	0	0	0	0	0	0	0	0	13	3	0	32	3	4
Helder MM Postiga	2003–04	9	10	1	2	0	0	1	2	1	0	0	0	6	1	2	18	13	4
Cec B Potter	1916–19	0	0	0	0	0	0	0	0	0	0	0	0	22	0	9	22	0	9
Herbert Powell	1916–17	0	0	0	0	0	0	0	0	0	0	0	0	1	0	0	1	0	0
J Powell	1918–19	0	0	0	0	0	0	0	0	0	0	0	0	1	0	0	1	0	0
Gus A Poyet	2001–04	66	16	18	6	1	3	8	1	2	0	0	0	11	10	8	91	28	31
Cecil Poynton	1922–33	152	0	3	6	0	0	0	0	0	0	0	0	21	0	0	179	0	3

NAME	SEASON	LEAGUE APPS	LEAGUE SUBS	LEAGUE GOALS	FA CUP APPS	FA CUP SUBS	FA CUP GOALS	FL CUP APPS	FL CUP SUBS	FL CUP GOALS	EURO APPS	EURO SUBS	EURO GOALS	OTHERS APPS	OTHERS SUBS	OTHERS GOALS	TOTAL APPS	TOTAL SUBS	TOTAL GOALS
John A Pratt	1968–86	307	24	39	23	5	2	27	4	7	24	1	1	81	11	15	462	45	64
I Haydn Price	1918–19	0	0	0	0	0	0	0	0	0	0	0	0	9	0	3	9	0	3
Jack D Price	1954–55	0	0	0	0	0	0	0	0	0	0	0	0	2	0	0	2	0	0
Owen Price	2004 Tour	0	0	0	0	0	0	0	0	0	0	0	0	0	1	0	0	1	0
Paul T Price	1981–84	35	4	0	6	0	0	7	0	0	10	0	0	13	3	0	71	7	0
R (Bob) I Pryde	1944–45	0	0	0	0	0	0	0	0	0	0	0	0	1	0	0	1	0	0
Predrag Radosavijec (Preki)	1991–92	0	0	0	0	0	0	0	0	0	0	0	0	1	0	0	1	0	0
Andy T Ralston	1915–19	0	0	0	0	0	0	0	0	0	0	0	0	104	0	0	104	0	0
A Ramsay	1915–16	0	0	0	0	0	0	0	0	0	0	0	0	1	0	0	1	0	0
Alf E Ramsey	1949–55	226	0	24	24	0	0	0	0	0	0	0	0	33	0	6	283	0	30
Charlie S Rance	1910–21	105	0	1	7	0	1	0	0	0	0	0	0	151	0	14	263	0	16
Grzegorz Rasiak	2005–06	4	4	0	1	0	0	0	0	0	0	0	0	0	0	0	5	4	0
Sergei Rebrov	2000–03	37	22	10	7	1	3	4	4	2	0	0	0	15	8	11	63	35	26
Jack Reddish	1928–32	6	0	0	1	0	0	0	0	0	0	0	0	3	0	0	10	0	0
Jamie F Redknapp	2002–05	37	11	4	0	0	0	1	0	0	0	0	0	15	2	1	53	13	5
Rees	1918–19	0	0	0	0	0	0	0	0	0	0	0	0	1	0	0	1	0	0
W (Billy) Rees	1949–50	11	0	3	2	0	0	0	0	0	0	0	0	1	0	0	14	0	3
Andy M Reid	2004–06	20	6	1	0	0	0	1	0	0	0	0	0	7	2	0	28	8	1
Charlie H Revell	1941–42	0	0	0	0	0	0	0	0	0	0	0	0	1	0	1	1	0	1
Ron SM Reynolds	1950–59	86	0	0	9	0	0	0	0	0	0	0	0	43	0	0	138	0	0
Dean J Richards	2001–05	73	0	4	5	0	0	3	0	0	0	0	0	8	1	2	89	1	6
Jock Richardson	1925–29	38	0	0	3	0	0	0	0	0	0	0	0	6	0	1	47	0	1
Rohan E Ricketts	2002–05	17	13	1	0	0	0	4	2	1	0	0	0	12	11	0	33	26	2
Chris Riley	2007–08	0	0	0	0	0	0	0	0	0	0	0	0	0	1	0	0	1	0
A (Bert) A Ringrose	1936–37	10	0	0	0	0	0	0	0	0	0	0	0	0	0		10	0	0
George W Robb	1951–59	182	0	53	18	0	5	0	0	0	0	0	0	24	0	7	224	0	65
Graham P Roberts	1979–88	200	9	23	27	0	2	24	1	5	25	1	5	81	6	10	357	17	45
R Roberts	1944–45	0	0	0	0	0	0	0	0	0	0	0	0	2	0	0	2	0	0
W (Tom) Roberts	1928–29	4	0	2	0	0	0	0	0	0	0	0	0	0	0	0	4	0	2
Jimmy G Robertson	1963–69	153	4	25	18	0	3	2	0	0	4	0	3	31	3	11	208	7	42
Robinson	1917–18	0	0	0	0	0	0	0	0	0	0	0	0	1	0	0	1	0	0
Martin J Robinson	1975–78	5	1	2	0	0	0	0	0	0	0	0	0	2	3	0	7	4	2
Paul W Robinson	2004–08	137	0	1	12	0	0	10	0	0	16	0	0	11	0	0	186	0	1
Steve Robinson	1993–95	1	1	0	0	0	0	0	0	0	0	0	0	0	3	1	1	4	1
Harry W Robshaw	1951–53	1	0	0	0	0	0	0	0	0	0	0	0	2	1	0	3	1	0
J Robson	1918–19	0	0	0	0	0	0	0	0	0	0	0	0	2	0	0	2	0	0
Mark A Robson	1987–92	3	5	0	0	0	0	1	0	0	0	0	0	5	13	0	9	18	0
Ricardo S Rocha	2006–08	13	1	0	3	0	0	0	1	0	0	0	0	5	1	0	21	3	0

NAME	SEASON	LEAGUE APPS	LEAGUE SUBS	LEAGUE GOALS	FA CUP APPS	FA CUP SUBS	FA CUP GOALS	FL CUP APPS	FL CUP SUBS	FL CUP GOALS	EURO APPS	EURO SUBS	EURO GOALS	OTHERS APPS	OTHERS SUBS	OTHERS GOALS	TOTAL APPS	TOTAL SUBS	TOTAL GOALS
Tommy W Roe	1925–27	7	0	4	0	0	0	0	0	0	0	0	0	2	0	1	9	0	5
Roper	1918–19	0	0	0	0	0	0	0	0	0	0	0	0	1	0	1	1	0	1
Danny Rose	2009–11	5	0	1	1	2	0	0	1	0	0	0	0	4	8	1	10	11	2
Ronny Rosenthal	1993–97	55	33	4	8	2	6	3	0	1	0	0	0	14	7	4	80	42	15
Jimmy D Ross	1920–24	7	0	0	0	0	0	0	0	0	0	0	0	2	0	0	9	0	0
Wayne NA Routledge	2005–08	3	2	0	0	0	0	0	0	0	0	0	0	12	7	1	15	9	1
Arthur S Rowe	1930–38	182	0	0	19	0	0	0	0	0	0	0	0	9	0	0	210	0	0
Jack F Rowley	1942–45	0	0	0	0	0	0	0	0	0	0	0	0	27	0	26	27	0	26
R (Dick) WM Rowley	1929–32	24	0	10	0	0	0	0	0	0	0	0	0	2	0	1	26	0	11
Neil Ruddock	1985–92	45	2	3	6	1	1	4	0	0	0	0	0	24	9	2	79	12	6
Charlie R Rundle	1945–50	28	0	12	1	0	0	0	0	0	0	0	0	10	0	3	39	0	15
John Rutherford	1914–19	0	0	0	0	0	0	0	0	0	0	0	0	2	0	0	2	0	0
John J Ryden	1955–59	63	0	2	5	0	0	0	0	0	0	0	0	21	0	1	89	0	3
W (Billy) Sage	1919–26	13	0	0	0	0	0	0	0	0	0	0	0	3	0	0	16	0	0
Moussa Saib	1997–99	3	10	1	0	0	0	0	0	0	0	0	0	7	1	2	10	11	3
R (Bobby) Sainsbury	1940–42	0	0	0	0	0	0	0	0	0	0	0	0	2	0	0	2	0	0
W (Billy) H Sainsbury	1941–44	0	0	0	0	0	0	0	0	0	0	0	0	5	0	1	5	0	1
Vinny Samways	1984–94	165	28	11	15	1	2	27	4	4	6	1	0	64	13	12	277	47	29
Cesar Sanchez	2008–09	0	0	0	0	0	0	0	1	0	0	0	0	0	0	0	0	1	0
Sandro (RG Cordeiro)	2010–11	11	8	1	2	0	0	1	0	0	3	1	0	0	0	0	17	9	1
Arthur W Sanders	1926–28	13	0	7	0	0	0	0	0	0	0	0	0	0	0	0	13	0	7
Fred A Sargent	1934–46	96	0	25	16	0	8	0	0	0	0	0	0	31	0	5	143	0	38
Frank L Saul	1959–68	112	4	37	7	0	6	1	0	0	5	0	2	33	6	15	158	10	60
Saunders	1917–18	0	0	0	0	0	0	0	0	0	0	0	0	1	0	0	1	0	0
Wilf W Saunders	1940–41	0	0	0	0	0	0	0	0	0	0	0	0	3	0	0	3	0	0
John R Scales	1996–00	29	4	0	0	0	0	4	0	1	0	0	0	5	3	0	38	7	1
Jimmy W Scarth	1949–52	7	0	3	0	0	0	0	0	0	0	0	0	5	0	4	12	0	7
Joe Scott	1928–31	18	0	4	0	0	0	0	0	0	0	0	0	3	0	2	21	0	6
Kevin W Scott	1993–96	16	2	1	0	0	0	0	1	0	0	0	0	4	7	1	20	10	2
Steve P Sedgley	1989–94	147	17	9	12	1	1	24	3	1	4	3	0	53	5	3	240	29	14
Max P Seeburg	1908–09	1	0	0	0	0	0	0	0	0	0	0	0	1	0	0	2	0	0
Jimmy M Seed	1919–27	230	0	65	25	0	12	0	0	0	0	0	0	31	0	8	286	0	85
Hans JCA Segers	1998–00	1	0	0	0	0	0	1	0	0	0	0	0	1	1	0	3	1	0
Buchanan Sharp	1922–25	3	0	0	0	0	0	0	0	0	0	0	0	2	0	1	5	0	1
Fred C Sharpe	1958–59	2	0	1	0	0	0	0	0	0	0	0	0	0	0	0	2	0	1
E (Teddy) P Sheringham	1992–03	230	6	97	21	0	14	20	1	13	0	0	0	30	1	20	301	8	144
Tim A Sherwood	1999–03	81	12	12	13	0	1	6	3	2	3	0	1	14	8	4	117	23	20
A (Joe) Sibley	1941–42	0	0	0	0	0	0	0	0	0	0	0	0	3	0	1	3	0	1

NAME	SEASON	LEAGUE APPS	LEAGUE SUBS	LEAGUE GOALS	FA CUP APPS	FA CUP SUBS	FA CUP GOALS	FL CUP APPS	FL CUP SUBS	FL CUP GOALS	EURO APPS	EURO SUBS	EURO GOALS	OTHERS APPS	OTHERS SUBS	OTHERS GOALS	TOTAL APPS	TOTAL SUBS	TOTAL GOALS
Edson Silva	2004–05	0	0	0	0	0	0	0	0	0	0	0	0	2	1	0	2	1	0
Simmonds	1979 Tour	0	0	0	0	0	0	0	0	0	0	0	0	0	1	0	0	1	0
H Tommy Simons	1918–19	0	0	0	0	0	0	0	0	0	0	0	0	4	0	2	4	0	2
Andy Sinton	1995–99	66	17	6	4	4	1	6	3	0	0	0	0	11	6	4	87	30	11
George EH Skinner	1940–47	1	0	0	0	0	0	0	0	0	0	0	0	15	0	3	16	0	3
Jimmy F Skinner	1919–26	88	0	3	6	0	0	0	0	0	0	0	0	17	0	0	111	0	3
Harry Skitt	1924–31	212	0	0	17	0	0	0	0	0	0	0	0	29	0	4	258	0	4
Jamie A Slabber	2002–04	0	1	0	0	0	0	0	0	0	0	0	0	1	3	0	1	4	0
HC Slade	1916–17	0	0	0	0	0	0	0	0	0	0	0	0	1	0	0	1	0	0
Steve A Slade	1994–96	1	4	0	0	2	0	0	1	0	0	0	0	3	1	0	4	8	0
Slender	1918–19	0	0	0	0	0	0	0	0	0	0	0	0	1	0	0	1	0	0
Tom Sloan	1978 Tours	0	0	0	0	0	0	0	0	0	0	0	0	2	0	0	2	0	0
Jimmy Smailes	1930–32	16	0	3	0	0	0	0	0	0	0	0	0	0	0	0	16	0	3
Adam Smith	2008–11	0	0	0	0	0	0	0	0	0	0	0	0	0	4	0	0	4	0
A (Tony) Smith	1959–65	0	0	0	0	0	0	0	0	0	0	0	0	2	0	0	2	0	0
Bert Smith	1916–29	291	0	9	28	0	1	0	0	0	0	0	0	52	0	3	371	0	13
George C Smith	1945–46	0	0	0	0	0	0	0	0	0	0	0	0	4	0	0	4	0	0
Gordon M Smith	1978–82	34	4	1	0	0	0	6	0	0	0	1	0	19	3	1	59	8	2
Ian R Smith	1975–76	2	0	0	0	0	0	0	0	0	0	0	0	1	3	0	3	3	0
JC Reg Smith	1943–44	0	0	0	0	0	0	0	0	0	0	0	0	1	0	0	1	0	0
JC Trevor Smith	1943–44	0	0	0	0	0	0	0	0	0	0	0	0	2	0	1	2	0	1
Jimmy MA Smith	1925–27	30	0	0	1	0	0	0	0	0	0	0	0	4	0	0	35	0	0
John Smith	1959–64	21	0	1	2	0	0	0	0	0	1	0	0	3	1	0	27	1	1
Ken Smith	1944–45	0	0	0	0	0	0	0	0	0	0	0	0	1	0	0	1	0	0
Neil J Smith	1990–01	0	0	0	0	0	0	0	0	0	0	0	0	0	1	0	0	1	0
P Smith	1918–19	0	0	0	0	0	0	0	0	0	0	0	0	4	0	0	4	0	0
R (Bobby) A Smith	1955–64	271	0	176	32	0	22	0	0	0	14	0	10	41	1	43	358	1	251
Roger A Smith	1965–66	0	0	0	0	0	0	0	0	0	0	0	0	1	0	0	1	0	0
Jimmy Smy	1928–31	17	0	6	0	0	0	0	0	0	0	0	0	2	0	0	19	0	6
George Snee	2002–03	0	0	0	0	0	0	0	0	0	0	0	0	0	1	0	0	1	0
Graeme J Souness	1971–72	0	0	0	0	0	0	0	0	0	0	1	0	0	0	0	0	1	0
Peter C Southey	1979–83	1	0	0	0	0	0	0	0	0	0	0	0	2	4	0	3	4	0
Harry Sparrow	1913–15	18	0	7	1	0	0	0	0	0	0	0	0	8	0	7	27	0	14
Isaac Spelman	1937–40	28	0	2	4	0	0	0	0	0	0	0	0	12	0	0	44	0	2
Alf Spencer	1917–18	0	0	0	0	0	0	0	0	0	0	0	0	1	0	1	1	0	1
Jimmy Sperrin	1940–42	0	0	0	0	0	0	0	0	0	0	0	0	16	0	4	16	0	4
W (Billy) T Sperrin	1940–44	0	0	0	0	0	0	0	0	0	0	0	0	28	0	6	28	0	6
Cyril H Spiers	1927–32	158	0	0	11	0	0	0	0	0	0	0	0	17	0	0	186	0	0

NAME	SEASON	LEAGUE APPS	LEAGUE SUBS	LEAGUE GOALS	FA CUP APPS	FA CUP SUBS	FA CUP GOALS	FL CUP APPS	FL CUP SUBS	FL CUP GOALS	EURO APPS	EURO SUBS	EURO GOALS	OTHERS APPS	OTHERS SUBS	OTHERS GOALS	TOTAL APPS	TOTAL SUBS	TOTAL GOALS
Doug Spivey	1954–55	0	0	0	0	0	0	0	0	0	0	0	0	1	0	0	1	0	0
Bert Sproston	1938–39	9	0	0	0	0	0	0	0	0	0	0	0	1	0	0	10	0	0
Ron Staley	1942–43	0	0	0	0	0	0	0	0	0	0	0	0	1	0	0	1	0	0
Paul A Stalteri	2005–08	37	5	2	3	2	1	3	0	0	4	2	0	5	2	0	52	11	3
Brian Statham	1987–91	20	4	0	0	1	0	2	0	0	0	0	0	13	5	0	35	10	0
Kevin Stead	1976–77	0	0	0	0	0	0	0	0	0	0	0	0	0	1	0	0	1	0
Micky J Stead	1975–78	14	1	0	0	0	0	0	0	0	0	0	0	17	9	3	31	10	3
Alex Steel	1909–10	1	0	0	0	0	0	0	0	0	0	0	0	0	0	0	1	0	0
Danny Steel	1908–12	131	0	3	12	0	0	0	0	0	0	0	0	24	0	1	167	0	4
R (Bobby) L Steel	1908–16	230	0	41	19	0	5	0	0	0	0	0	0	69	0	16	318	0	62
Gary A Stevens	1983–90	140	7	6	13	4	0	19	2	0	15	0	2	36	7	4	223	20	12
Les WG Stevens	1939–49	54	0	5	5	0	0	0	0	0	0	0	0	33	0	9	92	0	14
Paul Stewart	1988–92	126	5	28	9	0	2	23	0	7	8	0	0	43	2	20	209	7	57
Mark N Stimson	1986–89	1	1	0	0	0	0	0	0	0	0	0	0	6	5	1	7	6	1
Alfie F Stokes	1952–59	65	0	40	4	0	2	0	0	0	0	0	0	20	0	20	89	0	62
L Sturgess	1942–43	0	0	0	0	0	0	0	0	0	0	0	0	1	0	0	1	0	0
ME Sturgess	1942–43	0	0	0	0	0	0	0	0	0	0	0	0	1	0	1	1	0	1
Neil Sullivan	2000–04	64	0	0	9	0	0	8	0	0	0	0	0	21	1	0	102	1	0
John Sutton	2002–03	0	0	0	0	0	0	0	0	0	0	0	0	0	1	0	0	1	0
W (Bill) N Swift	1944–45	0	0	0	0	0	0	0	0	0	0	0	0	1	0	0	1	0	0
Adel Taarabt	2006–09	0	9	0	0	2	0	0	1	0	0	3	0	6	7	1	6	22	1
Teemu Tainio	2005–08	48	13	3	5	2	0	3	3	0	7	2	0	11	3	2	74	23	5
Mauricio R Taricco	1998–05	125	5	2	9	2	0	12	0	0	3	0	0	28	15	0	177	22	2
John A Tate	1912–14	4	0	0	0	0	0	0	0	0	0	0	0	2	0	0	6	0	0
Walter S Tattersall	1911–15	45	0	3	3	0	2	0	0	0	0	0	0	16	0	3	64	0	8
Alan Taylor	1929–36	60	0	0	10	0	0	0	0	0	0	0	0	7	0	0	77	0	0
Peter J Taylor	1976–90	116	7	31	8	3	2	4	2	0	0	0	0	27	6	13	155	18	46
Jan Telesnikov	1998–99	0	0	0	0	0	0	0	0	0	0	0	0	0	1	0	0	1	0
Ben D Thatcher	2000–03	29	7	0	3	0	0	6	1	0	0	0	0	11	3	0	49	11	0
Alton A Thelwell	1999–03	13	5	0	0	3	0	0	0	0	0	0	0	4	2	0	17	10	0
Andy Theodosiou	1988–89	0	0	0	0	0	0	0	0	0	0	0	0	0	1	0	0	1	0
Danny J Thomas	1983–87	80	7	1	4	0	0	11	2	0	8	4	0	48	8	4	151	21	5
Martin R Thomas	1982–83	0	0	0	0	0	0	0	0	0	0	0	0	0	1	0	0	1	0
Mitchell A Thomas	1986–91	136	21	6	12	0	1	28	1	1	0	0	0	31	11	2	207	33	10
W (Bill) SL Thomas	1915–19	0	0	0	0	0	0	0	0	0	0	0	0	26	0	6	26	0	6
Andy Thompson	1920–31	153	0	19	13	0	2	0	0	0	0	0	0	38	0	12	204	0	33
Erik Thorstvedt	1988–96	171	2	0	14	0	0	25	0	0	6	0	0	40	5	0	256	7	0
AW Thwaites	1916–19	0	0	0	0	0	0	0	0	0	0	0	0	12	0	3	12	0	3

NAME	SEASON	LEAGUE APPS	LEAGUE SUBS	LEAGUE GOALS	FA CUP APPS	FA CUP SUBS	FA CUP GOALS	FL CUP APPS	FL CUP SUBS	FL CUP GOALS	EURO APPS	EURO SUBS	EURO GOALS	OTHERS APPS	OTHERS SUBS	OTHERS GOALS	TOTAL APPS	TOTAL SUBS	TOTAL GOALS
Sid Tickridge	1941–51	96	0	0	6	0	0	0	0	0	0	0	0	49	0	0	151	0	0
Kazu Toda	2002–04	2	2	0	0	0	0	0	0	0	0	0	0	5	1	0	7	3	0
Albert H Tomkin	1938–40	4	0	0	0	0	0	0	0	0	0	0	0	2	0	0	6	0	0
Eric F Tomkins	1917–19	0	0	0	0	0	0	0	0	0	0	0	0	39	0	0	39	0	0
Ciaran Toner	2001–02	0	0	0	0	0	0	0	0	0	0	0	0	1	0	0	1	0	0
Cyril H Toulouse	1948–49	2	0	0	0	0	0	0	0	0	0	0	0	0	0	0	2	0	0
Jimmy C Townley	1927–28	3	0	2	0	0	0	0	0	0	0	0	0	2	0	2	5	0	4
Andros D Townsend	2008–11	0	0	0	1	0	1	0	0	0	0	0	0	1	6	0	2	6	1
Cyril Trailor	1941–49	11	0	0	1	0	0	0	0	0	0	0	0	7	0	0	19	0	0
Paolo Tramezzani	1998–99	6	0	0	0	0	0	1	0	0	0	0	0	10	0	1	17	0	1
George EJ Travers	1915–17	0	0	0	0	0	0	0	0	0	0	0	0	6	0	2	6	0	2
Sid Trigg	1942–43	0	0	0	0	0	0	0	0	0	0	0	0	1	0	0	1	0	0
Walter DJ Tull	1908–11	10	0	2	0	0	0	0	0	0	0	0	0	8	0	6	18	0	8
Ed L Tunney	1944–45	0	0	0	0	0	0	0	0	0	0	0	0	1	0	0	1	0	0
Andy P Turner	1991–96	8	12	3	0	1	0	0	2	1	0	0	0	13	10	3	21	25	7
David P Tuttle	1989–93	10	3	0	0	0	0	3	1	0	1	0	1	8	9	0	22	13	1
Dick Upex	1918–19	0	0	0	0	0	0	0	0	0	0	0	0	1	0	0	1	0	0
E Dennis H Uphill	1950–53	6	0	2	0	0	0	0	0	0	0	0	0	2	1	4	8	1	6
Soloman Upton	1912–13	2	0	0	0	0	0	0	0	0	0	0	0	2	0	0	4	0	0
Pat WR Van den Hauwe	1989–93	110	6	0	7	0	0	16	0	0	6	0	0	15	1	0	154	7	0
Rafael Van der Vaart	2010–11	28	0	13	1	0	0	0	0	0	7	0	2	0	0	0	36	0	15
R (Dick) T Vanner	1925–26	0	0	0	0	0	0	0	0	0	0	0	0	1	0	0	1	0	0
Mike Varney	1979 Tour	0	0	0	0	0	0	0	0	0	0	0	0	1	0	0	1	0	0
Ramon Vega	1996–01	53	11	7	8	1	0	9	2	1	0	0	0	17	5	5	87	19	13
Terry F Venables	1965–69	114	1	5	15	1	2	6	0	1	4	0	1	28	1	4	167	3	13
Ricky J Villa	1978–88	124	9	18	21	0	3	15	1	3	8	1	1	43	2	15	211	13	40
Stefano Visi	1998–99	0	0	0	0	0	0	0	0	0	0	0	0	1	0	0	1	0	0
Chris R Waddle	1985–03	137	1	33	14	0	5	21	0	4	0	0	0	41	4	11	213	5	53
F (Fanny) I Walden	1912–24	214	0	21	22	0	4	0	0	0	0	0	0	87	0	21	323	0	46
Steve J Walford	1975–76	1	1	0	0	0	0	0	0	0	0	0	0	7	4	0	8	5	0
David Walker	1944–45	0	0	0	0	0	0	0	0	0	0	0	0	1	0	0	1	0	0
Ian M Walker	1990–01	257	2	0	26	0	0	22	1	0	6	0	0	66	8	0	377	11	0
Kyle Walker	2009–11	2	1	0	0	0	0	0	0	0	0	0	0	4	2	0	6	3	0
Ernie Walley	1954–58	5	0	0	0	0	0	0	0	0	0	0	0	7	2	1	12	2	1
Johnny C Wallis	1940–45	0	0	0	0	0	0	0	0	0	0	0	0	9	0	1	9	0	1
Paul A Walsh	1987–92	84	44	19	4	4	0	9	7	2	1	3	0	40	12	15	138	70	36
Charlie Walters	1919–26	106	0	0	11	0	0	0	0	0	0	0	0	17	0	0	134	0	0
Joey Walters	1918–19	0	0	0	0	0	0	0	0	0	0	0	0	1	0	0	1	0	0

NAME	SEASON	LEAGUE APPS	LEAGUE SUBS	LEAGUE GOALS	FA CUP APPS	FA CUP SUBS	FA CUP GOALS	FL CUP APPS	FL CUP SUBS	FL CUP GOALS	EURO APPS	EURO SUBS	EURO GOALS	OTHERS APPS	OTHERS SUBS	OTHERS GOALS	TOTAL APPS	TOTAL SUBS	TOTAL GOALS
W (Sonny) E Walters	1943–56	211	0	66	23	0	5	0	0	0	0	0	0	112	0	38	346	0	109
Joe Walton	1908–09	24	0	2	4	0	0	0	0	0	0	0	0	2	0	1	30	0	3
A (Tony) G Want	1967–72	46	4	0	3	0	0	3	0	0	0	0	0	18	2	0	70	6	0
Ralph A Ward	1935–46	118	0	10	17	0	1	0	0	0	0	0	0	244	0	17	379	0	28
George Watkins	1914–15	0	0	0	0	0	0	0	0	0	0	0	0	1	0	0	1	0	0
W Watkins	1915–17	0	0	0	0	0	0	0	0	0	0	0	0	3	0	0	3	0	0
Kevin E Watson	1992–95	4	1	0	0	1	0	1	1	1	0	0	0	2	11	0	7	14	1
Fred J Webster	1911–15	83	0	0	4	0	0	0	0	0	0	0	0	16	0	0	103	0	0
Simon P Webster	1982–84	2	1	0	0	0	0	0	0	0	0	0	0	0	2	0	2	3	0
W Findlay Weir	1912–17	97	0	2	5	0	0	0	0	0	0	0	0	18	0	0	120	0	2
Keith Weller	1964–67	19	2	1	0	0	0	0	0	0	0	0	0	13	5	5	32	7	6
Johnny Westwood	1948–49	0	0	0	0	0	0	0	0	0	0	0	0	1	0	0	1	0	0
Ralph Wetton	1951–55	45	0	0	1	0	0	0	0	0	0	0	0	18	0	3	64	0	3
Gareth Whalley	1997 Tour	0	0	0	0	0	0	0	0	0	0	0	0	1	2	0	1	2	0
W (Bill) J Whatley	1932–47	226	0	2	28	0	0	0	0	0	0	0	0	139	0	0	393	0	2
Jack R Whent	1943–44	0	0	0	0	0	0	0	0	0	0	0	0	3	0	1	3	0	1
Charlie H Whitchurch	1945–47	8	0	2	0	0	0	0	0	0	0	0	0	19	0	5	27	0	7
John A White	1959–64	183	0	40	19	0	1	0	0	0	17	0	6	14	0	6	233	0	53
Roy BW White	1940–46	0	0	0	2	0	0	0	0	0	0	0	0	167	0	4	169	0	4
Sid E White	1923–26	20	0	0	2	0	0	0	0	0	0	0	0	3	0	1	25	0	1
Tom White	1964–65	0	0	0	0	0	0	0	0	0	0	0	0	1	0	1	1	0	1
Alf Whittingham	1944–45	0	0	0	0	0	0	0	0	0	0	0	0	1	0	0	1	0	0
W (Bill) A Whitton	1921–23	0	0	0	0	0	0	0	0	0	0	0	0	2	0	1	2	0	1
George N Wilbert	1939–40	0	0	0	0	0	0	0	0	0	0	0	0	1	0	0	1	0	0
Harry TO Wilding	1928–29	12	0	1	0	0	0	0	0	0	0	0	0	0	0	0	12	0	1
Fred Wilkes	1908–12	57	0	0	3	0	0	0	0	0	0	0	0	12	0	0	72	0	0
R (Bert) Wilkie	1956–57	1	0	0	0	0	0	0	0	0	0	0	0	1	1	1	2	1	1
Cyril E Williams	1941–42	0	0	0	0	0	0	0	0	0	0	0	0	3	0	0	3	0	0
Jack LJ Williams	1912–13	0	0	0	0	0	0	0	0	0	0	0	0	1	0	0	1	0	0
Ernie C Williamson	1916–17	0	0	0	0	0	0	0	0	0	0	0	0	1	0	0	1	0	0
Arthur Willis	1942–54	145	0	1	16	0	0	0	0	0	0	0	0	111	0	1	272	0	2
Archie Wilson	1915–16	0	0	0	0	0	0	0	0	0	0	0	0	10	0	0	10	0	0
Charlie Wilson	1918–23	55	0	27	7	0	6	0	0	0	0	0	0	18	0	15	80	0	48
Clive EA Wilson	1995–99	67	3	1	8	1	1	7	1	0	0	0	0	2	6	0	84	11	2
Joe A Wilson	1943–44	0	0	0	0	0	0	0	0	0	0	0	0	1	0	0	1	0	0
Charlie F Withers	1947–56	153	0	0	11	0	2	0	0	0	0	0	0	37	3	0	201	3	2
Norman A Wood	1908–09	0	0	0	0	0	0	0	0	0	0	0	0	1	0	0	1	0	0
Jonathan Woodgate	2007–11	49	0	2	1	0	0	5	0	1	9	1	0	3	0	0	67	1	3

NAME	SEASON	LEAGUE APPS	LEAGUE SUBS	LEAGUE GOALS	FA CUP APPS	FA CUP SUBS	FA CUP GOALS	FL CUP APPS	FL CUP SUBS	FL CUP GOALS	EURO APPS	EURO SUBS	EURO GOALS	OTHERS APPS	OTHERS SUBS	OTHERS GOALS	TOTAL APPS	TOTAL SUBS	TOTAL GOALS
George Woodger	1914–15	0	0	0	0	0	0	0	0	0	0	0	0	2	0	0	2	0	0
Vic R Woodley	1939–40	0	0	0	0	0	0	0	0	0	0	0	0	1	0	0	1	0	0
Charlie L Woodruff	1908–10	10	0	1	0	0	0	0	0	0	0	0	0	4	0	0	14	0	1
Alan E Woods	1954–55	6	0	0	0	0	0	0	0	0	0	0	0	0	1	0	6	1	0
H Johnny Woodward	1941–49	63	0	1	4	0	0	0	0	0	0	0	0	9	0	1	76	0	2
Vivian J Woodward	1908–09	27	0	18	4	0	0	0	0	0	0	0	0	1	0	0	32	0	18
Roy A Woolcott	1969–70	1	0	0	0	0	0	0	0	0	0	0	0	0	0	0	1	0	0
Len F Worley	1959–60	1	0	0	0	0	0	0	0	0	0	0	0	0	0	0	1	0	0
JE (Ted) Worrall	1918–19	0	0	0	0	0	0	0	0	0	0	0	0	11	0	0	11	0	0
George C Wren	1917–18	0	0	0	0	0	0	0	0	0	0	0	0	1	0	0	1	0	0
Alex M Wright	1950–51	2	0	1	0	0	0	0	0	0	0	0	0	0	0	0	2	0	1
Mark SA Yeates	2003–06	1	2	0	0	1	0	0	0	0	0	0	0	7	4	0	8	7	0
Terry C Yorath	1979–81	44	4	1	7	0	0	7	0	0	0	0	0	7	1	0	65	5	1
Albert E Young	1943–45	0	0	0	0	0	0	0	0	0	0	0	0	3	0	0	3	0	0
Alex S Young	1911–12	5	0	3	0	0	0	0	0	0	0	0	0	0	0	0	5	0	3
Chris Young	1912–13	4	0	0	0	0	0	0	0	0	0	0	0	2	0	0	6	0	0
Luke P Young	1998–02	44	14	0	9	2	0	1	3	0	2	1	0	7	7	0	63	27	0
Willie D Young	1975–77	54	0	3	2	0	0	8	0	1	0	0	0	24	0	3	88	0	7
R (Bobby) L Zamora	2003–04	6	10	0	0	1	0	1	0	1	0	0	0	1	2	3	8	13	4
Christian Ziege	2001–04	44	3	7	3	0	2	5	0	1	0	0	0	10	2	0	62	5	10
Reto P Ziegler	2004–07	12	12	1	5	0	0	4	0	0	1	1	0	3	5	0	25	18	1
A Didier Zokora	2006–09	74	13	0	8	0	0	11	1	0	26	0	0	11	1	0	130	15	0
Own Goals	1910–2010	0	0	89	0	0	16	0	0	11	0	0	7	0	0	33	0	0	156

ROLL OF HONOUR

Kelly Murphy
Mr Sean Mylod
Mr Anthony Winston Drake
Mohd Ridzuan Lu B Abdullah
Benjamin David Charles Moore
Mr Emanuel Cordina
Mr Michael John Grant
Mr Keith Preston
Paul Smith
Mr David Atkinson
Darren Curran
Paul Terrington
Michael McCann
Mr Calvin Carpenter
Lucas Riley
Mr Jon Allen
Mr John Riwai
Mr Daren Burney
Mr Michael Mears
Angelo Zachariades
Mr David G McCourt
Mr David Gary Whitaker
Mr Goran Ahlqvist
Mr Per Ahlqvist
Mr Brian Thorpe
Mr Michael Cloke
Mr Peder Brix Kjelgaard
Mr Michael Joseph Logue
Jan Gunnar Larkerod
Felix Boeni
Steve Martin
Soren Gronberg
Mr Keith Head
Mr Robert C Duffy
Gavin Clay
Kenneth Simmonds

Mr Stephen Doyle
Nigel Grace
Mr Adam L J Foot
Mr Gert Houtevels
Peter Womersley
Mr Idham Ramadi
Andy Gavey
Mr Stephen Garner
Marianne Vigo-Odinolfi
Mr Kai Mejland
Mr Keith Durkin
Mr Christopher Dennis Evoy
Mr Michael Buckler
Miss Emily Jayne Macaulay
Mr Gwyn Shoulders Williams
Apaloo Aime-Junior Jules Lily
Mr Philip Bayley
Mr Svein Erik Dalbak
Mr Jeff Lightfoot
Mr Paul Dark-Padre
Mr Andrew Keith Malloch
Mr Dean Russell Smith
Mr Christopher Cullinane
Thomas R J Harper
Mr Derry Locke
John Donaghy
Mr Clive Raymond Cook
Mr Aly Shiraz Maherali
Ian James Trueman
James Neil Trueman
Jim Taylor
Alastair Benn
Mr Douglas Norfolk
Graham Heywood
Michael Newman
Mr Darren Morrow

Mr David Johns
Mr Paul Wright
Bill Dawney
Miss Sarah Bassett
Ian Blaskett
Fabius Chen
Mr Joseph Camilleri Bowman
David J Stanford
Mr John Hollis
Euan Knowles
Miss Abigail Coggin
Mr Rick Pare
Mr Stephen Smith
Fernando Pina Jorge
Martyn Oxley
Dave William Bosher
Franco Wakefield
Mr Colin E Nix
Mark Spry
Mr Ian Macdonald
Kate Miller
Anthony James Foster
Simon James Jenkins
Johnny Deltin
John MacCabe
Mr Noel F Devitt
Mr Terry O'Brien
Mr Kenny Vervaeck
Mr Jamie Baxter
Mr Alan Hoppen
Alexander Macleod
Mr John Douglas
Mr Kelvin Walker
Mr Simon Durban
Benjy Randall
Mr Lance Epstein
Mr Piers Elsdon
Mr Matt Saul

Mr Stian Smaage
Mr Colin Mabey
Master Kade George Simmonds
Miss Kirsty Sims
Sam Matthew Christian Bellamy
Mr Richard John Reynolds
Mr Richard Gale
Mr James Comper
Danny Hartley
David Parfitt
Mr Robert Russell
Mr Patrick Kelly
Mr Jamie Titcombe
Mr Mark Peter Binns
Charlie Barret
Mr Ben Astaire
Mr Max Astaire
Mr Sam Astaire
Clifff Martin
Mr Noah Bear Dickens
Jeremy Reed
Mr Daniel Sims
Mr Ross James Chapman
Ian Pleace
Mr Peter Masters
Miles Patterson
Mr Stuart Tresham
Mr George Georgiou
Mr Simon Digby-Worsley
Mr Paul Burket
Mr Lawrence V Patrick
Ross Coker
Master Alex Robson
Mr Trevor Morrish
Mr Dan Neilson
Mr Harry Spencer
Paul Andrew Combes
Anthony G Lippett

Tara Maria Frances Quinn
Mr Bryan Carl Williams
Mr Chris J Grist
Mr Russell Edwards
Mr Philip Bracken
Tony McLoughlin
Mick Stephens
Mr Jean Michel Dethier
Mr Paul H Silson
Mr Christian Silson
Mr Michael J Silson
Mr Piers W Neal
Mr Ragnar Granum
Mr Jimmy Barnett
Mr Tim Gooch
Steve Walker
Mr Michael Hughes
Mr Barry Lancaster
John Devine
Geoff Keen
Mr Rishi Chowdhury
Mr Glenn Gibbs
Joseph James Mills
Mr Geoffrey R Hales
Mr Colin Salmon
Christian van Rooij
Glenn Richardson
Mr Stephen D Wade
Mr Ricky J Garrard
Mr Chris R Wheeler
Jonathan N Middlebrook
Adele Keenan
Mr William Sutton
Mr Richard Knights
Mr John Raymond Cox
Nick Reece Barrett
Alex Thomson
Mr Simon Wade

Marcus B Duckworth
Mr Darren Gale
Mr Brian Hunt
Mr Brett R Nurse
David Ingram
Mr Stephen C Moss
Mr Robert Edward Smith
Mr Eddie Clark
Mr William Victor Fudge
Daniel C Graham
Mr Joseph Grant-Evans
Mr Paul Alan Simon
Mrs Julie-Anne Simon
Master Teddy Fleming
Mr Chris Eaton
David Senner
Mr Mark Bradley
Mr Tom Symonds
Mr Jonathan R Davis BDA
Adrian Hughes
Monika De Borger
David Thomas
Colin Carter
Adrian Thomas
Mr Joshua Stewart-Boyadjian
Neil George Barry Edwards
Mr Dave King
James Macaulay
Stewart James Monks
Mr Rick V R Morgan
Andy Brooks
Master George Paynter
Mr Graham Little
Mr Victor Gregory
Mr Kristian Mo
Master Harry Joseph Dark
John Benfield
Mr Peter Fecser Jr

Louise Neligan
Mr Robert Parker
Steve Grubb
Mr Ian Barry Brewer
Mr Graham Antony Peers
Mr David Gettleson
Michael Phelvin
Tim Dumbleton
Mr James Martin
Frank Kercza Carlsen
Mr Nick Forsyth
Linus K Fenton
Mr Kenneth H D Ranson
Tony Cape
David Michael Kirston
Mr Thomas Bierig
Mr Peter Batchelor
Mr Michael Dewsall
Mr Michael Lee Swindells
Mr Robert Presland
Mr Simon Fisher
Mr Gary Lille
Mr Dennis Francis Gepp
Mr Phil Porter
Mr Kevin Evans
Mr James Bellchambers
Mr Colin James Bellchambers
Alan G M Campbell
David Carter
Samuel Carter
Martin Ostle
Mr Billy Spearen
Mr Marcel Bonnefin
Mr Barry Couchman
Mr Bashar Alfulaij
Mr Abdulwahab Alghanim
Mr Peter John Gladwell
Timothy Wraight

Andrew Pycock
Evan Jenkins
Rachel L Mason
Mr Cliff Jenkins
Mr Andrew Jenkins
Mr Steve Taylor
Samuel Hill
Jeff Kaye
Mr Grant G J Barry
Mr Mick Peebles
Mr Wayne Gonsalves
Neil James Read
Ben James Read
Miss Megan Luxford
Mr Chas Thornton
Mr Ian Steventon
Mr Henry Earey
Mr Alan R Whitehead
Mr Darrell Preece
Mr Michael Horton
Mr Val O'Flynn
Mr Glen A Mills
Mr Dave Bojko
Mr Ben Adams
Marcus Anthony Edwards
Mr Simon Graham King
Matti Aro ja Sanna Repo
Mr Stewart Sims
Mikkel Birlo
Jamie Blake
Mr Michael Shenouda
Mr Stuart George Smithies
Mr Kimberley Louise Smithies
Alan Dagless
Mr Luke Russell
Mr David John Cox
Mr Edmund Tackley
Mr Roger Lane

Mr Gordon Lee Jarvis
Elliot Benopoulos-Jones
Mr Chris CD Skinner
Max Waterman
Jack W Brigden
Dave Whitton
Mr Terry Borg
Mr Matthew Holder-Biziou
Mr Christopher Holder
Mr Harold Stern
Mr Bryan Harvey
Mr John Fidgett
Mr Terry Sandle
Simon Gaydon
David Ling
Michael T Fox
Stuart Roy Baker
Mr Darryl Telles
Mr Danny Cross
Mr Steven Seymour
David S Faubel
Mr Barry Dunkley
Mr Colin Robinson
Alex McLean
Mr Simon Knightley
Mr Ian Manning
Mr Edward Cockayne
Mr Tony E Emerson
Tahir Shazad Malik
David Relf
Mr Derek Wardhaugh
Mr Martin R Clark
Nicolas Klerck
Kent Stian Jacobsen
Mr Per-Ole Thorvaldsen
Martin Elliott
Mr Tony E Emerson
Mr Brandon Banyard

Isaac Hyman
Mr Barry Smyth
Tommy Moxham
Matthew Cooper
Michael Kaufman
George S Banes
Mr Anthony Bonello
John Wellman
Denis Collins
Mr Anthony James Thompson
Mr Keith Gordon Lane
Mr David Smith
Mr Ian Rogers
Mr Arnold Rosen
Mr Brian Shingleton
Mr Terry Norris
Shaun O'Dea
Mr Luke Bradley
Mr Ian Clive Underwood
Alan Buglass
Andrew Graham Mackie Fielding
Mr Phil Grainger
Mr Robert Lazarus
Mr Nick M Georgiou
Mr Geraint Davies
Mr Henry Piotr
Mr David Arthur Mills
Chris Gray
John J Kelly II
Mr Brian L Porter
Craig Whitley
Simon Fisher
Mr Alistair Crichton-Smith
Mrs Vanessa Andrews
Tomas Waag Helmeriksen
Geoff Seal
Steve Hurst
Mr Thomas Langoergen

Daley Knowles
Steven Anderson
Mr Torvald Eriksen
David Storer
Jason Palmer
John Cardnell
John Jackson
Fiona Howells
Mr Darrell John Frank Hill
Mr Matthew Robert Hill
Dave Chaplin
Derek Aldridge
Miss D Hainsworh
Don Turner
John O'Connor
Thomas O'Connor
Chris Smith
Paul Smith
Mr Al Terry
Melvin Marks
Leonard Paul Specterman
Kevin Hawes
Mr Vincent Cox
John Austin
Mr Steve Spiegel
Mr Howard Christopher
Mr Vernon William Elias Lloyd
Barry Sullivan
Tony Friend
Mr Patrick Peter Banham
Mr Geoffrey Evans
Mr Bryan Abraham
Akiva Solemani
Andrew Beardwell
Anna Solemani
James Stephen Wilson Smyth
Jay Nicholson Beacher
Mr Mark Gibbons
Mr Michael Dawson
David W Davidson
Mr Eddie Bassant
Mr Harry Bassant
Ciprian Moscu
Mr Julian D Goodwin
Mr Carl R Harper
Daniel Charles O'Rourke
Mr Jake Fryer
Mr Glen Hoddle
Mr Dave Spicer
Simon Holdsworth
Charlie Davis
James Stanbridge
Mr Kabir Singh Bhasin
Kenneth G. E. Hamilton
Mr James Gilmour Strachen
Miss Rose J Stather
Geoff Humphrey
David Livingstone
Mr Christopher Roy Clark
Mr Oystein Haugen
Benjo Lourie
Mr Benjamin Chan
Kevin Vaughn Roberts
Mr Bob Allcock
Simon Lixenberg
Julie Joseph
Mr Mads Fruergaard Nielsen
Keith Grose
Colin James
Dennis Sau Yiu Law
Jonathan Shooter
Mr Andrew Saunders
Mr Neil Saunders
Mr Steve Harvey
Peter Dale
Robert Wightwick

Chris Lloyd
Lucy Madsen
Miss Rebecca Modd
Mr Christopher Modd
Ryan Pavey
Steve Caron
James Caron
Matthew Caron
Daniel Caron
Steve Booth
Harry Booth
Thomas Booth
Mr Michael Shafkou
Mr Derek Kitts
Peter Oleinik
Mr Scott Robert Taylor
John Robert Taylor
Roy Sampson
Mr Alan John Thatcher
Mr Jamie Bristow
Jon Letch
Tom Delaney
Mr Terry Merryman
Peter James Dunn
Mr Malcolm Clixby
Mrs Dawn Clixby
Alison Pearce
Andy Wright
Lewis James Forecast
David William Oakley
Paul David Oakley
John Stewart Oakley
David James Oakley
Scott John Oakley
Mr Bryan Harvey
Reginald Churcher
Joe Delaney